D0000760

# COLLINS GEM

# DICTIONARY
## AND
# THESAURUS

# COLLINS GEM

# DICTIONARY

## AND

# THESAURUS

HarperCollins*Publishers*

First Edition 1990

Second Edition 1997

**Reprinted 1997**

© HarperCollins Publishers 1990, 1997

ISBN 0 00 472034-2

9 8 7 6 5 4 3 2 1

A catalogue record for this book
is available from the British Library.

Typeset by Morton Word Processing Ltd.
Scarborough, England

Printed and bound in Great Britain by
Caledonian International Book Manufacturing Ltd,
Glasgow, G64

# CONTENTS

Editorial Staff                                      vii

Features of the Dictionary and Thesaurus            viii

Abbreviations Used in the Text                         x

**Dictionary and Thesaurus**                          1


SUPPLEMENTS

Chemical Elements                                   679

Group Names and Collective Nouns                    680

Planets of the Solar System                         681

Characters in Classical Mythology                   682

Wedding Anniversaries                               684

Books of the Bible                                  685

Countries, Currencies and Capitals                  686

Types of Calendar                                   692

# EDITORIAL STAFF

# FEATURES OF THE DICTIONARY AND THESAURUS

**Short, clear definitions**

**peripatetic** *adj* travelling about
**periphery** *n* circumference; outside **peripheral** *adj* unimportant
**periscope** *n* instrument used for giving view of objects on different level
**perish** *v* die; rot **perishable** *adj* that will not last long **perishing** *adj Inf* very cold
**perjure** *v* be guilty of perjury **perjury** *n* crime of false testimony on oath
**perk** *n* incidental benefit from employment
**perky** *adj* lively, cheerful
**perm** *n* long-lasting curly hairstyle ~*v* give a perm
**permanent** *adj* continuing in same state; lasting **permanence** *n*
**permeate** *v* pervade; pass through pores of **permeable** *adj*

**Spelling help** with changes in form of entry word

**permit** *v* -mitting, -mitted allow; give leave to ~*n* warrant or licence to do something **permissible** *adj*

──────── THESA

**perish** be killed, die, expire, lose one's life, pass away; decay, decompose, rot, waste
**perjury** false statement, forswearing, oath breaking
**permanent** abiding, constant, durable, enduring, eternal, everlasting, fixed, immutable, invariable, lasting, perpetual, persistent, stable, unchanging
**permeate** fill, impregnate, penetrate, pervade, saturate
**permissible** acceptable, allowable, all right, authorized, lawful, legal, legitimate, O.K. *or* okay *Inf*, permitted

**Restrictive labels** show context of use

**permission** assent, authorization, consent, freedom, go-ahead *Inf*, green light, leave, licence, permit, sanction

# FEATURES OF THE DICTIONARY AND THESAURUS

**permission** *n* **permissive** *adj* (too) tolerant, esp. sexually

**permutation** *n Maths* arrangement of a number of quantities in every possible order — Restrictive labels

**pernicious** *adj* wicked; harmful

**pernickety** *adj Inf* fussy

**peroxide** *n* short for HYDROGEN PEROX-IDE

**perpendicular** *adj/n* (line) at right angles to another; (something) exactly upright — Parts of speech

**perpetrate** *v* perform or be responsible for (something bad)

**perpetual** *adj* continuous; lasting forever **perpetuate** *v* make perpetual; not to allow to be forgotten **perpetuity** *n*

**perplex** *v* puzzle; bewilder **perplexity** *n*

**persecute** *v* oppress because of race, religion etc. **persecution** *n*

**persevere** *v* persist, maintain effort **perseverance** *n*

---

URUS ————

**permissive** free, lax, liberal, tolerant

**permit** *v* agree, allow, authorize, consent, give leave or permission, let, license, sanction ~*n* licence, pass, passport, warrant — Parts of speech

**perpetrate** carry out, commit, do, execute, perform

**perpetual** abiding, endless, enduring, eternal, everlasting, immortal, lasting, perennial, permanent — Generous choice of **synonyms**

**perpetuate** maintain, preserve, sustain

**perplex** baffle, bewilder, confound, confuse, mystify, puzzle, stump

**persecute** harass, ill-treat, maltreat, oppress, torment, victimize

**perseverance** dedication, determination, doggedness, persistence,

ix

# ABBREVIATIONS USED IN THE TEXT

| | | | |
|---|---|---|---|
| abbrev | abbreviation | Lit | Literary |
| adj | adjective | | |
| adv | adverb | masc | masculine |
| Afr | African | Maths | Mathematics |
| Amer | American | Med | Medicine |
| Anat | Anatomy | Mil | Military |
| Arch | Archaic | Mus | Music |
| Aust | Australian | Myth | Mythology |
| | | | |
| Bot | Botany | n | noun |
| Brit | Britain, British | N | North(ern) |
| | | Naut | Nautical |
| Canad | Canadian | NZ | New Zealand |
| cap. | capital | | |
| Chem | Chemistry | Obs | Obsolete |
| comb. | combining | Offens | Offensive |
| conj | conjunction | oft. | often |
| Dial | Dialect | orig. | originally |
| | | | |
| E | East(ern) | Pathol | Pathology |
| Eng | England, English | pert. | pertaining |
| e.g. | for example | Photog | Photography |
| esp. | especially | pl | plural |
| etc. | et cetera | Poet | Poetic |
| | | prep | preposition |
| fem | feminine | pron | pronoun |
| Fig | Figurative | | |
| Fr | French | S | South(ern) |
| | | Scot. | Scottish |
| Geog | Geography | sing. | singular |
| | | Sl | Slang |
| Hist | History | | |
| | | US(A) | United States |
| Inf | Informal | | (of America) |
| interj | interjection | usu. | usually |
| | | | |
| kg | kilogram(s) | v | verb |
| km | kilometre(s) | Vulg | Vulgar |
| | | | |
| Lat | Latin | W | West(ern) |
| lb(s) | pound(s) | | |

# A a

**a, an** *adj* the indefinite article meaning one; *an* is used before vowels

**AA** Alcoholics Anonymous; Automobile Association

**aardvark** *n* S Afr. anteater

**aback** *adv* **taken aback** startled

**abacus** *n* counting device of beads on wire frame

**abandon** *v* desert; give up ~ *n* freedom from inhibitions etc. **abandoned** *adj* deserted; uninhibited; wicked

**abase** *v* humiliate, degrade

**abashed** *adj* ashamed

**abate** *v* make or become less

**abattoir** *n* slaughterhouse

**abbey** *n* community of monks or nuns; abbey church **abbot** *n* head of monastery

**abbreviate** *v* shorten **abbreviation** *n* shortened word or phrase

**abdicate** *v* give up (throne etc.)

**abdomen** *n* belly **abdominal** *adj*

**abduct** *v* carry off, kidnap

**aberration** *n* deviation from normal; lapse

**abet** *v* abetting, abetted help, esp. in doing wrong

**abeyance** *n* **in abeyance** not in use

**abhor** *v* abhorring, abhorred loathe **abhorrence** *n* **abhorrent** *adj*

**abide** *v* abiding, abode *or* abided endure; *Obs* reside **abide by** obey

**ability** *n* competence, power

**abject** *adj* wretched; servile

**ablaze** *adj* burning

**able** *adj* capable, competent, or tal-

---

## THESAURUS

**abandon** *v* desert, forsake, jilt, leave, leave behind ~ *n* dash, wantonness, wildness

**abbey** cloister, convent, friary, monastery, nunnery, priory

**abbreviate** abridge, abstract, compress, condense, contract, curtail, cut, reduce, shorten, summarize, trim, truncate

**abbreviation** abridgment, abstract, compendium, compression, condensation, contraction, curtailment, digest, epitome, précis, reduction, résumé, shortening, summary, synopsis, trimming, truncation

**abdicate** abandon, abjure, abnegate, cede, forgo, give up, quit, relinquish, renounce, resign, retire, step down *Inf*, surrender, vacate, waive, yield

**abduct** carry off, kidnap, run off with, seize, snatch *Sl*

**abeyance in abeyance** hanging fire, pending, shelved, suspended

**abhor** abominate, detest, hate, loathe, shrink from, shudder at

**abhorrent** abominable, detestable, disgusting, distasteful, hated, horrible, horrid, loathsome, odious, offensive, repulsive

**abide** accept, bear, brook, endure, put up with, stand, submit to, suffer, tolerate

**abide by** agree to, conform to, follow, obey, observe, submit to

**ability** aptitude, capability, capacity, competence, competency, expertise, facility, faculty, flair, force, gift, knack, power, proficiency, skill, talent

**abject** base, cringing, despicable, dishonourable, fawning, grovelling, ignominious, low, mean, servile,

ented **ably** adv

**abnormal** adj not usual or typical; odd **abnormally** adv **abnormality** n

**aboard** adv on, onto ship, train, or aircraft

**abode** n home; dwelling

**abolish** v do away with **abolition** n

**abominate** v detest **abominable** adj **abomination** n loathing; the object loathed

**Aborigine** n original inhabitant of Australia

**abort** v terminate (a pregnancy) prematurely; end prematurely and unsuccessfully **abortion** n **abortive** adj unsuccessful

**abound** v be plentiful

**about** adv on all sides; nearly; astir ~prep round; near; concerning

**about-turn** n turn to the opposite direction

**above** adv higher up ~prep over; higher than, more than; beyond

**abrasion** n place scraped (e.g. on skin); a wearing down **abrasive** n substance for grinding, polishing etc. ~adj causing abrasion; grating

**abreast** adv side by side

**abridge** v shorten

**abroad** adv to or in a foreign country; at large

**abrupt** adj sudden; blunt; steep **abruptly** adv

**abscess** n gathering of pus

slavish, submissive, vile, worthless

**able** accomplished, adept, adequate, capable, clever, competent, effective, efficient, experienced, expert, fit, gifted, proficient, qualified, skilful, skilled, talented

**abnormal** atypical, curious, deviant, eccentric, exceptional, extraordinary, irregular, odd, oddball Inf, peculiar, queer, singular, strange, uncommon, unusual, weird

**abnormality** deformity, deviation, eccentricity, exception, flaw, irregularity, oddity, peculiarity, strangeness, weirdness

**abolish** annul, axe Inf, blot out, cancel, destroy, do away with, eliminate, end, eradicate, extinguish, invalidate, nullify, obliterate, overthrow, overturn, put an end to, quash, rescind, revoke, suppress, terminate, void, wipe out

**abolition** cancellation, destruction, elimination, end, ending, eradication, extermination, extinction, obliteration, overthrow, overturning, revocation, suppression, termination, wiping out

**abominable** base, contemptible, despicable, detestable, disgusting, execrable, foul, horrible, horrid, loathsome, obnoxious, odious, repellent, repugnant, repulsive, revolting, terrible, vile

**abomination** antipathy, aversion, detestation, disgust, distaste, hate, hatred, repugnance, revulsion

**abound** be plentiful, crowd, flourish, increase, luxuriate, overflow, proliferate, swarm, swell, teem, thrive

**about** prep as regards, concerned with, concerning, dealing with, on, re, referring to, regarding, relative to; adjacent, beside, circa used with dates, close to, near, nearby; around, encircling, on all sides, round, surrounding ~adv almost, approaching, approximately, around, close to, more or less, nearing, nearly, roughly

**above** prep beyond, exceeding, higher than, on top of, over, upon

**abroad** in foreign lands, out of the

**abscond** *v* leave secretly

**absent** *adj* away; missing ~*v* keep away **absence** *n* **absentee** *n* one who stays away **absently** *adv*

**absolute** *adj* complete; unrestricted; pure **absolutely** *adv* completely ~*interj* certainly

**absolve** *v* free from, pardon

**absorb** *v* suck up; engross; take in **absorption** *n* **absorbent** *adj*

**abstain** *v* refrain **abstention** *n* **abstinence** *n*

**abstemious** *adj* sparing in eating and drinking

**abstract** *adj* existing only in the mind; not concrete ~*n* summary ~*v* remove; summarize **abstracted** *adj* preoccupied **abstraction** *n*

**abstruse** *adj* hard to understand

**absurd** *adj* ridiculous **absurdity** *n*

**abundant** *adj* plentiful **abundantly** *adv* **abundance** *n* great amount

**abuse** *v* misuse; address rudely ~*n* wrong treatment; insulting comments **abusive** *adj* **abusively** *adv*

**abut** *v* **abutting, abutted** adjoin

———————— THESAURUS ————————

**abrupt** blunt, brisk, brusque, curt, direct, gruff, impolite, rough, rude, short, terse

**absence** absenteeism, truancy; default, defect, deficiency, lack, need, omission, privation, want

**absent** away, elsewhere, gone, lacking, missing, not present, out, truant, unavailable, wanting

**absolute** complete, downright, entire, out-and-out, outright, perfect, pure, sheer, thorough, total, unqualified, utter; autocratic, despotic, dictatorial, full, sovereign, supreme, unbounded, unconditional, unlimited, unrestricted

**absorb** consume, devour, digest, drink in, exhaust, imbibe, receive, soak up, suck up, take in; captivate, engage, engross, fascinate, fill, fill up, fix, hold, immerse, occupy, preoccupy, rivet

**abstain** avoid, cease, desist, forbear, forgo, give up, keep from, refrain, refuse, renounce, shun, stop, withhold

**abstention** abstaining, abstinence, avoidance, forbearance, refraining, refusal, self-control, self-denial

**abstinence** forbearance, moderation, self-denial, self-restraint, soberness, sobriety, temperance

**abstract** *adj* abstruse, complex, conceptual, deep, general, occult, philosophical, profound, separate, subtle, theoretical ~*n* digest, epitome, essence, outline, précis, résumé, summary, synopsis ~*v* detach, extract, isolate, remove, separate, steal, take away, withdraw

**absurd** crazy, farcical, foolish, idiotic, illogical, irrational, laughable, ludicrous, nonsensical, preposterous, ridiculous, senseless, silly, stupid

**abundant** ample, bountiful, copious, exuberant, filled, full, lavish, luxuriant, overflowing, plenteous, plentiful, profuse, rich, teeming

**abuse** *v* damage, exploit, harm, hurt, ill-treat, injure, maltreat, mar, misapply, misuse, oppress, spoil, wrong; curse, defame, disparage, insult, libel, malign, revile, scold, slander, smear, swear at, vilify ~*n* damage, exploitation, harm, hurt, ill-treatment, imposition, maltreatment, misapplication, misuse, oppression, spoiling, wrong; blame, castigation, censure, cursing, defamation, disparagement, insults, in-

**abysmal** *adj* immeasurable, very great; *Inf* extremely bad **abysmally** *adv*

**abyss** *n* very deep gulf or pit

**AC** alternating current

**acacia** *n* gum-yielding tree or shrub

**academy** *n* society to advance arts or sciences; institution for specialized training; *Scot* secondary school

**academic** *adj* of a place of learning; theoretical ~*n* member of college or university

**accede** *v* agree; attain (office etc.)

**accelerate** *v* (cause to) increase speed **acceleration** *n* **accelerator** *n* mechanism to increase speed

**accent** *n* stress or pitch in speaking; mark to show this; style of pronunciation ~*v* emphasize

**accentuate** *v* stress, emphasize

**accept** *v* take, receive; admit, believe; agree to **acceptable** *adj* **acceptance** *n*

**access** *n* right or means of entry ~*v* *Computers* obtain (data) **accessible** *adj* easy to approach **accessibility** *n*

**accession** *n* attaining of office, right etc.; addition

**accessory** *n* supplementary part of

——————— THESAURUS ———————

vective, libel, reproach, revilement, scolding, slander, swearing, tirade, vilification

**academic** *adj* bookish, erudite, highbrow, learned, lettered, literary, scholarly, scholastic, school, studious, conjectural, notional, speculative, theoretical ~*n* don, fellow, lecturer, master, professor, tutor

**accede** accept, acquiesce, admit, agree, assent, comply, concede, concur, consent, endorse, grant, yield; assume, attain, come to, enter upon, inherit, succeed, succeed to *as heir*

**accelerate** expedite, forward, further, hasten, hurry, quicken, speed, speed up, spur

**acceleration** expedition, hastening, hurrying, quickening, speeding up, spurring, stimulation

**accent** *n* beat, emphasis, force, rhythm, stress; inflection, intonation, modulation, pronunciation, tone ~*v* accentuate, stress, underline, underscore

**accept** obtain, receive, secure, take; accede, acknowledge, acqui-

esce, admit, adopt, affirm, agree to, approve, believe, buy *Sl*, consent to, recognize, swallow *Inf*; acknowledge, admit, assume, take on, undertake

**acceptable** agreeable, gratifying, pleasant, pleasing, welcome; adequate, admissible, all right, fair, moderate, passable, satisfactory, so-so *Inf*, tolerable

**acceptance** obtaining, receipt, securing, taking; accession, acknowledgment, acquiescence, admission, adoption, affirmation, agreement, approbation, approval, assent, belief, compliance, concession, concurrence, consent, cooperation, O.K. *or* okay *Inf*, permission, recognition, seal of approval; deference, standing, submission; acknowledgment, admission, assumption, undertaking

**access** admission, admittance, course, door, entrance, entrée, entry, key, path, road

**accessible** achievable, at hand, attainable, available, handy, near, nearby, obtainable, on hand, possible, reachable, ready

car, woman's dress etc.; person assisting crime

**accident** *n* event happening by chance; mishap, esp. causing injury **accidental** *adj* **accidentally** *adv*

**acclaim** *v* applaud, praise ~*n* applause **acclamation** *n*

**acclimatize** *v* accustom to new climate or environment

**accolade** *n* public approval; honour; token of knighthood

**accommodate** *v* supply, esp. with lodging; oblige; adapt **accommodating** *adj* obliging **accommodation** *n* lodgings

**accompany** *v* -nying, -nied go with; supplement; occur with; play music to support a soloist **accompaniment** *n*

**accomplice** *n* one assisting another in crime

**accomplish** *v* carry out; finish **accomplished** *adj* complete; proficient

**accord** *n* (*esp.* **in accord with**) agreement, harmony ~*v* (cause to) be in accord with; grant **according to** as stated by; in conformity with **accordingly** *adv* as the circumstances suggest; therefore

———————— THESAURUS ————————

**accessory** addition, adornment, attachment, component, decoration, extra, frill, trim, trimming

**accident** calamity, casualty, chance, collision, crash, disaster, misadventure, mischance, misfortune, mishap, pile-up; chance, fate, fortune, hazard, luck

**accidental** casual, chance, fortuitous, haphazard, incidental, random, uncertain, unexpected, unforeseen, unintended, unintentional, unplanned

**acclaim** *v* applaud, approve, celebrate, cheer, clap, commend, exalt, extol, hail, honour, laud, praise, salute, welcome ~*n* acclamation, applause, approbation, approval, celebration, commendation, exaltation, honour, plaudits, praise, welcome

**acclimatize** accommodate, accustom, adapt, adjust, become seasoned to, get used to, inure, naturalize

**accommodate** billet, board, cater for, harbour, house, lodge, put up, quarter, shelter; aid, assist, furnish, help, oblige, provide, serve, supply

**accommodating** complaisant, considerate, cooperative, friendly, helpful, hospitable, kind, obliging, polite, unselfish, willing

**accommodation** board, digs *Brit inf*, harbouring, house, housing, lodging(s), quartering, quarters, shelter, sheltering

**accompany** attend, conduct, convoy, escort, go with, usher

**accomplice** accessory, ally, assistant, associate, collaborator, colleague, confederate, helper, henchman, partner

**accomplish** achieve, attain, bring off *Inf*, carry out, complete, conclude, do, effect, execute, finish, fulfil, manage, perform, produce, realize

**accomplished** adept, cultivated, expert, gifted, masterly, polished, practised, proficient, skilful, skilled, talented

**accordingly** as a result, consequently, ergo, hence, in consequence, so, therefore, thus

**according to** as maintained by, as stated by, in the light of; after, after the manner of,

**accordion** n musical instrument with bellows and reeds

**accost** v approach and speak to

**account** n report; importance; statement of moneys received, paid, or owed; person's money held in bank ~v regard as; give reason, answer (for) **accountable** adj responsible **accountancy** n keeping, preparation of business accounts **accountant** n **accounting** n

**accoutrements** pl n equipment, esp. military; trappings

**accredited** adj authorized, officially recognized

**accrue** v be added; result

**accumulate** v gather; collect accu-

mulation n

**accurate** adj exact, correct **accurately** adv **accuracy** n

**accursed** adj under a curse; detestable

**accuse** v charge with wrongdoing; blame **accusation** n

**accustom** v make used to, familiarize **accustomed** adj usual; used (to); in the habit (of)

**ace** n one at dice, cards, dominoes; Tennis winning serve; Inf expert

**acetylene** n colourless, flammable gas

**ache** n continuous pain ~v to be in pain **aching** adj

**achieve** v accomplish, gain

————— THESAURUS —————

in accordance with, in keeping with, in line with, in step with, in the manner of

**account** n chronicle, description, history, narration, narrative, recital, record, relation, report, statement, story, tale, version; Commerce balance, bill, book, books, charge, inventory, invoice, ledger, reckoning, register, score, statement, tally ~v assess, believe, calculate, consider, count, deem, esteem, estimate, hold, judge, rate, reckon, regard, think, value

**accountable** amenable, answerable, charged with, liable, obliged, responsible

**accredited** appointed, certified, commissioned, endorsed, guaranteed, licensed, official, recognized, sanctioned, vouched for

**accumulate** accrue, amass, build up, collect, gather, grow, hoard, increase, pile up, stockpile, store

**accumulation** aggregation, build-up, collection, gathering, heap, hoard, increase, mass, pile,

stack, stock, stockpile, store

**accuracy** carefulness, correctness, exactitude, precision, strictness, truth, truthfulness, veracity

**accurate** close, correct, exact, faithful, faultless, just, meticulous, precise, proper, regular, right, scrupulous, spot-on Brit inf, strict, true, truthful, unerring

**accusation** allegation, attribution, charge, complaint, imputation, incrimination, indictment, recrimination

**accuse** blame, censure, charge, impute, incriminate, indict, recriminate, tax

**accustom** acclimatize, adapt, familiarize, habituate, inure, season, train

**accustomed** acclimatized, adapted, familiar, given to, habituated, in the habit of, inured, seasoned, trained, used; common, conventional, customary, established, everyday, expected, habitual, normal, ordinary, regular, routine, set

**ache** v hurt, pain, smart, suffer,

**achievement** n

**acid** adj sharp, sour ~n Chem compound which combines with bases to form salts **acidic** adj **acidity** n

**acknowledge** v admit, recognize; say one has received **acknowledgment** n

**acme** n highest point

**acne** n pimply skin disease

**acorn** n fruit of the oak tree

**acoustic** adj of sound and hearing **acoustics** pl n science of sounds; features of room or building as regards sounds heard in it

**acquaint** v make familiar, inform **acquaintance** n person known; personal knowledge

**acquiesce** v agree, consent **acqui-**

**escence** n

**acquire** v gain, get **acquisition** n act of getting; material gain

**acquit** v **-quitting, -quitted** declare innocent; settle (a debt); behave (oneself) **acquittal** n

**acre** n measure of land, 4840 square yards

**acrid** adj pungent, sharp

**acrimony** n bitter feeling or language **acrimonious** adj

**acrobat** n one skilled in gymnastic feats, esp. in circus etc. **acrobatic** adj **acrobatics** pl n

**acronym** n word formed from initial letters of other words

**across** adv/prep crosswise; from side to side; on or to the other side

——————————— THESAURUS ———————————

throb, twinge

**achieve** accomplish, attain, bring about, carry out, complete, do, earn, effect, execute, finish, fulfil, gain, get, obtain, perform, procure, reach, win

**achievement** accomplishment, attainment, completion, execution, fulfilment, performance, production, realization

**acid** acrid, biting, pungent, sharp, sour, tart

**acidity** acridity, bitterness, pungency, sharpness, sourness, tartness

**acknowledge** accept, acquiesce, admit, allow, concede, confess, declare, grant, own, profess, recognize, yield; answer, notice, react to, recognize, reply to, respond to, return

**acquaint** announce, apprise, disclose, divulge, enlighten, inform, let (someone) know, notify, reveal, tell

**acquaintance** associate, colleague, contact

**acquiesce** accept, agree, assent, bow to, comply, concur, conform, consent, give in, submit, yield

**acquiescence** acceptance, agreement, assent, compliance, concurrence, conformity, consent, giving in, submission, yielding

**acquire** amass, achieve, buy, collect, earn, gain, gather, get, obtain, pick up, procure, realize, receive, score Sl, secure, win

**acquisition** buy, gain, possession, prize, property, purchase

**acquit** absolve, clear, deliver, discharge, exculpate, exonerate, free, fulfil, liberate, release, relieve, vindicate

**acquittal** absolution, clearance, discharge, exculpation, exoneration, liberation, release, relief, vindication

**acrimonious** astringent, bitter, caustic, censorious, cutting, irascible, mordant, petulant, pungent, rancorous, sarcastic, severe, sharp, spiteful, tart, testy, trenchant,

**acrylic** n synthetic fibre

**act** n thing done, deed; doing; law or decree; section of a play ~v perform, as in a play; exert force, work, as mechanism; behave **acting** n ~adj temporary **action** n operation; deed; gesture; expenditure of energy; battle; lawsuit **active** adj in operation; busy, occupied; brisk, energetic **activate** v **actively** adv **activity** n **actor**, **actress** n one who acts in a play, film etc.

**actual** adj existing in the present; real **actuality** n **actually** adv really, indeed

**actuary** n expert in insurance statistics

**actuate** v activate

**acumen** n keen discernment

**acupuncture** n medical treatment by insertion of needles into the body

**acute** adj shrewd; sharp; severe ~n accent (´) over letter **acutely** adv

─────── THESAURUS ───────

**act** n action, blow, deed, doing, execution, exertion, exploit, feat, operation, performance, step, stroke, undertaking; bill, decree, edict, enactment, law, measure, ordinance, resolution, statute; performance, routine, show, sketch, turn ~v acquit, bear, behave, carry, carry out, comport, conduct, do, enact, execute, exert, function, go about, make, move, operate, perform, react, serve, strike, take effect, undertake, work; act out, characterize, enact, impersonate, mime, mimic, perform, personate, personify, play, play or take the part of, portray, represent

**acting** adj interim, provisional, substitute, surrogate, temporary ~n dramatics, impersonation, performance, performing, portrayal, portraying

**action** accomplishment, achievement, act, deed, feat, move, operation, performance, step, stroke, undertaking; battle, combat, conflict, fighting, warfare; case, cause, lawsuit, litigation, proceeding, prosecution, suit

**activate** actuate, animate, arouse, energize, galvanize, get going, impel, initiate, kick-start, mobilize, motivate, move, prod, prompt, propel, rouse, set going, set in motion, set off, start, stimulate, stir, switch on, trigger (off), turn on

**active** acting, astir, at work, doing, functioning, in action, in force, in operation, live, moving, operative, running, working; bustling, busy, engaged, full, involved, occupied, on the go Inf, on the move; alert, animated, diligent, energetic, industrious, lively, nimble, on the go Inf, quick, spirited, sprightly, spry, vibrant, vigorous, vital, vivacious

**activity** action, animation, bustle, exertion, hurly-burly, hustle, labour, life, liveliness, motion, movement, stir, work

**actual** absolute, categorical, certain, definite, factual, indisputable, indubitable, physical, positive, real, substantial, tangible, undeniable, unquestionable; current, existent, extant, live, living, present, present-day, prevailing

**actually** as a matter of fact, de facto, essentially, indeed, in fact, in reality, in truth, literally, really, truly

**acute** clever, discerning, discriminating, incisive, intuitive, keen, observant, perceptive, perspicacious,

## DICTIONARY

**AD** anno Domini

**ad** n abbrev. of ADVERTISEMENT

**adage** n proverb

**adagio** adj/n Mus slow (passage)

**adamant** adj unyielding

**Adam's apple** projecting part at front of throat

**adapt** v alter for new use; modify; change **adaptable** adj **adaptation** n **adaptor, -er** n device for connecting two electrical appliances to a single socket

**add** v join; increase by; say further **addition** n **additional** adj **additionally** adv **additive** n something added, esp. to foodstuffs

**addendum** n (pl **-da**) thing to be added

**adder** n small poisonous snake

**addict** n one who has become dependent on something **addicted** adj **addiction** n

**address** n direction on letter; place where one lives; speech ~v mark destination; speak to; direct

**adenoids** pl n tissue at back of nose

**adept** adj skilled ~n expert

**adequate** adj sufficient, suitable; not outstanding **adequacy** n ad-

## THESAURUS

sharp, smart, subtle; pointed, sharp, sharpened

**adamant** determined, firm, fixed, immovable, inexorable, inflexible, insistent, intransigent, obdurate, relentless, resolute, rigid, set, stiff, stubborn, unbending, uncompromising, unrelenting, unyielding

**adapt** accommodate, adjust, alter, apply, change, comply, conform, convert, fit, habituate, make, match, modify, prepare, qualify, remodel, shape, suit, tailor

**adaptable** adjustable, compliant, easy-going, flexible, malleable, modifiable, plastic, pliant, resilient, versatile

**adaptation** adjustment, alteration, change, conversion, modification, refitting, shift, transformation, variation, version

**add** amplify, append, attach, augment, enlarge by, include, increase by, supplement; add up, compute, count up, reckon, sum up, total, tot up

**addict** dope-fiend Sl, freak Inf, junkie Inf, user Inf

**addicted** dedicated, dependent, devoted, hooked Sl, obsessed, prone

**addiction** craving, dependence, habit, obsession

**addition** adding, adjoining, affixing, amplification, attachment, augmentation, enlargement, extension, inclusion; addendum, adjunct, appendage, appendix, extension, extra, gain, increase, increment, supplement

**additional** added, add-on, extra, fresh, further, more, new, other, spare, supplementary

**address** n abode, domicile, dwelling, home, house, location, lodging, pad Sl, place, residence; discourse, dissertation, lecture, oration, sermon, speech, talk ~v discourse, give a speech, give a talk, harangue, lecture, orate, sermonize, speak, talk

**adept** able, accomplished, adroit, dexterous, expert, practised, proficient, skilful, skilled, versed

**adequacy** competence, fairness, sufficiency, tolerability

equately *adv*

**adhere** *v* stick to; be firm in opinion etc. **adherence** *n* **adherent** *n* **adhesion** *n* **adhesive** *adj*

**ad hoc** *adj/adv* for a particular occasion only

**adieu** *interj* farewell

**adjacent** *adj* lying near, next (to)

**adjective** *n* word which qualifies a noun

**adjoin** *v* be next to; join

**adjourn** *v* close (meeting etc.) temporarily; *Inf* move elsewhere **adjournment** *n*

**adjudge** *v* declare; decide

**adjudicate** *v* judge; sit in judgment **adjudication** *n* **adjudicator** *n*

**adjunct** *n* person or thing added or

subordinate

**adjure** *v* earnestly entreat

**adjust** *v* adapt; alter slightly, regulate **adjustable** *adj* **adjustment** *n*

**adjutant** *n* military officer who assists superiors

**ad-lib** *v* improvise ~*n* improvised remark

**administer** *v* manage; dispense, as justice etc.

**administrate** *v* manage (an organization) **administration** *n* management, supervision; governing body **administrative** *adj* **administrator** *n*

**admiral** *n* naval officer of highest rank

**admire** *v* regard with approval, re-

— THESAURUS —

**adequate** capable, competent, enough, fair, passable, satisfactory, sufficient, suitable, tolerable

**adhere** attach, cement, cling, fasten, fix, glue, glue on, hold fast, paste, stick, stick fast

**adhesive** *adj* clinging, gummy, holding, sticking, sticky, tacky, tenacious ~*n* glue, gum, paste

**adjacent** adjoining, alongside, beside, bordering, close, near, neighbouring, next door, touching

**adjourn** defer, delay, discontinue, interrupt, postpone, prorogue, put off, put on the back burner *Inf,* recess, stay, suspend

**adjournment** deferment, delay, discontinuation, interruption, recess, stay, suspension

**adjudicate** adjudge, arbitrate, decide, determine, judge, referee, settle, umpire

**adjudication** arbitration, decision, determination, finding, judgment, pronouncement, ruling, settlement, verdict

**adjust** adapt, alter, arrange, compose, convert, dispose, fit, fix, harmonize, make conform, measure, modify, order, reconcile, redress, regulate, remodel, set, settle, suit

**adjustable** flexible, malleable, modifiable, movable, tractable

**adjustment** adaptation, alteration, arrangement, arranging, fitting, fixing, modification, ordering, rectification, redress, regulation, remodelling, setting, tuning

**administer** conduct, control, direct, govern, handle, manage, oversee, run, superintend, supervise

**administration** conduct, control, direction, execution, government, management, overseeing, performance, provision, running, superintendence, supervision; executive, governing body, government, management, ministry, term of office

**admirable** commendable, estimable, excellent, exquisite, fine, laudable, meritorious, praiseworthy, rare, superior, valuable

spect, or wonder **admirable** adj **admirably** adv **admiration** n **admirer** n **admiring** adj

**admit** v -mitting, -mitted confess; accept as true; allow; let in **admissible** adj **admission** n permission to enter; entrance fee; confession **admittance** n permission to enter **admittedly** adv

**admonish** v reprove; exhort **admonition** n

**ad nauseam** Lat to a boring or disgusting extent

**ado** n fuss

**adolescence** n period of life just before maturity **adolescent** n/adj

young (person)

**adopt** v take as one's child; take up, as principle, resolution **adoption** n

**adore** v love intensely; worship **adorable** adj **adoration** n **adoring** adj

**adorn** v decorate

**adrenal** adj near the kidney **adrenalin** n hormone secreted by adrenal glands

**adrift** adj/adv drifting; Inf detached; Inf off course

**adroit** adj skilful; clever **adroitly** adv

**adulation** n flattery

wonderful, worthy

**admiration** adoration, affection, amazement, appreciation, approval, astonishment, delight, esteem, pleasure, praise, regard, respect, surprise, wonder

**admire** adore, appreciate, approve, esteem, idolize, look up to, praise, prize, respect, think highly of, value, worship

**admirer** beau, boyfriend, lover, suitor, sweetheart, wooer; devotee, disciple, enthusiast, fan, follower, partisan, supporter, worshipper

**admissible** acceptable, allowable, allowed, passable, permissible, permitted, tolerable, tolerated

**admission** access, entrance, entrée, entry, initiation, introduction; acknowledgment, allowance, avowal, concession, confession, declaration, disclosure, divulgence, profession, revelation

**admit** allow, allow to enter, give access, initiate, introduce, let in, receive, take in; acknowledge, affirm, avow, concede, confess, declare, disclose, divulge, own, profess, reveal; agree, allow, grant, let, permit, recognize

**adolescence** boyhood, girlhood, minority, teens, youth

**adolescent** adj boyish, girlish, growing, immature, juvenile, puerile, teenage, young, youthful ~n juvenile, minor, teenager, youngster, youth

**adopt** accept, appropriate, approve, assume, choose, embrace, endorse, espouse, follow, maintain, ratify, select, support, take on, take over, take up; foster, take in

**adoption** acceptance, approbation, appropriation, approval, assumption, choice, embracing, endorsement, espousal, ratification, support, taking on, taking over, taking up; adopting, fosterage, fostering, taking in

**adore** admire, cherish, dote on, esteem, exalt, glorify, honour, idolize, love, revere, reverence, venerate, worship

**adorn** array, bedeck, beautify, deck, decorate, embellish, enhance, enrich, festoon, garnish, grace, or-

**adult** *adj* grown-up; mature ~*n* mature person, animal or plant

**adulterate** *v* make impure by addition **adulteration** *n*

**adultery** *n* sexual unfaithfulness of a husband or wife **adulterer** *n* **adulterous** *adj*

**advance** *v* bring forward; suggest; lend (money); go forward; improve in position or value ~*n* progress; movement forward; improvement; a loan ~*adj* ahead in time or position **advanced** *adj* at a late stage; not elementary; ahead of the times

**advancement** *n*

**advantage** *n* more favourable position or state **advantageous** *adj*

**advent** *n* arrival, coming; (with *cap.*) the four weeks before Christmas

**adventure** *n* exciting undertaking or happening **adventurous** *adj*

**adverb** *n* word added to verb etc. to modify meaning

**adverse** *adj* hostile; unfavourable

**adversary** *n* enemy **adversely** *adv* **adversity** *n* distress, misfortune

**advert** *n Inf* advertisement

nament, trim

**adulation** blandishment, fawning, fulsome praise, servile flattery, sycophancy, worship

**adult** *adj* full grown, fully developed, fully grown, grown-up, mature, of age, ripe ~*n* grown-up

**advance** *v* accelerate, bring forward, bring up, come forward, elevate, go ahead, go forward, go on, hasten, move onward, move up, press on, proceed, progress, promote, send forward, send up, speed, upgrade; adduce, allege, cite, offer, present, proffer, put forward, submit, suggest; lend, pay beforehand, raise *price*, supply on credit ~*n* advancement, amelioration, betterment, breakthrough, furtherance, gain, growth, improvement, progress, promotion, step; appreciation, credit, deposit, down payment, increase *in price*, loan, prepayment, retainer, rise *in price* ~*adj* beforehand, early, foremost, forward, in front, leading, prior

**advanced** avant-garde, extreme, forward, higher, late, leading, precocious, progressive

**advantage** aid, ascendancy, asset,

assistance, avail, benefit, blessing, boon, convenience, edge, gain, good, help, interest, lead, profit, service, start, superiority, sway, upper hand, use, utility, welfare

**advantageous** dominant, favourable, superior

**adventure** chance, contingency, enterprise, escapade, experience, exploit, hazard, incident, occurrence, risk, speculation, undertaking, venture

**adventurous** adventuresome, audacious, bold, dangerous, daredevil, daring, enterprising, foolhardy, have-a-go *Inf*, hazardous, headstrong, intrepid, rash, reckless, risky

**adverse** conflicting, contrary, detrimental, disadvantageous, hostile, inexpedient, inopportune, negative, opposing, opposite, reluctant, repugnant, unfavourable, unfortunate, unfriendly, unlucky, unwilling

**adversity** affliction, bad luck, calamity, disaster, distress, hardship, hard times, ill-fortune, ill-luck, misery, misfortune, mishap, reverse, sorrow, suffering, trial, trouble, woe

**advertise** v publicize; give notice of, esp. in newspapers etc.; make public request (for) **advertisement** n advertising adj/n

**advice** n counsel; notification

**advise** v offer advice; give notice (of) **advisable** adj expedient **advisedly** adv deliberately **adviser, -or** n **advisory** adj

**advocate** n one who pleads the cause of another, esp. in court of law; Scot barrister ~v recommend **advocacy** n

**aeon** n long period of time

**aerate** v charge liquid with gas; expose to air

**aerial** adj operating in the air; pertaining to aircraft ~n part of radio etc. receiving or sending radio waves

**aerobatics** pl n stunt flying

**aerobics** pl n (with sing v) exercise system designed to increase oxygen in the blood **aerobic** adj

**aerodrome** n airfield

**aerodynamics** pl n (with sing v) study of air flow, esp. round moving solid bodies **aerodynamic** adj

**aeronautics** pl n (with sing v) science of air navigation and flying in general **aeronautical** adj

**aeroplane** n heavier-than-air flying machine

**aerosol** n (substance dispensed from) pressurized can

**aerospace** n earth's atmosphere and space beyond

**aesthetic** adj relating to principles of beauty **aesthetics** pl n study of beauty **aesthetically** adv **aesthete** n

**afar** adv from, at, or to, a great distance

**affable** adj polite and friendly

**affair** n thing done or attended to; business; happening; sexual liaison; pl personal or business interests; matters of public interest

**affect** v act on; move feelings;

---

THESAURUS

**advertise** advise, announce, declare, display, inform, make known, notify, praise, proclaim, promote, promulgate, publicize, publish, puff, tout

**advertisement** ad Inf, advert Brit inf, announcement, bill, blurb, circular, commercial, display, notice, placard, poster, promotion, publicity, puff

**advice** admonition, caution, counsel, guidance, help, injunction, opinion, recommendation, suggestion, view

**advisable** apt, desirable, expedient, fit, fitting, judicious, politic, profitable, proper, prudent, seemly, sensible, sound, suitable, wise

**advise** admonish, caution, commend, counsel, enjoin, recommend, suggest, urge

**advocate** v advise, argue for, campaign for, champion, defend, encourage, espouse, favour, plead for, press for, promote, propose, recommend, speak for, support, uphold, urge ~n backer, campaigner, champion, counsellor, defender, promoter, proposer, speaker, spokesman, supporter, upholder

**affable** amiable, benevolent, benign, civil, congenial, cordial, courteous, friendly, genial, good-humoured, good-natured, kindly, mild, obliging, pleasant, sociable, urbane

**affair** activity, business, circumstance, concern, episode, event, happening, incident, interest, matter, occurrence, proceeding, proj-

make show of **affectation** n show, pretence **affected** adj making a pretence; moved; acted upon **affection** n fondness, love **affectionate** adj **affectionately** adv

**affidavit** n written statement on oath

**affiliate** v/n (join as an) associate **affiliation** n

**affinity** n natural liking; resemblance; chemical attraction

**affirm** v assert positively; make solemn declaration **affirmation** n **affirmative** adj/n positive (statement)

**affix** v fasten (to)

**afflict** v cause to suffer **affliction** n

**affluent** adj wealthy **affluence** n

**afford** v to be able to (buy, do); provide **affordable** adj

**affront** v/n insult

**afield** adv **far afield** far away

**aflame** adv/adj burning

**afloat** adv floating; at sea

**afoot** adv astir; on foot

**aforesaid** adj previously mentioned

**afraid** adj frightened; regretful

**afresh** adv again, anew

**African** adj of Africa **African violet** house plant with pink or purple flowers

**aft** adv towards stern of ship

**after** adv later; behind ~prep behind; later than; on the model of;

———— THESAURUS ————

ect, question, subject, transaction, undertaking; amour, intrigue, liaison, relationship, romance

**affect** act on, alter, bear upon, change, concern, influence, interest, involve, modify, regard, relate to, sway, transform; assume, contrive, feign, imitate, pretend, sham, simulate

**affectation** appearance, artificiality, façade, false display, insincerity, mannerism, pose, pretence, pretentiousness, sham, show, simulation

**affected** artificial, assumed, conceited, contrived, counterfeit, feigned, insincere, mannered, precious, pretended, pretentious, put-on, sham, simulated, stiff, studied, unnatural

**affection** attachment, care, desire, feeling, fondness, friendliness, good will, inclination, kindness, liking, love, tenderness, warmth

**affectionate** attached, caring, devoted, doting, fond, friendly, kind, loving, tender, warm, warm-hearted

**affinity** analogy, closeness, compatibility, connection, correspondence, kinship, likeness, relation, relationship, resemblance, similarity

**affirm** assert, attest, aver, avouch, avow, certify, confirm, declare, maintain, state, swear, testify

**affirmation** assertion, averment, avouchment, avowal, confirmation, declaration, oath, pronouncement, ratification, statement, testimony

**affirmative** agreeing, approving, assenting, concurring, confirming, consenting, positive

**afflict** burden, distress, grieve, harass, hurt, oppress, pain, plague, trouble, try, wound

**affluence** abundance, fortune, opulence, plenty, profusion, prosperity, riches, wealth

**affluent** moneyed, opulent, prosperous, rich, wealthy, well-off, well-to-do

**afford** bear, spare, stand, sustain

**afraid** alarmed, anxious, apprehensive, cowardly, faint-hearted, fearful, frightened, intimidated, nerv-

pursuing *~conj* later than **afters** *pl n* dessert

**afterbirth** *n* membrane expelled after a birth

**aftermath** *n* result, consequence

**afternoon** *n* time from noon to evening

**aftershave** *n* lotion applied to face after shaving

**afterwards, afterward** *adv* later

**again** *adv* once more; in addition

**against** *prep* in opposition to; in contact with; opposite

**agape** *adj/adv* open-mouthed

**agate** *n* semiprecious quartz

**age** *n* length of time person or thing has existed; time of life; period of history; long time; maturity, old age *~v* make or grow old **aged** *adj* old *~pl n* old people **ageing** *n/*

*adj*

**agenda** *pl n* (*with sing v*) list of things to be attended to

**agent** *n* one authorized to act for another; person or thing producing effect **agency** *n* organization providing service; business, premises of agent

**aggrandize** *v* make greater in size, power, or rank

**aggravate** *v* make worse or more severe; *Inf* annoy **aggravation** *n*

**aggregate** *v* gather into mass *~adj* gathered thus *~n* mass, sum total; gravel etc. for concrete

**aggression** *n* unprovoked attack; hostile activity **aggressive** *adj* **aggressively** *adv*

**aggrieved** *adj* upset, angry

**aghast** *adj* appalled

──────── THESAURUS ────────

ous, scared, timid, timorous

**after** afterwards, behind, below, following, later, subsequently, succeeding, thereafter

**again** afresh, anew, another time, once more; also, besides, furthermore, in addition, moreover, on the contrary, on the other hand

**against** anti *Inf*, contra *Inf*, counter, hostile to, in contrast to, in defiance of, in opposition to, in the face of, opposed to, opposing, resisting, versus; abutting, close up to, facing, fronting, in contact with, on, opposite to, touching, upon

**age** *n* date, day(s), duration, epoch, era, generation, lifetime, period, span, time; advancing years, decline *of life,* majority, maturity, old age, senescence, senility, seniority *~v* decline, deteriorate, grow old, mature, mellow, ripen

**aged** age-old, ancient, antique, elderly, getting on, grey, hoary, old,

superannuated

**agency** bureau, business, department, office, organization

**agenda** calendar, diary, list, plan, programme, schedule, timetable

**agent** advocate, deputy, emissary, envoy, factor, go-between, negotiator, rep *Inf*, representative, substitute, surrogate; agency, cause, force, instrument, means, power, vehicle

**aggravate** exacerbate, exaggerate, heighten, increase, inflame, intensify, magnify, make worse, worsen; *Inf* annoy, exasperate, gall, get on one's nerves *Inf*, hassle *Inf*, irk, irritate, nark *Brit, Aust, & NZ sl,* needle *Inf*, nettle, pester, provoke, tease, vex

**aggression** assault, attack, encroachment, injury, invasion, offence, offensive, onslaught, raid

**aggressive** belligerent, destructive, hostile, offensive, pugnacious,

**agile** *adj* nimble; quick **agility** *n*

**agitate** *v* stir, shake up; trouble; stir up public opinion (for or against) **agitation** *n* **agitator** *n*

**aglow** *adj* glowing

**AGM** Annual General Meeting

**agnostic** *n* one who believes that we cannot know whether God exists

**ago** *adv* in the past

**agog** *adj/adv* eager, astir

**agony** *n* extreme suffering **agonize** *v* suffer agony; worry greatly ago-

nizing *adj*

**agoraphobia** *n* fear of open spaces **agoraphobic** *adj/n*

**agree** *v* agreeing, agreed be of same opinion; consent; harmonize; approve **agreeable** *adj* willing; pleasant **agreeably** *adv* **agreement** *n*

**agriculture** *n* (science of) farming **agricultural** *adj*

**aground** *adv* (of boat) touching bottom

**ahead** *adv* in front; onwards

——————— THESAURUS ———————

quarrelsome

**agile** active, acute, alert, brisk, clever, lithe, lively, nimble, quick, sharp, sprightly, spry, supple, swift

**agitate** beat, convulse, disturb, rock, rouse, shake, stir, toss; alarm, arouse, confuse, disquiet, distract, disturb, excite, faze, ferment, fluster, incite, inflame, perturb, rouse, trouble, unnerve, upset, work up, worry

**agitation** convulsion, disturbance, rocking, shake, shaking, stir, stirring, tossing, turbulence, upheaval; alarm, arousal, clamour, commotion, confusion, discomposure, disquiet, distraction, disturbance, excitement, ferment, flurry, fluster, incitement, outcry, stimulation, trouble, tumult, turmoil, upheaval, upset, worry

**agitator** demagogue, firebrand, inciter, rabble-rouser, revolutionary, stirrer *Inf*, troublemaker

**agony** affliction, anguish, distress, misery, pain, pangs, suffering, throes, torment, torture, woe

**agree** accede, acquiesce, admit, allow, assent, be of the same mind, comply, concede, concur, consent, engage, grant, permit, see eye to eye, settle; accord, answer, chime, coincide, conform, correspond, fit, get on (together), harmonize, match, square, suit, tally

**agreeable** acceptable, congenial, delightful, enjoyable, gratifying, pleasant, pleasing, pleasurable, satisfying, to one's liking, to one's taste; acquiescent, amenable, approving, complying, concurring, consenting, in accord, responsive, sympathetic, well-disposed, willing

**agreement** accord, accordance, compatibility, compliance, concert, concord, concurrence, conformity, congruity, consistency, correspondence, harmony, similarity, union, unison; arrangement, bargain, compact, contract, covenant, deal *Inf*, pact, settlement, treaty, understanding

**agriculture** culture, farming, husbandry, tillage

**aground** ashore, beached, foundered, grounded, high and dry, on the rocks, stranded, stuck

**ahead** along, at an advantage, at the head, before, forwards, in advance, in front, in the foreground, in the lead, leading, on, onwards, winning

**ahoy** *interj* ship's hailing cry

**aid** *v/n* help, support

**aide** *n* assistant

**AIDS** *n* disease that destroys the body's immune system

**ail** *v* trouble; be ill **ailing** *adj* **ailment** *n* illness

**aim** *v* direct (weapon etc.); intend *~n* aiming; intention **aimless** *adj* without purpose **aimlessly** *adv*

**ain't** *Nonstandard* am not; is not; are not; has not; have not

**air** *n* (gases of) earth's atmosphere; breeze; tune; manner; *pl* affected manners *~v* expose to air; communicate, make known **airless** *adj* stuffy **airy** *adj* well-ventilated; jaunty, nonchalant **air bed** inflatable mattress **air conditioning** control of temperature and humidity in build-ing **aircraft** *n* flying machines gener-ally; aeroplane **airfield** *n* landing and taking-off area for aircraft **air force** armed force using aircraft **air gun** gun discharged by compressed air **airline** *n* company operating aircraft **airliner** *n* large passenger aircraft **air mail** mail sent by aircraft **airman** *n* member of air force **air-play** *n* performances of a record on radio **airport** *n* station for civilian aircraft **air raid** attack by aircraft **airship** *n* lighter-than-air flying ma-chine with means of propulsion **air-strip** *n* strip of ground where air-craft can take off and land **airtight** *adj* not allowing passage of air **air-worthy** *adj* fit to fly

**aisle** *n* passage between rows of seats

---

THESAURUS

**aid** *v* abet, assist, befriend, encour-age, favour, help, promote, relieve, second, serve, subsidize, succour, support, sustain *~n* assistance, ben-efit, encouragement, favour, help, promotion, relief, service, succour, support

**aim** *v* aspire, attempt, design, di-rect, endeavour, intend, level, mean, plan, point, propose, pur-pose, resolve, seek, set one's sights on, sight, strive, take aim (at), train, try, want, wish *~n* ambition, aspiration, course, design, desire, direction, end, goal, intent, inten-tion, mark, object, objective, plan, purpose, scheme, target, wish

**aimless** chance, erratic, haphaz-ard, pointless, purposeless, ran-dom, stray, undirected, unguided, unpredictable, wayward

**air** *n* atmosphere, heavens; sky; blast, breath, breeze, draught, puff, waft, whiff, wind, zephyr; ambi-ence, appearance, atmosphere, aura, bearing, character, demean-our, effect, feeling, flavour, impres-sion, look, manner, mood, quality, style, tone, vibes *Sl* *~v* aerate, expo-se, freshen, ventilate; circulate, communicate, declare, disclose, display, disseminate, divulge, ex-hibit, expose, express, give vent to, make known, make public, pro-claim, publicize, reveal, tell, utter, voice

**airless** breathless, close, heavy, muggy, oppressive, stale, stifling, stuffy, suffocating, sultry, unventi-lated

**airy** blowy, breezy, draughty, fresh, gusty, light, lofty, open, spacious, uncluttered, well-ventilated, windy; animated, blithe, buoyant, cheerful, cheery, chirpy *Inf*, debonair, gay, happy, high-spirited, jaunty, light, light-hearted, lively, merry, non-chalant

**ajar** *adv* partly open

**akimbo** *adv* with hands on hips

**akin** *n* related by blood; alike

**alabaster** *n* white, decorative stone

**à la carte** *Fr* selected freely from the menu

**alacrity** *n* eager willingness

**à la mode** *Fr* fashionable

**alarm** *n* fright; apprehension; danger signal ~*v* frighten; alert **alarming** *adj*

**alas** *interj* cry of grief

**albatross** *n* large sea bird

**albino** *n* (*pl* **-nos**) individual lacking pigmentation

**album** *n* book for photographs, stamps etc.; collection of items in book or record form

**alchemy** *n* medieval form of chemistry **alchemist** *n*

**alcohol** *n* intoxicating fermented liquor; class of organic chemical substances **alcoholic** *adj* of alcohol ~*n* person addicted to alcoholic

drink **alcoholism** *n*

**alcove** *n* recess

**alder** *n* tree related to the birch

**alderman** *n* formerly, senior local councillor

**ale** *n* kind of beer

**alert** *adj* watchful; brisk ~*n* warning ~*v* warn; draw attention to **alertness** *n*

**alfresco** *adv/adj* in the open air

**algae** *pl n* (*sing* **alga**) various water plants

**algebra** *n* method of calculating, using symbols to represent quantities

**alias** *adv* otherwise ~*n* (*pl* **aliases**) assumed name

**alibi** *n* plea of being elsewhere at time of crime

**alien** *adj* foreign; different in nature; repugnant (to) ~*n* foreigner **alienate** *v* estrange; transfer **alienation** *n*

**alight**[1] *v* get down; land

**alight**[2] *adj* burning; lit up

—————————————— THESAURUS ——————————————

**alarm** *v* distress, frighten, panic, scare, startle, terrify, unnerve; alert, arouse, signal, warn ~*n* anxiety, dismay, distress, fear, fright, panic, scare, terror, unease; alarm-bell, alert, bell, danger signal, distress signal, siren, warning

**alarming** dismaying, distressing, disturbing, frightening, scaring, shocking, startling, terrifying

**alcoholic** *n* boozer *Inf*, dipsomaniac, drunk, drunkard, hard drinker, inebriate, soak *Sl*, sop, sponge *Inf*, toper, wino *Inf*

**alert** *adj* agile, attentive, brisk, careful, heedful, lively, nimble, observant, on guard, on the ball *Inf*, perceptive, quick, ready, spirited, sprightly, vigilant, wary, watchful,

wide-awake ~*n* alarm, signal, siren, warning ~*v* alarm, forewarn, inform, notify, signal, warn

**alias** *adv* also called, also known as, otherwise, otherwise known as ~*n* assumed name, *nom de guerre*, nom de plume, pen name, pseudonym, stage name

**alibi** defence, explanation, plea

**alien** *adj* adverse, exotic, foreign, inappropriate, incompatible, not native, opposed, outlandish, remote, repugnant, separated, strange, unfamiliar ~*n* foreigner, outsider, stranger

**alight**[1] *v* come down, descend, disembark, dismount, get down, get off, land, light, perch, settle, touch down

**align** *v* bring into line or agreement; ally, side (with) **alignment** *n*

**alike** *adj/adv* similar(ly)

**alimentary canal** food passage in body

**alimony** *n* allowance paid to separated or divorced spouse

**alive** *adj* living; active; aware; swarming

**alkali** *n* (*pl* **-lis**) substance which combines with acid and neutralizes it, forming a salt **alkaline** *adj*

**all** *adj* the whole of, every one of ~*adv* entirely ~*n* the whole; everything, everyone **all right** *adj* adequate, satisfactory; unharmed ~*interj* expression of approval

**allay** *v* relieve, soothe

**allege** *v* state without proof **allegation** *n* **allegedly** *adv*

**allegiance** *n* loyalty, esp. to one's country

**allegory** *n* symbolic story, poem **allegorical** *adj*

**allegro** *adv/adj/n Mus* fast (passage)

**allergy** *n* abnormal sensitivity to a specific substance **allergic** *adj*

**alleviate** *v* ease, lessen

**alley** *n* narrow street; enclosure for skittles

**alliance** *n* union, e.g. by treaty, agreement, or marriage

**alligator** *n* animal of crocodile family found in America

**alliteration** *n* beginning of successive words with same sound

**allocate** *v* assign as a share **allocation** *n*

**allot** *v* **-lotting, -lotted** allocate **allotment** *n* distribution; portion of land rented for cultivation; portion allotted

**allow** *v* permit; set aside; acknowl-

**alight²** *adj* ablaze, aflame, blazing, burning, fiery, flaming, flaring, lighted, lit, on fire

**alike** analogous, corresponding, equal, equivalent, even, identical, parallel, similar, the same, uniform

**alive** animate, breathing, having life, living, subsisting; active, existent, existing, extant, functioning, in existence, in force, operative; active, alert, animated, awake, brisk, cheerful, chirpy *Inf*, eager, energetic, full of life, lively, quick, spirited, sprightly, spry, vigorous, vital, vivacious

**all** *adj* every bit of, the complete, the entire, the sum of, the total of, the whole of; each, each and every, every, every one of, every single ~*n* aggregate, entirety, everything, sum, sum total, total, total amount, totality, whole ~*adv* altogether,

completely, entirely, fully, totally, utterly, wholly

**allege** advance, affirm, assert, aver, avow, charge, claim, declare, maintain, plead, profess, put forward, state

**allergic** affected by, sensitive, susceptible

**allergy** antipathy, hypersensitivity, sensitivity, susceptibility

**alley** alleyway, backstreet, lane, passage, passageway, pathway, walk

**alliance** affinity, agreement, association, coalition, combination, confederation, federation, league, marriage, pact, treaty, union

**allied** affiliated, associated, bound, combined, confederate, connected, in league, joined, kindred, married, related, unified, united, wed

**allot** allocate, apportion, assign,

edge **allowable** adj **allowance** n

**alloy** n metallic mixture

**allude** v refer (to) **allusion** n

**allure** v entice ~n attractiveness **alluring** adj

**ally** v -lying, -lied join by treaty, friendship etc. ~n friend **allied** adj

**almanac** n calendar of tides, events etc.

**almighty** adj all-powerful; Inf very great

**almond** n tree of peach family; its edible seed

**almost** adv very nearly

**alms** pl n gifts to the poor

**aloft** adv on high; overhead

**alone** adj/adv by oneself, by itself;

without equal, unique

**along** adv lengthwise; together (with); forward ~prep over the length of **alongside** adv/prep beside

**aloof** adj indifferent; at a distance

**aloud** adv loudly; audibly

**alphabet** n set of letters used in writing a language

**already** adv previously; sooner than expected

**Alsatian** n large wolflike dog

**also** adv besides, moreover **also-ran** n loser in a contest

**altar** n Communion table; sacrificial table

**alter** v change, make or become different **alterable** adj **alteration** n

—————— THESAURUS ——————

budget, designate, earmark, set aside, share out

**allotment** allocation, grant, lot, measure, portion, quota, ration, share, stint; kitchen garden, patch, plot, tract

**allow** approve, authorize, endure, let, permit, sanction, stand, suffer, tolerate; allocate, allot, assign, deduct, give, grant, provide, set aside, spare; acknowledge, acquiesce, admit, concede, confess, grant, own

**allowable** acceptable, admissible, all right, appropriate, approved, permissable, suitable, tolerable

**allowance** admission, concession, sanction, sufferance, toleration; allocation, amount, grant, lot, measure, pension, portion, quota, ration, share, stint, stipend, subsidy; concession, deduction, discount, rebate, reduction

**all right** adj acceptable, adequate, fair, O.K. or okay Inf, passable, satisfactory

**allusion** glance, hint, indirect reference, innuendo, intimation, mention, suggestion

**ally** accessory, accomplice, associate, colleague, confederate, friend, helper, partner

**almighty** absolute, all-powerful, omnipotent, supreme

**almost** about, all but, approximately, as good as, close to, just about, nearly, not quite, practically, virtually

**alone** abandoned, apart, deserted, desolate, detached, forsaken, isolated, lonely, lonesome, only, separate, single, sole, solitary, unaccompanied, unaided, unassisted, unattended, unescorted

**aloud** audibly, clearly, distinctly, intelligibly, out loud, plainly

**already** as of now, at present, before now, by now, by that time, by then, by this time, even now, previously

**also** additionally, along with, and, as well, as well as, besides, further, furthermore, in addition, including, into the bargain, moreover, on top of that, plus, to boot, too

**altercation** n quarrel

**alternate** v (cause to) occur by turns ~adj in turn; every second **alternately** adv **alternative** n one of two choices ~adj replacing **alternatively** adv

**although** conj despite the fact that

**altitude** n height, elevation

**alto** n (pl **-tos**) Mus male singing voice or instrument above tenor; contralto

**altogether** adv entirely; in total

**altruism** n unselfish concern for others

**aluminium** n light nonrusting silvery metal

**always** adv at all times; for ever

**am** first person sing. of BE

**a.m.** before noon

**amalgamate** v mix, (cause to) combine **amalgamation** n

**amass** v collect in quantity

**amateur** n one who does something for interest not money; unskilled practitioner **amateurish** adj

**amaze** v surprise greatly, astound **amazing** adj **amazement** n

**ambassador** n senior diplomatic representative overseas

**amber** n yellow fossil resin

**ambidextrous** adj able to use both hands with equal ease

**ambience** n atmosphere of a place

**ambiguous** adj having more than one meaning; obscure **ambiguity** n

**ambition** n desire for success;

———— T H E S A U R U S ————

**alter** adapt, adjust, amend, change, convert, modify, recast, reform, remodel, reshape, revise, shift, transform, turn, vary

**alteration** amendment, change, difference, diversification, metamorphosis, modification, revision, shift, transformation, variance, variation

**alternate** v act reciprocally, fluctuate, follow in turn, interchange, intersperse, oscillate, rotate, substitute, take turns, vary ~adj alternating, every other, every second

**alternative** n choice, option, other of two, preference, recourse, selection, substitute

**although** albeit, despite the fact that, even if, even supposing, even though, notwithstanding, tho' US or poet, though, while

**altogether** absolutely, completely, fully, perfectly, quite, thoroughly, totally, utterly, wholly; all in all, all things considered, as a whole, collectively, generally, in general, in toto, on the whole

**always** consistently, continually, ever, evermore, every time, forever, in perpetuum, invariably, perpetually, repeatedly, unceasingly, without exception

**amass** accumulate, aggregate, assemble, collect, compile, garner, gather, heap up, hoard, pile up, rake up, scrape together

**amateur** dabbler, dilettante, layman, nonprofessional

**amaze** alarm, astonish, astound, bewilder, bowl over Inf, daze, shock, stagger, startle, stun, stupefy, surprise

**amazement** astonishment, bewilderment, confusion, marvel, perplexity, shock, surprise, wonder

**ambassador** agent, consul, deputy, diplomat, emissary, envoy, legate, minister, plenipotentiary, representative

**ambiguous** doubtful, dubious, equivocal, inconclusive, indefinite, indeterminate, obscure, puzzling,

goal, aim **ambitious** *adj*

**ambivalence** *n* simultaneous existence of conflicting emotions

**amble** *v/n* (move at an) easy pace

**ambulance** *n* conveyance for sick or injured people

**ambush** *v/n* attack from hiding

**ameliorate** *v* improve

**amen** *interj* so be it

**amenable** *adj* easily controlled; answerable

**amend** *v* correct; alter **amendment** *n*

**amenity** *n* (*oft. pl*) useful or pleasant facility or service

**amiable** *adj* friendly, kindly

**amicable** *adj* friendly **amicably** *adv*

**amid, amidst** *prep* among

**amiss** *adj* wrong ~*adv* faultily

**ammonia** *n* pungent alkaline gas

**ammunition** *n* projectiles that can be discharged from weapon; facts that can be used in argument

**amnesia** *n* loss of memory

**amnesty** *n* general pardon

**amoeba** *n* (pl **-bas, -bae**) microscopic single-celled animal

**amok** *adv* **run amok** run about in a violent frenzy

**among, amongst** *prep* in the midst of; of the number of; between; with one another

**amoral** *adj* having no moral standards

**amorous** *adj* inclined to love

**amorphous** *adj* without distinct shape

**amount** *v* come, be equal (to) ~*n* quantity; sum total

uncertain, unclear, vague

**ambition** aspiration, desire, drive, eagerness, enterprise, longing, striving, yearning, zeal; aim, aspiration, desire, dream, end, goal, hope, intent, objective, purpose, wish

**ambitious** aspiring, avid, desirous, driving, eager, enterprising, hopeful, intent, purposeful, striving, zealous

**ambush** *n* cover, hiding, hiding place, lying in wait, retreat, shelter, trap

**amenable** acquiescent, agreeable, open, persuadable, responsive, susceptible, tractable

**amend** alter, ameliorate, better, change, correct, enhance, fix, improve, mend, modify, rectify, reform, remedy, repair, revise

**amendment** alteration, amelioration, change, correction, emendation, improvement, modification,

reform, remedy, repair, revision; addendum, addition, adjunct, alteration, attachment, clarification

**amenity** advantage, comfort, convenience, facility, service

**amiable** affable, agreeable, benign, charming, cheerful, engaging, friendly, genial, kind, kindly, lovable, obliging, pleasant, pleasing, sociable, winsome

**ammunition** armaments, explosives, munitions, powder, rounds, shot and shell

**amnesty** absolution, dispensation, forgiveness, general pardon, immunity, oblivion, remission of *penalty*, reprieve

**among, amongst** amid, amidst, in association with, in the middle of, in the midst of, midst, with; between, to each of; in the company of, in the group of, in the number of, out of; by all of, by the joint action of, by the whole of, mutually,

**amp** n ampere; *Inf* amplifier

**ampere** n unit of electric current

**ampersand** n sign (&) meaning *and*

**amphetamine** n synthetic medicinal stimulant

**amphibian** n animal that lives first in water then on land; vehicle, plane adapted to land and water **amphibious** adj

**amphitheatre** n arena surrounded by rising tiers of seats

**ample** adj big enough; large, spacious **amply** adv

**amplify** v **-fying, -fied** increase; make bigger, louder etc. **amplification** n **amplifier** n

**amplitude** n spaciousness, width

**amputate** v cut off (limb etc.) **amputation** n

**amulet** n thing worn as a charm against evil

**amuse** v entertain; cause to laugh or smile **amusing** adj **amusement** n

**an** *see* A

**anachronism** n something put in wrong historical period

**anaconda** n large snake which kills by constriction

**anaemia** n deficiency of red blood cells **anaemic** adj pale, sickly

**anaesthetic** n/adj (drug) causing loss of sensation **anaesthetist** n **anaesthetize** v

**anagram** n word(s) whose letters can be rearranged to make new word(s)

**anal** *see* ANUS

**analgesic** adj/n (drug) relieving pain

**analogy** n likeness in certain respects **analogous** adj similar

**analysis** n (pl **-ses**) separation into elements or components; evaluation, study **analyse** v examine critically; determine constituent parts **analyst** n **analytical** adj

**anarchy** n absence of government and law; disorder **anarchic** adj **anarchist** n one who opposes all forms

with one another

**amount** expanse, extent, magnitude, mass, measure, number, quantity, supply, volume; addition, aggregate, extent, sum total, total, whole

**ample** abounding, abundant, big, bountiful, broad, capacious, commodious, copious, expansive, extensive, full, generous, great, large, lavish, liberal, plenteous, plentiful, plenty, profuse, rich, roomy, spacious, substantial, wide

**amuse** beguile, charm, cheer, divert, enliven, entertain, occupy, please, recreate, regale

**amusement** cheer, delight, diversion, enjoyment, entertainment, fun, gratification, interest, laughter,

merriment, mirth, pleasure, recreation, sport; distraction, diversion, entertainment, game, hobby, joke, lark, pastime, prank, recreation, sport

**amusing** charming, cheerful, comical, delightful, diverting, droll, enjoyable, entertaining, funny, humorous, interesting, jocular, laughable, lively, merry, pleasant, pleasing, witty

**analyse** estimate, evaluate, examine, investigate, judge, test; break down, consider, dissect, dissolve, divide, resolve, separate, study

**analysis** breakdown, dissection, dissolution, division, enquiry, examination, investigation, scrutiny, separation, sifting, test; estimation,

of government

**anathema** n anything detested; curse of excommunication or denunciation

**anatomy** n (study of) bodily structure; detailed analysis **anatomical** adj **anatomist** n

**ancestor** n person from whom another is descended; forerunner **ancestral** adj **ancestry** n

**anchor** n heavy implement dropped to stop vessel drifting; any similar device ~v secure with anchor **anchorage** n act, place of anchoring

**anchovy** n small savoury fish of herring family

**ancient** adj belonging to former age; very old

**ancillary** adj subordinate, auxiliary

**and** conj word used to join words and sentences, introduce a consequence etc.

**andante** adv/adj/n Mus moderately slow (passage)

**androgynous** adj having male

and female characteristics

**android** n robot resembling a human

**anecdote** n short account of a single incident **anecdotal** adj

**anemone** n flower related to buttercup

**anew** adv afresh, again

**angel** n divine messenger; guardian spirit; very kind person **angelic** adj

**anger** n extreme annoyance; wrath ~v make angry **angry** adj **angrily** adv

**angina** n severe pain accompanying heart disease

**angle** n meeting of two lines or surfaces; point of view ~v bend at an angle; fish **angler** n one who fishes for sport **angling** n

**Anglican** adj/n (member) of the Church of England

**Anglo-** comb. form English or British, as in **Anglo-Scottish, Anglo-American**

**angora** n goat with long white silky hair; cloth or wool of this

———— THESAURUS ————

evaluation, opinion, study

**ancestor** forebear, forefather, precursor, progenitor

**ancient** aged, antediluvian, antiquated, antique, archaic, early, hoary, old, olden, old-fashioned, out-of-date, superannuated, time-worn

**and** along with, also, as well as, furthermore, in addition to, including, moreover, plus, together with

**anecdote** reminiscence, short story, sketch, story, tale, yarn

**angel** archangel, cherub, divine messenger, guardian spirit, seraph

**anger** n annoyance, displeasure, exasperation, fury, ill humour, ill temper, indignation, ire, irritability,

irritation, outrage, passion, pique, rage, resentment, spleen, temper, vexation, wrath ~v affront, annoy, displease, enrage, exasperate, excite, gall, incense, infuriate, irritate, madden, nettle, offend, outrage, pique, provoke, rile, vex

**angle** n bend, corner, crook, crotch, cusp, edge, elbow, intersection, knee, nook, point; approach, aspect, outlook, perspective, point of view, position, side, slant, standpoint, viewpoint ~v cast, fish

**angler** fisher, fisherman

**angry** annoyed, choleric, displeased, enraged, exasperated, furious, heated, hot, ill-tempered, incensed, indignant, infuriated, iras-

**anguish** *n* great mental or bodily pain **anguished** *adj*

**angular** *adj* (of people) bony; having angles; measured by an angle

**animal** *n* living creature that can move at will; beast ~*adj* of animals; sensual

**animate** *v* give life to; enliven; inspire; actuate; make cartoon film of **animated** *adj* **animation** *n* **animator** *n*

**animosity** *n* hostility, enmity

**animus** *n* hatred; animosity

**aniseed** *n* liquorice-flavoured seed of plant

**ankle** *n* joint between foot and leg

**annals** *pl n* yearly records

**annex** *v* append, attach; take possession of **annexation** *n*

**annexe** *n* extension to a building; nearby building used as an extension

**annihilate** *v* reduce to nothing, destroy utterly **annihilation** *n*

**anniversary** *n* yearly return of a date; celebration of this

**anno Domini** *Lat* in the year of our Lord

**annotate** *v* make notes upon **annotation** *n*

**announce** *v* make known, proclaim **announcement** *n* **announcer** *n*

**annoy** *v* vex; irritate **annoyance** *n*

———————— THESAURUS ————————

cible, irate, ireful, irritable, irritated, nettled, outraged, passionate, piqued, provoked, raging, resentful, wrathful

**animal** *n* beast, brute, creature ~*adj* bestial, bodily, brutish, carnal, fleshly, gross, physical, sensual

**animate** *v* activate, embolden, encourage, enliven, excite, fire, impel, incite, inspire, invigorate, kindle, move, quicken, revive, rouse, spark, spur, stimulate, stir, urge

**animated** *adj* active, airy, ardent, brisk, buoyant, dynamic, ebullient, elated, energetic, enthusiastic, excited, fervent, lively, passionate, quick, sparky, spirited, sprightly, vibrant, vigorous, vital, vivacious, vivid, zealous, zestful

**animation** *n* action, activity, airiness, ardour, briskness, buoyancy, dynamism, ebullience, elation, energy, enthusiasm, excitement, exhilaration, fervour, gaiety, high spirits, life, liveliness, passion, pep, sparkle, spirit, sprightliness, verve, vibrancy, vigour, vitality, vivacity,

zeal, zest

**animosity** animus, antagonism, antipathy, bad blood, bitterness, enmity, hate, hatred, hostility, ill will, malice, rancour, resentment

**annihilate** abolish, destroy, eradicate, exterminate, extinguish, obliterate, wipe out

**announce** advertise, broadcast, declare, disclose, give out, intimate, make known, proclaim, promulgate, publish, report, reveal, tell

**announcement** advertisement, broadcast, bulletin, communiqué, declaration, disclosure, intimation, proclamation, publication, report, statement

**annoy** aggravate *Inf*, anger, bedevil, bore, bother, displease, disturb, exasperate, get on one's nerves *Inf*, harass, harry, hassle *Inf*, irk, irritate, madden, molest, nark *Brit*, *Aust, & NZ sl*, needle *Inf*, nettle, pester, plague, provoke, rile, ruffle, tease, trouble, vex

**annoyance** anger, bother, displeasure, disturbance, exaspera-

**annual** adj yearly ~n plant which completes its life cycle in a year; book published each year **annually** adv

**annul** v -nulling, -nulled make void, cancel **annulment** n

**anodyne** n thing that relieves pain or distress ~adj relieving pain or distress

**anoint** v smear with oil or ointment; consecrate with oil

**anomaly** n irregular or abnormal thing **anomalous** adj

**anon.** anonymous

**anonymous** adj without (author's) name **anonymously** adv **anonymity** n

**anorak** n waterproof hooded jacket

**anorexia** n loss of appetite **anorexic** adj/n

**another** pron/adj one other; a different one; one more

**answer** v reply (to); be accountable (for, to); match; suit ~n reply; solution **answerable** adj

**ant** n small social insect **anteater** n animal which feeds on ants

**antagonist** n opponent **antagonism** n **antagonistic** adj **antagonize**

v arouse hostility in

**Antarctic** adj/n (of) south polar regions

**ante-** comb. form before, as in **antechamber**

**antecedent** adj/n (thing) going before

**antelope** n deerlike animal

**antenatal** adj of care etc. during pregnancy

**antenna** n (pl -nae) insect's feeler; aerial

**anterior** adj to the front; before

**anthem** n song of loyalty; sacred choral piece

**anther** n pollen sac of flower

**anthology** n collection of poems

**anthracite** n slow-burning coal

**anthrax** n infectious disease of cattle and sheep

**anthropoid** adj/n manlike (ape)

**anthropology** n study of origins, development of human race

**anti-** comb. form against, as in **anti-aircraft**

**antibiotic** n/adj (of) substance used against bacterial infection

**antibody** n substance which counteracts bacteria

tion, hassle Inf, irritation, nuisance, provocation, trouble, vexation

**anomaly** abnormality, departure, eccentricity, exception, incongruity, inconsistency, irregularity, oddity, peculiarity, rarity

**anonymous** incognito, nameless, unacknowledged, unidentified, unknown, unnamed, unsigned

**answer** n acknowledgment, defence, explanation, reaction, refutation, rejoinder, reply, report, response, retort, return, riposte ~v acknowledge, explain, react, rejoin, reply, resolve, respond, retort, re-

turn, solve

**answerable** accountable, chargeable, liable, responsible, subject, to blame

**antagonism** antipathy, conflict, contention, discord, dissension, friction, hostility, rivalry

**antagonize** aggravate Inf, alienate, anger, annoy, disaffect, estrange, gall, insult, irritate, nark Brit, Aust, & NZ sl, offend, repel, rub (someone) up the wrong way Inf

**anthem** canticle, chant, chorale, hymn, psalm

**anticipate** v expect; look forward to; foresee **anticipation** n

**anticlimax** n sudden descent to the trivial or ludicrous

**anticlockwise** adv/adj in the opposite direction to the rotation of the hands of a clock

**antics** pl n absurd behaviour

**anticyclone** n high-pressure area and associated winds

**antidote** n counteracting remedy

**antifreeze** n liquid added to water to prevent freezing

**antihistamine** n drug used esp. to treat allergies

**antimony** n brittle, bluish-white metal

**antipathy** n dislike, aversion

**antiperspirant** n substance used to reduce sweating

**antipodes** pl n regions on opposite side of the globe **antipodean** adj

**antique** n object valued because of its age ~adj ancient; old-fashioned

**antiquarian** n collector of antiques

**antiquated** adj out-of-date antiq-

uity n great age; former times

**antiseptic** n/adj (substance) preventing infection ~adj free from infection

**antisocial** adj avoiding company; (of behaviour) harmful to society

**antithesis** n (pl -ses) direct opposite; contrast

**antler** n branching horn of certain deer

**antonym** n word of opposite meaning to another

**anus** n open end of rectum **anal** adj

**anvil** n heavy iron block on which a smith hammers metal

**anxious** adj uneasy; concerned **anxiety** n **anxiously** adv

**any** adj/pron one indefinitely; some; every **anybody** n **anyhow** adv **anyone** n **anything** n **anyway** adv **anywhere** adv

**aorta** n main artery carrying blood from the heart

**apace** adv swiftly

**apart** adv separately, aside; in pieces

**anticipate** await, count upon, expect, forecast, foresee, foretell, hope for, look for, predict

**anticipation** awaiting, expectancy, expectation, foresight, foretaste, forethought, hope, premonition

**anticlimax** bathos, disappointment, letdown

**antipathy** antagonism, aversion, bad blood, disgust, dislike, distaste, enmity, hatred, hostility, ill will, loathing, rancour, repugnance

**antique** adj aged, ancient, elderly, old, archaic, obsolete, old-fashioned, outdated ~n bygone, heirloom, relic

**antiquity** age, elderliness, old age, oldness; ancient times, distant past,

olden days

**antiseptic** adj aseptic, clean, hygienic, pure, sanitary, sterile, unpolluted ~n bactericide, disinfectant, germicide, purifier

**antisocial** alienated, misanthropic, reserved, retiring, unfriendly, unsociable, withdrawn

**anxiety** apprehension, care, concern, disquiet, distress, misgiving, nervousness, restlessness, solicitude, suspense, tension, unease, uneasiness, worry

**anxious** apprehensive, careful, concerned, distressed, disturbed, fearful, fretful, in suspense, nervous, restless, solicitous, tense, troubled, uneasy, watchful, worried

**apartheid** *n* (esp. formerly in S Africa) official policy of segregation

**apartment** *n* room; flat

**apathy** *n* indifference; lack of emotion **apathetic** *adj*

**ape** *n* tailless monkey; imitator ~*v* imitate

**aperitif** *n* alcoholic appetizer

**aperture** *n* opening, hole

**apex** *n* (*pl* **apexes**, **apices**) top, peak; vertex

**aphid** *n* small insect which sucks the sap from plants

**aphorism** *n* maxim, clever saying

**aphrodisiac** *adj/n* (substance) exciting sexual desire

**apiece** *adv* for each

**aplomb** *n* assurance

**apocalypse** *n* prophetic revelation, esp. of the end of the world **apocalyptic** *adj*

**apocryphal** *adj* of questionable authenticity

**apology** *n* expression of regret for a fault; poor substitute (for) **apologetic** *adj* **apologetically** *adv* **apologize** *v*

**apoplexy** *n* paralysis caused by broken or blocked blood vessel in the brain **apoplectic** *adj* of apoplexy; *Inf* furious

**Apostle** *n* one of the first disciples of Jesus; (*without cap*.) enthusiastic supporter of a cause

**apostrophe** *n* mark (') showing omission of letter(s)

**appal** *v* **-palling**, **-palled** dismay, terrify **appalling** *adj Inf* terrible

**apparatus** *n* equipment for performing experiment, operation etc.

**apparel** *n* clothing

**apparent** *adj* seeming; obvious; acknowledged **apparently** *adv*

**apparition** *n* ghost

————————— THESAURUS —————————

**apart** afar, alone, aside, away, cut off, distant, distinct, divorced, excluded, independent, isolated, separate, singly, to itself, to oneself, to one side; asunder, in bits, in pieces, into parts, to bits, to pieces

**apartment** accommodation, compartment, quarters, room, rooms, suite

**apathetic** cool, emotionless, impassive, insensible, passive, stoic, stoical, torpid, unconcerned, unemotional, unfeeling, uninterested, unmoved, unresponsive

**apathy** coolness, impassivity, indifference, listlessness, passivity, stoicism, torpor, unconcern, unresponsiveness

**apocryphal** doubtful, dubious, equivocal, fictitious, legendary, mythical, questionable, spurious, unsubstantiated, unverified

**apologetic** contrite, penitent, sorry

**apologize** ask forgiveness, beg pardon, express regret, say sorry

**apology** confession, defence, excuse, extenuation, vindication

**appal** alarm, astound, daunt, dismay, harrow, horrify, outrage, petrify, scare, shock, terrify, unnerve

**appalling** alarming, astounding, awful, daunting, dire, dreadful, fearful, frightful, ghastly, godawful *Sl*, grim, harrowing, hellacious *US sl*, hideous, horrible, horrid, horrifying, intimidating, petrifying, scaring, shocking, terrible, terrifying

**apparatus** appliance, device, equipment, gear, implements, machine, machinery, materials, means, mechanism, outfit, tackle, tools, utensils

**apparent** blatant, clear, conspicu-

**appeal** v (*with* to) make earnest request; be attractive; apply to higher court ~n request; attractiveness **appealing** adj

**appear** v become visible or present; seem, be plain; be seen in public; perform **appearance** n an appearing; aspect; pretence

**appease** v pacify, satisfy **appeasement** n

**append** v join on, add

**appendicitis** n inflammation of the appendix

**appendix** n (pl **-dixes**, **-dices**) supplement; *Anat* small worm-shaped part of the intestine

**appertain** v belong, relate to

**appetite** n desire, inclination, esp. for food **appetizer** n something stimulating appetite **appetizing** adj

**applaud** v praise by clapping; praise loudly **applause** n

**apple** n round, firm fleshy fruit; tree bearing it

**appliance** n piece of equipment, esp. electrical

——————— THESAURUS ———————

ous, discernible, distinct, evident, indubitable, manifest, marked, obvious, open, overt, patent, plain, understandable, unmistakable, visible

**apparently** it appears that, it seems that, on the face of it, ostensibly, outwardly, seemingly, superficially

**appeal** n entreaty, invocation, petition, plea, prayer, request, suit, supplication; allure, attraction, beauty, charm, fascination ~v adjure, apply, ask, beg, beseech, call, call upon, entreat, implore, petition, plead, pray, refer, request, solicit, sue, supplicate; allure, attract, charm, engage, entice, fascinate, interest, invite, please, tempt

**appear** arise, arrive, attend, be present, come forth, come into sight, come out, come to light, develop, emerge, issue, loom, materialize, occur, surface, turn out, turn up; look (like *or* as if), occur, seem, strike one as; be apparent, be clear, be evident, be obvious, be plain; act, enter, perform, play, play a part, take part

**appearance** advent, arrival, debut, emergence, introduction, presence; air, aspect, bearing, demeanour, expression, face, figure, form, image, look, looks, manner; front, guise, image, impression, outward show, pretence

**appendix** addition, adjunct, postscript, supplement

**appetite** craving, demand, desire, hunger, liking, longing, passion, relish, stomach, taste, zeal, zest

**appetizing** delicious, inviting, mouthwatering, palatable, savoury

**applaud** approve, cheer, clap, commend, eulogize, extol, laud, praise

**applause** acclamation, approval, cheering, cheers, hand-clapping, laudation, ovation, plaudit, praise

**appliance** apparatus, device, gadget, implement, instrument, machine, mechanism, tool

**applicable** apposite, appropriate, apt, fit, fitting, germane, pertinent, relevant, suitable, useful

**applicant** candidate, inquirer, petitioner, suitor, suppliant

**application** function, pertinence, practice, purpose, relevance, use, value; appeal, claim, inquiry, petition, request, requisition, suit; assiduity, attentiveness, commitment,

**apply** v **-plying, -plied** utilize; lay or place on; devote; have reference (to); make request (to) **applicable** adj relevant **applicant** n **application** n request for a job etc.; diligence; use, function **applied** adj put to practical use

**appoint** v assign to a job or position; fix, equip **appointment** n engagement to meet; (selection for a) job

**apportion** v divide out in shares

**apposite** adj appropriate

**appraise** v estimate value of **appraisal** n

**appreciate** v value at true worth; be grateful for; understand; rise in value **appreciable** adj noticeable **appreciably** adv **appreciation** n **appreciative** adj

**apprehend** v arrest; understand; dread **apprehension** n anxiety **apprehensive** adj

**apprentice** n person learning a

———— THESAURUS ————

dedication, diligence, effort, hard work, industry, perseverance, study

**apply** bring into play, bring to bear, carry out, employ, engage, execute, exercise, exert, practise, put to use, use, utilize; appertain, be applicable, be appropriate, bear upon, be fitting, be relevant, fit, pertain, refer, relate, suit; anoint, bring into contact with, cover with, lay on, paint, place, put on, smear, spread on, touch to; claim, inquire, make application, petition, put in, request, requisition, solicit, sue; be diligent, be industrious, commit, concentrate, dedicate, devote, direct, give, pay attention, persevere, study, try, work hard

**appoint** assign, choose, commission, delegate, elect, install, name, nominate, select

**appointment** arrangement, assignation, consultation, date, engagement, interview, meeting, rendezvous, session; assignment, job, office, place, position, post, situation

**apportion** allocate, allot, assign, deal, dispense, distribute, divide, dole out, measure out, mete out, share

**appreciate** be appreciative, be grateful for, be indebted, be

obliged, be thankful for, give thanks for; acknowledge, be alive to, know, perceive, realize, recognize, take account of, understand; esteem, like, prize, rate highly, regard, relish, respect, savour, treasure, value; gain, grow, improve, increase, inflate, rise

**appreciation** acknowledgment, gratitude, indebtedness, obligation, thanks; admiration, assessment, awareness, cognizance, enjoyment, esteem, knowledge, liking, perception, realization, recognition, regard, relish, respect, sensitivity, sympathy, valuation; gain, growth, improvement, increase, rise

**appreciative** beholden, grateful, indebted, obliged, thankful; admiring, aware, cognizant, conscious, enthusiastic, mindful, perceptive, pleased, respectful, responsive, sensitive, sympathetic, understanding

**apprehend** arrest, capture, catch, lift Sl, pinch Inf, run in Sl, seize, take, take prisoner; appreciate, comprehend, conceive, grasp, know, perceive, realize, recognize, think, understand

**apprehension** alarm, anxiety, concern, disquiet, doubt, dread, fear, foreboding, misgiving, mis-

trade; novice

**apprise** v inform

**approach** v draw near (to); set about; address request to; approximate to ~n a drawing near; means of reaching or doing; approximation **approachable** adj

**approbation** n approval

**appropriate** adj suitable, fitting ~v

**approve** v think well of, commend; authorize **approval** n

**approx.** approximate(ly)

**approximate** v nearly correct; inexact ~v come or bring close; be almost the same as **approximately** adv **approximation** n

take for oneself; allocate **appropriately** adv

trust, trepidation, unease, uneasiness, worry

**apprehensive** afraid, alarmed, anxious, concerned, fearful, foreboding, mistrustful, uneasy, worried

**apprentice** beginner, learner, novice, pupil, student

**approach** v advance, catch up, come close, come near, come to, draw near, gain on, meet, move towards, near, push forward, reach; appeal to, apply to, make advances to, make a proposal to, make overtures to, sound out; approximate, be comparable to, be like, come close to, come near to, compare with, resemble ~n access, advance, advent, arrival, avenue, coming, drawing near, entrance, nearing, passage, road, way; approximation, likeness, semblance; attitude, course, manner, means, method, mode, procedure, style, technique, way

**appropriate** adj apposite, apropos, apt, becoming, befitting, belonging, congruous, correct, felicitous, fit, fitting, opportune, pertinent, proper, relevant, right, seemly, suitable, to the point, to the purpose, well-suited, well-timed ~v annex, arrogate, assume, commandeer, confiscate, expropriate, impound, seize, take, take over, take

possession of, usurp

**approval** acquiescence, agreement, assent, authorization, blessing, compliance, confirmation, consent, countenance, endorsement, leave, licence, mandate, O.K. or okay Inf, permission, sanction, the go-ahead Inf, the green light Inf; acclaim, admiration, applause, appreciation, approbation, commendation, esteem, favour, good opinion, liking, praise, regard, respect

**approve** acclaim, admire, applaud, appreciate, be pleased with, commend, esteem, favour, have a good opinion of, like, praise, regard highly, respect, think highly of; accede to, accept, advocate, agree to, allow, assent to, authorize, bless, concur in, confirm, consent to, countenance, endorse, give the go-ahead Inf, give the green light Inf, go along with, mandate, O.K. or okay Inf, pass, permit, ratify, recommend, uphold

**approximate** adj close, near; estimated, inexact, loose, rough ~v approach, border on, come close, come near, resemble, touch, verge on

**approximately** about, almost, around, circa used with dates, close to, generally, just about, loosely, more or less, nearly, not far off,

**Apr.** April

**après-ski** n social activities after skiing

**apricot** n orange-coloured fruit related to plum

**April** n fourth month

**apron** n covering worn in front to protect clothes; in theatre, strip of stage before curtain; on airfield, tarmac area where aircraft stand, are loaded etc.

**apropos** adv with reference to ~adj appropriate

**apt** adj suitable; likely; quick-witted **aptitude** n **aptly** adv

**aqualung** n breathing apparatus used in underwater swimming

**aquamarine** n precious stone ~adj greenish-blue

**aquarium** n (pl **aquariums**, **aquaria**) tank for water animals or plants

**aquatic** adj living, growing, done in or on water

**aqueduct** n artificial channel for water, esp. one like a bridge

**aquiline** adj like an eagle

**arable** adj suitable for growing crops

**arbiter** n judge, umpire **arbitrary** adj despotic; random **arbitrate** v settle (dispute) impartially **arbitration** n **arbitrator** n

**arboreal** adj of or living in trees

**arc** n part of circumference of circle or similar curve

**arcade** n row of arches on pillars; covered walk or avenue

**arcane** adj secret

**arch¹** n curved structure spanning an opening; a curved shape; curved part of the sole of the foot ~v form, make into, an arch

**arch²** adj knowingly playful

**arch-** comb. form chief, as in **arch-angel**, **archenemy**

**archaeology** n study of ancient times from remains **archaeologist** n

——————————— THESAURUS ———————————

relatively, roughly

**approximation** conjecture, estimate, estimation, guess, guesswork, rough calculation, rough idea

**apt** applicable, apposite, appropriate, befitting, correct, fit, fitting, germane, pertinent, proper, relevant, seemly, suitable, to the point, to the purpose; disposed, given, inclined, liable, likely, of a mind, prone, ready; astute, bright, clever, expert, gifted, ingenious, intelligent, prompt, quick, sharp, skilful, smart, talented, teachable

**aptitude** bent, disposition, inclination, leaning, predilection, proclivity, proneness, propensity, tendency; ability, aptness, capability, capacity, cleverness, faculty, flair, gift, giftedness, intelligence, knack, pro-

ficiency, quickness, talent; applicability, appositeness, appropriateness, fitness, relevance, suitability, suitableness

**arbitrary** capricious, erratic, fanciful, inconsistent, optional, personal, random, subjective, unreasonable, whimsical, wilful

**arbitrate** adjudge, adjudicate, decide, determine, judge, mediate, referee, settle, umpire

**arbitration** adjudication, decision, judgment, settlement

**arc** arch, bend, bow, crescent, curve, half-moon

**arch¹** archway, curve, dome, span, vault

**arch²** artful, frolicsome, knowing, mischievous, pert, playful, roguish, saucy, sly, waggish, wily

**archaic** *adj* old, primitive **archaism** *n* word no longer in use

**archbishop** *n* chief bishop

**archery** *n* skill, sport of shooting with bow and arrow **archer** *n*

**archetype** *n* prototype; perfect specimen **archetypal** *adj*

**archipelago** *n* (*pl* **-go(e)s**) group of islands

**architect** *n* person qualified to design buildings; contriver **architecture** *n*

**archives** *pl n* collection of records, documents etc.

**Arctic** *adj* of north polar region; (*without cap.*) very cold *~n* north polar region

**ardent** *adj* intensely enthusiastic;

passionate **ardently** *adv*

**ardour** *n* enthusiasm; zeal

**arduous** *adj* hard to accomplish

**are** *pres. tense of* BE (*used with you, we and they*)

**area** *n* surface extent; two-dimensional expanse enclosed by boundary; region; part; field of activity

**arena** *n* space in middle of amphitheatre or stadium; sphere; territory

**argon** *n* gas found in the air

**argue** *v* quarrel, offer reasons (for); debate **arguable** *adj* **arguably** *adv* **argument** *n* **argumentative** *adj*

**aria** *n* song in opera etc.

**arid** *adj* dry; dull

**arise** *v* **arising, arose, arisen** get up;

---

## THESAURUS

**architect** designer, master builder, planner

**architecture** building, construction, design, planning

**archives** annals, chronicles, documents, papers, records, registers, rolls

**ardent** avid, eager, enthusiastic, fervent, fiery, hot, impassioned, intense, keen, passionate, spirited, vehement, warm, zealous

**ardour** avidity, eagerness, enthusiasm, feeling, fervour, fire, heat, intensity, keenness, passion, spirit, vehemence, warmth, zeal

**arduous** burdensome, difficult, exhausting, fatiguing, hard, harsh, heavy, onerous, painful, punishing, rigorous, severe, steep, strenuous, taxing, tiring, tough, troublesome

**area** district, locality, neighbourhood, patch, plot, realm, region, sector, sphere, stretch, territory, tract, turf *US sl,* zone; part, portion, section, sector

**arena** amphitheatre, field, ground,

park *US & Canad,* ring, stadium, stage; battleground, domain, field, lists, province, realm, scene, scope, sphere, territory, theatre

**argue** altercate, bandy words, bicker, disagree, dispute, fall out *Inf,* feud, fight, have an argument, quarrel, squabble, wrangle; assert, claim, contend, controvert, debate, discuss, dispute, expostulate, hold, maintain, plead, question, reason, remonstrate; demonstrate, evince, exhibit, imply, indicate, point to, show, suggest

**argument** altercation, barney *Inf,* clash, controversy, difference of opinion, disagreement, dispute, feud, fight, quarrel, row, squabble, wrangle; assertion, claim, contention, debate, discussion, dispute, plea, pleading, remonstrance, remonstration; case, defence, dialectic, ground(s), logic, polemic, reason, reasoning

**argumentative** belligerent, combative, contrary, opinionated,

rise (up); come about

**aristocracy** n upper classes **aristocrat** n **aristocratic** adj

**arithmetic** n science of numbers

**ark** n Noah's vessel

**arm**[1] n upper limb from shoulder to wrist; anything similar, as branch of sea, supporting rail of chair etc.; sleeve **armful** n **armhole** n **armpit** n hollow under arm at shoulder

**arm**[2] v supply with weapons; take up arms ~pl n weapons; war; heraldic emblem

**armada** n large fleet

**armadillo** n (pl **-los**) S Amer. animal protected by bony plates

**armistice** n truce

**armour** n defensive covering; plating of tanks, warships etc.; armoured fighting vehicles **armoury** n

**army** n military land force; great number

**aroma** n sweet smell **aromatic** adj

**around** prep/adv on all sides (of); somewhere in or near; approximately; in a circle; here and there

**arouse** v awaken, stimulate

**arraign** v accuse, indict

**arrange** v set in proper order; make agreement; plan; adapt music

————— THESAURUS —————

**quarrelsome**

**arid** barren, desert, dried up, dry, parched, sterile, torrid, waterless

**arise** appear, begin, come to light, commence, crop up *Inf*, emanate, emerge, ensue, follow, happen, issue, occur, originate, proceed, result, set in, spring, start, stem; ascend, climb, lift, mount, move upward, rise, soar, tower

**aristocracy** elite, gentry, *haut monde*, nobility, noblesse *Lit*, patricians, peerage, upper class

**aristocrat** aristo *Inf*, grandee, lady, lord, noble, nobleman, patrician, peer

**aristocratic** blue-blooded, elite, gentlemanly, highborn, lordly, noble, patrician, titled, upper-class, well-born

**arm**[1] n appendage, limb, upper limb; bough, branch, department, division, extension, offshoot, section, sector

**arm**[2] v *esp. with weapons* array, deck out, equip, furnish, issue with, outfit, provide, rig, supply; mobilize, muster forces, prepare for war, take up arms

**armour** armour plate, covering, protection, sheathing, shield

**army** armed force, land forces, legions, military, soldiers, soldiery, troops; array, horde, host, multitude, pack, swarm, throng, vast number

**aroma** bouquet, fragrance, odour, perfume, redolence, savour, scent, smell

**aromatic** balmy, fragrant, perfumed, pungent, redolent, savoury, spicy

**around** *prep* about, encircling, enclosing, on all sides of, surrounding; about, approximately, circa *used with dates*, roughly ~*adv* about, all over, everywhere, here and there, in all directions, on all sides, throughout, to and fro; at hand, close, close at hand, close by, near, nearby, nigh *Arch or dial*

**arouse** agitate, awaken, call forth, enliven, excite, foster, goad, incite, inflame, instigate, kindle, move, provoke, quicken, rouse, sharpen, spark, spur, stimulate, stir up, summon up, waken, wake up, warm, whet, whip up

**arrangement** n

**array** n order, esp. military; dress; imposing show ~v set out; dress richly

**arrears** pl n money owed

**arrest** v detain by legal authority; stop; catch attention ~n seizure by warrant **arresting** adj striking

**arrive** v reach destination; (with at) reach, attain; Inf succeed **arrival** n

**arrogance** n conceit **arrogant** adj **arrogantly** adv

**arrow** n shaft shot from bow

**arsenal** n stores for guns etc.

**arsenic** n soft, grey, very poisonous metallic element

**arson** n crime of intentionally setting property on fire

**art** n human skill as opposed to nature; creative skill in painting, poetry, music etc.; any of the works produced thus; craft; knack; pl branches of learning other than science; wiles **artful** adj wily **artfully** adv **artist** n one who practises fine art, esp. painting **artiste** n professional entertainer **artistic** adj **artistry** n **artless** adj natural, frank **arty** adj ostentatiously artistic

**artefact**, **artifact** n something made by man

**artery** n tube carrying blood from heart; any main channel of communications

**arthritis** n painful inflammation of joint(s) **arthritic** adj/n

———————— THESAURUS ————————

**arrange** array, class, dispose, file, form, group, line up, marshal, order, organize, position, range, rank, set out, sort; adjust, agree to, come to terms, compromise, construct, contrive, determine, devise, plan, prepare, schedule, settle; adapt, instrument, orchestrate, score

**arrangement** array, classification, design, display, disposition, form, line-up, order, organization, rank, setup Inf, structure, system; adaptation, instrumentation, interpretation, orchestration, score, version

**array** arrangement, collection, display, disposition, exhibition, formation, line-up, marshalling, muster, order, parade, show, supply

**arrest** v apprehend, capture, catch, detain, lay hold of, lift Sl, run in Sl, seize, take, take into custody, take prisoner ~n apprehension, capture, cop Sl, detention, seizure

**arrival** advent, appearance, entrance, occurrence, taking place

**arrive** appear, befall, come, enter, get to, happen, occur, reach, show up Inf, take place, turn up

**arrogance** bluster, conceit, hauteur, insolence, loftiness, lordliness, pomposity, pompousness, presumption, pretentiousness, pride, scornfulness, superciliousness, swagger

**arrogant** assuming, blustering, conceited, contemptuous, disdainful, haughty, high-handed, imperious, insolent, lordly, overbearing, pompous, presumptuous, pretentious, proud, scornful, supercilious

**arsenal** ammunition dump, armoury, arms depot, magazine, ordnance depot, stock, stockpile, store, storehouse, supply

**art** adroitness, aptitude, artistry, craft, craftsmanship, dexterity, expertise, facility, ingenuity, knack, knowledge, mastery, method, profession, skill, trade, virtuosity

**artful** crafty, cunning, deceitful, designing, intriguing, sharp, shrewd, sly, tricky, wily

**artichoke** *n* thistle-like plant with edible flower

**article** *n* item, object; short written piece; *Grammar* words *the*, *a*, *an*; clause in a contract **articled** *adj* bound as an apprentice

**articulate** *adj* fluent; clear, distinct ~*v* utter distinctly **articulated** *adj* jointed

**artifice** *n* contrivance, trick **artificial** *adj* synthetic; insincere **artificially** *adv*

**artillery** *n* large guns on wheels; troops who use them

**artisan** *n* craftsman

**artiste** *see* ART

**as** *adv/conj* denoting: comparison; similarity; equality; identity; concurrence; reason

**asbestos** *n* fibrous mineral which does not burn

**ascend** *v* go, come up; climb **ascendancy** *n* dominance **ascent** *n*

**ascertain** *v* find out

**ascetic** *n/adj* (person) practising severe self-denial

**ascribe** *v* attribute, assign

**asexual** *adj* without sex

**ash**¹ *n* remains of anything burnt **ashen** *adj* pale

**ash**² *n* deciduous timber tree; its wood

**ashamed** *adj* feeling shame

**ashore** *adv* on shore

**aside** *adv* to, on one side; privately ~*n* words spoken so as not to be

——— THESAURUS ———

**article** commodity, item, object, piece, substance, thing, unit; composition, discourse, essay, feature, item, paper, piece, story, treatise

**articulate** *adj* clear, coherent, comprehensible, eloquent, expressive, fluent, intelligible, lucid, meaningful, vocal ~*v* enunciate, express, pronounce, say, speak, state, talk, utter, voice

**artificial** man-made, manufactured, plastic, synthetic; bogus, counterfeit, ersatz, fake, imitation, mock, sham, simulated, specious, spurious

**artistic** aesthetic, beautiful, creative, cultivated, cultured, decorative, elegant, exquisite, graceful, imaginative, refined, sensitive, stylish

**as** *conj* at the time that, during the time that, just as, when, while; in the manner that, in the way that, like; because, considering that, seeing that, since; in the same manner with, in the same way that, like; for

instance, like, such as ~*prep* being, in the character of, in the role of, under the name of

**ascend** climb, float up, fly up, go up, lift off, mount, move up, rise, scale, slope upwards, soar, take off, tower

**ascent** climb, climbing, mounting, rise, rising, scaling, upward movement; gradient, incline, ramp, rise, upward slope

**ascetic** abstainer, hermit, monk, nun, recluse ~*adj* abstemious, abstinent, austere, celibate, frugal, harsh, plain, puritanical, rigorous, self-denying, self-disciplined, severe, Spartan, stern

**ascribe** assign, attribute, charge, credit, impute, put down, refer, set down

**ashamed** bashful, blushing, crestfallen, discomfited, distressed, embarrassed, guilty, humiliated, mortified, prudish, reluctant, remorseful, shamefaced, sheepish, shy, sorry

heard by all

**asinine** *adj* stupid, silly

**ask** *v* make request or inquiry; invite; require

**askance** *adv* with mistrust

**askew** *adv* awry

**asleep** *adj/adv* sleeping

**asp** *n* small poisonous snake

**asparagus** *n* plant with edible young shoots

**aspect** *n* appearance; outlook; side

**aspen** *n* type of poplar tree

**aspersion** *n* (*usu. pl*) malicious remark

**asphalt** *n* covering for road surfaces etc.

**asphyxiate** *v* suffocate **asphyxiation** *n*

**aspic** *n* jelly used to coat meat, eggs, fish etc.

**aspidistra** *n* plant with long tapered leaves

**aspire** *v* have great ambition **aspiration** *n* **aspiring** *adj*

**aspirin** *n* (tablet of) drug used to relieve pain and fever

**ass** *n* donkey; fool

**assail** *v* attack, assault; criticize **assailable** *adj* **assailant** *n*

**assassin** *n* one who kills for money or political reasons **assassinate** *v* **assassination** *n*

**assault** *n/v* attack

**assemble** *v* meet, bring together; put together **assembly** *n*

**assent** *v* agree ~*n* agreement

———————————— THESAURUS ————————————

**aside** alone, alongside, apart, away, beside, in reserve, on one side, out of mind, privately, separately, to one side, to the side

**ask** inquire, interrogate, query, question, quiz, appeal, apply, beg, beseech, claim, crave, demand, entreat, implore, petition, plead, pray, request, seek, solicit, sue, supplicate; bid, invite, summon

**asleep** dead to the world *Inf*, dormant, dozing, sleeping, slumbering

**aspect** air, appearance, attitude, bearing, condition, countenance, demeanour, expression, look, manner; angle, facet, feature, side

**aspire** aim, crave, desire, dream, hanker, hope, long, pursue, seek, wish

**aspiring** *adj* ambitious, eager, hopeful, wishful, would-be

**assassin** executioner, hatchet man *Sl*, hit man *Sl*, killer, murderer

**assassinate** blow away *Sl*, *chiefly US*, eliminate *Sl*, hit *Sl*, kill, liquidate, murder, slay

**assault** *n* aggression, attack, charge, invasion, offensive, storm, storming, strike ~*v* attack, charge, invade, lay into *Inf*, set about, set upon, storm

**assemble** accumulate, amass, bring together, call together, collect, come together, congregate, convene, convoke, flock, forgather, gather, marshal, meet, muster, rally, summon; connect, construct, erect, fabricate, fit together, join, make, piece together, set up

**assembly** accumulation, aggregation, body, collection, company, conference, congregation, council, crowd, diet, flock, gathering, group, house, mass, meeting, rally, throng; construction, erection, fabrication, manufacture

**assent** *v* accede, accept, acquiesce, agree, allow, approve, comply, concur, consent, grant, permit ~*n* acceptance, accord, acquiescence, agreement, approval, consent, permission, sanction

**assert** v declare strongly, insist upon **assertion** n **assertive** adj **assertively** adv

**assess** v fix value or amount of; evaluate **assessment** n **assessor** n

**asset** n valuable or useful person, thing; pl things that can be used to raise money

**assiduous** adj persevering **assiduously** adv

**assign** v appoint; allot; transfer as-

**signation** n secret meeting **assignment** n

**assimilate** v take in; incorporate; (cause to) become similar **assimilation** n

**assist** v give help to **assistance** n **assistant** n

**associate** v link, connect; join; keep company; combine, unite ~n partner; friend; subordinate member ~adj affiliated **association** n

—————— THESAURUS ——————

**assert** affirm, allege, avow, contend, declare, maintain, profess, state, swear

**assertion** affirmation, allegation, attestation, avowal, contention, declaration, profession, pronouncement, statement, defence, insistence, maintenance, stressing, vindication

**assertive** aggressive, confident, decided, decisive, demanding, dogmatic, domineering, emphatic, firm, forceful, forward, insistent, overbearing, positive, self-assured, strong-willed

**assess** compute, determine, estimate, evaluate, fix, gauge, judge, rate, value, weigh; fix, impose, levy, rate, tax, value

**assessment** determination, estimate, judgment, rating, valuation; charge, demand, duty, evaluation, impost, levy, rate, rating, tax, taxation, toll

**asset** advantage, aid, benefit, blessing, boon, help, resource, service; pl capital, estate, funds, goods, holdings, means, money, possessions, property, reserves, resources, valuables, wealth

**assign** appoint, choose, name, nominate, select; allocate, allot, consign, give, grant

**assignment** appointment, charge, commission, duty, job, mission, position, post, responsibility, task

**assist** aid, back, boost, collaborate, cooperate, expedite, facilitate, further, help, reinforce, second, serve, succour, support, sustain, work for, work with

**assistance** aid, backing, boost, collaboration, cooperation, furtherance, help, helping hand, reinforcement, relief, service, succour, support

**assistant** accessory, accomplice, aide, ally, associate, auxiliary, backer, collaborator, colleague, helper, helpmate, henchman, partner

**associate** v affiliate, ally, combine, connect, couple, join, league, link, mix, pair, relate, unite, yoke ~n ally, colleague, companion, comrade, co-worker, follower, friend, mate, partner

**association** alliance, band, clique, club, company, confederacy, confederation, cooperative, corporation, federation, fraternity, group, league, order, partnership, society, syndicate, union; blend, bond, combination, concomitance, connection, correlation, identification, mixture, pairing, relation, tie, union

**assonance** n rhyming of vowel sounds but not consonants

**assorted** adj mixed **assortment** n mixture

**assume** v take for granted; pretend; take on **assumption** n

**assure** v tell positively, promise; make sure; insure against loss, esp. of life **assurance** n **assured** adj sure; confident, self-possessed

**aster** n plant with starlike flowers

**asterisk** n star (*) used in printing

**astern** adv in, behind the stern; backwards

**asteroid** n small planet

**asthma** n illness in which one has difficulty breathing **asthmatic** adj/n

**astigmatism** n inability of lens (esp. of eye) to focus properly

**astir** adv on the move

**astonish** v amaze, surprise, stun

**astonishment** n

**astound** v astonish greatly **astounding** adj

**astral** adj of the stars

**astray** adv/adj off the right path; into error or sin

**astride** adv with legs apart

**astringent** adj sharp; stopping bleeding ~n astringent substance

**astrology** n foretelling of events by stars **astrologer** n **astrological** adj

**astronaut** n one trained for travel in space

**astronomy** n scientific study of heavenly bodies **astronomer** n astronomical adj very large; of astronomy **astronomically** adv

**astute** adj perceptive, shrewd **astutely** adv

**asunder** adv apart; in pieces

**asylum** n refuge, place of safety;

─────────────── THESAURUS ───────────────

**assorted** different, diverse, diversified, heterogeneous, mixed, motley, sundry, varied, various

**assortment** array, choice, collection, diversity, hotchpotch, jumble, medley, *mélange*, miscellany, mishmash, mixture, selection, variety

**assume** accept, believe, expect, fancy, imagine, presuppose, suppose, surmise, suspect, take for granted, think; affect, feign, imitate, impersonate, mimic, put on, sham, simulate; accept, enter upon, put on, set about, shoulder, take on, take over, take responsibility for, take up, undertake

**assumption** belief, conjecture, inference, premise, premiss, presumption, surmise

**assurance** affirmation, declaration, guarantee, oath, pledge, promise, vow, word, word of honour

**assure** guarantee, pledge, promise, swear, vow; make certain, make sure, seal, secure

**astonish** amaze, astound, bewilder, confound, daze, stagger, stupefy, surprise

**astonishment** amazement, awe, bewilderment, stupefaction, surprise, wonder

**astounding** amazing, astonishing, bewildering, breathtaking, impressive, staggering, striking, stunning, stupefying, surprising

**astray** adj/adv adrift, afield, amiss, lost, off, off course, off the mark, off the right track, off the subject; into error, into sin, to the bad, wrong

**astute** adroit, artful, bright, calculating, canny, clever, crafty, cunning, intelligent, keen, knowing, perceptive, sagacious, sharp, shrewd, sly, subtle, wily

*Obs* mental hospital

**asymmetry** *n* lack of symmetry **asymmetrical** *adj*

**at** *prep/adv* denoting: location in space or time; rate; condition or state; amount; direction; cause

**atheism** *n* belief that there is no God **atheist** *n*

**athletics** *pl n* sports such as running, jumping, throwing etc. **athlete** *n* **athletic** *adj* **athleticism** *n*

**atlas** *n* book of maps

**atmosphere** *n* gases surrounding earth etc.; prevailing mood **atmospheric** *adj* **atmospherics** *pl n* radio interference

**atoll** *n* ring-shaped coral island enclosing lagoon

**atom** *n* smallest unit of matter which can enter into chemical combination; any very small particle **atomic** *adj* **atomizer** *n* instrument for discharging liquids in a fine spray **atomic bomb** bomb with immense power derived from nuclear fission or fusion **atomic energy** nuclear energy

**atonal** *adj* (of music) not in an established key

**atone** *v* make amends (for) **atonement** *n*

**atop** *prep* on top of

**atrocious** *adj* extremely cruel; horrifying; *Inf* very bad **atrociously** *adv* **atrocity** *n*

**atrophy** *n* wasting away ~*v* -phying, -phied waste away

**attach** *v* join; fasten; attribute **attached** *adj* (with to) fond of **attachment** *n*

**attaché** *n* specialist attached to diplomatic mission **attaché case** flat rectangular briefcase

**attack** *v* take action against; criti-

**asylum** harbour, haven, refuge, retreat, safety, sanctuary, shelter; *Old-fashioned* funny farm *Facetious*, hospital, institution, loony bin *Sl*, madhouse *Inf*, mental hospital, nuthouse *Sl*, psychiatric hospital

**atheism** godlessness, paganism, scepticism

**atheist** pagan, sceptic, unbeliever

**athlete** competitor, contender, contestant, runner, sportsman

**athletic** *adj* able-bodied, active, energetic, fit, muscular, powerful, robust, strapping, strong, sturdy, vigorous ~*pl n* contests, exercises, gymnastics, races, sports

**atmosphere** air, heavens, sky; air, aura, character, climate, feel, feeling, flavour, mood, quality, spirit, surroundings, tone, vibes *Sl*

**atom** fragment, grain, iota, jot, mite, molecule, particle, scrap, shred, speck, spot, tittle, trace, whit

**atone** (with for) answer for, compensate, do penance for, make amends for, make redress, make reparation for, make up for, pay for, recompense, redress

**atrocious** barbaric, brutal, cruel, fiendish, infamous, infernal, inhuman, monstrous, ruthless, savage, vicious, wicked

**atrocity** abomination, barbarity, brutality, crime, cruelty, enormity, evil, horror, outrage, villainy

**attach** add, adhere, bind, connect, couple, fasten, fix, join, link, secure, stick, tie, unite

**attached** affectionate towards, devoted, fond of, possessive

**attachment** bond, clamp, connection, connector, coupling, fastening, joint, junction, link, tie

cize; set about with vigour; affect adversely ~n attacking action; bout **attacker** n

**attain** v arrive at; achieve **attainable** adj **attainment** n

**attempt** v/n try

**attend** v be present at; accompany; (with **to**) take care of; pay attention to **attendance** n an attending; persons attending **attendant** n/adj **attention** n notice; heed; care; cour-

tesy **attentive** adj giving attention; considerably helpful

**attest** v bear witness to

**attic** n space within roof

**attire** v/n dress, array

**attitude** n mental view, opinion; posture, pose; disposition, behaviour

**attorney** n person legally appointed to act for another, esp. a lawyer

**attract** v draw (attention etc.);

---

THESAURUS

**attack** n assault, charge, foray, incursion, inroad, invasion, offensive, onset, onslaught, raid, rush, strike; access, bout, convulsion, fit, paroxysm, seizure, spasm, spell, stroke ~v assault, charge, fall upon, invade, raid, rush, set about, set upon, storm; abuse, blame, blast, censure, criticize, impugn, malign, put down, revile, vilify

**attacker** aggressor, assailant, assaulter, intruder, invader, raider

**attain** accomplish, achieve, arrive at, bring off, complete, earn, fulfil, gain, get, grasp, reach, realize, secure, win

**attainment** accomplishment, achievement, acquirement, acquisition, arrival at, completion, feat, fulfilment, gaining, getting, obtaining, procurement, reaching, realization, reaping, winning; ability, accomplishment, achievement, art, capability, competence, gift, mastery, proficiency, skill, talent

**attempt** n assault, bid, crack Inf, endeavour, go Inf, shot Inf, stab Inf, try, undertaking, venture ~v endeavour, essay, experiment, have a crack Inf, have a go Inf, have a shot Inf, have a stab Inf, seek, strive, tackle, take on, try, undertake, venture

**attend** appear, be at, be here, be present, be there, frequent, go to, haunt, show oneself, show up Inf, turn up, visit; hear, heed, listen, look on, mark, mind, note, notice, observe, pay attention, pay heed, regard, watch (with **to**) apply oneself to, concentrate on, devote oneself to, look after, see to, take care of

**attendance** audience, crowd, gate, house, number present, turnout

**attendant** aide, assistant, auxiliary, companion, escort, flunky, follower, guard, guide, helper, servant, steward, usher, waiter

**attention** concentration, consideration, heed, mind, scrutiny, thinking, thought, thoughtfulness; consideration, notice, recognition, regard; care, concern, looking after, ministration, treatment

**attentive** alert, careful, concentrating, heedful, mindful, observant, regardful, studious, watchful

**attic** garret, loft

**attitude** approach, frame of mind, mood, opinion, outlook, position, posture, stance, standing, view; air, aspect, bearing, carriage, condition, demeanour, manner, pose, position, posture, stance

arouse interest of; cause to come closer (as magnet etc.) **attraction** *n*

**attractive** *adj*

**attribute** *v* regard as belonging to or produced by ~*n* quality or characteristic **attributable** *adj* **attribution** *n*

**attrition** *n* wearing away

**attune** *v* tune; adjust

**atypical** *adj* not typical

**aubergine** *n* purple fruit eaten as vegetable

**auburn** *adj/n* reddish brown

**auction** *n* public sale in which goods are sold to the highest bidder ~*v* sell by auction **auctioneer** *n*

**audacious** *adj* bold; impudent **audaciously** *adv* **audacity** *n*

**audible** *adj* able to be heard **audibly** *adv*

**audience** *n* people assembled to listen or watch; formal interview

**audio-** *comb. form* relating to sound or hearing **audio** *adj* of, for sound or hearing

**audiovisual** *adj* involving both sight and hearing

**audit** *n* formal examination of accounts ~*v* examine accounts **auditor** *n*

**audition** *n* test of prospective performer ~*v* set, perform such a test

**auditorium** *n* (*pl* **-toriums, -toria**) place where audience sits

**Aug.** August

**augment** *v* increase, enlarge

**augur** *v* foretell

**August** *n* eighth month

**auk** *n* northern sea bird

**aunt** *n* father's or mother's sister; uncle's wife **auntie** *n Inf* aunt

**au pair** *n* young foreigner who receives board and lodging in return for housework etc.

**aura** *n* atmosphere considered distinctive of person or thing

**aural** *adj* of, by ear

**auricle** *n* outside ear; an upper cavity of heart

**aurora** *n* (*pl* **-ras, -rae**) lights in the sky radiating from polar regions; dawn

**auspices** *pl n* patronage **auspicious** *adj* giving hope of future suc-

———————— THESAURUS ————————

**attract** allure, charm, decoy, draw, enchant, endear, engage, entice, incline, interest, invite, lure, tempt

**attraction** allure, charm, draw, enticement, fascination, interest, lure, magnetism

**attractive** agreeable, appealing, beautiful, captivating, charming, engaging, fair, fetching, good-looking, gorgeous, handsome, interesting, inviting, lovely, magnetic, pleasing, pretty, seductive, tempting

**attribute** *v* apply, assign, blame, charge, lay at the door of, refer ~*n* aspect, characteristic, facet, feature, indication, mark, note, point, prop-

erty, quality, quirk, sign, symbol, trait, virtue

**audacious** adventurous, bold, brave, courageous, daredevil, daring, fearless, intrepid, rash, reckless, risky

**audacity** adventurousness, boldness, bravery, courage, daring, nerve, rashness, recklessness; cheek, chutzpah *US & Canad inf*, defiance, effrontery, impertinence, impudence, insolence, nerve

**audible** clear, discernible, distinct

**audience** congregation, crowd, gathering, house, listeners, viewers; consultation, hearing, interview, reception

cess **auspiciously** adv

**austere** adj severe; without luxury **austerity** n

**authentic** adj genuine **authentically** adv **authenticate** v make valid **authenticity** n

**author** n (fem **authoress**) writer; originator

**authority** n legal power or right; delegated power; influence; permission; expert; board in control **authoritarian** n/adj (person) insisting on strict obedience **authoritative** adj **authorize** v empower; permit **authorization** n

**autism** n disorder causing children to become withdrawn and divorced from reality **autistic** adj

**auto-** comb. form self, as in **autosuggestion**

**autobiography** n life of person written by himself **autobiographical** adj

**autocrat** n absolute ruler; despotic person **autocratic** adj **autocracy** n

**Autocue** n Trademark electronic television device displaying speaker's script unseen by audience

**autogiro, autogyro** n (pl -ros) self-propelled aircraft with unpowered rotor

**autograph** n signature ~v sign

**automatic** adj operated or controlled mechanically; done without conscious thought ~adj/n self-loading (weapon) **automatically** adv **automation** n introduction of automatic devices in industry **automaton** n robot; person who acts mechanically

———————— THESAURUS ————————

**auspicious** bright, encouraging, favourable, fortunate, happy, hopeful, lucky, promising, propitious, rosy

**austere** cold, forbidding, grave, grim, hard, serious, severe, solemn, stern, stiff; abstemious, abstinent, puritanical, sober, solemn, Spartan

**austerity** coldness, harshness, inflexibility, rigour, solemnity, sternness; economy, rigidity, self-denial

**authentic** actual, authoritative, faithful, genuine, real, reliable, true, valid

**authenticity** actuality, genuineness, truth, truthfulness, validity

**author** composer, creator, father, founder, inventor, maker, mover, originator, parent, planner, producer, writer

**authoritarian** autocratic, despotic, dictatorial, disciplinarian, doctrinaire, domineering, harsh, imperious, rigid, severe, strict, tyrannical

**authority** charge, command, control, domination, dominion, force, government, influence, might, power, prerogative, right, rule, strength, supremacy, sway, weight; authorization, licence, permission, permit, sanction, warrant; arbiter, expert, master, professional, scholar, specialist, textbook

**authorize** empower, enable, entitle, give authority; allow, approve, confirm, countenance, give leave, license, permit, ratify, sanction, warrant

**autocracy** absolutism, despotism, dictatorship, tyranny

**autocratic** absolute, all-powerful, despotic, dictatorial, domineering, imperious, tyrannical, tyrannous, unlimited

**automatic** mechanical, pushbutton, robot, self-activating, self-propelling, self-regulating; habitual, mechanical, perfunctory, routine,

**automobile** n motorcar

**autonomy** n self-government **autonomous** adj

**autopsy** n postmortem

**autumn** n season after summer **autumnal** adj

**auxiliary** adj/n (person) helping, subsidiary

**avail** v be of use, advantage ~n benefit **available** adj obtainable; accessible **availability** n

**avalanche** n mass of snow, ice, sliding down mountain; any great quantity

**avant-garde** adj innovative and progressive

**avarice** n greed for wealth **avaricious** adj

**avenge** v take vengeance for

**avenue** n wide street; approach; double row of trees

**aver** v averring, averred affirm, assert

**average** n middle or usual value ~adj ordinary ~v calculate an average; form an average

**averse** adj disinclined **aversion** n (object of) dislike

**avert** v turn away; ward off

**aviary** n enclosure for birds

**aviation** n art of flying aircraft **aviator** n

**avid** adj keen; greedy (for) **avidly** adv

**avocado** n (pl -dos) tropical pear-shaped fruit

**avoid** v keep away from; refrain from; not allow to happen **avoidable** adj **avoidance** n

**avow** v declare; admit **avowal** n

——— THESAURUS ———

unconscious

**autonomous** free, independent, self-governing, sovereign

**autonomy** freedom, home rule, independence, self-determination, self-government, self-rule, sovereignty

**auxiliary** accessory, aiding, ancillary, assisting, helping, reserve, secondary, subsidiary, substitute, supplementary

**available** accessible, applicable, at hand, free, handy, obtainable, on hand, on tap, ready, to hand, vacant

**avalanche** landslide, landslip, snow-slide, snow-slip; barrage, deluge, flood, inundation, torrent

**avant-garde** adj experimental, ground-breaking, innovative, innovatory, pioneering, progressive, unconventional

**avaricious** close-fisted, covetous, grasping, greedy, mean, miserly,

parsimonious, penurious, stingy

**avenge** hit back, punish, repay, requite, retaliate, revenge, take satisfaction for, take vengeance

**avenue** access, approach, boulevard, channel, course, drive, entrance, entry, pass, path, road, route, street, way

**average** n mean, medium, midpoint, norm, normal, par, rule, run, standard ~adj fair, general, indifferent, mediocre, middling, moderate, normal, not bad, ordinary, regular, so-so Inf, standard, tolerable, typical

**averse** disinclined, hostile, ill-disposed, loath, opposed, reluctant, unfavourable, unwilling

**avid** keen, devoted, eager, enthusiastic, fanatical, fervent, intense, keen, passionate, zealous

**avoid** avert, bypass, circumvent, dodge, elude, escape, evade, keep away from, prevent, shirk, shun,

**avowed** adj

**await** v wait or stay for; be in store for

**awake** v awaking, awoke, awoken emerge or rouse from sleep; (cause to) become alert ~adj not sleeping; alert **awaken** v awake **awakening** n

**award** v give formally ~n thing awarded

**aware** adj informed, conscious **awareness** n

**awash** adv covered by water

**away** adv absent, apart, at a dis-

tance, out of the way ~adj not present

**awe** n dread mingled with reverence ~v astonish, frighten **awesome** adj

**awful** adj dreadful; Inf very great **awfully** adv in an unpleasant way; Inf very much

**awhile** adv for a time

**awkward** adj clumsy; difficult; inconvenient; embarrassed **awkwardly** adv **awkwardness** n

**awl** n tool for boring wood etc.

─────────────── THESAURUS ───────────────

sidestep, steer clear of

**await** anticipate, expect, look for, stay for, wait for; attend, be in readiness for, be in store for, be ready for, wait for

**awake** alert, alive, aroused, attentive, aware, conscious, not sleeping, observant, on guard, on the alert, on the lookout, vigilant, wakeful, waking, watchful, wide-awake

**awaken** activate, alert, arouse, awake, call forth, excite, incite, kindle, provoke, revive, rouse, stimulate, stir up, wake

**awakening** n activation, arousal, awaking, revival, rousing, stimulation, stirring up, waking, waking up

**award** v accord, allot, apportion, assign, bestow, confer, decree, endow, gift, give, grant, hand out, render ~n decoration, gift, grant, prize, trophy, verdict

**aware** alive to, apprised, attentive, cognizant, conscious, conversant, familiar, knowing, mindful, sensible, wise Inf

**awareness** appreciation, attention, consciousness, familiarity, knowledge, mindfulness, perception, realization, recognition, understanding

**away** adv abroad, elsewhere, from here, from home, hence, off; apart, at a distance, far, remote; aside, out of the way, to one side ~adj abroad, elsewhere, gone, not here, not present, not there, out

**awe** n admiration, amazement, astonishment, dread, fear, horror, respect, reverence, terror, veneration, wonder ~v amaze, astonish, cow, daunt, frighten, horrify, impress, intimidate, stun, terrify

**awesome** alarming, amazing, astonishing, awe-inspiring, awful, breathtaking, daunting, dreadful, fearful, fearsome, formidable, frightening, horrible, horrifying, imposing, impressive, intimidating, magnificent, majestic, overwhelming, redoubtable, shocking, solemn, stunning, stupefying, terrible, terrifying, wonderful

**awful** alarming, appalling, deplorable, dire, distressing, dreadful, fearful, frightful, ghastly, gruesome, hideous, horrible, nasty, shocking, terrible, ugly, unpleasant

**awfully** badly, disgracefully, disreputably, dreadfully, unforgivably, unpleasantly, wickedly, woefully, wretchedly

**awning** ———— DICTIONARY ———— 46

**awning** n (canvas) roof to protect from weather

**AWOL** adj Mil absent without leave

**awry** adv crookedly; amiss ~adj crooked; wrong

**axe** n tool for chopping; Inf dismissal from employment ~v Inf dismiss from employment

**axiom** n accepted principle axio-

**matic** adj

**axis** n (pl **axes**) (imaginary) line round which body spins

**axle** n shaft on which wheels turn

**aye** interj yes ~n affirmative answer or vote

**azalea** n genus of shrubby flowering plants

**azure** adj sky-blue

———— THESAURUS ————

**awkward** artless, blundering, bungling, clownish, clumsy, coarse, gauche, gawky, graceless, hamfisted, inelegant, inept, inexpert, lumbering, maladroit, oafish, rude, stiff, uncoordinated, uncouth, ungainly, ungraceful, unpolished, unrefined, unskilful, unskilled; cumbersome, difficult, inconvenient, troublesome, unhandy, unmanageable, unwieldy; annoying, difficult, disobliging, exasperating, intractable, irritable, perverse, prickly, stubborn, touchy, troublesome, trying, unhelpful

**awkwardness** clumsiness, coarseness, gaucheness, gaucherie, gawkiness, gracelessness, inelegance, ineptness, inexpertness, maladroitness, oafishness, rudeness, stiffness, uncoordination, un-

couthness, ungainliness; delicacy, embarrassment, inconvenience; difficulty, stubbornness, touchiness, unhelpfulness

**axe** n chopper, hatchet **the axe** Inf cancellation, cutback, discharge, dismissal, termination, the boot Sl, the chop Sl, the order of the boot Sl, the sack Inf, wind-up ~v chop, cut down, fell, hew

**axiom** adage, aphorism, dictum, fundamental, maxim, postulate, precept, principle, truism

**axiomatic** accepted, assumed, fundamental, given, granted, manifest, self-evident, understood, unquestioned

**axis** axle, centre line, pivot, shaft, spindle

**axle** axis, pin, pivot, rod, shaft, spindle

# B b

**BA** Bachelor of Arts
**babble** *v/n* (make) foolish, incoherent speech
**babe** *n* baby
**baboon** *n* large monkey
**baby** *n* infant **baby-sitter** *n* one who cares for children when parents are out **baby-sit** *v*
**bachelor** *n* unmarried man
**bacillus** *n* (*pl* **bacilli**) minute organism sometimes causing disease
**back** *n* hind part of anything, e.g. human body; part opposite front; part further away or less used; (position of) player in ball games —*adj* situated behind; earlier —*adv* at to, the back; in, into the past; in return ~*v* move backwards; support; put wager on; provide with back; provide with musical accompaniment **backer** *n* **backward** *adj* behind in education **backwardness** *n* **backwards** *adv* to rear, past, worse state

**backbite** *v* slander absent person
**backbone** *n* spinal column; strength of character **backcloth, backdrop** *n* painted cloth at back of stage **backdate** *v* make effective from earlier date **backfire** *v* (of plan, scheme, etc.) fail to work; ignite wrongly **backgammon** *n* game played with draughtsmen and dice **background** *n* space behind chief figures of picture etc.; past history of person **backhand** *n* stroke made with hand turned backwards **backlash** *n* sudden adverse reaction **backside** *n* rump
**bacon** *n* cured pig's flesh
**bacteria** *pl n* (*sing* **bacterium**) microscopic organisms **bacterial** *adj* **bacteriology** *n*
**bad** *adj* **worse, worst** faulty; harmful; evil; severe; rotten; *Sl* very good **badly** *adv*
**badge** *n* distinguishing emblem

--- THESAURUS ---

**baby** babe, bairn *Scot*, child, infant, newborn child

**back** *n* backside, end, far end, hind part, hindquarters, posterior, rear, reverse, stern, tail end —*adj* end, hind, hindmost, posterior, rear, tail ~*v* backtrack, go back, regress, retire, retreat, reverse, turn tail, withdraw; abet, advocate, assist, champion, countenance, encourage, endorse, favour, finance, sanction, second, side with, sponsor, subsidize, support, sustain, underwrite

**backer** advocate, benefactor, patron, promoter, second, sponsor, subscriber, supporter, underwriter, well-wisher

**backfire** boomerang, disappoint,

fail, flop *Inf*, miscarry, rebound, recoil

**background** breeding, circumstances, credentials, culture, education, environment, experience, history, qualifications, tradition, upbringing

**backlash** backfire, reaction, recoil, repercussion, resentment, response, retaliation

**backward** behind, behindhand, dense, dull, retarded, slow, stupid, subnormal, undeveloped

**bad** defective, deficient, faulty, imperfect, inadequate, incorrect, inferior, poor, substandard, unsatisfactory; damaging, dangerous, detrimental, harmful, hurtful, injurious,

**badger** *n* burrowing night animal *~v* pester, worry

**badminton** *n* game played with rackets and shuttlecocks

**baffle** *v* check, frustrate, bewilder *~n* device to regulate flow of liquid etc.

**bag** *n* sack; measure of quantity; woman's handbag *~v* **bagging, bagged** bulge; sag; put in bag; kill as game, etc. **baggy** *adj* loose

**bagatelle** *n* trifle; game like pin-ball

**baggage** *n* suitcases, luggage

**bagpipes** *pl n* musical wind instrument

**bail**¹ *n Law* security given for person's reappearance in court *~v* (obtain) release on security

**bail**² *n Cricket* crosspiece on wicket

**bail**³ *also* **bale** *v* empty water from boat **bail out** parachute

**bailiff** *n* land steward, agent

**bait** *n* food to entice fish; any lure *~v* lure; persecute

**baize** *n* smooth woollen cloth

**bake** *v* cook or harden by dry heat *~v* make bread, cakes etc. **baker** *n*

**bakery** *n* **baking powder** raising agent used in cooking

**balalaika** *n* Russian musical instrument; like guitar

**balance** *n* pair of scales; equilibrium; surplus; sum due on an account; difference between two sums *~v* weigh; bring to equilibrium

**balcony** *n* platform outside window; upper seats in theatre

**bald** *adj* hairless; plain; bare **balding** *adj*

**bale** *n/v* bundle or package

**baleful** *adj* menacing

**balk** *v* swerve, pull up; thwart; shirk *~n* hindrance

**ball**¹ *n* anything round; globe,

———— THESAURUS ————

ruinous, unhealthy; base, corrupt, criminal, delinquent, evil, immoral, mean, sinful, vile, villainous, wicked, wrong; decayed, mouldy, off, putrid, rancid, rotten, sour, spoiled

**badge** *n* brand, device, emblem, mark, sign, token

**badly** carelessly, defectively, faultily, imperfectly, inadequately, incorrectly, ineptly, poorly, shoddily, wrong, wrongly

**bag** *v* acquire, capture, catch, gain, get, kill, land, shoot, take, trap

**baggage** bags, belongings, equipment, gear, luggage, suitcases

**baggy** billowing, bulging, droopy, floppy, ill-fitting, loose, oversize, roomy, sagging, seated, slack

**bail**¹ *n* bond, guarantee, guaranty, pledge, security, surety, warranty

**bail**², **bale** *v* dip, drain off, ladle,

scoop

**bait** *n* allurement, attraction, bribe, decoy, enticement, inducement, lure, snare, temptation *~v* entice, lure, seduce, tempt; irritate, needle *Inf.* persecute, provoke, tease, torment

**balance** *n* correspondence, equilibrium, equipoise, equity, equivalence, evenness, parity, symmetry; difference, remainder, residue, rest, surplus *~v* adjust, compensate for, counteract, counterbalance, equalize, equate, make up for, neutralize, offset

**bald** baldheaded, depilated, hairless; uncovered

**balk** demur, evade, flinch, hesitate, jib, recoil, refuse, resist, shirk; baffle, bar, check, defeat, hinder, obstruct, prevent, thwart

sphere, esp. as used in games ~v gather into a mass **ball bearings** steel balls used to lessen friction

**ball²** n assembly for dancing **ballroom** n

**ballad** n narrative poem; simple song

**ballast** n heavy material put in ship to steady it

**ballet** n theatrical presentation of dancing and miming **ballerina** n

**ballistics** pl n (with sing v) scientific study of motion of projectiles

**balloon** n large bag filled with air or gas ~v puff out

**ballot** n voting, usually by paper ~v vote

**balm** n healing or soothing (ointment)

**balmy** adj (of weather) mild and pleasant

**balsa** n Amer. tree with light but strong wood

**balsam** n resinous aromatic substance

**bamboo** n large tropical treelike reed

**bamboozle** v mystify, hoax

**ban** v banning, banned prohibit, forbid, outlaw **~n** prohibition; proclamation

**banal** adj commonplace, trite **banality** n

**banana** n tropical treelike plant; its fruit

**band¹** n strip used to bind; range of frequencies **bandage** n/v (apply) strip of cloth for binding wound

**band²** n company; company of musicians ~v bind together

**bandanna** n handkerchief

**bandit** n outlaw; robber

**bandwagon** n **jump on the bandwagon** join something that seems assured of success

**bandy** v bandying, bandied toss from one to another **bandy-legged** adj curving outwards

**bane** n person or thing causing misery or distress **baneful** adj

**bang** n sudden loud noise; heavy

━━━━━ THESAURUS ━━━━━

**ball** globe, orb, pellet, sphere

**ballast** balance, equilibrium, sandbag, stabilizer, weight

**ballot** election, poll, polling, vote, voting

**balm** balsam, cream, lotion, ointment, salve

**balmy** clement, mild, pleasant, summery, temperate

**ban** v banish, debar, disallow, exclude, forbid, outlaw, prohibit, proscribe, restrict, suppress **~n** boycott, censorship, embargo, prohibition, proscription, restriction, suppression, taboo

**banal** clichéd, commonplace, everyday, hackneyed, humdrum, old hat, ordinary, pedestrian, platitudinous, stale, stereotyped, stock, threadbare, tired, trite, vapid

**band¹** bandage, belt, bond, chain, cord, fetter, ribbon, shackle, strap, strip, tie

**band²** assembly, association, body, clique, club, company, coterie, crew Inf, gang, horde, party, society, troop; ensemble, group, orchestra

**bandage** compress, dressing, gauze, plaster

**bandit** brigand, crook, desperado, freebooter, gangster, gunman, hijacker, marauder, outlaw, pirate, robber, thief

**bane** affliction, bête noire, blight, burden, calamity, curse, despair,

blow ~v make loud noise; beat; slam

**banger** n Sl sausage; Inf old car; loud firework

**bangle** n ring worn on arm or leg

**banish** v exile; drive away

**banisters** pl n railing on staircase

**banjo** n (pl **-jos**) musical instrument like guitar

**bank¹** n mound of earth; edge of river etc. ~v enclose with ridge; pile up

**bank²** n establishment for keeping, lending, exchanging etc. money ~v put in bank; keep with bank **banker** n **banking** n **banknote** n written promise of payment **bank on** rely on

**bankrupt** n one who fails in business, insolvent debtor ~adj financially ruined ~v make bankrupt

**bankruptcy** n

**banner** n placard; flag

**banns** pl n public declaration of intended marriage

**banquet** n/v feast

**banshee** n spirit whose wailing warns of death

**bantam** n small chicken; very light boxing weight

**banter** v make fun of ~n light, teasing language

**baptize** v immerse in, sprinkle with water ceremoniously; christen **baptism** n

**bar** n rod or block of any substance; obstacle; rail in law court; body of lawyers; counter where drinks are served; unit of music ~v **barring**, **barred** fasten; obstruct; exclude ~prep except **barman** n (fem **barmaid**)

destruction, disaster, downfall, plague, ruin, scourge, torment, trial, trouble

**bang** n boom, burst, clang, clap, clash, detonation, explosion, peal, pop, shot, slam, thud, thump; blow, box, bump, cuff, hit, knock, punch, smack, stroke, wallop Inf, whack ~v bash Inf, beat, bump, clatter, crash, hammer, knock, pound, rap, slam, strike, thump

**banish** v deport, drive away, eject, evict, exclude, exile, expel, ostracize, outlaw

**bank¹** n embankment, heap, mass, mound, pile, ridge; brink, edge, margin, shore, side ~v amass, heap, mass, mound, pile, stack

**bank²** n depository, fund, hoard, repository, reserve, savings, store, storehouse ~v deal with, deposit, keep, save

**bankrupt** broke Inf, destitute, ex-

hausted, failed, impoverished, insolvent, lacking, ruined, spent

**banner** colours, ensign, flag, pennant, standard, streamer

**banquet** dinner, feast, meal, repast, revel, treat

**banter** v chaff, deride, jeer, jest, joke, kid Inf, make fun of, rib Inf, ridicule, taunt, tease ~n badinage, derision, jeering, jesting, joking, kidding Inf, mockery, repartee, ribbing Inf, ridicule

**baptism** christening; beginning, debut, dedication, initiation, introduction

**bar** n batten, crosspiece, paling, pole, rail, rod, shaft, stake, stick; deterrent, hindrance, impediment, obstacle, rail, railing, stop; bench, court, courtroom, dock, law court; Law barristers, counsel, court, tribunal; canteen, counter, inn, lounge, pub Inf, public house, sa-

**barb** n sharp point curving backwards; cutting remark **barbed** adj

**barbarous** adj savage, brutal, uncivilized **barbarian** n **barbaric** adj **barbarism** n **barbarity** n

**barbecue** n meal cooked outdoors over open fire ~v cook thus

**barber** n person who shaves beards and cuts hair

**barbiturate** n derivative of barbituric acid used as drug

**bard** n poet

**bare** adj uncovered; naked; plain; scanty ~v make bare **barely** adv only just **barefaced** adj shameless

**bargain** n something bought at a favourable price; agreement ~v haggle, negotiate

**barge** n flat-bottomed freight boat ~v Inf bump (into), push

**baritone** n (singer with) second lowest adult male voice ~adj of, for this voice

**barium** n white metallic element

**bark**¹ n/v (utter) sharp loud cry of dog etc.

**bark**² n outer layer of tree

**barley** n grain used for food and making malt

**barmy** adj Sl insane

**barn** n building to store grain, hay etc. **barnyard** n

**barnacle** n shellfish which sticks to rocks and ships

**barometer** n instrument to measure pressure of atmosphere **barometric** adj

**baron** n (fem **baroness**) member of lowest rank of peerage; powerful businessman **baronial** adj

**baronet** n lowest British hereditary title

**baroque** adj extravagantly ornamented

**barque** n sailing ship

**barracks** pl n building for lodging soldiers

**barrage** n heavy artillery fire; continuous heavy delivery of questions etc.; dam across river

**barrel** n round wooden vessel; tube of gun etc.

**barren** adj sterile; unprofitable

**barricade** n improvised barrier ~v

———— T H E S A U R U S ————

loon, tavern ~v barricade, bolt, fasten, latch, lock, secure; ban, exclude, forbid, hinder, keep out, obstruct, prevent, prohibit, restrain

**barb** bristle, point, prickle, prong, quill, spike, spur, thorn; cut, dig, gibe, insult, sarcasm, scoff, sneer

**barbarian** n hooligan, lout, ruffian, savage, vandal

**barbaric** primitive, rude, uncivilized, wild

**barbarism** coarseness, crudity, savagery

**bare** denuded, exposed, naked, nude, peeled, shorn, stripped, unclothed, undressed; barren, blank, empty, lacking, mean, open, poor,

scanty, scarce, unfurnished, vacant, void, wanting

**bargain** n (cheap) purchase, discount, giveaway, good buy, good deal, good value, reduction, snip Inf; agreement, business, compact, contract, negotiation, pact, pledge, promise, stipulation, transaction, treaty, understanding ~v barter, buy, deal, haggle, sell, trade, traffic

**bark**¹ n/v bay, growl, howl, snarl, woof, yap, yelp

**bark**² n casing, cortex Anat & Bot, covering, crust, husk, rind, skin

**barrage** battery, bombardment, gunfire, salvo, shelling, volley

**barren** childless, infertile, sterile;

block

**barrier** *n* fence, obstruction

**barrister** *n* advocate in the higher law courts

**barrow** *n* small wheeled handcart; wheelbarrow

**barter** *v/n* (trade by) exchange of goods

**base**¹ *n* bottom, foundation; starting point; centre of operations ~*v* found, establish **baseless** *adj* **basement** *n* lowest storey of building

**base**² low, mean; despicable

**baseball** *n* game played with bat and ball

**bash** *Inf v* strike violently ~*n* blow; attempt

**bashful** *adj* shy, modest

**basic** *adj* relating to, serving as base; fundamental; necessary **basically** *adv* **basics** *pl n* fundamental principles, facts etc.

**basil** *n* aromatic herb

**basin** *n* deep circular dish; harbour; land drained by river

**basis** *n* (*pl* **-ses**) foundation; principal constituent

**bask** *v* lie in warmth and sunshine

**basket** *n* vessel made of woven cane, straw etc. **basketball** *n* ball game played by two teams

**bass**¹ *n* lowest part in music; bass singer or voice ~*adj* of bass

**bass**² *n* sea fish

───────── THESAURUS ─────────

arid, desert, desolate, dry, empty, unfruitful, unproductive, unprofitable, waste

**barricade** *n* barrier, blockade, bulwark, fence, obstruction, palisade, rampart, stockade ~*v* bar, block, blockade, defend, fortify, obstruct, protect, shut in

**barrier** bar, barricade, blockade, boundary, ditch, fence, obstacle, obstruction, railing, rampart, stop, wall; difficulty, drawback, hindrance, impediment, limitation, obstacle, restriction, stumbling block

**barter** bargain, exchange, haggle, sell, swap, trade, traffic

**base**¹ *n* bed, bottom, foot, foundation, groundwork, pedestal, rest, stand, support; basis, core, essence, essential, fundamental, heart, key, origin, principle, root, source; camp, centre, headquarters, home, post, settlement, starting point, station ~*v* build, construct, depend, derive, establish, found, ground, hinge, locate, station

**base**² contemptible, corrupt, depraved, despicable, dishonourable, disreputable, evil, ignoble, immoral, infamous, scandalous, shameful, sordid, vile, villainous, wicked

**baseless** groundless, unfounded, unjustified, unsubstantiated

**bash** *v* belt *Inf*, biff *Sl*, break, crash, crush, deck *Sl*, hit, punch, slosh *Brit Sl*, smash, sock *Sl*, strike, wallop *Inf*

**bashful** blushing, coy, diffident, nervous, reserved, retiring, self-conscious, sheepish, shrinking, shy, timid, timorous

**basic** central, essential, fundamental, indispensable, intrinsic, key, necessary, primary, underlying, vital

**basics** brass tacks *Inf*, core, essentials, facts, hard facts, nitty-gritty *Inf*, practicalities, principles, rudiments

**basis** base, bottom, footing, foundation, ground, groundwork, support

**bask** laze, lie in, loll, lounge, relax, sunbathe

**basset** n type of smooth-haired dog

**bassoon** n woodwind instrument of low tone

**bastard** n child born of unmarried parents; Inf unpleasant person ~adj illegitimate; spurious

**bastion** n projecting part of fortification; defence

**bat**¹ n club used to hit ball in cricket etc. ~v **batting, batted** strike with bat

**bat**² n nocturnal mouselike flying animal

**batch** n group or set of similar objects

**bated** adj **with bated breath** anxiously

**bath** n vessel or place to bathe in; water for bathing; act of bathing ~v wash **bathroom** n

**bathe** v **bathing, bathed** swim; apply liquid; wash; immerse in water ~n swim; wash **bather** n

**baton** n stick, esp. of policeman, conductor, marshal

**battalion** n military unit of three companies

**batten** n strip of wood ~v (esp. with **down**) fasten

**batter** v strike continuously ~n mixture of flour, eggs, milk, used in cooking

**battery** n connected group of electrical cells; accumulator; number of similar things occurring together; Law assault by beating; number of guns

**battle** n fight between armies ~v fight **battle-axe** n large heavy axe; Inf domineering woman

**battlement** n wall with openings for shooting

**battleship** n heavily armed and armoured fighting ship

**batty** adj Inf crazy, silly

**bauble** n showy trinket

**bawdy** adj obscene, lewd

**bawl** v/n cry; shout

**bay**¹ n wide inlet of sea

**bay**² n space between two columns; recess

─────────── **THESAURUS** ───────────

**bastard** n illegitimate (child), love child ~adj counterfeit, false, illegitimate, imperfect, impure, irregular, misbegotten, sham, spurious

**bastion** bulwark, citadel, defence, fortress, prop, rock, stronghold, support

**bat** bang, hit, rap, smack, strike, swat, thump, wallop Inf, whack

**batch** accumulation, amount, collection, crowd, group, lot, pack, set

**bath** n ablution, douche, shower, soak, tub, wash ~v bathe, clean, scrub down, soak, soap, sponge, tub, wash

**bathe** v cleanse, immerse, moisten, rinse, soak, steep, wash, wet ~n dip, swim

**baton** club, mace, rod, staff, stick, truncheon, wand

**batten** board up, clamp down, cover up, fasten down, fix, nail down, secure

**batter** assault, bash Inf, beat, belabour, break, buffet, clobber Sl, lash, pelt, pound, pummel, smash, smite, thrash

**battery** assault, attack, beating, mayhem, onslaught, physical violence, thumping

**battle** action, attack, combat, encounter, engagement, fight, fray, hostilities, skirmish, war, warfare

**bawl** bellow, call, clamour, howl, roar, shout, yell

**bay³** n/v bark **at bay** cornered; at a distance

**bayonet** n stabbing weapon fixed to rifle ~v **bayonetting, bayonetted** stab with this

**bazaar** n market (esp. in the East); sale for charity

**bazooka** n powerful rocket launcher

**B & B** bed and breakfast

**BBC** British Broadcasting Corporation

**BC** before Christ

**be** v (present tense I **am**, he, she **is**, we, you, they **are**; present participle **being**; past tense I, he, she **was**, we, you, they **were**; past participle **been**) live; exist; have a state or quality

**beach** n shore of sea ~v run boat on shore

**beacon** n fire used to give signal; lighthouse, buoy

**bead** n little ball pierced for thread-

ing; drop of liquid **beaded** adj **beady** adj small and glittering

**beagle** n small hound

**beak** n projecting horny jaws of bird; anything similar; Sl magistrate

**beaker** n large drinking cup; glass vessel used by chemists

**beam** n long thick piece of wood; ray of light etc. ~v aim light, radio waves etc. (to); shine; smile broadly

**bean** n edible seed of various leguminous plants

**bear¹** v beating, **bore, born** or **borne** carry; support; produce; endure; press (upon) **bearer** n

**bear²** n heavy carnivorous animal

**beard** n hair on chin ~v oppose boldly

**bearing** n support for mechanical part; relevance; behaviour; direction; relative position

**beast** n four-footed animal; brutal man **beastly** adj

**beat** v beating, **beat, beaten** strike

**bay¹** cove, gulf, inlet, sound

**bay²** alcove, niche, nook, opening, recess

**bay³** bark, bell, clamour, cry, growl, howl, yelp

**bazaar** exchange, market, marketplace, mart; bring-and-buy, fair, fête

**be** be alive, breathe, exist, inhabit, live

**beach** coast, sands, seashore, seaside, shingle, shore, strand

**beacon** beam, bonfire, flare, lighthouse, sign, signal, watchtower

**bead** blob, bubble, dot, drop, droplet, globule, pill

**beak** bill, neb Arch or dial, nib

**beam** n girder, joist, plank, rafter, spar, support, timber; gleam, glimmer, glint, glow, radiation, ray,

shaft, streak, stream ~v glare, gleam, glitter, glow, radiate, shine, transmit; grin, laugh, smile

**bear** bring, carry, convey, move, take, tote, transport; beget, breed, bring forth, generate, give birth to, produce, yield; allow, endure, permit, put up with Inf, stomach, suffer, tolerate, undergo

**bearing** air, aspect, attitude, behaviour, carriage, demeanour, deportment, manner, mien, posture; connection, import, pertinence, relation, relevance; Naut course, direction, point of compass

**beast** animal, brute, creature; barbarian, brute, fiend, monster, ogre, sadist, savage, swine

**beastly** barbarous, bestial, brutal, brutish, coarse, cruel, depraved, in-

repeatedly; overcome; surpass; stir vigorously; flap (wings); make, wear (path); throb ~*n* stroke; pulsation; appointed course; basic rhythmic unit of music ~*adj Sl* exhausted **beater** *n*

**beau** *n* (*pl* **beaux**) suitor

**beauty** *n* loveliness, grace; beautiful person or thing **beautiful** *adj* **beautifully** *adv* **beautician** *n* person who gives beauty treatments

**beaver** *n* amphibious rodent; its fur ~*v* work industriously

**becalmed** *adj* (of ship) motionless through lack of wind

**because** *adv/conj* by reason of, since

**beckon** *v* summon by signal

**become** *v* **becoming, became, become** come to be; suit **becoming**

*adj* suitable

**bed** *n* piece of furniture for sleeping on; garden plot; bottom of river; layer, stratum ~*v* **bedding, bedded** lay in a bed; plant **bedding** *n* **bedpan** *n* container used as lavatory by bedridden people **bedridden** *adj* confined to bed **bedroom** *n* **bedsit** *n* one-roomed flat **bedstead** *n*

**bedevil** *v* -**illing,** -**illed** harass or torment

**bedlam** *n* noisy confused scene

**bedraggled** *adj* messy and wet

**bee** *n* insect that makes honey

**beech** *n* European tree with smooth greyish bark and small nuts

**beef** *n* flesh of cattle for eating; *Inf* complaint ~*v Inf* complain **beefy** *adj* muscular **beefburger** *n* flat grilled or fried cake of minced beef

——————————————— THESAURUS ———————————————

human, monstrous, sadistic, savage; awful, foul, mean, nasty, unpleasant

**beat** *v* bang, batter, break, buffet, cane, clobber *Sl*, cudgel, drub, flog, hit, knock, lambast(e), lash, maul, pound, punch, strike, thrash, whip; conquer, defeat, excel, master, outdo, outrun, overcome, subdue, surpass, vanquish ~*n* blow, hit, lash, punch, slap, strike, stroke, swing, thump; flutter, palpitation, pulsation, pulse, throb; circuit, course, path, rounds, route, way; accent, cadence, measure, metre, rhythm, stress, time

**beautiful** appealing, attractive, charming, comely, delightful, exquisite, fair, fine, good-looking, gorgeous, graceful, handsome, lovely, pleasing, radiant, stunning *Inf*

**beauty** attractiveness, bloom, charm, elegance, fairness, glamour,

grace; belle, charmer, cracker *Sl*, good-looker, stunner *Inf*, Venus

**because** as, by reason of, in that, on account of, owing to, since, thanks to

**beckon** bid, gesticulate, gesture, motion, nod, signal, summon, wave at

**become** alter to, be transformed into, change into, evolve into, grow into, mature into, ripen into; embellish, enhance, fit, flatter, grace, harmonize, ornament, set off, suit

**becoming** attractive, comely, flattering, graceful, neat, pretty, tasteful

**bed** bedstead, berth, bunk, cot, couch, divan, pallet; area, border, garden, patch, plot, row, strip

**bedlam** chaos, clamour, commotion, confusion, furore, hubbub, noise, pandemonium, tumult, turmoil, uproar

**bedridden** confined, incapacitat-

**beer** *n* fermented alcoholic drink made from hops and malt **beer parlour** *Canad* licensed place where beer is sold to the public

**beet** *n* any of various plants with root used for food **beetroot** *n* type of beet plant with a dark red root

**beetle** *n* class of insect with hard upper-wing cases

**befall** *v* befalling, befell, befallen happen (to)

**befit** *v* befitting, befitted be suitable to

**before** *prep* in front of; in presence of; in preference to; earlier than ~*adv* earlier; in front ~*conj* sooner than **beforehand** *adv* previously

**befriend** *v* become a friend to

**beg** *v* begging, begged ask earnestly; ask for money or food **beggar** *n*

**begin** *v* -ginning, -gan, -gun (cause to) start **beginner** *n* **beginning** *n*

**begonia** *n* tropical plant

**begrudge** *v* grudge, envy anyone the possession of

**beguile** *v* charm, fascinate; amuse; deceive

**behalf** *n* **on behalf of** in the interest of

**behave** *v* act in particular way; act properly **behaviour** *n* conduct

**behead** *v* cut off the head of

**behest** *n* charge, command

**behind** *prep* further back or earlier than ~*adv* in the rear

**behold** *v* beheld, behold *or* beholden watch, see

**beholden** *adj* bound in gratitude

——————— THESAURUS ———————

ed, laid up *Inf*

**beef** *Inf* brawn, flesh, muscle, physique, robustness, sinew, strength

**before** *prep* earlier than, in advance of, in front of, in the presence of, prior to ~*adv* ahead, earlier, formerly, in advance, in front, previously, sooner

**beforehand** before now, earlier, in advance, previously, sooner

**befriend** advise, aid, assist, back, benefit, favour, help, patronize, side with, stand by, succour, support, sustain, uphold, welcome

**beg** beseech, crave, desire, entreat, implore, importune, petition, plead, pray, request, solicit, supplicate; cadge, call for alms, sponge on

**beggar** cadger, mendicant, scrounger *Inf*, sponger *Inf*, supplicant, tramp, vagrant

**begin** commence, embark on, initiate, instigate, institute, prepare, set about, set on foot, start

**beginner** amateur, apprentice, fledgling, freshman, greenhorn *Inf*, initiate, learner, neophyte, novice, recruit, starter, student, trainee, tyro

**beginning** birth, commencement, inauguration, inception, initiation, onset, opening, origin, outset, preface, prelude, rise, rudiments, source, start

**begrudge** be jealous, envy, grudge, resent

**behave** act, function, operate, perform, run, work; conduct oneself properly, mind one's manners

**behaviour** actions, bearing, carriage, conduct, demeanour, deportment, manner, manners, manners, ways

**behind** *prep* after, at the back of, at the rear of, following, later than ~*adv* after, afterwards, following, in the wake (of), next, subsequently

**behold** observe, contemplate, discern, eye, look at, observe, regard, scan, view, watch, witness

**beige** n undyed woollen cloth; its colour

**being** n existence; that which exists; creature; *present participle of* BE

**belated** adj late; too late

**belch** v expel wind by mouth; eject violently ~n this act

**beleaguered** adj besieged; surrounded or beset

**belfry** n bell tower

**belie** v show to be untrue

**believe** v regard as true or real; have faith **belief** n **believable** adj **believer** n

**belittle** v regard, speak of, as having little worth

**bell** n hollow metal instrument giving ringing sound when struck; electrical device emitting ring

**belle** n beautiful woman

**bellicose** adj warlike

**belligerent** adj hostile, aggressive;

**bellow** v/n roar; shout

**bellows** pl n instrument for creating stream of air

**belly** n stomach ~v bellying, bellied swell out

**belong** v be property of; be member of; have an allotted place; pertain to **belongings** pl n personal possessions

**beloved** adj much loved ~n dear one

**below** adv beneath ~prep lower than

**belt** n band; girdle; zone ~v Inf thrash

**bemoan** v grieve over

**bemuse** v confuse, bewilder

**bench** n long seat; seat or body of judges etc.

**bend** v bending, bent (cause to) form a curve

making war **belligerence** n

—————————— THESAURUS ——————————

**being** actuality, existence, life, living, reality; entity, essence, nature, soul, spirit, substance; animal, beast, body, creature, human being, individual, living thing, mortal, thing

**belated** delayed, late, overdue, tardy

**belief** admission, assurance, confidence, conviction, credit, feeling, impression, judgment, notion, opinion, persuasion, reliance, theory, trust, view; credence, credo, creed, doctrine, dogma, faith, ideology, principles, tenet

**believable** acceptable, credible, creditable, imaginable, likely, plausible, possible, reliable, trustworthy

**believe** accept, be certain of, be convinced of, buy Sl, count on, credit, depend on, have faith in, hold, swallow Inf, swear by, trust

**believer** adherent, convert, devotee, disciple, follower, proselyte, supporter

**belong** be at the disposal of, be held by, be owned by; be allied to; be a member of, be associated with, be included in

**belongings** effects, gear, goods, personal property, possessions, stuff, things

**beloved** adored, cherished, darling, dear, dearest, loved, precious, sweet

**below** adv beneath, down, lower, under, underneath ~prep inferior, lesser, lesser than, subject, subordinate

**belt** band, girdle, girth, sash, waistband

**bench** form, pew, seat, settle; court, courtroom, judge, judges, judiciary, magistrate, magistrates

**beneath** *prep* under, lower than ~*adv* below

**benefit** *n* advantage, profit; money paid to unemployed etc. ~*v* -**fiting**, -**fited** do good to; receive good **benefactor** *n* (*fem* **benefactress**) one who helps or does good to others; patron **beneficial** *adj*

**benevolent** *adj* kindly, charitable **benevolence** *n*

**benign** *adj* kindly, favourable

**bent** *adj* curved; resolved (on); *Inf* corrupt; *Inf* deviant ~*n* inclination

**benzene** *n* one of group of flammable liquids used as solvents etc.

**bequeath** *v* leave property etc. by will **bequest** *n* bequeathing; legacy

**berate** *v* scold harshly

**bereave** *v* -**reaved** or -**reft** deprive of, esp. by death **bereavement** *n*

**beret** *n* round, close-fitting hat

**beriberi** *n* tropical disease caused by vitamin B deficiency

**berry** *n* small juicy stoneless fruit

**berserk** *adj* frenzied

**berth** *n* ship's mooring place; place to sleep in ship ~*v* moor

**beryl** *n* variety of crystalline mineral, e.g. aquamarine, emerald

**beseech** *v* **beseeching, besought** entreat, implore

**beset** *v* **besetting, beset** surround with danger, problems

**beside** *prep* by the side of, near; distinct from **besides** *adv/prep* in addition (to)

**besiege** *v* surround

**besotted** *adj* drunk; foolish; infatuated

**best** *adj/adv* superlative of GOOD and WELL ~*v* defeat **best man** groom's attendant at wedding **bestseller** *n*

**bend** *v* bow, buckle, contort, curve, diverge, flex, incline, lean, stoop, swerve, turn, twist, veer, warp ~*n* angle, arc, bow, corner, crook, curve, hook, loop, turn, twist

**beneath** *prep* below, inferior to, less than, lower than, unbefitting, underneath, unworthy of ~*adv* below, in a lower place, underneath

**beneficial** advantageous, favourable, healthful, helpful, useful, valuable, wholesome

**benefit** *n* advantage, aid, asset, blessing, boon, favour, gain, good, help, interest, profit, use ~*v* advance, aid, assist, avail, better, enhance, further, improve, profit, promote, serve

**bent** *adj* angled, arched, bowed, crooked, curved, hunched, twisted; (with **on**) determined, inclined, insistent, resolved, set ~*n* ability, aptitude, flair, forte, inclination,

knack, penchant, proclivity, propensity, talent

**bequeath** bestow, commit, endow, entrust, give, grant, hand down, leave to by will, pass on, will

**bereavement** death, deprivation, loss

**berserk** crazy, frenzied, insane, mad, manic, rabid, raging, violent, wild

**berth** *n* anchorage, dock, harbour, haven, pier, port, quay, wharf; bed, billet, bunk

**beside** abreast of, adjacent to, alongside, at the side of, close to, near, nearby, neighbouring, next door to, next to, overlooking

**besides** *adv* also, as well, further, furthermore, in addition, moreover, otherwise, too, what's more

**besiege** beleaguer, beset, blockade, encircle, encompass, hedge in, hem in, lay siege to, shut in,

book sold in great numbers

**bestial** *adj* like a beast, brutish

**bestir** *v* **bestirring, bestirred** rouse to activity

**bestow** *v* give, confer

**bet** *v* **betting, bet** *or* **betted** agree to pay money if wrong in guessing result of contest ~*n* money so risked

**bête noire** *n* (*pl* **bêtes noires**) particular dislike

**betray** *v* be disloyal to; reveal, divulge; show signs of **betrayal** *n*

**better** *adj/adv* comparative of GOOD and WELL ~*v* improve

**between** *prep/adv* in the intermediate part, in space or time; indicating reciprocal relation or comparison

**bevel** *n* angled surface ~*v* **-elling, -elled** slope, slant

**beverage** *n* drink

**bevy** *n* flock or group

**bewail** *v* lament

**beware** *v* be on one's guard

**bewilder** *v* puzzle, confuse

**bewitch** *v* charm, fascinate

**beyond** *adv* farther away ~*prep* on the farther side of; out of reach of

surround

**best** *adj* chief, finest, first, first-class, foremost, highest, leading, outstanding, perfect, pre-eminent, superlative, supreme; apt, correct, most desirable, most fitting, right; greatest, largest, most ~*adv* advantageously, excellently, most fortunately; extremely, greatly, most deeply, most fully, most highly

**bestial** animal, beastly, brutal, brutish, carnal, depraved, gross, inhuman, low, savage, sensual, sordid, vile

**bestow** accord, allot, award, commit, confer, donate, entrust, give, grant, impart, lavish, present

**bet** *v* chance, gamble, hazard, pledge, risk, speculate, stake, venture, wager ~*n* ante, gamble, hazard, pledge, risk, speculation, stake, venture, wager

**betray** be disloyal, break with, double-cross *Inf*, inform on, sell out *Inf*; disclose, divulge, evince, expose, give away, lay bare, let slip, reveal, show, tell, tell on, uncover, unmask

**betrayal** disloyalty, double-cross *Inf*, double-dealing, duplicity, false-

ness, perfidy, sell-out *Inf*, treachery, treason, trickery; disclosure, revelation, telling

**better** *adj* bigger, excelling, finer, fitter, greater, higher quality, larger, preferable, superior, surpassing, worthier; cured, fitter, healthier, improving, more healthy, on the mend *Inf*, progressing, recovering, stronger, well; bigger, greater, larger, longer ~*adv* in a more excellent manner, in a superior way, to a greater degree

**between** amidst, among, halfway, in the middle of, mid

**beverage** draught, drink, liquid, liquor, refreshment

**beware** avoid, be careful, be cautious, be wary, guard against, heed, look out, mind, shun, steer clear of, take heed, watch out

**bewilder** bemuse, confound, confuse, daze, flummox, mix up, mystify, perplex, puzzle

**bewitch** allure, beguile, charm, enchant, entrance, fascinate, spellbind

**beyond** above, apart from, at a distance, away from, before, farther, out of range, out of reach, over,

**bias** *n* (*pl* **biases**) slant; inclination
~*v* -**asing**, -**ased** influence; affect **bi-ased** *adj* prejudiced

**bib** *n* cloth put under child's chin when eating; top of apron

**Bible** *n* sacred writings of the Christian religion **biblical** *adj*

**bibliography** *n* list of books on a subject

**bicentenary** *n* 200th anniversary

**biceps** *n* two-headed muscle, esp. of upper arm

**bicker** *v/n* quarrel over petty things

**bicycle** *n* vehicle with two wheels **bicyclist** *n*

**bid** *v* **bidding, bid** or **bade, bid** or **bidden** offer; say; command; invite ~*n* offer, esp. of price; try; *Card games* call **bidder** *n* **bidding** *n* command

**bide** *v* remain; dwell; await

**bier** *n* frame for coffin

**bifocal** *adj* having two focal lengths **bifocals** *pl n* spectacles having bifo-cal lenses

**big** *adj* bigger, biggest of great size, height, number, power etc. **bighead** *n Inf* conceited person **big-headed** *adj*

**bigamy** *n* crime of marrying a person while one is still legally married to someone else **bigamist** *n*

**bigot** *n* person intolerant of ideas of others **bigoted** *adj* **bigotry** *n*

**bike** *n* short for BICYCLE or MOTORBIKE

**bikini** *n* (*pl* -**nis**) woman's two-piece swimming costume

**bilberry** *n* small moorland plant with edible blue berries

**bile** *n* fluid secreted by the liver; ill temper **bilious** *adj* nauseous, nauseating

**bilge** *n* bottom of ship's hull; dirty water collecting there; *Inf* nonsense

**bilingual** *adj* speaking, or written in, two languages

**bill**[1] *n* written account of charges; draft of Act of Parliament; poster;

——————— THESAURUS ———————

**bias** favouritism, inclination, leaning, narrow-mindedness, one-sidedness, partiality, prejudice, proneness, propensity, tendency, turn, unfairness

**biased** distorted, one-sided, partial, prejudiced, slanted, swayed, twisted, warped, weighted

**bicker** argue, disagree, dispute, fight, quarrel, squabble

**bid** *v* offer, proffer, propose, submit, tender; call, greet, say, tell, wish; ask, call, charge, command, desire, direct, enjoin, instruct, invite, require, solicit, summon, tell ~*n* offer, price, proposal, proposition, sum, tender; attempt, effort, try, venture

**bidding** behest, call, charge, com-mand, demand, invitation, order, request, summons

**big** bulky, burly, colossal, enormous, extensive, gigantic, great, huge, hulking, immense, large, mammoth, massive, prodigious, sizable, spacious, substantial, vast, voluminous; eminent, important, leading, main, powerful, principal, prominent, serious, significant, valuable, weighty; generous, gracious, heroic, magnanimous, noble, princely

**bigoted** biased, dogmatic, illiberal, intolerant, narrow-minded, opinionated, prejudiced, sectarian

**bigotry** bias, discrimination, dogmatism, fanaticism, intolerance, narrow-mindedness, prejudice, racialism, racism, sectarianism

commercial document ~*v* present account of charges; announce by advertisement

**bill²** *n* bird's beak

**billet** *n/v* (provide) civilian quarters for troops

**billiards** *n* game played on table with balls and cues

**billion** *n* thousand million, 10⁹; *Obs* million million, 10¹²

**billow** *n* swelling wave ~*v* swell

**bin** *n* receptacle for corn, refuse etc.

**binary** *adj* composed of, characterized by, two; dual

**bind** *v* binding, bound tie fast; tie round; oblige; seal; constrain; bandage; cohere; put (book) into cover **binder** *n* **binding** *n* cover of book; tape for hem etc.

**binge** *n Inf* spree

**bingo** *n* game of chance in which numbers drawn are matched with those on a card

**binoculars** *pl n* telescope made for both eyes

**bio-** *comb. form* life, living, as in **biochemistry**

**biodegradable** *adj* capable of decomposition by natural means

**biography** *n* story of one person's life **biographer** *n* **biographical** *adj*

**biology** *n* study of living organisms **biological** *adj* **biologist** *n*

**bionic** *adj* having physical functions aided by electronic equipment

**biopsy** *n* examination of tissue from a living body

**biped** *n* two-footed animal

**birch** *n* tree with silvery bark; rod for punishment ~*v* flog

**bird** *n* feathered animal

**birdie** *n Golf* score of one stroke under par

**Biro** *n Trademark* ballpoint pen

**birth** *n* bearing, or the being born, of offspring; parentage; origin **birthday** *n* **birthmark** *n* blemish on the skin

**biscuit** *n* dry, small, thin variety of cake

**bisect** *v* divide into two equal parts

**bisexual** *adj* sexually attracted to both men and women

**bishop** *n* clergyman governing dio-

──────── THESAURUS ────────

**bill¹** *n* account, charges, invoice, reckoning, score, statement, tally; measure, projected law, proposal; advertisement, broadsheet, circular, handbill, handout, leaflet, notice, placard, playbill, poster ~*v* charge, debit, figure, invoice

**bill²** *n* beak, mandible, neb *Arch or dial*, nib

**billet** *n* accommodation, barracks, lodging, quarters ~*v* accommodate, berth, quarter, station

**billow** *n* breaker, surge, swell, tide, wave ~*v* balloon, puff up, rise up, roll, surge, swell

**bind** *v* attach, fasten, glue, hitch, lash, paste, rope, secure, stick,

strap, tie, tie up; compel, constrain, force, necessitate, oblige

**binding** *adj* compulsory, indissoluble, irrevocable, mandatory, obligatory, unalterable

**biography** *n* account, curriculum vitae, CV, life, life story, memoirs, profile, record

**birth** childbirth, delivery, nativity, parturition; ancestry, background, blood, breeding, descent, genealogy, line, lineage, nobility, pedigree, race, stock, strain; beginning, emergence, genesis, origin, rise, source

**bisect** cut in half, cut in two, divide in two, halve

cese; chess piece

**bison** n large wild ox; Amer. buffalo

**bistro** n small restaurant

**bit**[1] n fragment, piece

**bit**[2] n biting, cutting part of tool; mouthpiece of horse's bridle

**bit**[3] n Computers smallest part of information

**bitch** n female dog, fox, or wolf; Offens sl spiteful woman **bitchy** adj

**bite** v biting, bit, bit or bitten cut into, esp. with teeth; grip; rise to the bait; corrode ~n act of biting; wound so made; mouthful **biting** adj piercing or keen; sarcastic

**bitter** adj sour tasting; (of person) resentful; sarcastic **bitterly** adv **bitterness** n

**bittern** n wading bird

**bitumen** n viscous substance occurring in asphalt, tar etc.

**bivouac** n temporary encampment of soldiers, hikers etc. ~v bivouac-

ing, bivouacked camp

**bizarre** adj unusual, weird

**blab** v blabbing, blabbed reveal secrets; chatter idly

**black** adj of the darkest colour; without light; dark; evil ~n dark colour; black dye, clothing etc.; (with cap.) person of dark-skinned race ~v boycott in industrial dispute **blacken** v make black; defame **blackball** v vote against, exclude **blackberry** n plant with dark juicy berries, bramble **blackbird** n common European songbird **blackboard** n dark surface for writing on with chalk **black box** Inf. name for FLIGHT RECORDER **blackhead** n small dark spot on skin **blackleg** n strikebreaker **blacklist** n list of people considered suspicious ~v put on such a list **black market** illegal buying and selling of goods **black spot** dangerous place, esp. on a road **blackguard** n scoundrel

———— THESAURUS ————

**bit**[1] chip, crumb, fragment, grain, iota, jot, mite, morsel, part, piece, scrap, slice, speck, tittle, whit

**bit**[2] brake, check, curb, restraint, snaffle

**bitchy** catty Inf, malicious, mean, nasty, rancorous, snide, spiteful, venomous, vicious, vindictive

**bite** v chew, clamp, crunch, crush, cut, gnaw, grip, hold, nibble, nip, pierce, pinch, rend, seize, snap, tear, wound ~n itch, nip, pinch, prick, sting, tooth marks, wound; food, light meal, morsel, mouthful, piece, snack

**biting** bitter, cold, cutting, freezing, harsh, penetrating, piercing, sharp; caustic, cutting, incisive, mordant, sarcastic, scathing, sharp, stinging, vitriolic, withering

**bitter** acid, acrid, astringent, sharp, sour, tart, unsweetened, vinegary, hostile, morose, rancorous, resentful, sore, sour, sullen

**bitterness** acerbity, acidity, sharpness, sourness, tartness; grudge, hostility, pique, rancour, resentment

**bizarre** curious, eccentric, extraordinary, fantastic, freakish, grotesque, ludicrous, odd, off-beat, outlandish, outré, peculiar, queer, strange, unusual, weird

**black** adj dark, dusky, ebony, inky, jet, murky, sable, starless, swarthy; bad, evil, iniquitous, nefarious, villainous, wicked

**blacken** befoul, cloud, darken, make black, smudge, soil; decry, defame, defile, denigrate, dishon-

**blackmail** v extort money by threats ~n extortion **blackmailer** n

**blackout** n complete failure of electricity supply; state of temporary unconsciousness; obscuring of lights as precaution against night air attack

**blacksmith** n person who works in iron

**bladder** n membranous bag to contain liquid

**blade** n edge, cutting part of knife or tool; leaf of grass etc.; sword

**blame** v censure; culpability ~v find fault with; censure **blameless** adj **blameworthy** adj

**blanch** v whiten, bleach; turn pale

**blancmange** n jellylike pudding made from milk

**bland** adj devoid of distinctive characteristics; smooth in manner **blandly** adv

**blank** adj without marks or writing; empty; vacant, confused ~n empty space; cartridge containing no bullet **blankly** adv

**blanket** n thick bed cover; concealing cover ~v cover, stifle

**blare** v sound loudly and harshly ~n such sound

**blarney** n flattering talk

**blasé** adj indifferent through familiarity; bored

**blaspheme** v show contempt for God, esp. in speech **blasphemous** adj **blasphemy** n

---

## THESAURUS

our, malign, slander, smear, smirch, stain, sully, taint, tarnish, vilify

**blacklist** v ban, bar, boycott, debar, exclude, expel, ostracize, preclude, proscribe, reject, snub, vote against

**blackmail** n bribe, exaction, extortion, hush money Sl, intimidation, protection Inf, ransom

**blackout** n power cut, power failure; coma, faint, oblivion, swoon, unconsciousness

**blame** n accusation, censure, charge, complaint, condemnation, criticism, recrimination, reproach, reproof; culpability, fault, guilt, incrimination, liability, onus, responsibility ~v accuse, admonish, censure, charge, chide, condemn, criticize, disapprove, find fault with, hold responsible, reprehend, reproach, reprove, tax, upbraid

**blameless** above suspicion, clean, faultless, guiltless, innocent, in the clear, irreproachable, perfect, stainless, unblemished, upright, virtuous

**blameworthy** discreditable, indefensible, inexcusable, iniquitous, reprehensible, reproachable, shameful

**bland** boring, dull, flat, humdrum, insipid, tasteless, tedious, vapid, weak

**blank** adj bare, clean, clear, empty, plain, spotless, unfilled, unmarked, void, white; at a loss, bewildered, confounded, confused, nonplussed, uncomprehending ~n emptiness, empty space, gap, nothingness, space, vacancy, vacuum, void

**blanket** n coverlet, rug; carpet, cloak, coat, coating, covering, envelope, film, layer, mantle, sheet, wrapper, wrapping ~v cloak, cloud, coat, conceal, cover, hide, mask, obscure

**blare** blast, boom, clang, honk, hoot, peal, resound, roar, trumpet

**blaspheme** curse, damn, desecrate, execrate, profane, swear

**blasphemous** godless, impious,

**blast** *n* explosion; shock wave; gust of wind; loud sound ~*v* blow up; blight

**blatant** *adj* obvious **blatantly** *adv*

**blaze¹** *n* strong fire or flame; brightness; outburst ~*v* burn strongly; be very angry

**blaze²** *v* establish trail ~*n* white mark on horse's face

**blazer** *n* type of jacket worn esp. for sports

**bleach** *v* make or become white ~*n* bleaching substance

**bleak** *adj* cold, exposed; dismal **bleakness** *n*

**bleary** *adj* with eyes dimmed, as with tears, sleep

**bleat** *v* cry, as sheep; say plaintively ~*n* sheep's cry

**bleed** *v* bleeding, bled lose blood; draw blood from

**bleep** *n* short high-pitched sound **bleeper** *n*

**blemish** *n* defect ~*v* make defective **blemished** *adj*

**blend** *v* mix ~*n* mixture **blender** *n* electrical appliance for mixing food

**bless** *v* blessing, blessed *or* blest consecrate; ask God's favour for; make happy **blessed** *adj* **blessing** *n*

**blether** *v* speak at length, esp. foolishly ~*n* foolish or babbling talk

———————— THESAURUS ————————

profane, sacrilegious, ungodly

**blasphemy** cursing, desecration, execration, impiety, impiousness, profanity, sacrilege, swearing

**blast** *n* bang, blow-up, burst, crash, explosion, outburst, salvo, volley; blow, clang, honk, peal, scream, toot, wail ~*v* blow up, break up, burst, demolish, destroy, explode, ruin, shatter

**blatant** brazen, conspicuous, flagrant, glaring, naked, obvious, ostentatious, outright, overt, prominent, sheer

**blaze** *n* bonfire, conflagration, fire, flame, flames; beam, brightness, flare, flash, glare, gleam, glitter, glow, light, radiance ~*v* beam, burn, fire, flame, flare, flash, glare, gleam, glow, shine

**bleach** blanch, fade, grow pale, lighten, peroxide, wash out, whiten

**bleak** bare, barren, chilly, cold, desolate, exposed, gaunt, open, raw, windswept, windy; cheerless, depressing, dismal, dreary, gloomy, grim, hopeless, joyless, sombre, unpromising

**bleed** exude, flow, gush, lose blood, ooze, run, seep, shed blood, spurt, trickle, weep; drain, draw or take blood, exhaust, extort, extract, fleece, milk, reduce, sap

**blemish** *n* blot, blotch, blur, defect, disfigurement, disgrace, dishonour, fault, flaw, imperfection, mark, smudge, speck, spot, stain, taint

**blend** *v* coalesce, combine, compound, fuse, intermix, merge, mingle, mix, unite ~*n* alloy, amalgam, composite, compound, concoction, fusion, mix, mixture, synthesis, union

**bless** consecrate, dedicate, exalt, extol, glorify, hallow, magnify, ordain, praise, sanctify, thank

**blessed** adored, beatified, divine, hallowed, holy, revered, sacred, sanctified; endowed, favoured, fortunate, lucky

**blessing** benediction, benison, consecration, dedication, grace, invocation, thanksgiving; advantage, benefit, boon, bounty, favour, gain, gift, godsend, good fortune, help,

**blight** n plant disease; harmful influence ~v injure

**blighter** n Inf irritating person

**blind** adj unable to see; heedless; closed at one end ~v deprive of sight ~n window screen; pretext

**blindly** adv **blindness** n **blindfold** v/n (cloth used to) cover the eyes

**blink** v wink; twinkle ~n gleam **blink at** ignore **on the blink** Inf not working

**blip** n repetitive sound or visible pulse, e.g. on radar screen

**bliss** n perfect happiness **blissful** adj **blissfully** adv

**blister** n bubble on skin; surface swelling ~v form blisters (on) **blistering** adj very hot; extremely harsh

**blithe** adj happy **blithely** adv

**blitz** n concentrated attack

**blizzard** n blinding storm of wind and snow

**bloated** adj swollen **bloater** n smoked herring

**blob** n soft mass or drop

**block** n solid (rectangular) piece of wood, stone etc.; obstacle; pulley with frame; large building of offices, flats etc. ~v obstruct, stop up; shape **blockage** n **blockhead** n stupid person **block letter** plain capital letter

**blockade** n physical prevention of access, esp. to port ~v prevent access

**bloke** n Inf fellow, chap

**blond** adj (fem **blonde**) (of hair) light-coloured ~n person with

——————— THESAURUS ———————

kindness, profit, service, windfall

**blight** n canker, decay, disease, fungus, infestation, mildew, pest, rot ~v blast, destroy, injure, nip in the bud, ruin, shrivel, wither

**blind** adj eyeless, sightless, unseeing, unsighted, visionless; careless, heedless, ignorant, inattentive, inconsiderate, indifferent, insensitive, neglectful, oblivious, prejudiced, thoughtless, unaware of, unconscious of, uncritical, undiscerning, unmindful of, unobservant, unreasoning ~n camouflage, cloak, cover, façade, feint, front, mask, screen, smoke screen

**blindly** aimlessly, at random, confusedly, frantically, indiscriminately, instinctively, madly, purposelessly, wildly

**bliss** beatitude, blessedness, ecstasy, euphoria, happiness, heaven, joy, paradise, rapture

**blissful** delighted, ecstatic, elated, enchanted, euphoric, happy, joyful, rapt, rapturous

**blister** abscess, boil, canker, carbuncle, cyst, pimple, sore, swelling, ulcer

**blithe** buoyant, carefree, cheerful, cheery, debonair, happy, jaunty, light-hearted, merry, sprightly, vivacious

**blitz** assault, attack, blitzkrieg, bombardment, offensive, onslaught, raid, strike

**blizzard** blast, gale, snowstorm, squall, storm, tempest

**blob** ball, bead, bubble, drop, droplet, globule, lump, mass, pearl

**block** n bar, brick, cake, chunk, cube, hunk, ingot, lump, mass, piece, square; bar, barrier, blockage, hindrance, impediment, jam, obstacle, obstruction, stoppage ~v choke, clog, close, obstruct, plug, stop up

**blockade** barricade, barrier, closure, hindrance, impediment, obstacle, obstruction, restriction,

light-coloured hair

**blood** n red fluid in veins; kindred ~v initiate (into hunting, war etc.)

**bloodless** adj lacking or covered in blood; savage; extreme ~adv Sl extremely ~v make bloody **blood bath** massacre **bloodhound** n large dog used for tracking **bloodshed** n slaughter **bloodshot** adj (of eyes) inflamed **bloodthirsty** adj cruel **bloody-minded** adj deliberately unhelpful

**bloom** n flower; prime; glow ~v be in flower; flourish

**bloomer** n Inf mistake

**bloomers** pl n wide, baggy knickers

**blossom** n flower ~v flower; flourish

**blot** n spot, stain ~v blotting, blot-

ted spot, stain; obliterate; soak up ink **blotter** n

**blotch** n dark spot ~v make spotted

**blouse** n light, loose upper garment

**blow**¹ v blowing, blew, blown make a current of air; pant; drive air upon or into; drive by current of air; make sound; Sl squander ~n blast; gale **blower** n **blowfly** n fly which infects food etc. **blowlamp** n small burner with very hot flame **blowout** n sudden puncture in tyre; uncontrolled escape of oil, gas, from well; Sl large meal **blow up** explode; fill with air; Inf enlarge photograph; Inf lose one's temper **blow**² n stroke, knock; sudden misfortune

———— THESAURUS ————

siege, stoppage

**blond, blonde** fair, fair-haired, flaxen, golden-haired, light

**blood** gore, lifeblood, vital fluid; ancestry, birth, descent, extraction, family, kindred, kinship, lineage, relations

**bloodshed** blood bath, butchery, carnage, gore, killing, massacre, murder, slaughter

**bloodthirsty** brutal, cruel, ferocious, inhuman, ruthless, savage, vicious, warlike

**bloody** bleeding, blood-soaked, bloodstained, raw; cruel, ferocious, fierce, savage

**bloom** n blossom, blossoming, bud, flower; beauty, flush, freshness, glow, health, heyday, lustre, perfection, prime, radiance, rosiness ~v blossom, blow, bud, burgeon, open, sprout

**blossom** n bloom, bud, flower, flowers ~v bloom, burgeon, flower;

bloom, develop, flourish, grow, mature, progress, prosper, thrive

**blot** n mark, patch, smear, smudge, speck, splodge, spot; blemish, blur, defect, disgrace, fault, flaw, spot, stain, taint ~v mark, smudge, spot, stain

**blow**¹ v blast, breathe, exhale, fan, pant, puff, waft; flow, rush, stream, whirl; bear, buffet, drive, fling, flutter, sweep, waft; pipe, play, sound, trumpet, vibrate ~n blast, draught, flurry, gale, gust, puff, strong breeze, tempest, wind

**blow**² n bang, bash Inf, buffet, knock, punch, rap, smack, stroke, thump, wallop Inf, whack; bombshell, calamity, catastrophe, disappointment, disaster, jolt, misfortune, reverse, setback, shock, upset

**blow up** blast, bomb, burst, detonate, explode, go off, rupture, shatter; distend, enlarge, expand, fill,

**blowzy** *adj* slovenly, sluttish

**blubber** *v* weep ~*n* whale fat

**bludgeon** *n* short thick club ~*v* strike with one; coerce

**blue** *adj* of the colour of sky; depressed; indecent ~*n* colour of sky; dye or pigment ~*pl Inf* depression; form of jazz music ~*v* blueing, blued make blue **blue** *adj* **bluebell** *n* wild spring flower **bluebottle** *n* blowfly **blueprint** *n* copy of drawing; original plan

**bluff**[1] *n* cliff, steep bank; *Canad* clump of trees ~*adj* hearty; blunt

**bluff**[2] *v/n* (deceive by) pretence

**blunder** *n/v* (make) clumsy mistake

**blunt** *adj* not sharp; (of speech) abrupt ~*v* make blunt **bluntly** *adv*

**blur** *v* blurring, blurred make, become less distinct ~*n* something distinct

**blurb** *n* statement recommending book etc.

**blurt** *v* utter suddenly

**blush** *v* become red in face; be ashamed ~*n* this effect **blusher** *n* cosmetic to give rosy colour to face

**bluster** *v/n* (indulge in) noisy, aggressive behaviour **blustery** *adj* (of wind) gusty

**BO** *Inf* body odour

**boa** *n* large, nonpoisonous snake; long scarf of fur or feathers

**boar** *n* male pig; wild pig

**board** *n* broad, flat piece of wood, card etc.; table; meals; group of people who administer company ~*v* cover with planks; supply board daily; enter ship etc.; take daily meals **boarder** *n* **boardroom** *n*

**boast** *v* speak too much in praise of oneself; brag of; have to show ~*n* thing boasted (of) **boastful** *adj*

THESAURUS

inflate, swell; blow up, enlarge, magnify

**blue** azure, cobalt, navy, sapphire, ultramarine; dejected, depressed, despondent, dismal, downcast, down-hearted, down in the mouth, fed up, gloomy, glum, low, melancholy, sad, unhappy

**blueprint** design, draft, layout, outline, pattern, pilot scheme, plan, project, prototype, scheme, sketch

**bluff** *v* deceive, delude, fake, feign, humbug, lie, mislead, pretend, sham ~*n* bluster, boast, deceit, deception, fake, feint, fraud, humbug, idle boast, lie, mere show, pretence, sham, show, subterfuge

**blunder** *n* error, fault, mistake, oversight, slip ~*v* botch, bungle, err

**blunt** dull, rounded, unsharpened; bluff, brusque, forthright, frank, impolite, outspoken, plain-spoken,

rude, tactless, trenchant

**blur** *v* cloud, darken, dim, fog, mask, obscure, soften ~*n* blear, confusion, dimness, fog, haze, indistinctness, obscurity

**blush** colour, crimson, flush, redden, turn red

**bluster** *v* boast, brag, bulldoze, bully, domineer, hector, rant, roar, storm, swagger, swell, vaunt ~*n* bombast, bragging, bravado, crowing, swagger

**board** *n* panel, plank, slat, timber; daily meals, food, meals, provisions; committee, conclave, council, directorate, directors, panel, trustees ~*v* accommodate, feed, house, lodge, put up, quarter, room; embark, embus, enplane, enter, entrain, mount

**boast** *v* be proud of, exhibit, flatter oneself, possess, show off; bluster,

**boat** *n* small open vessel; ship *~v* sail about in boat **boater** *n* flat straw hat **boatswain** *n* ship's officer in charge of equipment

**bob** *v* **bobbing, bobbed** move up and down; move jerkily; cut (women's) hair short *~n* jerking motion; short hairstyle; weight on pendulum etc.

**bobbin** *n* reel for thread

**bobble** *n* small, tufted ball

**bobby** *n* *Inf* police officer

**bobsleigh** *n* sledge for racing *~v* ride on this

**bode** *v* be an omen of

**bodice** *n* upper part of woman's dress

**bodkin** *n* large blunt needle

**body** *n* whole frame of man or animal; corpse; main part; substance; group regarded as single entity **bodily** *adj/adv* **bodyguard** *n* escort

to protect important person **bodywork** *n* outer shell of motor vehicle

**boffin** *n* *Inf* scientist

**bog** *n* wet, soft ground **boggy** *adj* **bog down** stick as in a bog

**bogey** *n* thing that causes fear; *Golf* score of one stroke over par

**boggle** *v* stare, be surprised

**bogus** *adj* sham, false

**bohemian** *n/adj* (person) leading unconventional life

**boil**[1] *v* (cause to) change from liquid to gas, esp. by heating; cook or become cooked by boiling; *Inf* be hot; *Inf* be angry *~n* boiling state **boiler** *n* equipment providing hot water

**boil**[2] *n* inflamed swelling on skin

**boisterous** *adj* wild; noisy

**bold** *adj* daring, presumptuous; prominent **boldly** *adv* **boldness** *n*

**bole** *n* tree trunk

————————— THESAURUS —————————

brag, crow, exaggerate, puff, strut, swagger, talk big *Sl*, vaunt *~n* avowal, brag, swank *Inf*, vaunt

**boastful** cocky, conceited, crowing, egotistical, puffed-up, swaggering

**bodily** *adj* carnal, corporeal, material, physical, tangible *~adv* altogether, collectively, completely, en masse, entirely, fully, totally, wholly

**body** build, figure, form, frame, physique, shape, torso, trunk; cadaver, carcass, corpse, dead body, remains; bulk, essence, main part, mass, material, matter, substance; association, band, collection, company, congress, corporation, society

**bog** fen, marsh, mire, morass, peat bog, quagmire, slough, swamp

**bogey** apparition, bogeyman, goblin, hobgoblin, imp, spectre, spirit,

spook *Inf*, sprite

**bogus** artificial, counterfeit, dummy, fake, false, forged, fraudulent, imitation, phoney *or* phony *Inf*, sham, spurious

**bohemian** avant-garde, eccentric, exotic, left bank, nonconformist, offbeat, unconventional, unorthodox

**boil** *v* agitate, bubble, churn, effervesce, fizz, foam, froth, seethe

**boisterous** bouncy, clamorous, impetuous, loud, noisy, riotous, rollicking, rowdy, rumbustious, unrestrained, unruly, uproarious, vociferous, wild

**bold** adventurous, audacious, brave, courageous, daring, dauntless, enterprising, fearless, gallant, heroic, intrepid, valiant; bright, colourful, conspicuous, eye-catching, flashy, lively, loud, prominent, spir-

**bolero** *n* (*pl* -ros) Spanish dance; short loose jacket

**bollard** *n* post to secure mooring lines; post in road as barrier

**bolster** *v* support, uphold ~*n* long pillow; pad, support

**bolt** *n* bar or pin (esp. with thread for nut); rush; lightning; roll of cloth ~*v* fasten; swallow hastily; rush away

**bomb** *n* explosive projectile; any explosive device ~*v* attack with bombs **bomber** *n* aircraft that drops bombs; person who throws or plants a bomb **bombard** *v* shell; attack (verbally) **bombshell** *n* shocking surprise

**bombastic** *adj* pompous

**bona fide** *Lat* genuine

**bonanza** *n* sudden wealth

**bond** *n* thing which binds; link; written promise ~*v* bind

**bondage** *n* slavery

**bone** *n* hard substance forming skeleton; piece of this ~*v* take out bone **bony** *adj* **bone-idle** *adj* extremely lazy

**bonfire** *n* large outdoor fire

**bongo** *n* (*pl* -gos, -goes) small drum played with fingers

**bonk** *v* *Inf* hit; have sexual intercourse (with)

**bonnet** *n* hat with strings; cap; cover of motor vehicle engine

**bonny** *adj* beautiful, handsome

**bonsai** *n* (art of growing) dwarf trees, shrubs

**bonus** *n* (*pl* **bonuses**) extra (unexpected) payment or gift

**boo** *interj* expression of disapproval; exclamation to surprise esp. child ~*v* make this sound

**boob** *n* *Sl* foolish mistake; female breast

**booby trap** harmless-looking object which explodes when disturbed

**boogie** *v* *Inf* dance quickly to pop music

**book** *n* sheets of paper bound together; literary work ~*v* reserve room, ticket etc.; charge with legal offence; enter name in book **booklet** *n* **book-keeping** *n* systematic recording of business transactions **bookmaker** *n* one who takes bets **bookworm** *n* person devoted to reading

**boom**[1] *n* sudden commercial activ-

ited, striking, strong, vivid

**bolt** *n* bar, catch, latch, lock; peg, pin, rivet, rod; spring, sprint ~*v* bar, fasten, latch, lock, secure; cram, devour, gobble, gorge, gulp, guzzle, stuff, wolf; abscond, bound, dash, escape, flee, fly, hurtle, jump, leap, run, rush, spring, sprint

**bomb** *n* bombshell, charge, device, explosive, grenade, mine, missile, projectile, rocket, shell, torpedo ~*v* attack, blow up, bombard, destroy, shell, strafe, torpedo

**bombard** assault, blast, blitz, bomb, fire upon, open fire, shell,

strafe; assail, attack, barrage, beset, besiege, harass, hound

**bond** *n* band, binding, chain, cord, fastening, fetter, link, shackle, tie; affinity, attachment, connection, link, relation, tie, union; compact, contract, covenant, guarantee, obligation, pledge, promise, word ~*v* bind, connect, fasten, fix together, fuse, glue, gum, paste

**bonus** benefit, bounty, commission, dividend, extra, gift, gratuity, hand-out, prize, reward

**book** *n* album, diary, jotter, notebook, pad; manual, publication,

ity; prosperity ~v prosper

**boom²** v/n (make) deep sound

**boom³** n long spar for bottom of sail

**boomerang** n curved wooden missile of Aust. Aborigines, which returns to the thrower

**boon** n something helpful, favour

**boor** n rude person **boorish** adj

**boost** n encouragement; upward push; increase ~v encourage; push **booster** n

**boot** n covering for the foot and ankle; luggage space in car; Inf kick ~v Inf kick

**booth** n stall; cubicle

**bootleg** v make, carry, sell illicit goods, esp. alcohol ~adj produced,

sold illicitly **bootlegger** n

**booty** n plunder, spoil

**booze** n/v Inf (consume) alcoholic drink

**border** n margin; frontier; limit; strip of garden ~v provide with border; adjoin

**bore¹** v pierce hole ~n hole; calibre of gun

**bore²** v make weary by repetition ~n tiresome person or thing **boredom** n **boring** adj

**boron** n chemical element used in hardening steel etc.

**borough** n town

**borrow** v obtain on loan; copy, steal **borrower** n

**borstal** n formerly prison for

---

roll, textbook, tome, tract, volume, work ~v arrange for, bill, charter, engage, line up, make reservations, organize, reserve, schedule

**boom¹** n advance, development, expansion, gain, growth, improvement, increase, spurt, upsurge ~v develop, expand, flourish, gain, grow, increase, intensify, prosper, spurt, succeed, swell, thrive

**boom²** v bang, blast, crash, explode, resound, reverberate, roar, roll, rumble, thunder ~n bang, blast, burst, clap, crash, explosion, roar, rumble, thunder

**boon** advantage, benefaction, benefit, blessing, favour, gift, grant, present, windfall

**boost** n encouragement, help, praise, promotion; addition, expansion, improvement, increase, increment, jump, rise ~v advance, advertise, assist, encourage, foster, further, improve, inspire, plug Inf, praise, promote, support, sustain; elevate, heave, hoist, lift, push,

raise, shove, thrust

**border** bound, boundary, bounds, brim, brink, confine, confines, edge, hem, limit, limits, lip, margin, rim, skirt, verge; borderline, boundary, frontier, line, march

**bore¹** v drill, mine, penetrate, pierce, sink, tunnel ~n borehole, calibre, drill hole, hole, shaft, tunnel

**bore²** v be tedious, bother, exhaust, fatigue, pall on, tire, trouble, vex, wear out, weary, worry ~n bother, drag Inf, nuisance, pain Inf, pest

**boredom** apathy, dullness, ennui, flatness, monotony, sameness, tediousness, tedium, weariness

**boring** dead, dull, flat, humdrum, insipid, monotonous, routine, stale, tedious, tiresome, tiring, unexciting, uninteresting, unvaried, wearisome

**borrow** take on loan, use temporarily; acquire, adopt, appropriate, copy, imitate, obtain, pilfer, pirate, simulate, steal, take, use, usurp

young criminals

**borzoi** n tall dog with long, silky coat

**bosom** n human breast

**boss** n person in charge of or employing others ~v be in charge of; be domineering over **bossy** adj overbearing

**botany** n study of plants **botanical** adj **botanist** n

**botch** v spoil by clumsiness ~n blunder

**both** adj/pron the two

**bother** v pester; perplex; trouble ~n fuss, trouble

**bottle** n vessel for holding liquid; its contents ~v put into bottle; restrain **bottleneck** n narrow outlet which impedes smooth flow

**bottom** n lowest part; bed of sea etc.; buttocks ~adj lowest ~v put bottom to; base (upon); get to bottom of **bottomless** adj

**boulder** n large rock

**boulevard** n broad street or promenade

**bounce** v (cause to) rebound on impact ~n rebounding; quality causing this; Inf vitality **bouncer** n person who removes unwanted people from nightclub etc. **bouncing** adj vigorous

**bound**[1] n (usu. pl) limit ~v restrict **boundary** n **boundless** adj

**bound**[2] v/n spring, leap

**bound**[3] adj on a specified course

**bound**[4] adj committed; certain; tied

**bounty** n liberality; gift; premium

——————————— THESAURUS ———————————

**bosom** breast, bust, chest

**boss** chief, director, employer, executive, foreman, gaffer Inf, chiefly Brit, governor Inf, head, leader, manager, master, overseer, owner, supervisor

**botch** v blunder, bungle, cobble, fumble, mar, mend, mess, muff, patch, screw up Inf, spoil

**bother** v alarm, annoy, concern, dismay, distress, disturb, harass, hassle Inf, inconvenience, irritate, molest, nag, pester, plague, put out, trouble, upset, vex, worry ~n annoyance, bustle, difficulty, flurry, fuss, hassle Inf, inconvenience, irritation, nuisance, pest, problem, strain, trouble, vexation, worry

**bottom** n base, basis, bed, deepest part, depths, floor, foot, foundation, groundwork, lowest part, pedestal, support ~adj base, basement, basic, fundamental, ground, last, lowest

**bounce** v bound, bump, jump, leap, rebound, recoil, ricochet, spring, thump ~n bound, elasticity, give, rebound, recoil, resilience, spring, springiness; animation, dynamism, energy, go Inf, life, liveliness, pep, vigour, vitality, vivacity, zip Inf

**bound**[1] n (usu. pl) border, boundary, confine, edge, extremity, fringe, limit, line, march, margin, rim, verge

**bound**[2] v/n bounce, caper, frisk, gambol, hurdle, jump, leap, pounce, prance, skip, spring, vault

**bound**[3] adj committed, compelled, forced, obligated, obliged, pledged, required; certain, destined, doomed, fated, sure; cased, fastened, fixed, secured, tied, tied up

**boundary** barrier, border, borderline, bounds, brink, confines, edge, extremity, fringe, frontier, limits, margin, precinct

**bounteous, bountiful** adj

**bouquet** n bunch of flowers; aroma; compliment

**bourbon** n US whisky made from maize

**bourgeois** n/adj middle class

**bout** n period of time spent doing something; contest, fight

**boutique** n small shop, esp. one selling clothes

**bow¹** n weapon for shooting arrows; implement for playing violin etc.; ornamental knot; bend ~v bend

**bow²** v bend body in respect, assent etc.; submit; bend downwards; crush ~n bowing

**bow³** n fore end of ship

**bowel** n (oft. pl) part of intestine; inside of anything

**bowl¹** n round vessel, deep basin; drinking cup; hollow

**bowl²** n wooden ball; pl game played with balls ~v roll or throw ball in various ways **bowler** n **bowling** n

**bowler** n man's low-crowned stiff felt hat

**box¹** n (wooden) container, usu. rectangular; its contents; any box-like cubicle or receptacle ~v put in box; confine **box office** place where tickets are sold

**box²** v fight with fists, esp. with padded gloves on; strike ~n blow **boxer** n one who boxes; large dog resembling bulldog **boxing** n

**box³** n evergreen shrub used for hedges

**boy** n male child; young man **boyish** adj **boyfriend** n woman's male companion

**boycott** v refuse to deal with or participate in ~n such refusal

**bra** n woman's undergarment, supporting breasts

**brace** n tool for boring; clamp; pair; support; pl straps to hold up trousers ~v steady (oneself) as before a blow; support **bracelet** n ornament for the arm **bracing** adj invigorating

**bracken** n large fern

———— THESAURUS ————

**boundless** endless, immense, incalculable, inexhaustible, infinite, measureless, unbounded, unending, unlimited, untold, vast

**bouquet** bunch of flowers, buttonhole, garland, nosegay, posy, wreath; aroma, fragrance, perfume, redolence, savour, scent

**bout** competition, contest, encounter, engagement, fight, match, set-to

**bow** v bend, droop, genuflect, incline, make obeisance, nod, stoop; accept, comply, concede, defer, give in, relent, submit, surrender, yield ~n bending, bob, genuflexion, nod

**box¹** carton, case, chest, container, pack, package, trunk

**box²** v exchange blows, fight, spar; buffet, clout Inf, cuff, hit, punch, slap, strike, wallop Inf, whack ~n blow, buffet, cuff, punch, slap, stroke, wallop Inf

**boxer** fighter, prizefighter, pugilist

**boy** fellow, junior, lad, schoolboy, stripling, youngster, youth

**boycott** ban, bar, black, blackball, blacklist, exclude, outlaw, prohibit, proscribe, refuse, reject, spurn

**boyfriend** admirer, date, follower, lover, man, suitor

**bracing** brisk, cool, crisp, exhilarating, fresh, invigorating, lively, refreshing, stimulating, tonic, vigorous

**bracket** *n* support for shelf etc.; group; *pl* marks, () used to enclose words etc. ~*v* enclose in brackets; connect

**brackish** *adj* (of water) slightly salty

**brag** *v* bragging, bragged boast ~*n* boastful talk **braggart** *n*

**braid** *v* interweave; trim with braid ~*n* anything plaited; ornamental tape

**Braille** *n* system of printing for blind, with raised dots

**brain** *n* mass of nerve tissue in head; intellect ~*v* kill by hitting on head **brainy** *adj* **brainchild** *n* creative idea of a person **brainwash** *v* force someone to change beliefs **brainwave** *n* sudden, clever idea

**braise** *v* stew in covered pan

**brake** *n* instrument for slowing motion of wheel on vehicle ~*v* apply brake to

**bramble** *n* prickly shrub

**bran** *n* sifted husks of corn

**branch** *n* limb of tree; local office ~*v* bear branches; diverge; spread

**brand** *n* trademark; class of goods; particular kind; mark made by hot iron; burning piece of wood ~*v* burn with iron; mark; stigmatize

**brand-new** *adj* absolutely new

**brandish** *v* flourish, wave

**brandy** *n* spirit distilled from wine

**brash** *adj* bold, impudent

**brass** *n* alloy of copper and zinc; group of brass wind instruments; *Inf* money; *Inf* (army) officers ~*adj* made of brass

**brassiere** *n* bra

**brat** *n* unruly child

**bravado** *n* showy display of boldness

**brave** *adj* courageous; splendid ~*n* warrior ~*v* defy, meet boldly **bravery** *n*

**bravo** *interj* well done!

**brawl** *v*/*n* (take part in) noisy fight

**brawn** *n* muscle; strength; pickled pork **brawny** *adj*

—————— THESAURUS ——————

**brainy** bright, brilliant, clever, intelligent, smart

**brake** *n* check, constraint, control, curb, rein, restraint ~*v* check, decelerate, halt, moderate, reduce speed, slacken, slow, stop

**branch** arm, bough, limb, offshoot, prong, ramification, shoot, spray, sprig; chapter, department, division, local office, office, part, section, subdivision, subsection, subsidiary, wing

**brand** *n* hallmark, label, mark, sign, stamp, symbol, trademark; cast, class, grade, kind, make, quality, sort, species, type, variety ~*v* burn, burn in, label, mark, scar, stamp; denounce, disgrace, expose, mark, stigmatize

**brandish** display, exhibit, flourish, raise, shake, swing, wield

**bravado** bluster, boastfulness, bombast, brag, swagger

**brave** bold, courageous, daring, fearless, gallant, heroic, intrepid, plucky, resolute, valiant

**bravery** boldness, courage, daring, fortitude, gallantry, grit, guts *Inf*, hardiness, heroism, intrepidity, mettle, pluck, spirit, valour

**brawl** *v* battle, dispute, fight, quarrel, row *Inf*, scrap *Inf*, scuffle, wrangle, wrestle ~*n* argument, battle, broil, clash, disorder, dispute, fight, fracas, fray, free-for-all *Inf*, quarrel, row *Inf*, rumpus, scrap *Inf*, uproar, wrangle

**brawny** athletic, beefy *Inf*, burly,

**bray** n/v (make) donkey's cry

**brazen** adj of, like brass; shameless ~v (usu. with out) face, carry through with impudence

**brazier** n pan for burning coals

**breach** n opening; breaking of rule etc. ~v make a gap in

**bread** n food make of flour baked; food; Sl money **breadwinner** n main earner in family

**breadth** n extent across, width; largeness of view, mind

**break** v breaking, broke, broken part by force; shatter; burst, destroy; become broken; fail to observe; disclose; interrupt; surpass; weaken; accustom (horse) to being ridden; decipher (code); open, appear; come suddenly ~n fracture; gap; opening; separation; interruption; respite; interval; Inf opportunity **breakable** adj **breakage** n

**breaker** n one that breaks; wave beating on shore **breakdown** n collapse; failure to function; analysis

**breakfast** n first meal of the day

**break-in** n illegal entering of building **breakneck** adj fast and dangerous **breakthrough** n important advance **breakwater** n barrier to break force of waves

**bream** n broad, thin fish

**breast** n human chest; milk-secreting gland on woman's chest; seat of the affections ~v face, oppose; reach summit of **breaststroke** n stroke in swimming

**breath** n air used by lungs; life; respiration; slight breeze **breathe** v inhale and exhale (air); live; rest; whisper **breather** n short rest **breathing** n **breathless** adj **breathtaking** adj causing awe or excitement

——————— THESAURUS ———————

hardy, lusty, muscular, powerful, robust, strapping, strong, sturdy, thickset, well-built

**breach** break, chasm, cleft, crack, fissure, gap, hole, opening, rent, rift, rupture, split; infringement, offence, transgression, trespass, violation

**bread** diet, fare, food, nourishment, nutriment, provisions, subsistence, sustenance

**breadth** latitude, span, spread, wideness, width; freedom, latitude, liberality, openness, permissiveness

**break** v batter, burst, crack, crash, demolish, destroy, fracture, fragment, part, rend, separate, shatter, shiver, smash, snap, splinter, split, tear; breach, disobey, disregard, infringe, transgress, violate; demoralize, dispirit, enfeeble, impair, incapacitate, subdue, tame,

undermine, weaken; of a record, etc. beat, better, cap Inf, exceed, excel, go beyond, outdo, outstrip, surpass, top; appear, burst out, emerge, erupt, happen, occur ~n breach, cleft, crack, division, fissure, fracture, gap, gash, hole, opening, rent, rift, rupture, split, tear; alienation, breach, disaffection, estrangement, rift, rupture, separation, split; breather Inf, halt, interlude, intermission, interruption, interval, let-up Inf, lull, pause, recess, respite, rest, suspension

**breakdown** collapse, disintegration, disruption, failure, stoppage; analysis, detailed list, diagnosis, dissection, itemization

**breakthrough** advance, development, discovery, find, gain, improvement, invention, leap, progress

**Breathalyser** n Trademark device that estimates amount of alcohol in breath **breathalyse** v

**breech** n buttocks; hind part of anything **breeches** pl n trousers

**breed** v **breeding, bred** generate; rear; be produced; be with young ~n offspring produced; race, kind **breeder** n **breeding** n result of good upbringing

**breeze** n gentle wind **breezy** adj windy; lively

**brethren** pl n brothers

**brevity** n conciseness of expression; short duration

**brew** v prepare liquor, as beer; make drink, as tea; plot; be in preparation; n beverage produced by brewing **brewer** n **brewery** n

**briar, brier** n prickly shrub

**bribe** n anything offered or given to gain favour ~v influence by bribe **bribery** n

**bric-a-brac** n small ornamental objects

**brick** n oblong mass of hardened clay used in building ~v build, block etc. with bricks **bricklayer** n

**bride** n (masc **bridegroom**) woman about to be, or just, married **bridal** adj **bridesmaid** n

**bridge**¹ structure for crossing river

━━━━━━━ THESAURUS ━━━━━━━

**breath** air, exhalation, gasp, gulp, inhalation, pant, respiration, wheeze; faint breeze, flutter, gust, puff, sigh, waft, zephyr

**breathe** draw in, gasp, gulp, inhale and exhale, pant, puff, respire, wheeze; articulate, express, murmur, say, sigh, utter, voice, whisper

**breathless** exhausted, gasping, gulping, out of breath, panting, spent, wheezing, winded

**breathtaking** amazing, astonishing, awe-inspiring, awesome, exciting, impressive, magnificent, moving, overwhelming, stunning Inf, thrilling

**breed** v bear, beget, bring forth, engender, generate, hatch, multiply, originate, procreate, produce, propagate, reproduce; bring up, cultivate, develop, instruct, nourish, nurture, raise, rear ~n brand, class, extraction, family, ilk, kind, line, lineage, pedigree, progeny, race, sort, species, stock, strain, type, variety

**breeding** civility, conduct, courtesy, cultivation, culture, gentility, manners, polish, refinement, urbanity

**breeze** air, draught, flurry, gust, waft, whiff, zephyr

**breezy** airy, blowy, blustery, fresh, gusty, squally, windy; airy, animated, blithe, carefree, casual, cheerful, chirpy Inf, debonair, easygoing, free and easy, jaunty, light, light-hearted, lively, spirited, sunny, upbeat Inf, vivacious

**brevity** conciseness, economy, pithiness, succinctness, terseness; impermanence, transience

**brew** v boil, ferment, infuse tea, make beer, seethe, soak, steep, stew; breed, concoct, contrive, develop, devise, excite, foment, form, gather, hatch, plan, plot, project, scheme, start, stir up

**bribe** n allurement, enticement, graft Inf, hush money Sl, incentive, inducement, kickback US, pay-off Inf ~v buy off, corrupt, get at, grease the palm or hand of Sl, lure, pay off Inf, reward, square, suborn

**bribery** buying off, corruption, graft, inducement, payola Inf

etc.; something joining or supporting other parts; raised narrow platform on ship; upper part of nose ~v make bridge over, span

**bridge²** n card game

**bridle** n headgear of horse; curb ~v put on bridle; restrain; show resentment

**brief** adj short in duration; concise; scanty ~n document containing facts of legal case; summary; pl underpants; panties ~v give instructions **briefly** adv **briefcase** n flat case for carrying papers, books etc.

**brier** see BRIAR

**brigade** n subdivision of army; organized band **brigadier** n high-ranking army officer

**brigand** n bandit

**bright** adj shining; full of light; cheerful; clever **brighten** v **brightly** adv **brightness** n

**brilliant** adj shining; sparkling; splendid; very clever; distinguished **brilliance, brilliancy** n

**brim** n margin, edge, esp. of river, cup, hat **brimful** adj

**brine** n salt water; pickle

**bring** v bringing, brought fetch; carry with one; cause to happen

<hr>

THESAURUS

**bridge** n flyover, overpass, span, viaduct; band, bond, connection, link, tie ~v arch over, attach, bind, connect, couple, cross, cross over, extend across, go over, join, link, reach across, span, traverse, unite

**bridle** v check, constrain, control, curb, govern, master, moderate, repress, restrain, subdue; bristle, get angry, raise one's hackles, rear up

**brief** adj fast, fleeting, little, momentary, quick, short, short-lived, swift, transitory; compressed, concise, crisp, curt, laconic, pithy, short, succinct, terse, to the point ~n case, contention, data, defence; abstract, digest, epitome, outline, précis, sketch, summary, synopsis ~v advise, explain, fill in Inf, instruct, prepare, prime

**briefly** concisely, cursorily, curtly, hastily, hurriedly, in brief, in outline, in passing, momentarily, precisely, quickly, shortly

**bright** adj beaming, blazing, brilliant, effulgent, flashing, gleaming, glistening, glittering, glowing, illuminated, intense, luminous, radiant, resplendent, shining, sparkling, twinkling, vivid; clear, clement, cloudless, fair, lucid, pleasant, sunny, unclouded; cheerful, chirpy Inf, gay, genial, glad, happy, jolly, joyful, joyous, lively, merry, vivacious; acute, astute, aware, brilliant, clever, ingenious, intelligent, inventive, keen, quick, quick-witted, sharp, smart

**brighten** clear up, enliven, gleam, glow, illuminate, lighten, light up, shine; become cheerful, gladden, hearten, perk up

**brilliant** ablaze, bright, dazzling, glittering, glossy, intense, luminous, radiant, refulgent, scintillating, shining, sparkling, vivid; accomplished, acute, astute, brainy, clever, discerning, expert, gifted, intellectual, intelligent, penetrating, profound, quick, talented; celebrated, distinguished, eminent, exceptional, famous, glorious, magnificent, outstanding, splendid, superb

**brim** border, brink, circumference, edge, lip, margin, rim, skirt, verge

**bring** accompany, bear, carry, conduct, convey, deliver, escort, fetch,

**brink** n edge of steep place

**brisk** adj active, vigorous **briskly** adv

**brisket** n meat from breast

**bristle** n short stiff hair ~v stand erect; show temper **bristly** adj

**Brit.** Britain; British

**brittle** adj easily broken; curt

**broach** v introduce (subject); open

**broad** adj wide, spacious, open; obvious; coarse; general **broaden** v **broadly** adv **broadcast** v transmit by radio or television; make widely known ~n radio or television programme **broadcaster** n **broadcasting** n **broad-minded** adj tolerant **broadside** n discharge of guns; strong (verbal) attack

**brocade** n rich woven fabric with raised design

**broccoli** n type of cabbage

**brochure** n pamphlet

**brogue** n stout shoe; dialect, esp.

Irish accent

**broil** v US grill

**broke** adj Inf having no money

**broker** n one employed to buy and sell for others

**bromide** n chemical compound used in medicine and photography

**bromine** n liquid element used in production of chemicals

**bronchial** adj of branches in the windpipe **bronchitis** n inflammation of bronchial tubes

**bronco** n (pl -cos) US wild pony

**brontosaurus** n large plant-eating dinosaur

**bronze** n alloy of copper and tin ~adj made of, or coloured like, bronze ~v give appearance of bronze to

**brooch** n ornamental pin

**brood** n family of young, esp. of birds ~v sit, as hen on eggs; fret over **broody** adj

———————— THESAURUS ————————

gather, guide, import, lead, take, transfer, transport, usher; cause, contribute to, create, effect, engender, inflict, occasion, produce, result in, wreak

**brink** border, brim, edge, fringe, frontier, limit, margin, point, rim, skirt

**brisk** active, agile, alert, bustling, busy, energetic, lively, nimble, quick, speedy, spry, vigorous, vivacious

**bristle** n barb, hair, prickle, spine, stubble, thorn, whisker ~v be angry, bridle, flare up, rage, see red, seethe

**brittle** breakable, crisp, crumbly, delicate, fragile, frail, shivery

**broad** ample, extensive, large, roomy, spacious, vast, voluminous, wide, widespread; comprehensive,

far-reaching, general, inclusive, sweeping, universal, unlimited, wide, wide-ranging

**broadcast** v air, beam, radio, relay, show, televise, transmit; advertise, announce, circulate, disseminate, make public, proclaim, promulgate, publish, report, spread ~n programme, show, transmission

**broaden** develop, enlarge, expand, extend, increase, open up, spread, stretch, swell, widen

**broad-minded** catholic, flexible, indulgent, liberal, open-minded, permissive, responsive, tolerant, unbiased, unprejudiced

**brochure** booklet, circular, folder, handbill, leaflet, pamphlet

**broker** agent, dealer, factor, go-between, intermediary, middleman

**bronze** brownish, chestnut, cop-

**brook¹** n small stream

**brook²** v put up with

**broom** n brush for sweeping; yellow-flowered shrub **broomstick** n handle of broom

**bros.** brothers

**broth** n thick soup

**brothel** n house of prostitution

**brother** n son of same parents; one closely united with another **brotherly** adj **brotherhood** n fellowship; association **brother-in-law** n. brother of husband or wife; husband of sister

**brow** n ridge over eyes; forehead; eyebrow; edge of hill **browbeat** v frighten with threats

**brown** adj of dark colour inclining to red or yellow ~n the colour ~v make, become brown

**Brownie** n junior Girl Guide

**browse** v look through (book etc.) in a casual manner; feed on shoots and leaves

**bruise** v injure without breaking skin ~n contusion, discoloration caused by blow **bruiser** n tough person

**brunch** n breakfast and lunch combined

**brunette** n woman of dark complexion and hair ~adj dark brown

**brunt** n chief shock of attack

**brush¹** n device with bristles, hairs etc. used for cleaning, painting etc.; act of brushing; brief contact; skirmish; bushy tail ~v apply, remove, clean, with brush; touch lightly

**brush²** n thick shrubbery

**brusque** adj curt

**Brussels sprout** vegetable like a tiny cabbage

per, reddish-brown, rust, tan

**brood** n breed, chicks, children, clutch, family, hatch, infants, issue, litter, offspring, progeny, young ~v agonize, dwell upon, fret, meditate, mope, muse, repine, ruminate, think upon

**brook** burn, stream, watercourse

**brother** kin, kinsman, relation, relative, sibling; associate, colleague, companion, comrade, fellow member, mate, partner

**brotherhood** camaraderie, companionship, comradeship, fellowship, friendliness, kinship; alliance, association, clan, clique, community, coterie, fraternity, guild, league, society, union

**brotherly** affectionate, amicable, benevolent, cordial, fraternal, friendly, kind, neighbourly, sympathetic

**brown** auburn, bronze, brunette,

chestnut, chocolate, coffee, dark, dun, dusky, hazel, rust, sunburnt, tan, tanned, tawny

**browse** dip into, leaf through, look through, peruse, scan, skim, survey; crop, eat, feed, graze, nibble, pasture

**bruise** v blacken, blemish, contuse, crush, damage, deface, discolour, injure, mar, mark ~n blemish, contusion, discoloration, injury, mark, swelling

**brush¹** n besom, broom, sweeper; clash, conflict, fight, fracas, scrap Inf, set-to Inf, skirmish, tussle ~v buff, clean, paint, polish, sweep, wash; contact, flick, glance, graze, kiss, scrape, stroke, sweep, touch

**brush²** n bushes, copse, scrub, shrubs, thicket, undergrowth

**brutal** bloodthirsty, cruel, ferocious, heartless, inhuman, merciless, pitiless, remorseless, ruthless,

**brute** *n* any animal except man; crude, vicious person ~*adj* animal; sensual; stupid; physical **brutal** *adj* **brutality** *n* **brutally** *adv*

**BSc** Bachelor of Science

**BST** British Summer Time

**bubble** *n* hollow globe of liquid, blown out with air; something insubstantial ~*v* rise in bubbles **bubbly** *adj*

**bubonic plague** acute infectious disease characterized by swellings

**buccaneer** *n* pirate

**buck** *n* male deer, or other male animal; act of bucking; *US & Aust sl* dollar ~*v* (of horse) attempt to throw rider **buckshot** *n* lead shot in shotgun shell

**bucket** *n* vessel, round with arched handle, for water etc. **bucketful** *n*

**buckle** *n* metal clasp for fastening belt, strap etc. ~*v* fasten with buckle; warp, bend

**bud** *n* shoot containing unopened leaf, flower etc. ~*v* **budding, budded** begin to grow

**budge** *v* move, stir

**budgerigar** *also* **budgie** *n* small Aust. parakeet

**budget** *n* annual financial statement; plan of systematic spending ~*v* make financial plan

**buff¹** *n* leather from buffalo hide; light yellow colour; polishing pad ~*v* polish

**buff²** *n* expert

**buffalo** *n* type of cattle

**buffer** *n* device to lessen impact

**buffet¹** *n* blow, slap ~*v* strike with blows; contend against

**buffet²** *n* refreshment bar; meal at which guests serve themselves; sideboard

**buffoon** *n* clown; fool

**bug** *n* any small insect; *Inf* disease, infection; concealed listening device ~*v* annoy; listen secretly

**bugbear** *n* object of needless terror; nuisance

**bugger** *n* *Sl* unpleasant person or thing

**bugle** *n* instrument like trumpet

**build** *v* **building, built** construct by putting together parts; develop ~*n*

─────────── THESAURUS ───────────

savage, uncivilized, vicious
**brute** animal, beast, creature, wild animal; barbarian, beast, devil, fiend, monster, ogre, sadist, savage, swine

**bubble** *n* bead, blister, drop, droplet, globule ~*v* boil, effervesce, fizz, foam, froth, seethe, sparkle

**buckle** *n* catch, clasp, clip, fastener ~*v* catch, clasp, close, fasten, hook, secure; bend, bulge, cave in, collapse, crumple, fold, twist, warp

**bud** *n* germ, shoot, sprout ~*v* burgeon, develop, grow, shoot, sprout

**budge** *v* dislodge, give way, inch, move, propel, push, remove, roll, shift, slide, stir

**budget** *n* allowance, cost, finances, funds, means, resources ~*v* apportion, cost, cost out, estimate, plan, ration

**buffer** bumper, cushion, fender, intermediary, safeguard, screen, shield

**buffet¹** *n* bang, blow, bump, cuff, jolt, knock, push, rap, shove, slap, smack ~*v* bang, batter, beat, box, bump, knock, pound, push, rap, shove, slap, strike, thump

**buffet²** *n* café, cafeteria, cold table, counter, cupboard, snack bar

**bug** *Inf* disease, germ, microorganism, virus ~*v* eavesdrop, listen in, spy, tap, wiretap

make, form **builder** n **building** n
**building society** organization where
money can be borrowed or invested

**bulb** n modified leaf bud emitting
roots from base, e.g. onion; globe
surrounding filament of electric
light **bulbous** adj

**bulge** n swelling; temporary increase ~v swell

**bulk** n size; volume; greater part;
cargo ~v be of weight or importance **bulky** adj

**bull** n male of cattle; male of various other animals **bulldog** n thickset breed of dog **bulldozer** n powerful tractor for excavating etc. **bull-
fight** n public show in which bull is
killed **bullock** n castrated bull
**bull's-eye** n centre of target

**bullet** n projectile discharged from
rifle, pistol etc.

**bulletin** n official report

**bullion** n gold or silver in mass

**bully** n one who hurts or intimi-
dates weaker people ~v **bullying**,
**bullied**

**bulrush** n tall reedlike marsh plant

**bulwark** n rampart; any defence

**bum** n Sl buttocks, anus

**bumble** v perform clumsily

**bumblebee** n large hairy bee

**bumf** also **bumph** n Inf official papers

**bump** n knock; thud; swelling ~v
strike or push against **bumper** n
horizontal bar on motor vehicle to
protect against damage ~adj abundant

**bumpkin** n simple country person

**bumptious** adj self-assertive

**bun** n small, round cake; round
knot of hair

**bunch** n number of things tied or
growing together; group, party ~v
gather together

**bundle** v package; number of

**build** v assemble, construct, erect,
fabricate, form, make, put up, raise;
base, begin, constitute, establish,
inaugurate, originate, set up, start
~n body, figure, form, frame, physique, shape

**building** dwelling, edifice, fabric,
house, pile, structure

**bulge** n bump, lump, protuberance, swelling; boost, increase, rise,
surge ~v dilate, distend, enlarge,
expand, project, protrude, sag,
stand out, stick out, swell

**bulk** immensity, largeness, magnitude, massiveness, size, substance,
volume, weight; body, greater part,
lion's share, main part, majority,
major part, mass, most

**bullet** missile, pellet, projectile,
shot, slug

**bulletin** announcement, commu-

niqué, dispatch, message, news
flash, notification, report, statement

**bully** v browbeat, bulldoze Inf, coerce, cow, domineer, hector, intimidate, oppress, persecute, push
around Sl, terrorize, tyrannize

**bulwark** bastion, buttress, defence, fortification, rampart, redoubt

**bump** n bang, blow, crash, hit, impact, jar, jolt, knock, rap, shock,
smash, thud, thump; bulge, contusion, knob, knot, lump, protuberance, swelling ~v bang, crash, hit,
knock, slam, smash into, strike

**bumptious** arrogant, boastful,
brash, cocky, conceited, egotistic,
forward, full of oneself, impudent,
overbearing, presumptuous, pushy
Inf

things tied together ~*v* tie in bundle; send (off) without ceremony

**bung** *n* stopper for cask ~*v* stop up *Sl* sling

**bungalow** *n* one-storeyed house

**bungle** *v/n* botch

**bunion** *n* inflamed swelling on foot or toe

**bunk** *n* narrow shelflike bed

**bunker** *n* large storage container for coal etc.; sandy hollow on golf course; underground defensive position

**bunny** *n Inf* rabbit

**bunting** *n* material for flags

**buoy** *n* floating marker anchored in sea ~*v* prevent from sinking **buoyancy** *n* **buoyant** *adj*

**burden** *n* load; weight, cargo; any-

thing difficult to bear ~*v* load, encumber **burdensome** *adj*

**bureau** *n* (*pl* **-reaus**) writing desk; office; government department **bureaucracy** *n* government by officials; body of officials **bureaucrat** *n*

**burgeon** *v* bud; flourish

**burglar** *n* one who enters building to commit crime esp. theft **burglary** *n* **burgle** *v*

**burgundy** *n* name of various wines, white and red

**burlesque** *n/v* caricature

**burly** *adj* sturdy, stout, robust

**burn** *v* burning, **burned** or **burnt** destroy or injure by fire; be on fire; be consumed by fire ~*n* injury, mark caused by fire **burning** *adj* intense; urgent

**bunch** *n* batch, bouquet, bundle, clump, cluster, collection, heap, lot, mass, parcel, pile, quantity, sheaf, spray, stack, tuft ~*v* assemble, bundle, cluster, collect, crowd, flock, group, herd, mass, pack

**bundle** *n* bag, bale, box, carton, crate, pack, package, packet, pallet, parcel, roll; assortment, batch, bunch, collection, group, heap, mass, pile, quantity ~*v* bale, bind, fasten, pack, tie, tie up, truss, wrap

**bungle** blunder, botch, butcher, make a mess of, mar, mess up, miscalculate, mismanage, muff, ruin, screw up *Inf*, spoil

**buoy** beacon, float, guide, marker, signal

**buoyant** afloat , floating, light

**burden** *n* affliction, anxiety, care, clog, load, onus, sorrow, strain, stress, trial, trouble, weight, worry ~*v* bother, encumber, load, oppress, overload, saddle with, strain, tax, weigh down, worry

**bureau** desk, writing desk; agency, branch, department, division, office, service

**bureaucracy** administration, civil service, government, ministry, officialdom

**bureaucrat** civil servant, mandarin, minister, officer, official, public servant

**burglar** housebreaker, pilferer, robber, sneak thief, thief

**burial** entombment, exequies, funeral, interment, obsequies

**burlesque** *n* caricature, mock, mockery, parody, satire, send-up *Brit inf*, spoof *Inf*, takeoff *Inf* ~*v* ape, caricature, exaggerate, imitate, lampoon, make fun of, mock, parody, ridicule, satirize, send up *Brit inf*, take off *Inf*

**burly** beefy, big, bulky, hefty, muscular, powerful, stocky, stout, strapping, strong, sturdy, well-built

**burn** be ablaze, be on fire, blaze, flame, flare, flash, flicker, glow,

burnish v/n polish

burp v/n Inf belch

burrow n hole dug by rabbit etc. ~v dig

bursar n official managing finances of college etc. bursary n scholarship

burst v break into pieces; break suddenly into some expression of feeling; shatter, break violently ~n bursting; explosion; outbreak; spurt

bury v burying, buried put underground; inter; conceal burial n/adj

bus n large motor vehicle for passengers

bush n shrub; uncleared country bushy adj shaggy bushbaby n tree-living, nocturnal Afr. animal

bushel n dry measure of eight gallons

business n occupation; commercial or industrial establishment; trade; responsibility; work businesslike adj businessman n businesswoman n

busker n street entertainer busk v

bust[1] n sculpture of head and shoulders; woman's breasts

bust[2] Inf v burst; make, become bankrupt; raid; arrest ~adj broken; bankrupt

bustle v be noisily busy ~n fuss, commotion

busy adj actively employed; full of activity ~v busying, busied occupy busily adv busybody n nosy person

but conj without; except; yet; still;

—————————— THESAURUS ——————————

smoke; char, ignite, incinerate, kindle, light, parch, scorch, set on fire, shrivel, singe, toast, wither

burning ardent, eager, earnest, fervent, frantic, intense, passionate, vehement, zealous

burrow n den, hole, lair, retreat, shelter, tunnel ~v delve, dig, excavate, hollow out, scoop out, tunnel

burst v blow up, break, crack, explode, fly open, fragment, puncture, rupture, shatter, shiver, split, tear apart ~n bang, blast, blowout, blow-up, breach, break, crack, discharge, explosion, rupture, split

bury embed, engulf, implant, sink, submerge; entomb, inearth, inhume, inter, lay to rest; conceal, cover, cover up, hide, secrete, stow away

bush hedge, plant, shrub, shrubbery, thicket; brush, scrub, the wild

busily actively, briskly, carefully, diligently, earnestly, energetically, industriously, intently, speedily, strenuously

business calling, career, craft, employment, function, job, line, métier, occupation, profession, pursuit, trade, vocation, work; company, concern, enterprise, firm, organization, venture; commerce, dealings, industry, manufacturing, selling, trade, trading, transaction

businesslike correct, efficient, methodical, orderly, organized, practical, professional, regular, systematic, thorough, well-ordered

businessman, businesswoman capitalist, employer, entrepreneur, executive, financier, industrialist, merchant, tradesman, tycoon

bust bosom, breast, chest, torso

bustle v bestir, dash, fuss, hasten, hurry, rush, scamper, scramble, scurry, stir ~n activity, ado, agitation, commotion, excitement, flurry, fuss, haste, hurry, stir, to-do, tumult

busy active, assiduous, brisk, diligent, employed, engaged, en-

besides; *adv* only

**butane** *n* gas used for fuel

**butch** *adj Inf* aggressively masculine

**butcher** *n* one who kills animals for food, or sells meat; savage man ~*v* slaughter **butchery** *n*

**butler** *n* chief male servant

**butt¹** *n* thick end; unused end

**butt²** *n* target; object of ridicule

**butt³** *v* strike with head; interrupt ~*n* blow made with head

**butter** *n* fatty substance got from cream by churning ~*v* spread with butter; flatter

**buttercup** *n* plant with glossy, yellow flowers

**butterfly** *n* insect with large wings

**butterscotch** *n* kind of hard, brittle toffee

**buttock** *n* (*usu. pl*) rump, protruding hind part

**button** *n* knob, stud for fastening dress; knob that operates doorbell, machine etc. ~*v* fasten with buttons

**buttonhole** *n* slit in garment to pass button through; flower worn on lapel etc. ~*v* detain (unwilling) person in conversation

**buttress** *n* structure to support wall; prop ~*v* support

**buxom** *adj* full of health, plump

**buy** *v* buying, **bought** get by payment, purchase; bribe ~*n* thing purchased **buyer** *n*

**buzz** *v/n* (make) humming sound **buzzer** *n* **buzzword** *n* fashionable word

**buzzard** *n* bird of prey

**by** *prep* near; along; past; during; not later than; through use or agency of; in units of ~*adv* near; aside; past **by and by** soon **by and large** on the whole

**by-** *comb. form* subsidiary, near, as in **byproduct, bystander**

**bye** *n Sport* situation where player or team wins by default of opponent

**bye-bye** *interj Inf* goodbye

**by-election** *n* election to fill vacant seat

**bygone** *adj* past, former ~*n* (*oft. pl*) past occurrence; small antique

—————— THESAURUS ——————

grossed, hard at work, industrious, occupied, on duty, slaving, working; active, energetic, full, hectic, hustling, lively, restless, tireless, tiring

**but** *conj* further, however, moreover, nevertheless, on the contrary, on the other hand, still, yet; bar, barring, except, excepting, excluding, notwithstanding, save, with the exception of ~*adv* just, merely, only, simply, singly, solely

**butcher** *n* destroyer, killer, murderer, slaughterer, slayer ~*v* carve, clean, cut, cut up, dress, joint, prepare, slaughter; assassinate, cut down, destroy, exterminate, kill, massacre, slaughter, slay

**butt¹** handle, hilt, shaft, shank, stock

**butt²** Aunt Sally, dupe, mark, object, point, subject, target, victim

**butt³** *v/n* With *or* of the head *or* horns buck, buffet, bump, jab, knock, poke, prod, punch, push, ram, shove, thrust

**buy** *v* get, invest in, obtain, pay for, procure, purchase, shop for ~*n* acquisition, bargain, deal, purchase

**by** *prep* along, beside, by way of, close to, near, next to, over, past, via; through, through the agency of, under the aegis of ~*adv* aside, at hand, away, beyond, close, handy,

**bylaw** n law, regulation made by local authority

**bypass** n road for diversion of traffic from overcrowded centres ~v make detour round

**byre** n cowshed

**byte** n Computers sequence of bits processed as single unit of information

**byway** n secondary or side road

**byword** n well-known name or saying

———— THESAURUS ————

in reach, near, past, to one side

**bypass** avoid, circumvent, depart from, detour round, deviate from, get round, go round, pass round

# C c

**C** *Chem* carbon; Celsius; Centigrade

**c.** circa

**cab** *n* taxi; driver's compartment on lorry etc.

**cabal** *n* small group of intriguers; secret plot

**cabaret** *n* floor show at a nightclub

**cabbage** *n* green vegetable

**cabin** *n* hut, shed; small room, esp. in ship

**cabinet** *n* piece of furniture with drawers or shelves; outer case of television, radio etc.; committee of politicians

**cable** *n* strong rope; wires conveying electric power, television signals etc.; telegraph ~*v* telegraph by cable **cable car** vehicle pulled up slope on cable

**cache** *n* secret hiding place; store of food etc.

**cackle** *v/n* (make) chattering noise, as of hen

**cacophony** *n* disagreeable sound; discord of sounds

**cactus** *n* (*pl* **cactuses, cacti**) spiny succulent plant

**cad** *n* unchivalrous person

**cadaver** *n* corpse **cadaverous** *adj*

**caddie, caddy** *n* golfer's attendant

**caddy** *n* small box for tea

**cadence** *n* fall or modulation of voice in music or verse

**cadenza** *n Mus* elaborate solo passage

**cadet** *n* youth in training, esp. for armed forces

**cadge** *v* get (food, money etc.) by begging

**cadmium** *n* metallic element

**caecum** *n* (*pl* **-ca**) part of large intestine

**Caesarean section** surgical operation to deliver a baby

**caesium** *n* metallic element

**café** *n* small restaurant serving light refreshments **cafeteria** *n* self-service restaurant

**caffeine** *n* stimulating chemical found in tea and coffee

**caftan** *n see* KAFTAN

**cage** *n* enclosure, box with bars or wires, esp. for keeping animals or birds ~*v* put in cage, confine **cagey** *adj* wary

**cagoule** *n* lightweight anorak

**cairn** *n* heap of stones, esp. as monument or landmark

**cajole** *v* persuade by flattery, wheedle

**cake** *n* baked, sweet, bread-like food; compact mass ~*v* harden (as of mud)

**calamine** *n* soothing ointment

**calamity** *n* disaster **calamitous** *adj*

---

THESAURUS

**cab** minicab, taxi, taxicab

**cabin** berth, chalet, cot, cottage, crib, hovel, hut, lodge, shack, shanty, shed; berth, compartment, deckhouse, quarters, room

**cabinet** case, closet, commode, cupboard, dresser, locker; administration, assembly, council, counsellors, ministry

**cage** *v* confine, coop up, fence in, impound, imprison, lock up, mew, pound, restrain, shut up

**cajole** beguile, coax, decoy, entice, flatter, inveigle, lure, mislead, seduce, tempt, wheedle

**cake** bar, block, cube, loaf, lump,

**calcium** *n* metallic element, the basis of lime

**calculate** *v* estimate; compute; make reckonings **calculable** *adj* **calculating** *adj* shrewd; scheming **calculation** *n* **calculator** *n* electronic device for making calculations

**calendar** *n* table of months and days in the year; list of events

**calf**[1] *n* (*pl* **calves**) young of cow and other animals; leather of calf's skin

**calf**[2] *n* (*pl* **calves**) fleshy back of leg below knee

**calibre** *n* size of bore of gun; capacity, character **calibrate** *v*

**calico** *n* (*pl* **-coes**, **-cos**) cotton cloth

**call** *v* speak loudly to attract attention; summon; telephone; name; shout; pay visit ~*n* shout; animal's cry; visit; inner urge; demand **caller** *n* **calling** *n* vocation, profession **call up** summon to serve in army; imagine

**calligraphy** *n* handwriting

**callipers** *pl n* instrument for measuring diameters

**callous** *adj* hardened, unfeeling

**callow** *adj* inexperienced

**callus** *n* area of hardened skin

**calm** *adj/v* (make, become) still, tranquil; (make) composed ~*n* absence of wind **calmly** *adv* **calmness** *n*

**calorie** *n* unit of heat; unit of energy from foods

**calypso** *n* (*pl* **-sos**) (West Indies) improvised song

**cam** *n* device to change rotary to reciprocating motion

—————————————— THESAURUS ——————————————

mass, slab

**calculate** adjust, compute, consider, count, determine, enumerate, estimate, figure, gauge, judge, rate, reckon, value, weigh, work out

**calculation** answer, computation, estimate, judgment, reckoning, result

**calibre** bore, diameter, gauge, measure; ability, capacity, endowment, faculty, force, gifts, merit, parts, quality, scope, stature, talent, worth

**call** *v* announce, arouse, awaken, cry, cry out, hail, proclaim, rouse, shout, waken, yell; assemble, bid, collect, contact, convene, convoke, gather, invite, muster, phone, rally, ring up *Inf*, *chiefly Brit*, summon, telephone; christen, describe as, designate, dub, entitle, label, name, style, term ~*n* cry, hail, shout, signal, whoop, yell

**calling** employment, life's work, line, métier, mission, occupation, profession, province, pursuit, trade, vocation, work

**callous** cold, hard-bitten, hardened, hardhearted, harsh, heartless, indifferent, insensitive, obdurate, soulless, thick-skinned, uncaring, unfeeling, unresponsive, unsympathetic

**calm** *adj* balmy, mild, pacific, peaceful, placid, quiet, restful, serene, smooth, still, tranquil, windless; collected, composed, cool, equable, impassive, imperturbable, relaxed, sedate, self-possessed, unemotional, unexcited, unfazed *Inf*, unmoved, unruffled ~*v* hush, mollify, placate, quieten, relax, soothe

**calmness** calm, composure, equability, hush, peace, peacefulness, placidity, quiet, repose, serenity, smoothness, stillness, tranquillity; composure, coolness, dispassion, equanimity, impassivity, self-

**camaraderie** n spirit of comradeship, trust

**camber** n curve on road surface

**cambric** n fine white linen or cotton cloth

**camcorder** n portable video camera and recorder

**camel** n animal of Asia and Africa, with humped back

**camellia** n ornamental shrub

**cameo** n (pl **cameos**) medallion, brooch etc. with design in relief; small part in film etc.

**camera** n apparatus used to make photographs **cameraman** n

**camisole** n underbodice

**camouflage** n disguise, means of avoiding enemy observation ~v disguise

**camp¹** n (place for) tents of hikers, army etc.; group supporting political party etc. ~v form or lodge in camp

**camp²** adj Inf homosexual; consciously artificial

**campaign** n/v (organize) series of coordinated activities for some purpose, e.g. political, military

**camphor** n solid essential oil with aromatic taste and smell

**campus** n grounds of university

**can¹** v (past tense **could**) be able; have the power; be allowed

**can²** n container, usu. metal, for liquids, foods ~v **canning, canned** put in can **canned** adj preserved in can; (of music) previously recorded

**canal** n artificial watercourse; duct in body

**canary** n yellow singing bird

**canasta** n card game played with two packs

**cancan** n high-kicking dance

**cancel** v **-celling, -celled** cross out; annul; call off **cancellation** n

**cancer** n malignant growth or tumour **cancerous** adj

**candid** adj frank, impartial **candour** n

**candidate** n one who seeks office etc.; person taking examination **candidacy, candidature** n

**candle** n stick of wax with wick; light **candelabrum** n (pl **-bra**) large, branched candle holder **candlestick** n

—— THESAURUS ——

possession

**camouflage** n blind, cloak, concealment, cover, deceptive markings, disguise, front, guise, mask, masquerade, mimicry, screen, subterfuge ~v cloak, conceal, cover, disguise, hide, mask, obscure, screen, veil

**camp¹** bivouac, camp site

**camp²** affected, artificial, effeminate, mannered, ostentatious, posturing

**campaign** attack, crusade, drive, expedition, offensive, push

**cancel** abolish, annul, blot out, call off, cross out, delete, efface, elimi-

nate, erase, expunge, obliterate, obviate, quash, repeal, repudiate, rescind, revoke

**cancer** blight, canker, carcinoma Pathol, corruption, evil, growth, malignancy, pestilence, rot, tumour

**candid** blunt, downright, fair, frank, free, impartial, just, open, outspoken, plain, straightforward, truthful, unprejudiced, upfront Inf

**candidate** applicant, aspirant, competitor, contender, contestant, entrant, nominee, runner

**candour** forthrightness, frankness, honesty, openness, outspokenness, truthfulness

**candy** n crystallized sugar; US confectionery in general ~v **candying, candied** preserve with sugar **candyfloss** n fluffy mass of spun sugar

**cane** n stem of small palm or large grass; walking stick ~v beat with cane

**canine** adj like, pert. to, dog ~n sharp pointed tooth

**canister** n container, usu. of metal, for storing dry food

**canker** n eating sore; thing that destroys, corrupts

**cannabis** n hemp plant; drug derived from this

**cannelloni** pl n tubular pieces of pasta filled with meat etc.

**cannibal** n one who eats human flesh **cannibalism** n

**cannon**[1] n (pl **-ons** or **-on**) large gun **cannonball** n heavy metal ball

**cannon**[2] n billiard stroke ~v make this stroke; rebound, collide

**cannot** negative form of CAN[1]

**canny** adj shrewd; cautious

**canoe** n (pl **-oes**) very light boat propelled with paddle ~v travel by canoe

**canon** n law or rule, esp. of church; standard; list of saints **canonize** v enrol in list of saints

**canopy** n covering over throne, bed etc. ~v **-opying, -opied** cover with canopy

**cant** n hypocritical speech; technical jargon; slang, esp. of thieves ~v use cant

**cantankerous** adj quarrelsome

**cantata** n choral work

**canteen** n place in factory, school etc. where meals are provided

**canter** n/v (move at) easy gallop

**cantilever** n beam, girder etc. fixed at one end only

**canvas** n coarse cloth used for sails, painting etc.

**canvass** v solicit votes, contributions etc.; discuss

**canyon** n deep gorge

**cap** n covering for head; lid, top ~v **capping, capped** put a cap on; outdo

**capable** adj able; competent; having the power **capability** n

**capacity** n power of holding; room; volume; function, role; ability

**cape**[1] n covering for shoulders

**cannon** big gun Inf, field gun, gun, mortar

**canny** acute, artful, astute, careful, cautious, circumspect, clever, judicious, knowing, prudent, sagacious, sharp, shrewd, subtle, wise

**canopy** awning, covering, shade, sunshade

**cant** n humbug, hypocrisy, insincerity, lip service, pretence

**cantankerous** bad-tempered, captious, contrary, crabby, crotchety Inf, crusty, difficult, disagreeable, grumpy, irascible, irritable, peevish, perverse, quarrelsome, testy, tetchy

**canter** n/v amble, jog, lope

**canvass** analyse, campaign, electioneer, examine, inspect, investigate, poll, scan, sift, solicit, study

**cap** v beat, better, cover, crown, exceed, excel, finish, outdo, outstrip, overtop, run rings around Inf, surpass, top, transcend

**capable** able, accomplished, adapted, adept, apt, clever, competent, efficient, fitted, gifted, masterly, proficient, skilful, suited, talented

**capacity** amplitude, compass, ex-

**cape²** *n* headland

**caper** *n* skip; frolic; escapade ~*v* skip, dance

**capillary** *n* small blood vessel

**capital** *n* chief town; money; large-sized letter ~*adj* involving or punishable by death; chief; excellent **capitalism** *n* economic system based on private ownership of industry **capitalist** *n/adj* **capitalize** *v* convert into capital; (with on) turn to advantage

**capitulate** *v* surrender

**capon** *n* a castrated cock fowl fattened for eating

**cappuccino** *n* (pl **-nos**) coffee with steamed milk

**caprice** *n* whim, freak **capricious** *adj*

**capsize** *v* (of boat) overturn accidentally

**capstan** *n* machine to wind cable

**capsule** *n* case for dose of medicine

**Capt.** Captain

**captain** *n* commander of vessel or company of soldiers; leader ~*v* be captain of **captaincy** *n*

**caption** *n* heading, title of article, picture etc.

**captive** *n* prisoner ~*adj* taken, imprisoned **captivate** *v* fascinate **captivity** *n*

**capture** *v* seize, make prisoner ~*n* seizure, taking **captor** *n*

**car** *n* road vehicle; passenger compartment

**carafe** *n* glass water bottle for the table, decanter

**caramel** *n* burnt sugar for cooking;

---

tent, range, room, scope, size, space, volume; function, office, position, post, province, role, service, sphere; ability, brains, cleverness, competence, competency, facility, faculty, forte, genius, gift, intelligence, power, readiness, strength

**cape** head, headland, point, promontory

**caper** *v* bounce, bound, cavort, dance, frisk, frolic, gambol, hop, jump, leap, romp, skip, spring

**capital** assets, cash, finances, funds, investment(s), means, money, principal, property, resources, stock, wealth, wherewithal ~*adj* cardinal, central, chief, foremost, important, leading, main, major, paramount, pre-eminent, prime, principal, vital

**capitalism** free enterprise, *laissez faire*, private enterprise, private ownership

**capsize** keel over, overturn, tip

over, turn over, turn turtle, upset

**capsule** lozenge, pill, tablet

**captain** boss, chief, commander, head, leader, master, officer, skipper

**captivate** allure, attract, beguile, bewitch, charm, dazzle, enchant, enslave, enthral, entrance, fascinate, infatuate, lure, mesmerize, seduce, win

**captive** convict, detainee, hostage, internee, prisoner, slave ~*adj* caged, confined, ensnared, imprisoned, incarcerated, locked up, restricted, subjugated

**captivity** confinement, custody, detention, imprisonment, incarceration, internment, servitude, slavery

**capture** *v* arrest, catch, nail *Inf*, secure, seize, take, take prisoner ~*n* arrest, imprisonment, seizure

**car** automobile, machine, motor, motorcar, vehicle

chewy sweet

**carat** *n* weight used for gold, diamonds etc.; measure used to state fineness of gold

**caravan** *n* large vehicle for living in, pulled by car etc.; company of merchants travelling together

**caraway** *n* plant with spicy seeds used in cakes etc.

**carbohydrate** *n* any compound containing carbon, hydrogen and oxygen, esp. sugars and starches

**carbon** *n* nonmetallic element, substance of pure charcoal, found in all organic matter **carbonate** *n* salt of carbonic acid **carbon copy** copy made with carbon paper; very similar person or thing **carbon dioxide** colourless gas exhaled in respiration

**carbuncle** *n* inflamed ulcer, boil or tumour

**carburettor** *n* device for mixing petrol with air in engine

**carcass, carcase** *n* dead animal body

**card** *n* thick, stiff paper; piece of this giving identification etc.; illustrated card sending greetings etc.; playing card; *pl* any card game **cardboard** *n* thin, stiff board made of paper pulp **cardsharp** *n* cheating card player

**cardiac** *adj* pert. to the heart **cardiograph** *n* instrument which records movements of the heart **cardiology** *n* study of heart diseases

**cardigan** *n* knitted jacket

**cardinal** *adj* chief, principal ~*n* rank next to the Pope in R.C. church **cardinal numbers** 1,2,3 etc.

**care** *v* be anxious; have regard or liking (for); look after; be disposed to ~*n* attention; protection; anxiety; caution **careful** *adj* **careless** *adj* **carefree** *adj* **caretaker** *n* person in charge of premises

**career** *n* course through life; profession; rapid motion ~*v* run or move at full speed

**caress** *v* fondle, embrace, treat with affection ~*n* affectionate em-

**carcass** body, cadaver *Med*, corpse, dead body, hulk, remains, shell, skeleton

**cardinal** capital, central, chief, essential, first, foremost, greatest, highest, important, leading, main, pre-eminent, primary, prime, principal

**care**; attention, caution, consideration, direction, forethought, heed, management, pains, prudence, regard, vigilance, watchfulness; charge, control, custody, keeping, management, protection, supervision, ward; anxiety, burden, concern, disquiet, interest, pressure, responsibility, solicitude, stress, trouble, vexation, woe, worry

**career** *n* calling, employment, life work, livelihood, occupation, pursuit, vocation

**careful** accurate, attentive, cautious, chary, circumspect, conscientious, discreet, fastidious, heedful, painstaking, precise, prudent, scrupulous, thoughtful, thrifty; alert, concerned, judicious, mindful, particular, protective, solicitous, vigilant, wary, watchful

**careless** absent-minded, forgetful, hasty, heedless, incautious, indiscreet, negligent, perfunctory, remiss, thoughtless, unconcerned, unguarded, unmindful, unthinking; inaccurate, irresponsible, lackadaisical, neglectful, offhand, slapdash,

brace or touch

**caret** *n* mark (∧) showing where to insert word etc.

**cargo** *n* (*pl* **-goes**) load, freight, carried by ship, plane etc.

**caribou** *n* reindeer

**caricature** *n* likeness exaggerated to appear ridiculous ~*v* portray in this way

**carnage** *n* slaughter

**carnal** *adj* fleshly, sensual

**carnation** *n* cultivated flower

**carnival** *n* festive occasion; travelling fair

**carnivorous** *adj* flesh-eating **carnivore** *n*

**carol** *n/v* **-olling, -olled** (sing) song or hymn of joy

**carouse** *v* have merry drinking spree **carousal** *n*

**carousel** *n* US merry-go-round; rotating device for holding slides

**carp**[1] *n* freshwater fish

**carp**[2] *v* find fault; nag

**carpenter** *n* worker in timber **carpentry** *n*

**carpet** *n* heavy fabric for covering floor

**carriage** *n* railway coach; bearing;

horse-drawn vehicle **carriageway** *n* part of road along which traffic passes in a single line

**carrion** *n* rotting dead flesh

**carrot** *n* plant with orange-red edible root; inducement

**carry** *v* **carrying, carried** convey, transport; capture, win; effect; behave; (of projectile, sound) reach **carrier** *n*

**cart** *n* open (two-wheeled) vehicle ~*v* carry in cart; carry with effort **carthorse** *n* heavily built horse **cartwheel** *n* sideways somersault

**carte blanche** *Fr* complete authority

**cartel** *n* industrial alliance for fixing prices etc.

**cartilage** *n* firm elastic tissue in the body; gristle

**cartography** *n* map making

**carton** *n* cardboard or plastic container

**cartoon** *n* drawing, esp. humorous or satirical; sequence of drawings telling story **cartoonist** *n*

**cartridge** *n* case containing charge for gun; container for film etc.

**carve** *v* cut; hew; sculpture; en-

slipshod, sloppy *Inf*

**caress** *v* cuddle, embrace, fondle, hug, kiss, pet, stroke ~*n* cuddle, embrace, hug, kiss, pat, stroke

**caretaker** concierge, curator, custodian, janitor, keeper, porter, warden, watchman

**cargo** baggage, consignment, contents, freight, goods, lading, load, merchandise, shipment, tonnage, ware

**caricature** *n* burlesque, cartoon, farce, lampoon, parody, satire, takeoff *Inf*, travesty ~*v* burlesque, distort, lampoon, mimic, mock,

parody, ridicule, satirize, send up *Brit inf*, take off *Inf*

**carnival** celebration, fair, festival, fête, fiesta, gala, holiday, revelry

**carriage** cab, coach, vehicle; air, bearing, behaviour, conduct, demeanour, gait, manner, mien, posture, presence

**carry** bear, bring, conduct, convey, fetch, haul, hump *Brit sl*, lift, lug, move, relay, take, transfer, transmit, transport

**carton** box, case, pack, package

**cartoon** animated film, animation, comic strip, lampoon, parody, sat-

grave; cut (meat) in pieces or slices
**carving** n

**cascade** n waterfall

**case¹** n instance; circumstance;
question at issue; arguments supporting particular action etc.; *Med*
patient; lawsuit **in case** so as to allow for eventualities

**case²** n box, sheath, covering; receptacle; box and contents ~v put
in a case

**cash** n money, banknotes and coins
~v turn into or exchange for money

**cashier** n one in charge of receiving
and paying of money

**cashier** v dismiss from office

**cashmere** n fine soft fabric made
from goat's wool

**casino** n (*pl* -**nos**) building, institution for gambling

**cask** n barrel

**casket** n small case for jewels etc.

**casserole** n fireproof cooking dish;
stew

**cassette** n plastic container for
film, magnetic tape etc.

**cassock** n clergyman's long tunic

**cast** v throw or fling; shed; deposit
(a vote); allot, as parts in play;
mould ~n throw; squint; mould;
that which is shed or ejected; set of
actors; type or quality **castaway** n
shipwrecked person **cast-iron** adj
made of hard, brittle type of iron;
rigid or unchallengeable **cast-off**
*adj/n* discarded (garment)

**castanets** pl n two small curved
pieces of wood clicked together in
hand

**caste** n section of society in India;
social rank

**caster sugar** also **castor sugar** n
finely powdered sugar

**castigate** v rebuke severely

**castle** n fortress

**castor** n bottle with perforated top;
small swivelled wheel on table leg
etc.

**castor oil** n vegetable medicinal oil

**castrate** v remove testicles **castra-
tion** n

**casual** adj accidental; unforeseen;
occasional; unconcerned; informal

**casually** adv **casualty** n person

———————— THESAURUS ————————

ire, sketch, takeoff

**cartridge** charge, round, shell

**carve** chip, chisel, cut, divide, engrave, etch, form, hack, hew, inscribe, mould, sculpt, sculpture,
slash, slice, whittle

**cascade** cataract, deluge, falls,
flood, fountain, outpouring, shower, torrent, waterfall

**case¹** example, illustration, instance, occasion, occurrence, specimen; circumstance(s), condition,
context, dilemma, event, plight, position, predicament, situation, state
*Law* action, cause, dispute, lawsuit,
proceedings, process, suit, trial

**case²** box, cabinet, capsule, carton,

cartridge, casket, chest, compact,
container, crate, holder, receptacle,
shell, suitcase, tray, trunk

**cash** bullion, charge, coin, coinage,
currency, dosh *Brit & Aust sl*,
dough *Sl*, funds, money, notes, payment, ready money, resources,
wherewithal

**cashier** n bank clerk, banker, bursar, clerk, teller

**cast** v chuck *Inf*, drive, drop, fling,
hurl, impel, launch, lob, pitch, project, shed, shy, sling, throw, thrust,
toss ~n fling, lob, throw, thrust,
toss; actors, characters, company,
players

**castle** chateau, citadel, fortress,

killed or injured in accident, war etc.

**cat** *n* any of various feline animals, esp. small domesticated furred animal **catty** *adj* spiteful **catcall** *n* derisive cry **catkin** *n* drooping flower spike **catnap** *v/n* doze **Catseye** *n* Trademark glass reflector set in road to indicate traffic lanes **catwalk** *n* narrow platform

**cataclysm** *n* (disastrous) upheaval; deluge

**catacomb** *n* underground chamber for burial

**catalogue** *n* descriptive list ~*v* make such list of

**catalyst** *n* substance causing or assisting a chemical reaction without taking part in it

**catamaran** *n* type of sailing boat with twin hulls

**catapult** *n* small forked stick with sling for throwing stones; launching device ~*v* launch with force

**cataract** *n* waterfall; downpour;

disease of eye

**catarrh** *n* inflammation of mucous membrane

**catastrophe** *n* great disaster **catastrophic** *adj*

**catch** *v* **catching, caught** take hold of; hear; contract disease; be in time for; detect; be contagious; get entangled; begin to burn ~*n* seizure; thing that holds, stops etc.; what is caught; *Inf* snag, disadvantage **catcher** *n* **catching** *adj* **catchy** *adj* (of tune) easily remembered

**catechism** *n* instruction by questions and answers

**category** *n* class, order **categorize** *v* **categorical** *adj* positive

**cater** *v* provide, esp. food **caterer** *n*

**caterpillar** *n* hairy grub of moth or butterfly

**catharsis** *n* relief of strong suppressed emotions **cathartic** *adj*

**cathedral** *n* principal church of diocese

**Catherine wheel** *n* rotating fire-

keep, mansion, stronghold, tower

**casual** accidental, chance, contingent, fortuitous, irregular, occasional, random, unexpected, unforeseen, unpremeditated; blasé, indifferent, informal, nonchalant, offhand, perfunctory, relaxed, unconcerned

**casualty** loss, sufferer, victim

**catalogue** directory, index, inventory, list, record, register, roll, roster, schedule

**catastrophe** adversity, affliction, blow, calamity, cataclysm, devastation, disaster, failure, fiasco, ill, mischance, misfortune, mishap, reverse, tragedy, trial, trouble

**catch** *v* apprehend, arrest, capture, clutch, ensnare, entrap, grab,

grasp, grip, lay hold of, lift *Sl*, nail *Inf*, seize, snare, snatch, take; detect, discover, expose, find out, surprise, unmask ~*n* bolt, clasp, clip, fastener, hasp, hook, hook and eye, latch; disadvantage, drawback, fly in the ointment, hitch, snag, stumbling block, trap, trick

**catching** contagious, infectious, infective, transferable, transmittable

**categorical** absolute, direct, downright, emphatic, explicit, express, positive, unequivocal, unqualified

**category** class, department, division, grade, head, heading, list, order, rank, section, sort, type

**cater** furnish, outfit, provide, pro-

work producing sparks

**catholic** *adj* universal; including whole body of Christians; (*with cap.*) relating to R.C. church *~n* (*with cap.*) adherent of R.C. church **Catholicism** *n*

**cattle** *pl n* pasture animals, esp. oxen, cows **cattleman** *n*

**cauldron** *n* large pot used for boiling

**cauliflower** *n* variety of cabbage with edible white flowering head

**cause** *n* that which produces an effect; reason; motive; charity, movement; lawsuit *~v* bring about, make happen

**causeway** *n* raised path over marsh etc.

**caustic** *adj* burning; bitter *~n* corrosive substance

**cauterize** *v* burn with caustic or hot iron

**caution** *n* heedfulness; care; warning *~v* warn **cautionary** *adj* **cautious** *adj*

**cavalcade** *n* procession

**cavalier** *adj* careless, disdainful *~n* courtly gentleman; *Obs* horseman; (*with cap.*) supporter of Charles I

**cavalry** *n* mounted troops

**cave** *n* hollow place in the earth; den **cavern** *n* deep cave **cavernous** *adj* **cavity** *n* hollow **caveman** *n* prehistoric cave dweller

**caviar, caviare** *n* salted sturgeon roe

**cavil** *v* **-illing, -illed** make trifling objections

**cavort** *v* prance, frisk

**CB** Citizens' Band

**CBE** Commander of the British Empire

**cc** cubic centimetre

**CD** compact disc **CD-ROM** compact disc storing written information, displayed on VDU

**cease** *v* bring or come to an end **ceaseless** *adj* **ceasefire** *n* temporary truce

**cedar** *n* large evergreen tree

————————————— T H E S A U R U S —————————————

vision, purvey, supply, victual

**cattle** beasts, cows, livestock, stock

**cause** *n* beginning, creator, genesis, maker, origin, prime mover, producer, root, source, spring; account, agency, aim, basis, consideration, end, grounds, incentive, inducement, motivation, motive, object, purpose, reason *~v* begin, bring about, compel, create, effect, engender, generate, give rise to, incite, induce, lead to, motivate, occasion, precipitate, produce, provoke, result in

**caustic** acrid, astringent, biting, burning, corroding, corrosive, keen, mordant

**caution** *n* care, carefulness, circumspection, discretion, fore-

thought, heed, prudence, vigilance, watchfulness; admonition, advice, counsel, injunction, warning *~v* admonish, advise, tip off, urge, warn

**cautious** alert, cagey *Inf*, careful, chary, circumspect, discreet, guarded, heedful, judicious, prudent, tentative, vigilant, wary, watchful

**cave** cavern, den, grotto, hollow

**cavern** cave, hollow, pothole

**cavity** crater, hole, hollow, pit

**cease** come to an end, conclude, desist, die away, end, fail, finish, halt, leave off, refrain, stay, stop, terminate

**ceaseless** constant, continuous, endless, eternal, everlasting, incessant, never-ending, nonstop, perpetual, unending, untiring

**cede** *v* yield, give up, transfer

**cedilla** *n* accent ( ‚ ) below letter

**ceilidh** *n* informal social gathering for dancing

**ceiling** *n* inner, upper surface of a room

**celebrate** *v* have festivities to mark (happy day, event etc.); observe (birthday etc.); perform (religious ceremony etc.); praise publicly **celebrated** *adj* famous **celebration** *n* **celebrity** *n* famous person; fame

**celery** *n* vegetable with long juicy edible stalks

**celestial** *adj* heavenly, divine

**celibacy** *n* unmarried state **celibate** *adj/n*

**cell** *n* small room in prison; small cavity; minute, basic unit of living matter; device converting chemical into electrical energy **cellular** *adj*

**cellar** *n* underground room for storage; stock of wine

**cello** *n* (*pl* **-los**) stringed instrument of violin family

**Cellophane** *n Trademark* transparent wrapping

**cellulose** *n* fibrous carbohydrate

**Celsius** *adj/n* (of) scale of temperature from 0° to 100°

**cement** *n* fine mortar; glue ~*v* unite as with cement

**cemetery** *n* burial ground

**cenotaph** *n* monument to one buried elsewhere

**censor** *n* one authorized to examine films, books etc. and suppress parts considered unacceptable ~*v* suppress **censorious** *adj* fault-finding **censorship** *n*

**censure** *n/v* blame

**census** *n* official counting of people, things etc.

**cent** *n* hundredth part of dollar etc.

**centaur** *n* mythical creature, half man, half horse

**centenary** *n* 100 years; celebration of hundredth anniversary ~*adj* pert. to a hundred

**centigrade** *adj/n* another name for CELSIUS

**centimetre** *n* hundredth part of metre

**centipede** *n* small segmented animal with many legs

**centre** *n* midpoint; pivot; place for

———— THESAURUS ————

**celebrate** commend, drink to, eulogize, exalt, extol, glorify, honour, keep, laud, observe, praise, proclaim, rejoice, reverence, toast

**celebrated** distinguished, eminent, famed, famous, glorious, illustrious, notable, popular, prominent, renowned, well-known

**celebration** carousal, festival, festivity, gala, jubilee, revelry

**celebrity** big name, dignitary, luminary, megastar *Inf*, name, personage, personality, star, superstar, V.I.P.

**cell** cavity, chamber, compartment, cubicle, dungeon, stall

**cement** *v* attach, bind, bond, glue, gum, join, plaster, seal, solder, stick together, unite, weld

**cemetery** burial ground, churchyard, graveyard

**censor** blue-pencil, bowdlerize, cut, expurgate

**censure** *n* blame, castigation, condemnation, criticism, disapproval, rebuke, remonstrance, reprimand, reproach, reproof, stricture ~*v* abuse, blame, castigate, condemn, criticize, denounce, lambast(e), rebuke, reprimand, reproach, reprove, scold, tear into *Inf*, upbraid

**central** chief, essential, fundamen-

specific organization or activity **central** adj **centralize** v **centrally** adv

**centurion** n Roman commander of 100 men

**century** n 100 years; any set of 100

**ceramics** pl n (with sing v) art, techniques of making clay, porcelain objects **ceramic** adj

**cereal** n any edible grain; (breakfast) food

**cerebral** adj pert. to brain

**ceremony** n formal observance; sacred rite; courteous act **ceremonial** adj/n

**certain** adj sure; inevitable; some, one; moderate (in quantity, degree etc.) **certainly** adv **certainty** n

**certify** v **-fying, -fied** declare formally; guarantee **certificate** n written declaration

**cervix** n (pl **-vixes, -vices**) neck, esp. of womb **cervical** adj

**cessation** n stop, pause

**cesspool, cesspit** n covered pit for sewage

**cf.** compare

**chafe** v make sore or worn by rubbing; warm; vex

**chaff** n husks of corn; worthless matter ~v tease

**chaffinch** n small songbird

**chagrin** n vexation, disappointment ~v embarrass

**chain** n series of connected rings; thing that binds; connected series of things or events; surveyor's measure ~v fasten with a chain; restrain

**chair** n movable seat, with back, for one person; seat of authority ~v preside over; carry in triumph **chairman** n one who presides over meeting **chairperson** n **chairwoman** n

**chalet** n Swiss wooden house

**chalice** n Poet cup

**chalk** n white substance, carbonate of lime; crayon ~v mark with chalk **chalky** adj

**challenge** v call to fight or account; dispute; stimulate ~n challenging **challenger** n

——— T H E S A U R U S ———

tal, inner, interior, main, mean, median, mid, middle, principal

**centralize** amalgamate, concentrate, condense, converge, incorporate, unify

**centre** core, crux, focus, heart, hub, mid, middle, pivot

**ceremonial** adj formal, ritual, solemn, stately ~n ceremony, formality, rite, ritual, solemnity

**ceremony** commemoration, function, observance, parade, rite, ritual, service, show

**certain** actual, ascertained, assured, constant, convinced, dependable, established, fixed, incontrovertible, indubitable, plain, positive, reliable, settled, true, undeni-

able, unmistakable

**certainty** assurance, confidence, conviction, faith, inevitability, positiveness, sureness, trust, validity

**certificate** credential(s), diploma, document, licence, testimonial

**certify** assure, attest, authenticate, aver, avow, confirm, declare, endorse, guarantee, show, testify, validate, verify, witness

**chain** n coupling, fetter, link, manacle, shackle, union; progression, sequence, series, set, string, succession, train ~v bind, enslave, fetter, handcuff, manacle, restrain, shackle, tether

**challenge** v brave, claim, dare, defy, demand, dispute, investigate,

**chamber** *n* (room for) assembly; compartment; cavity; *pl* office or apartment of barrister **chambermaid** *n* woman who cleans bedrooms

**chameleon** *n* lizard with power of changing colour

**chamois** *n* goatlike mountain antelope; soft pliable leather

**champ** *n* munch noisily; be impatient

**champagne** *n* light, sparkling white wine

**champion** *n* one that excels all others; defender of a cause *~v* fight for **championship** *n*

**chance** *n* unpredictable course of events; luck; opportunity; possibility; risk; probability *~v* risk; happen *~adj* casual, unexpected **chancy** *adj*

**chancel** *n* part of a church where altar is

**chancellor** *n* high officer of state; head of university

**chandelier** *n* hanging frame with branches for lights

**change** *v* alter, make or become different; put on (different clothes, fresh coverings); put or give for another; exchange *~n* alteration; variety; coins; balance received on payment **changeable** *adj*

**channel** *n* bed of stream; strait; deeper part of strait; groove; means of conveying; band of radio frequencies; television broadcasting station *~v* groove; guide

**chant** *n* simple song or melody; rhythmic slogan *~v* utter chant; speak monotonously

——————— THESAURUS ———————

object to, provoke, question, require, stimulate, summon, tax, try

**chamber** bedroom, compartment, cubicle, enclosure, hall, hollow, room

**champion** conqueror, defender, guardian, hero, patron, protector, title holder, upholder, victor, warrior, winner

**chance** *n* accident, casualty, coincidence, destiny, fate, fortune, luck, misfortune, peril, providence; likelihood, occasion, odds, opening, opportunity, possibility, probability, prospect, scope, time, window; gamble, hazard, risk, speculation, uncertainty *~v* endanger, gamble, hazard, risk, stake, try, venture, wager; befall, betide, come about, come to pass, fall out, happen, occur

**change** *v* alter, convert, diversify, fluctuate, metamorphose, moderate, modify, mutate, reform, re-

model, reorganize, restyle, shift, transform, vary, veer; barter, convert, displace, exchange, interchange, remove, replace, substitute, swap *Inf.* trade, transmit *~n* alteration, difference, innovation, metamorphosis, modification, mutation, permutation, revolution, transformation, transition

**changeable** capricious, erratic, fickle, fitful, fluid, inconstant, irregular, mercurial, mobile, protean, shifting, temperamental, uncertain, uneven, unpredictable, unreliable, unsettled, unstable, unsteady, vacillating, variable, versatile, volatile, wavering

**channel** *n* canal, duct, furrow, groove, gutter, main, passage, route, strait *~v* conduct, convey, direct, guide, transmit

**chant** *n* carol, chorus, melody, psalm, song *~v* intone, recite, sing, warble

**chaos** *n* disorder, confusion **chaotic** *adj*

**chap**[1] *v* **chapping, chapped** (of skin) become raw and cracked

**chap**[2] *n Inf* fellow, man

**chapati** *n* thin unleavened bread used in Indian cookery

**chapel** *n* place of worship; division of church with its own altar

**chaperon, chaperone** *n* one who attends young unmarried lady in public ~*v* attend in this way

**chaplain** *n* clergyman attached to prison, college etc.

**chapter** *n* division of book; assembly of clergy; organized branch of society

**char** *v* **charring, charred** scorch

**character** *n* nature; qualities making up individuality; moral qualities; eccentric person; fictional person **characteristic** *adj* typical ~*n* distinguishing feature **characterize** *v* mark out; describe

**charade** *n* absurd act; *pl* word-guessing game

**charcoal** *n* charred wood

**charge** *v* ask as price; bring accusation against; lay task on; attack; fill (with electricity); make onrush, attack ~*n* price; accusation; attack; command; accumulation of electricity **chargeable** *adj* **charger** *n* that which charges, esp. electrically; warhorse

**chargé d'affaires** head of small diplomatic mission

**chariot** *n* two-wheeled vehicle used in ancient fighting; state carriage **charioteer** *n*

**charisma** *n* special power of individual to inspire fascination, loyalty etc. **charismatic** *adj*

**charity** *n* giving of help, money to needy; organization for this; love, kindness **charitable** *adj*

**charlatan** *n* impostor

**charm** *n* attractiveness; anything

——————————— THESAURUS ———————————

**chaos** anarchy, bedlam, confusion, disorder, pandemonium, tumult

**chaotic** anarchic, confused, deranged, disordered, disorganized, lawless, purposeless, riotous, topsy-turvy, tumultuous, uncontrolled

**chapter** clause, division, episode, part, period, phase, section, stage, topic

**character** calibre, cast, complexion, constitution, disposition, make-up, nature, personality, quality, reputation, temper, temperament, type; honour, integrity, rectitude, strength, uprightness; card *Inf*, eccentric, nut *Sl*, oddball *Inf*, oddity, original, queer fish *Brit inf*, part, persona, portrayal, role

**characteristic** *adj* distinctive, distinguishing, individual, peculiar, representative, singular, special, specific, symbolic, typical ~*n* attribute, faculty, feature, mark, peculiarity, property, quality, trait

**charge** *v* accuse, arraign, blame, impeach, indict, involve; bid, command, enjoin, exhort, instruct, order, require ~*n* amount, cost, expenditure, expense, outlay, payment, price, rate; accusation, allegation, imputation, indictment; assault, attack, onset, rush, sortie

**charitable** benevolent, bountiful, generous, kind, lavish, liberal, philanthropic

**charity** alms-giving, assistance, benefaction, donations, fund, gift, hand-out, largess *or* largesse, philanthropy, relief

that fascinates; amulet; magic spell ~v bewitch; delight **charmer** n **charming** adj

**chart** n map of sea; tabulated statement ~v map

**charter** n document granting privileges etc. ~v let or hire; establish by charter **chartered** adj officially qualified

**charwoman** n woman paid to clean office, house etc.

**chary** adj cautious, sparing

**chase** v hunt, pursue; drive from, away, into etc. ~n pursuit, hunting

**chasm** n deep cleft

**chassis** n (pl **chassis**) framework of motor vehicle

**chaste** adj virginal; pure; modest; virtuous **chastity** n

**chasten** v correct by punishment; subdue **chastise** v inflict punish-

ment on

**chat** v chatting, chatted talk idly or rapidly ~n such talk **chatty** adj

**chateau** n (pl **-teaux** or **-teaus**) (esp. in France) castle, country house

**chattel** n any movable property

**chatter** v talk idly or rapidly; rattle teeth ~n idle talk **chatterbox** n person who chatters incessantly

**chauffeur** n (fem **chauffeuse**) paid driver of motorcar

**chauvinism** n irrational feeling of superiority **chauvinist** n/adj

**cheap** adj low in price; of little value; inferior **cheaply** adv **cheapen** v **cheapskate** n Inf miserly person

**cheat** v deceive; practise deceit to gain advantage ~n fraud

**check** v stop; control; examine ~n stoppage; restraint; brief examina-

———————————— T H E S A U R U S ————————————

**charm** n allure, appeal, attraction, desirability, enchantment, fascination, magic, magnetism, sorcery, spell ~v allure, attract, beguile, bewitch, cajole, captivate, delight, enchant, entrance, fascinate, mesmerize, please

**charming** appealing, attractive, bewitching, captivating, delightful, engaging, lovely, pleasant, pleasing, seductive, winning, winsome

**chart** n blueprint, diagram, graph, map, plan, table ~v graph, map out, outline, plot, shape, sketch

**charter** n contract, deed, document, franchise, indenture, privilege, right

**chase** course, drive, drive away, expel, follow, hound, hunt, pursue, put to flight, run after, track

**chaste** austere, decent, elegant, immaculate, incorrupt, innocent, modest, moral, neat, pure, quiet,

refined, restrained, simple, unaffected, undefiled, virtuous, wholesome

**chat** v chatter, gossip ~n chatter, gossip, talk, tête-à-tête

**chatter** v/n babble, blather, chat, gossip, natter, prattle

**cheap** bargain, cut-price, economical, inexpensive, keen, low-priced, reduced, sale; common, dime-a-dozen Inf, inferior, paltry, poor, second-rate, shoddy, tatty, tawdry, worthless

**cheat** v beguile, con Inf, deceive, defraud, double-cross Inf, dupe, fleece, fool, hoax, hoodwink, mislead, rip off Sl, swindle, thwart, trick, victimize; baffle, check, defeat, deprive, foil, frustrate, prevent, thwart ~n charlatan, cheater, con man Inf, deceiver, dodger, double-crosser Inf, impostor, knave, rogue, shark, sharper,

tion; pattern of squares; threat to king at chess **checkmate** n/v (make) final winning move **checkout** n counter in supermarket where customers pay **check-up** n examination (esp. medical) to see if all is in order

**Cheddar** n smooth hard cheese

**cheek** n side of face below eye; Inf impudence **cheeky** adj

**cheep** v/n (utter) high-pitched cry, as of young bird

**cheer** v comfort; gladden; encourage by shouts; shout applause ~n shout of approval; happiness; mood **cheerful** adj **cheerless** adj **cheery** adj

**cheerio** interj Inf goodbye

**cheese** n food made from solidified curd of milk **cheesy** adj **cheesecake** n dessert made from biscuits and cream cheese

**cheetah** n large, swift, spotted feline animal

**chef** n head cook

**chemistry** n science concerned with properties of substances and their combinations and reactions **chemical** n/adj **chemically** adv **chemist** n dispenser of medicines; shop that sells medicines etc.; one trained in chemistry

**chemotherapy** n treatment of disease by chemicals

**chenille** n soft cord, fabric of silk or worsted

**cheque** n written order to banker to pay money from one's account; printed slip of paper used for this **chequebook** n **cheque card** banker's card

**chequer** n marking as on chessboard; marble, peg etc. used in games ~v mark in squares; variegate **chequered** adj

**cherish** v treat tenderly

**cherry** n small red fruit with stone; tree bearing it

———— THESAURUS ————

swindler, trickster

**check** v bar, bridle, control, curb, delay, halt, hinder, impede, inhibit, limit, obstruct, pause, repress, restrain, retard, stop, thwart; compare, confirm, enquire into, examine, inspect, investigate, look at, look over, make sure, monitor, note, probe, scrutinize, study, test, tick, verify ~n constraint, control, curb, damper, hindrance, impediment, limitation, obstruction, rein, restraint, stoppage; examination, inspection, investigation, research, scrutiny, test

**cheek** n audacity, brazenness, disrespect, effrontery, gall Inf, impertinence, impudence, insolence, nerve, temerity

**cheer** v brighten, buoy up, cheer up, comfort, console, elate, elevate, encourage, enliven, exhilarate, gladden, hearten, incite, inspirit, solace, uplift, warm; acclaim, applaud, clap, hail, hurrah ~n cheerfulness, comfort, gaiety, gladness, glee, hopefulness, joy, liveliness, merriment, merry-making, mirth, optimism, solace

**cheerful** adj blithe, bright, buoyant, cheery, chirpy Inf, contented, enthusiastic, gay, glad, happy, hearty, jaunty, jolly, joyful, light-hearted, merry, optimistic, pleasant, sparkling, sprightly, sunny, upbeat Inf

**cherish** v care for, cling to, comfort, encourage, entertain, foster, harbour, hold dear, nourish, nurse, prize, shelter, support, sustain, treasure

**cherub** n (pl **cherubim**, **cherubs**) winged creature with human face; angel **cherubic** adj

**chess** n game played on chequered board **chessman** n piece used in chess

**chest** n upper part of trunk of body; large, strong box **chest of drawers** piece of furniture containing drawers

**chestnut** n tree bearing large nut in prickly husk; Inf old joke ~adj reddish-brown

**chevron** n Mil V-shaped braid designating rank

**chew** v grind with teeth ~n chewing **chewy** adj chewing gum flavoured gum

**chianti** n red Italian wine

**chic** adj stylish ~n stylishness

**chicane** n obstacle on racing circuit **chicanery** n trickery

**chick** n young of birds, esp. of hen; Sl girl, young woman **chickpea** n edible pealike seed

**chicken** n domestic fowl; Sl cow-ard ~adj cowardly **chickenpox** n infectious disease

**chicory** n salad plant whose root is used instead of coffee

**chide** v chiding, chid, chid or chidden scold

**chief** n head or principal person ~adj principal, foremost **chiefly** adv **chieftain** n leader of tribe

**chiffon** n gauzy material

**chihuahua** n breed of tiny dog

**chilblain** n inflamed sore on hands, legs etc. due to cold

**child** n (pl **children**) young human being; offspring **childish** adj silly **childlike** adj of or like a child; innocent **childhood** n

**chill** n coldness; cold with shivering; anything that discourages ~v make, become cold **chilly** adj cold; unfriendly

**chilli** n small red hot-tasting seed pod

**chime** n sound of bell ~v ring harmoniously; agree; strike (bells)

**chimney** n (pl **-neys**) vertical pas-

**chest** box, case, casket, crate, trunk

**chew** bite, champ, crunch, gnaw, grind, masticate, munch

**chief** n boss Inf, captain, commander, director, governor, head, leader, lord, manager, master, principal, ruler, superintendent ~adj capital, cardinal, central, especial, essential, foremost, grand, highest, key, leading, main, most important, outstanding, predominant, preeminent, premier, prevailing, principal, superior, supreme, uppermost, vital

**chiefly** especially, essentially, in general, in the main, largely, mainly, mostly, on the whole, principal-ly, usually

**child** baby, brat, descendant, infant, issue, juvenile, kid Inf, little one, minor, offspring, progeny, sprog Sl, toddler, tot, youngster Inf

**childhood** boyhood, girlhood, immaturity, infancy, minority, schooldays, youth

**childlike** artless, credulous, guileless, ingenuous, innocent, naive, simple, trustful, trusting, unfeigned

**chill** v congeal, cool, freeze, refrigerate ~adj bleak, chilly, cold, freezing, raw, sharp, wintry

**chilly** breezy, brisk, cold, crisp, draughty, fresh, nippy, sharp; hostile, unfriendly, unsympathetic, unwelcoming

sage for smoke

**chimpanzee** *n* ape of Africa

**chin** *n* part of face below mouth

**chinwag** *n Inf* chat

**china** *n* fine earthenware, porcelain; cups, saucers etc.

**chinchilla** *n* S Amer. rodent with soft, grey fur

**chink** *n* cleft, crack

**chintz** *n* cotton cloth printed in coloured designs

**chip** *n* splinter; place where piece has been broken off; thin strip of potato, fried; tiny wafer of silicon forming integrated circuit ~*v* **chipping**, **chipped** chop into small pieces; break small pieces from; break off **chip in** interrupt; contribute

**chipmunk** *n* small, striped N Amer. squirrel

**chiropodist** *n* one who treats disorders of feet **chiropody** *n*

**chirp, chirrup** *n/v* (make) short, sharp cry **chirpy** *adj Inf* happy

**chisel** *n* cutting tool ~*v* **-elling**, **-elled** cut with chisel; *Sl* cheat

**chit** *n* informal note

**chitchat** *n* gossip

**chivalry** *n* bravery and courtesy; medieval system of knighthood **chivalrous** *adj*

**chive** *n* herb with onion flavour

**chlorine** *n* nonmetallic element, yellowish-green poison gas **chloride** *n* bleaching agent **chlorinate** *v* disinfect

**chloroform** *n* volatile liquid formerly used as anaesthetic

**chlorophyll** *n* green colouring matter in plants

**chock** *n* block or wedge

**chocolate** *n* confectionery, drink made from ground cacao seeds

**choice** *n* act or power of choosing; alternative; thing or person chosen ~*adj* select, fine

**choir** *n* band of singers

**choke** *v* hinder, stop the breathing of; smother, stifle; obstruct; suffer choking ~*n* act, result of choking; device to increase richness of petrol-air mixture **choker** *n* tight-fitting necklace

**cholera** *n* deadly infectious disease

**choleric** *adj* bad-tempered

**cholesterol** *n* substance found in animal tissue and fat

**choose** *v* choosing, chose, chosen pick out, select; take by preference; decide, think fit **choosy** *adj*

**chop** *v* chopping, chopped cut with blow; hack ~*n* cutting blow; cut of meat with bone **chopper** *n* short

———— THESAURUS ————

**chip** *n* dent, flake, flaw, fragment, nick, notch, paring, scrap, scratch, shaving, wafer

**chivalrous** bold, brave, courteous, courtly, gallant, gentlemanly, heroic, high-minded, honourable, knightly, true, valiant

**chivalry** courage, courtesy, courtliness, gallantry, politeness

**choice** *n* alternative, election, option, pick, preference, say, selection, variety ~*adj* best, dainty, elect,

elite, excellent, exclusive, exquisite, hand-picked, nice, precious, prize, rare, select, special, uncommon, valuable

**choke** bar, block, bung, clog, close, congest, constrict, dam, gag, obstruct, occlude, overpower, smother, stifle, stop, strangle, suffocate, suppress, throttle

**choose** adopt, designate, elect, fix on, opt for, pick, prefer, see fit, select, settle upon, single out,

axe; *Inf* helicopter **choppy** *adj* (of sea) having short, broken waves

**chopsticks** *pl n* implements used by Chinese for eating food

**choral** *adj* of, for a choir

**chorale** *n* slow, stately hymn tune

**chord** *n* simultaneous sounding of musical notes

**chore** *n* (unpleasant) task

**choreography** *n* art of arranging dances, esp. ballet **choreographer** *n*

**chorister** *n* singer in choir

**chortle** *v/n* (make) happy chuckling sound

**chorus** *n* (music for) band of singers; refrain *~v* sing or say together

**chow**[1] *n Inf* food

**chow**[2] *n* thick-coated dog with curled tail, orig. from China

**Christ** *n* Jesus of Nazareth

**Christian** *n/adj* (person) following, believing in Christ **christen** *v* baptize, give name to **christening** *n* **Christianity** *n*

**Christmas** *n* festival of birth of Christ

**chrome, chromium** *n* metal used in alloys and for plating

**chromosome** *n* microscopic gene-carrying body in the tissue of a cell

**chronic** *adj* lasting a long time; habitual; *Inf* serious; *Inf* of bad quality

**chronicle** *n/v* (write) record of historical events

**chronological** *adj* arranged in order of time

**chrysalis** *n* (*pl* **chrysalises**) resting state of insect; case enclosing it

**chrysanthemum** *n* garden flower of various colours

**chub** *n* freshwater fish

**chubby** *adj* plump

**chuck** *v Inf* throw; pat affectionately (under chin); give up

**chuckle** *v/n* (make) soft laugh

**chuffed** *adj Inf* pleased, delighted

**chum** *n Inf* close friend **chummy** *adj*

**chunk** *n* thick, solid piece **chunky** *adj*

**church** *n* building for Christian worship; (*with cap.*) whole body or sect of Christians; clergy

**churlish** *adj* rude or surly

**churn** *n* large container for milk; vessel for making butter *~v* shake up, stir; (*with out*) produce rapidly

**chute** *n* slide for sending down parcels, coal etc.

**chutney** *n* pickle of fruit, spices etc.

**CIA** *US* Central Intelligence Agency

**CID** Criminal Investigation Department

**cider** *n* fermented drink made from apples

**cigar** *n* roll of tobacco leaves for smoking **cigarette** *n* finely-cut tobacco rolled in paper for smoking

──────── T H E S A U R U S ────────

take, wish

**chore** burden, duty, job, task

**chortle** cackle, chuckle, crow, guffaw

**chorus** choir, choristers, ensemble, singers, vocalists

**chronicle** *n* account, annals, diary, history, journal, narrative, record, story *~v* enter, narrate, record, re-

count, register, relate, report, set down, tell

**chuck** cast, discard, fling, heave, hurl, pitch, shy, sling, throw, toss

**chunk** block, hunk, lump, mass, piece, portion, slab, wad

**churlish** boorish, crabbed, harsh, ill-tempered, impolite, morose, oafish, rude, sullen, surly, uncivil,

**cinch** *n Inf* easy task

**cinder** *n* remains of burned coal

**cinema** *n* building used for showing of films; films generally

**cinnamon** *n* spice from bark of Asian tree

**cipher, cypher** *n* secret writing; arithmetical symbol; person of no importance

**circa** *Lat* about, approximately

**circle** *n* perfectly round figure; ring; *Theatre* section of seats above main level of auditorium; group, society with common interest ~*v* surround; move round **circular** *adj* round ~*n* letter sent to several persons **circulate** *v* move round; pass round; send round **circulation** *n* flow of blood; act of moving round; extent of sale of newspaper etc.

**circuit** *n* complete round or course; area; path of electric current; round of visitation **circuitous** *adj* indirect

**circumcise** *v* cut off foreskin of **circumcision** *n*

**circumference** *n* boundary line, esp. of circle

**circumflex** *n* accent (ˆ) over a letter

**circumnavigate** *v* sail right round

**circumscribe** *v* confine, bound, limit

**circumspect** *adj* cautious

**circumstance** *n* detail; event; *pl* state of affairs; condition in life, esp. financial; surroundings or things accompanying an action **circumstantial** *adj*

**circumvent** *v* outwit, evade, get round

**circus** *n* (*pl* **-cuses**) (performance of) acrobats, clowns, performing animals etc.

**cirrhosis** *n* disease of liver

**cirrus** *n* (*pl* **-ri**) high wispy cloud

**cistern** *n* water tank

**citadel** *n* city fortress

**cite** *v* quote; bring forward as proof **citation** *n* quoting; commendation for bravery etc.

**citizen** *n* member of state, nation etc.; inhabitant of city **citizenship** *n*

————————— THESAURUS —————————

uncouth, unmannerly, vulgar

**cinema** big screen *Inf*, films, flicks *Sl*, movies, pictures

**circle** *n* band, circumference, coil, cordon, cycle, disc, globe, lap, loop, orb, perimeter, revolution, ring, round, sphere, turn; assembly, clique, club, company, coterie, crowd, fellowship, fraternity, group, set, society ~*v* circumnavigate, coil, compass, curve, encircle, enclose, encompass, envelop, gird, hem in, revolve, ring, rotate, surround, tour

**circuit** area, compass, course, journey, lap, orbit, revolution, round, route, tour, track

**circulate** broadcast, diffuse, dis-

tribute, issue, make known, promulgate, propagate, publicize, publish, spread

**circulation** circling, flow, motion, rotation; currency, distribution, spread

**circumference** border, boundary, bounds, circuit, edge, extremity, fringe, limits, outline, perimeter, rim, verge

**circumstance** accident, condition, contingency, detail, element, event, fact, factor, happening, incident, item, occurrence, particular, position, respect, situation

**cite** adduce, advance, allude to, enumerate, evidence, extract, mention, name, quote, specify; *Law*

**citrus fruit** lemons, oranges etc.

**city** *n* large town

**civic** *adj* pert. to city or citizen

**civil** *adj* relating to citizens; not military; refined, polite; *Law* not criminal **civilian** *n* nonmilitary person **civility** *n*

**civilize** *v* bring out of barbarism; refine **civilization** *n* refinement; cultured society **civilized** *adj*

**claim** *v* demand as right; assert; call for ~ *n* demand for thing supposed due; right; thing claimed **claimant** *n*

**clairvoyance** *n* power of seeing things not present to senses **clairvoyant** *n/adj*

**clam** *n* edible mollusc

**clamber** *v* to climb awkwardly

**clammy** *adj* moist and sticky

**clamour** *n/v* (make) loud outcry **clamorous** *adj*

**clamp** *n* tool for holding ~ *v* fasten with or as with clamp; (*with* **down**) become stricter

**clan** *n* collection of families of common ancestry; group

**clandestine** *adj* secret; sly

**clang** *v* (cause to) make loud ringing sound ~ *n* this sound

**clap** *v* **clapping, clapped** (cause to) strike with noise; strike (hands) together; applaud; pat; place or put quickly ~ *n* hard, explosive sound; slap

**claret** *n* dry red wine

**clarify** *v* **-fying, -fied** make or become clear **clarification** *n* **clarity** *n*

**clarinet** *n* woodwind instrument

**clash** *n* loud noise; conflict, collision ~ *v* make clash; come into conflict; strike together

**clasp** *n* hook or fastening; embrace ~ *v* fasten; embrace, grasp

———————— THESAURUS ————————

**call**, subpoena, summon

**citizen** burgher, dweller, freeman, inhabitant, ratepayer, resident

**city** conurbation, megalopolis, metropolis, municipality

**civic** community, municipal, public

**civil** civic, domestic, home, interior, municipal, political; affable, civilized, courteous, courtly, obliging, polished, polite, refined, urbane, well-bred, well-mannered

**civilization** culture, development, education, enlightenment, progress, refinement, sophistication; community, nation, people, polity, society

**civilize** cultivate, educate, enlighten, improve, polish, refine, tame

**civilized** cultured, educated, enlightened, humane, polite, tolerant

**claim** *v* allege, ask, assert, call for, collect, demand, exact, hold, insist,

maintain, need, pick up, profess, require, take, uphold ~ *n* application, assertion, call, demand, petition, privilege, protestation, request, requirement, right, title

**clan** band, brotherhood, clique, faction, family, fraternity, group, race, sect, sept, set, society, tribe

**clap** acclaim, applaud, cheer

**clarify** clear up, elucidate, explain, make plain, resolve, shed light on, simplify

**clarity** definition, explicitness, intelligibility, lucidity, precision, simplicity, transparency

**clash** *n* brush, collision, conflict, confrontation, difference of opinion, disagreement, fight ~ *v* conflict, cross swords, feud, grapple, quarrel, war, wrangle

**clasp** *n* brooch, buckle, catch, clip, grip, hasp, hook, pin, snap ~ *v*

**class** *n* any division, order, kind, sort; rank; group of school pupils; division by merit; quality ~*v* assign to proper division **classy** *adj Inf* stylish, elegant **classify** *v* -**fying**, -**fied** arrange methodically in classes **classification** *n*

**classic** *adj* of highest rank, esp. of art; typical; famous ~*n* (literary) work of recognized excellence; *pl* ancient Greek and Latin literature

**classical** *adj* refined, elegant; of ancient Greek and Latin music

**clatter** *n* rattling noise ~*v* (cause to) make clatter

**clause** *n* part of sentence; article in formal document

**claustrophobia** *n* abnormal fear of confined spaces **claustrophobic** *adj*

**clavicle** *n* collarbone

**claw** *n* sharp hooked nail of animal ~*v* tear with claws

**clay** *n* fine-grained earth, plastic when wet, hardening when baked; earth **clayey** *adj*

**clean** *adj* free from dirt; pure; guiltless; trim ~*adv* so as to leave no dirt; entirely ~*v* free from dirt **cleaner** *n* **cleanliness** *n* **cleanly** *adv* **cleanse** *v* make clean

**clear** *adj* pure, bright; free from cloud; transparent; plain, distinct; without defect; unimpeded ~*adv* brightly; wholly, quite ~*v* make clear; acquit; pass over; make as profit; free from obstruction, difficulty; become clear, bright, free, transparent **clearly** *adv* **clearance** *n* **clearing** *n* land cleared of trees

clutch, connect, embrace, enfold, fasten, grapple, grasp, grip, hold, hug, press, seize, squeeze

**class** caste, category, collection, department, division, genus, grade, group, grouping, kind, league, order, rank, set, sort, species, sphere, status, type, value

**classic** *adj* best, finest, first-rate, masterly; archetypal, definitive, exemplary, ideal, master, model, standard, typical ~*n* exemplar, masterpiece, model, standard

**classical** chaste, elegant, pure, refined, restrained, symmetrical, well-proportioned; Attic, Augustan, Grecian, Greek, Hellenic, Latin, Roman

**classification** analysis, arrangement, codification, grading, sorting, taxonomy

**classify** arrange, catalogue, codify, dispose, distribute, file, grade, rank, sort

**clause** article, chapter, condition, paragraph, part, passage, section; heading, item, point, rider, stipulation

**claw** nail, nipper, pincer, talon, tentacle

**clean** *adj* faultless, fresh, hygienic, immaculate, pure, sanitary, spotless, squeaky-clean, unsoiled, unstained, unsullied, washed; chaste, decent, exemplary, good, honourable, impeccable, innocent, moral, pure, respectable, undefiled, upright, virtuous ~*v* bath, cleanse, disinfect, do up, dust, launder, mop, purge, purify, rinse, scour, scrub, sponge, swab, sweep, wash, wipe

**clear** *adj* bright, cloudless, fair, fine, light, luminous, shining, sunny, unclouded, undimmed; apparent, audible, blatant, coherent, definite, distinct, evident, explicit, express, lucid, manifest, obvious,

**cleave¹** *v* cleaving, clove *or* cleft, cloven *or* cleft (cause to) split **cleavage** *n* **cleaver** *n* short chopper

**cleave²** *v* cleaving, cleaved stick, adhere; be loyal

**clef** *n* Mus mark to show pitch

**clematis** *n* climbing plant

**clement** *adj* merciful; gentle; mild **clemency** *n*

**clench** *v* set firmly together; grasp, close (fist)

**clergy** *n* body of ministers of Christian church **clergyman** *n*

**clerical** *adj* of clergy; of office work **cleric** *n* clergyman

**clerk** *n* subordinate who keeps files etc.; officer in charge of records, correspondence etc.

**clever** *adj* intelligent; able, skilful, adroit **cleverly** *adv*

**cliché** *n* (*pl* **-s**) stereotyped hackneyed phrase

**click** *n/v* (make) short, sharp sound

**client** *n* customer **clientele** *n* clients

**cliff** *n* steep rock face **cliffhanger** *n* thing which is exciting and full of suspense

**climate** *n* condition of country with regard to weather **climatic** *adj*

**climax** *n* highest point, culmination **climactic** *adj*

**climb** *v* go up or ascend **climber** *n*

**clinch** *v* conclude (agreement)

**cling** *v* clinging, clung adhere; be firmly attached to **clingfilm** *n* thin polythene wrapping material

**clinic** *n* place for medical examination, advice or treatment **clinical** *adj*

**clink** *n* sharp metallic sound ~*v* (cause to) make this sound

**clip¹** *v* clipping, clipped cut with scissors; cut short ~*n* Inf sharp blow **clipping** *n* thing cut out, esp. newspaper article

**clip²** *n/v* clipping, clipped (attach with) gripping device

**clipper** *n* fast sailing ship

——————— THESAURUS ———————

palpable, patent, plain, pronounced, recognizable, unambiguous, unequivocal; empty, free, open, smooth, unhampered, unhindered, unimpeded, unlimited, unobstructed ~*v* clean, erase, purify, refine, sweep away, tidy (up), wipe; absolve, acquit, excuse, exonerate, justify, vindicate; jump, leap, miss, pass over, vault; break up, brighten, clarify, lighten

**clearly** beyond doubt, distinctly, evidently, obviously, openly, overtly, seemingly, undeniably, undoubtedly

**clever** able, adroit, apt, astute, brainy Inf, bright, canny, capable, cunning, deep, discerning, expert, gifted, ingenious, intelligent, inventive, keen, knowing, quick, rational,

sagacious, sensible, shrewd, skilful, smart, talented, witty

**client** applicant, buyer, consumer, customer, dependant, habitué, patient, protégé, shopper

**clientele** clients, customers, following, market, regulars, trade

**cliff** bluff, crag, escarpment, face, overhang, precipice, rock face, scar, scarp

**climate** region, temperature, weather

**climax** acme, apogee, culmination, head, height, highlight, high spot Inf, peak, summit, top, zenith

**climb** ascend, clamber, mount, rise, scale, shin up, soar, top

**cling** adhere, be true to, clasp, cleave to, clutch, embrace, fasten, grasp, grip, hug, stick, twine round

**clique** *n* small exclusive set; faction, group of people

**clitoris** *n* part of female genitals **clitoral** *adj*

**cloak** *n/v* (cover with) loose outer garment; disguise **cloakroom** *n*

**clobber** *v Inf* beat, batter

**clock** *n* instrument for measuring time **clockwise** *adv/adj* in the direction that the hands of a clock rotate **clockwork** *n* wind-up mechanism for clocks, toys etc.

**clod** *n* lump of earth

**clog** *v* **clogging, clogged** hamper, impede, choke up ~*n* wooden-soled shoe

**cloister** *n* covered pillared arcade; monastery or convent **cloistered** *adj* secluded

**clone** *n* cells of same genetic constitution as another, derived by asexual reproduction; *Inf* lookalike

~*v* replicate

**close¹** *adj* near; compact; crowded; intimate; almost equal; careful, searching; confined; secret; unventilated; niggardly; restricted ~*adv* nearly; tightly **closely** *adv* **close-up** *n* close view

**close²** *v* shut; stop up; prevent access to; finish; come together; grapple ~*n* end; shut-in place; precinct of cathedral **closure** *n*

**closet** *n* small private room; *US* cupboard ~*adj* secret ~*v* **closeting, closeted** shut away in private

**clot** *n* mass or lump (of blood); *Inf* fool ~*v* **clotting, clotted** (cause to) form into lumps

**cloth** *n* woven fabric **clothe** *v* **clothing, clothed** or **clad** put clothes on **clothes** *pl n* dress; bed coverings **clothing** *n*

**cloud** *n* vapour floating in air; state

———— THESAURUS ————

**clip¹** crop, curtail, cut, cut short, dock, pare, prune, shear, shorten, snip, trim

**clip²** *v* attach, fasten, fix, hold, pin, staple

**cloak** *n* blind, cape, coat, cover, front, mantle, mask, pretext, shield, wrap ~*v* camouflage, conceal, cover, disguise, hide, mask, obscure, screen, veil

**clog** block, bung, burden, congest, dam up, hamper, hinder, impede, jam, obstruct, occlude, shackle, stop up

**close¹** adjacent, adjoining, approaching, at hand, handy, hard by, imminent, impending, near, nearby, neighbouring, nigh, upcoming, compact, congested, cramped, cropped, crowded, dense, impenetrable, jam-packed, packed, short, solid, thick, tight; attached, confi-

dential, dear, devoted, familiar, inseparable, intimate, loving; airless, heavy, humid, muggy, oppressive, stale, stifling, stuffy, suffocating, sweltering, thick

**close²** *v* bar, block, choke, clog, confine, cork, fill, lock, obstruct, plug, seal, secure, shut, shut up, stop up; axe *Inf*, cease, complete, conclude, discontinue, end, finish, shut down, terminate, wind up ~*n* cessation, completion, conclusion, culmination, denouement, end, ending, finale, finish, termination

**cloth** dry goods, fabric, material, stuff, textiles

**clothe** attire, dress, fit out, outfit, rig, robe

**clothes, clothing** attire, costume, dress, ensemble, garb, garments, gear *Inf*, get-up *Inf*, habits, outfit, togs *Inf*, wardrobe, wear

of gloom ~v darken; become cloudy **cloudy** adj

**clout** n Inf blow; influence, power ~v strike

**clove** n pungent spice

**clover** n forage plant

**clown** n circus comic

**club** n thick stick; bat; association; suit at cards ~v clubbing, clubbed strike; join

**cluck** v/n (make) noise of hen

**clue** n indication, esp. of solution of mystery or puzzle **clueless** adj stupid

**clump**¹ n cluster of plants

**clump**² v/n (move with) heavy tread

**clumsy** adj awkward **clumsily** adv **clumsiness** n

**cluster** n/v group, bunch

**clutch** v grasp eagerly; snatch (at)

~n grasp, tight grip; device enabling two revolving shafts to be (dis)connected at will

**clutter** v cause obstruction, disorder ~n disordered mass

**cm** centimetre

**Co.** Company; County

**co-** comb. form together, jointly, as in coproduction

**c/o** care of; carried over

**coach** n long-distance bus; large four-wheeled carriage; railway carriage; tutor; instructor ~v instruct

**coagulate** v curdle, clot

**coal** n mineral used as fuel; glowing ember

**coalesce** v unite

**coalition** n alliance

**coarse** adj rough; unrefined; indecent **coarsely** adv **coarseness** n

**coast** n sea shore ~v move under

─────── THESAURUS ───────

**cloud** n billow, darkness, fog, gloom, haze, mist, murk, obscurity, vapour ~v darken, dim, eclipse, obscure, overcast, overshadow, shade, shadow, veil

**cloudy** blurred, confused, dark, dim, dismal, dull, dusky, gloomy, hazy, leaden, muddy, murky, overcast, sombre, sullen, sunless

**clown** n buffoon, comedian, dolt, fool, harlequin, jester, joker, pierrot, prankster

**club** n bat, bludgeon, cosh Brit, cudgel, stick, truncheon; association, circle, clique, company, fraternity, group, guild, lodge, order, set, society, union

**clue** n evidence, hint, indication, inkling, intimation, lead, pointer, sign, suggestion, suspicion, tip, tip-off, trace

**clumsy** awkward, blundering, bumbling, bungling, gauche,

gawky, heavy, ill-shaped, inept, klutzy US & Canad sl, lumbering, maladroit, ponderous, uncoordinated

**cluster** n batch, bunch, clump, collection, gathering, group, knot ~v assemble, bunch, collect, flock, gather

**clutch** catch, clasp, cling to, embrace, grab, grapple, grasp, grip, seize

**coach** n bus, car, carriage, vehicle; instructor, teacher, trainer, tutor ~v cram, drill, instruct, prepare, train, tutor

**coalition** alliance, amalgamation, association, bloc, combination, compact, confederacy, confederation, integration, league, merger, union

**coarse** boorish, brutish, foulmouthed, gruff, loutish, rough, rude, uncivil

momentum **coastal** adj **coaster** n small ship; small mat

**coat** n sleeved outer garment; animal's fur; covering layer ~v cover **coating** n covering layer

**coax** v persuade

**cob** n short-legged stout horse; male swan; head of corn

**cobalt** n metallic element; blue pigment from it

**cobble** n patch roughly; mend shoes ~n round stone **cobbler** n

**cobra** n poisonous, hooded snake

**cobweb** n spider's web

**cocaine** n addictive narcotic drug used medicinally

**cochineal** n scarlet dye

**cock** n male bird, esp. of domestic fowl; tap; hammer of gun ~v draw back to firing position; raise, turn **cockerel** n young cock

**cockatoo** n crested parrot

**cockle** n shellfish

**cockpit** n pilot's seat, compartment in small aircraft

**cockroach** n insect pest

**cocktail** n mixed drink of spirits; appetizer

**cocky** adj conceited, pert

**cocoa** n powdered seed of cacao tree; drink made from this

**coconut** n large, hard nut

**cocoon** n sheath of insect in chrysalis stage

**COD** cash on delivery

**cod** n large sea fish

**coda** n Mus final part of musical composition

**code** n system of letters, symbols to transmit messages secretly; scheme of conduct; collection of laws **codify** v **-fying, -fied**

**codeine** n pain-killing drug

**coerce** v compel, force **coercion** n

**coexist** v exist together **coexistence** n

**C of E** Church of England

**coffee** n seeds of tropical shrub; drink made from these

**coffer** n chest for valuables

**coffin** n box for corpse

**cog** n one of teeth on rim of wheel **cogwheel** n

**cogent** adj convincing

**cogitate** v think, reflect, ponder **cogitation** n

**cognac** n French brandy

**cognizance** n knowledge **cognizant** adj

**cohabit** v live together as husband and wife

**cohere** v stick together, be consistent **coherent** adj capable of logical speech, thought; connected, making sense **cohesion** n tendency to unite **cohesive** adj

**cohort** n troop; associate

**coiffure** n hairstyle

**coarseness** bawdiness, crudity, indelicacy, poor taste, ribaldry, roughness, smut, uncouthness, unevenness

**coast** n beach, border, coastline, seaside, shore, strand ~v cruise, drift, freewheel, get by, glide, sail, taxi

**coat** n fleece, fur, hair, hide, pelt, skin, wool; coating, covering, layer, overlay ~v apply, cover, plaster, smear, spread

**coax** allure, beguile, cajole, decoy, entice, flatter, persuade, prevail upon, soothe, talk into, wheedle

**cocky** arrogant, brash, cocksure, conceited, lordly, swaggering, vain

**code** cipher; canon, convention, custom, ethics, etiquette, manners, maxim, rules, system

**coil** v twist into winding shape ~n series of rings; anything coiled

**coin** n piece of money; money ~v stamp; invent **coinage** n

**coincide** v happen together **coincidence** n chance happening **coincidental** adj

**coke¹** n residue left from distillation of coal, used as fuel

**coke²** n Coca-Cola; Sl cocaine

**Col.** Colonel

**cola** n flavoured soft drink

**colander** n strainer for food

**cold** adj lacking heat; indifferent, unmoved; unfriendly ~n lack of heat; illness, marked by runny nose etc. **coldly** adv **cold-blooded** adj lacking pity

**coleslaw** n cabbage salad

**colic** n severe pains in the intestines

**collaborate** v work with another **collaboration** n **collaborator** n

**collage** n (artistic) composition of bits and pieces stuck together on background

**collapse** v fall; fail ~n act of collapsing; breakdown **collapsible** adj

**collar** n band, part of garment, worn round neck ~v seize **collarbone** n bone joining shoulder blade to breast bone

**collate** v compare carefully

**collateral** n security pledged for loan

**colleague** n fellow worker

**collect** v gather, bring, come together **collected** adj calm **collection** n **collective** n owned by its workers ~adj shared **collectively** adv **collector** n

**college** n place of higher education **collegiate** adj

**collide** v crash together **collision** n

**collie** n breed of sheepdog

---

**THESAURUS**

**coil** curl, entwine, loop, snake, spiral, twine, twist, wind, wreathe

**coincide** be concurrent, coexist, synchronize

**coincidence** accident, chance, eventuality, fluke, luck, stroke of luck

**cold** adj arctic, biting, bitter, bleak, chill, chilly, cool, freezing, frigid, frosty, frozen, harsh, icy, parky Brit inf, raw, wintry; aloof, distant, frigid, indifferent, reserved, standoffish, unfeeling, unmoved ~n chill, chilliness, coldness, frigidity, frostiness, iciness, inclemency

**collaborate** cooperate, join forces, participate, team up, work together

**collaborator** associate, colleague, confederate, co-worker, partner, team-mate

**collapse** v break down, cave in, come to nothing, crumple, fail,

faint, fall, fold, founder, give way, subside ~n breakdown, cave-in, disintegration, downfall, exhaustion, failure, faint

**colleague** ally, assistant, associate, auxiliary, collaborator, companion, comrade, fellow worker, helper, partner, team-mate, workmate

**collect** accumulate, amass, assemble, gather, heap, hoard, save, stockpile; assemble, congregate, convene, converge, rally

**collected** calm, composed, cool, placid, poised, self-possessed, serene, unfazed Inf, unruffled

**collection** accumulation, anthology, compilation, heap, hoard, mass, pile, set, stockpile, store; assembly, assortment, cluster, company, crowd, gathering, group

**collide** clash, conflict, crash, meet head-on

**colliery** n coal mine

**colloquial** adj pert. to, or used in, informal conversation **colloquialism** n

**collusion** n secret agreement for a fraudulent purpose **collude** v

**cologne** n perfumed liquid

**colon¹** n mark (:) indicating break in a sentence

**colon²** n part of large intestine

**colonel** n commander of regiment or battalion

**colonnade** n row of columns

**colony** n body of people who settle in new country; country so settled **colonial** adj **colonist** n **colonize** v **colonization** n

**colossal** adj huge, gigantic

**colour** n hue, tint; complexion; paint; pigment; Fig semblance, pretext; timbre, quality; pl flag; Sport distinguishing badge, symbol ~v

stain, paint; disguise; influence or distort; blush **colourful** adj bright; interesting **colourless** adj **colour-blind** adj unable to distinguish between certain colours

**colt** n young male horse

**columbine** n garden flower

**column** n long vertical pillar; division of page; body of troops **columnist** n journalist writing regular feature

**coma** n unconsciousness **comatose** adj

**comb** n toothed instrument for tidying hair; cock's crest; mass of honey cells ~v use comb on; search

**combat** v/n fight, contest **combatant** n **combative** adj

**combine** v join together ~n syndicate, esp. of businesses **combination** n **combine harvester** machine to harvest and thresh grain

**collision** accident, bump, crash, impact, pile-up Inf, smash

**colony** community, outpost, province, settlement, territory

**colour** n complexion, dye, hue, paint, pigment, shade, tincture, tinge, tint ~v dye, paint, stain, tinge, tint; disguise, distort, embroider, falsify, garble, gloss over, misrepresent, pervert, prejudice, slant, taint; blush, burn, crimson, flush, go crimson, redden

**colourful** bright, brilliant, intense, motley, multicoloured, rich, variegated, vivid; characterful, distinctive, graphic, interesting, lively, picturesque, rich, stimulating, unusual, vivid

**colourless** characterless, dreary, insipid, lacklustre, tame, uninteresting, vapid

**column** pillar, post, shaft, sup-

port, upright; cavalcade, file, line, list, procession, queue, rank, row, string, train

**coma** insensibility, oblivion, somnolence, stupor, trance, unconsciousness

**comb** v dress, groom, untangle; hunt, rake, ransack, rummage, scour, screen, search, sift, sweep

**combat** action, battle, conflict, contest, encounter, engagement, fight, skirmish, struggle, war, warfare

**combination** amalgam, blend, coalescence, composite, meld, mix, mixture

**combine** amalgamate, bind, blend, bond, compound, connect, cooperate, fuse, incorporate, integrate, join (together), link, marry, meld, merge, mix, pool, unify, unite

**combustion** n process of burning **combustible** adj

**come** v coming, came, come approach, arrive, move towards; reach; occur; originate (from); become **comeback** n Inf return to active life; retort **comedown** n decline in status; disappointment **comeuppance** n Inf deserved punishment

**comedy** n light, amusing play; humour **comedian** n (fem **comedienne**) entertainer who tells jokes

**comely** adj good-looking

**comet** n luminous heavenly body

**comfort** n ease; (means of) consolation ~v soothe; console **comfortable** adj giving comfort; well-off

**comfortably** adv **comforter** n

**comic** adj relating to comedy; funny ~n comedian; magazine of strip cartoons **comical** adj

**comma** n punctuation mark (,)

**command** v order; rule; compel; have in one's power ~n order; power of controlling; mastery; post of one commanding; jurisdiction **commandant** n **commander** v seize for military use **commander** n **commandment** n

**commando** n (pl **-dos**) (member of) special military unit

**commemorate** v keep in memory by ceremony **commemoration** n **commemorative** adj

**come** advance, appear, approach, arrive, become, draw near, enter, happen, materialize, move, move towards, near, occur, originate, turn out, turn up Inf; appear, arrive, attain, enter, materialize, reach, show up Inf, turn up Inf; fall, happen, occur, take place; arise, emanate, emerge, end up, flow, issue, originate, result, turn out

**comeback** rally, rebound, recovery, resurgence, return, revival, triumph

**comedown** anticlimax, blow, decline, demotion, disappointment, humiliation, reverse

**comedy** chaffing, drollery, facetiousness, farce, fun, hilarity, humour, jesting, joking, slapstick, witticisms

**comfort** n cosiness, creature comforts, ease, luxury, wellbeing; aid, alleviation, cheer, consolation, ease, encouragement, help, relief, succour, support ~v cheer, commiserate with, console, encourage, gladden, hearten, reassure, relieve, solace, soothe

**comfortable** agreeable, ample, commodious, convenient, cosy, delightful, easy, enjoyable, homely, loose, pleasant, relaxing, restful, roomy, snug; affluent, prosperous, well-off, well-to-do

**comic** adj amusing, comical, droll, facetious, farcical, funny, humorous, joking, light, witty

**command** v bid, charge, compel, demand, direct, enjoin, order, require; administer, control, dominate, govern, handle, head, lead, manage, reign over, rule, supervise, sway ~n behest, bidding, decree, direction, directive, edict, fiat, injunction, instruction, mandate, order, precept, requirement

**commander** boss, captain, chief, C in C, C.O., commanding officer, director, head, leader, officer, ruler

**commemorate** celebrate, honour, immortalize, keep, observe, pay tribute to, remember, salute

**commemoration** ceremony, honouring, memorial service, ob-

**commence** *v* begin

**commend** *v* praise; entrust **commendable** *adj* **commendation** *n*

**commensurate** *adj* equal; in proportion

**comment** *n/v* remark; gossip; note

**commentary** *n* explanatory notes; spoken accompaniment to film etc.

**commentate** *v* **commentator** *n*

**commerce** *n* trade **commercial** *adj* of business, trade etc. ~*n* advertisement, esp. on radio or television

**commiserate** *v* sympathize with **commiseration** *n*

**commission** *n* authority; (body entrusted with) some special duty; agent's payment by percentage; document appointing to officer's rank; committing ~*v* charge with duty; *Mil* confer a rank; give order for **commissioner** *n*

**commissionaire** *n* uniformed doorman

**commit** *v* -**mitting**, -**mitted** give in charge; be guilty of; pledge; send for trial **commitment** *n* **committal** *n*

**committee** *n* body appointed, elected for special business

**commode** *n* chest of drawers; stool containing chamber pot

**commodity** *n* article of trade

**commodore** *n* senior naval or air officer; president of yacht club

**common** *adj* shared by all; public; ordinary; inferior ~*n* land belonging to community; *pl* ordinary people; (*with cap.*) House of Commons **commoner** *n* one not of the nobility **commonly** *adv* **commonplace** *adj* ordinary ~*n* trite remark **commonwealth** *n* republic; (*with cap.*) federation of self-governing states

**commotion** *n* stir, disturbance

————————— THESAURUS —————————

servance, remembrance, tribute

**commence** begin, embark on, enter upon, initiate, open, originate, start

**commend** acclaim, applaud, approve, compliment, eulogize, extol, praise, recommend

**comment** *n* observation, remark, statement; commentary, criticism, elucidation, explanation, exposition, note ~*v* mention, note, observe, opine, point out, remark, say, utter

**commentary** analysis, critique, description, exegesis, explanation, narration, notes, review, treatise, voice-over

**commentator** reporter, sportscaster; annotator, critic, expositor, interpreter, scholiast

**commerce** business, dealing, exchange, trade, traffic

**commercial** business, mercantile, sales, trade, trading

**commission** *n* appointment, authority, charge, duty, employment, errand, function, mandate, mission, task, trust, warrant; board, committee, delegation, deputation, representative; allowance, cut, fee, percentage, royalties ~*v* appoint, authorize, contract, delegate, depute, empower, engage, nominate, order, select, send

**commit** carry out, do, enact, execute, perform, perpetrate

**commitment** duty, engagement, liability, obligation, responsibility, tie; assurance, guarantee, pledge, promise, undertaking, vow, word

**common** accepted, general, popular, prevailing, universal, widespread; average, conventional, customary, daily, everyday, familiar,

**commune**[1] v converse intimately **communion** n sharing of thoughts, feelings etc.; (with cap.) (participation in) sacrament of the Lord's Supper

**commune**[2] n group living together and sharing property, responsibility etc. **communal** adj for common use

**communicate** v impart, convey; reveal ~v give or exchange information; have connecting door **communicable** adj **communication** n giving information; message; (usu. pl) means of exchanging messages **communicative** adj willing to talk

**communiqué** n official announcement

**communism** n doctrine that all means of production etc. should be

property of community **communist** n/adj

**community** n body of people living in one district; the public; joint ownership; similarity

**commute** v travel daily some distance to work; exchange; reduce (punishment) **commuter** n

**compact**[1] adj closely packed; solid; terse ~v make, become compact **compact disc** small audio disc played by laser

**compact**[2] n small case to hold face powder etc.

**compact**[3] n agreement

**companion** n comrade

**company** n gathering of persons; companionship; guests; business firm; division of regiment

─────────── THESAURUS ───────────

frequent, general, humdrum, obscure, ordinary, plain, regular, routine, run-of-the-mill, simple, standard, stock, usual, workaday; coarse, hackneyed, inferior, low, pedestrian, plebeian, stale, trite, undistinguished, vulgar

**commotion** ado, agitation, bustle, disorder, disturbance, excitement, ferment, furore, fuss, hubbub, racket, riot, rumpus, to-do, tumult, turmoil, upheaval, uproar

**communal** collective, community, general, joint, public, shared

**commune** n collective, community, cooperative, kibbutz

**communicate** acquaint, announce, be in contact, be in touch, connect, convey, correspond, declare, disclose, divulge, impart, inform, make known, pass on, phone, proclaim, publish, report, reveal, ring up Inf, chiefly Brit, signify, spread, transmit, unfold

**communication** connection, con-

tact, conversation, correspondence, link, transmission; disclosure, dispatch, information, intelligence, message, news, report, statement, word

**communism** Bolshevism, collectivism, Marxism, socialism, state socialism

**community** association, body politic, brotherhood, commonwealth, company, district, general public, locality, people, populace, population, public, residents, society, state

**compact** close, compressed, condensed, dense, firm, impenetrable, impermeable, pressed together, solid; thick; brief, concise, epigrammatic, laconic, pithy, pointed, succinct, terse, to the point

**companion** accomplice, ally, associate, colleague, comrade, confederate, consort, crony, friend, partner

**company** assemblage, assembly,

**compare** v notice likenesses and differences; liken; be like; compete with **comparability** n **comparable** adj **comparative** adj relative; *Grammar* denoting form of adjective, adverb meaning *more* **comparison** n act of comparing

**compartment** n part divided off

**compass** n instrument for showing north; (*usu. pl*) instrument for drawing circles; scope ~v surround; comprehend; attain

**compassion** n pity, sympathy **compassionate** adj

**compatible** adj agreeing with **compatibility** n

**compatriot** n fellow countryman

**compel** v **-pelling, -pelled** force

**compendium** n (*pl* **-diums, -dia**) collection of different games; summary **compendious** adj brief but inclusive

**compensate** v make up for; recompense **compensation** n

**compere** n one who introduces cabaret, television shows etc. ~v act as compere

**compete** v (*oft.* with **with**) strive in rivalry, contend for **competition** n rivalry; contest **competitive** adj **competitor** n

**competent** adj able; properly qualified; sufficient **competence** n

**compile** v make up from various

———— THESAURUS ————

band, body, circle, collection, convention, coterie, crew, crowd, ensemble, gathering, group, league, party, set, throng, troop, troupe, turnout; association, business, concern, corporation, establishment, firm, house, partnership, syndicate

**comparable** a match for, as good as, commensurate, equal, equivalent, in a class with, on a par, proportionate, tantamount; akin, alike, corresponding, related, similar

**compare** (with **with**) balance, collate, contrast, juxtapose, set against, weigh

**comparison** contrast, distinction, juxtaposition

**compartment** alcove, bay, berth, booth, carriage, cell, chamber, cubicle, locker, niche, pigeonhole, section

**compassion** commiseration, condolence, fellow feeling, heart, humanity, kindness, mercy, pity, soft-heartedness, sorrow, sympathy, tenderness

**compatible** accordant, adaptable,

agreeable, congenial, congruent, congruous, consistent, consonant, harmonious, in harmony, in keeping, like-minded, reconcilable, suitable

**compel** coerce, constrain, dragoon, drive, enforce, exact, force, impel, make, oblige, railroad *Inf*, restrain, squeeze, urge

**compensate** balance, cancel (out), counteract, make up for, offset, redress, atone, indemnify, make good, make restitution, recompense, refund, reimburse, remunerate, repay, requite, reward, satisfy

**compensation** amends, atonement, damages, indemnity, payment, remuneration, reparation, restitution, reward, satisfaction

**compete** be in the running, challenge, contend, contest, emulate, fight, pit oneself against, rival, strive, struggle, vie

**competent** able, adapted, appropriate, capable, clever, equal, fit, proficient, qualified, sufficient,

sources **compilation** n

**complacent** adj self-satisfied **complacency** n

**complain** v grumble; make known a grievance; (with of) make known that one is suffering from **complaint** n grievance; illness

**complement** n something making up a whole; complete amount ~v add to, make complete **complementary** adj

**complete** adj perfect; ended; entire; thorough ~v make whole; fin-

ish completely adv **completion** n

**complex** adj intricate, compound, involved ~n group of related buildings; obsession **complexity** n

**complexion** n look, colour of skin, esp. of face; aspect, character

**complicate** v make involved, difficult **complication** n

**complicity** n partnership in wrongdoing

**compliment** n/v praise **complimentary** adj expressing praise; free of charge

————— THESAURUS —————

suitable

**competition** contention, contest, emulation, opposition, rivalry, strife, struggle; championship, contest, event, head-to-head, puzzle, quiz, tournament

**competitive** aggressive, ambitious, antagonistic, at odds, combative, cutthroat, dog-eat-dog, opposing, rival, vying

**competitor** adversary, antagonist, challenger, competition, contestant, opponent, opposition, rival

**compile** amass, collect, cull, garner, gather, organize, put together

**complacent** contented, gratified, pleased, satisfied, self-assured, self-righteous, self-satisfied, serene, smug, unconcerned

**complain** bemoan, bewail, bleat, carp, deplore, find fault, fuss, grieve, groan, grouch Inf, grouse, growl, grumble, lament, moan, whine, whinge Inf

**complaint** accusation, annoyance, charge, criticism, dissatisfaction, fault-finding, grievance, grouch Inf, grouse, grumble, lament, moan, plaint, protest, remonstrance, trouble, wail; affliction, ailment, disease, disorder, illness, malady,

sickness

**complete** adj accomplished, achieved, concluded, ended, finished; all, entire, full, intact, integral, unabridged, unbroken, undivided, whole; consummate, deep-dyed usu. derog, perfect, thorough, total, utter ~v accomplish, achieve, cap, close, conclude, crown, discharge, do, end, execute, fill in, finalize, finish, fulfil, perfect, perform, realize, round off, settle, terminate

**completely** absolutely, altogether, en masse, entirely, from beginning to end, fully, heart and soul, in full, in toto, perfectly, quite, solidly, thoroughly, totally, utterly, wholly

**complex** circuitous, complicated, intricate, involved, knotty, labyrinthine, mingled, mixed, tangled, tortuous

**complexion** colour, colouring, hue, pigmentation, skin, skin tone

**complicate** confuse, entangle, interweave, involve, make intricate, muddle, snarl up

**complication** complexity, confusion, entanglement, intricacy, mixture, web

**compliment** n admiration, bou-

**comply** v complying, complied do as asked **compliance** n **compliant** adj

**component** n part, constituent of whole

**compose** v put in order; write, invent; make up; calm **composer** n one who composes, esp. music **composite** adj made up of distinct parts **composition** n **composure** n calmness

**compos mentis** Lat sane

**compost** n decayed vegetable matter for fertilizing soil

**compound¹** n substance, word,

made up of parts ~adj not simple; composite ~v mix, make up; make worse; compromise

**compound²** n enclosure containing houses etc.

**comprehend** v understand; include **comprehensible** adj **comprehension** n **comprehensive** adj taking in much; pert. to education of children of all abilities

**compress** v squeeze together; make smaller ~n pad of lint applied to wound, inflamed part etc. **compressible** adj **compression** n **compressor** n

———————— THESAURUS ————————

quiet, commendation, congratulations, courtesy, eulogy, favour, flattery, honour, praise, tribute ~v commend, congratulate, extol, felicitate, flatter, laud, pay tribute to, praise, salute

**complimentary** appreciative, approving, commendatory, congratulatory, eulogistic, flattering, panegyrical; courtesy, free, free of charge, giveaway, gratis, gratuitous

**comply** accede, accord, acquiesce, adhere to, agree to, conform to, consent to, discharge, follow, fulfil, obey, observe, perform, respect, satisfy

**component** constituent, element, ingredient, item, part, piece, unit

**compose** build, compound, comprise, constitute, construct, fashion, form, make, make up, put together

**composition** arrangement, configuration, constitution, design, form, formation, layout, make-up, structure; creation, essay, exercise, literary work, opus, piece, study, treatise, work, writing

**composure** aplomb, calm, calmness, collectedness, coolness, dig-

nity, ease, equanimity, placidity, poise, sedateness, self-assurance, self-possession, serenity, tranquillity

**compound** n alloy, amalgam, blend, combination, composite, composition, conglomerate, fusion, medley, meld, mixture, synthesis ~adj complex, composite, conglomerate, intricate, multiple, not simple ~v amalgamate, blend, coalesce, combine, concoct, fuse, intermingle, meld, mingle, mix, synthesize, unite

**comprehend** assimilate, conceive, discern, fathom, grasp, know, make out, perceive, see, take in, understand

**comprehension** discernment, grasp, intelligence, judgment, knowledge, perception, realization, sense, understanding

**comprehensive** all-embracing, all-inclusive, blanket, broad, catholic, complete, encyclopedic, exhaustive, extensive, full, inclusive, sweeping, thorough, umbrella, wide

**compress** compact, concentrate,

**comprise** *v* include, contain

**compromise** *n* coming to terms by giving up part of claim ~*v* settle by making concessions; expose to suspicion

**compulsion** *n* act of compelling; urge **compulsive** *adj* **compulsory** *adj* not optional

**compunction** *n* regret

**compute** *v* calculate **computation** *n* **computer** *n* electronic machine for processing information **computerize** *v*

**comrade** *n* friend

**con**[1] *v* **conning, conned** *Inf* swindle

**con**[2] *v* vote against

**concave** *adj* rounded inwards

**conceal** *v* hide **concealment** *n*

**concede** *v* admit truth of; give up

**conceit** *n* vanity **conceited** *adj*

**conceive** *v* believe; become pregnant; devise **conceivable** *adj*

**concentrate** *v* focus (one's efforts etc.); increase in strength; devote all attention ~*n* concentrated substance **concentration** *n*

**concentric** *adj* having the same centre

**concept** *n* abstract idea **conceptual** *adj*

**conception** *n* idea, notion; act of conceiving

**concern** *v* relate to; worry; (*with* **in** or **with**) involve (oneself) ~*n* affair; worry; business, enterprise **concerned** *adj* worried; involved **concerning** *prep* about

**concert** *n* musical entertainment;

───── THESAURUS ─────

condense, constrict, cram, crowd, crush, press, shorten, summarize

**comprise** be composed of, consist of, contain, embrace, encompass, include, take in

**compromise** *n* accommodation, accord, adjustment, agreement, concession, give-and-take, settlement, trade-off ~*v* adjust, agree, concede, give and take, go fifty-fifty *Inf*, meet halfway, settle, strike a balance

**compulsive** compelling, driving, irresistible, obsessive, uncontrollable, urgent

**compulsory** binding, forced, imperative, mandatory, required, requisite

**comrade** ally, associate, colleague, companion, confederate, crony, fellow, friend, partner

**concave** cupped, depressed, excavated, hollowed, indented, sunken

**conceal** bury, cover, disguise, dissemble, hide, keep dark, keep se-

cret, mask, obscure, screen, secrete, shelter, stash *Inf*

**concede** acknowledge, admit, allow, confess, grant, own; cede, give up, hand over, surrender, yield

**conceit** arrogance, complacency, egotism, narcissism, pride, swagger, vainglory, vanity

**conceited** arrogant, cocky, egotistical, immodest, overweening, puffed up, self-important, swollen-headed, vain

**conceivable** believable, credible, imaginable, possible, thinkable

**conceive** apprehend, believe, comprehend, envisage, fancy, grasp, imagine, realize, suppose, understand; create, design, devise, form, formulate, produce, project, purpose, think up

**concentrate** consider closely, focus attention on, put one's mind to, rack one's brains

**concept** hypothesis, idea, image, impression, notion, theory, view

agreement **concerted** adj mutually planned **concertina** n musical instrument with bellows **concerto** n (pl **-tos, -ti**) composition for solo instrument and orchestra

**concession** n act of conceding; thing conceded

**conch** n seashell

**conciliate** v win over from hostility **conciliation** n **conciliatory** adj

**concise** adj brief, terse

**conclave** n private meeting

**conclude** v finish; deduce; settle; decide **conclusion** n **conclusive** adj decisive

**concoct** v make mixture; contrive

**concoction** n

**concord** n agreement; harmony

**concourse** n crowd; large, open place in public area

**concrete** n mixture of sand, cement etc. ~adj specific; actual; solid

**concubine** n woman cohabiting with man; secondary wife

**concur** v **-curring, -curred** agree; happen together **concurrent** adj **concurrently** adv

**concussion** n brain injury

**condemn** v blame; find guilty; doom; declare unfit **condemnation** n

**condense** v concentrate; turn from

—— THESAURUS ——

**concern** v affect, apply to, bear on, be relevant to, interest, involve, pertain to, regard, touch; bother, disquiet, distress, disturb, make anxious, make uneasy, perturb, trouble, worry ~n affair, business, charge, field, interest, involvement, job, matter, mission, responsibility, task; anxiety, attention, burden, care, consideration, disquiet, distress, heed, responsibility, solicitude, worry; business, company, enterprise, establishment, firm, house, organization

**concerned** anxious, bothered, distressed, disturbed, exercised, troubled, uneasy, upset, worried; active, implicated, interested, involved, mixed up, privy to

**concerning** about, apropos of, as regards, as to, in the matter of, on the subject of, re, regarding, relating to, respecting, touching, with reference to

**conciliate** appease, disarm, mediate, mollify, pacify, placate, propitiate, reconcile, restore harmony, soothe, win over

**concise** brief, compact, compressed, condensed, laconic, pithy, short, succinct, summary, terse, to the point

**conclude** cease, close, come to an end, complete, end, finish, round off, terminate; assume, decide, deduce, gather, infer, judge, suppose, surmise

**conclusion** close, completion, end, finale, finish, result; agreement, conviction, decision, deduction, inference, judgment, opinion, resolution, settlement, verdict

**conclusive** clinching, convincing, decisive, definite, definitive, final, irrefutable, ultimate, unanswerable

**concoction** blend, brew, compound, creation, mixture, preparation

**concrete** adj actual, definite, explicit, factual, material, real, sensible, specific, substantial, tangible

**concur** accord, acquiesce, agree, approve, assent, coincide, combine, consent, cooperate, harmonize, join

**condemn** blame, censure, damn, denounce, disapprove, reproach,

gas to liquid **condensation** n

**condescend** v treat graciously one regarded as inferior; stoop **condescension** n

**condiment** n seasoning for food

**condition** n state or circumstances; thing on which something else depends; prerequisite; physical fitness ~v accustom; regulate; make fit **conditional** adj dependent on events **conditioner** n liquid to make hair or clothes feel softer

**condolence** n sympathy

**condom** n sheathlike rubber contraceptive worn by man

**condone** v overlook, forgive

**conducive** adj leading (to)

**conduct** n behaviour; management ~v guide; direct; manage; transmit (heat etc.) **conduction** n **conductor**

n person in charge of bus etc.; director of orchestra; substance capable of transmitting heat etc.

**conduit** n channel or pipe for water, cables etc.

**cone** n tapering figure with circular base; fruit of pine, fir etc. **conical** adj

**confectionery** n sweets, cakes etc. **confectioner** n

**confederate** n ally; accomplice ~v unite **confederation** n alliance of political units

**confer** v -ferring, -ferred grant; talk with **conference** n meeting for consultation

**confess** v admit; declare one's sins orally to priest **confession** n **confessional** n confessor's box **confessor** n priest who hears confessions

──────── THESAURUS ────────

reprove, upbraid; convict, damn, doom, proscribe, sentence

**condemnation** blame, censure, denouncement, denunciation, disapproval, reproach, reprobation, reproof, stricture; conviction, damnation, doom, judgment, proscription, sentence

**condense** abridge, compact, compress, concentrate, contract, curtail, epitomize, précis, shorten, summarize

**condescend** patronize, talk down to; bend, deign, lower oneself, see fit, stoop, submit, unbend Inf

**condition** n case, circumstances, plight, position, predicament, shape, situation, state, state of affairs, status quo; arrangement, article, demand, limitation, modification, prerequisite, provision, proviso, qualification, requirement, requisite, restriction, rider, rule, stipulation, terms; fettle, fitness,

health, kilter, order, shape, state of health, trim ~v accustom, adapt, educate, equip, habituate, inure, make ready, prepare, ready, tone up, train, work out

**conditional** contingent, dependent, limited, provisional, qualified, subject to, with reservations

**conduct** n attitude, bearing, behaviour, carriage, comportment, demeanour, deportment, manners, mien Lit, ways; administration, control, direction, guidance, leadership, management, organization, running, supervision ~v administer, carry on, control, direct, govern, handle, lead, manage, organize, preside over, regulate, run, supervise

**confer** consult, converse, deliberate, discourse, parley, talk

**conference** congress, consultation, convention, convocation, discussion, forum, meeting, seminar,

**confetti** *pl n* bits of coloured paper thrown at weddings

**confide** *v* (*with* in) tell secrets; entrust **confidence** *n* trust; assurance; intimacy; secret **confident** *adj* certain; self-assured **confidential** *adj* private; secret

**configuration** *n* shape

**confine** *v* keep within bounds; shut up **confines** *pl n* limits **confinement** *n* being confined; childbirth

**confirm** *v* make sure; strengthen; make valid; admit as member of

church **confirmation** *n* confirmed *adj* long-established

**confiscate** *v* seize by authority **confiscation** *n*

**conflict** *n* struggle; disagreement ~v be at odds with; clash

**conform** *v* comply with accepted standards etc.; adapt to rule, pattern, custom etc. **conformist** *n* conformity *n*

**confound** *v* perplex; confuse **confounded** *adj* Inf damned

**confront** *v* face; bring face to face

—————— THESAURUS ——————

symposium, teach-in

**confess** acknowledge, admit, allow, concede, confide, disclose, divulge, grant, own, own up, recognize; reveal

**confession** acknowledgment, admission, avowal, disclosure, revelation

**confide** admit, breathe, confess, disclose, divulge, impart, reveal, whisper

**confidence** belief, credence, dependence, faith, reliance, trust; aplomb, assurance, boldness, courage, firmness, nerve, self-possession, self-reliance

**confident** certain, convinced, counting on, positive, satisfied, secure, sure; assured, bold, dauntless, fearless, self-assured, self-reliant

**confidential** classified, intimate, off the record, private, privy, secret

**confine** bind, bound, cage, enclose, hem in, hold back, imprison, incarcerate, intern, keep, limit, repress, restrain, restrict, shut up, straiten

**confirm** assure, buttress, clinch, establish, fix, fortify, reinforce, settle, strengthen; approve, authenticate, bear out, corroborate, en-

dorse, ratify, sanction, substantiate, validate, verify

**confirmation** evidence, proof, substantiation, testimony, verification; acceptance, agreement, approval, assent, endorsement, ratification, sanction

**confirmed** chronic, habitual, hardened, ingrained, inured, inveterate, long-established, rooted, seasoned

**conflict** *n* battle, clash, combat, contention, contest, encounter, engagement, fight, head-to-head, strife, struggle, war, warfare; antagonism, bad blood, difference, disagreement, discord, dissension, friction, hostility, interference, opposition, strife, variance ~v be at variance, clash, collide, combat, contend, contest, differ, disagree, fight, interfere, strive, struggle

**conform** adapt, adjust, comply, fall in with, follow, follow the crowd, obey, run with the pack, yield

**conformity** allegiance, compliance, observance, orthodoxy

**confound** amaze, astonish, astound, baffle, bewilder, confuse, dumbfound, flummox, mix up,

with **confrontation** *n*

**confuse** *v* bewilder; jumble; make unclear; mistake **confusion** *n*

**conga** *n* dance by people in single file; large drum

**congeal** *v* solidify

**congenial** *adj* pleasant

**congenital** *adj* existing at birth; dating from birth

**conger** *n* sea eel

**congest** *v* overcrowd or clog **congestion** *n*

**conglomerate** *n* substance composed of smaller elements; business organization comprising many companies **conglomeration** *n*

**congratulate** *v* express pleasure at good fortune, success etc. **congratulations** *pl n*

**congregate** *v* assemble; flock together **congregation** *n* assembly, esp. for worship

**congress** *n* formal assembly; legislative body

**conifer** *n* cone-bearing tree **coniferous** *adj*

**conjecture** *n/v* guess **conjectural** *adj*

**conjugal** *adj* of marriage

**conjugate** *v Grammar* inflect verb in its various forms **conjugation** *n*

**conjunction** *n* union; simultaneous happening; part of speech joining words, phrases etc. **conjunctive** *adj*

**conjunctivitis** *n* inflammation of membrane of eye

**conjure** *v* produce magic effects; perform tricks **conjuror, -er** *n*

**conker** *n Inf* horse chestnut

**connect** *v* join together, unite; associate in the mind **connection**, **connexion** *n* association; connecting thing; relation

——————— THESAURUS ———————

**mystify**, nonplus, perplex, startle, surprise

**confrontation** conflict, contest, crisis, encounter, head-to-head, set-to *Inf*, showdown *Inf*

**confuse** baffle, bemuse, bewilder, flummox, mystify, nonplus, obscure, perplex, puzzle

**confusion** bemusement, bewilderment, mystification, perplexity, puzzlement; bustle, chaos, clutter, commotion, disarrangement, disorder, disorganization, hodgepodge *US*, hotchpotch, jumble, mess, muddle, pig's breakfast *Inf*, shambles, tangle, turmoil, untidiness, upheaval

**congenial** adapted, affable, agreeable, compatible, favourable, fit, friendly, genial, kindly, kindred, like-minded, pleasant, pleasing, suitable, sympathetic, well-suited

**congestion** bottleneck, clogging, crowding, jam, mass, overcrowding, surfeit

**congratulate** compliment, felicitate

**congratulations** best wishes, compliments, felicitations, good wishes, greetings

**congregate** assemble, collect, come together, convene, converge, convoke, flock, forgather, gather, mass, meet, muster, rally, rendezvous, throng

**congregation** assembly, brethren, crowd, fellowship, flock, host, laity, multitude, parish, parishioners, throng

**congress** assembly, conclave, conference, convention, convocation, council, delegates, diet, house, legislature, meeting, parliament, representatives

**connive** v conspire

**connoisseur** n expert in fine arts

**connote** v imply, mean in addition **connotation** n

**conquer** v overcome; defeat; be victorious **conqueror** n **conquest** n

**conscience** n sense of right or wrong **conscientious** adj

**conscious** adj aware; awake; intentional **consciousness** n

**conscript** n one compulsorily enlisted for military service ~v enlist thus **conscription** n

**consecrate** v make sacred **consecration** n

**consecutive** adj in unbroken suc-

cession **consecutively** adv

**consensus** n widespread agreement

**consent** v agree to ~n permission; agreement

**consequence** n result, outcome; importance **consequent** adj **consequential** adj important **consequently** adv therefore

**conserve** v keep from change etc.; preserve ~n jam **conservation** n protection of environment **conservationist** n **conservative** adj/n (person) tending to avoid change; moderate (person) **conservatory** n greenhouse

─────── THESAURUS ───────

**connect** affix, ally, cohere, combine, couple, fasten, join, link, relate, unite

**connoisseur** aficionado, arbiter, authority, buff *Inf*, devotee, expert, judge, savant, specialist

**conquer** beat, crush, defeat, get the better of, humble, master, overcome, overpower, overthrow, quell, rout, subdue, triumph, vanquish

**conqueror** champion, hero, master, vanquisher, victor, winner

**conquest** annexation, appropriation, coup, invasion, occupation, subjection, takeover, defeat, discomfiture, mastery, overthrow, rout, triumph, victory

**conscience** moral sense, principles, scruples, still small voice

**conscientious** careful, diligent, exact, faithful, meticulous, painstaking, particular, punctilious, thorough

**conscious** alert, alive to, awake, aware, clued-up *Inf*, cognizant, percipient, responsive, sensible, sentient, wise to *Sl*; calculated, deliberate, intentional, knowing, premedi-

tated, studied, wilful

**consciousness** apprehension, awareness, knowledge, realization, recognition, sensibility

**consecrate** dedicate, devote, exalt, hallow, ordain, sanctify, set apart

**consecutive** following, in sequence, in turn, running, sequential, successive, uninterrupted

**consent** v accede, acquiesce, agree, allow, approve, assent, comply, concede, concur, permit, yield ~n agreement, approval, assent, compliance, go-ahead *Inf*, O.K. or okay *Inf*, permission, sanction

**consequent** ensuing, following, resultant, resulting, subsequent, successive

**conservation** custody, economy, maintenance, preservation, protection, safeguarding, safekeeping, saving, upkeep

**conservative** cautious, conventional, hidebound, reactionary, right-wing, sober, traditional

**conserve** hoard, husband, keep, nurse, preserve, protect, save, store

**consider** v think over; examine; make allowance for; be of opinion that **considerable** *adj* important; large **considerably** *adv* **considerate** *adj* thoughtful towards others **consideration** *n* act of considering; recompense **considering** *prep* taking into account

**consign** v hand over; entrust **consignment** *n* goods consigned **consignor** *n*

**consist** v be composed of **consistency** *n* agreement; degree of firmness **consistent** *adj* consistently *adv*

**console**¹ v comfort, cheer in distress **consolation** *n*

**console**² *n* bracket; keyboard etc. of organ; cabinet for television, radio etc.

**consolidate** v combine; make firm **consolidation** *n*

**consommé** *n* clear meat soup

**consonant** *n* sound, letter other than a vowel ~*adj* agreeing with, in accord **consonance** *n*

**consort** v associate ~*n* husband, wife, esp. of ruler **consortium** *n* (*pl* -tia) association of banks, companies etc.

**conspicuous** *adj* noticeable

**conspire** v plot together **conspiracy** *n* **conspirator** *n*

**constable** *n* policeman **constabulary** *n* police force

**constant** *adj* unchanging; steadfast; continual ~*n* quantity that does not vary **constancy** *n* loyalty **constantly** *adv*

——————— THESAURUS ———————

up, take care of

**consider** chew over, cogitate, consult, contemplate, deliberate, discuss, meditate, ponder, reflect, revolve, ruminate, study, weigh

**considerable** important, influential, noteworthy, renowned, significant; abundant, ample, appreciable, goodly, great, large, lavish, marked, much, plentiful, reasonable, substantial, tidy, tolerable

**considerate** concerned, discreet, kind, kindly, mindful, obliging, patient, tactful, thoughtful, unselfish

**consideration** attention, contemplation, deliberation, discussion, examination, perusal, reflection, regard, review, scrutiny, study, thought

**considering** all in all, in the light of, in view of

**consignment** batch, delivery, goods, shipment

**consist** (*with* of) amount to, be composed of, be made up of, comprise, contain, embody, include, incorporate, involve

**consistent** constant, dependable, regular, steady, true to type, unchanging, undeviating

**consolation** cheer, comfort, ease, encouragement, help, relief, solace, succour, support

**console** cheer, comfort, encourage, relieve, solace, soothe

**consolidate** fortify, reinforce, secure, stabilize, strengthen

**conspicuous** clear, discernible, easily seen, evident, manifest, noticeable, obvious, patent, perceptible, visible

**conspiracy** collusion, confederacy, frame-up *Sl*, intrigue, machination, plot, scheme, treason

**conspirator** intriguer, plotter, schemer, traitor

**conspire** contrive, devise, hatch treason, intrigue, machinate, manoeuvre, plot, scheme

**constant** even, firm, fixed, habitu-

**constellation** *n* group of stars

**consternation** *n* alarm, dismay

**constipation** *n* difficulty in emptying bowels **constipated** *adj*

**constituent** *adj* making up whole ~*n* component part; elector **constituency** *n* body of electors; parliamentary division

**constitute** *v* form; found **constitution** *n* composition; health; principles on which state is governed **constitutional** *adj* inborn; statutory ~*n* walk for good of health

**constrain** *v* force **constraint** *n* compulsion; restriction

**constriction** *n* squeezing together

**constrict** *v* **constrictor** *n* snake that squeezes its prey

**construct** *v* build; put together **construction** *n* **constructive** *adj* positive

**construe** *v* interpret

**consul** *n* government representative in a foreign country **consulate** *n* consul's office

**consult** *v* seek advice, information from **consultancy** *n* **consultant** *n* specialist, expert **consultation** *n* **consultative** *adj*

**consume** *v* eat or drink; engross; use up; destroy **consumer** *n* **consumption** *n*

———————— THESAURUS ————————

al, immutable, invariable, permanent, perpetual, regular, stable, steadfast, steady, unbroken, unvarying; ceaseless, continual, endless, eternal, everlasting, incessant, interminable, nonstop, perpetual, persistent, relentless, sustained, unrelenting

**consternation** alarm, anxiety, awe, bewilderment, confusion, dismay, distress, dread, fear, fright, horror, panic, shock, terror

**constituent** *adj* basic, component, elemental, essential, integral ~*n* component, element, essential, factor, ingredient, part, principle, unit

**constitute** comprise, create, enact, establish, fix, form, found, make, make up, set up

**constitution** establishment, formation, organization

**constitutional** *adj* congenital, inborn, inherent, intrinsic, organic; chartered, statutory, vested

**constrain** bind, compel, drive, force, impel, oblige, pressure, urge

**constraint** compulsion, force, necessity, pressure, restraint; check,

curb, damper, deterrent, hindrance, limitation, rein, restriction

**construct** assemble, build, compose, create, design, erect, establish, fabricate, fashion, form, formulate, found, frame, make, manufacture, organize, put up, raise, set up, shape

**construction** assembly, building, composition, creation, edifice, erection, fabric, fabrication, figure, form, shape, structure

**constructive** helpful, positive, practical, productive, useful, valuable

**consult** ask, compare notes, confer, consider, debate, deliberate, interrogate, question, refer to, take counsel, turn to

**consultant** adviser, authority, specialist

**consultation** appointment, conference, council, deliberation, dialogue, discussion, examination, hearing, interview, meeting, session

**consume** absorb, deplete, drain, eat up, employ, exhaust, expend, finish up, lavish, lessen, spend, use,

**consummate** v/adj perfect; complete **consummation** n

**cont.** continued

**contact** n touching; being in touch; useful acquaintance ~v get in touch with **contact lens** lens fitting over the eyeball

**contagious** adj communicable by contact, catching

**contain** v hold; have room for; comprise; restrain **container** n

**contaminate** v pollute **contamination** n

**contemplate** v meditate on; gaze upon; intend **contemplation** n

**contemporary** adj existing at same time; modern ~n of same age **contemporaneous** adj

**contempt** n scorn, disgrace; wilful disrespect of authority **contemptible** adj **contemptuous** adj showing contempt

**contend** v strive, dispute; maintain (that) **contender** n competitor **contention** n **contentious** adj

**content¹** adj satisfied; willing (to) ~v satisfy ~n satisfaction **contented** adj **contentment** n

**content²** n thing contained; pl index of topics

——————— T H E S A U R U S ———————

use up, utilize, vanish, waste, wear out

**consumer** buyer, customer, purchaser, shopper, user

**contact** n approximation, contiguity, junction, juxtaposition, touch, union; acquaintance, connection ~v approach, call, communicate with, get hold of, get or be in touch with, reach, ring (up) Inf, chiefly Brit, speak to, write to

**contagious** catching, epidemic, infectious, spreading

**contain** accommodate, enclose, have capacity for, hold, incorporate, seat

**container** holder, receptacle, vessel

**contemplate** brood over, consider, deliberate, meditate, observe, ponder, reflect upon study; consider, design, envisage, expect, foresee, intend, mean, plan, propose, think of

**contemporary** adj coexistent, synchronous; à la mode, current, happening Inf, in fashion, latest, modern, newfangled, present, present-day, recent, up-to-date ~n

compeer, fellow, peer

**contempt** derision, disdain, disrespect, mockery, neglect, scorn

**contemptible** abject, base, despicable, ignominious, low, mean, shameful, vile

**contemptuous** arrogant, condescending, derisive, disdainful, haughty, scornful

**contend** clash, compete, contest, cope, emulate, grapple, jostle, litigate, skirmish, strive, struggle, vie; affirm, allege, argue, assert, aver, avow, debate, dispute, hold, maintain

**content¹** adj agreeable, at ease, comfortable, contented, fulfilled, satisfied, willing to accept ~v appease, delight, gladden, gratify, humour, indulge, mollify, placate, please, reconcile, satisfy, suffice ~n comfort, ease, gratification, peace, peace of mind, pleasure, satisfaction

**content²** burden, essence, gist, ideas, matter, meaning, significance, substance, text, thoughts

**contented** at ease, at peace, cheerful, comfortable, glad, gratified,

**contest** n competition ~v dispute; compete for **contestant** n

**context** n words coming before and after a word or passage

**continent¹** n large continuous mass of land **continental** adj

**continent²** adj in control of bodily functions

**contingent** adj depending (on) ~n group part of larger group **contingency** n

**continue** v remain; carry on; resume; prolong **continual** adj **continually** adv **continuation** n **continuity** n logical sequence **continuous** adj

**contort** v twist out of normal shape

**contortion** n **contortionist** n

**contour** n outline, shape, esp. mountains, coast etc.

**contra-** comb. form against

**contraband** n/adj smuggled (goods)

**contraception** n prevention of conception **contraceptive** adj/n

**contract** v make or become smaller; enter into agreement; incur ~n agreement **contraction** n **contractor** n one making contract, esp. builder **contractual** adj

**contradict** v deny; be inconsistent with **contradiction** n **contradictory** adj

—————————— THESAURUS ——————————

happy, pleased, satisfied, serene, thankful

**contentment** comfort, ease, equanimity, fulfilment, gladness, gratification, happiness, peace, pleasure, repletion, satisfaction, serenity

**contest** n competition, game, head-to-head, match, tournament, trial ~v argue, challenge, debate, dispute, doubt, oppose, question; compete, contend, fight, fight over, strive, vie

**contestant** aspirant, candidate, competitor, contender, player

**context** background, connection, frame of reference, framework, relation

**contingency** accident, chance, eventuality, happening, incident, possibility, uncertainty

**continual** constant, endless, eternal, everlasting, frequent, incessant, interminable, perpetual, recurrent, regular, unceasing

**continually** all the time, always, constantly, endlessly, eternally, incessantly, interminably, repeatedly

**continuation** extension, furtherance, sequel, supplement

**continue** abide, carry on, endure, last, live on, persist, remain, rest, stay, stay on, survive

**continuity** cohesion, connection, flow, progression, sequence, succession

**continuous** connected, constant, extended, prolonged, unbroken, unceasing, undivided, uninterrupted

**contract** v abridge, compress, condense, curtail, dwindle, lessen, narrow, reduce, shrink, shrivel, tighten; agree, arrange, bargain, clinch, close, come to terms, covenant, engage, enter into, negotiate, pledge, stipulate ~n agreement, arrangement, bargain, bond, compact, convention, covenant, deal Inf, engagement, pact, settlement, treaty, understanding

**contradict** be at variance with, belie, challenge, contravene, counter, counteract, deny, dispute, negate, oppose

**contradiction** conflict, contraven-

**contraflow** n flow of traffic in opposite direction

**contralto** n (pl -tos) lowest female voice

**contraption** n gadget; device

**contrary** adj opposed; perverse ~n the exact opposite ~adv in opposition

**contrast** v bring out, show difference ~n striking difference

**contravene** v infringe

**contribute** v give, pay to common fund; help to occur; write for the press **contribution** n **contributor** n

**contrite** adj remorseful **contrition** n

**contrive** v arrange; devise, invent **contrivance** n

**control** v -trolling, -trolled command; regulate; direct, check ~n power to direct or determine; curb, check; pl instruments to control car, aircraft etc. **controller** n

**controversy** n debate **controversial** adj

**contusion** n bruise

**conundrum** n riddle

**conurbation** n large built-up area

**convalesce** v recover health after illness, operation etc. **convalescence** n **convalescent** adj/n

**convection** n transmission of heat

———— THESAURUS ————

tion, denial, inconsistency, opposite

**contradictory** antagonistic, antithetical, conflicting, contrary, incompatible, inconsistent, opposite, paradoxical

**contrary** adj adverse, anti, clashing, contradictory, counter, discordant, hostile, inimical, opposed, opposite

**contrast** v compare, differ, differentiate, distinguish, oppose, set in opposition, set off ~n comparison, difference, disparity, dissimilarity, distinction, divergence, foil, opposition

**contribute** v add, afford, bestow, chip in, donate, furnish, give, provide, subscribe, supply

**contribution** n addition, bestowal, donation, gift, grant, subscription

**contributor** n freelance, journalist, journo Sl, reporter

**contrite** humble, penitent, regretful, remorseful, repentant, sorrowful, sorry

**contrive** concoct, construct, create, design, devise, engineer, fabricate, frame, improvise, invent,

manufacture; arrange, bring about

**control** v command, conduct, direct, dominate, govern, handle, have charge of, lead, manage, manipulate, oversee, pilot, reign over, rule, steer, superintend, supervise; bridle, check, constrain, contain, curb, hold back, limit, master, rein in, repress, restrain, subdue ~n authority, charge, command, direction, discipline, government, guidance, jurisdiction, management, mastery, oversight, rule, supervision, supremacy; brake, check, curb, limitation, regulation, restraint

**controversial** at issue, contentious, debatable, disputable, disputed, open to question, under discussion

**controversy** n argument, contention, debate, discussion, dispute, dissension, polemic, quarrel, row, squabble, strife, wrangle

**convalescence** improvement, recovery, recuperation, rehabilitation, return to health

**convalescent** adj on the mend,

by currents

**convene** v call together, assemble **convenor, -er** n **convention** n assembly; treaty; accepted usage **conventional** adj (slavishly) observing customs of society; customary; (of weapons, war etc.) not nuclear

**convenient** adj handy; favourable to needs, comfort **convenience** n ease, comfort, suitability; public toilet ~adj (of food) quick to prepare **conveniently** adv

**convent** n religious community, esp. of nuns

**convention** see CONVENE

**converge** v tend to meet

**conversant** adj familiar (with), versed in

**converse**[1] v talk (with) ~n talk **conversation** n **conversational** adj

**converse**[2] adj opposite, reversed ~n the opposite **conversely** adv

**convert** v apply to another purpose; change; transform; cause to adopt (another) religion, opinion ~n converted person **conversion** n

**convertible** n car with folding roof ~adj capable of being converted

**convex** adj curved outwards

**convey** v transport; impart; Law transfer **conveyance** n **conveyancer** n one skilled in legal forms of transferring property **conveyancing** n **conveyor belt** continuous moving belt

**convict** v prove or declare guilty ~n criminal serving prison sentence **conviction** n verdict of guilty; being convinced, firm belief

**convince** v persuade by evidence

———— THESAURUS ————

recovering, recuperating

**convene** assemble, bring together, call, come together, congregate, gather, meet, muster, rally

**convenience** accessibility, appropriateness, availability, fitness, handiness, opportuneness, serviceability, suitability, usefulness, utility

**convenient** accessible, at hand, available, close at hand, handy; appropriate, beneficial, commodious, fitted, helpful, labour-saving, opportune, seasonable, suitable, suited, timely, useful, well-timed

**convention** assembly, conference, congress, convocation, council, delegates, meeting; code, custom, etiquette, formality, practice, propriety, protocol, tradition, usage

**converge** combine, come together, focus, gather, join, meet, merge, mingle

**conversation** chat, colloquy, communion, conference, converse, dialogue, discourse, discussion, exchange, gossip, talk, tête-à-tête

**converse** n antithesis, contrary, obverse, opposite, reverse

**conversion** adaptation, alteration, modification, reconstruction, reorganization; change, transformation, transmutation; change of heart, rebirth, reformation, regeneration

**convert** v adapt, apply, modify, remodel, reorganize, restyle, revise; alter, change, transform, transmute, transpose, turn

**convey** bear, bring, carry, conduct, fetch, forward, grant, guide, move, send, support, transmit, transport

**convict** v condemn, find guilty, imprison, sentence ~n convict, culprit, felon, lag Sl, malefactor, prisoner

**conviction** assurance, certainty, confidence, firmness, reliance

or argument **convincing** adj

**convivial** adj sociable

**convoluted** adj involved; coiled **convolution** n

**convoy** n party (of ships etc.) travelling together for protection ~v escort

**convulse** v shake violently; affect with spasms **convulsion** n

**coo** n/v cooing, cooed (make) cry of doves

**cook** v prepare food, esp. by heat; undergo cooking ~n one who prepares food **cooker** n apparatus for cooking **cookery** n **cookie** n US biscuit

**cool** adj moderately cold; calm; lacking friendliness ~v make, become cool **coolly** adv

**coop**[1] n/v (shut up in) cage

**coop**[2], **co-op** n cooperative society or shop run by one

**cooperate** v work together **co-**

**operation** n **cooperative** adj willing to cooperate; (of an enterprise) owned collectively ~n collectively owned enterprise

**co-opt** v add to group

**coordinate** v bring into order, harmony ~adj equal in degree, status etc. **coordination** n **coordinator** n

**coot** n small black water bird

**cop** n Sl policeman

**cope** v deal successfully (with); manage

**coping** n sloping top course of wall

**copious** adj abundant

**copper**[1] n reddish-brown metal; coin

**copper**[2] n Inf policeman

**coppice, copse** n small wood

**copulate** v unite sexually **copulation** n

**copy** n imitation; single specimen of book ~v copying, copied make copy of, imitate **copyright** n legal

---

THESAURUS

**convince** assure, bring round, persuade, satisfy, sway, win over

**convincing** believable, cogent, conclusive, credible, impressive, incontrovertible, likely, persuasive, plausible, powerful, probable, telling

**convoy** n armed guard, attendance, attendant, escort, guard, protection

**cool** adj chilled, chilly, nippy; calm, collected, composed, deliberate, imperturbable, level-headed, placid, quiet, relaxed, self-possessed, serene, unemotional, unexcited, unfazed Inf, unruffled; aloof, distant, frigid, indifferent, lukewarm, offhand, reserved, unfriendly ~v chill, cool off, freeze, lose heat, refrigerate

**cooperate** aid, assist, collaborate,

combine, concur, conspire, contribute, help, join forces, pitch in, pull together, work together

**cooperation** assistance, collaboration, give-and-take, helpfulness, participation, responsiveness, teamwork, unity

**cooperative** accommodating, helpful, obliging, responsive, supportive

**coordinate** correlate, harmonize, integrate, match, mesh, organize, relate

**cope cope with** deal, encounter, handle, struggle, tangle, tussle, weather, wrestle; carry on, manage, struggle through, survive

**copious** abundant, ample, bountiful, extensive, exuberant, full, generous, lavish, liberal, luxuriant, overflowing, plenteous, plentiful,

exclusive right to print and publish book, work of art etc. ~v protect by copyright

**coquette** n flirt

**coracle** n small round boat

**coral** n hard substance made by sea polyps

**cord** n thin rope or thick string; ribbed fabric

**cordial** adj sincere, warm ~n fruit-flavoured drink

**cordon** n chain of troops or police ~v form barrier round

**cordon bleu** (of cookery) of the highest standard

**corduroy** n cotton fabric with velvety, ribbed surface

**core** n seed case of apple; innermost part ~v take out core

**corgi** n small Welsh dog

**coriander** n herb

**cork** n bark of an evergreen Mediterranean oak tree; stopper for bottle etc. ~v stop up with cork **corkscrew** n tool for pulling out corks

**corm** n underground stem like a bulb

**cormorant** n large voracious sea bird

**corn**[1] n grain, fruit of cereals **corny** adj Inf trite, oversentimental **corned beef** beef preserved in salt

**cornflakes** pl n breakfast cereal

**cornflour** n finely ground maize

**cornflower** n blue flower growing in cornfields

**corn**[2] n horny growth on foot

**cornea** n transparent membrane covering front of eye

**corner** n part where two sides meet; remote or humble place; Business monopoly ~v drive into position of no escape; establish monopoly; move round corner **cornerstone** n indispensable part

**cornet** n trumpet with valves; cone-shaped ice cream wafer

**cornice** n moulding below ceiling

**cornucopia** n horn overflowing with fruit and flowers

**corollary** n inference from a preceding statement; deduction

**coronary** adj of blood vessels surrounding heart ~n coronary thrombosis **coronary thrombosis** disease of the heart

**coronation** n ceremony of crowning a sovereign

**coroner** n officer who holds inquests on unnatural deaths

**coronet** n small crown

**corporal**[1] adj of the body

**corporal**[2] n noncommissioned officer below sergeant

——————— THESAURUS ———————

profuse, rich

**copy** n counterfeit, duplicate, facsimile, forgery, image, imitation, likeness, model, pattern, photocopy, print, replica, replication, representation, reproduction ~v counterfeit, duplicate, photocopy, reproduce, transcribe; ape, echo, emulate, follow, imitate, mimic, mirror, repeat, simulate

**cord** line, rope, string, twine

**cordial** affable, affectionate, agree-able, cheerful, congenial, friendly, genial, hearty, sociable, warm, warm-hearted, welcoming, whole-hearted

**core** centre, crux, essence, gist, heart, kernel, nub, nucleus, pith

**corner** n angle, bend, crook, joint; cavity, cranny, hideaway, hide-out, hole, niche, nook, recess, retreat ~v bring to bay, run to earth, trap

**corny** banal, commonplace, dull, feeble, hackneyed, maudlin, mawk-

**corporation** n body of persons legally authorized to act as an individual **corporate** adj

**corps** n (pl **corps**) military force; any organized body of persons

**corpse** n dead body

**corpulent** adj fat **corpulence** n

**corpus** n (pl **corpora**) main part or body of something

**corpuscle** n minute particle, esp. of blood

**corral** n US enclosure for cattle

**correct** v set right; indicate errors in; punish ~adj right, accurate **correctly** adv **correction** n **corrective** n/adj

**correlate** v bring into reciprocal relation **correlation** n

**correspond** v be similar (to); exchange letters **correspondence** n **correspondent** n writer of letters; one employed by newspaper etc. to report on particular topic

**corridor** n passage

**corroborate** v confirm

**corrode** v eat into **corrosion** n **corrosive** adj

**corrugated** adj ridged

**corrupt** adj lacking integrity; involving bribery; wicked ~v make evil; bribe; make rotten **corruption** n

——————— THESAURUS ———————

ish, sentimental, stale, trite

**corporation** association, corporate body, society

**corps** band, body, company, crew, detachment, division, regiment, squadron, troop, unit

**corpse** body, cadaver, carcass

**correct** v adjust, amend, cure, improve, rectify, redress, reform, remedy, right; admonish, chastise, chide, discipline, punish, reprimand, reprove ~adj accurate, exact, faultless, flawless, just, precise, regular, right, strict, true

**correction** adjustment, alteration, amendment, improvement, modification; admonition, castigation, chastisement, discipline, punishment, reproof

**correctly** accurately, perfectly, precisely, properly, rightly

**correspond** accord, agree, be consistent, coincide, conform, dovetail, fit, harmonize, match, square, tally; communicate, exchange letters

**correspondence** agreement, analogy, coincidence, comparison, conformity, congruity, correlation,

fitness, harmony, match, relation, similarity; communication, letters, mail, post, writing

**correspondent** n letter writer, pen friend or pal; contributor, journalist, journo Sl, reporter

**corridor** aisle, hallway, passage, passageway

**corrode** canker, consume, corrupt, eat away, erode, rust, waste, wear away

**corrosive** acrid, caustic, erosive, virulent, wasting, wearing

**corrupt** adj dishonest, fraudulent, rotten, shady Inf, unprincipled, unscrupulous, venal; decadent, degenerate, depraved, evil, immoral, perverted, sinful, wicked ~v bribe, debauch, demoralize, deprave, entice, fix Inf, lure, pervert, subvert

**corruption** breach of trust, bribery, bribing, demoralization, dishonesty, extortion, fraud, graft Inf, jobbery, profiteering, shadiness, venality; decadence, degeneration, depravity, evil, immorality, impurity, iniquity, perversion, sinfulness, vice, viciousness, wickedness

**corsage** *n* (flower worn on) bodice of woman's dress

**corset** *n* close-fitting undergarment to support the body

**cortege** *n* formal (funeral) procession

**cortex** *n* (*pl* **-tices**) outer layer of brain etc.

**cortisone** *n* synthetic hormone used medically

**cosh** *n* blunt weapon ~*v* strike with one

**cosine** *n* in a right-angled triangle, ratio of adjacent side to hypotenuse

**cosmetic** *n/adj* (preparation) to improve appearance only

**cosmic** *adj* relating to the universe; vast

**cosmopolitan** *adj/n* (person) familiar with many countries

**cosmos** *n* the universe considered as an ordered system

**cosset** *v* pamper, pet

**cost** *n* price; expenditure of time, labour etc.; damage ~*v* have as price; entail payment, or loss of

**costly** *adj* valuable; expensive

**costume** *n* style of dress of particular place or time

**cosy** *adj* snug, comfortable

**cot** *n* child's bed

**cote** *n* shelter for animals or birds

**coterie** *n* social clique

**cottage** *n* small house **cottage cheese** mild, soft cheese **cottage pie** dish of minced meat and potato

**cotton** *n* plant with white downy fibres; cloth of this

**couch** *n* piece of furniture for reclining on ~*v* put into (words)

**cougar** *n* puma

**cough** *v* expel air from lungs with sudden effort and noise ~*n* act of coughing

**could** *past tense of* CAN[1]

**coulomb** *n* unit of electric charge

**council** *n* deliberative or administrative body; local governing authority of town etc. **councillor** *n*

**counsel** *n* **-selling, -selled** advice; barrister(s) ~*v* advise, recommend **counsellor** *n*

**corset** belt, bodice, girdle

**cosmetic** *adj* beautifying, superficial, surface

**cosmopolitan** sophisticated, universal, urbane, well-travelled, worldly, worldly-wise

**cost** *n* amount, charge, expenditure, expense, figure, outlay, payment, price, rate, worth; damage, detriment, expense, harm, hurt, injury, loss, penalty, sacrifice, suffering ~*v* come to, sell at

**costly** dear, excessive, expensive, extortionate, highly-priced, steep *Inf*, valuable

**costume** attire, clothing, dress, ensemble, garb, get-up *Inf*, livery, outfit, uniform

**cosy** comfortable, homely, intimate, secure, sheltered, snug, warm

**cottage** cabin, chalet, hut, lodge, shack

**cough** *v* bark, clear one's throat, hack, hawk ~*n* bark, hack

**council** assembly, board, cabinet, chamber, conference, congress, convention, diet, house, parliament, synod

**counsel** *n* admonition, advice, caution, consideration, direction, forethought, guidance, information, recommendation, suggestion, warning; advocate, attorney, barrister, lawyer, legal adviser, solicitor ~*v* admonish, advise, advocate,

**count¹** v reckon, number; consider to be; be reckoned in; depend (on); be of importance ~n reckoning; total number; act of counting **countless** adj too many to be counted **countdown** n counting of the seconds before an event

**count²** n nobleman **countess** n noblewoman

**countenance** n face, its expression ~v support, approve

**counter¹** n horizontal surface in bank, shop etc., on which business is transacted

**counter²** adv in opposite direction ~v oppose

**counter-** comb. form reversed, opposite, rival, retaliatory, as in **counterclaim, counterproductive**

**counteract** v neutralize

**counterattack** v/n attack in response to attack

**counterbalance** n weight balancing another ~v act as balance

**counterfeit** adj sham, forged ~n imitation, forgery ~v imitate with intent to deceive; forge

**counterfoil** n part of cheque, receipt etc. kept as record

**countermand** v cancel (previous order)

**counterpane** n bed covering

**counterpart** n something complementary to another

**counterpoint** n melody added as accompaniment to given melody

**countersign** v sign document already signed by another

**countersink** v enlarge top of hole to take head of screw, bolt etc. below surface

**countertenor** n male alto

**country** n region; nation; people of nation; land of birth; rural districts **countryman** n (fem **countrywoman**) **countryside** n

**county** n division of country

**coup** n successful stroke; (short for

─────────── THESAURUS ───────────

caution, exhort, instruct, recommend, urge, warn

**count** add (up), calculate, cast up, check, compute, enumerate, estimate, number, reckon, score, tally, tot up; carry weight, matter, rate, signify, tell, weigh

**counter** adv against, contrarily, conversely, in defiance of, versus ~v answer, hit back, meet, offset, parry, resist, respond, retaliate, return, ward off

**counterbalance** balance, compensate, make up for, offset, set off

**counterfeit** adj bogus, copied, faked, false, feigned, forged, fraudulent, imitation, phoney or phony Inf, pseudo Inf, sham, simulated, spurious ~n copy, fake, forgery, fraud, imitation, reproduc-

tion, sham ~v copy, fabricate, fake, feign, forge, imitate, impersonate, pretend, sham, simulate

**counterpart** complement, copy, duplicate, equal, fellow, match, mate, supplement, tally, twin

**countless** endless, incalculable, infinite, legion, limitless, measureless, myriad, uncounted, untold

**country** n land, part, region, terrain, territory; commonwealth, kingdom, nation, people, realm, sovereign state, state; citizens, community, electors, inhabitants, nation, people, populace, public, society, voters; fatherland, homeland, motherland, nationality, native land; backwoods, farmland, green belt, outdoors, provinces, rural areas, wide open spaces Inf

**coup d'état** *n* sudden, violent seizure of government

**coup de grace** *Fr* decisive action

**coupé** *n* sporty style of motorcar

**couple** *n* two, pair; husband and wife ~*v* connect, fasten together; join, associate **couplet** *n* two lines of verse **coupling** *n* connecting device

**coupon** *n* ticket entitling holder to discount, gift etc.

**courage** *n* bravery, boldness **courageous** *adj* **courageously** *adv*

**courgette** *n* type of small vegetable marrow

**courier** *n* messenger; person who guides travellers

**course** *n* movement in space or time; direction; sequence; line of action; series of lectures etc.; any of successive parts of meal; area where golf is played; racetrack ~*v* hunt; run swiftly; (of blood) circulate

**court** *n* space enclosed by buildings, yard; area for playing various games; royal household; body with judicial powers, place where it meets, one of its sittings ~*v* woo; seek, invite **courtier** *n* one who frequents royal court **courtly** *adj* ceremoniously polite; characteristic of a court **court card** king, queen or jack at cards **court martial** court for trying naval or military offences **courtship** *n* wooing **courtyard** *n* enclosed paved area

**courtesy** *n* politeness **courteous** *adj*

—— THESAURUS ——

**county** province, shire

**coup** action, deed, exploit, feat, manoeuvre, stratagem, stroke, stunt, *tour de force*

**couple** brace, duo, pair, twosome ~*v* buckle, clasp, conjoin, connect, hitch, join, link, marry, pair, unite, wed, yoke

**courage** balls *Taboo sl,* boldness, bottle *Brit sl,* bravery, daring, fearlessness, fortitude, gallantry, guts *Inf,* mettle, nerve, pluck, valour

**courageous** audacious, bold, brave, daring, fearless, gallant, hardy, heroic, indomitable, intrepid, plucky, valiant

**course** advance, continuity, development, flow, march, movement, order, progress, sequence, succession; channel, direction, line, orbit, passage, path, road, route, track, track, trail, trajectory, way; lapse, passage, passing, sweep, term, time; conduct, manner, method, mode, plan, policy, procedure, programme; classes, course of study, curriculum, lectures, programme, schedule, studies; circuit, lap, race, racecourse

**court** *n* cloister, courtyard, piazza, plaza, quadrangle, square; yard; hall, manor, palace; attendants, royal household, suite, train; bar, bench, court of justice, lawcourt, tribunal ~*v* chase, date, go (out) with, serenade, take out, walk out with, woo; cultivate, curry favour with, fawn upon, flatter, pander to, solicit

**courteous** affable, attentive, civil, courtly, elegant, gallant, gracious, mannerly, polished, polite, refined, respectful, urbane, well-bred, well-mannered

**courtesy** affability, civility, elegance, gallantry, good breeding, good manners, graciousness, polish, politeness, urbanity

**courtier** attendant, follower, squire, train-bearer

**cousin** *n* son or daughter of uncle or aunt

**cove** *n* small inlet of coast

**coven** *n* gathering of witches

**covenant** *n* agreement; compact ~*v* agree to a covenant

**cover** *v* place over; extend, spread; bring upon (oneself); protect; travel over; include; be sufficient; report over; ~*n* covering thing; shelter; insurance **coverage** *n* **coverlet** *n* top covering of bed

**covert** *adj* secret, sly

**covet** *v* long to possess, esp. what belongs to another **covetous** *adj*

**cow¹** *n* (*pl* **cows**) female of bovine and other animals **cowboy** *n* ranch worker who herds cattle; *Inf* irresponsible worker

**cow²** *v* frighten, overawe

**coward** *n* one who lacks courage **cowardice** *n* **cowardly** *adj*

**cower** *v* crouch in fear

**cowl** *n* monk's hooded cloak; hooded top for chimney

**cowslip** *n* wild primrose

**coxswain, cox** *n* steersman of boat

**coy** *adj* (pretending to be) shy, modest **coyly** *adv*

**coyote** *n* prairie wolf

**coypu** *n* aquatic rodent

**crab** *n* edible crustacean **crabbed** *adj* (of handwriting) hard to read **crabby** *adj* bad-tempered

**crab apple** wild sour apple

**crack** *v* split partially; break with sharp noise; break down, yield; *Inf* tell (joke); solve, decipher; make sharp noise ~*n* sharp explosive noise; split; flaw; *Inf* joke; chat; *Sl* highly addictive form of cocaine; *adj Inf* very skilful **cracker** *n* decorated paper tube, pulled apart with

**courtyard** area, enclosure, playground, quad, quadrangle, yard

**covenant** bargain, commitment, compact, concordat, contract, convention, pact, promise, stipulation, treaty, trust

**cover** *v* cloak, conceal, cover up, curtain, disguise, eclipse, hide, hood, house, mask, obscure, screen, secrete, shade, shroud, veil; defend, guard, protect, reinforce, shelter, shield; describe, detail, investigate, narrate, recount, relate, report, tell of, write up ~*n* cloak, cover-up, disguise, façade, front, mask, pretence, screen, smoke screen, veil; concealment, defence, guard, hiding place, protection, refuge, sanctuary, shelter, shield; compensation, indemnity, insurance, payment, protection

**covet** begrudge, crave, desire, envy, fancy *Inf*, hanker after, long for, lust after, thirst for, yearn for

**covetous** avaricious, envious, grasping, greedy, jealous, mercenary, yearning

**coward** chicken *Sl*, craven, faint-heart, poltroon, renegade, sneak, wimp *Inf*

**cowardly** base, craven, faint-hearted, fearful, lily-livered, scared, shrinking, soft, spineless, weak, yellow *Inf*

**cowboy** cattleman, cowhand, drover, gaucho *S Amer*, herder, herdsman, rancher, stockman

**cower** cringe, crouch, draw back, fawn, flinch, grovel, quail, shrink, skulk, sneak, tremble

**coy** arch, backward, bashful, demure, evasive, modest, prudish, reserved, retiring, self-effacing, shrinking, shy, skittish, timid

a bang, containing toy etc.; explosive firework; thin dry biscuit **crackers** *adj Sl* crazy **cracking** *adj* very good **crackle** *n/v* (make) sound of repeated small cracks **crackpot** *n Inf* eccentric person

**cradle** *n* infant's bed ~*v* hold or rock as in a cradle; cherish

**craft**[1] *n* skilled trade; skill, ability; cunning **crafty** *adj* cunning, shrewd **craftsman** *n* (*fem* **craftswoman**) **craftsmanship** *n*

**craft**[2] *n* vessel; ship

**crag** *n* steep rugged rock

**cram** *v* **cramming**, **crammed** stuff; prepare quickly for examination

**cramp**[1] *v* hinder

**cramp**[2] *n* painful muscular contraction

**cranberry** *n* edible red berry

**crane** *n* wading bird with long legs; machine for moving heavy weights ~*v* stretch neck **crane fly** long-legged insect

**cranium** *n* (*pl* **-niums, -nia**) skull **cranial** *adj*

**crank** *n* arm at right angles to axis, for turning main shaft; *Inf* eccentric person ~*v* start (engine) by turning crank **cranky** *adj* eccentric

**cranny** *n* small opening

**crash** *v* (cause to) make loud noise; (cause to) fall with crash; smash; collapse; cause (aircraft) to hit land or water; collide with; move noisily ~*n* loud, violent fall or impact; collision; uncontrolled descent of aircraft; sudden collapse; bankruptcy **crash helmet** protective helmet

**crass** *adj* grossly stupid

——————— THESAURUS ———————

**crack** *v* break, burst, chip, chop, fracture, snap, splinter, split; break down, collapse, give way, go to pieces, lose control, succumb, yield ~*n* burst, clap, crash, explosion, pop, report, snap; breach, break, chink, chip, cleft, cranny, crevice, fissure, fracture, gap, rift, split; *Sl* dig, gag *Inf*, insult, jibe, joke, quip, witticism; *adj Sl* ace, choice, elite, excellent, first-class, first-rate, hand-picked, superior, world-class

**cradle** *n* cot, crib, Moses basket ~*v* hold, lull, nestle, nurse, rock, support

**craft**[1] business, calling, line, occupation, trade, vocation, work; ability, aptitude, art, artistry, cleverness, dexterity, expertise, ingenuity, skill, technique, workmanship

**craft**[2] aircraft, barque, boat, plane, ship, spacecraft, vessel

**craftsman** artificer, artisan, maker, master, skilled worker, smith, technician, wright

**craftsmanship** artistry, expertise, mastery, technique, workmanship

**crafty** artful, astute, calculating, canny, cunning, deceitful, devious, foxy, scheming, sharp, shrewd, sly, subtle, tricky, wily

**cram** compact, compress, crowd, crush, force, jam, overcrowd, overfill, pack, pack in, press, ram, shove, squeeze, stuff

**cramp**[1] *v* check, clog, confine, encumber, hamper, handicap, hinder, impede, inhibit, obstruct, restrict, shackle

**cramp**[2] *n* ache, crick, pain, pang, shooting pain, spasm, stiffness, twinge

**cranny** breach, chink, cleft, crack, crevice, fissure, gap, hole, interstice, nook, opening, rift

**crash** *v* come a cropper *Inf*, dash, fall, give way, hurtle, lurch, overbalance, pitch, plunge, topple;

**crate** n large (usu. wooden) container for packing goods

**crater** n mouth of volcano; bowl-shaped cavity

**cravat** n man's neckcloth

**crave** v have very strong desire for; beg **craving** n

**craven** adj cowardly

**crawl** v move on hands and knees; move very slowly; ingratiate oneself; swim with crawl stroke; be overrun (with) ~n crawling motion; racing stroke at swimming

**crayfish** n edible freshwater crustacean

**crayon** n stick or pencil of coloured wax etc.

**craze** n short-lived fashion; strong desire; madness **crazed** adj **crazy** adj insane; very foolish; madly eager (for)

**creak** n/v (make) grating noise

**cream** n fatty part of milk; food like this; cosmetic like this; yellowish-white colour; best part ~v take cream from; take best part from; beat to creamy consistency **creamy** adj

**crease** n line made by folding; wrinkle ~v make, develop creases

**create** v bring into being; make; Inf make a fuss **creation** n **creative** adj imaginative, inventive **creativity** n **creator** n

——————— THESAURUS ———————

bang, bump (into), collide, crash-land an aircraft, drive into, have an accident, hit, plough into, wreck ~n bang, boom, clang, clash, racket, smash; accident, bump, collision, jar, jolt, pile-up Inf, smash, thud, thump, wreck; bankruptcy, collapse, debacle, depression, downfall, failure, ruin, smash

**crass** asinine, boorish, bovine, coarse, dense, doltish, gross, insensitive, obtuse, stupid, unrefined

**crate** n box, case, container, packing case, tea chest

**crater** depression, dip, hollow, shell hole

**crave** cry out for Inf, desire, fancy Inf, hanker after, hope for, hunger after, long for, lust after, need, pine for, thirst for, want, yearn for; ask, beg, beseech, entreat, implore, petition, plead for, pray for, seek, solicit, supplicate

**crawl** advance slowly, creep, drag, go on all fours, inch, pull or drag oneself along, slither, wriggle, writhe; cringe, fawn, grovel, hum-

ble oneself, ingratiate oneself, toady

**craze** enthusiasm, fad, fashion, infatuation, mania, mode, novelty, passion, rage, thing, trend, vogue

**crazy** barking mad Sl, berserk, cuckoo Inf, delirious, demented, deranged, idiotic, insane, loopy Inf, mad, mental Sl, nuts Sl, off one's head Sl, of unsound mind, potty Inf, round the bend Sl, unbalanced, unhinged; bizarre, eccentric, fantastic, odd, oddball Inf, outrageous, peculiar, ridiculous, silly, strange, wacko Sl, weird

**creak** v grate, grind, groan, rasp, scrape, scratch, screech, squeak, squeal

**cream** n cosmetic, liniment, lotion, ointment, salve; best, crème de la crème, elite, flower, pick, prime

**crease** n bulge, fold, groove, line, overlap, pucker, ridge, ruck, tuck, wrinkle ~v crinkle, crumple, double up, fold, pucker, ridge, ruck up, rumple, screw up, wrinkle

**create** beget, bring into being, coin, compose, concoct, design, de-

**creature** n living being

**crèche** n day nursery for very young children

**credentials** pl n testimonials; letters of introduction

**credible** adj worthy of belief **credibility** n

**credit** n commendation; source of honour; trust; good name; system of allowing customers to pay later; money at one's disposal in bank etc. ~v attribute, believe; put on credit side of account **creditable** adj bringing honour **creditor** n one to whom debt is due

**credulous** adj too easy of belief, gullible **credulity** n

**creed** n statement of belief

**creek** n narrow inlet on coast

**creep** v **creeping, crept** move slowly, stealthily; crawl; act in servile way; (of flesh) feel shrinking sensation ~n creeping; Sl repulsive person; pl feeling of fear or repugnance **creeper** n creeping or climbing plant **creepy** adj

**cremation** n burning of corpses **cremate** v **crematorium** n building where corpses are cremated

**creole** n language developed from mixture of languages

**creosote** n oily liquid used for preserving wood

**crepe** n fabric with crimped surface

**crescendo** n (pl **-dos**) Mus gradual increase of loudness

velop, devise, form, formulate, generate, hatch, initiate, invent, make, originate, produce, spawn

**creation** establishment, formation, foundation, inception, institution, laying down, origination, production, setting up; formation, generation, genesis, making, procreation, siring

**creative** artistic, clever, fertile, gifted, imaginative, ingenious, inspired, inventive, original, productive, stimulating, visionary

**creator** architect, author, begetter, designer, father, God, inventor, maker, originator, prime mover

**creature** animal, beast, being, brute, dumb animal, living thing, lower animal, quadruped

**credentials** authorization, card, certificate, deed, diploma, docket, licence, missive, passport, recommendation, reference(s), testimonial, title, voucher, warrant

**credibility** believability, integrity, plausibility, reliability, tenability, trustworthiness

**credible** believable, conceivable, imaginable, likely, plausible, possible, probable, reasonable, tenable, thinkable

**credit** n acclaim, acknowledgment, approval, commendation, fame, glory, honour, kudos, merit, praise, recognition, thanks, tribute v (with with) accredit, ascribe to, assign to, attribute to, impute to, refer to; accept, bank on, believe, depend on, have faith in, rely on, trust

**creditable** admirable, commendable, deserving, estimable, exemplary, honourable, laudable, meritorious, praiseworthy, reputable, respectable, worthy

**credulity** blind faith, gullibility, naiveté, silliness, simplicity

**creed** articles of faith, belief, canon, catechism, confession, credo, doctrine, dogma, principles

**creek** bay, bight, cove, inlet

**creep** skulk, slink, sneak, steal, tiptoe; crawl, glide, insinuate, slither,

**crescent** *n* (shape of) moon seen in first or last quarter

**cress** *n* various plants with edible pungent leaves

**crest** *n* tuft on bird's or animal's head; top of mountain, wave etc.; badge above shield of coat of arms **crestfallen** *adj* disheartened

**cretin** *n* person afflicted by retardation; *Inf* stupid person **cretinous** *adj*

**crevasse** *n* deep open chasm

**crevice** *n* cleft, fissure

**crew** *n* ship's, aircraft's company; *Inf* gang

**crib** *n* child's cot; rack for fodder; plagiarism ~*v* copy dishonestly

**cribbage** *n* card game

**crick** *n* cramp esp. in neck

**cricket**[1] *n* chirping insect

**cricket**[2] *n* game played with bats, ball and wickets **cricketer** *n*

**crime** *n* violation of law; wicked act **criminal** *adj/n*

**crimson** *adj/n* (of) rich deep red

**cringe** *v* shrink, cower; behave obsequiously

**crinkle** *v/n* wrinkle

**crinoline** *n* hooped petticoat or skirt

**cripple** *n* disabled person ~*v* disable

**crisis** *n* (*pl* **crises**) turning point; time of acute danger

**crisp** *adj* brittle; brisk; clear-cut; fresh ~*n* very thin, fried slice of potato **crispy** *adj* **crispbread** *n* thin dry biscuit

**crisscross** *v* go in crosswise pattern ~*adj* crossing in different directions

**criterion** *n* (*pl* **-ria**) standard of judgment

——————————— THESAURUS ———————————

**crescent** half-moon, new moon, old moon, sickle

**crest** apex, crown, head, peak, pinnacle, ridge, summit, top

**crestfallen** dejected, depressed, despondent, disappointed, disconsolate, downcast, downhearted

**crevice** chink, cleft, crack, cranny, fissure, fracture, gap, hole, rent, rift, slit, split

**crew** hands, (ship's) company, (ship's) complement; company, corps, gang, party, posse, squad, team, working party

**crib** *v Inf* cheat, pilfer, pirate, plagiarize, purloin, steal

**crime** fault, felony, misdeed, misdemeanour, offence, outrage, transgression, trespass, unlawful act, violation, wrong

**criminal** *adj* bent *Sl*, corrupt, crooked *Inf*, culpable, felonious, il-

legal, illicit, immoral, indictable, lawless, nefarious, unlawful, unrighteous, vicious, villainous, wicked, wrong ~*n* convict, crook *Inf*, culprit, delinquent, evildoer, felon, lag *Sl*, lawbreaker, malefactor, offender, villain

**cripple** *v* disable, enfeeble, incapacitate, lame, maim, paralyse, weaken

**crisis** climax, crunch *Inf*, crux, height, turning point; catastrophe, dilemma, dire straits, disaster, emergency, exigency, mess, plight, predicament, quandary, strait, trouble

**crisp** brittle, crispy, crumbly, crunchy, firm, fresh, unwilted

**criterion** canon, gauge, measure, norm, principle, rule, standard, test, yardstick

**critic** analyst, authority, commentator, connoisseur, expert, judge,

**critical** *adj* fault-finding; discerning; skilled in judging; crucial, decisive **critically** *adv* **critic** *n* one who passes judgment; writer expert in judging works of literature, art etc. **criticism** *n* **criticize** *v*

**croak** *v/n* (utter) deep hoarse cry

**crochet** *n/v* (do) handicraft like knitting

**crock** *n* earthenware pot **crockery** *n* earthenware dishes etc.

**crocodile** *n* large amphibious reptile

**crocus** *n* small bulbous plant

**croft** *n* small farm

**croissant** *n* crescent-shaped bread roll

**crone** *n* witchlike old woman

**crony** *n* intimate friend

**crook** *n* hooked staff; *Inf* swindler, criminal, **crooked** *adj* twisted; deformed; dishonest

**croon** *v* sing in soft tone

**crop** *n* produce of cultivated plants; harvest; pouch in bird's gullet; whip; short haircut ~*v* **cropping**, **cropped** cut short; produce crop; (of animals) bite, eat down **cropper** *n Inf* heavy fall; disastrous failure **crop up** *Inf* happen unexpectedly

**croquet** *n* lawn game played with balls and hoops

**croquette** *n* fried ball of minced meat, fish etc.

**cross** *n* structure or symbol of two intersecting lines or pieces; such a structure as means of execution; symbol of Christian faith; any thing in shape of cross; affliction; hybrid ~*v* move or go across (something); intersect; meet and pass; mark with lines across; (*with out*) delete; place in form of cross; make sign of cross; breed by intermixture; thwart ~*adj* angry; transverse; contrary **crossing** *n* intersection of roads, rails etc.; part of street where pedestrians are expected to cross **cross-country**

———— T H E S A U R U S ————

pundit, reviewer

**critical** carping, censorious, derogatory, disapproving, disparaging, fault-finding, scathing; accurate, analytical, diagnostic, discerning, discriminating, fastidious, judicious, penetrating, perceptive, precise; crucial, dangerous, deciding, decisive, grave, momentous, perilous, precarious, risky, serious, urgent, vital

**criticism** bad press, censure, character assassination, disapproval, disparagement, fault-finding, stick *Sl*, stricture; analysis, appraisal, appreciation, assessment, comment, commentary, critique, evaluation, judgment, notice, review

**criticize** censure, condemn, disapprove of, disparage, lambast(e),

slate *Inf*, tear into *Inf*

**croak** *v* caw, gasp, grunt, squawk

**crook** cheat, criminal, racketeer, robber, shark, swindler, thief, villain

**crooked** bent, bowed, crippled, curved, deformed, disfigured, distorted, hooked, irregular, misshapen, tortuous, twisted, twisting, warped, winding, zigzag; *Inf* bent *Sl*, corrupt, criminal, deceitful, dishonest, dishonourable, dubious, fraudulent, illegal, questionable, shady *Inf*, shifty, underhand, under-the-table, unlawful, unscrupulous

**crop** *n* fruits, gathering, harvest, produce, reaping, vintage, yield

**crop up** appear, arise, emerge, happen, occur, spring up, turn up

*adj/adv* by way of open fields
**cross-examine** *v* examine witness
already examined by other side
**cross-examination** *n* **cross-eyed** *adj*
having eyes turning inward **cross-ply** *adj* (of tyre) having fabric cords
in outer casing running diagonally.
**cross-reference** *n* reference within
text to another part of text **crossroads** *n* **crossword** puzzle puzzle
built up of intersecting words, indicated by clues **The Cross** cross on
which Jesus Christ was executed
**crotch** *n* angle between legs
**crotchet** *n* musical note
**crotchety** *adj Inf* bad-tempered
**crouch** *v* bend low; huddle down
close to ground; stoop
**croupier** *n* person dealing cards,
collecting money etc. at gambling
table
**crouton** *n* piece of toasted bread

served in soup
**crow¹** *n* large black carrion-eating
bird
**crow²** *v* utter cock's cry; boast ~*n*
cock's cry
**crowbar** *n* iron bar
**crowd** *n* throng, mass ~*v* flock together; cram, pack; fill with people
**crown** *n* monarch's headdress;
royal power; various coins; top of
head; summit, top; perfection of
thing ~*v* put crown on; occur as
culmination; *Inf* hit on head
**crucial** *adj* decisive, critical; *Inf*
very important **crucially** *adv*
**crucible** *n* small melting pot
**crucifix** *n* (*pl* -es) cross; image of
(Christ on the) Cross **crucifixion** *n*
**crucify** *v*
**crude** *adj* vulgar; in natural or raw
state; rough **crudely** *adv* **crudity** *n*
**cruel** *adj* causing pain or suffering

——————— THESAURUS ———————

**cross** *n* crucifix, rood; crossing,
crossroads, intersection, junction;
blend, combination, crossbreed,
cur, hybrid, mixture, mongrel ~*v*
bridge, cut across, extend over,
ford, meet, pass over, ply, span,
traverse, zigzag; crisscross, intersect, intertwine, lace; blend, crossbreed, hybridize, interbreed, mix
~*adj* angry, annoyed, churlish, disagreeable, fractious, ill-humoured,
ill-tempered, impatient, irascible,
irritable, peevish, petulant, querulous, ratty *Brit & NZ inf*, short,
snappy, sullen, surly, tetchy; crosswise, intersecting, oblique, transverse

**cross-examine** catechize, grill *Inf*,
interrogate, pump, question, quiz

**crouch** bend down, bow, duck,
hunch, kneel, squat, stoop

**crow** boast, brag, exult, gloat, glory

in, strut, swagger, triumph, vaunt
**crowd** *n* army, assembly, bevy,
company, flock, herd, horde, host,
mass, mob, multitude, pack, press,
rabble, swarm, throng ~*v* cluster,
congregate, flock, gather, huddle,
mass, muster, surge, swarm, throng
**crown** *n* circlet, coronet, tiara; emperor, empress, king, monarch,
monarchy, queen, royalty, ruler,
sovereign, sovereignty ~*v* adorn,
dignify, festoon, honour, invest, reward; cap, complete, consummate,
finish, fulfil, perfect, round off, surmount, terminate, top
**crucial** central, critical, decisive,
pivotal, searching, testing, trying
**crude** boorish, coarse, crass, dirty,
gross, indecent, lewd, obscene,
smutty, tactless, tasteless, uncouth,
vulgar; natural, raw, unprocessed,
unrefined; clumsy, makeshift,

**cruelly** adv **cruelty** n

**cruet** n small container for salt, pepper etc.

**cruise** v travel about in a ship ~n voyage **cruiser** n ship that cruises; warship

**crumb** n fragment of bread

**crumble** v break into small fragments; collapse **crumbly** adj

**crumpet** n flat, soft cake eaten with butter; Sl sexually desirable woman or women

**crumple** v (cause to) collapse; make or become creased

**crunch** n sound made by chewing crisp food, treading on gravel etc.; Inf critical situation ~v make crunching sound **crunchy** adj

**crusade** n medieval Christian war; concerted action to further a cause

~v take part in crusade **crusader** n

**crush** v compress so as to break; break to small pieces; defeat utterly ~n act of crushing; crowd of people etc.

**crust** n hard outer part of bread; similar casing **crusty** adj having crust; bad-tempered

**crustacean** n hard-shelled animal, e.g. crab, lobster

**crutch** n staff with crosspiece to go under armpit of lame person; support; crotch

**crux** n (pl **cruxes**, **cruces**) that on which a decision turns

**cry** v **crying**, **cried** weep; utter call; shout; beg (for); proclaim ~n loud utterance; call of animal; fit of weeping

**crypt** n vault, esp. under church

——————— THESAURUS ———————

primitive, rough, rough-hewn, rude, rudimentary, sketchy, undeveloped, unfinished, unpolished

**crudity** coarseness, crudeness, impropriety, indelicacy, lewdness, obscenity, vulgarity

**cruel** barbarous, brutal, callous, cold-blooded, ferocious, fierce, hard, hard-hearted, harsh, heartless, inhuman, inhumane, malevolent, painful, remorseless, sadistic, savage, severe, spiteful, unfeeling, unkind, vengeful, vicious

**cruelty** bestiality, brutality, callousness, depravity, ferocity, harshness, inhumanity, sadism, savagery, severity, spite, spitefulness, venom

**cruise** v coast, sail, voyage ~n boat trip, sail, sea trip, voyage

**crumb** atom, bit, grain, mite, morsel, particle, scrap, shred, sliver, snippet, soupçon, speck

**crumble** bruise, crush, crumb, fragment, granulate, grind, pound,

powder; break up, collapse, come to dust, decay, decompose, degenerate, deteriorate, disintegrate, fall apart, go to pieces, moulder, perish

**crumple** break down, cave in, collapse, fall, give way, go to pieces; crease, crush, pucker, rumple, screw up, wrinkle

**crusade** campaign, cause, drive, holy war, movement

**crush** break, bruise, compress, crease, crumble, crumple, crunch, mash, pound, pulverize, smash, squeeze, wrinkle; conquer, overcome, overpower, overwhelm, put down, quell, stamp out, subdue, vanquish

**crust** coat, coating, covering, layer, outside, shell, skin, surface

**crusty** brittle, crisp, crispy, friable, hard, short, well-baked, well-done

**cry** v bawl, bewail, blubber, lament, shed tears, snivel, sob, wail, weep,

**cryptic** adj secret, mysterious

**crystal** n transparent mineral; very clear glass; cut-glass ware; form with symmetrically arranged plane surfaces **crystalline** adj **crystallize** v form into crystals; become definite

**cu.** cubic

**cub** n young of fox and other animals; (with cap.) junior Scout

**cubbyhole** n small enclosed space

**cube** n solid figure with six equal square sides; cube-shaped block; product obtained by multiplying number by itself twice ~v multiply thus **cubic** adj

**cubicle** n enclosed section of room

**cuckoo** n (pl -oos) migratory bird; its call

**cucumber** n long fleshy green fruit used in salad

**cud** n food which ruminant animal brings back into mouth to chew again

**cuddle** v hug; lie close and snug, nestle ~n hug **cuddly** adj

**cudgel** n short thick stick ~v -elling, -elled beat with cudgel

**cue¹** n signal to act or speak; hint

**cue²** n long tapering rod used in billiards

**cuff¹** n ending of sleeve

**cuff²** v strike with open hand ~n blow with hand

**cuisine** n style of cooking; food cooked

**cul-de-sac** n (pl culs-de-sac) street open only at one end

**culinary** adj of, for, suitable for, cooking or kitchen

**cull** v select; take out animals from herd

**culminate** v reach highest point; come to a head **culmination** n

**culottes** pl n women's trousers flared like skirt

**culpable** adj blameworthy

**culprit** n one guilty of offence

**cult** n system of worship; devotion to some person, thing

**cultivate** v till and prepare (ground); develop, improve; devote attention to **cultivated** adj cultured **cultivation** n

**culture** n state of manners, taste

——————— THESAURUS ———————

whimper, whine, whinge Inf; bawl, bellow, call, call out, exclaim, howl, roar, scream, screech, shout, shriek, whoop, yell ~n howl, lament, lamentation, snivel, snivelling, sob, sobbing, wailing, weep, weeping

**cub** offspring, whelp, young

**cue** hint, key, nod, prompting, reminder, sign, signal, suggestion

**cul-de-sac** blind alley, dead end

**culminate** climax, close, conclude, end, end up, finish, terminate

**culmination** acme, apex, apogee, climax, completion, conclusion, consummation, crown, finale, height, peak, perfection, pinnacle, summit, top, zenith

**culpable** answerable, at fault, blameworthy, guilty, in the wrong, liable, reprehensible, sinful, to blame, wrong

**culprit** criminal, delinquent, felon, guilty party, miscreant, offender, sinner, villain, wrongdoer

**cult** body, church faction, clique, denomination, faith, following, party, religion, school, sect; admiration, craze, devotion, reverence, veneration, worship

**cultivate** farm, harvest, plant, plough, prepare, tend, till, work; better, bring on, cherish, civilize, develop, foster, improve, promote,

and intellectual development; cultivating **cultural** adj **cultured** adj

**culvert** n drain under road

**cumbersome** adj unwieldy

**cummerbund** n sash worn round waist

**cumulative** adj becoming greater by successive additions

**cumulus** n (pl **-li**) round billowing cloud

**cunning** adj crafty, sly ~n skill in deceit or evasion

**cup** n small drinking vessel with handle; various cup-shaped formations; cup-shaped trophy as prize ~v **cupping, cupped** shape as cup (hands etc.) **cupful** n **cupboard** n piece of furniture with door, for storage

**cur** n dog of mixed breed; con-

temptible person

**curate** n parish priest's appointed assistant

**curator** n custodian, esp. of museum

**curb** n check, restraint ~v restrain; apply curb to

**curd** n coagulated milk **curdle** v turn into curd, coagulate

**cure** v heal, restore to health; remedy; preserve (fish, skins etc.) ~n remedy; course of medical treatment; restoration to health **curable** adj

**curfew** n official regulation prohibiting movement of people, esp. at night; deadline for this

**curio** n (pl **curios**) rare or curious thing sought for collections

**curious** adj eager to know, inquisi-

——————— THESAURUS ———————

refine, train

**cultivation** advancement, advocacy, development, encouragement, enhancement, fostering, furtherance, help, nurture, patronage, promotion, support

**cultural** artistic, broadening, civilizing, edifying, educational, educative, elevating, enriching, humane, humanizing, liberal

**culture** civilization, customs, life style, mores, society, the arts, way of life; accomplishment, breeding, education, elevation, enlightenment, erudition, good taste, improvement, refinement, sophistication, urbanity

**cultured** accomplished, advanced, educated, enlightened, erudite, genteel, knowledgeable, polished, refined, scholarly, urbane, versed, well-bred, well-informed, well-read

**cumbersome** awkward, bulky, clumsy, heavy, unmanageable, un-

wieldy, weighty

**cunning** adj artful, astute, canny, crafty, devious, guileful, knowing, Machiavellian, sharp, shifty, shrewd, subtle, tricky, wily ~n artfulness, astuteness, craftiness, deceitfulness, deviousness, guile, shrewdness, slyness, trickery

**cup** beaker, chalice, draught, drink, goblet, teacup

**curb** n brake, bridle, check, control, deterrent, limitation, restraint ~v bite back, bridle, check, constrain, contain, control, hinder, impede, inhibit, moderate, muzzle, repress, restrain, restrict, subdue, suppress

**cure** v alleviate, ease, heal, help, make better, mend, rehabilitate, relieve, remedy; dry, kipper, pickle, preserve, salt, smoke ~n antidote, healing, medicine, panacea, remedy, restorative, treatment

**curiosity** interest, prying; freak,

tive; puzzling, odd **curiosity** n curiously adv

**curl** v take, bend into spiral or curved shape ~n spiral lock of hair; spiral **curly** adj

**curlew** n large long-billed wading bird

**curmudgeon** n bad-tempered person

**currant** n dried type of grape; fruit of various plants allied to gooseberry

**current** adj of immediate present; in general use ~n body of water or air in motion; transmission of electricity **currently** adv **currency** n money in use; state of being in use

**curriculum** n (pl -lums, -la) specified course of study **curriculum vitae** outline of career

**curry** n highly-flavoured, pungent condiment; dish flavoured with it

~v **currying, curried** prepare, flavour dish with curry

**curse** n profane or obscene expression of anger etc.; magic spell; affliction ~v utter curse, swear (at); afflict

**cursor** n movable point showing position on computer screen

**cursory** adj hasty, superficial

**curt** adj rudely brief, abrupt

**curtail** v cut short

**curtain** n hanging drapery at window etc. ~v provide, cover with curtain

**curtsy, curtsey** n/v (perform) woman's bow

**curve** n line of which no part is straight ~v bend into curve

**cushion** n bag filled with soft stuffing or air, to support or ease body ~v provide, protect with cushion; lessen effects of

———————————— THESAURUS ————————————

marvel, novelty, oddity, phenomenon, rarity, sight, spectacle, wonder

**curious** inquiring, inquisitive, interested, puzzled, questioning, searching; bizarre, exotic, extraordinary, mysterious, novel, odd, peculiar, puzzling, quaint, queer, rare, singular, strange, unconventional, unique, unorthodox, unusual

**curl** v bend, coil, corkscrew, crimp, crinkle, crisp, curve, entwine, loop, meander, ripple, spiral, turn, twine, twirl, twist, wind, wreathe, writhe

**currency** bills, coinage, coins, money, notes

**current** adj accepted, circulating, common, customary, general, in the news, ongoing, popular, present, prevailing, prevalent, rife, widespread ~n course, draught, flow, jet, river, stream, tide

**curse** n blasphemy, expletive, oath, obscenity, swearword; evil eye, execration, hoodoo Inf; jinx; affliction, bane, burden, calamity, disaster, evil, hardship, misfortune, ordeal, plague, scourge, torment, tribulation, trouble, vexation ~v blaspheme, swear, use bad language

**curt** abrupt, blunt, brief, brusque, gruff, offhand, rude, sharp, short, snappish, tart, terse

**curtail** abbreviate, abridge, contract, cut, cut back, decrease, dock, lessen, lop, pare down, reduce, shorten, trim, truncate

**curtain** n drape chiefly US, hanging ~v conceal, drape, hide, screen, shroud, shut off, shutter, veil

**curve** n arc, bend, camber, loop, turn ~v arc, arch, bend, bow, coil, hook, inflect, turn, twist, wind

**cushy** *adj Inf* easy

**custard** *n* dish made of eggs and milk; sweet sauce of milk and cornflour

**custody** *n* guardianship, imprisonment **custodian** *n* keeper, curator

**custom** *n* habit; practice; usage; business patronage; *pl* taxes levied on imports **customary** *adj* usual, habitual **customer** *n* one who enters shop to buy, esp. regularly; purchaser

**cut** *v* cutting, cut sever, wound, divide; pare, detach, trim; intersect; reduce, decrease; abridge; *Inf* ignore (person) ~*n* act of cutting; stroke; blow; wound; reduction; fashion, shape; *Inf* share **cutter** *n* **cutting** *n* piece cut from plant; article from newspaper; passage for railway ~*adj* keen, piercing; hurtful

**cutthroat** *n* killer; murderous; fiercely competitive

**cute** *adj* appealing, pretty

**cuticle** *n* dead skin, esp. at base of fingernail

**cutlass** *n* curved sword

**cutlery** *n* knives, forks etc.

**cutlet** *n* small piece of meat

**cuttlefish** *n* sea mollusc like squid

**CV** curriculum vitae

**cwt.** hundredweight

**cyanide** *n* extremely poisonous chemical compound

**cybernetics** *pl n (with sing v)* comparative study of control mechanisms of electronic and biological systems

**cyclamen** *n* plant with flowers having turned-back petals

**cycle** *n* recurrent, complete series or period; bicycle ~*v* ride bicycle **cyclical** *adj* **cyclist** *n* bicycle rider

**cyclone** *n* circular storm

**cygnet** *n* young swan

**cylinder** *n* roller-shaped body, of

---

**cushion** *n* beanbag, hassock, headrest, pad, pillow ~*v* bolster, buttress, cradle, dampen, deaden, muffle, soften, stifle, support

**custody** arrest, confinement, detention, imprisonment, incarceration

**custom** habit, manner, routine, way, wont

**customary** accepted, accustomed, acknowledged, common, confirmed, conventional, everyday, familiar, fashionable, general, normal, ordinary, popular, regular, routine, traditional, usual

**customer** buyer, client, consumer, patron, regular *Inf,* shopper

**cut** *v* chop, cleave, divide, gash, incise, lacerate, nick, notch, pierce, score, sever, slash, slice, slit, wound; contract, cut back, decrease, lower, rationalize, reduce, slash, slim (down); abbreviate, abridge, condense, curtail, delete, edit out, excise, shorten ~*n* gash, graze, groove, incision, laceration, nick, rip, slash, slit, stroke, wound; cutback, decrease, economy, fall, lowering, reduction, saving

**cutthroat** *n* assassin, butcher, executioner, hit man *Sl,* killer, murderer, thug ~*adj* barbarous, bloodthirsty, bloody, cruel, ferocious, homicidal, murderous, savage, thuggish, violent; competitive, dog-eat-dog, fierce, relentless, ruthless, unprincipled

**cutting** *adj* biting, bitter, chill, keen, numbing, penetrating, piercing, raw, sharp, stinging

**cycle** age, circle, era, period, phase, revolution, rotation

uniform diameter **cylindrical** *adj*
**cymbal** *n* one of two brass plates
struck together to produce clashing
sound
**cynic** *n* one who believes the worst
about people or outcome of events
**cynical** *adj* **cynicism** *n* being cynical

**cypress** *n* coniferous tree with very
dark foliage
**cyst** *n* sac containing liquid secretion or pus **cystitis** *n* inflammation
of bladder
**Czar, Tsar** *n* emperor, esp. of Rus-
sia 1547-1917

——————— THESAURUS ———————

**cynic** doubter, pessimist, sceptic,
scoffer
**cynical** derisive, ironic, misan-
thropical, mocking, pessimistic,
sarcastic, sardonic, sceptical, scornful, sneering
**cynicism** disbelief, doubt, misan-
thropy, pessimism, sarcasm, scepticism

# D d

**dab** v **dabbing, dabbed** apply with momentary pressure ~n small mass

**dabble** v splash about; be amateur (in)

**dachshund** n short-legged long-bodied dog

**dad, daddy** n Inf father **daddylonglegs** n Inf fly with long thin legs

**daffodil** n yellow spring flower

**daft** adj foolish, crazy

**dagger** n short stabbing weapon

**dahlia** n garden plant of various colours

**daily** adj/adv (done) every day ~n daily newspaper; charwoman

**dainty** adj delicate; choice; fastidious ~n delicacy **daintiness** n

**dairy** n place for processing milk and its products

**dais** n raised platform

**daisy** n flower with yellow centre and white petals

**dale** n valley

**dally** v **-lying, -lied** trifle; loiter

**Dalmatian** n white dog with black spots

**dam** n/v **damming, dammed** (barrier to) hold back flow of waters

**damage** n injury, harm; pl compensation for injury ~v harm

**damask** n patterned woven material; velvety red

**dame** n Obs lady; (with cap.) title of lady in Order of the British Empire; Sl woman

**damn** v **damning, damned** condemn; curse ~interj expression of annoyance etc. **damnable** adj **damnation** n

**damp** adj moist ~n moisture ~v make damp; deaden **dampen** v damp **damper** n anything that discourages; plate in flue

**damson** n small dark-purple plum

--- THESAURUS ---

**dabble** dally, dip into, play at, potter, tinker, trifle (with)

**dagger** bayonet, dirk, poniard, skean

**daily** adj diurnal, everyday, quotidian; common, commonplace, day-to-day, everyday, ordinary, regular, routine ~adv day after day, every day, often, once a day, regularly

**dainty** adj charming, delicate, elegant, fine, graceful, neat, petite, pretty

**dam** n barrage, barrier, hindrance, obstruction, wall ~v barricade, block, check, choke, confine, hold back, hold in, obstruct, restrict

**damage** n destruction, devastation, harm, hurt, injury, loss, suffering; pl fine, indemnity, reimbursement, reparation, satisfaction

~v deface, harm, hurt, impair, injure, mar, mutilate, ruin, spoil, tamper with, wreck

**damn** v blast, castigate, censure, condemn, criticize, denounce, denunciate, lambast(e), pan Inf, slam Sl, slate Inf; abuse, curse, execrate, imprecate, revile, swear; condemn, doom, sentence

**damp** adj clammy, dank, dewy, dripping, drizzly, humid, misty, moist, muggy, sodden, soggy, sopping, wet ~n dampness, darkness, dew, drizzle, fog, humidity, mist, moisture, vapour ~v dampen, moisten, wet; allay, check, chill, cool, curb, dash, deaden, deject, diminish, discourage, dull, inhibit, moderate, restrain, stifle

**dance** v move with rhythmic steps, to music; bob up and down; perform (dance) ~n rhythmical movement; social gathering **dancer** n

**dandelion** n yellow-flowered wild plant

**dandruff** n dead skin in small scales among the hair

**dandy** n man excessively concerned with smartness of dress ~adj Inf excellent

**danger** n exposure to harm; peril **dangerous** adj **dangerously** adv

**dangle** v hang loosely

**dank** adj damp and chilly

**dapper** adj neat, spruce

**dappled** adj marked with spots

**dare** v have courage (to); challenge ~n challenge **daring** adj/n **daredevil**

adj/n reckless (person)

**dark** adj without light; gloomy; deep in tint; unenlightened ~n absence of light **darken** v **darkly** adv

**darkness** n **dark horse** person, thing about whom little is known

**darling** adj/n beloved (person)

**darn** v mend (hole) by sewing

**dart** n small pointed missile; darting motion; small seam pl indoor game played with numbered target ~v throw, go rapidly

**dash** v move hastily; throw, strike violently; frustrate ~n rush; small amount; smartness; punctuation mark (-) showing change of subject **dashing** adj lively, stylish **dashboard** n instrument panel

**dastardly** adj mean

**dance** v caper, frolic, gambol, hop, jig, prance, rock, skip, spin, sway, swing, trip ~n ball, dancing party, knees-up Brit inf, social

**danger** n hazard, insecurity, jeopardy, menace, peril, risk, threat, venture, vulnerability

**dangerous** alarming, exposed, hazardous, insecure, menacing, nasty, perilous, risky, threatening, treacherous, ugly, unsafe

**dangle** v depend, flap, hang, hang down, sway, swing, trail

**dare** v brave, gamble, hazard, make bold, presume, risk, stake, venture; challenge, defy, goad, provoke, taunt ~n challenge, defiance, provocation, taunt

**daring** adj adventurous, bold, brave, fearless, game Inf, impulsive, intrepid, plucky, rash, reckless, valiant, venturesome ~n balls Taboo sl, boldness, bottle Brit sl, bravery, courage, fearlessness, grit, guts Inf, nerve Inf, pluck, spirit, temerity

**dark** adj black, dusky, ebony, sable, swarthy; cloudy, dim, dingy, gloomy, indistinct, murky, overcast, pitch-black, pitchy, shadowy, shady, sunless, unlit ~n darkness, dimness, dusk, gloom, murk

**darkness** n dark, dimness, dusk, gloom, murk, nightfall, obscurity, shade, shadiness, shadows

**darling** adj adored, beloved, cherished, dear, precious, treasured ~n beloved, dear, dearest, love, sweetheart

**darn** mend, patch, repair, sew up, stitch

**dart** v bound, dash, flash, flit, fly, race, run, rush, shoot, spring, sprint, tear, whiz

**dash** v bolt, bound, dart, fly, haste, hasten, hurry, race, run, rush, speed, spring, sprint, tear; break, crash, destroy, shatter, shiver, smash; confound, dampen, disappoint, discourage, frustrate, thwart

**dashing** bold, daring, debonair,

**data** pl n (oft. with sing v) series of facts; information **database** n store of information

**date**[1] n day of the month; time of occurrence; appointment ~v mark with date; reveal age of; exist (from); become old-fashioned **dated** adj

**date**[2] n fruit of palm

**daub** v paint roughly

**daughter** n one's female child **daughter-in-law** n son's wife

**daunt** v frighten into giving up purpose **daunting** adj

**dawdle** v idle, loiter

**dawn** n daybreak; beginning ~v begin to grow light; (begin to) be understood

**day** n period of 24 hours; time when sun is above horizon; time period **daybreak** n dawn **daydream** n idle fancy ~v have such fancies

**daydreamer** n **daylight** n natural light; dawn

**daze** v stun, bewilder ~n bewildered state **dazed** adj

**dazzle** v blind, confuse with brightness; impress greatly **dazzling** adj

**DC** direct current

**de-** comb. form removal of, from, reversal of, as in **delouse, desegregate**

**deacon** n (fem **deaconess**) one who assists in a church

**dead** adj no longer alive; obsolete; numb; lacking vigour; complete ~n (oft. pl **the dead**) dead person(s) ~adv utterly **deaden** v **deadly** adj fatal; deathlike ~adv as if dead; extremely **deadline** n limit of time allowed **deadlock** n standstill **deadpan** adj expressionless

**deaf** adj without hearing; unwilling

exuberant, gallant, plucky, spirited, swashbuckling

**data** details, documents, facts, figures, information, input, materials, statistics

**date** age, epoch, era, period, stage, time; appointment, assignation, engagement, meeting, rendezvous, tryst

**dated** antiquated, archaic, obsolete, old-fashioned, old hat, out, outdated, out of date, passé, unfashionable

**daub** v coat, cover, paint, plaster, slap on Inf, smear

**daunt** v alarm, appal, cow, dismay, frighten, intimidate, overawe, scare, subdue, terrify

**dawdle** v dally, delay, hang about, idle, lag, loaf, loiter, potter, waste time

**dawn** n daybreak, daylight, morning, sunrise ~v break, brighten, gleam, glimmer, lighten

**day** daylight, daytime, twenty-four hours, working day; date, particular day, point in time, set time, time

**daybreak** break of day, cockcrow, crack of dawn, dawn, first light, morning, sunrise, sunup

**daydream** n dream, fancy, fantasy, pipe dream, wish ~v dream, fancy, fantasize, imagine, muse

**daylight** sunlight, sunshine

**dazed** baffled, bemused, bewildered, confused, dizzy, fuddled, light-headed, muddled, numbed, perplexed, shocked, staggered, stunned, stupefied

**dazzle** bedazzle, blind, blur, confuse, daze; amaze, astonish, awe, bowl over Inf, impress, overawe, overpower, overwhelm, strike dumb, stupefy

to listen **deafen** v make deaf **deafness** n

**deal**[1] v dealing, dealt distribute; act; treat; do business (with, in) ~n agreement; treatment; share **dealer** n

**deal**[2] n (plank of) pine wood

**dean** n university official; head of cathedral chapter

**dear** adj beloved; precious; expensive ~n beloved one **dearly** adv

**dearth** n scarcity

**death** n dying; end of life; end **deathly** adj/adv

**debacle** n utter collapse, rout, disaster

**debase** v lower in value

**debate** v argue, esp. formally ~n formal discussion **debatable** adj **debater** n

**debauched** adj leading life of depraved self-indulgence **debauchery** n

**debilitate** v weaken

**debit** Accounting n entry in account of sum owed ~v enter as due

**debonair** adj suave, genial

**debrief** v report result of mission

———— THESAURUS ————

**dead** deceased, defunct, departed, extinct, gone, inanimate, late, lifeless, passed away, perished; callous, cold, dull, frigid, glassy, glazed, indifferent, spiritless, torpid, unresponsive, wooden; boring, dull, flat, ho-hum *Inf*, insipid, stale, tasteless, uninteresting, vapid

**deadlock** dead heat, draw, full stop, halt, impasse, stalemate, tie

**deadly** baleful, baneful, dangerous, deathly, destructive, fatal, lethal, malignant, mortal, noxious, pernicious, poisonous, venomous

**deaf** hard of hearing, stone deaf; oblivious, unconcerned, unhearing, unmoved

**deafen** din, drown out, make deaf, split the eardrums

**deal** v bargain, buy and sell, do business, negotiate, dispense, stock, trade, traffic; allot, apportion, assign, bestow, dispense, distribute, divide, dole out, give, reward, share ~n agreement, arrangement, bargain, contract, pact, transaction, understanding

**dealer** merchant, purveyor, supplier, trader, tradesman, wholesaler

**dear** adj beloved, cherished, close, darling, esteemed, familiar, favourite, intimate, precious, prized, respected, treasured; costly, expensive, high-priced ~n angel, beloved, darling, loved one, precious, treasure

**dearly** extremely, greatly, profoundly, very much

**death** bereavement, decease, demise, departure, dying, end, exit, expiration, loss, passing, release; destruction, downfall, end, extinction, finish, grave, ruin, undoing

**deathly** gaunt, ghastly, grim, haggard, pale, pallid, wan; deadly, extreme, fatal, intense, mortal, terrible

**debase** cheapen, degrade, demean, devalue, disgrace, dishonour, drag down, humble, lower, reduce, shame

**debatable** arguable, borderline, controversial, disputable, doubtful, dubious, in dispute, moot, open to question, questionable, uncertain, unsettled

**debate** v argue, contend, discuss, dispute, question, wrangle ~n argument, contention, controversy, discussion, disputation,

**debris** n rubbish

**debt** n what is owed; state of owing **debtor** n

**debunk** v expose falseness of, esp. by ridicule

**debut** n first appearance in public **debutante** n girl making society debut

**Dec.** December

**deca-** comb. form ten, as in **decalitre**

**decade** n period of ten years

**decadent** adj deteriorating; morally corrupt **decadence** n

**decaffeinated** adj (of tea, coffee) with caffeine removed

**decant** v pour off (wine) **decanter** n stoppered bottle

**decapitate** v behead

**decathlon** n athletic contest with ten events

**decay** v rot; decline ~n rotting

**decease** n death ~v die **deceased** adj/n dead (person)

**deceive** v mislead, delude **deceit** n fraud; duplicity **deceitful** adj

**decelerate** v slow down

**December** n twelfth month

**decent** adj respectable; fitting; adequate; Inf kind **decency** n

**deception** n deceiving; trick **deceptive** adj misleading

———————— THESAURUS ————————

dispute

**debris** bits, dross, fragments, litter, pieces, remains, rubbish, rubble, ruins, waste, wreck, wreckage

**debt** arrears, bill, commitment, debit, due, duty, liability, obligation, score

**debtor** borrower, defaulter, insolvent

**debunk** cut down to size, deflate, disparage, expose, lampoon, mock, puncture, ridicule, show up

**debut** beginning, bow, coming out, entrance, inauguration, initiation, introduction, launching

**decadent** corrupt, debased, decaying, declining, degenerate, degraded, depraved, dissolute, immoral

**decay** v crumble, decline, degenerate, deteriorate, disintegrate, dissolve, dwindle, moulder, shrivel, sink, spoil, wane, wither; decompose, mortify, perish, putrefy, rot

**deceased** adj dead, defunct, departed, expired, finished, former, gone, late

**deceit** artifice, cheating, cunning, dissimulation, double-dealing, du-

plicity, fraud, hypocrisy, pretence, slyness, treachery, trickery

**deceitful** crafty, designing, dishonest, disingenuous, double-dealing, duplicitous, fallacious, false, fraudulent, hypocritical, illusory, insincere, treacherous, two-faced, underhand, untrustworthy

**deceive** betray, cheat, con Inf, delude, double-cross Inf, dupe, ensnare, entrap, fool, hoax, hoodwink, mislead, outwit, swindle, take in Inf, trick

**decency** correctness, courtesy, decorum, etiquette, good form, good manners, modesty, propriety, seemliness

**decent** becoming, chaste, comely, decorous, delicate, fit, modest, nice, polite, presentable, proper, pure, respectable, seemly, suitable

**deception** cunning, deceit, duplicity, fraud, fraudulence, guile, hypocrisy, imposition, insincerity, treachery, trickery

**deceptive** deceitful, delusive, dishonest, fake, false, fraudulent, illusory, misleading, mock, specious,

**decibel** n unit for measuring intensity of sound

**decide** v settle; give judgement; come to a decision **decided** adj unmistakable; resolute **decidedly** adv

**decision** n **decisive** adj final; able to make (quick) decisions **decisiveness** n

**deciduous** adj (of trees) losing leaves annually

**decimal** adj relating to tenths ~n decimal fraction **decimalization** n **decimal point** dot between unit and fraction

**decimate** v destroy or kill a tenth of, large proportion of

**decipher** v make out meaning of; decode

**deck** n floor, esp. one covering ship's hull; turntable of record play-

er ~v decorate **deck chair** folding canvas chair

**declaim** v speak rhetorically

**declare** v announce formally; state emphatically **declaration** n

**decline** v refuse; slope downwards; deteriorate; diminish ~n deterioration; diminution; downward slope

**decode** v convert from code into ordinary language **decoder** n

**decompose** v rot

**decongestant** adj/n (drug) relieving (esp. nasal) congestion

**decontaminate** v render harmless

**decor** n decorative scheme

**decorate** v beautify; paint room etc.; invest (with medal etc.) **decoration** n **decorative** adj **decorator** n

**decorum** n propriety, decency **decorous** adj

——————— THESAURUS ———————

spurious, unreliable

**decide** adjudicate, choose, commit oneself, conclude, decree, determine, elect, end, purpose, resolve, settle

**decipher** construe, crack, decode, explain, interpret, make out, read, reveal, solve, understand, unfold, unravel

**decision** conclusion, finding, judgment, outcome, resolution, result, ruling, sentence, settlement, verdict

**decisive** absolute, conclusive, critical, crucial, definite, definitive, fateful, final, influential, significant; determined, firm, forceful, incisive, resolute, strong-minded

**deck** v adorn, array, attire, beautify, bedeck, bedight, clothe, decorate, dress, embellish, festoon, grace, ornament

**declaim** harangue, hold forth, lecture, proclaim, rant, recite, speak

**declaration** announcement, edict,

manifesto, notification, promulgation, pronouncement; affirmation, assertion, disclosure, revelation, statement, testimony

**declare** affirm, announce, assert, attest, aver, avow, claim, confirm, maintain, proclaim, profess, pronounce, state, swear, testify

**decline** v abstain, avoid, deny, forgo, refuse, reject, say 'no', turn down; decrease, diminish, drop, dwindle, ebb, fade, fail, fall, fall off, flag, lessen, shrink, sink, wane ~n deterioration, downturn, dwindling, falling off, lessening, recession, slump

**decorate** adorn, beautify, deck, embellish, enrich, festoon, grace, ornament, trim; colour, furbish, paint, paper, renovate; cite, honour

**decoration** adornment, embellishment, enrichment, ornamentation, trimming; award, badge, colours, emblem, garter, medal, order, rib-

**decoy** n bait, lure ~v lure, be lured as with decoy

**decrease** v diminish, lessen ~n diminishing

**decree** n/v **-creeing, -creed** (give) order having the force of law

**decrepit** adj old; worn out

**decry** v **-crying, -cried** disparage

**dedicate** v commit wholly to special purpose; inscribe or address; devote **dedicated** adj **dedication** n

**deduce** v draw as conclusion

**deduct** v subtract **deductible** adj **deduction** n deducting;. amount subtracted; conclusion

**deed** n action; exploit; legal document

**deem** v judge, consider, regard

**deep** adj extending far down; at, of given depth; profound; hard to fathom; (of colour) dark; (of sound) low ~n deep place; the sea ~adv far down etc. **deeply** adv **deepen** v

**deer** n (pl **deer**) ruminant animal typically with antlers in male

**deface** v spoil or mar surface

**defame** v speak ill of **defamation** n **defamatory** adj

**default** n failure to act, appear or pay ~v fail (to pay)

**defeat** v vanquish; thwart ~n overthrow

**defecate** v empty the bowels

—————— THESAURUS ——————

bon, star

**decorum** behaviour, breeding, decency, dignity, etiquette, gentility, good grace, good manners, gravity, politeness, propriety, protocol, respectability, seemliness

**decoy** n attraction, bait, enticement, inducement, lure, pretence, trap ~v allure, bait, deceive, ensnare, entice, entrap, inveigle, lure, seduce, tempt

**decrease** v abate, contract, curtail, cut down, decline, diminish, drop, dwindle, ease, fall off, lessen, lower, reduce, shrink, wane ~n cutback, decline, ebb, falling off, loss, reduction, shrinkage

**decree** n act, canon, command, edict, enactment, law, mandate, order, precept, proclamation, regulation, ruling, statute ~v command, decide, determine, dictate, enact, lay down, ordain, order, prescribe, proclaim

**decrepit** aged, crippled, debilitated, feeble, frail, incapacitated, infirm, weak

**dedicate** commit, devote, give over to, pledge, surrender

**dedicated** committed, devoted, enthusiastic, purposeful, single-minded, wholehearted, zealous

**deduce** conclude, derive, draw, gather, glean, infer, reason, understand

**deduct** decrease by, reduce by, remove, subtract, take away, take from, withdraw

**deduction** decrease, diminution, discount, reduction, subtraction; conclusion, consequence, finding, inference, reasoning, result

**deed** act, action, exploit, fact, feat, reality

**deep** adj bottomless, broad, far, profound, wide, yawning; extreme, grave, great, intense, profound; of a sound bass, booming, full-toned, low, low-pitched, resonant, sonorous

**default** n absence, defect, failure, lack, lapse, neglect, nonpayment, omission, want ~v defraud, dodge, evade, fail, neglect

**defect** n lack, blemish ~v desert

**defection** n defective adj defector n

**defend** v protect, ward off attack; support by argument **defence** n protection; justification; statement by accused person in court **defenceless** adj **defendant** n person accused in court **defender** n **defensible** adj **defensive** adj serving for defence ~n attitude of defence

**defer**[1] v -ferring, -ferred postpone

**defer**[2] v -ferring, -ferred submit to

opinion or judgement of another **deference** n obedience; respect **deferential** adj

**deficient** adj lacking in something **deficiency** n **deficit** n amount by which sum of money is too small

**define** v state meaning of; mark out **definition** n **definite** adj exact; clear; certain **definitely** adv **definition** n **definitive** adj conclusive

**deflate** v (cause to) collapse by re-

———————— THESAURUS ————————

**defeat** v beat, conquer, crush, master, overpower, overthrow, overwhelm, quell, repulse, rout, subdue, subjugate, vanquish ~n conquest, debacle, overthrow, repulse, rout

**defect** n blemish, blotch, error, failing, fault, flaw, imperfection, mistake, spot, taint, want ~v change sides, desert, go over, rebel, revolt

**defective** broken, faulty, flawed, imperfect, inadequate, incomplete, insufficient, not working, out of order

**defence** armament, cover, deterrence, guard, immunity, protection, resistance, safeguard, security, shelter; apologia, argument, excuse, exoneration, explanation, justification, plea, vindication; Law alibi, case, denial, plea, rebuttal, testimony

**defend** cover, fortify, guard, keep safe, preserve, protect, screen, secure, shelter, shield; assert, champion, endorse, espouse, justify, maintain, plead, stand by, stand up for, support, sustain, uphold, vindicate

**defender** bodyguard, escort, guard, protector; advocate, cham-

pion, patron, sponsor, supporter, vindicator

**defer**[1] adjourn, delay, hold over, postpone, protract, put off, set aside, shelve, suspend, table

**defer**[2] accede, bow, capitulate, comply, give in, give way to, respect, submit, yield

**defiance** challenge, contempt, disobedience, disregard, insolence, insubordination, opposition, rebelliousness, spite

**deficiency** defect, demerit, failing, fault, flaw, frailty, shortcoming, weakness

**deficit** arrears, default, deficiency, loss, shortage, shortfall

**define** describe, designate, detail, determine, explain, expound, interpret, specify, spell out

**definite** clear, clear-cut, determined, exact, explicit, express, fixed, marked, obvious, particular, precise, specific

**definitely** absolutely, categorically, certainly, clearly, easily, finally, indubitably, obviously, plainly, positively, surely, undeniably, unequivocally, unmistakably, unquestionably, without doubt

**definition** clarification, description, elucidation, explanation,

lease of gas from **deflation** n Economics reduction of economic and industrial activity

**deflect** v (cause to) turn from straight course **deflection** n

**deform** v spoil shape of; disfigure **deformity** n

**defraud** v cheat, swindle

**defrost** v make, become free of frost, ice; thaw

**deft** adj skilful, adroit

**defunct** adj dead, obsolete

**defuse** v remove fuse of bomb etc.; remove tension

**defy** v **-fying, -fied** challenge, resist successfully **defiance** n resistance **defiant** adj openly and aggressively hostile

**degenerate** v deteriorate to lower level ~adj fallen away in quality ~n degenerate person **degeneration** n

**degenerative** adj

**degrade** v dishonour; debase; reduce; decompose chemically **degradable** n **degradation** n

**degree** n step, stage in process; university rank; unit of measurement

**dehydrate** v remove moisture from

**deify** v **-fying, -fied** make a god of **deity** n god

**deign** v condescend

**déjà vu** Fr feeling of having experienced something before

**dejected** adj miserable **dejection** n

**delay** v delaying, delayed postpone; linger ~n delaying

**delectable** adj delightful

**delegate** n representative ~v send as deputy; entrust **delegation** n

**delete** v remove, erase **deletion** n

——————— THESAURUS ———————

exposition

**deflate** collapse, contract, exhaust, flatten, puncture, shrink, void

**deflect** bend, diverge, glance off, shy, sidetrack, swerve, turn, twist, veer, wind

**defraud** cheat, delude, dupe, embezzle, fleece, outwit, swindle, trick

**deft** able, adept, adroit, agile, clever, dexterous, expert, handy, neat, nimble, proficient, skilful

**defy** beard, brave, challenge, confront, dare, despise, disregard, face, flout, provoke, scorn, slight, spurn

**degenerate** v decay, decline, deteriorate, fall off, lapse, regress, rot, sink, slip, worsen ~adj base, corrupt, debased, debauched, decadent, degraded, depraved, dissolute, fallen, immoral, low, mean

**degrade** cheapen, corrupt, debase, demean, discredit, disgrace, dishonour, humble, humiliate, impair,

pervert, shame

**degree** class, grade, level, order, position, rank, standing, station, status

**dejected** cast down, crestfallen, depressed, despondent, disconsolate, disheartened, downcast, gloomy, glum, low, melancholy, miserable, morose, sad, wretched

**delay** v defer, hold over, postpone, procrastinate, prolong, protract, put off, shelve, stall, suspend ~n check, deferment, hindrance, hold-up, postponement, procrastination, stay, stoppage, suspension, wait

**delegate** n agent, ambassador, commissioner, deputy, envoy, legate, representative, vicar

**delegation** commission, contingent, deputation, embassy, envoys, legation, mission

**deliberate** *adj* intentional; well-considered; slow ~*v* consider **deliberately** *adv* **deliberation** *n*

**delicate** *adj* exquisite; fragile; requiring tact **delicacy** *n* elegance; delicious food

**delicatessen** *n* shop selling esp. imported or unusual foods

**delicious** *adj* delightful, pleasing to taste

**delight** *v* please greatly; take great pleasure (in) ~*n* great pleasure **delightful** *adj* charming

**delinquent** *n/adj* (one) guilty of delinquency **delinquency** *n* (minor) offence or misdeed

**delirium** *n* disorder of mind, esp. in feverish illness; violent excitement **delirious** *adj*

**deliver** *v* carry to destination; hand over; release; give birth or assist in birth (of); utter **deliverance** *n* rescue **delivery** *n*

**dell** *n* wooded hollow

**delta** *n* alluvial tract at river mouth

**delude** *v* deceive; mislead **delusion** *n*

**deluge** *n* flood, downpour ~*v* flood, overwhelm

**de luxe** rich, sumptuous; superior in quality

**delve** *v* (with *into*) search inten-

───────────────── THESAURUS ─────────────────

**delete** blot out, cancel, cross out, cut out, dele, edit, efface, erase, expunge, obliterate, remove, rub out

**deliberate** *adj* calculated, conscious, considered, designed, intentional, planned, premeditated, purposeful, studied, thoughtful, wilful ~*v* cogitate, consider, consult, debate, discuss, meditate, mull over, ponder, reflect, think, weigh

**deliberation** care, carefulness, caution, circumspection, consideration, coolness, forethought, meditation, prudence, purpose, reflection, speculation, study, thought, wariness

**delicacy** elegance, exquisiteness, fineness, lightness, nicety, precision, subtlety; dainty, luxury, relish, savoury, titbit, treat

**delicate** accurate, deft, detailed, exquisite, minute, precise, skilled; ailing, debilitated, flimsy, fragile, frail, sickly, slender, slight, tender, weak; considerate, diplomatic, discreet, sensitive, tactful

**delicious** appetizing, choice, dainty, luscious, mouthwatering, sa-

voury, tasty, toothsome

**delight** *v* amuse, charm, cheer, divert, enchant, gratify, please, ravish, rejoice, satisfy, thrill ~*n* ecstasy, enjoyment, gladness, gratification, happiness, joy, pleasure, rapture, transport

**delightful** agreeable, amusing, captivating, charming, delectable, engaging, enjoyable, entertaining, heavenly, pleasant, pleasurable, thrilling

**deliver** bear, bring, carry, cart, convey, distribute, transport; cede, commit, give up, grant, hand over, make over, relinquish, resign, surrender, transfer, turn over, yield

**delivery** consignment, conveyance, dispatch, distribution, handing over, surrender, transfer, transmission, transmittal

**delude** beguile, cheat, con *Inf*, deceive, dupe, fool, hoax, hoodwink, kid *Inf*, misguide, mislead, take in *Inf*, trick

**deluge** cataclysm, downpour, flood, overflowing, spate, torrent

**de luxe** choice, costly, elegant, ex-

sively; dig

**demagogue** *n* mob leader or agitator

**demand** *v* ask as giving an order; call for as due, necessary ~*n* urgent request; call for **demanding** *adj* requiring effort

**demean** *v* degrade, lower

**demeanour** *n* conduct, bearing

**demented** *adj* mad, crazy **dementia** *n* mental deterioration

**demerit** *n* undesirable quality

**demi-** *comb. form* half, as in **demigod**

**demijohn** *n* large bottle

**demilitarize** *v* prohibit military presence

**demise** *n* death; conveyance by will or lease

**demobilize** *v* disband (troops);

discharge (soldier)

**democracy** *n* government by the people or their elected representatives; state so governed **democrat** *n* advocate of democracy **democratic** *adj*

**demolish** *v* knock to pieces; destroy utterly **demolition** *n*

**demon** *n* devil, evil spirit

**demonstrate** *v* show by reasoning, prove; describe, explain; make exhibition of support, protest etc.

**demonstrable** *adj* **demonstration** *n* **demonstrative** *adj* expressing feelings; pointing out; conclusive **demonstrator** *n* one who takes part in a public demonstration; assistant in laboratory etc.

**demoralize** *v* deprive of courage; undermine morally

———— T H E S A U R U S ————

clusive, expensive, grand, opulent, palatial, rich, select, special, splendid, splendiferous *Facetious,* sumptuous, superior

**demand** *v* ask, challenge, inquire, interrogate, question, request; call for, cry out for, entail, involve, necessitate, need, require, take, want ~*n* bidding, charge, inquiry, interrogation, order, question, request, requisition

**demanding** challenging, difficult, exacting, exhausting, hard, taxing, tough, trying

**demeanour** air, bearing, behaviour, carriage, conduct, deportment, manner, mien

**democracy** commonwealth, government by the people, representative government, republic

**democratic** autonomous, egalitarian, popular, populist, representative, republican, self-governing

**demolish** bulldoze, destroy, dis-

mantle, flatten, knock down, level, overthrow, pulverize, raze, ruin, tear down, trash *Sl;* annihilate, defeat, destroy, overthrow, overturn, undo, wreck

**demonstrable** attestable, certain, evident, evincible, incontrovertible, indubitable, irrefutable, obvious, positive, self-evident, undeniable, unmistakable, verifiable

**demonstrate** display, establish, evidence, exhibit, indicate, prove, show, testify to; describe, explain, illustrate, make clear, show how, teach; march, parade, picket, protest, rally

**demonstration** confirmation, display, evidence, exhibition, expression, illustration, manifestation, proof, testimony, validation; explanation, exposition, presentation, test, trial; march, mass lobby, parade, picket, protest, rally, sit-in

**demoralize** cripple, daunt, deject,

**demote** v reduce in rank **demotion** n

**demur** v -murring, -murred make difficulties, object ~n demurring

**demure** adj reserved

**den** n hole of wild beast; small room, esp. study

**denigrate** v belittle

**denim** n strong cotton fabric

**denizen** n inhabitant

**denomination** n particular sect or church; name, esp. of class or group **denominator** n divisor in fraction

**denote** v stand for; show

**denouement** n unravelling of plot

**denounce** v speak violently against; accuse **denunciation** n

**dense** adj thick, compact; stupid **density** n

**dent** n/v (make) hollow or mark by blow or pressure

**dental** adj of teeth or dentistry

**dentist** n surgeon who attends to teeth **dentistry** n art of dentist **denture** n (usu. pl) set of false teeth

**denude** v strip, make bare

**deny** v -nying, -nied declare untrue; contradict; reject; refuse to give **denial** n

**deodorant** n substance to mask odour

**depart** v go away; start out; vary; die **departure** n

**department** n division; branch **departmental** adj

——————— THESAURUS ———————

**depress,** disconcert, discourage, dishearten, dispirit, undermine, unnerve, weaken

**demure** decorous, diffident, grave, modest, reserved, reticent, retiring, sedate, shy, sober, staid, unassuming

**den** cave, cavern, haunt, hide-out, hole, lair, shelter

**denial** contradiction, disavowal, disclaimer, dismissal, dissent, negation, prohibition, rebuff, refusal, renunciation, repudiation, repulse, retraction, veto

**denigrate** belittle, besmirch, blacken, calumniate, decry, defame, disparage, impugn, knock Inf, malign, revile, rubbish Inf, run down, slag (off) Sl, slander, vilify

**denote** betoken, designate, express, imply, import, indicate, mark, mean, show, signify, typify

**denounce** accuse, attack, castigate, censure, condemn, decry, impugn, proscribe, revile, stigmatize, vilify

**dense** close, compact, compressed, condensed, heavy, impenetrable, opaque, solid, substantial, thick, thickset

**dent** n chip, crater, depression, dimple, dip, hollow, impression, indentation, pit ~v depress, dint, hollow, imprint, press in, push in

**deny** contradict, disagree with, disprove, oppose, rebuff, refute; abjure, disavow, discard, disclaim, disown, recant, reject, renege, renounce, repudiate, retract, revoke

**depart** decamp, disappear, escape, exit, go, go away, leave, migrate, quit, remove, retire, retreat, set forth, start out, vanish, withdraw

**department** district, division, province, region, sector; branch, bureau, division, office, section, station, subdivision, unit

**departure** exit, exodus, going, leave-taking, leaving, removal, retirement, withdrawal; branching out, change, difference, innovation, novelty, shift, variation

**depend** v (usu. with on) rely entirely; live; be contingent **dependable** adj reliable **dependant** n one who relies on another **dependent** adj depending on **dependence, dependency** n

**depict** v give picture of; describe **depiction** n

**deplete** v empty; reduce **depletion** n

**deplore** v lament, regret; denounce **deplorable** adj

**deploy** v organize (troops) in battle formation **deployment** n

**depopulate** v (cause to) be reduced in population **depopulation** n

**deport** v expel, banish **deportation** n

**deportment** n behaviour

**depose** v remove from office; make statement on oath

**deposit** v set down; give into safe keeping; fall ~n thing deposited; money given in part payment; sediment **deposition** n statement written and attested; act of deposing or depositing **depositor** n **depository** n

**depot** n storehouse

**deprave** v make bad, corrupt **depravity** n

**deprecate** v express disapproval of

**depreciate** v (cause to) fall in value, price; belittle **depreciation** n

**depress** v affect with low spirits; lower **depression** n hollow; low spirits; low state of trade

**deprive** v dispossess **deprivation** n

——— THESAURUS ———

**depend** bank on, build upon, calculate on, confide in, count on, lean on, reckon on, rely upon, trust in, turn to; to be based on, be contingent on, be determined by, be subject to, hinge on, rest on

**dependent** counting on, defenceless, helpless, immature, reliant, relying on, vulnerable, weak; conditional, contingent, depending, determined by, liable to, relative, subject to

**deplete** consume, decrease, drain, empty, evacuate, exhaust, expend, impoverish, lessen, milk, reduce, use up

**deplorable** calamitous, dire, disastrous, distressing, grievous, lamentable, melancholy, miserable, pitiable, regrettable, sad, unfortunate, wretched; disgraceful, disreputable, execrable, opprobrious, reprehensible, scandalous, shameful

**deplore** bemoan, bewail, grieve for, lament, mourn, regret, rue, sorrow over; abhor, censure, condemn, denounce, deprecate, disapprove of, object to

**depose** break, cashier, degrade, demote, dethrone, dismiss, displace, downgrade, remove from office

**deposit** v drop, lay, locate, place, precipitate, put, settle, sit down ~n down payment, instalment, money (in bank), part payment, pledge, retainer, security, stake, warranty

**depot** repository, storehouse, warehouse

**deprave** corrupt, debase, debauch, degrade, demoralize, pervert, seduce, vitiate

**depreciate** decrease, deflate, devalue, lessen, lose value, lower, reduce

**depreciation** depression, devaluation, drop, fall, slump; belittlement, derogation, detraction, disparagement

**depress** cast down, chill, damp,

**deprived** *adj* lacking adequate food, care, amenities etc.

**dept.** department

**depth** *n* (degree of) deepness; deep place; intensity

**deputy** *n* assistant; delegate **deputation** *n* **deputize** *v* act as deputy

**derange** *v* put out of place, order; make insane

**deregulate** *v* remove regulations or controls from

**derelict** *adj* abandoned; falling into ruins **dereliction** *n* neglect of duty; abandonment

**deride** *v* treat with contempt, ridicule **derision** *n* **derisive** *adj*

**derisory** *adj*

**derive** *v* get, come from **derivation** *n* **derivative** *adj*

**dermatitis** *n* inflammation of skin

**derogatory** *adj* belittling

**derv** *n* diesel oil for road vehicles

**descant** *n Mus* decorative variation to basic melody

**descend** *v* come or go down; spring from; be transmitted; attack **descendant** *n* person descended from an ancestor **descent** *n*

**describe** *v* give detailed account of **description** *n* **descriptive** *adj*

**desecrate** *v* violate sanctity of; profane

—————————————— THESAURUS ——————————————

**deject**, desolate, discourage, dishearten, dispirit, oppress, sadden, weigh down

**depression** dejection, despair, despondency, dolefulness, downheartedness, gloominess, hopelessness, low spirits, melancholy, sadness; *Commerce* downturn, economic decline, hard *or* bad times, inactivity, lowness, recession, slump, stagnation

**deprive** bereave, despoil, dispossess, divest, expropriate, rob, strip, wrest

**deprived** bereft, denuded, destitute, disadvantaged, forlorn, in need, in want, lacking, needy, poor

**depth** abyss, deepness, drop, extent, measure, profundity

**deputation** commission, delegates, delegation, embassy, envoys, legation

**deputize** act for, stand in for, understudy

**deputy** agent, ambassador, commissioner, legate, lieutenant, proxy, representative, substitute, surrogate

**derelict** abandoned, deserted, discarded, forsaken, neglected, ruined

**derisory** contemptible, insulting, laughable, ludicrous, outrageous, preposterous, ridiculous

**derivation** ancestry, basis, beginning, descent, etymology, foundation, genealogy, origin, root, source

**derive** collect, deduce, draw, elicit, extract, follow, gain, gather, get, glean, infer, obtain, procure, receive, trace

**descend** alight, dismount, drop, fall, go down, move down, plunge, sink, subside, tumble; be handed down, be passed down, derive, issue, originate, proceed, spring

**descent** coming down, drop, fall, plunge, swoop; ancestry, extraction, family tree, genealogy, heredity, lineage, origin, parentage

**describe** characterize, define, depict, detail, explain, express, illustrate, narrate, portray, recount, relate, report, specify, tell

**description** account, characterization, detail, explanation, narrative, portrayal, report, representation, sketch

**desert**[1] *n* uninhabited and barren region

**desert**[2] *v* abandon, leave; run away from service **deserter** *n* **desertion** *n*

**desert**[3] *n* (*usu. pl*) what is due as reward or punishment

**deserve** *v* show oneself worthy of

**design** *v* sketch; plan; intend ~*n* sketch; plan; decorative pattern; project **designer** *n/adj*

**designate** *v* name, appoint ~*adj* appointed but not yet installed

**desire** *v* wish, long for; ask for ~*n* longing; expressed wish; sexual ap-

petite **desirable** *n* worth having; attractive **desirability** *n* **desirous** *adj*

**desist** *v* cease, stop

**desk** *n* writing table

**desolate** *adj* uninhabited; neglected; solitary; forlorn ~*v* lay waste; overwhelm with grief **desolation** *n*

**despair** *v* lose hope ~*n* loss of all hope; cause of this

**desperate** *adj* reckless from despair; hopelessly bad **desperately** *adv* **desperation** *n* **desperado** *n* (*pl* **-does**) reckless, lawless person

**despise** *v* look down on as inferior

---

## THESAURUS

**desert**[1] solitude, waste, wasteland, wilderness, wilds

**desert**[2] *v* abandon, abscond, betray, decamp, defect, forsake, give up, jilt, leave, leave stranded, maroon, quit, rat (on), relinquish, renounce, resign, throw over, vacate, walk out on *Inf*

**deserter** absconder, defector, escapee, fugitive, runaway, traitor, truant

**deserve** be entitled to, be worthy of, earn, gain, justify, merit, procure, rate, warrant, win

**design** *v* describe, draft, draw, outline, plan, sketch, trace; aim, conceive, contrive, create, devise, intend, make, originate, plan, project, propose, purpose, scheme, think up ~*n* blueprint, draft, drawing, model, outline, plan, scheme, sketch

**designer** artificer, creator, deviser, inventor, originator, stylist

**desirable** advisable, agreeable, beneficial, eligible, enviable, good, pleasing, preferable, profitable, worthwhile; alluring, attractive, fascinating, fetching, seductive

**desire** *v* aspire to, covet, crave, fancy, hanker after, hope for, long for,

thirst for, want, wish for, yearn for; ask, entreat, importune, petition, request, solicit ~*n* appetite, craving, hankering, longing, need, thirst, want, wish; appetite, concupiscence, lasciviousness, lechery, libido, lust, lustfulness, passion

**desist** abstain, break off, cease, discontinue, end, forbear, give up, kick *Inf*, leave off, pause, refrain from, stop, suspend

**desolate** bare, barren, bleak, desert, dreary, godforsaken, ruined, solitary, uninhabited, waste, wild; abandoned, bereft, comfortless, dejected, depressing, despondent, dismal, downcast, forlorn, forsaken, gloomy, lonely, melancholy, miserable, wretched

**desolation** destruction, devastation, havoc, ravages, ruin, ruination

**despair** *v* despond, give up, lose heart, lose hope ~*n* anguish, depression, desperation, gloom, hopelessness, melancholy, misery, wretchedness

**desperate** dangerous, daring, determined, foolhardy, frantic, furious, hasty, headstrong, impetuous, madcap, rash, reckless, risky, vio-

**despicable** *adj* base, contemptible, vile

**despite** *prep* in spite of

**despoil** *v* plunder, rob

**despondent** *adj* dejected, depressed

**despot** *n* tyrant, oppressor **despotic** *adj* **despotism** *n*

**dessert** *n* sweet course, or fruit, served at end of meal

**destination** *n* place one is bound for

**destine** *v* ordain beforehand; set

apart **destiny** *n* fate

**destitute** *adj* in absolute want

**destroy** *v* ruin; put an end to; demolish **destroyer** *n* small, swift warship **destructible** *adj* **destruction** *n* ruin **destructive** *adj*

**desultory** *adj* aimless; unmethodical

**detach** *v* unfasten, separate **detachable** *adj* **detached** *adj* standing apart; disinterested **detachment** *n* aloofness; detaching; body of troops on special duty

———————— THESAURUS ————————

lent, wild; despairing, forlorn, hopeless, irrecoverable, irretrievable, wretched

**desperately** badly, dangerously, gravely, perilously, seriously, severely

**despise** abhor, deride, detest, disdain, disregard, flout, loathe, look down on, neglect, revile, scorn, slight

**despite** *prep* against, even with, in spite of, in the face of, notwithstanding, regardless of

**despondent** blue, dejected, depressed, despairing, disconsolate, discouraged, disheartened, dismal, doleful, down, downcast, gloomy, glum, hopeless, in despair, low, melancholy, miserable, morose, sad, sorrowful, wretched

**despotic** absolute, arbitrary, arrogant, authoritarian, autocratic, dictatorial, domineering, imperious, oppressive, tyrannical, unconstitutional

**destination** harbour, haven, journey's end, landing-place, resting-place, station, stop, terminus

**destine** allot, appoint, assign, consecrate, decree, design, devote, doom, earmark, fate, intend, mark

out, ordain, predetermine, purpose, reserve

**destiny** doom, fate, fortune, lot, portion

**destitute** distressed, down and out, flat broke *Inf*, impoverished, indigent, insolvent, moneyless, needy, penniless, poor

**destroy** annihilate, blow to bits, crush, demolish, desolate, devastate, dismantle, eradicate, kill, ravage, raze, ruin, shatter, slay, smash, trash *Sl*, wipe out, wreck

**destruction** demolition, devastation, downfall, end, extermination, havoc, liquidation, massacre, ruin, ruination, slaughter, wreckage, wrecking

**destructive** baleful, baneful, calamitous, cataclysmic, catastrophic, damaging, deadly, deleterious, detrimental, devastating, fatal, harmful, hurtful, injurious, lethal, pernicious, ruinous

**detach** cut off, disconnect, disengage, disentangle, disjoin, disunite, divide, free, isolate, loosen, remove, separate, sever, tear off, uncouple, unfasten

**detachment** aloofness, coolness, indifference, remoteness; detail, pa-

**detail** n particular; small or unimportant part; treatment of anything item by item; soldier assigned for duty ~v relate in full; appoint

**detain** v keep under restraint; keep waiting **detention** n

**detect** v find out or discover **detection** n **detective** n policeman detecting crime **detector** n

**détente** n lessening of international tension

**deter** v -terring, -terred discourage; prevent **deterrent** adj/n

**detergent** n/adj cleaning (substance)

**deteriorate** v become or make worse **deterioration** n

**determine** v decide; fix; be deciding factor in; come to an end; come to a decision **determination** n determining; resolute conduct; resolve **determined** adj resolute

**detest** v hate, loathe **detestable** adj

**dethrone** v remove from position of authority

**detonate** v (cause to) explode **detonation** n **detonator** n

**detour** n roundabout way

**detract** v take away (a part) from, diminish **detractor** n

**detriment** n harm done, loss, damage **detrimental** adj

———— THESAURUS ————

trol squad, unit

**detail** n aspect, component, count, element, fact, factor, feature, item, particular, point, respect, specific, technicality ~v allocate, appoint, assign, charge, commission, delegate, detach, send

**detain** check, delay, hinder, hold up, impede, keep, keep back, retard, slow up (or down), stay, stop; arrest, confine, hold, intern, restrain

**detect** catch, descry, distinguish, identify, note, notice, observe, recognize, scent, spot

**detective** C.I.D. man, constable, investigator, private eye, sleuth Inf

**detention** confinement, custody, delay, hindrance, holding back, imprisonment, restraint

**deter** caution, check, damp, daunt, debar, discourage, dissuade, frighten, hinder, inhibit from, intimidate, prevent, prohibit, put off, restrain, stop, talk out of

**detergent** n cleaner, cleanser ~adj cleaning, cleansing, purifying

**deteriorate** decline, degenerate,

degrade, deprave, depreciate, go downhill Inf, lower, spoil, worsen

**determination** backbone, constancy, conviction, dedication, doggedness, drive, firmness, fortitude, perseverance, persistence, resolution, resolve, single-mindedness, steadfastness, tenacity, willpower

**determine** arbitrate, conclude, decide, end, finish, fix upon, ordain, regulate, settle

**determined** bent on, constant, dogged, firm, fixed, intent, persistent, purposeful, resolute, set on, single-minded, steadfast, tenacious, unflinching, unwavering

**deterrent** check, curb, discouragement, disincentive, hindrance, impediment, obstacle, restraint

**detest** abominate, despise, execrate, hate, loathe

**detour** bypass, byway, diversion

**detract** diminish, lessen, lower, reduce, take away from

**detriment** damage, disservice, harm, hurt, injury, loss, mischief, prejudice

**detrimental** adverse, baleful, del-

**deuce** *n* card with two spots; *Tennis* forty all; in exclamatory phrases, the devil

**devalue, devaluate** *v* reduce in value **devaluation** *n*

**devastate** *v* lay waste; ravage **devastated** *adj* extremely shocked **devastation** *n*

**develop** *v* developing, developed bring to maturity; elaborate; evolve; treat photographic film to bring out image; improve or change use of (land); grow to maturer state **developer** *n* **development** *n*

**deviate** *v* diverge **deviant** *n/adj* (person) deviating from normal, esp. in sexual practices **deviation** *n*

**devious** *adj* deceitful; roundabout **deviousness** *n*

**device** *n* contrivance; scheme

**devil** *n* personified spirit of evil; person of great wickedness, cruelty etc.; *Inf* fellow; *Inf* something difficult or annoying **devilish** *adj* **devilment** *n* **devilry** *n* **devil-may-care** *adj* happy-go-lucky

**devise** *v* plan

**devoid** *adj* (*usu. with* **of**) empty

—————————————— THESAURUS ——————————————

eterious, destructive, harmful, inimical, injurious, pernicious, prejudicial, unfavourable

**devastate** demolish, desolate, despoil, destroy, lay waste, level, pillage, plunder, ravage, raze, ruin, sack, spoil, total *Sl*, trash *Sl*, waste, wreck

**devastation** demolition, depredation, desolation, destruction, havoc, pillage, plunder, ravages, ruin, ruination

**develop** advance, cultivate, evolve, foster, grow, mature, progress, promote, prosper, ripen; amplify, augment, broaden, dilate upon, elaborate, enlarge, expand, unfold, work out

**development** advance, advancement, evolution, expansion, growth, improvement, increase, maturity, progress, progression, spread, unfolding; change, circumstance, event, happening, incident, issue, occurrence, outcome, result, situation, upshot

**deviate** avert, bend, deflect, depart, differ, digress, diverge, drift, err, part, stray, swerve, turn, turn aside, vary, veer, wander

**deviation** alteration, change, deflection, departure, digression, discrepancy, disparity, divergence, inconsistency, irregularity, shift, variance, variation

**device** apparatus, appliance, contraption, contrivance, gadget, gimmick, gismo *or* gizmo *Sl*, implement, instrument, invention, tool, utensil; artifice, design, dodge, expedient, gambit, manoeuvre, plan, ploy, project, purpose, ruse, scheme, shift, stratagem, stunt, trick

**devil** demon, fiend, Satan; beast, brute, demon, monster, ogre, rogue, savage, terror, villain

**devious** calculating, deceitful, dishonest, evasive, indirect, insidious, insincere, scheming, sly, surreptitious, treacherous, tricky, underhand, wily

**devise** arrange, conceive, concoct, construct, contrive, design, dream up, form, formulate, frame, imagine, invent, plan, plot, prepare, project, scheme, think up

**devoid** barren, bereft, deficient, denuded, destitute, empty, free from, lacking, unprovided with, va-

## DICTIONARY

**devolve** v (cause to) pass on to another **devolution** n devolving

**devote** v give up exclusively (to person, purpose etc.) **devoted** adj loving **devotee** n ardent enthusiast **devotion** n deep affection; dedication; pl prayers

**devour** v eat greedily

**devout** adj deeply religious

**dew** n moisture from air deposited as small drops at night

**dexterity** n manual skill **dexterous** adj

**diabetes** n various disorders characterized by excretion of abnormal amount of urine **diabetic** n/adj

**diabolic** adj devilish **diabolical** adj Inf extremely bad

**diadem** n crown

**diagnosis** n (pl -ses) identification of disease from symptoms **diagnose** v

**diagonal** adj/n (line) from corner to corner

**diagram** n drawing, figure, to illustrate something

**dial** n face of clock etc.; plate marked with graduations on which pointer moves; numbered disc on front of telephone ~v dialling, **dialled** operate telephone

**dialect** n characteristic speech of district

**dialogue** n conversation

**dialysis** n (pl **dialyses**) Med filtering of blood through membrane to remove waste products

**diameter** n (length of) straight line through centre of circle **diametrically** adv completely

**diamond** n very hard and brilliant precious stone; rhomboid figure; suit at cards

**diaphragm** n muscle between abdomen and chest

**diarrhoea** n excessive looseness of the bowels

**diary** n daily record of events; book for this

**diatribe** n violently bitter verbal

## THESAURUS

cant, void, wanting, without

**devote** allot, apply, appropriate, assign, commit, concern oneself, dedicate, enshrine, give, pledge, reserve

**devoted** ardent, caring, committed, concerned, constant, dedicated, devout, faithful, fond, loving, loyal, staunch, steadfast, true

**devour** bolt, consume, cram, eat, gobble, gorge, gulp, guzzle, pig out on Sl, stuff, swallow, wolf

**devout** godly, holy, orthodox, pious, prayerful, pure, religious, reverent, saintly

**dexterity** adroitness, artistry, deftness, expertise, facility, finesse, handiness, knack, mastery, neatness, nimbleness, proficiency, skill,

smoothness, touch

**diagnose** analyse, determine, distinguish, identify, interpret, pinpoint, pronounce, recognize

**diagnosis** analysis, examination

**diagonal** adj angled, cross, crossways, crosswise, oblique, slanting

**diagram** chart, drawing, figure, layout, outline, plan, representation, sketch

**dialect** accent, idiom, jargon, language, patois, pronunciation, provincialism, speech, tongue, vernacular

**dialogue** communication, conference, conversation, converse, discourse, discussion, interlocution

**diary** appointment book, chronicle, daily record, day-to-day account,

attack, denunciation

**dice** pl n (sing **dice**, **die**) cubes each with six sides marked one to six for games of chance ~v gamble with dice; Cookery cut vegetables into small cubes

**dichotomy** n division into two parts

**dictate** v say or read for another to transcribe; prescribe; impose ~n bidding **dictation** n **dictator** n absolute ruler **dictatorial** adj **dictatorship** n

**diction** n choice and use of words; enunciation

**dictionary** n book listing, alphabetically, words with meanings etc.

**did** past tense of DO

**die**[1] v dying, died cease to live; end; Inf look forward (to) **die-hard** n/adj (person) resisting change

**die**[2] n shaped block to form metal in forge, press etc.

**diesel** adj pert. to internal-combustion engine using oil as fuel ~n this engine; the fuel

**diet** n restricted or regulated course of feeding; kind of food lived on ~v follow a diet, as to lose weight **dietary** adj

**differ** v be unlike; disagree **difference** n unlikeness; point of unlikeness; disagreement; remainder left after subtraction **different** adj **differently** adv

**differential** adj varying with cir-

engagement book, journal

**dictate** read out, say, speak, transmit, utter; command, decree, direct, enjoin, impose, lay down, ordain, order, prescribe

**dictator** absolute ruler, autocrat, despot, oppressor, tyrant

**diction** language, phraseology, phrasing, style, usage; articulation, delivery, elocution, enunciation, inflection, intonation, pronunciation, speech

**dictionary** concordance, encyclopedia, glossary, lexicon, vocabulary, wordbook

**die** croak Sl, decease, depart, expire, finish, kick the bucket Sl, pass away, perish; decay, decline, disappear, dwindle, ebb, end, fade, lapse, pass, sink, vanish, wane, wilt, wither

**die-hard** n fanatic, old fogy, reactionary, zealot ~adj dyed-in-the-wool, immovable, inflexible, intransigent, reactionary

**diet** n abstinence, dietary, fast, re-

gime, regimen; commons, fare, food, nourishment, provisions, rations, sustenance ~v fast, lose weight, reduce, slim

**differ** be dissimilar, be distinct, contradict, contrast, depart from, diverge, run counter to, stand apart, vary

**difference** alteration, change, contrast, deviation, differentiation, discrepancy, disparity, dissimilarity, distinction, divergence, diversity, variation, variety; contention, exception, idiosyncrasy, peculiarity, singularity; argument, clash, conflict, contention, contretemps, controversy, debate, disagreement, discordance, dispute, quarrel, row, strife, tiff, wrangle

**different** altered, at variance, changed, clashing, contrasting, deviating, disparate, dissimilar, divergent, diverse, inconsistent, opposed, unlike; assorted, diverse, manifold, many, miscellaneous, multifarious, numerous, several,

cumstances ~n mechanism in car etc. allowing back wheels to revolve at different speeds; difference between two rates of pay **differentiate** v serve to distinguish between, make different; discriminate

**difficult** adj requiring effort, skill etc.; not easy; obscure **difficulty** n difficult task, problem; embarrassment; hindrance; trouble

**diffident** adj lacking confidence

**diffuse** v spread slowly ~adj widely spread; loose, wordy **diffusion** n

**dig** v digging, dug work with spade; turn up with spade; excavate; thrust into ~n piece of digging; thrust; jibe; pl Inf lodgings

**digest** v prepare (food) in stomach etc. for assimilation; bring into

handy form by summarizing ~n methodical summary **digestible** adj **digestion** n **digestive** adj

**digit** n finger or toe; numeral **digital** adj

**dignity** n stateliness, gravity; worthiness **dignify** v **-fying, -fied** give dignity to **dignitary** n holder of high office

**digress** v deviate from subject **digression** n

**dike** n see DYKE

**dilapidated** adj in ruins

**dilate** v widen, expand **dilation** n

**dilemma** n position offering choice only between unwelcome alternatives

**dilettante** n (pl dilettanti, -tes) person who enjoys fine arts as pas-

———————— THESAURUS ————————

some, sundry, varied, various

**differentiate** contrast, discern, discriminate, distinguish, mark off, separate, tell apart

**difficult** arduous, demanding, formidable, hard, laborious, onerous, painful, strenuous, toilsome, uphill, wearisome

**difficulty** awkwardness, hardship, labour, pain, painfulness, strain, tribulation; deep water, dilemma, distress, fix Inf, hot water Inf, jam Inf, mess, pickle Inf, plight, predicament, quandary, spot Inf, tight spot, trial, trouble

**diffident** backward, bashful, doubtful, hesitant, insecure, meek, modest, reluctant, reserved, self-conscious, sheepish, shrinking, shy, timid, unsure, withdrawn

**dig** v break up, burrow, delve, excavate, grub, hoe, hollow out, mine, penetrate, pierce, quarry, scoop, till, tunnel, turn over ~n jab, poke, prod, punch, thrust; barb, cutting

remark, gibe, insult, jeer, quip, taunt, wisecrack Inf

**digest** absorb, assimilate, concoct, dissolve, incorporate; absorb, assimilate, consider, contemplate, grasp, master, meditate, ponder, study, take in, understand

**dignitary** notability, notable, personage, public figure, V.I.P., worthy

**dignity** decorum, grandeur, gravity, majesty, nobility, propriety, solemnity, stateliness

**digress** depart, deviate, diverge, drift, expatiate, ramble, stray, turn aside, wander

**dilapidated** battered, broken-down, crumbling, decayed, decaying, decrepit, falling apart, in ruins, neglected, ramshackle, rickety, ruined, run-down, shabby, shaky, tumble-down, worn-out

**dilemma** difficulty, embarrassment, mess, perplexity, plight, predicament, problem, puzzle, quan-

time; dabbler

**diligent** *adj* hard-working **diligently** *adv* **diligence** *n*

**dill** *n* herb with medicinal seeds

**dilute** *v* reduce (liquid) in strength, esp. by adding water **dilution** *n*

**dim** *adj* **dimmer, dimmest** faint, not bright; mentally dull; unfavourable ~*v* **dimming, dimmed** make, grow dim **dimly** *adv*

**dime** *n* US 10-cent piece

**dimension** *n* measurement, size

**diminish** *v* lessen **diminutive** *adj* very small

**diminuendo** *adj/adv Mus* (of sound) dying away

**dimple** *n* small hollow in surface of skin, esp. of cheek

**din** *n* continuous roar of confused noises ~*v* **dinning, dinned** ram (fact, opinion etc.) into

**dine** *v* eat dinner **diner** *n*

**dinghy** *n* small open boat; collapsible rubber boat

**dingo** *n* (*pl* **-goes**) Aust. wild dog

**dingy** *adj* dirty-looking, dull

**dinner** *n* chief meal of the day; official banquet

**dinosaur** *n* extinct reptile, often of gigantic size

**dint** *n* **by dint of** by means of current

**diocese** *n* district, jurisdiction of bishop

**diode** *n Electronics* device for converting alternating current to direct current

**dip** *v* **dipping, dipped** plunge or be plunged partly or for a moment into liquid; take up in ladle, bucket etc.; direct headlights of vehicle downwards; go down; slope downwards ~*n* act of dipping; bathe; downward slope; hollow

**diphtheria** *n* infectious disease

---

## THESAURUS

dary, spot *Inf,* strait

**diligence** activity, application, assiduity, attention, attentiveness, care, constancy, industry, perseverance

**diligent** active, assiduous, attentive, busy, careful, conscientious, constant, earnest, hard-working, indefatigable, industrious, laborious, persevering, persistent, studious, tireless

**dilute** *v* adulterate, cut, thin (out), water down, weaken

**dim** *adj* cloudy, dark, darkish, dusky, grey, overcast, poorly lit, shadowy; dense, doltish, dozy *Brit inf,* dull, obtuse, slow, stupid, thick ~*v* blur, cloud, darken, dull, fade, lower, obscure, tarnish, turn down

**diminish** abate, contract, curtail, cut, decrease, lessen, lower, reduce, retrench, shrink, weaken

**diminutive** little, midget, miniature, minute, petite, pygmy *or* pigmy, small, teensy-weensy, tiny, wee

**din** babel, clamour, clangour, clash, clatter, commotion, crash, hullabaloo, noise, outcry, pandemonium, racket, row, shout, uproar

**dingy** colourless, dark, dim, dirty, discoloured, drab, dreary, dull, dusky, faded, gloomy, grimy, murky, obscure, seedy, shabby, soiled, sombre

**dinner** banquet, collation, feast, meal, refection, repast, spread *Inf*

**dip** *v* bathe, douse, duck, dunk, immerse, plunge, rinse, souse; ladle, scoop, spoon ~*n* douche, drenching, ducking, immersion, plunge, soaking; bathe, dive, plunge, swim; basin, concavity, depression, hole, hollow, incline, slope; decline, drop, fall, lowering, sag, slip, slump

causing breathing difficulties

**diphthong** *n* union of two vowel sounds

**diploma** *n* document vouching for person's proficiency

**diplomacy** *n* management of international relations; tactful dealing **diplomat** *n* **diplomatic** *adj*

**dipper** *n* ladle, scoop; bird (water ouzel)

**dipsomania** *n* uncontrollable craving for alcohol **dipsomaniac** *n/adj*

**dire** *adj* terrible; urgent

**direct** *v* control, manage, order; point out the way; aim ~*adj* frank; straight; immediate; lineal **direction** *n* directing; aim; instruction **direc-**

**tive** *adj/n* **directly** *adj* **directness** *n*

**director** *n* one who directs, esp. a film; member of board managing company **directorial** *adj* **directorship** *n* **directory** *n* book of names, addresses, streets etc.

**dirge** *n* song of mourning

**dirk** *n* short dagger

**dirt** *n* filth; soil; obscene material **dirty** *adj* unclean; obscene; unfair; dishonest

**dis-** *comb. form* negation, opposition, deprivation; in many verbs indicates undoing of the action of simple verb

**disable** *v* make unable; cripple, maim **disabled** *adj* **disability** *n*

**disabuse** *v* undeceive, disillusion;

——— THESAURUS ———

**diplomacy** statecraft, statesmanship; craft, delicacy, discretion, finesse, savoir-faire, skill, subtlety, tact

**diplomat** go-between, mediator, moderator, negotiator, politician

**diplomatic** adept, discreet, polite, politic, prudent, sensitive, subtle, tactful

**dire** alarming, awful, calamitous, cataclysmic, catastrophic, cruel, disastrous, horrible, ruinous, terrible, woeful; dismal, dreadful, fearful, gloomy, grim, ominous, portentous

**direct** *v* administer, advise, conduct, control, govern, guide, lead, manage, oversee, preside over, regulate, rule, run, superintend, supervise; guide, indicate, lead, show ~*adj* candid, frank, honest, open, outspoken, sincere, straight, upfront *Inf*

**direction** administration, charge, command, control, government, guidance, leadership, management,

order, oversight, supervision; aim, bearing, course, line, path, road, route, track, way

**directly** exactly, precisely, straight, unswervingly; candidly, face-to-face, honestly, in person, openly, personally, plainly, point-blank, straightforwardly, truthfully, unequivocally

**director** administrator, chairman, chief, controller, executive, governor, head, leader, manager, organizer, principal, producer

**dirt** dust, filth, grime, impurity, mire, muck, mud, slime, smudge, stain, tarnish; clay, earth, loam, soil

**dirty** filthy, foul, grimy, grotty *Sl*, grubby, messy, mucky, muddy, nasty, polluted, soiled, sullied, unclean; corrupt, crooked, dishonest, fraudulent, illegal, treacherous, unfair, unscrupulous, unsporting

**disability** affliction, ailment, defect, disorder, handicap, impairment, infirmity, malady

**disable** cripple, damage, handicap,

free from error

**disadvantage** n drawback; hindrance ~v handicap **disadvantaged** adj deprived, discriminated against **disadvantageous** adj

**disaffected** adj ill-disposed **disaffection** n

**disagree** v -greeing, -greed be at variance; conflict; (of food etc.) have bad effect on **disagreeable** adj **disagreement** n

**disallow** v reject as invalid

**disappear** v cease to be visible; cease to exist **disappearance** n

**disappoint** v fail to fulfil (hope) **disappointment** n

**disarm** v deprive of weapons; win over **disarming** adj removing hostility, suspicion **disarmament** n

**disarray** v throw into disorder ~n disorderliness

**disaster** n sudden or great misfortune **disastrous** adj

**disband** v (cause to) cease to function as a group

**disbelieve** v reject as false

**disburse** v pay out money

**disc** n thin, flat, circular object; record **disc jockey** announcer playing records

**discard** v reject; cast off

**discern** v make out; distinguish

─────────── THESAURUS ───────────

immobilize, impair, incapacitate, paralyse, prostrate, unfit, unman, weaken

**disabled** bedridden, crippled, handicapped, incapacitated, infirm, lame, mangled, mutilated, paralysed, weak

**disadvantage** damage, detriment, disservice, harm, hurt, injury, loss, prejudice

**disagree** be discordant, be dissimilar, conflict, contradict, counter, depart, deviate, differ, diverge, vary

**disagreeable** bad-tempered, brusque, churlish, cross, difficult, disobliging, ill-natured, irritable, peevish, rude, surly, unfriendly, unlikable, unpleasant

**disagreement** difference, discrepancy, disparity, divergence, incompatibility, incongruity, variance; argument, clash, conflict, debate, difference, discord, dispute, dissent, division, falling out, quarrel, row, squabble, wrangle

**disappear** abscond, depart, drop out of sight, ebb, escape, fade away,

flee, fly, go, pass, recede, retire, wane, withdraw; cease, die out, dissolve, end, evaporate, expire, fade, pass away, perish, vanish

**disappearance** departure, desertion, eclipse, evanescence, evaporation, fading, flight, loss, passing, vanishing

**disappoint** dash, deceive, disenchant, dishearten, disillusion, dismay, dissatisfy, fail, let down, sadden, vex

**disappointment** discontent, disenchantment, disillusionment, distress, failure, frustration, regret

**disarray** confusion, dismay, disorder, disunity, indiscipline, unruliness, upset

**disaster** accident, adversity, blow, calamity, catastrophe, misadventure, mischance, misfortune, mishap, reverse, ruin, stroke, tragedy, trouble

**disastrous** adverse, catastrophic, destructive, detrimental, devastating, dire, dreadful, fatal, hapless, harmful, ill-fated, ill-starred, ruinous, terrible, tragic, unfortunate,

**discernible** adj **discerning** adj discriminating

**discharge** v release; dismiss; emit; perform (duties), fulfil (obligations); fire off; unload; pay ~n discharging; being discharged

**disciple** n follower of a teacher

**discipline** n training that produces orderliness, obedience, self-control; system of rules etc.; punishment ~v train; punish **disciplinarian** n person practising strict discipline **disciplinary** adj

**disclaim** v deny, renounce **disclaimer** n

**disclose** v make known **disclosure** n

**disco** n club etc. for dancing to recorded music

**discolour** v stain

**discomfit** v embarrass

**discomfort** n inconvenience

**disconcert** v ruffle, upset

**disconnect** v break connection; stop supply of electricity, gas etc.

**disconsolate** adj very unhappy

**discontent** n lack of contentment

**discontinue** v bring to an end

**discord** n strife; disagreement of sounds **discordant** adj

——————— THESAURUS ———————

unlucky, untoward

**discard** abandon, cast aside, dispense with, dispose of, ditch *Sl*, drop, get rid of, jettison, reject, scrap, shed

**discharge** v absolve, acquit, allow to go, clear, free, liberate, pardon, release, set free; discard, dismiss, expel, oust; accomplish, carry out, do, execute, fulfil, observe, perform; detonate, explode, fire, let off, set off, shoot ~n blast, burst, discharging, explosion, firing, report, salvo, shot, volley; acquittal, clearance, liberation, pardon, release, remittance

**disciple** apostle, believer, convert, devotee, follower, learner, partisan, proselyte, pupil, student, supporter

**disciplinarian** despot, martinet, stickler, taskmaster, tyrant

**discipline** n drill, exercise, method, practice, regulation; conduct, control, orderliness, regulation, restraint, strictness; chastisement, correction, punishment ~v break in, bring up, check, control, drill, educate, exercise, form, govern, instruct, prepare, regulate,

restrain, train

**disclose** broadcast, communicate, confess, divulge, impart, leak, let slip, make known, make public, publish, relate, reveal, tell, unveil, utter

**discolour** fade, mar, mark, rust, soil, stain, streak, tarnish, tinge

**discomfort** ache, annoyance, disquiet, distress, hardship, hurt, irritation, nuisance, pain, soreness, trouble, uneasiness, vexation

**disconcert** abash, agitate, disturb, fluster, nonplus, perplex, perturb, rattle *Inf*, ruffle, take aback, trouble, unnerve, unsettle, upset, worry

**disconnect** cut off, detach, divide, part, separate, sever, take apart, uncouple

**disconsolate** dejected, desolate, despairing, dismal, forlorn, gloomy, heartbroken, hopeless, inconsolable, melancholy, miserable, sad, unhappy, wretched

**discontinue** abandon, axe *Inf*, break off, cease, drop, end, finish, give up, halt, interrupt, pause, put an end to, quit, refrain from, stop, suspend, terminate

**discount** v reject as unsuitable; deduct from usual price ~n amount deducted from cost

**discourage** v reduce confidence of; deter; show disapproval of **discouragement** n

**discourse** n conversation; speech ~v speak, converse

**discourteous** adj showing bad manners

**discover** v (be the first to) find; learn about for first time **discovery** n

**discredit** v damage reputation of; cast doubt on; reject as untrue ~n disgrace; doubt

**discreet** adj prudent, circumspect

**discrepancy** n variation, as between figures

**discrete** adj separate, distinct

─────────── THESAURUS ───────────

**discord** clashing, conflict, contention, difference, dispute, dissension, disunity, division, friction, opposition, row, rupture, strife, variance, wrangling; cacophony, din, dissonance, harshness, jangle, jarring

**discount** v disbelieve, disregard, ignore, overlook, pass over; lower, mark down, rebate, reduce, take off ~n allowance, concession, cut, cut price, deduction, rebate, reduction

**discourage** abash, awe, cast down, damp, dampen, dash, daunt, deject, demoralize, depress, dishearten, dismay, frighten, intimidate, overawe, psych out *Inf,* scare, unnerve

**discouragement** dejection, depression, despair, despondency, disappointment, dismay, hopelessness, low spirits, pessimism

**discourse** n chat, communication, conversation, converse, dialogue, discussion, speech, talk ~v confer, converse, debate, declaim, discuss, speak, talk

**discourteous** abrupt, badmannered, brusque, curt, illmannered, impolite, insolent, offhand, rude, uncivil, ungentlemanly, ungracious, unmannerly

**discover** come across, come upon, dig up, find, light upon, locate, turn up, uncover, unearth; ascertain, descry, detect, determine, discern, disclose, espy, find out, learn, notice, perceive, realize, recognize, reveal, see, spot, suss (out) *Sl,* uncover

**discovery** ascertainment, detection, disclosure, exploration, finding, introduction, location, origination, revelation; breakthrough, coup, find, findings, innovation, invention, secret

**discredit** v blame, bring into disrepute, censure, defame, degrade, detract from, disgrace, dishonour, disparage, reproach, slander, slur, smear, vilify; challenge, deny, disbelieve, discount, dispute, distrust, doubt, mistrust, question ~n aspersion, censure, disgrace, dishonour, disrepute, ignominy, ill-repute, odium, reproach, scandal, shame, slur, smear, stigma; distrust, doubt, mistrust, question, scepticism, suspicion

**discreet** careful, cautious, circumspect, considerate, diplomatic, discerning, guarded, judicious, politic, prudent, reserved, tactful, wary

**discrepancy** conflict, difference, disagreement, disparity, dissimilarity, dissonance, divergence, incongruity, inconsistency, variance, variation

**discretion** n quality of being discreet; freedom to act as one chooses **discretionary** adj

**discriminate** v show prejudice; distinguish between **discriminating** adj showing good taste **discrimination** n

**discursive** adj rambling

**discus** n disc-shaped object thrown in athletic competition

**discuss** v exchange opinions about; debate **discussion** n

**disdain** n/v scorn **disdainful** adj

**disease** n illness

**disembark** v land from ship etc.

**disembodied** adj (of spirit) released from bodily form

**disembowel** v -elling, -elled remove the entrails of

**disenchanted** adj disillusioned **disenchantment** n

**disengage** v release

**disfavour** n disapproval

**disfigure** v mar appearance of

**disgrace** n shame, dishonour ~v bring shame upon **disgraceful** adj **disgracefully** adv

**disgruntled** adj vexed; put out

**discretion** acumen, care, carefulness, caution, consideration, diplomacy, discernment, good sense, judgment, maturity, prudence, sagacity, tact, wariness

**discriminate** favour, show bias, show prejudice, single out, treat differently, victimize; assess, differentiate, discern, distinguish, evaluate, separate, sift

**discriminating** acute, astute, critical, cultivated, discerning, fastidious, keen, particular, refined, selective, sensitive, tasteful

**discrimination** bias, bigotry, favouritism, inequity, intolerance, prejudice, unfairness

**discuss** argue, confer, consider, converse, debate, deliberate, examine, go into, review, sift, thrash out, ventilate

**discussion** analysis, argument, colloquy, conference, consideration, consultation, conversation, debate, deliberation, dialogue, discourse, examination, exchange, review, scrutiny, symposium

**disdain** n arrogance, contempt, derision, dislike, hauteur, indifference, scorn, sneering

**disease** affliction, ailment, complaint, condition, disorder, ill health, illness, indisposition, infection, infirmity, malady, sickness, upset

**disembark** alight, arrive, get off, go ashore, land

**disfavour** disapprobation, disapproval, dislike, displeasure

**disfigure** blemish, damage, deface, deform, distort, injure, maim, mutilate, scar

**disgrace** n baseness, degradation, dishonour, disrepute, ignominy, infamy, odium, opprobrium, shame ~v abase, bring shame upon, defame, degrade, discredit, disfavour, dishonour, disparage, humiliate, reproach, shame, slur, stain, stigmatize, sully, taint

**disgraceful** contemptible, degrading, detestable, discreditable, dishonourable, disreputable, ignominious, infamous, low, mean, scandalous, shameful, shocking, unworthy

**disgruntled** annoyed, discontented, displeased, dissatisfied, grumpy, irritated, malcontent, peeved, peevish, petulant, put out,

**disguise** v change appearance of, make unrecognizable; conceal ~n device to conceal identity

**disgust** n/v (affect with) violent distaste, loathing

**dish** n shallow vessel for food; portion or variety of food ~v serve (up)

**dishearten** v weaken hope, enthusiasm etc.

**dishevelled** adj untidy

**dishonest** adj not honest or fair **dishonesty** n

**dishonour** v treat with disrespect ~n lack of respect; shame, disgrace **dishonourable** adj

**disillusion** v destroy ideals of ~n disenchantment

**disinfectant** n substance that prevents or removes infection **disinfect** v

**disinformation** n false information intended to mislead

**disingenuous** adj not sincere

**disinherit** v deprive of inheritance

**disintegrate** v fall to pieces

**disinterested** adj free from bias or partiality

**disjoint** v put out of joint; break the natural order of **disjointed** adj (of language) incoherent; disconnected

**disk** n computer storage device

**dislike** v consider unpleasant or disagreeable ~n feeling of not liking

———————— THESAURUS ————————

sulky, sullen

**disguise** v deceive, dissemble, dissimulate, fake, falsify, fudge, gloss over, misrepresent; cloak, conceal, cover, hide, mask, screen, secrete, shroud, veil ~n cloak, costume, cover, mask, screen, veil

**disgust** n abhorrence, abomination, antipathy, aversion, detestation, dislike, distaste, hatred, loathing, nausea, repugnance, repulsion, revulsion ~v nauseate, offend, outrage, put off, repel, revolt, sicken

**dish** bowl, plate, platter, salver; fare, food, recipe

**dishearten** cast down, crush, damp, dampen, dash, daunt, deject, depress, deter, discourage, dismay, dispirit

**dishonest** corrupt, crafty, deceitful, deceiving, designing, disreputable, double-dealing, false, fraudulent, lying, mendacious, perfidious, treacherous, unfair, unprincipled, unscrupulous, untrustworthy

**dishonesty** corruption, deceit, duplicity, falsehood, fraud, fraudulence, graft Inf, mendacity, sharp practice, treachery

**dishonour** v abase, blacken, corrupt, debase, debauch, defame, degrade, discredit, disgrace, shame, sully ~n discredit, disfavour, disgrace, disrepute, ignominy, infamy, obloquy, odium, opprobrium, reproach, scandal, shame

**dishonourable** base, despicable, discreditable, disgraceful, ignoble, infamous, scandalous, shameful

**disinfect** clean, cleanse, decontaminate, fumigate, purify, sterilize

**disinfectant** antiseptic, germicide, sterilizer

**disinherit** cut off, disown, dispossess, oust, repudiate

**disintegrate** break up, crumble, disunite, fall apart, fall to pieces, separate, shatter, splinter

**disinterested** detached, equitable, even-handed, impartial, impersonal, neutral, unbiased

**dislike** v abhor, abominate, be averse to, despise, detest, disapprove, disfavour, hate, loathe, ob-

**dislocate** v put out of joint **dislocation** n

**dislodge** v drive out from previous position

**disloyal** adj deserting one's allegiance **disloyalty** n

**dismal** adj depressing

**dismantle** v take apart

**dismay** v dishearten, daunt ~n consternation

**dismember** v tear limb from limb

**dismiss** v discharge from employment; send away; reject **dismissal** n

**dismissive** adj scornful

**dismount** v get off horse, bicycle

**disobey** v refuse or fail to obey **disobedience** n **disobedient** adj

**disorder** n confusion; ailment **disorderly** adj disorganized; unruly

**disorganized** adj lacking order, arrangement

**disorientate** v cause (someone) to lose his bearings, confuse **disorientation** n

**disown** v refuse to acknowledge

**disparage** v belittle

**disparity** n inequality; incongruity

**disparate** adj utterly different

**dispassionate** adj impartial

**dispatch, despatch** v send off

ject to, scorn, shun ~n animosity, animus, antagonism, antipathy, aversion, detestation, disapproval, disgust, distaste, enmity, hatred, hostility, loathing, repugnance

**disloyal** disaffected, faithless, false, perfidious, seditious, subversive, traitorous, treacherous, two-faced, unfaithful, unpatriotic, untrustworthy

**disloyalty** deceitfulness, double-dealing, falseness, falsity, inconstancy, infidelity, perfidy, treachery, treason

**dismal** bleak, cheerless, dark, depressing, despondent, discouraging, dreary, forlorn, gloomy, lugubrious, melancholy, sad, sombre, sorrowful

**dismay** v affright, alarm, appal, distress, frighten, horrify, paralyse, scare, terrify, unnerve ~n agitation, alarm, anxiety, apprehension, distress, dread, fear, fright, horror, panic, terror

**dismiss** cashier, discharge, lay off, oust, remove; disband, disperse, dissolve, free, let go, release, send away

**dismissal** discharge, expulsion, notice, removal, the (old) heave-ho Inf, the sack Inf; adjournment, end, release

**disobedience** insubordination, mutiny, noncompliance, recalcitrance, revolt, unruliness, waywardness

**disobedient** contrary, defiant, disorderly, insubordinate, intractable, mischievous, naughty, obstreperous, refractory, undisciplined, unruly, wilful

**disobey** defy, disregard, flout, ignore, infringe, overstep, rebel, resist, transgress, violate

**disorderly** chaotic, confused, disorganized, indiscriminate, irregular, jumbled, messy, untidy; disruptive, lawless, obstreperous, rebellious, riotous, rowdy, ungovernable, unlawful, unmanageable, unruly

**disown** cast off, deny, disallow, disavow, disclaim, reject, renounce, repudiate

**dispassionate** calm, collected, composed, cool, imperturbable, moderate, quiet, serene, sober,

promptly; finish off ~n speed; official message

**dispel** v -pelling, -pelled drive away

**dispense** v deal out; make up (medicine); administer (justice) **dispensable** adj **dispensary** n place where medicine is made up **dispensation** n **dispense with** do away with; manage without

**disperse** v scatter **dispersal** n

**dispirited** adj dejected

**displace** v move from its place;

take place of **displacement** n

**display** v/n show

**displease** v offend; annoy **displeasure** n

**dispose** v arrange; distribute; deal with **disposable** adj designed to be thrown away after use **disposal** n **disposition** n temperament; arrangement **dispose of** sell; get rid of

**disprove** v show to be incorrect

**dispute** v debate, discuss; call into question; contest ~n disagreement

─────── THESAURUS ───────

temperate, unemotional, unexcitable, unfazed *Inf*, unmoved

**dispatch, despatch** v conclude, discharge, dispose of, expedite, finish, perform, settle ~n account, bulletin, communication, communiqué, document, instruction, item, letter, message, missive, news, piece, report, story

**dispense** allocate, allot, apportion, assign, deal out, disburse, distribute, dole out, mete out, share; administer, apply, carry out, direct, discharge, enforce, execute, implement, operate, undertake

**disperse** broadcast, circulate, diffuse, disseminate, dissipate, distribute, scatter, spread, strew

**dispirited** crestfallen, dejected, depressed, despondent, discouraged, disheartened, down, downcast, gloomy, glum, in the doldrums, low, morose, sad

**displace** derange, disarrange, disturb, misplace, move, shift, transpose; crowd out, oust, replace, succeed, supersede, supplant, take the place of

**display** v betray, demonstrate, disclose, evidence, evince, exhibit, expose, manifest, open, present, reveal, show, unveil; expand, extend,

model, open out, spread out, unfold, unfurl ~n array, demonstration, exhibition, exposition, exposure, manifestation, presentation, revelation, show; pageant, parade, pomp, show, spectacle

**displease** anger, annoy, disgust, dissatisfy, exasperate, incense, irk, irritate, offend, pique, provoke, put out, rile, upset, vex

**displeasure** anger, annoyance, disapproval, dislike, dissatisfaction, distaste, indignation, irritation, offence, pique, resentment, vexation, wrath

**disposal** clearance, discarding, ejection, relinquishment, removal, riddance, scrapping, throwing away

**dispose** adjust, arrange, array, determine, distribute, fix, group, marshal, order, place, put, range, rank, regulate, set, settle, stand

**dispose of** bestow, give, make over, part with, sell, transfer; bin *Inf*, chuck *Inf*, destroy, discard, dump *Inf*, get rid of, jettison, junk *Inf*, scrap, unload

**disposition** character, constitution, make-up, nature, spirit, temper, temperament

**disprove** confute, controvert, discredit, expose, invalidate, negate,

**disputable** adj

**disqualify** v make ineligible **disqualification** n

**disquiet** n anxiety, uneasiness

**disregard** v ignore ~n lack of attention, respect

**disrepair** n state of bad repair, neglect

**disrepute** n bad reputation **disreputable** adj

**disrespect** n lack of respect **disre-**

**spectful** adj

**disrupt** v throw into disorder **disruption** n **disruptive** adj

**dissatisfied** adj not pleased, disappointed **dissatisfaction** n

**dissect** v cut up (body) for detailed examination

**dissemble** v pretend, disguise

**disseminate** v spread abroad

**dissent** v differ in opinion ~n such difference **dissension** n

---

THESAURUS

prove false, rebut, refute

**dispute** v argue, brawl, clash, contend, debate, discuss, quarrel, row, squabble, wrangle; challenge, contest, contradict, controvert, deny, doubt, impugn, question ~n argument, brawl, conflict, disagreement, discord, disturbance, feud, friction, quarrel, strife, wrangle

**disqualification** disenablement, disentitlement, elimination, exclusion, incompetence, ineligibility, rejection

**disqualify** debar, declare ineligible, disentitle, preclude, prohibit, rule out

**disquiet** alarm, anxiety, concern, disquietude, distress, fear, foreboding, fretfulness, restlessness, trepidation, trouble, uneasiness, unrest, worry

**disregard** discount, disobey, ignore, laugh off, make light of, neglect, overlook, pass over

**disreputable** base, contemptible, derogatory, discreditable, disgraceful, dishonourable, disorderly, ignominious, infamous, low, mean, notorious, scandalous, shameful, shocking, unprincipled, vicious, vile

**disrepute** disesteem, disfavour, disgrace, dishonour, ignominy, in-

famy, shame, unpopularity

**disrespect** contempt, discourtesy, dishonour, disregard, impertinence, impoliteness, impudence, insolence, irreverence, rudeness

**disrespectful** bad-mannered, cheeky, contemptuous, discourteous, ill-bred, impertinent, impolite, impudent, insolent, insulting, irreverent, misbehaved, rude, uncivil

**disrupt** agitate, confuse, disorder, disorganize, disturb, spoil, throw into disorder, upset

**dissatisfaction** annoyance, disappointment, discontent, dismay, displeasure, distress, exasperation, frustration, irritation, regret, unhappiness

**dissatisfied** disappointed, discontented, disgruntled, displeased, fed up, frustrated, unfulfilled, unhappy

**dissect** anatomize, cut up or apart, dismember, lay open

**disseminate** broadcast, circulate, diffuse, disperse, distribute, propagate, publish, scatter, sow, spread

**dissension** conflict, contention, difference, disagreement, discord, dispute, dissent, quarrel, strife

**dissent** v decline, differ, disagree, object, protest, refuse, withhold approval ~n difference, disagreement,

**dissertation** n written thesis

**disservice** n ill turn, injury

**dissident** n/adj (one) not in agreement, esp. with government

**dissimilar** adj not alike, different

**dissipate** v scatter; waste, squander **dissipated** adj **dissipation** n

**dissociate** v separate, sever

**dissolute** adj lax in morals

**dissolution** n break up; termination

**dissolve** v absorb or melt in fluid; annul; disappear; scatter **dissolvable**, **dissoluble** adj

**dissuade** v advise to refrain, persuade not to

**distance** n amount of space between two things; remoteness; aloofness **distant** adj

**distaste** n dislike **distasteful** adj

**distemper** n disease of dogs; paint

**distend** v swell out **distension** n

**distil** v -tilling, -tilled vaporize and recondense a liquid; purify **distillation** n **distiller** n maker of alcoholic drinks **distillery** n

**distinct** adj easily seen; definite; separate **distinctly** adv **distinction** n point of difference; act of distinguishing; repute, high honour dis-

discord, nonconformity, objection, opposition, refusal, resistance

**dissertation** discourse, essay, exposition, thesis, treatise

**disservice** bad turn, disfavour, harm, ill turn, injury, injustice, wrong

**dissident** n agitator, dissenter, rebel, recusant ~adj discordant, heterodox, nonconformist, schismatic

**dissimilar** different, disparate, divergent, diverse

**dissipate** burn up, deplete, expend, fritter away, lavish, misspend, run through, spend, squander, waste

**dissociate** detach, disconnect, distance, divorce, isolate, segregate, separate, set apart

**dissolute** abandoned, corrupt, debauched, degenerate, depraved, immoral, lax, lewd, libertine, licentious, loose, profligate, vicious, wanton, wild

**dissolution** breaking up, disintegration, division, divorce, parting, resolution, separation

**dissolve** flux, fuse, melt, soften,

thaw; crumble, decompose, diffuse, disappear, disintegrate, disperse, dissipate, dwindle, evaporate, fade, melt away, perish, vanish, waste away

**dissuade** deter, discourage, disincline, divert, expostulate, put off, remonstrate, urge not to, warn

**distance** absence, extent, gap, interval, lapse, length, range, reach, remoteness, remove, separation, space, span, stretch, width

**distant** abroad, afar, far, faraway, far-flung, far-off, outlying, out-of-the-way, remote, removed; aloof, cold, cool, formal, haughty, reserved, restrained, standoffish, stiff, unapproachable, unfriendly

**distaste** abhorrence, antipathy, aversion, disfavour, disgust, dislike, displeasure, horror, loathing, repugnance, revulsion

**distasteful** abhorrent, disagreeable, displeasing, obnoxious, offensive, repugnant, repulsive, undesirable, uninviting, unpalatable, unpleasant, unsavoury

**distil** condense, evaporate, express, purify, rectify, refine, vaporize

**tinctive** adj characteristic

**distinguish** v make difference in; recognize; honour; (usu. with between or among) draw distinction, grasp difference **distinguishable** adj **distinguished** adj

**distort** v put out of shape; misrepresent **distortion** n

**distract** v draw attention away; divert; perplex, drive mad **distraction** n agitation; amusement

**distraught** adj frantic, distracted

**distress** n trouble, pain ~v afflict

**distribute** v deal out; spread **distribution** n

**district** n region, locality; portion of territory

**distrust** v regard as untrustworthy ~n suspicion, doubt

**disturb** v intrude on; trouble, agitate, unsettle **disturbance** n

**disuse** n state of being no longer

---

THESAURUS

---

**distinct** apparent, clear, clear-cut, decided, definite, evident, lucid, manifest, marked, noticeable, obvious, patent, plain, recognizable, sharp, well-defined; different, dissimilar, individual, separate, unconnected

**distinction** contrast, difference, differential, division, separation; discernment, discrimination, penetration, perception, separation; credit, eminence, honour, importance, merit, name, note, prominence, quality, rank, renown, reputation, repute, worth

**distinguish** decide, determine, differentiate, discriminate, judge, tell apart; discern, know, make out, perceive, pick out, recognize, see, tell

**distinguished** celebrated, eminent, famed, famous, illustrious, notable, noted, well-known

**distort** bend, buckle, contort, deform, disfigure, misshape, twist, warp, wrench, wrest; bias, colour, falsify, garble, misrepresent, pervert, slant, twist

**distract** divert, draw away, sidetrack, turn aside; agitate, bewilder, confound, confuse, disturb, harass, madden, perplex, puzzle, torment, trouble

**distraction** agitation, bewilderment, commotion, confusion, discord, disorder, disturbance; amusement, beguilement, diversion, entertainment, pastime, recreation

**distress** n affliction, agony, anguish, anxiety, desolation, discomfort, grief, heartache, misery, pain, sadness, sorrow, torment, torture, woe, worry ~v afflict, agonize, bother, disturb, grieve, harass, harrow, pain, sadden, torment, trouble, upset, worry, wound

**distribute** administer, allocate, allot, assign, deal, dispense, dispose, divide, dole out, give, measure out, mete, share, spread

**distribution** allocation, allotment, division, dole, partition, sharing

**district** area, community, locality, neighbourhood, parish, quarter, region, sector, vicinity, ward

**distrust** v be sceptical of, be suspicious of, disbelieve, discredit, doubt, misbelieve, question, suspect ~n disbelief, doubt, misgiving, mistrust, qualm, question, scepticism, suspicion, wariness

**disturb** bother, disrupt, interfere with, interrupt, intrude on, pester, rouse, startle; agitate, alarm, annoy, distract, distress, excite, fluster, harass, hassle Inf, perturb, ruffle,

used **disused** adj

**ditch** n long narrow hollow dug in ground for drainage etc. ~v Inf abandon

**dither** v be uncertain or indecisive ~n this state

**ditto** n (pl **-tos**) the same

**ditty** n simple song

**divan** n bed, couch without back or head

**dive** v plunge under surface of water; descend suddenly; go deep down into ~n act of diving; Sl disreputable bar or club **diver** n

**diverge** v get farther apart; separate

**diverse** adj different, varied **diver**-

**sify** v -fying, -fied make varied **diversity** n

**divert** v turn aside; amuse **diversion** n

**divide** v make into parts, split up; distribute, share; become separated ~n watershed **dividend** n share of profits

**divine** adj of, pert. to God; sacred ~v guess; predict **divinity** n being divine; study of theology

**division** n act of dividing; part of whole; barrier; section; difference in opinion etc.; Maths method of finding how many times one number is contained in another; army unit **divisible** adj **divisive** adj caus-

──────── T H E S A U R U S ────────

shake, trouble, unnerve, unsettle, upset, worry

**disturbance** agitation, bother, confusion, disorder, distraction, hindrance, interruption, intrusion, perturbation, upset

**disuse** decay, discontinuance, idleness, neglect

**ditch** n channel, drain, dyke, furrow, gully, moat, trench, watercourse ~v chuck Inf, discard, dispose of, drop, get rid of, jettison, junk Inf, scrap

**dither** v falter, haver, hesitate, oscillate, waver

**dive** v dip, disappear, drop, duck, fall, jump, leap, pitch, plummet, plunge, submerge, swoop ~n dash, jump, leap, lunge, plunge, spring

**diverge** v branch, divide, fork, part, radiate, separate, split, spread

**diverse** adj different, dissimilar, distinct, separate, unlike, varying; assorted, miscellaneous, several, sundry, varied, various

**diversion** change, deflection, detour, deviation, digression, vari-

ation; amusement, delight, distraction, enjoyment, entertainment, game, pastime, play, pleasure, recreation, relaxation, sport

**diversity** assortment, difference, heterogeneity, medley, multiplicity, range, variance, variegation, variety

**divert** deflect, redirect, switch, turn aside

**divide** cut (up), detach, disconnect, part, partition, segregate, separate, sever, shear, split, subdivide; allocate, allot, apportion, deal out, dispense, distribute, dole out, measure out, portion, share

**dividend** bonus, extra, gain, plus, portion, share, surplus

**divine** adj celestial, godlike, heavenly, holy, spiritual, superhuman, supernatural ~v conjecture, deduce, discern, foretell, guess, infer, intuit, perceive, suppose, surmise, suspect, understand

**divinity** deity, divine nature, godliness, holiness, sanctity; religion, religious studies, theology

**divisible** fractional, separable,

ing disagreement

**divorce** n/v (make) legal dissolution of marriage; split **divorcé** n (fem **divorcée**) divorced person

**divulge** v reveal

**DIY** do-it-yourself

**dizzy** adj feeling dazed, unsteady **dizziness** n

**DJ** disc jockey

**DNA** n abbrev. for deoxyribonucleic acid, main constituent of the chromosomes of all organisms

**do** v doing, did, done perform, effect, finish; work at; solve; suit; provide; Sl cheat; act; fare; suffice; makes negative and interrogative sentences and expresses emphasis ~n Inf celebration **do away with** destroy **do up** fasten; renovate

**Doberman pinscher** large

black-and-tan dog

**docile** adj willing to obey, submissive **docility** n

**dock**[1] n artificial enclosure for loading or repairing ships ~v put or go into dock **docker** n **dockyard** n

**dock**[2] n solid part of tail; stump ~v cut short; deduct (an amount) from

**dock**[3] n enclosure in criminal court for prisoner

**dock**[4] n coarse weed

**docket** n piece of paper sent with package etc.

**doctor** n medical practitioner; one holding university's highest degree ~v treat medically; repair; falsify (accounts etc.)

**doctrine** n what is taught; belief; dogma **doctrinaire** adj stubbornly insistent about applying theories

——— THESAURUS ———

splittable

**division** cutting up, detaching, dividing, partition, separation; branch, category, class, compartment, department, group, head, part, portion, section, sector, segment

**divorce** n breach, break, decree nisi, dissolution, disunion, rupture, separation, severance, split-up ~v annul, disconnect, dissociate, disunite, divide, part, separate, sever, split up

**divulge** betray, confess, declare, disclose, exhibit, expose, impart, leak, let slip, make known, proclaim, publish, reveal, tell, uncover

**dizzy** faint, giddy, reeling, shaky, staggering, swimming, wobbly

**do** v accomplish, achieve, act, carry out, complete, conclude, discharge, end, execute, finish, perform, produce, work; bring about, cause, create, effect, produce; Inf cheat, con

Inf, deceive, defraud, dupe, fleece, hoax, swindle, trick; act, behave, carry oneself, conduct oneself; fare, get along, get on, make out, manage, proceed ~n Inf affair, event, function, gathering, occasion, party **do away with** destroy, exterminate, kill, liquidate, murder, slay

**docile** biddable, compliant, manageable, obedient, pliant, submissive, tractable

**docility** compliance, meekness, obedience, pliancy, submissiveness

**dock** n harbour, pier, quay, waterfront, wharf ~v anchor, berth, drop anchor, land, moor, put in, tie up

**doctor** n general practitioner, G.P., medical practitioner, physician ~v treat; botch, cobble, fix, mend, patch up, repair; alter, change, disguise, falsify, fudge, pervert, tamper with

**doctrine** article, belief, canon, concept, conviction, creed, dogma,

**document** n piece of paper etc. providing information ~v furnish with proofs

**documentary** adj (-v) of) type of film dealing with real life

**dodder** v totter, as with age

**dodge** v (attempt to) avoid by moving quickly; evade ~n trick, act of dodging **dodgy** adj Inf untrustworthy

**Dodgem** n Trademark car used for bumping other cars in rink at funfair

**dodo** n (pl dodos, dodoes) large extinct bird

**doe** n female of deer, hare, rabbit

**does** third person sing. of DO

**doff** v take off

**dog** n domesticated carnivorous four-legged mammal; male of wolf, fox and other animals; person (in contempt, abuse or playfully) ~v **dogging, dogged** follow closely **dogged** adj persistent, tenacious **dog-ear** n turned-down corner of

page in book **dog-end** n Inf cigarette end; rejected piece of anything **dogfight** n close combat between fighter aircraft; rough fight **dogleg** n sharp bend **dogsbody** n Inf one carrying out menial tasks

**doggerel** n trivial verse

**dogma** n article of belief **dogmatic** adj asserting opinions with arrogance

**doily** n small lacy mat to place under cake, dish etc.

**doldrums** pl n state of depression; region of light winds and calms near the equator

**dole** n Inf payment made to unemployed ~v (usu. with out) distribute **doleful** adj dreary, mournful

**doll** n child's toy image of human being

**dollar** n standard monetary unit of many countries, esp. USA

**dollop** n Inf semisolid lump

**dolly** n doll; wheeled support for film, TV camera

---

**THESAURUS**

**document** n certificate, legal form, paper, record, report ~v authenticate, back up, certify, cite, corroborate, detail, instance, substantiate, support, validate, verify

**dodge** v dart, duck, shift, sidestep, swerve, turn aside; avoid, deceive, elude, evade, fend off, get out of, shirk, shuffle, trick ~n device, feint, ploy, ruse, scheme, stratagem, subterfuge, trick, wile

**dog** n bitch, canine, cur, hound, man's best friend, mongrel, pup, puppy ~v follow, haunt, hound, plague, pursue, shadow, track, trail, trouble

**dogged** determined, firm, immov-

opinion, precept, principle, teaching, tenet

able, persevering, persistent, resolute, staunch, steadfast, steady, tenacious, unflagging, unshakable

**dogma** article, belief, creed, doctrine, precept, principle, tenet

**dogmatic** arbitrary, arrogant, assertive, categorical, dictatorial, downright, emphatic, imperious, obdurate, overbearing, peremptory

**doldrums** blues, boredom, depression, dullness, ennui, gloom, inertia, listlessness, malaise, stagnation, tedium

**dole** n allowance, alms, benefit, gift, grant, parcel, pittance, portion, quota, share v (usu. with out) administer, allocate, allot, assign, deal, dispense, distribute, divide, give, hand out, share

**dolphin** n sea mammal with beak-like snout

**domain** n lands held or ruled over; sphere of influence

**dome** n rounded roof; something of this shape

**domestic** adj of, in the home; home-loving; (of animals) tamed; of, in one's own country ~n house servant **domesticate** v tame

**domicile** n person's regular place of abode

**dominate** v rule, control; (of heights) overlook; be most influential **dominance** n **dominant** adj **domination** n **domineering** adj imperious

**dominion** n sovereignty; rule; territory of government

**dominoes** pl n game played with 28 oblong flat pieces marked with spots

**don¹** v donning, donned put on (clothes)

**don²** n fellow or tutor of college; Spanish title, Sir

**donate** v give **donation** n **donor** n

**done** past participle of DO

**donkey** n (pl -eys) ass

**doodle** v/n scribble

**doom** n fate; ruin; judicial sentence ~v condemn; destine **doomsday** n day of Last Judgment; dreaded day

**door** n hinged barrier to close entrance **doorway** n

**dope** n narcotic drug; Inf stupid person ~v drug **dopey, dopy** adj

**dormant** adj not active; sleeping

**dormitory** n sleeping room with many beds

**dormouse** n small hibernating mouselike rodent

**dorsal** adj of, on back

**dose** n amount (of drug etc.) ~v give doses to **dosage** n

———————— THESAURUS ————————

**domestic** family, home, household, private; house, house-trained, pet, tame, trained; indigenous, internal, native, not foreign

**dominant** ascendant, assertive, commanding, controlling, governing, leading, presiding, ruling, superior, supreme

**dominate** control, direct, govern, lead, master, monopolize, overbear, rule, tyrannize; bestride, loom over, overlook, stand over, survey, tower above

**domination** authority, command, control, influence, mastery, power, rule, superiority, supremacy, sway

**dominion** ascendancy, authority, command, control, government, mastery, power, rule, sovereignty, supremacy, sway

**don** dress in, get into, pull on, put on, slip on or in to

**donate** bestow, gift, give, present, subscribe

**donation** alms, benefaction, boon, contribution, gift, grant, gratuity, largess or largesse, offering, present, subscription

**donor** almsgiver, benefactor, contributor, donator, giver

**doom** n catastrophe, death, destiny, destruction, downfall, fate, fortune, lot, portion, ruin ~v condemn, consign, damn, decree, destine, judge, sentence

**door** egress, entrance, entry, exit, ingress, opening

**dope** drugs, narcotic, opiate

**dormant** asleep, inactive, inert, latent, quiescent, sleeping, sluggish, slumbering, suspended

**dose** draught, drench, measure,

**dossier** *n* set of papers on particular subject

**dot** *n* small spot, mark ~*v* **dotting, dotted** mark with dots; sprinkle

**dote** *v* (*with* **on** *or* **upon**) be passionately fond of **dotage** *n* senility

**double** *adj* of two parts, layers etc.; twice as much or many; designed for two users ~*adv* twice; to twice the amount or extent; in a pair ~*n* person or thing exactly like another; quantity twice as much as another; sharp turn; running pace ~*v* make, become double; increase twofold; fold in two; turn sharply **doubly** *adv* **double bass** lowest member of violin family **double-cross** *v* betray

**doubt** *v* suspect; hesitate to believe; call in question ~*n* (state of) uncertainty **doubtful** *adj* **doubtless** *adv* certainly; presumably

**dough** *n* flour or meal kneaded with water; *Sl* money **doughnut** *n* sweetened and fried piece of dough

**doughty** *adj* hardy, resolute

**dour** *adj* grim, severe

**douse** *v* thrust into water; extinguish (light)

**dove** *n* bird of pigeon family **dovetail** *v* fit closely, neatly together

**dowager** *n* widow with title or property from husband

**dowdy** *adj* shabbily dressed

**dowel** *n* wooden, metal peg

**down**[1] *adv* to, in, or towards, lower position; of (payment) on the spot ~*prep* from higher to lower part of; along ~*adj* depressed ~*v* knock, pull, push down; *Inf* drink **downward** *adj*/*adv* **downwards** *adv* **downbeat** *adj Inf* gloomy **downcast** *adj* dejected; looking down **downfall** *n* sudden loss of position **downpour** *n* heavy fall of rain **downright**

─────── THESAURUS ───────

portion, potion, prescription, quantity

**dot** *n* atom, circle, dab, fleck, full stop, iota, jot, mark, mite, mote, point, speck, speckle, spot

**dotage** feebleness, imbecility, old age, second childhood, senility, weakness

**double** *adj* coupled, doubled, dual, duplicate, in pairs, paired, twice, twin, twofold ~*v* duplicate, enlarge, fold, grow, increase, magnify, multiply, plait, repeat

**double-cross** betray, cheat, defraud, hoodwink, mislead, swindle, trick

**doubt** *v* discredit, distrust, fear, misgive, mistrust, query, question, suspect; be dubious, be uncertain, demur, fluctuate, hesitate, scruple, vacillate, waver ~*n* apprehension, disquiet, distrust, fear, incredulity,

misgiving, mistrust, qualm, scepticism, suspicion

**doubtful** hesitating, irresolute, perplexed, sceptical, suspicious, tentative, uncertain, unconvinced, undecided, unresolved, unsettled, unsure, vacillating, wavering; ambiguous, debatable, dodgy *Brit, Aust, & NZ inf*, dubious, equivocal, hazardous, iffy *Inf*, indefinite, obscure, problematic, questionable, unclear, unconfirmed, unsettled, vague

**doubtless** assuredly, certainly, clearly, of course, precisely, surely, truly, unquestionably; apparently, most likely, ostensibly, presumably, probably, seemingly

**dour** dismal, dreary, forbidding, gloomy, grim, morose, sour, sullen, unfriendly

**dowdy** dingy, drab, old-fashioned,

*adj* straightforward ~*adv* quite, thoroughly **down-and-out** *adj/n* destitute, homeless (person)

**down²** *n* soft underfeathers, hair; fluff **downy** *adj*

**downs** *pl n* open high land

**dowry** *n* property wife brings to husband

**doyen** *n* (*fem* **doyenne**) senior, respected member of group

**doze** *v/n* sleep, nap **dozy** *adj*

**dozen** *n* (set of) twelve

**Dr.** Doctor; Drive

**drab** *adj* dull, monotonous

**draconian** *adj* very harsh, cruel

**draft¹** *n* sketch; rough copy of document; order for money; detachment of troops; ~*v* make sketch of; make rough copy of; send detached party

**draft²** *v* US select for compulsory military service

**drag** *v* **dragging, dragged** pull along with difficulty; trail; sweep with net; protract; lag, trail; be tediously protracted ~*n* check on progress; checked motion

**dragon** *n* mythical fire-breathing monster **dragonfly** *n* long-bodied insect with gauzy wings

**dragoon** *n* cavalryman ~*v* coerce

**drain** *v* draw off (liquid) by pipes, ditches etc.; dry; empty; exhaust; flow off or away ~*n* channel; sewer; depletion; strain **drainage** *n*

**drake** *n* male duck

**dram** *n* small draught of strong drink

**drama** *n* stage play; art or literature of plays; playlike series of events **dramatic** *adj* of drama; striking or effective **dramatist** *n* writer of plays **dramatize** *v* adapt for acting

**drape** *v* cover, adorn with cloth

shabby, unfashionable

**down** *adj* blue, dejected, depressed, disheartened, downcast, low, miserable, sad, unhappy

**downcast** cheerless, dejected, depressed, despondent, disconsolate, discouraged, disheartened, dismayed, dispirited, miserable, sad, unhappy

**downfall** breakdown, collapse, debacle, descent, destruction, disgrace, fall, overthrow, ruin, undoing

**downpour** cloudburst, deluge, flood, inundation, rainstorm

**downward** *adj* declining, descending, earthward, heading down, slipping

**doze** *v* catnap, drowse, kip *Brit sl*, nap, nod, sleep, slumber, zizz *Brit inf*

**drab** cheerless, colourless, dingy,

dismal, dreary, dull, flat, gloomy, grey, lacklustre, shabby, sombre, uninspired

**draft** *n* outline, plan, rough, sketch, version ~*v* compose, design, draw, draw up, formulate, outline, plan, sketch

**drag** draw, hale, haul, lug, pull, tow, trail, tug, yank

**drain** *v* bleed, draw off, dry, empty, milk, remove, tap, withdraw; consume, deplete, dissipate, empty, exhaust, sap, strain, tax, use up, weary ~*n* channel, conduit, culvert, ditch, duct, outlet, pipe, sewer, sink, trench, watercourse; depletion, drag, exhaustion, reduction, sap, strain, withdrawal

**drama** play, show; acting, dramaturgy, stagecraft, theatre; crisis, excitement, scene, spectacle, theatrics, turmoil

**draper** *n* dealer in cloth, linen etc. **drapery** *n*

**drastic** *adj* extreme; severe

**draught** *n* current of air; act of drawing; act of drinking; quantity drunk at once; *pl* game played on chessboard with flat round pieces ~*adj* for drawing; drawn **draughty** *adj* full of air currents **draughtsman** *n* one who makes drawings, plans etc. **draughtsmanship** *n*

**draw** *v* drawing, drew, drawn portray with pencil etc.; pull, haul; attract; come (near); entice; take from (well, barrel etc.); receive (money); get by lot; make, current of air; (of game) tie ~*n* act of drawing; casting of lots; tie **drawer** *n* one who or that which draws;

sliding box in table or chest **drawing** *n* art of depicting in line; sketch so done **drawback** *n* snag **drawbridge** *n* hinged bridge to pull up **drawing room** living room, sitting room **draw up** arrange in order; stop

**drawl** *v* speak slowly ~*n* such speech

**drawn** *adj* haggard

**dread** *v* fear greatly ~*n* awe, terror ~*adj* feared, awful **dreadful** *adj* disagreeable, shocking or bad **dreadfully** *adv*

**dream** *n* vision during sleep; fancy, reverie, aspiration ~*v* **dreaming, dreamt** or **dreamed** have dreams; see, imagine in dreams; think of as possible **dreamer** *n* **dreamy** *adj*

**dramatic** theatrical; breathtaking, electrifying, emotional, exciting, melodramatic, sensational, startling, sudden, tense, thrilling

**dramatist** playwright, scriptwriter

**dramatize** act, overdo, overstate, play-act

**drastic** desperate, dire, extreme, forceful, harsh, radical, severe, strong

**draught** of air current, flow, movement; cup, dose, drench, drink, potion, quantity

**draw** *v* drag, haul, pull, tow, tug; allure, attract, bring forth, elicit, engage, entice, evoke, induce, influence, invite, persuade; depict, design, map out, mark out, outline, paint, portray, sketch, trace ~*n Inf* attraction, enticement, lure; dead heat, stalemate, tie

**drawback** defect, difficulty, disadvantage, downside, fault, flaw, handicap, hindrance, hitch, impediment, nuisance, obstacle, snag,

stumbling block, trouble

**drawing** cartoon, depiction, illustration, outline, picture, portrayal, representation, sketch, study

**drawn** fatigued, fraught, harassed, harrowed, pinched, sapped, strained, stressed, taut, tense, tired, worn

**draw up** compose, draft, formulate, frame, prepare, write out

**dread** *v* fear, quail, shrink from, shudder, tremble ~*n* alarm, apprehension, aversion, awe, dismay, fear, fright, horror, terror, trepidation

**dreadful** alarming, appalling, awful, distressing, fearful, formidable, frightful, ghastly, hideous, horrible, monstrous, shocking, terrible, tragic

**dream** *n* daydream, delusion, fantasy, illusion, imagination, reverie, speculation, trance, vision; ambition, aspiration, design, desire, goal, hope, notion, wish ~*v* day-

**dreary** *adj* dismal, dull **drearily** *adv*

**dredge** *v* bring up mud etc. from sea bottom ~*n* scoop **dredger** *n* boat with machinery for dredging

**dregs** *pl n* sediment, grounds

**drench** *v* wet thoroughly, soak

**dress** *v* put on clothes; array for show; prepare; put dressing on (wound) ~*n* one-piece garment for woman; clothing; evening wear

**dresser** *n* one who dresses; kitchen sideboard **dressing** *n* something applied, as sauce to food, ointment to wound etc. **dressing-down** *Inf* severe scolding **dressing gown** robe worn before dressing **dressy** *adj* stylish

**dressage** *n* method of training horse

**drey** *n* squirrel's nest

**dribble** *v* flow in drops, trickle; run at the mouth ~*n* trickle, drop

**drift** *v* be carried as by current of air, water ~*n* process of being driv-

en by current; tendency; meaning; wind-heaped mass of snow, sand etc. **drifter** *n* **driftwood** *n* wood washed ashore by sea

**drill**[1] *n* boring tool; exercise of soldiers; routine teaching ~*v* bore hole; exercise in routine; practise routine

**drill**[2] *v/n* (machine to) sow seed in furrows

**drink** *v* **drinking, drank, drunk** swallow liquid ~*n* liquid for drinking; intoxicating liquor **drinkable** *adj* **drinker** *n*

**drip** *v* **dripping, dripped** fall or let fall in drops ~*n* *Med* intravenous administration of solution; *Inf* insipid person **dripping** *n* melted fat from roasting meat ~*adj* very wet

**drip-dry** *adj* (of fabric) drying free of creases if hung up while wet

**drive** *v* **driving, drove, driven** urge in some direction; make move and steer (vehicle, animal etc.); be con-

dream, envisage, fancy, imagine, stargaze, think, visualize

**dreamer** daydreamer, fantasist, fantasizer, idealist, utopian, visionary

**dreamy** chimerical, fantastic, misty, shadowy, unreal

**dreary** bleak, cheerless, comfortless, depressing, dismal, doleful, downcast, drear, forlorn, funereal, gloomy, glum, lonely, melancholy, mournful, sad, solitary, sombre, sorrowful, wretched; boring, drab, dull, ho-hum *Inf*, mind-numbing, monotonous, routine, tedious

**dregs** deposit, dross, grounds, residue, scum, sediment, trash, waste

**drench** drown, flood, inundate, saturate, soak, souse, steep, wet

**dress** *v* attire, change, clothe, don,

garb, put on, robe; bandage, bind up, plaster, treat ~*n* costume, ensemble, frock, garment, gown, outfit, robe, suit; attire, clothes, clothing, costume, garb, garments, guise

**dribble** drop, drip, leak, ooze, run, seep, trickle

**drift** coast, float, meander, stray, waft, wander

**drill** *n* bit, borer, gimlet; discipline, exercise, practice, preparation, repetition, training ~*v* bore, pierce, puncture, sink in; exercise, instruct, practise, rehearse, teach, train

**drink** *v* drain, gulp, guzzle, imbibe, partake of, quaff, sip, suck, sup, swallow, swig *Inf*, swill, wash down ~*n* beverage, liquid, potion, refreshment; alcohol, liquor, spirits

**drip** *v* drop, exude, filter, splash,

veyed in vehicle; hit with force ~n act, action of driving; journey in vehicle; united effort, campaign; energy; forceful stroke **driver** n

**drivel** v -elling, -elled run at the mouth; talk nonsense ~n silly nonsense

**drizzle** v/n rain in fine drops

**droll** adj funny, odd

**dromedary** n one-humped camel

**drone** n male bee; lazy idler; deep humming ~v hum; talk in monotonous tone

**drool** v slaver, drivel

**droop** v hang down; wilt, flag ~n **droopy** adj

**drop** n globule of liquid; very small quantity; fall, descent; distance to fall ~v **dropping, dropped** (let) fall; utter casually; set down; discontinue; come or go casually **droplet** n

**dropout** n person who fails to complete course of study or one who rejects conventional society **drop-**

**pings** pl n dung of rabbits, sheep, birds etc.

**dropsy** n disease causing watery fluid to collect in the body

**dross** n scum of molten metal; impurity, refuse

**drought** n long spell of dry weather

**drove** n herd, flock, esp. in motion **drover** n driver of cattle etc.

**drown** v die or be killed by immersion in liquid; make sound inaudible by louder sound

**drowsy** adj half-asleep; lulling; dull **drowsiness** n **drowse** v

**drub** v **drubbing, drubbed** thrash, beat **drubbing** n beating

**drudge** v work at menial or distasteful tasks ~n one who drudges **drudgery** n

**drug** n medical substance; narcotic ~v **drugging, drugged** mix drugs with; administer drug to

**druid** n (also with cap.) member of

sprinkle, trickle

**drive** v herd, hurl, impel, propel, push, send, urge; direct, go, guide, handle, manage, motor, operate, ride, steer, travel ~n excursion, jaunt, journey, outing, ride, run, trip, turn; effort, energy, enterprise, initiative, vigour

**drizzle** v rain, shower, spray, sprinkle ~n fine rain, Scotch mist

**droll** amusing, comic, comical, diverting, eccentric, entertaining, funny, humorous, jocular, whimsical

**droop** bend, drop, fall down, hang (down), sag, sink

**drop** n bead, drip, globule, pearl, tear; dab, dash, nip, pinch, sip, taste, tot, trace; decline, decrease, downturn, fall-off, reduction ~v

abandon, cease, desert, discontinue, forsake, give up, leave, relinquish, terminate; decline, depress, descend, diminish, dive, droop, fall, lower, plunge, sink, tumble

**drought** dry spell, dry weather

**drove** collection, company, crowd, flock, gathering, herd, horde, mob, multitude, press, swarm, throng

**drown** deluge, drench, engulf, flood, go down, go under, immerse, inundate, sink, submerge, swamp

**drudge** factotum, hack, menial, plodder, servant, slave, toiler, worker

**drudgery** chore, hack work, hard work, labour, slavery, slog, toil

**drug** n medicine, physic, poison, remedy; narcotic, opiate ~v dose, medicate, treat

ancient order of Celtic priests

**drum** n percussion instrument of skin stretched over round hollow frame; thing shaped like drum ~v **drumming, drummed** play drum; tap, thump continuously **drummer** n **drum major** leader of military band **drumstick** n stick for beating drum; lower joint of cooked fowl's leg

**drunk** adj/n (person) overcome by strong drink **drunkard** n **drunken** adj **drunkenness** n

**dry** adj **drier** or **dryer, driest** or **dryest** without moisture; not yielding liquid; unfriendly; caustically witty; uninteresting; lacking sweetness ~v **drying, dried** remove water, moisture; become dry; evaporate **dryer, drier** n person or thing that dries; apparatus for removing moisture **dryly, drily** adv **dry-clean** v clean clothes with solvent **dry-cleaner** n **dry-cleaning** n

**dual** adj twofold

**dub** v **dubbing, dubbed** confer knighthood on; give title to; provide film with soundtrack

**dubious** adj causing doubt

**duchess** n duke's wife or widow

**duck** n (masc **drake**) common swimming bird ~v plunge (someone) under water; bob down; Inf avoid **duckling** n young duck

**duct** n channel, tube

**dud** n futile, worthless person or thing ~adj worthless

**due** adj owing; proper, expected; timed for ~adv (with points of compass) exactly ~n person's right; (usu. pl) charge, fee etc. **duly** adj properly; punctually **due to** attributable to; caused by

**duel** n arranged fight with deadly weapons, between two persons ~v **duelling, duelled** fight in duel

**duet** n piece of music for two performers

**duffel, duffle** n coarse woollen cloth; coat of this

**duffer** n stupid inefficient person

**dugout** n covered excavation to provide shelter; canoe of hollowed-out tree; Sport covered bench for players when not on the field

——————— THESAURUS ———————

**drum** v beat, pulsate, rap, reverberate, tap, tattoo, throb

**drunk** adj blitzed Sl, blotto Sl, drunken, fuddled, inebriated, intoxicated, legless Inf, merry Inf, paralytic Inf, tipsy, well-oiled Sl ~n drunkard, inebriate, sot, toper

**drunkenness** n alcoholism, dipsomania, insobriety, intemperance, intoxication, tipsiness

**dry** adj arid, barren, dehydrated, dried up, parched, sapless, thirsty, torrid, waterless ~v dehydrate, desiccate, drain, make dry, parch, sear

**dual** adj coupled, double, duplicate, matched, paired, twin, twofold

**dubious** doubtful, hesitant, uncertain, unconvinced, undecided, unsure, wavering

**duck** v bend, bow, crouch, dodge, drop, lower, stoop; Inf avoid, dodge, escape, evade, shirk, sidestep

**due** adj outstanding, owed, owing, payable, unpaid; appropriate, becoming, bounden, deserved, fit, fitting, just, justified, merited, obligatory, proper, right, rightful, suitable; expected, expected to arrive, scheduled ~adv dead, direct, directly, exactly, straight

**duel** affair of honour, single combat

**duke** *n* peer of rank next below prince **dukedom** *n*

**dulcet** *adj* (of sounds) sweet, melodious

**dulcimer** *n* stringed instrument played with hammers

**dull** *adj* stupid; sluggish; tedious; overcast ~*v* make or become dull **dullard** *n* **dully** *adj*

**dumb** *adj* incapable of speech; silent; *Inf* stupid **dumbbell** *n* weight for exercises **dumbfound** *v* confound into silence

**dummy** *n* tailor's or dressmaker's model; imitation object; baby's dummy teat ~*adj* sham, bogus

**dump** *v* throw down in mass; deposit; unload ~*n* rubbish heap; temporary depot of stores; *Inf* squalid place; *pl* low spirits **dumpling** *n* small round pudding of dough **dumpy** *adj* short, stout

**dunce** *n* stupid pupil

**dune** *n* sandhill

**dung** *n* excrement of animals

**dungarees** *pl n* overalls made of coarse cotton fabric

**dungeon** *n* underground cell for prisoners

**dunk** *v* dip bread etc. into liquid before eating it

**duo** *n* (*pl* **duos**) pair of performers

**duodenum** *n* upper part of small intestine **duodenal** *adj*

**dupe** *n* victim of delusion or sharp practice ~*v* deceive

**duplicate** *v* make exact copy of ~*adj* double ~*n* exact copy **duplication** *n* **duplicator** *n* **duplicity** *n* deceitfulness, double-dealing

**durable** *adj* lasting, resisting wear **durability** *n*

**duration** *n* time things last

**duress** *n* compulsion

**during** *prep* throughout, in the time of, in the course of

**dusk** *n* darker stage of twilight **dusky** *adj*

--- THESAURUS ---

**dull** dense, dim, dozy *Brit inf*, slow, stupid, thick; apathetic, blank, dead, empty, heavy, indifferent, lifeless, listless, slow, sluggish; boring, commonplace, dreary, dry, flat, ho-hum *Inf*, mind-numbing, plain, prosaic, tedious, tiresome, uninteresting; cloudy, dim, gloomy, overcast

**duly** accordingly, befittingly, correctly, deservedly, fittingly, properly, rightfully, suitably; on time, punctually

**dumb** inarticulate, mute, silent, soundless, speechless, tongue-tied, voiceless, wordless

**dummy** *n* figure, form, model; copy, counterfeit, duplicate, imitation, sham, substitute ~*adj* artificial, bogus, fake, false, imitation, mock, sham, simulated

**dump** *v* deposit, drop, fling down, let fall, throw down ~*n* junkyard, refuse heap, rubbish tip; *Inf* hovel, mess, pigsty, shack, shanty, slum

**dungeon** cage, cell, lockup, prison

**duplicate** *v* copy, double, echo, photocopy, repeat, reproduce ~*adj* corresponding, identical, matched, twin, twofold ~*n* carbon copy, copy, double, likeness, match, mate, replica, reproduction, twin

**durable** abiding, constant, dependable, enduring, fast, firm, hard-wearing, persistent, reliable, resistant, sound, stable, strong, sturdy, substantial, tough

**dusk** dark, evening, nightfall, sundown, sunset, twilight

**dusky** dark, dark-hued, sable,

**dust** n fine particles, powder of earth or other matter; ashes of the dead ~v sprinkle with powder; rid of dust **duster** n cloth for removing dust **dusty** adj covered with dust **dustbin** n container for household rubbish

**Dutch** adj pert. to the Netherlands, its inhabitants, its language

**duty** n moral or legal obligation; that which is due; tax on goods **duteous** adj **dutiful** adj

**duvet** n quilt filled with down or artificial fibre

**dwarf** n (pl **dwarfs, dwarves**) very undersized person; mythological, small, manlike creature ~adj unusually small ~v make seem small; make stunted

**dwell** v **dwelling, dwelt** or **dwelled** live, make one's home (in); think, speak at length (on) **dwelling** n house

**dwindle** v waste away

**dye** v **dyeing, dyed** impregnate (cloth etc.) with colouring matter;

colour thus ~n colouring matter in solution

**dyke** n embankment to prevent flooding; ditch

**dynamics** pl n (with sing v) branch of physics dealing with force as producing or affecting motion **dynamic** adj energetic and forceful

**dynamite** n high explosive mixture ~v blow up with this

**dynamo** n (pl **-mos**) machine to convert mechanical into electrical energy, generator of electricity

**dynasty** n line, family of hereditary rulers

**dysentery** n infection of intestine causing severe diarrhoea

**dysfunction** n abnormal, impaired functioning

**dyslexia** n impaired ability to read **dyslexic** adj

**dyspepsia** n indigestion **dyspeptic** adj/n

**dystrophy** n wasting of bodily tissues, esp. muscles

**dust** n grime, grit, particles, powder

**dusty** dirty, grubby, sooty, unclean, undusted, unswept

**dutiful** compliant, conscientious, devoted, docile, obedient, punctilious, respectful, submissive

**duty** business, calling, charge, engagement, function, mission, obligation, office, onus, responsibility, role, service, task, work; customs, excise, impost, levy, tariff, tax, toll

**dwarf** n bantam, midget, pygmy or pigmy ~adj baby, diminutive, miniature, petite, pocket, small, teensy-weensy, tiny, undersized ~v dominate, overshadow, tower

above or over

**dwell** abide, inhabit, live, lodge, remain, reside, rest, settle, sojourn, stay, stop

**dwelling** abode, domicile, establishment, habitation, home, house, pad SI, quarters, residence

**dye** v colour, pigment, stain, tincture, tinge, tint ~n colour, colouring, pigment, stain, tinge, tint

**dynamic** active, driving, energetic, forceful, go-ahead, high-powered, lively, magnetic, powerful, vigorous, vital

**dynasty** ascendancy, dominion, empire, government, house, regime, rule, sovereignty, sway

# E e

**E** East; Eastern; English

**each** *adj/pron* every one taken separately

**eager** *adj* having a strong wish; keen, impatient

**eagle** *n* large bird of prey

**ear**[1] *n* organ of hearing; sense of hearing; sensitiveness to sounds; attention **earache** *n* pain in ear **eardrum** *n* thin piece of skin inside the ear **earmark** *v* assign for definite purpose **earphone** *n* receiver for radio etc. held or put in ear **earring** *n* ornament for lobe of the ear **earshot** *n* hearing distance **earwig** *n* small insect with pincer-like tail

**ear**[2] *n* spike, head of corn

**earl** *n* British nobleman

**early** *adj/adv* before expected or usual time; in first part, near beginning

**earn** *v* obtain by work or merit; gain **earnings** *pl n*

**earnest** *adj* serious, sincere

**earth** *n* planet we live on; ground; soil; electrical connection to earth ~*v* cover, connect with earth **earthly** *adj* possible **earthy** *adj* of earth; uninhibited **earthenware** *n* (vessels of) baked clay **earthquake** *n* convulsion of earth's surface **earthworm** *n*

**ease** *n* comfort; freedom from constraint, awkwardness or trouble; idleness ~*v* reduce burden; give ease to; slacken; (cause to) move carefully **easily** *adv* **easy** *adj* not difficult; free from pain, care, or anxiety; compliant; comfortable **easygoing** *adj* not fussy; indolent

**easel** *n* frame to support picture etc.

**east** *n* part of horizon where sun rises; eastern lands, orient ~*adj* on, in, or near, east; coming from east ~*adv* from, or to, east **easterly** *adj/*

---

## THESAURUS

**each** *adj* every ~*pron* every one, one and all

**eager** agog, anxious, ardent, athirst, earnest, enthusiastic, fervent, greedy, hungry, intent, keen, longing, raring, zealous

**early** *adj* forward, premature, untimely ~*adv* beforehand, in advance, in good time, prematurely, too soon

**earn** *v* deserve, merit, rate, warrant, win; collect, draw, gain, get, gross, make, net, obtain, procure, reap, receive

**earnest** close, constant, determined, firm, fixed, grave, intent, resolute, serious, sincere, solemn, stable, staid, steady

**earnings** gain, income, pay, proceeds, profits, receipts, remuneration, return, reward, salary, stipend, wages

**earth** globe, orb, planet, sphere, world; clay, dirt, ground, land, loam, sod, soil, topsoil, turf

**earthenware** ceramics, crockery, crocks, pots, pottery, terra cotta

**ease** *n* affluence, calmness, comfort, contentment, enjoyment, happiness, leisure, peace, quiet, relaxation, repose, rest, serenity, tranquillity ~*v* abate, allay, alleviate, assuage, calm, comfort, lessen, lighten, moderate, pacify, quiet, relax, relent, relieve, soothe, still

**easily** comfortably, effortlessly,

*adv* **eastern** *adj* **eastward** *adj/adv* **eastwards** *adv*

**Easter** *n* festival of the Resurrection of Christ

**easy** *see* EASE

**eat** *v* **eating, ate, eaten** chew and swallow; destroy; gnaw; wear away **eatable** *adj*

**eau de Cologne** *Fr* light perfume

**eaves** *pl n* overhanging edges of roof **eavesdropping** *v* **-dropping, -dropped** listen secretly

**ebb** *v* flow back; decay ~*n* flowing back of tide; decline, decay

**ebony** *n/adj* (made of) hard black wood

**ebullient** *adj* exuberant **ebullience** *n*

**eccentric** *adj* odd, unconventional; irregular; not placed centrally ~*n*

odd, unconventional person **eccentricity** *n*

**echo** *n* (*pl* **echoes**) repetition of sounds by reflection; imitation ~*v* **echoing, echoed** repeat as echo; imitate; resound; be repeated

**éclair** *n* finger-shaped iced cake filled with cream

**eclectic** *adj* selecting from various sources

**eclipse** *n* blotting out of sun, moon etc. by another heavenly body; obscurity ~*v* obscure; surpass

**ecology** *n* science of plants and animals in relation to their environment **ecological** *adj* **ecologist** *n*

**economy** *n* careful management of resources to avoid unnecessary expenditure; system of interrelationship of money, industry and

——————————————— THESAURUS ———————————————

**easy** child's play, clear, effortless, facile, light, no bother, no trouble, painless, simple, smooth, straightforward, uncomplicated, undemanding

**easy-going** amenable, calm, carefree, casual, even-tempered, flexible, laid-back *Inf*, lenient, liberal, mild, moderate, placid, relaxed, serene, tolerant, uncritical, undemanding

**eat** chew, consume, devour, munch, scoff *Sl*, swallow

**eavesdrop** listen in, monitor, overhear, spy

**ebb** *v* abate, fall away, flow back, go out, recede, retire, retreat, sink, subside, wane, withdraw; decay, decline, decrease, degenerate, deteriorate, diminish, drop, dwindle, fade away, flag, lessen, peter out, shrink, weaken

**eccentric** abnormal, anomalous,

bizarre, capricious, erratic, idiosyncratic, irregular, odd, peculiar, queer *Inf*, strange, uncommon, unconventional, weird

**eccentricity** abnormality, anomaly, caprice, foible, idiosyncrasy, irregularity, nonconformity, oddity, peculiarity, quirk, singularity, strangeness, weirdness

**echo** *n* answer, repetition, reverberation; copy, imitation, parallel, reflection, reproduction, ringing ~*v* repeat, resound, reverberate

**eclipse** *v* blot out, cloud, darken, dim, obscure, overshadow, shroud, veil ~*n* dimming, extinction, shading

**economic** productive, profitable, profit-making, solvent, viable; business, commercial, financial, industrial, mercantile, trade

**economical** careful, frugal, prudent, thrifty

**economize** cut back, retrench,

employment **economic** adj economical adj frugal **economics** pl n (with sing v) study of economies of nations; (used as pl) financial aspects **economist** n **economize** v

**ecstasy** n exalted state of feeling **ecstatic** adj

**eczema** n skin disease

**eddy** n small whirl in water, smoke etc. ~v eddying, eddied move in whirls

**edge** n border, boundary; cutting side of blade; sharpness; advantage ~v sharpen; give edge or border to; move gradually **edgy** adj irritable on edge nervy; excited

**edible** adj eatable

**edict** n order, decree

**edifice** n building

**edify** v -fying, -fied improve morally, instruct

**edit** v prepare book, film, tape etc. **edition** n form in which something is published; number of copies **editor** n **editorial** adj ~n article stating opinion of newspaper etc.

**educate** v provide schooling for, teach; train **education** n **educational** adj

**eel** n snakelike fish

**eerie** adj weird, uncanny

**efface** v wipe or rub out

**effect** n result; impression; condition of being operative pl property; lighting, sounds etc. ~v bring about **effective** adj useful; in force **effectual** adj

**effeminate** adj womanish, un-

————————— THESAURUS —————————

save, scrimp, tighten one's belt

**economy** frugality, husbandry, parsimony, providence, prudence, restraint, saving, thrift

**ecstasy** bliss, delight, elation, euphoria, exaltation, fervour, frenzy, joy, rapture

**ecstatic** blissful, delirious, elated, enthusiastic, euphoric, fervent, frenzied, joyful, joyous, overjoyed, raptured

**eddy** n swirl, vortex, whirlpool ~v swirl, whirl

**edge** border, bound, boundary, brim, brink, fringe, limit, line, lip, margin, outline, perimeter, rim, side, threshold, verge; bite, force, incisiveness, interest, keenness, point, pungency, sharpness, sting, urgency, zest

**edible** eatable, fit to eat, good, harmless, palatable, wholesome

**edict** act, command, decree, dictate, dictum, fiat, injunction, law, mandate, manifesto, order, pro-

nouncement, regulation, ruling, statute

**edify** educate, elevate, enlighten, guide, improve, inform, instruct, nurture, school, teach, uplift

**edit** adapt, annotate, censor, check, condense, correct, emend, polish, revise, rewrite

**edition** copy, impression, issue, number, printing, version, volume

**educate** civilize, coach, cultivate, develop, discipline, drill, edify, enlighten, exercise, foster, improve, inform, instruct, school, teach, train

**education** breeding, civilization, cultivation, culture, development, discipline, edification, enlightenment, erudition, improvement, indoctrination, instruction, knowledge, scholarship, training, tutoring

**eerie** creepy Inf, frightening, ghostly, mysterious, scary Inf, spectral, spooky Inf, strange, uncanny, unearthly, weird

manly, womanish

**effervesce** *v* give off bubbles **effervescent** *adj*

**efficient** *adj* capable, competent **efficiency** *n*

**effigy** *n* image, likeness

**effluent** *n* liquid discharged as waste

**effort** *n* exertion, endeavour, attempt or something achieved **effortless** *adj*

**effrontery** *n* impudence

**e.g.** for example

**egalitarian** *adj* believing that all people should be equal

**egg**[1] *n* oval or round object from which young emerge

**egg**[2] *v* egg on urge

**ego** *n* (pl **egos**) the self **egotism**, **egoism** *n* selfishness; self-conceit **egotist, egoist** *n* **egotistic, -ical** *adj* **egocentric** *adj* self-centred

**egregious** *adj* blatant

**eider** *n* Arctic duck **eiderdown** *n* its breast feathers; quilt

**eight** *adj/n* cardinal number one above seven **eighteen** *adj/n* eight more than ten **eighteenth** *adj/n* **eighth** *adj/n* **eightieth** *adj/n* **eighty** *adj/n* ten times eight

**either** *adj/n* one or the other; one of two; each *~adv/conj* bringing in first of alternatives

**ejaculate** *v* eject (semen); exclaim **ejaculation** *n*

**eject** *v* throw out; expel **ejection** *n* **ejector** *n*

**eke out** make (supply) last

**elaborate** *adj* detailed; complicated *~v* expand (upon); work out in detail **elaboration** *n*

**élan** *n* style and vigour

**elapse** *v* (of time) pass

**elastic** *adj* springy; flexible *~n* tape

———————— THESAURUS ————————

**effect** *n* conclusion, consequence, event, fruit, issue, outcome, result, upshot *~v* accomplish, achieve, bring about, carry out, cause, complete, create, execute, fulfil, give rise to, initiate, make, perform, produce

**effective** able, active, capable, competent, effectual, efficient, energetic, operative, productive, serviceable, useful; active, current, in force, in operation, operative, real

**effervesce** ferment, fizz, foam, sparkle

**effervescent** bubbling, bubbly, foaming, foamy, frothing, sparkling

**efficiency** adeptness, capability, competence, economy, effectiveness, power, skill

**efficient** able, adept, businesslike, capable, competent, economic, productive, proficient, ready, skil-

ful, workmanlike

**effort** endeavour, energy, exertion, force, labour, power, striving, struggle, toil, trouble, work

**effortless** easy, facile, painless, simple, smooth, uncomplicated, undemanding

**egocentric** egotistic, self-centred, selfish

**eject** discharge, dislodge, dismiss, get rid of, oust, throw out; cast out, discharge, disgorge, emit, expel, throw out

**elaborate** *adj* careful, detailed, exact, intricate, laboured, minute, painstaking, precise, skilful, thorough; complex, complicated, detailed, fussy, involved, ornamented, showy *~v* add detail, amplify, decorate, develop, devise, enhance, enlarge, expand upon, garnish, improve, polish, refine

containing strands of rubber **elasticity** n

**elation** n high spirits **elate** v (*usu. passive*) make happy

**elbow** n joint between fore and upper parts of arm; part of sleeve covering this ~v shove with elbow **elbowroom** n room to move

**elder**[1] adj older, senior ~n person of greater age; official of certain churches **elderly** adj **eldest** adj oldest

**elder**[2] n tree with black berries

**elect** v choose by vote; choose ~adj appointed but not yet in office; chosen **election** n **elective** adj appointed by election **elector** n **electoral** adj **electorate** n body of electors

**electricity** n form of energy; electric current **electric** adj of, transmitting or powered by electricity **electrical** adj **electrician** n one trained in installation etc. of electrical devices **electrify** v **-fying, -fied electrifi-**cation n

**electro-** *comb. form* by, caused by electricity, as in **electrotherapy**

**electrocute** v kill by electricity **electrocution** n

**electrode** n conductor of electric current

**electron** n one of fundamental components of atom, charged with negative electricity **electronic** adj **electronics** pl n (with sing v) technology of electronic devices and circuits

**elegant** adj graceful, tasteful; refined **elegance** n

**elegy** n lament for the dead in poem **elegiac** adj

**element** n substance which cannot be separated by ordinary chemical techniques; component part; trace; heating wire in electric kettle etc.; proper sphere; pl powers of atmosphere; rudiments **elemental** adj **elementary** adj rudimentary, simple

**elephant** n huge animal with ivory

**elapse** go, go by, lapse, pass, pass by, slip away

**elastic** flexible, plastic, pliable, resilient, rubbery, springy, supple, yielding

**elbow** n angle, bend, corner, joint, turn ~v bump, crowd, hustle, jostle, knock, nudge, push, shoulder, shove

**elder** adj ancient, first-born, older, senior ~n older person, senior

**elect** appoint, choose, decide upon, determine, opt for, pick, pick out, prefer, select, settle on, vote

**election** choice, choosing, decision, judgment, preference, selection, vote

**elector** constituent, voter

**electric** charged, dynamic, rousing, stimulating, stirring, tense, thrilling

**electrify** amaze, animate, astonish, astound, excite, fire, invigorate, jolt, rouse, shock, startle, stimulate, stir, thrill

**elegance** beauty, dignity, gentility, grace, gracefulness, grandeur, polish, refinement

**elegant** artistic, beautiful, chic, choice, cultivated, delicate, exquisite, fashionable, fine, genteel, graceful, handsome, luxurious, refined, stylish, sumptuous, tasteful

**element** basis, component, constituent, factor, feature, ingredient, member, part, section, unit

**elementary** clear, easy, facile, plain, rudimentary, simple, straight-

tusks and long trunk

**elevate** v raise, exalt **elevation** n raising; height, esp. above sea level; drawing of one side of building etc.

**elevator** n US lift

**eleven** adj/n number next above 10 **eleventh** adj

**elf** n (pl **elves**) fairy **elfin, elvish** adj

**elicit** v draw out

**eligible** adj qualified; desirable **eligibility** n

**eliminate** v remove, get rid of, set aside **elimination** n

**elite** n the pick or best part of society

**elixir** n remedy

**elk** n large deer

**ellipse** n oval **elliptical** adj

**elm** n tree with serrated leaves

**elocution** n art of public speaking

**elongate** v lengthen

**elope** v run away from home with lover **elopement** n

**eloquence** n fluent, powerful use of language **eloquent** adj **eloquently** adv

**else** adv besides, instead; otherwise

**elsewhere** adv in or to some other place

**elucidate** v explain

**elude** v escape; baffle **elusive** ad' difficult to catch

**emaciated** adj abnormally thin

**emanate** v issue, proceed from **emanation** n

**emancipate** v set free **emancipa tion** n

**emasculate** v castrate; enfeeble

————————————— THESAURUS —————————————

forward, uncomplicated

**elevate** heighten, hoist, lift up, raise, uplift, upraise; advance, aggrandize, exalt, prefer, promote, upgrade

**elevation** altitude, height

**elicit** bring out, call forth, cause, derive, draw out, educe, evoke, evolve, exact, extort, extract, obtain, wrest

**eligible** fit, preferable, proper, qualified, suitable, suited, worthy

**eliminate** cut out, dispose of, do away with, exterminate, get rid of, remove, stamp out, take out

**elite** aristocracy, best, cream, elect, gentry, high society, nobility, upper class

**elocution** articulation, delivery, diction, enunciation, oratory, public speaking, rhetoric, speech, utterance

**elope** abscond, bolt, decamp, disappear, escape, leave, run away, run off, slip away, steal away

**eloquence** expressiveness, fluency, oratory, persuasiveness, rhetoric

**eloquent** articulate, fluent, forceful, graceful, moving, persuasive, well-expressed

**elsewhere** abroad, absent, away, not here, somewhere else

**elucidate** clarify, clear up, explain, expound, gloss, illuminate, make plain, spell out, unfold

**elude** avoid, dodge, escape, evade, flee, shirk, shun

**elusive** shifty, slippery, tricky

**emaciated** attenuated, cadaverous, gaunt, haggard, lank, lean, meagre, pinched, thin, wasted

**emanate** arise, derive, emerge, flow, issue, originate, proceed, spring, stem

**emancipate** deliver, discharge, enfranchise, free, liberate, release, set free, unshackle

**emancipation** deliverance, enfranchisement, freedom, liberation, liberty

weaken **emasculation** n

**embalm** v preserve corpse

**embankment** n artificial mound carrying road, railway, or to dam water

**embargo** n (pl **-goes**) order stopping movement of ships; ban **~v -goes, -going, -goed** put under embargo; requisition

**embark** v board ship, aircraft etc.; (with **on** or **upon**) commence new project etc.

**embarrass** v disconcert; abash; confuse **embarrassment** n

**embassy** n office or official residence of ambassador

**embattled** adj having many difficulties

**embed** v **-bedding, -bedded** fix fast (in)

**embellish** v adorn, enrich **embellishment** n

**ember** n glowing cinder

**embezzle** v misappropriate (money in trust etc.) **embezzlement** n **embezzler** n

**embitter** v make bitter

**emblem** n symbol; badge **emblematic** adj

**embody** v embodying, embodied represent, include, be expression of **embodiment** n

**embolism** n Med obstruction of artery

**emboss** v carve in relief

**embrace** v clasp in arms, hug; accept; comprise **~n** hug

**embrocation** n lotion for rubbing limbs etc. to relieve pain

**embroider** v ornament with needlework **embroidery** n

**embroil** v involve (someone) in problems

**embryo** n (pl **-bryos**) undeveloped offspring, germ **embryonic** adj

**emend** v to remove errors from, correct **emendation** n

**emerald** n bright green gem

**embargo** ban, bar, boycott, check, interdict, prohibition, restraint, restriction

**embark** board ship, go aboard, take ship (with **on** or **upon**) begin, broach, commence, engage, enter, initiate, launch, plunge into, set about, set out, start, take up, undertake

**embarrass** chagrin, discompose, disconcert, distress, fluster, mortify

**embarrassment** awkwardness, bashfulness, chagrin, confusion, distress, humiliation, mortification, shame

**embellish** adorn, beautify, bedeck, deck, decorate, dress up, elaborate, embroider, enhance, enrich, garnish, gild, grace, ornament

**embezzle** abstract, appropriate, filch, misapply, misappropriate, misuse, peculate, pilfer, purloin, steal

**embitter** anger, disaffect, disillusion, envenom, poison, sour

**emblem** badge, crest, device, figure, image, insignia, mark, representation, sign, symbol, token, type

**embrace** v clasp, cuddle, encircle, enfold, grasp, hold, hug, seize, squeeze; accept, adopt, espouse, grab, receive, seize, take up, welcome **~n** clasp, cuddle, hug, squeeze

**embroil** complicate, confound, confuse, enmesh, entangle, implicate, incriminate, involve, mire, mix up

**embryo** germ, nucleus, root

**emend** amend, correct, edit, im-

**emerge** v come up, out; rise to notice **emergence** n

**emergency** n sudden unforeseen event needing prompt action

**emery** n hard mineral used for polishing

**emigrate** v go and settle in another country **emigrant** n **emigration** n

**eminent** adj distinguished **eminently** adv **eminence** n

**emissary** n agent, representative sent on mission

**emit** v emitting, emitted give out, put forth **emission** n

**emollient** adj softening, soothing ~n ointment

**emotion** n excited state of feeling,

as joy, fear etc. **emotional** adj emotive **adj** arousing emotion

**empathy** n understanding of another's feelings

**emperor** n (fem **empress**) ruler of an empire

**emphasis** n (pl **-ses**) importance attached; stress on words **emphasize** v **emphatic** adj forceful

**emphysema** n disease of lungs, causing breathlessness

**empire** n group of states under supreme leader

**empirical** adj relying on experiment or experience

**emplacement** n position for gun

**employ** v employing, employed

———— THESAURUS ————

prove, revise

**emerge** appear, arise, come forth, come out, come up, emanate, issue, proceed, rise, spring up, surface

**emergency** crisis, danger, difficulty, extremity, necessity, pass, pinch, plight, predicament, quandary, strait

**emigrate** migrate, move, move abroad, remove

**eminence** celebrity, dignity, distinction, esteem, fame, greatness, importance, notability, note, prestige, rank, renown, reputation, repute, superiority

**eminent** celebrated, distinguished, esteemed, exalted, famous, illustrious, important, notable, noted, outstanding, prestigious, renowned, well-known

**emission** diffusion, discharge, ejection, exhalation, issuance, issue, radiation

**emit** diffuse, discharge, eject, emanate, exhale, exude, give off, give out, issue, radiate, send out, shed, throw out, transmit, utter, vent

**emotion** ardour, excitement, feeling, fervour, passion, sensation, sentiment, warmth

**emotional** demonstrative, excitable, hot-blooded, passionate, sensitive, susceptible, temperamental, tender, warm

**emotive** affecting, emotional, heart-warming, moving, pathetic, poignant, sentimental, tear-jerking Inf. touching

**emphasis** accent, attention, force, importance, insistence, intensity, moment, priority, prominence, significance, strength, stress, weight

**emphasize** accent, dwell on, highlight, insist on, play up, press home, stress, underline, underscore, weight

**emphatic** absolute, certain, decided, definite, direct, distinct, earnest, forceful, forcible, important, impressive, insistent, marked, positive, powerful, resounding, significant, striking, strong, telling, vigorous

**empire** commonwealth, domain,

provide work for in return for money; keep busy; use **employee** n **employer** n **employment** n employing, being employed; work; occupation

**empower** v authorize

**empress** SEE EMPEROR

**empty** adj containing nothing; unoccupied; senseless ~v emptying, emptied make, become devoid of content; discharge (contents) into **empties** pl n empty bottles etc. **emptiness** n

**emu** n large Aust. flightless bird

**emulate** v strive to equal or excel; imitate **emulation** n

**emulsion** n light-sensitive coating of film; liquid with oily particles in suspension; paint in this form

**emulsifier** n

**enable** v make able

**enact** v make law; act part

**enamel** n glasslike coating applied to metal etc.; coating of teeth; any hard coating ~v -elling, -elled cover with this

**enamour** v inspire with love

**encapsulate** v summarize; enclose

**enchant** v bewitch, delight **enchantment** n

**encircle** v surround; enfold

**enclave** n part of country entirely surrounded by foreign territory

**enclose** v shut in; surround; place in with letter **enclosure** n

**encompass** v surround, contain

**encore** interj again ~n (call for)

———————————— T H E S A U R U S ————————————

kingdom, realm

**employ** engage, enlist, hire, retain, take on; engage, fill, occupy, spend, take up, use up

**employee** hand, staff member, wage-earner, worker, workman

**employer** boss Inf, business, company, establishment, firm, organization, owner, patron, proprietor

**employment** application, exercise, exertion, use; engagement, enlistment, hire; business, calling, craft, employ, job, line, métier, occupation, profession, pursuit, service, trade, vocation, work

**empower** allow, authorize, commission, delegate, enable, entitle, license, permit, qualify, sanction, warrant

**emptiness** bareness, blankness, desolation, vacancy, vacuum, void, waste

**empty** adj bare, blank, clear, deserted, desolate, hollow, unfurnished, uninhabited, unoccupied, vacant, void, waste; aimless, banal,

frivolous, fruitless, futile, hollow, inane, ineffective, meaningless, silly, unreal, vain, valueless, worthless ~v clear, consume, deplete, discharge, drain, evacuate, exhaust, pour out, unburden, unload, use up, vacate, void

**enable** allow, authorize, commission, empower, fit, license, permit, prepare, qualify, sanction, warrant

**enact** authorize, command, decree, legislate, ordain, order, pass, proclaim, ratify, sanction

**enamour** bewitch, charm, enchant, endear, enrapture, entrance, fascinate

**enchant** beguile, bewitch, captivate, charm, delight, enamour, enrapture, enthral, fascinate, hypnotize, spellbind

**enclose** bound, cover, encase, encircle, encompass, fence, hedge, hem in, pen, shut in, wall in, wrap; include, insert, put in, send with

**encompass** circle, encircle, enclose, envelop, girdle, hem in, ring,

repetition of song etc.

**encounter** *v* meet unexpectedly; meet in conflict ~*n* encountering

**encourage** *v* inspire with hope; embolden **encouragement** *n*

**encroach** *v* intrude (on) **encroachment** *n*

**encrust** *v* cover with layer

**encumber** *v* hamper; burden **encumbrance** *n*

**encyclopedia, encyclopaedia** *n* book, set of books of information on one or all subjects **encyclopedic, -paedic** *adj*

**end** *n* limit; extremity; conclusion;

fragment; latter part; death; event; aim ~*v* put an end to; come to an end, finish **ending** *n* **endless** *adj*

**endanger** *v* put in danger

**endear** *v* make beloved **endearment** *n* loving word

**endeavour** *v* try, strive after ~*n* attempt

**endorse** *v* sanction; confirm; sign back of; record conviction on driving licence **endorsement** *n*

**endow** *v* provide permanent income for; furnish (with) **endowment** *n*

**endure** *v* undergo; tolerate; bear;

———— THESAURUS ————

surround

**encounter** *v* chance upon, come upon, confront, experience, face, meet, run across, run into *Inf*; attack, combat, contend, engage, fight, grapple with, strive, struggle ~*n* brush, confrontation, meeting

**encourage** buoy up, cheer, comfort, console, embolden, hearten, incite, inspire, rally, reassure, rouse, stimulate

**encouragement** aid, boost, cheer, consolation, favour, help, inspiration, reassurance, stimulation, stimulus, succour, support, urging

**encroach** impinge, infringe, intrude, invade, make inroads, overstep, trench, trespass, usurp

**end** *n* boundary, edge, extent, extremity, limit, terminus; close, closure, completion, conclusion, consequence, culmination, denouement, ending, expiry, finale, finish, outcome, resolution, result, stop, termination, upshot; death, demise, destruction, dissolution, doom, extinction, ruin, ruination; aim, aspiration, design, drift, goal, intention, object, objective, point, purpose,

reason ~*v* cease, close, complete, conclude, culminate, dissolve, expire, finish, resolve, stop, terminate, wind up

**endanger** compromise, hazard, imperil, jeopardize, put at risk, risk, threaten

**endeavour** *v* aim, aspire, attempt, essay, strive, struggle, try, undertake ~*n* aim, attempt, effort, enterprise, essay, go *Inf*, trial, try, venture

**ending** close, completion, conclusion, denouement, finale, finish, resolution, termination

**endless** ceaseless, constant, continual, eternal, everlasting, immortal, incessant, infinite, interminable, perpetual, unbounded, unbroken, undying, unlimited; continuous, unbroken, undivided, whole

**endorse** advocate, affirm, approve, authorize, back, champion, confirm, favour, O.K. or okay *Inf*, ratify, recommend, sanction, support, sustain, warrant

**endowment** award, benefaction, bequest, bestowal, boon, donation,

last **endurable** adj **endurance** n

**enema** n medicine, liquid injected into rectum

**enemy** n hostile person; opponent; armed foe

**energy** n vigour, force, activity; source of power, as oil, coal etc.; capacity of machine, battery etc. for work **energetic** adj **energize** v

**enervate** v weaken

**enfeeble** v weaken

**enfold** v cover by wrapping something around

**enforce** v compel obedience to; impose (action) upon **enforceable** adj **enforcement** n

**enfranchise** v give right of voting

to; give parliamentary representation to; set free

**engage** v participate; involve; employ; bring into operation; begin conflict **engaged** adj pledged to be married; in use **engagement** n appointment; pledge of marriage **engaging** adj charming

**engender** v give rise to

**engine** n any machine to convert energy into mechanical work; railway locomotive **engineer** n one who is in charge of engines, machinery etc.; one who originates, organizes ~v construct as engineer; contrive **engineering** n

**engrave** v cut in lines on metal for

fund, gift, grant, income, largess, legacy, presentation, property, provision, revenue

**endurance** bearing, fortitude, patience, perseverance, resignation, resolution, stamina, staying power, strength, submission, sufferance, tenacity, toleration

**endure** bear, brave, cope with, experience, go through, stand, suffer, support, sustain, undergo, weather, withstand; abide, allow, bear, brook, countenance, permit, stand, stick *Sl*, stomach, suffer, swallow, take patiently, tolerate

**enemy** adversary, antagonist, competitor, foe, opponent, rival

**energetic** active, brisk, dynamic, forceful, forcible, indefatigable, lively, potent, powerful, spirited, strenuous, strong, tireless, vigorous

**energy** activity, ardour, drive, efficiency, élan, exertion, fire, force, intensity, life, liveliness, power, spirit, stamina, strength, verve, vigour, vitality, vivacity, zeal, zest

**enforce** apply, carry out, coerce,

compel, constrain, exact, execute, impose, insist on, oblige, prosecute, reinforce, require, urge

**enfranchise** give the vote to; emancipate, free, liberate, manumit, release, set free

**engage** absorb, busy, engross, grip, involve, occupy, preoccupy, tie up; appoint, commission, employ, enlist, enrol, hire, retain, take on; activate, apply, energize, set going, switch on; assail, attack, combat, fall on, fight with, meet, take on

**engaged** affianced, pledged, promised, spoken for

**engagement** appointment, commitment, date, meeting; betrothal, bond, compact, contract, oath, obligation, pact, pledge, promise, vow, word

**engine** machine, mechanism, motor

**engineer** n contriver, designer, deviser, director, inventor, manipulator, originator, planner, schemer ~v bring about, cause, concoct, con-

## DICTIONARY

printing; carve, incise; impress deeply **engraving** n

**engross** v absorb (attention); occupy wholly

**engulf** v swallow up

**enhance** v intensify value or attractiveness of **enhancement** n

**enigma** n puzzling thing or person **enigmatic** adj

**enjoy** v delight in; have benefit of **enjoy oneself** be happy **enjoyable** adj **enjoyment** n

**enlarge** v make bigger; grow bigger; talk in greater detail **enlargement** n

**enlighten** v give information to **enlightenment** n

**enlist** v engage as soldier or helper

**enliven** v animate

**enmesh** v entangle

**enmity** n ill will, hostility

**enormous** adj very big, vast **enormity** n gross offence

**enough** adj/n/adv as much as need be

**enquire** SEE INQUIRE

**enrich** v make rich; add to

**enrol** v -rolling, -rolled write name of on roll; enlist; become member of

**en route** Fr on the way

## THESAURUS

trive, control, create, devise, effect, manage, mastermind, originate, plan, plot, scheme

**engrave** carve, chase, chisel, cut, etch, inscribe

**enigma** conundrum, mystery, problem, puzzle, riddle

**enigmatic** cryptic, Delphic, inscrutable, mysterious, obscure, perplexing, puzzling

**enjoy** appreciate, delight in, like, rejoice in, relish, revel in, take joy in; experience, own, possess, use

**enjoyable** agreeable, amusing, delicious, delightful, entertaining, pleasant, pleasing, pleasurable, satisfying

**enjoyment** amusement, delight, entertainment, fun, gladness, gratification, gusto, happiness, indulgence, joy, pleasure, recreation, relish, satisfaction, zest

**enlarge** add to, augment, broaden, diffuse, dilate, distend, elongate, expand, extend, grow, heighten, increase, inflate, lengthen, magnify, multiply, stretch, swell, widen

**enlighten** advise, apprise, civilize, counsel, edify, educate, inform, in-

struct, make aware, teach

**enlist** engage, enrol, gather, join, join up, muster, obtain, procure, recruit, register, secure, sign up

**enliven** brighten, buoy up, cheer up, excite, exhilarate, fire, gladden, hearten, inspire, inspirit, invigorate, quicken, rouse, spark, stimulate, vitalize, wake up

**enmity** animosity, animus, antagonism, antipathy, aversion, bad blood, bitterness, hate, hatred, hostility, ill will, malevolence, malice, rancour, spite, venom

**enormity** atrocity, depravity, disgrace, evilness, turpitude, viciousness, villainy, wickedness

**enormous** astronomic, colossal, gigantic, gross, huge, immense, jumbo Inf, mammoth, massive, monstrous, prodigious, tremendous, vast

**enough** adj abundant, adequate, ample, plenty, sufficient ~adv abundantly, adequately, amply, fairly, moderately, passably, reasonably, satisfactorily, sufficiently, tolerably

**en route** in transit, on the way

**ensemble** n all parts taken together; woman's complete outfit; *Mus* group of soloists performing together

**enshrine** v preserve with sacred affection

**ensign** n naval or military flag; badge

**enslave** v make into slave

**ensnare** v trap; entangle

**ensue** v follow, happen after

**ensure** v make certain

**entail** v necessitate

**entangle** v ensnare; perplex

**entente** n friendly understanding between nations

**enter** v go, come into; penetrate;
join; write in; begin **entrance** n going, coming in; door, passage; right to enter; fee **entrant** n one who enters **entry** n

**enterprise** n bold undertaking; bold spirit; business **enterprising** adj

**entertain** v amuse, receive as guest; consider **entertainer** n **entertainment** n

**enthral** v -thralling, -thralled captivate

**enthusiasm** n ardent eagerness **enthuse** v **enthusiast** n **enthusiastic** adj

**entice** v allure, attract

**entire** adj whole, complete **entirely**

——— THESAURUS ———

**ensemble** costume, get-up *Inf,* outfit, suit; band, cast, chorus, company, group, troupe

**ensue** arise, attend, be consequent on, befall, come after, derive, flow, follow, issue, proceed, result, stem, succeed, supervene

**entail** bring about, call for, cause, demand, give rise to, impose, involve, lead to, necessitate, occasion, require, result in

**entangle** catch, embroil, enmesh, ensnare, implicate, involve, knot, mix up, snag, snare, tangle, trap; complicate, confuse, mix up, muddle, perplex, puzzle, snarl, twist

**enter** arrive, come *or* go in *or* into, insert, introduce, penetrate, pierce; begin, commence, embark upon, enlist, enrol, join, sign up, start, take up; list, log, note, record, register, set down, take down, write down

**enterprise** adventure, effort, endeavour, essay, operation, plan, programme, project, undertaking, venture; activity, daring, dash,
drive, energy, enthusiasm, initiative, readiness, resource, spirit, vigour, zeal; business, company, concern, establishment, firm, operation

**enterprising** active, adventurous, bold, daring, dashing, eager, go-ahead, intrepid, keen, ready, resourceful, vigorous, zealous

**entertain** amuse, charm, cheer, delight, divert, occupy, please

**entertainment** amusement, cheer, distraction, diversion, enjoyment, fun, good time, play, pleasure, recreation, satisfaction, sport, treat

**enthusiasm** ardour, eagerness, earnestness, excitement, fervour, frenzy, interest, keenness, passion, relish, vehemence, warmth, zeal, zest

**enthusiast** admirer, aficionado, buff *Inf,* devotee, fan, fanatic, fiend *Inf,* follower, freak *Inf,* lover, zealot

**enthusiastic** ardent, avid, devoted, eager, earnest, ebullient, excited, fervent, fervid, hearty, keen, lively, spirited, unstinting, vigor-

*adv* **entirety** *n*
**entitle** *v* qualify; name **entitlement** *n*
**entity** *n* thing's being or existence; reality
**entomology** *n* study of insects
**entourage** *n* group of people assisting important person
**entrails** *pl n* intestines
**entrance**[1] *SEE* ENTER
**entrance**[2] *v* delight
**entreat** *v* ask earnestly; beg, implore **entreaty** *n*
**entrench** *v* establish firmly
**entrepreneur** *n* businessman who

attempts to profit by risk and initiative
**entrust** *v* commit, charge with
**entwine** *v* plait, interweave
**enumerate** *v* mention one by one
**enunciate** *v* state clearly
**envelop** *v* wrap up, surround
**envelope** *n* cover of letter
**environment** *n* surroundings; conditions of life or growth **environmental** *adj* **environs** *pl n* outskirts
**envisage** *v* visualize
**envoy** *n* diplomat
**envy** *v* **envying, envied** grudge

——————— THESAURUS ———————

ous, warm, wholehearted, zealous
**entice** allure, attract, beguile, cajole, coax, decoy, draw, inveigle, lead on, lure, persuade, seduce, tempt, wheedle
**entire** complete, full, total, whole
**entirely** absolutely, altogether, completely, fully, perfectly, thoroughly, totally, unreservedly, utterly, wholly, without exception, without reservation
**entitle** allow, authorize, empower, enable, fit for, license, permit, qualify for, warrant; call, christen, designate, dub, label, name, style, term, title
**entity** being, body, creature, individual, object, organism, presence, thing
**entrance**[1] *n* access, door, doorway, entry, gate, inlet, opening, passage, way in; arrival, entry, ingress, introduction; access, admission, admittance, entrée, entry, ingress
**entrance**[2] *v* bewitch, captivate, charm, delight, enchant, enthral, fascinate, ravish, transport
**entrant** candidate, competitor,

contestant, entry, participant, player
**entrust** assign, charge, commend, commit, confide, consign, delegate, deliver, hand over, invest, trust
**entry** access, door, doorway, entrance, gate, inlet, opening, passageway, portal, way in; access, admission, entrance, entrée; attempt, candidate, competitor, contestant, effort, entrant, participant, player, submission
**envelop** blanket, cloak, conceal, cover, embrace, encase, enclose, enfold, engulf, hide, obscure, sheathe, shroud, surround, swathe, veil, wrap
**envelope** case, casing, coating, cover, covering, jacket, sheath, shell, skin, wrapping
**enviable** blessed, desirable, favoured, fortunate, lucky, privileged
**envious** covetous, grudging, jaundiced, jealous, malicious, resentful, spiteful
**environment** atmosphere, background, conditions, context, element, habitat, locale, medium, milieu, scene, setting, situation,

another's good fortune ~n (object of) this feeling **enviable** adj **envious** adj

**enzyme** n any of group of proteins produced by living cells and acting as catalysts

**epaulette** n shoulder ornament on uniform

**ephemeral** adj short-lived

**epic** n long poem telling of achievements of hero ~adj on grand scale

**epicentre** n point immediately above origin of earthquake

**epicure** n one delighting in eating and drinking **epicurean** adj/n

**epidemic** adj (esp. of disease) prevalent and spreading rapidly ~n serious outbreak

**epidermis** n outer skin

**epidural** n spinal anaesthetic

**epigram** n witty saying

**epigraph** n quotation at start of book; inscription

**epilepsy** n disorder of nervous system causing fits **epileptic** n/adj

**epilogue** n closing speech

**episcopal** adj of, ruled by bishop

**episode** n incident; section of (serialized) book etc. **episodic** adj

**epistle** n letter

**epitaph** n inscription on tomb

**epithet** n descriptive word

**epitome** n typical example **epitomize** v

**epoch** n period, era

**equable** adj even-tempered, placid

**equal** adj the same in number, size, merit etc.; fit ~n one equal to another ~v equalling, **equalled** be equal to **equally** adv **equality** n **equalize** v

**equanimity** n composure

**equate** v make equal **equation** n equating of two mathematical expressions

**equator** n imaginary circle round

——— T H E S A U R U S ———

surroundings

**envoy** agent, ambassador, courier, delegate, diplomat, emissary, intermediary, messenger, minister, representative

**envy** v begrudge, be jealous (of), covet, grudge, resent ~n covetousness, grudge, hatred, ill will, jealousy, malice, resentment, spite

**epidemic** adj general, prevailing, rampant, rife, sweeping, widespread ~n outbreak, plague, rash, spread, wave

**epigram** bon mot, quip, witticism

**epilogue** coda, conclusion, postscript

**episode** adventure, affair, event, experience, happening, incident, matter, occurrence; chapter, instalment, part, passage, scene, section

**epistle** communication, letter,

message, missive, note

**epitome** embodiment, essence, exemplar, personification, type

**equable** agreeable, calm, composed, easy-going, even-tempered, placid, serene, unflappable Inf

**equal** adj alike, commensurate, equivalent, identical, like, proportionate, tantamount, uniform; able, adequate, capable, competent, fit, ready, suitable, up to ~n brother, compeer, equivalent, fellow, match, mate, peer, rival, twin

**equality** balance, egalitarianism, equivalence, evenness, fairness, identity, likeness, parity, sameness, similarity, uniformity

**equate** agree, balance, compare, correspond with, liken, match, offset, pair, square, tally

**equation** agreement, balancing,

earth equidistant from the poles

**equestrian** *adj* of horse-riding

**equilateral** *adj* having equal sides

**equilibrium** *n* (*pl* **-riums, -ria**) state of steadiness

**equinox** *n* time when sun crosses equator and day and night are equal

**equip** *v* **equipping, equipped** supply, fit out **equipment** *n*

**equitable** *adj* fair, reasonable, just **equity** *n*

**equivalent** *adj* equal in value

**equivocal** *adj* of double or doubtful meaning **equivocate** *v*

**era** *n* period of time

**eradicate** *v* wipe out

**erase** *v* rub out; remove

**ere** *prep/conj Poet* before

**erect** *adj* upright ~*v* set up; build **erection** *n*

**ermine** *n* stoat in northern regions

**erode** *v* wear away; eat into **erosion** *n*

**erotic** *adj* of sexual pleasure

**err** *v* make mistakes; be wrong; sin

**erratic** *adj* irregular **erratum** *n* (*pl* **-ta**) error, esp. in printing **erroneous** *adj* wrong **error** *n* mistake

**errand** *n* short journey for simple business

**errant** *adj* wandering

— THESAURUS —

comparison, correspondence, equivalence, likeness, match, pairing, parallel

**equilibrium** balance, counterpoise, equipoise, evenness, rest, stability, steadiness

**equip** accoutre, arm, array, attire, endow, fit out, furnish, kit out, outfit, prepare, provide, rig, stock, supply

**equipment** accoutrements, apparatus, baggage, furnishings, gear, outfit, stuff, supplies, tackle, tools

**equivalent** alike, commensurate, comparable, corresponding, equal, even, interchangeable, of a kind, same, similar, synonymous, tantamount

**equivocal** ambiguous, ambivalent, doubtful, dubious, evasive, indefinite, indeterminate, misleading, obscure, questionable, suspicious, uncertain

**era** age, cycle, date, day *or* days, epoch, generation, period, stage, time

**eradicate** annihilate, destroy, efface, eliminate, erase, expunge, ex-

tinguish, obliterate, remove, root out, stamp out, uproot, weed out, wipe out

**erect** *adj* firm, raised, rigid, standing, stiff, straight, upright, vertical ~*v* build, construct, lift, mount, pitch, put up, raise

**erode** consume, corrode, destroy, deteriorate, eat away, grind down, spoil

**erotic** carnal, erogenous, seductive, sensual, sexy *Inf*, titillating, voluptuous

**err** be inaccurate, be incorrect, blunder, go wrong, make a mistake, miscalculate, misjudge, mistake

**errand** charge, commission, job, message, mission, task

**erratic** aberrant, abnormal, capricious, changeable, desultory, fitful, inconsistent, irregular, shifting, unreliable, unstable, variable, wayward

**erroneous** amiss, fallacious, false, inaccurate, incorrect, inexact, invalid, mistaken, spurious, untrue, wrong

**error** bloomer *Brit inf*, blunder,

**erstwhile** adj former

**erudite** adj learned

**erupt** v burst out **eruption** n

**escalate** v increase, be increased, in extent, intensity etc. **escalation** n

**escalator** n moving staircase

**escape** v get free; get off safely; find way out; elude; leak ~n escaping **escapade** n wild adventure **escapism** n taking refuge in fantasy

**escarpment** n steep hillside

**eschew** v avoid, shun

**escort** n person accompanying another to guard, guide etc. ~v accompany

**esoteric** adj obscure

**ESP** extrasensory perception

**especial** adj pre-eminent; particular **especially** adv

**espionage** n spying

**esplanade** n promenade

**espouse** v support; Obs marry **espousal** v

**espy** v espying, espied catch sight of

**Esq.** Esquire, title used on letters

**essay** n prose composition; attempt ~v essaying, essayed try

**essence** n all that makes thing what it is; extract got by distillation **essential** adj vitally important; basic ~n essential thing

— THESAURUS —

**boob** Brit sl, delusion, erratum, fallacy, fault, flaw, inaccuracy, miscalculation, mistake, oversight, slip, solecism

**erudite** cultivated, educated, knowledgeable, learned, lettered, literate, scholarly, well-educated, well-read

**erupt** belch forth, blow up, break out, burst forth, burst out, discharge, explode, flare up, gush, pour forth or out, spit out, spout, throw off, vent, vomit

**eruption** discharge, ejection, explosion, flare-up, outbreak, outburst

**escalate** ascend, be increased, enlarge, expand, extend, grow, heighten, increase, intensify, mount, raise, rise

**escapade** adventure, antic, caper, fling, mischief, spree, stunt, trick

**escape** v bolt, break free, decamp, flee, fly, get away, run away or off, skedaddle Inf, skip, slip away; avoid, dodge, duck, elude, evade, pass, shun, slip; drain, emanate, flow, gush, issue, leak, seep, spurt

~n break, break-out, flight, getaway

**escort** n bodyguard, company, convoy, cortege, entourage, guard, protection, retinue, safeguard, train ~v accompany, conduct, convoy, guard, guide, lead, partner, protect, squire, usher

**especially** chiefly, conspicuously, exceptionally, extraordinarily, mainly, markedly, notably, principally, remarkably, specially, strikingly, supremely, uncommonly, usually

**essay** article, composition, discourse, disquisition, dissertation, paper, piece, tract

**essence** being, core, entity, heart, kernel, life, lifeblood, nature, pith, principle, soul, spirit, substance; concentrate, distillate, extract, spirits, tincture

**essential** adj crucial, important, indispensable, necessary, needed, requisite, vital; basic, cardinal, fundamental, inherent, innate, intrinsic, key, main, principal ~n basic, fundamental, must, necessity, requisite, rudiment

**establish** *v* set up; settle; prove **establishment** *n*

**estate** *n* landed property; person's property; area of property development **estate agent** one who values, leases and sells property

**esteem** *v/n* regard, respect

**ester** *n Chem* organic compound

**estimate** *v/n* (form) approximate idea of (amounts, measurements etc.) **estimable** *adj* worthy of regard **estimation** *n* opinion

**estranged** *adj* no longer living with one's spouse

**estuary** *n* mouth of river

**etc.** *et cetera*

**et cetera** *Lat* and the rest, and others, and so on

**etch** *v* make engraving on metal plate with acids etc. **etching** *n*

**eternal** *adj* everlasting **eternity** *n*

**ether** *n* colourless liquid used as anaesthetic; clear sky **ethereal** *adj* airy; heavenly

**ethics** *pl n* (science of) morals **ethical** *adj*

**ethnic** *adj* of race or relating to classification of humans into different groups

**ethos** *n* distinctive spirit of people, culture etc.

**etiquette** *n* conventional code of conduct

**étude** *n* short musical composition, exercise

**etymology** *n* tracing, account of word's origin, development

**eucalyptus, eucalypt** *n* Aust. tree, providing timber and gum

**Eucharist** *n* Christian sacrament of the Lord's Supper

**eugenics** *pl n* (with *sing v*) science of improving the human race by selective breeding

———————————— THESAURUS ————————————

**establish** base, constitute, create, decree, enact, entrench, fix, form, found, ground, implant, inaugurate, install, institute, plant, root, secure, settle, set up, start

**establishment** business, company, concern, enterprise, firm, house, institution, organization, outfit *Inf*, setup *Inf*, structure, system

**estate** area, domain, holdings, lands, manor, property

**esteem** *v* admire, be fond of, cherish, honour, like, love, prize, respect, revere, reverence, treasure, value ~*n* credit, good opinion, honour, regard, respect, reverence

**estimate** *v* assess, calculate roughly, evaluate, gauge, guess, judge, number, reckon, value ~*n* approximate calculation, assessment, evaluation, guess, judgment, reckoning, valuation

**estuary** creek, firth, fjord, inlet, mouth

**et cetera** and others, and so forth, and so on, and the like, and the rest

**eternal** abiding, ceaseless, constant, deathless, endless, everlasting, immortal, infinite, interminable, never-ending, perennial, perpetual, timeless, unceasing, undying, unending, without end

**ethical** correct, fitting, good, honest, honourable, just, moral, principled, proper, right, upright

**ethics** conscience, moral code, morality, moral philosophy, moral values, principles, standards

**ethnic** cultural, folk, indigenous, national, native, racial, traditional

**etiquette** civility, code, convention, courtesy, customs, decorum, manners, politeness, propriety,

eulogy n praise eulogize v

eunuch n castrated man

euphemism n substitution of mild term for offensive one euphemistic adj

euphoria n sense of elation euphoric adj

eureka interj exclamation of triumph

euthanasia n painless putting to death to relieve suffering

evacuate v empty; withdraw from evacuation n evacuee n

evade v avoid; elude evasion n evasive adj

evaluate v find or judge value of evaluation n

evangelical adj of, or according to, gospel teaching evangelism n evangelist n

evaporate v turn into vapour evaporation n

evasion SEE EVADE

eve n evening before; time just before evensong n evening service

even adj flat; smooth; uniform; equal; divisible by two; impartial ~v smooth; equalize ~adv equally; simply; notwithstanding

evening n close of day

event n happening; notable occurrence; result; any one contest in sporting programme eventful adj full of exciting events eventual adj resulting in the end eventuality n possible event

ever adv always; at any time evergreen n/adj (tree or shrub) bearing foliage throughout the year evermore adv for all time to come

——————— THESAURUS ———————

protocol, rules, usage

evacuate abandon, clear, decamp, depart, desert, forsake, leave, move out, pull out, quit, relinquish, remove, vacate, withdraw

evade avoid, circumvent, decline, dodge, duck, elude, escape, shirk, shun, sidestep

evaluate appraise, assay, assess, estimate, gauge, judge, rank, rate, reckon, size up Inf, value, weigh

evaporate dry, dry up, vaporize; dematerialize, disappear, disperse, dissipate, dissolve, fade away, melt, vanish

evasion avoidance, cunning, dodge, equivocation, escape, evasiveness, excuse, prevarication, ruse, shift, shuffling, sophistry, subterfuge, trickery

evasive cagey Inf, cunning, devious, elusive, equivocating, indirect, misleading, oblique, prevaricating, shifty

eve day before, night before, vigil

even adj flat, flush, level, plane, plumb, smooth, steady, straight, true, uniform; balanced, disinterested, dispassionate, equitable, fair, impartial, just, unbiased, unprejudiced ~adv all the more, much, still, yet

event affair, business, circumstance, episode, experience, fact, happening, incident, matter, milestone, occasion, occurrence

eventful active, busy, critical, crucial, decisive, exciting, fateful, full, historic, important, lively, memorable, momentous, notable, significant

eventual concluding, consequent, ensuing, final, future, later, resulting, ultimate

eventuality case, chance, contingency, event, likelihood, possibility, probability

ever always, at all times, constant-

**every** adj each of all; all possible

**everybody** n **everyday** adj usual, ordinary **everyone** n **everything** n

**everywhere** adv in all places

**evict** v expel by legal process, turn out **eviction** n

**evidence** n ground of belief; sign; testimony ~v indicate, prove **evident** adj plain, obvious

**evil** adj/n (what is) bad or harmful

**evoke** v call to mind; bring about **evocation** n **evocative** adj

**evolve** v (cause to) develop gradually; undergo slow changes **evolution** n development of species from earlier forms

**ewe** n female sheep

**ex-** comb. form out from, from, out of, formerly, as in **exclaim, exodus**

**exacerbate** v aggravate, make worse

**exact** adj precise, strictly correct ~v demand, extort **exacting** adj making rigorous demands **exactly** adv

**exaggerate** v magnify beyond

———————— THESAURUS ————————

ly, continually, endlessly, eternally, incessantly, perpetually, relentlessly, unceasingly; at all, at any period, at any point, at any time, in any case, on any occasion

**evermore** always, eternally, ever, for ever, *in perpetuum*, to the end of time

**every** all, each, each one, the whole number

**everyday** accustomed, common, commonplace, conventional, dull, familiar, frequent, habitual, informal, mundane, ordinary, routine, stock, usual, wonted

**evict** boot out *Inf*, chuck out *Inf*, dislodge, dispossess, eject, expel, kick out *Inf*, oust, put out, remove, show the door (to), throw on to the streets, throw out, turf out *Inf*, turn out

**evidence** affirmation, confirmation, data, declaration, demonstration, grounds, indication, mark, proof, sign, substantiation, testimony, token, witness

**evident** apparent, clear, incontestable, indisputable, manifest, noticeable, obvious, patent, perceptible, plain, visible

**evil** adj bad, base, corrupt, depraved, malicious, malignant, sinful, vicious, vile, villainous, wicked, wrong; calamitous, catastrophic, destructive, dire, harmful, hurtful, injurious, mischievous, painful, pernicious, ruinous, sorrowful, unfortunate, unlucky, woeful ~n badness, baseness, corruption, immorality, vice, villainy, wickedness, wrong, wrongdoing

**evoke** arouse, awaken, call, excite, induce, recall, stimulate, stir up, summon up; bring about, call forth, elicit, produce, provoke

**evolution** development, enlargement, expansion, growth, increase, progress, unrolling

**evolve** develop, disclose, educe, elaborate, enlarge, expand, grow, increase, mature, open, progress, unfold, unroll, work out

**exact** adj accurate, careful, correct, definite, explicit, faithful, faultless, identical, literal, methodical, orderly, particular, precise, right, specific, true, unequivocal, unerring, veracious, very; careful, meticulous, painstaking, punctilious, rigorous, scrupulous, severe, strict ~v call for, claim, command, compel, demand, extort, extract, force,

truth, overstate **exaggeration** n

**exalt** v raise up; praise

**exam** n examination

**examine** v investigate; look at closely; ask questions of; test knowledge of **examination** n **examiner** n

**example** n specimen; model

**exasperate** v irritate **exasperation** n

**excavate** v hollow out; dig; un-

earth **excavator** n

**exceed** v be greater than; go beyond **exceedingly** adv very

**excel** v -celling, -celled surpass; be very good **excellence** n **excellent** adj very good

**except** prep not including ~v exclude **exception** n thing not included in a rule; objection **exceptional** adj above average

**excerpt** n passage from book etc.

—————————— T H E S A U R U S ——————————

impose, insist upon, require

**exactly** accurately, carefully, correctly, definitely, explicitly, faithfully, faultlessly, literally, precisely, severely, strictly, truly, truthfully, veraciously

**exaggerate** amplify, embroider, emphasize, enlarge, exalt, inflate, magnify, overdo, overestimate, overstate

**exaggeration** embellishment, emphasis, enlargement, excess, hyperbole, inflation, overstatement, pretension, pretentiousness

**exalt** advance, dignify, elevate, ennoble, honour, promote, raise, upgrade

**examination** analysis, catechism, checkup, exploration, inquiry, inquisition, inspection, interrogation, investigation, once-over Inf, perusal, probe, questioning, quiz, review, scrutiny, search, study, survey, test, trial

**examine** analyse, appraise, check out, consider, explore, inspect, investigate, look over, peruse, ponder, probe, review, scan, scrutinize, sift, study, survey, test, vet, weigh

**example** case, illustration, instance, sample, specimen

**exasperate** anger, annoy, enrage, exacerbate, gall, get Inf, incense,

inflame, infuriate, irk, irritate, madden, pique, provoke, rankle, vex

**exasperation** anger, annoyance, fury, irritation, passion, pique, rage, vexation, wrath

**excavate** burrow, delve, dig, dig out, dig up, gouge, hollow, mine, quarry, scoop, trench, tunnel, uncover, unearth

**exceed** beat, better, cap Inf, eclipse, excel, outdistance, outdo, outreach, outrun, outshine, outstrip, overtake, pass, surmount, surpass, top, transcend

**excel** beat, be superior, better, cap Inf, eclipse, exceed, go beyond, outdo, outrival, outshine, pass, surmount, surpass, top, transcend

**excellence** distinction, eminence, goodness, greatness, high quality, merit, perfection, superiority, supremacy, virtue, worth

**excellent** admirable, capital, champion, choice, cracking Brit inf, distinguished, exemplary, exquisite, fine, first-class, first-rate, good, great, meritorious, outstanding, prime, select, superb, superior, superlative, top-notch Inf, worthy

**except, except for** apart from, bar, barring, besides, but, excepting, excluding, exclusive of, omitting, other than

**excess** n too great amount; intemperance **excessive** adj

**exchange** v give (something) in return for something else; barter ~n giving one thing and receiving another; thing given; building where merchants meet for business; central telephone office **exchangeable** adj

**exchequer** n government department in charge of revenue

**excise**[1] n duty charged on home goods

**excise**[2] v cut away

**excite** v arouse to strong emotion, stimulate; set in motion **excitable** adj **excitement** n **exciting** adj

**exclaim** v speak suddenly, cry out **exclamation** n **exclamation mark** punctuation mark (!), used after exclamations

**exclude** v shut out; debar from; reject, not consider **exclusion** n **exclusive** adj excluding; select **exclusiveness, exclusivity** n

**excommunicate** v cut off from sacraments of the Church **excommunication** n

———————————— THESAURUS ————————————

**exception** anomaly, deviation, freak, irregularity, oddity, peculiarity, quirk, special case

**exceptional** excellent, extraordinary, marvellous, outstanding, phenomenal, prodigious, remarkable, special, superior

**excess** glut, leftover, overdose, overflow, plethora, remainder, superfluity, surfeit, surplus, too much; debauchery, dissipation, dissoluteness, extravagance, intemperance, overindulgence, prodigality

**excessive** enormous, exaggerated, extravagant, extreme, inordinate, needless, overdone, overmuch, prodigal, profligate, superfluous, too much, undue, unreasonable

**exchange** v bandy, barter, change, commute, swap Inf, switch, trade, truck ~n barter, dealing, substitution, swap Inf, switch, trade, traffic, truck

**excitable** edgy, hasty, highly strung, hot-headed, nervous, passionate, sensitive, temperamental, testy, touchy, violent, volatile

**excite** agitate, arouse, awaken, disturb, evoke, fire, foment, galvanize, incite, inflame, inspire, move, provoke, quicken, rouse, stimulate, stir up, thrill, waken

**excitement** action, ado, adventure, animation, commotion, elation, ferment, kicks Inf, passion, thrill, tumult, warmth

**exciting** exhilarating, inspiring, intoxicating, moving, provocative, rip-roaring Inf, rousing, sensational, stimulating, stirring, thrilling

**exclaim** call, call out, cry, cry out, declare, proclaim, shout, utter, yell

**exclamation** call, cry, expletive, interjection, outcry, shout, utterance, yell

**exclude** ban, bar, blackball, debar, disallow, forbid, interdict, keep out, ostracize, prohibit, proscribe, refuse, shut out, veto; eliminate, except, ignore, leave out, omit, pass over, preclude, reject, repudiate, rule out

**exclusive** aristocratic, chic, choice, clannish, closed, elegant, fashionable, limited, narrow, posh Inf, chiefly Brit, private, restricted, select, selfish, snobbish

**excommunicate** anathematize, ban, banish, cast out, denounce, eject, exclude, expel, proscribe, re-

**excrement** *n* waste matter from bowels **excrete** *v* discharge from the system **excretion** *n* **excretory** *adj*

**excruciating** *adj* unbearably painful

**excursion** *n* trip for pleasure

**excuse** *v* overlook; try to clear from blame; gain exemption; set free ~*n* that which serves to excuse; apology **excusable** *adj*

**execrable** *adj* hatefully bad

**execute** *v* inflict capital punishment on, kill; carry out, perform; make **execution** *n* **execution** *n* **executive** *n/adj* (of) person in admin-

istrative position; (of) branch of government enforcing laws **executor** *n* (*fem* **executrix**) person appointed to carry out provisions of a will

**exemplary** *adj* serving as example

**exemplify** *v* **-fying, -fied** serve as example of

**exempt** *v* free from; excuse ~*adj* freed from, not liable for **exemption** *n*

**exercise** *n* use of limbs for health; practice; task; use ~*v* use; carry out; take exercise

**exert** *v* make effort **exertion** *n*

move, repudiate, unchurch

**excursion** airing, day trip, expedition, jaunt, journey, outing, pleasure trip, tour, trip

**excuse** *v* absolve, acquit, bear with, exculpate, exonerate, forgive, indulge, overlook, pardon, pass over, tolerate, wink at; absolve, discharge, exempt, free, let off, liberate, release, relieve, spare ~*n* apology, defence, explanation, grounds, justification, mitigation, plea, pretext, reason, vindication

**execute** behead, electrocute, guillotine, hang, kill, put to death, shoot

**execution** capital punishment, hanging, killing; accomplishment, achievement, administration, carrying out, completion, discharge, effect, enactment, enforcement, implementation, performance, prosecution, realization, rendering

**executive** *n* administrator, director, manager, official; administration, directorate, directors, government, leadership, management ~*adj* administrative, controlling, decision-making, directing, govern-

ing, managerial

**exemplary** admirable, commendable, correct, estimable, excellent, good, ideal, laudable, meritorious, model, praiseworthy, sterling

**exemplify** demonstrate, depict, display, embody, evidence, exhibit, illustrate, instance, represent, show

**exempt** *v* absolve, discharge, except, excuse, exonerate, free, let off, liberate, release, relieve, spare ~*adj* absolved, clear, discharged, excused, favoured, free, immune, liberated, not liable, not subject, privileged, released, spared

**exercise** *n* action, activity, discipline, drill, drilling, effort, labour, toil, training, work, work-out; drill, lesson, practice, problem, schooling, task, work ~*v* apply, bring to bear, employ, enjoy, exert, practise, put to use, use, utilize, wield; drill, inure, practise, train, work out

**exert** bring into play, bring to bear, employ, exercise, expend, use, utilize, wield

**exertion** action, application, attempt, effort, industry, strain, stretch, struggle, toil, trial, use

**exhale** v breathe out

**exhaust** v tire out; use up; empty ~n waste gases from engine; passage for this **exhaustible** adj **exhaustion** n state of extreme fatigue **exhaustive** adj comprehensive

**exhibit** v show, display ~n thing shown **exhibition** n display; public show **exhibitionist** n one with compulsive desire to attract attention **exhibitor** n

**exhilarate** v enliven, gladden **exhilaration** n

**exhort** v urge

**exhume** v dig up (corpse etc.)

**exigency** n urgent need

**exile** n banishment, expulsion from one's own country; one banished ~v banish

**exist** v be, have being, live **existence** n **existent** adj

**exit** n way out; going out ~v go out

**exodus** n departure

**exonerate** v free, declare free, from blame

**exorbitant** adj excessive

**exorcize** v cast out (evil spirits) by invocation **exorcism** n **exorcist** n

**exotic** adj foreign; unusual

**expand** v increase, spread out **expandable** adj **expanse** n wide space **expansion** n **expansive** adj extensive; friendly

**expatiate** v speak or write at great length (on)

**expatriate** adj/n (one) living in exile

**expect** v regard as probable; look

——————— THESAURUS ———————

**exhaust** bankrupt, cripple, debilitate, disable, drain, enervate, fatigue, impoverish, prostrate, sap, tire, weaken, wear out; consume, deplete, dissipate, expend, finish, run through, spend, squander, use up, waste; drain, dry, empty, strain, void

**exhibit** v display, expose, express, indicate, manifest, offer, parade, present, put on view, reveal, show ~n display, exhibition, model, show

**exhort** advise, beseech, bid, call upon, encourage, entreat, goad, incite, persuade, spur, urge, warn

**exile** n banishment, expatriation, expulsion, ostracism, proscription, separation; émigré, expatriate, outcast, refugee ~v banish, deport, drive out, eject, expel, oust, proscribe

**exist** abide, be, be living, be present, breathe, endure, happen, last, live, occur, prevail, remain, stand, survive

**existence** actuality, animation, being, breath, continuance, continuation, duration, endurance, life, subsistence, survival

**exit** door, egress, gate, outlet, passage out, vent, way out

**exotic** alien, foreign, imported, introduced, not native; bizarre, colourful, curious, different, extraordinary, outlandish, peculiar, strange, striking, unfamiliar, unusual

**expand** amplify, augment, bloat, blow up, broaden, develop, dilate, distend, enlarge, extend, fatten, fill out, grow, heighten, increase, inflate, lengthen, magnify, multiply, prolong, protract, swell, thicken, wax, widen

**expanse** area, breadth, extent, field, plain, range, space, stretch, sweep, tract

**expansive** affable, communicative, effusive, free, friendly, garrulous, genial, loquacious, open, outgoing, sociable, talkative, warm

forward to **expectant** adj **expectation** n

**expedient** adj fitting; politic; convenient ~n something suitable, useful **expediency** n

**expedite** v help on, hasten **expedition** n journey for definite purpose; people, equipment comprising expedition

**expel** v **-pelling, -pelled** drive out; exclude **expulsion** n

**expend** v spend, pay out; use up **expendable** adj likely to be used up **expenditure** n **expense** n cost; pl charges incurred **expensive** adj

**experience** n observation of facts as source of knowledge; being affected by event; the event; knowledge, skill gained ~v undergo, suffer, meet with **experienced** adj

**experiment** n/v test to discover or prove something **experimental** adj

———— THESAURUS ————

**expect** assume, believe, calculate, conjecture, forecast, foresee, imagine, presume, reckon, suppose, surmise, think, trust; anticipate, await, contemplate, envisage, hope for, look ahead to, look for, look forward to, predict, watch for

**expectation** assumption, assurance, belief, calculation, confidence, conjecture, forecast, likelihood, presumption, probability, supposition, surmise, trust

**expedient** advantageous, advisable, appropriate, beneficial, convenient, desirable, effective, fit, helpful, meet, opportune, politic, practical, pragmatic, profitable, proper, prudent, suitable, useful, worthwhile

**expedition** enterprise, excursion, exploration, journey, mission, quest, safari, tour, trek, trip, undertaking, voyage

**expel** cast out, discharge, dislodge, drive out, eject, remove, throw out; ban, banish, bar, discharge, dismiss, evict, exclude, exile, oust, proscribe, throw out

**expend** consume, disburse, dissipate, employ, exhaust, go through, lay out Inf, pay out, shell out Inf, spend, use (up)

**expendable** inessential, replaceable, unimportant

**expenditure** charge, cost, disbursement, expense, outgoings, outlay, output, payment, spending, use

**expense** charge, cost, disbursement, loss, outlay, output, payment, sacrifice, spending, toll, use

**expensive** costly, dear, excessive, exorbitant, overpriced, rich, steep Inf, stiff

**experience** n contact, doing, evidence, exposure, familiarity, knowledge, observation, participation, practice, proof, training, trial, understanding; affair, encounter, episode, event, happening, incident, ordeal, test, trial ~v behold, encounter, endure, face, feel, go through, have, know, live through, meet, observe, perceive, sample, sense, suffer, sustain, taste, try, undergo

**experienced** accomplished, adept, capable, competent, expert, familiar, knowledgeable, practised, professional, qualified, seasoned, skilful, tested, trained, tried, veteran, well-versed

**experiment** n assay, attempt, investigation, procedure, proof, research, test, trial, trial run, venture ~v examine, investigate, research,

**expert** n/adj (one) skilful, knowledgeable, in something **expertise** n

**expiate** v make amends for

**expire** v come to an end; die; breathe out **expiry** n end

**explain** v make clear, intelligible; account for **explanation** n **explanatory** adj

**expletive** n exclamation; oath

**explicable** adj explainable

**explicit** adj clearly stated

**explode** v (make) burst violently; (of population) increase rapidly; discredit **explosion** n **explosive** adj/n

**exploit** n brilliant feat, deed ~v turn to advantage; make use of for one's own ends **exploitation** n

**explore** v investigate; examine (country etc.) by going through it **exploration** n **exploratory** adj **explorer** n

**exponent** SEE EXPOUND

**export** v send (goods) out of the country ~n exporting; product sold abroad

**expose** v display; reveal (scandalous) truth; leave unprotected **exposure** n

**exposé** n bringing of scandal,

——————————— THESAURUS ———————————

sample, test, try, verify

**experimental** empirical, exploratory, pilot, preliminary, provisional, speculative, tentative, test, trial

**expert** n ace Inf, adept, authority, buff Inf, dab hand Brit inf, master, past master, professional, specialist, virtuoso, whiz Inf, wizard ~adj able, adept, adroit, apt, clever, deft, experienced, handy, knowledgeable, masterly, practised, proficient, qualified, skilful, trained

**expertise** aptness, cleverness, command, deftness, dexterity, facility, judgment, knack, knowledge, mastery, proficiency, skilfulness, skill

**expire** cease, close, come to an end, conclude, end, finish, lapse, run out, stop, terminate; depart, die, pass away or on, perish

**explain** clarify, clear up, define, demonstrate, describe, disclose, elucidate, expound, interpret, resolve, solve, teach, unfold

**explanation** elucidation, exposition, interpretation, resolution; account, answer, cause, excuse, meaning, motive, reason, sense,

vindication

**explicit** categorical, certain, clear, definite, direct, distinct, exact, express, frank, open, patent, plain, positive, precise, specific, stated, unqualified, unreserved

**explode** blow up, burst, detonate, discharge, go off, set off, shatter, shiver; debunk, discredit, disprove, invalidate, refute, repudiate

**exploit** n achievement, adventure, attainment, deed, feat, stunt ~v abuse, manipulate, misuse, play on or upon, take advantage of

**exploration** examination, inquiry, inspection, investigation, probe, research, scrutiny, search, study

**explore** analyse, examine, inquire into, inspect, investigate, look into, probe, prospect, research, scrutinize, search

**explosion** bang, blast, burst, clap, crack, detonation, discharge, outburst, report

**explosive** unstable, volatile

**exponent** advocate, backer, champion, defender, promoter, spokesman, supporter, upholder

**expose** display, exhibit, manifest,

crime etc, to public notice.

**expound** v explain, interpret **exponent** n one who expounds or promotes (idea, cause etc.); performer **exposition** n explanation; exhibition of goods etc.

**express** v put into words; make known or understood; adj definitely stated; specially designed; speedy ~adv with speed ~n express train; rapid parcel delivery service **expression** n expressing; word, phrase; look **expressive** adj

**expropriate** v dispossess

**expunge** v delete, blot out

**expurgate** v remove objectionable

parts (from book etc.)

**exquisite** adj of extreme beauty or delicacy

**extempore** adj/adv without previous preparation **extemporary** adj **extemporize** v

**extend** v stretch out; prolong; widen; accord, grant; reach; cover area; have range or scope **extension** n extending; additional part **extensive** adj wide **extent** n space; scope; size

**extenuate** v make less blameworthy; lessen; mitigate

**exterior** n outside ~adj outer, external

**exterminate** v destroy completely

———— THESAURUS ————

present, put on view, reveal, show, uncover, unveil; air, betray, bring to light, denounce, detect, disclose, divulge, lay bare, let out, make known, reveal, show up, uncover, unmask

**exposure** baring, display, manifestation, publicity, revelation, showing, uncovering, unveiling; airing, denunciation, detection, disclosure, divulgence, revelation, unmasking

**expound** describe, elucidate, explain, illustrate, interpret, spell out

**express** v articulate, assert, asseverate, communicate, couch, declare, phrase, pronounce, put, say, speak, state, tell, utter, voice, word ~adj clearcut, especial, particular, singular, special; direct, fast, high-speed, nonstop, quick, rapid, speedy, swift

**expression** assertion, communication, declaration, mention, pronouncement, speaking, statement, utterance; idiom, locution, phrase, remark, term, turn of phrase, word; air, appearance, countenance, face, look

**expulsion** banishment, discharge, dismissal, ejection, eviction, exclusion, exile, proscription, removal

**exquisite** beautiful, dainty, delicate, elegant, fine, lovely, precious

**extend** carry on, continue, drag out, draw out, lengthen, prolong, protract, spin out, spread out, stretch, unfurl, unroll; add to, augment, broaden, develop, dilate, enhance, enlarge, expand, increase, spread, widen

**extension** addendum, addition, adjunct, annexe, branch, supplement, wing

**extensive** broad, capacious, commodious, comprehensive, far-flung, far-reaching, general, great, huge, large, lengthy, long, prevalent, protracted, spacious, sweeping, thorough, universal, vast, wholesale, wide, widespread

**extent** bounds, compass, play, range, reach, scope, sphere, sweep; amount, amplitude, area, breadth, bulk, degree, duration, expanse, expansion, length, magnitude, measure, quantity, size, stretch, term,

**extermination** n

**external** adj outside, outward **externally** adv

**extinct** adj having died out; quenched **extinction** n

**extinguish** v put out, quench; wipe out

**extol** v **-tolling, -tolled** praise highly

**extort** v get by force or threats **extortion** n **extortionate** adj excessive

**extra** adj additional; more than usual ~adv more than usually ~n extra person or thing; something charged as additional

**extra-** comb. form beyond, as in

**extradition, extramural**

**extract** v take out, esp. by force; get by distillation etc.; derive; quote ~n passage from book, film etc.; concentrated solution **extraction** n extracting; ancestry

**extradition** n delivery of foreign fugitive **extradite** v

**extramural** adj outside normal courses etc. of university or college

**extraneous** adj not essential; added from without

**extraordinary** adj very unusual **extraordinarily** adv

**extrapolate** v make inference

——————— THESAURUS ———————

time, volume, width

**exterior** n appearance, aspect, coating, covering, façade, face, finish, outside, shell, skin, surface ~adj external, outer, outermost, outside, outward, superficial, surface

**exterminate** abolish, annihilate, destroy, eliminate, eradicate, extirpate

**external** apparent, exterior, outer, outermost, outside, outward, superficial, surface, visible

**extinct** dead, defunct, gone, lost, vanished

**extinction** abolition, annihilation, death, dying out, excision, extermination, obliteration, oblivion

**extinguish** blow out, douse, put out, quench, smother, snuff out, stifle; abolish, destroy, eliminate, end, expunge, exterminate, kill, obscure, remove, suppress, wipe out

**extol** acclaim, applaud, celebrate, commend, eulogize, exalt, glorify, laud, praise

**extort** blackmail, bleed *Inf*, bully, exact, extract, force, squeeze, wrest, wring

**extortionate** excessive, exorbitant, immoderate, inflated, inordinate, outrageous, preposterous, sky-high, unreasonable

**extra** adj accessory, added, additional, auxiliary, fresh, further, more, new, other, supplemental, supplementary ~adv especially, exceptionally, extraordinarily, extremely, particularly, remarkably, uncommonly, unusually ~n addendum, addition, appurtenance, attachment, bonus, complement, extension, supernumerary, supplement

**extract** v draw, pluck out, pull, pull out, remove, take out, uproot, withdraw; derive, draw, elicit, evoke, exact, gather, get, glean, obtain, reap, wrest, wring ~n abstract, citation, clipping, cutting, excerpt, passage, quotation, selection

**extraordinary** amazing, bizarre, curious, exceptional, fantastic, odd, outstanding, particular, peculiar, phenomenal, rare, remarkable, singular, special, strange, surprising, uncommon, unfamiliar, unheard-of, unique, unprecedented, un-

from known facts

**extrasensory** *adj* of perception apparently gained without use of known senses

**extravagant** *adj* wasteful; exorbitant **extravagance** *n* **extravaganza** *n* elaborate entertainment

**extreme** *adj* of high or highest degree; severe; going beyond moderation; outermost *~n* utmost degree; thing at either end **extremely** *adv* **extremist** *n* (one) favouring immoderate methods **extremity** *n* end; *pl* hands and feet

**extricate** *v* disentangle

**extrovert** *n* lively, outgoing person

**extrude** *v* squeeze, force out

**exuberant** *adj* high-spirited **exuberance** *n*

**exude** *v* ooze out; give off

**exult** *v* rejoice, triumph **exultant** *adj* **exultation** *n*

**eye** *n* organ of sight; look; glance; attention; aperture; thing resembling eye *~v* look at; observe **eyebrow** *n* fringe of hair above eye **eyelash** *n* hair fringing eyelid **eyelet** *n* small hole **eyelid** *n* eye shadow coloured cosmetic worn on upper eyelids **eyesore** *n* ugly object **eyetooth** *n* canine tooth **eyewitness** *n* one who was present at an event

usual, unwonted, weird, wonderful

**extravagance** improvidence, lavishness, overspending, prodigality, profligacy, profusion, squandering, waste

**extravagant** excessive, improvident, imprudent, lavish, prodigal, profligate, spendthrift, wasteful; costly, excessive, exorbitant, expensive, extortionate, inordinate, overpriced, steep *Inf*, unreasonable

**extreme** acute, great, greatest, high, highest, intense, maximum, severe, supreme, ultimate, utmost, uttermost, worst; faraway, far-off, farthest, final, last, outermost, remotest, terminal, ultimate, utmost *~n* acme, apex, boundary, climax, depth, edge, end, excess, extremity, height, limit, maximum, minimum, nadir, pinnacle, pole, termination, top, ultimate, zenith

**extremely** acutely, awfully *Inf*, exceedingly, exceptionally, excessively, extraordinarily, greatly, highly, inordinately, intensely, markedly, quite, severely, uncommonly, unusually, utterly, very

**extremity** acme, apex, apogee, border, bound, boundary, brim, brink, edge, end, frontier, limit, margin, maximum, minimum, nadir, pinnacle, pole, rim, terminal, tip, top, ultimate, verge, zenith

**extricate** clear, deliver, disengage, disentangle, free, get out, liberate, release, relieve, remove, rescue, withdraw

**exuberance** cheerfulness, eagerness, ebullience, effervescence, energy, enthusiasm, excitement, exhilaration, high spirits, life, liveliness, pep, spirit, sprightliness, vigour, vitality, vivacity, zest

**exuberant** animated, buoyant, cheerful, chirpy *Inf*, eager, ebullient, effervescent, elated, energetic, enthusiastic, excited, exhilarated, high-spirited, lively, sparkling, spirited, sprightly, vigorous, vivacious, zestful

**exult** be delighted, be elated, be joyful, be jubilant, be overjoyed, celebrate, jubilate, make merry, rejoice

**eye** *n* eyeball; appreciation, dis-

**eyrie** *n* nest of bird of prey, esp. eagle

———————————— THESAURUS ————————————

cernment, discrimination, judgment, perception, recognition, taste ~*v* contemplate, gaze at, inspect, look at, peruse, regard, scan, scrutinize, stare at, study, survey, view, watch

**eyesore** atrocity, blemish, blight, blot, disgrace, horror, mess, monstrosity, sight *Inf*

**eyewitness** looker-on, observer, onlooker, spectator, viewer, witness

# F f

**F** Fahrenheit

**f** *Mus* forte

**fable** *n* short story with moral **fabulous** *adj* amazing; *Inf* extremely good

**fabric** *n* cloth; structure **fabricate** *v* construct; invent (lie etc.)

**façade** *n* front of building; outward appearance

**face** *n* front of head; distorted expression; outward appearance; chief side of anything; dignity ~*v* look or front towards; meet (boldly); give a covering surface; turn **faceless** *adj* anonymous **face-lift** *n* operation to remove wrinkles **face-saving** *adj* maintaining dignity **facet** *n* one side of cut gem; one aspect **face value** apparent worth **facial** *adj* of

cosmetic treatment for face ~*adj* of face

**facetious** *adj* given to joking

**facia** *see* FASCIA

**facile** *adj* easy; superficial **facilitate** *v* make easy **facility** *n* easiness; dexterity; *pl* opportunities, good conditions; means, equipment for doing something

**facsimile** *n* exact copy

**fact** *n* thing known to be true; reality **factual** *adj*

**faction** *n* (dissenting) minority group; dissension

**factor** *n* something contributing to a result; one of numbers which multiplied together give a given number; agent

**factory** *n* building where things are

---

## THESAURUS

**fable** allegory, legend, myth, parable, story, tale

**fabric** cloth, material, stuff, textile, web; constitution, framework, make-up, organization, structure

**fabulous** amazing, astounding, breathtaking, fictitious, inconceivable, incredible, legendary, phenomenal, unbelievable

**face** *n* countenance, features, physiognomy, visage; appearance, aspect, expression, frown, grimace, look, pout, scowl, smirk ~*v* be opposite, front onto, look onto, overlook; brave, confront, deal with, defy, encounter, experience, meet, oppose

**facet** angle, aspect, face, part, phase, plane, side, slant, surface

**facetious** amusing, comical, droll, flippant, frivolous, funny, humorous, jesting, jocular, merry, playful,

waggish, witty

**facile** adept, adroit, easy, effortless, fluent, light, quick, ready, simple, skilful, smooth, uncomplicated

**facilitate** ease, expedite, forward, further, help, make easy, promote, speed up

**facility** ability, adroitness, dexterity, ease, efficiency, effortlessness, fluency, knack, proficiency, quickness, readiness, skilfulness, skill, smoothness

**facsimile** copy, duplicate, photocopy, print, replica, reproduction, transcript

**fact** act, deed, event, happening, incident, occurrence, performance; actuality, certainty, reality, truth

**faction** bloc, cabal, camp, caucus, clique, coalition, confederacy, division, lobby, minority, party, pressure group, schism, section, set,

manufactured

**faculty** *n* inherent power; ability; aptitude; department of university

**fad** *n* short-lived fashion

**fade** *v* lose colour, strength; cause to fade

**faeces** *pl n* excrement

**fag** *n Inf* boring task; *Sl* cigarette ~*v* **fagging, fagged** *Inf* (esp. with **out**) tire

**faggot** *n* ball of chopped liver; bundle of sticks

**Fahrenheit** *adj* measured by thermometric scale with freezing point of water 32°, boiling point 212°

**fail** *v* be unsuccessful; stop working; (judge to) be below the required standard; disappoint, give no help to; be insufficient; become bankrupt; neglect, forget to do **failing** *n* deficiency; fault ~*prep* in default of **failure** *n* **without fail** certainly

**faint** *adj* feeble, dim, pale; weak; dizzy ~*v* lose consciousness temporarily

**fair**[1] *adj* just; according to rules; blond; beautiful; of moderate quality or amount; favourable ~*adv* honestly **fairly** *adv* **fairness** *n* **fairway** *n* smooth area on golf course between tee and green

**fair**[2] *n* travelling entertainment with sideshows etc.; trade exhibition **fairground** *n*

——————— T H E S A U R U S ———————

splinter group

**factor** aspect, cause, circumstance, component, consideration, element, influence, item, part, point, thing

**factory** mill, plant, works

**factual** accurate, authentic, close, correct, credible, exact, faithful, genuine, literal, objective, precise, real, sure, true, true-to-life, unadorned, unbiased, veritable

**faculty** department, discipline, profession, school, teaching staff

**fad** affectation, craze, fancy, fashion, mania, mode, rage, trend, vogue, whim

**fade** blanch, bleach, blench, dim, discolour, dull, grow dim, pale, wash out; decline, die out, dim, disperse, dissolve, droop, dwindle, ebb, fail, fall, flag, melt away, perish, shrivel, vanish, waste away, wilt, wither

**fail** be defeated, be unsuccessful, break down, come to grief, come to naught, fall short, founder, go astray, go down, miscarry, misfire,

miss, run aground; abandon, desert, disappoint, forget, forsake, let down, neglect, omit

**failing** *n* blemish, blind spot, defect, deficiency, drawback, error, failure, fault, flaw, imperfection, lapse, misfortune, shortcoming, weakness

**failure** breakdown, collapse, defeat, downfall, fiasco, miscarriage, overthrow, wreck; default, neglect, negligence, nonsuccess, omission, remissness, shortcoming; bankruptcy, crash, downfall, insolvency, ruin

**faint** *adj* delicate, dim, distant, dull, faltering, feeble, hazy, hushed, ill-defined, indistinct, light, low, muted, soft, subdued, thin, vague, whispered; feeble, remote, slight, weak; dizzy, drooping, exhausted, fatigued, giddy, lethargic, lightheaded, muzzy, vertiginous, weak ~*v* black out, collapse, fade, fail, languish, pass out, weaken

**fair**[1] *adj* above board, clean, disinterested, dispassionate, equal, even-handed, honest, honourable,

**fairy** n imaginary small creature with powers of magic ~adj of fairies; delicate, imaginary

**faith** n trust; belief (without proof); religion; loyalty **faithful** adj constant, true **faithfully** adv **faithless** adj

**fake** v touch up; counterfeit ~n/adj fraudulent (thing or person)

**falcon** n small bird of prey

**fall** v **falling, fell, fallen** drop; become lower; hang down; cease to stand; perish; collapse; be cap-tured; become; happen ~n falling; amount that falls; decrease; collapse; drop; (oft. pl) cascade; yield-ing to temptation; US autumn **fall-out** n radioactive particles spread as result of nuclear explosion

**fallacy** n incorrect opinion or argu-ment **fallacious** adj **fallible** adj liable to error

**fallow** adj ploughed but left with-out crop

**false** adj wrong; deceptive; faith-less; artificial **falsely** adv **falsehood**

—————————— THESAURUS ——————————

impartial, just, lawful, legitimate, objective, proper, unbiased, upright; blond, light; beautiful, comely, handsome, lovely, pretty, well-favoured; adequate, all right, average, decent, mediocre, mid-dling, moderate, not bad, O.K. or okay, passable, reasonable, respect-able, satisfactory, tolerable

**fair²** n bazaar, carnival, festival, fête, gala, market, show

**fairly** deservedly, equitably, hon-estly, justly, objectively, properly; adequately, moderately, pretty well, quite, rather, reasonably, some-what, tolerably

**fairness** decency, equity, impar-tiality, justice, legitimacy, rightfulness, uprightness

**fairy** brownie, elf, hob, sprite

**faith** assurance, confidence, con-viction, credence, credit, reliance, trust; allegiance, constancy, faith-fulness, fealty, fidelity, loyalty, truth, truthfulness

**faithful** constant, dependable, de-voted, loyal, reliable, staunch, steadfast, true, trusty, truthful, un-wavering

**faithless** disloyal, doubting, false, fickle, inconstant, perfidious, trai-torous, treacherous, unbelieving, unfaithful, unreliable, untrue, un-trustworthy, untruthful

**fake** v copy, counterfeit, fabricate, feign, forge, pretend, put on, sham, simulate ~n charlatan, copy, for-gery, fraud, hoax, imitation, impos-tor, mountebank, phoney or phony Inf. reproduction, sham

**fall** v cascade, collapse, crash, de-scend, dive, drop, drop down, keel over, nose-dive, pitch, plummet, plunge, settle, sink, stumble, sub-side, topple, trip, trip over, tumble; abate, decline, decrease, depreci-ate, diminish, drop, dwindle, ebb, fall off, flag, go down, lessen, slump, subside; capitulate, give in or up, give way, go out of office, re-sign, succumb, surrender, yield ~n cut, decline, decrease, dip, drop, dwindling, falling off, lessening, lowering, reduction, slump; de-scent, dive, drop, plummet, plunge, slip, spill, tumble

**fallacy** deceit, deception, delusion, error, falsehood, flaw, illusion, mis-conception, sophism

**fallible** erring, frail, ignorant, im-perfect, mortal, uncertain, weak

**fallow** dormant, idle, inert, resting,

*n* **falsify** *v* **-fying, -fied** alter fraudulently

**falsetto** *n* (*pl* **-tos**) forced voice above natural range

**falter** *v* hesitate; waver; stumble

**fame** *n* renown **famed** *adj* famous *adj* widely known **famously** *adv Inf* excellently

**familiar** *adj* well-known; customary; intimate; acquainted; impertinent ~*n* friend; demon **familiarity** *n* **familiarize** *v*

**family** *n* parents and children, relatives; group of allied objects

**famine** *n* extreme scarcity of food; starvation **famished** *adj* very hungry

**fan**[1] *n* instrument for producing current of air; folding object of paper etc., for cooling the face ~*v* **fanning, fanned** blow or cool with fan; spread out

**fan**[2] *n Inf* devoted admirer

**fanatic** *adj/n* (person) filled with abnormal enthusiasm **fanatical** *adj* **fanaticism** *n*

**fancy** *adj* **-cier, -ciest** ornamental; *n* whim; liking; imagination; mental image ~*v* **-cying, -cied** imagine; be

─── THESAURUS ───

uncultivated, undeveloped

**false** concocted, erroneous, faulty, fictitious, improper, inaccurate, incorrect, inexact, invalid, mistaken, unfounded, unreal, wrong; lying, mendacious, unreliable, unsound, untrue, untrustworthy, untruthful; artificial, bogus, feigned, forged, imitation, mock, pretended, sham

**falsehood** deceit, deception, dishonesty, mendacity, perjury, prevarication; fib, fiction, lie, story, untruth

**falsify** alter, belie, counterfeit, distort, doctor, fake, forge, misrepresent, pervert

**falter** hesitate, shake, stammer, stutter, tremble, waver

**fame** celebrity, credit, eminence, glory, honour, name, prominence, renown, reputation, repute, stardom

**familiar** common, conventional, customary, domestic, everyday, frequent, household, mundane, ordinary, recognizable, repeated, routine, stock, well-known; amicable, close, confidential, cordial, easy, free, friendly, informal, intimate, near, open, relaxed, unreserved

**familiarity** acquaintance, awareness, experience, grasp; closeness, ease, fellowship, freedom, friendliness, intimacy, naturalness, openness, sociability

**family** brood, children, household, issue, kin, offspring, people, progeny, relations, relatives

**famine** dearth, hunger, scarcity, starvation

**famous** celebrated, conspicuous, eminent, glorious, honoured, illustrious, legendary, notable, noted, prominent, remarkable, renowned, well-known

**fan**[1] *v*; air-condition, air-cool, blow, cool, refresh, ventilate ~*n* air conditioner, blade, blower, propeller, vane, ventilator

**fan**[2] adherent, admirer, aficionado, buff *Inf*, devotee, enthusiast, follower, lover, supporter, zealot

**fanatic** *n* addict, bigot, buff *Inf*, devotee, enthusiast, extremist, visionary, zealot

**fanciful** capricious, chimerical, curious, extravagant, fabulous, fairy-tale, fantastic, ideal, imaginary, imaginative, mythical, poetic, romantic, unreal, visionary, whimsical,

inclined to believe; *Inf* have a liking for **fancier** *n* one with special interest in something **fanciful** *adj*

**fanfare** *n* flourish of trumpets; ostentatious display

**fang** *n* snake's tooth, injecting poison; long, pointed tooth

**fantasy** *n* power of imagination; mental image; fanciful invention **fantasize** *v* **fantastic** *adj* quaint, extremely fanciful, wild; *Inf* very good; *Inf* very large

**far** *adv* **farther** *or* **further**, **farthest** *or* **furthest** at or to a great distance or a remote time; by very much ~*adj* distant; more distant **far-fetched** *adj* incredible

**farce** *n* comedy of boisterous humour; absurd and futile proceeding **farcical** *adj*

**fare** *n* charge for transport; passenger; food ~*v* get on; happen **fare-**

**well** *interj* goodbye ~*n* leave-taking

**farm** *n* tract of land for cultivation or rearing livestock ~*v* cultivate (land); rear livestock (on farm) **farmer** *n* **farmhouse** *n* **farmyard** *n*

**fart** *Vulg* *n* (audible) emission of gas from anus ~*v* break wind

**farther** *adv/adj* further; *comparative of FAR* **farthest** *adv/adj* furthest; *superlative of FAR*

**farthing** *n* formerly, coin worth a quarter of a penny

**fascia, facia** *n* (*pl* **-ciae**) flat surface above shop window; dashboard

**fascinate** *v* attract and delight **fascination** *n*

**fascism** *n* authoritarian political system opposed to democracy and liberalism **fascist** *adj/n*

**fashion** *n* (latest) style, esp. of dress etc.; manner; type ~*v* shape,

──────── THESAURUS ────────

**fancy** *adj* decorated, elaborate, elegant, intricate, ornamental, ornate ~*v* believe, conceive, guess, imagine, infer, reckon, suppose, surmise, think, think likely; crave, desire, dream of, long for, relish, wish for, would like, yearn for

**fantastic** eccentric, exotic, fanciful, freakish, grotesque, imaginative, odd, peculiar, quaint, queer, rococo, strange, unreal, weird, whimsical

**far** *adv* afar, a good way, a great distance, a long way, deep; considerably, decidedly, extremely, greatly, incomparably, much ~*adj* distant, long, outlying, remote, removed

**farce** buffoonery, comedy, satire, slapstick; absurdity, joke, mockery, nonsense, parody, sham, travesty

**fare** *n* charge, price, ticket money,

transport cost; diet, eatables, food, meals, menu, provisions, rations ~*v* do, get along, get on, make out, manage, prosper

**farewell** adieu, departure, goodbye, parting, valediction

**far-fetched** doubtful, dubious, improbable, incredible, preposterous, strained, unbelievable, unconvincing, unlikely, unnatural, unrealistic

**farm** *n* grange, holding, homestead, land, plantation, smallholding ~*v* cultivate, operate, plant, work

**fascinate** absorb, allure, beguile, bewitch, captivate, charm, delight, enchant, engross, enthral, entrance, hypnotize, rivet, transfix

**fascination** allure, attraction, charm, enchantment, glamour, lure, magic, magnetism, pull, sorcery, spell

make **fashionable** adj

**fast¹** adj (capable of) moving quickly; ahead of true time; *Obs* dissipated; firm, steady ~adv rapidly; tightly **fast food** food, esp. hamburgers etc., served very quickly

**fast²** v go without food ~n **fasting fasting** n

**fasten** v attach, fix, secure; become joined **fastener, fastening** n

**fastidious** adj hard to please

**fat** n oily animal substance; fat part ~adj **fatter, fattest** having too much fat; greasy; profitable **fatten** v **fatty** adj

**fate** n power supposed to predetermine events; destiny; person's appointed lot; death or destruction **fatal** adj ending in death **fatality** n death **fatally** adv **fated** n destined **fateful** adj

**father** n male parent; ancestor; (with cap.) God; originator; priest ~v beget; originate **fatherhood** n **father-in-law** n husband's or wife's father **fatherland** n native country

**fathom** n measure of six feet of water ~v sound (water); understand

**fatigue** v tire ~n weariness; toil; weakness of metals etc.

**fatuous** adj very silly, idiotic

**fault** n defect; misdeed; blame ~v find fault in; (cause to) commit

**fashion** n convention, craze, custom, fad, latest, latest style, look, mode, rage, style, trend, usage, vogue; attitude, demeanour, manner, method, mode, style, way ~v construct, contrive, create, design, forge, form, make, manufacture, mould, shape, work

**fashionable** à la mode, chic, current, customary, genteel, happening *Inf*, in vogue, latest, modern, modish, popular, prevailing, smart, stylish, up-to-date, usual

**fast¹** adj brisk, fleet, flying, hasty, hurried, nippy *Brit inf*, quick, quickie *Inf*, rapid, speedy, swiftly, winged; dissipated, dissolute, intemperate, licentious, loose, profligate, promiscuous, wild ~adv quickly, rapidly, speedily, swiftly

**fast²** v abstain, deny oneself, go hungry, go without food, practise abstention ~n abstinence, fasting

**fasten** affix, anchor, attach, bind, bolt, chain, connect, fix, grip, join, lace, link, lock, make fast, make firm, seal, secure, tie, unite

**fat** n beef *Inf*, blubber, bulk, corpulence, flesh, obesity, overweight, paunch ~adj corpulent, fleshy, gross, heavy, obese, overweight, plump, podgy, portly, rotund, solid, stout, tubby

**fatal** deadly, final, incurable, killing, lethal, malignant, mortal, pernicious

**fate** n chance, destiny, divine will, fortune, predestination, providence; end, future, issue, outcome, upshot

**fated** destined, doomed, foreordained, marked down, predestined, preordained, sure, written

**fateful** critical, crucial, decisive, important, significant

**father** n begetter, pater, patriarch, sire; ancestor, forebear, forefather, predecessor, progenitor; abbé, confessor, curé, pastor, priest ~v beget, get, procreate, sire

**fatigue** v drain, exhaust, jade, overtire, tire, weaken, wear out, weary ~n debility, heaviness, languor, lethargy, tiredness

fault **faultily** adv **faultless** adj **faulty**
adj

**faun** n mythological woodland being with tail and horns

**fauna** n (pl **-nas**, **-nae**) animals of
region collectively

**faux pas** n social blunder or indiscretion

**favour** n goodwill; approval; especial kindness; partiality ~v regard or
treat with favour; oblige; treat with
partiality; support **favourable** adj
**favourite** n favoured person or
thing ~adj chosen, preferred **favouritism** n practice of showing undue preference

**fawn**[1] n young deer ~adj light yel-

lowish brown

**fawn**[2] v (oft. with **on** or **upon**)
cringe, court favour servilely

**fax** n facsimile ~v send by telegraphic facsimile system

**FBI** US Federal Bureau of Investigation

**fear** n unpleasant emotion caused
by coming danger ~v be afraid; regard with fear **fearful** adj **fearless**
adj **fearsome** adj

**feasible** adj able to be done **feasibility** n

**feast** n banquet; religious anniversary ~v eat banquet; entertain with
feast; delight

**feat** n notable deed

──────── THESAURUS ────────

**fault** n blemish, defect, demerit,
drawback, failing, flaw, imperfection, lack, shortcoming, snag,
weakness, weak point; lapse, misconduct, misdeed, misdemeanour,
offence, sin, trespass, wrong

**faultless** accurate, classic, correct,
exemplary, faithful, foolproof, impeccable, model, perfect; above reproach, blameless, guiltless, immaculate, impeccable, innocent,
pure, sinless, spotless, stainless

**faulty** bad, broken, damaged, defective, erroneous, impaired, imperfect, inaccurate, incorrect, invalid, malfunctioning, unsound, weak,
wrong

**favour** n approval, backing, bias,
esteem, good opinion, goodwill,
grace, kindness, partiality, patronage, support; benefit, boon, courtesy, good turn, indulgence, kindness, service ~v be partial to, esteem, indulge, pamper, reward,
smile upon, spoil, value

**favourable** advantageous, appropriate, auspicious, beneficial, con-

venient, fair, fit, good, helpful,
hopeful, opportune, promising,
propitious, suitable, timely

**favourite** n choice, darling, dear,
idol, pet, pick, preference ~adj
best-loved, choice, dearest, esteemed, preferred

**fawn**[1] adj beige, buff, neutral

**fawn**[2] v (oft. with **on** or **upon**) be
obsequious, be servile, court, crawl,
creep, cringe, flatter, grovel, kneel,
kowtow, pander to, toady

**fear** n alarm, awe, dread, fright,
horror, panic, qualms, terror, trepidation ~v dare not, dread, shudder
at, take fright, tremble at

**fearful** afraid, alarmed, anxious,
apprehensive, diffident, frightened,
hesitant, intimidated, nervous, panicky, scared, shrinking, tense, timid, timorous, uneasy

**fearless** bold, brave, confident,
courageous, daring, gallant, heroic,
indomitable, intrepid, plucky, unafraid, valiant, valorous

**feasible** attainable, likely, possible,
practicable, reasonable, viable,

**feather** n one of the barbed shafts which form covering of birds; anything resembling this ~v provide with feathers; grow feathers **feathery** adj

**feature** n (usu. pl) part of face; notable part of anything; main or special item ~v portray; be prominent (in) **featureless** adj without striking features

**Feb.** February

**February** n second month

**feckless** adj ineffectual, irresponsible

**federal** adj of the government of states which are united but retain internal independence **federalism** n **federalist** n **federate** v form into, become, a federation **federation** n league; federal union

**fee** n payment for services

**feeble** adj weak; not effective or

convincing

**feed** v **feeding, fed** give food to; supply, support; take food ~n feeding; fodder **feedback** n response **fed up** Inf bored, dissatisfied

**feel** v **feeling, felt** touch; experience; find (one's way) cautiously; be sensitive to; show emotion (for); believe, consider ~n feeling; impression perceived by feeling; sense of touch **feeler** n **feeling** n sense of touch; sensation; emotion; sympathy; opinion pl susceptibilities **feel like** have an inclination for

**feet** see FOOT

**feign** v pretend, sham

**feint** n sham attack; pretence ~v make feint

**felicity** n great happiness; apt wording **felicitations** pl n congratulations **felicitous** adj

**feline** adj of cats; catlike

workable

**feast** n banquet, carousal, dinner, entertainment, junket, repast, revels, treat

**feat** achievement, act, attainment, deed, exploit, performance

**feature** n aspect, attribute, characteristic, facet, factor, hallmark, mark, peculiarity, point, property, quality, trait; article, column, comment, item, piece, report, story ~v accentuate, emphasize, headline, play up, present, promote, set off, spotlight, star

**federation** alliance, amalgamation, association, coalition, combination, confederacy, entente, federacy, league, syndicate, union

**fee** account, bill, charge, compensation, emolument, pay, payment, remuneration, reward, toll

**feeble** delicate, doddering, effete,

enervated, enfeebled, exhausted, failing, faint, frail, infirm, languid, powerless, puny, sickly, weak, weakened

**feed** v cater for, nourish, provide for, supply, sustain, victual; devour, eat, fare, graze, live on, nurture, pasture, subsist

**feel** v caress, finger, fondle, handle, manipulate, maul, paw, stroke, touch; be aware of, endure, enjoy, experience, go through, have, know, notice, observe, perceive, suffer, undergo; explore, fumble, grope, sound, test, try; believe, consider, deem, hold, judge, think

**feeling** n feel, perception, sensation, sense, sense of touch, touch; consciousness, hunch, idea, impression, inkling, notion, presentiment, sense, suspicion; inclination, instinct, opinion, view

**fell¹** v knock down; cut down (tree)
**feller** n

**fell²** n mountain, moor

**fellow** n Inf man, boy; associate; counterpart; member (of society, college etc.) ~adj of the same class, associated **fellowship** n

**felon** n one guilty of felony **felony** n serious crime

**felt** n soft, matted fabric ~v make into, or cover with, felt; become matted **felt-tip pen** pen with writing point of pressed fibres

**female** adj of sex which bears offspring; relating to this sex ~n one of this sex

**feminine** adj of women; womanly **feminism** n advocacy of equal rights for women **feminist** n/adj **femininity** n

**fen** n tract of marshy land

**fence** n structure of wire, wood etc. enclosing an area; Sl dealer in stolen property ~v erect fence; fight

with swords; Sl deal in stolen property **fencing** n art of swordplay

**fend** v ward off; repel; provide (for oneself etc.) **fender** n low metal frame in front of fireplace

**fennel** n fragrant plant

**feral** adj wild

**ferment** n substance causing thing to ferment; excitement ~v (cause to) undergo chemical change with effervescence and alteration of properties **fermentation** n

**fern** n plant with feathery fronds

**ferocious** adj fierce, savage, cruel **ferocity** n

**ferret** n tamed animal like weasel ~v drive out with ferrets; search about

**ferric, ferrous** adj pert. to, containing, iron

**ferry** n boat etc. for transporting people, vehicles, across water ~v **-rying, -ried** carry, travel, by ferry

**fertile** adj (capable of) producing

**fell** v cut, cut down, demolish, flatten, floor, hew, knock down, level, raze

**fellow** n boy, character, individual, man, person; associate, colleague, companion, compeer, comrade, co-worker, equal, friend, member, partner, peer

**fellowship** brotherhood, camaraderie, communion, familiarity, intercourse, intimacy, kindliness, sociability

**feminine** delicate, gentle, girlish, graceful, ladylike, modest, soft, tender, womanly

**fen** bog, marsh, morass, quagmire, slough, swamp

**fence** n barricade, barrier, defence, guard, hedge, paling, palisade, railings, rampart, shield, stockade, wall

v (oft. with in or off) bound, confine, coop, defend, enclose, guard, hedge, pen, pound, protect, restrict, secure, separate, surround

**ferment** v boil, brew, bubble, concoct, foam, froth, heat, leaven, rise, seethe, work; agitate, boil, excite, fester, foment, heat, incite, inflame, provoke, rouse, seethe, smoulder, stir up ~n agitation, commotion, excitement, fever, frenzy, glow, heat, stew, stir, tumult, turmoil, unrest, uproar

**ferocious** fierce, predatory, rapacious, ravening, savage, violent, wild

**ferocity** brutality, cruelty, inhumanity, rapacity, ruthlessness, savagery, wildness

**ferry** n ferryboat, packet ~v carry,

offspring, bearing crops etc.; producing abundantly **fertility** *n* **fertilize** *v* make fertile **fertilization** *n* **fertilizer** *n*

**fervent, fervid** *adj* ardent, intense **fervour** *n*

**fester** *v* (cause to) form pus; rankle; become embittered

**festival** *n* day, period of celebration; organized series of events, performances etc. **festive** *adj* joyous, merry **festivity** *n* gaiety; rejoicing; *pl* festive proceedings

**festoon** *n* loop of flowers, ribbons etc. ~*v* form, adorn with festoons

**fetch** *v* go and bring; draw forth; be sold for **fetching** *adj* attractive

**fete, fête** *n* gala, bazaar etc., esp. one held out of doors ~*v* honour

with festive entertainment

**fetid, foetid** *adj* stinking

**fetish** *n* object believed to have magical powers; object, activity, to which excessive devotion is paid

**fetter** *n* chain for feet; check; *pl* captivity ~*v* chain up; restrain

**fettle** *n* state of health

**fetus, foetus** *n* fully developed embryo **fetal, foetal** *adj*

**feud** *n* long bitter hostility ~*v* carry on feud

**fever** *n* condition of illness with high body temperature; intense nervous excitement **fevered** *adj* **feverish** *adj*

**few** *adj* not many ~*pron* small number

**fez** *n* (*pl* **fezzes**) red, brimless cap

convey, ship, shuttle, transport

**fertile** abundant, fat, fecund, flowering, fruitful, luxuriant, plentiful, productive, prolific, rich, teeming, yielding

**fertility** abundance, fecundity, fruitfulness, productiveness, richness

**fervent, fervid** ardent, devout, eager, earnest, emotional, enthusiastic, excited, fiery, flaming, heartfelt, impassioned, intense, vehement, warm

**fervour** ardour, eagerness, earnestness, enthusiasm, excitement, intensity, passion, vehemence, warmth, zeal

**festival** commemoration, feast, fête, fiesta, holiday, saint's day; carnival, celebration, festivities, fête, field day, gala, jubilee, treat

**festive** back-slapping, carnival, celebratory, cheery, convivial, festal, gala, gay, happy, hearty, holiday, jolly, jovial, joyful, jubilant,

light-hearted, merry, mirthful, sportive

**festoon** array, bedeck, deck, decorate, drape, garland, hang, swathe, wreathe

**fetch** bring, carry, conduct, convey, deliver, escort, get, go for, lead, obtain, retrieve, transport; draw forth, elicit, give rise to, produce; bring in, earn, go for, make, realize, sell for, yield

**feud** argument, bad blood, broil, conflict, disagreement, discord, dissension, enmity, faction, grudge, hostility, quarrel, rivalry, strife, vendetta ~*v* bicker, brawl, clash, contend, dispute, duel, fall out, quarrel, row, squabble, war

**fever** agitation, delirium, ecstasy, excitement, ferment, fervour, flush, frenzy, heat, passion, turmoil, unrest

**few** *adj* inconsiderable, infrequent, insufficient, meagre, negligible, rare, scant, scanty, scarce, scat-

with tassel

**fiancé** n (fem **fiancée**) person engaged to be married

**fiasco** n (pl **-cos**) breakdown, total failure

**fib** n/v **fibbing, fibbed** (tell) trivial lie

**fibre** n filament forming part of animal or plant tissue; substance that can be spun **fibrous** adj **fibreglass** n material made of fine glass fibres

**fickle** adj changeable

**fiction** n literary works of the imagination **fictional** adj **fictitious** adj false; imaginary

**fiddle** n violin; Inf fraudulent arrangement ~v play fiddle; fidget; Sl cheat **fiddling** adj trivial **fiddly** adj small, awkward to handle

**fidelity** n faithfulness

**fidget** v move restlessly ~n (oft. pl) restless mood; one who fidgets **fidgety** adj

**field** n area of (farming) land; tract of land rich in specific product; players in a game or sport collectively; battlefield; sphere of knowledge ~v Cricket etc. stop and return ball; send player, team, on to sports field **fielder** n **field day** exciting occasion **fieldwork** n investigation made away from classroom or laboratory

**fiend** n devil; person addicted to something **fiendish** adj

**fierce** adj savage, wild, violent; intense **fiercely** adv

**fiery** adj **fierier, fieriest** consisting of, or like, fire; irritable **fierily** adv

**fiesta** n carnival

**fifteen, fifth, fifty** SEE FIVE

**fig** n soft, pear-shaped fruit; tree bearing this

**fight** v **fighting, fought** contend in battle; maintain against opponent; settle by combat ~n fight-

──────── THESAURUS ────────

tered, sparse, sporadic, thin ~pron handful, scarcely any, scattering, small number, some

**fiasco** catastrophe, cock-up Brit sl, debacle, disaster, failure, mess, rout, ruin

**fib** n fiction, lie, prevarication, story, untruth, white lie

**fibre** pile, staple, strand, texture, thread

**fickle** capricious, changeable, faithless, fitful, flighty, inconstant, irresolute, mercurial, temperamental, unfaithful, unstable, unsteady, vacillating, volatile

**fiction** fable, fantasy, legend, myth, novel, romance, story, tale, urban legend

**fictitious** apocryphal, artificial, assumed, bogus, false, fanciful, feigned, imaginary, imagined, im-

provised, invented, made-up, mythical, spurious, unreal, untrue

**fidelity** constancy, devotion, faithfulness, integrity, loyalty, staunchness, trustworthiness

**fidget** bustle, chafe, fret, squirm, twitch, worry

**fidgety** impatient, jerky, nervous, on edge, restive, restless, uneasy

**field** n grassland, green, meadow, pasture ~v catch, pick up, retrieve, return, stop

**fiend** demon, devil, evil spirit; addict, enthusiast, fanatic

**fierce** brutal, cruel, dangerous, feral, ferocious, menacing, murderous, passionate, savage, threatening, truculent, uncontrollable, untamed, vicious, wild

**fiercely** frenziedly, furiously, menacingly, passionately, savagely,

## DICTIONARY

ing **fighter** n person or aircraft that fights

**figment** n imaginary thing

**figure** n numerical symbol; amount, number; (bodily) shape; (conspicuous) appearance; space enclosed by lines; diagram, illustration ~v calculate; (oft. with in) show **figurative** adj (of language) symbolic **figurine** n statuette **figurehead** n nominal leader

**filament** n fine wire; threadlike body

**filch** v steal, pilfer

**file¹** n (box, folder etc. holding) papers for reference; orderly line ~v arrange (papers etc.) and put them away for reference; march in file **filing** n

**file²** n/v (use) roughened tool for smoothing or shaping **filing** n scrap of metal removed by file

**filial** adj of, befitting, son or daughter

**filibuster** v obstruct legislation by making long speeches ~n filibustering

**filigree** n fine tracery or openwork of metal

**fill** v make full; occupy completely; discharge duties of; stop up; satisfy; fulfil; become full ~n full supply; as much as desired **filling** n/adj

**fillet** n boneless slice of meat, fish; narrow strip ~v cut into fillets, bone **filleted** adj

**fillip** n stimulus

**filly** n young female horse

**film** n sequence of images projected on screen, creating illusion of movement; sensitized celluloid roll used in photography, cinematography; thin skin or layer ~adj connected with cinema ~v photograph with cine camera; make cine film of; cover, become covered, with film **filmy** adj gauzy

**filter** n device permitting fluids to

## THESAURUS

tempestuously, tigerishly, viciously

**fight** v assault, battle, box, brawl, clash, close, combat, conflict, contend, engage, feud, grapple, joust, row, spar, struggle, tilt, tussle, war, wrestle; contest, defy, dispute, oppose, resist, strive, struggle, withstand ~n altercation, battle, bout, brawl, brush, clash, combat, conflict, contest, dispute, duel, encounter, engagement, fracas, fray, hostilities, joust, melee, riot, row, scuffle, skirmish, struggle, tussle, war

**fighter** fighting man, soldier, warrior

**figure** n character, cipher, digit, number, numeral, symbol; amount, cost, price, sum, total, value; form, outline, shadow, shape, silhouette;

body, build, frame, physique, proportions, shape, torso

**figurehead** cipher, dummy, mouthpiece, name, nonentity, puppet

**file¹** n case, data, documents, dossier, folder, information, portfolio ~v enter, record, register, slot in *Inf*

**file²** v abrade, burnish, furbish, polish, rasp, refine, rub, rub down, scrape, shape, smooth

**fill** brim over, cram, crowd, furnish, glut, gorge, pack, pervade, replenish, sate, satiate, satisfy, stock, store, stuff, supply, swell

**filling** n contents, insides, padding, stuffing, wadding ~adj ample, heavy, satisfying, square, substantial

**film** n motion picture, movie *US*

pass but retaining solid particles; anything similar ~v act as filter, or as if passing through filter; pass slowly (through)

**filth** n disgusting dirt; obscenity **filthiness** n **filthy** adj

**fin** n propelling organ of fish; anything like this

**final** adj at the end; conclusive ~n game, heat, examination etc., coming at end of series **finale** n closing part of musical composition **finalist** n competitor in a final **finalize** v **finally** adv

**finance** n management of money; (also pl) money resources ~v find

capital for **financial** adj **financier** n

**finch** n one of family of small singing birds

**find** v finding, found come across; experience, discover; Law give verdict ~n (valuable) thing found **finding** n conclusion from investigation

**fine**[1] adj of high quality; not rainy; delicate; subtle; pure; in small particles; Inf healthy, at ease; satisfactory **finery** n showy dress **finesse** n skilful management **fine art** art produced for its aesthetic value **finetune** v make small adjustments

**fine**[2] n sum fixed as penalty ~v punish by fine

─────────── THESAURUS ───────────

inf; coating, covering, gauze, layer, membrane, scum, skin, tissue ~v photograph, shoot, take

**filter** n gauze, mesh, riddle, sieve, strainer ~v clarify, filtrate, purify, refine, screen, sieve, sift, strain, winnow

**filth** contamination, crap Sl, dirt, dung, excrement, excreta, faeces, filthiness, foulness, garbage, grime, muck, nastiness, ordure, pollution, refuse, sewage, shit Taboo sl; corruption, dirty-mindedness, impurity, indecency, obscenity, pornography, smut, vileness, vulgarity

**filthy** dirty, faecal, feculent, foul, nasty, polluted, slimy, putrid, squalid, unclean, vile; begrimed, black, blackened, grimy, grubby, miry, mucky, muddy, smoky, sooty, unwashed; bawdy, coarse, corrupt, depraved, foul, impure, indecent, lewd, licentious, obscene, pornographic, smutty, suggestive

**final** closing, end, eventual, last, latest, terminating, ultimate; absolute, conclusive, decided, decisive, definite, definitive, determinate,

finished, incontrovertible, irrevocable, settled

**finalize** agree, complete, conclude, decide, settle, tie up, work out

**finally** at last, at length, at long last, at the last, eventually, in the end, lastly, ultimately

**finance** n accounts, banking, business, commerce, economics, investment, money ~v back, float, fund, guarantee, pay for, subsidize, support, underwrite

**financial** budgeting, economic, fiscal, monetary, money, pecuniary

**find** v chance upon, come across, descry, discover, encounter, espy, expose, ferret out, hit upon, locate, meet, recognize, spot, turn up, uncover, unearth ~n acquisition, asset, bargain, catch, discovery, good buy

**fine**[1] adj admirable, beautiful, choice, excellent, exceptional, exquisite, first-class, first-rate, great, magnificent, masterly, ornate, outstanding, rare, select, skilful, splendid, sterling, superior, supreme, world-class; balmy, bright, clear,

**finger** *n* one of the jointed branches of the hand; various things like this *~n* touch with fingers **fingerprint** *n* impression of tip of finger

**finicky** *adj* fussy

**finish** *v* bring, come to an end, conclude; complete; perfect *~n* end; way in which thing is finished; final appearance

**finite** *adj* bounded, limited

**fiord** *see FJORD*

**fir** *n* coniferous tree

**fire** *n* state of burning; mass of burning fuel; destructive burning; device for heating a room etc.; shooting of guns; ardour *~v* discharge (firearm); *Inf* dismiss from employment; bake; make burn; inspire; explode; begin to burn; be-

come excited **firearm** *n* gun, rifle, pistol etc. **fire brigade** organized body to put out fires **fire engine** vehicle with apparatus for extinguishing fires **fire escape** means, esp. stairs, for escaping from burning buildings **firefly** *n* beetle that glows in dark **fireguard** *n* protective grating in front of fire **fireman** *n* member of fire brigade **fireplace** *n* recess in room for fire **fire station** building housing fire-fighting vehicles and equipment **firework** *n* device to give spectacular effects by explosions and coloured sparks; *pl* outburst of temper **firing squad** group of soldiers ordered to execute offender

**firm** *adj* solid, fixed, stable *~v* make, become firm *~n* commercial enterprise

cloudless, dry, fair, pleasant, sunny; dainty, delicate, elegant, exquisite, fragile; abstruse, acute, critical, fastidious, hairsplitting, intelligent, keen, minute, precise, quick, refined, sensitive, sharp, subtle, tasteful, tenuous; clear, pure, refined, solid, sterling, unadulterated, unalloyed, unpolluted; acceptable, agreeable, all right, convenient, good, O.K. *or* okay, satisfactory, suitable

**fine²** *v* mulct, penalize, punish *~n* damages, forfeit, penalty, punishment

**finesse** adroitness, artfulness, cleverness, craft, delicacy, diplomacy, discretion, polish, quickness, savoir-faire, skill, subtlety, tact

**finger** *v* feel, handle, manipulate, maul, meddle with, touch, toy with

**finish** *v* accomplish, achieve, cease, close, complete, conclude, deal with, discharge, do, end, execute,

finalize, fulfil, get done, round off, settle, stop, terminate; elaborate, perfect, polish, refine *~n* cessation, close, closing, completion, conclusion, culmination, dénouement, end, ending, finale; appearance, grain, lustre, patina, polish, shine, smoothness, surface, texture

**finite** bounded, conditioned, limited, restricted, terminable

**fire** *n* blaze, combustion, conflagration, flames, inferno; barrage, hail, salvo, shelling, sniping, volley; ardent, eager, enthusiastic, excited, inspired, passionate *~v* ignite, kindle, light, set ablaze, set aflame, set alight, set fire to, set on fire; detonate, discharge, eject, explode, hurl, launch, let off, loose, set off, shell, shoot

**firm¹** *adj* compact, compressed, concentrated, dense, hard, inelastic, inflexible, rigid, set, solid, solidified, stiff, unyielding, braced,

**first** adj earlier in time or order; foremost in rank or position ~n beginning; first occurrence of something ~adv before others in time, order etc. **firstly** adv **first aid** help given to injured person before arrival of doctor **first-class** adj of highest quality **first-hand** adj obtained directly from original source **first-rate** adj of highest class or quality

**fiscal** adj of government finances

**fish** n (pl **fish, fishes**) vertebrate cold-blooded animal with gills, living in water ~v (attempt to) catch fish; try to get information indirectly **fishy** adj of, like, or full of fish; Inf suspicious **fisherman** n **fish-**

**monger** n seller of fish

**fissure** n cleft, split **fission** n splitting; reproduction by division of living cells; splitting of atomic nucleus

**fist** n clenched hand **fisticuffs** pl n fighting

**fit¹** v **fitting, fitted** be suited to; be properly adjusted; adjust; supply ~adj **fitter, fittest** well-suited; proper; in good health ~n way anything fits **fitness** n **fitter** n **fitting** adj appropriate ~n attachment; action of fitting

**fit²** n seizure with convulsions; passing state, mood **fitful** adj spasmodic

———————— THESAURUS ————————

embedded, fast, fastened, fixed, immovable, motionless, riveted, robust, rooted, secure, secured, stable, stationary, steady, strong, sturdy, taut, tight, unshakable; adamant, constant, definite, fixed, immovable, inflexible, obdurate, resolute, resolved, set on, settled, stalwart, staunch, steadfast, strict, true, unflinching, unwavering, unyielding

**firm²** n association, business, company, concern, corporation, enterprise, house, organization, partnership

**first** adj earliest, initial, maiden, opening, original, premier, primitive, primordial, pristine; chief, foremost, head, highest, leading, pre-eminent, prime, principal, ruling ~adv beforehand, firstly, initially

**first-rate** admirable, cracking Brit inf, elite, excellent, exceptional, first class, outstanding, prime, sovereign, superb, superlative, world-class

**fissure** breach, break, chink, crack, cranny, crevice, fault, fracture, gap, hole, opening, rent, rift, rupture, slit, split

**fit¹** v accord, agree, belong, concur, conform, correspond, dovetail, go, interlock, join, match, meet, suit, tally; adapt, adjust, alter, arrange, dispose, fashion, modify, place, position, shape ~adj able, adequate, apposite, appropriate, apt, becoming, capable, competent, convenient, correct, deserving, equipped, expedient, good enough, prepared, proper, qualified, ready, right, seemly, suitable, trained, worthy; hale, healthy, robust, strapping, toned up, trim, well

**fit²** n attack, bout, convulsion, paroxysm, seizure, spasm; caprice, fancy, humour, mood, whim

**fitful** broken, desultory, erratic, fluctuating, haphazard, impulsive, inconstant, intermittent, irregular, spasmodic, sporadic, variable

**fitness** adaptation, applicability, appropriateness, aptness, compe-

**five** *adj/n* cardinal number after four **fifth** *adj* ordinal number **fifteen** *adj/n* ten plus five **fifteenth** *adj/n* **fiftieth** *adj* **fifty** *adj/n* five tens

**fix** *v* fasten, make firm; determine; repair; *Inf* influence unfairly ~*n* difficult situation; position of ship, aircraft ascertained by radar, observation etc.; *Sl* dose of narcotic drug **fixation** *n* obsession **fixed** *adj* **fixture** *n* thing fixed in position; (date for) sporting event

**fizz** *v* hiss ~*n* hissing noise; effervescent liquid **fizzy** *adj*

**fizzle** *v* splutter weakly **fizzle out** *Inf* fail

**fjord, fiord** *n* (esp. in Norway) long, narrow inlet of sea

**flabbergast** *v* overwhelm with astonishment

**flabby** *adj* limp; too fat; weak and

lacking purpose **flabbiness** *n*

**flag**[1] *n* banner, piece of bunting as standard or signal ~*v* **flagging, flagged** inform by flag signals **flagpole, flagstaff** *n* pole for flag **flagship** *n* admiral's ship; most important item

**flag**[2] *n* flat slab of stone **flagstone** *n*

**flag**[3] *v* **flagging, flagged** lose vigour

**flagon** *n* large bottle

**flagrant** *adj* blatant

**flail** *n* instrument for threshing corn by hand ~*v* beat with, move as, flail

**flair** *n* natural ability; elegant style

**flak** *n* anti-aircraft fire; *Inf* adverse criticism

**flake** *n* small, thin piece; piece chipped off ~*v* (cause to) peel off in flakes **flaky** *adj*

**flambé** *v* **flambéing, flambéed** cook in flaming brandy

———— THESAURUS ————

tence, eligibility, pertinence, preparedness, propriety, qualifications, readiness, seemliness, suitability; good condition, good health, health, robustness, strength, vigour

**fitting** *adj* appropriate, becoming, correct, decent, decorous, desirable, proper, right, seemly, suitable ~*n* attachment, component, connection, part, piece, unit

**fix** *v* attach, bind, cement, connect, couple, fasten, glue, link, pin, secure, stick, tie; anchor, embed, establish, implant, install, locate, place, plant, position, root, set, settle; agree on, appoint, arrange, arrive at, conclude, decide, define, determine, establish, limit, name, resolve, set, settle, specify ~*n Inf* difficulty, dilemma, embarrassment, hot water *Inf*, mess, plight, predicament, quandary, spot *Inf*, tight spot

**fixed** attached, established, im-

movable, made fast, permanent, rigid, rooted, secure, set; agreed, arranged, decided, definite, established, planned, resolved, settled

**flag**[1] banner, colours, ensign, jack, pennant, pennon, standard, streamer

**flag**[2] *v* abate, decline, die, droop, ebb, fade, fail, faint, fall, fall off, languish, pine, sag, sink, slump, succumb, wane, weaken, weary, wilt

**flagrant** awful, barefaced, blatant, bold, brazen, crying, dreadful, egregious, enormous, flaunting, glaring, immodest, infamous, notorious, open, ostentatious, outrageous, scandalous, shameless

**flail** *v* beat, thrash, thresh, windmill

**flair** *n* ability, aptitude, faculty, feel, genius, gift, knack, mastery, talent; chic, dash, discernment, elegance, panache, style, stylishness, taste

**flamboyant** *adj* showy **flamboyance** *n*

**flame** *n* burning gas, esp. above fire ~*v* give out flames

**flamenco** *n* (*pl* -**cos**) rhythmical Spanish dance

**flamingo** *n* (*pl* -**gos**) large pink bird with long neck and legs

**flammable** *adj* liable to catch fire

**flan** *n* open sweet or savoury tart

**flange** *n* projecting rim

**flank** *n* part of side between hips and ribs; side of anything ~*v* be at, move along either side of

**flannel** *n* soft woollen fabric; small piece of cloth for washing face

**flap** *v* **flapping**, **flapped** move (wings, arms etc.) as bird flying ~*n* act of flapping; broad piece of anything hanging from one side; *Inf* state of panic

**flapjack** *n* chewy biscuit

**flare** *v* blaze with unsteady flame; spread outwards ~*n* instance of flaring; signal light

**flash** *n* sudden burst of light or flame; very short time ~*v* break into sudden flame; move very fast; (cause to) gleam **flash**, **flashy** *adj* showy, sham **flashback** *n* break in narrative to introduce what has taken place previously

**flask** *n* type of bottle

**flat**[1] *adj* **flatter**, **flattest** level; at full length; smooth; downright; dull; *Mus* have true pitch; (of tyre) deflated; (of battery) dead ~*n* what is flat; *Mus* note half tone below natural pitch **flatly** *adv* **flatten** *v* **flatfish** *n* type of fish with broad, flat body **flat out** with maximum speed or effort

**flat**[2] *n* suite of rooms in larger building

**flatter** *v* praise insincerely; gratify **flatterer** *n* **flattery** *n*

**flatulent** *adj* suffering from, gener-

**flamboyant** elaborate, florid, ornate, rich, rococo, showy, theatrical

**flame** *n* blaze, fire, light ~*v* blaze, burn, flare, flash, glare, glow, shine

**flap** *v* agitate, beat, flail, flutter, shake, swing, swish, thrash, thresh, vibrate, wag, wave ~*n* apron, cover, fly, fold, lapel, skirt, tab, tail

**flare** blaze, burn up, dazzle, flicker, flutter, glare, waver

**flash** *n* blaze, burst, dazzle, flare, flicker, gleam, ray, shaft, shimmer, spark, sparkle, streak, twinkle; instant, moment, second, shake, split second, trice, twinkling ~*v* blaze, flare, flicker, gleam, glean, glint, glisten, glitter, light, shimmer, sparkle, twinkle; bolt, dart, fly, race, shoot, speed, sprint, streak, sweep, zoom

**flat**[1] even, horizontal, level, levelled, low, plane, smooth, unbroken; laid low, outstretched, prone, prostrate, reclining, recumbent, supine; boring, dead, dull, ho-hum *Inf*, insipid, lacklustre, lifeless, monotonous, prosaic, spiritless, stale, tedious, uninteresting, vapid, watery, weak

**flat**[2] apartment, rooms

**flatly** absolutely, categorically, completely, positively, unhesitatingly

**flatten** compress, even out, iron out, level, plaster, raze, roll, squash, trample

**flatter** blandish, butter up, cajole, compliment, court, fawn, humour, inveigle, pander to, praise, puff, wheedle

ating (excess) gases from intestines **flatulence** n

**flaunt** v show off

**flavour** n distinctive taste, savour ~v give flavour to **flavouring** n

**flaw** n defect, blemish **flawless** adj

**flax** n plant grown for its fibres, spun into linen thread **flaxen** adj of flax; light yellow

**flay** v strip skin off; criticize severely

**flea** n small, wingless, jumping, blood-sucking insect

**fleck** n/v (make) small mark(s)

**fledgling, fledgeling** n young bird; inexperienced person

**flee** v **fleeing, fled** run away from

**fleece** n sheep's wool ~v rob **fleecy** adj

**fleet**[1] n number of warships organized as unit; number of ships, cars etc.

**fleet**[2] adj swift; nimble **fleeting** adj

passing quickly

**flesh** n soft part, muscular substance, between skin and bone; in plants, pulp; fat; sensual appetites **fleshy** adj plump, pulpy **in the flesh** in person, actually present

**flex** n flexible insulated electric cable ~v bend, be bent **flexible** adj easily bent; manageable; adaptable **flexibility** n

**flick** v strike lightly, jerk ~n light blow; jerk; pl Sl cinema

**flicker** v burn, shine, unsteadily ~n unsteady light or movement; slight trace

**flight**[1] n act or manner of flying through air; group of flying birds or aircraft; power of flying; stairs between two landings **flighty** adj frivolous **flight recorder** electronic device in aircraft storing information about its flight

**flight**[2] n running away

———— THESAURUS ————

**flattery** blandishment, cajolery, fawning, obsequiousness, servility

**flavour** n aroma, essence, extract, odour, piquancy, relish, savour, seasoning, smack, tang, taste, zest ~v imbue, infuse, lace, leaven, season, spice

**flaw** blemish, defect, failing, fault, imperfection, speck, spot, weakness, weak spot

**flawless** faultless, impeccable, perfect, spotless, unblemished, unsullied

**flee** avoid, bolt, decamp, depart, do a runner Sl, escape, fly, get away, leave, shun, take flight, vanish

**fleet** n armada, flotilla, navy, squadron, task force, vessels, warships

**fleeting** brief, ephemeral, flying, fugitive, momentary, passing,

short, short-lived, temporary, transient, transitory

**flesh** body, brawn, fatness, food, meat, tissue, weight; body, human nature, sensuality

**flexibility** adaptability, complaisance, elasticity, resilience, springiness

**flexible** ductile, elastic, limber, lissom(e), lithe, plastic, pliable, springy, stretchy, supple; amenable, biddable, docile, gentle, manageable, responsive, tractable; adaptable, adjustable, open, variable

**flicker** v flutter, quiver, vibrate, waver ~n flare, flash, gleam, glimmer, spark; breath, drop, glimmer, spark, trace, vestige

**flight**[1] mounting, soaring, winging; journey, trip, voyage; cloud, flock,

**flimsy** *adj* delicate; weak, thin

**flinch** *v* draw back, wince

**fling** *v* **flinging, flung** throw, send, move with force ~*n* throw; spell of indulgence; vigorous dance

**flint** *n* hard steel-grey stone

**flip** *v* **flipping, flipped** flick lightly; turn over **flippant** *adj* treating serious things lightly **flipper** *n* limb, fin for swimming

**flirt** *v* play with another's affections ~*n* person who flirts **flirtation** *n* **flirtatious** *adj*

**flit** *v* **flitting, flitted** pass lightly and rapidly

**float** *v* rest on surface of liquid; be suspended freely; in commerce, get (company) started; obtain loan ~*n* anything small that floats; small de-

livery vehicle; motor vehicle carrying tableau etc.; sum of money used to provide change **floating** *adj* moving about, changing **flotation** *n*

**flock** *n* number of animals of one kind together; religious congregation ~*v* gather in a crowd

**floe** *n* floating ice

**flog** *v* **flogging, flogged** beat with whip, stick etc.; *Sl* sell

**flood** *n* inundation, overflow of water; rising of tide; outpouring ~*v* inundate; cover, fill with water; arrive, move etc. in great numbers **floodlight** *n* broad, intense beam of artificial light **floodlit** *adj*

**floor** *n* lower surface of room; set of rooms on one level; (right to speak in) legislative hall ~*v* supply with

—————————————— THESAURUS ——————————————

formation, squadron, swarm, unit, wing

**flight²** escape, exit, exodus, fleeing, getaway, retreat

**flimsy** delicate, fragile, frail, insubstantial, makeshift, rickety, shaky, shallow, slight, superficial, unsubstantial; feeble, frivolous, implausible, inadequate, pathetic, poor, thin, transparent, trivial, unconvincing, unsatisfactory, weak

**flinch** baulk, blench, cower, cringe, duck, flee, quail, recoil, retreat, shirk, shrink, start, swerve, wince, withdraw

**fling** *v* cast, heave, hurl, jerk, pitch, precipitate, propel, send, shy, sling, throw, toss

**flippant** disrespectful, frivolous, glib, impertinent, impudent, irreverent, pert, rude

**flirt** *v* coquet, dally, make advances, philander ~*n* coquette, heartbreaker, philanderer, tease

**float** *v* be buoyant, hang, hover,

poise; bob, drift, glide, move gently, sail, slide, slip along; launch, promote, set up

**floating** fluctuating, free, migratory, movable, unattached, uncommitted, variable, wandering

**flock** *n* drove, flight, gaggle, herd, skein; collection, company, congregation, convoy, crowd, gathering, group, herd, host, mass, multitude, throng ~*v* collect, congregate, converge, crowd, gather, group, herd, huddle, mass, throng, troop

**flog** beat, chastise, flay, lash, scourge, thrash, trounce, whack, whip

**flood** *n* deluge, downpour, flash flood, inundation, overflow, spate, tide, torrent; abundance, flow, glut, outpouring, profusion, rush, stream, torrent ~*v* engulf, flow, gush, inundate, overwhelm, rush, surge, swarm, sweep; deluge, drown, immerse, overflow, submerge, swamp

floor; knock down; confound **flooring** n material for floors

**flop** v **flopping, flopped** bend, fall, collapse loosely; fall flat on water etc.; Inf fail ~n flopping movement or sound; Inf failure **floppy** adj **floppy disk** Computers flexible magnetic disk that stores information

**flora** n (pl **-ras, -rae**) plants of a region **floral** adj of flowers **florist** n dealer in flowers

**floret** n small flower

**florid** adj with red, flushed complexion; ornate

**floss** n mass of fine, silky fibres

**flotilla** n fleet of small vessels; group of destroyers

**flotsam** n floating wreckage

**flounce**[1] v go, move abruptly and impatiently ~n fling, jerk of body or limb

**flounce**[2] n ornamental gathered strip on woman's garment

**flounder**[1] v plunge and struggle,

esp. in water or mud

**flounder**[2] n flatfish

**flour** n powder prepared by sifting and grinding wheat etc.

**flourish** v thrive; brandish; wave about ~n ornamental curve; showy gesture; fanfare

**flout** v show contempt for

**flow** v glide along as stream; circulate, as the blood; hang loose; be present in abundance ~n act, instance of flowing; quantity that flows; rise of tide

**flower** n brightly coloured part of plant from which fruit is developed; bloom, blossom; choicest part ~v produce flowers; come to prime condition **flowery** adj **flowerbed** n ground for growing flowers

**fl. oz.** fluid ounce

**flu** n short for INFLUENZA

**fluctuate** v vary, rise and fall, undulate **fluctuation** n

**flue** n chimney

——— THESAURUS ———

**floor** n level, stage, storey, tier ~v baffle, beat, bewilder, confound, conquer, defeat, discomfit, disconcert, dumbfound, faze, nonplus, overthrow, perplex, puzzle, stump

**flop** v collapse, dangle, droop, drop, fall, hang limply, sag, slump, topple, tumble; Inf close, come to nothing, fail, fall flat, fall short, founder, misfire ~n Inf debacle, disaster, failure, fiasco, loser, nonstarter, washout Inf

**florid** flushed, high-coloured, rubicund, ruddy; baroque, busy, embellished, flamboyant, flowery, fussy, high-flown, ornate

**flounder** v blunder, fumble, grope, muddle, plunge, struggle, stumble, toss, tumble, wallow

**flourish** v bear fruit, be successful,

bloom, blossom, boom, burgeon, develop, flower, increase, prosper, succeed, thrive ~n dash, display, fanfare, parade, shaking, show, twirling, wave

**flow** v circulate, course, glide, gush, move, pour, purl, ripple, roll, run, rush, slide, surge, sweep, swirl, whirl

**flower** n bloom, blossom, efflorescence; best, cream, elite, freshness, height, pick, vigour ~v bloom, blossom, burgeon, effloresce, flourish, mature, open, unfold

**flowery** embellished, fancy, figurative, florid, ornate, rhetorical

**fluctuate** alternate, change, hesitate, oscillate, seesaw, shift, swing, undulate, vacillate, vary, veer, waver

**fluent** adj speaking, writing easily and well **fluency** n

**fluff** n soft, feathery stuff ~v make or become soft, light; *Inf* make mistake **fluffy** adj

**fluid** adj flowing easily; flexible ~n gas or liquid **fluid ounce** unit of capacity 1/20 of pint

**fluke** n stroke of luck

**flummox** v bewilder, perplex

**flunky, flunkey** n liveried manservant; servile person

**fluorescent** adj giving off a special type of bright light

**fluoride** n salt containing fluorine

**fluorine** n nonmetallic element, yellowish gas

**flurry** n gust; bustle; fluttering ~v -rying, -ried agitate

**flush**¹ v blush; flow suddenly or violently; be excited; cleanse (e.g. toilet) by rush of water; excite ~n blush; rush of water; excitement; freshness

**flush**² adj level with surrounding surface; overflowing

**fluster** v make or become nervous, agitated ~n agitation

**flute** n wind instrument with blowhole in side; groove; v play on flute; make grooves in

**flutter** v flap (as wings) rapidly; quiver; be or make agitated ~n flapping movement; agitation; *Inf* modest wager

**flux** n discharge; constant succession of changes; substance mixed with metal in soldering etc.

**fly**¹ v flying, flew, flown move through air on wings or in aircraft; pass quickly; float loosely; run away; operate aircraft; cause to fly; set flying ~n (zip or buttons fastening) opening in trousers **flyer, flier** n small advertising leaflet; aviator **flying** adj hurried, brief **flying colours** conspicuous success **flying saucer** unidentified disc-shaped flying object **flying squad** special detachment of police, soldiers etc., ready

**fluency** assurance, command, control, ease, facility, glibness, slickness, smoothness

**fluent** articulate, easy, effortless, facile, flowing, natural, ready, smooth, voluble

**fluid** adj flowing, liquefied, liquid, melted, molten, runny, watery; adaptable, adjustable, changeable, flexible, floating, indefinite, mercurial, mobile, mutable, shifting ~n liquid, liquor, solution

**flurry** agitation, bustle, commotion, disturbance, excitement, ferment, flap, fluster, flutter, furore, fuss, hurry, stir, to-do, tumult, whirl

**flush**¹ v blush, burn, colour, colour up, crimson, flame, glow, go red, redden, suffuse ~n bloom, blush, colour, freshness, glow, redness, rosiness

**flush**² adj even, flat, level, plane, square, true; abundant, affluent, full, generous, lavish, liberal, overflowing, prodigal

**fluster** v agitate, bother, bustle, confound, confuse, disturb, excite, flurry, heat, hurry, perturb, ruffle, unnerve, upset ~n bustle, commotion, disturbance, dither *chiefly Brit,* flurry, flutter, furore, ruffle, turmoil

**flutter** v agitate, beat, flap, flicker, fluctuate, hover, palpitate, quiver, ripple, ruffle, shiver, tremble, vibrate, waver ~n palpitation, quiver, shiver, shudder, tremble, tremor,

to act quickly **flying start** very good start **flyover** n road passing over another by bridge **flywheel** n heavy wheel regulating speed of machine

**fly²** n (pl **flies**) two-winged insect, esp. common housefly

**foal** n young of horse

**foam** n collection of small bubbles on liquid; light cellular solid ~v (cause to) produce foam **foamy** adj

**fob** v **fobbing, fobbed** (with off) ignore, dismiss in offhand manner

**focus** n (pl **-cuses, -ci**) point at which rays meet; state of optical image when it is clearly defined; point on which interest, activity is centred ~v **-cusing, -cused** bring to focus; concentrate **focal** adj

**fodder** n bulk food for livestock

**foe** n enemy

**fog** n thick mist ~v **fogging, fogged** cover in fog; puzzle **foggy** adj **foghorn** n large horn to warn ships

**fogey** n old-fashioned person

**foible** n minor weakness, slight pe-

culiarity of character

**foil¹** v baffle, frustrate ~n blunt sword for fencing

**foil²** n metal in thin sheet; anything which sets off another thing to advantage

**foist** v (usually with on) force, impose on

**fold¹** v double up, bend part of; interlace (arms); clasp (in arms); Cookery mix gently; become folded; admit of being folded; Inf fail ~n folding; line made by folding **folder** n binder, file for loose papers

**fold²** n enclosure for sheep

**foliage** n leaves collectively

**folio** n (pl **-lios**) sheet of paper folded in half to make two leaves of book; book of largest common size

**folk** n people in general; family, relative; race of people **folksy** adj simple, unpretentious **folklore** n tradition, customs, beliefs popularly held

**follicle** n small sac

twitching, vibration

**fly** v flit, flutter, hover, mount, sail, soar, take wing, wing; aviate, control, manoeuvre, operate, pilot; elapse, flit, glide, pass, run quickly, roll on, run its course, slip away; display, float, show, wave; bolt, career, dart, dash, hasten, hurry, race, rush, scamper, scoot, shoot, speed, sprint, tear

**flying** adj brief, fleeting, hasty, hurried, rushed

**foam** n bubbles, froth, head, lather, spray, spume, suds ~v boil, bubble, effervesce, fizz, froth, lather

**focus** n centre, core, cynosure, headquarters, heart, hub, meeting place, target

**foe** adversary, antagonist, enemy,

opponent, rival

**fog** n gloom, miasma, mist, murk, murkiness, smog

**foggy** adj blurred, cloudy, dim, grey, hazy, indistinct, misty, murky, nebulous, obscure, vaporous

**foil¹** v baffle, balk, check, counter, defeat, elude, frustrate, nullify, outwit, stop, thwart

**foil²** antithesis, background, complement, contrast, setting

**fold** v bend, crease, crumple, double, gather, intertwine, overlap, pleat, tuck, turn under; do up, enclose, enfold, entwine, envelop, wrap, wrap up ~n bend, crease, furrow, layer, overlap, pleat, turn, wrinkle

**folder** binder, envelope, file,

**follow** v go or come after; accompany; keep to; be a consequence of; take as guide; grasp meaning of; have keen interest in **follower** n disciple, supporter **following** adj about to be mentioned ~n body of supporters

**folly** n foolishness

**foment** v foster, stir up

**fond** adj tender, loving **fondness** n **fond of** having liking for

**fondant** n flavoured paste of sugar and water

**fondle** v caress

**font** n bowl for baptismal water

**fontanelle** n soft, membraneous gap between bones of baby's skull

**food** n solid nourishment; what one eats

**fool**[1] n silly, empty-headed person; Hist jester ~v delude; dupe; act as fool **foolhardy** adj foolishly adventurous **foolish** adj silly, stupid; unwise **foolishness** n **foolproof** adj unable to fail **foolscap** n size of paper

**fool**[2] n dessert made from fruit and cream

**foot** n (pl **feet**) lowest part of leg,

— THESAURUS —

portfolio

**folk** clan, family, kin, people, race, tribe

**follow** succeed, supersede, supplant; accompany, attend, escort, tag along; comply, conform, heed, mind, note, obey, observe, regard, watch

**follower** adherent, admirer, apostle, backer, believer, convert, devotee, disciple, fan, fancier, habitué, partisan, pupil, supporter, votary, worshipper

**following** adj consequent, ensuing, later, next, specified, subsequent, succeeding, successive ~n audience, entourage, fans, public, supporters

**folly** absurdity, foolishness, idiocy, imbecility, imprudence, indiscretion, irrationality, lunacy, madness, nonsense, recklessness, silliness, stupidity

**fond** adoring, affectionate, amorous, caring, devoted, doting, indulgent, loving, tender, warm

**fondle** caress, cuddle, dandle, pat, pet, stroke

**fondness** attachment, fancy, liking, love, partiality, penchant, predilection, preference, soft spot, taste, weakness

**food** board, bread, cooking, cuisine, diet, edibles, fare, feed, foodstuffs, larder, meat, menu, nourishment, nutrition, provisions, rations, refreshment, stores, sustenance, table

**fool** n ass, berk Brit sl, charlie Brit inf, dolt, dunce, dunderhead, halfwit, idiot, ignoramus, illiterate, jackass, jerk Sl, chiefly US & Canad, lamebrain Inf, loon, moron, nerd or nurd Sl, nitwit, numskull or numbskull, silly, simpleton, wally Sl; buffoon, clown, comic, harlequin, jester, motley, pierrot ~v beguile, bluff, cheat, deceive, delude, dupe, hoax, hoodwink, mislead, take in, trick

**foolhardy** bold, hot-headed, impetuous, imprudent, incautious, irresponsible, madcap, precipitate, rash, reckless, venturesome, venturous

**foolish** brainless, crackpot Inf, crazy, doltish, fatuous, half-witted, harebrained, idiotic, imbecilic, inane, ludicrous, mad, ridiculous, senseless, silly, simple, stupid, weak, witless; absurd, ill-

from ankle down; lower part of anything, base, stand; end of bed etc.; measure of twelve inches ~v pay cost of **footage** n amount of film used **footing** n basis, foundation **football** n game played with large blown-up ball; the ball **footballer** n **foothills** pl n hills at foot of mountain **foothold** n place giving secure grip for the foot **footlights** pl n lights across front of stage **footloose** adj free from ties **footman** n male servant in livery **footnote** n note of reference or explanation printed at foot of page **footprint** n mark left by foot **footstep** n step in walking; sound made by walking **footwear** n anything worn to cover feet **footwork** n skilful use of the feet in football etc.

**footle** v Inf loiter aimlessly **footling** adj trivial

**for** prep directed to; because of; instead of; towards; on account of; in favour of; respecting; during; in search of; in payment of; in

character of; in spite of ~conj because

**forage** n food for cattle and horses ~v collect forage; make roving search

**foray** n raid, inroad

**forbear** v forbearing, forbore, forborne (esp. with from) cease; refrain (from); be patient **forbearance** n

**forbid** v forbidding, forbade, forbidden prohibit; refuse to allow **forbidden** adj forbidding **adj** uninviting, threatening

**force** n strength, power; compulsion; that which tends to produce a change in a physical system; body of troops, police etc.; group of people organized for particular task; validity; vigour ~v compel; produce by effort, strength; break open; hasten maturity of **forced** adj compulsory; unnatural **forceful** adj powerful, persuasive **forcible** adj done by force

**forceps** pl n surgical pincers

──── THESAURUS ────

considered, inane, nonsensical, short-sighted, unwise

**foolishness** absurdity, folly, idiocy, imprudence, inanity, indiscretion, irresponsibility, silliness, stupidity, weakness

**foolproof** certain, guaranteed, infallible, safe, unassailable

**footing** basis, establishment, foothold, foundation, ground, groundwork, installation, settlement

**footstep** footmark, footprint, trace, track; footfall, step, tread

**forage** n feed, fodder, food, foodstuffs, provender

**forbear** abstain, avoid, cease, decline, desist, eschew, omit, pause, refrain, stop, withhold

**forbearance** indulgence, leniency lenity, mildness, moderation, patience, resignation, restraint, self-control, temperance, tolerance

**forbid** ban, debar, disallow, exclude, hinder, inhibit, outlaw, preclude, prohibit, proscribe, rule out veto

**forbidden** banned, outlawed, prohibited, proscribed, taboo, vetoed

**force** n energy, impact, impulse, life, might, muscle, potency, power, pressure, stimulus, strength, stress, vigour; coercion, compulsion, constraint, duress, enforcement, pressure, violence; bite, cogency, effect effectiveness, efficacy, influence power, strength, validity, weight

## DICTIONARY

**ford** n shallow place where river may be crossed ~v cross river

**fore** adj in front ~n front part

**forearm** n arm between wrist and elbow ~v arm beforehand

**forebear** n ancestor

**forebode** v indicate in advance

**foreboding** n anticipation of evil

**forecast** v estimate beforehand (esp. weather) ~n prediction

**forecastle** n forward raised part of ship

**foreclose** v take away power of redeeming (mortgage)

**forecourt** n open space in front of building

**forefather** n ancestor

**forefinger** n finger next to thumb

**forefront** n most active or prominent position

**foregoing** adj going before, preceding **foregone** adj determined beforehand

**foreground** n part of view nearest observer

**forehand** adj (of stroke in racket games) made with inner side of wrist leading

**forehead** n part of face above eyebrows and between temples

**foreign** adj not of, or in, one's own country; relating to other countries; strange **foreigner** n

**foreman** n one in charge of work; leader of jury

**foremost** adj/adv first in time, place, importance etc.

**forensic** adj connected with a court

## THESAURUS

drive, emphasis, fierceness, intensity, persistence, vehemence, vigour ~v coerce, compel, constrain, dragoon, drive, impel, impose, make, necessitate, obligate, oblige, overcome, press, press-gang, pressure, pressurize, railroad Inf, urge; blast, break open, prise, propel, push, thrust, use violence on, wrench, wrest

**forced** compulsory, involuntary, mandatory, obligatory, slave, unwilling; affected, artificial, contrived, false, insincere, laboured, stiff, strained, unnatural, wooden

**forceful** cogent, compelling, convincing, dynamic, effective, pithy, potent, powerful, telling, vigorous, weighty

**forcible** active, cogent, compelling, effective, efficient, energetic, forceful, impressive, mighty, potent, powerful, strong, telling, valid, weighty

**forebear** ancestor, father, fore-

father, forerunner, predecessor, progenitor

**foreboding** anxiety, apprehension, apprehensiveness, chill, dread, fear, misgiving, premonition, presentiment

**forecast** v augur, calculate, divine, estimate, foresee, foretell, plan, predict, prophesy ~n anticipation, conjecture, foresight, forethought, guess, outlook, planning, prediction, prognosis, projection, prophecy

**forefather** ancestor, father, forebear, forerunner, predecessor

**foregoing** above, antecedent, former, preceding, previous, prior

**foreign** alien, borrowed, distant, exotic, external, imported, outlandish, outside, overseas, remote, strange, unfamiliar, unknown

**foreigner** alien, immigrant, incomer, newcomer, outlander, stranger

**foremost** chief, first, front, high-

of law **forensic medicine** application of medical knowledge in legal matters

**forerunner** *n* one who goes before, precursor

**foresee** *v* **-seeing, -saw, -seen** see beforehand

**foreshadow** *v* show, suggest beforehand

**foresight** *n* foreseeing; care for future

**foreskin** *n* skin that covers the tip of the penis

**forest** *n* area with heavy growth of trees **forestry** *n*

**forestall** *v* prevent, guard against in advance

**foretaste** *n* experience of something to come

**foretell** *v* **-telling, -told** prophesy

**forethought** *n* thoughtful consideration of future events

**forever** *adv* always; eternally; *Inf* for a long time

**forewarn** *v* warn, caution in advance

**foreword** *n* preface

**forge**[1] *n* place where metal is worked, smithy *v* shape (metal) by heating and hammering; counterfeit **forger** *n* **forgery** *n* counterfeiting; counterfeit thing

**forge**[2] *v* advance steadily

**forget** *v* **-getting, -got, -gotten** lose memory of, neglect, overlook **forgetful** *adj* **forget-me-not** *n* plant with small blue flowers

**forgive** *v* cease to blame or hold resentment against; pardon **forgiveness** *n*

**forgo** *v* **-going, -went, -gone** go without; give up

**fork** *n* pronged instrument used for

est, initial, leading, pre-eminent, principal, supreme

**forerunner** ancestor, envoy, forebear, foregoer, harbinger, herald, precursor, predecessor, progenitor, prototype

**foresee** anticipate, divine, envisage, forebode, forecast, foretell, predict, prophesy

**foreshadow** augur, betoken, bode, forebode, imply, indicate, portend, predict, presage, promise, signal

**foresight** anticipation, care, caution, forethought, precaution, preparedness, prescience, provision

**foretell** adumbrate, augur, forecast, foreshadow, forewarn, portend, predict, presage, prophesy, signify

**forethought** anticipation, precau-

tion, providence, provision, prudence

**forewarn** admonish, advise, alert, caution, tip off

**forfeit** damages, fine, loss, penalty ~v be deprived of, be stripped of, give up, lose, relinquish, surrender

**forge** coin, copy, counterfeit, fake, falsify, feign, imitate

**forget** lose sight of, omit, overlook

**forgetful** absent-minded, apt to forget, careless, dreamy, heedless, inattentive, lax, neglectful, negligent, oblivious, slapdash, slipshod, unmindful

**forgive** absolve, acquit, condone, excuse, exonerate, pardon, remit

**forgo, forego** abandon, cede, do without, give up, relinquish, renounce, resign, sacrifice, surrender, waive, yield

eating food; pronged tool for digging or lifting; division into branches ~v branch; dig, lift, throw, with fork; make fork-shaped

**forlorn** *adj* forsaken; desperate

**form** *n* shape, visible appearance; structure; nature; species, kind; regularly drawn up document; condition; class in school; customary way of doing things; bench ~v shape, organize; conceive; make part of; come into existence or shape **formation** *n* forming; thing formed **formative** *adj*

**formal** *adj* ceremonial, according to rule; of outward form; stiff **formality** *n* observance required by custom; condition of being formal

**formalize** *v* make official **formally** *adv*

**format** *n* size and shape of book etc.

**former** *adj* earlier in time; of past times; first named ~*pron* first named thing or person or fact **formerly** *adv* previously

**Formica** *n Trademark* material used for heat-resistant surfaces

**formidable** *adj* to be feared; overwhelming; likely to be difficult

**formula** *n* (*pl* **-las, -lae**) set form of words, rule; *Science, Maths* rule, fact expressed in symbols and figures **formulate** *v*

**fornication** *n* sexual intercourse outside marriage

───────────── THESAURUS ─────────────

**forlorn** abandoned, cheerless, comfortless, deserted, desolate, destitute, disconsolate, helpless, homeless, hopeless, lonely, lost, miserable, pathetic, pitiable, pitiful, unhappy, wretched

**form** *n* appearance, cast, cut, fashion, formation, model, mould, pattern, shape, stamp, structure; format, framework, harmony, order, orderliness, organization, plan, proportion, structure, symmetry; application, document, paper, sheet ~*v* assemble, bring about, build, concoct, construct, contrive, create, devise, establish, fabricate, fashion, forge, found, invent, make, model, mould, produce, set up, shape, stamp; arrange, combine, design, dispose, draw up, frame, organize, pattern, plan

**formal** approved, ceremonial, explicit, express, fixed, lawful, legal, methodical, official, prescribed, regular, rigid, ritualistic, set, solemn, strict

**formality** ceremony, convention, custom, gesture, procedure, red tape, rite, ritual; correctness, decorum, etiquette, protocol

**formation** accumulation, composition, development, establishment, evolution, generation, genesis, manufacture, organization, production; arrangement, configuration, design, disposition, figure, grouping, pattern, rank, structure

**former** ancient, bygone, departed, of yore, old, old-time, past; above, aforesaid, foregoing, preceding

**formerly** already, before, lately, once, previously

**formidable** daunting, dreadful, fearful, frightful, horrible, intimidating, menacing, shocking, terrifying, threatening; arduous, challenging, colossal, difficult, onerous, overwhelming, toilsome

**formula** blueprint, method, precept, prescription, principle, procedure, recipe, rule, way

**formulate** codify, define, detail,

**forsake** v -saking, -sook, -saken abandon, desert; give up

**forswear** v -swearing, -swore, -sworn renounce, deny; perjure

**fort** n stronghold

**forte**[1] n one's strong point, that in which one excels

**forte**[2] adv Mus loudly

**forth** adv onwards, into view **forthcoming** adj about to come; ready when wanted; willing to talk **forthwith** adv at once

**forthright** adj outspoken

**fortify** v -fying, -fied strengthen **fortification** n

**fortitude** n endurance

**fortnight** n two weeks

**fortress** n fortified place

**fortuitous** adj accidental

**fortune** n good luck; wealth; chance **fortunate** adj **fortunately** adv

**forty** SEE FOUR

**forum** n (place or medium for) meeting, discussion or debate

**forward** adj lying in front of; onward; presumptuous; advanced; relating to the future ~n player in various team games ~adv towards the future; towards the front, to the front, into view ~v help forward; send, dispatch **forwards** adv

**fossil** n remnant or impression of animal or plant, preserved in earth **fossilize** v turn into fossil; petrify

**foster** v promote development of; bring up child, esp. not one's own

**foul** adj loathsome, offensive; stink-

———— THESAURUS ————

express, frame, specify, systematize

**forsake** abandon, cast off, desert, disown, jilt, kick Inf, leave, quit, repudiate, throw over

**fort** blockhouse, camp, castle, citadel, fortress, garrison, redoubt, station, stronghold

**forthcoming** approaching, coming, expected, future, imminent, impending, prospective, upcoming; chatty, communicative, expansive, free, informative, open, sociable, talkative, unreserved

**forthright** above-board, blunt, candid, direct, downright, frank, open, outspoken, straightforward, upfront Inf

**forthwith** at once, directly, immediately, instantly, quickly, right away, straightaway

**fortification** bulwark, castle, citadel, defence, fastness, fort, fortress, keep, protection, stronghold

**fortify** brace, cheer, confirm, embolden, encourage, hearten, invig-

orate, reassure, stiffen, strengthen, sustain

**fortress** castle, citadel, fort, redoubt

**fortunate** bright, favoured, golden, happy, jammy Brit sl, lucky, prosperous, rosy, successful, well-off

**fortunately** by good luck, happily, luckily, providentially

**fortune** accident, chance, destiny, fate, hazard, kismet, luck, providence; affluence, gold mine, possessions, property, prosperity, riches, treasure, wealth

**forward** adj advanced, early, onward, precocious, premature, progressive, well-developed adv (also **forwards**) ahead, forth, on, onward ~v advance, aid, assist, back, encourage, expedite, favour, foster, further, hasten, help, hurry, promote, speed, support

**foster** cultivate, encourage, feed, nurture, promote, stimulate, sup-

ing; dirty; unfair; obscene ~*n* act of unfair play; breaking of a rule ~*v* make, become foul; jam; collide with

**found**[1] *v* establish; lay base of; base **foundation** *n* basis; lowest part of building; founding; endowed institution etc. **founder** *n*

**found**[2] *v* melt and run into mould; cast **foundry** *n* place for casting

**founder** *v* collapse; sink

**foundling** *n* deserted infant

**fount** *n* fountain; source

**fountain** *n* jet of water, esp. ornamental one; spring; source

**four** *n/adj* cardinal number next after three **fourth** *adj* ordinal number **fourteen** *n/adj* four plus ten **fourteenth** *adj* **forty** *n/adj* four tens **fortieth** *adj* **foursome** *n* group of four people

**fowl** *n* domestic cock or hen; bird; its flesh

**fox** *n* red bushy-tailed animal; its fur; cunning person ~*v* perplex; act craftily **foxy** *adj* **foxglove** *n* tall flowering plant **foxtrot** *n* (music for) ballroom dance

**foyer** *n* entrance hall in theatres, hotels etc.

**fracas** *n* noisy quarrel

**fraction** *n* numerical quantity not an integer; fragment

**fractious** *adj* irritable

**fracture** *n* breakage; breaking of bone ~*v* break

**fragile** *adj* breakable; delicate **fragility** *n*

**fragment** *n* piece broken off ~*v* shatter **fragmentary** *adj*

———————————— THESAURUS ————————————

port, uphold; bring up mother, nurse, raise, rear, take care of

**foul** *adj* contaminated, dirty, disgusting, fetid, filthy, impure, loathsome, nasty, nauseating, offensive, polluted, putrid, rank, repulsive, revolting, rotten, squalid, stinking, sullied, tainted, unclean ~*v* besmear, besmirch, contaminate, defile, dirty, pollute, smear, smirch, soil, stain, sully, taint

**found** constitute, construct, create, endow, erect, establish, fix, inaugurate, institute, organize, originate, plant, raise, settle, set up, start

**foundation** base, basis, bedrock, bottom, footing, substructure, underpinning; endowment, establishment, inauguration, institution, settlement

**founder**[1] *n* author, beginner, benefactor, builder, designer, establisher, father, framer, generator, initiator, inventor, maker, organizer,

originator, patriarch

**founder**[2] *v* be lost, go down, go to the bottom, sink, submerge

**fountain** fount, jet, reservoir, spout, spray, spring, well

**foyer** anteroom, entrance hall, lobby, vestibule

**fracas** brawl, disturbance, fight, melee, quarrel, riot, row, rumpus, scrimmage, scuffle, shindig *Inf*, shindy *Inf*, trouble, uproar

**fractious** awkward, captious, crabby, cross, fretful, irritable, peevish, recalcitrant, testy, touchy, unruly

**fracture** *n* breach, break, cleft, crack, fissure, gap, opening, rent, rift, rupture, schism, split ~*v* break, crack, rupture, splinter, split

**fragile** breakable, brittle, dainty, delicate, feeble, fine, flimsy, frail, infirm, slight, weak

**fragment** bit, chip, fraction, morsel, oddment, part, piece, portion, remnant, scrap, shiver, sliver

**fragrant** adj sweet-smelling **fragrance** n

**frail** adj fragile; in weak health **frailty** n

**frame** n that in which thing is set, as square of wood round picture etc.; structure; build of body ~v make; put into words; put into frame; bring false charge against

**framework** n supporting structure

**franc** n monetary unit in France, Switzerland etc.

**franchise** n right of voting; citizenship; privilege or right

**frank** adj candid, outspoken; sincere ~n official mark on letter either cancelling stamp or ensuring delivery without stamp ~v mark letter thus

**frankfurter** n smoked sausage

**frankincense** n aromatic gum resin burned as incense

**frantic** adj distracted with rage, grief, joy etc.; frenzied **frantically** adv

**fraternal** adj of brother, brotherly

**fraternity** n brotherliness; brotherhood **fraternize** v associate; make friends

**fraud** n criminal deception; impostor **fraudulent** adj

**fraught** adj filled (with), involving

———————— THESAURUS ————————

**fragmentary** bitty, broken, disconnected, discrete, disjointed, incoherent, incomplete, partial, piecemeal

**fragrance** aroma, balm, bouquet, perfume, scent, smell

**fragrant** aromatic, balmy, odorous, perfumed, sweet-scented, sweet-smelling

**frail** breakable, brittle, decrepit, delicate, feeble, flimsy, fragile, infirm, insubstantial, puny, slight, tender, unsound, vulnerable, weak

**frailty** feebleness, puniness, susceptibility, weakness

**frame** n mount, mounting, setting; casing, fabric, form, scheme, shell, structure, system; anatomy, body, build, physique, skeleton ~v assemble, build, constitute, construct, fabricate, fashion, forge, form, institute, invent, make, model, mould, set up; compose, contrive, devise, draft, draw up, form, formulate, hatch, plan, shape, sketch; case, enclose, mount, surround

**framework** core, fabric, foundation, groundwork, plan, schema,

shell, skeleton, structure

**frank** artless, blunt, candid, direct, downright, forthright, free, honest, open, outright, outspoken, plain, sincere, straightforward, transparent, truthful, unconcealed, undisguised, unreserved, unrestricted, upfront *Inf*

**frantic** berserk, desperate, distracted, distraught, frenetic, frenzied, furious, hectic, mad, overwrought, raging, raving, wild

**fraternity** association, brotherhood, circle, clan, club, companionship, company, comradeship, fellowship, guild, kinship, league, order, set, sodality, union

**fraud** artifice, cheat, chicanery, craft, deceit, deception, doubledealing, duplicity, guile, hoax, humbug, imposture, scam *Sl*, spuriousness, stratagems, swindling, treachery, trickery; bluffer, charlatan, cheat, counterfeit, doubledealer, fake, forgery, hoax, hoaxer, impostor, mountebank, pretender, quack, sham, swindler

**fraudulent** crafty, criminal, deceit-

**fray¹** n fight; noisy quarrel

**fray²** v make, become ragged at edge

**frazzle** Inf v make or become exhausted ~n exhausted state

**freak** n/adj abnormal (person or thing)

**freckle** n light brown spot on skin, esp. caused by sun

**free** adj freer, freest able to act at will, not under compulsion or restraint; self-ruling; not restricted or affected by; not subject to cost or tax; not in use; (of person) not occupied; loose, not fixed ~v freeing, freed set at liberty; remove (obstacles, pain etc.); rid (of) **freedom** n **free-for-all** n brawl **freehold** n tenure of land without obligation of

service or rent **freelance** adj/n (of) self-employed person **freeloader** n Sl scrounger **free-range** adj kept, produced in natural, nonintensive conditions **free speech** right to express opinions publicly **freewheel** v travel downhill on bicycle without pedalling

**freeze** v freezing, froze, frozen change (by reduction of temperature) from liquid to solid, as water to ice; preserve (food etc.) by extreme cold; fix (prices etc.); feel very cold; become rigid **freezer** n insulated cabinet for long-term storage of perishable foodstuffs

**freight** n commercial transport (esp. by railway, ship); cost of this; goods so carried ~v send as or by

————————————— THESAURUS —————————————

ful, deceptive, dishonest, false, knavish, sham, spurious, swindling, treacherous

**fray** v chafe, fret, rub, wear, wear away, wear thin

**freak** n aberration, abnormality, anomaly, malformation, monster, oddity ~adj aberrant, abnormal, atypical, bizarre, erratic, exceptional, fortuitous, odd, queer, unexpected, unforeseen, unpredictable, unusual

**free** adj at large, at liberty, footloose, independent, liberated, loose, uncommitted, unconstrained, unfettered, unrestrained; autarchic, autonomous, democratic, emancipated, independent, self-governing, self-ruling, sovereign; complimentary, for nothing, gratis, gratuitous, unpaid; able, allowed, clear, disengaged, free, open, permitted, unattached, unhampered, unimpeded, unobstructed, unregulated, unrestricted, un-

trammelled; available, empty, extra, idle, not tied down, spare, unemployed, uninhabited, unoccupied, unused, vacant ~v deliver, discharge, emancipate, let go, let out, liberate, loose, manumit, release, turn loose, unbridle, uncage, unchain, unfetter, unleash, untie; clear, cut loose, deliver, disengage, disentangle, exempt, extricate, ransom, redeem, relieve, rescue, rid, unburden, undo

**freedom** autonomy, deliverance, emancipation, home rule, independence, liberty, release, self-government; exemption, immunity, impunity, privilege; ability, carte blanche, discretion, elbowroom, facility, flexibility, free rein, latitude, leeway, licence, opportunity, play, power, range, scope

**freeze** benumb, chill, congeal, glaciate, harden, ice over or up, stiffen; fix, hold up, inhibit, peg, stop, suspend

freight **freighter** n

**French** n language spoken by people of France ~adj of, pert. to France **French dressing** salad dressing **French fries** potato chips **French horn** musical wind instrument

**frenetic** adj frenzied

**frenzy** n violent mental derangement; wild excitement **frenzied** adj

**frequent** adj happening often; common; numerous ~v go often to

**frequency** n rate of occurrence; in radio etc., cycles per second of alternating current

**fresco** n (pl **-coes**) (method of) painting on wet plaster

**fresh** adj not stale; new; additional; different; recent; inexperienced; pure; not pickled, frozen etc.; not faded; not tired; (of wind) strong

**freshen** v **freshman, fresher** n first-year student

**fret**[1] v fretting, fretted be irritated, worry ~n irritation **fretful** adj

**fret**[2] n repetitive geometrical pattern ~v fretting, fretted ornament with carved pattern **fretwork** n

**friable** adj easily crumbled

**friar** n member of religious order

**fricassee** n dish of stewed pieces of meat

**friction** n rubbing; resistance met with by body moving over another; clash of wills etc.

**Friday** n sixth day of the week

**fridge** n Inf refrigerator

**friend** n one well known to another and regarded with affection and loyalty **friendly** adj kind; favourable **friendship** n

——————— THESAURUS ———————

**freight** n bales, bulk, burden, cargo, consignment, contents, goods, haul, lading, load, merchandise, payload, tonnage

**frenzied** agitated, convulsive, distracted, distraught, excited, frantic, frenetic, furious, hysterical, mad, maniacal, rabid, uncontrolled, wild

**frequent** adj common, constant, continual, customary, everyday, familiar, habitual, numerous, persistent, recurrent, repeated, usual ~v attend, be found at, haunt, patronize, resort, visit

**fresh** added, additional, extra, further, more, other, renewed; different, latest, modern, new, novel, original, recent, unusual, up-to-date ; artless, callow, green, inexperienced, natural, new, raw, untrained, untried, youthful; bracing, bright, brisk, clean, clear, cool, crisp, invigorating, pure, refreshing, sparkling, stiff, sweet; blooming,

clear, fair, florid, glowing, good, hardy, healthy, rosy, wholesome

**freshen** enliven, liven up, refresh, restore, revitalize, rouse, spruce up, titivate

**fret** affront, agonize, anguish, annoy, brood, chagrin, goad, grieve, harass, irritate, provoke, ruffle, torment, worry

**friction** abrasion, erosion, fretting, grating, irritation, resistance, rubbing, scraping

**friend** chum, companion, comrade, confidant, crony, familiar, intimate, pal, partner, playmate, soul mate

**friendly** affectionate, amiable, amicable, attentive, beneficial, benevolent, benign, close, companionable, comradely, convivial, cordial, familiar, favourable, fond, genial, good, helpful, intimate, kind, kindly, neighbourly, outgoing, peaceable, propitious, receptive, socia-

**frieze** n ornamental band, strip (on wall)

**frigate** n fast warship

**fright** n sudden fear; shock; alarm; grotesque or ludicrous person or thing **frighten** v cause fear, fright in

**frightening** adj **frightful** adj terrible, calamitous; shocking; Inf very great, very large **frightfully** adv

**frigid** adj formal; (sexually) unfeeling; cold

**frill** n strip of fabric gathered at one edge; ruff of hair, feathers around neck of dog, bird etc.; unnecessary words; superfluous thing; adornment **frilly** adj

**fringe** n ornamental edge of hanging threads, tassels etc.; hair cut in front and falling over brow; edge ~adj (of theatre etc.) unofficial

**frisk** v move, leap, playfully; Inf search (person) **frisky** adj

**frisson** n shiver of excitement

**fritter**[1] v waste

**fritter**[2] n piece of food fried in batter

**frivolous** adj not serious, unimportant; flippant **frivolity** n

**frizz** v crisp, curl into small curls ~n frizzed hair **frizzy** adj

**frock** n woman's dress; various similar garments

**frog** n tailless amphibious animal developed from tadpole **frogman** n underwater swimmer with rubber suit

──────────────── T H E S A U R U S ────────────────

ble, sympathetic, welcoming, well-disposed

**friendship** affection, affinity, alliance, amity, attachment, benevolence, closeness, concord, familiarity, fondness, good-fellowship, good will, harmony, intimacy, love, rapport, regard

**fright** alarm, apprehension, dismay, dread, fear, horror, panic, quaking, scare, shock, terror, trepidation

**frighten** alarm, appal, cow, daunt, dismay, intimidate, petrify, scare, shock, startle, terrify, terrorize, unman, unnerve

**frightening** alarming, appalling, dismaying, dreadful, fearful, fearsome, hair-raising, harrowing, horrifying, intimidating, menacing, shocking, terrifying, unnerving

**frightful** appalling, awful, dire, dreadful, fearful, ghastly, grim, grisly, gruesome, harrowing, hideous, horrible, lurid, macabre, petrifying, shocking, terrible, terrifying, traumatic, unnerving, unspeakable

**frigid** aloof, austere, forbidding, formal, icy, lifeless, passionless, passive, repellent, rigid, stiff, unapproachable, unbending, unfeeling, unloving, unresponsive; arctic, chill, cold, cool, frost-bound, frosty, frozen, gelid, glacial, hyperboreal, icy, Siberian, wintry

**fringe** binding, border, edging, hem, tassel, trimming; borderline, edge, limits, march, marches, margin, outskirts, perimeter, periphery

**frisky** bouncy, frolicsome, full of beans Inf, high-spirited, in high spirits, kittenish, lively, playful, rollicking, romping, spirited, sportive

**frivolity** childishness, flippancy, folly, fun, gaiety, giddiness, jest, levity, lightness, nonsense, puerility, shallowness, silliness, superficiality, trifling, triviality

**frivolous** childish, dizzy, empty-headed, flighty, flippant, foolish, giddy, idle, juvenile, puerile, silly,

**frolic** n merrymaking ~v **-icking, -icked** behave playfully

**from** prep expressing point of departure, source, distance, cause, change of state etc.

**frond** n plant organ consisting of stem and foliage

**front** n fore part; position directly before or ahead; seaside promenade; outward aspect; Inf thing serving as respectable cover ~v look, face; Inf be a cover for ~adj of, at the front **frontal** adj **frontage** n façade of building; extent of front **frontier** n part of country which borders on another **frontispiece** n illustration facing title page of book

**frost** n frozen dew or mist; act or state of freezing ~v cover, be covered with frost or something similar in appearance **frosted** adj (of glass)

opaque **frosty** adj accompanied by frost; cold; unfriendly **frostbite** n destruction of tissue by cold

**froth** n collection of small bubbles, foam ~v (cause to) foam **frothy** adj

**frown** v wrinkle brows; (with on) disapprove of ~n expression of disapproval

**frugal** adj sparing; thrifty, economical; meagre

**fruit** n seed and its envelope, esp. edible one; vegetable product; (usu. pl) result, benefit ~v bear fruit **fruitful** adj **fruition** n enjoyment; realization of hopes **fruitless** adj **fruity** adj

**frump** n dowdy woman **frumpy** adj

**frustrate** v thwart; disappoint **frustration** n

**fry**[1] v **frying, fried** cook with fat; be cooked thus

**fry**[2] pl n young fishes

——————— THESAURUS ———————

superficial

**frolic** n amusement, fun, gaiety, high jinks, sport ~v caper, cavort, cut capers, frisk, gambol, lark, make merry, play, rollick, romp, sport

**front** n exterior, façade, face, facing, foreground, fore part, frontage, obverse; beginning, fore, forefront, head, lead, top, van, vanguard; blind, cover, cover-up, disguise, façade, mask, pretext, show ~v face (onto), look over or onto, overlook ~adj first, foremost, head, headmost, lead, leading, topmost

**frontier** borderland, borderline, bound, boundary, confines, edge, limit, marches, perimeter, verge

**frosty** chilly, cold, frozen, icy, parky Brit inf, rimy, wintry; discouraging, frigid, standoffish, unfriendly, unwelcoming

**frown** glare, glower, lour or lower,

scowl (with on) disapprove of, discourage, dislike

**frugal** abstemious, careful, economical, meagre, niggardly, parsimonious, prudent, saving, sparing, thrifty

**fruit** crop, harvest, produce, product, yield; advantage, benefit, consequence, effect, outcome, profit, result, return, reward

**fruitful** fecund, fertile; abundant, copious, flush, plenteous, plentiful, productive, profuse, prolific, rich, spawning

**fruitless** abortive, barren, futile, idle, ineffectual, in vain, pointless, profitless, unavailing, unproductive, unprofitable, unsuccessful, useless, vain

**frustrate** baffle, balk, block, check, confront, counter, defeat, disappoint, foil, forestall, inhibit, neutralize, nullify, stymie, thwart

**ft.** feet; foot

**fuchsia** *n* shrub with purple-red flowers

**fuddle** *v* (cause to) be intoxicated, confused

**fuddy-duddy** *n Inf* (elderly) dull person

**fudge**[1] *n* soft, variously flavoured sweet

**fudge**[2] *v* avoid definite decision

**fuel** *n* material for burning as source of heat or power ~*v* **fuelling, fuelled** provide with fuel

**fugitive** *n* one who flees, esp. from arrest ~*adj* elusive

**fugue** *n* musical composition in which themes are repeated in different parts

**fulcrum** *n* (*pl* **-crums, -cra**) point on which a lever is placed for support

**fulfil** *v* **-filling, -filled** satisfy; carry out **fulfilment** *n*

**full** *adj* containing as much as possible; abundant; complete; ample; plump ~*adv* very; quite; exactly **fully** *adv* **full-blooded** *adj* vigorous, enthusiastic **full-blown** *adj* fully developed **full stop** punctuation mark (.) at end of sentence

**fulminate** *v* (*esp. with against*) criticize harshly

**fulsome** *adj* insincerely excessive

**fumble** *v* grope about; handle awkwardly ~*n* awkward attempt

**fume** *v* be angry; emit smoke or vapour ~*n* smoke; vapour **fumigate** *v* apply fumes or smoke to, esp. for disinfection

**fun** *n* anything enjoyable, amusing etc. **funny** *adj* comical; odd **funnily** *adv* **funfair** *n* entertainment with rides and stalls

**function** *n* work a thing is de-

——————— THESAURUS ———————

**fuel** ammunition, encouragement, fodder, food, incitement, material, means, nourishment, provocation

**fugitive** runaway

**fulfil** accomplish, achieve, answer, carry out, complete, conclude, conform to, discharge, effect, execute, fill, finish, keep, meet, obey, observe, perform, realize, satisfy

**fulfilment** accomplishment, achievement, attainment, completion, consummation, crowning, discharge, end, implementation, observance, perfection, realization

**full** brimful, complete, entire, filled, gorged, intact, loaded, replete, sated, satiated, satisfied, saturated, stocked, sufficient; abundant, ample, broad, comprehensive, copious, detailed, exhaustive, extensive, generous, maximum, plenary, plenteous, plentiful, thorough, unabridged

**fully** absolutely, altogether, completely, entirely, intimately, perfectly, positively, thoroughly, totally, utterly, wholly; abundantly, adequately, amply, enough, plentifully, satisfactorily, sufficiently

**fulsome** adulatory, excessive, extravagant, fawning, gross, ingratiating, inordinate, insincere, nauseating, saccharine, sickening, sycophantic, unctuous

**fumble** botch, bungle, make a hash of *Inf*, mess up, mishandle, mismanage, muff, spoil

**fume** boil, chafe, rage, rant, rave, see red *Inf*, seethe, smoulder, storm

**fumigate** cleanse, disinfect, purify, sterilize

**fun** amusement, cheer, distraction, diversion, enjoyment, entertain-

signed to do; (large) social event; duty; profession ~v operate, work **functional** adj

**fund** n stock or sum of money; supply; pl money resources ~v provide or obtain funds

**fundamental** adj of, affecting, or serving as, the base; essential, primary ~n basic rule or fact **fundamentalism** n strict interpretation of religion **fundamentalist** n/adj

**funeral** n (ceremony associated with) burial or cremation of dead **funereal** adj like a funeral; dark; gloomy

**fungus** n (pl **-gi, -guses**) plant without leaves, flowers, or roots, as mushroom, mould **fungicide** n substance that destroys fungi

**funk** n style of dance music **funky** adj

**funnel** n cone-shaped vessel or tube; chimney of locomotive or ship ~v **-nelling, -nelled** (cause to) move as through funnel

**funny** adj SEE FUN

**fur** n soft hair of animal; garment of this **furry** adj

**furious** adj extremely angry; violent

**furl** v roll up and bind

**furlong** n eighth of mile

**furnace** n apparatus for applying great heat to metals

**furnish** v fit up house with furniture; supply **furnishings** pl n **furniture** n

**furore** n very angry or excited reac-

ment, frolic, gaiety, good time, jollity, joy, merriment, mirth, pleasure, recreation, romp, sport, treat

**function** n activity, business, capacity, charge, concern, duty, employment, exercise, job, mission, occupation, office, operation, part, post, province, purpose, responsibility, role, situation, task; affair, do Inf, gathering, reception, social occasion ~v act, behave, do duty, go, officiate, operate, perform, run, serve, work

**functional** practical, serviceable, useful, utilitarian, utility, working

**fund** n hoard, mine, repository, reserve, reservoir, source, storehouse, treasury, vein; capital, endowment, foundation, kitty, pool, reserve, stock, store, supply ~v capitalize, endow, finance, float, pay for, promote, stake, subsidize, support

**fundamental** adj basic, cardinal, central, crucial, elementary, essential, first, important, indispensable,

integral, intrinsic, key, necessary, prime, principal, radical, underlying, vital

**funeral** burial, interment, obsequies

**funny** absurd, amusing, comic, comical, diverting, droll, entertaining, facetious, farcical, hilarious, humorous, jocular, jolly, laughable, ludicrous, rich, ridiculous, riotous, risible, silly, slapstick, waggish, witty; curious, dubious, mysterious, odd, peculiar, perplexing, puzzling, queer, remarkable, rum Brit sl, strange, suspicious, unusual, weird

**furious** angry, beside oneself, boiling, enraged, frantic, frenzied, fuming, incensed, infuriated, mad, maddened, raging, wrathful

**furnish** appoint, decorate, equip, fit out, fit up, outfit, provide, purvey, rig, stock, store, supply; afford, bestow, endow, give, grant, hand out, offer, present, provide, reveal, supply

tion to something

**furrow** *n* trench; groove *~v* make furrows in

**further** *adv* more; in addition; at or to a greater distance or extent *~adj* more distant; additional; *comparative of FAR ~v* promote **furthermore** *adv* besides **furthermost** *adj* furthest *adj/adv superlative of FAR*

**furtive** *adj* stealthy, sly, secret

**fury** *n* wild rage, violence

**fuse** *v* blend by melting; melt with heat; (cause to) fail as a result of blown fuse *~n* soft wire used as safety device in electrical systems; device for igniting bomb etc. **fusion** *n*

**fuselage** *n* body of aircraft

**fuss** *n* needless bustle or concern; complaint; objection *~v* make fuss **fussy** *adj*

**fusty** *adj* mouldy; smelling of damp; old-fashioned

**futile** *adj* useless, ineffectual, trifling **futility** *n*

**futon** *n* Japanese padded quilt

**future** *n* time to come; what will happen *~adj* that will be; of, relating to, time to come **futuristic** *adj* appearing to belong to some future time

**fuzz** *n* fluff; frizzed hair; blur; *Sl* police **fuzzy** *adj*

——————————— THESAURUS ———————————

**furniture** appointments, chattels, effects, equipment, fittings, furnishings, goods, household goods, possessions

**furrow** channel, crease, fluting, groove, hollow, line, rut, seam, trench, wrinkle

**further** *adv* additionally, also, as well as, besides, furthermore, in addition, moreover, on top of, what's more, yet *~adj* additional, extra, fresh, more, new, other, supplementary *~v* advance, aid, assist, champion, encourage, expedite, facilitate, forward, foster, hasten, help, patronize, promote, push, speed, succour, work for

**furthermore** additionally, as well, besides, in addition, moreover, to boot, too

**furthest** extreme, farthest, most distant, outermost, outmost, remotest, ultimate, uttermost

**furtive** clandestine, cloaked, covert, hidden, secret, secretive, skulking, slinking, sly, sneaking, sneaky, stealthy, surreptitious, underhand

**fury** anger, frenzy, ire, madness, passion, rage, wrath; ferocity, force, intensity, power, savagery, severity, turbulence, vehemence, violence

**fuss** *n* ado, agitation, bother, bustle, commotion, confusion, excitement, fidget, flurry, fluster, flutter, hurry, stir, to-do, upset, worry; argument, bother, complaint, difficulty, display, furore, objection, row, squabble, trouble, unrest, upset *~v* bustle, fidget, fret, fume

**fussy** choosy, difficult, exacting, faddy, fastidious, finicky, particular, pernickety, picky *Inf*

**futile** abortive, barren, bootless, empty, forlorn, fruitless, hollow, ineffectual, nugatory, profitless, sterile, unavailing, unproductive, unprofitable, unsuccessful, useless, vain, valueless, worthless

**future** *n* expectation, hereafter, outlook, prospect, time to come *~adj* approaching, coming, destined, eventual, expected, fated, forthcoming, impending, later, prospective, subsequent, to come

# G g

**g** gram

**gabardine, gaberdine** *n* fine twill cloth like serge

**gabble** *v* **gabbling, gabbled** talk, utter inarticulately or too fast

**gable** *n* triangular upper part of wall at end of ridged roof

**gad** *v* **gadding, gadded** (*esp.* with **about**) go around in search of pleasure

**gadget** *n* small mechanical device

**gaffe** *n* tactless remark

**gaffer** *n* old man; *Inf* foreman, boss

**gag¹** *v* **gagging, gagged** stop up (person's mouth); *Sl* retch, choke ~*n* cloth etc. tied across mouth

**gag²** *n* joke, funny story

**gaggle** *n* flock of geese

**gain** *v* obtain (as profit); earn; reach; increase, improve; get nearer ~*n* profit; increase, improvement

**gainsay** *v* **gainsaying, gainsaid** deny, contradict

**gait** *n* manner of walking

**gala** *n* festive occasion; show; sporting event

**galaxy** *n* system of stars **galactic** *adj*

**gale** *n* strong wind; *Inf* outburst, esp. of laughter

**gall¹** *n* *Inf* impudence; bitterness **gall bladder** sac for bile

**gall²** *v* make sore by rubbing; irritate

**gallant** *adj* fine, stately; brave; chivalrous **gallantry** *n*

---
## THESAURUS
---

**gadget** appliance, contrivance, device, gimmick, invention, novelty, tool

**gaffe** blunder, boob *Brit sl*, clanger *Inf*, faux pas, howler, indiscretion

**gag¹** *v* curb, muffle, muzzle, quiet, silence, stifle, suppress, throttle

**gag²** crack *Sl*, funny *Inf*, hoax, jest, joke, wisecrack *Inf*, witticism

**gaiety** blitheness, cheerfulness, elation, glee, good humour, high spirits, *joie de vivre*, jollity, joviality, joyousness, liveliness, merriment, mirth, vivacity

**gaily** blithely, cheerfully, gleefully, happily, joyfully, light-heartedly, merrily

**gain** *v* achieve, acquire, advance, attain, capture, collect, gather, get, glean, harvest, increase, net, obtain, pick up, procure, profit, realize, reap, secure, win, win over; *acquire*, bring in, clear, earn, get,

make, net, obtain, produce, realize, win, yield ~*n* acquisition, advance, advantage, attainment, benefit, dividend, earnings, emolument, growth, headway, improvement, income, increase, increment, proceeds, produce, profit, return, rise, winnings, yield

**gait** bearing, carriage, pace, step, stride, tread, walk

**gala** carnival, celebration, festival, festivity, fête, jamboree, pageant, party

**gale** blast, hurricane, squall, storm, tempest, tornado, typhoon

**gallant** *adj* bold, brave, courageous, daring, dashing, doughty, fearless, heroic, honourable, intrepid, manly, noble, plucky, valiant, valorous; attentive, chivalrous, courteous, courtly, gentlemanly, gracious, magnanimous, noble, polite

**galleon** *n* large sailing ship

**gallery** *n* projecting upper floor in church, theatre etc.; place for showing works of art

**galley** *n* one-decked vessel with sails and oars; kitchen of ship or aircraft

**gallivant** *v* gad about

**gallon** *n* liquid measure of eight pints (4.55 litres)

**gallop** *n* horse's fastest pace; ride at this pace ~*v* go, ride at gallop; move fast

**gallows** *n* structure for hanging criminals

**galore** *adv* in plenty

**galoshes** *pl n* waterproof over-shoes

**galvanize** *v* stimulate to action; coat (iron etc.) with zinc

**gambit** *n* opening move, comment etc. intended to secure an advantage

**gamble** *v* play games of chance to win money; act on expectation of ~*n* risky undertaking; bet **gambler** *n* gambling

**gambol** *v* -bolling, -bolled skip, jump playfully

**game**[1] *n* pastime; jest; contest for amusement; scheme; animals or birds hunted; their flesh ~*adj* brave; willing **gaming** *n* gambling **gamekeeper** *n* man employed to breed game, prevent poaching

**game**[2], **gammy** *adj* lame

**gammon** *n* cured or smoked ham

**gamut** *n* whole range or scale

**gander** *n* male goose

**gang** *n* (criminal) group; organized group of workmen ~*v* (*esp. with together*) form gang

**gangling** *adj* lanky

**gangplank** *n* portable bridge for boarding or leaving vessel

**gangrene** *n* death or decay of body tissue as a result of disease or injury

**gangster** *n* member of criminal gang

**gangway** *n* bridge from ship to shore; anything similar; passage between rows of seats

**gannet** *n* predatory sea bird

——————— **THESAURUS** ———————

**gallantry** audacity, boldness, bravery, courage, daring, fearlessness, heroism, manliness, mettle, nerve, pluck, prowess, spirit, valiance, valour

**gallop** bolt, career, dart, dash, fly, hasten, hurry, race, run, rush, shoot, speed, sprint

**gamble** *v* back, bet, game, play, punt, stake, wager; back, chance, hazard, risk, speculate, stake, venture ~*n* chance, lottery, risk, speculation, uncertainty, venture; bet, flutter *Inf*, punt, wager

**gambol** caper, cavort, frisk, frolic, hop, jump, prance, rollick, skip

**game** *n* amusement, distraction,

diversion, entertainment, pastime, fun, jest, joke, merriment, pastime, play, recreation, romp, sport; contest, event, match, meeting, round; chase, prey, quarry ~*adj* bold, brave, courageous, dogged, fearless, gallant, heroic, intrepid, persistent, plucky, resolute, spirited, valiant

**gang** band, circle, clique, club, company, coterie, crew *Inf*, crowd, group, herd, horde, lot, mob, pack, party, ring, set, shift, squad, team, troupe

**gangster** bandit, brigand, crook *Inf*, desperado, hoodlum *chiefly US*, racketeer, robber, ruffian, thug,

## DICTIONARY

**gantry** n structure to support crane, railway signals etc.

**gaol** n see JAIL

**gap** n opening, interval

**gape** v stare in wonder; open mouth wide; be, become wide open

**garage** n (part of) building to house cars; refuelling and repair centre for cars

**garb** n/v dress

**garbage** n rubbish

**garble** v jumble or distort story, account etc.

**garden** n ground for cultivation ~v cultivate garden **gardener** n **gardening** n

**gargantuan** adj immense

**gargle** v wash throat with liquid kept moving by the breath ~n gargling; preparation for this purpose

**gargoyle** n grotesque carving on church etc.

**garish** adj showy; gaudy

**garland** n wreath of flowers as decoration

**garlic** n (bulb of) plant with strong smell and taste, used in cooking and seasoning

**garment** n article of clothing

**garner** v store, collect

**garnet** n red semiprecious stone

**garnish** v decorate (esp. food) ~n material for this

**garret** n attic

**garrison** n troops stationed in town, fort etc.; fortified place ~v occupy with garrison

**garrotte** v execute by strangling

**garrulous** adj talkative

**garter** n band worn round leg to hold up sock or stocking

**gas** n (pl **gases**) airlike substance; fossil fuel in form of gas; gaseous anaesthetic; gaseous poison or irritant; Inf, esp. US petrol ~v **gassing**, **gassed** poison with gas; talk idly, boastfully **gaseous** adj of, like gas

**gash** n gaping wound, slash ~v cut deeply

**gasket** n seal between metal faces,

## THESAURUS

**gap** blank, breach, break, chink, cleft, crack, cranny, crevice, divide, hiatus, hole, intermission, interruption, interstice, interval, lacuna, lull, opening, pause, recess, rent, rift, space, void

**gape** gawk, goggle, stare, wonder; crack, open, split, yawn

**garbage** debris, detritus, junk, litter, rubbish, scraps

**garble** confuse, jumble, mix up; distort, doctor, falsify, misquote, misreport, misrepresent, mistranslate, slant, tamper with, twist

**garish** brassy, cheap, flash Inf, flashy, gaudy, glaring, glittering, loud, showy, tacky Inf, tasteless, vulgar

**garland** bays, chaplet, crown, festoon, honours, laurels, wreath

**garner** accumulate, amass, assemble, collect, deposit, gather, hoard, put by, reserve, save, stockpile, store

**garnish** adorn, beautify, bedeck, deck, decorate, embellish, enhance, grace, ornament, set off, trim

**garrison** armed force, command, detachment, troops, unit; base, camp, encampment, fort, fortification, fortress, post, station, stronghold

**gash** n cleft, cut, incision, laceration, rent, slash, slit, split, tear, wound ~v cleave, cut, incise, lacerate, rend, slash, slit, split, tear, wound

esp. in engines

**gasp** v catch breath as in exhaustion or surprise ~n gasping

**gastric** adj of stomach

**gastroenteritis** n inflammation of stomach and intestines **gastronomy** n art of good eating

**gate** n opening in wall, fence etc.; barrier for closing it; any entrance or way out **gate-crash** v enter social function etc. uninvited **gateway** n entrance with gate; means of access

**gâteau** n (pl **-eaux**) elaborate, rich cake

**gather** v (cause to) assemble; increase gradually; draw together; collect; learn, understand **gathering** n assembly

**gaudy** adj showy in tasteless way

**gauge** n standard measure, as of

diameter of wire etc.; distance between rails of railway; instrument for measuring ~v measure; estimate

**gaunt** adj lean, haggard

**gauntlet** n (armoured) glove covering part of arm

**gauze** n thin transparent fabric of silk, wire etc.

**gavel** n auctioneer's mallet

**gay** adj homosexual; merry; bright **gaiety** n **gaily** adv

**gaze** v look fixedly ~n fixed look

**gazebo** n (pl **-bos**) summerhouse

**gazelle** n small graceful antelope

**gazette** n official newspaper for announcements **gazetteer** n geographical dictionary

**GB** Great Britain

**GBH** grievous bodily harm

**GC** George Cross

— THESAURUS —

**gasp** v blow, choke, gulp, pant, puff ~n blow, ejaculation, exclamation, gulp, pant, puff

**gate** access, barrier, door, doorway, egress, entrance, exit, passage, portal

**gather** accumulate, amass, assemble, collect, congregate, convene, flock, garner, group, heap, hoard, marshal, mass, muster, pile up, round up, stack up, stockpile; collect, crop, cull, garner, glean, harvest, pick, pluck, reap, select; assume, conclude, deduce, draw, hear, infer, learn, make, surmise, understand

**gathering** assembly, company, conclave, concourse, congregation, congress, convention, crowd, flock, group, knot, meeting, muster, party, rally, throng, turnout

**gaudy** bright, flash Inf, flashy, florid, garish, gay, glaring, loud, ostentatious, raffish, showy, tacky Inf,

tasteless, tawdry, vulgar

**gauge** v ascertain, calculate, check, compute, count, determine, measure, weigh; adjudge, appraise, assess, estimate, evaluate, guess, judge, rate, reckon, value ~n basis, example, guide, indicator, measure, meter, model, pattern, rule, sample, standard, test, yardstick

**gaunt** angular, bony, cadaverous, emaciated, haggard, lank, lean, meagre, pinched, rawboned, scraggy, scrawny, skinny, spare, thin, wasted

**gay** animated, blithe, carefree, cheerful, debonair, glad, gleeful, happy, hilarious, jolly, jovial, joyful, joyous, lively, merry, sparkling, sunny, vivacious; bright, brilliant, colourful, flamboyant, flashy, fresh, garish, gaudy, rich, showy, vivid

**gaze** v contemplate, gape, look, regard, stare, view, watch, wonder ~n fixed look, look, stare

**GCE** General Certificate of Education

**GCSE** General Certificate of Secondary Education

**gear** n set of wheels working together, esp. by engaging cogs; equipment; clothing; *Sl* drugs ~**v** adapt (one thing) so as to conform with another **gearbox** n case protecting gearing of bicycle, car etc.

**geese** pl of GOOSE

**geezer** n *Inf* (old or eccentric) man

**geisha** n in Japan, professional female companion for men

**gel** n jelly-like substance

**gelatine, gelatin** n substance prepared from animal bones etc., producing edible jelly

**geld** v castrate **gelding** n castrated horse

**gelignite** n powerful explosive consisting of dynamite in gelatine form

**gem** n precious stone, esp. when cut and polished

**gen** n *Inf* information

**gender** n sex, male or female

**gene** n biological factor determining inherited characteristics

**genealogy** n study or account of descent from ancestors

**general** adj widespread; not particular or specific; usual; miscellaneous ~**n** army officer of rank above colonel **generally** adv **generalize** v draw general conclusions

**general practitioner** doctor serving local area

**generate** v bring into being; produce **generation** n bringing into being; all persons born about same time; time between generations (about 30 years) **generator** n apparatus for producing (steam, electricity etc.)

**generous** adj free in giving; abundant **generosity** n

**genesis** n (pl **-eses**) origin; mode of formation

**genetics** pl n (with sing v)

---

THESAURUS

---

**gear** cog, cogwheel, toothed wheel; accessories, accoutrements, apparatus, equipment, harness, instruments, outfit, rigging, supplies, tackle, tools, trappings; apparel, attire, clothes, dress, garb, outfit

**gem** jewel, precious stone, stone

**general** accepted, broad, common, extensive, popular, prevailing, prevalent, public, universal, widespread; approximate, ill-defined, imprecise, inaccurate, indefinite, inexact, loose, undetailed, unspecific, vague; accustomed, conventional, customary, everyday, habitual, normal, ordinary, regular, typical, usual

**generally** almost always, as a rule, by and large, conventionally, customarily, habitually, mainly, normally, ordinarily, regularly, typically, usually; commonly, extensively, popularly, publicly, universally, widely

**generate** beget, breed, cause, create, engender, form, initiate, make, originate, procreate, produce, propagate, spawn

**generation** begetting, breeding, creation, formation, genesis, procreation, production, propagation, reproduction; age, day, days, epoch, era, period, time, times

**generosity** benevolence, bounty, charity, kindness, liberality

**generous** benevolent, bounteous, bountiful, charitable, free, hospitable, kind, lavish, liberal, princely,

scientific study of heredity **genetic** *adj*

**genial** *adj* cheerful; mild

**genie** *n* in fairy tales, servant appearing by, and working, magic

**genital** *adj* relating to sexual organs or reproduction **genitals** *pl n* sexual organs

**genius** *n* (person with) exceptional power or ability

**genocide** *n* murder of entire race of people

**genre** *n* style of literary work

**gent** *Inf* = gentleman **gents** *n* men's public lavatory

**genteel** *adj* well-bred; affectedly proper **gentility** *n* respectability

**gentile** *adj n*; (person) of race other than Jewish

**gentle** *adj* mild, not rough or severe; moderate; well-born **gently** *adv* **gentleness** *n* quality of being gentle **gentleman** *n* chivalrous well-bred man; man (used as a mark of politeness)

**gentry** *n* people just below nobility

in social rank

**genuine** *adj* real; sincere

**genus** *n* (*pl* **genera**) class, order, group (esp. of insects, animals etc.) with common characteristics

**geography** *n* science of earth's form, physical features, climate, population etc. **geographer** *n* **geographical** *adj*

**geology** *n* science of earth's crust, rocks, strata etc. **geological** *adj* **geologist** *n*

**geometry** *n* science of properties and relations of lines, surfaces etc. **geometrical, -metric** *adj*

**geranium** *n* plant with red, pink or white flowers

**gerbil** *n* desert rodent of Asia and Africa

**geriatrics** *n* science of old age and its diseases **geriatric** *adj/n* old (person)

**germ** *n* microbe, esp. causing disease; rudiment

**German** *n* language spoken by people of Germany ~*adj* of, pert. to

—————————— THESAURUS ——————————

ungrudging, unstinting

**genial** affable, agreeable, amiable, cheerful, cheery, convivial, cordial, easygoing, friendly, happy, hearty, jolly, jovial, kind, kindly, pleasant, sunny, warm

**genius** adept, expert, maestro, master, virtuoso, whiz *Inf*; ability, aptitude, bent, brilliance, capacity, endowment, faculty, flair, gift, inclination, knack, talent, turn

**genteel** aristocratic, civil, courteous, courtly, cultured, elegant, fashionable, formal, gentlemanly, ladylike, mannerly, polished, polite, refined, respectable, stylish, urbane, well-mannered

**gentility** civility, courtesy, culture,

decorum, elegance, etiquette, formality, good manners, polish, politeness, propriety, refinement, respectability

**gentle** amiable, benign, bland, humane, kind, kindly, lenient, meek, merciful, mild, peaceful, placid, quiet, soft, tender; balmy, calm, clement, easy, light, low, mild, moderate, muted, placid, quiet, serene, slight, smooth, soft, soothing, temperate, tranquil, untroubled

**genuine** actual, authentic, honest, legitimate, natural, original, pure, real, sound, sterling, true, veritable

**germ** bug *Inf*, microbe, microorganism, virus; beginning, bud, cause, embryo, origin, root, rudi-

Germany **German measles** contagious disease accompanied by red spots

**germinate** v (cause to) sprout or begin to grow

**gestation** n carrying of young in womb

**gesticulate** v use expressive movements of hands and arms when speaking

**gesture** n/v (make) movement to convey meaning

**get** v **getting, got** obtain; catch; cause to go or come; bring into position or state; induce; be in possession of, have (to do); become

**geyser** n hot spring throwing up spout of water; water heater

**ghastly** adj deathlike; Inf horrible ~adv sickly

**gherkin** n small pickled cucumber

**ghetto** n (pl **-tos**) densely populated (esp. by one racial group) slum area **ghetto blaster** Inf large portable cassette recorder

**ghost** n dead person appearing again; spectre; faint trace **ghostly** adj

**ghoul** n malevolent spirit; person with morbid interests **ghoulish** adj

**giant** n mythical being of superhuman size; very tall person, plant etc. ~adj huge **gigantic** adj enormous, huge

**gibber** v make meaningless sounds with mouth **gibberish** n meaningless speech or words

**gibbon** n type of ape

**gibe, jibe** v/n jeer

**giblets** pl n internal edible parts of fowl

**giddy** adj dizzy; liable to cause dizziness; flighty

**gift** n thing given, present; faculty,

---

ment, seed, source, spark

**germinate** bud, develop, grow, originate, shoot, sprout, swell

**gesture** n action, indication, motion, sign, signal ~v indicate, motion, sign, signal, wave

**get** achieve, acquire, attain, bring, come by, earn, fetch, gain, glean, inherit, make, net, obtain, pick up, procure, realize, reap, receive, secure, succeed to, win; arrest, capture, catch, collar Inf, grab, nab Inf, nail Inf, seize, take, trap; arrive, come, reach; arrange, contrive, fix, manage, succeed; coax, convince, induce, influence, persuade, sway, wheedle, win over; become, come to be, grow, turn, wax

**ghastly** ashen, cadaverous, deathlike, dreadful, frightful, grim, grisly, gruesome, hideous, horrible, livid, loathsome, pale, pallid, repellent, shocking, spectral, terrible, terrifying, wan

**ghost** apparition, phantom, revenant, soul, spectre, spirit, spook Inf, wraith

**ghostly** eerie, illusory, insubstantial, phantom, spectral, spooky Inf, supernatural, uncanny, unearthly, weird

**giant** n colossus, leviathan, monster, titan ~adj colossal, elephantine, enormous, gargantuan, gigantic, huge, immense, large, mammoth, monstrous, prodigious, vast

**gibberish** babble, balderdash, double talk, drivel, garbage Inf, gobbledegook Inf, jabber, jargon, mumbo jumbo, nonsense, twaddle

**gibe, jibe** n barb, crack Sl, derision, dig, jeer, mockery, ridicule, sarcasm, scoffing, sneer, taunt

**giddy** dizzy, faint, light-headed,

power **gifted** *adj* talented

**gig** *n* performance by pop or jazz musicians

**gigantic** *see* GIANT

**giggle** *v* laugh nervously, foolishly ~*n* such a laugh

**gild** *v* gilding, gilded, gilt *or* gilded put thin layer of gold on **gilt** *n* thin layer of gold put on **gilt-edged** *adj* guaranteed

**gill**¹ *n* (*usu. pl*) breathing organs in fish

**gill**² *n* liquid measure, quarter of pint (0.142 litres)

**gimmick** *n* stratagem etc., esp. designed to attract attention or publicity

**gin** *n* spirit flavoured with juniper berries

**ginger** *n* plant with hot-tasting spicy root; the root ~*v* stimulate

**gingerbread** *n* cake flavoured with ginger

**gingerly** *adv* cautiously

**gingham** *n* cotton cloth, usu.

checked

**gingivitis** *n* inflammation of gums

**ginseng** *n* plant root used as tonic

**Gipsy** *see* GYPSY

**giraffe** *n* Afr. animal with very long neck

**gird** *v* girding, girded *or* girt put belt round; prepare (oneself) **girder** *n* large beam

**girdle** *n* corset; waistband

**girl** *n* female child; young (unmarried) woman **girlfriend** *n* man's female companion

**giro** *n* system operated by banks and post offices for the transfer of money

**girth** *n* measurement round thing; band put round horse to hold saddle etc.

**gist** *n* substance, main point (of remarks etc.)

**give** *v* giving, gave, given make present of; deliver; assign; utter; yield, give way ~*n* yielding, elasticity

reeling, unsteady, vertiginous

**gift** benefaction, bequest, bounty, contribution, donation, grant, gratuity, hand-out, legacy, offering, present; ability, aptitude, attribute, bent, capability, capacity, faculty, flair, genius, knack, power, talent

**gifted** able, accomplished, adroit, brilliant, capable, clever, expert, ingenious, intelligent, masterly, skilled, talented

**gigantic** colossal, elephantine, enormous, gargantuan, giant, huge, immense, mammoth, monstrous, prodigious, stupendous, tremendous, vast

**giggle** *v/n* chortle, chuckle, laugh, snigger, titter

**gimmick** contrivance, device,

dodge, gadget, gambit, ploy, scheme, stratagem, stunt, trick

**gird** belt, bind, girdle

**girdle** band, belt, cummerbund, fillet, sash, waistband

**girl** bird *Sl*, damsel, daughter, female child, lass, lassie *Inf*, maid, maiden, miss, wench

**girth** bulk, measure, size

**gist** core, drift, essence, force, idea, import, marrow, meaning, nub, pith, point, sense, substance

**give** accord, administer, allow, award, bestow, commit, confer, consign, contribute, deliver, donate, entrust, furnish, grant, permit, present, provide, supply; allow, cede, concede, devote, grant, hand over, lend, relinquish, surren-

**glacé** *adj* crystallized; iced

**glacier** *n* slow-moving river of ice **glacial** *adj*

**glad** *adj* pleased; happy **gladden** *v* make glad **gladly** *adv*

**glade** *n* grassy space in forest

**gladiator** *n* trained fighter in Roman arena

**gladiolus** *n* (*pl* -li) kind of iris, with sword-shaped leaves

**glamour** *n* alluring charm, fascination **glamorous** *adj*

**glance** *v* look rapidly or briefly; glide off something struck ~*n* brief look

**gland** *n* organ controlling different bodily functions by chemical means **glandular** *adj*

**glare** *v* look fiercely; shine intensely ~*n* glaring **glaring** *adj* conspicuous

**glass** *n* hard transparent substance; things made of it; tumbler; its contents; *pl* spectacles **glassy** *adj* like glass; expressionless

**glaucoma** *n* eye disease

**glaze** *v* furnish with glass; cover with glassy substance; become glassy ~*n* transparent coating; substance used for this **glazier** *n* one who glazes windows

**gleam** *n/v* (give out) slight or passing beam of light

**glean** *v* pick up; gather

**glee** *n* mirth; merriment **gleeful** *adj*

**glen** *n* narrow valley

**glib** *adj* fluent but insincere or superficial

**glide** *v* pass smoothly and continu-

———————— THESAURUS ————————

der, yield

**glad** cheerful, chuffed *Sl*, contented, delighted, gay, gleeful, gratified, happy, jocund, jovial, joyful, overjoyed, pleased, willing

**gladden** cheer, delight, enliven, exhilarate, hearten, please, rejoice

**gladly** cheerfully, freely, gaily, gleefully, happily, joyfully, merrily, readily, willingly

**glamorous** alluring, attractive, beautiful, captivating, charming, dazzling, elegant, enchanting, entrancing, exciting, fascinating, glittering, glossy, lovely, prestigious, smart

**glamour** allure, appeal, attraction, beauty, charm, enchantment, fascination, prestige

**glance** *v* gaze, glimpse, look, peep, scan, view ~*n* dekko *Sl*, gander *Inf*, glimpse, look, peek, peep, quick look, squint, view

**glare** *v* frown, glower, lower, scowl; blaze, dazzle, flame, flare ~*n* black look, dirty look, frown, glower, lower, scowl; blaze, brilliance, dazzle, flame, glow

**glaring** audacious, blatant, conspicuous, flagrant, gross, manifest, obvious, open, outstanding, overt, patent, rank, visible

**glassy** clear, glossy, icy, shiny, slick, slippery, smooth, transparent

**glaze** *v* burnish, coat, enamel, gloss, lacquer, polish, varnish ~*n* coat, enamel, finish, gloss, lacquer, lustre, patina, polish, shine, varnish

**gleam** *n* beam, flash, glow, ray, sparkle ~*v* flare, flash, glance, glimmer, glint, glisten, glitter, glow, shimmer, shine, sparkle

**glee** cheerfulness, delight, elation, exultation, fun, gaiety, gladness, hilarity, jollity, joy, joyfulness, liveliness, merriment, mirth, triumph, verve

**gleeful** cheerful, chirpy *Inf*, cock-a-hoop, delighted, elated, exuberant, exultant, gay, happy, jovial,

ously ~n smooth, silent movement
**glider** n aircraft without engine
**glimmer** v shine faintly ~n faint
light
**glimpse** n brief view ~v catch
glimpse of
**glint** v/n flash
**glisten** v gleam by reflecting light
**glitter** v shine with bright quivering
light, sparkle ~n lustre; sparkle

**gloat** v regard with smugness or
malicious satisfaction
**globe** n sphere with map of earth
or stars; ball **global** adj relating to
whole world; total, comprehensive
**globule** n small round drop
**glockenspiel** n percussion instrument played with hammers
**gloom** n darkness; melancholy
**gloomy** adj

———————— THESAURUS ————————

joyful, jubilant, merry, overjoyed
**glib** artful, easy, fluent, plausible,
quick, ready, slick, smooth, suave,
voluble
**glide** coast, drift, float, flow, fly,
roll, run, sail, skate, skim, slide,
slip, soar
**glimmer** v blink, flicker, gleam,
glisten, glitter, glow, shimmer,
shine, sparkle, twinkle ~n blink,
flicker, gleam, glow, shimmer, sparkle, twinkle
**glimpse** n brief view, gander Inf,
glance, look, peek, peep, quick
look, sight, sighting ~v espy, sight,
spot, spy, view
**glint** v flash, gleam, glimmer, glitter, shine, sparkle, twinkle ~n flash,
gleam, glimmer, glitter, shine, sparkle
**glisten** flash, gleam, glimmer,
glint, glitter, shimmer, shine, sparkle, twinkle
**glitter** v coruscate, flare, flash,
gleam, glimmer, glint, glisten, scin-
tillate, shimmer, shine, sparkle,
twinkle ~n beam, brightness, flash,
glare, lustre, radiance,
sheen, shimmer, shine, sparkle
**gloat** crow, exult, glory, relish, revel in, rub it in Inf, triumph, vaunt
**global** international, planetary,
universal, worldwide; all-inclusive,
all-out, comprehensive, encyclo-

pedic, exhaustive, general, thorough, total, unbounded, unlimited
**globe** ball, earth, orb, planet,
round, sphere, world
**globule** bead, bubble, drop, droplet, particle
**gloom** blackness, cloud, cloudi-
ness, dark, darkness, dimness, dullness, dusk, murk, murkiness, obscurity, shade, shadow, twilight;
blues, dejection, depression, despair, despondency, low spirits, melancholy, misery, sadness, sorrow,
unhappiness, woe
**gloomy** black, dark, dim, dismal,
dreary, dull, dusky, murky, obscure, overcast, shadowy, sombre;
bad, black, cheerless, depressing,
disheartening, dispiriting, dreary,
joyless, sad, sombre; blue, cheerless, dejected, despondent, dispirited, down, downcast, downhearted,
glum, melancholy, miserable,
moody, morose, pessimistic, sad
**glorify** adorn, augment, dignify, elevate, enhance, ennoble, illuminate, immortalize, lift up, magnify,
raise; celebrate, eulogize, extol,
hymn, laud, lionize, magnify, praise
**glorious** celebrated, distinguished,
elevated, eminent, excellent,
famed, famous, grand, honoured,
illustrious, magnificent, majestic,
noble, noted, renowned, sublime,

**glory** n renown; splendour; heavenly bliss ~v **glorying**, **gloried** take pride (in) **glorify** v **-ifying**, **-ified** make glorious; praise **glorious** adj illustrious; splendid; Inf delightful **gloriously** adv

**gloss**[1] n surface shine, lustre ~v put gloss on; (esp. with **over**) (try to) cover up, pass over (fault, error) **glossy** adj smooth, shiny

**gloss**[2] n interpretation of word; comment ~v interpret; comment **glossary** n dictionary of special words

**glove** n covering for the hand ~v cover as with glove

**glow** v give out light and heat without flames; be or look hot ~n shining heat **glow-worm** n insect giving out light

**glower** v/n scowl

**glucose** n type of sugar found in fruit etc.

**glue** n/v (fasten with) sticky substance **gluey** adj

**glum** adj sullen, gloomy

**glut** n surfeit, excessive amount ~v glutting, glutted feed, gratify to the full or to excess

**glutton** n greedy person; one with great liking or capacity for something **gluttonous** adj **gluttony** n

**glycerine**, **glycerol** n colourless sweet liquid

**GMT** Greenwich Mean Time

**gnarled** adj knobby, twisted

**gnash** v grind (teeth) together as in anger or pain

**gnat** n small, biting fly

**gnaw** v bite or chew steadily

——————— THESAURUS ———————

triumphant; Inf delightful, enjoyable, excellent, fine, great, heavenly Inf, marvellous, pleasurable, splendid, wonderful

**glory** n celebrity, dignity, distinction, eminence, exaltation, fame, honour, immortality, kudos, praise, prestige, renown; grandeur, greatness, magnificence, majesty, nobility, pageantry, pomp, splendour, sublimity, triumph ~v boast, crow, exult, gloat, relish, revel, triumph

**gloss**[1] n brightness, brilliance, burnish, gleam, lustre, polish, sheen, shine, varnish, veneer ~v camouflage, conceal, cover up, disguise, hide, mask, veil

**gloss**[2] n annotation, commentary, explanation, footnote, note, scholium, translation

**glossy** bright, brilliant, burnished, glassy, glazed, lustrous, polished, shining, shiny, sleek, smooth

**glow** v brighten, burn, gleam,

glimmer, redden, shine, smoulder; blush, colour, fill, flush, radiate, thrill, tingle ~n brightness, brilliance, burning, effulgence, gleam, glimmer, light, radiance, splendour, vividness

**glower** frown, glare, lour or lower, scowl

**glue** n adhesive, cement, gum, paste ~v affix, cement, fix, gum, paste, seal, stick

**glum** crestfallen, crusty, dejected, doleful, down, gloomy, gruff, grumpy, ill-humoured, low, moody, morose, saturnine, sour, sulky, sullen

**glut** excess, oversupply, saturation, superfluity, surfeit, surplus

**glutton** gannet Sl, gobbler, gorger, gormandizer, gourmand, pig Inf

**gluttony** greed, piggishness, rapacity, voraciousness, voracity

**gnaw** bite, chew, munch, nibble, worry

**gnome** *n* legendary creature like small old man

**gnu** *n* oxlike antelope

**go** *v* **going, went, gone** move along; depart; function; fare; fail; elapse; be able to be put; become ~*n* going; energy; attempt; turn **go-between** *n* intermediary

**goad** *n* spiked stick for driving cattle; anything that urges to action ~*v* urge on; torment

**goal** *n* end of race; object of effort; posts through which ball is to be driven in football etc.; the score so made

**goat** *n* animal with long hair, horns and beard **goatee** *n* small pointed beard

**gobble**¹ *v* eat hastily, noisily or greedily

**gobble**² *n/v* (make) cry of turkey

**gobbledegook, gobbledygook** *n* intelligible language

**goblet** *n* drinking cup

**goblin** *n* Folklore small, usu. malevolent being

**god** *n* (*fem* **goddess**) superhuman being worshipped as having supernatural power; object of worship, idol; (*with cap.*) the Supreme Being, creator and ruler of universe **godly** *adj* devout, pious **godfather** *n* (*fem* **godmother**) sponsor at baptism **godforsaken** *adj* desolate, dismal **godsend** *n* something unexpected but welcome

**goggle** *v* (of eyes) bulge; stare ~*pl n* protective spectacles

**go-kart** *or* **go-cart** *n* miniature, low-powered racing car

**gold** *n* yellow precious metal; coins of this; colour of gold ~*adj* of, like gold **golden** *adj* **golden wedding** fiftieth wedding anniversary **goldfinch** *n* bird with yellow feathers **goldfish** *n* any of various ornamental pond or aquarium fish

**golf** *n* outdoor game in which small ball is struck into holes **golfer** *n*

**gondola** *n* Venetian canal boat **gondolier** *n* rower of gondola

**gong** *n* metal plate which sounds

———————— THESAURUS ————————

**go** *v* advance, decamp, depart, journey, leave, move, pass, proceed, repair, set off, travel, withdraw; function, move, operate, perform, run, work; develop, eventuate, fall out, fare, happen, proceed, result, turn out, work out; elapse, expire, flow, lapse, pass, slip away ~*n* attempt, bid, effort, essay, shot *Inf*, stab *Inf*, try, turn, whack *Inf*

**goad** *n* impetus, incentive, incitement, irritation, motivation, pressure, spur, stimulation, stimulus, urge ~*v* annoy, arouse, drive, egg on, exhort, harass, hound, impel, incite, instigate, irritate, lash, prick, prod, prompt, propel, spur, stimulate, sting, urge, worry

**goal** aim, ambition, design, destination, end, intention, limit, mark, object, objective, purpose, target

**gobble** bolt, cram, devour, gorge, gulp, guzzle, stuff, swallow, wolf

**go-between** agent, broker, dealer, factor, intermediary, liaison, mediator

**godforsaken** abandoned, backward, bleak, deserted, desolate, dismal, dreary, forlorn, gloomy, lonely, remote

**godly** devout, god-fearing, good, holy, pious, religious, righteous, saintly

**godsend** blessing, windfall

**golden** blond *or* blonde, bright, brilliant, flaxen, shining, yellow

when struck with soft mallet

**good** adj **better, best** commendable; right; beneficial; well-behaved; virtuous; sound; valid ~n benefit; wellbeing; profit; pl property; wares **goodly** adj large, considerable **goodness** n **goodwill** n kindly feeling

**goodbye** interj/n form of address on parting

**gooey** adj Inf sticky, soft

**goose** n (pl **geese**) web-footed bird; its flesh; simpleton

**gooseberry** n thorny shrub; its hairy fruit

**gore**¹ n (dried) blood from wound **gory** adj

**gore**² v pierce with horns

**gorge** n ravine; disgust, resentment ~v feed greedily

**gorgeous** adj splendid, showy

**gorilla** n largest anthropoid ape, found in Africa

**gormless** adj Inf stupid

**gorse** n prickly shrub

**gosling** n young goose

**gospel** n unquestionable truth; (with cap.) any of first four books of New Testament

**gossamer** n filmy substance like spider's web

**gossip** n idle (malicious) talk about other persons; one who talks thus ~v engage in gossip

**gouge** v scoop out; force out ~n chisel with curved cutting edge

**goulash** n stew seasoned with paprika

**gourd** n large fleshy fruit; its rind as vessel

---

THESAURUS

---

**good** adj admirable, capital, choice, commendable, excellent, fine, first-class, first-rate, great, pleasant, pleasing, splendid, superior, valuable, worthy; decorous, dutiful, mannerly, obedient, orderly, polite, proper, seemly, well-behaved; admirable, estimable, ethical, exemplary, honest, honourable, moral, praiseworthy, right, righteous, upright, virtuous, worthy; able, accomplished, adept, adroit, capable, clever, competent, dexterous, efficient, expert, first-rate, proficient, reliable, satisfactory, serviceable, skilled, sound, suitable, talented, thorough, useful; authentic, bona fide, dependable, genuine, honest, legitimate, proper, real, reliable, sound, true, trustworthy, valid ~n advantage, avail, behalf, benefit, gain, interest, profit, service, use, usefulness, welfare, wellbeing, worth

**goodbye** adieu, farewell, parting

**goodness** excellence, merit, quality, superiority, value, worth; benevolence, friendliness, generosity, good will, graciousness, kindness, mercy; honesty, honour, integrity, merit, morality, probity, rectitude, uprightness, virtue

**gorge**¹ n canyon, cleft, defile, fissure, pass, ravine ~v bolt, cram, devour, feed, fill, glut, gobble, gulp, guzzle, overeat, surfeit, swallow, wolf

**gorgeous** beautiful, brilliant, dazzling, elegant, glittering, grand, luxuriant, magnificent, opulent, ravishing, showy, splendid, stunning Inf, sumptuous, superb

**gossip** n chitchat, hearsay, idle talk, prattle, scandal, small talk, tittle-tattle; blether, busybody, chatterbox Inf, scandalmonger, tattler, telltale ~v blether, chat, gabble, prate, prattle, tattle

**gourmand** *n* glutton

**gourmet** *n* connoisseur of wine, food; epicure

**gout** *n* disease with inflammation, esp. of joints

**govern** *v* rule, control; determine **governess** *n* woman teacher, esp. in private household **government** *n* exercise of political authority in directing a people, state etc.; system by which community is ruled; governing group; control **governor** *n* one who governs; chief administrator of an institution; member of committee responsible for an organization or institution

**gown** *n* loose flowing outer garment; woman's (long) dress; official robe

**GP** General Practitioner

**grab** *v* grabbing, grabbed grasp suddenly; snatch ~*n* sudden clutch; quick attempt to seize

**grace** *n* charm, elegance; goodwill, favour; sense of propriety; postponement granted; short thanksgiving for meal ~*v* add grace to, honour **graceful** *adj* **gracious** *adj* kind; condescending

**grade** *n* step, stage; class; rating; slope ~*v* arrange in classes; assign grade to **gradation** *n* series of steps; each of them

**gradient** *n* (degree of) slope

——————— THESAURUS ———————

**govern** administer, command, conduct, control, direct, guide, hold sway, lead, manage, order, oversee, pilot, reign, rule, steer, supervise

**government** administration, authority, dominion, law, rule, sovereignty, state, statecraft; administration, executive, ministry, regime; authority, command, control, direction, domination, guidance, management, regulation, restraint, supervision, sway

**governor** administrator, chief, commander, controller, director, executive, head, leader, manager, overseer, ruler, supervisor

**gown** costume, dress, frock, garb, garment, habit, robe

**grab** bag, capture, catch, clutch, grasp, grip, pluck, seize, snap up, snatch

**grace** *n* beauty, charm, ease, elegance, finesse, loveliness, pleasantness, poise, polish, refinement; benefaction, beneficence, benevolence, favour, generosity, goodness, good will, kindness; cultivation, decency, decorum, etiquette, manners, propriety, tact; charity, clemency, compassion, forgiveness, indulgence, leniency, mercy, pardon, quarter, reprieve; benediction, blessing, prayer, thanks, thanksgiving ~*v* adorn, beautify, bedeck, deck, decorate, dignify, distinguish, elevate, embellish, enhance, enrich, favour, garnish, glorify, honour, ornament, set off

**graceful** agile, beautiful, becoming, charming, comely, easy, elegant, fine, flowing, natural, pleasing, smooth, tasteful

**gracious** affable, amiable, beneficent, benevolent, benign, charitable, chivalrous, civil, compassionate, considerate, cordial, courteous, friendly, hospitable, indulgent, kind, lenient, loving, merciful, mild, obliging, pleasing, polite, well-mannered

**grade** *n* brand, category, class, condition, degree, echelon, group, level, mark, notch, order, place, po-

**gradual** adj taking place by degrees; slow and steady; not steep **gradually** adv

**graduate** v take university degree; divide into degrees ~n holder of university degree **graduation** n

**graffiti** pl n (oft. obscene) writing, drawing on walls

**graft**[1] n shoot of plant set in stalk of another; the process; surgical transplant of skin, tissue ~v insert (shoot) in another stalk; transplant (living tissue in surgery)

**graft**[2] n Inf hard work; self-advancement, profit by unfair means

**grain** n (seed, fruit of) cereal plant; small hard particle; very small unit of weight; arrangement of fibres; any very small amount

**gram, gramme** n one thousandth of a kilogram

**grammar** n science of structure and usages of language; use of words **grammatical** adj **grammar school** state-maintained secondary school providing academic education

**gramophone** n record player

**gran, granny** n Inf grandmother

**granary** n storehouse for grain

**grand** adj magnificent; noble; splendid; eminent **grandeur** n nobility; magnificence; dignity **grandiose** adj imposing; affectedly grand **grandchild** n child of one's child **grandson, granddaughter** n **grandparent** n parent of parent **grandfather, grandmother** n **grandstand** n structure with tiered seats for spectators

**granite** n hard crystalline rock

**grant** v consent to fulfil (request); permit; admit ~n sum of money provided for specific purpose, esp. education; gift; allowance, concession

**granule** n small grain

————————— THESAURUS —————————

sition, quality, rank, rung, size, stage, station, step ~v arrange, brand, class, classify, evaluate, group, order, range, rank, rate, sort, value

**gradient** bank, grade, hill, incline, rise, slope

**gradual** even, gentle, graduated, moderate, piecemeal, progressive, regular, slow, steady, unhurried

**gradually** bit by bit, by degrees, evenly, gently, moderately, piecemeal, progressively, slowly, steadily

**graduate** v calibrate, grade, mark off, measure out, proportion, regulate

**grain** cereals, corn; grist, kernel, seed

**grand** ambitious, august, dignified, elevated, eminent, exalted, fine,

glorious, great, haughty, illustrious, imposing, impressive, lofty, lordly, luxurious, magnificent, majestic, noble, opulent, palatial, pompous, princely, regal, splendid, stately

**grandeur** dignity, greatness, importance, loftiness, magnificence, majesty, nobility, pomp, splendour, state

**grandiose** affected, ambitious, bombastic, extravagant, flamboyant, pompous, pretentious, showy

**grant** v accede to, accord, acknowledge, admit, agree to, allocate, allot, allow, assign, award, bestow, cede, concede, confer, consent to, donate, give, impart, permit, present, yield ~n admission, allocation, allotment, allowance, award, bequest, bounty, conces-

**grape** n small fruit, used to make wine **grapevine** n grape-bearing plant; Inf unofficial way of spreading news

**grapefruit** n subtropical citrus fruit

**graph** n drawing depicting relation of different numbers, quantities etc. **graphic** adj vividly descriptive; of writing, drawing, painting etc. ~pl n diagrams etc. used on television, computer screen etc.

**graphite** n form of carbon (used in pencils)

**grapple** v wrestle; struggle

**grasp** v (try, struggle to) seize hold; understand ~n grip; comprehension **grasping** adj greedy, avaricious

**grass** n common type of plant with jointed stems and long narrow leaves; such plants grown as lawn; pasture; Sl marijuana; Sl informer **grassy** adj **grasshopper** n jumping, chirping insect **grass roots** ordinary members of group

**grate**[1] n framework of metal bars for holding fuel in fireplace **grating** n framework of bars covering opening

**grate**[2] v rub into small bits on rough surface; rub with harsh noise; irritate **grater** n utensil with rough surface for reducing substance to small particles **grating** adj harsh; irritating

**grateful** adj thankful; appreciative; pleasing **gratefully** adv **gratitude** n sense of being thankful

**gratify** v -ifying, -ified satisfy; please **gratification** n

**gratis** adv/adj free, for nothing

**gratuitous** adj given free; uncalled for **gratuity** n gift of money for services rendered; tip

**grave**[1] n hole dug to bury corpse **graveyard** n

**grave**[2] adj serious; solemn

**grave**[3] n accent (`) over letter

———— THESAURUS ————

sion, donation, endowment, gift, present, subsidy

**graphic** clear, descriptive, detailed, explicit, expressive, forcible, illustrative, lively, lucid, picturesque, striking, telling, vivid, well-drawn; diagrammatic, drawn, illustrative, pictorial, representational, seen, visible, visual

**grasp** v catch, clasp, clinch, clutch, grab, grapple, grip, hold, lay or take hold of, seize, snatch; comprehend, follow, realize, see, take in, understand ~n clasp, clutches, embrace, grip, hold, possession, tenure; comprehension, knowledge, mastery, perception, realization, understanding

**grasping** acquisitive, avaricious, covetous, greedy, mean, miserly, niggardly, penny-pinching Inf, rapacious, selfish, stingy, tightfisted, venal

**grate** creak, grind, rasp, rub, scrape, scratch; annoy, chafe, exasperate, fret, gall, irk, irritate, jar, nettle, peeve, rankle, vex

**grateful** appreciative, indebted, obliged, thankful

**gratify** delight, favour, fulfil, give pleasure, gladden, humour, indulge, pander to, please, recompense, thrill

**gratitude** appreciation, indebtedness, obligation, recognition, thanks

**gratuitous** free, unasked-for, unpaid, unrewarded, voluntary

**gratuity** benefaction, bonus, bounty, donation, gift, largess or

**gravel** *n* small stones; coarse sand **gravelly** *adj*

**graven** *adj* carved, engraved

**gravitate** *v* move by gravity; tend (towards) centre of attraction; sink, settle down

**gravity** *n* force of attraction of one body for another, esp. of objects to the earth; heaviness; importance; seriousness

**gravy** *n* juices from meat in cooking; sauce made from these

**graze**¹ *v* feed on grass, pasture

**graze**² *v* touch lightly in passing, scratch, scrape ~*n* grazing; abrasion

**grease** *n* soft melted fat of animals; thick oil as lubricant ~*v* apply grease to **greasy** *adj* **greasepaint** *n*

theatrical make-up

**great** *adj* large; important; pre-eminent; *Inf* excellent ~*comb. form* one degree further removed in relationship, as in **great-grandfather** **greatly** *adv*

**greed** *n* excessive consumption of, desire for, food, wealth **greedy** *adj*

**green** *adj* of colour between blue and yellow; grass-coloured; unripe; inexperienced; envious ~*n* colour; area of grass, esp. for playing bowls etc; *pl* green vegetables **greenery** *n* vegetation **greenfly** *n* aphid, small green garden pest **greengrocer** *n* dealer in vegetables and fruit **greenhouse** *n* glass building for rearing plants

largesse, present, reward, tip

**grave**¹ *n* crypt, mausoleum, pit, sepulchre, tomb, vault

**grave**² acute, critical, crucial, dangerous, hazardous, important, momentous, perilous, pressing, serious, severe, threatening, vital, weighty; dignified, dour, dull, earnest, gloomy, muted, quiet, serious, sober, solemn, sombre, staid, subdued, thoughtful

**graveyard** burial ground, cemetery, churchyard, necropolis

**gravity** acuteness, exigency, importance, moment, seriousness, severity, significance, urgency, weightiness

**greasy** fatty, oily, slick, slimy, slippery

**great** big, bulky, colossal, enormous, extensive, gigantic, huge, immense, large, mammoth, stupendous, tremendous, vast, voluminous; consequential, critical, crucial, grave, important, momentous, serious, significant, weighty; cel-

ebrated, distinguished, eminent, exalted, excellent, famed, famous, glorious, illustrious, notable, outstanding, pre-eminent, prominent, remarkable, renowned; admirable, cracking *Brit inf*, excellent, fantastic *Inf*, fine, first-rate, good, marvellous *Inf*, superb, terrific *Inf*, tremendous *Inf*, wonderful

**greatly** abundantly, by much, considerably, enormously, exceedingly, extremely, highly, hugely, immensely, mightily, much, notably, powerfully, remarkably, vastly, very much

**greed** gluttony, hunger, piggishness, ravenousness, voracity; avidity, covetousness, cupidity, desire, eagerness, longing, rapacity, selfishness

**greedy** gluttonous, hungry, insatiable, piggish, ravenous, voracious; acquisitive, avaricious, avid, covetous, craving, desirous, eager, grasping, hungry, impatient, rapacious, selfish

**greet** v meet with expressions of welcome; salute; receive **greeting** n

**gregarious** adj sociable

**gremlin** n imaginary being blamed for mechanical malfunctions

**grenade** n bomb thrown by hand or shot from rifle **grenadier** n soldier of Grenadier Guards

**grenadine** n syrup made from pomegranate juice, for sweetening and colouring drinks

**grey** adj between black and white; clouded; turning white; aged; intermediate, indeterminate ~n grey colour

**greyhound** n swift slender dog

**grid** n network of horizontal and vertical lines, bars etc.; any interconnecting system of links

**griddle** n flat iron plate for cooking

**gridiron** n frame of metal bars for grilling

**grief** n deep sorrow **grievance** n real or imaginary cause for complaint **grieve** v feel grief; cause grief to **grievous** adj painful, oppressive; very serious

**grill** n device on cooker to radiate heat downwards; food cooked under grill; gridiron ~v cook (food) under grill; subject to severe questioning

**grille** n grating

**grim** adj stern; relentless; joyless

**grimace** n/v (pull) wry face

**grime** n ingrained dirt, soot **grimy** n

**grin** v/n **grinning, grinned** (give)

**green** adj blooming, budding, fresh, grassy, leafy, new, undecayed, verdant; fresh, immature, new, raw, recent, unripe ~n common, grassplot, lawn, sward, turf

**greet** accost, address, hail, meet, receive, salute, welcome

**greeting** address, hail, reception, salute, welcome

**grey** ashen, bloodless, colourless, livid, pale, pallid, wan; cheerless, clouded, cloudy, dark, depressing, dim, dismal, drab, dreary, dull, foggy, gloomy, misty, murky, overcast, sunless; aged, ancient, elderly, mature, old, venerable

**grief** agony, anguish, bereavement, dejection, distress, grievance, heartache, heartbreak, misery, mourning, pain, regret, remorse, sadness, sorrow, suffering, trial, tribulation, woe

**grievance** complaint, damage, distress, gripe Inf, hardship, injury, injustice, resentment, sorrow, trial, tribulation, trouble, wrong

**grieve** ache, bemoan, bewail, complain, deplore, lament, mourn, regret, rue, sorrow, suffer, wail, weep; afflict, agonize, crush, distress, hurt, injure, pain, sadden, wound

**grievous** calamitous, damaging, distressing, dreadful, grave, harmful, heavy, hurtful, injurious, lamentable, oppressive, painful, severe; deplorable, dreadful, flagrant, glaring, heinous, intolerable, lamentable, monstrous, offensive, outrageous, shameful, shocking, unbearable

**grim** cruel, ferocious, fierce, forbidding, formidable, frightful, ghastly, grisly, gruesome, harsh, hideous, horrible, horrid, merciless, morose, relentless, resolute, ruthless, severe, shocking, sinister, stern, sullen, surly, terrible

**grimace** face, frown, mouth, scowl, sneer, wry face

broad smile

**grind** v **grinding, ground** crush to powder; make sharp, smooth; grate ~n Inf hard work; action of grinding

**grip** n firm hold; mastery; handle; travelling bag ~v **gripping, gripped** hold tightly; hold attention of

**gripe** v Inf complain (persistently) ~n intestinal pain (esp. in infants); Inf complaint

**grisly** adj causing terror

**grist** n corn to be ground

**gristle** n cartilage, tough flexible tissue

**grit** n rough particles of sand; courage ~v **gritting, gritted** clench (teeth)

**grizzle** v Inf whine

**grizzled** adj grey (haired)

**grizzly** n large Amer. bear

**groan** v/n (make) low, deep sound of grief or pain

**grocer** n dealer in foodstuffs **groceries** pl n commodities sold by a grocer **grocery** n trade, premises of grocer

**grog** n spirit (esp. rum) and water

**groggy** adj Inf shaky, weak

**groin** n fold where legs meet abdomen

**groom** n person caring for horses; bridegroom ~v tend or look after; brush or clean (esp. horse); train

**groove** n narrow channel; routine ~v cut groove in

**grope** v feel about, search blindly

**gross** adj very fat; total, not net; coarse; flagrant ~n twelve dozen

**grotesque** adj (horribly) distorted;

**grime** dirt, filth, smut, soot

**grimy** begrimed, besmeared, besmirched, dirty, filthy, foul, grubby, smutty, soiled, sooty, unclean

**grind** v crush, granulate, grate, mill, pound, powder, pulverize; gnash, grate, grit, scrape ~n chore, drudgery, hard work, labour, task, toil

**grip** n clasp, purchase; control, domination, grasp, hold, influence, mastery, perception, possession, power, tenure, understanding ~v clasp, clutch, grasp, hold, seize; absorb, catch up, compel, engross, enthral, entrance, fascinate, hold, involve, mesmerize, rivet, spellbind

**grisly** abominable, appalling, awful, dreadful, frightful, ghastly, grim, gruesome, hideous, horrid, macabre, terrible

**grit** n dust, gravel, sand; backbone, courage, fortitude, gameness, guts Inf, mettle, nerve, perseverance, pluck, resolution, spirit, tenacity, toughness

**groan** v cry, grumble, moan, sigh, whine ~n cry, moan, sigh, whine

**groggy** confused, dazed, dizzy, faint, muzzy, punch-drunk, reeling, shaky, stunned, unsteady, weak, woozy Inf

**groom** n stableboy, stableman ~v clean, dress, smarten up, spruce up, tidy, turn out; coach, drill, educate, make ready, nurture, prepare, prime, ready, train

**groove** channel, cutting, flute, furrow, gutter, hollow, rut, score, trench

**grope** feel, finger, fish, flounder, fumble, grabble, search

**gross** adj big, bulky, corpulent, fat, great, heavy, hulking, large, massive, obese, overweight; aggregate, entire, total, whole; coarse, crude, improper, impure, indecent, indelicate, lewd, low, obscene, offensive,

ugly *or* repulsive

**grotto** *n* (*pl* **-oes**) cave

**grotty** *adj Inf* nasty, in bad condition

**grouch** *Inf n* persistent grumbler; discontented mood ~*v* grumble

**ground** *n* surface of earth; soil, earth; reason; special area; *pl* dregs; enclosed land round house ~*v* establish; instruct; place on ground; run ashore **grounded** *adj* (of aircraft) unable or not permitted to fly **grounding** *n* basic knowledge of subject **groundless** *adj* without reason **groundwork** *n* preliminary work

**group** *n* number of persons or things together; small musical band; class ~*v* place, fall into group

**grouse¹** *n* (*pl* **grouse**) game bird; its flesh

**grouse²** *v* grumble, complain ~*n* complaint

**grout** *n* thin fluid mortar ~*v* fill up with grout

**grove** *n* small group of trees

**grovel** *v* **-elling, -elled** abase oneself; lie face down

**grow** *v* **growing, grew, grown** develop naturally; increase; be produced; become by degrees; produce by cultivation **growth** *n* growing; increase; what has grown or is growing **grown-up** *adj/n* adult

**growl** *v/n* (make) low guttural sound of anger

**grub** *v* **grubbing, grubbed** dig; root up; rummage ~*n* short, legless larva

——————— THESAURUS ———————

ribald, rude, sensual, unseemly, vulgar

**grotesque** bizarre, deformed, distorted, fantastic, freakish, incongruous, malformed, misshapen, odd, outlandish, ridiculous, strange, unnatural, weird

**ground** *n* clod, dirt, dry land, dust, earth, field, land, mould, sod, soil, terra firma, terrain, turf (*oft. pl*) area, country, district, domain, estate, fields, gardens, land, property, realm, terrain, tract ~*v* base, establish, fix, found, set, settle

**groundless** baseless, empty, false, idle, imaginary, uncalled-for, unfounded, unjustified, unsupported, unwarranted

**groundwork** base, basis, footing, foundation, fundamentals, preliminaries, preparation, spadework

**group** *n* association, band, batch, bevy, bunch, category, circle, class, clique, clump, cluster, collection, company, coterie, crowd, faction,

formation, gang, gathering, organization, pack, party, set, troop ~*v* arrange, assemble, associate, assort, bracket, class, classify, dispose, gather, marshal, order, organize, put together, range, sort

**grovel** abase oneself, bow and scrape, cower, crawl, creep, cringe, demean oneself, fawn, flatter, humble oneself, kowtow, pander to, toady

**grow** develop, flourish, shoot, spring up, sprout, vegetate; develop, enlarge, expand, extend, fill out, heighten, increase, multiply, spread, stretch, swell, thicken, widen; breed, cultivate, farm, produce, raise

**grown-up** adult, fully-grown, mature

**growth** development, enlargement, evolution, expansion, extension, growing, increase, multiplication; crop, cultivation, development, produce, shooting, sprout-

of certain insects; *Sl* food

**grubby** *adj* dirty

**grudge** *v* be unwilling to give, allow ~*n* ill will

**gruel** *n* food of oatmeal etc., boiled in milk or water

**gruelling** *adj* exhausting

**gruesome** *adj* horrible, grisly

**gruff** *adj* rough-voiced, surly

**grumble** *v* complain; rumble ~*n* complaint

**grumpy** *adj* ill-tempered, surly

**grunt** *v/n* (make) sound characteristic of pig

**G-string** *n* very small covering for genitals

**guarantee** *n* formal assurance (esp. in writing) that product etc.

will meet certain standards ~*v* **guaranteeing, guaranteed** give guarantee; secure (against risk etc.) **guarantor** *n*

**guard** *v* protect, defend; take precautions (against) ~*n* person, group that protects; sentry; official in charge of train; protection **guarded** *adj* cautious, noncommittal **guardian** *n* keeper, protector; person having custody of infant etc.

**guava** *n* tropical tree with fruit used to make jelly

**guerrilla, guerilla** *n* member of irregular armed force

**guess** *v* estimate; conjecture; *US* think ~*n* conclusion reached by guessing

——————— THESAURUS ———————

ing, vegetation

**grubby** dirty, filthy, grimy, messy, mucky, scruffy, seedy, shabby, slovenly, smutty, soiled, sordid, squalid, unkempt, untidy, unwashed

**grudge** *v* begrudge, complain, covet, envy, mind, resent, stint ~*n* antipathy, aversion, bitterness, dislike, enmity, grievance, hate, ill will, malevolence, malice, pique, rancour, resentment, spite, venom

**gruelling** arduous, brutal, crushing, demanding, difficult, fierce, grinding, hard, harsh, laborious, punishing, severe, stiff, strenuous, taxing, tiring, trying

**gruesome** abominable, awful, fearful, ghastly, grim, grisly, horrendous, horrific, horrifying, macabre, repugnant, repulsive, shocking, terrible

**gruff** bearish, blunt, brusque, churlish, crabbed, crusty, curt, discourteous, grumpy, ill-humoured, ill-natured, impolite, rough, rude, sour, sullen, surly, uncivil, ungra-

cious, unmannerly

**grumble** *v* beef *Sl,* bitch *Sl,* carp, complain, find fault, gripe *Inf,* grouse, moan, whine ~*n* beef *Sl,* complaint, grievance, gripe *Inf,* grouse, moan, objection

**guarantee** *n* assurance, bond, certainty, covenant, earnest, pledge, promise, security, surety, undertaking, warranty, word ~*v* answer for, assure, certify, insure, maintain, pledge, promise, protect, secure, swear, vouch for, warrant

**guard** *v* cover, defend, escort, keep, mind, oversee, patrol, police, protect, safeguard, save, screen, secure, shelter, shield, tend, watch, watch over ~*n* custodian, defender, lookout, picket, sentinel, sentry, warder, watch, watchman; buffer, bulwark, bumper, defence, pad, protection, rampart, safeguard, screen, security, shield

**guardian** champion, curator, custodian, defender, escort, guard, keeper, preserver, protector, trus-

**guest** *n* one entertained at another's house; one living in hotel

**guffaw** *n/v* (make) burst of boisterous laughter

**guide** *n* one who shows the way; adviser; book of instruction or information ~*v* lead, act as guide to **guidance** *n* **guideline** *n* set principle

**guild** *n* organization for mutual help, or with common object

**guile** *n* cunning, deceit

**guillotine** *n* machine for beheading; machine for cutting paper ~*v* use guillotine on

**guilt** *n* fact, state of having done wrong; responsibility for wrong **guiltless** *adj* innocent **guilty** *adj* having committed an offence

**guinea** *n* formerly, sum of 21 shillings **guinea pig** rodent originating in S Amer; *Inf* person or animal used in experiments

**guise** *n* external appearance, esp. one assumed

**guitar** *n* stringed instrument played by plucking or strumming **guitarist** *n*

**gulf** *n* large inlet of the sea; chasm; large gap

**gull** *n* long-winged web-footed sea bird

**gullet** *n* food passage from mouth to stomach

**gullible** *adj* easily imposed on, credulous

**gully** *n* channel or ravine worn by

—————————————— THESAURUS ——————————————

tee, warden, warder

**guess** *v* conjecture, estimate, fathom, predict, solve, speculate, work out ~*n* conjecture, feeling, hypothesis, judgment, notion, prediction, reckoning, speculation, supposition, surmise, suspicion, theory

**guest** boarder, company, lodger, visitor

**guidance** advice, conduct, control, counsel, direction, government, help, instruction, intelligence, leadership, management, teaching

**guide** *n* adviser, attendant, conductor, counsellor, director, escort, leader, mentor, monitor, pilot, steersman, teacher; catalogue, directory, handbook, instructions, key, manual ~*v* accompany, attend, conduct, convoy, direct, escort, lead, pilot, shepherd, steer, usher; advise, counsel, educate, govern, influence, instruct, regulate, rule, superintend, supervise, sway, teach, train

**guild** brotherhood, club, company, corporation, fellowship, fraternity, league, lodge, order, society, union

**guile** art, artifice, cleverness, craft, craftiness, cunning, deceit, deception, duplicity, knavery, ruse, treachery, trickery

**guilt** blame, delinquency, iniquity, misconduct, responsibility, sinfulness, wickedness, wrong, wrongdoing; bad conscience, contrition, disgrace, dishonour, infamy, regret, remorse, self-reproach, shame, stigma

**guiltless** blameless, clean *Sl*, clear, impeccable, innocent, irreproachable, pure, sinless, spotless, untainted, untarnished

**guilty** at fault, convicted, criminal, culpable, delinquent, erring, evil, felonious, offending, responsible, sinful, to blame, wicked, wrong

**gulf** bay, bight, sea inlet; abyss, breach, chasm, cleft, gap, rent, rift, split, void

**gullible** credulous, foolish, green,

action of water

**gulp** v/n swallow; gasp

**gum¹** n firm fixture in which teeth are set

**gum²** n sticky substance issuing from certain trees; adhesive; chewing gum ~v **gumming, gummed** stick with gum **gumboots** pl n boots of rubber **gumtree** n any species of eucalypt

**gumption** n resourcefulness; shrewdness, sense

**gun** n weapon with metal tube from which missiles are discharged by explosion; cannon, pistol etc. ~v shoot; pursue vigorously **gunner** n **gunpowder** n explosive mixture of saltpetre, sulphur, charcoal **gunshot** n shot or range of gun ~adj caused by missile from gun

**gunge** n Inf any sticky, unpleasant substance

**gunwale, gunnel** n upper edge of ship's side

**guppy** n small colourful aquarium fish

**gurgle** n/v (make) bubbling noise

**guru** n spiritual teacher, esp. in India

**gush** v flow out suddenly and copiously, spurt ~n sudden and copious flow

**gusset** n triangle or diamond-shaped piece of material let into garment

**gust** n sudden blast of wind; burst of rain, anger, passion etc.

**gusto** n enjoyment, zest

**gut** n (oft. pl) intestines; material made from guts of animals, e.g. for violin strings etc. pl Inf courage ~v remove guts from (fish etc.); remove, destroy contents of (house)

**gutter** n shallow trough for carrying off water from roof or side of street

**guttural** adj harsh-sounding, as if produced in the throat

**guy¹** n effigy of Guy Fawkes burnt on Nov. 5th; Inf person (usu. male) ~v make fun of; ridicule

**guy²** n rope, chain to steady, secure something, e.g. tent

**guzzle** v eat or drink greedily

───────────── THESAURUS ─────────────

innocent, naive, silly, simple, trusting, unsophisticated, unsuspecting

**gulp** v bolt, devour, gobble, guzzle, knock back Inf, quaff, swallow, swig Inf, swill, toss off, wolf ~n draught, mouthful, swallow

**gum** adhesive, cement, exudate, glue, mucilage, paste, resin

**gumption** ability, acumen, common sense, enterprise, initiative, resourcefulness, sagacity, savvy Sl, shrewdness, spirit, wit(s)

**gurgle** n murmur, ripple ~v babble, bubble, burble, crow, lap, murmur, plash, purl, ripple, splash

**gush** v burst, cascade, flood, flow, jet, pour, run, rush, spout, spurt,

stream ~n burst, cascade, flood, flow, jet, outburst, outflow, rush, spout, spurt, stream, torrent

**gust** blast, blow, breeze, flurry, gale, puff, rush, squall

**gusto** appetite, brio, delight, enjoyment, enthusiasm, fervour, liking, pleasure, relish, verve, zeal, zest

**gutter** channel, conduit, ditch, drain, duct, pipe, sluice, trench, trough, tube

**guttural** deep, gravelly, gruff, hoarse, husky, low, rasping, rough, thick, throaty

**guy** n Inf bloke Brit inf, chap, fellow, lad, man, person, youth

**gym** *n* short for GYMNASIUM *or* GYMNASTICS

**gymkhana** *n* competition or display of horse riding

**gymnasium** *n* (*pl* **-nasiums, -nasia**) place equipped for muscular exercises, athletic training **gymnastics** *pl n* muscular exercises **gymnast** *n*

**gynaecology** *n* branch of medicine dealing with functions and diseases of women **gynaecologist** *n*

**gypsum** *n* chalklike mineral, used for making plaster

**Gypsy** *n* one of wandering race orig. from NW India

**gyrate** *v* move in circle, spiral

**gyroscope** *n* disc rotating on axis that can turn in any direction

———— THESAURUS ————

**guzzle** bolt, cram, devour, drink, gobble, gorge, quaff, stuff (oneself), swill, wolf

# H h

**haberdasher** *n* dealer in articles of dress, ribbons, pins, needles etc. **haberdashery** *n*

**habit** *n* settled tendency or practice; customary apparel, esp. of nun or monk **habitual** *adj* formed or acquired by habit; usual, customary

**habitable** *adj* fit to live in **habitat** *n* natural home (of animal etc.) **habitation** *n* abode

**hack¹** *v* cut, chop (at) violently; *Inf* utter harsh, dry cough ~*n* violent blow **hacker** *n* *Sl* computer enthusiast who breaks into computer system of company or government

**hack²** *n* horse for ordinary riding; inferior writer

**hackles** *pl n* hairs on back of neck of dog and other animals which are raised in anger

**hackneyed** *adj* (of words etc.) stale, trite because of overuse

**hacksaw** *n* handsaw for cutting metal

**haddock** *n* large, edible sea fish

**haemoglobin** *n* colouring and oxygen-bearing matter of red blood corpuscles

**haemophilia** *n* illness in which blood does not clot **haemophiliac** *n*

**haemorrhage** *n* profuse bleeding

**haemorrhoids** *pl n* swollen veins in rectum

**hag** *n* ugly old woman; witch

**haggard** *adj* anxious, careworn

**haggis** *n* Scottish dish made from sheep's offal, oatmeal etc.

**haggle** *v* bargain over price

**hail¹** *n* (shower of) pellets of ice; barrage ~*v* pour down as shower of hail **hailstone** *n*

**hail²** *v* greet; acclaim; call

**hair** *n* filament growing from skin of animal, as covering of man's head; such filaments collectively **hairy** *adj* **hairdo** *n* (*pl* **-os**) way of dressing hair **hairdresser** *n* one who cuts and styles hair **hairgrip** *n* small,

---

## THESAURUS

**habit** bent, custom, disposition, manner, practice, propensity, quirk, tendency, way; custom, mode, practice, routine, rule, second nature, tradition, usage, wont; dress, garb, garment, riding dress

**habitation** abode, domicile, dwelling, home, house, lodging, pad *Sl*, quarters, residence

**habitual** accustomed, common, customary, familiar, fixed, natural, normal, ordinary, regular, routine, standard, traditional, usual

**hack¹** chop, cut, gash, hew, kick, lacerate, mangle, mutilate, notch, slash

**hack²** penny-a-liner, scribbler

**hackneyed** banal, common, commonplace, overworked, stale, stereotyped, stock, threadbare, timeworn, tired, trite, unoriginal, worn-out

**hag** crone, fury, harridan, shrew, virago, vixen, witch

**haggard** careworn, drawn, emaciated, gaunt, pinched, shrunken, thin, wan, wasted

**haggle** bargain, barter

**hail¹** *n* barrage, pelting, rain, shower, storm, volley ~*v* barrage, batter, pelt, rain, shower, storm, volley

**hail²** acclaim, acknowledge, applaud, cheer, exalt, glorify, greet,

tightly bent metal hairpin **hairpin** n
pin for keeping hair in place **hairpin
bend** U-shaped turn of road

**hale** adj robust, healthy

**half** n (pl **halves**) either of two
equal parts of thing ~adj forming
half ~adv to the extent of half **half-
baked** adj Inf poorly planned **half-
breed**, **half-caste** n person with parents of different races **half-brother,
-sister** n brother (or sister) by one
parent only **half-hearted** adj unenthusiastic **halfwit** n feeble-minded
person

**halibut** n large edible flatfish

**halitosis** n bad-smelling breath

**hall** n (entrance) passage; large
room or building used for esp. public assembly

**hallelujah** n/interj exclamation of
praise to God

**hallmark** n mark used to indicate
standard of tested gold and silver;
mark of excellence; distinguishing
feature

**hallo** interj SEE HELLO

**hallowed** adj holy

**hallucinate** v suffer illusions **hallu-**
**cination** n **hallucinatory** adj

**halo** n (pl **-loes**) circle of light

**halt** n interruption or end to progress etc. (esp. as command to stop
marching) ~v (cause to) stop **halting** adj hesitant, lame

**halter** n rope with headgear to fasten horse; low-cut dress style with
strap passing behind neck; noose
for hanging person

**halve** v cut in half; reduce to half;
share

**ham** n meat (esp. salted or
smoked) from thigh of pig; actor
adopting exaggerated style; amateur radio enthusiast **ham-fisted** adj
clumsy

**hamburger** n fried cake of minced
beef

**hamlet** n small village

**hammer** n tool usu. with heavy
head at end of handle, for beating,
driving nails etc. ~v strike as with
hammer

**hammock** n bed of canvas etc.,
hung on cords

**hamper**[1] n large covered basket

**hamper**[2] v impede, obstruct

honour, salute, welcome

**hair** locks, mane, mop, shock,
tresses

**hale** blooming, fit, flourishing,
healthy, hearty, robust, sound,
strong, vigorous

**half** n division, equal part, fifty per
cent, fraction, portion, section ~adj
divided, fractional, halved, incomplete, limited, moderate, partial
~adv all but, barely, inadequately,
incompletely, in part, partially,
partly, slightly

**half-hearted** cool, indifferent, listless, lukewarm, perfunctory, spiritless, uninterested

**hall** corridor, entry, foyer, lobby,
passage, vestibule; auditorium,
chamber, meeting place

**halt** n arrest, break, close, end,
pause, stand, standstill, stop, stoppage, termination ~v break off,
cease, close down, desist, draw up,
pull up, rest, stand still, stop, wait

**halting** awkward, faltering, hesitant, laboured, stumbling, stutter-
ing

**halve** bisect, cut in half, divide
equally, split in two

**hammer** v bang, beat, drive, hit,
knock, strike

**hamper** v bind, cramp, curb, em-

**hamster** n type of rodent, sometimes kept as pet

**hamstring** n tendon at back of knee

**hand** n extremity of arm beyond wrist; side; style of writing; cards dealt to player; manual worker; help; pointer of dial; applause ~v pass; deliver; hold out **handful** n (pl **-fuls**) small quantity; Inf person, thing causing problems **handiness** n dexterity; state of being near, available **handy** adj convenient; clever with hands **handbag** n woman's bag **handbook** n small instruction book **handcuff** n fetter for wrist, usu. joined in pair ~v secure thus **handicraft** n manual occupation or skill **handiwork** n thing done by particular person **handkerchief** n small square of fabric for wiping nose etc. **hand-out** n thing given free; written information given out at talk etc. **handwriting** n way person writes **handyman** n man employed to do various tasks

**handicap** n something that hampers or hinders; race, contest in which chances are equalized; any physical disability ~v **-capping, -capped** hamper, impose handicaps on

**handle** n part of thing to hold it by; ~v touch, feel with hands; manage; deal with; trade **handler** n person who controls animal **handlebars** pl n curved metal bar to steer cycle

**handsome** adj of fine appearance; generous; ample

**hang** v **hanging, hung** suspend; attach, set up (wallpaper, doors etc.); be suspended, cling; (past **hanged**)

barrass, encumber, fetter, frustrate, handicap, hinder, hold up, impede, obstruct, prevent, restrict, slow down, thwart

**hand** n fist, palm; aid, assistance, help, support ~v deliver, pass; aid, assist, conduct, convey, give, guide, help, lead, present, transmit

**handbook** guide, instruction book, manual

**handcuff** fetter, manacle, shackle

**handful** few, small number, small quantity, smattering, sprinkling

**handicap** barrier, block, disadvantage, drawback, encumbrance, hindrance, impediment, limitation, obstacle, restriction, shortcoming; advantage, edge, head start, odds, penalty, upper hand; defect, disability, impairment

**handicraft** art, craft, handiwork, skill, workmanship

**handiwork** achievement, artefact, craft, creation, design, invention, product, production, result

**handle** n grip, haft, helve, hilt, knob, stock ~v feel, finger, fondle, grasp, hold, maul, poke, touch; control, direct, guide, manage, manipulate, manoeuvre, operate, steer, use, wield; administer, conduct, cope with, deal with, manage, supervise, treat

**hand-out** alms, charity, dole; bulletin, circular, leaflet

**handsome** admirable, attractive, becoming, comely, elegant, fine, good-looking, graceful

**handwriting** calligraphy, fist, hand, longhand, scrawl, script

**handy** accessible, available, close, convenient, near, nearby, within reach; convenient, helpful, manageable, neat, practical, serviceable, useful; adept, adroit, clever, deft, dexterous, expert, nimble, ready,

kill by suspension by neck **hanger** n frame on which clothes etc. can be hung **hangdog** adj sullen, dejected **hang-glider** n glider with light frame from which pilot hangs in harness **hangman** n person who executes people by hanging **hangover** n aftereffects of too much drinking **hang-up** n Inf emotional or psychological problem

**hangar** n large shed for aircraft

**hanker** v crave

**hanky** n Inf handkerchief

**haphazard** adj random, careless

**hapless** adj unlucky

**happen** v come about, occur; chance to do **happening** n occurrence, event

**happy** adj glad, content; lucky **happily** adv **happiness** n

**harangue** n vehement speech; tirade ~v address vehemently

**harass** v worry, torment **harassment** n

**harbour** n shelter for ships ~v give shelter; maintain (secretly)

**hard** adj firm, resisting pressure; solid; difficult to do, understand; unfeeling; heavy ~adv vigorously; persistently; close **harden** v **hardly** adv unkindly, harshly; scarcely; not quite; only just **hardship** n ill luck; severe toil, suffering; instance of this **hard-headed** adj shrewd **hard-hearted** adj unfeeling **hard shoulder** motorway verge for emergency stops **hardware** n tools, implements; Computers mechanical and electronic parts **hardwood** n wood from deciduous trees

——————— THESAURUS ———————

skilful, skilled

**hang** dangle, depend, droop, incline, suspend; attach, cover, deck, decorate, drape, fasten, fix, furnish; adhere, cling, hold, rest, stick

**happen** appear, arise, come about, come to pass, develop, ensue, follow, materialize, occur, result, transpire; chance, fall out, pan out Inf, supervene, turn out

**happening** accident, adventure, affair, case, chance, episode, event, experience, incident, occurrence, phenomenon

**happily** agreeably, contentedly, delightedly, enthusiastically, freely, gladly, heartily, willingly, with pleasure; auspiciously, favourably, fortunately, luckily, propitiously

**happiness** bliss, cheer, cheerfulness, contentment, delight, ecstasy, elation, enjoyment, gaiety, gladness, high spirits, joy, jubilation, merriment, satisfaction

**happy** blessed, blithe, cheerful, cock-a-hoop, content, contented, delighted, ecstatic, elated, glad, gratified, jolly, joyful, jubilant, merry, overjoyed, pleased, rapt, thrilled

**harass** annoy, badger, bait, bother, disturb, exasperate, exhaust, fatigue, harry, hound, perplex, persecute, pester, plague, tease, tire, torment, trouble, vex, weary, worry

**harbour** n destination, haven, port ~v conceal, hide, lodge, protect, provide refuge, relieve, secrete, shelter, shield

**hard** adj compact, dense, firm, inflexible, rigid, rocklike, solid, stiff, stony, strong, tough, unyielding; arduous, backbreaking, exacting, exhausting, fatiguing, formidable, laborious, rigorous, strenuous, tough, uphill, wearying; baffling, complex, complicated, difficult, intricate, involved, knotty, perplexing, puzzling, tangled, thorny; cal-

**hardy** *adj* robust, vigorous; bold; (of plants) able to grow in the open all the year round

**hare** *n* animal like large rabbit **harebell** *n* round-leaved bell-shaped flower **harebrained** *adj* rash, wild **harelip** *n* fissure of upper lip

**harem** *n* women's part of Muslim dwelling; one man's wives

**hark** *v* listen

**harlequin** *n* masked clown in diamond-patterned costume

**harlot** *n* whore, prostitute

**harm** *n/v* damage **harmful** *adj* **harmless** *adj* unable or unlikely to hurt

**harmony** *n* agreement; combina-

tion of notes to make chords; melodious sound **harmonic** *adj* of harmony **harmonica** *n* mouth organ **harmonious** *adj* **harmonium** *n* small organ **harmonize** *v* bring into harmony; cause to agree; reconcile; be in harmony

**harness** *n* equipment for attaching horse to cart, plough etc. ~*v* put on, in harness; utilize energy or power of

**harp** *n* musical instrument of strings played by hand ~*v* play on harp; dwell on continuously **harpsichord** *n* stringed instrument like piano

**harpoon** *n/v* (use) barbed spear for

lous, cold, cruel, exacting, grim, harsh, implacable, obdurate, pitiless, ruthless, severe, stern, strict, stubborn, unkind ~*adv* energetically, fiercely, forcefully, forcibly, heavily, intensely, powerfully, severely, sharply, strongly, vigorously, violently; assiduously, determinedly, diligently, doggedly, earnestly, industriously, intently, persistently, steadily, strenuously

**harden** bake, cake, freeze, set, solidify, stiffen; brace, buttress, fortify, gird, indurate, nerve, reinforce, steel, strengthen, toughen

**hardly** almost not, barely, by no means, faintly, infrequently, just, not at all, not quite, no way, only, only just, scarcely, with difficulty

**hardship** adversity, affliction, austerity, burden, calamity, destitution, difficulty, fatigue, grievance, labour, misery, misfortune, need, suffering, toil, torment, tribulation, trouble, want

**hardy** firm, fit, hale, healthy, hearty, lusty, robust, rugged,

sound, stalwart, stout, strong, sturdy, tough, vigorous

**harm** *n* abuse, damage, detriment, hurt, ill, impairment, injury, loss, mischief, misfortune ~*v* abuse, blemish, damage, hurt, ill-treat, ill-use, impair, injure, maltreat, mar, molest, ruin, spoil, wound

**harmful** baleful, baneful, destructive, detrimental, evil, hurtful, injurious, noxious, pernicious

**harmless** gentle, innocent, innocuous, inoffensive, safe

**harmonious** agreeable, compatible, concordant, congruous, coordinated, dulcet, euphonious, matching, melodious, musical, tuneful

**harmony** accord, agreement, amicability, amity, assent, compatibility, concord, conformity, cooperation, friendship, like-mindedness, peace, rapport, sympathy, unity; euphony, melody, tune, tunefulness

**harness** *n* equipment, gear, tack, tackle, trappings ~*v* couple, hitch up, saddle, yoke; apply, channel,

catching whales

**harrier** n hound used in hunting hares; falcon

**harrow** n implement for smoothing, levelling or stirring up soil ~v draw harrow over; distress greatly **harrowing** adj distressful

**harry** v **harrying, harried** harass; ravage

**harsh** adj rough, discordant; severe; unfeeling **harshly** adv

**harvest** n (season for) gathering grain; gathering; crop ~v reap and gather in **harvester** n

**has** third person sing. of HAVE **has-been** n Inf one who is no longer successful

**hash** n dish of chopped meat etc.; mess ~v cut up small, chop; mix up

**hashish, hasheesh** n resinous extract of Indian hemp, esp. used as hallucinogen

**hassle** ~n Inf quarrel; a lot of bother, trouble ~v bother

**hassock** n kneeling cushion

**haste** n speed, hurry ~v hasten **hasten** v (cause to) hurry **hastily** adv **hasty** adj

**hat** n head covering usu. with brim

**hat trick** set of three achievements

**hatch**[1] v (of young birds etc.) (cause to) emerge from egg; contrive, devise **hatchery** n

**hatch**[2] n hatchway; trapdoor over it; opening in wall, to facilitate service of meals etc. **hatchback** n car with lifting rear door **hatchway** n opening in deck of ship etc.

**hatchet** n small axe

**hate** v dislike strongly; bear malice towards ~n this feeling; that which is hated **hateful** adj detestable **hatred** n

**haughty** adj proud, arrogant

---

THESAURUS

control, employ, exploit, utilize

**harsh** coarse, croaking, crude, discordant, dissonant, glaring, grating, guttural, jarring, rasping, raucous, rough, strident; abusive, austere, bitter, bleak, brutal, cruel, dour, grim, hard, relentless, ruthless, severe, sharp, stern, unfeeling, unkind, unpleasant

**harvest** ingathering, reaping; crop, produce, yield

**hash** hotchpotch, jumble, mess, mix-up, muddle, pig's ear Inf, shambles

**haste** briskness, celerity, dispatch, expedition, fleetness, quickness, rapidity, speed, swiftness, urgency; bustle, hurry, hustle, impetuosity, rashness, recklessness, rush

**hasten** bolt, dash, fly, haste, race, run, rush, scurry, scuttle, speed, sprint

**hastily** apace, fast, promptly, quickly, rapidly, speedily; hurriedly, impetuously, impulsively, rashly, recklessly, too quickly

**hasty** brisk, eager, fast, fleet, hurried, prompt, rapid, speedy, swift, urgent; foolhardy, headlong, heedless, impetuous, impulsive, precipitate, rash, reckless

**hatch** breed, brood, incubate; conceive, concoct, contrive, design, devise, manufacture, plan, plot, project, scheme

**hate** v abhor, abominate, despise, detest, dislike, execrate ~n abhorrence, abomination, antagonism, antipathy, aversion, detestation, dislike, enmity, execration, hatred, hostility, loathing, odium

**hateful** abominable, despicable, detestable, disgusting, execrable, foul, horrible, loathsome, obnox-

**haughtily** *adv*

**haul** *v* pull, drag with effort ~*n* hauling; what is hauled **haulage** *n* **haulier** *n*

**haunch** *n* human hip or fleshy hindquarter of animal

**haunt** *v* visit regularly; visit in form of ghost; recur to ~*n* place frequently visited **haunted** *adj* frequented by ghosts; worried **haunting** *adj* extremely beautiful or sad

**have** *v* (*present tense I, we, you, they* **have**, *he, she* **has**; *present participle* **having**; *past tense and past participle* **had**) hold, possess; be affected with; be obliged (to do); cheat; obtain; contain; allow; cause to be done; give birth to; as auxiliary, forms perfect and other tenses

**haven** *n* place of safety

**haversack** *n* canvas bag for provi-sions etc. carried on back

**havoc** *n* devastation, ruin; *Inf* confusion, chaos

**hawk**[1] *n* bird of prey smaller than eagle; advocate of warlike policies

**hawk**[2] *v* offer (goods) for sale, esp. in street **hawker** *n*

**hawthorn** *n* thorny shrub or tree

**hay** *n* grass mown and dried **hay fever** *n* allergic reaction to pollen, dust etc. **haystack** *n* large pile of hay **haywire** *adj* crazy; disorganized

**hazard** *n* chance; risk, danger ~*v* expose to risk; run risk of **hazardous** *adj* risky

**haze** *n* mist; obscurity **hazy** *adj* misty; vague

**hazel** *n* bush bearing nuts ~*adj* light brown

**he** *pron* (*third person masc*) person, animal already referred to; *comb.*

———————— THESAURUS ————————

ious, offensive, repellent, repugnant, repulsive, revolting, vile

**hatred** animosity, animus, antagonism, antipathy, aversion, detestation, dislike, enmity, execration, hate, ill will, odium, repugnance, revulsion

**haughty** arrogant, conceited, disdainful, high, imperious, lofty, overweening, proud, scornful, snobbish, supercilious

**haul** drag, draw, hale, heave, lug, pull, tow, trail, tug ~*n* booty, catch, find, gain, harvest, loot, spoils, takings, yield

**haunt** *v* frequent, repair, resort, visit; beset, come back, obsess, plague, possess, prey on, recur, torment, trouble ~*n* rendezvous, resort

**haunting** eerie, evocative, nostalgic, poignant, unforgettable

**have** hold, keep, obtain, occupy, own, possess, retain; endure, enjoy, experience, feel, meet with, suffer, sustain, undergo **have to** be bound, be compelled, be forced, be obliged, must, ought, should

**haven** asylum, refuge, retreat, sanctuary, shelter

**havoc** damage, desolation, destruction, devastation, ravages, ruin, slaughter, waste, wreck; chaos, confusion, disorder, disruption, mayhem, shambles

**hazardous** dangerous, difficult, insecure, perilous, precarious, risky, unsafe

**haze** cloud, film, fog, mist, obscurity, smokiness, steam, vapour

**hazy** blurry, cloudy, dim, dull, faint, foggy, misty, nebulous, obscure, overcast, smoky, veiled; fuzzy, indefinite, indistinct, loose, muddled, nebulous, uncertain, unclear, vague

*form* male, as in **he-goat**
**head** *n* upper part of body, containing mouth, sense organs and brain; upper part of anything; chief of organization, school etc.; chief part; aptitude, capacity; crisis; person, animal considered as unit ~*adj* chief, principal; (of wind) contrary ~*v* be at the top; lead; provide with head; hit (ball) with head; make for; form a head **heading** *n* title **heady** *adj* apt to intoxicate or excite **headache** *n* continuous pain in head **headland** *n* area of land jutting into sea **headlight** *n* powerful lamp on front of vehicle etc. **headline** *n* news summary, in large type in newspaper **headlong** *adv* in rush **headphones** *pl n* two small loud-

speakers strapped against ears **headquarters** *pl n* centre of operations **head start** advantage **headstrong** *adj* self-willed **headway** *n* progress

**heal** *v* make or become well **health** *n* soundness of body; condition of body; toast drunk in person's honour **healthy** *adj* **health food** vegetarian food etc., eaten for dietary value **heap** *n* pile; great quantity ~*v* pile, load with

**hear** *v* **hearing, heard** perceive sound by ear; listen to; *Law* try (case); heed; learn **hearing** *n* ability to hear; earshot; judicial examination **hearsay** *n* rumour

**hearken** *v* listen

**hearse** *n* funeral carriage for coffin

**head** *n* pate, skull; apex, crest, crown, height, peak, pitch, summit, tip, top, vertex; captain, chief, chieftain, commander, director, leader, manager, master, principal, supervisor; ability, aptitude, brain, capacity, faculty, flair, intellect, mind, talent, thought ~*adj* arch, chief, first, foremost, front, highest, leading, main, premier, prime, principal, supreme, topmost ~*v* be or go first, cap, crown, lead, precede, top; command, control, direct, govern, guide, lead, manage, rule, run, supervise

**heading** caption, headline, name, rubric, title

**headlong** hastily, heedlessly, helter-skelter, hurriedly, pell-mell, precipitately, rashly, wildly

**headstrong** contrary, heedless, impulsive, intractable, obstinate, perverse, rash, reckless, self-willed, stiff-necked, stubborn, ungovernable, unruly, wilful

**headway** advance, improvement, progress, way

**heal** cure, make well, mend, remedy, restore, treat

**health** fitness, robustness, soundness, strength, vigour, wellbeing

**healthy** active, blooming, fit, flourishing, hale, hardy, robust, sound, strong, sturdy, vigorous, well

**heap** *n* accumulation, collection, hoard, lot, mass, mound, mountain, pile, stack, store ~*v* accumulate, amass, augment, bank, collect, gather, hoard, increase, mound, pile, stack, stockpile, store

**hear** attend, catch, eavesdrop, hark, heed, listen to, overhear; *Law* examine, investigate, judge, try; ascertain, be informed, discover, find out, gather, learn, pick up, understand

**hearing** audition, ear, perception; audience, audition, interview; inquiry, investigation, review, trial

**hearsay** buzz, gossip, report,

**heart** *n* organ which makes blood circulate; seat of emotions and affections; mind, soul, courage; central part; suit at cards **hearten** *v* make, become cheerful **heartless** *adj* unfeeling **hearty** *adj* friendly; vigorous; in good health; satisfying **heart attack** sudden severe malfunction of heart **heartbeat** *n* single pulsation of heart **heartbreak** *n* intense grief **heartfelt** *adj* felt sincerely **heart-rending** *adj* agonizing **by heart** by memory

**hearth** *n* part of room where fire is made; home

**heat** *n* hotness; sensation of this; hot weather; warmth of feeling, anger etc.; sexual excitement in female animals; one of many eliminating races etc. ~*v* make, become hot **heated** *adj* angry **heater** *n*

**heath** *n* tract of waste land

**heathen** *adj/n* (*pl* **heathens, heathen**) (one) not adhering to a religious system; pagan

**heather** *n* shrub growing on heaths and mountains

**heave** *v* lift (and throw) with effort; utter (sigh); swell, rise; feel nausea ~*n* act of heaving

**heaven** *n* abode of God; place of bliss; (*also pl*) sky **heavenly** *adj*

**heavy** *adj* weighty; dense; sluggish; severe; sorrowful; serious; dull **heavily** *adv*

**heckle** *v* interrupt (speaker) by

─────── THESAURUS ───────

rumour, talk

**heart** affection, benevolence, compassion, concern, humanity, love, pity, tenderness, understanding; boldness, bravery, courage, mettle, mind, nerve, pluck, purpose, resolution, spirit, will; centre, core, crux, essence, hub, kernel, marrow, middle, nucleus, pith, quintessence, root

**heartfelt** ardent, cordial, deep, devout, earnest, fervent, genuine, honest, profound, sincere, unfeigned, warm

**heartless** brutal, callous, cold, cruel, hard, harsh, inhuman, merciless, pitiless, uncaring, unfeeling, unkind

**hearty** affable, ardent, cordial, eager, effusive, friendly, generous, genial, jovial, unreserved, warm; active, energetic, hale, hardy, healthy, robust, sound, strong, vigorous, well

**heat** *n* fever, sultriness, swelter, torridity, warmness, warmth; agita-

tion, ardour, excitement, fervour, fever, fury, intensity, passion, vehemence, violence, warmth, zeal ~*v* flush, glow, grow hot, make hot, reheat, warm up

**heated** angry, bitter, excited, fierce, fiery, frenzied, furious, intense, passionate, raging, stormy, vehement, violent

**heathen** *adj* godless, heathenish, idolatrous, infidel, irreligious, pagan ~*n* idolater, infidel, pagan, unbeliever

**heave** drag, elevate, haul, hoist, lever, lift, pull, raise, tug; cast, fling, hurl, pitch, send, sling, throw, toss

**heaven** bliss, dreamland, ecstasy, enchantment, happiness, paradise, rapture, transport, utopia

**heavenly** *Inf* beautiful, blissful, delightful, entrancing, exquisite, glorious, lovely, rapturous, ravishing, sublime, wonderful

**heavy** bulky, massive, ponderous, portly, weighty; apathetic, drowsy, dull, inactive, indolent, inert, list-

questions, taunts etc.

**hectare** n one hundred ares or 10,000 square metres (2,471 acres)

**hectic** adj rushed, busy

**hedge** n fence of bushes ~v surround with hedge; be evasive; secure against loss **hedgehog** n small animal covered with spines

**hedonism** n pursuit of pleasure **hedonist** n

**heed** v take notice of **heedless** adj careless

**heel**[1] n hind part of foot; part of shoe supporting this; Sl undesirable person ~v supply with heel

**heel**[2] v lean to one side

**hefty** adj bulky; weighty; strong

**heifer** n young cow

**height** n measure from base to top; quality of being high; elevation; highest degree; (oft. pl) hilltop **heighten** v make higher; intensify

**heinous** adj atrocious, extremely wicked, detestable

**heir** n (fem **heiress**) person entitled to inherit property or rank **heirloom** n thing that has been in family for generations

**helicopter** n aircraft lifted by rotating blades

**helium** n very light, nonflammable gaseous element

**helix** n (pl **helices, helixes**) spiral

**hell** n abode of the damned; abode of the dead generally; place of torture **hellish** adj **hell-bent** adj intent

**hello** also **hallo** interj expression of greeting

**helm** n tiller, wheel for turning ship's rudder

**helmet** n defensive or protective covering for head

**help** v/n aid; support; remedy **helper** n **helpful** adj **helping** n single portion of food **helpless** adj incompetent; unaided; unable to help

————— THESAURUS —————

less, slow, sluggish, stupid, torpid, wooden; burdensome, difficult, grievous, hard, harsh, intolerable, laborious, onerous, oppressive, severe, tedious, vexatious, wearisome

**heckle** boo, disrupt, interrupt, jeer, pester, shout down, taunt

**hectic** boisterous, chaotic, excited, fevered, feverish, flurrying, frantic, frenetic, frenzied, heated, riotous, turbulent, wild

**hedge** n hedgerow, quickset ~v border, edge, enclose, fence, surround; dodge, duck, equivocate, evade, flannel Brit inf, prevaricate, quibble, sidestep, temporize

**heed** v attend, consider, follow, listen to, mark, mind, note, obey, observe, regard

**heedless** careless, imprudent, inattentive, negligent, oblivious, rash, reckless, thoughtless

**height** altitude, elevation, highness, loftiness, stature; apex, apogee, crest, crown, hill, mountain, peak, pinnacle, summit, top, vertex, zenith; acme, dignity, eminence, exaltation, grandeur, loftiness, prominence

**heighten** add to, aggravate, amplify, augment, enhance, improve, increase, intensify, magnify, sharpen, strengthen

**hell** abyss, infernal regions, inferno, underworld; agony, anguish, martyrdom, misery, nightmare, ordeal, suffering, torment, trial, wretchedness

**hellish** damnable, damned, devilish, diabolical, fiendish, infernal

**help** v abet, aid, assist, back, befriend, cooperate, encourage, pro-

**helter-skelter** *adv/adj/n* (in) hurry and confusion *~n* high spiral slide at fairground

**hem** *n* edge of cloth, folded and sewn down *~v* **hemming, hemmed** sew thus; confine, shut in

**hemisphere** *n* half sphere; half of the earth

**hemlock** *n* poisonous plant

**hemp** *n* Indian plant; its fibre used for rope etc.; any of several narcotic drugs

**hen** *n* female of domestic fowl and others **henpecked** *adj* (of man) dominated by wife

**hence** *adv* from this point; for this reason **henceforward, henceforth** *adv* from now onwards

**henchman** *n* trusty follower

**henna** *n* flowering shrub; reddish dye made from it

**hepatitis** *n* inflammation of the liver

**heptagon** *n* figure with seven angles

**her** *pron* object of SHE *~adj* of, belonging to her **hers** *pron* of her **herself** *pron* emphatic or reflexive form of SHE

**herald** *n* messenger, envoy *~v* announce **heraldic** *adj* **heraldry** *n* study of (right to have) heraldic bearings

**herb** *n* plant used in cookery or medicine **herbaceous** *adj* of, like herbs; perennial flowering **herbal** *adj* **herbicide** *n* chemical which destroys plants **herbivore** *n* animal that feeds on plants **herbivorous** *adj*

**herd** *n* company of animals feeding together *~v* crowd together; tend (herd) **herdsman** *n*

**here** *adv* in this place; at or to this point **hereabouts** *adv* near here **hereafter** *adv* in time to come *~n* future existence **hereby** *adv* as a result of this **herein** *adv* in this place **herewith** *adv* with this

**heredity** *n* tendency of organism to transmit its nature to its de-

mote, relieve, save, second, serve, stand by, succour, support; alleviate, ameliorate, cure, ease, facilitate, heal, improve, mitigate, relieve, remedy, restore *~n* advice, aid, assistance, avail, benefit, co-operation, guidance, service, support, use, utility

**helper** aide, ally, assistant, attendant, collaborator, colleague, deputy, helpmate, mate, partner, second, supporter

**helpful** beneficial, constructive, favourable, fortunate, practical, productive, profitable, serviceable, timely, useful; beneficent, benevolent, caring, friendly, kind, supportive, sympathetic

**helping** *n* piece, plateful, portion, ration, serving

**helpless** disabled, feeble, impotent, incapable, incompetent, infirm, paralysed, powerless, unfit, weak

**hem** border, edge, fringe, margin, trimming

**herald** *n* crier, messenger *~v* advertise, announce, broadcast, proclaim, publish, trumpet

**herd** *n* collection, crowd, crush, drove, flock, horde, mass, mob, multitude, press, swarm, throng *~v* assemble, associate, collect, congregate, flock, gather, huddle, muster, rally

**hereafter** after this, from now on, henceforth, in future

**hereditary** family, genetic, inborn,

scendants **hereditary** adj descending by inheritance or heredity

**heresy** n unorthodox opinion or belief **heretic** n **heretical** adj

**heritage** n what may be or is inherited

**hermaphrodite** n person or animal with characteristics, or reproductive organs, of both sexes

**hermetic** adj sealed so as to be airtight **hermetically** adj

**hermit** n one living in solitude **hermitage** n hermit's dwelling

**hernia** n projection of organ through lining

**hero** n (pl **heroes**, fem **heroine**) one greatly regarded for achievements or qualities; principal character in story **heroic** adj **heroism** n

**heroin** n highly addictive drug

**heron** n long-legged wading bird

**herring** n important food fish

**hertz** n (pl **hertz**) SI unit of frequency

**hesitate** v hold back; feel, or show indecision; be reluctant **hesitancy**, **hesitation** n **hesitant** adj

**hessian** n coarse jute cloth

**heterogeneous** adj composed of diverse elements **heterogeneity** n

**heterosexual** n/adj (person) sexually attracted to members of the opposite sex

**hew** v hewing, hewed, hewed or hewn chop, cut with axe; carve

**hexagon** n figure with six angles **hexagonal** adj

**hey** interj expression of surprise or for catching attention

**heyday** n bloom, prime

**hiatus** n (pl **hiatuses, hiatus**) break or gap

**hibernate** v pass the winter, esp. in a torpid state **hibernation** n

**hiccup, hiccough** n/v (have) spasm of the breathing organs with an abrupt sound

**hickory** n N Amer. nut-bearing tree; its tough wood

**hide**¹ v hiding, hid, hidden or hid put, keep out of sight; conceal oneself

**hide**² n skin of animal **hiding** n Sl thrashing **hidebound** adj restricted; narrow-minded

**hideous** adj repulsive, revolting

————— THESAURUS —————

inbred, inheritable

**heresy** apostasy, error, impiety, schism, unorthodoxy

**heretic** apostate, dissenter, renegade, sectarian, separatist

**heritage** bequest, birthright, endowment, estate, inheritance, legacy, lot, patrimony, portion, share, tradition

**hermit** anchorite, eremite, monk, recluse, solitary

**hero** celebrity, champion, exemplar, great man, idol, star, superstar, victor; leading man, male lead, protagonist

**heroic** bold, brave, courageous,

daring, doughty, fearless, gallant, intrepid, undaunted, valiant

**heroism** boldness, bravery, courage, daring, fearlessness, fortitude, gallantry, prowess, spirit, valour

**hesitant** diffident, doubtful, halfhearted, halting, irresolute, reluctant, sceptical, shy, timid, uncertain, unsure, vacillating, wavering

**hesitate** be uncertain, delay, dither chiefly Brit, doubt, pause, vacillate, wait, waver

**hew** axe, chop, cut, hack, lop, split; carve, fashion, form, make, model, sculpt, sculpture, shape, smooth

**heyday** bloom, flowering, pink,

**hierarchy** *n* system of persons or things arranged in graded order **hierarchical** *adj*

**hieroglyphic** *adj* of picture writing, as used in ancient Egypt ~*n* symbol representing object, concept or sound

**hi-fi** *adj* short for HIGH-FIDELITY ~*n* high-fidelity equipment

**high** *adj* tall, lofty; far up; (of sound) acute in pitch; expensive; of great importance, quality, or rank; *Inf* in state of euphoria ~*adv* at, to a height **highly** *adv* **highness** *n* quality of being high; (*with cap.*) title of royal person **highbrow** *n/adj* intellectual **high-fidelity** *adj* of high-quality sound reproducing equipment **high-handed** *adj* domineering

**highlands** *pl n* area of relatively high ground **highlight** *n* outstanding feature ~*v* emphasize **highly strung** excitable, nervous **high-rise** *adj* of building that has many stories **high-tech** *adj* using sophisticated technology **high time** latest possible time **highway** *n* main road; ordinary route **highwayman** *n* formerly, horseman who robbed travellers

**hijack** *v* divert or wrongfully take command of a vehicle (esp. aircraft) **hijacker** *n*

**hike** *v* walk a long way (for pleasure) in country; pull (up), hitch **hiker** *n*

**hilarity** *n* cheerfulness, gaiety **hilarious** *adj*

——————— THESAURUS ———————

prime, salad days

**hide** cache, conceal, hole up, lie low, secrete, stash *Inf,* take cover; bury, cloak, conceal, cover, disguise, eclipse, mask, obscure, screen, shelter, shroud, veil

**hidebound** conventional, narrow-minded, rigid, set

**hideous** ghastly, grim, grisly, grotesque, gruesome, monstrous, repulsive, revolting, ugly, unsightly

**hiding** *n* beating, caning, drubbing, flogging, spanking, thrashing, whipping

**high** *adj* elevated, lofty, soaring, steep, tall, towering; arch, chief, eminent, exalted, important, influential, leading, notable, powerful, prominent, ruling, significant, superior; acute, penetrating, piercing, piping, sharp, shrill, soprano, strident, treble; costly, dear, expensive, high-priced ~*adv* aloft, at great height, far up, way up

**highbrow** *n* aesthete, intellectual,

mastermind, savant, scholar ~*adj* bookish, cultivated, cultured, deep

**high-handed** arbitrary, autocratic, despotic, domineering, imperious, oppressive, overbearing

**highlight** *n* climax, feature, focus, peak ~*v* accent, emphasize, feature, set off, show up, spotlight, stress, underline

**highly** decidedly, eminently, extraordinarily, extremely, greatly, immensely, supremely, tremendously, vastly, very, very much

**hijack** commandeer, expropriate, seize, skyjack, take over

**hike** *v* back-pack, ramble, tramp, walk ~*n* march, ramble, tramp, trek, walk

**hilarious** amusing, comical, convivial, entertaining, funny, gay, happy, humorous, jolly, jovial, joyful, merry, noisy

**hilarity** amusement, cheerfulness, exhilaration, exuberance, gaiety, glee, high spirits, jollity, joyousness,

**hill** n natural elevation, small mountain; mound **hillock** n little hill **hilly** adj

**hilt** n handle of sword etc.

**him** pron object of HE **himself** pron emphatic form of HE

**hind¹** n female of deer

**hind²** adj at the back, posterior

**hinder** v obstruct, impede, delay **hindrance** n

**hinge** n movable joint, as that on which door hangs ~v attach with hinge; depend on

**hint** n slight indication; piece of advice; small amount ~v give hint

**hinterland** n district lying behind coast, port etc.

**hip** n either side of body below waist and above thigh; fruit of rose

**hippie** n person who rejects conventional dress and lifestyle

**hippopotamus** n (pl -muses, -mi) large Afr. animal living in rivers

**hire** v obtain temporary use of by payment; engage for wage ~n hiring or being hired; payment for use of thing **hire-purchase** n purchase of goods by instalments

**hirsute** adj hairy

**his** pron/adj belonging to him

**hiss** v make sharp sound of letter s; express disapproval thus ~n hissing

**history** n (record of) past events; study of these **historian** n **historic** n **historic** adj **historical** adj

**histrionic** adj excessively theatrical, insincere, artificial in manner **histrionics** pl n behaviour like this

**hit** v hitting, **hit** strike with blow or missile; affect injuriously; find; light (upon) ~n blow; success **hit man** hired assassin

───────── THESAURUS ─────────

laughter, merriment, mirth

**hill** elevation, eminence, fell, height, knoll, mound, mount, prominence, tor

**hinder** v arrest, check, debar, delay, deter, encumber, hamper, handicap, impede, interrupt, obstruct, oppose, prevent, retard, stop, thwart

**hindrance** n bar, barrier, block, check, deterrent, difficulty, drag, drawback, encumbrance, handicap, hitch, impediment, limitation, obstacle, snag, stoppage

**hinge** v depend, hang, pivot, rest, turn

**hint** n clue, implication, indication, inkling, innuendo, intimation, mention, reminder, suggestion, tip-off; advice, help, pointer, suggestion, tip; breath, dash, soupçon, speck, suggestion, suspicion, taste, tinge, touch, trace, whiff, whisper

~v allude, cue, imply, indicate, intimate, mention, prompt, suggest, tip off

**hire** v charter, engage, lease, let, rent; appoint, employ, engage, sign up, take on ~n charge, cost, fee, price, rent, rental

**hiss** n rasp, shrill, sibilate, wheeze, whirr, whistle, whiz; boo, catcall, condemn, damn, decry, deride, hoot, jeer, mock, revile, ridicule ~n buzz, hissing, sibilance; boo, catcall, contempt, derision, jeer

**historic** celebrated, extraordinary, famous, momentous, notable, outstanding, remarkable, significant

**history** n account, annals, chronicle, memoirs, narration, narrative, recital, record, relation, saga, story

**hit** v bang, batter, beat, cuff, deck Sl, flog, knock, lay one on Sl, lob, punch, slap, smack, sock Sl, strike, swat, thump, whack ~n blow,

**hitch** v fasten with loop etc.; raise with jerk; be caught or fastened ~n difficulty; knot; jerk **hitchhike** v travel by begging free rides **hitchhiker** n

**hither** adv to this place **hitherto** adv up to now

**HIV** human immunodeficiency virus

**hive** n structure in which bees live **hive off** transfer

**hives** pl n eruptive skin disease

**HM** His (or Her) Majesty

**HMS** His (or Her) Majesty's Service or Ship

**hoard** n store, esp. hidden ~v amass and hide

**hoarding** n large board for displaying advertisements

**hoarse** adj sounding husky

**hoary** adj grey with age; greyish-white; very old **hoarfrost** n frozen dew

**hoax** n practical joke ~v play trick upon

**hob** n top area of cooking stove

**hobble** v walk lamely; tie legs together ~n limping gait

**hobby** n favourite occupation as pastime **hobbyhorse** n favourite topic; toy horse

**hobgoblin** n mischievous fairy

**hobnob** v -nobbing, -nobbed drink together; be familiar (with)

**hobo** n (pl -bos) US & Canad shiftless, wandering person

**hock¹** n backward-pointing joint on leg of horse etc.

**hock²** n dry white wine

**hockey** n team game played on a field with ball and curved sticks; US & Canad ice hockey

**hod** n small trough for carrying bricks etc.; coal scuttle

**hoe** n tool for weeding, breaking ground etc. ~v hoeing, hoed work with hoe

**hog** n pig; greedy person ~v hogging, hogged Inf eat, use (something) selfishly

**hoist** v raise aloft, raise with tackle etc.

**hold¹** v holding, held keep in hands; maintain in position; contain; occupy; carry on; detain; be in force; occur ~n grasp; influence **holdall** n large travelling bag **holder** n holding n (oft. pl) property hold-

bump, clash, cuff, impact, knock, rap, shot, slap, smack, stroke; Inf sellout, sensation, success, triumph, winner

**hitch** v attach, connect, couple, fasten, harness, join, make fast, tether, tie, unite, yoke ~n catch, check, delay, difficulty, drawback, hassle Inf, hindrance, hold-up, impediment, mishap, obstacle, problem, snag, stoppage, trouble

**hitherto** heretofore, previously, so far, thus far, till now, until now, up to now

**hoard** n cache, fund, heap, mass, pile, reserve, stockpile, store, supply ~v accumulate, amass, buy up, cache, collect, deposit, garner, gather, hive, lay up, put by, save, stockpile, store, treasure

**hoarse** croaky, grating, gravelly, growling, gruff, guttural, harsh, husky, rasping, raucous, rough, throaty

**hoax** cheat, deception, fraud, imposture, joke, practical joke, prank, ruse, swindle, trick

**hobby** activity, diversion, pastime, relaxation, sideline

**hoist** elevate, erect, heave, lift,

**up** n armed robbery; delay

**hold²** n space in ship or aircraft for cargo

**hole** n hollow place; perforation; opening; *Inf* unattractive place **holey** adj

**holiday** n day(s) of rest from work etc., esp. spent away from home

**holistic** adj considering the complete person, esp. in treatment of disease

**hollow** adj having a cavity, not solid; empty; insincere ~n cavity, hole, valley ~v make hollow; excavate

**holly** n evergreen shrub with prickly leaves and red berries

**hollyhock** n tall plant bearing many large flowers

**holocaust** n great destruction of life, esp. by fire

**hologram** n three-dimensional photographic image

**holster** n leather case for pistol, hung from belt etc.

**holy** adj belonging, devoted to God; free from sin; divine; consecrated **holily** adv **holiness** n

**homage** n tribute, respect

**home** n dwelling-place; residence ~adj of home; native; in home ~adv to, at one's home; to the point ~v direct or be directed onto a point or target **homeless** adj **homelessness** n **homely** adv unpretentious; domesticated **homeward** adj/adv **homewards** adv **home-made** adj **homesick** adj depressed by absence from home **homesickness** n **homespun** adj domestic; simple **homestead** n house with outbuildings, esp. on farm **homework** n school work done at home

**homeopathy** n treatment of disease by small doses of drug that produces symptoms of the disease in healthy people **homeopathic** adj

———— THESAURUS ————

raise, rear

**hold** v adhere, clasp, cleave, clinch, cling, clutch, cradle, embrace, enfold, grasp, grip, stick; have, keep, maintain, occupy, own, possess, retain; accommodate, comprise, contain, seat, take; assemble, call, carry on, celebrate, conduct, convene, have, run; arrest, bind, check, confine, curb, detain, imprison, pound, restrain, stay, stop, suspend ~n clasp, clutch, grasp, grip; authority, control, dominance, influence, sway

**holder** bearer, custodian, incumbent, keeper, occupant, owner, possessor, proprietor, purchaser

**hold-up** bottleneck, delay, difficulty, hitch, obstruction, setback, snag, stoppage, trouble, wait

**hole** breach, break, crack, fissure, gap, opening, outlet, puncture, rent, split, tear, vent

**holiday** break, leave, recess, time off, vacation

**holiness** devoutness, divinity, godliness, piety, purity, sanctity, spirituality

**hollow** adj empty, unfilled, vacant, void; concave, depressed, indented, sunken; empty, fruitless, futile, pointless, useless, vain, worthless ~n basin, bowl, cave, cavern, cavity, crater, cup, dent, depression, hole, indentation, pit, trough; bottom, dale, dell, dingle, glen, valley

**holy** devout, divine, faithful, godly, hallowed, pious, pure, religious, righteous, saintly, sublime, virtuous

**home** abode, dwelling, habitation, house, pad *Sl*, residence

**homespun** artless, coarse, home-

**homicide** *n* killing of human being; killer **homicidal** *adj*

**homily** *n* sermon

**homogeneous** *adj* formed of uniform parts; similar **homogeneity** *n*

**homogenize** ~*v* break up fat globules in milk and cream to distribute them evenly

**homonym** *n* word of same form as another, but of different sense

**homosexual** *n/adj* (person) sexually attracted to members of the same sex **homosexuality** *n*

**hone** *v* sharpen (on whetstone)

**honest** *adj* not cheating, lying, stealing etc.; genuine **honestly** *adv* **honesty** *n*

**honey** *n* sweet fluid made by bees **honeycomb** *n* wax structure in hexagonal cells ~*v* fill with cells or perforations **honeymoon** *n* holiday tak-

en by newly wedded pair **honeysuckle** *n* climbing plant

**honk** *n* call of wild goose; sound of motor-horn ~*v* make this sound

**honour** *n* personal integrity; renown; reputation ~*v* respect highly; confer honour on; accept or pay (bill etc.) when due **honourable** *adj*

**honorary** *adj* conferred for the sake of honour only

**hood** *n* covering for head and neck; hoodlike thing **hoodwink** ~*v* deceive

**hoodlum** *n* gangster

**hoof** *n* (*pl* **hoofs** or **hooves**) horny casing of foot of horse etc.

**hook** *n* bent piece of metal etc., for catching hold, hanging up etc.; something resembling hook in shape or function ~*v* grasp, catch, hold, as with hook **hooked** *adj*

——————— THESAURUS ———————

ly, inelegant, plain, rough, rude, rustic, unpolished

**homicidal** deadly, lethal, mortal, murderous

**homicide** bloodshed, killing, manslaughter, murder, slaying

**homogeneous** akin, alike, cognate, comparable, consistent, identical, kindred, similar, uniform, unvarying

**honest** decent, ethical, highminded, honourable, law-abiding, reliable, reputable, scrupulous, trustworthy, trusty, truthful, upright, veracious, virtuous; candid, direct, forthright, frank, genuine, open, outright, plain, sincere, upfront *Inf*

**honestly** by fair means, cleanly, ethically, honourably, in good faith, lawfully, legally, legitimately; candidly, frankly, in all sincerity, in plain English, plainly, straight

(out), to one's face, truthfully

**honesty** fidelity, honour, integrity, morality, probity, rectitude, trustworthiness, uprightness, virtue

**honour** *n* decency, fairness, goodness, integrity, morality, probity, rectitude, uprightness; credit, dignity, distinction, eminence, esteem, fame, glory, prestige, rank, renown, reputation, repute ~*v* admire, adore, appreciate, esteem, exalt, glorify, hallow, prize, respect, revere, reverence, value, venerate, worship

**honourable** ethical, fair, honest, just, moral, principled, true, trustworthy, trusty, upright, upstanding, virtuous; eminent, great, illustrious, noble, notable, noted, prestigious, renowned, venerable

**hoodwink** befool, cheat, cozen, delude, dupe, fool, hoax, impose, kid *Inf*, mislead, swindle, trick

shaped like hook; caught; *Sl* addicted

**hooligan** *n* violent, irresponsible (young) person **hooliganism** *n*

**hoop** *n* rigid circular band of metal, wood etc.

**hooray** *interj see* HURRAH

**hoot** *n* owl's cry or similar sound; cry of derision; *Inf* funny person or thing ~*v* utter hoot **hooter** *n* device (e.g. horn) to emit hooting sound

**Hoover** *n Trademark* vacuum cleaner ~*v* (*without cap.*) vacuum

**hop**[1] *v* **hopping, hopped** spring on one foot ~*n* leap, skip

**hop**[2] *n* climbing plant with bitter cones used to flavour beer etc.; *pl* the cones

**hope** *n* expectation of something desired; thing that gives, or object of, this feeling ~*v* feel hope for **hopeful** *adj* **hopefully** *adv* **hopeless** *adj*

**hopper** *n* one who hops; device for feeding material into mill

**hopscotch** *n* children's game of hopping in pattern drawn on ground

**horde** *n* large crowd

**horizon** *n* line where earth and sky seem to meet **horizontal** *adj* parallel with horizon, level

**hormone** *n* substance secreted from gland which stimulates organs of the body

**horn** *n* hard projection on heads of certain animals; various things made of, or resembling it; wind instrument; device (esp. in car) emitting sound **horny** *adj* **hornpipe** *n* sailor's lively dance

**hornet** *n* large insect of wasp family

**horoscope** *n* telling of person's fortune by studying positions of planets etc. at his or her birth

**horrendous** *adj* horrific

**horror** *n* terror; loathing, fear of; its

——————— THESAURUS ———————

**hook** *n* catch, clasp, fastener, hasp, holder, link, lock, peg; noose, snare, springe, trap ~*v* catch, clasp, fasten, fix, hasp, secure

**hooligan** delinquent, rowdy, ruffian, tough, vandal

**hoop** band, circlet, girdle, loop, ring, wheel

**hoot** *n* call, cry, toot; boo, catcall, hiss, jeer, yell ~*v* cry, scream, shout, shriek, toot, whoop, yell; boo, catcall, condemn, decry, denounce, hiss, howl down, jeer, yell at

**hop** *v* bound, caper, dance, jump, leap, skip, spring, trip, vault ~*n* bounce, bound, jump, leap, skip, spring, step, vault

**hope** *n* ambition, anticipation, assumption, belief, confidence, desire, dream, expectancy, faith, longing ~*v* anticipate, aspire, await, believe, desire, expect, foresee, long, rely, trust

**hopeful** assured, buoyant, confident, expectant, optimistic, sanguine; auspicious, bright, cheerful, encouraging, heartening, promising, propitious, reassuring, rosy

**hopefully** confidently, expectantly, optimistically, sanguinely; conceivably, expectedly, feasibly, probably

**hopeless** forlorn, futile, impossible, impracticable, pointless, unattainable, useless, vain

**horde** band, crew, crowd, drove, gang, host, mob, multitude, pack, press, swarm, throng, troop

**horizon** skyline, vista

**horrible** abominable, appalling,

cause **horrible** *adj* exciting horror, hideous, shocking; disagreeable **horribly** *adv* **horrid** *adj* unpleasant, repulsive; *Inf* unkind **horrific** *adj* particularly horrible **horrify** *v* **-ifying, -ified** cause horror (in); shock

**hors d'oeuvre** *n* small dish served before main meal

**horse** *n* four-footed animal used for riding; cavalry; frame for support etc. **horsy** *adj* devoted to horses; like a horse **horse chestnut** tree with white or pink flowers and large nuts **horsefly** *n* large bloodsucking fly **horseman** *n* (*fem* **horsewoman**) rider on horse **horsepower** *n* unit of power of engine etc. **horseradish** *n* plant with pungent root **horseshoe** *n* protective U-shaped piece of iron nailed to horse's hoof

**horticulture** *n* art or science of gardening

**hose** *n* flexible tube for conveying liquid or gas; stockings ~*v* water with hose **hosiery** *n* stockings

**hospice** *n* home for care of the terminally ill

**hospital** *n* institution for care of sick **hospitalize** *v* send or admit to hospital

**hospitality** *n* friendly and liberal reception of strangers or guests **hospitable** *adj*

**host**[1] *n* (*fem* **hostess**) one who entertains another; innkeeper; compere of show ~*v* act as a host

**host**[2] *n* large number

**hostage** *n* person taken or given as pledge or security

**hostel** *n* building providing accommodation at low cost for students etc.

**hostile** *adj* antagonistic; warlike; of an enemy **hostility** *n* enmity; *pl* acts of warfare

**hot** *adj* **hotter, hottest** of high tem-

awful, dreadful, fearful, frightful, ghastly, grim, grisly, gruesome, heinous, hideous, horrid, repulsive, revolting, shameful, shocking, terrible; awful, cruel, disagreeable, dreadful, horrid, mean, nasty, terrible, unkind, unpleasant

**horrid** awful, disgusting, dreadful, horrible, nasty, offensive, terrible, unpleasant

**horrify** alarm, frighten, intimidate, petrify, scare, terrify; appal, disgust, dismay, gross out *US sl*, outrage, shock, sicken

**horror** alarm, apprehension, awe, consternation, dismay, dread, fear, fright, panic, terror; aversion, disgust, hatred, loathing, repugnance, revulsion

**hospitable** amicable, bountiful,

cordial, friendly, generous, genial, gracious, kind, liberal, sociable, welcoming

**hospitality** cheer, conviviality, cordiality, friendliness, sociability, warmth, welcome

**host**[1] entertainer, innkeeper, landlord, proprietor

**host**[2] army, array, drove, horde, legion, multitude, myriad, swarm, throng

**hostage** captive, gage, pawn, pledge, prisoner, security, surety

**hostile** antagonistic, contrary, inimical, malevolent, opposed, unkind, warlike

**hostility** animosity, antagonism, antipathy, aversion, detestation, enmity, hatred, ill will, malevolence, malice, opposition

perature; angry; new; spicy **hotly**
*adv* **hot air** *Inf* empty talk **hotbed** *n*
bed of heated earth for young
plants; any place encouraging
growth **hot-blooded** *adj* excitable
**hot dog** hot sausage in split bread
roll **hotfoot** *v/adv* (go) quickly **hothead** *n* intemperate person **hot-
house** *n* heated greenhouse **hotline**
*n* direct telephone link for emergency use **hotplate** *n* heated plate
on electric cooker

**hotchpotch** *n* medley; dish of
many ingredients

**hotel** *n* commercial establishment
providing lodging and meals **hotelier** *n*

**hound** *n* hunting dog ~*v* chase,
urge, pursue

**hour** *n* twenty-fourth part of day;
sixty minutes; appointed time; *pl*
fixed periods for work etc. **hourly**
*adv/adj* **hourglass** *n* timing device
in which sand trickles between two
glass compartments

tation; legislative assembly; family;
business firm ~*v* give or receive
shelter, lodging, or storage; cover
or contain **housing** *n* (providing of)
houses; part designed to cover, protect, contain **houseboat** *n* boat used
as home **household** *n* inmates of
house collectively **housekeeper** *n*
person managing affairs of household **housekeeping** *n* (money for)
running household **housewife** *n*
woman who runs her own household

**hovel** *n* lowly dwelling

**hover** *v* hang in the air; loiter; be in
state of indecision **hovercraft** *n* type
of craft which can travel over both
land and sea on a cushion of air

**how** *adv* in what way; by what
means; in what condition; to what
degree **however** *conj* nevertheless
~*adv* in whatever way, degree; all
the same

**howl** *v/n* (utter) long loud cry
**howler** *n* *Inf* stupid mistake

**HP** hire-purchase

———— THESAURUS ————

**hot** boiling, burning, fiery, flaming,
heated, roasting, scalding, scorching, searing, steaming, sultry, sweltering, torrid, warm; acrid, biting,
peppery, piquant, pungent, sharp,
spicy

**hot air** bombast, bunkum *or* buncombe *chiefly US*, rant, verbiage,
wind

**hotchpotch** hash, jumble, medley,
*mélange*, mess, mishmash, mixture,
potpourri

**hothead** daredevil, desperado,
tearaway

**hound** *v* chase, drive, give chase,
hunt, hunt down, pursue

**house** *n* abode, building, dwelling,
edifice, home, pad *Sl*, residence;

family, household, ménage; business, company, concern, establishment, firm, organization ~*v* accommodate, billet, board, domicile,
harbour, lodge, put up, quarter,
take in

**household** *n* family, home, house,
ménage

**housing** dwellings, houses, houses

**hovel** cabin, den, hole, hut, shack,
shanty, shed

**hover** drift, float, flutter, fly, hang,
poise; linger

**however** after all, anyhow, but,
even though, nevertheless, nonetheless, notwithstanding, still,
though, yet

**howl** *v* bellow, cry, cry out, lament,

**HQ** headquarters

**HRH** His (*or* Her) Royal Highness

**hub** *n* middle part of wheel; central point of activity

**hubbub** *n* confused noise

**huddle** *n* crowded mass; *Inf* impromptu conference ~*v* heap, crowd together; hunch

**hue** *n* colour

**huff** *n* passing mood of anger ~*v* make or become angry; blow

**hug** *v* hugging, hugged clasp tightly in the arms; keep close to ~*n* fond embrace

**huge** *adj* very big **hugely** *adv* very much

**hulk** *n* body of abandoned vessel; large, unwieldy person or thing **hulking** *adj*

**hull** *n* frame, body of ship; calyx of strawberry etc. ~*v* remove shell,

hull from (fruit, seeds)

**hullabaloo** *n* uproar; clamour

**hum** *v* humming, hummed make low continuous sound; sing with closed lips ~*n* humming sound **hummingbird** *n* very small Amer. bird whose wings make humming noise

**human** *adj* of man; relating to, characteristic of, man's nature **humane** *adj* kind; merciful **humanism** *n* belief in human effort rather than religion **humanitarian** *n* philanthropist ~*adj* philanthropic **humanity** *n* human nature; human race; kindliness; *pl* study of literature, philosophy, the arts **humanize** *v*

**humble** *adj* lowly, modest ~*v* humiliate **humbly** *adv*

**humbug** *n* imposter; sham, nonsense; sweet of boiled sugar

——————————————— T H E S A U R U S ———————————————

roar, scream, shout, shriek, wail, weep, yell, yelp ~*n* bay, bellow, clamour, cry, groan, hoot, outcry, roar, scream, shriek, wail, yelp

**howler** blunder, error, malapropism, mistake

**huddle** *n* crowd, disorder, heap, jumble, mass, mess, muddle; conference, discussion, meeting ~*v* cluster, converge, crowd, flock, gather, press, throng

**hue** colour, dye, shade, tincture, tinge, tint, tone

**hug** *v* clasp, cuddle, embrace, enfold, hold close, squeeze; cherish, cling, hold onto, nurse, retain ~*n* clasp, clinch *Sl*, embrace, squeeze

**huge** colossal, elephantine, enormous, gargantuan, giant, gigantic, great, immense, large, massive, prodigious, stupendous, tremendous, vast

**hulk** derelict, frame, hull, shell,

shipwreck, wreck

**hull** *n* body, casing, covering, frame, framework, skeleton; husk, peel, pod, rind, shell, shuck, skin

**hum** buzz, drone, mumble, murmur, purr, sing, throb, thrum, vibrate, whir

**human** fleshly, manlike, mortal

**humane** benign, charitable, clement, compassionate, forbearing, forgiving, gentle, good, kind, lenient, merciful, mild, sympathetic, tender, understanding

**humanity** flesh, man, mankind, men, mortality, people

**humble** meek, modest, submissive, unostentatious; common, commonplace, insignificant, low, low-born, lowly, mean, modest, obscure, ordinary, poor, simple

**humbug** charlatan, cheat, fraud, impostor, phoney *or* phony *Inf*, quack, swindler, trickster; bluff,

**humdrum** *adj* commonplace, dull

**humid** *adj* moist, damp **humidifier** *n* device for increasing amount of water vapour in air in room etc. **humidity** *n*

**humiliate** *v* lower dignity of, abase, mortify **humiliation** *n*

**humility** *n* state of being humble; meekness

**hummock** *n* low knoll, hillock

**humour** *n* faculty of saying or perceiving what excites amusement; amusing speech, writing etc.; state of mind, mood *~v* gratify, indulge **humorist** *n* person who acts, speaks, writes humorously **humorous** *adj*

**hump** *n* normal or deforming lump, esp. on back *~v* make hump-shaped; *Sl* carry or heave

**humpback** *n* person with hump

**humus** *n* decayed vegetable and animal mould

**hunch** *n Inf* intuition; hump *~v* bend into hump **hunchback** *n* humpback

**hundred** *n/adj* cardinal number, ten times ten **hundredth** *adj* ordinal number **hundredweight** *n* weight of 112 lbs (50.8 kg), 20th part of ton

**hunger** *n/v* (have) discomfort from lack of food; (have) strong desire **hungrily** *adv* **hungry** *adj* having keen appetite

**hunk** *n* thick piece

**hunt** *v* seek out to kill or capture for sport or food; search (for) *~n* chase, search; (party organized for) hunting **hunter** *n*

**hurdle** *n* portable frame of bars for

——————— THESAURUS ———————

cheat, deceit, dodge, feint, fraud, hoax, ruse, sham, swindle, trick, trickery, wile

**humdrum** banal, boring, dreary, dull, ho-hum *Inf*, mind-numbing, mundane, ordinary, repetitious, routine, tedious, tiresome, unvaried

**humid** clammy, damp, dank, moist, muggy, steamy, sticky, sultry, wet

**humiliate** abase, bring low, chagrin, chasten, crush, debase, degrade, discomfit, disgrace, embarrass, humble, shame, subdue

**humility** diffidence, lowliness, meekness, modesty, servility, submissiveness

**humorist** card *Inf*, comedian, comic, droll, jester, joker, wag, wit

**humorous** amusing, comic, comical, entertaining, facetious, farcical, funny, hilarious, laughable, ludicrous, merry, playful, pleasant, witty

**humour** *n* amusement, comedy, drollery, facetiousness, fun, funniness, wit; comedy, farce, jesting, jests, jokes, joking, pleasantry, wit, wittiness; mood, spirits, temper *~v* accommodate, cosset, favour, flatter, gratify, indulge, mollify, pamper, pander to, spoil

**hump** bulge, bump, knob, mound, projection, swelling

**hunch** feeling, idea, impression, inkling, intuition, premonition, presentiment, suspicion

**hunger** *n* appetite, emptiness, famine, ravenousness, starvation, voracity; appetite, craving, desire, itch, lust, yearning *~v* crave, desire, hanker, itch, long, pine, starve, thirst, want, wish, yearn

**hungry** empty, famishing, hollow, ravenous, starved, starving, voracious

**hunk** block, chunk, lump, mass, piece, slab, wedge

temporary fences or for jumping over; obstacle ~v race over hurdles

**hurdy-gurdy** n mechanical musical instrument

**hurl** v throw violently

**hurly-burly** n loud confusion

**hurrah, hooray** interj exclamation of joy or applause

**hurricane** n very strong, violent wind or storm

**hurry** v hurrying, hurried (cause to) move or act in great haste ~n in undue haste; eagerness **hurriedly** adv

**hurt** v hurting, hurt injure, damage, give pain to; feel pain ~n wound, injury, harm **hurtful** adj

**hurtle** v rush violently

**husband** n married man ~v economize; use to best advantage **husbandry** n farming; economy

**hush** v make or be silent ~n stillness; quietness

**husk** n dry covering of certain seeds and fruits ~v remove husk from **husky** adj rough in tone;

hoarse, throaty

**husky** n Arctic sledge dog

**hussy** n cheeky young woman

**hustings** pl n political campaigning

**hustle** v push about, jostle, hurry ~n lively activity

**hut** n small house or shelter

**hutch** n cage for rabbits etc.

**hyacinth** n bulbous plant with bell-shaped flowers

**hybrid** n offspring of two plants or animals of different species ~adj crossbred

**hydrangea** n ornamental shrub

**hydrant** n water-pipe with nozzle for hose

**hydraulic** adj concerned with, operated by, pressure transmitted through liquid in pipe

**hydrochloric acid** strong colourless acid

**hydroelectric** adj pert. to generation of electricity by use of water

**hydrofoil** n fast, light vessel with

———— THESAURUS ————

**hunt** v chase, hound, pursue, stalk, track, trail; forage, look, scour, search, seek ~n chase, hunting, investigation, pursuit, quest, search

**hurdle** n barricade, barrier, block, fence, hedge, wall; barrier, block, difficulty, hindrance, impediment, obstacle, snag

**hurl** v cast, fire, fling, heave, launch, pitch, project, propel, send, shy, sling, throw, toss

**hurricane** cyclone, gale, storm, tempest, tornado, typhoon, windstorm

**hurry** v dash, fly, rush, scurry; accelerate, expedite, goad, hasten, hustle, push on, quicken, urge ~n bustle, celerity, commotion, dispatch, flurry, haste, quickness,

rush, speed, urgency

**hurt** v bruise, damage, disable, harm, impair, injure, mar, spoil, wound; afflict, aggrieve, annoy, distress, grieve, pain, sadden, sting, upset, wound; ache, be sore, burn, pain, smart, sting, throb ~n bruise, sore, wound; discomfort, distress, pain, pang, soreness, suffering

**hush** v mute, quieten, silence, still, suppress ~n calm, peace, quiet, silence, stillness, tranquillity

**husky** croaking, croaky, gruff, guttural, harsh, hoarse, rasping, raucous, rough, throaty

**hustle** bustle, crowd, elbow, force, haste, hasten, hurry, impel, jog, jostle, push, rush, shove, thrust

**hut** cabin, den, hovel, lean-to, ref-

hull raised out of water at speed

**hydrogen** *n* colourless gas which combines with oxygen to form water **hydrogen bomb** atom bomb of enormous power **hydrogen peroxide** colourless liquid used as antiseptic and bleach

**hydrophobia** *n* aversion to water, esp. as symptom of rabies

**hyena** *n* wild animal related to dog

**hygiene** *n* (study of) principles and practice of health and cleanliness **hygienic** *adj*

**hymen** *n* membrane partly covering vagina of virgin

**hymn** *n* song of praise, esp. to God ~*v* praise in song

**hype** *n* intensive publicity ~*v* publicize

**hyperbole** *n* rhetorical exaggeration

**hypermarket** *n* huge self-service store

**hypertension** *n* abnormally high blood pressure

**hyphen** *n* short line (-) indicating that two words or syllables are to be connected **hyphenate** *v* **hyphenated** *adj*

**hypnosis** *n* (*pl* **-ses**) induced state like deep sleep in which subject acts on external suggestion **hypnotic** *adj* **hypnotism** *n* **hypnotize** *v* affect with hypnosis

**hypochondria** *n* morbid depression without cause, about one's own health **hypochondriac** *adj/n*

**hypocrisy** *n* assuming of false appearance of virtue; insincerity **hypocrite** *n* **hypocritical** *adj*

**hypodermic** *adj* introduced, injected beneath the skin ~*n* hypodermic syringe or needle

**hypotenuse** *n* side of right-angled triangle opposite the right angle

**hypothermia** *n* condition of having body temperature reduced to dangerously low level

**hypothesis** *n* (*pl* **-eses**) suggested explanation of something; assumption as basis of reasoning **hypothetical** *adj*

**hysterectomy** *n* surgical operation for removing uterus

**hysteria** *n* mental disorder with emotional outbursts; fit of crying or laughing **hysterical** *adj* **hysterics** *pl n* fits of hysteria

———————— THESAURUS ————————

uge, shanty, shed, shelter

**hygiene** cleanliness, sanitation

**hygienic** aseptic, clean, germ-free, healthy, pure, sanitary, sterile

**hypnotic** mesmeric, mesmerizing, narcotic, sleep-inducing, soporific, spellbinding

**hypnotize** entrance, fascinate, magnetize, mesmerize, spellbind

**hypocrisy** cant, deceit, deception, dissembling, duplicity, falsity, insincerity, pharisaism, pretence, two-facedness

**hypocrite** charlatan, deceiver, dissembler, fraud, impostor, pharisee,

phoney *or* phony *Inf*, pretender

**hypocritical** deceitful, deceptive, duplicitous, false, fraudulent, hollow, insincere, phoney *or* phony *Inf*, sanctimonious, two-faced

**hypothesis** assumption, postulate, premise, proposition, theory, thesis

**hypothetical** academic, assumed, conjectural, imaginary, putative

**hysteria** agitation, delirium, frenzy, hysterics, madness, panic, unreason

**hysterical** berserk, convulsive, crazed, distracted, distraught, frantic, frenzied, mad, raving

# I i

**I** *pron* the pronoun of the first person singular

**ibis** *n* storklike bird

**ice** *n* frozen water; **ice cream** ~*v* cover, become covered with ice; cool with ice; cover with icing **icicle** *n* hanging spike of ice **icing** *n* mixture of sugar and water etc. used to decorate cakes **icy** *adj* covered with ice; cold; unfriendly **iceberg** *n* large floating mass of ice **ice cream** sweet creamy frozen dessert **ice hockey** team game played on ice with puck **ice skate** boot with steel blade for gliding over ice **ice-skate** *v*

**icon** *n* religious image **iconoclast** *n* one who attacks established ideas

**idea** *n* notion; conception; plan, aim **ideal** *n* idea of perfection; perfect person or thing ~*adj* perfect **idealism** *n* tendency to seek perfection in everything **idealist** *n* one who strives after the ideal; impractical person **idealistic** *adj* **idealization** *n* **idealize** *v* portray as ideal **ideally** *adv*

**identity** *n* individuality; state of being exactly alike **identical** *adj* very same **identifiable** *adj* **identification** *n* recognition; identifying document **identify** *v* identifying, identified establish identity of; associate (oneself) with; treat as identical

**ideology** *n* body of ideas, beliefs of group, nation etc. **ideological** *adj*

**idiom** *n* expression peculiar to a language or group **idiomatic** *adj*

**idiosyncrasy** *n* peculiarity of mind

**idiot** *n* mentally deficient person; stupid person **idiocy** *n* **idiotic** *adj* utterly stupid

--- THESAURUS ---

**icy** arctic, biting, bitter, chilly, cold, freezing, frosty, frozen over, ice-cold, parky *Brit inf*, raw

**idea** belief, conviction, doctrine, interpretation, notion, opinion, teaching, view, viewpoint; conception, conclusion, fancy, impression, judgment, perception, thought, understanding

**ideal** *n* archetype, criterion, epitome, example, exemplar, last word, model, paradigm, paragon, pattern, perfection, prototype, standard ~*adj* classic, complete, model, perfect, quintessential, supreme

**idealist** *n* romantic, visionary

**identical** alike, duplicate, equal, equivalent, indistinguishable, interchangeable, like, selfsame, the same, twin

**identification** cataloguing, labelling, naming, pinpointing, recognition; credentials, ID, identity card, papers

**identify** catalogue, classify, diagnose, label, make out, name, pick out, pinpoint, place, recognize, spot, tag

**identity** distinctiveness, existence, individuality, oneness, particularity, personality, self, selfhood, singularity, uniqueness

**idiocy** fatuity, fatuousness, foolishness, imbecility, insanity, lunacy

**idiom** expression, locution, phrase

**idiosyncrasy** characteristic, eccentricity, habit, mannerism, peculiarity, quirk, trick

**idiot** ass, berk *Brit sl*, cretin, dunderhead, fool, halfwit, imbecile,

**idle** *adj* unemployed; lazy; useless; groundless ~*v* be idle; run slowly in neutral gear **idleness** *n* **idler** *n* **idly** *adv*

**idol** *n* image worshipped as deity; object of excessive devotion **idolatry** *n* **idolize** *v* love or admire to excess

**idyll** *n* (poem describing) picturesque or charming scene or episode **idyllic** *adj* delightful

**i.e.** that is

**if** *conj* on condition or supposition that; whether; although

**igloo** *n* (*pl* **-loos**) domed house made of snow

**ignite** *v* (cause to) burn **ignition** *n* act of kindling or setting on fire; car's electrical firing system

**ignoble** *adj* mean, base; of low birth

**ignominy** *n* public disgrace; shameful act **ignominious** *adj*

**ignore** *v* disregard, leave out of account **ignoramus** *n* ignorant person **ignorance** *n* lack of knowledge **ignorant** *adj* lacking knowledge; uneducated

**iguana** *n* large tropical American lizard

**ill** *adj* not in good health; bad, evil; harmful ~*n* evil, harm ~*adv* badly; hardly **illness** *n* **ill-advised** *adj* imprudent **ill-disposed** *adj* unsympathetic **ill-fated** *adj* unfortunate **ill-gotten** *adj* obtained dishonestly **ill-treat** *v* treat cruelly **ill will** hostility **illegal** *adj* against the law

──────── THESAURUS ────────

jerk *Sl, chiefly US & Canad*, moron, nerd *or* nurd *Sl*, nitwit *Inf*, numskull *or* numbskull, prat *Sl*, simpleton, twit *Inf, chiefly Brit*, wally *Sl*

**idiotic** asinine, crackpot *Inf*, crazy, fatuous, foolish, halfwitted, imbecile, insane, lunatic, moronic, senseless, stupid

**idle** *adj* dead, empty, inactive, jobless, out of work, redundant, stationary, unemployed, unoccupied, unused, vacant; indolent, lazy, shiftless, slothful, sluggish ~*v* coast, drift, mark time, shirk, slack, slow down, vegetate

**idleness** inaction, inactivity, leisure, unemployment; lazing, loafing, pottering, time-wasting, trifling

**idol** deity, god, graven image, image, pagan symbol

**idolize** admire, adore, deify, dote upon, exalt, glorify, hero-worship, look up to, love, revere, venerate, worship

**ignite** burn, catch fire, fire, inflame, kindle, light, set fire to

**ignominious** abject, disgraceful, dishonourable, disreputable, humiliating, indecorous, inglorious, scandalous, shameful, sorry, undignified

**ignorance** benightedness, blindness, illiteracy, unenlightenment, unintelligence

**ignorant** benighted, blind to, inexperienced, innocent, oblivious, unaware, unconscious, unenlightened, uninformed, unknowing, unwitting; green, illiterate, naive, unaware, uneducated, unlettered, unread, untaught, untrained, untutored

**ignore** cold-shoulder, discount, disregard, neglect, overlook, pass over, reject

**ill** *adj* ailing, diseased, indisposed, infirm, off-colour, queasy, queer, sick, unwell; bad, damaging, evil, foul, harmful, injurious, ruinous,

**illegible** *adj* unable to be read

**illegitimate** *adj* born to unmarried parents; irregular **illegitimacy** *n*

**illicit** *adj* illegal; prohibited, forbidden

**illiterate** *adj* unable to read or write ~*n* illiterate person **illiteracy** *n*

**illogical** *adj* not logical

**illuminate** *v* light up; clarify; decorate with lights or colours **illumination** *n*

**illusion** *n* deceptive appearance or belief **illusionist** *n* conjuror **illusory** *adj*

**illustrate** *v* provide with pictures or examples; explain by examples **illustration** *n* picture, diagram; example

———— THESAURUS ————

unfortunate, unlucky, vile, wicked, wrong ~*n* abuse, badness, cruelty, damage, destruction, evil, malice, mischief, suffering, wickedness; affliction, hardship, harm, hurt, injury, misery, misfortune, pain, trial, tribulation, trouble, unpleasantness, woe ~*adv* badly, hard, poorly, unfavourably, unfortunately, unluckily

**ill-advised** foolish, impolitic, imprudent, inappropriate, incautious, indiscreet, misguided, overhasty, rash, reckless, unseemly, unwise

**illegal** banned, black-market, bootleg, criminal, felonious, forbidden, illicit, lawless, outlawed, prohibited, proscribed, unauthorized, unconstitutional, under-the-table, unlawful, unlicensed, unofficial, wrongful

**illegible** faint, indecipherable, obscure, scrawled, unreadable

**illegitimate** bastard, fatherless, natural; illegal, illicit, improper, unconstitutional, under-the-table, unlawful

**ill-fated** blighted, doomed, hapless, ill-omened, luckless, unfortunate, unhappy, unlucky

**illicit** bootleg, contraband, criminal, felonious, illegal, prohibited, unlawful, unlicensed; forbidden, furtive, guilty, immoral, improper, wrong

**illiterate** benighted, ignorant, uncultured, uneducated

**illness** affliction, ailment, attack, complaint, disability, disease, disorder, indisposition, infirmity, malady, malaise, poor health, sickness

**illogical** absurd, fallacious, faulty, inconsistent, incorrect, invalid, irrational, meaningless, senseless, specious, spurious, unreasonable, unsound

**ill-treat** abuse, damage, harass, harm, harry, injure, maltreat, mishandle, misuse, oppress, wrong

**illuminate** brighten, light, light up; clarify, clear up, elucidate, enlighten, explain, instruct, make clear

**illumination** awareness, clarification, enlightenment, perception, revelation, understanding

**illusion** chimera, daydream, fantasy, hallucination, mirage, mockery, phantasm, semblance

**illusory** apparent, beguiling, deceitful, delusive, fallacious, false, misleading, mistaken, sham, unreal, untrue

**illustrate** adorn, decorate, depict, draw, picture, sketch; bring home, clarify, demonstrate, elucidate, emphasize, exhibit, explain, interpret, show

**illustration** adornment, decoration, figure, picture, plate, sketch;

**illustrious** *adj* famous; glorious
**image** *n* likeness; optical counterpart; double; copy; general impression; word picture **imagery** *n* images collectively
**imagine** *v* picture to oneself; think; conjecture **imaginable** *adj* imaginary *adj* existing only in fantasy **imagination** *n* faculty of making mental images of things not present; fancy **imaginative** *adj*
**imbalance** *n* lack of balance in

emphasis or proportion
**imbecile** *n* idiot ~*adj* idiotic
**imbibe** *v* drink (in)
**imbue** *v* instil, fill
**imitate** *v* take as model; copy **imitation** *n* act of imitating; copy; counterfeit ~*adj* synthetic **imitative** *adj*
**immaculate** *adj* spotless; pure
**immaterial** *adj* unimportant; not consisting of matter
**immature** *adj* not fully developed; lacking wisdom because of youth

analogy, case, clarification, demonstration, elucidation, example, explanation, instance, specimen
**illustrious** brilliant, celebrated, distinguished, eminent, famous, glorious, great, noble, notable, noted, prominent, remarkable, renowned, signal, splendid
**ill will** acrimony, animosity, antagonism, antipathy, aversion, dislike, enmity, envy, grudge, hatred, hostility, malice, rancour, resentment, spite, unfriendliness, venom
**image** appearance, effigy, figure, icon, idol, likeness, picture, portrait, reflection, statue; conceit, concept, figure, idea, impression, perception
**imaginable** conceivable, credible, likely, plausible, possible, thinkable
**imaginary** assumed, dreamlike, fanciful, fictional, ideal, illusive, illusory, imagined, invented, legendary, made-up, mythological, nonexistent, shadowy, supposed, unreal, unsubstantial, visionary
**imagination** creativity, enterprise, fancy, ingenuity, insight, inspiration, inventiveness, originality, vision, wit
**imaginative** clever, creative, dreamy, enterprising, fanciful, in-
genious, inspired, inventive, original, poetical, visionary, vivid
**imagine** conceive, conjure up, create, devise, envisage, frame, invent, jerk, picture, plan, project, scheme, think of, think up, visualize
**imitate** affect, ape, burlesque, copy, counterfeit, duplicate, echo, emulate, follow, impersonate, mimic, mirror, mock, parody, personate, repeat, simulate
**imitation** *n* fake, forgery, impersonation, impression, mockery, parody, reflection, reproduction, sham, substitution, travesty; aping, copy, counterfeit, echoing, likeness, mimicry, resemblance, simulation ~*adj* artificial, dummy, ersatz, mock, reproduction, sham, simulated, synthetic
**immaculate** clean, impeccable, neat, spotless, spruce, squeaky-clean, trim; faultless, flawless, guiltless, impeccable, incorrupt, innocent, perfect, pure, sinless, squeaky-clean, stainless, unpolluted, unsullied, untarnished, virtuous
**immaterial** extraneous, impertinent, inapposite, inconsequential, inessential, insignificant, irrelevant, trifling, trivial, unimportant
**immature** adolescent, crude,

**immediate** *adj* occurring at once; closest **immediately** *adv*

**immense** *adj* huge, vast **immensely** *adv* **immensity** *n*

**immerse** *v* submerge in liquid; involve; engross **immersion** *n*

**immigrant** *n* settler in foreign country **immigration** *n*

**imminent** *adj* liable to happen soon **imminence** *n*

**immobile** *adj* unable to move **immobility** *n* **immobilize** *v*

**immolate** *v* kill, sacrifice

**immoral** *adj* corrupt; promiscuous

**immorality** *n*

**immortal** *adj* deathless; famed for all time ~*n* person living forever **immortality** *n* **immortalize** *v*

**immune** *adj* protected (against a disease etc.); exempt **immunity** *n*

**immunization** *n* process of making immune to disease **immunize** *v*

**imp** *n* little devil; mischievous child

**impact** *n* collision; profound effect **impacted** *adj* wedged

**impair** *v* weaken, damage **impairment** *n*

**impala** *n* S Afr. antelope

---

THESAURUS

---

green, premature, raw, undeveloped, unformed, unripe, unseasonable, untimely, young; callow, childish, inexperienced, infantile, jejune, juvenile, puerile

**immediate** instant, instantaneous; adjacent, close, direct, near, nearest, next, recent

**immediately** at once, directly, forthwith, instantly, now, posthaste, promptly, right away, this instant, unhesitatingly, without delay

**immense** colossal, enormous, extensive, giant, gigantic, great, huge, infinite, large, mammoth, massive, monumental, prodigious, titanic, tremendous, vast

**immigrant** incomer, newcomer, settler

**imminent** at hand, close, coming, forthcoming, gathering, impending, looming, menacing, near, threatening

**immobile** fixed, frozen, immovable, motionless, rigid, riveted, rooted, stable, static, stationary, stiff, still, unmoving

**immobilize** cripple, disable, freeze, halt, paralyse, stop, transfix

**immoral** abandoned, bad, corrupt, debauched, degenerate, depraved, evil, impure, indecent, sinful, unchaste, unethical, vile, wicked, wrong

**immorality** corruption, debauchery, depravity, dissoluteness, evil, licentiousness, profligacy, sin, vice, wickedness

**immortal** *adj* abiding, constant, deathless, endless, enduring, eternal, everlasting, indestructible, perennial, perpetual, timeless, undying, unfading ~*n* god, goddess; hero

**immortality** deathlessness, endlessness, eternity, perpetuity; celebrity, fame, glorification, greatness, renown

**immune** clear, exempt, free, invulnerable, proof (against), protected, resistant, safe, unaffected

**immunity** amnesty, charter, exemption, franchise, freedom, indemnity, liberty, prerogative, privilege, release, right

**immunize** inoculate, protect, safeguard, vaccinate

**impact** bang, blow, bump, collision, contact, crash, force, jolt, knock, shock, smash, stroke, thump

**impale** v pierce with sharp instrument

**impart** v communicate; give

**impartial** adj unbiased; fair **impartiality** n

**impassable** adj blocked

**impasse** n deadlock

**impassioned** adj full of feeling, ardent

**impassive** adj showing no emotion; calm

**impatient** adj irritable; restless **impatience** n

**impeach** v charge, esp. with treason or crime in office; denounce **impeachable** adj **impeachment** n

**impeccable** adj faultless

**impede** v hinder **impediment** n obstruction; defect

**impel** v -pelling, -pelled induce; drive

**impending** adj imminent

**imperative** adj necessary; peremptory; *Grammar* expressing command ~n *Grammar* imperative mood

**imperfect** adj having faults; not complete **imperfection** n

**imperial** adj of empire, or emperor; majestic; denoting weights and measures formerly official in Brit. **imperialism** n policy of acquiring empire

**imperil** v -illing, -illed endanger

——————————— THESAURUS ———————————

**impair** blunt, damage, deteriorate, diminish, enfeeble, harm, hinder, injure, lessen, mar, reduce, spoil, undermine, weaken, worsen

**impartial** detached, disinterested, equal, equitable, even-handed, fair, just, neutral, objective, open-minded, unbiased, unprejudiced

**impartiality** detachment, disinterest, dispassion, equality, equity, fairness, neutrality, objectivity

**impasse** deadlock, stalemate

**impassioned** ardent, blazing, excited, fervent, fiery, furious, glowing, heated, inflamed, inspired, intense, passionate, rousing, stirring, violent, vivid, warm

**impatient** abrupt, brusque, curt, demanding, edgy, hasty, intolerant, irritable, sudden, testy; eager, fretful, headlong, impetuous, restless

**impeach** accuse, arraign, blame, censure, charge, denounce, indict, tax

**impeccable** exact, exquisite, faultless, flawless, incorrupt, innocent, perfect, precise, pure, sinless,

stainless, unblemished

**impediment** bar, barrier, block, check, clog, curb, defect, difficulty, hindrance, obstacle, snag

**impel** drive, force, incite, induce, influence, instigate, motivate, move, oblige, power, prod, prompt, propel, push, require, spur, stimulate, urge

**impending** approaching, coming, gathering, imminent, looming, menacing, near, nearing, threatening, upcoming

**imperative** compulsory, crucial, essential, insistent, obligatory, pressing, urgent, vital

**imperfect** broken, damaged, defective, faulty, flawed, immature, impaired, incomplete, inexact, limited, partial, patchy, sketchy, unfinished

**imperfection** blemish, defect, deficiency, failing, fault, flaw, frailty, infirmity, shortcoming, stain, taint, weakness

**imperial** kingly, majestic, princely, queenly, regal, royal, sovereign

**imperious** *adj* domineering

**impersonal** *adj* objective

**impersonate** *v* pretend to be impersonation *n* impersonator *n*

**impertinent** *adj* insolent, rude impertinence *n*

**imperturbable** *adj* calm, not excitable

**impervious** *adj* impossible to penetrate; unaffected by

**impetigo** *n* contagious skin disease

**impetuous** *adj* rash impetuosity *n*

**impetus** *n* incentive; momentum

**impinge** *v* encroach (upon)

**impious** *adj* irreverent

**implacable** *adj* not to be placated

**implant** *v* insert firmly

**implement** *n* tool, instrument ~*v* carry out

**implore** *v* entreat earnestly

**imply** *v* implying, implied hint; mean implicate *v* involve implication *n* something implied implicit *adj* implied; absolute

**import** *v* bring in ~*n* thing imported; meaning importation *n* importer *n*

**important** *adj* of great consequence; eminent, powerful importance *n*

**imperil** endanger, expose, hazard, jeopardize, risk

**impersonal** cold, detached, dispassionate, formal, inhuman, neutral, remote

**impersonate** act, ape, enact, imitate, mimic, personate

**impetuous** ardent, eager, fierce, furious, hasty, headlong, impulsive, precipitate, rash, spontaneous, unplanned, unthinking, vehement, violent

**impetus** goad, impulse, incentive, push, spur, stimulus; energy, force, momentum, power

**implant** inculcate, infix, infuse, instil, sow

**implement** *n* apparatus, appliance, device, gadget, instrument, tool ~*v* bring about, carry out, complete, effect, enforce, execute, fulfil, perform, realize

**implicate** associate, compromise, concern, embroil, entangle, imply, include, incriminate, involve, mire

**implication** inference, innuendo, meaning, overtone, presumption, signification, suggestion

**implicit** contained, implied, inferred, inherent, latent, tacit, understood, unspoken

**implore** beg, beseech, crave, entreat, importune, plead with, pray, solicit, supplicate

**imply** connote, hint, insinuate, intimate, signify, suggest; betoken, denote, entail, evidence, import, include, indicate, involve, mean, point to, presuppose

**import** *v* bring in, introduce, land ~*n* bearing, drift, gist, implication, intention, meaning, message, purport, sense, significance, thrust

**importance** concern, consequence, import, interest, moment, significance, substance, value, weight; distinction, eminence, esteem, influence, mark, preeminence, prestige, prominence, standing, status, worth

**important** far-reaching, grave, large, material, momentous, primary, salient, serious, signal, significant, substantial, urgent, weighty; eminent, foremost, high-level, high-ranking, influential, leading, notable, noteworthy, outstanding,

**impose** v place (upon); take advantage (of) **imposing** adj impressive **imposition** n

**impossible** adj not possible; unreasonable **impossibility** n **impossibly** adv

**impostor** n one who assumes false identity

**impotent** adj powerless; (of males) incapable of sexual intercourse **impotence** n

**impound** v seize legally

**impoverish** v make poor or weak

**impractical** adj not sensible

**impregnable** adj proof against attack

**impregnate** v saturate; make pregnant

**impresario** n (pl **-ios**) organizer of public entertainment; manager of opera, ballet etc.

**impress** v affect deeply, usu. favourably; imprint, stamp **impression** n effect; notion, belief; imprint; comic impersonation **impressionable** adj susceptible **impressive** adj making deep impression

**imprint** n mark made by pressure ~v stamp; fix in mind

**imprison** v put in prison **imprisonment** n

**improbable** adj unlikely

───── THESAURUS ─────

powerful, pre-eminent, prominent, seminal

**impose** decree, establish, exact, fix, institute, introduce, lay, levy, ordain, place, promulgate, put, set

**imposing** august, commanding, dignified, effective, grand, impressive, majestic, stately, striking

**imposition** application, decree, laying on, levying, promulgation; encroachment, intrusion, liberty, presumption

**impossible** hopeless, impracticable, inconceivable, unattainable, unobtainable, unthinkable

**impostor** charlatan, cheat, deceiver, fake, fraud, hypocrite, phoney or phony *Inf*, pretender, quack, rogue, sham, trickster

**impotence** disability, feebleness, frailty, inability, inadequacy, incapacity, incompetence, ineffectiveness, infirmity, paralysis, powerlessness, uselessness, weakness

**impotent** disabled, feeble, frail, helpless, incapable, ineffective, infirm, nerveless, paralysed, powerless, unable, weak

**impoverish** bankrupt, beggar, break, ruin; deplete, diminish, drain, exhaust, reduce, sap

**impractical** impossible, unrealistic, unserviceable, unworkable, visionary, wild

**impress** affect, excite, influence, inspire, move, stir, strike, sway, touch

**impression** effect, feeling, impact, influence, reaction, sway; belief, concept, conviction, fancy, feeling, hunch, idea, memory, notion, opinion, sense, suspicion; imitation, impersonation, parody

**impressive** exciting, forcible, moving, powerful, stirring, striking, touching

**imprint** n impression, mark, print, sign, stamp ~v engrave, establish, etch, fix, impress, print, stamp

**imprison** confine, constrain, detain, immure, jail, lock up, put away

**imprisonment** confinement, custody, detention, duress, incarceration

**improbability** doubt, dubiety, un-

**impromptu** adv/adj without preparation ~*n* improvisation

**improper** adj indecent; incorrect **impropriety** *n*

**improve** *v* make or become better **improvement** *n*

**improvident** adj thriftless

**improvise** *v* make use of materials at hand; perform, speak without preparation **improvisation** *n*

**impudent** adj impertinent **impudence** *n*

**impugn** *v* call in question, challenge

**impulse** *n* sudden inclination to act; impetus **impulsive** adj rash

**impunity** *n* exemption from consequences

**impure** adj having unwanted substances mixed in; immoral, obscene **impurity** *n*

**impute** *v* attribute to **imputation** *n* reproach

**in** prep expresses inclusion within limits of space, time, circumstance, sphere etc. ~adv in or into some state, place etc.; **Inf** in vogue etc. ~adj **Inf** fashionable

**inability** *n* lack of means or skill to do something

**inaccurate** adj not correct **inaccuracy** *n*

————————— THESAURUS —————————

certainty, unlikelihood

**improbable** doubtful, dubious, fanciful, far-fetched, implausible, questionable, unbelievable, unlikely

**impromptu** ad-lib, extempore, improvised, offhand, spontaneous, unprepared, unrehearsed, unscripted

**improper** impolite, indecent, indecorous, indelicate, risqué, smutty, suggestive, unfitting, unseemly, untoward, vulgar; abnormal, false, inaccurate, incorrect, irregular, wrong

**impropriety** bad taste, indecency, vulgarity; bloomer Brit inf, blunder, faux pas, gaffe, gaucherie, mistake, slip, solecism

**improve** advance, amend, augment, better, correct, help, mend, polish, rectify, touch up, upgrade; develop, enhance, increase, pick up, progress, rally, reform, rise

**improvement** amelioration, amendment, betterment, correction, gain, rectification; advance, development, enhancement, increase, progress, rally, recovery, rise, upswing

**improvise** concoct, contrive, devise, make do; ad-lib, busk, extemporize, invent, vamp, wing it Inf

**impudent** audacious, bold, boldfaced, brazen, forward, impertinent, insolent, presumptuous, rude

**impulse** force, impetus, momentum, movement, pressure, push, stimulus, surge, thrust

**impulsive** emotional, hasty, headlong, impetuous, instinctive, intuitive, passionate, precipitate, quick, rash

**impure** adulterated, alloyed, debased, mixed, unrefined; contaminated, defiled, dirty, filthy, foul, infected, polluted, sullied, tainted, unclean

**impurity** adulteration, mixture; contamination, defilement, dirtiness, filth, foulness, infection, pollution, taint, uncleanness

**imputation** accusation, attribution, blame, censure, charge, insinuation, reproach, slander, slur

**inability** impotence, inadequacy, incapability, incapacity, incompe-

**inadequate** adj not enough; incapable **inadequacy** n

**inane** adj foolish

**inanimate** adj lifeless

**inappropriate** adj not suitable

**inarticulate** adj unable to express oneself clearly

**inaugurate** v initiate; admit to office **inaugural** adj **inauguration** n formal initiation (to office etc.)

**inauspicious** adj unlucky

**inborn** adj existing from birth

**incalculable** adj beyond calculation; very great

**incandescent** adj glowing; produced by glowing filament

**incantation** n magic spell

**incapable** adj helpless

**incapacitate** v disable; disqualify

**incarcerate** v imprison

**incarnate** adj in human form; typified **incarnation** n

**incendiary** adj designed to cause fires; inflammatory ~n fire-bomb

**incense¹** v enrage

**incense²** n gum, spice giving perfume when burned; its smoke

**incentive** n something that stimulates effort

**inception** n beginning

**incessant** adj unceasing

**incest** n sexual intercourse between close relatives **incestuous** adj

**inch** n one twelfth of a foot, or 0.0254 metre ~v move very slowly

**incident** n event or occurrence;

———————— THESAURUS ————————

tence, ineptitude, powerlessness

**inaccurate** careless, defective, faulty, imprecise, incorrect, in error, inexact, mistaken , out, unfaithful, unreliable, unsound, wild, wrong

**inadequate** defective, deficient, faulty, imperfect, incomplete, insubstantial, insufficient, meagre, niggardly, scant, scanty, short, sketchy, skimpy, sparse; inapt, incapable, incompetent, unequal, unfitted, unqualified

**inane** empty, fatuous, frivolous, futile, idiotic, mindless, puerile, senseless, silly, stupid, trifling, vacuous, vain, vapid, worthless

**inanimate** cold, dead, defunct, extinct, inactive, inert, lifeless, quiescent, soulless, spiritless

**inappropriate** ill-suited, ill-timed, improper, incongruous, malapropos, tasteless, unbecoming, unbefitting, unfit, unfitting, unseemly, unsuitable, untimely

**inarticulate** faltering, halting,

hesitant, poorly spoken

**inaugurate** begin, commence, initiate, institute, introduce, launch, originate, set in motion, set up; induct, install, instate, invest

**inauguration** initiation, institution, launch, launching, opening

**incalculable** boundless, countless, enormous, immense, inestimable, infinite, limitless, measureless, numberless, untold, vast

**incapable** feeble, incompetent, ineffective, inept, insufficient, unfit, unfitted, unqualified, weak

**incapacitate** cripple, disable, disqualify, immobilize, paralyse, prostrate

**incentive** bait, encouragement, goad, impetus, impulse, inducement, lure, motivation, motive, spur, stimulus

**incessant** ceaseless, constant, continuous, endless, eternal, everlasting, interminable, perpetual, persistent, relentless, unending, unrelenting, unremitting

public disturbance **incidence** n extent or frequency of occurrence **incidental** adj occurring as a minor, inevitable, or chance accompaniment **incidentally** adv by chance; by the way **incidentals** pl n accompanying items

**incinerate** v burn up completely **incinerator** n

**incipient** adj beginning

**incise** v cut into **incision** n **incisive** adj sharp **incisor** n cutting tooth

**incite** v urge, stir up

**inclement** adj severe

**incline** v lean, slope; (cause to) be disposed ~n slope **inclination** n liking, tendency; degree of deviation

**include** v have as (part of) contents; add in **inclusion** n **inclusive** adj including (everything)

**incognito** adv/adj under an assumed identity ~n (pl -tos) assumed identity

**incoherent** adj lacking clarity; inarticulate **incoherence** n

**income** n money received from salary, investments etc.

**incoming** adj coming in; about to come into office; next

**incomparable** adj beyond comparison

**incompatible** adj inconsistent, conflicting

**incompetent** adj lacking neces-

**incident** adventure, circumstance, episode, event, fact, happening, matter, occurrence; brush, clash, commotion, mishap, scene, skirmish

**incidental** accidental, casual, chance, fortuitous, odd, random

**incipient** beginning, developing, embryonic, inceptive, inchoate, starting

**incision** cut, gash, slash, slit

**incisive** acute, keen, piercing, sharp, trenchant

**incite** animate, drive, egg on, encourage, excite, goad, impel, inflame, instigate, prod, prompt, provoke, rouse, spur, stimulate, urge

**inclement** bitter, boisterous, foul, harsh, intemperate, rigorous, rough, severe, stormy, tempestuous

**inclination** affection, aptitude, bent, bias, desire, disposition, fancy, fondness, leaning, liking, partiality, penchant, predilection, proclivity, propensity, stomach, taste, tendency, turn, wish

**incline** v bend, bevel, cant, deviate,

diverge, heel, lean, slant, slope, tend, tilt, tip, veer; be disposed, bias, influence, persuade, prejudice, sway, tend, turn ~n ascent, descent, dip, grade, gradient, ramp, rise, slope

**include** comprehend, comprise, contain, cover, embody, embrace, encompass, incorporate, involve, take in

**inclusion** incorporation, insertion

**inclusive** all in, all together, blanket, comprehensive, full, general, overall, sweeping, umbrella

**incoherent** confused, disjointed, inarticulate, inconsistent, loose, muddled, rambling, uncoordinated, unintelligible, wandering, wild

**income** earnings, gains, interest, means, pay, proceeds, profits, receipts, revenue, salary, takings, wages

**incomparable** inimitable, matchless, paramount, peerless, superlative, supreme, unequalled, unmatched, unrivalled

**incompatible** antipathetic, con-

sary ability **incompetence** n

**inconceivable** adj impossible to imagine

**inconclusive** adj not giving a final decision

**incongruous** adj not appropriate **incongruity** n

**inconsequential** adj trivial; haphazard

**incontinent** adj not able to control bladder or bowels

**incontrovertible** adj undeniable

**inconvenience** n trouble, difficulty **inconvenient** adj

**incorporate** v include; form into corporation

**incorrigible** adj beyond correction or reform

**increase** v make or become greater in size, number etc. ~n growth, enlargement **increasingly** adv more and more

**incredible** adj unbelievable; Inf amazing **incredibly** adv

**incredulous** adj unbelieving **incredulity** n

**increment** n increase

**incriminate** v imply guilt of

———————————— THESAURUS ————————————

flicting, contradictory, discordant, disparate, incongruous, inconsistent, mismatched, uncongenial, unsuitable

**incompetent** cowboy Inf, incapable, ineffectual, inept, inexpert, insufficient, unable, unfit, unfitted, unskilful, useless

**inconceivable** impossible, incredible, unbelievable, unheard-of, unimaginable, unknowable, unthinkable

**inconclusive** ambiguous, indecisive, indeterminate, open, uncertain, undecided, unsettled, vague

**incongruous** absurd, conflicting, contradictory, contrary, discordant, extraneous, improper, inapt, incoherent, inconsistent, unbecoming, unsuitable, unsuited

**inconvenience** n annoyance, awkwardness, bother, difficulty, disadvantage, disruption, disturbance, drawback, fuss, hassle Inf, hindrance, nuisance, trouble, uneasiness, upset

**inconvenient** annoying, awkward, bothersome, disturbing, embarrassing, inopportune, tiresome, troublesome, unsuitable, untimely

**incorporate** absorb, amalgamate, assimilate, blend, coalesce, combine, consolidate, embody, fuse, include, integrate, meld, merge, mix, unite

**incorrigible** hardened, hopeless, incurable, intractable, inveterate

**increase** v add to, advance, amplify, augment, boost, build up, develop, dilate, enhance, enlarge, escalate, expand, extend, grow, heighten, inflate, intensify, magnify, mount, multiply, proliferate, prolong, raise, spread, strengthen, swell ~n addition, boost, development, enlargement, escalation, expansion, extension, gain, growth, increment, intensification, rise, upsurge, upturn

**incredible** absurd, beyond belief, far-fetched, implausible, impossible, improbable, inconceivable, preposterous, unbelievable, unimaginable, unthinkable

**incredulous** disbelieving, doubtful, doubting, dubious, sceptical, suspicious, unbelieving

**incriminate** accuse, arraign, blame, charge, impeach, implicate, indict, involve

**incubate** v provide eggs, bacteria etc. with heat for development; develop in this way **incubation** n **incubator** n apparatus for hatching eggs or rearing premature babies

**inculcate** v fix in the mind

**incumbent** adj not subject to others; self-reliant; free; valid in itself **independence** n being independent; self-reliance; self-support

**indescribable** adj beyond description

**incur** v -curring, -curred bring upon oneself **incursion** n invasion

**indebted** adj owing gratitude or money

**indecent** adj offensive; unseemly

**indeed** adv really; in fact ~interj denoting surprise, doubt etc.

**indefatigable** adj untiring

**indefensible** adj not justifiable

**indefinite** adj without exact limits

**indelible** adj that cannot be blotted out **indelibly** adv

**indelicate** adj coarse, embarrassing

**indemnity** n compensation; security against loss **indemnify** v **indemnifying, indemnified** give indemnity to

**indent** v set in (from margin etc.); notch; order by indent ~n notch; requisition **indentation** n

**independent** adj not subject to others; self-reliant; free; valid in itself **independence** n being independent; self-reliance; self-support

**indescribable** adj beyond description

**indeterminate** adj uncertain

**index** n (pl indexes, indices) alphabetical list of references; indicator; Maths exponent; forefinger ~v provide with, insert in index

**indicate** v point out; state briefly; signify **indication** n **indicative** adj pointing to; Grammar stating fact **indicator** n

**indict** v accuse, esp. by legal pro-

**incur** arouse, contract, draw, earn, gain, induce, meet with, provoke

**indebted** beholden, grateful, obligated, obliged

**indecent** blue, coarse, crude, dirty, filthy, foul, gross, improper, impure, indelicate, lewd, licentious, pornographic, salacious, scatological, smutty, vile

**indeed** actually, certainly, doubtlessly, positively, really, strictly, truly, undeniably, undoubtedly, veritably

**indefensible** inexcusable, unforgivable, unpardonable, wrong

**indefinite** confused, doubtful, equivocal, evasive, general, imprecise, indeterminate, indistinct, inexact, loose, obscure, uncertain, unclear, undetermined, unfixed, unknown, unlimited, unsettled, vague

**indelible** enduring, indestructible, ineffaceable, ineradicable, permanent

**indelicate** blue, coarse, crude, embarrassing, gross, immodest, improper, indecent, low, obscene, off-colour, offensive, risqué, rude, suggestive, tasteless, vulgar

**independence** autarchy, autonomy, freedom, home rule, liberty, self-government, self-rule, sovereignty

**independent** absolute, free, liberated, separate, unconnected, uncontrolled, unrelated

**indescribable** ineffable, inexpressible, unutterable

**index** director, forefinger, hand, indicator, needle, pointer

**indicate** betoken, denote, evince, imply, manifest, point to, reveal, show, signify, suggest

cess **indictment** n

**indifferent** adj uninterested; mediocre **indifference** n

**indigenous** adj native

**indigent** adj poor, needy

**indigestion** n (discomfort caused by) poor digestion

**indignant** adj angered by injury or injustice **indignation** n **indignity** n humiliation, insult, slight

**indigo** n (pl **-gos**) blue dye obtained from plant; the plant ~adj deep blue

**indirect** adj done, caused by someone or something else; not by straight route

**indiscreet** adj tactless in revealing

secrets **indiscretion** n

**indiscriminate** adj lacking discrimination; jumbled

**indispensable** adj essential

**indisposed** adj unwell; disinclined

**indisputable** adj without doubt

**indissoluble** adj permanent

**individual** adj single; distinctive ~n single person or thing **individuality** n distinctive personality **individually** adv singly

**indoctrinate** v implant beliefs in the mind of

**indolent** adj lazy **indolence** n

**indoor** adj within doors; under cover **indoors** adv

**indubitable** adj beyond doubt

———— THESAURUS ————

**indication** clue, evidence, explanation, hint, index, manifestation, mark, note, omen, portent, sign, signal, symptom, warning

**indicator** display, gauge, guide, index, mark, marker, meter, pointer, sign, signal, signpost, symbol

**indictment** accusation, allegation, charge, impeachment, prosecution, summons

**indifferent** aloof, apathetic, callous, careless, cold, cool, detached, distant, heedless, inattentive, regardless, unconcerned, unimpressed, unresponsive; average, fair, mediocre, middling, moderate, ordinary, passable, perfunctory, undistinguished, uninspired

**indignant** angry, annoyed, disgruntled, exasperated, furious, heated, incensed, irate, resentful, riled, scornful, wrathful

**indignation** anger, fury, rage, resentment, scorn, umbrage, wrath

**indirect** circuitous, crooked, devious, meandering, oblique, rambling, roundabout, tortuous, wan-

dering, winding, zigzag

**indiscreet** foolish, hasty, illadvised, ill-considered, ill-judged, imprudent, naive, rash, reckless, tactless, unwise

**indiscriminate** aimless, careless, desultory, general, random, sweeping, wholesale

**indispensable** crucial, essential, imperative, key, necessary, needed, needful, requisite, vital

**indisposed** ailing, ill, sick, unwell

**indisputable** absolute, beyond doubt, certain, evident, incontrovertible, positive, sure, undeniable

**individual** adj characteristic, discrete, distinct, exclusive, identical, own, particular, peculiar, personal, proper, respective, separate, several, single, singular, special, specific, unique ~n being, character, creature, mortal, party, person, soul, type, unit

**individuality** character, distinction, originality, uniqueness

**indubitable** certain, evident, incontrovertible, indisputable, obvi-

**induce** v persuade; bring on **inducement** n incentive

**induct** v install in office **induction** n inducting; general inference from particular inferences; production of electric or magnetic state by proximity

**indulge** v gratify; pamper **indulgence** n indulging; extravagance; favour, privilege **indulgent** adj

**industry** n manufacture, processing etc. of goods; branch of this; diligence **industrial** adj of industries, trades **industrialize** v **industrious** adj diligent

**inebriated** adj drunk

**inedible** adj not eatable

**ineffable** adj unutterable

**ineligible** adj not fit or qualified (for something)

**inept** adj absurd; out of place; clumsy **ineptitude** n

**inert** adj without power of motion; sluggish; unreactive **inertia** n inactivity; tendency to continue at rest or in uniform motion

**inescapable** adj unavoidable

**inestimable** adj immeasurable

**inevitable** adj unavoidable; sure to happen **inevitability** n

**inexorable** adj relentless

**inexplicable** adj impossible to explain

**infallible** adj not liable to fail or err

**infamous** adj notorious; shocking **infamy** n

ous, sure, undeniable

**induce** actuate, convince, draw, encourage, get, impel, incite, influence, move, persuade, press, prompt

**inducement** attraction, bait, cause, consideration, encouragement, impulse, incentive, incitement, influence, lure, motive, reward, spur, stimulus, urge

**indulge** cater to, feed, give way to, gratify, pander to, regale, satiate, satisfy, yield to

**indulgence** excess, fondness, intemperance, kindness, leniency, partiality, profligacy, spoiling

**indulgent** compliant, easy-going, favourable, fond, forbearing, gentle, kind, lenient, liberal, mild, permissive, tender, tolerant

**industrious** active, busy, diligent, energetic, hard-working, productive, tireless

**industry** business, commerce, manufacturing, production, trade; activity, application, assiduity, de-

termination, diligence, effort, labour, perseverance, persistence, toil, vigour, zeal

**ineligible** disqualified, ruled out, unacceptable, undesirable, unfit, unqualified, unsuitable

**inept** awkward, bungling, clumsy, gauche, maladroit, unskilful

**inert** dead, dormant, dull, idle, immobile, inactive, inanimate, leaden, lifeless, motionless, passive, quiescent, slack, sluggish, static, still, torpid, unresponsive

**inertia** apathy, deadness, drowsiness, dullness, idleness, immobility, laziness, lethargy, listlessness, passivity, sloth, stillness, stupor, torpor

**inescapable** certain, destined, fated, inevitable, inexorable, sure

**inevitable** assured, certain, decreed, destined, fixed, necessary, ordained, settled, sure, unavoidable

**inexplicable** baffling, enigmatic, inscrutable, insoluble, mysterious, strange, unaccountable

**infallible** faultless, impeccable,

**infant** *n* very young child **infancy** *n* babyhood; early stage of development **infantile** *adj* childish

**infantry** *n* foot soldiers

**infatuated** *adj* foolishly enamoured **infatuation** *n*

**infect** *v* affect (with disease); contaminate **infection** *n* **infectious** *adj* catching

**infer** *v* -ferring, -ferred deduce, conclude **inference** *n*

**inferior** *adj* of poor quality; lower ~**n** one lower (in rank etc.) **inferiority** *n*

**infernal** *adj* devilish; hellish; *Inf* irritating, confounded

**inferno** *n* (*pl* -nos) intense, raging fire; hell

**infertile** *adj* barren, not productive

**infest** *v* inhabit or overrun in dangerously or unpleasantly large numbers

**infidelity** *n* unfaithfulness; religious disbelief **infidel** *n* unbeliever

**infiltrate** *v* trickle through; gain access surreptitiously

**infinite** *adj* boundless **infinitely** *adv* exceedingly **infinitesimal** *adj* extremely small **infinity** *n* unlimited extent

**infinitive** *n* form of verb without tense, person, or number

**infirm** *adj* physically or mentally weak; **infirmary** *n* hospital; sick

——————— THESAURUS ———————

perfect, unerring

**infamous** base, disgraceful, dishonourable, heinous, ignominious, loathsome, monstrous, nefarious, notorious, odious, outrageous, scandalous, shameful, shocking, villainous, wicked

**infancy** babyhood, early childhood; beginnings, cradle, dawn, early stages, emergence, inception, origins, outset, start

**infant** *n* baby, child, toddler, tot

**infantile** babyish, childish, immature, puerile, tender, weak, young

**infatuated** beguiled, besotted, bewitched, captivated, enraptured, fascinated, inflamed, intoxicated, obsessed, possessed, spellbound

**infect** blight, contaminate, corrupt, defile, influence, poison, pollute, taint, touch

**infection** contagion, contamination, corruption, poison, pollution

**infectious** catching, communicable, contagious, contaminating, corrupting, infective, pestilential,

poisoning, virulent

**infer** conclude, conjecture, deduce, derive, gather, presume, understand

**inference** assumption, conclusion, conjecture, consequence, corollary, deduction, presumption, surmise

**inferior** junior, lesser, lower, menial, minor, secondary, subordinate, subsidiary, underneath

**inferiority** imperfection, inadequacy, meanness, mediocrity, shoddiness

**infertile** barren, sterile, unfruitful

**infest** beset, flood, invade, overrun, ravage, swarm, throng

**infiltrate** creep in, penetrate, percolate, permeate, pervade

**infinite** *adj* absolute, all-embracing, boundless, eternal, immense, inestimable, inexhaustible, interminable, limitless, measureless, numberless, perpetual, total, unbounded, uncounted, untold, vast, wide, without end

**infinity** boundlessness, endlessness, eternity, immensity, vastness

quarters **infirmity** n

**inflame** v rouse to anger, excitement; cause inflammation in **inflammable** adj easily set on fire; excitable **inflammation** n painful infected swelling **inflammatory** adj

**inflate** v blow up with air, gas; swell; raise price, esp. artificially **inflatable** adj **inflation** n increase in prices and fall in value of money

**inflection**, **inflexion** n modification of word; modulation of voice

**inflexible** adj incapable of being bent; stubborn

**inflict** v impose, deliver forcibly **infliction** n

**influence** n power to affect other people, events etc.; person, thing possessing such power ~v sway; induce; affect **influential** adj

**influenza** n contagious viral disease

**influx** n flowing in; inflow

**inform** v give information (about) **informant** n one who tells **information** n what is told, knowledge **informative** adj **informer** n

**informal** adj relaxed and friendly; appropriate for everyday use **informally** adv **informality** n

**infrared** adj below visible spectrum

**infrastructure** n basic structure or fixed capital items of an organization or economic system

**infringe** v transgress, break

**infuriate** v enrage

——————— THESAURUS ———————

**infirm** decrepit, doddering, doddery, failing, feeble, frail, lame, weak

**inflame** anger, arouse, enrage, excite, fire, heat, ignite, incense, infuriate, kindle, madden, provoke, rile, rouse, stimulate

**inflammable** combustible, flammable, incendiary

**inflate** amplify, balloon, blow up, boost, dilate, distend, enlarge, escalate, exaggerate, expand, increase, swell

**inflation** blowing up, distension, enlargement, escalation, expansion, increase, rise, spread, swelling

**inflection** accentuation, intonation, modulation; *Grammar* conjugation, declension

**inflexible** adamant, firm, fixed, immovable, implacable, intractable, obdurate, relentless, resolute, rigorous, set, steadfast, strict, stringent, stubborn

**inflict** apply, deliver, exact, impose, levy, visit, wreak

**influence** n agency, authority, control, credit, direction, domination, effect, guidance, mastery, power, pressure, rule, spell, sway, weight ~v affect, arouse, control, count, direct, dispose, guide, impel, impress, induce, instigate, manipulate, modify, move, persuade, predispose, prompt, rouse, sway

**inform** acquaint, advise, apprise, communicate, enlighten, instruct, notify, teach, tell, tip off

**informal** casual, easy, familiar, natural, relaxed, simple

**information** advice, counsel, data, facts, instruction, intelligence, knowledge, latest *Inf.*, material, message, news, notice, report, tidings, word

**informer** accuser, betrayer, sneak, stool pigeon

**infringe** break, contravene, disobey, transgress, violate

**infuriate** anger, enrage, exasperate, gall, incense, irritate, madden, provoke, rile

**infuse** v soak to extract flavour etc.; instil **infusion** n infusing; extract obtained

**ingenious** adj clever at contriving; cleverly contrived **ingenuity** n

**ingenuous** adj frank; innocent

**ingot** n block of cast metal, esp. gold

**ingrained** adj deep-rooted; inveterate

**ingratiate** v get (oneself) into favour

**ingredient** n component part of a mixture

**inhabit** v dwell in **inhabitant** n

**inhale** v breathe in (air etc.) **inhalation** n **inhaler** n container with medical preparation inhaled to help breathing

**inherent** adj existing as an inseparable part

**inherit** v receive, succeed as heir;

derive from parents **inheritance** n

**inhibit** v restrain; hinder **inhibition** n repression of emotion, instinct

**inhospitable** adj unfriendly; harsh

**inhuman** adj cruel, brutal; not human

**inhumane** adj cruel, brutal **inhumanity** n

**inimical** adj unfavourable, hostile

**inimitable** adj defying imitation

**iniquity** n gross injustice; sin **iniquitous** adj

**initial** adj of, occurring at the beginning ~n initial letter, esp. of person's name ~v -tialling, -tialled mark, sign with one's initials **initially** adv

**initiate** v originate; admit into closed society; instruct **initiation** n

**initiative** n lead; ability to act independently

**inject** v put (fluid, medicine etc.)

———————————— THESAURUS ————————————

**ingenious** adroit, bright, brilliant, clever, crafty, creative, dexterous, fertile, inventive, masterly, original, ready, resourceful, shrewd, skilful, subtle

**ingenuous** artless, candid, childlike, frank, honest, innocent, naive, open, plain, simple, sincere, trustful, unsophisticated

**ingredient** component, constituent, element, part

**inhabit** abide, dwell, live, lodge, occupy, people, populate, possess, reside, tenant

**inhabitant** citizen, denizen, inmate, native, occupant, occupier, resident, tenant

**inherit** accede to, be left, fall heir to, succeed to

**inheritance** bequest, birthright, heritage, legacy, patrimony

**inhibit** arrest, bar, bridle, check,

constrain, curb, debar, discourage, forbid, frustrate, hinder, impede, obstruct, prevent, restrain, stop

**inhibition** bar, check, embargo, hindrance, interdict, obstacle, prohibition, reserve, restraint, restriction, reticence, shyness

**inhospitable** unfriendly, ungenerous, unwelcoming; bare, barren, bleak, desolate, empty, godforsaken, harsh, hostile, lonely

**inhuman** animal, barbaric, bestial, brutal, cruel, heartless, merciless, pitiless, ruthless, savage, unfeeling, vicious

**inhumane** brutal, cruel, heartless, pitiless, unfeeling, unkind

**initial** adj beginning, early, first, inaugural, introductory, opening, primary

**initially** at first, at or in the beginning, first, firstly, originally,

into body with syringe; introduce (new element) **injection** *n*

**injunction** *n* (judicial) order

**injury** *n* physical damage; wrong **injure** *v* do harm or damage to

**injustice** *n* want of justice; wrong; unjust act

**ink** *n* fluid used for writing or printing ~*v* mark, cover with ink **inky** *adj*

**inkling** *n* hint, vague idea

**inland** *adj/adv* in, towards the interior; away from the sea

**in-law** *n* relative by marriage

**inlay** *v* **inlaying, inlaid** embed; decorate with inset pattern ~*n* inlaid piece or pattern

**inlet** *n* entrance; mouth of creek; piece inserted

**inmate** *n* occupant, esp. of prison, hospital, etc.

**inmost** *adj* most inward, deepest

**inn** *n* public house providing food and accommodation; hotel **innkeeper** *n*

**innards** *pl n Inf* internal parts, esp. of body

**innate** *adj* inborn; inherent

**inner** *adj* lying within **innermost** *adj*

**innings** *n Sport* player's or side's turn of batting; turn

**innocent** *adj* guiltless; without experience of evil ~*n* innocent person **innocence** *n*

**innocuous** *adj* harmless

**innovate** *v* introduce new things **innovation** *n*

**innuendo** *n* (*pl* -**does**) indirect accusation

**innumerable** *adj* countless

——— THESAURUS ———

primarily

**initiate** begin, break the ice, inaugurate, institute, kick-start, launch, open, originate, pioneer, start; indoctrinate, induct, instate, instruct, introduce, invest, teach, train

**initiative** advantage, beginning, first move, first step, lead

**inject** inoculate, vaccinate; infuse, insert, instil, interject, introduce

**injunction** command, dictate, mandate, order, precept, ruling

**injure** abuse, blemish, blight, break, damage, deface, disable, harm, hurt, impair, maltreat, mar, ruin, spoil, tarnish, undermine, weaken, wound

**injury** abuse, damage, evil, grievance, harm, hurt, ill, injustice, mischief, ruin, wound, wrong

**injustice** bias, favouritism, inequality, oppression, partiality, partisanship, prejudice, unfairness,

unlawfulness, wrong

**inland** interior, internal, upcountry

**inlet** arm (of the sea), bay, bight, cove, creek, entrance

**inmost** basic, buried, central, deep, deepest, essential, intimate, personal, private, secret

**innate** congenital, essential, inborn, inbred, inherent, instinctive, intrinsic, intuitive, native, natural

**inner** central, essential, inside, interior, internal, intestinal, inward, middle

**innocence** blamelessness, faultlessness, guiltlessness, righteousness; artlessness, gullibility, naïveté, simplicity

**innocent** blameless, clear, faultless, guiltless, honest; artless, childlike, credulous, frank, guileless, gullible, ingenuous, naive, open, simple

**innovation** change, departure, introduction, novelty, variation

**inoculate** v immunize by injecting vaccine **inoculation** n

**inoperable** adj Med not able to be operated on **inoperative** adj not operative

**inordinate** adj excessive

**inorganic** adj not organic; not containing carbon

**input** n material, data, current etc. fed into a system

**inquest** n coroner's inquiry into cause of death; detailed inquiry

**inquire, enquire** v seek information **inquirer, enquirer** n **inquiry, enquiry** n question; investigation

**inquisition** n searching investigation; Hist (with cap.) tribunal for suppression of heresy **inquisitor** n

**inquisitive** adj curious; prying

**insane** adj mentally deranged; crazy **insanely** adv madly; excessively

**insanity** n

**insatiable** adj incapable of being satisfied

**inscribe** v write, engrave (in or on something) **inscription** n words inscribed

**inscrutable** adj enigmatic; incomprehensible

**insect** n small, usu. winged animal with six legs **insecticide** n preparation for killing insects

**insecure** adj not safe or firm; anxious

**inseminate** v implant semen into

**insensible** adj unconscious; without feeling; not aware **insensibly** adv imperceptibly

**insensitive** adj unaware of other people's feelings

**insert** v put into or between ~n something inserted **insertion** n

——————————— THESAURUS ———————————

**innuendo** aspersion, hint, implication, insinuation, suggestion, whisper

**innumerable** countless, incalculable, infinite, many, myriad, untold

**inordinate** excessive, exorbitant, extravagant, unreasonable

**inquest** inquiry, inquisition, investigation, probe

**inquire** examine, explore, inspect, investigate, make inquiries, probe, scrutinize, search

**inquisition** cross-examination, examination, inquest, inquiry, investigation, question

**inquisitive** curious, inquiring, intrusive, peering, probing, prying, questioning

**insane** barking mad Sl, crackpot Inf, crazed, crazy, demented, deranged, mad, unhinged

**insanity** dementia, frenzy, mad-

ness, mental illness

**insatiable** greedy, intemperate, rapacious, ravenous, voracious

**inscribe** address, dedicate, write; carve, cut, engrave, etch, impress, imprint

**inscription** dedication, engraving, label, legend, lettering, saying, words

**inscrutable** blank, deadpan, enigmatic; hidden, incomprehensible, mysterious, unintelligible

**insecure** flimsy, frail, insubstantial, loose, precarious, rickety, rocky, shaky, unreliable, unsound, unstable, unsteady, weak; afraid, anxious, uncertain, unsure

**insensible** dull, inert, numbed, stupid, torpid

**insensitive** callous, crass, indifferent, obtuse, tactless, thick-skinned, unfeeling

**insert** enter, interpolate, interpose,

**inset** n something extra inserted **in-set** v -setting, -set

**inshore** adv/adj near shore

**inside** n inner part; pl Inf stomach, entrails ~adj/adv/prep in, on, into the inside

**insidious** adj unseen but deadly

**insight** n discernment

**insignia** pl n badges, emblems

**insignificant** adj not important **insignificance** n

**insincere** adj pretending what one does not feel **insincerity** n

**insinuate** v hint; introduce subtly **insinuation** n

**insipid** adj dull, tasteless

**insist** v demand persistently; maintain; emphasize **insistence** n **insistent** adj

**insole** n inner sole of shoe or boot

**insolent** adj impudent **insolence** n

**insoluble** adj incapable of being solved; incapable of being dissolved

**insolvent** adj unable to pay one's debts **insolvency** n

**insomnia** n inability to sleep **insomniac** adj/n

**inspect** v examine (closely or officially) **inspection** n **inspector** n

**inspire** v arouse creatively; give rise

——————— THESAURUS ———————

introduce, place, put, set, stick in, tuck in

**insertion** addition, implant, inclusion, inset, introduction

**inside** n contents, inner part, interior; (oft. pl) Inf belly, bowels, entrails, guts, guts, stomach ~adj inner, innermost, interior, internal, inward ~adv indoors, under cover, within

**insidious** artful, crafty, cunning, deceptive, duplicitous, slick, sly, smooth, stealthy, subtle, tricky, wily

**insight** awareness, discernment, intuition, judgment, observation, perception, understanding, vision

**insignia** badge, crest, emblem, ensign, symbol

**insignificant** flimsy, irrelevant, meaningless, minor, negligible, paltry, petty, scanty, trifling, trivial, unimportant

**insincere** devious, dishonest, double-dealing, duplicitous, evasive, false, hollow, hypocritical, lying, two-faced, untruthful, untrue

**insinuate** allude, hint, imply, indicate, intimate, suggest; infiltrate,

infuse, inject, instil, introduce

**insinuation** allusion, aspersion, hint, implication, innuendo, slur, suggestion

**insist** be firm, demand, persist, require; aver, claim, contend, hold, maintain, reiterate, repeat, swear, urge, vow

**insistence** assertion, contention, emphasis, reiteration, stress, urging

**insistent** demanding, dogged, emphatic, exigent, forceful, incessant, unrelenting, urgent

**insolence** abuse, audacity, boldness, disrespect, effrontery, front, gall, impertinence, impudence, insubordination, rudeness

**insolent** abusive, bold, contemptuous, impertinent, impudent, insubordinate, insulting, pert, rude, uncivil

**insoluble** baffling, inexplicable, mysterious, mystifying, obscure, unfathomable

**insolvent** bankrupt, failed, ruined

**insomnia** sleeplessness, wakefulness

**inspect** check, check out Inf, examine, investigate, look over, over-

to **inspiration** n good idea; creative influence

**install** v place in position; formally place (person) in position or rank **installation** n act of installing; equipment installed

**instalment** n part payment; one of a series of parts

**instance** n example ~v cite

**instant** n moment ~adj immediate; (of foods) requiring little preparation **instantaneous** adj happening in an instant **instantly** adv at once

**instead** adv in place (of)

**instep** n top of foot between toes and ankle

**instigate** v incite, urge **instigation** n **instigator** n

**instil** v -stilling, -stilled implant; inculcate

**instinct** n inborn impulse; unconscious skill **instinctive** adj

**institute** v establish; set going ~n society for promoting science etc. **institution** n setting up; establishment for care or education; established custom, law etc. **institutional** adj of institutions; routine

—————————————— THESAURUS ——————————————

see, scan, scrutinize, search, supervise, survey, vet

**inspection** check, examination, investigation, review, scan, scrutiny, search, supervision, surveillance, survey

**inspector** censor, checker, critic, examiner, investigator, overseer, scrutineer, supervisor

**inspiration** arousal, awakening, encouragement, influence, muse, spur, stimulus

**inspire** animate, encourage, enliven, galvanize, hearten, imbue, influence, infuse, inspirit, instil, rouse, spark off, spur, stimulate

**install** fix, lay, lodge, place, position, put in, set up, station; establish, induct, institute, introduce, invest, set up

**installation** inauguration, induction, investiture; equipment, machinery, plant, system

**instalment** chapter, division, episode, part, portion, repayment, section

**instance** n case, example, illustration, occasion, occurrence, precedent, situation, time ~v adduce, cite, mention, name, quote, specify

**instant** n flash, moment, second, split second, trice, twinkling ~adj direct, immediate, instantaneous, prompt, quick, quickie Inf, urgent

**instantaneous** direct, immediate, instant, on-the-spot

**instantly** at once, directly, forthwith, immediately, instantaneously, now, without delay

**instead** alternatively, preferably, rather

**instigate** actuate, encourage, get going, impel, incite, influence, initiate, kick-start, kindle, move, prompt, provoke, rouse, set off, set on, spur, start, stimulate, stir up, trigger

**instil** engender, implant, impress, infix, infuse, insinuate

**instinct** aptitude, faculty, feeling, gift, impulse, intuition, knack, proclivity, talent, tendency, urge

**instinctive** inborn, inherent, innate, intuitional, intuitive, natural, reflex

**institute** v appoint, begin, enact, establish, fix, found, induct, initiate, install, introduce, invest, ordain, organize, pioneer, settle, set up, start ~n academy, college, con-

**instruct** v teach; inform; order **instruction** n teaching, order; pl directions **instructive** adj informative **instructor** n

**instrument** n thing used to make, do, measure etc.; mechanism for producing musical sound **instrumental** adj acting as instrument or means; produced by musical instruments

**insubordinate** adj mutinous, rebellious **insubordination** n

**insufferable** adj unbearable

**insular** adj of an island; narrowminded

**insulate** v prevent or reduce trans-

fer of electricity, heat, sound etc.; isolate, detach **insulation** n insula- **tor** n

**insulin** n hormone used in treatment of diabetes

**insult** v behave rudely to; offend ~n affront **insulting** adj

**insuperable** adj not able to be overcome

**insure** v contract for payment in event of loss, death etc.; make safe (against) **insurance** n

**insurrection** n revolt

**intact** adj untouched; uninjured

**intake** n thing, amount taken in; opening

———— THESAURUS ————

servatory, foundation, guild, school, seminary, society

**institution** creation, establishment, foundation, investiture; academy, college, foundation, hospital, institute, school, seminary, society, university; custom, fixture, law, practice, ritual, rule, tradition

**instruct** coach, discipline, drill, educate, ground, guide, inform, school, teach, train, tutor, bid, charge, direct, enjoin, order, tell

**instruction** coaching, discipline, drilling, education, grounding, guidance, information, lesson(s), schooling, teaching, training, tuition

**instructor** adviser, coach, guide, master, mentor, pedagogue, teacher, trainer, tutor

**instrument** appliance, contrivance, device, gadget, implement, mechanism, tool, utensil

**instrumental** active, assisting, auxiliary, conducive, helpful, involved, subsidiary, useful

**insubordinate** defiant, disobedient, disorderly, rebellious, riotous,

seditious, turbulent, undisciplined, unruly

**insubordination** defiance, disobedience, indiscipline, insurrection, mutiny, rebellion, revolt, sedition

**insufferable** detestable, impossible, intolerable, outrageous, unbearable, unendurable

**insular** blinkered, closed, limited, narrow, parochial, petty, provincial

**insulate** close off, cut off, isolate, protect

**insult** v abuse, injure, offend, outrage, put down, revile, slander, slight ~n abuse, indignity, insolence, outrage, put-down, rudeness, slight, snub

**insurance** cover, guarantee, indemnity, protection, provision, safeguard, security, warranty

**insure** assure, cover, guarantee, indemnify, underwrite, warrant

**intact** complete, entire, perfect, sound, together, unbroken, undamaged, unharmed, unhurt, untouched, virgin, whole

**integer** n whole number

**integral** adj essential **integrate** v combine into one whole **integration** n

**integrity** n honesty

**intellect** n power of thinking and reasoning **intellectual** adj of, appealing to intellect; having good intellect ~n intellectual person

**intelligent** adj clever **intelligence** n intellect; information, esp. military

**intelligible** adj understandable

**intemperate** adj drinking alcohol to excess; immoderate

**intend** v propose, mean

**intense** adj very strong or acute; emotional **intensify** v intensifying, intensified increase intensity n intensive adj

**intent** n purpose ~adj concentrating (on); resolved **intention** n purpose, aim **intentional** adj

———————— THESAURUS ————————

**integral** basic, component, constituent, essential

**integrate** accommodate, assimilate, blend, coalesce, combine, fuse, harmonize, join, knit, merge, unite

**integration** amalgamation, assimilation, blending, combining, fusing, harmony, incorporation, mixing, unification

**integrity** goodness, honesty, honour, rectitude, righteousness, virtue

**intellect** brains Inf, intelligence, judgment, mind, reason, sense, understanding

**intellectual** adj bookish, highbrow, intelligent, mental, rational, scholarly, studious, thoughtful ~n academic, highbrow

**intelligence** acumen, alertness, brightness, capacity, cleverness, discernment, intellect, mind, perception, quickness, reason, understanding; advice, data, disclosure, facts, findings, information, knowledge, news, notice, report, rumour, tidings, tip-off, word

**intelligent** acute, alert, apt, bright, clever, discerning, knowing, perspicacious, quick, rational, sharp, smart

**intelligible** clear, distinct, lucid, open, plain, understandable

**intend** aim, contemplate, determine, mean, meditate, plan, propose, purpose, scheme

**intense** acute, close, concentrated, deep, drastic, extreme, fierce, forceful, great, harsh, powerful, profound, protracted, severe, strained; ardent, burning, eager, earnest, emotional, fanatical, fervent, fierce, heightened, impassioned, keen, passionate, vehement

**intensify** add to, aggravate, augment, boost, concentrate, deepen, emphasize, enhance, heighten, increase, magnify, quicken, reinforce, set off, sharpen, strengthen

**intensity** ardour, concentration, depth, emotion, energy, excess, fervour, fire, force, keenness, passion, potency, power, severity, strength, vehemence, vigour

**intensive** all-out, concentrated, demanding, exhaustive, thorough

**intent** absorbed, alert, attentive, committed, concentrated, determined, eager, earnest, fixed, occupied, preoccupied, rapt, resolute, resolved, steadfast, steady, watchful, wrapped up

**intention** aim, design, end, goal, idea, object, objective, point, purpose, scope, target, view

**intentional** deliberate, designed,

**inter** v interring, interred bury interment n

**inter-** comb. form between, among, mutually, as in **interglacial, interrelation**

**interact** v act on each other **interaction** n **interactive** adj

**intercede** v plead in favour of, mediate **intercession** n

**intercept** v cut off; seize, stop in transit **interception** n

**interchange** v (cause to) exchange places ~n motorway junction **interchangeable** adj able to be exchanged in position or use

**inter-city** adj denoting fast rail service between main towns

**intercom** n internal communication system

**intercontinental** adj connecting continents; (of missile) able to reach one continent from another

**intercourse** n act of having sex; communications or dealings between individuals or groups

**interdict** n formal prohibition ~v prohibit

**interest** n concern, curiosity; thing exciting this; sum paid for borrowed money; advantage; right, share ~v excite, cause to feel interest **interested** adj **interesting** adj

**interface** n area, surface, boundary linking two systems

**interfere** v meddle, intervene; clash **interference** n act of interfering; Radio atmospherics

**interim** n meantime ~adj temporary

**interior** adj inner; inland; indoors ~n inside; inland region

**interject** v interpose (remark etc.) **interjection** n exclamation; interjected remark

**interlock** v lock together firmly

**interloper** n intruder

**interlude** n interval; something filling an interval

meant, planned, premeditated, purposed, studied

**intercept** arrest, block, catch, check, cut off, deflect, head off, stop, take

**interchangeable** equivalent, identical, reciprocal, synonymous, the same

**intercourse** association, commerce, communion, connection, contact, converse, dealings, trade, traffic, truck; carnal knowledge, coitus, copulation, sex, sexual intercourse

**interest** n affection, attention, attraction, concern, curiosity, notice, regard, suspicion, sympathy; activity, diversion, hobby, pastime, pursuit, relaxation; advantage, benefit, gain, good, profit ~v amuse, attract,

divert, engross, excite, fascinate; affect, concern, engage, involve

**interested** affected, attentive, attracted, curious, drawn, excited, fascinated, intent, into Inf, keen, moved, stimulated

**interesting** absorbing, compelling, engaging, engrossing, entertaining, gripping, intriguing, stimulating

**interfere** butt in, intervene, intrude, meddle, tamper

**interference** intervention, intrusion, meddling

**interior** adj inner, inside, internal, inward; Geog central, inland, remote ~n Geog centre, heartland, upcountry

**interlude** break, delay, episode, halt, hiatus, intermission, interval,

**intermarry** v (of families, races, religions) become linked by marriage; marry within one's family **intermarriage** n

**intermediate** adj coming between; interposed **intermediary** n

**interminable** adj endless

**intermission** n interval **intermittent** adj occurring at intervals

**intern** v confine to special area or camp **internment** n

**internal** adj inward; interior; within (a country, organization)

**international** adj of relations between nations ~n game or match between teams of different countries

**internecine** adj mutually destructive; deadly

**interplanetary** adj of, linking planets

**interplay** n action and reaction of things upon each other

**interpolate** v insert new matter; interject

**interpose** v insert; say as interruption

**interpret** v explain; translate, esp. orally; represent **interpretation** n **interpreter** n

**interrogate** v question, esp. closely or officially **interrogation** n **interrogative** n word used in asking question **interrogator** n

**interrupt** v break in (upon); stop; block **interruption** n

**intersect** v divide by passing across or through; meet and cross **intersection** n

**intersperse** v sprinkle among or in

**interstellar** adj between stars

**interstice** n slit, crevice

**intertwine** v twist together

**interval** n intervening time or

———————— THESAURUS ————————

pause, respite, rest, spell, stop, stoppage, wait

**intermediate** halfway, intervening, mean, mid, middle, midway

**intermittent** broken, discontinuous, fitful, irregular, occasional, periodic, punctuated, recurrent, spasmodic, sporadic

**internal** inner, inside, interior, intimate, private

**international** cosmopolitan, global, intercontinental, universal, worldwide

**interpose** insert, interject, introduce; interfere, intervene, intrude, step in

**interpret** adapt, clarify, construe, decipher, decode, define, elucidate, explain, expound, paraphrase, read, render, solve, take, translate

**interpretation** analysis, diagnosis, elucidation, explanation, meaning, performance, reading, rendering, sense, translation, version

**interpreter** annotator, exponent, scholiast, translator

**interrogate** ask, cross-examine, enquire, examine, inquire, investigate, pump, question, quiz

**interrogation** cross-examination, cross-questioning, enquiry, examination, inquisition, probing, questioning

**interrupt** break in, butt in, disturb, divide, heckle, hinder, hold up, intrude, obstruct, separate, sever, stay, stop, suspend

**interruption** break, disconnection, disruption, disturbance, division, halt, hiatus, hitch, impediment, intrusion, obstacle, obstruction, pause, stop, stoppage

**intersection** crossing, crossroads, interchange, junction

space; pause, break; difference (of pitch)

**intervene** v come into a situation in order to change it; be, come between or among; occur in the meantime; interpose **intervention** n

**interview** n meeting, esp. one involving questioning ~v have interview with **interviewee** n **interviewer** n

**intestate** adj not having made a will

**intestine** n (usu. pl) lower part of alimentary canal between stomach and anus **intestinal** adj

**intimate**[1] adj closely acquainted, familiar; private; having cosy atmosphere ~n intimate friend **intimacy** n

**intimate**[2] v announce; imply in indirect way **intimation** n

**intimidate** v frighten into submission **intimidation** n

**into** prep expresses motion to a point within; indicates change of state; indicates coming up against, encountering; indicates arithmetical division

**intolerable** adj more than can be endured

**intolerant** adj narrow-minded

**intone** v chant **intonation** n accent

**intoxicate** v make drunk

**intractable** adj difficult

**intransigent** adj uncompromising

**intravenous** adj into a vein

**intrepid** adj fearless, undaunted

**intricate** adj complex **intricacy** n

**intrigue** n underhand plot; secret love affair; v carry on intrigue; in-

————— THESAURUS —————

**interval** break, delay, gap, interlude, intermission, meantime, meanwhile, opening, pause, period, playtime, respite, rest, season, space, spell, term, time, wait

**intervene** arbitrate, intercede, interfere, intrude, mediate

**intervention** agency, interference, intrusion, mediation

**interview** n audience, conference, consultation, dialogue, meeting, talk ~v examine, interrogate, question, talk to

**intimacy** closeness, confidence, familiarity, understanding

**intimate**[1] adj bosom, cherished, close, confidential, dear, friendly, near, warm; personal, private, privy, secret; comfy, cosy, friendly, informal, snug ~n bosom friend, companion, comrade, confidant, crony, familiar, friend, pal

**intimate**[2] v allude, communicate, declare, hint, impart, imply, indicate, insinuate, remind, state, suggest, warn

**intimidate** alarm, appal, bully, coerce, dishearten, dismay, frighten, overawe, scare, subdue, terrify, terrorize, threaten

**intimidation** browbeating, bullying, fear, menaces, pressure, terror, threat

**intolerable** excruciating, impossible, insufferable, painful, unbearable, unendurable

**intolerant** chauvinistic, fanatical, narrow, narrow-minded, one-sided, prejudiced, small-minded

**intrepid** bold, brave, courageous, daring, doughty, fearless, gallant, have-a-go Inf, heroic, plucky, resolute, stalwart, unafraid, unflinching, valiant, valorous

**intricate** complex, complicated, difficult, elaborate, fancy, involved, knotty, obscure, perplexing, tangled, tortuous

terest, puzzle

**intrinsic** *adj* inherent, essential

**introduce** *v* make acquainted; present; bring in; insert **introduction** *n* introducing; preliminary part of book etc. **introductory** *adj* preliminary

**introvert** *n Psychoanalysis* one who looks inward **introverted** *adj*

**intrude** *v* thrust (oneself) in **intruder** *n* **intrusion** *n* **intrusive** *adj*

**intuition** *n* spontaneous insight **intuitive** *adj*

**inundate** *v* flood; overwhelm **inundation** *n*

**inured** *adj* hardened

**invade** *v* enter by force; overrun **invader** *n* **invasion** *n*

**invalid**[1] *n* one suffering from ill health ~*v* retire because of illness etc.

**invalid**[2] *adj* having no legal force **invalidate** *v*

**invaluable** *adj* priceless

**invasion** *SEE* INVADE

**invective** *n* bitter verbal attack

**inveigle** *v* entice

**invent** *v* devise, originate; fabricate **invention** *n* that which is invented; ability to invent **inventive** *adj* resourceful; creative **inventor** *n*

**inventory** *n* detailed list

———————— THESAURUS ————————

**intrigue** *n* collusion, conspiracy, double-dealing, knavery, manipulation, manoeuvre, plot, ruse, scheme, stratagem, trickery, wile; affair, amour, liaison, romance ~*v* connive, conspire, machinate, plot, scheme; attract, charm, fascinate, interest, rivet, titillate

**intrinsic** *adj* basic, built-in, central, congenital, essential, genuine, inborn, inbred, inherent, native, natural, real, true

**introduce** *v* acquaint, familiarize, make known, present; begin, bring in, commence, establish, found, inaugurate, initiate, institute, launch, organize, pioneer, set up, start, usher in

**introduction** *n* baptism, debut, inauguration, induction, initiation, institution, launch, presentation; foreword, lead-in, opening, overture, preamble, preface, prelude, proem, prologue

**introductory** *adj* early, elementary, first, inaugural, initial, opening, preliminary, preparatory

**intrude** *v* encroach, infringe, inter-

fere, interrupt, obtrude, trespass, violate

**intruder** *n* burglar, interloper, invader, prowler, raider, thief, trespasser

**intrusion** *n* infringement, interruption, invasion, trespass, violation

**intuition** *n* hunch, insight, instinct, perception, presentiment

**invade** *v* assail, assault, attack, burst in, encroach, infringe, occupy, raid, violate

**invader** *n* aggressor, attacker, plunderer, raider, trespasser

**invalid**[1] *adj* ailing, disabled, feeble, frail, ill, infirm, sick, sickly

**invalid**[2] *adj* baseless, false, ill-founded, illogical, irrational, null and void, unfounded, unsound, untrue, void, worthless

**invaluable** *adj* costly, inestimable, precious, priceless, valuable

**invasion** *n* assault, attack, foray, incursion, inroad, irruption, offensive, onslaught, raid

**invent** *v* coin, conceive, contrive, create, design, devise, discover, formulate, imagine, improvise, manufacture, originate, think up

**invert** v turn upside down; reverse **inverse** adj inverted; opposite **inversion** n

**invertebrate** n/adj (animal) without backbone

**invest** v lay out (money, time, effort etc.) for profit or advantage; install; endow **investiture** n formal installation in office or rank **investment** n investing; money invested; stocks and shares bought **investor** n

**investigate** v inquire into; examine **investigation** n **investigative** adj **investigator** n

**inveterate** adj deep-rooted; confirmed

**invidious** adj likely to cause ill will

**invigilate** v supervise examination candidates **invigilator** n

**invigorate** v give vigour to

**invincible** adj unconquerable

**inviolable** adj not to be violated **inviolate** adj not violated

**invisible** adj not able to be seen

**invite** v request the company of; ask courteously; ask for; attract, call forth **invitation** n

**invoice** n list of goods or services sold, with prices ~v make, present an invoice

**invoke** v call on; appeal to; ask earnestly for; summon **invocation** n

————— THESAURUS —————

**invention** contraption, contrivance, creation, design, development, device, discovery, gadget

**inventive** creative, fertile, gifted, ground-breaking, imaginative, ingenious, resourceful

**inventor** author, coiner, creator, designer, father, maker, originator

**inventory** n account, catalogue, list, record, register, roll, roster, schedule

**inverse** adj contrary, inverted, opposite, reverse, transposed

**invert** capsize, overturn, reverse, transpose, upset, upturn

**invest** advance, devote, lay out, put in, sink, spend; endow, endue, provide, supply

**investigate** consider, enquire into, examine, explore, inspect, probe, scrutinize, search, sift, study

**investigation** analysis, enquiry, examination, exploration, hearing, inquest, inquiry, inspection, probe, recce, research, review, scrutiny, search, study, survey

**investigator** examiner, inquirer, (private) detective, researcher, reviewer, sleuth

**investment** asset, speculation, transaction, venture

**inveterate** chronic, confirmed, entrenched, established, hardened, incorrigible, long-standing

**invigorate** brace, energize, enliven, exhilarate, fortify, galvanize, harden, quicken, refresh, rejuvenate, stimulate, strengthen

**invincible** indestructible, unassailable, unbeatable

**invisible** indiscernible, out of sight, unseen; concealed, disguised, hidden, inconspicuous

**invitation** asking, begging, bidding, call, request, solicitation, summons; coquetry, enticement, incitement, inducement, overture, provocation, temptation

**invite** ask, beg, bid, call, request, solicit, summon; allure, attract, bring on, court, draw, encourage, entice, lead, provoke, solicit, tempt, welcome

**invocation** appeal, entreaty, petition, prayer, supplication

**invoke** adjure, beg, beseech, call

**involuntary** adj unintentional; instinctive

**involve** v include; entail; implicate (person); concern; entangle **involved** adj complicated; concerned (in)

**inward** adj internal; situated within; mental ~adv (also **inwards**) towards the inside; into the mind **inwardly** adv in the mind; internally

**iodine** n nonmetallic element found in seaweed

**ion** n electrically charged atom

**IOU** n signed paper acknowledging debt

**IQ** intelligence quotient

**IRA** Irish Republican Army

**ire** n anger **irascible** adj hot-tempered **irate** adj angry

**iridescent** adj exhibiting changing colours

**iris** n circular membrane of eye containing pupil; plant with sword-shaped leaves and showy flowers

**irk** v irritate, vex **irksome** adj tiresome

**iron** n common metallic element; tool etc. of this metal; appliance used to smooth cloth; metal-headed golf club; pl fetters ~adj of, like, iron; unyielding; robust ~v press **ironmonger** n dealer in hardware

**irony** n use of words to mean the opposite of what is said; event, situation opposite of that expected **ironic, ironical** adj of, using, irony

**irradiate** v treat with light or beams of particles; shine upon **irradiation** n

**irrational** adj not based on logic

**irregular** adj not regular or even; unconventional **irregularity** n

——————— THESAURUS ———————

**involuntary** compulsory, forced, obligatory, reluctant, unwilling

**involve** entail, imply, mean, necessitate, presuppose, require; affect, associate, concern, connect, draw in, implicate, incriminate, inculpate, touch

**involvement** association, commitment, concern, connection, interest, responsibility

**inward** adj entering, incoming, ingoing, penetrating; confidential, hidden, inmost, innermost, inside, interior, internal, personal, private, secret

**irksome** annoying, boring, burdensome, disagreeable, exasperating, tedious, tiresome, troublesome, unwelcome, vexatious, vexing, wearisome

**iron** adj adamant, cruel, hard, heavy, immovable, implacable, inflexible, obdurate, rigid, steel, strong, tough, unbending, unyielding

**irony** mockery, sarcasm, satire; incongruity, paradox

**irrational** absurd, crackpot Inf, crazy, foolish, illogical, silly, unreasonable, unsound, unthinking, unwise

**irregular** asymmetrical, broken, bumpy, craggy, crooked, jagged, lopsided, pitted, ragged, rough, unequal, uneven; eccentric, erratic, fitful, fluctuating, fragmentary, haphazard, inconstant, intermittent, occasional, patchy, random, shifting, spasmodic, sporadic, unsteady, variable, wavering

**irregularity** asymmetry, bumpiness, crookedness, lopsidedness,

**irrelevant** *adj* not connected with the matter in hand **irrelevance** *n*

**irreparable** *adj* not able to be repaired or remedied

**irresistible** *adj* too strong to resist; enchanting, seductive

**irrespective** *adj* without taking account (of)

**irreverence** *n* lack of respect **irreverent** *adj*

**irrevocable** *adj* not able to be changed

**irrigate** *v* water by artificial channels, pipes etc. **irrigation** *n*

**irritate** *v* annoy; inflame **irritable** *adj* easily annoyed **irritant** *adj/n* (person or thing) causing irritation **irritation** *n*

**is** third person sing. of BE

**Islam** *n* Muslim faith or world **Islamic** *adj*

**island** *n* piece of land surrounded by water; anything like this **islander**

*n* inhabitant of island

**isle** *n* island **islet** *n* little island

**isobar** *n* line on map connecting places of equal mean barometric pressure

**isolate** *v* place apart or alone **isolation** *n*

**isomer** *n* substance with same molecules as another but different atomic arrangement

**isometric** *adj* having equal dimensions; relating to muscular contraction without movement **isometrics** *pl n* (with *sing v*) system of isometric exercises

**isosceles** *adj* (of triangle) having two sides equal

**isotope** *n* atom having different atomic weight from other atoms of same element

**issue** *n* topic of discussion or dispute; edition of newspaper etc.; offspring; outcome ~*v* go out; result

─────── THESAURUS ───────

patchiness, raggedness, roughness, spottiness, unevenness; aberration, anomaly, breach, deviation, eccentricity, freak, malfunction, malpractice, oddity, peculiarity

**irrelevant** extraneous, immaterial, impertinent, inapplicable, inappropriate, unrelated

**irreparable** beyond repair, irretrievable, irreversible

**irresistible** compelling, imperative, overpowering, overwhelming, potent, urgent; alluring, enchanting, fascinating, ravishing, seductive, tempting

**irreverent** derisive, disrespectful, flippant, impertinent, mocking

**irrevocable** changeless, fated, fixed, irreversible, predestined, settled

**irrigate** flood, inundate, moisten,

water, wet

**irritable** bad-tempered, cantankerous, choleric, crabbed, cross, dyspeptic, edgy, exasperated, ill-tempered, irascible, peevish, petulant, prickly, testy, touchy

**irritate** anger, annoy, bother, enrage, exasperate, fret, gall, harass, incense, infuriate, nettle, offend, pester, provoke; aggravate, chafe, fret, inflame, intensify, pain, rub

**irritation** anger, annoyance, displeasure, exasperation, impatience, indignation, irritability, resentment

**isolate** cut off, detach, disconnect, divorce, insulate, quarantine, segregate, separate, set apart

**isolation** aloofness, detachment, exile, loneliness, quarantine, seclusion, separation, solitude, withdrawal

in; arise (from); give, send out; publish

**isthmus** *n* neck of land between two seas

**it** *pron* neuter pronoun of the third person **its** *adj* belonging to it **it's** it is **itself** *pron emphatic form of IT*

**italic** *adj* (of type) sloping **italics** *pl n* this type, used for emphasis etc. **italicize** *v* put in italics

**itch** *v/n* (feel) irritation in the skin **itchy** *adj*

**item** *n* single thing; piece of information; entry **itemize** *v*

**itinerant** *adj* travelling from place to place **itinerary** *n* plan of journey; route

**ivory** *n* hard white substance of the tusks of elephants etc.

**ivy** *n* climbing evergreen plant

———————————— THESAURUS ————————————

**issue** *n* affair, argument, concern, matter, point, problem, question, subject, topic; copy, edition, instalment, number ~*v* arise, emanate, emerge, flow, originate, proceed, rise, spring, stem; announce, broadcast, circulate, deliver, distribute, emit, give out, promulgate, publish, release

**itch** *v* irritate, prickle, tickle, tingle

~*n* irritation, prickling, tingling

**item** *n* account, article, bulletin, dispatch, feature, note, paragraph, piece, report; article, aspect, component, consideration, detail, entry, matter, particular, point, thing

**itinerary** circuit, journey, line, programme, route, schedule, timetable, tour

# ℐ j

**jab** v **jabbing, jabbed** poke roughly; thrust, stab ~n poke; *Inf* injection

**jabber** v chatter; talk incoherently

**jack** n device for lifting heavy weight, esp. motorcar; lowest court card; *Bowls* ball aimed at; socket and plug connection in electronic equipment; small flag, esp. national, at sea ~v (*usu. with* **up**) lift with a jack

**jackal** n doglike scavenging animal of Asia and Africa

**jackass** n male ass; blockhead

**jackboot** n large military boot

**jackdaw** n small kind of crow

**jacket** n outer garment, short coat; outer casing, cover

**jackknife** n (pl **-knives**) clasp knife ~v angle sharply, esp. the parts of an articulated lorry

**jackpot** n large prize, accumulated stake, as pool in poker

**Jacuzzi** n *Trademark* bath with device that swirls water

**jade** n ornamental semiprecious stone, usu. dark green; this colour

~*adj* of this colour

**jaded** *adj* tired; off colour

**jagged** *adj* having sharp points

**jaguar** n large S Amer. cat

**jail** n building for confinement of criminals or suspects ~v send to, confine in prison **jailer** n

**jam** v **jamming, jammed** pack together; (cause) to stick and become unworkable; *Radio* block (another station) ~n fruit preserved by boiling with sugar; crush; hold-up of traffic; awkward situation

**jamb** n side post of door, fireplace etc.

**jamboree** n large gathering or rally of Scouts

**Jan.** January

**jangle** v (cause) to sound harshly, as bell; (of nerves) be irritated

**janitor** n caretaker

**January** n first month

**jar¹** n round vessel of glass, earthenware etc.; *Inf* glass of esp. beer

**jar²** v **jarring, jarred** grate, jolt; have distressing effect on ~n jarring

---
**THESAURUS**
---

**jab** v/n dig, lunge, nudge, poke, prod, punch, stab, tap, thrust

**jacket** case, casing, coat, covering, envelope, folder, sheath, skin, wrapper

**jackpot** award, bonanza, kitty, pool, pot, prize, reward, winnings

**jaded** exhausted, fatigued, spent, tired, weary

**jagged** barbed, broken, craggy, pointed, ragged, ridged, rough, serrated, spiked, toothed, uneven

**jail** n nick *Brit sl*, prison, slammer *Sl* ~v confine, detain, impound, imprison, incarcerate, lock up

**jailer** captor, guard, keeper, warder

**jam** v cram, crowd, crush, force, pack, press, squeeze, stuff, throng, wedge; block, clog, congest, halt, obstruct, stall, stick ~n crowd, crush, horde, mass, mob, multitude, pack, press, swarm, throng; bind, dilemma, hot water, plight, predicament, quandary, strait, tight spot, trouble

**jangle** v chime, clank, clash, rattle, vibrate ~n clang, clangour, clash, din, dissonance, jar, racket, rattle

**janitor** caretaker, concierge, custodian, doorkeeper, porter

sound; shock etc.

**jargon** *n* special vocabulary for particular subject; pretentious language

**jasmine** *n* shrub with sweet-smelling flowers

**jaundice** *n* disease marked by yellowness of skin **jaundiced** *adj* prejudiced, bitter etc.

**jaunt** *n/v* (make) short pleasure excursion

**jaunty** *adj* sprightly; brisk

**javelin** *n* spear, esp. for throwing in sporting events

**jaw** *n* one of bones in which teeth are set; *pl* mouth; gripping part of vice etc.

**jay** *n* noisy bird of brilliant plumage

**jazz** *n* syncopated music and dance ~*v* (*with* up) make more lively **jazzy** *adj* flashy, showy

**jealous** *adj* envious; suspiciously watchful **jealousy** *n*

**jeans** *pl n* casual trousers, esp. of denim

**Jeep** *n Trademark* light four-wheel-drive motor vehicle

**jeer** *v/n* scoff, taunt

**jell** *v* congeal; *Inf* assume definite form

**jelly** *n* sweet, preserve etc. becoming softly stiff as it cools; anything of similar consistency **jellyfish** *n* small jelly-like sea animal

**jemmy** *n* short steel crowbar

**jeopardy** *n* danger **jeopardize** *v* endanger

**jerk** *n* sharp push or pull; *Sl* stupid person ~*v* move or throw with a jerk **jerky** *adj* uneven; spasmodic

**jerkin** *n* sleeveless jacket

**jersey** *n* knitted jumper; machine-knitted fabric

**jest** *n/v* joke **jester** *n* joker; *Hist* professional fool at court

**jet**[1] *n* aircraft driven by jet propulsion; stream of liquid, gas etc.; spout, nozzle ~*v* **jetting, jetted** throw out; shoot forth **jet lag** fatigue caused by crossing time zones

---

**THESAURUS**

**jar**[1] *n* crock, flagon, jug, pitcher, pot, urn, vase, vessel

**jar**[2] *v* agitate, disturb, grate, irritate, jolt, rasp, rock, shake, vibrate; annoy, clash, gall, grate, grind, irk, irritate, nettle

**jargon** argot, cant, dialect, idiom, parlance, patois, slang, tongue, usage

**jaunt** airing, excursion, expedition, outing, ramble, stroll, tour, trip

**jaunty** airy, breezy, buoyant, carefree, gay, high-spirited, lively, perky, smart, sprightly, spruce, trim

**jealous** covetous, desirous, envious, green, grudging, intolerant, resentful, rival

**jealousy** covetousness, distrust, envy, ill-will, mistrust, resentment,

spite, suspicion

**jeer** *v* banter, barrack, deride, flout, gibe, heckle, hector, mock, ridicule, scoff, sneer, taunt

**jeopardize** chance, endanger, gamble, hazard, imperil, risk, stake, venture

**jeopardy** danger, exposure, hazard, peril, pitfall, risk, venture

**jerk** *n/v* jolt, lurch, pull, throw, thrust, tug, tweak, twitch, wrench, yank

**jest** *n* banter, bon mot, fun, hoax, jape, joke, play, prank, quip, sally, sport, witticism ~*v* banter, chaff, deride, gibe, jeer, joke, mock, quip, scoff, sneer, tease

**jester** comedian, comic, humorist, joker, wag, wit; buffoon, clown,

in aircraft **jet propulsion** propulsion by jet of gas or liquid **jet-propelled** *adj*

**jet²** *n* hard black mineral **jet-black** *adj* glossy black

**jetsam** *n* goods thrown overboard

**jettison** *v* abandon; throw overboard

**jetty** *n* small pier, wharf

**Jew** *n* one of Hebrew religion or ancestry **Jewish** *adj*

**jewel** *n* precious stone; ornament containing one; precious thing **jeweller** *n* dealer in jewels **jewellery** *n*

**jib** *n* triangular sail set forward of mast; arm of crane ~*v* **jibbing**, **jibbed** (of horse, person) stop and refuse to go on

**jibe** *SEE* GIBE

**jig** *n* lively dance; music for it; guide for cutting etc. ~*v* **jigging**, **jigged** dance jig; make jerky up-and-down movements **jigsaw** *n* machine fret saw **jigsaw puzzle** picture cut into pieces, which the user tries to fit together again

**jilt** *v* reject (lover)

**jingle** *n* light metallic noise; catchy rhythmic verse, song etc. ~*v* (cause to) make jingling sound

**jingoism** *n* aggressive nationalism

**jinks** *pl n* **high jinks** boisterous merrymaking

**jinx** *n* force, person, thing bringing bad luck ~*v* cause bad luck

**jitters** *pl n* worried nervousness, anxiety **jittery** *adj* nervous

**jive** *n* (dance performed to) popular music, esp. of 1950s ~*v* do this dance

**job** *n* piece of work, task; post; *Inf* difficult task **jobbing** *adj* doing single, particular jobs for payment **jobless** *adj/pl n* unemployed (people)

**jockey** *n* (*pl* **jockeys**) rider in horse races ~*v* **jockeying, jockeyed** (*esp. with* for) manoeuvre

**jockstrap** *n* belt with pouch to support genitals

**jocular** *adj* joking; given to joking **jocularity** *n*

**jodhpurs** *pl n* tight-legged riding breeches

**jog** *v* **jogging, jogged** run slowly,

fool, madcap

**jet¹** *n* flow, fountain, gush, spout, spray, spring, stream; nozzle, rose, spout, sprinkler ~*v* flow, gush, issue, rush, shoot, spout, squirt, stream, surge

**jet²** black, ebony, inky, raven, sable

**jettison** abandon, discard, dump, eject, expel, heave, scrap, unload

**jetty** breakwater, dock, mole, pier, quay, wharf

**jewel** brilliant, ornament, precious stone, trinket; charm, gem, paragon, pearl, prize, rarity, wonder

**jig** *v* bounce, caper, prance, shake, skip, twitch, wobble

**jingle** *n* clang, clink, rattle, ringing,

tinkle; chorus, ditty, doggerel, melody, song, tune ~*v* chime, clatter, clink, rattle, ring, tinkle

**jinx** *n* curse, evil eye, hoodoo *Inf*, plague, voodoo ~*v* bewitch, curse

**job** affair, charge, chore, concern, duty, errand, function, pursuit, responsibility, role, stint, task, undertaking, venture, work; business, calling, capacity, career, craft, employment, function, livelihood, métier, occupation, office, position, post, profession, situation, trade, vocation

**jocular** amusing, comical, droll, facetious, funny, humorous, jolly, jovial, playful, roguish, sportive, teas-

trot, esp. for exercise; nudge; stimulate ~n jogging **jogger** n **jogging** n

**join** v fasten, unite; become a member (of); become connected; (*with* *up*) enlist; take part (in) ~n (place of) joining **joiner** n maker of finished woodwork **joinery** n joiner's work

**joint** n arrangement by which two things fit together; place of this; meat for roasting, oft. with bone; *Sl* disreputable bar or nightclub; *Sl* marijuana cigarette ~*adj* shared ~v connect by joints; divide at the joints **jointly** *adv* **out of joint** dislocated; disorganized

**joist** n beam supporting floor or ceiling

**joke** n thing said or done to cause laughter; ridiculous thing ~v make

jokes **joker** n one who jokes; *Sl* fellow; extra card in pack **jokey** *adj*

**jolly** *adj* jovial; merry ~v **jollying, jollied** make person, occasion happier **jollification** n **jollity** n

**jolt** n/v jerk; jar; shock

**joss stick** incense stick

**jostle** v knock or push

**jot** n small amount ~v **jotting, jotted** note **jotter** n notebook

**joule** n *Electricity* unit of work or energy

**journal** n newspaper or other periodical; daily record **journalism** n editing, writing in periodicals **journalist** n

**journey** n going to a place, excursion; distance travelled ~v travel

**journeyman** n qualified craftsman

**jovial** *adj* convivial, merry **joviality** n

——————— THESAURUS ———————

ing, waggish, witty

**jog** canter, lope, run, trot; arouse, nudge, prod, prompt, push, remind, shake, stimulate, stir, suggest

**join** accompany, add, adhere, annex, append, attack, cement, combine, connect, couple, fasten, knit, link, marry, splice, tie, unite, yoke; enlist, enrol, enter, sign up

**joint** n connection, hinge, junction, knot, nexus, node, seam, union ~*adj* collective, combined, communal, concerted, cooperative, joined, mutual, shared, united

**joke** n frolic, fun, jape, jest, lark, play, prank, pun, quip, quirk, sally, sport, witticism, yarn ~v banter, frolic, gambol, jest, mock, quip, ridicule, taunt, tease

**jolly** carefree, cheerful, funny, gay, hilarious, jocund, jovial, joyful, jubilant, merry, mirthful, playful

**jolt** n bump, jar, jerk, jump, quiver,

shake, start; blow, bombshell, reversal, setback, shock, surprise ~v jar, jerk, knock, push, shake, shove; astonish, disturb, perturb, shock, stagger, startle, stun, surprise, upset

**jostle** bump, butt, crowd, elbow, jog, jolt, press, push, shove, squeeze, throng, thrust

**journal** daily, gazette, magazine, monthly, newspaper, paper, periodical, record, register, review, tabloid, weekly; diary, log, record

**journalist** broadcaster, columnist, commentator, contributor, correspondent, hack, newspaperman, pressman, reporter

**journey** excursion, expedition, jaunt, odyssey, outing, passage, pilgrimage, tour, travel, trek, trip, voyage

**jovial** airy, blithe, buoyant, cheery, convivial, cordial, gay, glad, happy,

**jowl** n (flesh hanging over) lower jaw

**joy** n gladness, pleasure, delight; cause of this **joyful** adj **joyous** adj extremely happy **joy ride** trip, esp. in stolen car **joystick** n control column of aircraft; control device for video game

**JP** Justice of the Peace

**jubilant** adj exultant **jubilation** n

**jubilee** n time of rejoicing, esp. 25th or 50th anniversary

**judder** v shake, vibrate ~n vibration

**judge** n officer appointed to try cases in law courts; one who decides in a dispute, contest etc.; one able to form a reliable opinion ~v act as judge (of, for); **judgement**, **judgment** n faculty of judging; sentence of court; opinion **judgmental, judgemental** adj

**judicial** adj of, by a court or judge

**judiciary** n judges collectively **judicious** adj well-judged, sensible

**judo** n modern sport derived from jujitsu

**jug** n vessel for liquids, with handle and small spout; its contents

**juggernaut** n large heavy lorry; irresistible, destructive force

**juggle** v keep several objects in the air simultaneously; manipulate to deceive **juggler** n

**jugular vein** one of three large veins of the neck returning blood from the head

**juice** n liquid part of vegetable, fruit or meat; Inf electric current; Inf petrol **juicy** adj succulent; interesting

**jujitsu, jujutsu** n Japanese art of wrestling and self-defence

**jukebox** n automatic, coin-operated record player

**July** n seventh month

———————— THESAURUS ————————

jolly, jubilant, merry

**joy** bliss, delight, ecstasy, elation, exultation, gaiety, gladness, glee, pleasure, rapture, satisfaction

**joyful** blithesome, delighted, glad, gratified, happy, jubilant, lighthearted, merry, pleased, satisfied

**jubilant** cock-a-hoop, elated, enraptured, excited, exuberant, exultant, glad, joyous, overjoyed, rejoicing, thrilled, triumphant

**jubilation** celebration, ecstasy, elation, excitement, exultation, joy, triumph

**jubilee** carnival, celebration, festival, festivity, fête, gala

**judge** n justice, magistrate; adjudicator, arbiter, moderator, referee, umpire; arbiter, assessor, authority, connoisseur, critic, evaluator, expert ~v adjudge, adjudicate, arbi-

trate, ascertain, conclude, decide, determine, discern, mediate, referee, umpire; appreciate, assess, consider, criticize, esteem, estimate, evaluate, examine, review, value

**judicial** judiciary, legal, official

**judicious** acute, astute, careful, cautious, circumspect, considered, diplomatic, discerning, discreet, expedient, informed, politic, prudent, rational, sage, sane, sensible, shrewd, skilful, sober, sound, thoughtful, wise

**jug** carafe, crock, ewer, jar, pitcher, urn, vessel

**juice** fluid, liquid, liquor, nectar, sap

**juicy** lush, moist, succulent, watery; colourful, interesting, racy, risqué, sensational, spicy Inf, sug-

**jumble** *v* mix in confused heap ~*n* confused heap or state **jumble sale** sale of miscellaneous, usu. second-hand, items

**jumbo** *n* (*pl* **jumbos**) *Inf* elephant; anything very large

**jump** *v* (cause to) spring, leap (over); move hastily; pass or skip (over); rise steeply; start (with astonishment etc.) ~*n* act of jumping; obstacle to be jumped; distance, height jumped; sudden rise **jumper** *n* sweater, pullover **jumpy** *adj* nervous

**junction** *n* place where routes meet; point of connection

**juncture** *n* state of affairs

**June** *n* sixth month

**jungle** *n* equatorial forest; tangled mass; condition of intense competition

**junior** *adj* younger; of lower standing ~*n* junior person

**juniper** *n* evergreen shrub

**junk**[1] *n* useless objects **junkie** *n* *Sl* drug addict **junk food** food of low nutritional value **junk mail** unsolicited mail

**junk**[2] *n* Chinese sailing vessel

**junket** *n* flavoured curdled milk; excursion

**junta** *n* group holding power in country

**jurisdiction** *n* authority; territory covered by it

**jury** *n* body of persons sworn to render verdict in court of law; judges of competition **juror** *n*

**just** *adj* fair; upright, honest; right, equitable ~*adv* exactly; barely; at this instant; merely; really **justice** *n* moral or legal fairness; judge, magistrate **justice of the peace** person who can act as judge in local court **justify** *v* **-ifying, -ified** prove right; vindicate **justifiable** *adj* **justification** *n*

**jut** *v* jutting, jutted project, stick

gestive, vivid

**jumble** *v* confound, confuse, disarrange, dishevel, disorder, disorganize, entangle, mix, muddle, shuffle, tangle ~*n* chaos, clutter, confusion, disarray, disorder, litter, medley, *mélange*, mess, miscellany, mixture, muddle

**jump** *v* bounce, bound, caper, clear, gambol, hop, hurdle, leap, skip, spring, vault; avoid, digress, evade, miss, omit, overshoot, skip, switch ~*n* bound, caper, hop, leap, skip, spring, vault; advance, boost, increase, increment, rise, upsurge, upturn

**jumpy** *adj* agitated, anxious, fidgety, jittery, nervous, restless, tense, twitchy *Inf*

**junction** alliance, combination,

connection, coupling, joint, juncture, linking, seam, union

**junior** inferior, lesser, lower, minor, secondary, subordinate, younger

**junk** clutter, debris, leavings, litter, oddments, refuse, rubbish, rummage, scrap, trash, waste

**jurisdiction** authority, command, control, dominion, influence, power, prerogative, rule, say, sway

**just** *adj* blameless, decent, equitable, fair, good, honest, honourable, impartial, lawful, pure, right, righteous, unbiased, upright, virtuous; appropriate, apt, deserved, due, fitting, justified, merited, proper, reasonable, right, suitable ~*adv* absolutely, completely, entirely, exactly, perfectly, precisely;

out, protrude

**jute** *n* plant fibre used for rope, canvas etc.

**juvenile** *adj* of, for young children; immature *~n* young person, child

**juxtapose** *v* put side by side **juxtaposition** *n*

barely, hardly, lately, only now, recently, scarcely

**justice** equity, fairness, honesty, impartiality, integrity, justness, law, legality, legitimacy, rectitude, right

**justifiable** acceptable, defensible, excusable, fit, lawful, legitimate, proper, right, sound, tenable, valid, warrantable, well-founded

**justification** apology, approval, defence, excuse, explanation, plea, vindication

**justify** absolve, acquit, approve, confirm, defend, establish, excuse, exonerate, explain, legalize, maintain, substantiate, support, sustain, uphold, validate, vindicate, warrant

**juvenile** adolescent, boy, child, girl, infant, minor, youth

# K k

**kaftan** n woman's long, loose dress with sleeves

**kaleidoscope** n optical toy producing changing patterns; any complex pattern **kaleidoscopic** adj

**kamikaze** n Japanese suicide pilot ~adj (of action) certain to kill or injure the doer

**kangaroo** n Aust. marsupial with strong hind legs for jumping

**karaoke** n entertainment involving singing over prerecorded backing tape

**karate** n Japanese system of unarmed combat

**karma** n person's actions affecting fate for next incarnation

**kasbah** n citadel of N Afr. town

**kayak** n Inuit canoe; any similar canoe

**kebab** n dish of small pieces of meat, tomatoes etc. grilled on skewers; grilled minced lamb served in split slice of unleavened bread

**kedgeree** n dish of fish cooked with rice, eggs etc.

**keel** n lowest longitudinal support on which ship is built **keel over** turn upside down; *Inf* collapse suddenly

**keen** adj sharp; acute; eager; shrewd; (of price) competitive

**keep** v keeping, kept retain possession of, not lose; hold; (cause to) remain; maintain; remain good; continue ~n maintenance; central tower of castle **keeper** n **keeping** n harmony; care, charge **keepsake** n gift treasured for sake of the giver

**keg** n small barrel; container for beer

**kelp** n large seaweed

**ken** n range of knowledge

**kennel** n shelter for dog

**kerb** n stone edging to footpath

**kernel** n inner seed of nut or fruit stone; central, essential part

**kerosene** n paraffin oil

**kestrel** n small falcon

**ketchup** n sauce of vinegar, tomatoes etc.

**kettle** n metal vessel with spout and handle, esp. for boiling water **kettledrum** n musical instrument made of membrane stretched over copper hemisphere

---
THESAURUS
---

**keen** ardent, avid, eager, earnest, enthusiastic, fervid, fierce, intense, zealous; acid, acute, biting, caustic, cutting, incisive, sardonic, satirical, sharp, vitriolic

**keep** v conserve, control, hold, maintain, possess, preserve, retain; amass, carry, deal in, deposit, furnish, garner, heap, hold, pile, stack, stock, store; care for, defend, guard, look after, maintain, manage, mind, operate, protect, safeguard, shelter, shield, tend, watch

over ~n board, food, livelihood, living, maintenance, means, nourishment, subsistence, support

**keeper** attendant, caretaker, curator, custodian, defender, governor, guard, jailer, steward, warden, warder

**keeping** care, charge, custody, patronage, possession, protection, safekeeping, trust

**keepsake** emblem, favour, memento, relic, remembrance, reminder, souvenir, symbol, token

**key** n instrument for operating lock, winding clock etc.; explanation, means of achieving an end etc.; Mus set of related notes; operating lever of typewriter, piano, organ etc. ~adj most important **keyboard** n set of keys on piano, computer etc. **keyhole** n opening for key **keynote** n dominant idea

**kg** kilogram

**khaki** adj dull, yellowish-brown ~n khaki cloth; military uniform

**kibbutz** n (pl **kibbutzim**) communal agricultural settlement in Israel

**kick** v strike (out) with foot; recoil; resist; Inf free oneself of (habit etc.) ~n blow with foot; thrill; strength (of flavour, alcoholic drink etc.); recoil **kick off** start (a game of football) **kick out** dismiss or expel forcibly

**kid** n young goat; leather of its skin; Inf child ~v **kidding, kidded** Inf tease, deceive; behave, speak in fun

**kidnap** v **-napping, -napped** seize and hold to ransom **kidnapper** n

**kidney** n (pl **-neys**) either of the pair of organs which secrete urine; animal kidney used as food

**kill** v deprive of life; put an end to; pass (time) ~n act of killing; animals etc. killed **killer** n **killing** adj Inf very tiring; very funny

**kiln** n furnace, oven

**kilo** n short for KILOGRAM

**kilo-** comb. form one thousand, as in **kilometre, kilowatt**

**kilogram, kilogramme** n 1000 grams

**kilohertz** n 1000 cycles per second

**kilt** n pleated tartan skirt orig. worn by Scottish Highlanders

**kimono** n (pl **-nos**) loose Japanese robe

**kin** n relatives **kindred** n relatives ~adj similar; related **kinsman** n (fem **kinswoman**)

**kind** n sort, type, class ~adj considerate; gentle **kindly** adj kind, genial ~adv gently **kindness** n **kindhearted** adj

**kindergarten** n class, school for

──────── THESAURUS ────────

**key** n latchkey, opener; answer, clue, cue, explanation, guide, interpretation, lead, means, pointer, sign, solution ~adj basic, chief, crucial, decisive, essential, fundamental, important, leading, main, major, pivotal, principal

**keynote** centre, core, essence, gist, kernel, marrow, substance

**kick** v boot, punt ~n force, intensity, pep, power, punch, pungency, sparkle, strength, tang, verve, vitality, zest

**kid** n baby, bairn, boy, child, girl, infant, lad, teenager, youngster, youth ~v bamboozle, fool, hoax, hoodwink, jest, mock, pretend, ridicule, tease, trick

**kidnap** abduct, capture, hijack, remove, seize, skyjack, steal

**kill** annihilate, assassinate, butcher, destroy, execute, exterminate, massacre, murder, slaughter, slay; cancel, cease, deaden, defeat, halt, quash, quell, ruin, scotch, smother, stifle, stop, suppress, veto

**killer** assassin, butcher, executioner, gunman, murderer, slaughterer, slayer

**killing** bloodshed, carnage, fatality, homicide, manslaughter, massacre, murder, slaughter, slaying

**kin** affinity, blood, connection, extraction, kinship, lineage, relationship, stock

**kind** n brand, breed, class, family,

children of about four to six years old

**kindle** v set alight; arouse; catch fire **kindling** n small wood to kindle fires

**kinetic** adj relating to motion

**king** n male ruler; chess piece; highest court card; Draughts crowned piece **kingdom** n state ruled by king; realm; sphere **kingpin** n Inf chief thing or person **king-size** adj Inf very large

**kingfisher** n small brightly-coloured bird

**kink** n tight twist in rope, wire, hair etc. ~v make, become kinked **kinky** adj full of kinks; Inf deviant

**kiosk** n small, sometimes movable booth; public telephone box

**kip** n/v **kipping, kipped** Inf sleep

**kipper** n smoked herring

**kirk** n in Scotland, church

**kismet** n fate, destiny

**kiss** n touch or caress with lips; light touch ~v touch with lips **kiss**

**of life** mouth-to-mouth resuscitation

**kit** n outfit, equipment; personal effects, esp. of traveller; set of pieces of equipment sold ready to be assembled ~v (with out) provide with kit **kitbag** n bag for soldier's or traveller's kit

**kitchen** n room used for cooking

**kite** n light papered frame flown in wind; large hawk

**kitsch** n vulgarized, pretentious art

**kitten** n young cat **kittenish** adj playful

**kitty** n in some card games, pool; communal fund

**kiwi** n (pl **kiwis**) NZ flightless bird; Inf New Zealander **kiwi fruit** edible fruit with green flesh

**klaxon** n loud horn

**kleptomania** n compulsion to steal **kleptomaniac** n

**km** kilometre

**knack** n acquired facility or dexterity; trick; habit

genus, race, set, sort, species, stamp, variety ~adj affectionate, amiable, beneficent, benevolent, benign, bounteous, charitable, compassionate, congenial, considerate, cordial, courteous, friendly, generous, gentle, good, gracious, humane, indulgent, lenient, loving, mild, neighbourly, obliging, thoughtful

**kindle** fire, ignite, inflame, light, set fire to

**kindly** adj affable, benevolent, compassionate, cordial, favourable, genial, gentle, good-natured, hearty, helpful, kind, mild, pleasant, polite, sympathetic, warm ~adv agreeably, graciously, politely, tenderly, thoughtfully

**kindness** affection, benevolence, charity, compassion, fellow-feeling, generosity, goodness, grace, humanity, indulgence, tenderness, tolerance, understanding

**king** emperor, majesty, monarch, overlord, prince, ruler, sovereign

**kingdom** dominion, dynasty, empire, monarchy, realm, reign, sovereignty

**kink** bend, coil, knot, tangle, twist, wrinkle

**kiosk** bookstall, booth, counter, newsstand, stall, stand

**kiss** v greet, osculate, salute

**kit** apparatus, effects, equipment, gear, outfit, rig, supplies, tackle, tools

**knack** ability, aptitude, bent, ca-

**knacker** n buyer of worn-out horses etc. for killing **knackered** adj Sl exhausted

**knapsack** n haversack

**knave** n jack at cards; Obs rogue **knavish** adj

**knead** v work into dough; massage

**knee** n joint between thigh and lower leg **kneecap** n bone in front of knee **kneejerk** adj (of reaction) automatic and predictable **knees-up** n Inf party

**kneel** v kneeling, knelt fall, rest on knees

**knell** n/v (ring) death bell

**knickers** pl n woman's undergarment for lower half of body

**knick-knack** n trinket

**knife** n (pl knives) cutting blade, esp. one in handle, used as implement or weapon ~v cut or stab with knife

**knight** n man of rank below baronet; member of medieval order of chivalry; piece in chess ~v confer knighthood on **knighthood** n

**knit** v knitting, knitted or knit form (garment etc.) by linking loops of

yarn; draw together; unite **knitter** n

**knitting** n knitted work; act of knitting

**knob** n rounded lump **knobbly** adj

**knock** v strike, hit; Inf disparage; rap audibly; (of engine) make metallic noise ~n blow, rap **knocker** n appliance for knocking on door **knock back** Inf drink quickly; reject **knock-kneed** adj having incurved legs **knock out** render unconscious; Inf overwhelm, amaze **knockout** n

**knoll** n small hill

**knot** n fastening of strands by looping and pulling tight; cluster; hard lump, esp. in timber; nautical miles per hour ~v **knotting, knotted** tie with knot, in knots **knotty** adj full of knots; puzzling, difficult

**know** v knowing, knew, known be aware (of), have information (about); be acquainted with; understand; feel certain **knowing** adj shrewd **knowingly** adv shrewdly; deliberately **knowledge** n knowing; what one knows; learning **knowledgable, knowledgeable** adj well-informed

pacity, dexterity, expertise, flair, forte, genius, gift, ingenuity, skill, talent, trick

**kneel** bow, curtsey, genuflect, kowtow, stoop

**knell** n chime, peal, toll ~v chime, herald, peal, resound, ring, sound, toll

**knickers** bloomers, briefs, drawers, panties, smalls, underwear

**knife** blade, cutter, cutting tool

**knit** affix, ally, bind, connect, contract, fasten, heal, intertwine, join, link, loop, mend, secure, tie, unite, weave

**knob** bump, knot, lump, projec-

tion, protrusion, snag, stud, swelling, tumour

**knock** v belt Inf, clap, cuff, hit, punch, rap, slap, smack, strike, thump, thwack ~n Inf, blow, box, clip, clout Inf, cuff, hammering, rap, slap, smack, thump

**knot** n bond, bow, braid, connection, joint, ligature, loop, tie ~v bind, entangle, knit, loop, secure, tether, tie, weave

**know** apprehend, experience, fathom, feel certain, learn, notice, perceive, realize, recognize, see, undergo, understand; be familiar with, have dealings with, have knowledge

**knuckle** *n* bone at finger joint
**knuckle down** get down (to work)
**knuckle-duster** *n* metal appliance on knuckles to add force to blow
**knuckle under** submit
**KO** knockout
**koala** *n* marsupial Aust. animal, native bear
**kohl** *n* cosmetic powder

**Koran** *n* sacred book of Muslims
**kosher** *adj* conforming to Jewish dietary law; *Inf* legitimate, authentic
**kowtow** *v* prostrate oneself; be obsequious
**krypton** *n* rare atmospheric gas
**kudos** *n* fame; credit
**kung fu** *n* Chinese martial art

─────────── THESAURUS ───────────

of, recognize
**knowing** astute, clever, competent, discerning, experienced, expert, intelligent, qualified, skilful, well-informed
**knowledge** ability, cognition, consciousness, discernment, grasp, judgment, recognition, understanding; enlightenment, erudition, instruction, intelligence, learning, scholarship, science, tuition, wisdom

# L l

**l** litre

**lab** *n Inf* short for LABORATORY

**label** *n* slip of paper, metal etc., giving information; descriptive phrase ~*v* **-elling, -elled** give label

**laboratory** *n* place for scientific investigations or for manufacture of chemicals

**labour** *n* exertion of body or mind; workers collectively; process of childbirth ~*v* work hard; strive; move with difficulty; stress to excess **laboured** *adj* uttered, done, with difficulty **labourer** *n* manual worker **laborious** *adj* tedious

**labrador** *n* breed of large, smooth-coated retriever dog

**laburnum** *n* tree with yellow hanging flowers

**labyrinth** *n* maze; perplexity

**lace** *n* patterned openwork fabric; cord, usu. one of pair, to draw edges together ~*v* fasten with laces; flavour with spirit **lacy** *adj* fine, like lace

**lacerate** *v* tear, mangle

**lachrymose** *adj* tearful

**lack** *n* deficiency ~*v* need, be short of

**lackadaisical** *adj* languid

**lackey** *n (pl -eys)* servile follower; footman

**lacklustre** *adj* lacking brilliance or vitality

**laconic** *adj* terse

**lacquer** *n* hard varnish ~*v* coat with this

**lacrosse** *n* ball game played with long-handled racket

**lad** *n* boy, young fellow

**ladder** *n* frame with rungs, for climbing; line of torn stitches, esp. in stockings

**laden** *adj* heavily loaded

**ladle** *n* spoon with long handle and large bowl ~*v* serve out liquid with a ladle

**lady** *n* female counterpart of gentleman; polite term for a woman; title of some women of rank **ladybird** *n* small red bettle with black spots **ladylike** *adj* polite and

─────────── THESAURUS ───────────

**label** *n* flag, marker, sticker, tag, tally, ticket ~*v* flag, mark, stamp, sticker, tag, tally

**labour** *n* industry, toil, work; employees, hands, labourers, workers, work force, workmen; childbirth, contractions, delivery, labour pains, pains, throes ~*v* dwell on, elaborate, overdo, overemphasize, strain

**laboured** awkward, difficult, forced, heavy, stiff, strained

**labourer** blue-collar worker, drudge, hand, labouring man, manual worker, worker, workman

**lacerate** cut, gash, jag, maim,

rend, rip, slash, tear, wound

**lack** *n* absence, dearth, deficiency, deprivation, destitution, need, scantiness, scarcity, shortage, want ~*v* miss, need, require, want

**lackey** creature, hanger-on, instrument, minion, parasite, sycophant, toady, tool, yes man; attendant, flunky, footman, manservant, valet

**lacklustre** boring, drab, dry, dull, flat, leaden, lifeless, prosaic, vapid

**lad** boy, fellow, juvenile, kid *Inf*, schoolboy, youngster, youth

**laden** burdened, charged, full, hampered, loaded, oppressed,

refined

**lag¹** v **lagging, lagged** go too slowly, fall behind **laggard** n one who lags

**lag²** v **lagging, lagged** wrap boiler, pipes etc. with insulating material **lagging** n this material

**lag³** n Sl convict

**lager** n light-bodied beer

**lagoon** n saltwater lake, enclosed by atoll or sandbank

**laid** see LAY² **laid-back** adj Inf relaxed

**lair** n den of animal

**laird** n Scottish landowner

**laissez-faire** n principle of non-intervention

**laity** n people not belonging to clergy

**lake** n expanse of inland water

**lama** n Buddhist priest in Tibet or Mongolia

**lamb** n young of the sheep; its meat; innocent or helpless creature ~v give birth to lamb

**lambast, lambaste** v beat, thrash; reprimand severely

**lame** adj crippled in leg; limping; unconvincing ~v cripple

**lamé** n/adj (fabric) interwoven with gold or silver thread

**lament** v express sorrow (for) ~n expression of grief; song of grief **lamentable** adj deplorable, disap-

pointing, **lamentation** n

**laminate** v make (sheet of material) by bonding together two or more thin sheets; cover with thin sheet ~n laminated sheet **lamination** n

**lamp** n appliance (esp. electrical) that produces, light, heat etc. **lamppost** n post supporting lamp in street

**lampoon** n/v (make subject of) a satire

**lamprey** n fish like an eel

**lance** n horseman's spear ~v pierce with lance or lancet **lancet** n pointed two-edged surgical knife **lance corporal** lowest noncommissioned army rank

**land** n solid part of earth's surface; ground; country; estate ~v come to land; disembark; arrive on ground; bring to land; Inf obtain; catch; Inf strike **landed** adj possessing, consisting of lands **landing** n act of landing; platform between flights of stairs **landlocked** adj completely surrounded by land **landlord** n (fem **landlady**) person who lets land or houses etc.; master or mistress of inn, boarding house etc. **landlubber** n person ignorant of the sea and ships **landmark** n conspicuous object; event, decision etc. considered as important stage in development

———— THESAURUS ————

taxed, weighed down

**lag** dawdle, delay, idle, linger, loiter, saunter, straggle, tarry, trail

**laid-back** at ease, casual, easygoing, relaxed, unhurried

**lame** crippled, disabled, game, hobbling, limping; feeble, flimsy, inadequate, pathetic, poor, thin, unconvincing, weak

**lament** v bemoan, bewail, com-

plain, deplore, grieve, mourn, regret, sorrow, wail, weep ~n complaint, moan, moaning, plaint, wail, wailing

**lamentable** deplorable, disappointing, low, meagre, mean, miserable, pitiful, poor, wretched

**lampoon** n burlesque, parody, satire, skit, squib ~v burlesque, caricature, make fun of, mock, parody,

of something **landscape** n piece of inland scenery; picture of this ~v create, arrange garden, park etc.

**landslide** n falling of soil, rock etc. down mountainside; overwhelming election victory

**lane** n narrow road or street; specified air, sea route; area of road for one stream of traffic

**language** n system of sounds, symbols etc. for communicating thought; style of speech or expression

**languish** v be or become weak or faint; droop, pine **languid** adj lacking energy, spiritless **languor** n lack of energy; tender mood **languorous** adj

**lank** adj lean; limp **lanky** adj

**lantern** n transparent case for lamp or candle

**lap**¹ n the part between waist and knees of a person when sitting; single circuit of track; stage or part of journey ~v **lapping, lapped** enfold, wrap round; overtake opponent to be one or more circuits ahead

**lap**² v **lapping, lapped** drink by scooping up with tongue; (of waves etc.) beat softly

**lapel** n part of front of coat folded back towards shoulders

**lapse** n fall (in standard, condition, virtue etc.); slip; passing (of time etc.) ~v fall away; end, esp. through disuse

**lapwing** n type of plover

**larceny** n theft

**larch** n deciduous conifer tree

**lard** n prepared pig's fat ~v insert strips of bacon in (meat); intersperse

**larder** n storeroom for food

**large** adj great in size, number etc. ~adv in a big way **largely** adv **largesse** n generosity; gift **at large**

--- THESAURUS ---

ridicule, satirize

**land** n earth, ground, terra firma; dirt, ground, loam, soil; country, district, nation, province, region, territory, tract; acres, estate, grounds, property, realty ~v alight, arrive, berth, debark, disembark, dock, touch down

**landlord** host, hotelier, hotelkeeper, innkeeper

**landmark** feature, monument; crisis, milestone, turning point, watershed

**landscape** countryside, outlook, panorama, prospect, scene, scenery, view, vista

**language** conversation, discourse, expression, parlance, speech, talk; dialect, idiom, speech, tongue, vernacular, vocabulary; diction, expression, phrasing, style, wording

**languid** drooping, faint, feeble, limp, pining, sickly, weak, weary; dull, inactive, lazy, lethargic, listless, sluggish, spiritless

**languish** decline, droop, fade, fail, faint, flag, sicken, waste, weaken, wilt, wither

**lank** dull, lifeless, limp, long, straggling

**lanky** angular, bony, gaunt, rangy, spare, tall, thin

**lap**¹ n circle, circuit, course, loop, orbit, round, tour ~v cover, enfold, fold, swathe, turn, twist, wrap

**lap**² drink, lick, sip, sup; ripple, slap, splash, swish, wash

**lapse** n error, failing, fault, indiscretion, mistake, omission, oversight, slip ~v decline, drop, fail, fall, sink, slide, slip; end, expire, run out, stop, terminate

free; in general **large-scale** *adj* wide-ranging, extensive

**largo** *adv/n Mus* (passage played) in slow and dignified manner

**lark**[1] *n* small, brown singing bird; skylark

**lark**[2] *n* frolic, spree ~*v* indulge in lark

**larva** *n* (*pl* **-vae**) immature insect **larval** *adj*

**larynx** *n* (*pl* **larynges**) part of throat containing vocal cords **laryngitis** *n* inflammation of this

**lasagne** *n* pasta formed in wide, flat sheets

**lascivious** *adj* lustful

**laser** *n* device for concentrating electromagnetic radiation in an intense, narrow beam

**lash**[1] *n* stroke with whip; flexible part of whip; eyelash ~*v* strike with whip etc.; dash against; attack verbally, ridicule; flick, wave sharply to and fro; (*with* **out**) hit, kick

**lash**[2] *v* fasten or bind tightly

**lashings** *pl n Inf* abundance

**lass, lassie** *n* girl

**lassitude** *n* weariness

**lasso** *n* (*pl* **-sos, -soes**) rope with noose for catching cattle etc. ~*v* **-soing, -soed** catch with this

**last**[1] *adj/adv* after all others; most recent(ly) ~*adj* remaining ~*n* last person or thing **lastly** *adv* finally **last-ditch** *adj* done as final resort **last straw** small irritation that, coming after others, is too much to bear **last word** final comment in argument; most recent or best example

**last**[2] *v* continue, hold out

**last**[3] *n* model of foot on which shoes are made, repaired

**latch** *n* fastening for door ~*v* fasten with latch; (*with* **onto**) become attached

**late** *adj* later, latest, last coming after the appointed time; recent; recently dead ~*adv* after proper time; recently; at, till late hour **lately** *adv* not long since

**latent** *adj* existing but not developed; hidden

**lateral** *adj* of, at, from the side

**latex** *n* sap or fluid of plants, esp. of rubber tree

———————————— THESAURUS ————————————

**large** big, bulky, enormous, giant, great, huge, immense, king-size, massive, monumental, sizable, substantial, vast

**largely** chiefly, generally, mainly, mostly, predominantly, primarily, principally, widely

**lark** antic, caper, fling, frolic, fun, gambol, game, jape, mischief, prank, romp, spree

**lash**[1] *n* blow, hit, stripe, stroke ~*v* beat, birch, flog, horsewhip, lambast(e), thrash, whip

**lash**[2] bind, fasten, join, make fast, rope, secure, strap, tie

**lass** damsel, girl, maid, maiden,

miss, young woman

**last**[1] aftermost, hindmost, rearmost; latest, most recent ~*adv* after, behind

**last**[2] *v* abide, continue, endure, keep, persist, remain, survive, wear

**latch** bar, bolt, catch, clamp, fastening, hasp, hook, lock

**late** behind, belated, delayed, overdue, slow, tardy, unpunctual; advanced, fresh, modern, new, recent; dead, deceased, defunct, departed

**lately** just now, latterly, of late, recently

**lateral** edgeways, flanking, side,

**lath** *n* thin strip of wood

**lathe** *n* machine for turning and shaping

**lather** *n* soapy froth; frothy sweat ~*v* make frothy

**Latin** *n* language of ancient Romans —*adj* of ancient Romans or their language

**latitude** *n* angular distance in degrees N or S of equator; scope; *pl* regions

**latrine** *n* in army etc., lavatory

**latter** *adj* second of two; later; more recent **latterly** *adv* **latter-day** *adj* modern

**lattice** *n* network of strips of wood, metal etc.; window so made

**laud** *v* praise **laudable** *adj* praiseworthy

**laudanum** *n* sedative from opium

**laugh** *v/n* (make) sound of amusement, merriment or scorn **laughable** *adj* ludicrous **laughter** *n* laughing **laughing stock** object of general derision

**launch**[1] *v* set afloat; set in motion; begin; propel (missile, spacecraft) into space

**launch**[2] *n* large power-driven boat

**laundry** *n* place for washing clothes; clothes etc. for washing **launder** *v* wash and iron **Launderette** *n* Trademark shop with coin-operated washing, drying machines

**laureate** *adj* crowned with laurels **poet laureate** poet with appointment to Royal Household

**laurel** *n* glossy-leaved shrub, bay tree; *pl* its leaves, emblem of victory or merit

**lava** *n* molten matter thrown out by volcano

**lavatory** *n* toilet, water closet

**lavender** *n* shrub with fragrant, pale-lilac flowers; this colour

**lavish** *adj* plentiful, rich; very generous ~*v* spend, bestow, profusely

**law** *n* rule binding on community; system of such rules; legal science; general principle deduced from facts **lawful** *adj* allowed by law **lawless** *adj* ignoring laws; violent **lawyer** *n* professional expert in law **lawsuit** *n* prosecution of claim in court

————————— THESAURUS —————————

sideways

**lather** bubbles, foam, froth, soap, soapsuds, suds

**latitude** breadth, compass, extent, range, room, scope, space, span, spread, sweep, width

**latter** closing, concluding, last, later, latest, modern, recent, second

**lattice** fretwork, grating, grid, grille, mesh, network, trellis, web

**laudable** admirable, creditable, excellent, meritorious, praiseworthy, worthy

**laugh** *v* chortle, chuckle, giggle, guffaw, snigger, titter ~*n* chortle, chuckle, giggle, guffaw, snigger, titter

**laughter** amusement, glee, hilarity, merriment, mirth

**launch** cast, discharge, dispatch, fire, project, propel, throw; begin, commence, embark upon, inaugurate, initiate, instigate, introduce, open, start

**lavatory** bathroom, convenience, loo, powder room, (public) convenience, toilet, washroom, water closet

**lavish** copious, exuberant, lush, opulent, plentiful, profuse, prolific, sumptuous; bountiful, free, generous, liberal, munificent, openhanded

**law** act, code, commandment, cov-

**lawn** *n* tended turf in garden etc.

**lawyer** *see* LAW

**lax** *adj* not strict; slack **laxative** *adj/n* (substance) having loosening effect on bowels **laxity, laxness** *n*

**lay**[1] *past tense of* LIE **layabout** *n* lazy person, loafer

**lay**[2] *v* **laying, laid** deposit, set, cause to lie; devise (plan); attribute (blame); place (bet); (of animal) produce eggs **layer** *n* single thickness as stratum or coating **~v** form layer **lay-by** *n* stopping place for traffic beside road **lay off** *v* dismiss staff during slack period **lay-off** *n* **layout** *n* arrangement

**lay**[3] *adj* not clerical or professional **layman** *n* ordinary person

**lay**[4] *n* narrative poem

**layette** *n* clothes for newborn child

**lazy** *adj* averse to work **laze** *v* be lazy **lazily** *adv*

**lb.** pound

**lbw** *Cricket* leg before wicket

**lead**[1] *v* **leading, led** guide, conduct; persuade; direct; be, go, play first; spend (one's life); result; give access to **~n** that which leads or is used to lead; example; front or principal place, role etc.; cable bringing current to electrical instrument **leader** *n* one who leads; editorial article in newspaper **leadership** *n*

**lead**[2] *n* soft, heavy grey metal; graphite in pencil; plummet **leaded** *adj* (of windows) made from small panes held together by lead strips **leaden** *adj* sluggish; dull grey; made from lead

━━━━━━━━━━━━━━━ THESAURUS ━━━━━━━━━━━━━━━

**enant**, decree, edict, enactment, order, ordinance, rule, statute

**lawful** allowable, authorized, constitutional, just, legal, legalized, legitimate, licit, permissible, proper, rightful, valid

**lawless** anarchic, chaotic, disorderly, insubordinate, insurgent, mutinous, rebellious, reckless, riotous, seditious, unruly, wild

**lawsuit** action, argument, case, cause, contest, dispute, litigation, proceedings, prosecution, suit, trial

**lawyer** advocate, attorney, barrister, legal adviser, solicitor

**lay**[1] deposit, establish, leave, place, plant, posit, put, set, set down, settle, spread; arrange, dispose, locate, organize, position, set out; concoct, contrive, design, devise, hatch, plan, plot, prepare, work out; bet, gamble, hazard, risk, stake, wager

**lay**[2] secular; amateur; inexpert

**layabout** good-for-nothing, idler,

laggard, loafer, lounger, shirker, vagrant, wastrel

**layer** bed, ply, row, seam, stratum, thickness, tier

**layman** amateur, lay person, nonprofessional, outsider

**lay off** discharge, dismiss, drop, let go, oust, pay off

**layout** arrangement, design, draft, outline, plan

**lazy** idle, inactive, indolent, inert, slack, slothful, slow

**lead** *v* conduct, escort, guide, pilot, precede, steer, usher; cause, dispose, draw, incline, induce, influence, persuade, prevail, prompt; command, direct, govern, head, manage, supervise; be ahead (of), exceed, excel, outdo, outstrip, surpass, transcend; have, live, pass, spend, undergo **~n** advantage, edge, first place, margin, precedence, priority, start, supremacy, van; direction, example, guidance,

**leaf** *n* (*pl* **leaves**) organ of photosynthesis in plants, consisting of a flat, usu. green blade on stem; two pages of book etc.; thin sheet ~*v* turn through (pages etc.) cursorily **leaflet** *n* small leaf; single printed and folded sheet, handbill **leafy** *adj*

**league**[1] *n* agreement for mutual help; parties to it; federation of clubs etc.; *Inf* class, level

**league**[2] *n* former measure of distance, about 3 miles

**leak** *n* defect that allows escape or entrance of liquid, gas, radiation etc.; disclosure ~*v* let fluid etc. in or out; (of fluid etc.) find its way through leak; (allow) to become known little by little **leakage** *n* leaking; gradual escape or loss **leaky** *adj*

**lean**[1] *adj* lacking fat; thin; meagre;

*n* lean part of meat

**lean**[2] *v* **leaning**, **leaned** or **leant** rest against; incline; tend (towards); rely (on) **leaning** *n* tendency **lean-to** *n* room, shed built against existing wall

**leap** *v* **leaping**, **leapt** or **leaped** spring, jump; spring over ~*n* jump **leapfrog** *n*/*v* vault over person bending down **leap year** year with extra day

**learn** *v* **learning**, **learnt** or **learned** gain skill, knowledge; memorize; find out **learned** *adj* showing much learning **learner** *n* learning knowledge got by study

**lease** *n* contract by which land or property is rented ~*v* let, rent by lease **leasehold** *n*/*v* held on lease **leash** *n* lead for dog

——————— THESAURUS ———————

leadership, model; leading role, principal, protagonist, star part

**leader** captain, chief, chieftain, commander, conductor, director, guide, head, principal, ruler, superior

**leadership** direction, domination, guidance, management, running; authority, command, control, influence, initiative, pre-eminence, supremacy, sway

**leaf** *n* blade, flag, needle, pad; folio, page, sheet

**leaflet** bill, booklet, circular, handbill, pamphlet

**league** alliance, association, coalition, compact, confederacy, fellowship, fraternity, guild, order, partnership, union

**leak** *n* chink, crack, crevice, fissure, hole, opening, puncture; drip, leakage, percolation, seepage; disclosure, divulgence ~*v* discharge, drip, escape, exude, pass, percolate,

seep, spill, trickle; disclose, divulge

**lean**[1] *adj* bony, emaciated, gaunt, lank, rangy, skinny, slender, slim, spare, thin, wiry; bare, barren, meagre, pitiful, poor, scanty, sparse

**lean**[2] *v* be supported, prop, recline, repose, rest; bend, incline, slant, slope, tilt, tip

**leaning** aptitude, bent, bias, inclination, liking, partiality, penchant, taste, tendency

**leap** *v* bounce, bound, caper, cavort, frisk, gambol, hop, jump, skip, spring ~*n* bound, caper, frisk, hop, jump, skip, spring, vault

**learn** acquire, attain, grasp, imbibe, master, pick up; get off pat, learn by heart, memorize; detect, discern, discover, find out, gain, gather, hear, understand

**learned** academic, cultured, erudite, expert, highbrow, literate, scholarly, skilled, versed, well-read

**learner** beginner, disciple, novice,

**least** adj smallest; *superlative of* LIT-TLE ~*n* smallest one ~*adv* in smallest degree

**leather** *n* prepared skin of animal **leathery** adj like leather, tough

**leave**[1] *v* leaving, left go away; allow to remain; entrust; bequeath

**leave**[2] *n* permission, esp. to be absent from duty; period of such absence; formal parting

**leaven** *n* yeast ~*v* raise with leaven

**lecherous** adj full of lust; lascivious **lecher** *n* lecherous man **lechery** *n*

**lectern** *n* reading desk

**lecture** *n* instructive discourse; speech of reproof ~*v* deliver discourse; reprove **lecturer** *n*

**ledge** *n* narrow shelf sticking out from wall, cliff etc.; ridge below surface of sea

**ledger** *n* book of debit and credit accounts

**lee** *n* shelter; side, esp. of ship, away from wind **leeward** adj/adv/n (on, towards) lee side **leeway** *n* lee-

ward drift of ship; room for movement within limits

**leech** *n* species of bloodsucking worm

**leek** *n* plant like onion with long bulb and thick stem

**leer** *v/n* glance with malign or lascivious expression

**lees** *pl n* sediment; dregs

**left**[1] adj on or to the west; opposite to the right; radical, socialist ~*adv* on or towards the left ~*n* the left hand or part; *Politics* reforming or radical party; (*also* **left wing**) **leftist** *n/adj* (person) of the political left

**left**[2] past tense past participle of LEAVE[1] **leftover** *n* unused portion

**leg** *n* one of limbs on which person or animal walks, runs, stands; part of garment covering leg; support, as leg of table; **leggings** *pl n* covering of leather or other material (for legs) **leggy** adj long-legged **legless** adj without legs; *Sl* very drunk

**legacy** *n* bequest; thing handed down to successor

pupil, scholar, student, trainee, tyro

**lease** *v* charter, hire, let, loan, rent

**least** fewest, last, lowest, meanest, minimum, poorest, smallest, tiniest

**leave**[1] *v* abandon, abscond, decamp, depart, desert, disappear, exit, forsake, go, move, quit, relinquish, retire, withdraw; abandon, cease, desert, desist, drop, give up, relinquish, renounce, stop; allot, assign, cede, commit, consign, entrust, refer; bequeath, transmit, will

**leave**[2] *n* allowance, concession, consent, freedom, liberty, permission, sanction; furlough, holiday, sabbatical, time off, vacation

**lecture** *n* address, discourse, harangue, instruction, lesson, speech,

talk; censure, chiding, rebuke, reprimand, reproof, scolding ~*v* address, discourse, expound, harangue, speak, spout, talk, teach; admonish, castigate, censure, chide, reprimand, reprove, scold

**leeway** latitude, margin, play, room, scope, space

**left** adj larboard *Naut*, left-hand, port, sinistral; communist, leftist, left-wing, socialist

**leftover** *pl* leavings, oddments, odds and ends, remains, remnants, scraps

**leg** limb, member; brace, prop, support, upright; lap, part, portion, section, segment, stage, stretch

**legacy** bequest, estate, gift, heir-

**legal** adj in accordance with law **legality** n **legalize** v make legal **legally** adv

**legate** n messenger, representative

**legatee** n recipient of legacy

**legato** adv Mus smoothly

**legend** n traditional story; notable person or event; inscription **legendary** adj

**legible** adj readable **legibility** n

**legion** n various military bodies; association of veterans; large number ~adj countless **legionary** adj/n **legionnaire** n member of legion **legionnaire's disease** serious bacterial disease similar to pneumonia

**legislate** v make laws **legislation** n act of legislating; laws which are made **legislative** adj

**legislator** n **legislature** n body that makes laws

**legitimate** adj born in wedlock; lawful, regular ~v make lawful **legitimacy** n **legitimize** v

**legume** n pod

**leisure** n spare time **leisurely** adj unhurried ~adv slowly

**lemming** n rodent of arctic regions

**lemon** n pale yellow fruit; its colour; Sl useless person or thing **lemonade** n drink made from lemon juice **lemon curd** creamy spread made of lemons, butter etc.

**lemur** n nocturnal animal like monkey

**lend** v **lending**, **lent** give temporary use of; let out at interest; bestow **lender** n

**length** n measurement from end to end; duration; extent; piece of a certain length **lengthen** v make, become, longer **lengthy** adj very long

———————— THESAURUS ————————

loom, inheritance; heritage; tradition

**legal** allowed, authorized, lawful, legalized, legitimate, licit, permissible, proper, rightful, sanctioned, valid

**legalize** allow, approve, license, permit, sanction, validate

**legend** fable, fiction, folk tale, myth, narrative, saga, story, tale

**legendary** fabled, fabulous, fanciful, fictitious, mythical, romantic, traditional

**legible** clear, distinct, neat, plain, readable

**legion** n army, brigade, horde, division, force, troop; drove, horde, host, mass, multitude, myriad, number, throng ~adj countless, myriad

**legislate** enact, establish, ordain, prescribe

**legislation** enactment, prescrip-

tion, regulation; act, bill, charter, law, measure

**legislative** adj congressional, judicial, ordaining, parliamentary

**legitimate** authentic, genuine, kosher Inf, lawful, legal, licit, proper, real, rightful, sanctioned, statutory, true

**leisure** ease, freedom, holiday, liberty, opportunity, pause, quiet, recreation, relaxation, respite, rest, retirement, spare time, vacation

**leisurely** comfortable, easy, gentle, lazy, relaxed, restful, slow, unhurried

**lend** advance, loan; add, afford, bestow, confer, contribute, furnish, give, grant, hand out, impart, present, provide, supply

**length** of linear extent distance, extent, measure, reach, span; of time duration, period, space, span, stretch, term

**lenient** *adj* not strict **leniency** *n*

**lens** *n* (*pl* **lenses**) glass etc. shaped to converge or diverge light rays

**Lent** *n* period of fasting from Ash Wednesday to Easter Eve

**lent** *see* LEND

**lentil** *n* edible seed of leguminous plant

**leopard** *n* (*fem* **leopardess**) large, spotted, carnivorous cat

**leotard** *n* tight-fitting garment covering most of body

**leper** *n* one ill with leprosy; person shunned **leprosy** *n* ulcerous skin disease

**leprechaun** *n* mischievous Irish elf

**lesbian** *n* homosexual woman ~*adj* (of woman) homosexual

**lesion** *n* harmful sore on bodily organ

**less** *adj comparative of* LITTLE not so much ~*n* smaller part, quantity; a lesser amount ~*adv* to a smaller ex-

tent ~*prep* minus **lessen** *v* diminish; reduce **lesser** *adj* smaller; minor

**lesson** *n* instalment of course of instruction; content of this; experience that teaches; portion of Scripture read in church

**lest** *conj* for fear that

**let**[1] *v* letting, let allow, enable, cause; rent; be leased **let down** disappoint; lower; deflate **let off** excuse; fire, explode; emit **let up** *v* diminish, stop

**let**[2] *n* hindrance; in some games, minor infringement or obstruction

**lethal** *adj* deadly

**lethargy** *n* apathy, lack of energy **lethargic** *adj*

**letter** *n* alphabetical symbol; written message; strict meaning, interpretation; *pl* literature ~*v* mark with, in, letters

**lettuce** *n* salad plant

**leukaemia** *n* progressive blood

————————————— THESAURUS —————————————

**lengthen** continue, draw out, elongate, expand, extend, increase, prolong, protract, stretch

**lengthy** diffuse, extended, interminable, long, prolix, tedious, verbose

**leniency, lenience** clemency, forbearance, gentleness, indulgence, mercy, mildness, tolerance

**lenient** forbearing, forgiving, gentle, indulgent, kind, merciful, mild, tender, tolerant

**less** *adj* shorter, slighter, smaller; inferior, minor, secondary, subordinate ~*adv* barely, little, meagrely

**lessen** abate, abridge, contract, curtail, decrease, diminish, ease, impair, lighten, lower, moderate, narrow, reduce, relax, shrink, slacken, weaken

**lesser** inferior, lower, minor, secondary, slighter, subordinate

**lesson** class, coaching, instruction, period, schooling, teaching, tutoring; deterrent, example, exemplar, message, model, moral, precept

**let** *v* allow, authorize, give leave, grant, permit, sanction, tolerate, warrant; hire, lease, rent

**lethal** baneful, deadly, destructive, devastating, fatal, mortal, murderous, pernicious, virulent

**lethargic** apathetic, comatose, drowsy, dull, heavy, inactive, inert, languid, lazy, listless, sleepy, slothful, slow, sluggish, torpid

**let off** absolve, discharge, excuse, exempt, exonerate, forgive, pardon, release, spare; discharge, emit, explode, fire, give off, leak, release

**letter** character, sign, symbol; acknowledgment, answer, communication, dispatch, epistle, line, mes-

disease

**level** *adj* horizontal; even, flat ~*n* horizontal line or surface; instrument for establishing horizontal plane; position on scale; grade ~*v* -elling, -elled make, become level; knock down; aim (gun, accusation etc.) **level crossing** point where railway and road cross **level-headed** *adj* not apt to be carried away by emotion

**lever** *n* rigid bar pivoted about a fulcrum to transfer a force with mechanical advantage; operating handle ~*v* prise, move, with lever **leverage** *n* action, power of lever; influence

**leveret** *n* young hare

**leviathan** *n* sea monster; anything huge or formidable

**levitation** *n* raising of solid body into the air supernaturally **levitate** *v* (cause to) do this

**levity** *n* (undue) frivolity

**levy** *v* levying, levied impose (tax); raise (troops) ~*n* (*pl* **levies**) imposition or collection of taxes

**lewd** *adj* lustful; indecent

**lexicon** *n* dictionary

**liable** *adj* answerable; exposed (to); subject (to); likely (to) **liability** *n* state of being liable; debt; hindrance, disadvantage; *pl* debts

**liaison** *n* union; connection; secret relationship **liaise** *v*

**liar** *n see* LIE²

**lib** *n Inf* short for LIBERATION

**libel** *n* published statement falsely damaging person's reputation ~*v* -belling, -belled defame falsely **libellous** *adj* defamatory

**liberal** *adj* (*also with cap.*) of politi-

sage, missive, note, reply

**let up** abate, decrease, diminish, moderate, relax, slacken, stop, subside

**level** *adj* even, flat, horizontal, plain, plane, smooth, uniform; balanced, comparable, equal, equivalent, even, flush, in line, on a par, proportionate ~*n* bed, floor, layer, storey, stratum; altitude, elevation, height ~*v* flatten, plane, smooth; bulldoze, demolish, destroy, flatten, raze, smooth, wreck

**level-headed** balanced, calm, collected, composed, cool, dependable, reasonable, sane, sensible, steady

**lever** *n* bar, crowbar, handle ~*v* force, move, prise, purchase, raise

**levy** *v* charge, collect, demand, exact, gather, impose, tax ~*n* assessment, collection, exaction, gathering, imposition

**lewd** bawdy, blue, dirty, indecent, libidinous, licentious, loose, obscene, pornographic, salacious, smutty, vile, vulgar

**liability** accountability, duty, obligation, onus, responsibility; arrear, debit, debt, obligation; burden, disadvantage, drag, drawback, encumbrance, handicap, hindrance, impediment, millstone, nuisance

**liable** accountable, answerable, bound, responsible; exposed, open, subject, susceptible, vulnerable

**liaison** communication, connection, contact, go-between, interchange; affair, amour, intrigue, romance

**liar** fibber, perjurer, prevaricator

**libel** *n* aspersion, defamation, slander, smear ~*v* blacken, defame, malign, revile, slander, slur, smear, traduce, vilify

**libellous** aspersive, defamatory,

cal party favouring democratic re-
forms and individual freedom; generous; tolerant; abundant ~n one
who has liberal ideas or opinions
**liberality** n generosity **liberalize** v
make (laws etc.) less restrictive **liberally** adv

**liberate** v set free **liberation** n **lib-
erator** n

**libertine** n morally dissolute person ~adj dissolute

**liberty** n freedom **libertarian** n/adj
(person) believing in freedom of
thought and action **at liberty** free;
having the right **take liberties** be
presumptuous

**libido** n psychic energy; sexual
drive **libidinous** adj lustful

**library** n room, building where
books are kept; collection of books,
records etc. **librarian** n keeper of library

**libretto** n (pl **-tos**, **-ti**) words of op-

era **librettist** n

**lice** n pl of LOUSE

**licence** n permit; permission; excessive liberty; dissoluteness **license**
v grant licence to **licensee** n holder
of licence

**licentious** adj dissolute

**lichen** n small flowerless plants on
rocks, trees etc.

**licit** adj lawful

**lick** v pass tongue over; touch
slightly; Sl defeat ~n act of licking;
small amount (esp. of paint etc.); Sl
speed **licking** n Sl beating

**licorice** n see LIQUORICE

**lid** n movable cover; eyelid

**lido** n (pl **-dos**) pleasure centre with
swimming and boating

**lie**[1] v lying, lay, lain be horizontal,
at rest; be situated; be in certain
state; exist ~n state (of affairs etc.)
**lie in** remain in bed late **lie-in** n

**lie**[2] v lying, lied make false state-

derogatory, false, injurious, malicious, scurrilous, slanderous, tra-
ducing, untrue

**liberal** libertarian, progressive,
radical, reformist; altruistic, bountiful, charitable, generous, kind,
open-handed, prodigal; abundant,
ample, bountiful, copious, handsome, lavish, munificent, plentiful,
profuse, rich

**liberalize** broaden, ease, expand,
extend, loosen, moderate, relax,
slacken, soften, stretch

**liberate** deliver, discharge, emancipate, free, redeem, release, rescue, set free

**liberation** deliverance, emancipation, freedom, release

**liberty** autonomy, emancipation,
freedom, immunity, independence,
release, self-determination, sover-

eignty

**libidinous** carnal, debauched, lascivious, lecherous, loose, lustful,
prurient, randy Inf, chiefly Brit, salacious, wanton, wicked

**licence** n authority, carte blanche,
certificate, charter, dispensation,
entitlement, exemption, immunity,
leave, liberty, permission, permit,
privilege, right, warrant; abandon,
anarchy, disorder, excess, indulgence, lawlessness

**license** v accredit, allow, authorize,
certify, commission, empower, entitle, permit, sanction, warrant

**licentious** abandoned, debauched,
dissolute, immoral, impure, lascivious, lewd, profligate, sensual, wanton

**lick** brush, lap, taste, tongue,
touch, wash

ment ~*n* deliberate falsehood **liar** *n* person who tells lies

**lieu** *n* **in lieu of** in place of

**lieutenant** *n* deputy; junior army or navy officer

**life** *n* (*pl* **lives**) active principle of existence; time that it lasts; story of a person's life; way of living; vigour, vivacity **lifeless** *adj* dead; insensible; dull **lifelike** *adj* **lifelong** *adj* lasting a lifetime **life belt, jacket** buoyant device to keep person afloat **lifeline** *n* means of help; rope thrown to person in danger **lifestyle** *n* particular habits, attitudes etc. of person or group **lifetime** *n* time person, animal or object lives or functions

**lift** *v* move upwards in position, status, mood, volume etc.; take up and remove; *Inf* steal; disappear ~*n* cage in vertical shaft for raising and lowering people or goods; act of lifting; ride in car etc., as passenger; boost **liftoff** *n* moment rocket leaves the ground

**ligament** *n* band of tissue joining bones **ligature** *n* anything which binds; thread for tying up artery

**light¹** *adj* of, or bearing, little weight; not severe; trivial; not clumsy; not serious or profound; (of industry) producing small, usu. consumer goods, using light machinery ~*adv* in light manner ~*v* **lighted, lit** come by chance (upon) **lighten** *v* reduce, remove (load etc.) **lightly** *adv* **lights** *pl n* lungs of animal **light-fingered** *adj* likely to steal **light-headed** *adj* dizzy, delirious **light-hearted** *adj* carefree **lightweight** *n/adj* (person) of little weight or importance

**light²** *n* electromagnetic radiation by which things are visible; source of this, lamp; window; means or act of setting fire to; understanding; *pl* traffic lights ~*adj* bright; pale, not dark ~*v* **lighting, lighted** *or* **lit** set on fire; give light to; brighten **lighten** *v* give light to **lighting** *n* apparatus for supplying artificial light **lightning** *n* visible discharge of electricity in atmosphere **lighthouse** *n* tower with a light to guide ships **light year** distance light travels in one year

**lie¹** *v* be prone, lounge, recline, repose, rest, sprawl, stretch out; be located, belong, be placed, be situated, exist, extend, remain

**lie²** *v* equivocate, fabricate, falsify, fib, invent, misrepresent, perjure, prevaricate ~*n* deceit, fabrication, falsehood, fib, fiction, invention, mendacity, prevarication, untruth

**life** being, breath, entity, growth, vitality; being, career, course, duration, existence, span, time; autobiography, biography, career, confessions, history, memoirs, story

**lifeless** cold, dead, deceased, defunct, extinct, inanimate, inert

**lifelike** authentic, exact, faithful, natural, real, realistic, vivid

**lifelong** constant, enduring, lasting, long-lasting, long-standing, perennial, permanent, persistent

**lift** *v* elevate, hoist, pick up, raise, rear, upheave, uplift, upraise; annul, cancel, end, relax, remove, rescind, revoke, stop, terminate; ascend, be dispelled, climb, disappear, disperse, dissipate, mount, rise, vanish ~*n* car ride, drive, ride, run, transport

**light¹** *adj* airy, delicate, easy, flimsy, portable, slight; easy, effortless, manageable, moderate, simple; mi-

# DICTIONARY

**lighter** *n* device for lighting cigarettes etc.; flat-bottomed boat for unloading ships

**like¹** *adj* resembling; similar; characteristic of ~*adv* in the manner of ~*pron* similar thing **likelihood** *n* probability **likely** *adj* probable; promising ~*adv* probably **liken** *v* compare **likeness** *n* resemblance; portrait **likewise** *adv* in like manner

**like²** *v* find agreeable, enjoy, love **likeable** *adj* **liking** *n* fondness; inclination, taste

**lilac** *n* shrub bearing pale mauve or white flowers

**lilt** *n* rhythmical swing **lilting** *adj*

**lily** *n* bulbous flowering plant **lily of the valley** small garden plant with fragrant white flowers

**limb** *n* arm or leg; wing; branch of tree

**limber** *adj* pliant, lithe **limber up** loosen stiff muscles by exercise

**limbo¹** *n* (*pl* -bos) region between Heaven and Hell for the unbaptized; indeterminate place or state

**limbo²** *n* (*pl* -bos) West Indian dance in which dancers lean backwards to pass under a bar

**lime¹** *n* calcium compound used in fertilizer, cement ~*v* treat (land) with lime **limelight** *n* glare of publicity **limestone** *n* sedimentary rock used in building

**lime²** *n* small acid fruit like lemon **lime-green** *adj* greenish-yellow

**lime³** *n* tree

**limerick** *n* humorous verse of five

## THESAURUS

nute, scanty, slight, small, thin, tiny, trifling, trivial; agile, airy, graceful, lithe, nimble; entertaining, frivolous, funny, pleasing, superficial, trifling, trivial, witty

**light²** *n* blaze, brilliance, flash, glare, gleam, glint, glow, illumination, radiance, ray, shine, sparkle; beacon, bulb, candle, flame, lamp, lantern, star, taper, torch; flame, lighter, match ~*adj* aglow, bright, glowing, shining, sunny ~*v* fire, ignite, inflame, kindle; brighten, clarify, illuminate, irradiate, put on, switch on, turn on

**lighten¹** *v* ease, unload; alleviate, assuage, ease, lessen, mitigate, reduce, relieve

**lighten²** brighten, flash, gleam, illuminate, irradiate, make bright, shine

**lightweight** *adj* insignificant, paltry, petty, slight, trifling, trivial, unimportant, worthless

**like¹** *adj* akin, alike, allied, analogous, corresponding, identical, relating, resembling, same, similar

**like²** *v* delight in, enjoy, love, relish, revel in; admire, appreciate, approve, cherish, esteem, prize

**likelihood** chance, liability, likeliness, possibility, probability, prospect

**likely** *adj* anticipated, apt, disposed, expected, inclined, liable, possible, probable, prone, tending ~*adv* doubtlessly, no doubt, presumably, probably

**likeness** affinity, resemblance, similarity; copy, depiction, effigy, facsimile, image, model, picture, portrait, replica, study

**liking** affection, appreciation, attraction, bias, desire, fondness, love, penchant, preference, stomach, taste, tendency, weakness

**limb** appendage, arm, extension, extremity, leg, member, part, wing

**limelight** attention, fame, prominence, publicity, public eye, recog-

lines

**limit** n utmost extent or duration; boundary ~v restrict, restrain, bound **limitation** n limited company one whose shareholders' liability is restricted

**limousine** n large, luxurious car

**limp**[1] adj without firmness or stiffness

**limp**[2] v walk lamely ~n limping walk

**limpet** n shellfish that sticks tightly to rocks

**limpid** adj clear; translucent

**linchpin** n pin to hold wheel on its axle; essential person or thing

**linctus** n syrupy cough medicine

**line** n long narrow mark; row; series; course; telephone connection; progeny; province of activity; shipping company; railway track; any class of goods; cord; approach, policy ~v cover inside; mark with lines; bring into line **lineage** n de-

scent from, descendants of an ancestor **lineament** n feature **linear** adj of, in lines **liner** n large ship or aircraft of passenger line **linesman** n sporting official who helps referee

**line-up** n people or things assembled for particular purpose

**linen** adj made of flax ~n linen cloth; linen articles collectively

**linger** v delay, loiter; remain long

**lingerie** n women's underwear or nightwear

**linguist** n one skilled in languages or language study **linguistic** adj of languages or their study **linguistics** pl n (with sing v) study, science of language

**liniment** n embrocation

**lining** n covering for inside of garment etc.

**link** n ring of chain; connection ~v join with, as with, link; intertwine **linkage** n

**links** pl n golf course

nition, stardom, the spotlight

**limit** n bound, deadline, end, termination, ultimate, utmost; ceiling, check, curb, maximum, restraint, restriction ~v bound, check, confine, curb, fix, hinder, ration, restrain, restrict, specify, straiten

**limitation** block, check, condition, constraint, control, curb, drawback, impediment, qualification, restraint, restriction, snag

**limp**[1] adj drooping, flabby, flaccid, floppy, lax, loose, relaxed, slack, soft

**limp**[2] v falter, hobble, hop, shamble, shuffle

**line** n band, bar, channel, groove, mark, rule, score, streak, stripe, stroke; column, file, procession, queue, rank, row, sequence, series;

ancestry, family, lineage, race, succession; activity, area, business, calling, department, employment, field, forte, interest, job, occupation, profession, pursuit, trade, vocation; axis, course, direction, path, route, track; cable, cord, filament, rope, strand, string, thread, wire ~v crease, cut, draw, furrow, inscribe, mark, rule, score, trace; border, bound, edge, fringe, rank, rim, skirt, verge

**line-up** arrangement, array, row, selection, team

**linger** loiter, remain, stay, stop, tarry, wait; abide, continue, endure, persist, remain, stay

**link** n component, element, member, part, piece; affiliation, affinity, association, attachment, bond, con-

**linnet** n songbird of finch family

**lino** n short for LINOLEUM

**linoleum** n floor covering of powdered cork, linseed oil etc. backed with hessian

**linseed** n seed of flax plant

**lint** n soft material for dressing wounds

**lintel** n top piece of door or window

**lion** n (fem **lioness**) large animal of cat family

**lip** n either edge of the mouth; edge or margin; Sl impudence **lip-reading** n method of understanding speech by interpreting lip movements **lip service** insincere tribute or respect **lipstick** n cosmetic for colouring lips

**liqueur** n alcoholic liquor flavoured and sweetened

**liquid** adj fluid, not solid or gaseous; flowing smoothly; (of assets) easily converted into money ~n substance in liquid form **liquefy** v **-fying, -fied** make or become liquid

**liquidity** n state of being able to meet debts **liquidize** v **liquidizer** n

**liquidate** v pay (debt); arrange affairs of, and dissolve (company); wipe out, kill **liquidation** n clearing up of financial affairs; bankruptcy

**liquidator** n official appointed to liquidate business

**liquor** n alcoholic liquid

**liquorice** n black substance used in medicine and as a sweet

**lira** n (pl **-re, -ras**) monetary unit of Italy and Turkey

**lisp** v/n (speak with) faulty pronunciation of s and z

**lissom, lissome** adj supple, agile

**list¹** n inventory, register; catalogue ~v place on list

**list²** v (of ship) lean to one side ~n inclination of ship

**listen** v try to hear, attend to **listener** n

**listless** adj indifferent, languid

**litany** n prayer with responses

**literal** adj according to the strict meaning of the words, not figurative; actual, true **literally** adv

**literate** adj able to read and write;

——————— THESAURUS ———————

nection, joint, knot, tie ~v attach, bind, connect, couple, fasten, join, tie, unite, yoke; associate, bracket, connect, identify

**lip** brim, brink, edge, margin, rim

**liquid** adj fluid, melted, molten, running, runny, thawed, wet; of assets convertible, negotiable ~n fluid, juice, liquor

**liquidate** clear, discharge, pay, settle, square; abolish, annul, cancel, dissolve, terminate; annihilate, destroy, dispatch, eliminate, exterminate, kill, murder

**liquor** alcohol, drink, intoxicant, spirits, strong drink

**list¹** n catalogue, directory, file, index, inventory, invoice, register, roll, schedule, tally ~v bill, book, catalogue, enrol, enter, enumerate, file, index, itemize, note, record, register, schedule

**list²** v cant, heel over, incline, lean, tilt, tip ~n cant, slant, tilt

**listen** attend, hark, hear

**listless** apathetic, heavy, indolent, inert, languid, lethargic, limp, sluggish, supine, torpid

**literal** close, exact, faithful, strict, verbatim; actual, genuine, plain, real, simple, true

**literally** actually, exactly, faithfully, plainly, precisely, really, simply, strictly, truly, verbatim

educated **literacy** n

**literature** n books and writings of a country, period or subject **literary** adj

**lithe** adj supple, pliant

**lithium** n metallic chemical element

**lithography** n method of printing using the antipathy of grease and water **lithograph** n print so produced ~v print thus

**litigation** n lawsuit

**litmus** n blue dye turned red by acids and restored to blue by alkali

**litre** n measure of volume of fluid, one cubic decimetre, about 1.75 pints

**litter** n untidy refuse; young of animal produced at one birth; kind of stretcher for wounded ~v strew with litter; give birth to young

**little** adj **less, least** small, not much; young ~n small quantity

~adv slightly

**liturgy** n prescribed form of public worship **liturgical** adj

**live**[1] v have life; pass one's life; continue in life; continue, last; dwell

**living** n action of being in life; people now alive; means of living; church benefice ~adj alive **living room** room in house for relaxation and entertainment

**live**[2] adj living, alive, active, vital; flaming; (of electrical conductor) carrying current; (of broadcast) transmitted during the actual performance **liveliness** n **lively** adj brisk, active, vivid **liven** v (esp. with up) make (more) lively

**livelihood** n means of living

**liver** n organ secreting bile; animal liver as food **liverish** adj unwell, as from liver upset; touchy, irritable

**livery** n distinctive dress, esp. servant's

—————— THESAURUS ——————

**literary** bookish, erudite, formal, learned, literate, well-read

**literate** cultivated, educated, erudite, informed, learned, lettered, scholarly

**literature** letters, lore, writings

**lithe** flexible, lissom(e), pliable, pliant, supple

**litigation** action, case, contending, disputing, lawsuit, process

**litter** n debris, fragments, muck, refuse, rubbish, shreds; brood, family, offspring, progeny, young; palanquin, stretcher ~v clutter, derange, disorder, scatter, strew

**little** adj diminutive, dwarf, elfin, mini, miniature, minute, petite, pygmy or pigmy, short, slender, small, teeny-weeny, tiny, wee; infant, junior, undeveloped, young ~adv barely, hardly, slightly; rarely,

scarcely, seldom

**live**[1] v be, breathe, exist, have life; endure, fare, feed, lead, pass, remain, subsist, survive; last, persist, prevail; abide, dwell, inhabit, lodge, occupy, reside, settle

**live**[2] adj alive, animate, breathing, existent, living, vital; active, burning, current, hot, pressing, prevalent, topical, unsettled, vital

**livelihood** job, living, maintenance, means, occupation, subsistence, work

**liveliness** activity, brio, dynamism, energy, gaiety, spirit, vitality, vivacity

**lively** active, agile, alert, brisk, chirpy Inf, energetic, keen, nimble, perky, quick, sprightly, spry, upbeat Inf, vigorous; bright, colourful, exciting, forceful, invigorating,

**livestock** n farm animals

**livid** adj Inf angry, furious; discoloured, as by bruising

**lizard** n four-footed reptile

**llama** n woolly animal of S America

**load** n something carried; quantity carried; burden; amount of power used ~v put load on or into; charge (gun); weigh down **loaded** adj carrying a load; (of dice) dishonestly weighted; (of question) containing hidden trap or implication; (of weapon) charged with ammunition; Sl wealthy; Sl drunk

**loaf**[1] n (pl **loaves**) mass of baked bread; shaped mass of food

**loaf**[2] v idle, loiter **loafer** n idler

**loam** n fertile soil

**loan** n act of lending; thing lent; money borrowed at interest ~v lend

**loath, loth** adj unwilling **loathe** v feel strong disgust for **loathing** n

disgust **loathsome** adj

**lob** n in tennis etc., shot pitched high in air ~v **lobbing, lobbed** throw, pitch shots thus

**lobby** n corridor into which rooms open; group which tries to influence legislature ~v try to enlist support (of)

**lobe** n soft, hanging part of ear; rounded segment **lobotomy** n surgical incision into lobe of brain

**lobelia** n garden plant with lobed flowers

**lobster** n shellfish with long tail and claws, turning red when boiled

**local** adj of, existing in particular place; confined to particular place ~n person from district; Inf (nearby) pub **locale** n scene of event **locality** n neighbourhood **localize** v assign, restrict to definite place **locally** adv

**locate** v find; situate **location** n

— THESAURUS —

racy, refreshing, stimulating, vivid

**livid**; enraged, fuming, furious, incensed, indignant; angry, blackand-blue, bruised, contused, discoloured

**living** n being, existence, life, subsistence; job, livelihood, maintenance, occupation, subsistence, sustenance, work ~adj active, alive, breathing, existing, strong, vigorous, vital

**load** n bale, cargo, freight, lading, shipment; burden, millstone, onus, oppression, pressure, trouble, weight, worry ~v cram, fill, freight, heap, lade, pack, pile, stack, stuff; charge, prime; burden, hamper, oppress, trouble, weigh down, worry

**loaded** burdened, charged, full, laden, weighted; biased, distorted, weighted; charged, primed; Sl afflu-

ent, moneyed, rich, wealthy, well off, well-to-do

**loan** advance, credit, mortgage

**loath, loth** against, averse, disinclined, indisposed, opposed, reluctant, resisting, unwilling

**loathing** abhorrence, antipathy, aversion, disgust, hatred, horror, odium, repugnance, repulsion, revulsion

**loathsome** abhorrent, disgusting, execrable, hateful, horrible, nasty, odious, offensive, repugnant, revolting, vile

**lobby** n corridor, foyer, hall, hallway, passage, porch, vestibule; pressure group ~v campaign for, influence, persuade, pressure, promote

**local** adj community, district, parish, regional; confined, limited,

placing; situation; site of film production away from studio

**loch** *n* Scottish lake or long narrow bay

**lock**¹ *n* appliance for fastening door, lid etc.; arrangement for moving boats from one level of canal to another; extent to which vehicle's front wheels will turn; block, jam ~*v* fasten, make secure with lock; place in locked container; join firmly; jam; embrace closely **locker** *n* small cupboard with lock **lockjaw** *n* tetanus **lockout** *n* exclusion of workers by employers as means of coercion **locksmith** *n* one who makes and mends locks **lockup** *n* garage, storage area away from main premises

**lock**² *n* tress of hair

**locket** *n* small hinged pendant for portrait etc.

**locomotive** *n* engine for pulling carriages on railway tracks **locomotion** *n* action, power of moving

**locum** *Lat* substitute, esp. for doctor or clergyman

**locus** *n* (*pl* **loci**) curve traced by all points satisfying specified mathematical condition

**locust** *n* destructive winged insect

**lodge** *n* house, cabin used seasonally or occasionally, e.g. for hunting, skiing; gatekeeper's house; branch of Freemasons etc. ~*v* house; deposit; bring (a charge etc.); live in another's house at fixed charge; come to rest (in, on) **lodger** *n* **lodgings** *pl n* rented accommodation in another person's house

**loft** *n* space under roof **loftily** *adv* haughtily **lofty** *adj* of great height; elevated; haughty

**log**¹ *n* trimmed portion of felled tree; record of voyages of ship, aircraft etc. ~*v* **logging, logged** enter in a log; record; cut logs **logbook** *n*

**log**² *n* logarithm

**loganberry** *n* purplish-red fruit

**logarithm** *n* one of series of arithmetical functions tabulated for use in calculation

**loggerheads** *pl n* **at loggerheads** quarrelling, disputing

**logic** *n* science of reasoning; rea-

———————————— THESAURUS ————————————

narrow, parish, parochial, provincial, restricted ~*n* inhabitant, native, resident

**locality** area, district, region, vicinity

**localize** circumscribe, concentrate, confine, contain, delimit, limit, restrain, restrict

**locate** detect, discover, find, pinpoint, unearth

**location** bearings, locale, place, point, site, situation, spot, venue

**lock**¹ *n* bolt, clasp, padlock ~*v* bolt, close, fasten, latch, seal, secure, shut

**lock**² curl, ringlet, strand, tress

**lodge** *n* cabin, chalet, cottage, gatehouse, house, hut, shelter; association, branch, club, group, society ~*v* accommodate, billet, board, entertain, harbour, put up, shelter, stay, stop; catch, imbed, implant, stick

**lodger** boarder, guest, paying guest, resident, tenant

**lofty** high, raised, soaring, tall, towering; distinguished, elevated, grand, illustrious, imposing, majestic, noble, stately, superior

**log** *n* block, chunk, stump, trunk; account, chart, journal, listing, record, tally ~*v* book, chart, note,

soned thought or argument; coherence of various facts, events etc.
**logical** *adj* of logic; according to reason; reasonable; apt to reason correctly
**logistics** *pl n* (*with sing or pl v*) the handling of supplies and personnel **logistical** *adj*
**logo** *n* company emblem or similar device
**loin** *n* part of body between ribs and hip; cut of meat from this; *pl* hips and lower abdomen **loincloth** *n* garment covering loins only
**loiter** *v* dawdle, hang about; idle **loiterer** *n*
**loll** *v* sit, lie lazily; (esp. of the tongue) hang out
**lollipop** *n* sweet on small wooden stick
**lolly** *n* Inf lollipop or ice lolly; Sl money
**lone** *adj* solitary **loneliness** *n* **lonely** *adj* sad because alone; unfrequented; solitary **loner** *n* one who prefers to be alone **lonesome** *adj*
**long¹** *adj* having length, esp. great

length, in space or time; extensive; protracted ~*adv* for a long time
**long-distance** *adj* going between places far apart **longhand** *n* words written in full **long-range** *adj* into the future; able to travel long distances without refuelling; (of weapons) designed to hit distant target **long shot** competitor, undertaking, bet etc. with small chance of success **long-sighted** *adj* able to see distant objects in focus but not nearby ones **long-standing** *adj* existing for a long time **long-suffering** *adj* enduring trouble or unhappiness without complaint **long-winded** *adj* tediously loquacious
**long²** *v* have keen desire, yearn (for) **longing** *n* yearning
**longevity** *n* long life
**longitude** *n* distance east or west from standard meridian
**loo** *n* Inf lavatory
**look** *v* direct eyes (at); face; seem; search (for); hope (for); (*with* **after**) take care of ~*n* looking; view; search; (*oft. pl*) appearance look-

record, register, tally
**logic** reason, sense, sound judgment; link, rationale, relationship
**logical** clear, cogent, coherent, consistent, rational, relevant, sound, valid
**loiter** dally, dawdle, delay, idle, lag, linger, loaf, stroll
**loll** flop, lean, loaf, lounge, recline, relax, slouch, slump, sprawl; dangle, droop, drop, flop, hang, hang loosely, sag
**lone** isolated, one, only, separate, single, sole, unaccompanied
**loneliness** desolation, isolation, seclusion, solitude
**lonely** abandoned, estranged, for-

lorn, forsaken, friendless, outcast; deserted, remote, secluded, solitary, unfrequented, uninhabited; alone, apart, single, solitary, withdrawn
**long¹** *adj* expanded, extended, lengthy, stretched
**long²** *v* covet, crave, desire, hanker, hunger, itch, lust, pine, want, yearn
**longing** ambition, aspiration, coveting, craving, desire, hungering, itch, thirst, urge, wish
**long-standing** enduring, established, fixed, time-honoured
**long-suffering** easygoing, patient, resigned, stoical, tolerant
**long-winded** garrulous, lengthy,

**alike** n person who is double of another **lookout** n watchman; place for watching; prospect

**loom**[1] n machine for weaving

**loom**[2] v appear dimly; seem ominously close

**loony** n/adj Sl foolish or insane (person)

**loop** n figure made by curved line crossing itself ~v form loop **loophole** n means of evading rule without infringing it

**loose** adj slack; not fixed or restrained; vague; dissolute ~v free; unfasten; slacken; (with off) shoot, let fly **loosen** v make loose **looseleaf** adj allowing addition or removal of pages

**loot** n/v plunder

**lop** v **lopping**, **lopped** cut away

twigs and branches; chop off

**lope** v run with long, easy strides

**lopsided** adj with one side lower than the other

**loquacious** adj talkative

**lord** n British nobleman; ruler; (with cap.) God ~v domineer **lordly** adj imperious; fit for a lord **lordship** n

**lore** n learning; body of facts and traditions

**lorry** n motor vehicle for heavy loads, truck

**lose** v **losing**, **lost** be deprived of, fail to retain or use; fail to get; (of clock etc.) run slow; be defeated in **loser** n **loss** n act of losing; what is lost **lost** adj unable to be found; unable to find one's way; bewildered; not won; not utilized

——————————— THESAURUS ———————————

rambling, verbose, wordy

**look** v consider, contemplate, examine, eye, gaze, glance, inspect, observe, peep, regard, scan, scrutinize, see, study, survey, view, watch; appear, display, evidence, exhibit, present, seem, show ~n gander Inf, gaze, glance, glimpse, inspection, observation, review, sight, survey, view; air, appearance, aspect, bearing, cast, complexion, demeanour, effect, expression, face, fashion, guise, manner

**lookout** guard, sentinel, sentry; beacon, citadel, post, watchtower

**loom** appear, bulk, emerge, hover, impend, menace, take shape, threaten

**loop** n bend, circle, coil, curl, curve, eyelet, kink, noose, ring, spiral, twirl, twist ~v bend, circle, coil, connect, curl, encircle, fold, join, knot, roll, turn, twist

**loophole** avoidance, escape, eva-

sion, excuse, plea, pretext

**loose** adj baggy, easy, relaxed, slack, sloppy; floating, free, insecure, movable, released, unattached, unfastened, unsecured, untied, wobbly; diffuse, ill-defined, imprecise, inaccurate, indefinite, inexact, rambling, random, vague ~v detach, disengage, ease, free, release, slacken, unbind, unbridle, undo, unfasten, unloose, untie

**loosen** detach, separate, slacken, undo, unstick, untie

**loot** booty, goods, haul, plunder, prize, spoils

**lopsided** askew, awry, crooked, off balance, squint, tilting, unbalanced, uneven

**lord** earl, noble, nobleman, peer, viscount; commander, governor, leader, master, potentate, prince, ruler, seigneur, sovereign, superior

**lore** beliefs, doctrine, folk-wisdom, teaching, wisdom

**lot** *pron* great number ~*n* collection; large quantity; share; fate; item at auction; object used to make decision by chance; area of land; *pl Inf* great numbers or quantity **a lot** *Inf* a great deal

**lotion** *n* liquid for washing wounds, improving skin etc.

**lottery** *n* method of raising funds by selling tickets that win prizes by chance; gamble

**lotus** *n* legendary plant whose fruits induce forgetfulness

**loud** *adj* strongly audible; noisy; *Fig* garish **loudly** *adv* **loudspeaker** *n* instrument for converting electrical signals into sound audible at a distance

**lounge** *v* recline, move at ease ~*n* living room of house; public room, area for sitting **lounge suit** man's suit for daytime wear

**lour** *see* LOWER

**louse** *n* (*pl* **lice**) parasitic insect **lousy** *adj Sl* bad; *Sl* nasty; having lice

**lout** *n* crude, oafish person

**louvre** *n* one of set of slats slanted to admit air but not rain

**love** *n* warm affection; benevolence; sexual passion; sweetheart; *Tennis etc.* score of nothing ~*v* admire passionately; delight in **lovable** *adj* **lovelorn** *adj* pining for a lover **lovely** *adj* beautiful, delightful **lover** *n* **loving** *adj* affectionate; tender **make love (to)** have sexual intercourse (with)

**lose** displace, drop, forget, mislay, misplace, miss; be defeated

**loser** also-ran, failure, underdog

**loss** deprivation, failure, losing, misfortune, privation, waste; cost, damage, defeat, destruction, detriment, harm, hurt, injury, ruin

**lost** disappeared, forfeited, mislaid, misplaced, missing, strayed, vanished, wayward; adrift, astray, at sea, disoriented, off-course; baffled, bewildered, confused, helpless, ignorant, mystified, perplexed, puzzled

**lot** batch, collection, crowd, group, quantity, set; accident, chance, destiny, doom, fate, fortune, hazard, plight, portion; allowance, parcel, part, piece, portion, quota, ration, share **lots** abundance, heap(s), number(s), piles *Inf*, plenty, scores

**lotion** balm, cream, liniment, solution

**lottery** draw, raffle, sweepstake; chance, gamble, hazard, risk

**loud** blaring, deafening, ear-piercing, noisy, piercing, resounding, stentorian, strident, thundering; brash, brassy, flamboyant, flashy, garish, gaudy, glaring, lurid, ostentatious, showy, tacky *Inf*, tasteless, vulgar

**lounge** *v* laze, loaf, loiter, recline, relax, saunter, sprawl

**lout** bear, boor, clod, dolt, oaf

**lovable** amiable, attractive, charming, cuddly, cute, delightful, enchanting, endearing, lovely, pleasing, sweet, winning

**love** *n* adulation, affection, ardour, devotion, fondness, friendship, infatuation, liking, passion, rapture, regard, tenderness, warmth ~*v* cherish, hold dear, idolize, prize, treasure, worship; appreciate, delight in, desire, enjoy, fancy, like, relish, savour

**lovely** attractive, beautiful, charming, comely, exquisite, graceful, handsome, pretty, sweet; agreeable,

**low¹** *adj* not tall, high or elevated; humble; unwell; below what is usual; not loud **lower** *v* cause, allow to move down; diminish, degrade ~*adj* below; at an early stage, period **lowly** *adj* modest, humble **lowbrow** *n/adj* nonintellectual (person) **lowdown** *n Inf* inside information **low-down** *adj Inf* mean, shabby **lower case** small letters **low-key** *adj* not intense **lowland** *n* low-lying country

**low²** *v/n* (utter) cry, bellow of cattle

**lower, lour** *v* (of sky) look threatening; scowl

**loyal** *adj* faithful, true to allegiance **loyalist** *n* **loyalty** *n*

**lozenge** *n* small sweet or tablet of medicine; diamond shape

**LP** long-playing record

**L-plate** *n* sign on car driven by learner driver

**LSD** lysergic acid diethylamide (hallucinogenic drug); pounds, shillings, and pence

**lubricate** *v* oil, grease; make slippery **lubricant** *n* substance used for this **lubrication** *n*

**lucerne** *n* fodder plant

**lucid** *adj* clear; easily understood; sane **lucidity** *n*

**luck** *n* chance, whether good or bad; good fortune **luckily** *adv* fortunately **luckless** *adj* having bad luck **lucky** *adj* having good luck

**lucrative** *adj* very profitable

**ludicrous** *adj* ridiculous

**lug¹** *v* lugging, lugged drag with

———————— THESAURUS ————————

delightful, enjoyable, gratifying, nice, pleasant

**lover** admirer, beau, beloved, boyfriend, girlfriend, mistress, paramour, suitor, sweetheart

**loving** affectionate, ardent, cordial, dear, devoted, doting, fond, friendly, kind, tender, warm

**low** little, short, small, squat, stunted; deep, shallow, subsided, sunken; humble, lowborn, lowly, meek, obscure, plain, plebeian, poor, simple; coarse, common, crude, disgraceful, dishonourable, disreputable, gross, obscene, rough, rude, unrefined, vulgar; abject, base, dastardly, degraded, depraved, despicable, ignoble, mean, nasty, sordid, unworthy, vile, vulgar; gentle, hushed, muffled, muted, quiet, soft, subdued, whispered

**lower** *v* depress, drop, fall, sink, submerge; abase, belittle, debase, degrade, deign, demean, devalue, disgrace, humiliate ~*adj* inferior,

junior, lesser, minor, secondary, smaller, subordinate

**loyal** attached, constant, dependable, devoted, dutiful, faithful, immovable, staunch, steadfast, true, trustworthy

**loyalty** allegiance, faithfulness, fidelity, patriotism

**lubricate** grease, oil, smear

**lucid** clear, distinct, evident, explicit, intelligible, limpid, obvious, plain, transparent; *compos mentis*, rational, sane

**luck** accident, chance, destiny, fate, fortune; advantage, blessing, fluke, prosperity, stroke, success, windfall

**luckily** favourably, fortunately, happily, opportunely

**lucky** blessed, charmed, favoured, fortunate, jammy *Brit sl*, prosperous, successful

**lucrative** fat, fruitful, gainful, paying, productive, profitable, remunerative, well-paid

**ludicrous** absurd, burlesque, com-

effort

**lug²** *n* projection, serving as handle or support; *Inf* ear

**luggage** *n* traveller's baggage

**lugubrious** *adj* doleful

**lukewarm** *adj* tepid; indifferent

**lull** *v* soothe, sing to sleep; calm; subside ~*n* quiet spell **lullaby** *n* lulling song, esp. for children

**lumbago** *n* rheumatism of the lower part of the back

**lumber¹** *n* disused articles, useless rubbish; sawn timber ~*v Inf* burden with something unpleasant **lumberjack** *n* US & Canad man who fells trees and prepares logs

**lumber²** *v* move heavily

**luminous** *adj* shedding light; glowing **luminary** *n* famous person **luminescence** *n* emission of light without heat

**lump¹** *n* shapeless piece or mass; swelling; large sum ~*v* throw together **lumpy** *adj* full of lumps; uneven

**lump²** *v Inf* tolerate

**lunar** *adj* relating to the moon

**lunatic** *adj/n* foolish or irresponsible (person); insane (person) **lunacy** *n*

**lunch** *n* meal taken in middle of day ~*v* eat, entertain to lunch **luncheon** *n* lunch **luncheon meat** tinned ground mixture of meat and cereal

**lung** *n* one of the two organs of respiration in vertebrates

**lunge** *v* thrust with sword etc. ~*n* thrust; sudden movement of body, plunge

**lupin** *n* leguminous plant with spikes of flowers

**lurch** *n* sudden roll to one side ~*v* stagger **leave in the lurch** leave in difficulties

**lure** *n* bait; power to attract ~*v* entice; attract

**lurid** *adj* sensational; garish

**lurk** *v* lie hidden **lurking** *adj* (of suspicion) not definite

───────── THESAURUS ─────────

ic, crazy, funny, laughable, odd, preposterous, ridiculous, silly

**luggage** baggage, bags, cases, gear, suitcases, trunks

**lull** *v* allay, calm, compose, hush, pacify, quell, quiet, soothe, still, subdue ~*n* calm, calmness, hush, pause, quiet, respite, silence

**lumber** clump, plod, shamble, shuffle, stump, trudge, trundle

**luminous** bright, brilliant, glowing, lighted, lit, lustrous, radiant, resplendent, shining, vivid

**lump** *n* ball, bunch, cake, chunk, gob, group, hunk, mass, piece, spot, wedge; bulge, bump, growth, hump, protrusion, protuberance, swelling, tumour ~*v* bunch, collect, combine, group, mass, pool, unite

**lunacy** absurdity, craziness, folly, foolishness, idiocy, madness, stupidity

**lunatic** *adj* barking mad *Sl*, crackpot *Inf*, crazy, daft, demented, deranged, insane, irrational, loopy *Inf*, mad, unhinged ~*n* madcap *Inf*, madman, maniac, psychopath

**lunge** *v* bound, charge, cut, dash, dive, jab, leap, poke, stab, thrust ~*n* charge, cut, jab, pass, spring, stab, swing, swipe, thrust

**lure** *n* attraction, bait, decoy, magnet, temptation ~*v* attract, beckon, decoy, draw, ensnare, entice, inveigle, invite, lead on, seduce, tempt

**lurid** graphic, melodramatic, sensational, shock-horror *Facetious*, shocking, startling, unrestrained,

**luscious** *adj* sweet, juicy; extremely attractive

**lush** *adj* (of plant growth) luxuriant; luxurious

**lust** *n* strong desire for sexual gratification; any strong desire ~*v* have passionate desire **lustful** *adj* **lusty** *adj* vigorous, healthy

**lustre** *n* gloss, sheen; renown; metallic pottery glaze **lustrous** *adj* shining

**lute** *n* old stringed musical instrument played like a guitar

**luxury** *n* possession and use of costly, choice things for enjoyment; enjoyable, comfortable surroundings; enjoyable but not essential thing **luxuriance** *n* abundance **luxu-**

**riant** *adj* growing thickly; abundant **luxuriate** *v* indulge in luxury; flourish profusely; take delight (in) **luxurious** *adj* fond of luxury; self-indulgent; sumptuous

**lychee** *n* Chinese fruit

**Lycra** *n Trademark* fabric used for tight-fitting garments

**lymph** *n* colourless body fluid, mainly white blood cells **lymphatic** *adj*

**lynch** *v* put to death without trial

**lynx** *n* animal of cat family

**lyre** *n* instrument like harp

**lyric** *n* songlike poem expressing personal feelings; *pl* words of popular song **lyrical** *adj* expressed in this style; enthusiastic **lyricist** *n*

——————— THESAURUS ———————

vivid

**lurk** crouch, hide, juicy, prowl, skulk, slink, sneak, snoop

**luscious** appetizing, delectable, delicious, honeyed, juicy, mouth-watering, palatable, rich, savoury, succulent, sweet

**lush** abundant, dense, green, lavish, prolific, rank, teeming, verdant

**lust** carnality, lechery, lewdness, libido, salaciousness, sensuality; appetite, avidity, craving, cupidity, desire, greed, longing, passion, thirst ~*v* covet, crave, desire, need, want, yearn

**lustre** burnish, gleam, glint, glitter, gloss, glow, sheen, shimmer, shine, sparkle; distinction, fame, glory, honour, prestige, renown

**lusty** hale, healthy, hearty, powerful, robust, stalwart, stout, strapping, strong, sturdy, vigorous, virile

**luxurious** comfortable, costly, expensive, lavish, opulent, rich, splendid, sumptuous

**luxury** affluence, opulence, richness, splendour; comfort, delight, enjoyment, gratification, indulgence, pleasure, satisfaction, wellbeing; extra, extravagance, treat

# M m

**m** metre
**MA** Master of Arts
**mac** n *Inf* mackintosh
**macabre** adj gruesome, ghastly
**macaroni** n pasta in thin tubes
**macaroon** n biscuit containing almonds
**macaw** n kind of parrot
**mace**[1] n staff of office
**mace**[2] n spice made of nutmeg shell
**machete** n broad, heavy knife
**Machiavellian** adj (politically) unprincipled, crafty
**machination** n (*usu. pl*) plotting, intrigue
**machine** n apparatus with several parts to apply mechanical force; controlling organization; mechanical appliance ~v shape etc. with machine **machinery** n machines or machine parts; procedures by which system functions **machinist** n
**machine gun** automatic gun firing repeatedly
**macho** adj exhibiting exaggerated pride in masculinity **machismo** n strong, exaggerated masculinity
**mackerel** n edible sea fish
**mackintosh** n waterproof raincoat

**macramé** n ornamental work of knotted cord
**macrocosm** n the universe; any large system
**mad** adj suffering from mental disease, foolish; enthusiastic (about); excited; *Inf* furious **madden** v make mad **madness** n
**madam** n polite title for a woman
**madcap** adj/n reckless (person)
**made** past tense and past participle of MAKE
**Madonna** n Virgin Mary
**madrigal** n unaccompanied part song
**maelstrom** n great whirlpool
**maestro** n (*pl* -tros, -tri) outstanding musician, conductor; master of any art
**magazine** n periodical publication; appliance for supplying cartridges to gun; storehouse for arms etc.
**magenta** adj/n (of) deep purplish-red
**maggot** n grub, larva **maggoty** adj
**magic** n art of supposedly invoking supernatural powers to influence events etc.; witchcraft, conjuring; fascinating quality or power ~adj

─────────── THESAURUS ───────────

**machine** apparatus, appliance, contraption, device, engine, instrument, tool; agency, organization, party, structure, system
**machinery** apparatus, equipment, gear, tackle, tools, works; agency, channels, organization, procedure, system
**mad** crazed, delirious, demented, deranged, insane, lunatic, psychotic, raving, unhinged; absurd, fool-

hardy, foolish, imprudent, inane, irrational, ludicrous, preposterous, unsound, wild
**madden** aggravate, annoy, craze, enrage, exasperate, infuriate, provoke, upset, vex
**madness** delusion, dementia, derangement, insanity, lunacy, mania, mental illness, psychosis; absurdity, folly, foolishness, idiocy, nonsense
**magazine** journal, pamphlet, pa-

of, using magic **magical** adj **magician** n wizard, conjuror

**magistrate** n civil officer administering law **magisterial** adj of magistrate; authoritative

**magnanimous** adj generous, not petty **magnanimity** n

**magnate** n influential person

**magnesium** n metallic element **magnesia** n white powder used in medicine

**magnet** n piece of iron, steel having properties of attracting iron, steel **magnetic** adj of magnet; exerting powerful attraction **magnetism** n **magnetize** v **magneto** n (pl **-tos**) apparatus for ignition in internal-combustion engine **magnetic tape** coated plastic strip for recording sound or video signals

**magnificent** adj splendid; imposing; excellent **magnificence** n

**magnify** v **-fying, -fied** increase apparent size of, as with lens; exaggerate **magnification** n

**magnitude** n importance; size

**magnolia** n tree with white, sweet-scented flowers

**magnum** n large wine bottle

**magpie** n black-and-white bird

**maharajah** n (fem **maharanee**) former title of some Indian princes

**mahogany** n tree yielding reddish-brown wood

**maiden** n Lit young unmarried woman **-ly** adj unmarried; first **maid** n woman servant; Lit maiden **maiden name** woman's surname before marriage

**mail¹** n letters etc. transported and

per, periodical

**magic** n enchantment, occultism, sorcery, spell, witchcraft; conjuring, illusion, trickery; allurement, charm, enchantment, fascination, glamour, magnetism, power adj also **magical** charming, enchanting, entrancing, fascinating, magnetic, marvellous, miraculous

**magician** conjurer, conjuror, enchanter, illusionist, sorcerer, warlock, witch, wizard

**magistrate** judge, justice

**magnanimous** big, charitable, free, generous, handsome, kind, munificent, noble, selfless, ungrudging, unselfish

**magnate** baron, chief, leader, mogul, plutocrat, tycoon

**magnetic** alluring, attractive, captivating, charming, enchanting, entrancing, hypnotic, irresistible, seductive

**magnetism** allure, appeal, attrac-tion, charisma, charm, draw, enchantment, fascination, magic, power, pull, spell

**magnificent** brilliant, elevated, exalted, excellent, glorious, gorgeous, grand, imposing, impressive, lavish, noble, opulent, princely, regal, rich, splendid, stately, sumptuous, superb, superior

**magnify** amplify, augment, boost, deepen, dilate, enlarge, expand, heighten, increase, intensify; blow up, dramatize, enhance, exaggerate

**magnitude** consequence, eminence, grandeur, greatness, importance, mark, moment, note, significance, weight; amount, amplitude, bulk, capacity, dimensions, expanse, extent, hugeness, immensity, largeness, mass, measure, quantity, size, space, strength, volume

**maid** housemaid, servant; damsel, girl, maiden, miss, wench

**maiden** n damsel, girl, maid, miss,

delivered by the post office; postal system; train etc. carrying mail ~v send by mail

**mail²** n armour of interlaced rings

**maim** v cripple, mutilate

**main** adj chief, principal ~n principal pipe, line carrying water etc.; Obs sea **mainframe** n high-speed general-purpose computer; central processing unit of computer **mainland** n stretch of land which forms main part of a country **mainstay** n chief support **mainstream** n prevailing cultural trend

**maintain** v carry on; support; assert; support by argument **maintenance** n maintaining; means of support; upkeep of buildings etc.

**maisonette** n part of house fitted as self-contained dwelling

**maize** n type of corn

**majesty** n stateliness; sovereignty **majestic** adj

**major** n army officer above captain; scale in music ~adj greater in number, extent etc. **majority** n greater number; coming of age

**make** v making, made construct; produce; create; establish; appoint; amount to; cause to do; reach; earn; tend; contribute ~n brand, type **maker** n **making** n **make-believe** n fantasy, pretence **make do** manage with inferior alternative **make it** Inf be successful **makeshift** adj serving as temporary substitute **make-up** n cosmetics; characteristics; layout

nymph, virgin, wench ~adj chaste, intact, pure, virgin; first, initial, introductory

**mail** n letters, packages, parcels, post; post, postal service ~v dispatch, forward, post, send

**maim** cripple, disable, hurt, incapacitate, injure, mutilate, wound

**main** adj central, chief, critical, crucial, essential, foremost, head, leading, paramount, pre-eminent, primary, prime, principal, special, supreme, vital ~n cable, channel, conduit, duct, line, pipe

**mainstay** anchor, backbone, bulwark, linchpin, pillar, prop

**maintain** conserve, continue, finance, keep, look after, nurture, perpetuate, preserve, prolong, provide, retain, supply, support, sustain, uphold; affirm, allege, assert, asseverate, aver, avow, claim, contend, declare, hold, insist, profess, state; back, champion, defend, justify, plead for, uphold, vindicate

**maintenance** care, conservation, continuation, nurture, preservation, provision, repairs, supply, support, upkeep

**majestic** awesome, elevated, exalted, grand, imperial, imposing, impressive, lofty, magnificent, monumental, noble, princely, regal, royal, splendid, stately, sublime, superb

**majesty** dignity, glory, grandeur, kingliness, magnificence, nobility, pomp, royalty, splendour, state, sublimity

**major** better, bigger, chief, elder, greater, head, higher, larger, lead, leading, main, most, senior, superior, supreme

**majority** best part, bulk, mass, more, most, plurality, preponderance, superiority; manhood, maturity, seniority

**make** v assemble, build, compose, constitute, construct, create, fabricate, fashion, forge, form, frame,

**mal-, male-** *comb. form* ill, badly, as in **malformation, malfunction**

**maladjusted** *adj* badly adjusted, as to society

**malady** *n* disease

**malaise** *n* vague feeling of discomfort

**malapropism** *n* ludicrous misuse of word

**malaria** *n* infectious disease transmitted by mosquitoes

**malcontent** *adj/n* discontented (person)

**male** *adj* of sex that fertilizes female; of men or male animals ~*n* male person or animal

**malevolent** *adj* full of ill will **malevolence** *n*

**malice** *n* ill will; spite **malicious** *adj* spiteful

**malign** *adj* causing evil ~*v* slander

**malignancy** *n* **malignant** *adj* feeling ill will; (of disease) resistant to therapy

**malinger** *v* feign illness to escape duty

**mall** *n* shopping centre

**mallard** *n* wild duck

**malleable** *adj* capable of being hammered into shape; adaptable

**mallet** *n* (wooden) hammer

**malnutrition** *n* inadequate nutrition

**malodorous** *adj* evil-smelling

**malpractice** *n* immoral, illegal or unethical conduct

———————— THESAURUS ————————

manufacture, originate, produce, shape, synthesize; accomplish, beget, cause, create, effect, generate, occasion, produce; appoint, assign, create, designate, elect, install, invest, nominate, ordain; draw up, enact, establish, fix, form, frame, pass; cause, coerce, compel, constrain, dragoon, drive, force, impel, induce, oblige, press, railroad *Inf,* require ~*n* brand, build, construction, cut, designation, form, kind, mark, model, shape, sort, style, type, variety

**make do** cope, improvise, manage

**maker** author, builder, director, framer, manufacturer, producer

**makeshift** expedient, provisional, stopgap, substitute, temporary

**make-up** cosmetics, powder; arrangement, assembly, composition, configuration, constitution, construction, format, formation, layout, organization, structure

**maladjusted** disturbed, neurotic, unstable

**malady** ailment, complaint, disease, illness, infirmity, sickness

**malcontent** agitator, complainer, grumbler, rebel, troublemaker

**male** manlike, manly, masculine, virile

**malevolent** baleful, evil-minded, hostile, malicious, malignant, pernicious, spiteful, vengeful, vicious, vindictive

**malice** animosity, bitterness, enmity, hate, hatred, rancour, spite, venom, vindictiveness

**malicious** baleful, bitter, hateful, injurious, malevolent, pernicious, rancorous, resentful, spiteful, vengeful, vicious

**malign** *adj* bad, baleful, baneful, evil, harmful, hostile, hurtful, pernicious, vicious, wicked ~*v* abuse, defame, denigrate, disparage, knock *Inf,* libel, revile, slag (off) *Sl,* slander, smear

**malignant** baleful, bitter, harmful, hostile, hurtful, malevolent, malicious, pernicious, spiteful, vicious

**malt** *n* grain used for brewing

**maltreat** *v* treat badly

**mammal** *n* animal of type that suckles its young **mammalian** *adj*

**mammary** *adj* of, relating to breast

**mammon** *n* wealth regarded as source of evil

**mammoth** *n* extinct animal like an elephant ~*adj* colossal

**man** (*pl* **men**) human being; human race; adult male; piece used in chess etc. ~*v* **manning, manned** supply with men **manful** *adj* brave **manly** *adj* **manhandle** *v* treat roughly **manhole** *n* opening through which man may pass to a sewer etc. **mankind** *n* human beings **manslaughter** *n* unintentional homicide

**manacle** *n/v* fetter

**manage** *v* be in charge of; succeed in doing; control; handle **manageable** *adj* **management** *n* those who manage; administration **manager** *n* **managerial** *adj*

**mandarin** *n* small orange; high-ranking bureaucrat

**mandate** *n* command of, or commission to act for, another; instruction from electorate to representative or government **mandatory** *adj* compulsory

**mandible** *n* lower jawbone

**mandolin** *n* stringed musical instrument

**mane** *n* long hair on neck of horse, lion etc.

**manganese** *n* metallic element

**mange** *n* skin disease of dogs etc. **mangy** *adj*

**manger** *n* eating trough in stable

**mangle**[1] *n* machine for rolling clothes etc. to remove water ~*v* press in mangle

**mangle**[2] *v* mutilate

**mango** (*pl* **-goes, -gos**) tropical fruit

**mangrove** *n* tropical tree which grows on muddy river banks

**mania** *n* madness; prevailing craze

———————————— THESAURUS ————————————

**malpractice** misbehaviour, misconduct, misdeed, offence

**maltreat** abuse, damage, harm, hurt, injure, mistreat

**man** *n* adult, being, body, human being, individual, one, person, personage, somebody, soul; humanity; human race, mankind, mortals, people; gentleman, male ~*v* crew, fill, garrison, occupy, people, staff

**manage** administer, command, concert, conduct, direct, govern, handle, oversee, rule, run, supervise; accomplish, arrange, contrive, cut it *Inf*, deal with, effect, engineer, succeed; control, guide, handle, influence, manipulate, operate, pilot, ply, steer, train, use, wield

**manageable** compliant, controllable, docile, easy, handy, submissive, tractable, wieldy

**management** administration, board, directorate, employers

**manager** conductor, controller, director, executive, governor, head, organizer, proprietor, supervisor

**mandate** authority, bidding, charge, command, decree, directive, edict, fiat, instruction, order, sanction, warrant

**mandatory** binding, compulsory, obligatory, required, requisite

**mangle** butcher, crush, cut, deform, destroy, distort, hack, maim, mar, mutilate, spoil, tear, trash *Sl*, wreck

**mangy** dirty, mean, scruffy, seedy, shabby, shoddy, squalid

**maniac** *adj/n* mad (person) **maniacal, manic** *adj* affected by mania

**manicure** *n* treatment and care of fingernails and hands ~*v* treat, care for hands

**manifest** *adj* clear, undoubted ~*v* make manifest **manifestation** *n*

**manifesto** *n* (*pl* **-tos**) declaration of policy by political party etc.

**manifold** *adj* numerous and varied ~*n* in engine, pipe with several outlets

**manila, manilla** *n* fibre used for ropes; type of paper

**manipulate** *v* handle skilfully; manage; falsify **manipulation** *n*

**manna** *n* nourishment; unexpected gift

**mannequin** *n* woman who models clothes

**manner** *n* way; style; bearing; sort, kind; *pl* social behaviour **mannered** *adj* affected **mannerism** *n* person's distinctive habit

**manoeuvre** *n* complicated, perhaps deceptive plan or action ~*v* employ stratagems; (cause to) perform manoeuvres

**manor** *n* large country house with land

**manse** *n* house of minister in some religious denominations

**mansion** *n* large house

**mantelpiece** *n* shelf at top of fireplace

**mantle** *n* loose cloak; covering ~*v* cover

**mantra** *n* sacred word or syllable in Hinduism and Buddhism

**manual** *adj* done with the hands; by human labour, not automatic ~*n* handbook

———— THESAURUS ————

**manhandle** maul, pull, push

**mania** craziness, delirium, derangement, disorder, frenzy, insanity, lunacy, madness

**maniac** headbanger *Inf*, headcase *Inf*, lunatic, madman, psychopath

**manifest** *adj* apparent, blatant, clear, distinct, evident, glaring, noticeable, obvious, open, patent, plain, visible

**manifestation** disclosure, display, exhibition, exposure, instance, mark, materialization, revelation, show, sign, symptom, token

**manifold** abundant, assorted, diverse, many, multiple, numerous, varied, various

**manipulate** employ, handle, operate, ply, use, wield, work

**mankind** humanity, human race, man, people

**manly** bold, brave, courageous, daring, fearless, gallant, hardy, heroic, male, masculine, noble, powerful, resolute, robust, strong, valiant, valorous, vigorous, virile

**manner** approach, custom, genre, habit, line, method, mode, practice, process, routine, style, tenor, usage, way, wont; air, appearance, aspect, bearing, behaviour, conduct, demeanour, deportment, look, presence, tone

**mannerism** foible, habit, peculiarity, quirk, trait, trick

**manoeuvre** *n* action, artifice, dodge, intrigue, machination, move, plan, plot, ploy, ruse, scheme, subterfuge, tactic, trick ~*v* contrive, devise, engineer, intrigue, manage, plan, plot, scheme; direct, drive, guide, handle, navigate, pilot, steer

**mansion** abode, dwelling, habitation, hall, manor, residence, seat, villa

**manufacture** v make (materials) into finished articles; concoct ~n making of articles, esp. in large quantities **manufacturer** n

**manure** n dung or chemical fertilizer used to enrich land

**manuscript** n book etc. written by hand; copy for printing

**many** adj **more, most** numerous ~n large number

**map** n flat representation of the earth ~v **mapping, mapped** make map of; (*with* out) plan

**maple** n tree of sycamore family

**mar** v **marring, marred** spoil

**Mar.** March

**maraca** n shaken percussion instrument

**marathon** n long-distance race; endurance contest

**maraud** v raid; plunder **marauder** n

**marble** n kind of limestone; small ball used in children's game

**March** n third month

**march** v walk with military step; go, progress ~n action of marching; distance marched; marching tune

**marchioness** n wife, widow of marquis

**mare** n female horse

**margarine** n butter substitute made from vegetable fats

**margin** n border, edge; space round printed page; amount allowed beyond what is necessary **marginal** adj

**marigold** n plant with yellow flowers

**marijuana, marihuana** n dried flowers and leaves of hemp plant, used as narcotic

**marina** n mooring facility for pleasure boats

**marinade** n liquid in which food is soaked before cooking **marinate** v soak in marinade

**marine** adj of the sea or shipping ~n soldier trained for land or sea combat; fleet **mariner** n sailor

**marionette** n puppet

**marital** adj of marriage

**maritime** adj of seafaring; near the sea

──────── T H E S A U R U S ────────

**manual** adj hand-operated, human, physical ~n bible, guide, handbook, instructions

**manufacture** v assemble, build, compose, construct, create, forge, form, make, mould, process, produce, shape, think up, trump up ~n assembly, construction, fabrication, production

**manure** n compost, droppings, dung, muck, ordure

**many** adj abundant, copious, countless, frequent, manifold, myriad, numerous, profuse, sundry, varied, various

**mar** v blemish, blight, blot, damage, deface, harm, hurt, injure, ruin, scar, spoil, stain, taint, tarnish, vitiate

**march** v file, pace, parade, stalk, stride, strut, tramp, tread, walk ~n demonstration, parade, procession

**margin** n border, bound, brim, brink, confine, edge, limit, rim, side, verge; allowance, extra, latitude, leeway, play, room, scope, space

**marginal** borderline, peripheral

**marine** maritime, nautical, naval, oceanic, seafaring

**mariner** hand, sailor, salt, seafarer, seaman, tar

**marital** conjugal, married, matrimonial, nuptial, wedded

**mark**[1] n dot, scar etc.; sign, token; letter, number showing evaluation of schoolwork etc.; indication; target ~v make mark on; distinguish; notice; assess; stay close to sporting opponent **marked** adj noticeable **marker** n **marksman** n skilled shot

**mark**[2] n German currency unit

**market** n place for buying and selling; demand for goods ~v offer for sale **marketable** adj **market garden** place where fruit and vegetables are grown for sale

**marmalade** n preserve made of oranges, lemons etc.

**marmoset** n small bushy-tailed monkey

**maroon**[1] adj/n (of) brownishcrimson colour

**maroon**[2] v leave on deserted island etc.; isolate

**marquee** n large tent

**marquetry** n inlaid work, wood mosaic

**marquis, marquess** n nobleman

of rank below duke

**marrow** n fatty substance inside bones; vital part; plant with long, green-striped fruit, eaten as vegetable

**marry** v marrying, married join as husband and wife; unite closely

**marriage** n being married; wedding

**marsh** n low-lying wet land **marshy** adj

**marshal** n high officer of state; US law enforcement officer; highranking officer in the army, air force ~v -shalling, -shalled arrange; conduct with ceremony

**marshmallow** n spongy pink or white sweet

**marsupial** n animal that carries its young in pouch

**marten** n weasel-like animal

**martial** adj of war; warlike

**martin** n species of swallow

**martinet** n strict disciplinarian

**martyr** n one who suffers or dies for his beliefs ~v make martyr of

**maritime** marine, nautical, naval, oceanic, sea, seafaring

**mark** n blot, bruise, dent, impression, line, nick, scar, scratch, smirch, smudge, spot, stain, streak; badge, blaze, brand, emblem, evidence, feature, hallmark, indication, label, note, print, proof, seal, sign, stamp, symbol, symptom, token ~v blemish, blot, blotch, brand, bruise, dent, impress, imprint, nick, scar, scratch, smirch, smudge, stain, streak; attend, mind, note, notice, observe, regard, remark, watch

**marked** apparent, blatant, clear, conspicuous, decided, distinct, evident, manifest, notable, noted, obvious, patent, remarkable, signal,

striking

**market** n bazaar, fair, mart ~v retail, sell, vend

**maroon** abandon, cast away, desert, leave, strand

**marriage** match, matrimony, wedding, wedlock

**marrow** core, cream, essence, gist, heart, kernel, pith, quick, substance

**marry** espouse, wed; ally, bond, join, knit, link, match, merge, tie, unite, yoke

**marsh** bog, fen, quagmire, slough, swamp

**marshal** align, arrange, array, assemble, collect, deploy, dispose, gather, group, muster, order, rank

**marshy** boggy, miry, spongy, swampy, wet

**marvel** v **-velling, -velled** wonder ~n wonderful thing **marvellous** adj

**marzipan** n paste of almonds, sugar etc.

**mascara** n cosmetic for darkening eyelashes

**mascot** n thing supposed to bring luck

**masculine** adj relating to males; manly

**mash** n/v (crush into) soft mass or pulp

**mask** n covering for face; disguise, pretence ~v disguise

**masochism** n abnormal condition where pleasure (esp. sexual) is derived from pain **masochist** n

**mason** n worker in stone **masonry** n stonework

**masquerade** n masked ball ~v appear in disguise

**Mass** n service in R.C. Church

**mass** n quantity of matter; *Physics* amount of matter in body; large quantity ~v form into mass **massive** adj large and heavy **mass-market**

adj appealing to many people

**mass-produce** v produce standardized articles in large quantities

**massacre** n indiscriminate, large-scale killing ~v kill indiscriminately

**massage** n rubbing and kneading of muscles etc. as curative treatment ~v perform massage **masseur** n (fem **masseuse**) one who practises massage

**mast** n pole for supporting ship's sails; tall support for aerial etc.

**mastectomy** n surgical removal of breast

**master** n one in control; employer; owner; document etc. from which copies are made; expert; teacher ~adj expert, skilled ~v overcome; acquire skill in **masterful** adj expert, skilled; domineering **masterly** adj showing great skill **mastery** n understanding (of); expertise; victory **mastermind** v plan, direct ~n one who directs complex operation **masterpiece** n outstanding work

**masticate** v chew

——————— THESAURUS ———————

**marvel** v gape, gaze, goggle, wonder ~n genius, miracle, phenomenon, portent, prodigy, wonder

**marvellous** adj amazing, astounding, breathtaking, brilliant, extraordinary, miraculous, prodigious, remarkable, sensational *Inf*, stupendous, wondrous

**masculine** adj male, manful, manlike, manly, virile; bold, brave, gallant, hardy, powerful, resolute, robust, strong, vigorous

**mask** n false face, visor; camouflage, cloak, cover, cover-up, disguise, façade, front, guise, screen, veil, veneer ~v camouflage, cloak, conceal, cover, disguise, hide, obscure, screen, veil

**mass** n block, chunk, hunk, lump, piece; bulk, dimension, magnitude, size ~v accumulate, assemble, collect, forgather, gather, mob, muster, rally, swarm, throng ~adj extensive, large-scale, popular, wholesale, widespread

**massacre** n butchery, carnage, killing, murder, slaughter ~v butcher, exterminate, kill, murder, slaughter, slay

**massage** n manipulation, rubdown ~v manipulate, rub down

**massive** adj big, bulky, enormous, extensive, gigantic, great, heavy, huge, hulking, immense, substantial, vast, weighty

**master** n captain, chief, com-

**mastiff** n large dog

**masturbate** v fondle genital organs **masturbation** n

**mat**[1] n small rug; piece of fabric to protect another surface; thick tangled mass ~v **matting, matted** form into such mass

**mat**[2], **matt** adj dull, lustreless

**matador** n man who kills bull in bullfights

**match**[1] n contest; game; equal; person, thing corresponding to another; marriage ~v get something corresponding to; oppose; put in competition (with); correspond **matchmaker** n person who schemes to bring about marriage

**match**[2] n small stick with head which ignites when rubbed **matchbox** n **matchstick** n

**mate** n comrade; husband, wife; one of pair; officer in merchant ship ~v marry; pair **matey** adj Inf friendly

**material** n substance from which thing is made; cloth; information on which piece of work is based ~adj of body; affecting physical wellbeing; important **materialism** n excessive interest in money and possessions; doctrine that nothing but matter exists **materialistic** adj **materialize** v come into existence or view **materially** adv appreciably

mander, controller, director, employer, governor, head, lord, manager, overlord, overseer, owner, principal, ruler; adept, expert, genius, maestro, virtuoso, wizard ~adj adept, expert, masterly, proficient, skilful, skilled ~v bridle, check, conquer, curb, defeat, overcome, quash, quell, subdue, subjugate, suppress, tame, vanquish; acquire, grasp, learn

**masterful** adept, adroit, clever, deft, expert, first-rate, skilful, skilled, superior, supreme; arrogant, dictatorial, domineering, high-handed

**masterly** adept, adroit, clever, fine, first-rate, skilful, superior

**mastermind** v conceive, devise, direct, manage, organize, plan ~n brain(s) Inf, brainbox, director, engineer, genius, intellect, manager, organizer, planner

**masterpiece** classic, jewel, tour de force

**mastery** command, familiarity, grasp, knowledge, understanding; ability, attainment, expertise, prowess, skill

**match** n bout, contest, game, head-to-head, test, trial; equal, peer, rival; affiliation, alliance, combination, couple, duet, marriage, pair, pairing, partnership, union ~v ally, combine, couple, join, link, marry, mate, pair, unite, yoke; compare, contend, equal, oppose, pit against, rival, vie; adapt, agree, blend, correspond, fit, go with, harmonize, suit, tally

**mate** n colleague, companion, comrade, fellow-worker; husband, partner, significant other US inf, spouse, wife ~v marry, match, wed; breed, copulate, couple, pair

**material** n body, element, matter, stuff, substance; cloth, fabric, stuff; data, evidence, facts, information, notes, work ~adj bodily, concrete, fleshly, physical, substantial, tangible, worldly

**materialize** appear, happen, occur, turn up

**materially** appreciably, consider-

**maternal** *adj* of mother **maternity** *n* motherhood

**mathematics** *pl n* (*with sing v*) science of number, quantity, shape and space **mathematical** *adj* **mathematician** *n*

**maths** *n* *Inf* mathematics

**matinée** *n* afternoon performance in theatre

**matins** *pl n* morning service

**matriarch** *n* mother as head of family **matriarchal** *adj*

**matriculate** *v* enrol, be enrolled in college or university

**matrimony** *n* marriage **matrimonial** *adj*

**matrix** *n* (*pl* **matrices**) substance, situation in which something originates, is enclosed; mould

**matron** *n* married woman; woman who superintends domestic arrangements of public institution; *former name for* NURSING OFFICER

**matter** *n* substance of which thing is made; affair; business; trouble; pus ~*v* be of importance

**mattress** *n* stuffed flat (sprung) case used as part of bed

**mature** *adj* ripe, completely developed; grown-up ~*v* bring, come to maturity **maturity** *n*

**maudlin** *adj* weakly sentimental

**maul** *v* handle roughly

**mausoleum** *n* (*pl* **-leums, -lea**) stately building as a tomb

**mauve** *adj/n* pale purple

**maverick** *n* independent, unorthodox person

**maw** *n* stomach

**mawkish** *adj* maudlin; sickly

**maxim** *n* general truth; rule of conduct

**maximum** *adj/n* (*pl* **-mums, -ma**) greatest (size or number) **maximize** *v* increase to maximum

**May** *n* fifth month; (*without cap.*) hawthorn or its flowers **mayfly** *n* short-lived aquatic insect

**may** *v* (*past tense* **might**) expresses possibility, permission, opportunity etc. **maybe** *adv* perhaps; possibly

**Mayday** *n* international distress signal

**mayhem** *n* violent destruction

ably, essentially, gravely, greatly, much, seriously, significantly, substantially

**matrimonial** conjugal, marital, married, nuptial, wedding

**matrimony** marriage, nuptials, wedlock

**matter** *n* body, stuff, substance; affair, business, concern, episode, event, incident, occurrence, question, situation, subject, topic ~*v* signify

**mature** *adj* adult, fit, grown, matured, mellow, of age, perfect, prepared, ready, ripe, seasoned ~*v* age, bloom, blossom, develop, mellow, perfect, ripen, season

**maturity** adulthood, experience, fullness, majority, manhood, perfection, ripeness, wisdom

**maudlin** lachrymose, sentimental, tearful

**maul** abuse, ill-treat, manhandle, molest, paw

**maxim** adage, aphorism, axiom, byword, dictum, motto, proverb, rule, saw, saying

**maximum** *adj* greatest, highest, most, topmost, utmost ~*n* ceiling, crest, extremity, height, most, peak, pinnacle, summit, top, utmost, zenith

**maybe** perchance, perhaps, possibly

**mayonnaise** *n* creamy sauce, esp. for salads

**mayor** *n* head of municipality

**mayoress** *n* mayor's wife; lady mayor

**maze** *n* labyrinth; network of paths, lines; state of confusion

**MBE** Member of the Order of the British Empire

**MD** Doctor of Medicine

**me** *pron object of* I

**mead** *n* alcoholic drink made from honey

**meadow** *n* piece of grassland

**meagre** *adj* lean, scanty

**meal**¹ *n* occasion when food is served and eaten; the food

**meal**² *n* grain ground to powder

**mealy-mouthed** *adj* not outspoken enough

**mean**¹ *v* **meaning, meant** intend; signify; have a meaning; have the intention of behaving **meaning** *n*

**mean**² *adj* ungenerous, petty; miserly; callous; shabby

**mean**³ *n* middle point; *pl* that by which thing is done; money; resources ~*adj* intermediate; average

**meantime, meanwhile** *advn* (during) time between one happening and another

**meander** *v* flow windingly; wander aimlessly ~*n* wandering course

**measles** *n* infectious disease producing rash of red spots **measly** *adj Inf* meagre

**measure** *n* size, quantity; unit, system of measuring; course of action; law ~*v* ascertain size, quantity of; be (so much) in size or quantity; indicate measurement of **measurable** *adj* **measured** *adj* slow and steady; carefully considered **measurement** *n* measuring; size

**meat** *n* animal flesh as food; food

**meaningful** *adj* of great significance

──── THESAURUS ────

**mayhem** chaos, commotion, confusion, destruction, disorder, fracas, havoc, trouble, violence

**maze** intricacy, labyrinth, meander, imbroglio, perplexity, puzzle, snarl, tangle, web

**meadow** field, grassland, pasture

**meagre** deficient, inadequate, little, measly, paltry, pathetic, poor, puny, scanty, short, slender, slight, small, spare, sparse

**mean**¹ *v* convey, denote, express, imply, indicate, purport, represent, say, signify, spell, suggest, symbolize; aim, aspire, desire, design, intend, plan, propose, purpose, set out, want, wish

**mean**² *adj* beggarly, close, mercenary, miserly, parsimonious, stingy, tight, ungenerous; abject, base, callous, contemptible, degraded, des-

picable, ignoble, shabby, shameful, sordid, vile, wretched

**mean**³ *n* average, balance, median, middle, mid-point, norm ~*adj* average, intermediate, medial, median, medium, middle, standard

**meander** *v* ramble, snake, stray, stroll, turn, wander, wind ~*n* bend, coil, curve, loop, turn, twist, zigzag

**meaning** drift, explanation, gist, implication, import, interpretation, message, purport, sense, significance, substance, upshot, value; aim, design, end, goal, idea, intention, object, plan, point, purpose, trend

**meaningful** important, material, purposeful, relevant, serious, significant, valid

**measurable** determinable, material, perceptible, quantifiable,

meaty *adj*

**mechanic** *n* one who works with machinery; *pl* scientific theory of motion **mechanical** *adj* of, by machine; acting without thought

**mechanism** *n* structure of machine; piece of machinery; process, technique **mechanization** *n* **mechanize** *v* equip with machinery; make automatic

**medal** *n* piece of metal with inscription etc. used as reward or memento **medallion** *n* (design like) large medal

**meddle** *v* interfere

**media** *n pl* of MEDIUM used esp. of the mass media, radio, television etc.

**median** *adj/n* middle (point or line)

**mediate** *v* intervene to reconcile **mediation** *n* **mediator** *n*

**medic** *n* *Inf* doctor or medical student

**medicine** *n* drug or remedy for treating disease; science of preventing, curing disease **medical** *adj* **medicate** *v* impregnate with medicinal substances **medication** *n* (treatment with) medicinal substance **medicinal** *adj* curative

**medieval, mediaeval** *adj* of Middle Ages

**mediocre** *adj* ordinary, middling; second-rate **mediocrity** *n* state of being mediocre; mediocre person

**meditate** *v* reflect deeply, esp. on spiritual matters; think about, plan **meditation** *n*

**medium** *adj* between two qualities, degrees etc. ~*n* (*pl* **mediums, media**) middle quality; means; agency of communicating news etc. to public; surroundings

significant

**measure** *n* allowance, amount, amplitude, capacity, degree, extent, proportion, quantity, quota, range, ration, reach, scope, share, size; gauge, metre, rule, scale; method, standard, system; act, action, course, deed, expedient, means, procedure, step; act, bill, enactment, law, resolution, statute ~*v* assess, calculate, calibrate, compute, determine, estimate, evaluate, gauge, judge, quantify, rate, size, sound, survey, value, weigh

**measurement** assessment, calculation, calibration, estimation, evaluation, mensuration, survey, valuation

**mechanical** automatic; cold, cursory, dead, habitual, impersonal, instinctive, lacklustre, lifeless, perfunctory, routine, unconscious, un-

feeling, unthinking

**mechanism** apparatus, appliance, contrivance, device, instrument, structure, system, tool; agency, execution, means, medium, method, operation, performance, procedure, system, technique

**meddle** interfere, intervene, intrude, pry

**mediate** arbitrate, conciliate, intercede, intervene, reconcile, referee, resolve, settle, umpire

**medicine** cure, drug, physic, remedy

**medieval** antiquated, archaic, old-fashioned, primitive

**mediocre** average, indifferent, inferior, mean, middling, ordinary, passable, pedestrian, tolerable, undistinguished, uninspired

**meditate** cogitate, consider, contemplate, deliberate, muse, ponder,

**medley** n (pl **-leys**) mixture

**meek** adj submissive, humble

**meet** v meeting, met come face to face (with); satisfy; pay; converge; assemble; come into contact **meeting** n

**megabyte** n Computers 1 048 576 bytes

**megalith** n great stone

**megalomania** n desire for, delusions of grandeur, power etc. **megalomaniac** adj/n

**megaphone** n cone-shaped instrument to amplify voice

**megaton** n explosive power of 1 000 000 tons of TNT

**melancholy** n sadness, dejection ~adj gloomy, dejected

**melanin** n dark pigment found in hair, skin etc.

**mêlée** n confused fight

**mellifluous** adj (of sound) smooth, sweet

**mellow** adj ripe; softened by age, experience; not harsh; genial ~v make, become mellow

**melodrama** n play full of sensational situations **melodramatic** adj

**melody** n series of musical notes which make tune; sweet sound **melodic** adj **melodious** adj

**melon** n large, fleshy, juicy fruit

**melt** v melting, melted, melted or molten (cause) to become liquid by heat; dissolve; soften; disappear

**member** n individual making up body or society; limb; any part of complex whole **membership** n

——— THESAURUS ———

reflect, study, think

**medium** adj average, fair, intermediate, mean, mediocre, middle ~n average, centre, mean, middle; agency, avenue, channel, form, instrument, means, mode, organ, vehicle, way

**medley** jumble, miscellany, mishmash, mixture, pastiche, patchwork

**meek** deferential, docile, gentle, humble, mild, modest, patient, peaceful, soft, submissive, yielding

**meet** confront, contact, encounter, find; answer, comply, discharge, equal, fulfil, gratify, handle, match, perform, satisfy; connect, converge, cross, intersect, join, touch, unite; assemble, collect, come together, gather, muster, rally

**meeting** assignation, encounter, engagement, introduction, rendezvous; concourse, confluence, convergence, crossing, intersection, junction, union; assembly, audience, company, conference, congregation, congress, convention, gathering, rally, reunion, session

**melancholy** n dejection, depression, despondency, gloom, sadness, sorrow, unhappiness, woe ~adj gloomy, glum, joyless, low, lugubrious, miserable, mournful, pensive, sad, sombre, sorrowful, unhappy

**mellow** adj delicate, juicy, mature, perfect, rich, ripe, soft, sweet; dulcet, full, melodious, rich, rounded, smooth, sweet, tuneful; cheerful, cordial, elevated, expansive, genial, happy, jolly, jovial, relaxed ~v develop, improve, mature, perfect, ripen, season, soften, sweeten

**melodious** dulcet, musical, silvery, sweet-sounding, tuneful

**melodramatic** extravagant, histrionic, overdramatic, theatrical

**melody** air, descant, music, refrain, song, strain, theme, tune

**melt** diffuse, dissolve, flux, fuse, liquefy, soften, thaw

**member** fellow, representative;

**membrane** n thin flexible tissue in plant or animal body

**memento** n (pl **-tos**) reminder, souvenir

**memo** n short for MEMORANDUM

**memoir** n autobiography, personal history

**memory** n faculty of recalling to mind; recollection; thing remembered; commemoration **memorable** adj worthy of remembrance **memorandum** n (pl **-dums, -da**) note to help the memory etc.; informal letter **memorial** n thing which serves to keep in memory ~adj serving as a memorial **memorize** v commit to memory

**men** n pl of MAN

**menace** n threat ~v threaten

**ménage** n household

**menagerie** n collection of wild animals

**mend** v repair; correct, put right;

improve ~n repaired breakage

**menial** adj requiring little skill; servile ~n servant

**meningitis** n inflammation of the membranes of the brain

**menopause** n final cessation of menstruation

**menstruation** n monthly discharge of blood from womb **menstrual** adj **menstruate** v

**mensuration** n measuring

**mental** adj of, by the mind; Inf mad **mentality** n way of thinking

**menthol** n substance found in peppermint

**mention** v refer to briefly ~n acknowledgment; reference to

**mentor** n wise adviser

**menu** n list of dishes served

**mercantile** adj of trade

**mercenary** adj influenced by greed; working merely for reward ~n hired soldier

───── THESAURUS ─────

arm, component, constituent, element, leg, limb, organ, part, portion

**memoir** account, biography, essay, journal, life, narrative

**memorable** celebrated, distinguished, famous, historic, illustrious, important, notable, remarkable, significant, striking, unforgettable

**memorial** n monument, plaque, record, souvenir ~adj commemorative, monumental

**memorize** learn, learn by heart, learn by rote, remember

**memory** recall, recollection, reminiscence; commemoration, honour, remembrance

**menace** n scare, threat, warning ~v alarm, browbeat, bully, frighten, impend, intimidate, loom, terror-

ize, threaten

**mend** v cure, darn, fix, heal, patch, rectify, refit, reform, remedy, renew, repair, restore; amend, better, correct, emend, improve, rectify, reform, revise ~n darn, patch, repair, stitch

**menial** adj boring, dull, humdrum, routine, unskilled

**mental** cerebral, intellectual

**mentality** attitude, disposition, outlook, personality, way of thinking

**mention** v adduce, broach, cite, communicate, declare, disclose, divulge, impart, intimate, name, recount, refer to, report, reveal, state, tell, touch upon ~n acknowledgment, citation, recognition, tribute; allusion, indication, reference, remark

**merchant** *n* one engaged in trade; wholesale trader **merchandise** *n* trader's wares **merchant navy** ships engaged in a nation's commerce

**mercury** *n* silvery metal, liquid at ordinary temperature **mercurial** *adj* lively, changeable

**mercy** *n* refraining from infliction of suffering by one who has right, power to inflict it; fortunate occurrence **merciful** *adj*

**mere** *adj* only; nothing but **merely** *adv*

**merge** *v* (cause to) lose identity or be absorbed **merger** *n* combination esp. of business firms

**meridian** *n* circle of the earth passing through poles; highest point

**meringue** *n* baked mixture of white of eggs and sugar

**merit** *n* excellence, worth; quality of deserving reward ~*v* deserve

**mermaid** *n* imaginary sea creature half woman, half fish

**merry** *adj* joyous, cheerful **merriment** *n* **merry-go-round** *n* roundabout

**mesh** *n* (one of the open spaces of, or wires etc. forming) network, net ~*v* (cause to) entangle, engage

**mesmerize** *v* hypnotize

**mess** *n* untidy confusion; trouble; (place where) group regularly eat together ~*v* potter (about); muddle **messy** *adj*

**message** *n* communication sent;

———————— THESAURUS ————————

**mercenary** *adj* avaricious, covetous, grasping, greedy, sordid, venal; bought, hired, paid, venal ~*n* soldier of fortune

**merchandise** goods, produce, stock, wares

**merchant** broker, dealer, purveyor, retailer, salesman, seller, shopkeeper, supplier, trader, tradesman, trafficker, vendor, wholesaler

**merciful** compassionate, forbearing, forgiving, generous, gracious, humane, kind, lenient, liberal, soft, sparing, sympathetic

**mercy** charity, clemency, compassion, favour, forbearance, forgiveness, grace, kindness, pity, quarter; boon, godsend, piece of luck, relief

**mere** *adj* absolute, bare, common, entire, plain, pure, sheer, simple, stark, unmixed, utter

**merge** amalgamate, blend, combine, fuse, join, meet, mingle, mix, unite

**merger** amalgamation, coalition, fusion, incorporation, union

**merit** *n* asset, excellence, good, goodness, integrity, quality, talent, value, virtue, worth, worthiness; claim, credit, desert, due, right ~*v* deserve, earn, incur, warrant

**merriment** amusement, conviviality, festivity, frolic, fun, gaiety, laughter, mirth, revelry, sport

**merry** blithe, carefree, cheerful, convivial, festive, gay, glad, gleeful, happy, jolly, joyful, joyous, lighthearted, rollicking, vivacious

**mesh** *n* net, network, web ~*v* catch, ensnare, entangle, net, snare, tangle, trap; combine, connect, dovetail, engage, harmonize, knit

**mess** *n* botch, chaos, clutter, cock-up *Brit sl,* confusion, disarray, disorder, hotchpotch, jumble, litter, shambles, state, untidiness; difficulty, hot water *Inf,* muddle, perplexity, plight, predicament, spot *Inf,* tight spot, trouble *v (often with up)* botch, bungle, clutter, dirty, disarrange, dishevel, foul, litter, muddle, pollute, scramble

meaning, moral **messenger** n

**Messiah** n promised saviour; Christ

**met** past tense past participle of MEET

**metabolism** n chemical process of living body **metabolic** adj

**metal** n mineral substance, malleable and capable of conducting heat and electricity **metallic** adj **metallurgist** n **metallurgy** n scientific study of metals

**metamorphosis** n (pl -phoses) change of shape, character etc.

**metaphor** n figure of speech in which term is transferred to something it does not literally apply to **metaphorical** adj

**metaphysical** adj philosophical; abstract, abstruse

**mete** v mete out distribute; allot

**meteor** n small, fast-moving celestial body, visible as streak of incandescence if it enters earth's atmosphere **meteoric** adj of meteor; brilliant but short-lived **meteorite** n fallen meteor

**meteorology** n study of climate, weather **meteorological** adj meteor-

ologist n

**meter** n instrument for recording, measuring

**methane** n flammable gas, compound of carbon and hydrogen

**method** n way, manner; technique; orderliness **methodical** adj orderly

**meths** n Inf methylated spirits

**methylated spirits** alcoholic mixture used as fuel etc.

**meticulous** adj particular about details

**metre** n unit of length in decimal system; SI unit of length; rhythm of poem **metric** adj of system of weights and measures in which metre is a unit **metrical** adj of measurement; of poetic metre

**metronome** n instrument which marks musical time by means of ticking pendulum

**metropolis** n (pl -lises) chief city of a region **metropolitan** adj

**mettle** n courage, spirit

**mew** n/v (utter) cry of cat

**mews** pl n (with sing or pl v) yard, street orig. of stables, now oft. converted to houses

———————— THESAURUS ————————

**message** bulletin, communication, dispatch, letter, missive, note, notice, tidings, word; idea, import, moral, point, theme

**messenger** agent, bearer, carrier, courier, emissary, envoy, go-between, herald, runner

**messy** chaotic, cluttered, confused, dirty, dishevelled, disordered, disorganized, grubby, littered, muddled

**metaphor** allegory, analogy, image, symbol

**mete** v administer, allot, assign, deal, dispense, distribute, divide,

dole, measure, portion, ration, share

**method** approach, course, fashion, form, manner, mode, plan, practice, procedure, programme, routine, rule, scheme, style, system, technique, way; design, form, order, pattern, planning, structure

**methodical** businesslike, deliberate, disciplined, efficient, meticulous, neat, organized, planned, precise, regular, tidy

**meticulous** detailed, exact, fastidious, painstaking, precise, scrupulous, strict, thorough

**mezzanine** n intermediate storey, balcony between two main storeys

**mezzo-soprano** n (pl -nos) voice, singer between soprano and contralto

**mg** milligram

**miasma** n (pl -mata, -mas) unwholesome atmosphere

**mica** n mineral found as glittering scales, plates

**microbe** n minute organism; disease germ

**microchip** n small wafer of silicon containing electronic circuits

**microcosm** n miniature representation of larger system

**microfiche** n microfilm in sheet form

**microfilm** n miniaturized recording of manuscript, book on roll of film

**microphone** n instrument for amplifying, transmitting sounds

**microprocessor** n integrated circuit acting as central processing unit in small computer

**microscope** n instrument by which very small body is magnified **microscopic** adj very small

**microwave** n electromagnetic wave with wavelength of a few cen-

timetres, used in radar, cooking etc.; oven using microwaves

**mid** adj intermediate **midday** n noon **midnight** n twelve o'clock at night **midway** adj/adv halfway

**middle** adj equidistant from two extremes ~n middle point or part **middling** adj mediocre; moderate **middle age** period of life between youth and old age **middle class** social class of businessmen, professional people etc. **middleman** n trader between producer and consumer **middle-of-the-road** adj moderate

**midge** n gnat or similar insect

**midget** n very small person or thing

**midriff** n middle part of body

**midst** prep in the middle of ~n middle

**midwife** n trained person who assists at childbirth **midwifery** n

**mien** n person's manner or appearance

**might¹** past tense of MAY

**might²** n power, strength **mightily** adv **mighty** adj

**migraine** n severe headache

**migrate** v move from one place to another **migrant** n/adj **migration** n

———— THESAURUS ————

**microscopic** imperceptible, infinitesimal, teensy-weensy, teenyweeny, tiny

**midday** noon, noonday, twelve o'clock

**middle** adj central, halfway, inner, inside, mean, medial, median, medium, mid ~n centre, focus, heart, inside, mean, midpoint, midst, thick

**midget** dwarf, gnome, pygmy or pigmy, teeny-weeny

**midst** bosom, centre, core, depths,

heart, hub, interior, middle, thick

**might** ability, capability, efficacy, energy, force, potency, power, prowess, strength, sway, valour, vigour

**mighty** forceful, hardy, potent, powerful, robust, stalwart, stout, strong, sturdy, vigorous

**migrant** drifter, gypsy, itinerant, nomad, rover, tinker, transient, vagrant, wanderer

**migrate** journey, move, roam, rove, shift, travel, trek, wander

**mike** n Inf microphone

**mild** adj not strongly flavoured; gentle; temperate **mildly** adv

**mildew** n destructive fungus on plants or things exposed to damp

**mile** n measure of length, 1760 yards, 1.609 km **mileage** n travelling expenses per mile; miles travelled (per gallon of petrol) **mileometer** n device that records miles travelled by vehicle **milestone** n significant event

**milieu** n (pl -lieux) environment

**militant** adj aggressive, vigorous in support of cause; prepared to fight **militancy** n

**military** adj of, for, soldiers, armies or war ~n armed forces **militarism** n enthusiasm for military force and methods **militia** n military force of citizens for home service

**militate** v (esp. with against) have strong influence, effect on

**milk** n white fluid with which mammals feed their young; fluid in some plants ~v draw milk from **milky** adj

**mill** n factory; machine for grinding, pulverizing corn, paper etc. ~v put through mill; cut fine grooves across edges of (e.g. coins); move in confused manner **miller** n **mill-**

**stone** n flat circular stone for grinding

**millennium** n (pl -iums, -ia) period of a thousand years; period of peace, happiness

**millet** n cereal grass

**milli-** comb. form thousandth part of, as in **milligram, millilitre, millimetre**

**milliner** n maker of women's hats

**million** n 1000 thousands **millionaire** n owner of a million pounds, dollars etc. **millionth** adj/n

**millipede, millepede** n small animal with many pairs of legs

**mime** n acting without words ~v perform mime

**mimic** v mimicking, mimicked imitate, esp. for satirical effect ~n one who does this **mimicry** n

**mimosa** n plant with fluffy, yellow flowers

**minaret** n tall slender tower of mosque

**mince** v cut, chop small; soften (words etc.) ~n minced meat **mincer** n **mincing** adj affected in manner **mincemeat** n mixture of currants, spices, suet etc. **mince pie** pie containing mincemeat

**mind** n intellectual faculties; memory; intention; taste; sanity ~v

———— THESAURUS ————

**migration** journey, movement, roving, shift, travel, trek, voyage

**mild** amiable, balmy, bland, calm, docile, easy, forbearing, forgiving, gentle, indulgent, kind, meek, mellow, merciful, moderate, peaceable, placid, pleasant, serene, smooth, soft, temperate, tender, tranquil, warm

**militant** active, aggressive, assertive, combative; belligerent, fighting

**military** adj armed, martial, soldierly, warlike ~n armed forces, army, forces, services

**milk** v drain, express, extract, press, tap

**mill** n factory, foundry, plant, shop, works; crusher, grinder

**mime** n dumb show, gesture ~v gesture, represent, simulate

**mimic** v ape, caricature, imitate, impersonate, parody ~n caricaturist, imitator, impersonator, paro-

take offence at; care for; attend to; heed **minder** n Sl bodyguard **mindful** adj heedful **mindless** adj stupid; requiring no thought; careless
**mine**[1] pron belonging to me
**mine**[2] n deep hole for digging out coal, metals etc.; hidden deposit of explosive to blow up ship etc.; profitable source ~v dig from mine; place explosive mines in, on **miner** n **minefield** n area of land or sea containing mines **minesweeper** n ship for clearing mines
**mineral** n/adj (of) naturally occurring inorganic substance **mineralogy** n science of minerals **mineral water** water containing dissolved mineral salts
**minestrone** n soup containing vegetables and pasta
**mingle** v mix, blend; mix socially
**mini** n something small or miniature; short skirt ~adj small
**miniature** n small painted portrait; anything on small scale ~adj on

small scale **miniaturize** v make to very small scale
**minibus** n small bus
**minim** n Mus note half the length of semibreve
**minimum** n (pl -mums, -ma) lowest size or quantity ~adj least possible **minimal** adj **minimize** v reduce to minimum
**minion** n servile dependant
**minister** n person in charge of department of State; diplomatic representative; clergyman ~v take care of **ministerial** adj **ministration** n rendering help **ministry** n office of clergyman; government department
**mink** n variety of weasel; its fur
**minnow** n small freshwater fish
**minor** adj lesser; under age ~n person below age of legal majority; scale in music **minority** n lesser number, group; state of being a minor
**minster** n cathedral, large church

dist, parrot
**mind** n intellect, mentality, reason, sense, spirit, understanding, wits; brain, head, imagination, psyche; memory, recollection, remembrance; bent, desire, disposition, fancy, inclination, intention, leaning, notion, purpose, tendency, urge, will, wish ~v care, disapprove, dislike, object, resent; guard, look after, take care of, tend, watch
**mindful** adj alert, attentive, aware, careful, chary, cognizant, conscious, heedful, wary, watchful
**mine** n colliery, deposit, lode, pit, shaft, vein; fund, hoard, reserve, source, stock, store, supply ~v delve, excavate, extract, hew, quarry, unearth

**mingle** alloy, blend, combine, compound, intermix, join, marry, merge, mix, unite; associate, circulate, fraternize, hobnob, socialize
**miniature** adj baby, diminutive, dwarf, little, midget, pocket, pygmy or pigmy, reduced, small, toy
**minimal** adj least, littlest, nominal, slightest, smallest, token
**minimum** n bottom, depth, least, lowest, nadir, slightest ~adj least, lowest, slightest, smallest
**minister** n ambassador, delegate, diplomat, envoy, executive, officeholder, official; churchman, clergyman, cleric, ecclesiastic, parson, pastor, preacher, priest, vicar ~v attend, tend
**ministry** administration, cabinet,

**minstrel** n medieval singer, musician, poet

**mint¹** n place where money is coined ~adj brand-new ~v coin, invent

**mint²** n aromatic plant

**minuet** n stately dance

**minus** prep/adj less; lacking; negative ~n the sign of subtraction (-)

**minuscule** adj very small

**minute¹** adj very small; precise

**minute²** n 60th part of hour or degree; pl record of proceedings of meeting etc.

**minx** n bold, flirtatious woman

**miracle** n supernatural event; marvel **miraculous** adj

**mirage** n deceptive image in atmosphere

**mire** n swampy ground, mud

**mirror** n glass or polished surface reflecting images ~v reflect in or as if in mirror

**mirth** n merriment, gaiety

**mis-** comb. form wrong, bad

**misadventure** n unlucky chance

**misanthrope, misanthropist** n hater of mankind

**misapprehension** n misunderstanding

**misappropriate** v put to dishonest use; embezzle

**miscarry** v expel fetus prematurely; fail **miscarriage** n

**miscellaneous** adj mixed **miscellany** n medley

**mischief** n annoying behaviour; inclination to tease; harm, annoyance **mischievous** adj

**misconception** n wrong idea

———— THESAURUS ————

council, government, holy orders

**minor** inconsiderable, inferior, junior, lesser, light, paltry, petty, secondary, slight, small, subordinate, trivial, younger

**mint** adj brand-new, excellent, first-class, fresh, perfect ~v cast, coin, make, produce, stamp, strike

**minute¹** adj fine, little, slender, small, teensy-weensy, teeny-weeny, tiny

**minute²** n flash, instant, moment, second

**minx** coquette, flirt, hoyden, hussy, jade, tomboy, wanton

**miracle** marvel, prodigy, wonder

**miraculous** amazing, astonishing, astounding, extraordinary, incredible, magical, marvellous, phenomenal, supernatural, wonderful

**mirage** illusion, phantasm

**mire** bog, marsh, morass, quagmire, swamp

**mirror** n glass, reflector ~v copy,

depict, echo, emulate, follow, reflect, represent, show

**mirth** amusement, cheerfulness, festivity, frolic, fun, gaiety, glee, laughter, levity, merriment, pleasure, rejoicing, revelry, sport

**misappropriate** embezzle, misapply, misuse, pocket, steal, swindle

**miscellaneous** assorted, diverse, indiscriminate, jumbled, manifold, many, mingled, mixed, motley, promiscuous, sundry, varied, various

**mischief** devilment, impishness, misbehaviour, naughtiness, roguery, trouble, waywardness; damage, detriment, disruption, evil, harm, hurt, injury, trouble

**mischievous** arch, bad, impish, naughty, playful, puckish, teasing; bad, damaging, destructive, evil, harmful, hurtful, injurious, malignant, pernicious, sinful, spiteful, wicked

**misconduct** *n* unethical behaviour

**miscreant** *n* evildoer

**misdemeanour** *n* minor offence

**miser** *n* hoarder of money

**miserable** *adj* very unhappy; causing misery; worthless; squalid **misery** *n*

**misfire** *v* fail to fire, start etc.

**misfit** *n* person not suited to environment

**misfortune** *n* (piece of) bad luck

**misgiving** *n* (*oft. pl*) feeling of fear, doubt etc.

**misguided** *adj* foolish

**mishap** *n* minor accident

**misjudge** *v* judge wrongly

**mislay** *v* put in place which cannot later be remembered

**mislead** *v* misleading, misled give false information to

**mismanage** *v* organize badly

**misnomer** *n* wrong name or term

**misogyny** *n* hatred of women **misogynist** *n*

**misprint** *n* printing error

**Miss** *n* title of unmarried woman; (*without cap.*) girl

**miss** *v* fail to hit, reach, catch etc.; not be in time for; notice or regret absence of; avoid; omit ~*n* fact, in-

————— T H E S A U R U S —————

**misconception** delusion, error, misunderstanding

**misconduct** delinquency, immorality, impropriety, malpractice, misbehaviour, transgression, wrongdoing

**misdemeanour** fault, misconduct, offence, peccadillo, transgression

**miser** niggard, skinflint

**miserable** afflicted, crestfallen, dejected, depressed, despondent, dismal, distressed, downcast, forlorn, gloomy, melancholy, mournful, sorrowful, unhappy, woebegone, wretched; abject, bad, contemptible, despicable, disgraceful, low, mean, pathetic, piteous, pitiable, shabby, shameful, sordid, sorry, squalid, vile, worthless, wretched

**misery** agony, anguish, depression, desolation, despair, discomfort, distress, gloom, grief, hardship, melancholy, sadness, sorrow, suffering, torment, torture, unhappiness, woe; affliction, burden, calamity, curse, disaster, hardship, load, misfortune, ordeal, sorrow,

trial, tribulation, trouble, woe

**misfire** fail, fall through, miscarry

**misfit** eccentric, nonconformist

**misfortune** bad luck, infelicity; accident, adversity, affliction, blow, calamity, disaster, hardship, harm, loss, misadventure, misery, reverse, setback, tragedy, trouble

**misgiving** anxiety, distrust, doubt, hesitation, reservation, suspicion, uncertainty, worry

**misguided** deluded, foolish, ill-advised, imprudent, misled, misplaced, mistaken, unreasonable, unwise

**mishap** accident, adversity, bad luck, hard luck, misadventure, misfortune

**misjudge** miscalculate, overestimate, overrate, underestimate, underrate

**mislay** lose, lose track of, misplace, miss

**mislead** beguile, bluff, deceive, delude, fool, hoodwink, misdirect, misguide, misinform

**mismanage** botch, bungle, maladminister, misdirect, misgovern, mishandle

stance of missing **missing** adj lost, absent

**missal** n book containing prayers, rites etc.

**missile** n that which may be thrown, shot etc. to damage or destroy

**mission** n specific duty; delegation; those sent **missionary** n one sent to a place, society to spread religion

**missive** n letter

**mist** n water vapour in fine drops **misty** adj

**mistake** n error ~v fail to understand; take (person or thing) for another **mistaken** adj

**mister** n (abbrev **Mr.**) title of cour-

tesy to man

**mistletoe** n evergreen parasitic plant

**mistress** n illicit lover of married man; woman with mastery or control; title formerly given to married woman

**mistrust** v not trust ~n lack of trust

**misunderstand** v fail to understand properly **misunderstanding** n

**misuse** n incorrect use ~v use wrongly; treat badly

**mite** n very small insect; anything very small

**mitigate** v make less severe **mitigation** n

**mitre** n bishop's headdress; right-

—————— THESAURUS ——————

**miss**[1] v avoid, blunder, err, escape, evade, fail, forego, lack, lose, miscarry, mistake, omit, overlook, skip, slip, trip; need, pine for, want, wish ~n blunder, error, failure, fault, loss, mistake, omission, oversight, want

**miss**[2] damsel, girl, maid, spinster

**missile** projectile, rocket, weapon

**missing** absent, astray, gone, lacking, lost, mislaid, misplaced

**mission** aim, assignment, business, calling, charge, duty, errand, goal, job, office, operation, purpose, pursuit, quest, task, trust, undertaking, vocation, work; delegation, deputation, task force

**missionary** converter, evangelist, preacher

**mist** cloud, dew, drizzle, film, fog, haze, smog, spray, steam, vapour

**mistake** n blunder, error, fault, gaffe, oversight, slip, solecism ~v misconceive, misconstrue, misjudge, misread, misunderstand

**mistaken** fallacious, false, faulty,

inaccurate, incorrect, misguided, misinformed, unfounded, wrong

**mistress** concubine, girlfriend, kept woman, lover, paramour

**mistrust** v beware, doubt, fear, suspect ~n doubt, fear, misgiving, scepticism, suspicion, uncertainty

**misty** bleary, cloudy, dark, dim, foggy, hazy, indistinct, obscure, vague

**misunderstand** misconceive, misconstrue, mishear, misinterpret, misjudge, mistake

**misunderstanding** error, misconstruction, misjudgment, misreading, mistake, mix-up

**misuse** n abuse, corruption, malapropism, perversion, profanation, solecism, waste ~v abuse, corrupt, desecrate, dissipate, misapply, pervert, profane, prostitute, squander, waste

**mitigate** abate, allay, appease, assuage, blunt, calm, check, dull, ease, extenuate, lessen, lighten, modify, mollify, pacify, palliate,

angled joint

**mitt** n covering for hand

**mitten** n glove with two compartments for thumb and fingers

**mix** v put together, combine, blend; be mixed; associate **mixed** adj of different elements, races etc. **mixer** n **mixture** n **mix-up** n confused situation

**ml** millilitre

**mm** millimetre

**mnemonic** n something to help the memory

**moan** v/n (utter) low murmur, usually of pain

**moat** n deep wide ditch, esp. round castle

**mob** n disorderly crowd ~v **mobbing, mobbed** attack in mob, hustle

**mobile** adj capable of movement;

easily changed ~n hanging structure designed to move in air currents **mobility** n

**mobilize** v prepare, esp. for military service **mobilization** n

**moccasin** n Amer. Indian soft shoe, usu. of deerskin

**mocha** n strong dark coffee; flavouring of coffee and chocolate

**mock** v ridicule; mimic ~adj sham **mockery** n derision; travesty

**mode** n manner; prevailing fashion **modish** adj fashionable

**model** n miniature representation; pattern; one worthy of imitation; person employed to pose, or display clothing ~adj made as (miniature) copy; exemplary ~v **-elling, -elled** make model of; mould; display (clothing)

## THESAURUS

placate, soften, soothe, subdue, temper

**mix** alloy, amalgamate, blend, coalesce, combine, compound, cross, fuse, incorporate, intermingle, join, meld, merge, mingle, unite; associate, consort, fraternize, join, mingle, socialize

**mixed** alloyed, amalgamated, blended, combined, composite, compound, fused, incorporated, joint, mingled, united; assorted, diverse, motley, varied

**mixture** alloy, amalgam, association, assortment, blend, brew, combine, compound, concoction, conglomeration, cross, fusion, medley, meld, miscellany, mix, union, variety

**mix-up** confusion, disorder, jumble, mess, mistake, muddle

**moan** v bewail, deplore, grieve, groan, lament, mourn, sigh, sob, whine ~n groan, lament, sigh, sob,

sough, wail, whine

**mob** n body, collection, crowd, drove, flock, gang, gathering, herd, horde, host, mass, pack, press, swarm, throng

**mobile** itinerant, migrant, movable, peripatetic, portable, travelling, wandering

**mobilize** call up, marshal, muster, organize, prepare, rally, ready

**mock** v chaff, deride, flout, insult, jeer, ridicule, scoff, scorn, sneer, taunt, tease ~adj artificial, bogus, counterfeit, dummy, fake, false, feigned, forged, fraudulent, imitation, pretended, sham, spurious

**mockery** contempt, contumely, derision, disdain, jeering, ridicule, scorn; burlesque, caricature, deception, farce, imitation, lampoon, mimicry, parody, pretence, sham, travesty

**model** n copy, facsimile, image, imitation, mock-up, replica, repre-

**modem** n device for connecting two computers by telephone line

**moderate** adj not going to extremes ~n person of moderate views ~v make, become less excessive; preside over **moderation** n **moderator** n arbitrator

**modern** adj of present or recent times; in, of current fashion **modernity** n **modernize** v bring up to date

**modest** adj not overrating one's qualities or achievements; moderate, decent **modesty** n

**modicum** n small quantity

**modify** v -fying, -fied change slightly **modification** n

**modulate** v regulate; vary in tone **modulation** n

**module** n (detachable) component with specific function

**mogul** n powerful person

**mohair** n cloth of goat's hair

**moist** adj slightly wet **moisten** v **moisture** n liquid, esp. diffused or in drops

**molar** n/adj (tooth) for grinding

**molasses** n syrup, by-product of sugar refining

**mole¹** n small dark spot on skin

**mole²** n small burrowing animal

**molecule** n simplest freely existing chemical unit **molecular** adj

**molest** v pester, interfere with so as to annoy or injure

**moll** n Sl gangster's female accomplice

——————— THESAURUS ———————

sentation; archetype, design, epitome, example, exemplar, gauge, ideal, mould, norm, original, paradigm, paragon, pattern, prototype, standard, type; poser, sitter, subject ~adj copy, dummy, facsimile, imitation, miniature; archetypal, exemplary, ideal, illustrative, paradigmatic, perfect, standard, typical ~v base, carve, cast, design, fashion, form, mould, pattern, plan, sculpt, shape, stamp; display, show off, wear

**moderate** adj cool, deliberate, equable, gentle, limited, mild, modest, peaceable, reasonable, restrained, sober, steady, temperate ~v abate, allay, appease, calm, control, curb, decrease, diminish, mitigate, pacify, quiet, restrain, soften, subdue, tame, temper

**moderation** calmness, composure, coolness, equanimity, fairness, justice, mildness, reasonableness, restraint, sedateness, temperance

**modern** contemporary, current, fresh, late, latest, new, novel, present, recent

**modernize** rejuvenate, remake, remodel, renew, renovate, revamp, update

**modest** bashful, coy, demure, discreet, humble, meek, quiet, reserved, reticent, retiring, shy, simple; fair, limited, moderate, ordinary, small

**modesty** demureness, diffidence, humility, meekness, propriety, reserve, reticence, shyness, timidity

**modify** adapt, adjust, alter, change, convert, recast, reform, reorganize, reshape, revise, transform, vary

**moist** clammy, damp, dank, dewy, drizzly, humid, rainy, wet, wettish

**moisten** damp, soak, water, wet

**moisture** damp, dew, humidity, liquid, sweat, water

**molest** abuse, afflict, annoy, badger, bother, disturb, harass, harry, hector, irritate, persecute, pester,

**mollify** v **-fying, -fied** calm down, placate **mollification** n

**mollusc** n soft-bodied, usu. hard-shelled animal, e.g. snail

**mollycoddle** v pamper

**molten** SEE MELT

**moment** n short space of, (present) point in, time **momentarily** adv

**momentary** adj lasting only a moment

**momentous** adj of great importance

**momentum** n (pl **-ta, -tums**) force of a moving body; impetus gained from motion

**monarch** n sovereign ruler **monarchist** n supporter of monarchy **monarchy** n state ruled by sovereign; government by sovereign

**monastery** n house occupied by religious order **monastic** adj

**Monday** n second day of the week

**money** n (pl **-eys, -ies**) banknotes, coins etc., used as medium of exchange **monetary** adj **moneyed, monied** adj rich

**mongoose** n (pl **-gooses**) small animal of Asia and Africa

**mongrel** n/adj (animal) of mixed breed; hybrid

**monitor** n person or device which checks, controls, warns, records; pupil assisting teacher with odd jobs; type of large lizard ~v watch, check on

**monk** n one of a religious community of men living apart under vows

**monkey** n long-tailed primate; mischievous child ~v meddle with

**mono-** comb. form single, as in monosyllabic

**monochrome** adj of one colour

**monocle** n single eyeglass

**monogamy** n custom of being married to one person at a time

**monogram** n design of letters interwoven

**monograph** n short book on single subject

**monolith** n large upright block of stone **monolithic** adj

**monologue** n long speech by one person

**monopoly** n exclusive possession

—————————— THESAURUS ——————————

torment, upset, vex, worry

**moment** flash, instant, minute, second, twinkling; hour, instant, juncture, point, stage, time

**momentous** critical, crucial, decisive, fateful, grave, historic, important, serious, significant, vital

**momentum** drive, energy, force, impetus, power, push, thrust

**monarch** n king, potentate, prince, princess, queen, ruler, sovereign

**monastery** abbey, cloister, convent, friary, house, nunnery, priory

**monastic** ascetic, austere, cloistered, recluse, secluded, withdrawn

**monetary** capital, cash, financial, fiscal

**money** banknotes, brass N Eng dial, capital, cash, coin, currency, dosh Brit & Aust sl, funds, hard cash, legal tender

**mongrel** n cross, crossbreed, hybrid ~adj crossbred, half-breed, hybrid

**monitor** n guide, overseer, supervisor, watchdog ~v check, follow, observe, record, scan, supervise, survey, watch

**monk** brother, monastic, religious

**monkey** n primate, simian; devil, imp, rascal, rogue, scamp ~v fool, interfere, meddle, mess, play, tamper, tinker, trifle

**monologue** harangue, lecture,

of trade, privilege etc. **monopolize** v claim, take exclusive possession of

**monotone** n speech on one note **monotonous** adj lacking variety, dull **monotony** n

**monsoon** n seasonal wind of SE Asia; very heavy rainfall season

**monster** n fantastic imaginary beast; huge or misshapen person, animal or thing ~adj huge **monstrosity** n monstrous being; deformity **monstrous** adj horrible; shocking; enormous

**month** n one of twelve periods into which the year is divided **monthly** adj/adv once a month

**monument** n anything that commemorates, esp. a building or statue **monumental** adj

**mooch** v Sl loaf, slouch

**mood¹** n state of mind and feelings; sulk **moody** adj gloomy; changeable in mood

**mood²** n Grammar form indicating function of verb

**moon** n satellite which revolves round earth; any secondary planet ~v go about dreamily **moonlight** n

**moor¹** n tract of open uncultivated land **moorhen** n small black water bird

**moor²** v secure (ship) with chains or ropes **moorings** pl n ropes etc. for mooring

**moose** n N Amer. deer

**moot** adj debatable

**mop** n yarn, cloth etc. on end of stick, used for cleaning; tangle (of

———— THESAURUS ————

sermon, speech

**monopolize** control, corner, dominate, engross, take up

**monotonous** boring, colourless, droning, dull, flat, ho-hum Inf, humdrum, mind-numbing, plodding, repetitious, repetitive, soporific, tedious, tiresome, toneless, unchanging, wearisome

**monster** n barbarian, beast, brute, demon, devil, fiend, ghoul, ogre, savage, villain ~adj colossal, enormous, giant, huge, immense, massive, tremendous

**monstrous** abnormal, dreadful, fiendish, freakish, frightful, grotesque, gruesome, hellish, hideous, horrible, obscene, terrible, unnatural; atrocious, cruel, diabolical, disgraceful, evil, fiendish, foul, horrifying, infamous, inhuman, loathsome, odious, satanic, scandalous, shocking, vicious, villainous; colossal, enormous, giant, gigantic, great, huge, immense, massive,

prodigious, stupendous, tremendous, vast

**monument** cairn, gravestone, mausoleum, memorial, obelisk, pillar, shrine, statue, tombstone

**monumental** awesome, classic, enduring, enormous, historic, immortal, important, lasting, majestic, memorable, outstanding, prodigious, unforgettable

**mood** disposition, humour, spirit, temper, tenor, vein; blues, depression, doldrums, melancholy, sulk

**moody** angry, broody, crabbed, crestfallen, cross, crusty, curt, dismal, doleful, dour, downcast, gloomy, glum, ill-tempered, irritable, lugubrious, melancholy, miserable, morose, pensive, petulant, sulky, sullen, temperamental, touchy

**moon** n satellite ~v daydream, idle, languish

**moor¹** heath, moorland

**moor²** anchor, berth, dock, fasten,

hair etc.) ~v **mopping, mopped**
clean, wipe as with mop
**mope** v be gloomy, apathetic
**moped** n light motorized bicycle
**moral** adj pert. to right and wrong
conduct; of good conduct ~n practical lesson, e.g. of fable; pl habits
with respect to right and wrong **morality** n good moral conduct; moral
goodness or badness **moralize** v
write, think about moral aspect of
things
**morale** n degree of confidence,
hope
**morass** n marsh; mess
**moratorium** n (pl -**ria**) authorized
postponement of payments etc.
**morbid** adj unduly interested in
death; gruesome; diseased
**mordant** adj biting; corrosive
**more** adj/pron greater or additional
(amount or number); comparative
of MANY and MUCH ~adv to a greater

extent; in addition **moreover** adv
besides
**mores** pl n customs and conventions of society
**morgue** n mortuary
**moribund** adj dying; without force
or vitality
**morning** n early part of day until
noon **morn** n Poet morning
**moron** n mentally deficient person
**morose** adj sullen, moody
**morphine, morphia** n extract of
opium used to relieve pain
**morrow** n Poet next day
**Morse** n telegraphic signalling in
which letters are represented by
dots and dashes
**morsel** n small piece
**mortal** adj subject to death; causing death ~n mortal creature **mortality** n state of being mortal; death
rate; great loss of life
**mortar** n mixture of lime, sand and

—————————————— THESAURUS ——————————————

fix, lash, secure
**moral** adj ethical; blameless,
chaste, decent, good, honest, innocent, just, noble, principled, proper, pure, right, righteous, upright,
virtuous ~n lesson, meaning, message, point, significance
**morale** confidence, heart, mettle,
spirit, temper
**morality** chastity, decency, goodness, honesty, integrity, justice,
principle, righteousness, virtue
**morbid** brooding, funereal,
gloomy, grim, pessimistic, sick,
sombre, unhealthy, unwholesome;
dreadful, ghastly, grisly, gruesome,
hideous, horrid, macabre
**more** adj added, extra, fresh, further, new, other, spare, supplementary ~adv better, further, longer
**moreover** additionally, also, be-

sides, further
**morning** dawn, daybreak, fore-
noon, sunrise
**moron** ass, berk Brit sl, blockhead,
cretin, dolt, dunce, fool, halfwit, idiot, imbecile, nitwit Inf, numbskull,
simpleton, thickhead, twit Inf, wally Sl
**morose** crabbed, cross, depressed,
dour, down, gloomy, glum, gruff,
ill-tempered, low, melancholy,
moody, mournful, perverse, pessimistic, sulky, sullen, surly, taciturn
**morsel** bit, bite, crumb, fraction,
fragment, grain, mouthful, piece,
scrap, segment, slice, soupçon, taste
**mortal** adj earthly, ephemeral, human, temporal, transient, worldly;
deadly, destructive, fatal, killing, lethal, murderous ~n being, body,
earthling, human, individual, man,

water for holding bricks together; small cannon; vessel in which substances are pounded **mortarboard** n square academic cap

**mortgage** n conveyance of property as security for debt ~v pledge as security

**mortify** v **-fying, -fied** humiliate; subdue by self-denial; (of flesh) be affected with gangrene **mortification** n

**mortise** n hole in piece of wood etc. to receive the tongue (tenon) and end of another piece

**mortuary** n building where corpses are kept before burial

**mosaic** n picture or pattern of small bits of coloured stone, glass etc.

**mosque** n Muslim temple

**mosquito** n **-toes, -tos** flying, biting insect

**moss** n small plant growing in masses on moist surfaces **mossy** adj

**most** adj/n (of) greatest number, amount or degree; superlative of

MUCH and MANY ~adv in the greatest degree **mostly** adv generally

**MOT** Ministry of Transport

**motel** n roadside hotel for motorists

**moth** n usu. nocturnal insect like butterfly **mothball** n small ball of chemical to repel moths from stored clothing etc. ~v store, postpone **moth-eaten** adj damaged by grub of moth; scruffy

**mother** n female parent; head of religious community of women ~adj inborn ~v act as mother to **motherhood** n **motherly** adj **mother-in-law** n mother of one's wife or husband **mother of pearl** iridescent lining of certain shells

**motif** n dominating theme

**motion** n process or action or way of moving; proposal in meeting ~v direct by sign

**motive** n that which makes person act in particular way **motivate** v incite **motivation** n

**motley** adj varied; multicoloured

person, woman

**mortality** n humanity, transience; bloodshed, carnage, death, destruction, fatality, killing

**mortify** v abase, abash, annoy, chasten, confound, crush, disappoint, displease, embarrass, humble, shame, vex

**mostly** adv chiefly, customarily, generally, largely, mainly, particularly, predominantly, principally, usually

**mother** n dam, mater ~adj inborn, innate, native, natural ~v bear, produce; cherish, nurse, nurture, protect, raise, rear, tend

**motherly** adj affectionate, caring, fond, gentle, kind, loving, maternal, tender

**motion** n action, change, flow, move, movement, passage, progress, travel; proposal, proposition, submission, suggestion ~v beckon, direct, gesture, nod, signal, wave

**motionless** adj calm, frozen, halted, immobile, lifeless, static, stationary, still, unmoving

**motivate** v actuate, arouse, bring, cause, draw, drive, impel, induce, inspire, instigate, lead, move, persuade, prod, prompt, stimulate, stir

**motivation** n ambition, desire, drive, hunger, inspiration, interest, wish

**motive** n cause, design, ground(s), incentive, inducement, influence, inspiration, intention, occasion,

**motocross** *n* motorcycle race over rough course

**motor** *n* that which imparts movement; machine to supply power to move ~*v* travel by car **motorist** *n* **motorize** *v* equip with a motor or motor transport **motorbike**, **motorcycle** *n* **motorcar** *n* **motorway** *n* main road for fast-moving traffic

**mottled** *adj* marked with blotches

**motto** *n* **-toes**, **-tos** saying adopted as rule of conduct

**mould**[1] *n* hollow object in which metal etc. is cast; character; shape ~*v* shape **moulding** *n* ornamental edging

**mould**[2] *n* fungoid growth caused by dampness **mouldy** *adj*

**mould**[3] *n* loose or surface earth **moulder** *v* decay

**moult** *v* cast or shed fur, feathers etc. ~*n* moulting

**mound** *n* heap; small hill

**mount** *v* rise; increase; get on (horse); frame (picture); set up ~*n* support; horse; hill

**mountain** *n* hill of great size **mountaineer** *n* one who lives among or climbs mountains **mountainous** *adj* **mountain bike** bicycle with straight handlebars and heavy-duty tyres

**mountebank** *n* charlatan, fake

**mourn** *v* feel, show sorrow (for) **mourner** *n* **mournful** *adj* sad; dismal **mourning** *n* grieving; clothes of mourner

**mouse** *n* (*pl* **mice**) small rodent **mousy** *adj* like mouse, esp. in colour

**mousse** *n* dish of flavoured cream

**moustache** *n* hair on upper lip

**mouth** *n* opening in head for eating, speaking etc.; opening, entrance ~*v* form (words) with lips without speaking **mouth organ**

purpose, reason, spur, stimulus

**motley** assorted, dissimilar, diversified, mingled, mixed, unlike, varied

**mottled** blotchy, chequered, dappled, flecked, marbled, piebald, pied, speckled, stippled, streaked, variegated

**motto** adage, cry, dictum, maxim, proverb, rule, saw, saying, slogan

**mould** *n* cast, die, form, pattern, shape, stamp; brand, build, cut, design, fashion, form, format, frame, kind, line, make, pattern, shape, stamp, style ~*v* carve, cast, construct, create, fashion, forge, form, make, model, sculpt, shape, stamp, work

**mouldy** bad, decaying, rotten, spoiled, stale

**mound** heap, pile, stack; bank,

dune, hill, hillock, knoll, rise

**mount** *v* arise, ascend, rise, soar, tower; build, grow, increase, intensify, multiply, pile up, swell; bestride, jump on; display, frame, set ~*n* backing, base, fixture, foil, frame, mounting, setting, stand, support; horse

**mountain** alp, elevation, eminence, height, mount, peak

**mountainous** alpine, high, highland, rocky, soaring, steep, towering, upland

**mourn** bewail, deplore, grieve, lament, miss, rue, sorrow, wail, weep

**mournful** afflicting, distressing, grievous, harrowing, lamentable, melancholy, painful, piteous, plaintive, sad, sorrowful, tragic, unhappy, woeful

**mourning** grief, lamentation,

small musical instrument **mouthpiece** n end of anything placed between lips

**move** v change position, place; (cause to) be in motion; stir emotions of; incite; propose; change one's dwelling etc. ~n a moving; motion **movement** n moving; moving parts; group with common aim; division of piece of music **movie** n Inf film

**mow** v mowing, mown cut (grass etc.) **mower** n

**MP** Member of Parliament; Military Police

**mph** miles per hour

**Mr.** mister

**Mrs.** title of married woman

**Ms.** title used instead of Miss or Mrs.

**much** adj more, most existing in quantity ~n large amount; important matter ~adv in a great degree; nearly

**muck** n dung; dirt **mucky** adj

**mucus** n fluid secreted by mucous membranes

**mud** n wet and soft earth **muddy** adj **mudguard** n cover over wheel **mudpack** n cosmetic paste to improve complexion

**muddle** v (esp. with up) confuse; bewilder; mismanage ~n confusion

**muesli** n mixture of grain, nuts, dried fruit etc.

**muff¹** n tube-shaped covering to keep hands warm

**muff²** v bungle, fail in

**muffin** n light round yeast cake

**muffle** v wrap up, esp. to deaden sound **muffler** n scarf

**mug¹** n drinking cup

**mug²** n Sl face; Sl fool, simpleton ~v mugging, mugged rob violently **mugger** n

**mug³** v mugging, mugged Inf (esp. with up) study hard

**muggy** adj damp and stifling

—————————— THESAURUS ——————————

weeping, woe

**mouth** n jaws, lips; door, entrance, gateway, inlet, opening, orifice, rim

**move** v carry, change, shift, switch, transfer, transport, transpose; advance, budge, drift, go, march, proceed, progress, shift, stir, walk; affect, agitate, cause, excite, incite, induce, influence, inspire, lead; advocate, propose, recommend, suggest, urge; leave, migrate, quit, relocate, remove ~n act, action, deed, measure, motion, ploy, shift, step, stratagem, stroke, turn

**movement** n act, action, activity, advance, agitation, change, exercise, flow, gesture, motion, operation, progress, shift, steps, stir, stirring, transfer; campaign, crusade, drive, faction, front, group, party;

Mus division, part, passage, section

**mow** v crop, cut, scythe, shear, trim

**much** adj abundant, ample, considerable, copious, great, plenteous, substantial ~adv a lot, considerably, decidedly, exceedingly, frequently, greatly, indeed, often, regularly

**mud** n clay, dirt, mire, ooze, silt, slime, sludge

**muddle** v confuse, disorder, mess, scramble, spoil, tangle; bewilder, confound, confuse, daze, perplex, stupefy ~n chaos, clutter, confusion, daze, disarray, disorder, hotchpotch, mess, mix-up, tangle

**muddy** boggy, dirty, marshy, soiled

**muffle** cloak, conceal, cover, disguise, envelop, hood, mask, shroud

**mulberry** n tree whose leaves are used to feed silkworms

**mulch** n straw, leaves etc. spread as protection for roots of plants ~v protect thus

**mule** n cross between horse and ass; hybrid **mulish** adj obstinate

**mull** v heat (wine) with sugar and spices; think (over)

**multi-** comb. form many, as in **multistorey**

**multifarious** adj of various kinds or parts

**multiple** adj having many parts ~n quantity which contains another an exact number of times **multiplication** n multiplicity n variety, greatness in number **multiply** v **-plying, -plied** (cause to) increase; combine (two numbers) by multiplication; increase by reproduction

**multitude** n great number

**mum** n Inf mother

**mumble** v speak indistinctly

**mummy¹** n embalmed body **mummify** v **-fying, -fied**

**mummy²** n Inf mother

**mumps** pl n infectious disease marked by swelling in neck

**munch** v chew vigorously

**mundane** adj ordinary, everyday; earthly

**municipal** adj belonging to affairs of city or town **municipality** n city or town with local self-government

**munificent** adj very generous **munificence** n

**munition** n (usu. pl) military stores

**mural** n painting on wall

**murder** n unlawful premeditated killing of human being ~v kill thus **murderer** n **murderous** adj

**murk** n darkness **murky** adj

**murmur** n low, indistinct sound ~v make, utter such a sound; complain

**mug¹** beaker, cup, flagon, jug, pot, tankard

**mug²** n charlie Brit inf, chump Inf, soft touch Sl, fool, muggins Brit sl, simpleton, sucker Sl ~v assail, assault, attack, beat up, duff up Brit sl, hold up, rob, set about

**muggy** close, damp, humid, sticky, stuffy, sultry

**multiple** collective, many, several, sundry, various

**multiply** augment, breed, expand, extend, increase, reproduce, spread

**multitude** army, assembly, collection, congregation, crowd, horde, host, legion, lot, mass, mob, myriad, sea, swarm, throng

**mundane** banal, everyday, humdrum, ordinary, prosaic, routine, workaday

**municipal** borough, city, civic, community, public, town, urban

**murder** n assassination, bloodshed, butchery, carnage, homicide, killing, manslaughter, massacre, slaying ~v assassinate, butcher, destroy, dispatch, kill, massacre, slaughter

**murderer** assassin, butcher, cutthroat, killer, slayer

**murderous** barbarous, bloodthirsty, bloody, brutal, cruel, deadly, fatal, lethal, savage

**murky** cheerless, cloudy, dark, dim, dreary, dull, dusky, foggy, gloomy, grey, misty, obscure, overcast

**murmur** n babble, drone, humming, mumble, muttering, purr, rumble, undertone, whisper ~v babble, buzz, drone, hum, mumble, mutter, purr, rumble, whisper

**muscle** n part of body which produces movement by contracting; system of muscles **muscular** adj strong; of muscle

**muse** v ponder; be lost in thought ~n musing; reverie; goddess inspiring creative artist

**museum** n (place housing) collection of historical etc. objects

**mush** n soft pulpy mass **mushy** adj

**mushroom** n fungoid growth, typically with stem and cap ~v shoot up rapidly

**music** n art form using harmonious combination of notes; composition in this art **musical** adj of, like, interested in music ~n show, film in which music plays essential part **musician** n

**musk** n scent obtained from gland of deer **musky** adj **muskrat** n N Amer. rodent found near water; its fur

**musket** n Hist infantryman's gun

**Muslim, Moslem** n follower of religion of Islam ~adj of Islam

**muslin** n fine cotton fabric

**mussel** n bivalve shellfish

**must** v be obliged to, or certain to ~n necessity

**mustang** n wild horse

**mustard** n powder made from the seeds of a plant, used in paste as a condiment

**muster** v assemble ~n assembly, esp. for exercise, inspection

**musty** adj mouldy, stale

**mutate** v (cause to) undergo mutation **mutant** n mutated animal, plant etc. **mutation** n change, esp. genetic change causing divergence from kind or racial type

**mute** adj dumb; silent ~n dumb person; Mus contrivance to soften tone of instruments **muted** adj muffled; subdued

**mutilate** v deprive of a limb etc.; damage

**mutiny** n rebellion against authority, esp. against officers of disciplined body ~v **mutinying**, **mutinied** commit mutiny **mutineer** n **mutinous** adj

**mutter** v speak, utter indistinctly;

--- THESAURUS ---

**muscle** sinew, tendon, thew; brawn, force, might, potency, power, stamina, strength, weight

**muscular** athletic, lusty, powerful, robust, sinewy, stalwart, strapping, strong, vigorous

**muse** brood, cogitate, deliberate, dream, meditate, ponder, reflect, ruminate, speculate, think, weigh

**musical** dulcet, lilting, lyrical, melodious, tuneful

**must** n duty, essential, imperative, necessity, obligation, requirement, requisite, sine qua non

**muster** v assemble, call up, collect, congregate, convene, convoke, enrol, gather, group, marshal, meet,

mobilize, rally, summon ~n assembly, collection, concourse, congregation, convention, gathering, meeting, rally

**musty** airless, dank, decayed, frowsty, fusty, mildewed, mouldy, old, smelly, stale, stuffy

**mute** adj dumb, silent, speechless, unspoken, wordless

**mutilate** butcher, cripple, damage, disable, disfigure, dismember, hack, injure, lacerate, lame, maim, mangle

**mutinous** disobedient, insubordinate, rebellious, refractory, revolutionary, seditious, subversive, unruly

grumble ~n muttered sound

**mutton** n flesh of sheep used as food

**mutual** adj done, possessed etc. by each of two with respect to the other; Inf common

**muzzle** n mouth and nose of animal; cover for these to prevent biting; open end of gun ~v put muzzle on

**muzzy** adj indistinct, confused

**my** adj belonging to me **myself** pron emphatic or reflexive form of I

**mynah** n Indian bird related to starling

**myopia** n short-sightedness **myopic** adj

**myriad** adj innumerable ~n large number

**myrrh** n aromatic gum, formerly used as incense

**myrtle** n flowering evergreen shrub

**myself** see MY

**mystery** n obscure or secret thing; anything strange or inexplicable **mysterious** adj

**mystic** n one who seeks divine, spiritual knowledge, esp. by prayer, contemplation etc. **mystical** adj

**mystify** v -fying, -fied bewilder, puzzle

**mystique** n aura of mystery, power etc.

**myth** n tale with supernatural characters or events; imaginary person or object **mythical** adj **mythology** n myths collectively

**myxomatosis** n contagious, fatal disease of rabbits

——————— THESAURUS ———————

**mutiny** n disobedience, insubordination, insurrection, rebellion, resistance, revolt, revolution, riot, rising, strike, uprising ~v disobey, rebel, resist, revolt, strike

**mutter** complain, mumble, murmur, rumble

**mutual** common, interactive, joint, reciprocal, returned, shared

**muzzle** censor, choke, curb, restrain, silence, stifle, suppress

**mysterious** abstruse, arcane, baffling, concealed, cryptic, curious, dark, furtive, hidden, inexplicable, inscrutable, obscure, recondite, se-

cret, strange, uncanny, unknown, weird

**mystery** conundrum, enigma, problem, puzzle, question, riddle, secrecy, secret

**mystify** baffle, bewilder, confound, confuse, escape, flummox, nonplus, perplex, puzzle, stump

**myth** allegory, fable, fiction, legend, parable, saga, story, tradition

**mythical** fabled, fairy-tale, legendary; fabricated, fanciful, fictitious, invented, unreal, untrue

**mythology** folklore, legend, stories, tradition

# N n

**nadir** n lowest point

**naff** adj Sl inferior or useless

**nag¹** v **nagging, nagged** scold or trouble constantly ~n nagging; one who nags

**nag²** n Inf horse

**nail** n horny shield at ends of fingers, toes; small metal spike for fixing wood etc. ~v fix with nails

**naïve, naive** adj simple, unaffected, ingenuous **naïveté, naivety** n

**naked** adj without clothes; exposed, bare; undisguised

**name** n word by which person, thing etc. is denoted; reputation ~v give name to; call by name; appoint; mention **nameless** adj without a name; unknown; indescribable **namely** adv that is to say

**namesake** n person with same name as another

**nanny** n child's nurse **nanny goat**
she-goat

**nap¹** v **napping, napped** take short sleep ~n short sleep

**nap²** n downy surface on cloth made by projecting fibres

**nape** n back of neck

**napkin** n cloth, paper for wiping fingers or lips at table; nappy

**nappy** n towelling cloth to absorb baby's excrement

**narcissism** n abnormal admiration for oneself

**narcissus** n (pl **-cissi**) genus of bulbous plants including daffodil, esp. one with white flowers

**narcotic** n/adj (drug) producing numbness and stupor

**nark** v Sl annoy, irritate

**narrate** v tell (story) **narration** n

**narrative** n account, story **narrator** n

**narrow** adj of little breadth; limit-

--- THESAURUS ---

**nadir** bottom, depths, zero

**nag** v annoy, badger, chivvy, goad, harass, harry, hassle Inf, henpeck, pester, plague, provoke, scold, vex, worry ~n harpy, scold, shrew, termagant, virago

**nail** v attach, beat, fasten, fix, hammer, join, pin, secure, tack

**naive** artless, candid, childlike, guileless, ingenuous, innocent, open, simple, trusting, unsophisticated

**naked** bare, divested, exposed, nude, stripped, undressed; defenceless, helpless, unarmed, unguarded, unprotected, vulnerable

**name** n denomination, designation, epithet, nickname, sobriquet, term, title; credit, reputation ~v

baptize, call, christen, dub, entitle, label, style, term; appoint, choose, commission, designate, identify, nominate, select, specify

**nameless** anonymous, untitled; incognito, obscure, unknown, unsung; horrible, indescribable, unmentionable, unspeakable

**namely** specifically, to wit, viz.

**narcissism** egotism, self-admiration, self-love, vanity

**narrate** describe, detail, recite, recount, rehearse, relate, repeat, report, tell

**narration** description, explanation, reading, recital, relation, storytelling

**narrative** account, chronicle, detail, history, report, statement, sto-

ed ~v make, become narrow **narrow-minded** adj illiberal; bigoted

**nasal** adj of nose ~n sound partly produced in nose

**nasturtium** n garden plant with red or orange flowers

**nasty** adj foul, unpleasant; spiteful

**nation** n people or race organized as a state **national** adj of, characteristic of, a nation ~n citizen **nationalism** n devotion to one's country; movement for independence **nationalist** n/adj **nationality** n fact of belonging to a particular nation **nationalization** n acquisition and management of industries by the state **nationalize** v **National Health Service** system of medical services financed mainly by taxation **national service** compulsory military service

**native** adj inborn; born in particular place ~n native person, animal or plant

**nativity** n birth; (with cap.) birth of Christ

**NATO** North Atlantic Treaty Organization

**natter** Inf v talk idly ~n idle talk

**natty** adj neat and smart

**nature** n innate qualities of person or thing; class, sort; (with cap.) power underlying all phenomena; natural unspoilt scenery **natural** adj of nature; inborn; normal; unaffected ~n something, somebody well suited for something; Mus character used to remove effect of sharp or flat preceding it **naturalist** n one who studies animals and plants **naturalize** v admit to citizenship **naturally** adv

**naturism** n nudism

———— THESAURUS ————

ry, tale

**narrator** author, bard, chronicler, commentator, reporter, storyteller

**narrow** adj close, confined, cramped, limited, meagre, near, pinched, restricted, scanty, straitened, tight ~v diminish, limit, reduce, simplify, straiten, tighten

**narrow-minded** biased, bigoted, hidebound, insular, intolerant, parochial, petty, strait-laced

**nasty** dirty, disagreeable, disgusting, filthy, foul, horrible, nauseating, obnoxious, odious, offensive, repellent, repugnant, sickening, unpleasant, vile; abusive, despicable, malicious, mean, spiteful, unpleasant, vicious, vile

**nation** community, country, people, race, realm, society, state

**national** civil, countrywide, governmental, public, state; domestic, internal, social

**nationalism** allegiance, chauvinism, loyalty, patriotism

**nationality** birth, race

**native** adj congenital, endemic, hereditary, inborn, inherited, innate, instinctive; domestic, home, home-made, indigenous, local ~n aborigine, citizen, countryman, dweller, inhabitant

**natural** characteristic, essential, inborn, inherent, innate, instinctive, intuitive; common, everyday, logical, normal, ordinary, regular, typical, usual; artless, candid, frank, genuine, ingenuous, open, real, simple, spontaneous, unaffected, unpretentious

**nature** character, complexion, essence, features, make-up, quality, traits; disposition, humour, mood, outlook, temper, temperament; cat-

**naughty** *adj* disobedient; *Inf* mildly indecent

**nausea** *n* feeling that precedes vomiting **nauseate** *v* sicken **nauseous** *adj*

**nautical** *adj* of seamen or ships **nautical mile** 1852 metres

**nave** *n* main part of church

**navel** *n* small depression in abdomen where umbilical cord was attached

**navigate** *v* direct, plot path of ship etc.; travel **navigable** *adj* **navigation** *n* **navigator** *n*

**navvy** *n* labourer employed on roads, railways etc.

**navy** *n* fleet; warships of country with their crews ~*adj* navy-blue **naval** *adj* of the navy **navy-blue** *adj* very dark blue

**nay** *adv Obs* no

**NB** note well

**near** *prep* close to ~*adv* at or to a short distance ~*adj* close at hand; closely related; stingy ~*v* approach **nearby** *adj* adjacent **nearly** *adv* closely; almost **nearside** *n* side of vehicle nearer kerb

**neat** *adj* tidy, orderly; deft; undiluted

**nebulous** *adj* vague

**necessary** *adj* that must be done; inevitable ~*n* what is needed **necessarily** *adv* **necessitate** *v* make necessary **necessity** *n* something needed; constraining power; compulsion; poverty

**neck** *n* part of body joining head to

———— THESAURUS ————

egory, description, kind, sort, species, style, type, variety; creation, earth, environment, universe, world; country, landscape

**naughty** bad, disobedient, impish, misbehaving, mischievous, wayward

**nausea** biliousness, qualm(s), sickness, vomiting

**nauseate** disgust, horrify, offend, repel, repulse, revolt, sicken

**nautical** maritime, naval, seafaring, yachting

**naval** marine, maritime, nautical

**navigable** clear, negotiable, passable, unobstructed

**navigate** cross, cruise, direct, drive, guide, handle, journey, manoeuvre, pilot, plan, plot, sail, steer, voyage

**navigation** cruising, pilotage, sailing, seamanship, steering, voyaging

**navy** fleet, flotilla, warships

**near** adjacent, adjoining, alongside, beside, bordering, close, contiguous, nearby, neighbouring,

nigh, touching; akin, allied, attached, connected, dear, familiar, intimate, related

**nearby** adjacent, adjoining, convenient, handy, neighbouring

**nearly** about, all but, almost, approaching, approximately, closely, not quite, practically, roughly, virtually, well-nigh

**neat** accurate, dainty, fastidious, methodical, nice, orderly, shipshape, smart, spruce, straight, systematic, tidy, trim; adept, adroit, agile, apt, clever, deft, dexterous, efficient, effortless, elegant, expert, graceful, handy, nimble, precise, skilful, stylish; *of alcoholic drinks* pure, straight, undiluted, unmixed

**necessarily** automatically, by definition, certainly, compulsorily, consequently, inevitably, inexorably, naturally, of course, perforce, willy-nilly

**necessary** compulsory, essential, imperative, mandatory, needful,

shoulders; narrow part of anything
**neckerchief** *n* cloth tied round the
neck **necklace** *n* ornament round
the neck
**nectar** *n* honey of flowers
**nectarine** *n* variety of peach
**née, nee** *adj* indicating maiden
name of married woman
**need** *v* want, require ~*n* (state, instance of) want; requirement; necessity; poverty **needful** *adj* necessary **needless** *adj* unnecessary
**needy** *adj* poor, in want
**needle** *n* thin pointed piece of metal for sewing, knitting; stylus for
record player; leaf of fir tree ~*v* *Inf*
goad, provoke **needlework** *n* sewing, embroidery

**nefarious** *adj* wicked
**negate** *v* deny, nullify **negation** *n*
**negative** *adj* expressing denial or
refusal; lacking enthusiasm; not
positive; of electrical charge having
the same polarity as the charge of
an electron ~*n* negative word or
statement; *Photog* picture in which
lights and shades are reversed
**neglect** *v* take no care of; fail to do
~*n* fact of neglecting or being neglected
**negligee, negligée** *v* woman's
light dressing gown
**negligence** *n* carelessness **negligent** *adj* **negligible** *adj* very small or
unimportant
**negotiate** *v* discuss with view to

——————————— THESAURUS ———————————

obligatory, required, vital
**necessitate** call for, coerce, compel, constrain, demand, entail,
force, oblige, require
**necessity** demand, exigency,
need, requirement; fundamental,
need, prerequisite, requirement,
requisite, *sine qua non*, want
**need** *v* call for, demand, entail,
lack, miss, necessitate, require,
want ~*n* longing, requisite, want,
wish; obligation, urgency, want;
destitution, distress, extremity, inadequacy, lack, neediness, paucity,
penury, poverty, privation, shortage
**needful** essential, indispensable,
necessary, needed, required, requisite, stipulated, vital
**needless** dispensable, excessive,
expendable, groundless, pointless,
redundant, superfluous, unwanted,
useless
**needy** deprived, destitute, impoverished, penniless, poor, under-
privileged
**negate** annul, cancel, invalidate,

neutralize, nullify, obviate, repeal,
rescind, retract, reverse, revoke,
void, wipe out
**negation** antithesis, contrary, converse, denial, disavowal, disclaimer,
inverse, opposite, rejection, reverse
**negative** *adj* contrary, denying,
dissenting, opposing, refusing, resisting; antagonistic, contrary, cynical, gloomy, jaundiced, neutral,
pessimistic, unenthusiastic, unwilling, weak; invalidating, neutraliz-
ing, nullifying ~*n* denial, refusal
**neglect** *v* disdain, disregard, ignore, overlook, rebuff, scorn, slight,
spurn; be remiss, evade, forget,
omit, procrastinate, shirk, skimp ~*n*
disdain, disregard, disrespect, indifference, slight, unconcern; carelessness, default, failure, forgetfulness,
laxity, oversight, slackness
**negligent** careless, forgetful, heedless, inadvertent, inattentive, indifferent, offhand, regardless, remiss,
slack, slapdash, slipshod, thoughtless, unthinking

mutual settlement; arrange by conference; transfer (bill, cheque etc.); get over (obstacle) **negotiable** adj **negotiation** n **negotiator** n

**neigh** n/v (utter) cry of horse

**neighbour** n one who lives near another **neighbourhood** n district; people of district **neighbouring** adj nearby **neighbourly** adj friendly; helpful

**neither** adj/pron not the one or the other ~adv not on the one hand; not either ~conj nor yet

**nemesis** n (pl **-ses**) retribution, vengeance

**neologism** n newly-coined word or phrase

**neon** n inert gas in the atmosphere, used to illuminate signs and lights

**nephew** n brother's or sister's son

**nepotism** n undue favouritism towards one's relations

**nerve** n bundle of fibres carrying feeling, impulses to motion etc. to and from brain; assurance; coolness in danger; audacity; pl sensitiveness

to fear, annoyance etc. ~v give courage to **nervous** adj excitable; apprehensive **nervy** adj nervous, jumpy **nerve-racking** adj very distressing

**nest** n place in which bird lays and hatches its eggs; animal's breeding place; snug retreat ~v make, have a nest **nest egg** (fund of) money in reserve

**nestle** v settle comfortably close to something

**net¹** n openwork fabric of meshes of cord etc. ~v **netting, netted** cover with, or catch in, net **netting** n string or wire net **netball** n game in which ball has to be thrown through high net

**net², nett** adj left after all deductions ~v **netting, netted** gain, yield as clear profit

**nether** adj lower

**nettle** n plant with stinging hairs ~v irritate

**network** n system of intersecting lines, roads etc.; interconnecting

———————————— THESAURUS ————————————

**negligible** insignificant, minor, minute, petty, small, trifling, trivial, unimportant

**negotiate** arbitrate, arrange, bargain, confer, consult, contract, deal, debate, discuss, handle, manage, mediate, parley, settle, transact, work out

**negotiation** arbitration, bargaining, debate, diplomacy, discussion

**neighbourhood** community, district, environs, locality, precincts, proximity, quarter, region, vicinity

**neighbouring** adjacent, adjoining, bordering, near, nearby, nearest, next, surrounding

**nerve** bravery, courage, daring, fearlessness, firmness, fortitude,

mettle, pluck, resolution, spirit, vigour, will; Inf audacity, boldness, brazenness, chutzpah US & Canad inf, effrontery, gall, impertinence, impudence, insolence

**nervous** agitated, anxious, apprehensive, edgy, fidgety, hysterical, jumpy, neurotic, shaky, tense, timid, twitchy Inf, uneasy, weak, worried

**nest** breeding-ground, den; den, haunt, refuge, resort, retreat

**nestle** cuddle, huddle, snuggle

**net¹** n lattice, mesh, tracery, web ~v bag, capture, catch, enmesh, ensnare, entangle, trap

**net², nett** adj clear, final, take-home ~v clear, earn, gain, make,

group; linked broadcasting stations

**neural** *adj* of the nerves

**neuralgia** *n* pain in, along nerves

**neurosis** *n* (*pl* **-ses**) relatively mild mental disorder **neurotic** *adj/n*

**neuter** *adj* neither masculine nor feminine ~*v* castrate (animals)

**neutral** *adj* taking neither side in war, dispute etc.; without marked qualities ~*n* neutral nation or subject of one; position of disengaged gears **neutrality** *n* **neutralize** *v* make ineffective

**neutron** *n* electrically neutral particle of nucleus of an atom

**never** *adv* at no time **nevertheless** *adv* for all that

**new** *adj* not existing before; fresh; unfamiliar ~*adv* newly **newly** *adv* recently, freshly **newcomer** *n* recent arrival **newfangled** *adj* objection-

ably or unnecessarily modern

**news** *n* report of recent happenings; interesting fact not previously known **newsagent** *n* shopkeeper selling newspapers, magazines etc.

**newsflash** *n* brief news item, oft. interrupting programme **newspaper** *n* periodical publication containing news **newsprint** *n* inexpensive paper **newsreel** *n* film giving news

**newt** *n* small, tailed amphibian

**newton** *n* unit of force

**next** *adj/adv* nearest; immediately following **next-of-kin** *n* closest relative

**NHS** National Health Service

**nib** *n* (split) pen point

**nibble** *v* take little bites of ~*n* little bite

**nice** *adj* pleasant; friendly; kind;

———————— THESAURUS ————————

realize, reap

**network** arrangement, channels, complex, grid, grill, maze, mesh, organization, structure, system, web

**neurosis** abnormality, deviation, instability, obsession, phobia

**neurotic** abnormal, anxious, compulsive, disordered, disturbed, nervous, unstable

**neuter** *v* castrate, geld, spay

**neutral** disinterested, dispassionate, impartial, unaligned, unbiased, uncommitted, undecided, unprejudiced

**neutralize** cancel, counteract, frustrate, nullify, offset, undo

**nevertheless** but, (even) though, however, notwithstanding, regardless, still, yet

**new** advanced, contemporary, current, different, fresh, happening *Inf*, latest, modern, newfangled, novel,

original, recent, topical, up-to-date

**newcomer** alien, arrival, beginner, foreigner, incomer, novice, outsider

**newfangled** contemporary, modern, new, new-fashioned, novel, recent

**newly** anew, freshly, just, lately, latterly, recently

**news** account, bulletin, dispatch, exposé, gossip, hearsay, information, intelligence, latest *Inf*, leak, release, report, revelation, rumour, scandal, statement, story, tidings, word

**next** *adj* adjacent, adjoining, closest, nearest, neighbouring; consequent, ensuing, following, later, subsequent, succeeding ~*adv* afterwards, closely, following, later, subsequently, thereafter

**nibble** *v* bite, eat, gnaw, munch, nip, pick at ~*n* bite, crumb, morsel,

subtle, fine; careful, exact **nicely** *adv* **nicety** *n* minute distinction or detail

**niche** *n* recess in wall

**nick** *v* make notch in, indent; *Sl* steal ~*n* notch; *Inf* condition; *Sl* prison

**nickel** *n* silver-white metal much used in alloys and plating; *US & Canad* five cent piece

**nickname** *n* familiar name

**nicotine** *n* poisonous oily liquid in tobacco

**niece** *n* brother's or sister's daughter

**nifty** *adj Inf* smart; quick

**niggard** *n* mean, stingy person **niggardly** *adj/adv*

**niggle** *v* find fault continually; annoy

**nigh** *adj/adv/prep Obs or poet* near

**night** *n* time of darkness between sunset and sunrise **nightly** *adv/adj* (happening, done) every night **nightcap** *n* drink taken before bedtime **nightclub** *n* place for dancing, music

etc., open late at night **nightdress** *n* woman's loose robe worn in bed

**nightingale** *n* small bird which sings at night **nightmare** *n* very bad dream; terrifying experience **nightshade** *n* various plants of potato family, some with very poisonous berries **night-time** *n*

**nil** *n* nothing, zero

**nimble** *adj* agile, quick, dexterous

**nimbus** *n* (*pl* **-bi, -buses**) rain or storm cloud; halo

**nincompoop** *n Inf* stupid person

**nine** *adj/n* cardinal number next above eight **ninth** *adj* ordinal number **nineteen** *adj/n* nine more than ten **nineteenth** *adj* **ninetieth** *adj* **ninety** *adj/n* nine tens

**nip** *v* nipping, nipped pinch sharply; detach by pinching, bite; check growth (of plants) thus; *Inf* hurry ~*n* pinch; sharp coldness of weather; short drink **nipper** *n* thing that nips; *Inf* small child **nippy** *adj Inf* cold; quick

**nipple** *n* point of breast, teat; anything like this

———————— THESAURUS ————————

snack, *soupçon*, taste, titbit

**nice** agreeable, amiable, attractive, charming, courteous, friendly, good, kind, likable *or* likeable, pleasant, polite, refined, well-mannered; dainty, fine, neat, tidy, trim; accurate, careful, critical, delicate, exact, fastidious, fine, meticulous, precise, rigorous, scrupulous, strict, subtle

**niche** alcove, corner, hollow, nook, opening, recess

**nick** chip, cut, damage, dent, mark, notch, scar, score, scratch

**nickname** diminutive, epithet, label, moniker *or* monicker *Sl*, pet name, sobriquet

**niggardly** close, covetous, frugal, grudging, mean, mercenary, miserly, parsimonious, penurious, sparing, stingy, tightfisted

**niggle** carp, cavil, criticize, find fault, fuss; annoy, irritate, rankle, worry

**night** dark, night-time

**nightmare** hallucination; horror, ordeal, torment, trial, tribulation

**nil** duck, love, none, nothing, zero

**nimble** active, agile, alert, brisk, deft, lively, prompt, quick, ready, smart, sprightly, spry, swift

**nip** *v* bite, catch, clip, grip, pinch, snap, snip, tweak, twitch ~*n* dram, draught, drop, finger, por-

**nit** n egg of louse or other parasite; Inf nitwit **nit-picking** adj Inf overconcerned with insignificant detail **nitwit** n Inf fool

**nitrogen** n one of the gases making up air **nitrate** n compound of nitric acid and an alkali **nitric** adj **nitroglycerine** n explosive liquid

**no** adj not any, not a; not at all ~adv expresses negative reply ~n (pl **noes**) refusal; denial; negative vote or voter **no-one, no one** nobody

**no.** number

**noble** adj of the nobility; having high moral qualities; impressive ~n member of the nobility **nobility** n class holding special rank; being noble **nobleman** n (fem **noblewoman**) **nobly** adv

**nobody** n no person; person of no importance

**nocturnal** adj of, in, by, night

**nod** v nodding, nodded bow head slightly and quickly in assent, command etc.; let head droop with sleep ~n act of nodding

**node** n knot or knob

**nodule** n little knot; rounded irregular mineral mass

**noise** n any sound, esp. disturbing one ~v rumour **noisy** adj

**nomad** n member of wandering tribe; wanderer **nomadic** adj

**nomenclature** n system of names

**nominal** adj in name only; (fee etc.) small

**nominate** v propose as candidate; appoint to office **nomination** n **nominee** n candidate

tion, sip, soupçon, taste

**nippy** biting, chilly, sharp, stinging

**nobility** aristocracy, elite, lords, nobles, peerage; dignity, eminence, excellence, grandeur, greatness, majesty, nobleness, superiority, worthiness

**noble** adj aristocratic, highborn, lordly; generous, honourable, upright, virtuous, worthy; august, dignified, distinguished, elevated, eminent, grand, great, imposing, impressive, lofty, splendid, stately ~n lord, nobleman, peer

**nobody** no-one; cipher, menial, nonentity

**nocturnal** night, nightly, nighttime

**nod** v bow, dip, duck, gesture, indicate, salute, signal; agree, assent, concur; doze, droop, drowse, kip Brit sl, nap, sleep, slump ~n beck, gesture, greeting, salute, sign, signal

**noise** babble, blare, clamour, clatter, commotion, cry, din, fracas, hubbub, outcry, pandemonium, racket, row, tumult, uproar

**noisy** boisterous, chattering, deafening, loud, piercing, riotous, strident, uproarious, vociferous

**nomad** drifter, migrant, rambler, rover, vagabond, wanderer

**nomadic** itinerant, migrant, roaming, roving, travelling, vagrant, wandering

**nominal** formal, ostensible, pretended, professed, puppet, selfstyled, so-called, supposed, theoretical, titular

**nominate** appoint, assign, choose, designate, elect, elevate, name, present, propose, recommend, select, submit, suggest, term

**nomination** appointment, choice, election, proposal, selection, suggestion

**nominee** aspirant, candidate, con-

**non-** *comb. form* indicates the negative of a word

**nonchalant** *adj* casually unconcerned, indifferent

**noncommissioned officer** *Mil* subordinate officer, risen from the ranks

**noncommittal** *adj* avoiding definite preference or pledge

**nonconformist** *n* dissenter, esp. from Established Church

**nondescript** *adj* lacking distinctive characteristics

**none** *pron* no-one, not any *~adv* in no way **nonetheless** *adv* despite that, however

**nonentity** *n* insignificant person, thing

**nonevent** *n* disappointing or insignificant occurrence

**nonflammable** *adj* not easily set on fire

**nonpareil** *n/adj* (person or thing) unequalled or unrivalled

**nonplussed** *adj* disconcerted

**nonsense** *n* absurd language; absurdity; silly conduct

**non sequitur** statement with little relation to what preceded it

**noodle** *n* strip of pasta served in soup etc.

**nook** *n* sheltered corner

**noon** *n* midday, twelve o'clock

**noose** *n* loop on end of rope; snare

**nor** *conj* and not

**norm** *n* average level; standard **normal** *adj* ordinary; usual; conforming to type **normality** *n* **normally** *adv*

**north** *n* direction to the right of person facing the sunset *~adv/adj* from, towards or in the north **northerly** *adj* *~n* wind from the north **northern** *adj* **northwards** *adv*

**nose** *n* organ of smell, used also in breathing; any projection resembling a nose *~v* (cause to) move forward slowly and carefully; touch with nose; smell, sniff; pry **nosy** *adj Inf* inquisitive **nose dive** sudden drop

**nosh** *Sl n* food *~v* eat

———————— T H E S A U R U S ————————

testant, entrant, runner

**nonchalant** airy, apathetic, calm, careless, casual, collected, cool, detached, indifferent, offhand, unconcerned

**noncommittal** careful, cautious, discreet, evasive, guarded, indefinite, neutral, politic, reserved, tactful, vague, wary

**nonconformist** dissenter, eccentric, heretic, maverick, protester, radical, rebel

**nondescript** characterless, dull, ordinary, undistinguished, uninspiring, uninteresting, unremarkable

**none** nil, nobody, no-one, nothing, not one, zero

**nonentity** cipher, mediocrity, nobody

**nonetheless** despite that, even so, however, nevertheless, yet

**nonsense** absurdity, balderdash, bilge *Inf*, bunkum, drivel, folly, garbage *Inf*, gibberish, inanity, jest, poppycock *Inf*, rot, rubbish, stupidity, trash, twaddle

**nook** alcove, cavity, corner, cranny, crevice, niche, opening, recess, retreat

**norm** average, criterion, mean, model, par, pattern, rule, standard, type

**normal** accustomed, average, common, natural, ordinary, popular, regular, routine, run-of-the-mill,

**nostalgia** *n* longing for past events **nostalgic** *adj*

**nostril** *n* one of the two external openings of the nose

**not** *adv* expressing negation, refusal, denial

**notable** *adj/n* remarkable (person) **notably** *adv*

**notary** *n* person authorized to draw up deeds, contracts

**notation** *n* representation of numbers, quantities by symbols

**notch** *n/v* (make) V-shaped cut

**note** *n* brief comment or record; short letter; banknote; symbol for musical sound; single tone; fame; notice ~*v* observe, record; heed **noted** *adj* well-known **notebook** *n*

small book with blank pages for writing

**nothing** *n* no thing; not anything, nought ~*adv* not at all, in no way

**notice** *n* observation; attention; warning, announcement ~*v* observe, mention; give attention to

**notify** *v* **-fying, -fied** give notice of or to

**notion** *n* concept; opinion; whim

**notorious** *adj* known for something bad **notoriety** *n*

**notwithstanding** *prep* in spite of ~*adv* all the same ~*conj* although

**nougat** *n* chewy sweet containing nuts, fruit etc.

**nought** *n* nothing; figure 0

**noun** *n* word used as name of per-

——— THESAURUS ———

standard, typical, usual

**nostalgia** homesickness, longing, yearning

**nostalgic** homesick, longing, regretful

**notable** *adj* celebrated, distinguished, eminent, famous, manifest, marked, memorable, noteworthy, noticeable, pre-eminent, pronounced, rare, remarkable, renowned, striking, uncommon, unusual, well-known ~*n* celebrity, dignitary, personage

**notation** characters, code, script, signs, symbols, system

**notch** cleft, cut, incision, mark, nick, score

**note** *n* comment, epistle, gloss, letter, memo, message, minute, record, remark, reminder; indication, mark, sign, symbol, token; heed, notice, observation, regard ~*v* designate, indicate, mark, mention, notice, observe, record, register, remark, see

**noted** acclaimed, celebrated, dis-

tinguished, eminent, famous, illustrious, prominent, recognized, well-known

**nothing** cipher, naught, nonentity, nonexistence, nought, void, zero

**notice** *n* heed, note, observation, regard; advice, announcement, instruction, intelligence, intimation, news, order, warning ~*v* detect, discern, distinguish, heed, mark, mind, note, observe, perceive, remark, see, spot

**notify** acquaint, advise, alert, announce, declare, inform, tell, warn

**notion** belief, concept, idea, impression, inkling, judgment, knowledge, opinion, view; caprice, desire, fancy, impulse, whim, wish

**notoriety** dishonour, disrepute, scandal

**notorious** disreputable, infamous, scandalous

**notwithstanding** although, despite, (even) though, however, nevertheless, nonetheless, though, yet

son, idea or thing

**nourish** v feed; nurture **nourishment** n

**Nov.** November

**novel¹** n fictitious tale in book form **novelist** n

**novel²** adj new, recent; strange

**novelty** n newness; something new; small trinket

**November** n eleventh month

**novice** n beginner

**now** adv at the present time; immediately; recently ~conj seeing that, since **nowadays** adv in these times

**nowhere** adv not in any place or state

**noxious** adj poisonous, harmful

**nozzle** n pointed spout, esp. at end of hose

**nuance** n delicate shade of difference

**nub** n small lump; main point

**nubile** adj sexually attractive; marriageable

**nucleus** n (pl **-clei**) centre, kernel; core of atom **nuclear** adj of, pert. to atomic nucleus **nuclear energy** energy released by nuclear fission **nuclear fission** disintegration of atom

**nude** n/adj naked (person) **nudism** n practice of nudity **nudist** n **nudity** n

**nudge** v touch slightly with elbow ~n such touch

**nugget** n lump of gold

**nuisance** n something or someone annoying

**nuke** v Sl attack or destroy with nuclear weapons

**null** adj of no effect, void **nullify** v **-fying, -fied** cancel; make useless

**numb** adj deprived of feeling ~v make numb

**number** n sum or aggregate; word or symbol saying how many; single issue of a paper etc.; company, collection; identifying number ~v count; class, reckon; give a number to **numberless** adj countless

————— THESAURUS —————

**nought** naught, nil, nothing, zero

**nourish** attend, feed, nurse, nurture, supply, sustain, tend

**nourishment** diet, food, nutrition, sustenance

**novel¹** fiction, romance, story, tale

**novel²** different, fresh, groundbreaking, new, original, rare, singular, strange, uncommon, unfamiliar, unusual

**novelty** freshness, newness, oddity, strangeness, surprise; bauble, curiosity, gadget, gimmick, memento, souvenir, trifle, trinket

**novice** amateur, apprentice, beginner, learner, newcomer, proselyte, pupil, trainee, tyro

**now** at once, immediately, instantly, promptly, straightaway

**nucleus** basis, centre, core, heart, kernel, pivot

**nude** bare, disrobed, exposed, naked, stripped, unclothed, undressed

**nudge** v bump, dig, elbow, jog, poke, prod, push, shove, touch

**nudity** bareness, nakedness, undress

**nugget** chunk, clump, hunk, lump

**nuisance** bore, bother, drag Inf, hassle Inf, irritation, offence, pest, plague, problem, trouble

**numb** adj dead, deadened, frozen, insensible, paralysed, stupefied, torpid ~v benumb, deaden, dull, freeze, paralyse, stun, stupefy

**number** n count, digit, figure, integer, numeral, sum, total, unit;

**numeral** *n* sign or word denoting a number **numeracy** *n* ability to use numbers in calculations **numerate** *adj* **numerator** *n* top part of fraction **numerical** *adj* of numbers **numerous** *adj* many

**numskull** *n* dolt, dunce

**nun** *n* woman living (in convent) under religious vows **nunnery** *n* convent of nuns

**nuptial** *adj* of marriage **nuptials** *pl n* wedding

**nurse** *n* person trained for care of sick or injured ~*v* act as nurse to; suckle **nursery** *n* room for children; rearing place for plants **nursing home** private hospital or home for old people **nursing officer** administrative head of nursing staff of hospital

**nurture** *n* bringing up; rearing ~*v* bring up; educate; nourish

**nut** *n* fruit consisting of hard shell and kernel; hollow metal collar into which a screw fits; *Inf* head; *Sl* crank, maniac **nutty** *adj* **nutmeg** *n* aromatic seed of Indian tree

**nutrient** *adj* nourishing ~*n* something nutritious

**nutrition** *n* receiving foods; act of nourishing **nutritional, nutritious, nutritive** *adj*

**nuzzle** *v* burrow, press with nose; nestle

**nylon** *n* synthetic material used for fabrics etc. *pl* stockings of this

**nymph** *n* legendary spirit of sea, woods etc.

**nymphomaniac** *n* woman with abnormally intense sexual desire

——————— THESAURUS ———————

copy, edition; amount, collection, company, crowd, horde, many, multitude, quantity ~*v* account, add, calculate, compute, count, reckon, tell, total

**numberless** countless, endless, infinite, untold

**numeral** character, cipher, digit, figure, integer, number, symbol

**numerous** abundant, copious, many, plentiful, profuse, several

**nurse** *v* tend, treat; feed, nourish, nurture, suckle

**nurture** *n* rearing ~*v* feed, nourish, nurse, support, sustain, tend; bring up, develop, educate, instruct, rear, school, train

**nutrition** food, nourishment, sustenance

# O o

**oaf** n lout; dolt

**oak** n common deciduous tree

**OAP** old age pensioner

**oar** n wooden lever with broad blade worked by the hands to propel boat

**oasis** n (pl **-ses**) fertile spot in desert

**oat** n (usu. pl) grain of cereal plant; the plant **oatmeal** n

**oath** n confirmation of truth of statement by naming something sacred; curse

**obdurate** adj stubborn, unyielding

**OBE** Officer of the Order of the British Empire

**obedience** n submission to authority **obedient** adj

**obelisk** n tapering rectangular stone column

**obese** adj very fat **obesity** n

**obey** v do the bidding of; do as ordered

**obituary** n notice, record of death; biographical sketch of deceased person

**object¹** n material thing; that to which feeling or action is directed; end or aim; *Grammar* word dependent on verb or preposition

**object²** v express or feel dislike or reluctance to something **objection** n **objectionable** adj

**objective** adj external to the mind; impartial ~n thing or place aimed at

**oblige** v compel; do favour for (someone) **obligate** v bind, esp. by legal contract **obligation** n binding duty, promise; debt of gratitude ob-

--- THESAURUS ---

**oasis** haven, island, refuge, retreat, sanctuary

**oath** affirmation, avowal, bond, pledge, promise, vow, word; curse, expletive, profanity

**obedience** acquiescence, agreement, compliance, deference, docility, duty, observance, respect

**obedient** acquiescent, amenable, biddable, compliant, docile, duteous, dutiful, regardful, respectful, submissive

**obese** corpulent, fat, heavy, plump, podgy, portly, rotund, stout, tubby

**obey** comply, conform, discharge, execute, follow, fulfil, heed, keep, mind, observe, perform, respond, serve

**object¹** n article, body, fact, item, reality, thing; design, end, goal,

idea, intent, motive, objective, point, purpose, reason

**object²** v demur, expostulate, oppose, protest

**objection** cavil, censure, demur, doubt, exception, opposition, protest, remonstrance, scruple

**objectionable** deplorable, distasteful, insufferable, intolerable, obnoxious, offensive, regrettable, repugnant, undesirable, unpleasant

**objective** adj detached, dispassionate, fair, impartial, impersonal, just, unprejudiced ~n aim, ambition, aspiration, design, end, goal, mark, object, purpose, target

**obligation** burden, charge, compulsion, duty, liability, must, onus, requirement, responsibility, trust

**obligatory** binding, compulsory, essential, imperative, mandatory,

ligatory *adj* required; binding **obliging** *adj* ready to serve others, helpful

**oblique** *adj* slanting; indirect

**obliterate** *v* blot out, efface; destroy completely

**oblivion** *n* forgetting or being forgotten **oblivious** *adj* forgetful; unaware

**oblong** *adj* rectangular, with adjacent sides unequal ~*n* oblong figure

**obnoxious** *adj* offensive, repulsive

**oboe** *n* woodwind instrument

**obscene** *adj* indecent, repulsive

**obscenity** *n*

**obscure** *adj* unclear; indistinct ~*v*
make unintelligible; dim; conceal
**obscurity** *n* indistinctness; lack of
intelligibility; obscure place or position

**obsequious** *adj* servile, fawning

**observe** *v* notice, remark; watch;
note systematically; keep; follow
**observance** *n* keeping of custom;
ritual, ceremony **observant** *adj*
quick to notice **observation** *n* ob-
servatory *n* place for watching stars
etc. **observer** *n*

necessary, required

**oblige** bind, compel, force, impel,
make, require; accommodate, benefit, favour, gratify, indulge, please,
serve

**obliging** agreeable, amiable, civil,
considerate, cooperative, courteous, helpful, kind, polite, willing

**oblique** angled, aslant, inclined,
slanted, slanting, sloped, sloping

**obliterate** cancel, delete, destroy,
efface, eradicate, erase, wipe out

**oblivious** blind, careless, deaf, forgetful, heedless, ignorant, neglectful, regardless, unaware

**obnoxious** abominable, detestable, disgusting, foul, insufferable,
nasty, odious, offensive, repellent,
repulsive, revolting, unpleasant

**obscene** bawdy, blue, coarse,
dirty, disgusting, filthy, foul, gross,
indecent, lewd, offensive, pornographic, salacious, suggestive

**obscure** *adj* ambiguous, arcane,
confusing, cryptic, deep, doubtful,
esoteric, hazy, hidden, involved,
mysterious, occult, opaque, unclear, vague; blurred, cloudy, dim,
dusky, faint, gloomy, indistinct,
murky, shadowy, shady, sombre,

tenebrous, unlit, veiled ~*v* blur,
cloak, cloud, darken, dim, dull,
eclipse, mask, overshadow, shade,
shroud; conceal, cover, disguise,
hide, screen, veil

**obscurity** darkness, dimness,
dusk, gloom, haze, murkiness,
shadows; ambiguity, complexity,
vagueness; insignificance, lowliness, unimportance

**observance** attention, celebration, discharge, notice, observation,
performance; ceremonial, custom,
fashion, form, practice, rite, ritual,
tradition

**observant** alert, attentive, heedful, mindful, perceptive, quick,
vigilant, watchful

**observation** attention, consideration, examination, experience, information, inspection, knowledge,
notice, review, scrutiny, study, surveillance

**observe** detect, discern, discover,
espy, note, notice, perceive, see,
spot, witness; check out *Inf.*, monitor, regard, scrutinize, study, survey, view, watch; comply, follow,
fulfil, heed, honour, keep, mind,
obey, respect; keep, remember, sol-

**obsess** v haunt, fill the mind **obsession** n

**obsolete** adj disused, out of date **obsolescent** adj going out of use

**obstacle** n obstruction

**obstetrics** pl n (with sing v) branch of medicine concerned with childbirth **obstetrician** n

**obstinate** adj stubborn; hard to overcome or cure **obstinacy** n

**obstreperous** adj unruly, noisy

**obstruct** v block up; hinder; impede **obstruction** n **obstructive** adj

**obtain** v get; acquire; be customary **obtainable** adj

**obtrude** v thrust forward unduly

**obtrusive** adj

**obtuse** adj dull of perception; stupid; greater than right angle; not pointed

**obverse** n complement; principal side of coin, medal etc.

**obviate** v remove, make unnecessary

**obvious** adj clear, evident **obviously** adv

**occasion** n time when thing happens; reason, need; opportunity; special event ~v cause **occasional** adj happening, found now and then **occasionally** adv

**Occident** n the West **Occidental** adj

——————— THESAURUS ———————

emnize; comment, declare, mention, note, opine, remark, say, state

**observer** commentator, eyewitness, onlooker, spectator, viewer, witness

**obsession** complex, fetish, fixation, hang-up Inf, infatuation, mania, phobia, preoccupation

**obsolescent** ageing, declining, waning

**obsolete** ancient, antiquated, archaic, bygone, dated, démodé, extinct, old, outmoded, outworn, passé

**obstacle** bar, barrier, block, check, hindrance, hitch, hurdle, interruption, obstruction, snag

**obstinate** determined, dogged, firm, immovable, inflexible, intractable, opinionated, perverse, recalcitrant, self-willed, stubborn, tenacious

**obstruct** arrest, bar, block, bung, check, choke, clog, curb, cut off, frustrate, hamper, hamstring, hide, hinder, impede, inhibit, interrupt, mask, obscure, prevent, restrict,

stop

**obstruction** bar, barrier, block, blockage, check, hindrance, impediment, obstacle, snag, stop, stoppage

**obstructive** awkward, preventative, restrictive, unhelpful

**obtain** achieve, acquire, earn, gain, get, procure, secure

**obtrusive** forward, meddling, nosy, officious, prying

**obvious** apparent, blatant, clear, conspicuous, distinct, evident, manifest, open, overt, palpable, patent, perceptible, plain, pronounced, recognizable, self-evident, straightforward, transparent, unmistakable, unsubtle, visible

**occasion** chance, incident, moment, occurrence, opening, time; call, cause, excuse, ground(s), motive, prompting, provocation, reason; affair, event, experience, occurrence

**occasional** casual, desultory, incidental, infrequent, irregular, odd, rare, sporadic

**occult** *adj* secret, mysterious; supernatural

**occupy** *v* **-pying, -pied** inhabit; fill; employ; take possession of **occupancy** *n* fact of occupying **occupant** *n* **occupation** *n* employment, pursuit; tenancy; military control of country by foreign power **occupational** *adj* **occupier** *n*

**occur** *v* **-curring, -curred** happen; come to mind **occurrence** *n* happening

**ocean** *n* great body of water; large division of this; the sea

**ochre** *n* earth used as yellow or brown pigment

**o'clock** *adv* by the clock

**Oct.** October

**octagon** *n* figure with eight angles **octagonal** *adj*

**octane** *n* chemical found in petrol

**octave** *n Mus* eighth note above or below given note; this space

**octet** *n* (music for) group of eight

**October** *n* tenth month

**octopus** *n* mollusc with eight arms covered with suckers

**odd** *adj* strange, queer; incidental, random; left over or additional; not even; not part of a set **oddity** *n* odd person or thing; quality of being odd **oddments** *pl n* things left over **odds** *pl n* advantage conceded in betting; likelihood **odds and ends** odd fragments or scraps

**ode** *n* lyric poem

**odium** *n* hatred, widespread dislike **odious** *adj*

**odour** *n* smell **odorous** *adj* fragrant; scented

**odyssey** *n* long eventful journey

**oesophagus** *n* (*pl* **-gi**) passage between mouth and stomach

**of** *prep* denotes removal, separation, ownership, attribute, material, quality

— THESAURUS —

**occupant** holder, indweller, inhabitant, inmate, lessee, occupier, resident, tenant, user

**occupation** activity, business, calling, craft, employment, job, post, profession, pursuit, trade, vocation, work; control, holding, occupancy, possession, residence, tenancy, tenure, use; conquest, invasion

**occupy** (*oft. passive*) absorb, amuse, busy, divert, employ, engage, engross, entertain, immerse, interest, involve, monopolize, preoccupy; capture, hold, invade, keep, seize

**occur** arise, befall, betide, chance, eventuate, happen, materialize, result

**occurrence** affair, circumstance, episode, event, happening, incident, proceeding

**odd** abnormal, bizarre, curious, deviant, different, eccentric, freak, irregular, peculiar, quaint, queer, remarkable, rum *Brit sl*, singular, strange, uncommon, unusual, weird, whimsical; lone, remaining, single, solitary, spare, unpaired

**oddity** abnormality, anomaly, freak, irregularity, peculiarity, phenomenon, quirk, rarity

**odds** edge, lead, superiority; balance, chances, likelihood, probability

**odious** abominable, detestable, disgusting, execrable, foul, hateful, horrible, loathsome, offensive, repellent, repugnant, repulsive, revolting, unpleasant

**odour** aroma, bouquet, essence, fragrance, perfume, scent, smell, stink

**off** adv away ~prep away from ~adj not operative; cancelled or postponed; bad, sour etc. **offhand** adj/adv without previous thought; curt **off-licence** n place where alcoholic drinks are sold for consumption elsewhere **offset** v counterbalance, compensate **offspring** n children, issue

**offal** n edible entrails of animal; refuse

**offend** v hurt feelings of, displease; do wrong; disgust **offence** n wrong; crime; insult **offender** n **offensive** adj causing displeasure; aggressive ~n position or movement of attack

**offer** v present for acceptance or refusal; tender; propose; attempt ~n offering, bid

**office** n room(s), building, in which business, clerical work etc. is done; commercial or professional organization; official position; service; duty; form of worship; pl task; service **officer** n one in command in army, navy, ship etc.; official

**official** adj with, by, authority ~n one holding office

**officiate** v perform duties of office, ceremony

**officious** adj importunate in offering service; interfering

**offside** adj/adv Sport illegally forward

——————— THESAURUS ———————

**off** adj absent, cancelled, finished, gone, inoperative, postponed, unavailable; bad, decomposed, high, mouldy, rancid, rotten, sour, turned

**offence** crime, fault, lapse, misdeed, misdemeanour, peccadillo, sin, transgression, trespass, wrong

**offend** affront, annoy, displease, fret, gall, insult, irritate, outrage, pain, pique, provoke, rile, slight, snub, upset, vex, wound

**offender** criminal, culprit, lawbreaker, malefactor, miscreant, transgressor, villain

**offensive** adj disagreeable, disgusting, loathsome, nasty, obnoxious, odious, repellent, revolting, sickening, unpleasant, unsavoury, vile, abusive, aggressive, annoying, detestable, displeasing, insolent, insulting, irritating, rude, uncivil ~n attack, drive, onslaught

**offer** v bid, extend, give, proffer, tender; advance, extend, move, propose, submit, suggest; afford, furnish, present, provide, show ~n

attempt, bid, essay, overture, proposal, suggestion, tender

**offhand** abrupt, aloof, brusque, careless, casual, cavalier, curt, glib, perfunctory

**office** appointment, business, capacity, charge, commission, duty, employment, obligation, occupation, place, post, responsibility, role, service, situation, station, trust, work

**officer** agent, bureaucrat, executive, representative

**official** adj authentic, authoritative, bona fide, certified, formal, legitimate, licensed, proper ~n agent, bureaucrat, executive, representative

**officiate** chair, conduct, manage, preside, serve

**officious** bustling, forward, impertinent, interfering, intrusive, meddlesome, obtrusive, opinionated, overzealous

**offset** counteract, counterbalance, counterpoise, countervail, neutralize

**oft** *adv Poet* often

**often** *adv* many times

**ogle** *v* stare, look (at) amorously ~*n* this look

**ogre** *n* man-eating giant; monster

**oh** *interj* exclamation of surprise, pain etc.

**ohm** *n* unit of electrical resistance

**oil** *n* any viscous liquid with smooth, sticky feel; petroleum ~*v* lubricate with oil **oily** *adj* **oilskin** *n* cloth treated with oil to make it waterproof

**ointment** *n* greasy preparation for healing or beautifying the skin

**O.K., okay** *Inf adj/adv/interj* all right ~*v* agree to, endorse

**old** *adj* aged, having lived or existed long; belonging to earlier period **olden** *adj* old **old-fashioned** *adj* in style of earlier period, out of date; fond of old ways

**olfactory** *adj* of smelling

**oligarchy** *n* government by small group

**olive** *n* evergreen tree; its oil-yielding fruit; its wood ~*adj* greyish-green

**ombudsman** *n* official who investigates complaints against government organizations

**omelette** *n* dish of eggs beaten and fried

**omen** *n* prophetic happening **ominous** *adj* boding evil, threatening

**omit** *v* **omitting, omitted** leave out, leave undone **omission** *n*

**omnibus** *n* book etc. containing several works; bus ~*adj* serving, containing several objects

**omnipotent** *adj* all-powerful

**omniscient** *adj* knowing everything

**omnivorous** *adj* eating both animals and plants **omnivore** *n*

**on** *prep* above and touching, at, near, towards etc.; attached to; concerning; performed upon; during; taking regularly ~*adj* operating; taking place ~*adv* so as to be on; forwards; continuously etc.; in progress **oncoming** *adj* approaching from the front **ongoing** *adj* in progress, continuing

**once** *adv* one time; formerly; ever **at once** immediately; simultaneously **once-over** *n Inf* quick examination

**one** *adj* lowest cardinal number; single; united; only, without others;

**often** frequently, generally, much, repeatedly

**oil** *v* grease, lubricate

**old** aged, ancient, decrepit, elderly, grey, mature, senile, venerable, antiquated, antique, cast-off, crumbling, dated, decayed, done, obsolete, old-fashioned, outdated, passé, stale, timeworn, unoriginal, worn-out; antique, archaic, bygone, early, immemorial, original, primeval, primitive, pristine, remote

**old-fashioned** ancient, antiquated, archaic, dated, dead, obsoles-

cent, past

**omen** augury, foreboding, indication, portent, presage, sign

**ominous** dark, fateful, menacing, portentous, sinister, threatening

**omission** default, failure, gap, lack, leaving out, neglect, oversight

**omit** disregard, drop, eliminate, exclude, fail, forget, miss (out), neglect, overlook, skip

**omnipotent** all-powerful, supreme

**once** long ago, previously **at once** directly, forthwith, immediately, in-

identical ~*n* number or figure 1; unity; single specimen ~*pron* particular but not stated person; any person **oneself** *pron* **one-sided** *adj* partial; uneven

**onerous** *adj* burdensome

**onion** *n* edible bulb of pungent flavour

**onlooker** *n* person who watches without taking part

**only** *adj* being the one specimen ~*adv* solely, merely, exclusively ~*conj* but then; excepting that

**onset** *n* beginning

**onslaught** *n* attack

**onto** *prep* on top of

**onus** *n* responsibility, burden

**onward** *adj* advanced or advancing ~*adv* in advance, ahead, forward **onwards** *adv*

**onyx** *n* variety of quartz

**ooze** *v* pass slowly out, exude ~*n*

sluggish flow; wet mud

**opal** *n* glassy gemstone displaying variegated colours

**opaque** *adj* not transparent

**open** *adj* not shut or blocked up; without lid or door; bare; undisguised; not enclosed, covered or exclusive; spread out, accessible; frank ~*v* make or become open; begin ~*n* clear space, unenclosed country **opening** *n* hole, gap; beginning; opportunity ~*adj* first; initial **openly** *adv* without concealment **open-minded** *adj* unprejudiced

**opera** *n* musical drama **operatic** *adj* **operetta** *n* light opera

**operation** *n* working, way things work; act of surgery; military campaign **operate** *v* cause to function; work; produce an effect; perform act of surgery **operative** *adj* working ~*n* worker **operator** *n*

stantly, now, right away

**one-sided** biased, coloured, lopsided, partial, partisan, prejudiced, unfair, unjust

**onlooker** bystander, eyewitness, observer, spectator, witness

**only** *adj* exclusive, individual, lone, single, sole, solitary, unique ~*adv* exclusively, just, merely, purely

**ooze** bleed, discharge, drain, drop, emit, escape, filter, leach, leak, seep, strain, sweat, weep

**opaque** cloudy, dim, dull, filmy, hazy, muddied, murky

**open** *adj* agape, ajar, extended, gaping, revealed, uncovered, unfastened, unlocked, yawning; airy, bare, clear, exposed, extensive, free, navigable, passable, rolling, spacious, sweeping, wide; accessible, available, free, general, public, unoccupied, vacant; artless,

candid, fair, frank, guileless, honest, innocent, natural, sincere ~*v* clear, crack, uncover, undo, unfasten, unlock, unseal, untie; begin, commence, inaugurate, initiate, launch, start

**opening** *n* aperture, breach, break, cleft, crack, gap, hole, rent, rupture, slot, space, split, vent; beginning, birth, dawn, inception, initiation, launch, onset, outset, start ~*adj* beginning, early, first, inaugural, initial, introductory, primary

**openly** candidly, forthrightly, frankly, overtly, plainly; blatantly, brazenly, publicly, shamelessly

**open-minded** dispassionate, enlightened, free, impartial, liberal, reasonable, tolerant, unbiased, unprejudiced

**operate** act, function, go, perform, run, work

**ophthalmic** adj of eyes

**opinion** n what one thinks about something; belief, judgment **opinionated** adj stubborn in one's opinions

**opium** n narcotic drug made from poppy **opiate** n drug containing opium

**opossum** n small Amer. and Aust. marsupial

**opponent** n adversary, antagonist

**opportune** adj seasonable, well-timed **opportunist** n one who grasps opportunities regardless of principle **opportunity** n favourable time or condition; good chance

**oppose** v resist, set against opposite adj contrary; facing **~n** the contrary **~prep/adv** facing; on the other side **opposition** n resistance; hostility; group opposing another

**oppress** v govern by tyranny; weigh down **oppression** n **oppressive** adj tyrannical; hard to bear; (of weather) hot and tiring

**opt** v make a choice

**optic** adj of eye or sight **optical** adj **optician** n maker of, dealer in spectacles, optical instruments

**optimism** n disposition to look on the bright side **optimist** n **optimistic** adj

**optimum** adj/n (pl -ma, -mums) the best, the most favourable

——————————— THESAURUS ———————————

**operation** action, affair, course, exercise, motion, movement, procedure, process, use, working; assault, campaign, exercise, manoeuvre

**operator** conductor, driver, handler, mechanic, technician, worker

**opinion** assessment, belief, conjecture, feeling, idea, judgment, mind, notion, persuasion, sentiment, theory, view

**opinionated** bigoted, doctrinaire, dogmatic, inflexible, obstinate, prejudiced, stubborn

**opponent** adversary, antagonist, challenger, competitor, contestant, disputant, enemy, foe, rival

**opportune** appropriate, apt, auspicious, convenient, favourable, fitting, lucky, seasonable, suitable, timely

**opportunity** chance, hour, moment, occasion, opening, scope, time

**oppose** bar, block, check, combat, counter, defy, face, fight, hinder, obstruct, prevent, resist, take on, withstand

**opposite** adj adverse, conflicting, contradictory, contrary, hostile, inimical, irreconcilable, opposed, inverse, unlike; corresponding, facing, fronting **~n** antithesis, contradiction, contrary, converse, inverse, reverse

**opposition** antagonism, competition, disapproval, hostility, prevention, resistance; antagonist, foe, other side, rival

**oppress** abuse, crush, harry, maltreat, overpower, persecute, subdue, subjugate, suppress, wrong

**oppression** abuse, brutality, cruelty, harshness, injury, injustice, misery, persecution, severity, tyranny

**oppressive** brutal, cruel, despotic, grinding, harsh, heavy, onerous, repressive, severe, tyrannical, unjust; airless, close, heavy, stifling, stuffy, sultry, torrid

**optimistic** assured, bright, buoyant, cheerful, confident, expectant, hopeful, positive

**option** n choice; thing chosen **optional** adj leaving to choice

**optometrist** n person testing eyesight, prescribing corrective lenses

**opulent** adj rich; copious **opulence** n

**opus** n work; musical composition

**or** conj introducing alternatives; if not

**oracle** n divine utterance, prophecy given at shrine of god; the shrine; wise adviser

**oral** adj spoken; by mouth ~n spoken examination

**orange** adj reddish-yellow ~n reddish-yellow citrus fruit

**orang-utan, orang-utang** n large reddish-brown ape

**orator** n maker of speech; skilful speaker **oration** n formal speech **oratory** n speeches; eloquence

**orb** n globe

**orbit** n track of planet, satellite, comet etc. around another heavenly body; field of influence ~v move in, or put into, an orbit

**orchard** n (area for) fruit trees

**orchestra** n band of musicians; place for such band in theatre etc. **orchestral** adj **orchestrate** v arrange (music) for orchestra; organize (something) to particular effect

**orchid** n genus of various flowering plants

**ordain** v confer holy orders upon; decree, enact

**ordeal** n severe, trying experience

**order** n regular, proper or peaceful arrangement or condition; class; species; command; request for something to be supplied; monastic society ~v command; request (something) to be supplied; arrange **orderly** adj tidy; well-behaved ~n hospital attendant

**ordinal number** number showing

───── THESAURUS ─────

**optimum** adj best, highest, ideal, peak, perfect, superlative

**option** alternative, choice, election, preference, selection

**optional** extra, open, possible, voluntary

**oracle** divination, prediction, prognostication, prophecy, revelation, vision; prophet, seer, sibyl, soothsayer

**oral** spoken, verbal, viva voce, vocal

**orator** declaimer, lecturer, rhetorician, speaker

**oratory** declamation, eloquence, rhetoric

**orbit** n circle, course, cycle, path, revolution, rotation, track, trajectory; compass, course, domain, influence, range, reach, scope, sphere, sweep ~v circle, encircle, revolve around

**ordain** anoint, appoint, call, consecrate, destine, elect, frock, invest, nominate; decree, dictate, enact, enjoin, establish, fix, lay down, order, prescribe, rule, set, will

**ordeal** affliction, agony, anguish, hardship, suffering, test, torture, trial

**order** n calm, control, discipline, law, peace; arrangement, method, pattern, plan, regularity, symmetry, system; caste, class, degree, grade, hierarchy, position, rank, status; breed, cast, class, family, genre, genus, ilk, kind, sort, species, tribe; application, booking, commission, request, reservation; brotherhood, community, company, fraternity, guild, league, lodge, sect, sisterhood, society, union ~v bid,

position in series

**ordinance** n decree, rule

**ordinary** adj usual, normal; commonplace **ordinarily** adv

**ordnance** n artillery; military stores **ordnance survey** official geographical survey of Britain

**ore** n mineral which yields metal

**oregano** n aromatic herb

**organ** n musical wind instrument of pipes and stops, played with keys; member of animal or plant with particular function; medium of information **organist** n organ player

**organism** n plant, animal **organic** adj of, derived from, living organisms; of bodily organs; Chem of compounds formed from carbon;

organized, systematic

**organize** v give definite structure; arrange; unite in a society **organization** n act of organizing; structure; association, group **organizer** n

**orgasm** n sexual climax

**orgy** n drunken or licentious revel; unrestrained bout

**orient** n (with cap.) East ~v determine (one's) position (also **orientate**) **oriental** adj/n **orientation** n

**orifice** n opening, mouth

**origami** n art of paper folding

**origin** n beginning; source; parentage **original** adj earliest; new, not copied; thinking or acting for oneself ~n thing from which another is copied **originality** n **originally** adv **originate** v come or bring into exist-

charge, command, decree, direct, enact, enjoin, instruct, ordain, prescribe, require; book, call for, engage, prescribe, request, reserve; adjust, align, arrange, catalogue, class, classify, conduct, control, dispose, group, manage, marshal, neaten, organize, regulate, systematize, tabulate, tidy

**orderly** adj businesslike, methodical, neat, shipshape, systematic, tidy; controlled, decorous, disciplined, law-abiding, restrained, well-behaved

**ordinarily** commonly, customarily, generally, habitually, normally, usually

**ordinary** accustomed, common, customary, established, everyday, mundane, normal, prevailing, regular, routine, settled, standard, stock, typical, usual; average, commonplace, fair, indifferent, inferior, pedestrian, unremarkable

**organ** element, member, part, pro-

cess, structure, unit; agency, channel, forum, medium, mouthpiece, newspaper, publication, vehicle, voice

**organism** animal, being, body, creature, entity

**organization** assembly, construction, disposal, formation, management, regulation, running, standardization; arrangement, chemistry, composition, constitution, design, format, framework, grouping, make-up, method, organism, pattern, plan, structure, system, unity, whole; association, body, combine, company, concern, consortium, group, institution, league, society, syndicate, union

**organize** arrange, catalogue, classify, codify, constitute, construct, coordinate, dispose, establish, form, frame, group, marshal, pigeonhole, set up, shape

**orgy** debauch, revelry; bout, excess, indulgence, spree, surfeit

ence, begin; create, pioneer

**ornament** *n* any object used to adorn or decorate *~v* adorn **ornamental** *adj*

**ornate** *adj* highly decorated or elaborate

**ornithology** *n* science of birds

**orphan** *n* child whose parents are dead **orphanage** *n* institution for care of orphans

**orthodox** *adj* holding accepted views; conventional **orthodoxy** *n*

**orthopaedic** *adj* for curing deformity, disorder of bones

**oscillate** *v* swing to and fro; waver

**osmosis** *n* movement of liquid through membrane from higher to lower concentration

**osprey** *n* fishing hawk

**ossify** *v* **-fying, -fied** turn into bone; grow rigid

**ostensible** *adj* apparent; professed

**ostentation** *n* show, pretentious display **ostentatious** *adj*

**osteopathy** *n* art of treating disease by manipulation of bones **osteopath** *n*

**ostracize** *v* exclude, banish from society **ostracism** *n*

**ostrich** *n* large flightless bird

**other** *adj* not this; not the same; alternative *~pron* other person or thing **otherwise** *adv* differently *~conj* or else, if not

─────────── THESAURUS ───────────

**origin** beginning, birth, dawning, emergence, foundation, genesis, inauguration, inception, launch, outset, start; base, cause, derivation, fount, fountain, occasion, roots, source, spring

**original** *adj* earliest, first, initial, introductory, opening, primary, pristine, rudimentary, starting; archetypal, authentic, first, genuine, master, primary; creative, fertile, fresh, ground-breaking, ingenious, inventive, new, novel, resourceful, untried, unusual *~n* archetype, master, model, pattern, precedent, prototype, standard, type

**originality** boldness, creativeness, creative spirit, creativity, daring, freshness, imagination, individuality, ingenuity, innovation, inventiveness, novelty

**originate** arise, begin, come, derive, emerge, flow, issue, result, rise, spring, start, stem; conceive, create, discover, evolve, formulate, generate, initiate, institute, introduce, invent, launch, pioneer, produce

**ornament** adornment, bauble, decoration, frill, garnish, trinket

**ornamental** attractive, decorative, showy

**ornate** busy, decorated, elaborate, elegant, fancy, florid, rococo

**orthodox** accepted, approved, conformist, conventional, doctrinal, established, official, received, traditional

**ostensible** alleged, apparent, manifest, outward, plausible, professed, seeming, specious

**ostentation** affectation, boasting, display, exhibitionism, flourish, parade, pomp, pretentiousness, show

**ostentatious** boastful, conspicuous, extravagant, flamboyant, gaudy, loud, pompous, pretentious, showy, vulgar

**ostracize** blackball, blacklist, boycott, cast out, cold-shoulder, exclude, expel, give (someone) the cold shoulder, reject, send to Coventry, shun, snub

**other** *adj* different, dissimilar, dis-

**otter** *n* furry aquatic fish-eating mammal

**ouch** *interj* exclamation of sudden pain

**ought** *v* expressing obligation or advisability or probability

**ounce** *n* unit of weight, sixteenth of pound (28.4 grams)

**our** *adj* belonging to us **ours** *pron* ourselves *pron emphatic or reflexive form of* WE

**oust** *v* put out, expel

**out** *adv/adj* from within, away; wrong; not burning; not allowed; *Sport* dismissed **outer** *adj* away from the inside **outermost**, **outmost** *adj* on extreme outside **outing** *n* pleasure excursion **outward** *adj/adv*

**outboard** *adj* (of boat's engine) mounted on, outside stern

**outbreak** *n* sudden occurrence

**outburst** *n* sudden expression of emotion

**outcast** *n* rejected person

**outcome** *n* result

**outcry** *n* expression of widespread protest

**outdoors** *adv* in the open air **outdoor** *adj*

**outfit** *n* equipment; clothes and accessories; group or association regarded as a unit

**outgoing** *adj* leaving; sociable **outgoings** *pl n* expenses

**outlandish** *adj* queer, extravagantly strange

**outlaw** *n* one beyond protection of the law ~*v* make (someone) an outlaw; ban

**outlay** *n* expenditure

**outlet** *n* means of release or escape; market

**outline** *n* rough sketch; general plan; lines enclosing visible figure ~*v* sketch; summarize

tinct, diverse, remaining; separate; added, alternative, extra, further, more, spare, supplementary

**otherwise** if not, or else, or then

**out** *adj* impossible, ruled out, unacceptable; abroad, absent, away, elsewhere, gone, not at home, outside

**outbreak** burst, explosion, flareup, flash, outburst, rash, spasm

**outcast** *n* castaway, exile, leper, pariah, refugee, untouchable, wretch

**outcome** aftermath, consequence, end, issue, result, upshot

**outcry** clamour, complaint, cry, howl, noise, outburst, protest, scream, screech, uproar, yell

**outdoor** alfresco, open-air, outside

**outer** exposed, exterior, external, outside, outward, peripheral, re-

mote, superficial, surface

**outfit** clothes, costume, ensemble, garb, gear *Inf*, kit, suit, trappings

**outgoing** departing, former, last, leaving, past, retiring

**outgoings** costs, expenditure, expenses, outlay, overheads

**outing** excursion, jaunt, trip

**outlandish** alien, barbarous, eccentric, exotic, foreign, grotesque, queer, strange, weird

**outlaw** *n* bandit, brigand, highwayman, marauder, robber ~*v* ban, banish, bar, condemn, forbid, prohibit, proscribe

**outlay** *n* cost, expenses, investment, outgoings

**outlet** avenue, channel, opening, release, vent

**outline** *n* draft, drawing, frame, layout, plan, rough, skeleton,

**outlook** n point of view; probable outcome

**outlying** adj remote

**outmoded** adj no longer fashionable or accepted

**outpatient** n patient who does not stay in hospital overnight

**outpost** n outlying settlement

**output** n quantity produced; *Computers* information produced

**outrage** n violation of others' rights; shocking act; anger arising from this ~v commit outrage **outrageous** adj shocking; offensive

**outright** adj complete; definite ~adv completely

**outset** n beginning

**outside** n exterior ~adv not inside ~adj on exterior; unlikely; greatest possible **outsider** n person outside specific group; contestant thought unlikely to win

**outsize, outsized** adj larger than normal

**outskirts** pl n outer areas, districts, esp. of city

**outspoken** adj frank, candid

**outstanding** adj excellent; remarkable; unsettled, unpaid

**outweigh** v be more important than

**outwit** v get the better of by

—————————————— THESAURUS ——————————————

sketch, tracing; résumé, rundown, summary, synopsis; contour, figure, form, profile, shape, silhouette ~v adumbrate, delineate, draft, plan, summarize, trace

**outlook** angle, attitude, perspective, slant, viewpoint, views; forecast, future, prospect

**output** manufacture, production, yield

**outrage** n abuse, affront, indignity, injury, insult, offence, shock, violation, violence; atrocity, enormity, evil, inhumanity; anger, fury, hurt, indignation, resentment, shock, wrath ~v affront, incense, offend, scandalize, shock

**outrageous** atrocious, beastly, flagrant, horrible, infamous, inhuman, scandalous, shocking, villainous, violent, wicked; disgraceful, offensive, over the top *Sl*, scandalous, shocking

**outright** adj absolute, arrant, complete, perfect, pure, thorough, total, undisputed, utter, wholesale; definite, direct, flat ~adv absolutely, completely, explicitly, openly,

overtly, straightforwardly, thoroughly

**outset** beginning, inception, opening, start

**outside** n exterior, façade, face, front, skin, surface, topside ~adj exterior, external, extramural, extreme, outdoor, outer, outward, surface; distant, faint, marginal, negligible, remote, slight, slim, small, unlikely

**outskirts** borders, boundary, edge, environs, suburbs, vicinity

**outspoken** abrupt, blunt, candid, direct, downright, explicit, frank, free, open, round

**outstanding** celebrated, distinguished, eminent, excellent, exceptional, great, important, impressive, special, superior, well-known; arresting, conspicuous, marked, memorable, notable, prominent, remarkable, salient, striking; due, open, owing, payable, pending, unpaid, unsettled

**outward** adj apparent, evident, exterior, external, obvious, ostensible, outer, outside, perceptible, superfi-

cunning

**oval** *adj/n* egg-shaped, elliptical (thing)

**ovary** *n* female egg-producing organ **ovarian** *adj*

**ovation** *n* enthusiastic burst of applause

**oven** *n* heated chamber for baking

**over** *adv* above; beyond; in excess; finished; in repetition; across; downwards ~*prep* above; upon; more than; along ~*n* Cricket delivery of six balls from one end

**over-** *comb. form* too, too much, in excess, above

**overall** *n* (also *pl*) loose garment worn as protection against dirt etc. ~*adj* total

**overbearing** *adj* domineering

**overboard** *adv* from a boat into water **go overboard** go to extremes

**overcast** *adj* cloudy

**overcome** *v* conquer; surmount; make incapable or powerless

**overdose** *n/v* (take) excessive dose of drug

**overdraft** *n* withdrawal of more money than is in bank account

**overdrive** *n* very high gear in motor vehicle

**overgrown** *adj* thickly covered with plants

**overhaul** *v* examine and set in order ~*n* examination and repair

**overhead** *adj/adv* over one's head, above

**overland** *adj/adv* by land

**overlap** *v* share part of same space or period of time ~*n* area overlapping

**overlook** *v* fail to notice; disregard

**overseas** *adj/adv* foreign; from or to a place over the sea

**overseer** *n* supervisor **oversee** *v* supervise

**overshadow** *v* reduce significance of

**oversight** *n* failure to notice; mistake

**overt** *adj* open, unconcealed

——————— THESAURUS ———————

cial, surface, visible

**outweigh** compensate for, eclipse, override, predominate

**outwit** cheat, deceive, defraud, dupe, outjockey, outmanoeuvre, swindle

**ovation** acclaim, applause, cheers, plaudits, tribute

**over** *adv* above, aloft, on high, overhead ~*prep* above, on, on top of, upon; above, exceeding, in excess of, more than

**overall** *adj* blanket, complete, general, inclusive, umbrella

**overbearing** arrogant, despotic, dogmatic, domineering, lordly, officious, oppressive, overweening, peremptory, superior

**overcast** clouded, darkened, dismal, dreary, dull, grey, hazy, lowering, murky, sombre, threatening

**overcome** beat, best, conquer, crush, defeat, master, overpower, prevail, subdue, subjugate, surmount, vanquish

**overhaul** *v* check, do up *Inf*, examine, inspect, recondition, reexamine, repair, restore, service, survey ~*n* checkup, examination, inspection, service

**overhead** *adj* overhanging, roof, upper ~*adv* above, skyward, up above, upward

**overlook** disregard, forget, ignore, miss, neglect, omit, pass, slight; condone, disregard, excuse, forgive

**overshadow** dominate, dwarf, eclipse, excel, outshine, surpass

**overtake** v move past; catch up

**overthrow** v overturn; defeat ~n ruin; fall

**overtime** n time at work, outside normal working hours; payment for this time

**overtone** n additional meaning

**overture** n Mus orchestral introduction; opening of negotiations

**overwhelm** v crush; submerge

**overwhelming** adj irresistible

**overwrought** adj overexcited

**owe** v be bound to repay, be indebted for **owing** adj owed, due

**owing to** caused by, as result of

**own** adj emphasizes possession ~v possess; acknowledge; confess **owner** n **ownership** n possession

**ox** n (pl **oxen**) castrated bull

**oxide** n compound of oxygen and one other element

**oxygen** n gas in atmosphere essential to life

**oyster** n edible mollusc

**oz.** ounce

**ozone** n form of oxygen with pungent odour

——————————— THESAURUS ———————————

**oversight** blunder, error, fault, lapse, laxity, mistake, neglect, omission, slip

**overt** apparent, blatant, manifest, obvious, open, patent, plain, unconcealed, undisguised, visible

**overtake** outdistance, outdo, outstrip, overhaul, pass

**overthrow** v demolish, destroy, level, overturn, raze, ruin, subvert, upend, upset; abolish, conquer, defeat, depose, dethrone, oust, overwhelm, topple, unseat ~n defeat, displacement, dispossession, downfall, end, fall, ousting, rout, ruin, undoing

**overture** (oft. pl) advance, approach, invitation, offer, proposal, signal, tender

**overwhelm** bury, crush, deluge, engulf, flood, inundate, submerge, swamp

**overwhelming** crushing, devastating, overpowering, shattering, stunning

**overwrought** agitated, distracted, excited, frantic, keyed up, on edge, tense, wired Sl

**owe** be beholden to, be in arrears, be in debt, be indebted, be under an obligation to

**owing** adj due, outstanding, overdue, owed, payable, unpaid, unsettled

**own** adj individual, particular, personal, private ~v enjoy, have, hold, keep, possess, retain; acknowledge, admit, allow, avow, concede, confess, disclose, grant, recognize

**owner** holder, landlord, lord, master, mistress, possessor, proprietor

**ownership** dominion, possession, proprietorship, title

# P p

**p** page; pence; penny; *Mus* piano (softly)

**pace** *n* step; rate of movement ~*v* step; set speed for; measure **pacemaker** *n* electronic device to regulate heartbeat; person who sets speed for race

**pacify** *v* -ifying, -ified calm **pacifism** *n* pacifist *n* advocate of abolition of war; one who refuses to help in war

**pack** *n* bundle; band of animals; large set of people or things ~*v* put together in suitcase etc.; make into a bundle; cram; fill **package** *n* parcel; set of items offered together ~*v* put into packages **packet** *n* small parcel; small container (and contents)

**pact** *n* covenant, agreement

**pad** *n* soft stuff used as a cushion, protection etc.; block of sheets of paper; foot or sole of various animals ~*v* **padding, padded** make soft, fill in, protect etc., with pad; walk with soft step

**paddle**[1] *n* short oar with broad blade ~*v* move by, as with, paddles

**paddle**[2] *v* walk with bare feet in shallow water

**paddock** *n* small grass enclosure

**paddy field** field where rice is grown

**padlock** *n/v* (fasten with) detachable lock with hinged hoop

**paediatrics** *pl n* (*with sing v*) branch of medicine dealing with diseases of children **paediatrician** *n*

**paella** *n* Spanish dish of rice, chicken, shellfish etc.

**pagan** *adj/n* heathen

**page**[1] *n* one side of leaf of book etc.

**page**[2] *n* boy attendant ~*v* summon by loudspeaker announcement or electronic device **pager** *n* small portable electronic signalling device

**pageant** *n* show of persons in costume in procession, dramatic scenes etc.

**pagoda** *n* pyramidal temple of Chinese or Indian type

**pail** *n* bucket

---

## THESAURUS

**pace** gait, measure, step, stride, tread, walk; progress, rate, speed, tempo, time, velocity ~*v* march, patrol, pound, stride; count, mark out, measure, step

**pack** *n* bale, bundle, load, package, packet, parcel; band, bunch, collection, company, crew, crowd, gang, group, lot, mob, troop ~*v* bundle, load, package, store, stow; compact, compress, cram, fill, jam, press, ram, stuff

**package** *n* box, carton, container, parcel; combination, unit, whole ~*v* box, pack, wrap

**packet** bag, carton, container, package, parcel

**pact** agreement, alliance, bargain, bond, contract, covenant, deal, treaty

**pad** *n* buffer, cushion, protection, stuffing, wad; jotter, notepad, tablet, writing pad; foot, paw, sole ~*v* cushion, pack, protect, stuff

**paddle**[1] *v* oar, propel, pull, row

**paddle**[2] dabble, plash, wade

**page**[1] folio, leaf, sheet, side

**page**[2] footboy, pageboy, squire ~*v* call, summon

**pageant** display, parade, proces-

**pain** n bodily or mental suffering; pl trouble ~v inflict pain upon **painful** adj **painkiller** n drug that reduces pain **painstaking** adj careful

**paint** n colouring matter spread on a surface ~v colour, coat, or make picture of, with paint **painter** n **painting** n

**pair** n set of two ~v arrange in twos

**pal** n Inf friend

**palace** n residence of king, bishop etc.; stately mansion **palatial** adj

**palate** n roof of mouth; sense of taste **palatable** adj agreeable to eat

**palaver** n fuss

**pale** adj wan, whitish ~v whiten; lose superiority

**palette** n artist's flat board for mixing colours on

**palindrome** n word etc., that is the same read backwards or forwards

**paling** n upright plank in fence

**pall**[1] n cloth spread over a coffin **pallbearer** n one carrying coffin at funeral

**pall**[2] v become tiresome; cloy

**pallet** n portable platform for storing and moving goods

**palliate** v relieve without curing; excuse **palliative** adj/n

**pallid** adj pale **pallor** n

**palm** n inner surface of hand; tropical tree; its leaf as symbol of victory **palmistry** n fortune-telling from lines on palm of hand

**palomino** n (pl -nos) golden horse with white mane and tail

**palpable** adj obvious

**palpitate** v throb

**palsy** n paralysis

**paltry** adj worthless

**pamper** v overindulge, spoil

**pamphlet** n thin unbound book

**pan-** comb. form all, as in **pan-**American

**pan**[1] n broad, shallow vessel; bowl of lavatory; depression in ground ~v panning, panned Inf criticize harshly

**pan**[2] v panning, panned move film camera slowly while filming

**panacea** n universal remedy

**panache** n dashing style

─────────────────── THESAURUS ───────────────────

**pain** n ache, hurt, pang, spasm, throb, twinge; affliction, agony, distress, grief, heartache, misery, suffering, torment, torture ~v chafe, hurt, smart, sting, throb; afflict, aggrieve, distress, grieve, hurt, sadden, torment, torture, wound

**painful** disagreeable, distasteful, grievous, unpleasant; agonizing, inflamed, raw, smarting, sore, tender

**painkiller** anaesthetic, analgesic, drug, sedative

**painstaking** assiduous, careful, conscientious, diligent, meticulous, scrupulous, thorough

**paint** n colour, colouring, dye, emulsion, pigment, stain, tint ~v delineate, depict, draw, picture, portray, represent, sketch; apply, coat, colour, cover, daub

**pair** n brace, couple, duo ~v couple, join, marry, match, mate, team, twin, wed

**pale** anaemic, ashen, bleached, colourless, faded, light, pallid, pasty, wan, white

**pamper** baby, coddle, cosset, indulge, pet, spoil

**pamphlet** booklet, brochure, circular, leaflet, tract

**pan** n container, pot, saucepan, vessel ~v Inf censure, criticize, knock Inf, slate Inf

**panama** *n* straw hat

**pancake** *n* thin cake of batter fried in pan

**pancreas** *n* digestive gland behind stomach

**panda** *n* large black and white bearlike mammal of China

**pandemonium** *n* din and uproar

**pander** *v* (*esp.* **with to**) give gratification to ~*n* pimp

**pane** *n* sheet of glass

**panegyric** *n* speech of praise

**panel** *n* compartment of surface, usu. raised or sunk, e.g. in door; team in quiz game etc.; list of jurors, doctors etc. ~*v* **-elling, -elled** adorn with panels

**pang** *n* sudden pain

**panic** *n* sudden and infectious fear ~*v* **-icking, -icked** (cause to) feel panic **panicky** *adj*

**pannier** *n* basket carried by beast of burden, bicycle etc.

**panoply** *n* magnificent array

**panorama** *n* wide view

**pansy** *n* flower, species of violet; *Inf* effeminate man

**pant** *v/n* gasp

**pantechnicon** *n* large van, esp. for carrying furniture

**panther** *n* variety of leopard

**pantomime** *n* theatrical show, usu. at Christmas time, often founded on a fairy tale

**pantry** *n* room for storing food or utensils

**pants** *pl n* undergarment for lower trunk; *US* trousers

**pap** *n* soft food

**papacy** *n* office of Pope **papal** *adj* of the Pope

**paper** *n* material made by pressing pulp of rags, wood etc., into thin sheets; sheet of paper; newspaper; essay; *pl* documents etc. ~*v* cover with paper **paperback** *n* book with flexible covers

**papier-mâché** *n* paper pulp mixed with paste, shaped and dried hard

**paprika** *n* red pepper

**papyrus** *n* (*pl* **papyri**) species of reed; paper made from this

**par** *n* equality of value or standing; face value; *Golf* estimated standard score **parity** *n* equality; analogy

**parable** *n* allegory, story with moral lesson

**parachute** *n* apparatus extending like umbrella used to slow the descent of falling body ~*v* drop by parachute

**parade** *n* display; muster of troops ~*v* march; display

**paradise** *n* Heaven; state of bliss; Garden of Eden

**panache** dash, élan, flamboyance, flourish, style

**pandemonium** bedlam, din, hullabaloo, racket, uproar

**pang** pain, spasm, stab, sting, twinge

**panic** alarm, consternation, fear, fright, scare, terror

**panorama** prospect, scenery, view, vista

**pant** blow, gasp, heave, huff, puff

**paper** *n* (*oft. pl*) certificate, deed, documents, record

**par** *n* average, level, mean, norm, standard, usual

**parable** allegory, fable, moral tale

**parade** *n* display, ostentation, show, spectacle; array, cavalcade, ceremony, march, pageant, procession, review, spectacle ~*v* display, exhibit, flaunt, show, show off *Inf*, strut, swagger

**paradox** *n* statement that seems self-contradictory **paradoxical** *adj*

**paraffin** *n* waxlike or liquid hydrocarbon mixture used as fuel, solvent, etc.

**paragon** *n* pattern or model of excellence

**paragraph** *n* section of chapter or book ~*v* arrange in paragraphs

**parakeet** *n* small parrot

**parallel** *adj/n* (line or lines) continuously at equal distances; (thing) precisely corresponding ~*v* represent as similar **parallelogram** *n* four-sided figure with opposite sides parallel

**paralysis** *n* (*pl* -yses) incapacity to move or feel **paralyse** *v* affect with paralysis; make immobile **paralytic** *adj/n*

**paramedic** *n* person working in support of medical profession

**parameter** *n* limiting factor

**paramilitary** *adj* organized on military lines

**paramount** *adj* supreme

**paranoia** *n* mental disease with delusions of persecution etc. **paranoid** *adj/n*

**parapet** *n* low wall along edge of bridge etc.

**paraphernalia** *pl n* (*used as sing*) belongings; equipment

**paraphrase** *v* express in other words

**paraplegia** *n* paralysis of lower body **paraplegic** *n/adj*

**parasite** *n* animal or plant living in or on another **parasitic** *adj*

**parasol** *n* sunshade

**paratroops, -troopers** *pl n* troops trained to descend by parachute

**parboil** *v* boil until partly cooked

**parcel** *n* packet ~*v* -celling, -celled wrap up; divide into parts

**parch** *v* make, become hot and dry

**parchment** *n* sheep, goat, calf skin prepared for writing

**pardon** *v* forgive, excuse ~*n* forgiveness; release from punishment

**pare** *v* peel, trim; decrease

—————— THESAURUS ——————

**paradise** bliss, delight, heaven

**paradox** ambiguity, contradiction, enigma, puzzle

**paragon** exemplar, ideal, model, nonpareil, pattern

**paragraph** clause, item, part, passage, portion, section, subdivision

**parallel** *adj* analogous, like, matching, similar ~*n* counterpart, equivalent, match, twin; analogy, comparison, likeness, resemblance, similarity

**paralyse** cripple, disable, incapacitate, lame; arrest, freeze, halt, immobilize, petrify

**parameter** framework, guideline, limit, limitation, restriction

**paramount** chief, first, foremost,

greatest, highest, pre-eminent, prime, principal, top

**paraphernalia** apparatus, belongings, effects, gear, stuff, tackle, trappings

**paraphrase** rephrase, restate, reword

**parasite** hanger-on, leech, scrounger, sponger *Inf*

**parcel** *n* bundle, carton, package *v* (*oft. with up*) do up, pack, package, tie up, wrap

**parch** dehydrate, desiccate, dry up, shrivel, wither

**pardon** *v* absolve, acquit, condone, excuse, exonerate, forgive, let off *Inf*, overlook, reprieve ~*n* absolution, acquittal, amnesty, forgive-

**parent** *n* father or mother **parentage** *n* descent, extraction **parental** *adj* **parenthood** *n*

**parenthesis** *n* word(s) inserted in passage **parentheses** *pl n* round brackets, (), used to mark this

**pariah** *n* social outcast

**parish** *n* district under one clergyman **parishioner** *n* inhabitant of parish

**parity** *SEE PAR*

**park** *n* large area of land in natural state for recreational use ~*v* leave for short time; manoeuvre (car) into suitable space

**parka** *n* warm waterproof coat

**parlance** *n* particular way of speaking

**parley** *v/n* (hold) discussion about terms

**parliament** *n* law-making assembly of country **parliamentary** *adj*

**parlour** *n* sitting room

**parochial** *adj* narrow, provincial; of a parish

**parody** *n/v* **-odying, -odied** (write) satirical, amusing imitation of a work

**parole** *n* release of prisoner on condition of good behaviour ~*v* release on parole

**paroxysm** *n* sudden attack of pain, rage, laughter

**parquet** *n* flooring of wooden blocks

**parrot** *n* brightly coloured bird which can imitate speaking ~*v* **parroting, parroted** repeat words without thinking

**parry** *v* **parrying, parried** ward off, turn aside

**parsimony** *n* stinginess **parsimonious** *adj*

**parsley** *n* herb used for seasoning, garnish etc.

**parsnip** *n* root vegetable

**parson** *n* clergyman

**part** *n* portion; role; duty; region; component ~*v* divide; separate

**parting** *n* division of hair on head; separation; leave-taking **partly** *adv* in part

**partake** *v* **partaking, partook** take or have share in; take food or drink

**partial** *adj* not complete; prejudiced; fond of **partially** *adv* partly

**participate** *v* share in; take part **participant** *n* **participation** *n*

ness, release, remission, reprieve

**parentage** ancestry, birth, descent, family, line, lineage, origin, pedigree, race, stock

**park** estate, garden, grounds, parkland

**parliament** assembly, congress, council, senate

**parlour** front room, lounge, sitting room

**parody** *n* burlesque, caricature, lampoon, satire, send-up *Brit inf*, skit, spoof *Inf*, takeoff *Inf* ~*v* burlesque, caricature, lampoon, satirize, send up *Brit inf*, travesty

**part** *n* bit, fraction, fragment, piece, portion, scrap, section, slice; capacity, duty, function, place, role, task, work; component, constituent, element, ingredient, member, unit ~*v* break, cleave, come apart, detach, divide, separate, split, tear

**partake (with in)** engage, participate, share, take part

**partial** incomplete, limited, uncompleted, unfinished; biased, one-sided, partisan, prejudiced, unfair, unjust

**participate** enter into, join in,

**participle** *n Grammar* verbal adjective

**particle** *n* minute portion

**particular** *adj* relating to one; distinct; fussy ~*n* detail, item; *pl* items of information **particularly** *adv*

**partisan** *n* adherent of a party; guerilla ~*adj* adhering to faction; prejudiced

**partition** *n* division; interior dividing wall ~*v* divide into sections

**partner** *n* ally or companion; spouse **partnership** *n*

**partridge** *n* game bird

**party** *n* social assembly; group of persons organized together, esp. with common political aim; person

**pass** *v* go by, beyond, through etc.; exceed; transfer; spend; elapse; undergo examination successfully; bring a law into force ~*n* way, esp. through mountains; permit; successful result **passable** *adj* (just) acceptable **passing** *adj* transitory; casual **pass away** die **pass out** faint

**passage** *n* opening; corridor; part of book etc.; voyage, fare

**passé** *adj* out-of-date

**passenger** *n* traveller, esp. by public conveyance

**passion** *n* ardent desire; any strong emotion; great enthusiasm **passionate** *adj*

**passive** *adj* submissive; inactive

————————————— THESAURUS —————————————

share, take part

**particle** atom, bit, crumb, grain, jot, piece, scrap, shred, speck

**particular** *adj* distinct, exact, peculiar, precise, special, specific; choosy *Inf*, demanding, discriminating, exacting, fastidious, finicky, fussy, pernickety *Inf*

**parting** adieu, farewell, goodbye; breaking, division, separation, split

**partisan** *n* adherent, backer, devotee, supporter, upholder ~*adj* biased, one-sided, partial, prejudiced, sectarian

**partition** *n* division, segregation, separation; barrier, screen, wall ~*v* apportion, cut up, divide, separate, share, split up, subdivide

**partner** ally, associate, colleague, helper, mate, team-mate; consort, helpmate, husband, mate, spouse, wife

**party** celebration, do *Inf*, festivity, function, knees-up *Brit inf*, reception, social; alliance, cabal, camp, clique, coalition, confederacy, league, set, side

**pass** *v* flow, go, move, proceed, roll, run; exceed, excel, go beyond, outdo, outstrip, surmount, surpass; convey, deliver, give, hand, send, transfer; get through, graduate, qualify, succeed; accept, approve, decree, ratify ~*n* authorization, identification, licence, passport, permission, permit, ticket, warrant

**passable** acceptable, adequate, all right, so-so *Inf,* tolerable

**passage** alley, avenue, channel, lane, thoroughfare, way; corridor, hall, lobby, vestibule; excerpt, extract, paragraph, piece, quotation, reading, section; crossing, journey, tour, trek, trip, voyage

**passing** *adj* brief, ephemeral, fleeting, momentary, short, transient, transitory; casual, cursory, quick, short, slight, superficial

**passion** ardour, emotion, feeling, fervour, fire, heat, intensity, spirit, zeal; ardour, desire, love, lust; bug *Inf*, craze, enthusiasm, fascination, infatuation, mania, obsession

**passionate** amorous, ardent, erot-

**passport** *n* official document granting permission to travel abroad etc.

**password** *n* secret word to ensure admission etc.

**past** *adj* ended; gone by; elapsed ~*n* bygone times ~*adv* by; along ~*prep* beyond; after

**pasta** *n* any of several preparations of dough, e.g. spaghetti

**paste** *n* soft mixture; adhesive ~*v* fasten with paste **pasting** *n Sl* defeat; strong criticism **pasty** *adj* like paste; white; sickly

**pastel** *n* coloured crayon; drawing with crayons; pale, delicate colour ~*adj* (of colour) pale

**pasteurize** *v* sterilize by heat

**pastiche** *n* work of art that mixes or copies styles

**pastille** *n* lozenge

**pastime** *n* recreation

**pastor** *n* clergyman **pastoral** *adj* of rural life; of pastor

**pastry** *n* article of food made chiefly of flour, fat and water

**pasture** *n* ground on which cattle

**graze** ~*v* (cause to) graze

**pasty** *n* small pie of meat and crust, baked without a dish

**pat¹** *v* patting, patted tap ~*n* tap; small mass, as of butter

**pat²** *adv* exactly; fluently

**patch** *n* piece of cloth sewed on garment; spot; plot of ground ~*v* mend; repair clumsily **patchy** *adj* of uneven quality **patchwork** *n* needlework of different pieces sewn together

**pate** *n* head; top of head

**pâté** *n* spread of finely minced liver etc.

**patent** *n* exclusive right to invention ~*adj* open; evident ~*v* secure a patent **patently** *adv* obviously

**paternal** *adj* fatherly; of a father **paternity** *n* fatherhood

**path** *n* way, track; course of action

**pathetic** *adj* moving to pity

**pathology** *n* science of diseases **pathological** *adj* **pathologist** *n*

**pathos** *n* power of exciting tender emotions

**patient** *adj* bearing troubles calmly

ic, hot, loving, lustful, sensual; ardent, emotional, fervent, fierce, impassioned, intense, strong, vehement, wild

**passive** compliant, docile, inactive, inert, quiescent, submissive

**past** *adj* completed, done, elapsed, ended, finished, gone, over; ancient, bygone, erstwhile, former, late, olden, previous ~*n* background, experience, history, life

**pastel** delicate, light, pale, soft

**pastiche** blend, hotchpotch, medley, *mélange,* miscellany, mixture

**pastime** activity, amusement, diversion, entertainment, game, hobby, recreation, sport

**pastoral** *adj* rural, rustic, simple; clerical, ecclesiastical, ministerial, priestly

**pat** *v* dab, slap, stroke, tap ~*n* clap, dab, light blow, slap, stroke, tap

**patch** *n* bit, scrap, shred, spot; area, ground, land, plot, tract

**patent** *adj* apparent, clear, conspicuous, downright, evident, manifest, obvious, open, unmistakable ~*n* copyright, licence

**path** footway, track, trail; avenue, course, direction, passage, road, route, way

**pathetic** affecting, moving, pitiable, poignant, sad, touching

**pathos** pitifulness, poignancy,

~*n* person under medical treatment

**patience** *n*

**patio** *n* (*pl* -**tios**) paved area adjoining house

**patriarch** *n* father and ruler of family

**patrician** *n/adj* (one) of noble birth

**patriot** *n* person that loves his or her country **patriotic** *adj* **patriotism** *n*

**patrol** *n* regular circuit by guard; person, small group patrolling ~*v* -**trolling**, -**trolled** go round on guard

**patron** *n* one who aids artists, charities etc.; regular customer; guardian saint **patronage** *n* support given by patron **patronize** *v* assume air of superiority towards; be regular customer

**patter** *n* quick succession of taps; *Inf* glib, rapid speech ~*v* make quick tapping noise

**pattern** *n* arrangement of repeated parts; design; plan for cutting cloth

etc.; model ~*v* (*with* **on** or **after**) model

**paunch** *n* belly

**pauper** *n* very poor person

**pause** *v/n* stop, rest

**pave** *v* form surface with stone **pavement** *n* paved footpath

**pavilion** *n* clubhouse on playing field etc.; building for exhibition etc.; large tent

**paw** *n* foot of animal ~*v* scrape with forefoot; maul

**pawn**[1] *v* deposit (article) as security for money borrowed **pawnbroker** *n* lender of money on goods deposited

**pawn**[2] *n* piece in chess; person used as mere tool

**pay** *v* **paying**, **paid** give money etc., for goods or services; give; be profitable to; (*with* **out**) spend ~*n* wages **payable** *adj* justly due **payee** *n* person to whom money is paid or due **payment** *n*

**PC** personal computer; Police Con-

─────── THESAURUS ───────

sadness

**patience** forbearance, sufferance, tolerance, toleration

**patient** *adj* long-suffering, philosophical, resigned, stoical, uncomplaining

**patron** advocate, backer, benefactor, champion, friend, helper, sponsor, supporter; buyer, client, customer, shopper

**patronage** aid, assistance, backing, encouragement, help, promotion, sponsorship, support

**patronize** look down on, talk down on; frequent, shop at

**pattern** *n* arrangement, decoration, design, device, figure, motif, design, diagram, guide, instructions, plan, template; example,

guide, model, norm, original, prototype, sample, specimen, standard ~*v* form, model, mould, shape, style

**pause** *v* break, cease, desist, discontinue, halt, interrupt, rest ~*n* break, breather *Inf*, gap, halt, interlude, intermission, interval, let-up *Inf*, lull, respite, rest

**pawn** *n* cat's-paw, instrument, puppet, stooge *Sl*, tool

**pay** *v* clear, compensate, discharge, foot, give, honour, meet, reimburse, requite, reward, settle; bestow, give, grant, hand out, present ~*n* earnings, fee, income, remuneration, salary, wages

**payment** discharge, paying, remittance, settlement; fee, remunera-

stable; Privy Councillor

**PE** physical education

**pea** *n* edible seed, growing in pods, of climbing plant; the plant

**peace** *n* freedom from war; harmony; calm **peaceable** *adj* disposed to peace **peaceful** *adj*

**peach** *n* fruit of delicate flavour

**peacock** *n* male bird with fanlike tail

**peak** *n* pointed end of anything, esp. hilltop; highest point

**peal** *n* (succession of) loud sound(s) ~*v* sound loudly

**peanut** *n* pea-shaped nut; *pl Inf* trifling amount of money

**pear** *n* tree yielding sweet, juicy fruit; the fruit **pear-shaped** *adj* shaped like a pear, heavier at the bottom than the top

**pearl** *n* hard, lustrous structure found esp. in oyster and used as jewel

**peasant** *n* member of low social class, esp. in rural district

**peat** *n* decomposed vegetable substance

**pebble** *n* small roundish stone

**peccadillo** *n* (*pl* **-los, -loes**) slight offence; petty crime

**peck** *v* strike with or as with beak; nibble at; *Inf* kiss quickly ~*n* pecking movement **peckish** *adj Inf* hungry

**pectoral** *adj* of the breast

**peculiar** *adj* strange; particular; belonging to **peculiarity** *n* oddity; characteristic; distinguishing feature

**pedal** *n* foot lever ~*v* **-alling, -alled** propel bicycle by using its pedals; use pedal

**pedant** *n* one who insists on petty details of book-learning, grammatical rules etc. **pedantic** *adj*

**peddle** *v* go round selling goods

**pedestal** *n* base of column

**pedestrian** *n* one who walks on foot ~*adj* going on foot; commonplace; dull **pedestrian crossing** place marked where pedestrians may cross road

**pedigree** *n* register of ancestors; genealogy

**pedlar** *n* one who sells; hawker

**peek** *v/n* peep, glance

———————— THESAURUS ————————

tion, wage

**peace** armistice, conciliation, treaty, truce; accord, agreement, concord, harmony; calm, calmness, quiet, silence, stillness, tranquillity

**peaceful** amicable, friendly, nonviolent; calm, placid, quiet, restful, serene, still, tranquil, undisturbed

**peak** *n* apex, crest, pinnacle, point, summit, tip, top; climax, crown, culmination, zenith

**peal** *n* chime, clang, clap, crash, ring, rumble ~*v* chime, crash, resonate, resound, ring, roll, rumble, toll

**peasant** countryman, hick *Inf*,

chiefly *US & Canad,* rustic, yokel

**peculiar** abnormal, bizarre, curious, eccentric, funny, odd, quaint, queer, strange, uncommon, unusual, weird

**peculiarity** abnormality, eccentricity, foible, mannerism, oddity, quirk

**pedantic** academic, fussy, hairsplitting, nit-picking *Inf*, particular, pompous, precise, punctilious

**pedestal** base, foot, plinth, stand, support

**pedigree** ancestry, blood, breed, descent, family, genealogy, heritage, line, lineage, race, stock

**peel** v strip off skin, rind or covering; flake off, as skin, rind ~n rind, skin

**peep** v look slyly or quickly ~n such a look

**peer**[1] n (fem **peeress**) nobleman; one of the same rank **peerage** n one of the same rank **peerage** n similar age, status etc.

**peerless** adj without match or equal **peer group** group of people of similar age, status etc.

**peer**[2] v look closely

**peeved** adj Inf sulky, irritated

**peevish** adj fretful; irritable

**peewit** n lapwing

**peg** n pin for joining, fastening, marking etc.; (mark of) level, standard etc. ~v **pegging, pegged** fasten with pegs; stabilize (prices); (with **away**) persevere

**pejorative** adj (of words etc.) with disparaging connotation

**pelican** n waterfowl with large pouch beneath its bill **pelican crossing** road crossing with pedestrian-operated traffic lights

**pellet** n little ball

**pelmet** n ornamental drapery or board, concealing curtain rail

**pelt**[1] v throw missiles; rain persistently; rush

**pelt**[2] n raw hide or skin

**pelvis** n bony cavity at base of human trunk **pelvic** adj

**pen**[1] n instrument for writing ~v **penning, penned** compose; write **pen friend** friend with whom one corresponds without meeting **penknife** n small knife with folding blade

**pen**[2] n/v **penning, penned** (put in) enclosure

**penal** adj of punishment **penalize** v impose penalty on **penalty** n punishment; forfeit; Sport handicap

**penance** n suffering submitted to as expression of penitence

**pence** n pl of PENNY

**penchant** n inclination, decided taste

**pencil** n instrument, esp. of graphite, for writing etc. ~v -**cilling**, -**cilled** draw; mark with pencil

**pendant** n hanging ornament **pendent** adj hanging

**pending** prep during, until ~adj awaiting settlement; imminent

**pendulous** adj hanging, swinging **pendulum** n suspended weight swinging to and fro

**penetrate** v enter into; pierce; arrive at meaning of **penetrating** adj sharp; easily heard; quick to under-

─────────── T H E S A U R U S ───────────

**peel** flake off, pare, scale, skin, strip off

**peer**[1] n aristocrat, noble, nobleman; equal, fellow

**peer**[2] v gaze, inspect, scan

**peerless** incomparable, matchless, unequalled, unrivalled

**peevish** cantankerous, cross, crotchety Inf, fractious, grumpy, irritable, querulous, snappy, testy, touchy

**pelt** batter, bombard, cast, hurl, shower, sling, throw

**pen** n cage, coop, enclosure, fold, hutch, sty ~v cage, coop up, enclose, fence in

**penal** corrective, disciplinary, punitive

**penalize** discipline, handicap, punish

**penalty** fine, forfeit, handicap, price, punishment

**penance** atonement, reparation

**penchant** bent, bias, fondness, inclination, leaning, liking, partiality, propensity, taste, tendency

stand **penetration** n
**penguin** n flightless bird
**penicillin** n antibiotic drug
**peninsula** n portion of land nearly surrounded by water **peninsular** adj
**penis** n male organ of copulation and urination
**penitent** adj affected by sense of guilt ~n one that repents **penitence** n sorrow for sin **penitentiary** adj ~n US prison
**pennant** n long narrow flag
**pennon** n small pointed flag
**penny** n (pl **pence**, **pennies**) Brit. bronze coin, 100th part of pound **penniless** adj having no money
**pension** n regular payment to old people, soldiers etc. ~v grant pension to **pensioner** n
**pensive** adj thoughtful
**pent** adj shut up, kept in
**pentacle**, **pentagram** n five-pointed star
**pentagon** n figure with five angles
**penthouse** n apartment, flat on top of building
**penultimate** adj next before the last
**penury** n extreme poverty

**peony** n plant with showy red, pink, or white flowers
**people** pl n persons generally, nation; race; family ~v populate
**pep** n Inf vigour; energy ~v **pepping**, **pepped** give energy, enthusiasm **pep talk** Inf talk designed to increase confidence, enthusiasm etc.
**pepper** n pungent aromatic spice; slightly pungent vegetable ~v season with pepper; sprinkle; pelt with missiles **peppermint** n plant noted for aromatic pungent liquor distilled from it; sweet flavoured with this
**per** prep for each; by; in manner of
**perambulate** v walk through or over; walk about **perambulator** n pram
**per annum** Lat by the year
**per capita** Lat for each person
**perceive** v obtain knowledge of through senses; understand **perceptible** adj **perception** n **perceptive** adj
**percentage** n proportion or rate per hundred **per cent** in each hundred
**perch¹** n freshwater fish

———————— THESAURUS ————————

**penetrate** bore, enter, go through, pierce, stab
**penitent** adj apologetic, contrite, regretful, remorseful, repentant, sorry
**penniless** broke Inf, destitute, down and out, impoverished, indigent, poor, poverty-stricken, skint Brit sl
**pension** allowance, annuity, benefit, superannuation
**pensive** contemplative, dreamy, meditative, musing, preoccupied, reflective, thoughtful
**people** pl n humanity, mankind,

persons; citizens, clan, community, family, folk, nation, population, public, race, tribe ~v colonize, inhabit, occupy, populate, settle
**perceive** discern, discover, note, notice, observe, recognize, remark, see, spot
**perceptible** apparent, appreciable, clear, detectable, discernible, evident, noticeable, observable, recognizable, visible
**perception** awareness, consciousness, discernment, feeling, idea, impression, insight, recognition, sensation, sense, understanding

**perch²** *n* resting place, as for bird ~v place, as on perch; alight on branch etc.; balance on

**perchance** *adv Obs* perhaps

**percolate** *v* pass through fine mesh as liquor; filter **percolator** *n* coffeepot with filter

**percussion** *n* striking of one thing against another

**peregrine** *n* type of falcon

**peremptory** *adj* imperious

**perennial** *adj* lasting through the years; perpetual ~n plant lasting more than two years

**perfect** *adj* complete; unspoilt; correct, precise; excellent ~v improve; make skilful **perfection** *n* **perfectionist** *n* one who demands highest standards **perfectly** *adv*

**perfidy** *n* treachery, disloyalty **perfidious** *adj*

**perforate** *v* make holes in, penetrate **perforation** *n*

**perform** *v* fulfil; function; act part; play, as on musical instrument **performance** *n*

**perfume** *n* agreeable scent ~v imbue with an agreeable odour

**perfunctory** *adj* done indifferently

**perhaps** *adv* possibly

**peril** *n* danger; exposure to injury **perilous** *adj*

**perimeter** *n* outer boundary of area; length of this

**period** *n* particular portion of time; series of years; single occurrence of menstruation; full stop ~*adj* (of furniture, dress etc.) belonging to a particular time in history **periodic** *adj* recurring at regular intervals **periodical** *adj* periodic ~n publication issued at regular intervals **periodic table** *Chem* chart showing relationship of elements to each other

——————— THESAURUS ———————

**perceptive** acute, alert, astute, discerning, observant, quick, sharp

**perch** *v* alight, balance, land, rest, roost, settle, sit on

**perennial** abiding, constant, continual, enduring, incessant, lasting, persistent, recurrent

**perfect** *adj* absolute, complete, consummate, finished, full, sheer, utter, whole; faultless, flawless, ideal, immaculate, impeccable, pure, spotless, unspoilt, untarnished ~v develop, hone, improve, polish, refine

**perfection** achievement, completion, consummation, fulfilment; completeness, exactness, faultlessness, purity, wholeness

**perform** accomplish, achieve, act, carry out, complete, discharge, do, effect, execute, fulfil, function, work; act, play

**performance** accomplishment, achievement, act, carrying out, completion, discharge, execution, fulfilment; acting, appearance, gig *Inf*, play, portrayal, production, show

**perfume** aroma, bouquet, fragrance, odour, scent, smell

**perfunctory** careless, cursory, indifferent, negligent, offhand, superficial

**perhaps** maybe, perchance *Arch*, possibly

**peril** danger, hazard, jeopardy, menace, risk

**perimeter** border, boundary, bounds, circumference, confines, edge, limit, margin

**period** interval, season, space, spell, term, time, while

**periodical** *n* journal, magazine, paper, publication, serial

**peripatetic** *adj* travelling about

**periphery** *n* circumference; outside **peripheral** *adj* unimportant

**periscope** *n* instrument used for giving view of objects on different level

**perish** *v* die; rot **perishable** *adj* that will not last long **perishing** *adj Inf* very cold

**perjure** *v* be guilty of perjury **perjury** *n* crime of false testimony on oath

**perk** *n* incidental benefit from employment

**perky** *adj* lively, cheerful

**perm** *n* long-lasting curly hairstyle ~*v* give a perm

**permanent** *adj* continuing in same state; lasting **permanence** *n*

**permeate** *v* pervade; pass through pores of **permeable** *adj*

**permit** *v* -mitting, -mitted allow; give leave to ~*n* warrant or licence to do something **permissible** *adj*

**permission** *n* **permissive** *adj* (too) tolerant, esp. sexually

**permutation** *n Maths* arrangement of a number of quantities in every possible order

**pernicious** *adj* wicked; harmful

**pernickety** *adj Inf* fussy

**peroxide** *n short for* HYDROGEN PEROX-IDE

**perpendicular** *adj/n* (line) at right angles to another; (something) exactly upright

**perpetrate** *v* perform or be responsible for (something bad)

**perpetual** *adj* continuous; lasting forever **perpetuate** *v* make perpetual; not to allow to be forgotten **perpetuity** *n*

**perplex** *v* puzzle; bewilder **perplexity** *n*

**persecute** *v* oppress because of race, religion etc. **persecution** *n*

**persevere** *v* persist, maintain effort **perseverance** *n*

———— THESAURUS ————

**perish** be killed, die, expire, lose one's life, pass away; decay, decompose, rot, waste

**perjury** false statement, forswearing, oath breaking

**permanent** abiding, constant, durable, enduring, eternal, everlasting, fixed, immutable, invariable, lasting, perpetual, persistent, stable, unchanging

**permeate** fill, impregnate, penetrate, pervade, saturate

**permissible** acceptable, allowable, all right, authorized, lawful, legal, legitimate, O.K. *or* okay *Inf*, permitted

**permission** assent, authorization, consent, freedom, go-ahead *Inf*, green light, leave, licence, permit, sanction

**permissive** free, lax, liberal, tolerant

**permit** *v* agree, allow, authorize, consent, give leave *or* permission, let, license, sanction ~*n* licence, pass, passport, warrant

**perpetrate** carry out, commit, do, execute, perform

**perpetual** abiding, endless, enduring, eternal, everlasting, immortal, lasting, perennial, permanent

**perpetuate** maintain, preserve, sustain

**perplex** baffle, bewilder, confound, confuse, mystify, puzzle, stump

**persecute** harass, ill-treat, maltreat, oppress, torment, victimize

**perseverance** dedication, determination, doggedness, persistence,

**persist** v continue in spite of obstacles or objections **persistence** n **persistent** adj

**person** n individual (human) being; body of human being; *Grammar* classification of pronouns and verb forms according to the person speaking, spoken to, or of **personable** adj pleasant in looks and personality **personal** adj individual, private; of grammatical person **personality** n distinctive character; celebrity **personally** adv independently; in one's own opinion **personal computer** small computer for word processing or computer games **personal stereo** portable cassette player with headphones

**persona** n (pl **-nae**) someone's personality as presented to others

**personify** v **-fying, -fied** represent as person; typify **personification** n

**personnel** n staff employed in organization

**perspective** n mental view; method of drawing on flat surface to give effect of relative distances and sizes

**Perspex** n *Trademark* transparent acrylic substitute for glass

**perspicacious** adj having quick mental insight

**perspire** v sweat **perspiration** n

**persuade** v make (one) do something by argument, charm etc.; convince **persuasion** n art, act of persuading; belief **persuasive** adj

**pert** adj forward, saucy

**pertain** v belong, relate, have reference (to)

**pertinacious** adj persistent

**pertinent** adj to the point **pertinence** n relevance

**perturb** v disturb; alarm

**peruse** v read in careful or leisurely manner **perusal** n

**pervade** v spread through **pervasive** adj

**pervert** v turn to wrong use; lead

———————— THESAURUS ————————

resolution, tenacity

**persevere** carry on, continue, go on, keep going, maintain, persist

**persist** continue, persevere; carry on, continue, keep up, last, remain

**persistence** doggedness, endurance, perseverance, tenacity

**persistent** determined, dogged, persevering, pertinacious, tenacious

**person** being, body, human, individual, soul

**personal** individual, own, particular, private, special

**personality** character, disposition, make-up, nature, temperament; celebrity, household name, star

**personification** embodiment, epitome, incarnation, representation

**personify** embody, epitomize, rep-

resent, symbolize, typify

**personnel** employees, people, staff, workers

**perspective** angle, attitude, context, outlook, way of looking

**persuade** coax, entice, induce, influence, prompt, sway, urge, win over

**persuasive** cogent, compelling, convincing, forceful, logical, moving, sound, telling, weighty

**pertain** apply, befit, belong, concern, regard, relate

**pertinent** apposite, appropriate, apt, fit, fitting, germane, material, relevant

**perturb** agitate, alarm, disquiet, disturb, fluster, trouble, unsettle, upset, vex

**pervade** fill, imbue, infuse, pen-

astray ~n one who practises sexual perversion **perverse** adj obstinately or unreasonably wrong; wayward **perversion** n sexual act considered abnormal; corruption **perversity** n

**peseta** n Spanish monetary unit

**pessimism** n tendency to see worst side of things **pessimist** n **pessimistic** adj

**pest** n troublesome or harmful thing, person or insect **pesticide** n chemical for killing pests, esp. insects

**pester** v vex; harass

**pestilence** n epidemic disease

**pestle** n instrument with which things are pounded

**pet** n animal or person kept or regarded with affection ~adj favourite ~v **petting, petted** make pet of; Inf fondle

**petal** n white or coloured leaflike part of flower

**peter** v peter out Inf lose power

gradually

**petite** adj small, dainty

**petition** n request, esp. to sovereign or parliament ~v present petition to

**petrel** n sea bird

**petrify** v **-fying, -fied** turn to stone; make motionless with fear

**petroleum** n mineral oil **petrol** n refined petroleum as used in motorcars etc.

**petticoat** n woman's underskirt

**pettifogging** adj overconcerned with unimportant detail

**petty** adj unimportant; small-minded **petty cash** cash kept to pay minor expenses **petty officer** non-commissioned officer in navy

**petulant** adj irritable; peevish

**petunia** n garden plant

**pew** n fixed seat in church

**pewter** n greyish alloy of tin and lead

**phallus** n (pl **-luses, -li**) penis; sym-

——————— THESAURUS ———————

etrate, permeate, spread through, suffuse

**perverse** contrary, obstinate, pig-headed, stiff-necked, stubborn, wayward

**perversion** aberration, abnormality, deviation, kink Brit inf, kinkiness Sl

**pervert** v distort, misuse, twist, warp; corrupt, debase, debauch, degrade, deprave, lead astray ~n degenerate, deviant

**pessimism** cynicism, gloom, hopelessness

**pessimist** cynic, defeatist, wet blanket Inf, worrier

**pessimistic** bleak, cynical, gloomy, glum, hopeless

**pest** annoyance, bother, drag Inf, irritation, nuisance; bane, blight,

curse, plague

**pester** aggravate Inf, annoy, badger, bother, bug Inf, harass, nag, plague, torment

**pet** n darling, favourite ~adj favourite, preferred, special ~v coddle, cosset, pamper, spoil; caress, fondle, pat, stroke

**petition** n appeal, entreaty, plea, prayer, request, supplication ~v adjure, appeal, ask, beg, beseech, entreat, plead, pray

**petty** inconsiderable, insignificant, negligible, paltry, slight, small, trifling, trivial, unimportant; cheap, mean, shabby, small-minded, ungenerous

**petulant** bad-tempered, cross, huffy, irritable, moody, peevish, querulous, sulky, sullen

bol of it used in primitive rites **phallic** adj

**phantom** n apparition; ghost

**Pharaoh** n title of ancient Egyptian kings

**pharmaceutical** adj of drugs or pharmacy **pharmacist** n person qualified to dispense drugs **pharmacology** n study of drugs **pharmacy** n preparation and dispensing of drugs; dispensary

**phase** n distinct stage in development **phase in, out** introduce or discontinue gradually

**PhD** Doctor of Philosophy

**pheasant** n game bird

**phenomenon** n (pl **phenomena**) anything observed; remarkable person or thing **phenomenal** adj

**phial** n small bottle

**philanthropy** n practice of doing good to one's fellow men **philanthropic** adj **philanthropist** n

**philately** n stamp collecting **philatelist** n

**philistine** n/adj ignorant (person)

**philosophy** n study of realities and general principles; system of theories on nature of things or on conduct **philosopher** n **philosophi-cal** adj of, like philosophy; wise, learned; calm, stoical

**phlegm** n thick yellowish substance formed in throat **phlegmatic** adj not easily agitated

**phobia** n fear or aversion

**phoenix** n legendary bird

**phone** n telephone; telephone call; v telephone **phonecard** n card used to operate some public telephones

**phonetic** adj of vocal sounds **phonetics** pl n (with sing v) science of vocal sounds

**phoney** Inf adj sham; suspect ~n phoney person or thing

**phosphorus** n nonmetallic element which appears luminous in the dark **phosphate** n compound of phosphorus **phosphorescence** n faint glow in the dark

**photo** n Inf photograph

**photocopy** n photographic reproduction ~v make photocopy of

**photogenic** adj tending to look attractive when photographed

**photograph** n picture made by chemical action of light on sensitive film ~v take photograph of **photographer** n **photographic** adj **photography** n

━━━━━━━ T H E S A U R U S ━━━━━━━

**phantom** apparition, ghost, phantasm, spectre, spirit

**phase** chapter, juncture, period, point, stage, step, time

**phenomenal** extraordinary, marvellous, miraculous, outstanding, prodigious, remarkable, sensational

**phenomenon** marvel, prodigy, rarity, sensation, wonder

**philanthropist** benefactor, humanitarian

**philistine** n boor, ignoramus, lout, lowbrow ~adj anti-intellectual, boorish, crass, ignorant, lowbrow, tasteless, uncultured, unrefined

**philosophical** calm, collected, composed, cool, imperturbable, resigned, stoical, unruffled

**philosophy** knowledge, reason, reasoning, thinking, thought, wisdom

**phobia** aversion, detestation, dread, fear, hatred, horror, loathing, revulsion, terror

**phoney** adj bogus, counterfeit, fake, false, forged, imitation, pseudo Inf, sham ~n counterfeit, fake, forgery, fraud, humbug, impostor,

**photosynthesis** *n* process by which green plant uses sun's energy to make carbohydrates

**phrase** *n* group of words; expression ~*v* express in words **phraseology** *n* choice of words

**physics** *pl n* (with *sing v*) science of properties of matter and energy **physical** *adj* bodily, as opposed to mental; material **physician** *n* qualified medical practitioner **physicist** *n* one skilled in, or student of, physics

**physiognomy** *n* face

**physiology** *n* science of living things

**physiotherapy** *n* therapeutic use of physical means, as massage etc. **physiotherapist** *n*

**physique** *n* bodily structure, constitution

**pi** *n* (*pl* **pis**) *Maths* ratio of circumference of circle to its diameter

**piano** *n* (*pl* **pianos**) musical instrument with keyboard ~*adj/adv Mus* softly **pianist** *n* performer on piano

**piazza** *n* square

**pic** *n* (*pl* **pics**, **pix**) *Inf* photograph or illustration

**picador** *n* mounted bullfighter with lance

**piccalilli** *n* pickle of vegetables in mustard sauce

**piccolo** *n* (*pl* **-los**) small flute

**pick**[1] *v* choose, select carefully; pluck, gather; find occasion for **~n** act of picking; choicest part **pick on** find fault with **pickpocket** *n* thief who steals from someone's pocket **pick up** lift; obtain; collect; get better; accelerate **pick-up** *n* small truck; device for conversion of mechanical energy into electric signals

**pick**[2] *n* tool with curved iron crossbar **pickaxe** *n* pick

**picket** *n* pointed stake; party of trade unionists posted to deter would-be workers during strike ~*v* post as picket

**pickle** *n* food preserved in brine, vinegar etc.; awkward situation ~*v* preserve in pickle

**picnic** *n* pleasure excursion including meal out of doors ~*v* **picnicking**, **picnicked** take part in picnic

**picture** *n* drawing or painting; mental image; film, movie; *pl* cinema ~*v* represent in, or as in, a picture **pictorial** *adj* of, in, with pictures ~*n* newspaper with pictures **picturesque** *adj* visually striking, vivid

**pidgin** *n* language made up of two

pretender, sham

**photograph** *n* photo *Inf*, picture, shot, slide, snap *Inf*, snapshot ~*v* film, record, shoot, snap *Inf*

**phrase** *n* expression, idiom, saying ~*v* couch, express, frame, put, put into words, say, word

**physical** bodily, corporal, corporeal, fleshly; material, real, solid, substantial, tangible

**physique** body, build, figure, form, frame, shape

**pick** *v* choose, decide upon, opt for,

select, single out; collect, gather, harvest, pluck, pull ~*n* choice, option, preference, selection; cream, elect, elite

**pick on** bait, bully, tease, torment

**pick up** hoist, lift, raise, take up, uplift; buy, obtain, purchase; call for, collect, get

**picture** *n* drawing, illustration, image, likeness, painting, photograph, portrait, print, representation, sketch; account, depiction, description, image; film, movie ~*v* see,

or more other languages

**pie** *n* baked dish of meat, fruit etc. usu. with pastry crust

**piebald** *adj* irregularly marked with black and white **pied** *adj* piebald; variegated

**piece** *n* bit, part, fragment; single object; literary or musical composition etc. ~*v* mend, put together **piecemeal** *adv* by, in, or into pieces, a bit at a time

**pier** *n* structure running into sea; piece of solid upright masonry

**pierce** *v* make hole in; make a way through **piercing** *adj* shrill; alert, probing

**piety** *n* godliness; devoutness

**pig** *n* wild or domesticated mammal killed for pork, ham, bacon; *Inf* greedy, dirty person **piggish, piggy** *adj* **pig-headed** *adj* obstinate

**pigeon** *n* bird of wild and domesticated varieties **pigeonhole** *n* compartment for papers in desk etc. ~*v* defer; classify

**piggyback** *n* ride on the back

**pigment** *n* colouring matter, paint or dye

**pigmy** *see* PYGMY

**pigtail** *n* plait of hair on either side of head

**pike¹** *n* predatory freshwater fish

**pike²** *n* long-handled spear

**pilau, pilaf** *n* Oriental dish of meat or fowl boiled with rice, spices etc.

**pilchard** *n* small sea fish like herring

**pile¹** *v* heap (up); (with **in, out, off** etc.) crowd ~*n* heap **pile-up** *n* *Inf* traffic accident with several vehicles

**pile²** *n* beam driven into the ground, esp. as foundation

**pile³** *n* nap of cloth

**piles** *pl n* haemorrhoids

**pilfer** *v* steal small items

**pilgrim** *n* one who journeys to sacred place **pilgrimage** *n*

**pill** *n* small ball of medicine swallowed whole **the pill** oral contraceptive

**pillage** *v/n* plunder

**pillar** *n* upright support; strong supporter **pillar box** red pillar-shaped letter box

**pillion** *n* seat behind rider of

———————— THESAURUS ————————

visualize

**picturesque** attractive, beautiful, charming, pretty, scenic, striking, vivid

**piebald** black and white, dappled, pied

**piece** bit, chunk, division, fraction, fragment, morsel, part, portion, scrap, section, segment, shred, slice; article, composition, item, study, work

**pierce** bore, drill, enter, penetrate, puncture, stab, transfix

**piercing** *usu. of sound* ear-splitting, high-pitched, penetrating, sharp, shrill, alert, keen, penetrat-

ing, sharp, shrewd

**piety** devotion, faith, godliness, holiness, religion, reverence, veneration

**pig-headed** inflexible, obstinate, perverse, self-willed, stiff-necked, stubborn, unyielding, wilful

**pigment** colour, dye, paint, stain, tint

**pile** *n* accumulation, heap, mass, mound, mountain, stack ~*v* accumulate, amass, heap, mass, stack

**pile-up** accident, collision, crash, smash

**pill** capsule, pellet, tablet

**pillage** *v* loot, plunder, raid, ran-

motorcycle or horse

**pillory** *n* frame with holes for head and hands in which offender was confined ~*v* **pillorying, pilloried** expose to ridicule and abuse

**pillow** *n* cushion for the head, esp. in bed **pillowcase** *n* removable cover for pillow

**pilot** *n* person qualified to fly an aircraft or spacecraft; one qualified to take charge of ship entering or leaving harbour etc.; guide ~*adj* experimental and preliminary ~*v* act as pilot to; steer **pilot light** small flame lighting main one in gas appliance

**pimento** or **pimiento** *n* (*pl* -**tos**) allspice; sweet red pepper

**pimp** *n* one who solicits for prostitute ~*v* act as pimp

**pimpernel** *n* plant with small scarlet, blue, or white flowers

**pimple** *n* small pus-filled spot on skin **pimply** *adj*

**pin** *n* piece of stiff wire with point and head, for fastening; wooden or metal peg or rivet ~*v* **pinning, pinned** fasten with pin; seize and hold fast **pinpoint** *v* identify exactly

**pinstripe** *n* very narrow stripe in fabric **pin-up** *n* picture of sexually attractive person

**pinafore** *n* apron; dress with bib top

**pincers** *pl n* tool for gripping; claws of lobster etc.

**pinch** *v* nip, squeeze; stint; *Inf* steal; *Inf* arrest ~*n* nip; small amount; emergency

**pine**[1] *n* evergreen coniferous tree; its wood

**pine**[2] *v* yearn; waste away with grief etc.

**pineapple** *n* tropical plant bearing large edible fruit

**pinion** *n* bird's wing ~*v* confine by binding wings, arms etc.

**pink** *n* pale red colour; garden plant; best condition ~*adj* of the colour pink ~*v* pierce; cut indented edge; (of engine) knock

**pinnacle** *n* highest point; mountain peak; pointed turret

**pint** *n* liquid measure; 1/8 gallon (.568 litre)

**pioneer** *n* explorer; early settler; originator ~*v* act as pioneer

**pious** *adj* devout; self-righteous

sack, sack, strip ~*n* plunder, sack

**pillar** column, post, prop, shaft, support, upright; mainstay, rock, supporter, upholder

**pilot** airman, aviator, helmsman, steersman ~*adj* model, test, trial ~*v* control, direct, drive, fly, guide, handle, manage, operate, steer

**pimple** boil, pustule, spot, zit *Sl*

**pin** *v* affix, attach, fasten, fix, secure; fix, hold fast, immobilize, pinion

**pinch** *v* nip, press, squeeze ~*n* nip, squeeze; dash, jot, mite, *soupçon*, speck; crisis, difficulty, emergency,

plight, predicament

**pine** (*oft. with* for) ache, crave, eat one's heart out over, hanker, hunger for, long, yearn; decline, fade, languish, waste

**pinnacle** apex, crest, crown, height, peak, summit, top, zenith

**pinpoint** define, distinguish, identify, locate

**pioneer** *n* colonist, explorer, settler; developer, founder, originator ~*v* create, develop, establish, initiate, institute, invent, originate

**pious** devout, God-fearing, godly, holy, religious, righteous, saintly

**pip¹** n seed in fruit

**pip²** n high-pitched sound as time signal on radio; spot on cards, dice etc.; *Inf* star on junior officer's shoulder showing rank

**pipe** n tube of metal or other material; tube with small bowl at end for smoking tobacco; musical instrument; *pl* bagpipes ~v play on pipe; utter in shrill tone; convey by pipe; ornament with piping **piper** n **piping** n system of pipes; decoration of icing on cake; fancy edging on clothes **pipeline** n long pipe for transporting oil, water etc.

**piquant** *adj* pungent

**pique** n feeling of injury ~v hurt pride of; irritate

**piranha** n fierce tropical Amer. fish

**pirate** n sea robber; publisher etc. who infringes copyright; person broadcasting illegally ~v use or reproduce (artistic work etc.) illicitly **piracy** n

**pirouette** n/v (perform) act of spinning round on toe

**pistachio** n (pl -os) small hard-shelled, sweet-tasting nut

**piste** n ski slope

**pistol** n small firearm for one hand

**piston** n in engine, cylindrical part propelled to and fro in hollow cylinder

**pit** n deep hole in ground; mine or its shaft; depression; part of theatre occupied by orchestra; servicing area on motor-racing track ~v **pitting, pitted** to set to fight; match; mark with small dents **pitfall** n hidden danger

**pitch¹** v throw; set up; set the key of (a tune); fall headlong ~n act of pitching; degree, height, intensity; slope; degree of highness or lowness of sound; *Sport* field of play **pitchfork** n fork for lifting hay etc. ~v throw with, as with, pitchfork

**pitch²** n dark sticky substance obtained from tar or turpentine

**pitcher** n large jug

**pith** n tissue in stems and branches of certain plants; essential part **pithy** *adj* terse, concise; consisting of pith

**pittance** n small amount of money

**pituitary** *adj* of, pert. to, endocrine

———————— THESAURUS ————————

**pipe** n conduit, duct, hose, line, main, tube

**pique** n huff, hurt feelings, offence, resentment, umbrage, wounded pride ~v affront, annoy, irk, mortify, nettle, offend, sting, wound

**pirate** v copy, crib *Inf*, plagiarize, poach, reproduce, steal

**pit** n abyss, cavity, chasm, crater, hole, hollow, pothole

**pitch** v cast, chuck *Inf*, fling, heave, hurl, sling, throw, toss; erect, put up, set up ~n degree, height, level, point, summit; angle, dip, gradient, incline, slope, tilt

**piteous** affecting, distressing, heartbreaking, heart-rending, moving, pathetic, pitiable, pitiful, poignant, sad

**pitfall** catch, danger, hazard, peril, snag, trap

**pitiful** distressing, heartbreaking, heart-rending, pathetic, piteous, pitiable, sad, wretched; contemptible, despicable, insignificant, low, mean, miserable, paltry, sorry, worthless

**pitiless** callous, cold-blooded, cold-hearted, cruel, hardhearted, harsh, heartless, merciless, ruthless, unmerciful

**pittance** chicken feed *Sl*, peanuts

gland at base of brain

**pity** n sympathy for others' suffering; regrettable fact ~v **pitying**, **pitied** feel pity for **piteous** adj **pitiful** adj woeful; contemptible **pitiless** adj feeling no pity; hard, merciless

**pivot** n shaft or pin on which thing turns ~v furnish with pivot; hinge on one

**pixie** n fairy

**pizza** n baked disc of dough covered with savoury topping

**pizzicato** adv/adj Mus played by plucking strings with finger

**pl.** place; plate; plural

**placard** n notice for posting up or carrying poster

**placate** v pacify, appease

**place** n locality, spot; position; duty; town, village, residence, buildings; employment; seat, space ~v put in particular place; identify; make (order, bet etc.)

**placebo** n (pl **-bos, -boes**) inactive

substance given to patient in place of active drug

**placenta** n (pl **-tas, -tae**) organ formed in uterus during pregnancy, providing nutrients for fetus; afterbirth

**placid** adj calm

**plagiarism** n presenting another's ideas, writing etc. as one's own **plagiarize** v

**plague** n highly contagious disease; Inf nuisance ~v trouble, annoy

**plaice** n flat fish

**plaid** n long Highland cloak or shawl; tartan pattern

**plain** adj flat, level; not intricate; clear, simple; candid, forthright; ordinary; without decoration; not beautiful ~n tract of level country ~adv clearly

**plaintiff** n Law one who sues in court

**plaintive** adj sad, mournful

Sl, slave wages

**pity** n clemency, compassion, condolence, sympathy, understanding ~v commiserate with, feel for, feel sorry for

**pivot** n axis, axle, fulcrum, swivel ~v revolve, rotate, spin, swivel, turn

**placate** appease, assuage, calm, mollify, pacify, propitiate

**place** n area, location, point, position, site, spot, station; district, hamlet, locale, locality, neighbourhood, quarter, region, vicinity; grade, position, rank, station, status; duty, function, responsibility, right, role; appointment, job, position, post ~v deposit, establish, fix, install, lay, locate, plant, position, put, rest, set, settle, situate, stand

**placid** calm, collected, composed,

cool, equable, even-tempered, quiet, unexcitable, unruffled

**plague** n disease, epidemic, infection, pestilence; Inf bother, hassle Inf, irritant, nuisance, pest, problem ~v annoy, badger, bother, harass, hassle Inf, pester, tease, torment, trouble

**plain** adj apparent, clear, distinct, evident, manifest, obvious, patent, unambiguous, unmistakable; artless, blunt, candid, direct, downright, forthright, frank, honest, open, outspoken, straightforward; common, commonplace, ordinary, simple, workaday; austere, bare, basic, severe, simple, stark, unadorned, unembellished; ugly, unattractive

**plaintive** doleful, grief-stricken,

**plait** n braid of hair, straw etc. ~v weave into plaits

**plan** n scheme; way of proceeding; project; drawing; map ~v **planning, planned** make plan of; arrange beforehand

**plane**[1] n smooth surface; level; tool for smoothing wood ~v make smooth with plane ~adj perfectly flat or level

**plane**[2] n aeroplane

**plane**[3] n tree with broad leaves

**planet** n heavenly body revolving round sun **planetary** adj

**planetarium** n (pl **-iums, -ia**) apparatus that shows movement of sun, moon, stars and planets by projecting lights on inside of dome

**plank** n long flat piece of timber

**plankton** n minute animal and vegetable organisms floating in ocean

**plant** n living organism without power of locomotion; building and equipment for manufacturing purposes ~v set in ground to grow; establish; Sl hide

**plantation** n estate for cultivation of tea, tobacco etc.; wood of planted trees

**plaque** n ornamental tablet; plate of brooch; deposit on teeth

**plasma** n clear, fluid portion of blood

**plaster** n mixture of lime, sand etc. for coating walls etc.; adhesive dressing for cut, wound etc. ~v apply plaster to; apply like plaster **plastered** adj Sl drunk

**plastic** n synthetic substance, easily moulded and extremely durable ~adj made of plastic; easily moulded **plastic surgery** repair, reconstruction of part of body for medical or cosmetic reasons

**Plasticine** n Trademark modelling material like clay

**plate** n shallow round dish; flat thin sheet of metal, glass etc.; utensils of gold or silver; device for printing illustration in book; device to straighten children's teeth; Inf denture ~v cover with thin coating of metal

**plateau** n (pl **-eaus, -eaux**) tract of level high land; period of stability

**platform** n raised level surface, stage; raised area in station from which passengers board trains

**platinum** n white heavy malleable metal

**platitude** n commonplace remark

**platonic** adj (of love) purely spiritual, friendly

——————— T H E S A U R U S ———————

melancholy, mournful, pathetic, piteous, sad, sorrowful, woebegone, woeful

**plan** n design, method, plot, procedure, programme, project, proposal, proposition, scheme, strategy, system; blueprint, chart, diagram, drawing, map, representation, sketch ~v arrange, contrive, design, devise, draft, formulate, organize, outline, plot, scheme, think out

**plane** adj even, flat, flush, horizontal, level, regular, smooth

**plant** v scatter, seed, set out, sow, transplant

**plaster** v coat, cover, smear, spread

**plastic** adj flexible, mouldable, pliable, pliant, soft, supple

**plate** dish, platter; layer, panel, sheet

**platform** dais, podium, rostrum, stage, stand

**platoon** n body of soldiers employed as unit

**platter** n flat dish

**platypus** also **duck-billed platypus** n Aust. egg-laying amphibious mammal

**plaudit** n act of applause

**plausible** adj apparently reasonable; persuasive

**play** v amuse oneself; contend with in game; take part in (game); trifle; act the part of; perform (music); perform on (instrument) ~n dramatic piece or performance; sport; amusement; activity; free movement; gambling **player** n lively **playboy** n rich man who lives for pleasure **playing card** one of set of 52 cards **playing fields** extensive piece of ground for open-air games **playwright** n author of plays

**plaza** n open space or square

**plc** public limited company

**plea** n entreaty; statement of prisoner or defendant; excuse **plead** v **pleading, pleaded** or US, Scots **pled** make earnest appeal; address court of law; bring forward as excuse or plea

**please** v be agreeable to; gratify; delight; be willing ~adv word of request **pleasant** adj pleasing, agreeable **pleasantry** n joke, humour **pleased** adj pleasing **pleasurable** adj giving pleasure **pleasure** n enjoyment; satisfaction

**pleat** n fold made by doubling material ~v make into pleats

**plebeian** adj/n (one) of the common people

**plectrum** n (pl **-trums, -tra**) small implement for plucking strings of guitar etc.

**pledge** n solemn promise; thing given as security ~v promise, swear

**plenary** adj complete

**plenipotentiary** adj/n (envoy) having full powers

———————— THESAURUS ————————

**platter** dish, plate, salver, tray

**plausible** believable, credible, glib, likely, persuasive, reasonable

**play** v challenge, compete, participate, take on, take part; act, perform, portray, represent ~n comedy, drama, dramatic piece, entertainment, performance, show, stage show, tragedy; fun, humour, jest, sport; amusement, diversion, entertainment, fun, game, pastime, recreation

**playboy** lady-killer Inf, philanderer, rake, womanizer

**player** competitor, contestant, participant; instrumentalist, musician, performer

**playful** frisky, frolicsome, gay, lively, merry, mischievous

**plea** appeal, entreaty, petition, prayer, request, supplication

**plead** ask, beg, beseech, crave, entreat, implore, petition

**pleasant** agreeable, delightful, enjoyable, fine, nice, pleasurable, satisfying; affable, agreeable, amiable, charming, congenial, friendly, genial, likable, nice

**please** charm, content, delight, gladden, gratify, humour, indulge, rejoice, satisfy, suit

**pleasure** bliss, comfort, contentment, delight, enjoyment, gladness, gratification, happiness, joy, satisfaction

**pledge** n assurance, covenant, oath, promise, undertaking, vow; bail, bond, collateral, deposit, guarantee, security ~v contract, engage, promise, swear, undertake, vow

**plenitude** n abundance

**plenty** n abundance; quite enough **plenteous** adj ample **plentiful** adj

**plethora** n oversupply

**pleurisy** n inflammation of membrane lining chest and covering lungs

**pliable** adj easily bent or influenced **pliant** adj pliable

**pliers** pl n tool with hinged arms and jaws for gripping

**plight**[1] n distressing state

**plight**[2] v promise

**plimsolls** pl n rubber-soled canvas shoes

**plinth** n slab as base of column etc.

**plod** v **plodding, plodded** walk or work doggedly

**plonk**[1] v put down heavily and carelessly

**plonk**[2] n Inf cheap inferior wine

**plop** n sound of object falling into water without splash ~v fall with this sound

**plot**[1] n secret plan, conspiracy; essence of story, play etc. ~v **plotting, plotted** plan secretly; mark position of; make map of

**plot**[2] n small piece of land

**plough** n implement for turning up soil ~v turn up with plough, furrow; work at slowly **ploughman** n

**plover** n shore bird with straight bill and long pointed wings

**ploy** n manoeuvre designed to gain advantage

**pluck** v pull, pick off; strip from; sound strings of (guitar etc.) with fingers, plectrum ~n courage; sudden pull or tug **plucky** adj brave

**plug** n thing fitting into and filling hole; Electricity device connecting appliance to electricity supply; Inf favourable mention of product etc. intended to promote it ~v **plugging, plugged** stop with plug; Inf advertise product etc. by frequently mentioning it

**plum** n fruit with stone; tree bearing it; choicest part, piece, position etc. ~adj choice

**plumb** n ball of lead attached to string used for sounding, finding the perpendicular etc. ~adj perpendicular ~adv exactly; perpendicularly ~v find depth of; equip with,

**plentiful** abundant, ample, bountiful, copious, generous, lavish, liberal

**plenty** abundance, lots Inf, mass, masses, oodles Inf, quantity

**pliable** bendy, flexible, malleable, plastic, pliant, supple, impressionable, pliant, susceptible, tractable, yielding

**plight** n difficulty, dilemma, jam Inf, pickle Inf, predicament, scrape Inf, spot Inf, trouble

**plod** tramp, tread, trudge

**plot**[1] n cabal, conspiracy, intrigue, plan, scheme, stratagem; outline, story, subject, theme ~v collude,

conspire, intrigue, plan, scheme; calculate, chart, draft, draw, locate, map, mark

**plot**[2] n allotment, area, ground, lot, patch

**plough** v cultivate, dig, till, turn over

**pluck** v catch, jerk, tug, tweak, yank ~n boldness, bravery, courage, grit, guts Inf, nerve

**plucky** bold, brave, courageous, daring, game, gutsy Sl

**plug** n bung, stopper; mention, publicity, puff, push ~v bung, close, cork, seal, stop, stop up; Inf advertise, mention, publicize, puff,

connect to plumbing system
**plumber** n worker who attends to
water and sewage systems **plumbing** n trade of plumber; system of
water and sewage pipes **plumb line**
cord with plumb attached

**plume** n feather; ornament of
feathers etc. ~v furnish with
plumes; pride oneself **plumage** n
bird's feathers

**plummet** v plunge headlong ~n
plumb line

**plump¹** adj fat, rounded ~v make,
become plump

**plump²** v drop, fall abruptly;
choose

**plunder** v take by force; rob ~n
booty, spoils

**plunge** v put forcibly, throw (into);
descend suddenly ~n dive **plunger**
n suction cap to unblock drains
**plunging** adj (of neckline) cut low

**plural** adj of, denoting more than
one ~n word in its plural form **plurality** n majority

**plus** prep with addition of (usu. indicated by the sign +) ~adj positive

**plush** n fabric with long nap ~adj
luxurious

**ply¹** v plying, plied wield; work at;
supply insistently; go to and fro
regularly

**ply²** n fold or thickness; strand of

yarn **plywood** n board of thin layers
of wood glued together

**PM** prime minister

**p.m.** after noon

**PMT** premenstrual tension

**pneumatic** adj of, worked by, inflated with wind or air

**pneumonia** n inflammation of the
lungs

**PO** Post Office

**poach¹** v take (game) illegally; encroach **poacher** n

**poach²** v simmer (eggs, fish etc.)
gently in water etc.

**pocket** n small bag inserted in garment; cavity, pouch or hollow; isolated group or area ~v put into
one's pocket; appropriate ~adj
small **pocket money** small allowance, esp. for children

**pod** n long seed vessel, as of peas,
beans etc.

**podgy** adj short and fat

**podium** n (pl -diums, -dia) small
raised platform

**poem** n imaginative composition
in rhythmic lines **poet** n writer of
poems **poetic** adj **poetry** n art or
work of poet, verse

**poignant** adj moving; keen **poignancy** n

**point** n dot; punctuation mark; detail; unit of value, scoring; degree;

push, write up

**plumb** v lead, weight ~v fathom,
gauge, measure, sound

**plump** buxom, chubby, fat, podgy,
roly-poly, rotund, round, tubby

**plunder** v loot, pillage, raid, ransack, rob, sack, strip ~n booty, loot,
pillage, spoils

**plunge** v cast, descend, dive, drop,
fall, immerse, nose-dive, pitch,
plummet, throw ~n descent, dive,

drop, fall

**plus** prep added to, and, with ~adj
added, additional, extra, positive

**poach** encroach, infringe, intrude,
steal, trespass

**pocket** n bag, compartment,
pouch, receptacle

**podgy** chubby, dumpy, fat, plump,
roly-poly, rotund, tubby

**poignant** affecting, moving, pathetic, sad, touching

stage; moment; gist; purpose; special quality; sharp end; headland; direction mark on compass; movable rail changing train to other rails; power point ~v show direction or position by extending finger; direct; sharpen; fill up joints with mortar **pointed** adj sharp; direct **pointer** n indicating rod etc. used for pointing; indication; breed of gun dog **pointless** adj futile **point-blank** adj at short range; blunt; direct ~adv bluntly

**poise** n composure; self-possession; balance **poised** adj ready; showing poise

**poison** n substance harmful or fatal to living organism ~v give poison to; infect **poisonous** adj

**poke** v push, thrust with finger, stick etc.; thrust forward; pry ~n act of poking **poker** n metal rod for

poking fire **poky** adj small, confined, cramped

**poker** n card game

**pole**[1] n long, rounded piece of wood etc.

**pole**[2] n each of the ends of axis of earth or celestial sphere; each of opposite ends of magnet, electric cell etc. **polar** adj **polarize** v (cause) to form into groups with opposite views **polar bear** white bear that lives around North Pole

**poleaxe** v stun with heavy blow

**polecat** n small animal of weasel family

**police** n civil force which maintains public order ~v keep in order **policeman** n (fem **policewoman**) member of police force

**policy**[1] n course of action adopted, esp. in state affairs

**policy**[2] n insurance contract

——————— THESAURUS ———————

**point** n dot, full stop, period, stop; condition, degree, extent, stage; instant, juncture, moment, time; location, place, position, site, spot, stage; aim, design, end, goal, intent, intention, motive, object, purpose, reason; aspect, attribute, characteristic, peculiarity, quality; apex, prong, spike, spur, summit, tip ~v direct, indicate, show, signify

**point-blank** adj abrupt, blunt, direct, downright, plain ~adv bluntly, frankly, openly, plainly, straight

**pointed** adj acute, barbed, sharp; biting, cutting, direct, incisive, pertinent, sharp

**pointer** n hand, indicator, needle; advice, hint, recommendation, suggestion, tip

**pointless** adj aimless, futile, meaningless, senseless, useless, vain, worthless

**poise** n aplomb, assurance, calmness, composure, cool Sl, sangfroid, self-possession

**poised** adj all set, prepared, ready, standing by, waiting; calm, collected, composed, self-confident, self-possessed

**poison** n bane, toxin, venom ~v contaminate, infect, pollute

**poisonous** adj noxious, toxic, venomous, virulent

**poke** v/n butt, dig, hit, jab, nudge, prod, push, shove, thrust

**poky** adj confined, cramped, narrow, small, tiny

**pole** n mast, post, rod, shaft, staff, stick

**police** n constabulary, fuzz Sl, the law Inf ~v control, guard, patrol, protect, watch

**policeman** n bobby Inf, constable, cop Sl, copper Sl, officer

**polio** *also* **poliomyelitis** *n* disease affecting spinal cord, often causing paralysis

**polish** *v* make smooth and glossy; refine ~*n* shine; polishing; substance for polishing; refinement

**polite** *adj* showing regard for others in manners, speech etc.; refined, cultured

**politics** *pl n* art of government; political affairs **politic** *adj* wise, shrewd **political** *adj* of the state or its affairs **politician** *n* one engaged in politics

**polka** *n* lively dance; music for it **polka dot** one of pattern of bold spots on fabric etc.

**poll** *n* voting; counting of votes; number of votes recorded; survey of opinion ~*v* receive (votes); take votes of; vote **polling booth** voting place

**pollen** *n* fertilizing dust of flower **pollinate** *v*

**pollute** *v* make foul; corrupt **pollution** *n*

**polo** *n* game like hockey played on horseback **polo neck** (sweater with) tight turned-over collar

**poltergeist** *n* spirit believed to move furniture, throw objects around etc.

**polyester** *n* synthetic material

**polygamy** *n* custom of being married to several persons at a time **polygamist** *n*

**polygon** *n* figure with many angles or sides

**polystyrene** *n* synthetic material used esp. as rigid foam for packing etc.

**polythene** *n* tough light plastic material

**polyunsaturated** *adj* pert. to fats that do not form cholesterol in blood

**polyurethane** *n* synthetic material used esp. in paints

**pomegranate** *n* tree; its fruit with thick rind containing many seeds in red pulp

**pommel** *n* front of saddle; knob of sword hilt

**pomp** *n* splendid display or ceremony

**pompom** *n* decorative tuft of ribbon, wool, feathers etc.

**pompous** *adj* self-important; ostentatious; (of language) inflated, stilted

**pond** *n* small body of still water

**ponder** *v* muse, think over

**ponderous** *adj* heavy, unwieldy; boring

—————— THESAURUS ——————

**policy** action, approach, course, custom, practice, programme

**polish** *v* brighten, buff, burnish, clean, rub, shine, smooth; brush up, refine ~*n* brightness, brilliance, finish, gloss, lustre, sheen; class *Inf*. finesse, refinement, style, suavity, urbanity

**polite** civil, courteous, gracious, mannerly, respectful, well-behaved, well-mannered

**poll** *n* ballot, canvass, census, count, survey

**pollute** contaminate, dirty, foul, infect, poison, soil, taint; besmirch, corrupt, debase, defile, desecrate, profane, sully

**pollution** contamination, corruption, impurity, taint, uncleanness

**pompous** affected, arrogant, grandiose, ostentatious, pretentious, showy

**ponder** cogitate, consider, contemplate, deliberate, meditate, mull

**pong** n/v Inf (give off) strong unpleasant smell

**pontiff** n Pope; bishop **pontificate**
v speak dogmatically

**pontoon**[1] n flat-bottomed boat or
metal drum for use in supporting
temporary bridge

**pontoon**[2] n gambling card game

**pony** n horse of small breed **pony-
tail** n long hair tied at back of head

**poodle** n pet dog with long curly
hair

**pool**[1] n small body of still water;
deep place in river or stream; puddle; swimming pool

**pool**[2] n common fund or resources;
group of people, e.g. typists, shared
by several employers; collective
stakes in various games ~v put in
common fund

**poop** n ship's stern

**poor** adj having little money; unproductive; inadequate; inferior;
miserable, pitiful **poorly** adj in not
good health ~adv in poor manner

**pop**[1] v popping, popped (cause to)
make small explosive sound; put or
place suddenly ~n small explosive
sound **popcorn** n maize that puffs
up when roasted

**pop**[2] n/adj (music) of general appeal, esp. to young people

**Pope** n bishop of Rome and head
of R.C. Church

**poplar** n tall slender tree

**poplin** n corded fabric, usu. of cotton

**poppadom** n thin round crisp Indian bread

**poppy** n bright-flowered plant
yielding opium

**populace** n the common people

**popular** adj finding general favour;
of, by the people **popularity** n **popu-
larize** v

**populate** v fill with inhabitants
**population** n (number of) inhabitants **populous** adj thickly populated

**porcelain** n fine earthenware, china

**porch** n covered approach to entrance of building

**porcupine** n rodent covered with
long, pointed quills

**pore**[1] v study closely

**pore**[2] n minute opening, esp. in
skin **porous** adj allowing liquid to
soak through; full of pores

——————————————— THESAURUS ———————————————

over, muse, reflect, think

**pool** n bank, funds, kitty, pot; collective, consortium, group, syndicate ~v amalgamate, combine,
merge, share

**poor** broke Inf, destitute, hard up
Inf, impecunious, impoverished, indigent, needy, penniless, poverty-
stricken, skint Brit sl, stony-broke
Brit sl; deficient, inadequate, insufficient, meagre, measly, miserable,
niggardly, scanty, skimpy, sparse;
inferior, low-grade, rotten Inf, rubbishy, sorry, substandard, unsatisfactory

**pop** v bang, burst, explode, go off;
insert, push, put, shove, slip, stick,
thrust ~n bang, burst, explosion

**populace** crowd, general public,
hoi polloi, masses, multitude, people

**popular** approved, fashionable, favourite, in, in demand, in favour,
liked, sought-after, well-liked; common, current, general, prevailing,
public, universal

**populate** colonize, inhabit, occupy, settle

**population** community, folk, inhabitants, natives, people, residents

**pork** *n* pig's flesh as food

**pornography** *n* indecent literature, films etc. **pornographic** *adj*

**porpoise** *n* blunt-nosed sea mammal like dolphin

**porridge** *n* soft food of oatmeal etc. boiled in water

**port¹** *n* (town with) harbour

**port²** *n* left side of ship

**port³** *n* strong red wine

**port⁴** *n* opening in side of ship **porthole** *n* small opening or window in side of ship

**portable** *adj* easily carried

**portcullis** *n* grating above gateway that can be lowered to block entrance

**portend** *v* foretell; be an omen of **portent** *n* omen

**porter** *n* person employed to carry luggage etc.; doorkeeper

**portfolio** *n* (*pl* **-os**) flat portable case for loose papers; collection of work, shares etc.

**portico** *n* (*pl* **-coes**) porch, covered walkway

**portion** *n* part, share, helping; destiny, lot ~*v* divide into shares

**portly** *adj* bulky, stout

**portmanteau** *n* (*pl* **-teaus, -teaux**) leather suitcase, esp. one opening into two compartments

**portray** *v* make pictures of, describe **portrait** *n* likeness of (face of) individual **portraiture** *n* **portrayal** *n* act of portraying

**pose** *v* place in attitude; put forward; assume attitude; affect or pretend to be a certain character ~*n* attitude, esp. one assumed for effect

**poser** *n* puzzling question

**posh** *adj* luxurious; upper-class

**position** *n* place; situation; attitude; status; employment ~*v* place in position

**pore¹** *v* brood, dwell on, examine, peruse, ponder, read, scrutinize, study

**pore²** *n* hole, opening, orifice, outlet

**pornographic** blue, dirty, filthy, indecent, lewd, obscene, salacious, smutty

**pornography** dirt, filth, indecency, obscenity, porn *Inf*, smut

**port** anchorage, harbour, haven

**portable** handy, light, manageable, movable

**portend** augur, betoken, bode, foreshadow, foretell, herald, indicate, omen, predict

**portent** augury, forewarning, indication, omen, premonition, sign, threat, warning

**porter** bearer, carrier; caretaker, concierge, doorman, gatekeeper

**portion** bit, part, piece, section, segment; allocation, allotment, allowance, lot, quota, ration, share; helping, piece

**portrait** image, likeness, painting, photograph, picture, representation

**portray** depict, draw, illustrate, paint, picture, represent, sketch; characterize, depict, describe

**pose** *v* arrange, position, sit; advance, present, propound, put, set, state, submit (*oft.* **with as**) affect, impersonate, masquerade as, sham; posture, show off *Inf* ~*n* attitude, position, posture, stance; act, air, façade, front, masquerade, pretence

**poser** enigma, problem, puzzle, question, riddle

**position** *n* area, location, place, point, post, site, situation, spot,

**positive** *adj* sure; definite; assertive; constructive; not negative *~n* something positive

**possess** *v* own; have mastery of **possession** *n* act of possessing; ownership; *pl* things a person possesses **possessive** *adj* of, indicating possession; with excessive desire to possess, control

**possible** *adj* that can, or may, be, exist, happen or be done; worthy of consideration **possibility** *n* feasibility; chance **possibly** *adv* perhaps

**possum** *see* OPOSSUM

**post**[1] *n* upright pole to support or mark something *~v* display; stick up (on notice board etc.) **poster** *n* large advertisement

**post**[2] *n* official carrying of letters or parcels; collection or delivery of these; office; situation; place of duty; fort *~v* put into official box for carriage by post; station (soldiers etc.) in particular spot **postage** *n* charge for carrying letter

**postal** *adj* **postal order** written order for payment of sum of money **postcard** *n* stamped card sent by post **postman** *n* (*fem* **postwoman**) person who collects and delivers post **postmark** *n* official mark stamped on letters **post office** place where postal business is conducted

**post-** *comb. form* after, later than, as in **postwar**

**posterior** *adj* later, hind *~n* buttocks

**posterity** *n* later generations; descendants

**posthaste** *adv* with great speed

**posthumous** *adj* occurring after death

**postmortem** *n* medical examination of dead body

**postpone** *v* put off to later time, defer

---

whereabouts; angle, attitude, outlook, point of view, stance, standpoint, view, viewpoint; prestige, rank, reputation, status; duty, employment, job, occupation, office, place, post, situation *~v* arrange, fix, lay out, locate, place, put, set, settle, stand

**positive** assured, certain, confident, convinced, sure; absolute, actual, categorical, certain, clear-cut, conclusive, concrete, definite, firm, real; beneficial, constructive, helpful, practical, productive, useful

**possess** have, hold, own; control, dominate, hold, occupy

**possession** control, custody, hold, occupation, ownership; *pl* assets, belongings, chattels, effects, property, things

**possessive** controlling, dominating, domineering, jealous

**possibility** feasibility, likelihood, plausibility, workableness; chance, hope, liability, odds, prospect, risk

**possible** conceivable, credible, likely, potential; attainable, feasible, practicable, realizable, viable, workable; hopeful, likely, potential, promising

**possibly** maybe, perchance *Arch,* perhaps

**post**[1] *n* column, picket, pillar, pole, shaft, stake, support, upright

**post**[2] *n* collection, delivery, mail; appointment, employment, job, office, place, position, situation *~v* dispatch, mail, send, transmit; assign, establish, locate, place, position, put, situate, station

**poster** advertisement, bill, notice,

**postscript** *n* addition to letter, book

**postulate** *v* take for granted ~*n* something postulated

**posture** *n* attitude, position of body ~*v* pose

**posy** *n* bunch of flowers

**pot** *n* round vessel; cooking vessel ~*v* **potting**, **potted** put into, preserve in pot **potluck** *n* whatever is available

**potassium** *n* white metallic element

**potato** *n* (*pl* **-toes**) plant with tubers grown for food; one of these tubers

**potent** *adj* powerful, influential **potency** *n*

**potentate** *n* ruler

**potential** *adj* that might exist or act but does not now ~*n* possibility

**pothole** *n* hole in surface of road; underground cave

**potion** *n* dose of medicine or poison

**potpourri** *n* fragrant mixture of dried flower petals; medley

**potter¹** *n* maker of earthenware

vessel **pottery** *n* earthenware; where it is made; art of making it

**potter²** *v* work, act in unsystematic way

**potty¹** *adj Inf* crazy, silly

**potty²** *n* bowl used by small child as toilet

**pouch** *n* small bag; pocket ~*v* put into pouch

**poultice** *n* soft composition of mustard, kaolin etc., applied hot to sore or inflamed parts of body

**poultry** *n* domestic fowls

**pounce** *v* spring (upon) suddenly, swoop (upon) ~*n* swoop, sudden descent

**pound¹** *v* beat, thump; crush to pieces or powder; walk, run heavily

**pound²** *n* British monetary unit; unit of weight equal to 0.454 kg

**pound³** *n* enclosure for stray animals or officially removed vehicles

**pour** *v* come out in a stream, crowd etc.; flow freely; rain heavily ~*v* give out thus

**pout** *v* thrust out lips to look sulky ~*n* act of pouting

**poverty** *n* state of being poor; lack

—————— THESAURUS ——————

placard

**postpone** adjourn, defer, delay, put back, shelve, suspend

**postscript** addition, afterthought, P.S.

**posture** attitude, bearing, carriage, set, stance ~*v* affect, pose, show off *Inf*

**potent** forceful, mighty, powerful, strong

**potential** *adj* future, hidden, latent, likely, possible, promising ~*n* ability, capability, capacity, possibility

**potion** brew, concoction, dose, draught, elixir, mixture

**potter** dabble, footle *Inf*, mess about, tinker

**pottery** ceramics, earthenware, stoneware, terra cotta

**pouch** bag, container, pocket, purse, sack

**pounce** *v* attack, drop, jump, spring, strike, swoop ~*n* attack, bound, jump, leap, spring, swoop

**pound¹** batter, beat, clobber *Sl*, hammer, strike, thump; crush, powder, pulverize

**pound²** *n* compound, enclosure, pen, yard

**pour** course, flow, gush, run, rush, spout, stream; bucket down *Inf*,

of, scarcity

**POW** prisoner of war

**powder** *n* solid matter in fine dry particles; medicine in this form; gunpowder; face powder etc. ~*v* apply powder to; reduce to powder **powdery** *adj*

**power** *n* ability to do or act; strength; authority; control; person or thing having authority; mechanical energy; electricity supply **powerful** *adj* **powerless** *adj*

**pp** pages

**PR** proportional representation; public relations

**practical** *adj* given to action rather than theory; sensible, realistic; skilled **practicable** *adj* that can be

done, used etc. **practically** *adv* all but; sensibly **practical joke** trick intended to make someone look foolish

**practise** *v* do repeatedly, work at to gain skill; do habitually; put into action; exercise profession **practice** *n* habit; exercise of art or profession; action, not theory

**pragmatic** *adj* concerned with practical consequences

**prairie** *n* large treeless tract of grassland

**praise** *n* commendation; fact of praising; expression of thanks to God ~*v* express approval, admiration of; express thanks to God **praiseworthy** *adj*

———————— THESAURUS ————————

pelt (down), teem

**poverty** beggary, destitution, hardship, insolvency, penury, privation, want; dearth, deficiency, insufficiency, lack, scarcity, shortage

**powder** *v* dredge, dust, scatter, sprinkle; crush, granulate, grind, pound, pulverize

**power** ability, capability, capacity, faculty, potential; energy, force, intensity, might, muscle, potency, strength; authority, authorization, licence, prerogative, right, warrant; authority, command, control, dominion, influence, mastery, rule, sovereignty, sway

**powerful** mighty, potent, strapping, strong, sturdy, vigorous; authoritative, commanding, dominant, influential

**powerless** feeble, frail, helpless, impotent, incapable, incapacitated, ineffectual, weak

**practicable** achievable, attainable, doable, feasible, possible, viable, workable

**practical** applied, empirical, functional, pragmatic, realistic; businesslike, down-to-earth, hardheaded, realistic, sensible

**practically** all but, almost, just about, nearly, virtually, well-nigh; rationally, realistically, sensibly

**practice** custom, habit, method, routine, system, tradition, usage, way, wont; drill, exercise, preparation, rehearsal, training, work-out

**practise** drill, go over, prepare, rehearse, study, train; apply, carry out, do, follow, observe, perform; carry on, engage in, pursue, undertake

**praise** *n* acclaim, acclamation, accolade, applause, approval, commendation, compliment, plaudit, tribute; adoration, glory, thanks, worship ~*v* acclaim, applaud, approve, compliment, congratulate, extol, laud; adore, glorify, worship

**praiseworthy** admirable, commendable, creditable, laudable, meritorious

**pram** n carriage for baby

**prance** v/n swagger; caper

**prank** n mischievous trick

**prattle** v talk like child

**prawn** n edible sea shellfish like shrimp

**pray** v ask earnestly; entreat; offer prayers, esp. to God **prayer** n action, practice of praying to God; earnest entreaty

**pre-** comb. form before, as in **prerecord, preshrunk**

**preach** v deliver sermon; give moral, religious advice; advocate **preacher** n

**preamble** n introductory part of story etc.

**precarious** adj insecure, unstable, perilous

**precaution** n previous care to prevent evil or secure good

**precede** v go, come before in rank, order, time etc. **precedence** n priority in position, rank, time etc. **prece-**

**edent** n previous case or occurrence taken as rule

**precept** n rule for conduct

**precinct** n enclosed, limited area; pl environs

**precious** adj beloved, cherished; of great value

**precipice** n very steep cliff or rock face

**precipitate** v hasten happening of; throw headlong; Chem cause to be deposited in solid form from solution ~adj too sudden; rash ~n substance chemically precipitated **precipitation** n rain, snow etc.

**precipitous** adj steep; rash, hurried

**précis** n (pl précis) summary ~v summarize

**precise** adj definite; exact; careful in observance **precisely** adv **precision** n

**preclude** v prevent

**precocious** adj developed, ma-

**prance** bound, caper, cavort, dance, frisk, gambol, skip

**prank** caper, escapade, jape, lark Inf, practical joke, trick

**prattle** babble, blether, chatter, gabble, jabber, rabbit (on) Brit inf, waffle Inf, chiefly Brit, witter Inf

**pray** ask, beg, beseech, entreat, implore, petition, plead, request

**prayer** devotion, litany, orison; appeal, entreaty, petition, plea, request

**preach** lecture, moralize, sermonize

**preacher** clergyman, evangelist, minister, missionary, parson

**precarious** dangerous, dicey Inf, chiefly Brit, dodgy Brit, Aust, & NZ inf, hazardous, insecure, perilous, risky, shaky, tricky, unsafe

**precaution** insurance, protection, safeguard

**precede** antedate, come first, go before, introduce, lead, preface

**precedence** primacy, priority, rank, seniority, superiority

**precedent** n antecedent, criterion, example, instance, model, pattern, standard

**precinct** area, district, quarter, section, sector, zone

**precious** adored, beloved, cherished, darling, dear, loved, prized, treasured, valued; costly, dear, invaluable, priceless, valuable

**precise** absolute, accurate, clear-cut, correct, definite, exact, literal, particular, specific, strict

**precision** accuracy, correctness, exactness, meticulousness

tured early or too soon

**preconceive** *v* form an idea beforehand **preconception** *n*

**precursor** *n* forerunner

**predatory** *adj* preying on other animals **predator** *n*

**predecessor** *n* one who precedes another in office or position

**predestined** *adj* decreed beforehand **predestination** *n*

**predicament** *n* difficult situation

**predict** *v* foretell, prophesy **predictable** *adj* **prediction** *n*

**predispose** *v* incline, influence; make susceptible

**predominate** *v* be main or controlling element **predominance** *n* **predominant** *adj*

**pre-eminent** *adj* excelling all others **pre-eminence** *n*

**pre-empt** *v* do in advance of or to exclusion of others

**preen** *v* trim (feather) with beak;

smarten oneself

**prefabricated** *adj* (of building) manufactured in shaped sections for rapid assembly

**preface** *n* introduction to book etc. ~*v* introduce

**prefect** *n* person put in authority; schoolchild in position of limited authority over others

**prefer** *v* -ferring, -ferred like better; promote **preferable** *adj* more desirable **preference** *n* **preferential** *adj* special, privileged **preferment** *n* promotion

**prefix** *n* group of letters put at beginning of word ~*v* put as introduction; put as prefix

**pregnant** *adj* carrying fetus in womb; full of meaning, significant **pregnancy** *n*

**prehistoric** *adj* before period in which written history begins

**prejudice** *n* preconceived opinion;

———————— THESAURUS ————————

**precocious** advanced, ahead, developed, forward

**preconception** bias, predisposition, prejudice, presupposition

**predecessor** antecedent, forerunner, precursor

**predicament** corner, fix *Inf*, jam *Inf*, mess, scrape *Inf*, situation, spot *Inf*

**predict** forecast, foretell, prophesy

**prediction** forecast, prognosis, prophecy

**predispose** dispose, incline, influence, lead, prompt

**predominant** chief, dominant, leading, main, prevailing, principal, ruling

**pre-eminent** excellent, foremost, outstanding, peerless, predominant, superior, supreme, unrivalled, unsurpassed

**preen** *of birds* clean, plume; *doll up Sl,* dress up, spruce up, titivate

**preface** *n* foreword, introduction, preamble, prelude, prologue ~*v* begin, introduce, open, precede, prefix

**prefer** be partial to, choose, elect, fancy, favour, incline towards, opt for, pick, select

**preference** choice, favourite, first choice, option, partiality, pick, selection

**preferential** better, favoured, privileged, special, superior

**pregnant** expectant, expecting *Inf,* in the club *Brit sl,* in the family way *Inf,* preggers *Brit inf,* with child; charged, expressive, loaded, meaningful, pointed, significant, telling

**prehistoric** earliest, early, primeval, primitive, primordial

unreasonable or unfair dislike ~*v* influence; bias; injure **prejudicial** *adj*

**preliminary** *adj/n* preparatory, introductory (action, statement)

**prelude** *n Mus* introductory movement; performance; event etc. serving as introduction

**premature** *adj* happening, done before proper time

**premeditated** *adj* planned beforehand

**premier** *n* prime minister ~*adj* chief, foremost; first

**première** *n* first performance of play etc.

**premise** *n Logic* proposition from which inference is drawn

**premises** *pl n* house, building with its belongings

**premium** *n* (*pl* **-iums**) bonus; sum paid for insurance; excess over nominal value; great value or regard

**premonition** *n* presentiment

**preoccupy** *v* **-pying, -pied** occupy to exclusion of other things **preoccupation** *n*

**preordained** *adj* determined in advance

**prepare** *v* make, get ready; concoct, make **preparation** *n* making ready beforehand; something prepared, as a medicine **preparatory** *adj* serving to prepare; introductory **prepared** *adj* ready; willing

**preponderate** *v* be of greater weight or power **preponderance** *n*

**preposition** *n* word marking relation between noun or pronoun and other words

**prepossessing** *v* impressive

**preposterous** *adj* utterly absurd, foolish

**prerequisite** *n/adj* (something) required as prior condition

———— THESAURUS ————

**prejudice** *n* preconception, prejudgment; bigotry, chauvinism, discrimination, intolerance, racism, sexism, unfairness ~*v* bias, colour, distort, influence, slant, sway; damage, harm, injure, spoil, undermine

**preliminary** *adj* first, initial, introductory, opening, preparatory, prior or ~*n* beginning, groundwork, introduction, opening, preamble, preface, prelude, start

**prelude** beginning, introduction, overture, preamble, preface, prologue, start

**premature** early, immature, undeveloped, unripe, untimely; hasty, impulsive, overhasty, precipitate, rash

**premeditated** calculated, considered, deliberate, intentional, planned

**premium** bonus, fee, remuneration, reward

**premonition** feeling, foreboding, hunch, idea, intuition, presentiment

**preparation** development, getting ready groundwork; anticipation, foresight, precaution, provision, readiness, safeguard

**preparatory** introductory, opening, prefatory, preliminary

**prepare** arrange, fit, make ready, prime; assemble, concoct, construct, contrive, fashion, make, produce

**prepared** in order, in readiness, ready, set; disposed, inclined, predisposed, willing

**preposterous** absurd, crazy, foolish, impossible, incredible, insane, laughable, ludicrous, ridiculous,

**prerogative** n peculiar power or right, esp. as vested in sovereign

**prescribe** v set out rules for; order use of (medicine) **prescription** n prescribing; thing prescribed; written statement of it

**present**[1] that is here; now existing or happening ~n present time or tense **presence** n being present; appearance, bearing **presently** adv soon; US at present

**present**[2] v introduce formally; show; give ~n gift **presentable** adj fit to be seen **presentation** n **presenter** n

**presentiment** n sense of something about to happen

**preserve** v keep from harm, injury or decay ~n special area; fruit preserved by cooking in sugar; place where game is kept for private fishing, shooting **preservation** n **preservative** n preserving agent ~adj preserving

**preside** v be in charge **presidency** n **president** n head of society, company, republic etc. **presidential** adj

**press** v subject to push or squeeze; smooth; urge; throng; hasten ~n machine for pressing, esp. printing machine; printing house; newspapers and journalists collectively; crowd **pressing** adj urgent; persistent

─────────── THESAURUS ───────────

senseless, unthinkable

**prerequisite** n condition, must, necessity, precondition, qualification, requirement ~adj essential, indispensable, mandatory, necessary, obligatory, required, vital

**prescribe** decree, define, dictate, direct, lay down, ordain, rule, set, specify, stipulate

**prescription** drug, medicine, mixture, preparation, remedy

**presence** attendance, existence, occupancy, residence; air, appearance, aspect, aura, bearing, demeanour

**present**[1] adj at hand, available, here, ready, there, to hand; contemporary, current, existing, immediate, instant ~n here and now, the time being, today

**present**[2] v acquaint with, introduce; advance, declare, extend, offer, put forward, state, submit, suggest, tender; display, exhibit, give, mount, put on, show, stage ~n donation, endowment, gift, grant, gratuity, hand-out, largess, offering

**presentable** acceptable, decent, fit to be seen, O.K. or okay Inf, passable, respectable, satisfactory, suitable

**presentation** award, bestowal, conferral, offering; demonstration, display, exhibition, performance, production, show

**presently** anon Arch, before long, by and by, shortly, soon

**preservation** conservation, maintenance, protection, safekeeping, safety

**preserve** v care for, conserve, guard, keep, protect, safeguard, save, shelter

**preside** administer, control, direct, govern, head, lead, manage, run

**press** v crush, depress, jam, mash, push, squeeze, stuff; flatten, iron, smooth; beg, entreat, exhort, implore, plead, urge n **the press** Fleet Street, fourth estate, journalism, news media, newspapers, the papers

**pressing** crucial, high-priority, imperative, important, serious,

**pressure** *n* act of pressing; compelling force; *Physics* thrust per unit area

**prestige** *n* reputation; influence depending on it **prestigious** *adj*

**presto** *adv Mus* very quickly

**presume** *v* take for granted; take liberties **presumably** *adv* **presumption** *n* forward, arrogant opinion or conduct; strong probability **presumptive** *adj* that may be assumed is true or valid until contrary is proved **presumptuous** *adj* forward, impudent

**presuppose** *v* assume or take for granted beforehand **presupposition** *n*

**pretend** *v* claim or allege (something untrue); make believe; lay claim (to) **pretence** *n* simulation

**pretender** *n* claimant (to throne)

**pretension** *n* pretentious *adj* making claim to special merit or importance; given to outward show

**pretext** *n* excuse; pretence

**pretty** *adj* appealing in a delicate way ~*adv* moderately

**prevail** *v* gain mastery; be generally established **prevalent** *adj* widespread; predominant

**prevaricate** *v* tell lies or speak evasively **prevaricator** *n*

**prevent** *v* stop, hinder **prevention** *n* **preventive** *adj/n*

————— THESAURUS —————

urgent, vital

**pressure** compression, crushing, force, squeezing, weight; coercion, compulsion, constraint, force, influence

**prestige** credit, honour, importance, influence, kudos, renown, reputation, standing, status

**presumably** apparently, it would seem, probably, seemingly

**presume** assume, believe, conjecture, guess *Inf, chiefly US & Canad,* infer, suppose, surmise, take for granted, take it, think

**presumption** audacity, cheek *Inf,* effrontery, gall *Inf,* impudence, insolence, nerve *Inf,* temerity

**presuppose** assume, postulate, presume, take as read, take for granted, take it

**pretence** acting, charade, feigning, sham, simulation

**pretend** affect, allege, assume, fake, falsify, feign, impersonate, profess, sham, simulate; imagine, play, suppose

**pretension** aspiration, assump-

tion, claim, profession; affectation, airs, conceit, pomposity, pretentiousness, self-importance, show, snobbery, vanity

**pretentious** affected, conceited, extravagant, grandiloquent, grandiose, ostentatious, pompous, showy, snobbish

**pretext** cloak, cover, excuse, guise, mask, ploy, pretence, ruse, semblance, show

**pretty** *adj* attractive, beautiful, bonny, comely, fair, good-looking, lovely

**prevail** be victorious, overcomee, succeed, triumph, win

**prevalent** common, current, customary, established, fashionable, general, ordinary, popular, usual, widespread

**prevaricate** dodge, equivocate, evade, flannel *Brit inf,* hedge, lie

**prevent** avert, bar, block, check, frustrate, hamper, hinder, impede, inhibit, obstruct, restrain, stop, thwart

**prevention** bar, check, hindrance,

**preview** n advance showing

**previous** adj preceding; happening before **previously** adv

**prey** n animal hunted by another for food; victim ~v (**with on**) treat as prey; worry, obsess

**price** n that for which thing is bought or sold; cost ~v fix, ask price for **priceless** adj invaluable **pricey** adj Inf expensive

**prick** v pierce slightly; cause to feel sharp pain ~n slight hole made by pricking; sting **prickle** n thorn, spike ~v feel pricking sensation **prickly** adj thorny; stinging; touchy

**pride** n too high an opinion of oneself; worthy self-esteem; great satis-

faction; something causing this; best part of something **pride oneself** take pride

**priest** n (fem **priestess**) official minister of religion **priesthood** n

**prig** n smug self-righteous person **priggish** adj

**prim** adj formal and prudish

**primacy** n supremacy

**prima donna** female opera singer

**primary** adj chief; earliest; elementary

**primate**¹ n one of order of mammals including monkeys and man

**primate**² n archbishop

**prime** adj fundamental; original; chief; best ~n first, best part of any-

---

impediment, interruption, obstacle, obstruction, stoppage

**previous** antecedent, earlier, erstwhile, former, past, preceding, prior

**previously** before, beforehand, earlier, formerly, hitherto, once

**prey** game, kill, quarry; dupe, target, victim

**price** n amount, assessment, charge, cost, expense, fee, figure, outlay, payment, rate, valuation, value, worth; consequences, cost, penalty, toll ~v assess, cost, estimate, evaluate, rate, value

**priceless** costly, dear, expensive, invaluable

**prick** v jab, lance, perforate, pierce, puncture, stab; prickle, smart, sting, tingle ~n hole, perforation, pinhole, puncture, wound

**prickle** barb, needle, point, spike, spine, spur, thorn

**prickly** barbed, spiny, thorny; itchy, scratchy, sharp, smarting, stinging, tingling; bad-tempered, cantankerous, grumpy, irritable,

peevish, snappish, tetchy, touchy

**pride** n arrogance, conceit, egotism, loftiness, pretension, pretentiousness, self-importance, snobbery, superciliousness, vanity; dignity, honour, self-esteem, self-respect, self-worth; delight, gratification, joy, pleasure, satisfaction ~v boast, brag, congratulate oneself, exult, glory in

**priest** clergyman, cleric, curate, divine, ecclesiastic, father, minister, padre Inf, pastor, vicar

**prig** goody-goody Inf, prude, puritan

**priggish** goody-goody Inf, holier-than-thou, prim, prudish, puritanical

**prim** demure, formal, fussy, precise, priggish, prissy Inf, proper, prudish, puritanical, strait-laced

**prima donna** diva, leading lady, star

**primary** cardinal, chief, first, greatest, highest, leading, main, paramount, prime, principal; basic, elemental, elementary, essential, fun-

thing ~v prepare for use **primer** n paint for preliminary coating **Prime Minister** leader of government

**primeval** adj of earliest age of the world

**primitive** adj of an early undeveloped kind; crude

**primrose** n pale yellow spring flower; this colour ~adj of this colour

**prince** n male member of royal family; ruler, chief **princely** adj generous; magnificent **princess** n female member of royal family

**principal** adj chief in importance ~n person for whom another is agent; head of institution, esp. school or college; sum of money lent and yielding interest **principality** n territory of prince

**principle** n moral rule; settled reason of action; uprightness; fundamental truth

**print** v reproduce (words, pictures etc.) by pressing inked types on blocks of paper etc.; write in imitation of this; *Photog* produce pictures from negatives; stamp (fabric) with design ~n printed matter; photograph; impression left by something pressing; printed cotton fabric **printer** n

**prior** adj earlier ~n (fem **prioress**) leader of religious house or order **priority** n precedence, something given special attention **priory** n monastery, nunnery under prior, prioress **prior to** before

**prise** v force open by levering

**prism** n transparent solid, usu. with triangular ends and rectangular sides, used to disperse light into spectrum

**prison** n jail **prisoner** n one kept in prison; captive

**pristine** adj completely new and

———————————————— THESAURUS ————————————————

damental

**prime** adj basic, fundamental, original, underlying; chief, leading, main, predominant, pre-eminent, principal, ruling; best, capital, choice, excellent, first-class, first-rate, highest, select, superior, top ~n bloom, flower, height, heyday, peak, zenith ~v get ready, make ready, prepare

**primeval, primaeval** ancient, early, first, old, prehistoric, primal, primitive, primordial

**primitive** earliest, early, elementary, first, primeval, primordial; crude, rough, rude, rudimentary, simple, uncivilized, unrefined

**prince** monarch, ruler, sovereign

**princely** bounteous, generous, lavish, liberal, munificent, rich

**principal** adj cardinal, chief, essential, first, foremost, highest, key, leading, main, paramount, pre-eminent, primary, prime ~n dean, head *Inf*, headmaster, headmistress, master, rector

**principle** axiom, canon, criterion, doctrine, dogma, law, maxim, precept, rule; belief, code, ethic, tenet; conscience, integrity, morals, rectitude, scruples, uprightness

**print** v engrave, impress, imprint, issue, publish, stamp ~n copy, engraving, photo *Inf*, photograph, picture, reproduction

**priority** precedence, preference, rank, seniority, superiority, supremacy

**priory** abbey, convent, monastery, nunnery

**prison** confinement, cooler *Sl*, dungeon, gaol, jail, jug *Sl*, lockup,

pure

**private** *adj* secret, not public; not general, individual; personal; excluded; denoting soldier of lowest rank ~*n* private soldier **privacy** *n* **privatize** *v* transfer (service etc.) from public to private ownership

**privation** *n* lack of comforts or necessities

**privet** *n* bushy evergreen shrub used for hedges

**privilege** *n* right, advantage granted or belonging only to few **privileged** *adj* enjoying privilege

**privy** *adj* admitted to knowledge of secret ~*n* lavatory

**prize** *n* reward given for success in competition; thing striven for; thing won, e.g. in lottery etc. ~*adj* thing winning or likely to win prize ~*v* value highly

**pro-** *comb. form* in favour of; in-

stead of

**pro¹** *adj/adv* in favour of **pros and cons** arguments for and against

**pro²** *n* professional

**probable** *adj* likely **probability** *n* likelihood; anything probable **probably** *adv*

**probate** *n* proving of authenticity of will; certificate of this

**probation** *n* system of dealing with lawbreakers by placing them under supervision; trial period **probationer** *n* person on probation

**probe** *v* search into, examine, question closely ~*n* that which probes, or is used to probe; thorough inquiry

**probity** *n* honesty, integrity

**problem** *n* matter etc. difficult to deal with or solve; question set for solution **problematical** *adj*

**proceed** *v* go forward, continue;

——————— THESAURUS ———————

nick *Brit sl*, penitentiary *US*

**prisoner** convict, jailbird, lag *Sl*; captive, detainee, hostage, internee

**privacy** isolation, retirement, retreat, seclusion, solitude

**private** confidential, in camera, secret; exclusive, individual, own, personal, special; isolated, secluded, secret, separate, sequestered

**privilege** advantage, birthright, claim, concession, due, entitlement, prerogative, right

**prize** *n* accolade, award, honour, trophy; aim, ambition, goal; jackpot, purse, stakes, winnings ~*adj* award-winning, best, champion, first-rate, outstanding, top ~*v* cherish, esteem, hold dear, treasure, value

**probability** chance(s), expectation, likelihood, likeliness, odds, prospect

**probable** credible, feasible, likely, presumable, reasonable

**probably** likely, maybe, perchance *Arch*, perhaps, possibly, presumably

**probation** apprenticeship, test, trial, trial period

**probe** *v* examine, explore, go into, investigate, look into, scrutinize, search, sift; explore, feel around, poke, prod ~*n* examination, exploration, inquiry, investigation, research, scrutiny, study

**problem** *n* complication, difficulty, dilemma, dispute, predicament, quandary, trouble; conundrum, enigma, poser, puzzle, question, riddle

**procedure** action, conduct, course, custom, method, modus operandi, policy, practice, process, routine, strategy, system

be carried on; arise from; go to law **procedure** n act, manner of proceeding **proceeding** n act or course of action; pl minutes of meeting; legal action **proceeds** pl n profit

**process** n series of actions or changes; method of operation; state of going on; action of law ~v handle, treat, prepare by special method of manufacture etc. **procession** n train of persons in formal order

**proclaim** v announce publicly, declare **proclamation** n

**procrastinate** v put off, delay **procrastination** n

**procreate** v produce offspring **procreation** n

**procure** v obtain, acquire; bring about; act as pimp **procurement** n

**procurer** n (fem **procuress**) one who procures; pimp

**prod** v prodding, prodded poke ~n prodding; pointed instrument

**prodigal** adj wasteful ~n spendthrift

**prodigy** n person with some marvellous gift; thing causing wonder **prodigious** adj very great; extraordinary

**produce** v bring into existence; yield; bring forward; manufacture; present on stage, film, television ~n that which is yielded or made **producer** n product n thing produced; consequence **production** n consequence; staging of play etc. **productive** adj fertile; creative **productivity** n

**Prof.** Professor

—————— THESAURUS ——————

**proceed** advance, carry on, continue, go ahead, go on, move on, progress; arise, come, emanate, ensue, flow, issue, originate, result, spring, stem

**proceeding** pl n business, dealings, doings, minutes, records, report, transactions

**proceeds** earnings, gain, income, profit, returns, revenue, takings

**process** n action, course, means, measure, method, mode, operation, performance, practice, procedure, system, transaction; advance, course, development, evolution, movement, progress, progression

**procession** cavalcade, column, file, parade, train

**proclaim** advertise, announce, circulate, declare, make known, profess, promulgate, publish

**proclamation** announcement, declaration, decree, edict, notice, notification, promulgation, pro-

nouncement, publication

**procrastinate** adjourn, defer, delay, postpone, put off, stall, temporize

**procure** acquire, appropriate, come by, find, gain, get, obtain, pick up, secure

**prod** v dig, jab, nudge, poke, push, shove ~n dig, jab, nudge, poke, push, shove; goad, spur

**prodigal** adj extravagant, immoderate, improvident, profligate, reckless, spendthrift, wasteful ~n profligate, spendthrift

**prodigy** genius, talent, whiz Inf. wizard; marvel, miracle, phenomenon, sensation, wonder

**produce** v bear, beget, breed, bring forth, deliver, give, render, yield; bring about, cause, effect, generate, give rise to, occasion, provoke, set off; compose, construct, create, develop, invent, make, manufacture, turn out; direct, present, put on, show, stage

**profane** *adj* irreverent, blasphemous; not sacred ~*v* treat irreverently **profanity** *n* profane talk

**profess** *v* affirm belief in; claim, pretend **profession** *n* calling or occupation, esp. learned, scientific or artistic; professing **professional** *adj* engaged in a profession; taking part in sport, music etc. for money; skilled ~*n* paid player **professor** *n* teacher of highest rank in university

**proffer** *v* offer

**proficient** *adj* skilled; expert **proficiency** *n*

**profile** *n* outline, esp. of face, as seen from side; brief biographical sketch

**profit** *n* money gained; benefit obtained ~*v* benefit; earn **profitable** *adj* **profiteer** *n* one who makes excessive profits at public's expense ~*v* profit thus

**profligate** *adj* recklessly extravagant; depraved, immoral

**profound** *adj* very learned; deep; heartfelt **profundity** *n*

——————— THESAURUS ———————

~*n* crop, harvest, product, yield

**producer** director, impresario, farmer, grower, maker, manufacturer

**product** artefact, commodity, creation, goods, merchandise, produce, work; consequence, effect, fruit, outcome, result, spin-off, upshot, yield

**production** construction, creation, fabrication, manufacture, origination; direction, management, presentation, staging

**productive** creative, fertile, fruitful, inventive, plentiful, prolific

**productivity** output, production, work rate, yield

**profane** *adj* blasphemous, disrespectful, impious, irreligious, irreverent, sacrilegious ~*v* abuse, debase, defile, desecrate, misuse, pervert, violate

**profanity** blasphemy, curse, foul language, impiety, malediction, obscenity, sacrilege, swearing, swearword

**profess** affirm, announce, assert, aver, avow, confirm, maintain, proclaim, state

**profession** business, calling, career, line, occupation, sphere, voca-

tion; affirmation, assertion, avowal, claim, declaration, statement, testimony, vow

**professional** *adj* adept, competent, efficient, expert, masterly, polished, practised, proficient, qualified, skilled

**proficiency** ability, accomplishment, competence, expertise, facility, knack, know-how *Inf,* mastery, skill, talent

**proficient** able, accomplished, adept, capable, competent, efficient, expert, gifted, masterly, skilful, talented

**profile** *n* contour, figure, form, outline, portrait, shape, silhouette, sketch; biography, characterization, sketch

**profit** *n (oft. pl)* earnings, gain, proceeds, return, revenue, takings, winnings, yield; advantage, avail, benefit, gain, good, use, value ~*v* aid, avail, benefit, gain, help, serve; clear, earn, gain, make money

**profitable** cost-effective, lucrative, money-making, paying; advantageous, beneficial, fruitful, productive, rewarding, useful, valuable, worthwhile

**profound** abstruse, deep, erudite,

**profuse** adj abundant **profusion** n

**progeny** n children **progenitor** n ancestor

**prognosis** n (pl **-noses**) forecast

**programme** n plan of intended proceedings; broadcast on radio or television **program** n instructions for computer ~v **-gramming**, **-grammed** feed program into (computer); arrange program

**progress** n onward movement; sequence ~v go forward; improve **progression** n moving forward; improvement **progressive** adj progressing by degrees; favouring political or social reform

**prohibit** v forbid **prohibition** n act of forbidding; ban on sale or drinking of alcohol **prohibitive** adj tending to forbid or exclude; (of cost) too high to be afforded

**project** n plan, scheme ~v plan; throw; cause to appear on distant background; stick out **projectile** n heavy missile **projection** n bulge; forecast **projector** n apparatus for projecting photographic images

**proletariat** n working class **proletarian** adj/n

**proliferate** v grow or reproduce rapidly **proliferation** n

**prolific** adj fruitful; producing

———— THESAURUS ————

learned, sagacious, serious; wise; abysmal, bottomless, cavernous, deep, fathomless, yawning; extreme, great, heartfelt, intense

**profuse** abundant, ample, copious, plentiful, prolific, teeming

**profusion** abundance, excess, glut, multitude, quantity, surplus, wealth

**programme** n design, plan, procedure, project, scheme; broadcast, performance, presentation, production, show ~v arrange, bill, book, engage, line up, plan, schedule

**progress** n advance, course, movement, passage, way ~v advance, continue, make headway, move on, proceed, travel; advance, develop, grow, improve, increase

**progression** advance, advancement, furtherance, headway; advance, development, growth, headway, improvement

**progressive** advancing, continuing, developing, growing, increasing, intensifying; avant-garde, forward-looking, liberal, radical, reformist, revolutionary

**prohibit** ban, debar, disallow, forbid, outlaw, proscribe, veto

**prohibition** exclusion, prevention, restriction; ban, bar, boycott, embargo, injunction, interdict, proscription, veto

**prohibitive** forbidding, repressive, restrictive, suppressive; esp. of prices excessive, exorbitant, extortionate, steep Inf

**project** n activity, assignment, enterprise, job, plan, programme, proposal, scheme, task, undertaking, venture, work ~v contrive, design, devise, draft, frame, outline, plan, propose, scheme; cast, fling, hurl, launch, propel, shoot, throw; bulge, extend, jut, overhang, protrude, stick out

**projectile** bullet, missile, rocket, shell

**projection** bulge, protrusion, protuberance, ridge; calculation, computation, estimate, estimation, forecast, reckoning

**proletariat** commoners, hoi polloi, labouring classes, the common people, the masses, wage-earners,

much
**prologue** *n* preface
**prolong** *v* lengthen
**promenade** *n* leisurely walk; place made or used for this ~*v* take leisurely walk
**prominent** *adj* sticking out; conspicuous; distinguished **prominence** *n*
**promiscuous** *adj* indiscriminate, esp. in sexual relations **promiscuity** *n*
**promise** *v* give undertaking or assurance; be likely to ~*n* undertak-

ing to do or not to do something; potential **promising** *adj* showing good signs, hopeful; likely to succeed
**promontory** *n* high land jutting out into sea
**promote** *v* help forward; move up to higher rank or position; encourage sale of **promoter** *n* **promotion** *n*
**prompt** *adj* done at once; punctual ~*adv* punctually ~*v* urge, suggest; help (actor or speaker) by suggesting next words ~*n* cue, reminder
**promulgate** *v* proclaim, publish

—————————————— THESAURUS ——————————————

working class
**prolific** bountiful, copious, fertile, fruitful, luxuriant, productive, profuse, rich, teeming
**prologue** foreword, introduction, preamble, preface, prelude
**prolong** continue, drag out, draw out, extend, lengthen, perpetuate, spin out, stretch
**promenade** *n* constitutional, saunter, stroll, turn, walk; esplanade, parade, prom, walkway ~*v* perambulate, saunter, stroll, walk
**prominence** distinction, eminence, fame, greatness, importance, prestige, rank, reputation, standing
**prominent** bulging, jutting, protruding, standing out; conspicuous, eye-catching, noticeable, obtrusive, obvious, salient, striking; chief, distinguished, eminent, famous, foremost, important, leading, main, notable, renowned, top, well-known
**promiscuous** abandoned, dissolute, fast, immoral, lax, licentious, loose, wanton, wild
**promise** *v* assure, give one's word, guarantee, pledge, swear, undertake, vouch, vow; augur, betoken,

denote, indicate, suggest ~*n* assurance, bond, commitment, guarantee, oath, pledge, undertaking, vow, word; aptitude, flair, potential, talent
**promising** auspicious, bright, encouraging, favourable, hopeful, likely, rosy; gifted, likely, rising, talented
**promote** advance, aid, assist, back, boost, develop, encourage, forward, foster, help, support; aggrandize, dignify, elevate, exalt, raise, upgrade; advertise, hype, plug *Inf*, push, sell
**promotion** advancement, aggrandizement, elevation, preferment, upgrading; advertising, hype, propaganda, publicity
**prompt** *adj* immediate, instant, punctual, quick, rapid, speedy, swift, timely, unhesitating ~*adv Inf* exactly, on the dot, punctually, sharp ~*v* impel, incite, induce, inspire, motivate, move, provoke, spur, stimulate, urge; cue, prod, remind ~*n* cue, help, hint, prod, reminder, spur, stimulus
**promptly** at once, directly, immediately, on the dot, on time,

**prone** *adj* lying face downwards; inclined (to)

**prong** *n* one spike of fork or similar instrument

**pronoun** *n* word used to replace noun

**pronounce** *v* utter (formally); give opinion **pronounced** *adj* strongly marked **pronouncement** *n* declaration **pronunciation** *n* way word etc. is pronounced

**proof** *n* evidence; thing which proves; test, demonstration; trial impression from type or engraved plate; standard of strength of alcoholic drink ~*adj* giving impenetrable defence against

**prop**[1] *n/v* propping, propped support

**prop**[2] *n* object used on set of film, play etc.

**propaganda** *n* organized dissemination of information to assist or damage political cause etc.

**propagate** *v* reproduce, breed; spread **propagation** *n*

**propel** *v* -**pelling**, -**pelled** cause to move forward **propeller** *n* revolving shaft with blades for driving ship or aircraft **propulsion** *n* act of driving forward

**propensity** *n* inclination; tendency

**proper** *adj* appropriate; correct; conforming to etiquette; strict; (of noun) denoting individual person or place **properly** *adv*

**property** *n* that which is owned; land, real estate; quality, attribute

**prophet** *n* (*fem* **prophetess**) in-

—————————————— THESAURUS ——————————————

punctually, quickly, speedily, swiftly, unhesitatingly

**prone** face down, flat, horizontal, prostrate, recumbent; apt, disposed, given, inclined, liable, subject, susceptible

**prong** point, spike, tine

**pronounce** articulate, enunciate, say, sound, speak, utter, voice; affirm, announce, declare, proclaim

**pronounced** conspicuous, decided, definite, distinct, marked, noticeable, obvious, striking

**pronouncement** announcement, declaration, proclamation, statement

**pronunciation** accent, articulation, diction, elocution, enunciation, inflection, intonation, stress

**proof** *n* authentication, confirmation, corroboration, demonstration, evidence, substantiation, testimony, verification ~*adj* impenetrable, impervious, repellent, resistant

**prop** *n* brace, buttress, mainstay, stay, support ~*v* bolster, brace, buttress, support, sustain, uphold

**propaganda** advertising, disinformation, hype, promotion, publicity

**propagate** breed, engender, increase, multiply, procreate, produce, proliferate, reproduce; broadcast, circulate, disseminate, promulgate, publicize, publish, spread, transmit

**propel** drive, force, push, send, shoot, shove, thrust

**proper** appropriate, apt, becoming, befitting, fit, fitting, right, suitable, suited; accepted, conventional, correct, established, exact, formal, orthodox, precise; decent, decorous, genteel, gentlemanly, ladylike, mannerly, polite, refined, seemly

**property** assets, belongings, capital, chattels, effects, estate, goods, holdings, means, possessions, re

spired teacher or revealer of God's word; foreteller of future **prophecy** *n* prediction, prophetic utterance

**prophesy** *v* foretell **prophetic** *adj*

**proponent** *n* one who argues in favour of something

**proportion** *n* relative size or number; due relation between connected things or parts; share; *pl* dimensions ~*v* arrange proportions of **proportional, proportionate** *adj* in due proportion

**propose** *v* put forward for consideration; intend; offer marriage **proposal** *n* **proposition** *n* offer; statement

**propound** *v* put forward for consideration

**proprietor** *n* (*fem* **proprietress**) owner

**propriety** *n* properness, correct conduct

**propulsion** *SEE* PROPEL.

**prosaic** *adj* commonplace, unromantic

**proscribe** *v* outlaw, condemn

**prose** *n* speech or writing not in verse

**prosecute** *v* carry on, bring legal proceedings against **prosecution** *n* **prosecutor** *n*

**prospect** *n* expectation, chance for success; view **prospective** *adj* anticipated; future **prospector** *n* **prospectus** *n* booklet giving details of university, company etc.

**prosper** *v* be successful **prosperity** *n* **prosperous** *adj* successful; welloff

**prostate** *n* gland around neck of

sources; estate, freehold, holding, land, real estate; attribute, characteristic, feature, hallmark, quality, trait, virtue

**prophecy** divination, forecast, prediction, prognosis, second sight

**prophesy** divine, forecast, foresee, foretell, predict

**prophet** clairvoyant, forecaster, oracle, seer, sibyl, soothsayer

**proportion** ratio, relationship, relative amount; agreement, balance, congruity, correspondence, harmony, symmetry; amount, part, percentage, quota, segment, share; *pl* amplitude, breadth, bulk, capacity, dimensions, expanse, extent, size, volume

**proposal** bid, motion, offer, plan, presentation, programme, project, recommendation, scheme, suggestion, tender

**propose** advance, present, proffer, propound, put forward, submit,

suggest, tender; aim, intend, mean, plan, purpose, scheme

**proposition** motion, offer, recommendation, suggestion

**propriety** aptness, correctness, fitness, rightness; courtesy, decency, decorum, etiquette, manners, politeness, respectability, seemliness

**propulsion** drive, impetus, impulse, power, push, thrust

**prosecute** arraign, indict, litigate, sue, try

**prospect** *n* anticipation, expectation, future, hope, odds, outlook, probability, promise; landscape, panorama, scene, sight, spectacle, view, vista

**prospective** anticipated, coming, destined, expected, future, imminent, intended, likely, potential

**prospectus** catalogue, list, programme, syllabus, synopsis

**prosper** do well, flourish, get on, succeed, thrive

male bladder

**prostitute** n one who offers sexual intercourse in return for payment ~v make a prostitute of; put to unworthy use **prostitution** n

**prostrate** adj lying flat; overcome ~v throw flat on ground; reduce to exhaustion

**protagonist** n leading character in story; proponent

**protect** v keep from harm **protection** n **protective** adj **protector** n

**protégé** n (fem **protégée**) one under another's patronage

**protein** n any of group of organic compounds which form essential part of food of living creatures

**protest** n declaration or demonstration of objection ~v object; make declaration against; assert formally **protestation** n strong declaration

**Protestant** adj relating to Christian church split from R.C. church ~n member of Protestant church

**protocol** n diplomatic etiquette

**proton** n positively charged particle in nucleus of atom

**prototype** n original, model, after which thing is copied

**protract** v lengthen; prolong **protractor** n instrument for measuring angles

**protrude** v stick out, project **protrusion** n

**protuberant** adj bulging out

**proud** adj pleased, satisfied; arrogant, haughty

**prove** v **proving, proved, proved** or **proven** establish validity of; demonstrate, test; turn out to be **proven** adj proved

**proverb** n short, pithy saying in common use **proverbial** adj

——— THESAURUS ———

**prosperity** affluence, plenty, prosperousness, riches, success, wealth

**prosperous** booming, flourishing, prospering, successful, thriving; affluent, moneyed, opulent, rich, wealthy, well-off, well-to-do

**prostitute** n call girl, courtesan, harlot, hooker, streetwalker, strumpet, tart Inf, trollop, whore ~v cheapen, debase, degrade, demean

**prostrate** adj flat, horizontal, prone; drained, exhausted, overcome, spent, worn out

**protect** care for, defend, guard, harbour, keep, look after, safeguard, save, screen, shelter, shield, stick up for Inf, watch over

**protection** care, charge, custody, defence, safeguard, safekeeping, safety, security; armour, barrier, cover, guard, screen, shelter, shield

**protector** bodyguard, champion, defender, guard, guardian, patron

**protest** n complaint, dissent, objection, outcry, remonstrance ~v complain, demonstrate, demur, disagree, disapprove, object, oppose

**protocol** decorum, etiquette, manners, propriety

**prototype** model, original, pattern, type

**protrude** bulge, come through, extend, jut, project, stand out, stick out

**proud**; appreciative, content, glad, gratified, pleased, satisfied; arrogant, conceited, disdainful, haughty, lordly, self-satisfied, snobbish, supercilious

**prove** authenticate, confirm, demonstrate, determine, establish, justify, show, substantiate, verify; analyse, assay, check, experiment, test,

**provide** v make preparation; supply, equip **provided that** on condition that

**provident** adj thrifty; showing foresight **providence** n kindly care of God or nature; foresight; economy

**province** n division of country; sphere of action; pl any part of country outside capital **provincial** adj of a province; narrow in outlook ~n unsophisticated person; inhabitant of province

**provision** n providing, esp. for the future; thing provided; pl food ~v supply with food **provisional** adj temporary

**proviso** n (pl -os) condition

**provoke** v anger; arouse; cause **provocation** n **provocative** adj

**prow** n bow of vessel

**prowess** n bravery; skill

**prowl** v roam stealthily, esp. in search of prey or booty ~n prowling **prowler** n

**proximity** n nearness

**proxy** n authorized agent or substitute; writing authorizing one to act as this

**prude** n one who is excessively modest or proper **prudish** adj

**prudent** adj careful, discreet; sensible; thrifty **prudence** n

**prune¹** n dried plum

───── THESAURUS ─────

try; end up, result, turn out

**proverb** adage, dictum, maxim, saying

**proverbial** axiomatic†, famed, famous, legendary, traditional, typical, well-known

**provide** cater, equip, furnish, outfit, purvey, stock up, supply

**providence** destiny, fate, fortune; care, caution, foresight, prudence

**provident** careful, cautious, farseeing, prudent, shrewd, thrifty, well-prepared, wise

**province** colony†, district, division, patch, region, section, tract, zone; area, business, capacity, concern, duty, field, function, line, responsibility, role, sphere, turf US sl

**provincial** adj insular, inward-looking, limited, narrow, narrow-minded, parochial, small-minded, small-town US

**provision** catering, equipping, furnishing, providing, supplying; arrangement, plan, precaution, preparation; pl food, rations, supplies

**provocation** cause, grounds, incitement, motivation, reason; affront, annoyance, grievance, offence, taunt

**provocative** annoying, goading, offensive, provoking

**provoke** anger, annoy, enrage, exasperate, infuriate, irk, irritate, madden, offend, rile, vex; cause, elicit, evoke, inspire, produce, rouse, stir

**prowess** adeptness, expertise, genius, mastery, skill, talent

**prowl** move stealthily, skulk, slink, stalk

**proximity** closeness, nearness, vicinity

**proxy** agent, delegate, deputy, representative, substitute

**prudence** care, caution, common sense, discretion, judgment, wisdom; foresight, planning, precaution, providence, thrift

**prudent** careful, cautious, discreet, judicious, politic, sensible, shrewd, wise; canny, careful, economical, far-sighted, provident, sparing,

**prune**[2] v cut out dead parts, excessive branches etc.; shorten, reduce

**pry** v **prying, pried** make furtive or impertinent inquiries

**PS** postscript

**psalm** n sacred song

**pseudo-** comb. form false

**pseudonym** n false, fictitious name; pen name

**psychic** adj of soul or mind; sensitive to phenomena lying outside range of normal experience **psychiatric** adj of psychiatry **psychiatrist** n **psychiatry** n medical treatment of mental diseases **psychoanalysis** n method of studying and treating mental disorders **psychoanalyse** v **psychoanalyst** n **psychological** adj of psychology; of the mind **psychologist** n **psychology** n study of mind; Inf person's mental make-up **psychopath** n person afflicted with severe mental disorder **psychopathic** adj **psychosis** n severe mental

disorder **psychosomatic** adj (of a physical disorder) thought to have psychological causes **psychotherapy** n treatment of disease by psychological, not physical, means

**PTO** please turn over

**pub** n public house, building with bar and licence to sell alcoholic drinks

**puberty** n sexual maturity

**pubic** adj of the lower abdomen

**public** adj of or concerning the community as a whole; not private ~n the community or its members **publican** n keeper of public house **public house** see PUB **public school** Brit private fee-paying school

**publicity** n process of attracting public attention; attention thus gained **publicize** v advertise

**publish** v prepare and issue for sale (books, music etc.); make generally known; proclaim **publication** n **publisher** n

——————— THESAURUS ———————

thrifty

**prudish** old-maidish Inf, priggish, prim, prissy Inf, proper, puritanical, schoolmarmish Brit inf, starchy Inf, strait-laced, stuffy, Victorian

**prune** clip, cut, snip, trim

**pry** intrude, meddle, peep, peer, poke

**psalm** chant, hymn

**pseudonym** alias, assumed name, incognito, pen name

**psychiatrist** analyst, psychoanalyst, psychologist

**psychic** extrasensory, mystic, occult, supernatural, telepathic

**psychopath** headbanger Inf, headcase Inf, lunatic, madman, maniac

**pub** also **public house** bar, inn, tavern

**puberty** adolescence, teenage, teens

**public** adj civic, common, general, national, popular, social, state, universal, widespread; accessible, communal, open, unrestricted; acknowledged, known, open, plain ~n citizens, community, nation, people, populace, society

**publication** brochure, handbill, leaflet, magazine, newspaper, pamphlet, periodical, title

**publicity** attention, boost, press, promotion

**publicize** advertise, broadcast, make known, promote, push

**publish** issue, print, produce, put out; advertise, announce, broadcast, circulate, declare, disclose, divulge, leak, proclaim, promulgate,

**puck** *n* rubber disc used instead of ball in ice hockey

**pucker** *v* gather into wrinkles ~*n* crease, fold

**pudding** *n* sweet, cooked dessert, often made from suet, flour etc.; sweet course of meal; soft savoury dish with pastry or batter; kind of sausage

**puddle** *n* small muddy pool

**puerile** *adj* childish

**puff** *n* short blast of breath, wind etc.; type of pastry; laudatory notice or advertisement ~*v* blow abruptly; breathe hard; send out in a puff; inflate; advertise; smoke hard **puffy** *adj* swollen

**puffin** *n* sea bird with large brightly-coloured beak

**pug** *n* small snub-nosed dog

**pugnacious** *adj* given to fighting **pugnacity** *n*

**pull** *v* exert force on object to move it towards source of force; remove; strain or stretch; attract ~*n* act of pulling; force exerted by act of pulling; *Inf* influence

**pulley** *n* wheel with groove in rim for cord, used to raise weights

**pullover** *n* jersey, sweater without fastening, to be pulled over head

**pulmonary** *adj* of lungs

**pulp** *n* soft, moist, vegetable or animal matter; flesh of fruit; any soft soggy mass ~*v* reduce to pulp

**pulpit** *n* (enclosed) platform for preacher

**pulse**[1] *n* movement of blood in arteries corresponding to heartbeat, discernible to touch, e.g. in wrist; any regular beat or vibration **pulsate** *v* throb, quiver **pulsation** *n*

**pulse**[2] *n* edible seed of pod-bearing plant

**pulverize** *v* reduce to powder

**puma** *n* large Amer. feline carnivore, cougar

**pumice** *n* light porous variety of lava

**pummel** *v* -melling, -melled strike repeatedly

**pump**[1] *n* appliance for raising water, or putting in or taking out air or liquid etc. ~*v* raise, put in, take out etc. with pump; work like pump

**pump**[2] *n* light shoe

**pumpkin** *n* edible gourd

**pun** *n* play on words ~*v* **punning, punned** make pun

**punch**[1] *n* tool for perforating or stamping; blow with fists; *Inf* vigour ~*v* stamp, perforate with punch; strike with fist

**punch**[2] *n* drink of spirits or wine

——— THESAURUS ———

publicize, reveal, spread

**puerile** babyish, childish, immature, juvenile

**puff** *n* blast, breath, draught, gust, whiff ~*v* blow, breathe, exhale, gasp, gulp, pant, wheeze (*usu.* with up) bloat, dilate, distend, expand, inflate, swell

**puffy** bloated, distended, enlarged, puffed up, swollen

**pull** *v* drag, draw, haul, jerk, tow, trail, tug, yank; dislocate, rip,

sprain, strain, stretch, tear, wrench *Inf* attract, draw, entice, lure ~*n* jerk, tug, twitch, yank; attraction, force, influence, lure, magnetism, power *Inf* influence, muscle, weight

**pulp** *n* flesh, soft part; mash, mush, paste ~*v* crush, mash, squash

**pulsate** beat, throb, vibrate

**pulse** *n* beat, beating, rhythm, throb, vibration

**pump** *v* drive, force, inject, pour, push, send

with fruit juice etc.

**punctilious** *adj* making much of details of etiquette; very exact, particular

**punctual** *adj* good time, not late **punctuality** *n*

**punctuate** *v* put in punctuation marks; interrupt at intervals **punctuation** *n* marks put in writing to assist in making sense clear

**puncture** *n* small hole made by sharp object, esp. in tyre ~*v* prick hole in, perforate

**pundit** *n* expert who speaks publicly on subject

**pungent** *adj* acrid, bitter

**punish** *v* cause to suffer for offence; inflict penalty on; use or treat roughly **punishable** *adj* **punishing** *adj* harsh, difficult **punishment** *n* **punitive** *adj* inflicting or intending to inflict punishment

**punnet** *n* small basket for fruit

**punt** *n* flat-bottomed square-ended boat, propelled by pushing with

pole ~*v* propel thus

**punter** *n* person who bets; member of public

**puny** *adj* small and feeble

**pup** *n* young of certain animals, e.g. dog, seal

**pupa** *n* (*pl* **pupae**) stage between larva and adult in metamorphosis of insect

**pupil** *n* person being taught; opening in iris of eye

**puppet** *n* small doll controlled by operator's hand; *Fig* stooge, pawn

**puppy** *n* young dog

**purchase** *v* buy ~*n* buying; what is bought; leverage, grip

**pure** *adj* unmixed, untainted; simple; faultless; innocent; concerned with theory only **purely** *adv* **purification** *n* **purify** *v* **-ifying, -ified** make, become pure, clear or clean **purist** *n* person obsessed with strict obedience to tradition **purity** *n* state of being pure

**purée** *n* pulp of cooked fruit or

---

**punch** *n* blow, hit, knock, thump; *Inf* bite, drive, forcefulness, impact, verve, vigour ~*v* bore, cut, drill, pierce, puncture, stamp; belt *Inf*, hit, slam, smash, strike

**punctual** exact, precise, prompt, timely

**punctuate** break, interrupt, pepper, sprinkle

**puncture** *n* hole, leak, nick, opening, slit ~*v* bore, cut, nick, penetrate, perforate, pierce, prick

**pungent** acid, acrid, bitter, hot, peppery, piquant, sharp, sour, spicy, strong, tart

**punish** beat, chastise, correct, discipline, flog, penalize, scourge, whip

**punishing** arduous, backbreaking,

exhausting, gruelling, strenuous, taxing, tiring, wearing

**punishment** chastisement, correction, discipline, penalty, penance, retribution

**punt** *n* bet, gamble, stake, wager ~*v* bet, gamble, lay, stake, wager

**puny** diminutive, feeble, frail, little, pygmy or pigmy, sickly, stunted, tiny, weak, weakly

**pupil** disciple, learner, scholar, schoolboy, schoolgirl, student, trainee

**puppet** doll, marionette; instrument, mouthpiece, pawn, stooge, tool

**purchase** *v* acquire, buy, get, invest in, obtain, pay for, pick up, procure, score *Sl* ~*n* asset, buy, in-

vegetables ~v reduce to pulp

**purgatory** n place or state of torment, pain or distress, esp. temporary

**purge** v make clean, purify; remove, get rid of; clear out ~n act, process of purging **purgative** adj/n

**puritan** n person with strict moral and religious principles ~adj strictly moral **puritanical** adj

**purl** n stitch that forms ridge in knitting ~v knit in purl

**purloin** v steal; pilfer

**purple** n/adj (of) colour between crimson and violet

**purport** v claim to be (true etc.); signify, imply ~n meaning; apparent meaning

**purpose** n reason, object; design; aim, intention; determination ~v intend **on purpose** intentionally

**purposely** adv

**purr** n pleased noise which cat makes ~v utter this

**purse** n small bag for money; resources; money as prize ~v pucker

**purser** n ship's officer who keeps accounts

**pursue** v chase; engage in; continue **pursuer** n **pursuit** n pursuing; occupation

**purvey** v supply (provisions)

**pus** n yellowish matter produced by suppuration

**push** v move, try to move away by pressure; drive or impel; make thrust; advance with steady effort ~n thrust; persevering self-assertion; big military advance **pusher** n seller of illegal drugs **pushy** adj assertive, ambitious **pushchair** n collapsible chair-

————— THESAURUS —————

vestment, possession, property

**pure** unadulterated, uncontaminated, unpolluted, untainted, wholesome; genuine, natural, perfect, real, simple, straight, unalloyed, unmixed; blameless, chaste, honest, impeccable, innocent, maidenly, virtuous

**purely** absolutely, completely, entirely, merely, only, simply, solely, wholly

**purge** v absolve, cleanse, clear, exonerate, forgive, pardon, purify; eradicate, expel, exterminate, kill, liquidate, oust, remove ~n cleanup, elimination, eradication, liquidation, removal, witch hunt

**purify** clarify, clean, cleanse, disinfect, filter, wash; absolve, cleanse, exonerate, redeem, sanctify

**purist** formalist, pedant, stickler

**puritanical** ascetic, austere, intolerant, narrow-minded, prudish, rig-

id, severe, strait-laced, strict

**purpose** n aim, design, end, goal, intention, object, plan, target; determination, resolution, resolve, tenacity, will **on purpose** deliberately, intentionally, knowingly ~v aim, aspire, decide, design, determine, intend, mean, plan, propose, resolve

**purposely** consciously, deliberately, intentionally, knowingly, wilfully, with intent

**purse** pouch, wallet; exchequer, funds, means, money, resources, treasury, wealth; award, gift, prize, reward

**pursue** chase, dog, follow, hound, hunt, hunt down, run after, shadow, stalk, tail Inf, track; adhere to, carry on, continue, maintain, persist in, proceed

**pursuit** chase, hunt, quest, search, trailing; activity, hobby, interest, occupation, pastime, pleasure

shaped carriage for baby
**puss** also **pussy** n cat
**pustule** n pimple containing pus
**put** v putting, put place; set; express; throw (esp. shot) ~n throw
**put off** postpone; disconcert; repel
**put up** accommodate
**putrid** adj decomposed; rotten **putrefy** v -efying, -efied make or become rotten
**putt** v strike (golf ball) along ground **putter** n golf club for putting
**putty** n paste used by glaziers
**puzzle** v perplex or be perplexed ~n bewildering, perplexing question, problem or toy
**PVC** polyvinyl chloride
**pygmy, pigmy** n abnormally

undersized person; (with cap.) member of one of dwarf peoples of Equatorial Africa ~adj very small
**pyjamas** pl n sleeping suit of trousers and jacket
**pylon** n tower-like erection, esp. to carry electric cables
**pyramid** n solid figure or structure with sloping sides meeting at apex, esp. in ancient Egypt
**pyre** n pile of wood for burning dead body
**pyromania** n urge to set things on fire **pyromaniac** n
**pyrotechnics** n (with sing v) manufacture, display of fireworks
**python** n large nonpoisonous snake that crushes its prey

———— THESAURUS ————

**push** v drive, press, propel, ram, shove, thrust; elbow, jostle, move, shoulder, shove ~n butt, jolt, nudge, shove, thrust; *Inf* ambition, determination, drive, dynamism, enterprise, initiative; *Inf* advance, assault, attack, charge, offensive, thrust

**put** bring, deposit, lay, place, position, rest, set, settle, situate

**put off** defer, delay, postpone, put on the back burner *Inf*, take a rain check on *US & Canad inf*; confuse, discomfit, disconcert, faze, nonplus, unsettle

**putrefy** corrupt, decay, decompose, go bad, rot, spoil

**putrid** bad, corrupt, decayed, de-

composed, off, putrefied, rancid, rotten, spoiled

**put up** build, construct, erect, raise; accommodate, board, house, lodge

**puzzle** v baffle, bewilder, mystify, perplex, stump; brood, muse, ponder, think hard, wonder ~n conundrum, enigma, mystery, paradox, poser, problem, question, riddle

**puzzlement** bafflement, bewilderment, confusion, mystification, perplexity

**pygmy, pigmy** adj baby, diminutive, dwarf, midget, miniature, small, stunted, teeny-weeny, tiny, undersized

# Q q

**QC** *Brit* Queen's Counsel

**quack** *n* harsh cry of duck; pretender to medical or other skill ~*v* (of duck) utter cry

**quadrangle** *n* four-sided figure; four-sided courtyard in a building

**quadrant** *n* quarter of circle

**quadrilateral** *adj/n* four-sided (figure)

**quadruped** *n* four-footed animal

**quadruple** *adj* fourfold ~*v* make, become four times as much

**quadruplet** *n* one of four offspring born at one birth

**quaff** *v* drink heartily or in one draught

**quagmire** *n* bog, swamp

**quail¹** *n* small bird of partridge family

**quail²** *v* flinch; cower

**quaint** *adj* interestingly old-fashioned or odd; curious

**quake** *v* shake, tremble

**qualify** *v* **-fying, -fied** make (oneself) competent; moderate; modifying or limiting quality to **qualification** *n* skill needed for activity; modifying condition **qualified** *adj* fully trained; conditional, restricted

**quality** *n* attribute; (degree of) excellence

**qualm** *n* misgiving; sudden feeling of sickness

**quandary** *n* state of perplexity, dilemma

**quango** *n* (*pl* **-gos**) partly independent official body, set up by government

**quantify** *v* **-fying, -fied** discover or express the quantity of

**quantity** *n* (specified or considerable) amount

---

## THESAURUS

**quack** *n* charlatan, fake, fraud, humbug, impostor, pretender

**quagmire** bog, fen, marsh, mire, quicksand, slough, swamp

**quaint** curious, eccentric, fanciful, old-fashioned, peculiar, queer, rum *Brit sl*, singular, strange, unusual, whimsical

**quake** move, quiver, rock, shake, shudder, throb, tremble, vibrate, waver

**qualification** ability, aptitude, capability, capacity, eligibility, fitness, skill, suitability; allowance, caveat, condition, exception, limitation, modification, requirement, reservation, rider, stipulation .

**qualified** able, adept, capable, certificated, competent, efficient, equipped, experienced, expert, fit,

practised, proficient, skilful, talented, trained; bounded, conditional, limited, modified, provisional, reserved, restricted

**qualify** certify, commission, condition, empower, endow, equip, fit, ground, permit, prepare, ready, sanction, train; abate, adapt, assuage, diminish, ease, lessen, limit, moderate, reduce, regulate, restrain, restrict, soften, temper, vary

**quality** aspect, attribute, condition, feature, mark, property, trait; calibre, distinction, excellence, grade, merit, position, rank, standing, status, superiority, value, worth

**quandary** difficulty, dilemma, doubt, impasse, plight, strait, uncertainty

**quarantine** *n/v* (place in) isolation to prevent spreading of infection

**quarrel** *n* angry dispute; argument ~*v* **-relling, -relled** argue; find fault with **quarrelsome** *adj*

**quarry**[1] *n* object of hunt or pursuit; prey

**quarry**[2] *n* excavation where stone etc. is dug for building etc. ~*v* **-rying, -ried** get from quarry

**quart** *n* liquid measure, quarter of gallon

**quarter** *n* fourth part; region, district; mercy; *pl* lodgings ~*v* divide into quarters; lodge **quarterly** *adj* happening, due etc. each quarter of year **quartermaster** *n* officer responsible for stores

**quartet** *n* (music for) group of four musicians

**quartz** *n* hard glossy mineral

**quash** *v* annul; reject

**quasi-** *comb. form* not really, as in quasi-religious

**quaver** *v* say or sing in quavering tones; tremble, shake, vibrate ~*n* musical note half length of crotchet

**quay** *n* solid, fixed landing stage; wharf

**queasy** *adj* inclined to, or causing, sickness

**queen** *n* female sovereign; king's wife; piece in chess; fertile female bee, wasp etc.; court card

**queer** *adj* odd, strange

**quell** *v* crush, put down; allay

**quench** *v* slake; extinguish

**querulous** *adj* peevish, whining

**query** *n/v* **-rying, -ried** question

**quest** *n/v* search

**question** *n* sentence seeking for answer; problem; point at issue; doubt ~*v* ask questions of; dispute; doubt **questionable** *adj* doubtful **questionnaire** *n* formal list of questions **question mark** punctuation mark (?) written at end of questions

**queue** *n* line of waiting persons,

——— THESAURUS ———

**quantity** allotment, amount, lot, number, part, sum, total

**quarrel** affray, argument, breach, controversy, disagreement, discord, dispute, dissension, feud, fight, row, squabble, tiff ~*v* argue, bicker, brawl, clash, differ, disagree, dispute, fight, row, wrangle

**quarrelsome** argumentative, combative, disputatious, fractious, irascible, irritable, peevish, petulant, querulous

**quarry** aim, game, goal, objective, prey, prize, victim

**quarter** *n* area, district, locality, neighbourhood, part, place, point, position, province, region, territory; favour, forgiveness, leniency, mercy, pity ~*v* accommodate, billet, board, house, install, lodge, place,

post, station

**quash** annul, cancel, invalidate, nullify, overrule, overthrow, rescind, reverse, revoke

**queen** consort, monarch, ruler, sovereign

**queer** abnormal, curious, droll, extraordinary, funny, odd, peculiar, remarkable, rum *Brit sl*, singular, strange, uncanny, uncommon, unnatural, weird

**quench** check, crush, douse, end, extinguish, put out, smother, stifle, suppress

**query** *n* demand, doubt, hesitation, inquiry, objection, problem, question, suspicion ~*v* ask, enquire, question; challenge, disbelieve, dispute, distrust, doubt, mistrust, suspect

vehicles ~v wait in queue

**quibble** n/v (make) trivial objection

**quiche** n savoury flan

**quick** adj fast; lively; hasty ~n sensitive flesh ~adv rapidly **quicken** v make, become faster or more lively **quickly** adj **quicksand** n loose wet sand that engulfs heavy objects **quicksilver** n mercury **quickstep** n fast ballroom dance

**quiet** adj with little noise; undisturbed; not showy or obtrusive ~n quietness ~v make, become quiet **quieten** v

**quiff** n tuft of brushed-up hair

**quill** n large feather; pen made from feather; spine of porcupine

**quilt** n padded coverlet ~v stitch (two pieces of cloth) with pad between

**quinine** n drug used to treat fever and as tonic

**quintessence** n most perfect representation of a quality **quintessential** adj

**quintet** n (music for) group of five musicians

**quintuplet** n one of five offspring born at one birth

**quip** n/v quipping, quipped (utter) witty saying

**quirk** n individual peculiarity of character; unexpected twist

—————————— THESAURUS ——————————

**question** n inquiry, investigation; argument, contention, controversy, debate, difficulty, dispute, doubt, misgiving, problem, query; issue, motion, point, proposal, proposition, subject, theme, topic ~v ask, cross-examine, enquire, examine, interrogate, interview, probe, quiz; challenge, disbelieve, dispute, doubt, mistrust, oppose, query, suspect

**questionable** controversial, debatable, dodgy Brit, Aust, & NZ inf, doubtful, equivocal, iffy Inf, moot, problematical, suspect, uncertain

**queue** chain, file, line, order, sequence, series, string, train

**quibble** n cavil, complaint, criticism, evasion, objection ~v carp, cavil

**quick** active, brief, brisk, express, fast, fleet, hasty, headlong, hurried, prompt, quickie Inf, rapid, speedy, swift; agile, alert, animated, energetic, flying, lively, nimble, spirited, spry, vivacious

**quicken** accelerate, expedite, has-

ten, hurry, impel, speed; arouse, excite, incite, inspire, revive, stimulate

**quickly** abruptly, apace, briskly, fast, hastily, hurriedly, promptly, pronto Inf, rapidly, soon, speedily, swiftly

**quiet** adj dumb, hushed, inaudible, low, peaceful, silent, soft, soundless; calm, contented, gentle, mild, pacific, peaceful, placid, restful, serene, smooth, tranquil; modest, plain, restrained, simple, sober, subdued, unobtrusive ~n calmness, ease, peace, quietness, repose, rest, serenity, silence, tranquillity

**quieten** allay, appease, blunt, calm, deaden, dull, hush, lull, muffle, mute, quell, quiet, silence, soothe, stifle, still, stop, subdue

**quip** n gibe, jest, joke, pleasantry, repartee, retort, witticism

**quirk** aberration, caprice, characteristic, eccentricity, fancy, fetish, foible, habit, idiosyncrasy, kink, mannerism, oddity, peculiarity, singularity, trait, vagary, whim

**quit** v **quitting, quit** stop doing (something); leave; give up

**quite** adv completely; somewhat ~interj expression of agreement

**quiver**[1] v/n shake, tremble

**quiver**[2] n case for arrows

**quiz** n (pl **quizzes**) entertainment in which knowledge of players is tested by questions; examination, interrogation ~v **quizzing, quizzed** question, interrogate **quizzical** adj questioning; mocking

**quoit** n ring for throwing at peg as a game; pl (with sing v) this game

**quorum** n least number that must be present to make meeting valid **quorate** adj

**quota** n share to be contributed or received

**quote** v repeat passages from; state price for **quotation** n

**quotient** n number resulting from dividing one number by another

———————— THESAURUS ————————

**quit** cease, discontinue, drop, end, halt, stop, suspend; abandon, decamp, depart, desert, exit, go, leave, resign, retire, step down Inf, surrender, withdraw

**quite** completely, entirely, fully, largely, totally, wholly; fairly, rather, somewhat

**quiver** v oscillate, palpitate, pulsate, shiver, shudder, tremble, vibrate

**quiz** n questioning, test ~v ask, examine, investigate, question

**quota** allowance, assignment, part, portion, ration, share, slice

**quotation** cutting, excerpt, extract, passage, reference; Commerce charge, cost, estimate, figure, price, rate, tender

**quote** attest, cite, detail, instance, name, proclaim, recall, recite, recollect, refer to, repeat, retell

# R r

**R** King; Queen; river

**rabbi** (*pl* **rabbis**) *n* Jewish learned man, spiritual leader

**rabbit** *n* small burrowing mammal

**rabble** *n* crowd of vulgar, noisy people

**rabid** *adj* of, having rabies; fanatical

**rabies** *n* infectious disease transmitted by dogs etc.

**raccoon** *n* small N Amer. mammal

**race**¹ *n* contest of speed; rivalry; strong current; *pl* meeting for horse racing ~*v* (cause to) run, move swiftly **racer** *n*

**race**² *n* group of people of common ancestry with distinguishing physical features; species **racial** *adj* **racism, racialism** *n* belief in superiority of particular race; antagonism towards members of different race based on this **racist, racialist** *adj/n*

**rack** *n* framework for displaying or holding things; instrument of torture ~*v* torture

**racket**¹ *n* uproar; occupation by which money is made illegally **racketeer** *n*

**racket**², **racquet** *n* bat used in tennis etc.; *pl* ball game

**raconteur** *n* skilled storyteller

**racquet** *see* RACKET²

**racy** *adj* lively; piquant

**radar** *n* device for locating objects by radio waves, which reflect back to their source

**radial** *see* RADIUS

**radiate** *v* emit, be emitted in rays; spread out from centre **radiance** *n* brightness; splendour **radiation** *n* transmission of heat, light etc. from one body to another; particles, rays emitted in nuclear decay **radiator** *n* heating apparatus for rooms; cooling apparatus of car engine

**radical** *adj* fundamental; extreme; *of root* ~*n* person of extreme (political) views

**radio** *n* use of electromagnetic waves for broadcasting, communi-

---

## THESAURUS

**rabble** crowd, herd, horde, mob, swarm, throng

**rabid** berserk, crazed, fanatical, frantic, furious, mad, raging

**race**¹ *n* chase, contest, dash, pursuit, rivalry ~*v* career, compete, contest, dart, dash, fly, gallop, hurry, run, speed, tear

**race**² blood, breed, clan, family, folk, house, issue, kin, kindred, line, nation, offspring, people, progeny, stock, tribe, type

**racial** ethnic, ethnological, folk, genealogical, genetic, national, tribal

**rack** *n* frame, framework, stand, structure

**racket** clamour, din, fuss, noise, outcry, row, shouting, tumult, uproar; fraud, scheme

**racy** animated, buoyant, energetic, entertaining, exciting, heady, lively, sparkling, spirited

**radiate** diffuse, emit, gleam, pour, scatter, send out, shed, shine, spread

**radical** *adj* basic, deep-seated, essential, fundamental, innate, native, natural, profound; complete, drastic, entire, excessive, extreme, extremist, fanatical, severe, sweeping, thorough, violent ~*n* extremist, fanatic, militant

cation etc.; device for receiving, amplifying radio signals; broadcasting of radio programmes ~v transmit message etc. by radio

**radioactive** adj emitting invisible rays that penetrate matter **radioactivity** n

**radiography** n production of image on film by radiation

**radiology** n science of use of rays in medicine

**radiotherapy** n diagnosis and treatment of disease by X-rays

**radish** n pungent root vegetable

**radium** n radioactive metallic element

**radius** n (pl **radii**, **radiuses**) straight line from centre to circumference of circle **radial** adj

**RAF** Royal Air Force

**raffia** n prepared palm fibre for making mats etc.

**raffle** n lottery in which article is won by one of those buying tickets ~v dispose of by raffle

**raft** n floating structure of logs, planks etc.

**rafter** n main beam of roof

**rag** n fragment of cloth; torn piece; pl tattered clothing **ragged** adj **ragtime** n style of jazz piano music

**ragamuffin** n ragged, dirty person, esp. child

**rage** n violent anger; fury ~v speak, act with fury; proceed violently, as storm

**raglan** adj (of sleeve) continuing in one piece to the neck

**raid** n attack; foray ~v make raid on

**rail**[1] n horizontal bar **railing** n fence, barrier made of rails supported by posts **railway** n track of iron rails on which trains run

**rail**[2] v utter abuse; scold

**rain** n moisture falling in drops from clouds ~v pour down as, like rain **rainy** adj **rainbow** n arch of colours in sky **rainforest** n dense forest in tropics

**raise** v lift up; set up; build; increase; heighten, as voice; breed; collect; propose, suggest

**raisin** n dried grape

**rake**[1] n tool with long handle and teeth for gathering leaves etc. ~v gather, smooth with rake; search over; sweep with shot

**rake**[2] n dissolute man

**rakish** adj dashing; speedy

**rally** v **rallying**, **rallied** bring together, esp. what has been scattered; come together; regain health or

————————————— THESAURUS —————————————

**rage** n anger, frenzy, fury, ire, madness, obsession, rampage, violence, wrath ~v blow a fuse Sl, fly off the handle Inf, fret, fume, go up the wall Sl, rave, seethe, storm

**ragged** mean, poor, rent, shabby, threadbare, torn, unkempt, worn-out

**raid** n attack, foray, incursion, inroad, invasion, sally, seizure, sortie ~v assault, attack, foray, invade, pillage, plunder, rifle, sack

**rain** n deluge, downpour, drizzle,

fall, showers ~v drizzle, fall, pelt (down), pour, shower, teem

**raise** build, elevate, erect, exalt, heave, hoist, lift, promote, rear, uplift; advance, aggravate, amplify, boost, enhance, enlarge, escalate, increase, inflate, intensify, magnify, strengthen

**rake**[1] v collect, gather, remove; harrow, hoe, scour, scrape, scratch, smooth

**rake**[2] n lech or letch Inf, lecher, libertine, playboy, profligate, roué

**strength** ~*n* assembly, esp. outdoor; **Tennis** lively exchange of strokes

**ram** *n* male sheep; hydraulic machine; battering engine ~*v* **ramming, rammed** force, drive; strike against with force; stuff

**ramble** *v* walk without definite route; talk incoherently ~*n* rambling walk

**ramify** *v* **-ifying, -ified** spread in branches; become complex **ramification** *n*

**ramp** *n* gradual slope joining two level surfaces

**rampage** *v* dash about violently ~*n* angry or destructive behaviour

**rampant** *adj* violent; rife; rearing

**rampart** *n* wall for defence

**ramshackle** *adj* rickety

**ran** *past tense of* RUN

**ranch** *n* Amer. cattle farm

**rancid** *adj* smelling or tasting offensively, like stale fat

**rancour** *n* bitter hate

**random** *adj* by chance, without plan

**randy** *adj* Sl sexually aroused

**rang** *past tense of* RING²

**range** *n* limits; row; scope, distance missile can travel; place for shooting practice; kitchen stove ~*v* set in row; extend; fluctuate **ranger** *n* official patrolling park etc. **rangy** *adj* with long, slender limbs

**rank**¹ *n* row, line; place where taxis wait; order; status; relative position; *pl* (also **rank and file**) common soldiers; great mass of people ~*v* draw up in rank; have rank, place

**rank**² *adj* growing too thickly; rancid; flagrant

**rankle** *v* continue to cause anger or

———— THESAURUS ————

**rally** *v* reassemble, re-form, regroup, reorganize, unite; assemble, collect, convene, gather, marshal, mobilize, muster, organize, round up, summon, unite; improve, pick up, recover, recuperate, revive ~*n* congress, convention, convocation, gathering, meeting, muster

**ram** butt, crash, dash, drive, force, hit, impact, smash, strike

**ramble** *v* drift, range, roam, rove, saunter, straggle, stray, stroll, walk, wander; chatter, digress, maunder, waffle *Inf, chiefly Brit,* wander ~*n* excursion, hike, saunter, stroll, tour, trip, walk

**ramification** branch, division, extension, offshoot; complication, consequence, development, result, sequel, upshot

**rampage** *v* rage, storm ~*n* fury, rage, storm, tempest, tumult, uproar, violence

**rampant** aggressive, flagrant, outrageous, raging, riotous, unbridled, wanton, wild

**rampart** bastion, bulwark, defence, fence, fort, guard, security, wall

**ramshackle** crumbling, decrepit, derelict, flimsy, rickety, shaky, unsafe

**rancid** bad, fetid, foul, off, putrid, rank, rotten, sour, tainted

**random** accidental, aimless, casual, chance, fortuitous, haphazard, hit or miss, incidental, spot

**range** *n* area, bounds, distance, extent, field, latitude, limits, orbit, province, radius, reach, scope, span, sphere, sweep ~*v* align, arrange, array, dispose, line up, order; cruise, explore, ramble, roam, rove, stray, stroll, sweep, wander

**rank**¹ *n* column, file, group, line, range, row, series, tier; caste, class,

bitterness

**ransack** v search thoroughly; pillage

**ransom** n release from captivity by payment; amount paid ~v pay ransom for

**rant** v rave in violent language

**rap** v **rapping, rapped** give smart slight blow to; utter abruptly; perform monologue to music ~n smart slight blow; punishment; monologue set to music

**rapacious** adj greedy; grasping

**rape**[1] v force (woman) to submit to sexual intercourse ~n act of raping **rapist** n

**rape**[2] n plant with oil-yielding seeds

**rapid** adj quick, swift ~n (esp. pl) part of river with fast, turbulent current

**rapier** n fine-bladed sword

**rapport** n harmony, agreement

**rapt** adj engrossed **rapture** n ecstasy

**rare**[1] adj uncommon; of exceptionally high quality **rarely** adv seldom **rarity** n

**rare**[2] adj (of meat) lightly cooked

**rarefy** v **-fying, -fied** make, become thin or less dense

**raring** adj enthusiastically willing, ready

**rascal** n rogue; naughty (young) person

**rash**[1] adj hasty, reckless

**rash**[2] n skin eruption; outbreak

**rasher** n slice of bacon

**rasp** n harsh, grating noise; coarse file ~v scrape with rasp; make scraping noise; irritate

**raspberry** n red, edible berry;

————— THESAURUS —————

degree, dignity, division, grade, level, order, position, quality, sort, station, status, type ~v align, arrange, array, class, classify, grade, locate, marshal, order, range, sort

**rank**[2] dense, lush, productive, profuse, vigorous; bad, fetid, foul, fusty, musty, off, putrid, rancid

**ransack** explore, rake, rove, search; despoil, gut, loot, pillage, plunder, raid, ravage, rifle, sack, strip

**ransom** n liberation, redemption, release, rescue; money, payment, payoff, price ~v deliver, liberate, redeem, release, rescue

**rant** bluster, cry, declaim, rave, roar, shout, yell

**rape** v ravish, sexually assault, violate ~n sexual assault, violation

**rapid** brisk, express, fast, fleet, flying, hasty, hurried, prompt, quick, swift

**rapt** absorbed, engrossed, enthralled, gripped, held, intent, spellbound

**rapture** bliss, delight, ecstasy, exaltation, happiness, joy, spell, transport

**rare** few, infrequent, scarce, singular, sparse, strange, uncommon, unusual; choice, extreme, fine, great, peerless, superb

**rarely** hardly, little, seldom

**rarity** curio, find, gem, pearl, treasure; infrequency, shortage

**rascal** blackguard, devil, disgrace, imp, rake, rogue, scamp, scoundrel, villain, wastrel

**rash**[1] brash, careless, foolhardy, hasty, heedless, hot-headed, ill-advised, impetuous, imprudent, impulsive, reckless

**rash**[2] eruption, outbreak; flood, outbreak, plague, series, spate, wave

plant which bears it

**Rastafarian** n (oft. shortened to **Rasta**) member of Jamaican cult ~adj of this cult

**rat** n small rodent ~v **ratting, ratted** inform (on); betray; desert **ratty** adj Inf irritable **rat race** continual hectic competitive activity

**ratchet** n set of teeth on bar or wheel allowing motion in one direction only

**rate** n proportion between two things; charge; degree of speed etc.; pl local tax on business property ~v value

**rather** adv to some extent; preferably; more willingly

**ratify** v **-ifying, -ified** confirm **ratification** n

**rating** n valuing; classification; (also **naval rating**) sailor

**ratio** n (pl **-tios**) proportion; relation

**ration** n fixed allowance of food

etc. ~v supply with, limit to certain amount

**rational** adj reasonable, capable of reasoning **rationale** n reason for decision **rationalize** v justify by plausible reasoning; reorganize to improve efficiency etc.

**rattle** v (cause to) give out succession of short sharp sounds ~n such sound; instrument for making it; set of horny rings in rattlesnake's tail **rattlesnake** n poisonous snake

**raucous** adj hoarse

**raunchy** adj Sl earthy, sexy

**ravage** v plunder ~n destruction

**rave** v talk wildly in delirium or enthusiasm ~n wild talk; large-scale party with electronic music **raving** adj delirious; Inf exceptional

**raven** n black bird ~adj jet-black

**ravenous** adj very hungry

**ravine** n narrow steep-sided valley

**ravioli** pl n small squares of pasta with filling

——————— THESAURUS ———————

**rate** n degree, proportion, ratio, scale, standard; charge, cost, dues, duty, fee, figure, hire, price, tariff, tax; measure, pace, speed, tempo, time ~v appraise, assess, class, consider, count, estimate, evaluate, grade, measure, rank, reckon, regard, value, weigh

**rather** a bit, a little, fairly, moderately, quite, relatively, slightly, somewhat, to some degree, to some extent; instead, preferably, sooner

**ratify** affirm, approve, bind, confirm, corroborate, endorse, establish, sanction, sign, uphold

**ratio** fraction, percentage, proportion, rate, relation

**ration** n allotment, allowance, dole, helping, measure, part, portion, provision, quota, share ~v al-

locate, allot, deal, distribute, dole, amount

**rational** enlightened, intelligent, logical, lucid, realistic, reasonable, sane, sensible, sound, wise

**rationalize** excuse, justify, vindicate; downsize, restructure

**rattle** v bang, clatter; bounce, jar, jolt, shake, vibrate

**raucous** grating, harsh, hoarse, husky, loud, noisy, rasping, rough, strident

**ravage** demolish, despoil, destroy, devastate, loot, pillage, plunder, ransack, ruin, sack, spoil

**rave** fume, go mad Inf, rage, rant, roar, splutter, storm, thunder

**ravenous** famished, starved

**ravine** canyon, defile, flume,

**ravish** v enrapture; rape **ravishing** adj lovely

**raw** adj uncooked; not manufactured or refined; skinned; inexperienced; chilly

**ray**[1] n narrow beam of light, heat etc.; any of set of radiating lines

**ray**[2] n marine flatfish

**rayon** n synthetic fibre

**raze** v destroy completely

**razor** n sharp instrument for shaving

**razzle-dazzle** also **razzmatazz** n showy activity

**RC** Roman Catholic

**RE** religious education

**re** prep concerning

**re-** comb. form again

**reach** v arrive at; extend; touch ~n act of reaching; grasp; range

**react** v act in return, opposition or

towards former state **reaction** n counter or backward tendency; response; chemical or nuclear change **reactionary** n/adj (person) opposed to change, esp. in politics etc. **reactive** adj chemically active **reactor** n apparatus to produce nuclear energy

**read** v reading, read understand written matter; learn by reading; read and utter; study; understand any indicating instrument **reader** n one who reads; university lecturer; school textbook **reading** n

**ready** adj prepared for action; willing **readiness** n

**real** adj happening; actual; genuine **realism** n regarding things as they are **realist** n **realistic** adj **reality** n real existence **really** adv **real estate** landed property

———— THESAURUS ————

gorge, gully, pass

**raw** fresh, natural, uncooked, undressed, unprepared; basic, coarse, crude, green, natural, organic, rough, unprocessed, unrefined, unripe; chafed, grazed, open, skinned, sore, tender

**ray** bar, beam, flash, gleam, shaft

**reach** v arrive at, attain, drop, fall, move, rise, sink; contact, extend to, grasp, stretch to, touch ~n ambit, capacity, command, compass, distance, extension, extent, grasp, influence, jurisdiction, mastery, power, range, scope

**react** answer, reply, respond; act, behave, function, operate, proceed, work

**reaction** recoil; answer, feedback, reply, response

**reactionary** n die-hard, obscurantist, rightist ~adj blimpish, conservative

**read** comprehend, construe, decipher, discover, interpret, see, understand; look at, peruse, pore over, scan, study; announce, declaim, deliver, recite, speak, utter

**readily** eagerly, freely, gladly, promptly, quickly, willingly; easily, effortlessly, quickly, smoothly, speedily, unhesitatingly

**reading** lecture, lesson, recital, rendering, sermon

**ready** arranged, completed, fit, organized, prepared, primed, ripe, set; agreeable, apt, disposed, eager, glad, happy, inclined, keen, prone, willing

**real** absolute, actual, authentic, certain, factual, genuine, honest, intrinsic, positive, right, rightful, sincere, true, unfeigned, valid, veritable

**realistic** common-sense, levelheaded, matter-of-fact, practical,

**realize** v grasp significance of; make real; convert into money

**realm** n kingdom

**ream** n twenty quires of paper; pl Inf large quantity of written matter

**reap** v cut and gather harvest

**rear[1]** n back part **rear admiral** high-ranking naval officer

**rear[2]** v care for and educate (children); breed; rise on hind feet

**reason** n motive; ability to think; sanity; sensible thought ~v think logically; persuade by logical argument **reasonable** adj sensible; suitable; logical

**reassure** v restore confidence to

**rebate** n discount, refund

**rebel** v **-belling, -belled** resist lawful authority ~n one who rebels ~adj rebelling **rebellion** n organized open resistance to authority **rebellious** adj

**rebound** v spring back; misfire, esp. so as to hurt perpetrator ~n recoiling

**rebuff** n/v repulse, snub

**rebuke** n/v reprimand

———————— THESAURUS ————————

**real**, sensible, sober; authentic, faithful, genuine, lifelike, natural, true, truthful

**reality** actuality, fact, realism, truth, validity, verity

**realize** appreciate, comprehend, conceive, grasp, imagine, recognize, understand; accomplish, bring off, complete, consummate, do, effect, fulfil, perform; acquire, clear, earn, gain, get, make, net, obtain, produce

**reap** acquire, collect, cut, derive, gain, garner, gather, get, harvest, win

**rear[1]** n back, end, rearguard, stern, tail and tail end

**rear[2]** v breed, cultivate, educate, foster, grow, nurse, nurture, raise, train

**reason** n aim, basis, cause, design, end, goal, grounds, impetus, incentive, inducement, intention, motive, object, purpose; brains, intellect, judgment, logic, mentality, mind, sanity, sense(s), soundness, understanding ~v conclude, deduce, infer, make out, ratiocinate, resolve, solve, think, work out

**reasonable** arguable, believable, credible, intelligent, logical, plausible, practical, sane, sensible, sober, sound, tenable, wise; average, equitable, fair, fit, honest, inexpensive, just, moderate, modest

**reassure** comfort, encourage, hearten, inspirit, restore confidence to

**rebel** v mutiny, resist, revolt; defy, disobey, dissent ~n insurgent, revolutionary, revolutionist, secessionist; apostate, dissenter, heretic, schismatic ~adj insurgent, rebellious

**rebellion** mutiny, resistance, revolt, revolution, rising, uprising

**rebellious** defiant, disloyal, disobedient, disorderly, insurgent, mutinous, rebel, revolutionary, unruly

**rebound** v bounce, recoil, return; backfire, boomerang, misfire, recoil ~n bounce, kickback, return, ricochet

**rebuff** n check, defeat, denial, discouragement, knock-back Sl, opposition, refusal, rejection, repulse, slight, snub ~v cold-shoulder, cut, decline, deny, discourage, refuse, reject, repulse, resist, slight, snub, spurn

**rebuke** n blame, censure, lecture,

**rebut** *v* **-butting, -butted** refute, disprove **rebuttal** *n*

**recalcitrant** *adj* wilfully disobedient

**recall** *v* remember; call back; restore ~*n* summons; ability to remember

**recant** *v* withdraw statement, opinion etc.

**recap** *v* **-capping, -capped** recapitulate ~*n* recapitulation

**recapitulate** *v* state again briefly **recapitulation** *n*

**recede** *v* go back; slope backward

**receipt** *n* written acknowledgment of money received; receiving

**receive** *v* accept, experience; greet (guests) **receiver** *n* officer appointed to take public money; one who knowingly takes stolen goods; equipment in telephone etc. to convert electrical signals into sound etc.

**recent** *adj* lately happened; new **recently** *adv*

**receptacle** *n* vessel to contain anything

**reception** *n* receiving; formal party; area for receiving guests etc.; in broadcasting, quality of signals received **receptionist** *n* person who receives clients etc.

**receptive** *adj* quick, willing to receive new ideas

**recess** *n* alcove; hollow; suspension of business

**recession** *n* period of reduction in trade; act of receding **recessive** *adj* receding

**recipe** *n* directions for cooking food

**recipient** *n* one that receives

**reciprocal** *adj* complementary; mutual; moving backwards and forwards **reciprocate** *v* give and receive mutually

**recite** *v* repeat aloud, esp. to audience **recital** *n* musical performance, usu. by one person; narration **recitation** *n*

———————— THESAURUS ————————

**reprimand**, reproach, reproof ~*v* admonish, blame, castigate, censure, chide, lecture, reprehend, reproach, reprove, scold

**recall** *v* evoke, recollect, remember; annul, cancel, countermand, repeal, retract, revoke, withdraw ~*n* cancellation, repeal, retraction, withdrawal; memory, remembrance

**recede** abate, ebb, fall back, regress, retire, retreat, return, subside, withdraw

**receipt** stub, voucher; acceptance, delivery, receiving, reception

**receive** accept, acquire, collect, derive, get, obtain, pick up, take; accommodate, admit, entertain, greet, meet, take in, welcome

**recent** current, fresh, late, latter,

modern, new, novel, young

**reception** admission, receipt; function, levee, party, soirée

**receptive** alert, bright, perceptive, responsive, sensitive

**recess** alcove, bay, corner, hollow, niche, nook, oriel; break, closure, holiday, interval, respite, rest, vacation

**recession** decline, depression, drop, slump

**recipe** ingredients, instructions

**reciprocate** barter, exchange, reply, requite, respond, return, swap, trade

**recital** account, narrative, performance, reading, rehearsal, rendering, statement, story, tale, telling

**recite** declaim, deliver, describe,

**reckless** *adj* incautious

**reckon** *v* count; include; think

**reclaim** *v* make fit for cultivation; bring back; reform; demand the return of

**recline** *v* sit, lie back

**recluse** *n* hermit

**recognize** *v* identify again; treat as valid; notice **recognition** *n*

**recoil** *v* draw back in horror; rebound ~*n* recoiling

**recollect** *v* remember **recollection** *n*

**recommend** *v* advise; praise; make acceptable **recommendation** *n*

**recompense** *v* reward; compensate ~*n* reward; compensation

**reconcile** *v* bring back into friendship; adjust, harmonize **reconciliation** *n*

**reconnoitre** *v* make survey of **reconnaissance** *n* survey, esp. for military purposes

**reconstitute** *v* restore (food) to former state, esp. by addition of water

**record** *n* document that records; disc with indentations which can be transformed into sound; best achievement; known facts ~*v* put in writing; preserve (sound etc.) on magnetic tape etc. for reproduction on playback device **recorder** *n* one that records; type of flute; judge in certain courts **record player** instru-

——————— THESAURUS ———————

detail, itemize, narrate, perform, recount, repeat, speak, tell

**reckless** careless, hasty, headlong, heedless, imprudent, indiscreet, mindless, precipitate, rash, thoughtless, wild

**reckon** add up, compute, count, figure, number, tally, total; assume, believe, imagine, suppose, surmise, think

**reclaim** recapture, recover, redeem, reform, regain, reinstate

**recline** lean, loll, lounge, repose, rest, sprawl

**recluse** anchoress, anchorite, ascetic, hermit, monk, solitary

**recognition** discovery, recall, remembrance; acceptance, admission, allowance, appreciation, avowal, confession, notice, perception, respect

**recognize** identify, know, notice, place, recall, recollect, remember, spot; accept, admit, allow, avow, concede, confess, grant, own, perceive, realize, respect, see, take on

board, understand

**recoil** *v* draw back, falter, quail, shrink; backfire, misfire, rebound ~*n* backlash, kick, reaction, rebound, repercussion

**recollect** place, recall, remember, summon up

**recollection** impression, memory, recall, reminiscence

**recommend** advance, advise, advocate, counsel, enjoin, exhort, prescribe, propose, put forward, suggest, urge

**recommendation** advice, counsel, proposal; advocacy, approval, blessing, endorsement, praise, reference, sanction, testimonial

**reconcile** appease, conciliate, propitiate, reunite; adjust, compose, harmonize, rectify, resolve, settle, square; accept, resign, submit, yield

**reconnaissance** exploration, observation, patrol, scan, survey

**reconnoitre** case *Sl*, explore, inspect, investigate, observe, patrol, scan, scout, spy out, survey

ment for reproducing sound on records

**recount** v tell in detail

**recoup** v recover what has been expended or lost

**recourse** n (resorting to) source of help

**recover** v get back; become healthy again **recovery** n

**recreation** n agreeable relaxation, amusement

**recrimination** n mutual abuse and blame

**recruit** n newly-enlisted soldier; one newly joining ~v enlist **recruitment** n

**rectangle** n oblong four-sided figure with four right angles **rectangular** adj

**rectify** v -fying, -fied correct

**rectitude** n honesty

**rector** n clergyman with care of parish; head of academic institution

**rectory** n rector's house

**rectum** n (pl -ta) final section of large intestine

**recumbent** adj lying down

**recuperate** v restore, be restored from illness etc.

**recur** v -curring, -curred happen again; go or come back in mind **recurrence** n **recurrent** adj

**recycle** v reprocess substance for use again

**red** adj/n (of) colour of blood; Inf communist **reddish** adj **reddish** n **red-blooded** adj Inf vigorous; virile **red carpet** special welcome for important guest **red-handed** adj Inf (caught) in the act **red herring** topic introduced to divert attention **red-hot** adj extremely hot; very keen **red tape** excessive adherence to rules **redwood** n giant coniferous tree of California

**redeem** v buy back; set free; free

**record** n account, chronicle, diary, entry, file, journal, log, memory, minute, register, report; album, disc, recording, release, single; background, career, history, performance ~v document, enrol, enter, inscribe, log, minute, note, register, report, transcribe

**recount** v depict, detail, enumerate, narrate, portray, recite, rehearse, relate, repeat, report, tell

**recover** v recapture, reclaim, redeem, regain, repair, repossess, restore, retrieve; convalesce, get better, get well, heal, improve, mend, rally, recuperate, revive

**recovery** n healing, improvement, mending, rally, revival; betterment, improvement, rally, restoration, revival, upturn

**recreation** n amusement, diversion,

enjoyment, exercise, fun, hobby, pastime, play, pleasure, relaxation, relief, sport

**recruit** n apprentice, beginner, convert, helper, initiate, learner, novice, trainee ~v draft, enlist, enrol, impress, levy, mobilize, muster, raise; engage, procure

**rectify** v adjust, amend, correct, emend, fix, improve, mend, redress, reform, remedy, repair, right, square

**recuperate** v convalesce, improve, mend, recover

**recur** v come again, happen again, persist, reappear, repeat, return, revert

**recurrent** adj continued, frequent, habitual, periodic

**red** cardinal, carmine, cherry, coral, crimson, rose, ruby, scarlet, ti-

from sin; make up for **redemption** n

**redolent** adj smelling strongly; reminiscent (of)

**redouble** v increase, intensify

**redoubtable** adj dreaded, formidable

**redress** v make amends for ~n compensation

**reduce** v lower; lessen; bring by necessity to some state; slim; simplify **reduction** n

**redundant** adj superfluous; (of worker) deprived of job because no longer needed **redundancy** n

**reed** n various water plants; tall straight stem of one; Mus vibrating strip of certain wind instruments

**reef** n ridge of rock or coral near surface of sea; part of sail which can be rolled up to reduce area

**reek** v/n (emit) strong unpleasant smell

**reel** n spool on which film, thread etc. is wound; Cinema portion of film; lively dance ~v wind on reel;

draw (in) by means of reel; stagger

**refectory** n room for meals in college etc.

**refer** v **-ferring, -ferred** relate (to); send to for information; ascribe to; submit for decision **reference** n act of referring; citation; appeal to judgment of another; testimonial; one to whom inquiries as to character etc. may be made

**referee** n arbitrator; umpire ~v act as referee

**referendum** n (pl **-dums, -da**) submitting of question to electorate

**refill** v fill again ~n subsequent filling; replacement supply

**refine** v purify **refined** adj cultured, polite; purified **refinement** n subtlety; elaboration; fineness of taste or manners **refinery** n place where sugar, oil etc. is refined

**reflect** v throw back, esp. light; cast (discredit etc.) upon; meditate **reflection** n reflecting; image of object given back by mirror etc.; thought;

─────── THESAURUS ───────

tian, vermilion, wine

**redeem** reclaim, recover, regain, repossess, repurchase, retrieve, win back; deliver, emancipate, free, liberate, ransom

**redress** make amends

**reduce** abate, abridge, curtail, decrease, dilute, diminish, impair, lessen, lower, moderate, shorten, truncate, weaken; cheapen, cut, discount, lower, slash; bring, conquer, drive, force, master, overpower, subdue, vanquish

**redundant** excessive, superfluous, supernumerary, surplus, unwanted

**reek** v smell, stink ~n odour, smell, stench, stink

**reel** revolve, spin, swim, swirl, twirl, whirl; lurch, pitch, rock, roll,

stagger, sway

**refer** advert, allude, cite, hint, invoke, mention; direct, guide, point, recommend, send; apply, consult, go, turn to

**referee** n arbiter, arbitrator, judge, umpire ~v adjudicate, arbitrate, judge, mediate, umpire

**reference** allusion, citation, mention, note, quotation, remark; character, recommendation, testimonial

**refine** clarify, cleanse, distil, filter, process, purify, rarefy

**refined** civilized, courtly, cultivated, elegant, gracious, ladylike, polished, polite, urbane

**refinement** fine point, nicety, nuance, subtlety; breeding, civility, courtesy, cultivation, culture, gen-

expression of thought **reflective** *adj* **reflector** *n*

**reflex** *n* involuntary action ~*adj* (of muscular action) involuntary; bent back **reflexive** *adj* *Grammar* describes verb denoting agent's action on himself

**reform** *v* improve; abandon evil practices ~*n* improvement **reformation** *n*

**refract** *v* change course of light etc. passing from one medium to another **refraction** *n*

**refractory** *adj* unmanageable

**refrain**[1] *v* abstain (from)

**refrain**[2] *n* chorus

**refresh** *v* revive; renew; brighten **refreshment** *n* that which refreshes, esp. food, drink

**refrigerate** *v* freeze; cool **refrigerant** *n/adj* **refrige'ration** *n* **refrigerator** *n* apparatus in which foods,

drinks are kept cool

**refuge** *n* shelter, sanctuary **refugee** *n* one who seeks refuge, esp. in foreign country

**refund** *v* pay back ~*n* repayment

**refurbish** *v* renovate and brighten up

**refuse**[1] *v* decline, deny, reject **refusal** *n*

**refuse**[2] *n* rubbish

**refute** *v* disprove **refutation** *n*

**regain** *v* get back, recover; reach again

**regal** *adj* of, like a king **regalia** *pl n* insignia of royalty; emblems of high office

**regale** *v* give pleasure to; feast

**regard** *v* look at; consider; relate to ~*n* look; attention; particular respect; esteem; *pl* expression of good will **regardless** *adj* heedless ~*adv* in spite of everything

———— THESAURUS ————

tility, polish

**reflect** echo, mirror, reproduce, return, throw back; cogitate, consider, meditate, muse, ponder, ruminate, think, wonder

**reflection** echo, image; cogitation, consideration, idea, meditation, musing, observation, opinion, pondering, study, thinking, view

**reform** *v* amend, correct, emend, improve, mend, rebuild, reclaim, regenerate, remodel, renovate, repair, restore ~*n* amendment, betterment, improvement, rehabilitation

**refrain** *v* abstain, avoid, cease, desist, forbear, kick *Inf*, renounce, stop

**refresh** brace, cheer, cool, enliven, freshen, reinvigorate, revitalize, revive, revivify, stimulate; prompt, renew, stimulate

**refreshment** enlivenment, freshening, renewal, repair, revival, stimulation; *pl* drinks, snacks, titbits

**refuge** asylum, harbour, haven, hide-out, resort, retreat, shelter

**refugee** émigré, escapee, exile, fugitive, runaway

**refund** *v* pay back, reimburse, repay, restore, return ~*n* repayment, return

**refusal** denial, rebuff, rejection, repudiation

**refuse** *v* decline, deny, reject, repel, repudiate, withhold

**regain** recapture, recoup, recover, repossess, retake, retrieve

**regard** *v* behold, check, check out *Inf*, eye, mark, notice, observe, remark, view, watch; adjudge, believe, consider, deem, esteem, hold, imagine, rate, see, sup-

**regatta** n meeting for boat races

**regenerate** v reform; re-create; re-organize **regeneration** n

**regent** n ruler of kingdom during absence, minority etc. of its monarch **regency** n

**reggae** n popular music with strong beat

**regime** n system of government

**regiment** n organized body of troops ~v discipline (too) strictly **regimental** adj

**region** n area, district; part; sphere **regional** adj

**register** n list; catalogue; device for registering; range of voice or instrument ~v show, be shown on meter, face etc.; enter in register; record **registrar** n keeper of a register; senior hospital doctor **registration** n registry; place where registers are kept

**regress** v revert to former place, condition etc. **regression** n

**regret** v -gretting, -gretted feel sorry, distressed for loss of or on account of ~n feeling of sorrow **regretful** adj **regrettable** adj

**regular** adj normal; habitual; according to rule; periodical; straight ~n soldier in standing army **regularity** n

**regulate** v adjust; arrange; govern **regulation** n

——— THESAURUS ———

pose, think, treat, value, view ~n attention, heed, interest, mind, notice; affection, care, concern, deference, esteem, honour, love, note, repute, respect, store, sympathy, thought

**regardless** adj heedless, inconsiderate, indifferent, neglectful, rash, reckless, remiss, unmindful ~adv anyway, nevertheless, nonetheless

**regime** government, leadership, management, reign, rule, system

**region** area, country, district, expanse, land, locality, part, patch, place, quarter, section, sector, territory, tract, zone

**regional** district, local, parochial, provincial, sectional, zonal

**register** n archives, catalogue, chronicle, diary, file, ledger, list, log, record, roll, roster, schedule ~v betray, display, exhibit, express, indicate, manifest, mark, read, record, reflect, reveal, say, show; catalogue, chronicle, enlist, enrol, enter, inscribe, list, note, record, take down

**regret** v bemoan, bewail, deplore, grieve, lament, miss, mourn, repent, rue ~n bitterness, compunction, contrition, disappointment, penitence, remorse, repentance, ruefulness, sorrow

**regrettable** disappointing, distressing, lamentable, pitiable, sad, shameful, unfortunate

**regular** common, customary, daily, everyday, habitual, normal, ordinary, routine, typical, usual; consistent, constant, even, fixed, ordered, periodical, set, stated, steady, systematic, uniform; balanced, even, flat, level, smooth, straight, symmetrical, uniform

**regulate** adjust, arrange, balance, conduct, control, direct, fit, govern, guide, handle, manage, monitor, order, rule, run, settle, supervise, tune

**regulation** n decree, dictate, direction, edict, law, order, precept, procedure, requirement, rule, statute; adjustment, control, direction, government, management, supervi-

**regurgitate** v vomit; bring back (swallowed food) into mouth

**rehabilitate** v help (person) to readjust to society after illness, imprisonment etc.; restore to former position **rehabilitation** n

**rehash** n old materials presented in new form ~v rework

**rehearse** v practise (play etc.); repeat; train **rehearsal** n

**reign** n period of sovereign's rule ~v rule

**reimburse** v pay back

**rein** n strap attached to bit to guide horse; instrument for governing

**reincarnation** n rebirth of soul in successive bodies

**reindeer** n (pl -deer, -deers) deer of cold regions

**reinforce** v strengthen with new support, material, force **reinforcement** n

**reinstate** v replace, restore

**reiterate** v repeat again

**reject** v refuse to accept; put aside; discard; renounce ~n person or thing rejected **rejection** n

**rejig** v -jigging, -jigged re-equip; rearrange

**rejoice** v make or be joyful

**rejoin** v reply **rejoinder** n

**rejuvenate** v restore to youth

**relapse** v fall back into evil, illness etc. ~n relapsing

**relate** v narrate; establish relation between; have reference to; (with **to**) form sympathetic relationship

**relation** n relative condition; connection by blood or marriage; connection between things; narrative **relationship** n **relative** adj dependent on relation to something else; having reference (to) ~n one connected by blood or marriage

───── THESAURUS ─────

sion, tuning

**rehearsal** drill, practice, preparation, reading

**rehearse** act, drill, practise, prepare, ready, recite, repeat, run through, study, train, try out

**reign** n command, control, dominion, empire, influence, monarchy, power, rule, sway ~v administer, command, govern, influence, rule

**reinforce** bolster, emphasize, fortify, harden, increase, prop, stiffen, strengthen, stress, support, toughen, underline

**reinforcement** enlargement, fortification, increase, strengthening, supplement; brace, buttress, prop, shore, stay, support

**reinstate** recall, rehabilitate, replace, restore, return

**reject** v decline, deny, despise, discard, jettison, rebuff, refuse, re-

nounce, repel, scrap, spurn, throw away or out, turn down, veto ~n castoff, discard, failure, second

**rejection** dismissal, exclusion, knock-back Sl, rebuff, refusal, repudiation, veto

**rejoice** celebrate, delight, exult, glory, joy, revel, triumph

**relapse** v degenerate, fail, lapse, regress, revert, weaken; deteriorate, fade, fail, sicken, sink, weaken, worsen ~n lapse, regression, retrogression, reversion; deterioration, weakening, worsening

**relate** describe, detail, narrate, present, recite, rehearse, report, tell; apply, concern, pertain, refer

**relation** affinity, kindred, kinship; kin, kinsman, relative; bearing, bond, comparison, connection, link, pertinence, reference, regard, similarity

**relax** v make, become loose or slack; ease up; relax, become less strict **relaxation** n recreation; abatement

**relay** n fresh set of people or animals relieving others; *Radio, Television* broadcasting station receiving programmes from another station ~v **relaying**, **relayed** pass on, as message **relay race** race between teams of which each runner races part of distance

**release** v set free; permit showing of (film etc.) ~n releasing; permission to show publicly; film, record etc. newly issued

**relegate** v put in less important position; demote **relegation** n

**relent** v become less severe **relentless** adj

**relevant** adj having to do with the matter in hand **relevance** n

**reliable, reliance** SEE RELY

**relic** n thing remaining

**relief** n alleviation of pain etc.; money, food given to victims of disaster; release from duty; one who relieves another; bus, plane etc. operating when a scheduled service is full; freeing of besieged city; projection of carved design from surface; prominence **relieve** v

**religion** n system of belief in, worship of a supernatural power or god

——————— THESAURUS ———————

**relationship** affair, affinity, bond, conjunction, connection, exchange, kinship, liaison, link, proportion, similarity, tie-up

**relative** adj allied, connected, contingent, dependent, reciprocal, related, respective; applicable, apposite, appropriate, appurtenant, apropos, germane, pertinent, relevant ~n kinsman

**relax** abate, ease, ebb, lessen, let up, loosen, lower, moderate, reduce, relieve, slacken, weaken; calm, chill out *Sl, chiefly US*, laze, soften, unwind

**relaxation** enjoyment, fun, leisure, pleasure, recreation, refreshment, rest

**relay** n relief, shift, turn; dispatch, message, transmission ~v broadcast, carry, hand on, pass on, send, spread, transmit

**release** v deliver, discharge, drop, extricate, free, liberate, loose, set free, unchain, undo, unfasten, untie; circulate, distribute, issue, launch, present, publish, put out,

unveil ~n acquittal, delivery, discharge, freedom, liberty, relief

**relent** be merciful, capitulate, forbear, melt, soften, unbend, yield

**relentless** cruel, fierce, grim, hard, harsh, pitiless, remorseless

**relevant** admissible, apposite, appropriate, apt, fitting, material, pertinent, proper, related, significant, suited

**reliable** dependable, faithful, honest, predictable, regular, responsible, safe, sound, stable, staunch, sure, true

**relic** fragment, keepsake, memento, remnant, scrap, token, trace, vestige

**relief** balm, comfort, cure, deliverance, ease, mitigation, release, remedy, solace; aid, assistance, help, succour, support; break, diversion, remission, respite, rest

**relieve** allay, alleviate, appease, assuage, calm, comfort, console, cure, dull, ease, mitigate, mollify, relax, soften, solace, soothe; aid, assist, help, succour, support, sustain;

**religious** *adj* of religion; pious; scrupulous

**relinquish** *v* give up

**relish** *v* enjoy ~*n* liking; savoury taste; sauce; pickle

**relocate** *v* move to new place, esp. to work

**reluctant** *adj* unwilling **reluctance** *n*

**rely** *v* **relying, relied** depend (on); trust **reliability** *n* **reliable** *adj* **reliance** *n* trust; confidence

**remain** *v* be left behind; continue; last **remainder** *n* **remains** *pl n* relics; dead body

**remand** *v* send back, esp. into cus-

tody **on remand** in custody

**remark** *v/n* (make) casual comment (on) **remarkable** *adj* unusual

**remedy** *n* means of curing ~*v* **-edying, -edied** put right **remedial** *adj*

**remember** *v* retain in, recall to memory **remembrance** *n*

**remind** *v* cause to remember **reminder** *n*

**reminisce** *v* talk, write of past times, experiences etc. **reminiscence** *n* **reminiscent** *adj*

**remiss** *adj* careless

**remit** *v* **-mitting, -mitted** send money for goods etc.; refrain from

——————— THESAURUS ———————

**religious** devotional, devout, faithful, godly, holy, pious, pure, reverent, righteous, sacred, spiritual

**relish** *v* delight in, enjoy, fancy, like, prefer, savour, taste ~*n* appreciation, enjoyment, fancy, fondness, gusto, liking, love, partiality, penchant, taste; flavour, savour, smack, spice, tang, taste, trace; condiment, sauce, seasoning

**reluctant** disinclined, grudging, hesitant, loath, slow, unwilling

**rely** bank, bet, count, depend, lean, reckon, trust

**remain** abide, cling, continue, delay, dwell, endure, last, linger, persist, prevail, rest, stand, stay, survive, tarry, wait

**remainder** balance, excess, leavings, residue, residuum, rest, surplus, trace

**remains** balance, crumbs, debris, dregs, fragments, leftovers, pieces, relics, remnants, residue, rest, scraps, traces, vestiges

**remark** *v* comment, declare, mention, observe, pass comment, re-

flect, say, state ~*n* comment, declaration, reflection, statement, thought, utterance, word

**remarkable** distinguished, extraordinary, famous, impressive, notable, outstanding, phenomenal, pre-eminent, rare, signal, singular, strange, striking, surprising, uncommon, unusual, wonderful

**remedy** *n* cure, medicine, nostrum, panacea, relief, treatment ~*v* alleviate, assuage, control, cure, ease, heal, help, relieve, restore, soothe, treat

**remember** call up, commemorate, recall, recognize, recollect, reminisce, retain

**remind** call up, prompt

**reminiscence** anecdote, memoir, recall, review

**reminiscent** remindful, similar, suggestive

**remission** abatement, alleviation, lull, moderation, reduction, relaxation, respite, suspension; absolution, amnesty, discharge, excuse, exemption, exoneration, forgiveness, pardon, release, reprieve

exacting; give up; return; slacken ~n area of authority **remission** n abatement; reduction of prison term; pardon **remittance** n sending of money; money sent

**remnant** n fragment

**remonstrate** v protest

**remorse** n regret and repentance **remorseful** adj **remorseless** adj pitiless

**remote** adj distant; aloof; slight **remote control** control of apparatus from distance by electrical device

**remove** v take, go away; transfer; withdraw **removal** n

**remunerate** v reward, pay **remuneration** n **remunerative** adj

**renaissance** n revival, rebirth

**renal** adj of the kidneys

**rend** v **rending, rent** tear apart; burst

**render** v submit; give in return; cause to become; represent; melt down; plaster

**rendezvous** n (pl **-vous**) meeting place; appointment

**rendition** n performance; translation

**renegade** n deserter

**renege** v go back on (promise etc.)

**renew** v begin again; make valid again; make new; restore; replenish **renewal** n

**renounce** v give up, disown; resign, as claim **renunciation** n

**renovate** v restore, repair **renovation** n

**renown** n fame

——————— THESAURUS ———————

**remit** v dispatch, forward, mail, post, send, transmit; cancel, desist, forbear, halt, refrain, repeal, rescind, stop ~n brief, guidelines, instructions, orders

**remorse** anguish, compassion, compunction, contrition, grief, guilt, pity, regret, shame

**remorseless** inexorable, relentless; callous, cruel, hard, harsh, inhumane, merciless, pitiless

**remote** distant, far, inaccessible, isolated, secluded; abstracted, aloof, cold, detached, distant, removed, reserved, standoffish, withdrawn

**removal** dislodgment, dismissal, dispossession, ejection, elimination, eradication, expulsion, extraction, stripping, subtraction, taking off, withdrawal; departure, move, relocation, transfer

**remove** abolish, delete, depose, detach, discharge, dismiss, displace, doff, efface, eject, eliminate,

erase, excise, expel, extract, move, oust, purge, relegate, shed, transfer, transport, unseat, withdraw; depart, move away, quit, relocate, shift, transfer, vacate

**render** deliver, furnish, give, hand out, pay, present, provide, show, submit, supply, tender, turn over, yield; exchange, give, return, swap, trade; act, depict, do, give, interpret, perform, play, portray, present, represent

**renew** continue, extend, mend, modernize, overhaul, reaffirm, recreate, refit, refurbish, rejuvenate, renovate, reopen, repair, replace, restore, transform

**renounce** abjure, abstain from, cast off, decline, deny, discard, disown, forgo, forsake, forswear, quit, recant, reject, relinquish, renege, repudiate, resign, retract, spurn, waive

**renovate** modernize, overhaul, recondition, refit, reform, renew, re-

**rent**[1] n payment for use of land, buildings etc. ~v hire

**rent**[2] n tear

**reorganize** v organize in new, more efficient way

**rep** n short for REPERTORY or REPRESENTATIVE

**repair**[1] v make whole again ~n repaired part **reparation** n compensation

**repair**[2] v go (to)

**repartee** n witty retort; interchange of them

**repatriate** v send (someone) back to his or her own country **repatriation** n

**repay** v **repaying, repaid** pay back; make return for **repayment** n

**repeal** v cancel ~n cancellation

**repeat** v say, do again; recur ~n act, instance of repeating **repetition** n act of repeating; thing repeated

**repetitive** adj

**repel** v **-pelling, -pelled** drive back; be repulsive to **repellent** adj/n

**repent** v feel regret for deed or omission **repentance** v **repentant** adj

**repercussion** n indirect effect, oft. unpleasant

**repertoire** n stock of plays, songs etc. that player or company can give **repertory** n repertoire

**repetition** SEE REPEAT

**replace** v substitute for; put back **replacement** n

**replay** n reshowing on TV of sporting incident, esp. in slow motion; second sports match, esp. following earlier draw ~v play (match, recording etc.) again

**replenish** v fill up again

**replete** adj filled, gorged

**replica** n exact copy **replicate** v

——————— THESAURUS ———————

pair, restore

**rent** n fee, hire, lease, payment, rental, tariff ~v charter, hire, lease, let

**repair** v fix, heal, mend, patch, patch up, recover, rectify, redress, renew, renovate, restore ~n darn, mend, overhaul, patch

**repay** compensate, refund, reimburse, requite, restore, square

**repeal** v abolish, annul, cancel, invalidate, nullify, recall, reverse, revoke, withdraw ~n abolition, annulment, invalidation, rescindment, withdrawal

**repeat** v echo, iterate, quote, recite, rehearse, reiterate, relate, renew, replay, reproduce, restate, retell ~n duplicate, echo, reiteration, repetition, replay, reproduction, reshowing

**repel** check, confront, decline,

fight, oppose, parry, rebuff, refuse, reject, repulse, resist; disgust, nauseate, offend, revolt, sicken

**repent** atone, deplore, regret, relent, rue, sorrow

**repentant** ashamed, chastened, contrite, rueful, sorry

**repercussion** backlash, consequence, echo, rebound, recoil, result, sequel

**repetition** echo, recital, recurrence, rehearsal, reiteration, relation, renewal, repeat, replication, restatement, return, tautology

**replace** follow, oust, re-establish, reinstate, restore, substitute, succeed, supersede, supplant, supply

**replacement** double, proxy, substitute, successor, surrogate, understudy

**replenish** fill, furnish, provide, refill, reload, replace, restore, supply,

make or be copy of

**reply** n/v **replying, replied** answer

**report** n account; written statement of child's progress at school; rumour; repute; bang ~v announce; give account of; complain about; make report; present oneself (to) **reporter** n

**repose** n; peace; composure; sleep ~v rest **repository** n place where valuables are deposited for safekeeping

**repossess** v take back property from one who is behind with payments

**reprehensible** adj deserving censure; unworthy

**represent** v stand for; deputize for; act; symbolize; make out to be; describe **representation** n **representative** n one chosen to stand for group; salesman ~adj typical

**repress** v keep down or under **repression** n **repressive** adj

**reprieve** v suspend execution of (condemned person) ~n postponement or cancellation of punishment; respite

**reprimand** n/v rebuke

**reprisal** n retaliation

——————— THESAURUS ———————

top up

**replica** carbon copy, copy, duplicate, facsimile, imitation, model, reproduction

**reply** n answer, counter, counterattack, echo, reaction, rejoinder, response, retort, return ~v answer, counter, echo, react, reciprocate, rejoin, respond, retaliate, retort, return

**report** n account, announcement, article, declaration, description, detail, dispatch, message, news, note, paper, piece, statement, story, tale, tidings, word, write-up; gossip, hearsay, rumour, talk; bang, blast, boom, crack, crash, detonation, discharge, explosion, noise, sound ~v air, broadcast, circulate, cover, declare, describe, detail, document, inform of, mention, narrate, note, pass on, proclaim, publish, recite, record, recount, relate, relay, state, tell; appear, arrive, come, turn up

**reporter** correspondent, journalist, newspaperman, pressman, writer

**reprehensible** bad, culpable, delinquent, disgraceful, errant, ignoble, remiss, shameful, unworthy

**represent** act for, be, betoken, express, mean, serve as, speak for, stand for, symbolize; embody, epitomize, exemplify, personify, symbolize, typify; act, enact, exhibit, perform, produce, put on, show, stage; denote, depict, describe, evoke, outline, picture, portray, render, reproduce, show, sketch

**representation** account, description, illustration, image, likeness, model, picture, portrait, portrayal, relation, sketch

**representative** n agent, councillor, delegate, deputy, member, proxy; agent, rep, salesman, traveller ~adj archetypal, characteristic, illustrative, symbolic, typical

**repress** chasten, check, control, crush, curb, inhibit, master, overpower, quash, quell, restrain, silence, stifle, subdue, suppress

**reprieve** v abate, allay, alleviate, mitigate, palliate, relieve, respite ~n amnesty, deferment, pardon, postponement, remission, suspension

**reprimand** n blame, censure, rebuke, reprehension, reproach, reproof, row ~v blame, censure,

**reproach** v blame, rebuke ~n scolding; thing bringing discredit **reproachful** adj

**reprobate** adj/n depraved (person)

**reproduce** v produce copy of; bring new individuals into existence **reproduction** n **reproductive** adj

**reprove** v censure, rebuke **reproof** n

**reptile** n cold-blooded, air breathing vertebrate, as snake

**republic** n state without monarch governed by elected representatives **republican** adj/n

**repudiate** v reject authority or validity of

**repugnant** adj offensive; distasteful; contrary

**repulse** v drive back; rebuff; repel

**repulsion** n **repulsive** adj disgusting

**repute** v consider ~n reputation **reputable** adj of good repute **reputation** n estimation in which person is held; character; good name

**request** n asking; thing asked for ~v ask

**Requiem** n Mass for the dead

**require** v need; demand **requirement** n

**requisite** adj/n essential

**requisition** n formal demand, e.g. for materials ~v demand (supplies); press into service

**requite** v repay

**rescind** v cancel

**rescue** v -cuing, -cued save, extricate ~n rescuing

**research** n investigation to gather

—————— THESAURUS ——————

check, chide, rebuke, reproach, scold, tear into *Inf*, upbraid

**reproach** v blame, censure, chide, condemn, criticize, discredit, find fault with, rebuke, reprimand, reprove, scold ~n abuse, blemish, censure, contempt, disgrace, disrepute, scorn, shame, slight, slur, stain, stigma

**reproduce** copy, echo, imitate, match, mirror, print, recreate, repeat; breed, multiply, proliferate, propagate, spawn

**reproduction** copy, duplicate, facsimile, imitation, picture, print, replica; generation, increase, multiplication

**repugnant** abhorrent, abominable, disgusting, distasteful, foul, hateful, horrid, loathsome, nauseating, objectionable, obnoxious, odious, offensive, repellent, revolting, sickening, vile

**repulsive** abominable, disagreeable, distasteful, foul, hateful, hid-

eous, objectionable, odious, revolting, sickening, ugly, vile

**reputable** creditable, excellent, good, honourable, legitimate, reliable, respectable, trustworthy, upright, worthy

**reputation** credit, eminence, esteem, fame, honour, name, opinion, stature

**request** n appeal, asking, begging, call, demand, desire, petition, prayer, suit ~v ask (for), beg, beseech, demand, desire, entreat, petition, pray, seek, solicit

**require** crave, desire, lack, miss, need, want, wish; ask, beg, bid, command, compel, constrain, demand, direct, enjoin, exact, insist upon, oblige, order

**requirement** demand, essential, lack, must, need, precondition, stipulation, want

**rescue** v deliver, free, get out, liberate, recover, redeem, release, salvage, save ~n deliverance,

or discover facts ~v investigate

**resemble** v be like; look like ~re-
semblance n

**resent** v show, feel indignation at
resentful *adj* resentment n

**reserve** v hold back, set aside ~n
(also pl) something, esp. troops,
kept for emergencies; (also reservation) area of land reserved for particular purpose or group; reticence
~adj auxiliary, substitute reservation n reserving; thing reserved;
doubt; limitation reserved *adj*
booked; not showing one's feelings

**reservoir** n enclosed area for storage of water; receptacle for liquid,

gas etc.

**reshuffle** n reorganization ~v reorganize

**reside** v dwell permanently residence n home resident *adj/n* residential *adj*

**residue** n remainder residual *adj*

**resign** v give up (esp. office, job);
reconcile (oneself) to resignation n

**resilient** *adj* elastic; (of person) recovering quickly from shock etc. resilience n

**resin** n sticky substance from
plants, esp. firs and pines

**resist** v withstand, oppose resistance n resisting; opposition resist-

——— THESAURUS ———

liberation, recovery, release, relief,
salvage, saving

**research** n examination, exploration, probe, study ~v analyse, examine, experiment, explore, investigate, probe, scrutinize, study,
work over

**resemblance** comparison, correspondence, facsimile, image, kinship, likeness, semblance

**resemble** duplicate, echo, look
like, remind one of, take after

**resent** begrudge, dislike, grudge,
take exception to

**resentful** angry, bitter, incensed,
indignant, irate, jealous, piqued

**resentment** anger, bitterness, displeasure, fury, grudge, hurt, ire,
malice, pique, rage, umbrage,
wrath

**reservation** condition, doubt, rider, scepticism, scruple, stipulation

**reserve** v hoard, hold, husband,
keep, preserve, put by, retain, save,
stockpile, store, withhold; book,
engage, prearrange, retain, secure
~n backlog, cache, capital, fall-
back, fund, hoard, reservoir, sav-

ings, stock, store, supply; park, preserve, reservation, sanctuary, tract;
coolness, formality, restraint, reticence, shyness, silence ~adj auxiliary, extra, fall-back, spare, substitute

**reserved** booked, engaged, held,
kept, retained, taken; cautious,
cold, cool, demure, modest, restrained, reticent, secretive, shy, silent

**reside** abide, dwell, inhabit, live,
lodge, remain, settle, sojourn, stay

**residence** domicile, dwelling, flat,
habitation, home, house, lodging,
place, quarters

**resident** citizen, inhabitant, local,
lodger, occupant, tenant

**resign** abandon, abdicate, cede,
forgo, forsake, hand over, leave,
quit, relinquish, renounce, step
down *Inf*, surrender, turn over, vacate, yield

**resignation** abdication, departure,
notice, retirement, surrender; acquiescence, compliance, endurance, fortitude, passivity, patience,
submission, sufferance

**resilient** buoyant, hardy, irrepress-

ant *adj* **resistor** *n* component of electrical circuit producing resistance to current

**resit** *v* retake (exam) ~*n* exam to be retaken

**resolute** *adj* determined **resolution** *n* resolving; firmness; thing resolved; decision; vote

**resolve** *v* decide; vote; separate component parts of; make clear ~*n* absolute determination

**resonance** *n* echoing, esp. in deep tone **resonant** *adj* **resonate** *v*

**resort** *v* have recourse ~*n* place of recreation, e.g. beach; recourse

**resound** *v* echo, go on sounding

**resource** *n* ingenuity; that to which one resorts for support; expedient; *pl* stock that can be drawn on; funds **resourceful** *adj*

**respect** *n* esteem; aspect; reference ~*v* treat with esteem; show consideration for **respectability** *n* **respectable** *adj* worthy of respect; fairly good **respectful** *adj* **respecting** *prep* concerning **respective** *adj* relating separately to each; separate **respectively** *adv*

**respiration** *n* breathing **respirator** *n* apparatus worn over mouth and breathed through **respiratory** *adj*

**respite** *n* pause, interval; reprieve

ible, quick to recover, strong, tough

**resist** battle, check, combat, confront, curb, defy, dispute, hinder, oppose, refuse, repel, thwart, weather, withstand

**resolute** bold, constant, determined, dogged, firm, fixed, immovable, obstinate, relentless, set, staunch, steadfast, stubborn, undaunted

**resolution** boldness, courage, dedication, determination, doggedness, earnestness, firmness, fortitude, purpose, resolve, sincerity, steadfastness, tenacity, willpower; aim, decision, declaration, intent, intention, judgment, motion, purpose, resolve, verdict

**resolve** *v* agree, conclude, decide, determine, fix, intend, purpose, settle, undertake; analyse, break down, clear, disintegrate ~*n* boldness, courage, determination, firmness, resoluteness, willpower

**resort** *v* employ, exercise, look to , turn to, use, utilize ~*n* haunt, refuge, retreat, spot, tourist centre

**resound** echo, re-echo, resonate,

reverberate, ring

**resource** ability, capability, cleverness, ingenuity, initiative, talent; hoard, reserve, source, stockpile, supply

**resourceful** able, bright, capable, clever, creative, ingenious, inventive, quick-witted, sharp, talented

**respect** *n* admiration, consideration, deference, esteem, honour, recognition, regard, veneration; aspect, detail, feature, matter, particular, point, sense, way; bearing, connection, reference, regard, relation ~*v* admire, adore, appreciate, defer to, esteem, honour, look up to, recognize, regard, value, venerate; abide by, adhere to, attend, follow, heed, honour, notice, obey, observe, regard

**respectable** decent, decorous, dignified, estimable, good, honest, proper, upright, venerable, worthy; ample, appreciable, decent, fair, goodly, presentable, reasonable, sizable, substantial, tolerable

**respective** individual, own, particular, personal, relevant, several,

**resplendent** adj brilliant, shining

**respond** v answer; react **respond-
ent** adj replying ~n one who answers; defendant **response** n **responsive** adj readily reacting

**responsible** adj in charge; liable
to answer for; dependable; involving responsibility **responsibility** n

**rest**[1] n repose; freedom from exertion etc.; pause; support ~v take,
give rest; support; be supported
**restful** adj **restless** adj unable to

rest or be still

**rest**[2] n remainder ~v remain

**restaurant** n commercial establishment serving food

**restitution** n giving back; compensation

**restive** adj restless

**restore** v repair, renew; give back
**restoration** n **restorative** adj/n

**restrain** v hold back; prevent restraint n self-control; anything that
restrains

———— THESAURUS ————

specific, various

**respite** break, cessation, halt, interval, lull, pause, recess, relaxation, relief, rest

**respond** answer, counter, react,
reciprocate, rejoin, reply, retort, return

**response** answer, counterattack,
feedback, reaction, rejoinder, reply,
retort, return, riposte

**responsibility** answerability, care,
charge, duty, liability, obligation,
onus, trust; authority, importance,
power; blame, burden, fault, guilt

**responsible** in charge, in control;
accountable, answerable, bound,
chargeable, duty-bound, liable,
subject; at fault, culpable, guilty, to
blame

**rest**[1] n calm, doze, kip Brit sl, leisure, nap, relaxation, relief, repose,
siesta, sleep, slumber, stillness,
tranquillity; break, cessation, halt,
holiday, interlude, intermission, interval, lull, pause, respite, stop,
time off, vacation; base, holder,
prop, shelf, stand, support, trestle
~v doze, drowse, kip Brit sl, nap,
relax, sit down, sleep, slumber; lay,
lean, lie, prop, recline, repose, sit,
stand

**rest**[2] balance, excess, others, re-

mainder, remnants, residue, rump,
surplus

**restful** calm, calming, pacific,
peaceful, quiet, relaxed, serene, sleepy, tranquil

**restive** agitated, edgy, fidgety, fretful, impatient, jumpy, nervous, uneasy, unquiet, unruly

**restless** agitated, disturbed, edgy,
fidgety, fitful, fretful, jumpy, nervous, restive, sleepless, troubled, uneasy, unquiet

**restore** fix, mend, recover, refurbish, renew, renovate, repair, re-
touch, touch up; give back, hand
back, recover, reinstate, replace, return, send back

**restrain** bridle, check, confine,
contain, control, curb, curtail, debar, govern, hamper, hinder, hold,
hold back, inhibit, keep, limit, prevent, rein, repress, restrict, subdue,
suppress

**restrained** calm, controlled, mild,
moderate, muted, reticent, soft,
steady

**restraint** compulsion, constraint,
control, curtailment, grip, hindrance, hold, inhibition, moderation, self-control, self-discipline,
suppression; ban, bridle, check,
curb, embargo, interdict, limit,

**restrict** v limit **restriction** n **restrictive** adj

**result** v follow as consequence; happen; end ~n outcome **resultant** adj

**resume** v begin again **résumé** n summary **resumption** n

**resurgence** n rising again **resurgent** adj

**resurrect** v restore to life, use **resurrection** n

**resuscitate** v restore to consciousness **resuscitation** n

**retail** n sale in small quantities ~adv by retail ~v sell, be sold, retail; recount **retailer** n

**retain** v keep; engage services of **retainer** n fee to retain esp. barrister; Hist follower of nobleman etc.

**retention** n **retentive** adj

**retaliate** v repay in kind **retaliation** n

**retard** v make slow; impede development of **retarded** adj

**retch** v try to vomit

**reticent** adj reserved; uncommunicative **reticence** n

**retina** n (pl -nas, -nae) light-sensitive membrane at back of eye

**retinue** n band of followers

**retire** v give up office or work; go away; go to bed **retirement** n **retiring** adj unobtrusive, shy

**retort** v reply; retaliate ~n vigorous reply; vessel with bent neck used for distilling

**retrace** v go back over

**retract** v draw in or back; withdraw

limitation, rein

**restrict** bound, confine, contain, hamper, handicap, hem in, impede, inhibit, limit, regulate, restrain

**restriction** check, condition, containment, control, handicap, inhibition, limitation, regulation, restraint, rule

**result** v appear, arise, derive, develop, emanate, ensue, flow, follow, happen, issue, spring, stem, turn out ~n consequence, decision, development, effect, end, event, fruit, issue, outcome, product, reaction, sequel, upshot

**resume** begin again, carry on, continue, go on, proceed, reopen, restart

**resurrect** bring back, reintroduce, renew, revive

**resurrection** reappearance, rebirth, renaissance, renewal, restoration, resurgence, resuscitation, return, revival

**retain** absorb, contain, grasp, grip,

hold, hold back, keep, maintain, preserve, reserve, restrain, save; employ, engage, hire, pay, reserve

**retainer** advance, deposit, fee; attendant, domestic, flunky, footman, lackey, servant, supporter, valet, vassal

**retaliate** give tit for tat, hit back, reciprocate, strike back, take revenge

**retaliation** reprisal, retribution, revenge, vengeance

**retard** arrest, brake, check, clog, decelerate, defer, delay, detain, encumber, handicap, hinder, hold back or up, impede, obstruct, set back, slow down, stall

**reticent** mum, quiet, reserved, secretive, silent

**retire** give up work, stop working; depart, exit, go away, leave, remove, withdraw

**retiring** coy, demure, diffident, humble, meek, modest, quiet, reserved, reticent, shy, timid,

statement **retraction** n

**retreat** v move back ~n withdrawal; place to which anyone retires; refuge

**retrench** v reduce expenditure

**retribution** n recompense, esp. for evil

**retrieve** v fetch back again; regain **retrieval** n **retriever** n dog trained to retrieve game

**retroactive** adj applying to the past

**retrograde** adj going backwards, reverting

**retrospect** n survey of past **retrospective** adj

**return** v go, come back; give, send back; report officially; elect ~n returning; profit; report **returning of-**ficer one conducting election

**reunion** n gathering of people who have been apart **reunite** v bring, come together again

**rev** n Inf revolution (of engine)

**Rev.** Reverend

**revalue** v adjust exchange value of currency upwards

**revamp** v renovate, restore

**reveal** v make known; show **revelation** n

**reveille** n morning bugle call etc. to waken soldiers

**revel** v -elling, -elled take pleasure (in); make merry ~n (usu. pl) merrymaking **revelry** n

**revenge** n retaliation for wrong done ~v avenge; make retaliation for

——————— THESAURUS ———————

unassuming

**retract** pull back, sheathe; cancel, deny, disavow, disclaim, disown, recall, recant, renege, repeal, repudiate, reverse, revoke, take back, unsay, withdraw

**retreat** v depart, draw back, ebb, fall back, go back, leave, pull back, recede, recoil, retire, shrink, turn tail, withdraw ~n ebb, flight, retirement, withdrawal

**retribution** compensation, justice, reckoning, redress, repayment, reprisal, requital, retaliation, revenge, reward, satisfaction, vengeance

**retrieve** recall, recapture, recoup, recover, redeem, regain, repair, rescue, restore, salvage, save, win back

**retrospect** hindsight, review, survey

**return** v come back, go back, reappear, rebound, recur, repair, retreat, revert, turn back; convey, give back, put back, re-establish, reinstate, remit, render, replace, restore, send, take back, transmit; give back, pay back, refund, reimburse, repay, requite; choose, elect, pick, vote in ~n homecoming, rebound, recoil, recurrence, retreat, returning, reversion

**reveal** betray, blow wide open Sl, broadcast, disclose, divulge, give away, give out, impart, leak, let on, let out, let slip, proclaim, publish, tell; bare, display, exhibit, manifest, open, show, uncover, unearth, unmask, unveil

**revel** v (with in) delight, gloat, indulge, joy, lap up, luxuriate, rejoice, relish, savour, wallow; carouse, celebrate n (oft. pl) carousal, celebration, debauch, festivity, gala, jollification, party, rave Brit sl, rave-up Brit sl

**revelation** disclosure, discovery, display, exhibition, exposition, giveaway, leak, news, publication, telling

**revenge** n reprisal, retaliation, ret-

**revenue** *n* income, esp. of state

**reverberate** *v* echo, resound **reverberation** *n*

**revere** *v* hold in great regard or religious respect **reverence** *n* **reverend** *adj* (esp. as prefix to clergyman's name) worthy of reverence **reverent** *adj*

**reverie** *n* daydream

**reverse** *v* move (vehicle) backwards; turn other way round; change completely ~*n* opposite; side opposite; defeat ~*adj* opposite **reversal** *n*

**revert** *v* return to former state,

**review** *v* examine; reconsider; hold, make, write review of ~*n* survey; critical notice of book etc.; periodical with critical articles; *Mil* inspection of troops

**revile** *v* abuse viciously

**revise** *v* look over and correct; study again (work done previously); change **revision** *n*

**revive** *v* bring, come back to life, vigour, use etc. **revival** *n*

**revoke** *v* withdraw; cancel **revocation** *n*

**revolt** *n* rebellion ~*v* rise in rebel-

— THESAURUS —

ribution, satisfaction ~*v* avenge, hit back, repay, requite, retaliate

**revenue** gain, income, proceeds, profits, receipts, returns, rewards, yield

**reverberate** echo, rebound, recoil, re-echo, resound, ring, vibrate

**revere** adore, defer to, exalt, honour, respect, reverence, venerate, worship

**reverence** admiration, adoration, awe, deference, devotion, homage, honour, respect, worship

**reverent** adoring, awed, deferential, devout, humble, loving, meek, pious, respectful, solemn

**reverse** *v* back, go backwards, move backwards, retreat; invert, transpose, turn back, turn over, turn round, turn upside down, upend; alter, annul, cancel, change, invalidate, overrule, overturn, quash, repeal, rescind, retract, revoke, undo ~*n* contrary, converse, inverse, opposite; adversity, affliction, blow, check, defeat, failure, hardship, mishap, repulse, reversal, setback, trial ~*adj* backward, contrary, inverted, opposite

**review** *v* assess, criticize, examine, inspect, judge, study, weigh; reassess, reconsider, re-examine, rethink, revise, think over ~*n* examination, report, scrutiny, study, survey; commentary, criticism, critique, evaluation, judgment, notice, study; journal, magazine, periodical; *Mil* display, inspection, march past, parade, procession

**revise** alter, amend, change, correct, edit, emend, review, rework, rewrite, update; go over, memorize, reread, run through, study

**revision** amendment, change, correction, emendation, modification, review, rewriting; homework, rereading, studying

**revival** reawakening, rebirth, recrudescence, renaissance, renewal, restoration, resurgence, resuscitation

**revive** awaken, bring round, cheer, comfort, invigorate, quicken, rally, reanimate, recover, refresh, rekindle, renew, renovate, restore, resuscitate, rouse

**revoke** abrogate, annul, cancel, countermand, disclaim, invalidate,

lion; feel disgust; affect with disgust

**revolting** *adj* disgusting

**revolve** *v* turn round; be centred on; rotate **revolution** *n* violent overthrow of government; great change; complete rotation **revolutionary** *adj/n* **revolutionize** *v*

**revolver** *n* pistol with revolving magazine

**revue** *n* entertainment with sketches and songs

**revulsion** *n* repugnance or abhorrence

**reward** *n* thing given in return for service, conduct etc. ~*v* give reward **rewarding** *adj*

**rewind** *v* run (tape, film etc.) back to earlier point

**rewire** *v* provide (house, engine etc.) with new wiring

**rhapsody** *n* enthusiastic (musical) piece or utterance **rhapsodic** *adj*

**rhapsodize** *v*

**rhesus** *n* small, long-tailed monkey **rhesus factor** feature distinguishing different types of human blood

**rhetoric** *n* art of effective speaking or writing; exaggerated language **rhetorical** *adj* (of question) not requiring an answer

**rheumatism** *n* painful inflammation of joints or muscles **rheumatic** *adj/n*

**rhinoceros** *n* (*pl* **-oses, -os**) large animal with one or two horns on nose

**rhododendron** *n* evergreen flowering shrub

**rhombus** *n* (*pl* **-buses, -bi**) diamond-shaped figure

**rhubarb** *n* garden plant with edible fleshy stalks

**rhyme** *n* identity of final sounds in words; word or syllable identical in

negate, nullify, quash, recall, recant, renege, renounce, repeal, repudiate, rescind, retract, reverse, withdraw

**revolt** *n* insurgency, insurrection, rebellion, revolution, rising, uprising ~*v* defect, mutiny, rebel, resist, rise; disgust, nauseate, offend, repel, sicken

**revolting** abhorrent, disgusting, foul, horrible, nasty, nauseating, obnoxious, obscene, offensive, repugnant, repulsive, shocking, sickening

**revolution** coup, insurgency, mutiny, rebellion, revolt, rising, uprising; innovation, reformation, shift, transformation, upheaval; circle, circuit, cycle, gyration, lap, orbit, rotation, spin, turn

**revolutionary** *adj* extremist, insurgent, radical, rebel, subversive;

different, drastic, experimental, fundamental, ground-breaking, innovative, new, novel, progressive, radical ~*n* insurgent, mutineer, rebel

**revolve** circle, gyrate, orbit, rotate, spin, turn, twist, wheel, whirl

**revulsion** abhorrence, abomination, aversion, disgust, distaste, loathing, repugnance

**reward** *v* honour, pay, recompense, repay ~*n* benefit, bonus, bounty, gain, honour, merit, payment, premium, prize, profit, return, wages

**rewarding** edifying, enriching, fulfilling, gainful, gratifying, pleasing, productive, profitable, satisfying, valuable

**rhetoric** eloquence, oratory; bombast, hyperbole, rant, verbosity, wordiness

final sound to another; verse marked by rhyme ~v (of words) have identical final sounds

**rhythm** n measured beat of words, music etc. **rhythmic, -ical** adj

**rib** n one of curved bones springing from spine and forming framework of upper part of body; raised series of rows in knitting etc. ~v **ribbing, ribbed** mark with ribs; knit to form a rib pattern

**ribald** adj irreverent, scurrilous

**ribbon** n narrow band of fabric; long strip of anything

**rice** n Eastern cereal plant; its seeds as food

**rich** adj wealthy; fertile; abounding, valuable; containing much fat or sugar; mellow; amusing **riches** pl n wealth **richly** adv elaborately; fully

**rick¹** n stack of hay etc.

**rick²** v/n sprain, wrench

**rickets** n disease of children marked by softening of bones **rickety** adj shaky, unstable

**rickshaw** n two-wheeled man-drawn Asian vehicle

**ricochet** v (of bullet) rebound or be deflected ~n rebound

**rid** v ridding, rid relieve of; free **riddance** n

**ridden** past participle of RIDE ~adj afflicted, as in **disease-ridden**

**riddle¹** n question made puzzling to test one's ingenuity; puzzling thing, person

**riddle²** v pierce with many holes ~n coarse sieve

**ride** v riding, rode, ridden sit on and control or propel; be carried on or across; go on horseback or in vehicle; lie at anchor ~n journey on horse, in vehicle **rider** n one who rides; supplementary clause; addition to document

**ridge** n long narrow hill; line of meeting of two sloping surfaces ~v form into ridges

**ridiculous** adj deserving to be laughed at, absurd **ridicule** v laugh at, deride ~n derision

**rife** adj prevalent, common

————— THESAURUS —————

**rhyme** n ode, poem, poetry, song, verse ~v harmonize, sound like

**rhythm** n accent, beat, cadence, flow, lilt, metre, movement, pattern, pulse, swing, tempo, time

**rich** affluent, moneyed, opulent, prosperous, wealthy, well-off; abounding, abundant, ample, copious, exuberant, fertile, fruitful, full, lush, luxurious, plentiful, productive, prolific; costly, elaborate, elegant, expensive, exquisite, fine, gorgeous, lavish, palatial, precious, priceless, splendid, superb, valuable; creamy, delicious, juicy, luscious, savoury, spicy, succulent, sweet, tasty

**riches** affluence, assets, fortune, gold, money, plenty, property, resources, substance, treasure, wealth

**rid** clear, deliver, disburden, disencumber, free, make free, purge, relieve, unburden

**riddle** brain-teaser Inf, conundrum, enigma, mystery, poser, problem, puzzle

**ride** v control, handle, manage, sit on; float, go, journey, move, progress, sit, travel ~n drive, jaunt, journey, lift, outing, trip

**ridicule** v banter, caricature, deride, humiliate, jeer, lampoon, mock, parody, pooh-pooh, satirize, scoff, sneer, taunt ~n banter, derision, gibe, irony, jeer, laughter, mockery, sarcasm, satire

**riff** n short repeated musical phrase

**riffraff** n rabble

**rifle** v search and rob ~n firearm with long barrel

**rift** n crack, split

**rig** v **rigging, rigged** provide (ship) with ropes etc.; equip; arrange in dishonest way ~n apparatus for drilling for oil **rigging** n ship's spars and ropes

**right** adj just; in accordance with truth and duty; true; correct; proper; of side that faces east when front is turned to north; *Politics* conservative; straight ~v make, become right ~n claim, title etc. allowed or due; what is right; conservative po-litical party ~adv straight; properly; very; on or to right side **rightful** adj

**right angle** angle of 90 degrees

**right-hand man** most valuable assistant

**righteous** adj virtuous; good **righteousness** n

**rigid** adj inflexible; stiff **rigidity** n

**rigmarole** n long, complicated procedure; nonsense

**rigor mortis** stiffening of body after death

**rigour** n severity; hardship **rigorous** adj

**rile** v anger

**rim** n edge

**rind** n outer coating of fruits etc.

———————— THESAURUS ————————

**ridiculous** absurd, comical, derisory, farcical, foolish, funny, incredible, laughable, outrageous, risible, silly, stupid

**rift** breach, break, chink, cleft, crack, crevice, fault, fissure, flaw, gap, space, split; breach, disagreement, division, quarrel, schism, separation, split

**rig** v equip, fit out, furnish, provision, supply, turn out; arrange, engineer, fake, falsify, gerrymander, juggle, manipulate ~n apparatus, equipment, fittings, fixtures, gear, machinery, outfit, tackle

**right** adj equitable, ethical, fair, good, honest, just, lawful, moral, proper, true, virtuous; accurate, admissible, authentic, correct, exact, factual, genuine, precise, sound, true, unerring, valid; appropriate, becoming, convenient, deserved, desirable, done, due, favourable, fit, ideal, proper, propitious, seemly, suitable ~adv directly, promptly, quickly, straight; ethically, fairly, honestly, justly, morally, properly;

absolutely, completely, entirely, perfectly, quite, thoroughly, totally, utterly, wholly ~v correct, fix, rectify, redress, repair, settle, sort out ~n business, claim, due, freedom, interest, liberty, licence, permission, power, prerogative, privilege, title; equity, good, goodness, honour, integrity, justice, lawfulness, legality, morality, propriety, reason, truth, virtue

**rigid** austere, exact, fixed, harsh, inflexible, rigorous, set, severe, stern, stiff, strict, unalterable, uncompromising

**rigorous** challenging, demanding, exacting, firm, hard, harsh, inflexible, severe, stern, strict, tough; bad, bleak, extreme, harsh, inclement, severe

**rigour** austerity, hardship, inflexibility, ordeal, sternness, suffering, trial

**rim** border, brim, brink, edge, lip, margin, verge

**rind** crust, husk, integument, outer layer, peel, skin

## DICTIONARY

**ring¹** n circular band, esp. for finger; circle of persons; enclosed area ~v put ring round **ringer** n Inf identical thing or person **ringleader** n instigator of mutiny, riot etc. **ringlet** n curly lock of hair **ring road** main road that bypasses a town (centre) **ringworm** n skin disease

**ring²** v **ringing, rang, rung** (cause to) give out resonant sound like bell; telephone ~n resonant sound

**rink** n sheet of ice for skating

**rinse** v remove soap from by applying water; wash lightly ~n rinsing; liquid to tint hair

**riot** n/v (engage in) tumult, disorder **riotous** adj

**RIP** rest in peace

**rip** v/n **ripping, ripped** cut, slash **ripcord** n cord pulled to open parachute **rip off** Sl cheat by overcharging

**ripe** adj ready to be harvested,

eaten etc. **ripen** v

**riposte** n verbal retort; counterattack ~v make riposte

**ripple** n slight wave; soft sound ~v form into little waves; (of sounds) rise and fall gently

**rise** v **rising, rose, risen** get up; move upwards; reach higher level; increase; rebel; have its source ~n rising; upslope; increase **rising** n revolt

**risk** n chance of disaster or loss ~v put in jeopardy; take chance of **risky** adj

**risotto** n (pl **-tos**) dish of rice with vegetables, meat etc.

**risqué** adj suggestive of indecency

**rissole** n cake of minced meat coated with breadcrumbs

**rite** n formal practice or custom, esp. religious **ritual** n prescribed order of rites; stereotyped behaviour ~adj concerning rites

## THESAURUS

**ring¹** n band, circle, circuit, halo, hoop, loop, round; association, band, cartel, clique, combine, coterie, gang, group, mob, syndicate; arena, circus, enclosure, rink ~v encircle, enclose, gird, girdle, hem in, surround

**ring²** v chime, clang, peal, reverberate, sound, toll; call, phone, telephone ~n chime, knell, peal; call, phone call

**rinse** v bathe, clean, cleanse, dip, splash, wash, wash out, wet ~n bath, dip, splash, wash, wetting

**riot** n anarchy, confusion, disorder, fray, lawlessness, quarrel, row, strife, tumult, turmoil, upheaval, uproar ~v rampage, run riot

**riotous** adj disorderly, lawless, rebellious, rowdy, unruly, violent

**ripe** fully developed, mature, mel-

low, ready, seasoned

**ripen** burgeon, develop, mature, prepare, season

**rise** v get up, stand up, surface; ascend, climb, enlarge, go up, grow, improve, increase, intensify, lift, mount, soar, swell, wax; advance, progress, prosper; appear, crop up, emanate, emerge, eventuate, flow, happen, issue, occur, originate, spring; mutiny, rebel, resist, revolt ~n ascent, incline, upward slope; increment, pay increase; advance, climb, improvement, increase, upsurge, upturn

**risk** n chance, danger, gamble, hazard, jeopardy, peril, pitfall, speculation, uncertainty, venture ~v chance, dare, endanger, gamble, hazard, imperil, jeopardize, venture

**ritual** n ceremonial, ceremony, lit-

**rival** n one that competes with another ~adj in position of rival ~v -valling, -valled vie with **rivalry** n

**river** n large natural stream of water

**rivet** n bolt for fastening metal plates, the end being put through holes and then beaten flat ~v fasten firmly **riveting** adj very interesting

**rivulet** n small stream

**RN** Royal Navy

**roach** n freshwater fish

**road** n track, way prepared for passengers, vehicles etc.; direction, way; street **roadblock** n barricade across road to stop traffic for inspection **roadworks** pl n repairs to road

**roam** v wander about, rove

**roar** v/n (utter) loud deep hoarse sound

**roast** v cook in oven or over open fire; make, be very hot ~n roasted joint ~adj roasted

**rob** v robbing, robbed steal from **robber** n **robbery** n

**robe** n long outer garment ~v dress; put on robes

**robin** n small brown bird with red breast

**robot** n automated machine, esp. performing functions in human manner

**robust** adj sturdy; strong

**rock¹** n stone; mass of stone; hard sweet in sticks **rockery** n mound of stones in garden **rocky** adj

**rock²** n (cause to) sway to and fro ~n popular music with heavy beat **rocker** n curved piece of wood etc. on which thing may rock; rocking chair **rock and roll** style of popular music

**rocket** n self-propelling device

———————— THESAURUS ————————

urgy, mystery, observance, rite, sacrament, service, solemnity; convention, custom, formality, habit, ordinance, practice, prescription, procedure, protocol, red tape, routine, stereotype, tradition, usage ~adj ceremonial, ceremonious, conventional, customary, formal, habitual, prescribed, procedural, routine

**rival** n adversary, challenger, competitor, contender, contestant, opponent ~adj competing, conflicting, opposed ~v come up to, compare with, compete, contend, equal, match, oppose, vie with

**rivalry** n antagonism, competition, conflict, contention, contest, duel, opposition

**road** avenue, course, highway, lane, motorway, path, pathway, roadway, route, street, thorough-

fare, track, way

**roam** prowl, ramble, range, rove, stray, stroll, travel, walk, wander

**roar** v bawl, bay, bellow, clamour, crash, cry, howl, rumble, shout, yell ~n bellow, clamour, crash, cry, howl, outcry, rumble, shout, thunder, yell

**rob** burgle, cheat, defraud, despoil, dispossess, gyp Sl, hold up, loot, pillage, plunder, raid, ransack, rifle, sack, skin Sl, strip, swindle

**robber** bandit, brigand, burglar, cheat, fraud, highwayman, pirate, plunderer, raider, stealer, thief

**robbery** burglary, fraud, hold-up, larceny, pillage, plunder, raid, rapine, stealing, swindle, theft

**robe** n costume, gown, habit ~v attire, clothe, drape, dress, garb

**robot** android, automaton, machine, mechanical man

powered by burning of explosive contents ~v move fast, esp. upwards, as rocket

**rod** n slender straight bar; stick; cane

**rodent** n gnawing animal

**rodeo** n (pl -deos) US & Canad display of bareback riding, cattle handling etc.

**roe¹** n small species of deer

**roe²** n mass of eggs in fish

**rogue** n scoundrel; mischief-loving person or child

**role, rôle** n actor's part; specific task or function

**roll** v move by turning over and over; wind round; smooth out with roller; move, sweep along; undulate ~n act of rolling; anything rolled up; list; small round piece of baked bread; continuous sound, as of drums, thunder etc. **roller** n cylinder of wood, stone, metal etc.; long wave of sea **roller coaster** narrow undulating railway at funfair **roller skate** skate with wheels instead of runner **rolling pin** cylindrical roller for pastry **rolling stock** locomotives, carriages etc. of railway

**rollicking** adj boisterously jovial and merry

**roly-poly** n pudding of suet pastry ~adj round, plump

**ROM** Computers read only memory

**Roman** adj of Rome or Church of Rome **Roman Catholic** member of that section of Christian Church which acknowledges supremacy of the Pope **Roman numerals** letters used to represent numbers

**romance** n love affair; mysterious or exciting quality; tale of chivalry; tale remote from ordinary life ~v exaggerate, fantasize **romantic** adj characterized by romance; of love; (of literature etc.) displaying passion and imagination ~n romantic person

**rock¹** boulder, stone

**rock²** lurch, pitch, reel, roll, sway, swing, toss

**rocky** craggy, rough, rugged, stony; firm, flinty, hard, rugged, solid, steady, tough

**rod** bar, baton, birch, cane, mace, pole, sceptre, shaft, staff, stick, wand

**rogue** charlatan, cheat, fraud, rascal, reprobate, scally NW Eng dial, scamp, scoundrel, swindler, villain

**role** character, part, portrayal, representation; capacity, duty, function, job, part, position, post, task

**roll** v flow, go round, gyrate, pass, pivot, reel, revolve, rock, rotate, run, spin, swivel, trundle, turn, twirl, wheel, whirl; bind, coil, curl, enfold, entwine, envelop, furl, swathe, twist, wind, wrap; flatten, level, press, smooth, spread ~n cycle, reel, revolution, rotation, run, spin, turn, twirl, wheel, whirl; annals, catalogue, census, chronicle, directory, index, inventory, list, record, register, schedule, scroll, table; boom, growl, grumble, resonance, reverberation, roar, rumble, thunder

**romance** affair, amour, attachment, intrigue, liaison, passion, relationship; charm, colour, excitement, fascination, glamour, mystery, sentiment; fantasy, fiction, idyll, legend, melodrama, novel, story, tale

**romantic** adj colourful, exciting, exotic, fascinating, glamorous, mysterious, nostalgic, picturesque;

**Romany** *n/adj* Gypsy

**romp** *v* run, play wildly ~*n* spell of romping **rompers** *pl n* child's overalls

**roof** *n* outside upper covering of building ~*v* put roof on, over

**rook** *n* bird of crow family

**rookie** *n Inf* new recruit

**room** *n* space; division of house; scope; *pl* lodgings **roomy** *adj* spacious

**roost** *n/v* perch **rooster** *n US* domestic cock

**root** *n* underground part of plant; source, origin; *Anat* embedded portion of tooth, hair etc.; *p* person's sense of belonging ~*v* (cause to) take root; pull by roots; dig, burrow

**rope** *n* thick cord ~*v* secure, mark off with rope

**rosary** *n* series of prayers; string of beads for counting these prayers

**rose** *n* shrub usu. with prickly stems and fragrant flowers; pink colour **rosette** *n* rose-shaped bunch of ribbon **rosy** *adj* flushed; promising **rose-coloured** *adj* having colour of rose; unjustifiably optimistic **rosehip** *n* berry-like fruit of rose plant

**rosé** *n* pink wine

**rosemary** *n* evergreen fragrant flowering shrub

**roster** *n* list of turns of duty

**rostrum** *n* (*pl* -trums, -tra) platform, stage

**rot** *v* rotting, rotted decompose, decay; deteriorate physically or mentally ~*n* decay; any disease producing decomposition of tissue; *Inf* nonsense **rotten** *adj* decomposed; very bad; corrupt **rotter** *n Inf* despicable person

**rota** *n* roster, list

**rotary** *adj* (of movement) circular **rotate** *v* (cause to) move round centre; (cause to) follow set sequence **rotation** *n*

─────────── THESAURUS ───────────

amorous, fond, loving, passionate, sentimental, tender; dreamy, high-flown, idealistic, quixotic, utopian, visionary, whimsical ~*n* dreamer, idealist, sentimentalist, visionary

**room** *n* area, capacity, compass, expanse, extent, leeway, margin, play, range, scope, space, territory, volume; apartment, chamber, office; chance, occasion, scope

**root** *n* rhizome, stem, tuber; base, bottom, cause, core, crux, derivation, foundation, fundamental, germ, heart, nucleus, occasion, origin, seat, seed, source; *pl* birthplace, cradle, family, heritage, home, origins ~*v* anchor, embed, entrench, establish, fasten, fix, ground, implant, moor, set, stick

**rope** *n* cable, cord, hawser, line, strand ~*v* bind, fasten, hitch, lash, lasso, moor, pinion, tether, tie

**roster** agenda, catalogue, list, register, roll, rota, scroll, table

**rosy** blooming, blushing, flushed, fresh, glowing, radiant, reddish, ruddy; auspicious, bright, cheerful, encouraging, favourable, hopeful, optimistic, promising, sunny

**rot** *v* corrupt, crumble, decay, decompose, deteriorate, go bad, moulder, perish, putrefy, spoil, taint; decline, deteriorate, waste away ~*n* blight, canker, corruption, decay, mould, putrefaction

**rotate** go round, gyrate, pivot, reel, revolve, spin, swivel, turn, wheel; alternate, interchange, switch

**rotation** orbit, reel, revolution, spin, spinning, turn, turning,

**rote** n mechanical repetition

**rotor** n revolving portion of dynamo motor or turbine

**Rottweiler** n large dog with black and tan coat

**rotund** adj round; plump

**rouge** n red powder, cream used to colour cheeks

**rough** adj not smooth; violent, stormy; rude; approximate; in preliminary form ~v make rough; plan ~n rough state or area; sketch **roughen** v **roughage** n unassimilated portion of food **rough it** live without usual comforts etc.

**roulette** n gambling game played with revolving wheel

**round** adj spherical, circular, curved; plump; complete; roughly correct; considerable ~adv with circular course ~n thing round in

shape; recurrent duties; stage in competition; customary course; game (of golf); period in boxing match etc.; cartridge for firearm ~prep about; on all sides of ~v make, become round; move round **rounders** pl n ball game **roundly** adv thoroughly **roundabout** n revolving circular platform on which people ride for amusement; road junction at which traffic passes round central island ~adj not straightforward **round trip** journey out and back again **round up** drive (cattle) together

**rouse** v wake up, stir up, excite; waken

**rout** n overwhelming defeat, disorderly retreat ~v put to flight

**route** n road, chosen way

**routine** n regularity of procedure

wheel; cycle, sequence, succession, switching

**rotten** bad, corrupt, crumbling, decayed, decomposed, festering, fetid, foul, mouldy, perished, putrid, rank, sour, stinking, tainted, unsound; bad, deplorable, disappointing, regrettable, unfortunate, unlucky; corrupt, deceitful, degenerate, dishonest, disloyal, faithless, immoral, perfidious, treacherous, venal, vicious

**rough** adj broken, bumpy, craggy, irregular, jagged, rocky, stony, uneven; bristly, bushy, coarse, disordered, tangled, uncut, unshorn; boisterous, choppy, squally, stormy, turbulent, wild; basic, crude, cursory, hasty, imperfect, incomplete, quick, raw, rudimentary, shapeless, sketchy, unpolished

**round** adj circular, curved, cylindrical, disc-shaped, globular, rotund, rounded, spherical; ample, fleshy, full, full-fleshed, plump, rotund ~n ball, band, circle, disc, globe, orb, ring, sphere; bout, cycle, sequence, series, session, succession; division, lap, level, period, session, stage, turn; ambit, beat, circuit, compass, course, routine, schedule, series, tour, turn; bullet, discharge, shell, shot ~v bypass, circle, encircle, flank, go round, skirt, turn

**rouse** agitate, anger, animate, disturb, excite, inflame, instigate, move, prod, provoke, startle, stimulate, stir, whip up; awaken, call, rise, wake, waken, wake up

**rout** n beating, debacle, defeat, drubbing, overthrow, pasting *Sl*, ruin, shambles, thrashing ~v beat, chase, clobber *Sl*, conquer, crush, defeat, destroy, dispel, overpower, overthrow, thrash

~*adj* ordinary, regular

**rove** *v* wander, roam

**row**¹ *n* number of things in a straight line

**row**² *v* propel boat by oars ~*n* spell of rowing

**row**³ *Inf n* dispute; disturbance ~*v* quarrel noisily

**rowan** *n* tree producing bright red berries, mountain ash

**rowdy** *adj/n* disorderly, noisy (person)

**rowlock** *n* device to hold oar on gunwale of boat

**royal** *adj* of king or queen **royalist** *n* supporter of monarchy **royalty** *n* royal power; royal persons; payment for right, use of invention or copyright

**rpm** revolutions per minute

**RSVP** please reply

**rub** *v* rubbing, rubbed apply pressure to with circular or backwards-and-forwards movement; clean, polish, dry thus; abrade, chafe; re-

move by friction; become frayed or worn by friction ~*v* rubbing

**rubber** *n* elastic dried sap of certain tropical trees; synthetic material resembling this; piece of rubber etc. used for erasing ~*adj* made of rubber **rubbery** *adj*

**rubbish** *n* refuse; anything worthless; nonsense ~*v Inf* criticize

**rubble** *n* fragments of stone

**rubella** *n* mild contagious viral disease, German measles

**ruby** *n* precious red gem; its colour ~*adj* of this colour

**ruck**¹ *n* crowd; common herd

**ruck**² *n/v* crease

**rucksack** *n* pack carried on back, knapsack

**ruction** *n Inf* noisy disturbance

**rudder** *n* steering device for boat, aircraft

**ruddy** *adj* of healthy red colour

**rude** *adj* impolite; coarse; vulgar; roughly made

**rudiments** *pl n* elements, first

**route** beat, circuit, course, direction, itinerary, journey, passage, path, road, round, run, way

**routine** *n* custom, formula, groove, method, order, pattern, practice, programme, usage, way ~*adj* customary, everyday, familiar, habitual, normal, ordinary, standard, typical, usual, workaday

**row**¹ *n* bank, column, file, line, queue, range, rank, sequence, series, string, tier

**row**² *n* brawl, dispute, disturbance, fray, fuss, noise, quarrel, racket, rumpus, squabble, tiff, trouble, tumult, uproar ~*v* argue, brawl, dispute, fight, spar, wrangle

**rowdy** disorderly, loud, noisy, rough, unruly, uproarious, wild

**royal** imperial, kingly, princely, queenly, regal, sovereign

**rub** *v* caress, chafe, clean, fray, grate, massage, polish, scour, scrape, shine, smooth, stroke, wipe; apply, put, smear, spread ~*n* caress, massage, polish, shine, stroke, wipe

**rubbish** debris, dregs, dross, garbage, junk *Inf*, litter, lumber, offal, refuse, scrap, trash, waste; drivel, gibberish, hot air *Inf*, nonsense, piffle *Inf*, rot, tripe *Inf*, twaddle

**ruddy** blooming, blushing, florid, flushed, fresh, glowing, healthy, radiant, red, reddish, rosy, rosy-cheeked, sanguine, sunburnt

**rude** abrupt, abusive, blunt, brusque, cheeky, curt, discourteous, ill-mannered, impertinent,

principles **rudimentary** adj

**rue** v grieve for; regret **rueful** adj

**ruff** n frilled collar; natural collar of feathers, fur etc. on some birds and animals **ruffle** v rumple, annoy, frill ~v frilled trimming

**ruffian** n violent, lawless person

**rug** n small floor mat; woollen coverlet

**rugby** n form of football in which the ball may be carried

**rugged** adj rough; strong-featured

**ruin** n destruction; downfall; fallen or broken state; loss of wealth etc.; pl ruined buildings etc. ~v bring or come to ruin **ruinous** adj

**rule** n principle; government; what is usual; measuring stick ~v govern; decide; mark with straight lines **ruler** n one who governs; stick for measuring or ruling lines **ruling** n formal decision

**rum** n spirit distilled from sugar cane

**rumba** n lively ballroom dance

**rumble** v/n (make) noise as of distant thunder

**ruminate** v chew cud; ponder over

─────────────── THESAURUS ───────────────

impolite, impudent, insolent, insulting, offhand, short, unmannerly; boorish, brutish, coarse, crude, graceless, loutish, oafish, rough, savage, uncivilised, uncouth, uncultured, vulgar; artless, crude, inartistic, inelegant, makeshift, primitive, raw, rough, simple

**rudiments** basics, beginnings, elements, essentials, first principles, foundation, fundamentals

**ruffle** derange, disarrange, discompose, disorder, rumple, tousle, wrinkle; agitate, annoy, confuse, disquiet, disturb, fluster, harass, hassle Inf, irritate, nettle, perturb, stir, torment, trouble, unnerve, unsettle, upset, worry

**rugged** broken, bumpy, craggy, difficult, jagged, ragged, rocky, rough, stark, uneven; furrowed, lined, rough-hewn, weathered, worn, wrinkled

**ruin** n bankruptcy, breakdown, collapse, crash, damage, decay, defeat, destruction, devastation, disrepair, downfall, failure, fall, wreckage ~v bankrupt, break, bring down, crush, defeat, demolish, destroy, devastate, impoverish, lay waste,

overthrow, raze, shatter, smash, wreck

**rule** n axiom, canon, decree, direction, guideline, law, maxim, order, ordinance, precept, principle, regulation, standard; ascendancy, authority, command, control, direction, domination, empire, government, influence, leadership, mastery, power, regime, reign, supremacy, sway; condition, convention, custom, form, habit, practice, procedure, routine, tradition, wont; course, formula, method, policy, procedure, way ~v administer, command, control, direct, dominate, govern, guide, hold sway, lead, manage, preside over, regulate, reign; decide, decree, determine, establish, find, judge, lay down, pronounce, resolve, settle

**ruler** commander, controller, emperor, empress, governor, king, leader, lord, monarch, potentate, prince, princess, queen, sovereign; measure, rule, straight edge, yardstick

**ruling** adjudication, decision, decree, finding, judgment, pronouncement, resolution, verdict

**ruminant** *adj/n* cud-chewing (animal)

**rummage** *v* search thoroughly

**rummy** *n* card game

**rumour** *n* hearsay, unproved statement ~*v* put around as rumour

**rump** *n* tail end; buttocks

**rumple** *v* make untidy, dishevelled

**rumpus** *n* disturbance

**run** *v* **running, ran, run** move with more rapid gait than walking; go quickly; flow; flee; compete in race, contest, election; cross by running; expose oneself (to risk etc.); cause to run; manage; operate ~*n* act, spell of running; rush; tendency; course; enclosure for domestic fowls; ride in car; unravelled stitches; score of one at cricket **runner** *n* racer; messenger; curved

piece of wood on which sleigh slides; stem of plant forming new roots; strip of cloth, carpet **running** *adj* continuous; consecutive; flowing ~*n* act of moving or flowing quickly; ride in car; continuous period or sequence **running jump, run-down** *n* summary **run-down** *adj* exhausted; decrepit; broken-down **run down** stop working; reduce; exhaust; denigrate **run-of-the-mill** *adj* ordinary **run out** be completely used up **runway** *n* level stretch where aircraft take off and land

**rune** *n* character of old Germanic alphabet

**rung** *n* crossbar in ladder

**runt** *n* unusually small animal

**rupture** *n* breaking, breach; hernia ~*v* break; burst; sever

───────── THESAURUS ─────────

**rumour** buzz, gossip, hearsay, news, report, story, talk, tidings, whisper, word

**run** *v* bolt, career, dart, dash, gallop, hare *Brit inf*, hasten, hotfoot, hurry, jog, race, rush, scamper, scramble, scurry, speed, sprint; discharge, flow, go, gush, leak, spill, spout, stream; abscond, bolt, decamp, depart, do a runner *Sl*, escape, flee; challenge, compete, contend, stand, take part; administer, carry on, conduct, control, coordinate, direct, handle, head, lead, manage, operate, oversee, own, regulate, supervise; function, go, operate, perform, tick, work ~*n* dash, gallop, jog, race, rush, sprint, spurt; drive, excursion, jaunt, journey, lift, outing, ride, round; course, cycle, passage, period, round, season, sequence, series, spell, stretch, string

**run down** curtail, cut, cut back,

decrease, drop, reduce, trim; exhaust, tire, weaken; belittle, decry, defame, disparage, put down, revile, rubbish *Inf*, slag (off) *Sl*

**run-down** below par, debilitated, drained, enervated, exhausted, unhealthy, weak, weary, worn-out; broken-down, decrepit, dilapidated, dingy, ramshackle, seedy, shabby, worn-out

**running** *adj* constant, continuous, incessant, perpetual, together, unbroken, uninterrupted; flowing, moving, streaming ~*n* charge, conduct, control, direction, leadership, management, organization, regulation, supervision

**run-of-the-mill** average, common, fair, mediocre, middling, ordinary, passable, tolerable, undistinguished

**rupture** *n* breach, break, burst, cleavage, cleft, crack, rent, split, tear ~*v* break, burst, cleave, crack, fracture, puncture, rend, separate,

**rural** adj of the country; rustic

**ruse** n stratagem, trick

**rush¹** v hurry or cause to hurry; move violently or rapidly ~n rushing ~adj done with speed **rush hour** period when many people travel to or from work

**rush²** n marsh plant with slender pithy stem

**rusk** n kind of biscuit

**russet** n/adj reddish-brown (colour)

**rust** n reddish-brown coating formed on iron; disease of plants ~v affect with rust **rusty** adj corroded; reddish-brown; out of practice

**rustic** adj simple, homespun; rural; uncouth. boorish ~n countryman

**rustle¹** v/n (make) sound as of blown dead leaves etc.

**rustle²** v US steal (cattle) **rustler** n

**rut** n furrow made by wheel; settled habit

**ruthless** adj merciless

**rye** n grain; plant bearing it

————————— THESAURUS —————————

sever, split, tear

**rural** agrarian, agricultural, bucolic, country, pastoral, rustic, sylvan

**rush** v bolt, career, dart, dash, fly, hasten, hurry, press, push, quicken, race, run, scramble, scurry, shoot, speed, sprint, stampede, tear ~n charge, dash, expedition, haste, hurry, race, scramble, speed, stampede, surge, swiftness, urgency

**rust** n corrosion, oxidation; blight, mildew, mould, must, rot ~v corrode, oxidize

**rustic** adj artless, homespun, plain, simple, unaffected, unpolished;

country, pastoral, rural, sylvan; awkward, boorish, churlish, clownish, coarse, crude, loutish, rough, uncouth ~n boor, bumpkin, clod, countryman, peasant, yokel

**rustle** v crackle, whisper ~n crackle, rustling, whisper

**rut** furrow, gouge, groove, indentation, score, track, wheelmark; dead end, groove, habit, pattern, routine, system

**ruthless** brutal, callous, cruel, ferocious, fierce, hard, harsh, heartless, inhuman, merciless, pitiless, relentless, savage, stern, unmerciful

# S s

**Sabbath** *n* day of worship and rest, observed on Saturday in Judaism, on Sunday by Christians **sabbatical** *adj/n* (pert. to) leave for study

**sabotage** *n* intentional damage done to roads, machines etc., esp. secretly in war – *v* damage intentionally **saboteur** *n*

**sabre** *n* curved cavalry sword

**sac** *n* pouchlike structure in animal or plant

**saccharin** *n* artificial sweetener

**sachet** *n* small envelope or bag, esp. one holding liquid

**sack** *n* large bag, esp. of coarse material; pillaging; *Inf* dismissal – *v* pillage (captured town); *Inf* dismiss **sackcloth** *n* coarse fabric used for sacks

**sacrament** *n* one of certain ceremonies of Christian Church

**sacred** *adj* dedicated, regarded as holy; revered; inviolable

**sacrifice** *n* giving something up for sake of something else; thing so given up; making of offering to a god; thing offered – *v* offer as sacrifice; give up **sacrificial** *adj*

**sacrilege** *n* misuse, desecration of something sacred **sacrilegious** *adj*

**sacrosanct** *adj* preserved by religious fear against desecration or violence

**sad** *adj* sorrowful; unsatisfactory, deplorable **sadden** *v* make sad **sadness** *n*

**saddle** *n* rider's seat on horse, bicycle etc.; joint of meat – *v* put saddle on; lay burden on

**sadism** *n* love of inflicting pain **sadist** *n* **sadistic** *adj*

**safari** *n* (*pl* -**ris**) expedition to hunt or observe wild animals, esp. in Africa

**safe** *adj* secure, protected; uninjured, out of danger; not involving risk; trustworthy; sure – *n* strong lockable container **safely** *adv* **safety** *n* **safeguard** *n* protection – *v* protect **safety pin** pin with guard over the point when closed

---

## THESAURUS

**sabotage** *n* damage, destruction, wrecking – *v* damage, destroy, disable, vandalize, wreck

**sack** *v* discharge, dismiss

**sacred**; holy, religious; blessed, divine, hallowed, holy, revered, sanctified, venerable; inviolable, sacrosanct

**sacrifice** *n* loss, renunciation, surrender – *v* give up, lose, surrender

**sacrilege** *n* blasphemy, desecration, impiety, violation

**sad** depressed, dismal, doleful, down, melancholy, mournful, sorrowful, unhappy, woebegone; bad, deplorable, lamentable, regrettable, serious, sorry

**sadden** deject, depress, grieve

**sadistic** barbarous, brutal, cruel, vicious

**sadness** depression, gloominess, grief, melancholy, misery, sorrow, unhappiness

**safe** *adj* guarded, protected, secure; intact, undamaged, unharmed, unhurt; dependable, reliable, sure, trustworthy – *n* coffer, safe-deposit box, strongbox

**safeguard** *n* defence, protection, shield – *v* defend, preserve, protect,

**saffron** n crocus; orange-coloured flavouring obtained from it; orange colour ~adj orange

**sag** v **sagging, sagged** sink in middle; curve downwards under pressure; hang loosely ~n droop

**saga** n legend of Norse heroes; any long (heroic) story

**sage¹** n very wise man ~adj wise

**sage²** n aromatic herb

**sago** n starchy cereal from powdered pith of palm tree

**said** past tense and past participle of SAY

**sail** n piece of fabric stretched to catch wind for propelling ship etc.; act of sailing; arm of windmill ~v travel by water; move smoothly; begin voyage **sailor** n seaman; one who sails

**saint** n person recognized as having gained a special place in heaven; exceptionally good person

**sake** n cause, account; end, purpose **for the sake of** on behalf of; to please or benefit

**salad** n mixed raw vegetables or fruit used as food

**salami** n variety of highly-spiced sausage

**salary** n fixed regular payment to persons employed usu. in non-manual work

**sale** n selling; selling of goods at unusually low prices; auction **salesman** n shop assistant; one travelling to sell goods

**salient** adj prominent, noticeable; jutting out

**saline** adj containing, consisting of a chemical salt, esp. common salt; salty

**saliva** n liquid which forms in mouth, spittle

**sallow** adj of unhealthy pale or yellowish colour

**sally** n (pl -lies) rushing out, esp. by troops; witty remark ~v -lying, -lied rush; set out

**salmon** n large silvery fish with orange-pink flesh valued as food; colour of its flesh ~adj of this colour

**salmonella** n (pl -lae) bacterium causing food poisoning

**salon** n (reception room for) guests in fashionable household; commercial premises of hairdressers, beauticians etc.

**saloon** n public room, esp. on passenger ship; car with fixed roof **saloon bar** first-class bar in hotel etc.

**salt** n white powdery or crystalline substance consisting mainly of sodium chloride, used to season or preserve food; chemical compound of acid and metal ~v season, sprinkle with, preserve with salt ~adj preserved in salt **salty** adj of, like salt **saltcellar** n small vessel for salt at table

**salubrious** adj favourable to health, beneficial

—————— THESAURUS ——————

shield

**safety** protection, refuge, sanctuary, security, shelter

**sail** v navigate, pilot, steer, voyage; drift, float, glide, scud, skim; embark, set sail

**sailor** marine, mariner, salt, sea dog, seafarer, seaman

**sake** account, behalf, good, interest, profit, welfare

**salary** earnings, income, pay, remuneration

**sale** deal, transaction

**sallow** pale, pasty, peely-wally Scot, sickly, wan, yellowish

**salt** n flavour, relish, seasoning

**salutary** adj producing beneficial result

**salute** v greet with words or sign; acknowledge with praise; perform military salute ~n word, sign by which one greets another; motion of arm as mark of respect to military superior; firing of guns as military greeting of honour

**salvage** n act of saving ship or other property from danger of loss; property so saved ~v save

**salvation** n fact or state of being saved, esp. of soul

**salve** n healing ointment ~v anoint with such, soothe

**salver** n (silver) tray for presentation of food, letters etc.

**salvo** n (pl **-vos**, **-voes**) simultaneous discharge of guns etc.

**same** adj identical, not different, unchanged; uniform; just mentioned previously

**sample** n specimen ~v take, give sample of; try **sampler** n beginner's exercise in embroidery

**sanatorium** n (pl **-riums**, **-ria**) hospital, esp. for chronically ill; health resort

**sanctify** v **-fying**, **-fied** set apart as holy; free from sin **sanctity** n sa-

credness **sanctuary** n holy place; place of refuge; nature reserve

**sanctimonious** adj making affected show of piety

**sanction** n permission, authorization; penalty for breaking law; pl boycott or other coercive measure, esp. by one state against another ~v allow, authorize

**sand** n substance consisting of small grains of rock or mineral, esp. on beach or in desert; pl stretches or banks of this ~v polish, smooth with sandpaper; cover, mix with sand **sandy** adj like sand; sand-coloured; consisting of, covered with sand **sandbag** n bag filled with sand or earth as protection against gunfire, floodwater etc. and as weapon ~v beat, hit with sandbag **sandpaper** n paper with sand stuck on it for scraping or polishing **sandpiper** n shore bird with long bill **sandstone** n rock composed of sand

**sandal** n shoe consisting of sole attached by straps

**sandwich** n two slices of bread with meat or other substance between ~v insert between two other things

---

**——————— THESAURUS ———————**

~adj brackish, briny, saline, salty

**salute** v address, greet, hail; acknowledge, honour, recognize ~n address, greeting, salutation

**salvage** v recover, rescue, retrieve, save

**salvation** deliverance, redemption, rescue, saving

**same** adj duplicate, equal, identical, twin; aforementioned, aforesaid

**sample** n example, illustration, instance, specimen ~v experience,

taste, test, try

**sanctify** bless, consecrate, hallow, set apart

**sanctimonious** hypocritical, pious, self-satisfied, smug

**sanction** n approval, authority, endorsement, support; (oft. pl) ban, boycott, embargo, penalty ~v allow, approve, authorize, endorse, permit, support

**sanctuary** altar, church, shrine, temple; asylum, haven, refuge, retreat, shelter

**sane** *adj* of sound mind; sensible, rational **sanity** *n*

**sang** past tense of SING

**sanguine** *adj* cheerful, confident; ruddy in complexion

**sanitary** *adj* helping protection of health against dirt etc. **sanitation** *n* measures, apparatus for preservation of public health

**sap**¹ *n* moisture which circulates in plants; *Inf* foolish person **sapling** *n* young tree

**sap**² *v* **sapping, sapped** undermine; weaken

**sapphire** *n* (usu. blue) precious stone; deep blue ~*adj* of deep blue colour

**sarcasm** *n* bitter or wounding ironic remark; (use of) such remarks **sarcastic** *adj*

**sarcophagus** *n* (*pl* **-gi, -guses**) stone coffin

**sardine** *n* small fish of herring family

**sardonic** *adj* characterized by irony, mockery or derision

**sari, saree** *n* long garment worn by Hindu women

**sartorial** *adj* of tailor, tailoring, or men's clothes

**sash** *n* decorative belt, ribbon, wound around the body

**Satan** *n* the devil **satanic** *adj* devilish

**satchel** *n* small bag, esp. for school books

**satellite** *n* celestial body or manmade projectile orbiting planet; person, country etc. dependent on another

**satin** *n* fabric (of silk, rayon etc.) with glossy surface on one side

**satire** *n* use of ridicule or sarcasm to expose vice and folly **satirical** *adj* **satirize** *v* make object of satire

**satisfy** *v* **-fying, -fied** please, meet wishes of; fulfil, supply adequately; convince **satisfaction** *n* **satisfactory** *adj*

**satsuma** *n* kind of small orange

**saturate** *v* soak thoroughly **saturation** *n* act, result of saturating

**Saturday** *n* seventh day of the week

─────────── THESAURUS ───────────

**sane** lucid, mentally sound, rational; balanced, judicious, levelheaded, reasonable, sensible

**sanitary** clean, germ-free, healthy, hygienic

**sanity** rationality, reason, stability; good sense, level-headedness, rationality, sense

**sarcasm** cynicism, derision, irony, mockery, satire

**sarcastic** cynical, ironical, mocking, sardonic, satirical

**Satan** Beelzebub, Lucifer, Mephistopheles, Old Nick *Inf*, Prince of Darkness, The Devil

**satanic** devilish, diabolic, evil, fiendish, hellish, wicked

**satire** burlesque, irony, lampoon, parody, ridicule

**satirical** biting, caustic, cutting, incisive, ironical, mocking

**satisfaction** content, contentment, enjoyment, happiness, pleasure; assuaging, fulfilment, gratification

**satisfactory** acceptable, adequate, all right, average, fair, passable, sufficient

**satisfy** assuage, content, feed, fill, gratify, please, sate, slake; do, fulfil, meet, serve, suffice; assure, convince, persuade, reassure

**saturate** drench, soak, souse, steep

**satyr** *n* woodland deity, part man, part goat; lustful man

**sauce** *n* liquid added to food to enhance flavour ~*v* add sauce to

**saucy** *adj* impudent **saucepan** *n* cooking pot with long handle

**saucer** *n* curved plate put under cup; shallow depression

**sauerkraut** *n* dish of shredded cabbage fermented in brine

**sauna** *n* steam bath

**saunter** *v* walk in leisurely manner, stroll ~*n* leisurely walk or stroll

**sausage** *n* minced meat enclosed in thin tube of animal intestine or synthetic material **sausage roll** pastry cylinder filled with sausage

**sauté** *v* fry quickly

**savage** *adj* wild; ferocious; brutal; uncivilized, primitive ~*n* member of savage tribe, barbarian ~*v* attack ferociously

**save** *v* rescue, preserve; keep for future; prevent need of; lay by money ~*n Sport* act of preventing goal etc. ~*prep* except **saving** *adj* redeeming ~*prep* excepting ~*n* economy; *pl* money put by for future use

**saviour** *n* person who rescues another; (*with cap.*) Christ

**savour** *n* characteristic taste or

smell ~*v* have particular taste or smell; give flavour to; have flavour of; enjoy **savoury** *adj* attractive to taste or smell; not sweet

**saw**[1] *n* tool with toothed edge for cutting wood etc. ~*v* **sawing**, **sawed** or **sawn** cut with saw; make movements of sawing **sawdust** *n* fine wood fragments made in sawing

**saw**[2] *past tense of* SEE

**saxophone** *n* keyed wind instrument

**say** *v* **saying**, **said** speak; pronounce; state; express; take as example or as near enough; form and deliver opinion ~*n* what one has to say; chance of saying it; share in decision **saying** *n* maxim, proverb

**scab** *n* crust formed over wound; skin disease; disease of plants

**scabbard** *n* sheath for sword or dagger

**scaffold** *n* temporary platform for workmen; gallows **scaffolding** *n* (material for building) scaffold

**scald** *v* burn with hot liquid or steam; heat (liquid) almost to boiling ~*n* injury by scalding

**scale**[1] *n* one of the thin, overlapping plates covering fishes and rep-

─────────── THESAURUS ───────────

store

**saving** *adj* qualifying, redeeming

**savour** *n* flavour, relish, smack, taste ~*v* appreciate, enjoy, relish

**savoury** delectable, delicious, luscious, palatable, tasty

**say** *v* announce, declare, mention, pronounce, remark, speak, state, utter, voice; communicate, convey, express ~*n* authority, influence, power, sway, weight

**saying** adage, aphorism, axiom, dictum, maxim, proverb

**saunter** *v* amble, meander, ramble, stroll ~*n* amble, promenade, ramble, stroll, walk

**savage** *adj* rough, untamed, wild; barbarous, bloody, brutal, cruel, ferocious, fierce, murderous, vicious; primitive, uncivilized ~*v* attack, maul

**save** deliver, free, liberate, recover, redeem, rescue, salvage; guard, keep safe, preserve, protect, screen, shield; economize, hoard, husband, lay by, put by, reserve, set aside,

tiles; thin flake; crust which forms in kettles etc. ~v remove scales from; come off in scales

**scale²** n (usu. pl) weighing instrument

**scale³** n graduated table or sequence of marks at regular intervals used as reference in making measurements; series of musical notes; ratio of size between a thing and a model or map of it; (relative) degree, extent ~v climb ~adj proportionate

**scallop** n edible shellfish; edging in small curves like scallop shell ~v shape like scallop shell

**scalp** n skin and hair of top of head ~v cut off scalp of

**scalpel** n small surgical knife

**scamp** n mischievous person

**scamper** v run about; run hastily ~n scampering

**scampi** pl n large prawns

**scan** v scanning, scanned look at carefully; examine, search using radar or sonar beam; glance over quickly; (of verse) conform to metrical rules ~n scanning **scanner** n device, esp. electronic, which scans

**scandal** n something disgraceful;

malicious gossip **scandalize** v shock **scandalous** adj

**scant** adj barely sufficient or not sufficient **scanty** adj

**scapegoat** n person bearing blame due to others

**scar** n mark left by healed wound, burn or sore; change resulting from emotional distress ~v scarring, scarred mark, heal with scar

**scarce** adj hard to find; existing or available in insufficient quantity; uncommon **scarcely** adv only just; not quite; definitely or probably not **scarcity, scarceness** n

**scare** v frighten ~n fright, sudden panic **scary** adj **scarecrow** n thing set up to frighten birds from crops; badly dressed person

**scarf** n (pl **scarves** or **scarfs**) long narrow strip of material to put round neck, head etc.

**scarlet** n brilliant red colour ~adj of this colour; immoral, esp. unchaste **scarlet fever** infectious fever with scarlet rash

**scathing** adj harshly critical

**scatter** v throw in various directions; put here and there; sprinkle; disperse **scatterbrain** n empty-

**scale** n gradation, graduation, hierarchy, ladder, series, steps; proportion, ratio; degree, extent, range, scope

**scamper** dash, fly, hurry, run, scoot

**scan** check, check out Inf, examine, glance over, scrutinize, search, skim, survey, sweep

**scandal** crime, disgrace, offence, sin, wrongdoing; dirt, gossip, rumours, slander, talk

**scandalous** atrocious, disgraceful, monstrous, outrageous, shameful,

shocking, unseemly; defamatory, libellous, scurrilous

**scanty** bare, deficient, inadequate, meagre, poor, short, thin

**scar** n injury, mark ~v damage, disfigure, mark

**scarce** deficient, few, infrequent, insufficient, rare, uncommon, unusual

**scare** v alarm, frighten, intimidate, shock, startle, terrify ~n alarm, fright, panic, shock, start

**scathing** biting, caustic, critical, cutting, harsh, scornful

headed person

**scavenge** v search for (anything usable), esp. among discarded material **scavenger** n person who scavenges; animal, bird which feeds on refuse

**scenario** n (pl **-rios**) summary of plot of play or film; imagined sequence of future events

**scene** n place of action of novel, play etc.; place of any action; subdivision of play; view; episode; display of strong emotion **scenery** n natural features of district; constructions used on stage to represent scene of action **scenic** adj picturesque

**scent** n distinctive smell, esp. pleasant one; trail; perfume ~v detect or track (by smell); sense; fill with fragrance

**sceptic** n one who maintains doubt or disbelief **sceptical** adj **scepticism** n

**sceptre** n ornamental staff as symbol of royal power

**schedule** n plan of procedure for project; list; timetable ~v enter into schedule; plan to occur at certain time

**scheme** n plan, design; project; outline ~v devise, plan, esp. in underhand manner **scheming** adj

**schism** n (group resulting from) division in political party, church etc.

**schizophrenia** n mental disorder involving deterioration of, confusion about personality **schizophrenic** adj/n

**school**[1] n institution for teaching children or for giving instruction in any subject; buildings of such institution; group of thinkers, writers, artists etc. with principles or methods in common ~v educate; bring under control, train **scholar** n learned person; one taught in school **scholarly** adj learned **scholarship** n learning; prize, grant to student for payment of school or college fees **scholastic** adj of schools or scholars

———————— THESAURUS ————————

**scatter** diffuse, disseminate, fling, shower, spread, sprinkle, strew; disband, dispel, disperse, dissipate

**scene** backdrop, location, set, setting; area, locality, place, position, setting, site, spot; landscape, panorama, prospect, view, vista; exhibition, fuss, performance, row, to-do, upset

**scenery** landscape, surroundings, view, vista

**scent** n aroma, bouquet, fragrance, odour, perfume, smell; spoor, track, trail ~v detect, discern, sense, smell

**sceptic** cynic, disbeliever, doubter

**sceptical** cynical, doubtful, dubious, incredulous

**schedule** n agenda, calendar, plan, programme, timetable ~v appoint, arrange, book, organize, plan, programme, time

**scheme** n design, plan, programme, project, proposal, strategy, system, tactics; blueprint, chart, diagram, draft, layout, outline, pattern ~v conspire, devise, intrigue, plan, plot

**scheming** calculating, conniving, cunning, sly, underhand

**scholar** academic, intellectual; learner, pupil, schoolboy, schoolgirl, student

**scholarship** book-learning, education, erudition, knowledge, learning; bursary, fellowship

**school²** *n* shoal (of fish, whales etc.)

**schooner** *n* fore-and-aft rigged vessel with two or more masts; tall glass

**science** *n* systematic study and knowledge of natural or physical phenomena; any branch of study concerned with observed material facts; skill, technique **scientific** *adj* of the principles of science; systematic **scientist** *n* **science fiction** stories making imaginative use of scientific knowledge

**scimitar** *n* curved oriental sword

**scintillating** *adj* sparkling; animated, witty, clever

**scissors** *pl n* (*esp.* **pair of scissors**) cutting instrument of two blades pivoted together

**scoff¹** *v* express derision for

**scoff²** *v Sl* eat rapidly

**scold** *v* find fault; reprimand

**scone** *n* small plain cake baked on griddle or in oven

**scoop** *n* shovel-like tool for ladling, hollowing out etc.; news story re-

ported in one newspaper before its rivals ~*v* use scoop

**scooter** *n* child's vehicle propelled by pushing on ground with one foot; light motorcycle (*also* **motor scooter**)

**scope** *n* range of activity or application; room, opportunity

**scorch** *v* burn, be burnt, on surface ~*n* slight burn

**score** *n* points gained in game, competition; group of 20; (*esp. pl*) a lot; musical notation; mark or notch, esp. to keep tally; reason, account; grievance ~*v* gain points in game; mark; cross out; arrange music (for); keep tally of points

**scorn** *n* contempt, derision ~*v* despise **scornful** *adj*

**scorpion** *n* small lobster-shaped animal with sting at end of jointed tail

**scotch** *v* put an end to

**scot-free** *adj* without harm or loss

**scoundrel** *n* villain, blackguard

**scour¹** *v* clean, polish by rubbing; clean or flush out **scourer** *n* rough

---

**school** *n* academy, college, institution, seminary ~*v* coach, discipline, drill, educate, instruct, prepare, prime, train, tutor

**scientific** accurate, controlled, exact, precise, systematic

**scoff** belittle, deride, jeer, mock, pooh-pooh, ridicule, scorn, sneer

**scold** *v* berate, castigate, chide, lecture, rebuke, reprimand, reproach, reprove, rate into *Inf*, tear (someone) off a strip *Brit inf*

**scope** area, capacity, extent, freedom, latitude, liberty, opportunity, orbit, range, reach, room, space, sphere

**scorch** blacken, burn, char, sear,

singe

**score** *n* grade, mark, outcome, points, result, total; account, cause, grounds, reason; grievance, grudge, injury ~*v* achieve, gain, win; cut, graze, scrape, scratch, slash; (*with out or through*) cancel, cross out, delete, strike out

**scorn** *n* contempt, derision, disdain, mockery ~*v* be above, disdain, reject, scoff at, slight, spurn

**scornful** contemptuous, derisive, disdainful, mocking, sneering

**scoundrel** bastard *Offens*, blackguard, good-for-nothing, heel *Sl*, rascal, reprobate, rogue, son-of-a-bitch *Sl, chiefly US & Canad*, villain

pad for cleaning pots and pans

**scour²** v move rapidly along or over (territory) in search of something

**scourge** n whip, lash; severe affliction ~v flog; punish severely

**scout** n one sent out to reconnoitre ~v act as scout

**scowl** v/n (make) gloomy or sullen frown

**scrabble** v scrape at with hands, claws in disorderly manner

**scrag** n lean person or animal; lean end of a neck of mutton **scraggy** adj thin, bony

**scram** v **scramming, scrammed** Inf go away hastily

**scramble** v move along or up by crawling, climbing etc.; struggle with others (for); mix up; cook (eggs) beaten up with milk ~n scrambling; rough climb; disorderly proceeding

**scrap** n small piece or fragment; leftover material; Inf fight; pl leftover food ~v **scrapping, scrapped** break up, discard as useless; Inf fight **scrappy** adj unequal in quality; badly finished **scrapbook** n

book in which newspaper cuttings or pictures are stuck

**scrape** v rub with something sharp; clean, smooth thus; grate; scratch; rub with harsh noise ~n act, sound of scraping **scraper** n instrument for scraping

**scratch** v score, make narrow surface mark or wound with something sharp; scrape (skin) with nails to relieve itching; remove, withdraw from list, race etc. ~n wound, mark or sound made by scratching

**scrawl** v write, draw untidily ~n thing scrawled

**scrawny** adj thin, bony

**scream** v utter piercing cry, esp. of fear, pain etc.; utter in a scream ~n shrill, piercing cry

**screech** v/n scream

**screed** n long (tedious) letter, passage or speech

**screen** n device to shelter from heat, light, draught, observation etc.; blank surface on which photographic images are projected; windscreen ~v shelter, hide; show (film); examine (group of people) for political motives or for presence of

**scour¹** buff, clean, polish, scrub

**scour²** comb, hunt, ransack, search

**scourge** n lash, switch, thong, whip; affliction, bane, curse, plague, torment ~v beat, cane, flog, horsewhip, lash, leather, thrash, whip

**scowl** v frown, glower, lour or lower ~n black look, frown, glower

**scramble** v climb, crawl; contend, struggle, strive, vie ~n climb, trek; melee, race, rush, struggle, tussle

**scrap** n atom, bit, crumb, fragment, grain, morsel, part, particle, piece, portion; junk, off cuts, waste;

pl bits, leavings, leftovers, remains ~v abandon, chuck Inf, discard, drop, jettison, write off

**scrape** v bark, graze, scratch, scuff, skin; clean, rub, scour, grate, grind, rasp, scratch

**scrappy** bitty, disjointed, fragmentary, piecemeal, sketchy, thrown together

**scratch** v claw, grate, graze, mark, score, scrape; cancel, eliminate, withdraw ~n graze, laceration, mark, scrape

**scrawl** doodle, scratch, scribble, writing

disease, weapons etc.

**screw** n metal pin with spiral thread, twisted into materials to pin or fasten; anything resembling a screw in shape ~v fasten with screw; twist around **screwdriver** n tool for turning screws

**scribble** v write, draw carelessly; make meaningless marks with pen or pencil ~n something scribbled

**scribe** n writer; copyist ~v scratch a line with pointed instrument

**scrimp** v make too small or short; treat meanly

**script** n (system or style of) handwriting; written text of film, play, radio or television programme

**scripture** n sacred writings; the Bible

**scroll** n roll of parchment or paper; ornament shaped thus

**scrotum** n (pl **-ta, -tums**) pouch of skin containing testicles

**scrounge** v Inf get without cost, by begging **scrounger** n

**scrub¹** v **scrubbing, scrubbed** clean with hard brush and water; scour; Inf delete, cancel ~n scrubbing

**scrub²** n stunted trees; brushwood

**scruff** n nape of neck

**scruffy** adj unkempt, shabby

**scrum, scrummage** n Rugby restarting of play in which opposing packs of forwards push against each other to gain possession of the ball; disorderly struggle

**scruple** n doubt or hesitation about what is morally right ~v hesitate **scrupulous** adj extremely conscientious; thorough

**scrutiny** n close examination; critical investigation **scrutinize** v examine closely

**scuba diving** sport of swimming under water using self-contained breathing apparatus

**scud** v **scudding, scudded** run fast; run before wind

**scuff** v drag, scrape with feet in walking; graze ~n act, sound of scuffing

**scuffle** v fight in disorderly manner; shuffle ~n scuffling

**scull** n oar used in stern of boat; short oar used in pairs ~v propel, move by means of sculls

**scullery** n place for washing dishes etc.

**sculpture** n art of forming solid figures; product of this art ~v represent by sculpture **sculptor** n (fem **sculptress**)

——————————————— THESAURUS ———————————————

**scream** v/n screech, shriek, squeal

**screen** n canopy, cover, guard, shade, shelter, shield ~v cloak, conceal, cover, hide, mask, shade, veil; defend, guard, protect, shelter, shield; examine, filter, scan, vet

**screw** v tighten, turn, twist

**scribble** v dash off, jot, scrawl

**script** n book, copy, dialogue, lines, text, words

**scrounge** beg, cadge, sponge Inf

**scrounger** cadger, parasite, sponger

**scrub** v clean, cleanse, rub, scour; Inf call off, cancel, delete, drop, give up

**scruffy** ragged, shabby, slovenly, tattered, untidy

**scrupulous** careful, exact, meticulous, precise, punctilious, rigorous, strict

**scrutinize** examine, inspect, peruse, scan, study

**scrutiny** examination, inspection, perusal, study

**scuffle** n brawl, fight, scrimmage,

**scum** *n* froth or other floating matter on liquid; waste part of anything; vile people **scummy** *adj*

**scurrilous** *adj* coarse, indecently abusive

**scurry** *v* -rying, -ried run hastily ~*n* bustling haste; flurry

**scurvy** *n* disease caused by lack of vitamin C

**scuttle**[1] *n* fireside container for coal

**scuttle**[2] *v* rush away; run hurriedly ~*n* hurried run

**scuttle**[3] *v* make hole in ship to sink it

**scythe** *n* manual implement with long curved blade for cutting grass ~*v* cut with scythe

**sea** *n* mass of salt water covering greater part of earth; broad tract of this; waves; vast expanse ~*adj* of the sea **seagull** *n* gull **sea horse** fish with bony-plated body and horse-like head **sea lion** kind of large seal **seaman** *n* sailor **seasick** *adj* seasickness *n* nausea caused by motion of ship **seaweed** *n* plant growing in sea **seaworthy** *adj* in fit condition to put to sea

**seal**[1] *n* piece of metal or stone engraved with device for impression on wax etc.; impression thus made (on letters etc.); device, material preventing passage of water, air, oil etc. ~*v* affix seal to ratify, authorize; mark with stamp as evidence of some quality; keep close or secret; settle; make watertight, airtight etc.

**seal**[2] *n* amphibious furred carnivorous mammal with flippers as limbs

**seam** *n* line of junction of two edges, e.g. of two pieces of cloth; thin layer, stratum ~*v* mark with furrows or wrinkles **seamless** *adj* **seamy** *adj* sordid

**seance** *n* meeting at which people attempt to communicate with the dead

**sear** *v* scorch

**search** *v* look over or through to find something ~*n* act of searching; quest **searching** *adj* thorough

**season** *n* one of four divisions of year; period during which thing happens etc. ~*v* flavour with salt, herbs etc.; make reliable or ready for use; make experienced **seasonable** *adj* appropriate for the season; opportune **seasonal** *adj* varying with seasons **seasoning** *n* flavouring

**seat** *n* thing for sitting on; buttocks; base; right to sit (e.g. in council etc.); place where something is located, centred; locality of disease, trouble etc.; country house ~*v* make to sit; provide sitting ac-

**shindig** *Inf*, shindy *Inf*, tussle

**scurry** *v* dash, hurry, race, scamper, scoot, scuttle

**sea** *n* main, ocean, the deep, the waves; expanse, mass, multitude ~*adj* marine, ocean, saltwater

**seal** *n* insignia, stamp ~*v* bung, plug, stop, stopper, waterproof; ratify, stamp, validate; clinch, finalize, settle

**seam** *n* layer, lode, stratum, vein

**search** *v* comb, examine, ferret, inquire, inspect, ransack, rummage through, probe, ransack, rummage through, scour ~*n* examination, hunt, inquiry, inspection, investigation, rummage

**searching** *adj* close, intent, keen, probing, thorough

**season** *n* period, spell, term, time ~*v* accustom, harden, mature, prepare, toughen, train

commodation for **seat belt** belt worn in vehicle to prevent injury in crash

**secateurs** pl n small pruning shears

**secede** v withdraw formally from federation, Church etc. **secession** n

**seclude** v guard from, remove from sight, view, contact with others **secluded** adj remote; private **seclusion** n

**second**[1] adj next after first; alternate, additional; of lower quality ~n person or thing coming second; attendant; sixtieth part of minute ~v support **second-class** adj inferior **second-hand** adj bought after use by another; not original **second sight** supposed ability to predict events

**second**[2] v transfer (employee, officer) temporarily

**secondary** adj of less importance; developed from something else; Education after primary stage

**secret** adj kept, meant to be kep from knowledge of others; hidden ~n thing kept secret **secrecy** n keeping or being kept secret **secretive** adj given to having secrets

**secretary** n one employed to deal with papers and correspondence keep records etc.; head of a state department **secretariat** n body of secretaries

**secrete** v hide; conceal; (of gland etc.) collect and supply particular substance in body **secretion** n

**sect** n group of people (within religious body etc.) with common interest; faction **sectarian** adj

**section** n division; portion; distinct part; cutting; drawing of anything as if cut through

**sector** n part or subdivision

**secular** adj worldly; lay, not religious

**secure** adj safe; firmly fixed; certain ~v gain possession of; make safe; make firm **security** n state of

---

**seasoning** condiment, flavouring

**seat** n bench, chair, pew, stool; base, bottom, cause, foundation, ground; capital, centre, cradle, heart, hub, site, source, station ~v fix, install, locate, place, set, settle, sit; accommodate, cater for, contain, hold, take

**secluded** cloistered, cut off, isolated, lonely, private, remote, sheltered

**second** adj following, next, subsequent, succeeding; additional, alternative, extra, further, other; inferior, lesser, lower ~n backer, helper, supporter ~v aid, assist, back, endorse, help, promote, support

**secondary** lesser, lower, minor, subordinate; backup, extra, reserve,

subsidiary, supporting

**second-hand** nearly new, used

**secret** concealed, disguised, furtive, hidden, underground, undisclosed, unknown, unseen; hidden private, secluded

**secretive** close, cryptic, deep, enigmatic

**secretly** furtively, privately, quietly, stealthily, surreptitiously

**sect** camp, denomination, division, faction, group, party, schism, splinter group, wing

**sectarian** exclusive, insular, limited, parochial, partisan

**section** division, fraction, instalment, part, passage, piece, portion, segment

**secular** earthly, lay, profane, tem

safety; protection; anything given as bond or pledge

**sedate**[1] *adj* calm, serious

**sedate**[2] *v* make calm by sedative **sedation** *n* **sedative** *adj* having soothing or calming effect ~*n* sedative drug

**sediment** *n* matter which settles to the bottom of liquid

**sedition** *n* stirring up of rebellion

**seduce** *v* persuade to commit some (wrong) deed, esp. sexual intercourse **seducer** *n* (*fem* **seductress**) **seduction** *n* **seductive** *adj* alluring

**see**[1] *v* **seeing, saw, seen** perceive with eyes or mentally; watch; find out; interview; make sure; accompany; consider **seeing** *conj* in view of the fact that

**see**[2] *n* diocese, office of bishop

**seed** *n* reproductive germs of plants; one grain of this; such grains saved or used for sowing; sperm; origin ~*v* sow with seed; produce seed **seedling** *n* young plant raised from seed **seedy** *adj* shabby; full of seed

**seek** *v* **seeking, sought** make search or enquiry (for)

**seem** *v* appear (to be or to do) **seemly** *adj* becoming and proper

**seep** *v* trickle through slowly

**seesaw** *n* plank on which children sit at opposite ends and swing up and down ~*v* move up and down

**seethe** *v* **seething, seethed** boil, foam; be very agitated; be in constant movement (as large crowd etc.)

**segment** *n* piece cut off; section ~*v* divide into segments

---

poral, worldly

**secure** *adj* immune, protected, safe, unassailable; fast, fastened, firm, fixed, immovable, stable, steady, tight; assured, certain, sure ~*v* acquire, gain, get, obtain, procure; fasten, fix, lash, moor, tie up

**security** asylum, refuge, retreat, safety; defence, protection, surveillance; collateral, guarantee, insurance, pledge

**sedate** calm, collected, composed, cool, quiet, serious, sober, solemn

**sedative** calming, relaxing, soothing ~*n* narcotic, opiate, tranquillizer

**sediment** deposit, dregs, grounds, lees, residue

**seduce** corrupt, deprave, dishonour; beguile, entice, lure, mislead, tempt

**seductive** alluring, bewitching, enticing, inviting, tempting

**see** *v* behold, discern, distinguish, espy, glimpse, look, mark, note, notice, observe, perceive, regard, sight, spot, view, witness; follow, get, grasp, know, realize, understand; ascertain, determine, discover, find out, learn; consider, decide, deliberate, judge; confer with, consult, interview, meet, speak to

**seed** germ, grain, kernel, pip; beginning, germ, nucleus, origin, source, start

**seedy** dilapidated, old, run-down, shabby, worn

**seek** hunt, pursue, search for

**seem** appear, look, pretend

**seemly** becoming, befitting, decent, decorous, fit, fitting, proper, suitable

**seethe** boil, bubble, foam, froth; be alive, swarm, teem

**segment** bit, division, part, piece, portion, section, slice, wedge

**segregate** v set apart from rest **segregation** n

**seize** v grasp; lay hold of; capture; (of machine part) stick tightly through overheating **seizure** n act of taking; sudden onset of disease

**seldom** adv not often, rarely

**select** v pick out, choose ~adj choice, picked; exclusive **selection** n option; assortment **selective** adj **selector** n

**self** n (pl **selves**) one's own person or individuality **selfish** adj unduly concerned with personal profit or pleasure; greedy **selfless** adj unselfish

**self-** comb. form of oneself or itself
**self-assured** adj confident
**self-conscious** adj unduly aware of oneself
**self-contained** adj containing everything needed
**self-made** adj having achieved wealth, status etc. by one's own efforts

**self-possessed** adj calm
**self-respect** n proper sense of one's own dignity and integrity
**self-righteous** adj smugly sure of one's own virtue
**selfsame** adj very same
**self-service** adj (of shop or restaurant) letting customers serve themselves
**self-sufficient** adj independent
**sell** v selling, sold hand over for a price; stock, have for sale; make someone accept; Inf betray, cheat; find purchasers **seller** n
**Sellotape** n Trademark type of adhesive tape ~v (without cap.) stick with Sellotape
**semaphore** n system of signalling by human or mechanical arms
**semblance** n (false) appearance; image, likeness
**semen** n fluid carrying sperm of male animals; sperm

**segregate** dissociate, isolate, separate, set apart

**seize** clutch, grab, grasp, grip, lay hands on; catch; get, nab Inf, nail Inf; annex, arrest, capture, commandeer, confiscate, impound

**seizure** arrest, capture, commandeering, grabbing, taking; attack, convulsion, fit, paroxysm, spasm

**seldom** infrequently, not often, occasionally, rarely

**select** v choose, pick ~adj choice, excellent, first-rate, hand-picked, picked, prime, special, superior

**selection** choice, choosing, option, pick; assortment, choice, collection, medley, range, variety

**selective** discerning, discriminating, particular

**self-conscious** awkward, bashful, embarrassed, ill at ease, insecure, nervous

**selfish** egoistic, egotistical, greedy, mean, self-seeking, ungenerous

**selfless** altruistic, generous, self-denying, self-sacrificing, unselfish

**self-possessed** collected, confident, cool, poised, self-assured, unruffled

**self-respect** dignity, pride, self-esteem

**self-righteous** complacent, priggish, sanctimonious, self-satisfied, smug, superior

**sell** barter, exchange, trade; deal in, market, peddle, stock, trade in, traffic in

**seller** agent, dealer, merchant, purveyor, rep, retailer, salesman, shopkeeper, supplier, tradesman,

**semi-** *comb. form* half, partly, not completely, as in **semicircle**

**semibreve** *n* musical note equal to four crotchets

**semicircle** *n* half of circle

**semicolon** *n* punctuation mark (;)

**semiconductor** *n* substance whose electrical conductivity increases with temperature, used in transistors, circuits etc.

**semidetached** *adj* (of house) joined to another by one side only

**semifinal** *n* match, round etc. before final

**seminal** *adj* capable of developing; influential; of semen or seed

**seminar** *n* meeting of group (of students) for discussion

**semiprecious** *adj* (of gemstones) having less value than precious stones

**semolina** *n* hard grains left after sifting of flour, used for puddings etc.

**senate** *n* upper council of state, university etc. **senator** *n*

**send** *v* **sending, sent** cause to go or

be conveyed; despatch; transmit (by radio)

**senile** *adj* showing weakness of old age **senility** *n*

**senior** *adj* superior in rank or standing; older ~*n* superior; elder person **seniority** *n*

**sensation** *n* operation of sense, feeling, awareness; excited feeling, state of excitement; exciting event **sensational** *adj* producing great excitement **sensationalism** *n* deliberate use of sensational material

**sense** *n* any of bodily faculties of perception or feeling; ability to perceive; consciousness; meaning; coherence; sound practical judgment ~*v* perceive **senseless** *adj*

**sensible** *adj* reasonable; wise; aware **sensibility** *n* ability to feel, esp. emotional or moral feelings

**sensitive** *adj* open to, acutely affected by, external impressions; easily affected or altered; easily upset by criticism; responsive to slight changes **sensitivity, sensitiveness** *n* **sensitize** *v* make sensitive

———— THESAURUS ————

vendor

**send** consign, convey, despatch, direct, forward, transmit

**senile** decrepit, doting, failing

**senior** *adj* elder, higher ranking, older, superior

**seniority** precedence, priority, rank, superiority

**sensation** consciousness, feeling, impression, perception, sense; agitation, commotion, excitement, furore, scandal, stir, surprise, thrill

**sensational** amazing, astounding, dramatic, electrifying, exciting, thrilling

**sense** *n* faculty, feeling, sensation, atmosphere, aura, feel, impression;

drift, gist, implication, import, meaning; (*sometimes pl*) brains *Inf*, cleverness, discernment, discrimination, intelligence, judgment, mother wit, reason, understanding, wisdom ~*v* appreciate, discern, divine, feel, grasp, notice, observe, perceive, pick up, realize, understand

**senseless** absurd, crazy, foolish, idiotic, inane, mad, mindless, nonsensical, stupid; cold, out, stunned, unconscious

**sensible** down-to-earth, intelligent, judicious, practical, prudent, rational, realistic, shrewd, sound, wise

**sensor** *n* device that detects or measures the presence of something

**sensory** *adj* relating to senses

**sensual** *adj* of senses only and not of mind; given to pursuit of pleasures of sense

**sensuous** *adj* stimulating, or apprehended by, senses, esp. in aesthetic manner

**sentence** *n* combination of words expressing a thought; judgment passed on criminal by court or judge ~*v* pass sentence on, condemn

**sentient** *adj* capable of feeling

**sentiment** *n* tendency to be moved by feeling rather than reason; mental feeling; opinion **sentimental** *adj* given to indulgence in sentiment and in its expression **sentimentality** *n*

**sentinel** *n* sentry

**sentry** *n* soldier on watch

**separate** *v* part; divide ~*adj* disconnected, distinct, individual

**separable** *adj* **separation** *n* disconnection; living apart of married couple

**sepia** *n* reddish-brown pigment ~*adj* of this colour

**Sept.** September

**September** *n* ninth month

**septet** *n* (music for) group of seven musicians

**septic** *adj* (of wound) infected; of, caused by pus-forming bacteria

**septicaemia** *n* blood poisoning

**sepulchre** *n* tomb; burial vault

**sequel** *n* consequence; continuation, e.g. of story

**sequence** *n* arrangement of things in successive order

**sequin** *n* small ornamental metal disc on dresses etc.

**seraph** *n* (*pl* **seraphim, seraphs**) angel

**serenade** *n* sentimental song addressed to woman by lover, esp. at evening ~*v* sing serenade (to someone)

**serendipity** *n* gift of making fortu-

————— THESAURUS —————

**sensitive** acute, delicate, fine, keen, perceptive, responsive, susceptible

**sensual** animal, bodily, carnal, fleshly, physical; erotic, lascivious, lustful, sexual

**sentence** *n* decision, decree, judgment, order, ruling, verdict

**sentiment** emotion, sensibility, tenderness; (*oft. pl*) belief, feeling, idea, opinion, view, way of thinking

**sentimental** emotional, impressionable, nostalgic, romantic, softhearted, tender, touching

**sentimentality** nostalgia, romanticism, tenderness

**separate** *v* break up, divorce, estrange, part, split up; isolate, segregate, single out; come away, detach, disconnect, divide, remove, sever, split, sunder ~*adj* apart, detached, disconnected, divided, divorced, isolated; distinct, independent, individual, particular, single, solitary

**separation** break, disconnection, dissociation, division, segregation, severance; break-up, divorce, parting, split

**septic** festering, infected, poisoned, suppurating

**sequel** continuation, follow-up; conclusion, end, outcome, result, upshot

**sequence** arrangement, chain, course, cycle, series, succession

nate discoveries by accident

**serene** *adj* calm, tranquil; unclouded **serenity** *n*

**serf** *n* one of class of medieval labourers bound to, and transferred with, land

**sergeant** *n* noncommissioned officer in army; police officer above constable **sergeant major** highest noncommissioned officer in regiment

**series** *n* (*pl* series) sequence; succession, set (e.g. of radio, TV programmes) **serial** *n* story or play produced in successive episodes **serialize** *v*

**serious** *adj* thoughtful, solemn; earnest, sincere; of importance; giving cause for concern

**sermon** *n* discourse of religious instruction or exhortation; any similar discourse

**serpent** *n* snake **serpentine** *adj* twisting, winding like a snake

**serrated** *adj* having notched, sawlike edge

**serum** *n* (*pl* **-rums, -ra**) watery animal fluid, esp. thin part of blood as used for inoculation or vaccination

**serve** *v* work for, under another; attend (to customers) in shop etc.; provide; help to (food etc.); present (food etc.) in particular way; be member of military unit, spend time doing; be useful, suitable enough **servant** *n* personal or domestic attendant **service** *n* act of serving; system organized to provide for needs of public; maintenance of vehicle; use; department of State employment; set of dishes etc.; form, session of public worship; *pl* armed forces **~v** overhaul **serviceable** *adj* in working order, usable; durable **serviceman** *n* member of armed forced **service station** place supplying fuel, oil, maintenance for motor vehicles

**serviette** *n* table napkin

**servile** *adj* slavish, without independence; fawning

**servitude** *n* bondage, slavery

**sesame** *n* plant whose seeds and oil are used in cooking

---

THESAURUS

**serene** calm, composed, peaceful, placid, tranquil, undisturbed, unruffled, untroubled; clear, cloudless, fair

**serenity** calm, calmness, composure, peace, peacefulness, peace of mind, placidity, quietness, stillness, tranquillity; brightness, clearness, fairness

**series** chain, course, run, sequence, set, string, succession

**serious** grave, sober, solemn, unsmiling; earnest, genuine, in earnest, sincere; crucial, important, momentous, pressing, significant, urgent, weighty; acute, critical, dangerous, grave, severe

**sermon** address, homily; harangue, lecture

**servant** attendant, domestic, maid, retainer, slave, vassal

**serve** aid, assist, help, minister to, wait on, work for; act, do, fulfil, officiate, perform; deal, dish up, distribute, provide, purvey, supply; be acceptable, be adequate, do, suffice, suit

**service** *n* assistance, benefit, help, use; check, maintenance, overhaul; business, duty, labour, office, work; ceremony, function, observance, rite, worship **~v** check, go over, maintain, overhaul, repair, tune (up)

**session** n meeting of court etc.; continuous series of such meetings; any period devoted to an activity

**set** v setting, set put or place in specified position or condition; make ready; become firm or fixed; establish; prescribe, allot; put to music; (of sun) go down ~adj fixed, established, deliberate; unvarying ~n act or state of being set; bearing, posture; Radio, Television complete apparatus for reception or transmission; Theatre, Cinema organized settings and equipment to form ensemble of scene; number of associated things, persons **setback** n anything that hinders or impedes **set up** establish

**sett** n badger's burrow

**settee** n couch

**setter** n gun dog

**setting** n background; surroundings; scenery and other stage accessories; decorative metalwork holding precious stone etc. in position; tableware and cutlery for (single place at) table; music for song

**settle** v arrange; establish; decide upon; end (dispute etc.); pay; make calm or stable; come to rest; subside; become clear; take up residence **settlement** n act of settling; place newly inhabited; money bestowed legally **settler** n colonist

**seven** adj/n cardinal number next after six **seventh** adj ordinal number **seventeen** adj/n ten plus seven **seventeenth** adj **seventieth** adj **seventy** adj/n ten times seven

**sever** v separate, divide; cut off **severance** n

**several** adj some, a few; separate; individual ~pron indefinite small number

**severe** adj strict; harsh; austere; extreme **severity** n

**session** assembly, conference, congress, hearing, period, sitting, term

**set** v aim, direct, fasten, fix, lay, locate, place, plant, put, rest, seat, situate; allocate, appoint, arrange, assign, decide, determine, establish, fix, schedule, settle, specify; congeal, harden, solidify, thicken; allot, impose, ordain, prescribe ~adj agreed, appointed, arranged, decided, definite, firm, fixed, prescribed, scheduled, settled; hidebound, inflexible, rigid, stubborn ~n band, circle, clique, company, coterie, crowd, gang, group; assortment, collection, compendium

**setback** blow, check, hitch, holdup, misfortune

**setting** backdrop, background, location, scene, scenery, set, site, surroundings

**settle** arrange, order, straighten out, work out; clear up, complete, conclude, decide, reconcile, resolve; clear, discharge, pay; allay, calm, pacify, quell, quieten, reassure, relieve, soothe; alight, descend, land, light; decline, fall, sink, subside; colonize, people, pioneer, populate

**settlement** agreement, arrangement, conclusion, resolution; colony, community, encampment, outpost

**settler** colonist, immigrant, pioneer

**set up** arrange, begin, establish, found, institute, organize; back, finance, subsidize

**several** adj many, some, sundry, various; different, distinct, individ-

**sew** v sewing, sewed, sewn join with needle and thread; make by sewing **sewing** n

**sewage** n refuse, waste matter, excrement conveyed in sewer **sewer** n underground drain

**sex** n state of being male or female; males or females collectively; sexual intercourse ~adj concerning sex ~v ascertain sex of **sexism** n discrimination on basis of sex **sexist** n/adj **sexual** adj **sexy** adj **sexual intercourse** act of procreation in which male's penis is inserted into female's vagina

**sextet** n (composition for) six musicians

**shabby** adj faded, worn; poorly dressed; mean, dishonourable

**shack** n rough hut

**shackle** n metal ring or fastening for prisoner's wrist or ankle ~v fasten with shackles; hamper

**shade** n partial darkness; shelter, place sheltered from light, heat etc.; darker part of anything; depth of colour; screen; US window blind ~v screen from light, darken; represent shades in drawing **shady** adj shielded from sun; Inf dishonest

**shadow** n dark figure projected by anything that intercepts rays of light; patch of shade; slight trace ~v cast shadow over; follow and watch closely **shadowy** adj

**shaft** n straight rod, stem, handle; arrow; ray, beam (of light); revolving rod for transmitting power

**shag** n long-napped cloth; coarse shredded tobacco **shaggy** adj covered with rough hair; unkempt

**shake** v shaking, shook, shaken (cause to) move with quick vibrations; tremble; grasp the hand (of

———————— THESAURUS ————————

ual, single

**severe** cruel, hard, harsh, oppressive, pitiless, relentless, strict, unrelenting; austere, classic, plain, restrained, simple, unfussy; acute, critical, dangerous, extreme, intense

**sex** gender; Inf coition, coitus, copulation, (sexual) intercourse, intimacy, lovemaking

**sexual** carnal, erotic, intimate, sexy

**sexual intercourse** carnal knowledge, coition, coitus, copulation, coupling, mating, union

**sexy** erotic, naughty, provocative, seductive, sensual, suggestive, titillating, voluptuous

**shabby** dilapidated, frayed, ragged, tattered, tatty, threadbare, worn-out; contemptible, despicable, dirty, dishonourable, low,

mean, shameful, shoddy

**shade** n dimness, dusk, gloom, obscurity, shadow; colour, hue, tint, tone; blind, canopy, cover, curtain, screen, shield, veil ~v cloud, conceal, cover, dim, hide, protect, screen, shadow, veil

**shadow** n cover, darkness, dimness, protection, shade, shelter; hint, suggestion, suspicion, trace ~v screen, shade, shield; follow, stalk, trail

**shadowy** dark, dim, indistinct, obscure, shaded; dim, nebulous, obscure, undefined, vague

**shady** cool, dim, leafy, shaded; Inf crooked, disreputable, dodgy Brit, Aust, & NZ inf; dubious, shifty, slippery, suspect

**shaft** handle, pole, rod, stem; beam, gleam, ray, streak

**shaggy** hairy, hirsute, long-haired,

another) in greeting; upset; wave, brandish ~n act of shaking; vibration; jolt; Inf short period of time **shaky** adj unsteady, insecure; questionable

**shale** n flaky fine-grained rock

**shall** v (past tense **should**) makes compound tenses or moods to express obligation, command, condition or intention

**shallow** adj not deep; superficial ~n shallow place

**sham** adj/n imitation, counterfeit ~v **shamming**, **shammed** pretend, feign

**shamble** v walk in shuffling, awkward way

**shambles** pl n messy, disorderly thing or place

**shame** n emotion caused by consciousness of guilt or dishonour in one's conduct or state; cause of dis-

grace; pity, hard luck ~v cause to feel shame; disgrace; force by shame (into) **shameful** adj **shameless** adj with no sense of shame; indecent **shamefaced** adj ashamed

**shampoo** n preparation of liquid soap for washing hair, carpets etc.; this process ~v use shampoo to wash

**shamrock** n clover leaf, esp. as Irish emblem

**shandy** n drink of beer and lemonade

**shanty**[1] n temporary wooden building; crude dwelling

**shanty**[2] n sailor's song

**shape** n external form or appearance; mould, pattern; Inf condition ~v shaping, **shaped** form, mould; develop **shapeless** adj **shapely** adj well-proportioned

**shard** n broken piece of pottery

———— THESAURUS ————

unkempt, unshorn

**shake** v quake, rock, shiver, shudder, totter, tremble, vibrate, waver; distress, disturb, frighten, intimidate, shock, unnerve, upset; brandish, flourish, wave ~n agitation, quaking, shiver, shudder, trembling, tremor, vibration

**shaky** insecure, precarious, quivery, rickety, trembling, unstable, unsteady; dubious, questionable, suspect

**shallow** empty, foolish, frivolous, idle, simple, slight, superficial, surface, trivial

**sham** adj artificial, bogus, counterfeit, false, feigned, imitation, mock, phoney or phony Inf, pretended, simulated ~n forgery, fraud, hoax, humbug, imitation, impostor, phoney or phony Inf, pretence ~v affect, assume, fake, feign, pretend,

put on, simulate

**shame** n blot, disgrace, disrepute, infamy, scandal, smear; abashment, humiliation, ignominy ~v abash, embarrass, humble; blot, disgrace, dishonour, smear, stain

**shameful** base, disgraceful, low, mean, scandalous; degrading, humiliating, shaming

**shameless** audacious, brash, brazen, flagrant, immodest, improper, indecent, wanton

**shape** n build, configuration, contours, cut, figure, form, lines, outline, profile; frame, model, mould, pattern; condition, fettle, health, state, trim ~v create, fashion, form, make, model, mould, produce; adapt, develop, devise, frame, plan

**shapeless** amorphous, formless, nebulous, undeveloped, unstructured

**share** *n* portion; quota; lot; unit of ownership in public company ~*v* give, take a share; join with others in doing, using, something **shareholder** *n*

**shark** *n* large usu. predatory sea fish; person who cheats others

**sharp** *adj* having keen cutting edge or fine point; not gradual or gentle; brisk; clever; harsh; dealing cleverly but unfairly; shrill; strongly marked, esp. in outline; sour ~*adv* promptly **sharpen** *v* make sharp **sharpshooter** *n* marksman

**shatter** *v* break in pieces; ruin (plans etc.); disturb (person) greatly **shattered** *adj Inf* completely exhausted

**shave** *v* **shaving, shaved, shaved** or **shaven** cut close, esp. hair of face or head; pare away; graze; reduce ~*n* shaving **shavings** *pl n* parings

**shawl** *n* piece of fabric to cover woman's shoulders or wrap baby

**she** *pron* (third person fem) person, animal already referred to; *comb. form* female, as in **she-wolf**

**sheaf** *n* (*pl* **sheaves**) bundle, esp. of corn; loose leaves of paper

**shear** *v* **shearing, sheared, sheared** or **shorn** clip hair, wool from; cut through; fracture **shears** *pl n* large pair of scissors

**sheath** *n* close-fitting cover, esp. for knife or sword **sheathe** *v* put into sheath

**shed** *n* roofed shelter used as store or workshop

**shed** *v* **shedding, shed** (cause to) pour forth (e.g. tears, blood); cast off

**sheen** *n* gloss

**sheep** *n* ruminant animal bred for wool or meat **sheepish** *adj* embarrassed, shy **sheepdog** *n* dog used for herding sheep

**sheer** *adj* perpendicular; (of material) very fine, transparent; absolute, unmitigated

**sheet** *n* large piece of cotton etc. to cover bed; broad piece of any thin material; large expanse

**sheikh** *n* Arab chief

**shelf** *n* (*pl* **shelves**) board fixed horizontally (on wall etc.) for holding things; ledge

**shell** *n* hard outer case (esp. of egg, nut etc.); explosive projectile; outer part of structure left when interior is removed ~*v* take shell from; take

**share** *n* allotment, allowance, contribution, lot, part, portion, quota, ration ~*v* distribute, divide, partake, participate, split

**sharp** *adj* acute, jagged, keen, pointed, serrated, spiky, abrupt, marked, sudden; alert, astute, bright, clever, observant, perceptive, quick, ready; caustic, cutting, harsh, hurtful, scathing, trenchant; clear, clear-cut, crisp, distinct, well-defined; acerbic, acid, sour, tart, vinegary ~*adv* exactly, on time, on the dot, precisely, prompt-

ly, punctually

**shatter** break, burst, crush, demolish, explode, smash; blast, demolish, destroy, ruin, torpedo, wreck; crush, devastate

**shed** *v* cast, emit, give, give forth, radiate, scatter, shower, spill; cast off, discard, moult, slough

**sheer** abrupt, precipitous, steep; complete, downright, pure, total, unqualified, utter

**sheet** area, expanse, stretch, sweep; blanket, coat, covering, film, layer, panel, piece, plate, slab

out of shell; fire at with shells **shell-fish** n mollusc; crustacean

**shelter** n place, structure giving protection; refuge ~v give protection to; take shelter

**shelve** v put on a shelf; put off; slope gradually

**shepherd** n (fem **shepherdess**) one who tends sheep ~v guide, watch over **shepherd's pie** dish of minced meat and potato

**sherbet** n fruit-flavoured effervescent powder

**sheriff** n US law enforcement officer; in England and Wales, chief executive officer of the crown in a county; in Scotland, chief judge of a district; Canad municipal officer who enforces court orders etc.

**sherry** n fortified wine

**shield** n piece of armour carried on arm; any protection used to stop blows, missiles etc. ~v cover, protect

**shift** v (cause to) move, change position ~n move, change of position; relay of workers; time of their working; woman's underskirt or dress ~v

**shiftless** adj lacking in resource or

character **shifty** adj evasive, of dubious character

**shilling** n former Brit. coin, now 5p

**shimmer** v shine with quivering light ~n such light

**shin** n front of lower leg ~v climb with arms and legs

**shine** v front of lower leg ~v climb with arms and legs

**shine** v shining, shone give out, reflect light; excel; polish ~n brightness, lustre; polishing **shiny** adj

**shingle** n mass of pebbles

**shingles** n disease causing rash of small blisters

**ship** n large seagoing vessel ~v shipping, shipped put on or send (esp. by ship) **shipment** n act of shipping; goods shipped **shipping** n freight transport business; ships collectively **shipshape** adj orderly, neat **shipwreck** n destruction of ship ~v cause shipwreck of **shipyard** n place for building and repair of ships

**shire** n county **shire horse** large powerful breed of horse

**shirk** v evade, try to avoid (duty etc.)

**shirt** n garment with sleeves and

———————— THESAURUS ————————

**shell** n case, husk, pod; frame, framework, hull ~v blitz, bomb, bombard

**shelter** n asylum, cover, haven, protection, refuge, retreat, safety, sanctuary ~v cover, harbour, protect, safeguard, shield

**shelve** v defer, postpone, put on the back burner Inf, take a rain check on US & Canad inf

**shield** n cover, defence, guard, protection, safeguard, screen, shelter ~v cover, defend, guard, protect, safeguard, screen, shelter

**shift** v budge, change, displace,

move, relocate, reposition, switch, transfer, transpose ~n change, move, shifting, switch, transfer

**shifty** devious, evasive, furtive, slippery, sly, tricky, underhand, untrustworthy

**shimmer** dance, gleam, glisten, twinkle

**shine** v beam, flash, glare, gleam, glisten, glitter, glow, radiate, sparkle, twinkle; be conspicuous, excel, stand out ~n brightness, glare, gleam, light, radiance, shimmer, sparkle

**shiny** bright, gleaming, glistening,

collar for upper part of body

**shirty** *adj Inf* annoyed

**shiver**[1] *v* tremble, usu. with cold or fear ~*n* act, state of shivering

**shiver**[2] *v/n* splinter

**shoal**[1] *n* large number of fish swimming together

**shoal**[2] *n* stretch of shallow water; sandbank

**shock**[1] *v* horrify, scandalize ~*n* violent or damaging blow; emotional disturbance; state of weakness, illness, caused by physical or mental shock; paralytic stroke; collision; effect on sensory nerves of electric discharge **shocking** *adj* causing horror, disgust or astonishment; *Inf* very bad

**shock**[2] *n* mass of hair

**shoddy** *adj* worthless, trashy

**shoe** *n* (*pl* **shoes**) covering for foot, not enclosing ankle; metal rim put on horse's hoof; various protective plates or undercoverings ~*v* **shoeing, shod** protect, furnish with shoe(s)

**shoo** *interj* go away!

**shoot** *v* **shooting, shot** wound, kill with missile fired from weapon; discharge weapon; send, slide, push

rapidly; photograph, film; hunt; sprout ~*n* young branch, sprout; hunting expedition

**shop** *n* place for retail sale of goods and services; workshop, works building ~*v* **shopping, shopped** visit shops to buy **shoplifter** *n* one who steals from shop **shopsoiled** *adj* damaged from being displayed in shop

**shore**[1] *n* edge of sea or lake

**shore**[2] *v* prop (up)

**short** *adj* not long; not tall; brief; not enough; lacking; abrupt ~*adv* abruptly; without reaching end ~*n* drink of spirits; short film; *pl* short trousers **shortage** *n* deficiency **shorten** *v* **shortly** *adv* soon; briefly **shortbread, shortcake** *n* crumbly biscuit made with butter **short circuit** *Electricity* connection, often accidental, of low resistance between two parts of circuit **shortcoming** *n* failing **short cut** quicker route or method **shorthand** *n* method of rapid writing **short list** list of candidates from which final choice will be made **short-sighted** *adj* unable to see faraway things clearly; lacking in foresight

——————— THESAURUS ———————

glossy, lustrous

**shirk** avoid, dodge, evade

**shock** *v* disgust, gross out *US sl*, horrify, nauseate, offend, outrage, revolt, shake, sicken, stagger ~*n* blow, bombshell, collapse, distress, stupor, trauma, upset

**shocking** appalling, atrocious, disgraceful, dreadful, ghastly, hideous, horrible, offensive, outrageous, revolting, scandalous, sickening

**shoddy** inferior, poor, second-rate, slipshod, trashy

**shoot** *v* bag, hit, open fire, pick off;

emit, fire, fling, hurl, launch, project, propel; bolt, charge, dart, dash, fly, hurtle, race, rush, speed, tear ~*n* branch, bud, sprig, sprout

**shore** beach, coast, sands, seashore

**short** *adj* dumpy, little, low, small, squat; brief, fleeting, momentary; brief, concise, laconic, pithy, succinct, summary, terse; (*oft. with of*) deficient, lacking, limited, meagre, poor, scant, scanty, scarce, tight, wanting ~*adv* abruptly, by surprise, suddenly, unaware

**shortage** dearth, deficit, lack, pov-

**shot** n act of shooting; small lead pellets; marksman; Inf attempt; photograph; dose; Inf injection

**shotgun** n gun for firing shot at short range **shot put** contest in which athletes throw heavy metal ball

**should** past tense of SHALL

**shoulder** n part of body to which arm or foreleg is attached; anything resembling shoulder; side of road ~v undertake; put on one's shoulder; make way by pushing

**shout** n/v (utter) loud cry

**shove** v/n push

**shovel** n instrument for scooping earth etc. ~v -elling, -elled lift, move (as) with shovel

**show** v showing, showed, shown or showed expose to view; point out; explain; prove; guide; appear; be noticeable ~n display; entertainment; ostentation; pretence **showy** adj gaudy; ostentatious **show business** the entertainment industry **showcase** n glass case to display

objects; situation in which thing is displayed to best advantage **showdown** n confrontation **showman** n one skilled at presenting anything effectively **show off** exhibit to invite admiration; behave in this way **show-off** n showroom n room in which goods for sale are displayed

**shower** n short fall of rain; anything falling like rain; kind of bath in which person stands under water spray ~v bestow liberally; take bath in shower

**shrapnel** n shell splinters

**shred** n fragment, torn strip ~v shredding, shredded or shred cut, tear to shreds

**shrew** n animal like mouse; bad-tempered woman

**shrewd** adj astute; crafty

**shriek** n/v (utter) piercing cry

**shrill** adj piercing, sharp in tone

**shrimp** n small edible crustacean; Inf undersized person

**shrine** n place of worship, usu. associated with saint

———————— THESAURUS ————————

erty, scarcity, want

**shortcoming** defect, failing, fault, flaw, imperfection, weakness

**shorten** abbreviate, cut, decrease, diminish, dock, lessen, reduce, trim

**shot** n Inf attempt, chance, effort, endeavour, essay, go Inf, opportunity, stab Inf, try, turn

**shoulder** v accept, assume, bear, be responsible for, carry, take on; elbow, jostle, push, shove, thrust

**shout** n/v bawl, bellow, call, cry, roar, scream, yell

**shove** v drive, elbow, impel, jostle, propel, push, thrust

**show** v disclose, display, divulge, exhibit, indicate, manifest, present, register, reveal; demonstrate, ex-

plain, instruct, prove, teach; conduct, escort, guide, lead ~n demonstration, display, exhibition, sight, spectacle, view; appearance, display, illusion, ostentation, pose, pretence, profession, semblance

**shower** n deluge, rain, stream, torrent, volley ~v deluge, heap, lavish, load, pour, rain, spray

**show off** advertise, display, exhibit, flaunt, parade; boast, brag

**shred** n bit, fragment, piece, rag, scrap, tatter

**shrewd** astute, canny, clever, crafty, cunning, discerning, keen, knowing, perceptive, sharp, smart

**shrill** high, penetrating, piercing, screeching, sharp

**shrink** v **shrinking, shrank, shrunk** or **shrunken** become smaller; recoil; make smaller **shrinkage** n

**shrivel** v **-elling, -elled** shrink and wither

**shroud** n wrapping for corpse; anything which envelops like a shroud ~v put shroud on; veil

**shrub** n bush **shrubbery** n

**shrug** v **shrugging, shrugged** raise (shoulders) as sign of indifference, ignorance etc. ~n shrugging

**shudder** v shake, tremble violently ~n shuddering

**shuffle** v move feet without lifting them; mix (cards) ~n shuffling; rearrangement

**shun** v **shunning, shunned** keep away from

**shunt** v push aside; move (train) from one line to another

**shut** v **shutting, shut** close; forbid entrance to **shutter** n movable window screen; device in camera admitting light as required

**shuttle** n bobbin-like device to hold thread in weaving, sewing etc.; plane, bus etc. travelling to and fro

**shuttlecock** n cone with feathers, struck to and fro in badminton

**shy**[1] adj timid, bashful; lacking ~v shying, shied start back in fear; show sudden reluctance ~n start of fear by horse

**shy**[2] v shying, shied throw

**Siamese twins** twins born joined to each other

**sibilant** adj/n hissing (sound)

**sibling** n brother or sister

**sick** adj inclined to vomit; not well or healthy; Inf macabre; Inf bored; Inf disgusted **sicken** v make, become sick; disgust **sickly** adj unhealthy; inducing nausea **sickness** n

**sickle** n reaping hook

**side** n one of the surfaces of object that is to right or left; aspect; faction ~adj at, in the side; subordinate ~v (usu. with **with**) take up cause of **siding** n short line of rails from main line **sideboard** n piece of dining room furniture **sideburns** pl n man's side whiskers **side effect** additional undesirable effect **sidekick** n Inf close associate **sidelong** adj not directly forward ~adv obliquely **sidestep** v avoid **sidetrack** v divert from main topic **sideways** adv to or from the side

**sidle** v move in furtive or stealthy

**shrink** contract, decrease, diminish, dwindle, lessen, shorten; cower, cringe, draw back, flinch, quail, recoil

**shrivel** desiccate, dwindle, shrink, wither

**shudder** v quake, quiver, shake, shiver, tremble ~n quiver, spasm, tremor

**shuffle** confuse, disarrange, disorder, mix, rearrange, shift

**shun** avoid, eschew, evade

**shut** bar, close, draw to, fasten, seal, secure

**shy** bashful, coy, diffident, modest, nervous, retiring, shrinking, timid

**sick** ill, nauseated, queasy; ailing, diseased, indisposed, unwell; Inf black, ghoulish, macabre, morbid, sadistic

**sicken** ail, fall ill, take sick; disgust, gross out US sl, nauseate, repel, revolt

**sickly** ailing, delicate, faint, feeble, infirm, peaky, unhealthy, weak

**sickness** nausea, vomiting; affliction, ailment, bug Inf, complaint, disease, disorder, illness, infirmity,

**siege** n besieging of town

**siesta** n rest, sleep in afternoon

**sieve** n device with perforated bottom ~v sift; strain

**sift** v separate coarser portion from finer

**sigh** v/n (utter) long audible breath

**sight** n faculty of seeing; thing seen; glimpse; device for guiding eye; spectacle ~v catch sight of; adjust sights on gun etc. **sightseeing** n visiting places of interest

**sign** n mark, gesture etc. to convey some meaning; (board bearing) notice etc.; symbol; omen ~v put one's signature to; make sign or gesture

**signal** n sign to convey order or information; *Radio etc.* sequence of electrical impulses transmitted or received ~adj remarkable ~v -nalling, -nalled make signals to; give orders etc. by signals

**signatory** n one of those who signs agreements, treaties

**signature** n person's name written by himself **signature tune** tune used to introduce television or radio programme

**signet** n small seal

**significant** adj revealing; designed to make something known; important **significance** n

**signify** v -fying, -fied mean; indicate; imply; be of importance

**silage** n fodder crop stored in state of partial fermentation

**silence** n absence of noise; refraining from speech ~v make silent; put a stop to **silencer** n device to reduce noise of engine exhaust, gun etc. **silent** adj

**silhouette** n outline of object seen against light ~v show in silhouette

**silica** n naturally occurring dioxide of silicon

**silicon** n brittle metal-like element found in sand, clay, stone **silicon chip** tiny wafer of silicon used in electronics

**silk** n fibre made by silkworms;

lurgi *Inf*, malady

**side** n border, edge, limit, margin, perimeter, rim, verge; aspect, face, facet, flank, part, surface, view; camp, faction, party, sect, team

**sidetrack** deflect, distract, divert

**sift** filter, separate, sieve

**sight** n eye, eyes, seeing, vision, display, exhibition, scene, show, spectacle, vista ~v observe, perceive, see, spot

**sign** n clue, evidence, gesture, hint, indication, proof, signal, symptom, token; board, notice, placard; badge, device, emblem, ensign, logo, mark, symbol; augury, auspice, omen, portent, warning ~v autograph, endorse, initial; beckon,

gesticulate, gesture, indicate, signal

**signal** n beacon, cue, gesture, indication, mark, sign ~v beckon, gesture, indicate, motion, sign

**significance** force, import, meaning, message, point; consequence, importance, relevance, weight

**significant** expressive, indicative, meaningful; critical, important, momentous, vital, weighty

**silence** n calm, hush, peace, quiet, stillness; dumbness, muteness, reticence, taciturnity ~v cut off, cut short, gag, muffle, quieten, still

**silent** hushed, quiet, soundless, still; dumb, mute, speechless, taciturn, voiceless, wordless

**silhouette** n form, outline, profile,

thread, fabric made from this **silky** *adj* **silkworm** *n* larva of certain moth

**sill** *n* ledge beneath window

**silly** *adj* foolish; trivial

**silo** *n* (*pl* **-los**) pit, tower for storing fodder

**silt** *n* mud deposited by water ~*v* fill, be choked with silt

**silver** *n* white precious metal; silver coins; cutlery ~*adj* made of silver; resembling silver or its colour **silvery** *adj*

**similar** *adj* resembling, like **similarity** *n* likeness

**simile** *n* comparison of one thing with another

**simmer** *v* keep or be just below boiling point; be in state of suppressed rage

**simper** *v* smile, utter in silly or affected way

**simple** *adj* not complicated; plain; not complex; ordinary; stupid **simpleton** *n* foolish person **simplicity** *n* **simplify** *v* **-fying, -fied** make simple, plain or easy **simply** *adv*

**simulate** *v* make pretence of; re-

produce **simulation** *n*

**simultaneous** *adj* occurring at the same time

**sin** *n* breaking of divine or moral law ~*v* **sinning, sinned** commit sin **sinful** *adj* **sinner** *n*

**since** *prep* during period of time after ~*conj* from time when; because ~*adv* from that time

**sincere** *adj* not hypocritical; genuine **sincerity** *n*

**sine** *n* in a right-angled triangle, ratio of opposite side to hypotenuse

**sinew** *n* tough, fibrous cord joining muscle to bone

**sing** *v* **singing, sang, sung** utter (sounds, words) with musical modulation; hum, ring; celebrate in song **singer** *n*

**singe** *v* **singeing, singed** burn surface of

**single** *adj* one only; unmarried; for one; denoting ticket for outward journey only ~*n* single thing ~*v* pick (out) single file persons in one line **single-handed** *adj* without assistance **single-minded** *adj* having one aim only

shape

**silly** absurd, asinine, fatuous, foolhardy, foolish, idiotic, inane, irresponsible, ridiculous, stupid

**similar** alike, comparable, resembling, uniform

**similarity** affinity, closeness, correspondence, likeness, resemblance

**simple** clear, easy, easy-peasy *Sl*, intelligible, lucid, plain, uncomplicated, understandable; natural, plain, unfussy; elementary, pure, single, uncombined, unmixed; brainless, dense, feeble, foolish, obtuse, slow, stupid, thick

**simplicity** clarity, clearness, ease;

naturalness, plainness, purity

**simultaneous** at the same time, coinciding, concurrent, contemporaneous

**sin** *n* crime, evil, guilt, iniquity, misdeed, offence, trespass, unrighteousness, wickedness ~*v* err, fall, lapse, offend, transgress

**sincere** artless, candid, earnest, frank, genuine, guileless, honest, open, real, true, unaffected

**sincerity** candour, frankness, genuineness, honesty, truth

**sinful** bad, corrupt, guilty, immoral, iniquitous, unrighteous, wicked

**sing** chant, croon, trill, warble

**singlet** *n* sleeveless undervest

**singular** *adj* remarkable; unique; denoting one person or thing

**sinister** *adj* threatening; evil-looking; wicked

**sink** *v* **sinking, sank, sunk** *or* **sunken** become submerged; drop; decline; penetrate (into); cause to sink; make by digging out; invest ~*n* fixed basin with waste pipe

**sinuous** *adj* curving

**sinus** *n* cavity in bone, esp. of skull

**sip** *v* **sipping, sipped** drink in very small portions ~*n* amount sipped

**siphon, syphon** *n/v* (device to) draw liquid from container

**sir** *n* polite term of address for man

**sire** *n* male parent, esp. of horse or domestic animal ~*v* father

**siren** *n* device making loud wailing noise

**sirloin** *n* prime cut of beef

**sissy** *adj/n* weak, cowardly (person)

**sister** *n* daughter of same parents; woman fellow-member; senior nurse **sister-in-law** *n* sister of husband or wife; brother's wife

**sit** *v* **sitting, sat** rest on buttocks, thighs; perch; pose for portrait; hold session; remain; take examination; keep watch over baby etc.

**sitar** *n* stringed musical instrument of India

**site** *n* place, space for building ~*v* provide with site

**situate** *v* place **situation** *n* position; state of affairs; employment

**six** *adj/n* cardinal number one more than five **sixth** *adj* ordinal number **sixteen** *n/adj* six and ten **sixteenth** *adj* **sixtieth** *adj* **sixty** *n/adj* six times ten

**size**[1] *n* dimensions; one of series of standard measurements ~*v* arrange according to size **sizable** *adj* quite large **size up** *v Inf* assess

**size**[2] *n* gluelike sealer, filler

**sizzle** *v/n* (make) hissing, spluttering sound as of frying

**skate**[1] *n* steel blade attached to boot ~*v* glide as on skates **skateboard** *n* small board mounted on roller-skate wheels

**skate**[2] *n* large marine ray

**skein** *n* quantity of yarn, wool etc. in loose knot

**skeleton** *n* bones of animal; framework ~*adj* reduced to a minimum

**sketch** *n* rough drawing; short humorous play ~*v* make sketch (of)

──── THESAURUS ────

**single** individual, lone, one, sole, solitary; free, unattached, unmarried, unwed

**single-minded** dedicated, determined, dogged, fixed, steadfast

**singular** exceptional, notable, noteworthy, outstanding, remarkable, unparalleled; individual, separate, single

**sinister** menacing, ominous, threatening

**sink** *v* decline, descend, dip, disappear, drop, ebb, fall, lower, plunge, submerge, subside; decay, decline, die, diminish, dwindle, fade, lessen

**sit** perch, rest, settle; assemble, convene, meet

**site** *n* ground, location, place, position, spot

**situation** location, place, position, setting, site, spot; case, circumstances, condition, plight, state; employment, job, place, position, post

**size** amount, bulk, dimensions, extent, mass, proportions, volume

**sketchy** adj

**skew** adj/v (make) slanting or crooked

**skewer** n pin to fasten meat

**ski** n (pl **skis**) long runner fastened to foot for sliding over snow or water ~v **skiing, skied** slide on skis

**skid** v **skidding, skidded** slide (sideways) ~n instance of this

**skill** n practical ability, cleverness, dexterity **skilful** adj **skilled** adj

**skim** v **skimming, skimmed** remove floating matter from surface of liquid; glide over lightly and rapidly; read quickly

**skimp** v give short measure; do imperfectly **skimpy** adj scanty

**skin** n outer covering of body; animal hide; fruit rind ~v **skinning, skinned** remove skin of **skinless** adj **skinny** adj thin **skinflint** n miser

**skint** adj Sl having no money

**skip**[1] v **skipping, skipped** leap lightly; jump over rope; pass over, omit ~n act of skipping

**skip**[2] n large open container for builders' rubbish etc.

**skipper** n captain of ship

**skirmish** n small battle ~v fight briefly

**skirt** n woman's garment hanging from waist; lower part of dress, coat etc. ~v border; go round **skirting board** narrow board round bottom of wall

**skit** n satire, esp. theatrical

**skittish** adj frisky, frivolous

**skittles** n game in which players try to knock over bottle-shaped objects

**skive** v evade work

**skivvy** n servant who does menial work

**skulduggery** n Inf trickery

**skulk** v sneak out of the way

**skull** n bony case enclosing brain

**skunk** n small N Amer. animal which emits evil-smelling fluid

**sky** n (pl **skies**) expanse extending upwards from the horizon; outer space **skylark** n bird that sings while soaring at great height **skylight** n window in roof or ceiling **skyscraper** n very tall building

**slab** n thick, broad piece

**slack** adj loose; careless; not busy

———————— THESAURUS ————————

**sketch** n design, draft, drawing, outline, plan ~v draft, draw, outline, plot, rough out

**sketchy** adj bitty, incomplete, rough, scrappy, skimpy, superficial, vague

**skilful** adj able, adept, adroit, expert, masterly, professional, proficient, skilled

**skill** n ability, adroitness, competence, craft, dexterity, expertise, knack, talent

**skilled** able, expert, masterly, professional, proficient, skilful

**skim** v coast, fly, glide, sail; (usu. with **through**) glance, run one's eye over, scan, skip Inf, thumb or leaf through

**skimp** be mean with, be niggardly, be sparing with, cut corners, scamp, stint

**skin** n hide, pelt; casing, coating, husk, peel, rind ~v bark, flay, graze, peel, scrape

**skinny** lean, thin

**skip** v caper, dance, frisk, gambol, hop, prance

**skirmish** n battle, brush, clash, combat, conflict, fracas, incident, tussle

**skirt** v border, edge, flank

**slab** chunk, lump, piece, portion, slice, wedge

~n loose part ~v be idle or lazy

**slacken** v become looser; become slower

**slacks** pl n casual trousers

**slag** n refuse of smelted metal

**slake** v satisfy (thirst)

**slalom** n skiing race over winding course

**slam** v **slamming, slammed** shut noisily; bang ~n (noise of) this action

**slander** n/v (utter) false or malicious statement about person **slanderous** adj

**slang** n colloquial language

**slant** v slope; write, present (news etc.) with bias ~n slope; point of view **slanting** adj

**slap** n blow with open hand or flat instrument ~v **slapping, slapped** strike thus; Inf put down carelessly **slapdash** adj careless, hasty **slapstick** n boisterous knockabout comedy

**slash** v/n gash; cut

**slat** n narrow strip

**slate** n stone which splits easily in flat sheets; piece of this for covering roof ~v cover with slates; abuse

**slaughter** n killing ~v kill **slaughterhouse** n place where animals are killed for food

**slave** n captive, person without freedom or personal rights ~v work like slave **slavery** n **slavish** adj servile

**slaver** v/n (dribble) saliva from mouth

**slay** v **slaying, slew, slain** kill

**sleazy** adj sordid

**sledge¹, sled** n carriage on runners for sliding on snow; toboggan ~v move on sledge

**sledge², sledgehammer** n heavy hammer with long handle

**sleek** adj glossy, smooth, shiny

**sleep** n unconscious state regularly occurring in man and animals; slumber, repose ~v **sleeping, slept** take rest in sleep **sleeper** n one who

———— THESAURUS ————

**slack** adj baggy, limp, loose, relaxed; idle, inactive, inattentive, lax, lazy, neglectful, negligent, slapdash, slipshod; inactive, quiet, slow, slow-moving, sluggish ~n excess, leeway, room

**slam** v/n bang, crash, smash

**slander** n calumny, libel, misrepresentation, scandal, smear ~v decry, defame, disparage, libel, malign, slur, smear, vilify

**slanderous** adj abusive, damaging, defamatory, libellous, malicious

**slant** v bear, cant, heel, incline, lean, list, slope, tilt; angle, bias, colour, distort, twist ~n camber, gradient, incline, pitch, slope, tilt; angle, bias, emphasis, one-sidedness, prejudice

**slanting** adj angled, bent, inclined, oblique, sloping, tilted, tilting

**slap** n/v clout, cuff, smack, spank, whack

**slapdash** adj careless, hasty, hurried, perfunctory, slipshod

**slash** v cut, gash, hack, lacerate, rip, score, slit ~n cut, gash, incision, laceration, rip, slit

**slate** v berate, censure, criticize, scold, tear into Inf

**slaughter** n bloodshed, butchery, carnage, killing, massacre, murder, slaying ~v butcher, destroy, kill, massacre, murder, slay

**slave** n drudge, serf, servant, skivvy chiefly Brit ~v drudge, slog, toil

**slavery** n bondage, captivity, serfdom, servitude

sleeps; beam supporting rails; railway sleeping car **sleepless** *adj* **sleepy** *adj*

**sleet** *n* rain and snow falling together

**sleeve** *n* part of garment which covers arm

**sleigh** *n* sledge

**sleight** *n* **sleight of hand** (manual dexterity in) conjuring

**slender** *adj* slim, slight; small in amount

**sleuth** *n* detective

**slice** *n* thin flat piece cut off; share ~*v* cut into slices

**slick** *adj* smooth; glib; skilful ~*v* make glossy, smooth ~*n* slippery area; patch of oil on water

**slide** *v* **sliding, slid** slip smoothly along; glide; pass ~*n* sliding; track for sliding; glass mount for object to be viewed under microscope; photographic transparency

**slight** *adj* small, trifling; slim ~*v* disregard ~*n* act of discourtesy

**slightly** *adv*

**slim** *adj* **slimmer, slimmest** thin; slight ~*v* **slimming, slimmed** reduce weight by diet and exercise

**slime** *n* thick, liquid mud **slimy** *adj* of, like, covered in slime; insincerely pleasant

**sling** *n* loop for hurling stone; bandage for supporting wounded limb; rope for hoisting weights ~*v* **slinging, slung** throw

**slink** *v* **slinking, slunk** move stealthily, sneak

**slip** *v* **slipping, slipped** (cause to) move smoothly; pass out of (mind etc.); lose balance by sliding; fall from person's grasp; (*usu. with up*) make mistake; put on or take off easily, quickly ~*n* act or occasion of slipping; mistake; petticoat; small piece of paper **slipshod** *adj* slovenly, careless **slipstream** *n* stream of air forced backwards by fast-moving object

**slipper** *n* light shoe for indoors

**sleep** *n* doze, kip *Brit sl,* nap, repose, siesta, slumber(s) ~*v* catnap, doze, drowse, kip *Brit sl,* slumber

**sleepless** restless, wakeful

**sleepy** drowsy, dull, heavy, inactive, lethargic, sluggish, torpid

**slender** lean, narrow, slight, slim, willowy; inadequate, insufficient, little, meagre, scant, scanty, small

**slice** *n* cut, piece, portion, segment, share, sliver, wedge ~*v* carve, cut, divide, sever

**slick** glib, plausible, smooth; adroit, deft, dextrous, polished, skilful

**slide** *v* coast, glide, skim, slip, slither

**slight** *adj* insignificant, meagre, minor, paltry, scanty, small, super-

ficial, trivial, unimportant; delicate, fragile, lightly-built, slim, small, spare ~*v* affront, disparage, ignore, insult, put down, scorn, snub ~*n* affront, disparagement, disdain, disrespect, insult, rebuff, snub

**slightly** a little, somewhat

**slim** *adj* lean, narrow, slender, slight, thin, trim; faint, poor, remote, slender, slight

**slimy** glutinous, miry, muddy, viscous; creeping, ingratiating, obsequious, oily, sycophantic, unctuous

**slink** creep, prowl, skulk, slip, sneak, steal

**slip** *v* glide, glide, skid; slither; creep, sneak, steal; fall, skid; (*sometimes with up*) blunder, err, miscalculate ~*n* blunder, error, indiscretion,

**slippery** *adj* so smooth as to cause slipping or to be difficult to hold; unreliable

**slit** *v* **slitting, slit** make long straight cut in ~*n* long straight cut

**slither** *v* slide unsteadily (down slope etc.)

**sliver** *n* splinter

**slob** *n Inf* lazy, untidy person

**slobber** *v/n* slaver

**slog** *v* **slogging, slogged** hit vigorously; work doggedly ~*n* struggle

**slogan** *n* distinctive phrase

**slop** *v* **slopping, slopped** spill, splash ~*n* liquid spilt; liquid food; *pl* **slops** liquid refuse **sloppy** *adj* careless, untidy

**slope** *v* be, place at slant ~*n* slant

**slot** *n* narrow hole; slit for coins; place in series ~*v* **slotting, slotted** put in slot; *Inf* place in series

**sloth** *n* S Amer. animal; sluggishness **slothful** *adj*

**slouch** *v* walk, sit etc. in drooping manner ~*n* drooping posture

**slovenly** *adj* dirty, untidy

**slow** *adj* lasting a long time; moving at low speed; dull ~*v* slacken speed (of) **slowly** *adv*

**sludge** *n* thick mud

**slug**[1] *n* land snail with no shell; bullet **sluggish** *adj* slow, inert; not functioning well

**slug**[2] *v* **slugging, slugged** hit, slog ~*n* heavy blow; portion of spirits

**sluice** *n* gate, door to control flow of water

**slum** *n* squalid street or neighbourhood

**slumber** *v/n* sleep

**slump** *v* fall heavily; relax ungracefully; decline suddenly ~*n* sudden decline

**slur** *v* **slurring, slurred** pass over lightly; run together (words); disparage ~*n* slight

**slurp** *Inf* *v* eat or drink noisily ~*n* slurping sound

**slurry** *n* muddy liquid mixture

**slush** *n* watery, muddy substance

**slut** *n* dirty (immoral) woman

**sly** *adj* cunning; deceitful

———— THESAURUS ————

mistake, omission, oversight

**slippery** glassy, greasy, icy, smooth; crafty, cunning, devious, dishonest, evasive, false, tricky, unreliable

**slit** *v* cut (open), gash, rip, slash ~*n* cut, gash, incision, opening, split, tear

**slither** *v* glide, slide, slip

**slog** *v* labour, plod, plough through, slave, toil, trudge, work ~*n* effort, exertion, labour, struggle, tramp, trudge

**slogan** catchphrase, motto

**slope** *v* drop away, fall, incline, lean, pitch, rise, slant, tilt ~*n* gradient, incline, rise, slant, tilt

**sloppy** *Inf* careless, inattentive,

messy, slipshod, slovenly, unkempt, untidy

**slot** *n* aperture, groove, hole, slit, vent *Inf* place, position, space, time, vacancy

**slouch** *v* droop, loll, slump, stoop

**slow** gradual, lingering, prolonged, protracted; deliberate, easy, leisurely, measured, unhurried; dense, dim, dozy *Brit inf,* dull, dull-witted, obtuse, stupid, thick

**sluggish** dull, heavy, inactive, inert, lethargic, slow, torpid

**slump** *v* collapse, crash, deteriorate, fall, fall off, plunge, sink ~*n* collapse, crash, decline, depression, downturn, drop, fall, low, recession

**slur** *n* blot, discredit, disgrace, in-

**smack¹** n taste, flavour ~v taste (of); suggest

**smack²** v slap; open and close (lips) loudly ~n slap; such sound; loud kiss ~adv Inf squarely

**small** adj little; unimportant; short ~n small slender part, esp. of the back **smallholding** n small area of farmland **smallpox** n contagious disease

**smart** adj astute; clever; well-dressed ~v feel, cause pain ~n sharp pain **smarten** v make or become smart

**smash** v break; ruin; destroy ~n heavy blow; collision **smashing** adj Inf excellent

**smattering** n slight superficial knowledge

**smear** v rub with grease etc.; smudge; slander ~n greasy mark; slander

**smell** v smelling, smelt or smelled perceive by nose; give out odour ~n faculty of perceiving odours; any-

thing detected by sense of smell **smelly** adj having nasty smell

**smelt** v extract metal from ore

**smile** n curving or parting of lips in pleased or amused expression ~v give smile

**smirk** n smile expressing scorn, smugness ~v give smirk

**smite** v smiting, smote, smitten strike; afflict

**smith** n worker in iron, gold etc.

**smithy** n blacksmith's workshop

**smithereens** pl n shattered fragments

**smock** n loose, outer garment

**smog** n mixture of smoke and fog

**smoke** n cloudy mass that rises from fire etc. ~v give off smoke; inhale and expel tobacco smoke; expose to smoke **smoker** n **smoky** adj **smoke screen** thing intended to hide truth

**smooth** adj not rough; even; calm; unctuous ~v make smooth

**smother** v suffocate

sult, smear, stain, stigma

**slut** scrubber Brit & Aust sl, tart, trollop

**sly** adj artful, crafty, cunning, devious, furtive, scheming, secret, shifty, stealthy, subtle, underhand

**smack** v clap, cuff, hit, slap ~n blow, crack, slap

**small** diminutive, little, miniature, minute, petite, pygmy or pigmy, slight, tiny, undersized, wee; insignificant, minor, negligible, paltry, petty, trifling, trivial, unimportant

**smart** adj acute, astute, bright, canny, clever, intelligent, keen, quick, shrewd; chic, elegant, neat, snappy, spruce, stylish, trim ~v hurt, pain, sting, tingle

**smash** v break, collide, crash,

crush, demolish, shatter; defeat, destroy, lay waste, ruin, trash Sl, wreck ~n accident, collision, crash

**smear** v bedaub, blur, coat, cover, daub, smirch, smudge, spread over, stain, sully; blacken, sully, tarnish ~n blot, blotch, daub, smirch, smudge, splotch, streak; calumny, libel, slander

**smell** v scent, sniff; niff Brit sl, reek, stink ~n aroma, fragrance, odour, perfume, scent, whiff

**smooth** adj even, flat, flush, horizontal, level; glossy, polished, shiny, silky, sleek; calm, glassy, peaceful, serene, tranquil, undisturbed, unruffled; glib, persuasive, silky, slick, suave, unctuous ~v flatten, iron, level, plane, press

**smoulder** v burn slowly; (of feelings) be suppressed

**smudge** v/n (make) smear, stain (on)

**smug** adj self-satisfied, complacent

**smuggle** v import, export without paying customs duties **smuggler** n

**smut** n piece of soot; obscene talk etc. **smutty** adj

**snack** n light, hasty meal

**snag** n difficulty; sharp protuberance; hole, loop in fabric ~v **snagging, snagged** catch, damage on snag

**snail** n slow-moving mollusc with shell

**snake** n long scaly limbless reptile ~v move like snake

**snap** v **snapping, snapped** break suddenly; make cracking sound; bite (at) suddenly; speak suddenly, angrily ~n act of snapping; fastener; card game; Inf snapshot ~adj sudden, unplanned **snappy** adj irritable; Sl quick; Sl fashionable **snapshot** n photograph

**snare** n/v trap

**snarl** n growl of angry dog; tangle ~v utter snarl

**snatch** v make quick grab (at); seize, catch ~n grab; fragment

**sneak** v move about furtively; act

in underhand manner ~n petty informer **sneaking** adj secret; slight but persistent

**sneer** n scornful, contemptuous expression or remark ~v give sneer

**sneeze** v emit breath through nose with sudden involuntary spasm and noise ~n act of sneezing

**snide** adj malicious, supercilious

**sniff** v inhale through nose with sharp hiss; smell; (with at) express disapproval etc. ~n act of sniffing

**sniffle** v sniff noisily, esp. when suffering from a cold

**snigger** n sly, disrespectful laugh, esp. partly stifled ~v produce snigger

**snip** v **snipping, snipped** cut with quick stroke ~n quick cut; Inf bargain **snippet** n small piece

**snipe** n wading bird ~v shoot at enemy from cover; (with at) criticize **sniper** n

**snivel** v -elling, -elled sniffle to show distress; whine

**snob** n one who pretentiously judges others by social rank etc. **snobbery** n **snobbish** adj

**snooker** n game played on table with balls and cues

**snoop** v pry, meddle; peer into

**snooty** adj Sl haughty

———— T H E S A U R U S ————

**smug** complacent, conceited, superior

**snack** bite, light meal, refreshment(s), tidbit

**snap** v break, crack, separate; click, crackle, pop ~adj immediate, instant, sudden

**snare** v catch, net, seize, trap

**snatch** v clutch, grab, grasp, grip, pluck, pull, seize, take ~n bit, fragment, part, piece, snippet

**sneak** v lurk, sidle, skulk, slink,

slip, steal ~n informer, telltale

**sneaking** hidden, private, secret; nagging, persistent

**sneer** n derision, gibe, jeer, mockery, ridicule, scorn ~v gibe, jeer, laugh, mock, ridicule, scoff, scorn

**sniff** v breathe, inhale, smell, snuffle

**snigger** giggle, laugh, titter

**snip** v clip, crop, cut, dock, trim ~n bit, clipping, fragment, piece, scrap, shred; Inf bargain, giveaway,

**snooze** *v/n* (take) nap

**snore** *v* breathe noisily when asleep ~*n* sound of snoring

**snorkel** *n* tube for breathing underwater

**snort** *v* make (contemptuous) noise by driving breath through nostrils ~*n* act of snorting

**snout** *n* animal's nose

**snow** *n* frozen vapour which falls in flakes ~*v* fall, sprinkle as snow **snowy** *adj* **snowball** *n* snow pressed into hard ball for throwing ~*v* increase rapidly **snowdrift** *n* bank of deep snow **snowdrop** *n* small, white, bell-shaped spring flower **snowman** *n* figure shaped out of snow **snowplough** *n* vehicle for clearing away snow **snowshoes** *pl n* racket-shaped shoes for travelling on snow

**snub** *v* **snubbing, snubbed** insult (esp. by ignoring) intentionally ~*n* snubbing ~*adj* short and blunt **snub-nosed** *adj*

**snuff**[1] *n* powdered tobacco

**snuff**[2] *v* extinguish (esp. candle)

**snuffle** *v* breathe noisily

**snug** *adj* warm, comfortable

**snuggle** *v* lie close to, nestle

**so** *adv* to such an extent; in such a manner; very ~*conj* therefore; in order that; with the result that ~*interj* well! **so-and-so** *n Inf* person whose name is not specified; unpleasant person **so-called** *adj* called by but doubtfully deserving that name

**soak** *v* steep; absorb; drench **soaking** *n/adj*

**soap** *n* compound of alkali and oil used in washing ~*v* apply soap to **soapy** *adj* **soap opera** television, radio serial dealing with domestic themes

**soar** *v* fly high; increase rapidly

**sob** *v* **sobbing, sobbed** catch breath, esp. in weeping ~*n* sobbing

**sober** *adj* not drunk; temperate; subdued; dull; solemn ~*v* make, become sober **sobriety** *n*

**soccer** *n* game of football, with spherical ball

**sociable** *adj* friendly; convivial

**social** *adj* living in communities; relating to society; sociable ~*n* informal gathering **socialize** *v*

**socialism** *n* political system which advocates public ownership of means of production **socialist** *n/adj*

**society** *n* living associated with

good buy, steal *Inf*

**snoop** interfere, poke one's nose in *Inf*, pry, spy

**snooze** *v* catnap, doze, nap ~*n* catnap, doze, nap, siesta

**snub** *v* cold-shoulder, rebuff, slight ~*n* affront, insult

**snug** comfortable, cosy, homely, warm

**snuggle** cuddle, nestle, nuzzle

**soak** drench, immerse, infuse, penetrate, permeate, saturate, steep

**soaking** drenched, dripping, saturated, sodden, sopping, water

logged, wringing wet

**soar** ascend, fly, rise, wing; climb, escalate, rise, rocket, shoot up

**sober** abstemious, abstinent, moderate, temperate; calm, composed, cool, dispassionate, grave, rational, reasonable, serious, solemn, steady, unexcited, unruffled

**so-called** alleged, professed, self-styled, supposed

**sociable** affable, companionable, convivial, friendly, gregarious, outgoing, social

**social** *adj* collective, communal,

others; those so living; companionship; association; fashionable people collectively

**sociology** *n* study of societies **sociological** *adj*

**sock**[1] *n* cloth covering for foot

**sock**[2] *Sl v* hit ~*n* blow

**socket** *n* hole or recess for something to fit into

**sod** *n* lump of earth with grass

**soda** *n* compound of sodium; soda water **soda water** water charged with carbon dioxide

**sodden** *adj* soaked

**sodium** *n* metallic alkaline element **sodium bicarbonate** compound used in baking powder

**sodomy** *n* anal intercourse

**sofa** *n* upholstered seat with back and arms

**soft** *adj* yielding easily to pressure; not hard; mild; easy; subdued; quiet; gentle; (too) lenient **soften** *v* make, become soft or softer **softly** *adv* **soft drink** nonalcoholic drink **software** *n* computer programs

**soggy** *adj* damp and heavy

**soil**[1] *n* earth, ground

**soil**[2] *v* make, become dirty

**solace** *n/v* comfort in distress

**solar** *adj* of the sun

**solarium** *n* (*pl* **-lariums, -laria**) place with beds and ultraviolet lights for acquiring artificial suntan

**solder** *n* easily-melted alloy used for joining metal ~*v* join with it

**soldier** *n* one serving in army ~*v* serve in army; (*with* **on**) persist doggedly

**sole**[1] *adj* one and only **solely** *adv* alone; only; entirely

**sole**[2] *n* underside of foot; underpart of boot etc. ~*v* fit with sole

**sole**[3] *n* small edible flatfish

**solemn** *adj* serious; formal **solemnity** *n* **solemnize** *v* celebrate, perform

**solicit** *v* request; accost **solicitor** *n* lawyer who prepares documents, advises clients **solicitous** *adj* anxious; eager **solicitude** *n*

**solid** *adj* not hollow; composed of one substance; firm; reliable ~*n* body of three dimensions; substance not liquid or gas **solidarity** *n* unity **solidify** *v* **-fying, -fied** harden

community, group, public

**socialize** fraternize, get about or around, get together, go out, mix

**society** civilization, culture, mankind, people, the community, the public; companionship, company, fellowship, friendship; association, club, fellowship, fraternity, group, guild, institute, league, union; gentry, high society, upper classes

**soft** yielding; spongy, squashy, yielding; elastic, flexible, plastic, pliable, supple; balmy, mild, temperate; dim, low, subdued; faint, gentle, low, muted, quiet; compassionate, gentle, kind, sensitive, sentimental,

sympathetic, tender

**soften** ease, lessen, lighten, mitigate, moderate, temper; abate, allay, appease, calm, soothe, still

**soil**[1] *n* clay, dirt, earth, ground, loam

**soil**[2] *v* defile, dirty, foul, pollute, smear, smirch, stain, sully, tarnish

**soldier** fighter, man-at-arms, serviceman, squaddie *or* squaddy *Brit sl*, trooper, warrior

**sole** alone, individual, one, single, solitary

**solemn** grave, serious, sober; ceremonial, formal, grand, stately

**solid** *adj* compact, concrete, dense,

**soliloquy** n (esp. in drama) thoughts spoken by person while alone

**solitary** adj alone, single **solitaire** n game for one person; single precious stone set by itself **solitude** n state of being alone

**solo** n (pl **-los**) music for one performer ~adj unaccompanied, alone **soloist** n

**solstice** n shortest (winter) or longest (summer) day

**solve** v work out; find answer to **soluble** adj capable of being dissolved in liquid; able to be solved **solution** n answer; dissolving; liquid with something dissolved in it **solvable** adj **solvency** n **solvent** adj able to meet financial obligations ~n liquid with power of dissolving

**sombre** adj dark, gloomy

**sombrero** n (pl **-ros**) wide-brimmed hat

**some** adj denoting an indefinite number, amount or extent; one or another; certain ~pron portion, quantity **somebody** pron some person ~n important person **somehow** adv by some means **someone** pron somebody **something** pron thing not clearly defined **sometime** adv at

some unspecified time ~adj former **sometimes** adv occasionally **somewhat** adv rather **somewhere** adv at some unspecified place

**somersault** n tumbling head over heels

**son** n male child **son-in-law** n daughter's husband

**sonar** n device for detecting underwater objects

**sonata** n piece of music in several movements

**song** n singing; poem etc. for singing

**sonic** adj pert. to sound waves

**sonnet** n fourteen-line poem with definite rhyme scheme

**sonorous** adj giving out (deep) sound, resonant

**soon** adv in a short time; before long; early, quickly

**soot** n black powdery substance formed by burning of coal etc. **sooty** adj

**soothe** v make calm, tranquil; relieve (pain etc.)

**sop** n piece of bread etc. soaked in liquid; bribe ~v sopping, sopped steep in water etc.; soak (up) **soppy** adj Inf oversentimental

**sophisticated** adj worldly wise;

—————————— THESAURUS ——————————

hard; firm, stable, strong, sturdy, unshakable; dependable, genuine, pure, reliable, sound

**solidarity** accord, concordance, harmony, team spirit, unanimity, unity

**solidify** cake, coagulate, congeal, harden, jell, set

**solitary** alone, lone, single, sole

**solitude** isolation, loneliness, privacy, seclusion

**solution** answer, explanation, key, resolution, result; blend, com-

pound, mix, mixture

**solve** answer, clear up, crack, decipher, disentangle, explain, resolve, suss (out) Sl

**sombre** dark, dim, drab, dull, gloomy, grave, shadowy, shady, sober

**sometimes** at times, occasionally

**soon** before long, in the near future, shortly

**soothe** allay, alleviate, appease, assuage, calm, ease, hush, lull, pacify, quiet, relieve, settle, still

complex, refined **sophistication** n

**soporific** adj causing sleep

**soprano** n (pl **-pranos**) highest voice in women and boys

**sorbet** n (fruit-flavoured) water ice

**sorcerer** n (fem **sorceress**) magician **sorcery** n

**sordid** adj mean, squalid; base

**sore** adj painful; causing annoyance ~n sore place **sorely** adv greatly

**sorrow** n/v (feel) grief, sadness **sorrowful** adj

**sorry** adj feeling pity or regret; miserable, wretched

**sort** n kind, class ~v classify

**sortie** n sally by besieged forces

**SOS** n international code signal of distress; call for help

**so-so** adj Inf mediocre

**soufflé** n dish of eggs beaten to froth, flavoured and baked

**soul** n spiritual and immortal part of human being; person; sensitivity; type of Black music **soulful** adj

**sound**¹ n what is heard; noise ~v make sound; give impression of; utter **soundproof** adj

**sound**² adj in good condition; solid; of good judgment; thorough; deep **soundly** adv thoroughly

**sound**³ v find depth of, as water; ascertain views of; probe

**sound**⁴ n channel; strait

**soup** n liquid food made by boiling meat, vegetables etc.

**sour** adj acid; gone bad; peevish; disagreeable ~v make, become sour

———— THESAURUS ————

**sophisticated** cultivated, cultured, refined, urbane, worldly; advanced, complex, complicated, elaborate, intricate, subtle

**sophistication** poise, savoir-faire, urbanity, worldliness, worldly wisdom

**soppy** corny Sl, mawkish, overemotional, schmaltzy Sl, sentimental, slushy Inf

**sorcerer** enchanter, magician, sorceress, warlock, witch, wizard

**sorcery** black art, black magic, magic, necromancy, witchcraft, wizardry

**sordid** dirty, filthy, foul, mean, seedy, squalid, unclean; base, low, shabby, shameful

**sore** painful, raw, sensitive, tender; annoying, troublesome

**sorrow** n anguish, distress, grief, heartache, misery, mourning, sadness, unhappiness, woe

**sorrowful** dejected, depressed, dismal, melancholy, miserable,

mournful, sad, unhappy, woebegone, woeful, wretched

**sorry** contrite, penitent, regretful, remorseful, repentant; abject, base, deplorable, distressing, mean, miserable, pathetic, pitiful, poor, sad, wretched

**sort** n brand, breed, category, character, class, kind, make, nature, order, race, species, style, type, variety ~v arrange, categorize, class, classify, divide, group, order, rank

**soul** essence, life, mind, psyche, spirit; being, creature, individual, mortal, person

**sound**¹ n din, noise, tone ~v echo, resound, reverberate

**sound**² adj complete, entire, firm, fit, hale, healthy, intact, perfect, robust, solid, whole; correct, rational, reasonable, reliable, responsible, right, sensible, trustworthy, valid, well-founded, wise

**sound**³ v fathom, plumb, probe

**sour** acid, bitter, sharp, tart;

**source** n origin, starting point; spring

**south** n point opposite north; region, part of country etc. lying to that side ~adj/adv from, towards or in the south **southerly** adj ~n wind from the south **southern** adj **southward** adj **southwards** adv

**souvenir** n keepsake, memento

**sou'wester** n seaman's waterproof headgear

**sovereign** n king, queen; former gold coin worth 20 shillings ~adj supreme; efficacious **sovereignty** n

**sow**[1] v sowing, sowed, sown or sowed scatter, plant seed

**sow**[2] n female adult pig

**soya** n plant yielding edible beans **soya bean** edible bean used for food and oil **soy sauce** sauce made from fermented soya beans

**spa** n medicinal spring; place, resort with one

**space** n extent; room; period; empty place; area; expanse; region beyond earth's atmosphere ~v place at intervals **spacious** adj roomy, extensive **spacecraft, spaceship** n ve-

hicle for travel beyond earth's atmosphere **spaceman** n astronaut

**spade**[1] n tool for digging

**spade**[2] n suit at cards

**spaghetti** n pasta in long strings

**span** n extent, space; stretch of arch etc.; space from thumb to little finger ~v spanning, spanned stretch over; measure with hand

**spangle** n small shiny metallic ornament ~v decorate with spangles

**spaniel** n breed of dog with long ears and silky hair

**spank** v slap with flat of hand, esp. on buttocks ~n spanking

**spanner** n tool for gripping nut or bolt head

**spar**[1] n pole, beam, esp. as part of ship's rigging

**spar**[2] v sparring, sparred box; dispute, esp. in fun ~n sparring

**spare** v leave unhurt; show mercy; do without; give away ~adj additional; in reserve; thin; lean ~n reserve copy **sparing** adj economical, careful

**spark** n small glowing or burning particle; flash of light produced by

───────── **THESAURUS** ─────────

cynical, disagreeable, embittered, grudging, ill-natured, peevish, tart, waspish

**source** beginning, cause, derivation, fount, origin, spring, wellspring

**souvenir** keepsake, memento, relic, reminder

**sovereign** n chief, emperor, empress, king, monarch, potentate, prince, queen, ruler, shah, tsar

**sovereignty** ascendancy, domination, kingship, primacy, supremacy, supreme power, sway

**space** capacity, expanse, leeway, margin, room, scope; blank, gap,

interval

**spacious** ample, broad, commodious, expansive, extensive, huge, large, roomy, sizable, vast

**span** n extent, length, reach, spread, stretch ~v bridge, cross, link, traverse

**spank** v slap, smack

**spare** v be merciful to, have mercy on, pardon, release; allow, bestow, give, grant; afford , dispense with, part with, relinquish ~adj additional, extra, free, leftover, odd, superfluous, surplus; gaunt, lean, meagre, slender, slight, slim

**sparing** careful, economical, fru-

electrical discharge; trace ~v emit sparks; kindle

**sparkle** v glitter; effervesce ~n glitter; vitality **sparkling** adj glittering; (of wines) effervescent

**sparrow** n small brownish bird

**sparrowhawk** n hawk that hunts small birds

**sparse** adj thinly scattered

**spartan** adj strict, austere

**spasm** n sudden convulsive (muscular) contraction; sudden burst of activity etc. **spasmodic** adj

**spastic** adj affected by spasms; suffering cerebral palsy ~n person with cerebral palsy

**spate** n rush, outpouring; flood

**spatial** adj of, in space

**spatter** v splash, cast drops over; be scattered in drops ~n spattering

**spatula** n utensil with broad, flat blade for various purposes

**spawn** n eggs of fish or frog ~v (of fish or frog) cast eggs

**spay** v remove ovaries from (female animal)

**speak** v speaking, spoke, spoken utter words; converse; express; communicate in; give speech

**speaker** n one who speaks; speech maker; loudspeaker

**spear** n long pointed weapon ~v pierce with spear **spearhead** v leading force in attack ~v lead attack

**spearmint** n type of mint

**special** adj beyond the usual; particular **specialist** n one who devotes himself to special subject **speciality** n special product, skill, characteristic etc. **specialization** n **specialize** v be specialist; make special

**species** n (pl **-cies**) group of plants or animals that are closely related

**specific** adj exact in detail; characteristic **specification** n detailed description of something **specify** v **-fying, -fied** state definitely or in detail

**specimen** n part typifying whole; individual example

**specious** adj deceptively plausible, but false

**speck** n small spot, particle ~v

gal, prudent, saving, thrifty

**spark** flare, flash, flicker, gleam, glint

**sparkle** v beam, dance, flash, gleam, glint, glitter, shimmer, shine, twinkle ~n flash, gleam, glint, glitter, twinkle; dash, élan, gaiety, life, spirit, vitality

**spasm** convulsion, paroxysm; burst, fit, frenzy, outburst, seizure

**speak** articulate, converse, discourse, express, pronounce, say, state, talk, tell, utter, voice

**speaker** n lecturer, orator, public speaker, spokesman

**special** especial, exceptional, extraordinary, important, significant, unique, unusual; appropriate,

certain, distinctive, individual, particular, peculiar

**specialist** n authority, buff Inf, connoisseur, consultant, expert, master, professional

**speciality** bag Sl, forte, métier

**species** category, class, group, kind, sort, type, variety

**specific** definite, exact, explicit, particular, precise; characteristic, especial, peculiar, special

**specification** detail, particular, requirement, stipulation

**specify** define, designate, detail, enumerate, indicate, mention

**specimen** copy, example, individual, instance, model, proof, sample, type

mark with spots **speckle** n/v speck

**spectacle** n show; thing exhibited; strange, interesting, or ridiculous sight; pl pair of lenses for correcting defective sight **spectacular** adj impressive; showy **spectate** v **spectator** n one who looks on

**spectre** n ghost; image of something unpleasant

**spectrum** n (pl -tra) band of colours into which light can be decomposed, e.g. by prism

**speculate** v guess, conjecture; engage in (risky) commercial transactions **speculation** n **speculative** adj **speculator** n

**speech** n act, faculty of speaking; words, language; (formal) talk given before audience **speechless** adj dumb; at a loss for words

**speed** n swiftness; rate of progress ~v speeding, sped or speeded move

quickly; drive vehicle at high speed; further **speeding** n driving at high speed, esp. over legal limit **speedy** adj **speedometer** n instrument to show speed of vehicle **speedwell** n plant with small blue flowers

**spell¹** v spelling, spelt or spelled give letters of in order; indicate, result in **spelling** n

**spell²** n magic formula; enchantment **spellbound** adj enchanted; entranced

**spell³** n (short) period of time, work

**spend** v spending, spent pay out; pass (time); use up completely **spendthrift** n wasteful person

**sperm** n male reproductive cell; semen

**spew** v vomit

**sphere** n ball, globe; field of action **spherical** adj

**speck** blemish, blot, dot, fleck, mark, speckle, spot, stain; atom, bit, grain, iota, jot, mite, particle

**spectacle** display, event, pageant, parade, performance, show, sight

**spectacular** dazzling, dramatic, grand, impressive, magnificent, splendid, striking

**spectator** bystander, eyewitness, looker-on, observer, onlooker, viewer, watcher, witness

**speculate** conjecture, guess, suppose, surmise, theorize; gamble, hazard, risk

**speech** communication, conversation, dialogue, discussion, talk; address, discourse, homily, lecture, oration

**speechless** dumb, inarticulate, mute, silent, wordless; aghast, amazed, astounded

**speed** n haste, hurry, quickness,

rapidity, swiftness, velocity ~v career, gallop, hasten, hurry, race, rush, sprint, tear, zoom; advance, aid, assist, expedite, facilitate, further, help

**speedy** express, fast, hasty, headlong, hurried, immediate, precipitate, prompt, quick, rapid, summary, swift

**spell¹** n charm, incantation

**spell²** n bout, course, interval, period, season, stint, stretch, term, time, turn

**spend** disburse, expend; fill, occupy, pass, while away; consume, drain, empty, exhaust, run through, use up

**sphere** ball, globe, orb; capacity, domain, field, function, patch, province, range, realm, scope, territory, turf US sl

**spherical** globe-shaped, globular,

**spice** *n* aromatic or pungent vegetable substance; spices collectively; anything that adds relish, interest etc. ~*v* season with spices **spicy** *adj*

**spick-and-span** *adj* neat, smart, new-looking

**spider** *n* small eight-legged creature which spins web to catch prey **spidery** *adj* thin and angular

**spike** *n* sharp point; long cluster with flowers attached directly to stalk ~*v* pierce, fasten with spike; render ineffective **spiky** *adj*

**spill** *v* **spilling, spilt** or **spilled** (cause to) pour from, flow over, fall out, esp. unintentionally ~*n* fall; amount spilt **spillage** *n*

**spin** *v* **spinning, spun** (cause to) revolve rapidly; twist into thread; prolong ~*n* spinning **spinning** *n* act, process of drawing out and twisting into threads **spin-dryer** *n* machine in which clothes are spun to remove excess water **spin-off** *n* incidental benefit

**spinach** *n* dark green leafy vegetable

**spindle** *n* rod, axis for spinning **spindly** *adj* long and slender

**spine** *n* backbone; thin spike, esp. on fish etc.; ridge; back of book **spinal** *adj* **spineless** *adj* lacking in spine; cowardly

**spinster** *n* unmarried woman

**spiral** *n* continuous curve drawn at ever increasing distance from fixed point; anything resembling this ~*adj* shaped like spiral

**spire** *n* pointed part of steeple

**spirit** *n* life principle animating body; disposition; liveliness; courage; essential character or meaning; soul; ghost; *pl* emotional state; strong alcoholic drink ~*v* carry away mysteriously **spirited** *adj* lively

**spiritual** *adj* given to, interested in things of the spirit ~*n* sacred song orig. sung by Black slaves in America **spiritualism** *n* belief that spirits of the dead communicate with the living **spiritualist** *n* **spirituality** *n*

**spit**[1] *v* **spitting, spat** eject saliva (from mouth) ~*n* spitting, saliva **spittle** *n* saliva

**spit**[2] *n* sharp rod to put through meat for roasting; sandy point projecting into the sea ~*v* **spitting, spitted** thrust through

**spite** *n* malice ~*v* thwart spitefully **spiteful** *adj* **in spite of** *prep* regardless of; notwithstanding

———— THESAURUS ————

rotund, round

**spice** colour, excitement, pep, piquancy, zest

**spike** *n* barb, point, prong, spine ~*v* impale, spear

**spill** disgorge, overflow, overturn, slop over, run over, upset

**spin** *v* revolve, rotate, turn, twirl, twist, wheel, whirl

**spirit** *n* life, soul, vital spark; attitude, character, disposition, outlook, temper, temperament; energy, enthusiasm, fire, force, liveli-

ness, mettle, sparkle, vigour, zest; essence, intent, intention, meaning, purpose, sense; apparition, ghost, phantom, spectre; *pl* feelings, mood, morale

**spirited** animated, energetic, feisty *Inf, chiefly US & Canad.*, high-spirited, lively, mettlesome, vivacious

**spite** malice, rancour, spitefulness, spleen, venom **in spite of** despite, (even) though, notwithstanding, regardless of

**splash** v scatter liquid about or on, over something; print (story, photo) prominently in newspaper ~n sound of splashing liquid; patch, esp. of colour; (effect of) extravagant display

**splatter** v/n spatter

**splay** adj spread out; turned outwards ~v spread out; twist outwards

**spleen** n organ in the abdomen

**splenetic** adj spiteful, irritable

**splendid** adj magnificent, excellent **splendour** n

**splice** v join by interweaving strands ~n spliced joint

**splint** n rigid support for broken limb etc.

**splinter** n thin fragment ~v break into fragments

**split** v **splitting, split** break asunder; separate; divide ~n crack; division **split second** very short period of time

**splutter** v make hissing, spitting sounds; utter incoherently with spitting sounds ~n spluttering

**spoil** v **spoiling, spoilt** or **spoiled** damage, injure; damage manners or behaviour of (esp. child) by indulgence; go bad **spoils** pl n booty

**spoilsport** n person who spoils others' enjoyment

**spoke** n radial bar of a wheel

**spokesman** n one deputed to speak for others

**sponge** n marine animal; its skeleton, or a synthetic substance like it, used to absorb liquids; type of light cake ~v wipe with sponge; live at the expense of others **spongy** adj spongelike; wet and soft

**sponsor** n one promoting something; one who agrees to give money to charity on completion of a specified activity by another; godparent ~v act as sponsor **sponsorship** n

**spontaneous** adj voluntary; natural **spontaneity** n

**spoof** n mildly satirical parody

**spook** n Inf ghost **spooky** adj

**spool** n reel, bobbin

**spoon** n implement with shallow

—————————— T H E S A U R U S ——————————

**spiteful** ill-natured, malicious, venomous, vindictive

**splash** shower, slop, spatter, spray, sprinkle, wet ~n burst, dash, patch, splodge, touch

**splendid** brilliant, glorious, grand, magnificent, outstanding, superb, supreme

**splendour** brilliance, glory, grandeur, magnificence

**splinter** n chip, flake, fragment ~v fracture, shatter, split

**split** v break, burst, cleave, crack, open, part, separate; disband, disunite, part, separate; branch, diverge, fork; divide, halve, parcel out, partition, share out ~n breach,

crack, division, fissure; breach, break-up, disunion, division, estrangement, rift, schism

**spoil** damage, destroy, harm, injure, mar, mess up, ruin, undo, upset, wreck; indulge, overindulge, pamper; curdle, decay, go bad, putrefy, rot, turn

**spoilsport** damper, dog in the manger, kill-joy, misery Brit inf, wet blanket Inf

**sponsor** n backer, patron, promoter ~v back, finance, fund, promote, subsidize

**spontaneous** free, impulsive, instinctive, natural, unforced, unprompted, voluntary

bowl at end of handle for carrying food to mouth etc. ~v lift with spoon **spoonful** n **spoon-feed** v give (someone) too much help

**sporadic** adj intermittent; scattered

**spore** n minute reproductive body of some plants

**sporran** n pouch worn in front of kilt

**sport** n game, activity for pleasure, competition; exercise; enjoyment; cheerful person, good loser ~v wear (esp. ostentatiously); frolic; play (sport) **sporting** adj of sport; behaving with fairness, generosity **sports car** fast low-built car **sportsman** n (fem **sportswoman**) one who engages in sport; good loser

**spot** n small mark, stain; blemish; pimple; place; (difficult) situation; Inf small quantity ~v **spotting**, **spotted** mark with spots; detect; observe **spotless** adj unblemished; pure **spotty** adj with spots; uneven **spotlight** n powerful light illuminating small area; centre of attention

**spouse** n husband or wife

**spout** v pour out ~n projecting tube or lip for pouring liquids; copious discharge

**sprain** v wrench, twist

**sprat** n small sea fish

**sprawl** v lie or sit about awkwardly; spread in rambling, unplanned way ~n sprawling

**spray**[1] n (device for producing) fine drops of liquid ~v sprinkle with shower of fine drops

**spray**[2] n branch, twig with buds, flowers etc.; ornament like this

**spread** v **spreading**, **spread** extend; stretch out; open out; scatter; distribute; unfold; cover ~n extent; increase; ample meal; food which can be spread on bread etc. **spread-eagled** adj with arms and legs outstretched

**spree** n session of overindulgence; romp

**sprig** n small twig

**sprightly** adj lively, brisk

**spring**[1] v **spreading**, **sprang**, **sprung** leap; shoot up or forth; come into being; appear; grow; become bent or split; produce unexpectedly; set off (trap) ~n leap; recoil; piece of

**sport** n amusement, diversion, game, pastime, play, recreation

**spot** n blemish, blot, blotch, flaw, mark, smudge, speck, stain; location, place, position, scene, site; Inf difficulty, hot water Inf, mess, plight, predicament, quandary ~v detect, discern, observe, recognize, see, sight

**spotless** clean, flawless, immaculate, impeccable, pure, unblemished, unstained, unsullied, untarnished

**spouse** consort, mate, partner, significant other US inf

**spout** v discharge, emit, erupt, gush, jet, shoot, stream

**sprawl** v flop, loll, lounge, slouch, slump, spread

**spray** v scatter, shower, sprinkle

**spread** v broaden, expand, extend, open, sprawl, stretch, unfold, unfurl, unroll, widen ~n extent, reach, span, stretch; advance, development, escalation, expansion, increase

**spree** bender Inf, binge Inf, carousal, carouse, fling, orgy

**sprightly** active, brisk, lively, spirited, spry

coiled or bent metal with much re-silience; flow of water from earth; first season of year **springy** *adj* elastic **spring-clean** *v* clean (house) thoroughly

**springbok** *n* S Afr. antelope

**sprinkle** *v* scatter small drops on, strew **sprinkler** *n* **sprinkling** *n* small quantity or number

**sprint** *v* run short distance at great speed ~*n* such run, race **sprinter** *n*

**sprite** *n* elf

**sprocket** *n* toothed wheel, attached to chain

**sprout** *v* put forth shoots, spring up ~*n* shoot

**spruce**[1] *n* variety of fir

**spruce**[2] *adj* neat in dress **spruce up** make neat and smart

**spry** *adj* nimble, vigorous

**spur** *n* pricking instrument attached to horseman's heel; incitement; stimulus ~*v* **spurring**, **spurred** urge on

**spurious** *adj* not genuine

**spurn** *v* reject with scorn

**spurt** *v* send, come out in jet; rush

suddenly ~*n* jet; short sudden effort

**spy** *n* one who watches (esp. in rival countries, companies etc.) and reports secretly ~*v* **spying, spied** act as spy; catch sight of

**squabble** *v/n* (engage in) petty, noisy quarrel

**squad** *n* small party, esp. of soldiers **squadron** *n* division of cavalry regiment, fleet or air force

**squalid** *adj* mean and dirty **squalor** *n*

**squall** *n* harsh cry; sudden gust of wind; short storm ~*v* yell

**squander** *v* spend wastefully

**square** *n* equilateral rectangle; area of this shape; in town, open space (of this shape); product of a number multiplied by itself; instrument for drawing right angles ~*adj* square in form; honest; straight; even; level, equal ~*v* make square; find square (of); pay; fit, suit

**squash** *v* crush flat; pulp; suppress ~*n* juice of crushed fruit; crowd; game played with rackets and ball in walled court

━━━━━━━━━ THESAURUS ━━━━━━━━━

**spring** *v* bounce, bound, jump, leap, vault (*oft. with from*) arise, come, emerge, grow, originate, start, stem (*with up*) appear, develop, grow, mushroom, shoot up ~*n* bound, jump, leap, vault

**sprinkle** *v* dredge, dust, pepper, powder, scatter

**sprout** *v* bud, develop, grow, shoot, spring

**spur** *v* goad, prick; impetus, impulse, incentive, inducement, motive, stimulus ~*v* drive, goad, impel, incite, prompt, stimulate, urge

**spurious** artificial, bogus, fake, false, forged, imitation, mock, phoney *or* phony *Inf.* pretended, sham

**spurn** disdain, rebuff, reject, scorn, slight, snub

**spy** *v* descry, espy, glimpse, notice, observe, spot

**squabble** *v* argue, bicker, fight, quarrel, row ~*n* argument, disagreement, fight, row, tiff

**squad** band, company, crew, force, team, troop

**squalid** dirty, filthy, seedy, slummy, sordid, unclean

**squalor** filth, meanness, squalidness

**squander** fritter away, lavish, misspend, misuse, spend, waste

**squash** *v* compress, crush, distort, flatten, pulp; crush, humiliate,

**squat** v **squatting, squatted** sit on heels; occupy unused premises illegally ~adj short and thick **squatter** n

**squawk** n short harsh cry, esp. of bird ~v utter this

**squeak** v/n (make) short shrill sound

**squeal** n long piercing squeak ~v make one

**squeamish** adj easily made sick; easily shocked

**squeeze** v press; wring; force; hug ~n act of squeezing

**squelch** v/n (make) wet sucking sound

**squid** n type of cuttlefish

**squiggle** n wavy line

**squint** v have the eyes turn in different directions; glance sideways ~n this eye disorder; glance

**squire** n country gentleman

**squirm** v wriggle; be embarrassed ~n squirming

**squirrel** n small graceful bushy-tailed tree animal

**squirt** v (of liquid) force, be forced through narrow opening ~n jet of liquid

**St.** Saint; Street

**st.** stone (weight)

**stab** v **stabbing, stabbed** pierce, strike (at) with pointed weapon ~n blow, wound so inflicted; sudden sensation; (pl of fear; attempt

**stabilize** v make or become stable **stabilizer** n device to maintain stability of ship, aircraft etc.

**stable**[1] n building for horses; race-horses of particular owner, establishment; such establishment ~v put into stable

**stable**[2] adj firmly fixed; steadfast, resolute **stability** n steadiness; ability to resist change

**staccato** adj/adv Mus with the notes sharply separated

**stack** n ordered pile, heap; chimney; v pile in stack

**stadium** n (pl -diums, -dia) open-air arena for athletics etc.

**staff** n body of officers or workers; pole ~v supply with personnel

**stag** n male deer

**stage** n period, division of development; (platform of) theatre; stopping-place on road, distance between two of them ~v put (play) on stage; arrange, bring about

**stagger** v walk unsteadily; astound; arrange in overlapping or alternating positions, times; distrib-

————— THESAURUS —————

quell, silence, suppress

**squeak** v peep, pipe, squeal

**squeamish** queasy, sick; delicate, fastidious, prudish, scrupulous, strait-laced

**squeeze** v compress, crush, press, squash; clasp, cuddle, embrace, hug ~n clasp, embrace, hug; crush, jam, press, squash

**squirm** twist, wriggle, writhe

**stab** v cut, injure, jab, knife, pierce, stick, thrust, wound ~n gash, jab, puncture, thrust, wound; pang,

prick, twinge; attempt, endeavour, essay, try

**stable** enduring, established, fast, firm, fixed, immovable, lasting, permanent, reliable, secure, sound, steady, strong, sturdy, well-founded

**stack** n heap, mound, mountain, pile ~v bank up, heap up, load, pile

**staff** n employees, personnel, workers, work force; cane, pole, rod, sceptre, stave

**stage** division, leg, length, level,

ute over a period

**stagnate** v cease to flow or develop **stagnant** adj sluggish; not flowing; foul, impure **stagnation** n

**staid** adj of sober and quiet character, sedate

**stain** v spot, mark; apply liquid colouring to (wood etc.) ~n discoloration or mark; moral blemish **stainless** adj **stainless steel** rustless steel alloy

**stairs** pl n set of steps, esp. as part of house **staircase, stairway** n structure enclosing stairs; stairs

**stake** n sharpened stick or post; bet; investment ~v secure, mark out with stakes; wager, risk

**stalactite** n lime deposit hanging from roof of cave

**stalagmite** n lime deposit sticking up from floor of cave

**stale** adj old, lacking freshness; lacking energy, interest through monotony **stalemate** n deadlock

**stalk¹** n plant's stem; anything like this

**stalk²** v follow stealthily; walk in stiff and stately manner

**stall** n compartment in stable etc.; erection for display and sale of

goods; front seat in theatre etc. ~v (of motor engine) unintentionally stop; delay

**stallion** n uncastrated male horse, esp. for breeding

**stalwart** adj strong, brave; staunch ~n stalwart person

**stamina** n power of endurance

**stammer** v speak, say with repetition of syllables ~n habit of so speaking

**stamp** v put down foot with force; impress mark on; affix postage stamp ~n stamping with foot; imprinted mark; appliance for marking; piece of gummed paper printed with device as evidence of postage etc.

**stampede** n sudden frightened rush, esp. of herd of cattle, crowd ~v rush

**stance** n manner, position of standing; attitude

**stanch** SEE STAUNCH¹

**stanchion** n upright bar used as support

**stand** v **standing, stood** have, take, set in upright position; be situated; remain firm or stationary; endure; offer oneself as a candidate; be

——————— THESAURUS ———————

period, phase, point, step

**stagger** lurch, reel, sway, waver, wobble; amaze, astonish, astound, overwhelm, stun, stupefy, surprise

**staid** quiet, sedate, serious, sober

**stain** v blemish, blot, dirty, discolour, mark, smirch, soil, spot, tarnish ~n blemish, spot; blemish, disgrace, dishonour, shame, slur, smirch, stigma

**stake** n concern, interest, investment, involvement, share ~v bet, gamble, hazard, risk, venture, wager

**stale** decayed, fetid, flat, fusty, insipid, musty, old, tasteless

**stalk** v follow, hunt, pursue, shadow, track

**stamina** energy, force, power, strength, vigour

**stammer** v falter, stutter

**stamp** v crush, trample; impress, imprint, mark, print ~n brand, hallmark, imprint, mark, mould, signature

**stance** bearing, carriage, deportment, posture; attitude, position, stand, standpoint, viewpoint

symbol etc. of; *Inf* provide free, treat to ~n holding firm; position; something on which thing may be placed; structure from which spectators can watch sport etc. **standing** n reputation, status; duration ~*adj* erect; lasting; stagnant **standoffish** *adj* reserved or haughty

**standard** n accepted example of something against which others are judged; degree, quality; flag ~*adj* usual; of recognized authority, accepted as correct **standardize** *v* regulate by a standard

**standpipe** n tap attached to water main to provide public water supply

**standpoint** n point of view

**standstill** n complete halt

**stanza** n group of lines of verse

**staple** n U-shaped piece of metal used to fasten; main product ~*adj* principal ~*v* fasten with staple **stapler** n

**star** n celestial object, seen as twinkling point of light; asterisk (*); celebrated player, actor ~*v* **starring starred** adorn with stars; mark

(with asterisk); feature as star performer ~*adj* most important **stardom** n **starry** *adj* covered with stars **starfish** n small star-shaped sea creature

**starboard** n right-hand side of ship

**starch** n substance forming the main food element in bread, potatoes etc., and used mixed with water, for stiffening linen etc. ~*v* stiffen thus **starchy** *adj* containing starch; stiff

**stare** *v* look fixedly (at) ~n staring gaze

**stark** *adj* blunt, bare; desolate; absolute; *adv* completely

**starling** n glossy black speckled songbird

**start** *v* begin; set going; make sudden movement ~n beginning; abrupt movement; advantage of a lead in a race **starter** n first course of meal; electric motor starting car engine; competitor in race; supervisor of start of race

**startle** *v* give a fright to

**starve** *v* (cause to) suffer or die

**stand** *v* be upright, erect, mount, place, position, put, rise, set; continue, exist, hold, pause, prevail, remain, rest, stay, stop; abide, allow, bear, countenance, endure, experience, handle, stomach, suffer, take, tolerate, undergo, weather, withstand ~n attitude, opinion, position, stance

**standard** n criterion, example, guide, measure, model, norm, par, sample, type ~*adj* average, basic, customary, normal, regular, typical, usual

**standpoint** angle, position, post, stance, station

**star** n celebrity, lead, luminary, megastar *Inf* ~*adj* leading, major, principal, prominent, well-known

**stare** *v* gape, gawk, glare, look

**stark** *adj* absolute, bare, blunt, downright, pure, sheer, utter; austere, bare, barren, bleak, desolate, plain, severe, unadorned ~*adv* absolutely, altogether, completely, entirely

**start** *v* arise, begin, commence, depart, originate, set off, set out; activate, initiate, kick-start, open, originate, trigger, turn on ~n beginning, birth, dawn, foundation, initiation, onset, outset; advantage, edge, lead

from hunger **starvation** n

**stash** v *Inf* store in secret place

**state** n condition; politically organized people; government; pomp ~v express in words **stately** adj dignified, lofty **statement** n expression in words; account **statesman** n (*fem* **stateswoman**) respected political leader **statesmanship** n

**static** adj motionless, inactive ~n electrical interference in radio reception

**station** n place where thing stops or is placed; stopping place for railway trains; local office for police force, fire brigade etc.; place equipped for radio or television transmission; bus garage; post; position in life ~v put in position **stationary** adj not moving; not changing

**stationer** n dealer in writing materials etc. **stationery** n

**statistics** pl n (*with sing* v) science of classifying and interpreting numerical information **statistic** n systematically collected fact **statistical** adj **statistician** n expert in statistics

**statue** n solid carved or cast image **statuesque** adj like statue; dignified **statuette** n small statue

**stature** n bodily height; greatness

**status** n position, rank; prestige; relation to others **status quo** existing state of affairs

**statute** n law **statutory** adj

**staunch**[1] v stop flow (of blood) from

**staunch**[2] adj trustworthy, loyal

**stave** n strip of wood in barrel ~v **staving, stove** or **staved** break hole in; ward (off)

**stay**[1] v remain; reside; endure; stop; postpone ~n remaining, residing; postponement

**stay**[2] n support, prop

**stead** n place **in stead** in place (of)

**steady** adj **steadier, steadiest** firm; regular; temperate ~v **steadying, steadied** make steady **steadily** adv **steadfast** adj firm, unyielding

**steak** n thick slice of meat

**startle** agitate, frighten, scare, shock

**state** n case, circumstances, condition, position, shape, situation; commonwealth, country, federation, kingdom, land, nation, republic, territory ~v affirm, assert, declare, explain, express, put, report, say, specify

**stately** august, dignified, lofty, majestic, noble

**statement** account, communiqué, declaration, explanation, proclamation, report

**station** n base, depot, headquarters, location, place, position, post, situation; appointment, business, calling, employment, grade, position, post, rank, situation, standing, status ~v establish, install, locate, post, set

**stationary** fixed, motionless, parked, standing

**status** condition, position, prestige, rank, standing

**stay** v abide, continue, delay, halt, linger, loiter, pause, remain, reside, stand, stop, wait ~n sojourn, stop, stopover, visit

**steadfast** constant, faithful, fast, firm, loyal, persevering, resolute, staunch, steady, unswerving, unwavering

**steady** adj firm, fixed, safe, stable; consistent, constant, even, regular, unbroken, uninterrupted, unvary-

**steal** *v* stealing, stole, stolen take without right or permission; move silently

**stealth** *n* secret or underhand procedure, behaviour **stealthy** *adj*

**steam** *n* vapour of boiling water ~*v* give off steam; move by steam power; cook or treat with steam **steamer** *n* steam-propelled ship **steam engine** *n* engine worked by steam **steamroller** *n* steam-powered vehicle with heavy rollers, used to level road surfaces

**steed** *n Lit* horse

**steel** *n* hard and malleable metal made by mixing carbon in iron ~*v* harden

**steep**¹ *adj* sloping abruptly; (of prices) very high

**steep**² *v* soak, saturate

**steeple** *n* church tower with spire **steeplechase** *n* race with obstacles to jump **steeplejack** *n* one who builds, repairs chimneys etc.

**steer**¹ *v* guide, direct course of vessel, motor vehicle etc.; direct one's course

**steer**² *n* castrated male ox

**stellar** *adj* of stars

**stem**¹ *n* stalk, trunk; part of word to which inflections are added

**stem**² *v* stemming, stemmed check, dam up

**stench** *n* foul smell

**stencil** *n* thin sheet pierced with pattern which is brushed over with paint or ink, leaving pattern on surface under it; the pattern ~*v* -cilling, -cilled make pattern thus

**step** *v* stepping, stepped move and set down foot; proceed (in this way); measure in paces ~*n* stepping; series of foot movements forming part of dance; measure, act, stage in proceeding; board, rung etc. to put foot on; degree in scale **stepladder** *n* folding portable ladder with supporting frame

**stepchild** *n* child of husband or wife by former marriage **stepbrother** *n* **stepfather** *n* **stepmother** *n* **stepsister** *n*

**stereophonic** *adj* (of sound) giving effect of coming from many directions **stereo** *n* stereophonic sound, record player etc. ~*adj* stereophonic

**stereotype** *n* something (monotonously) familiar, conventional ~*v* form stereotype of

**sterile** *adj* unable to produce fruit, crops, young etc.; free from (harm-

———— THESAURUS ————

ing; balanced, calm, equable, imperturbable, level-headed, sensible, temperate ~*v* balance, brace, stabilize

**steal** appropriate, embezzle, filch, nick *Sl, chiefly Brit*, pilfer, purloin, take, thieve; creep, slink, slip, sneak

**stealth** secrecy, slyness, surreptitiousness

**stealthy** clandestine, furtive, secret, secretive, sly, sneaking, surreptitious

**steep** *adj* abrupt, precipitous,

sheer; *Inf* exorbitant, extortionate, high, unreasonable

**steer** conduct, control, direct, govern, guide, handle, pilot

**stem**¹ *n* branch, shoot, stalk, trunk

**stem**² *v* check, contain, curb, dam, staunch, stop

**step** *v* move, pace, tread, walk ~*n* footfall, footstep, gait, pace, stride, walk; act, action, deed, measure, move; degree, level, rank

**stereotype** *n* formula, mould, pattern ~*v* categorize, typecast

ful) germs **sterility** n **sterilize** v render sterile

**sterling** adj genuine, true; of solid worth; in British money ~n British money

**stern**[1] adj severe, strict

**stern**[2] n rear part of ship

**sternum** n (pl **-na**, **-nums**) breast bone

**steroid** n organic compound, oft. used to increase body strength

**stethoscope** n instrument for listening to action of heart, lungs etc.

**stew** n food cooked slowly in closed vessel ~v cook slowly

**steward** n (fem **stewardess**) one who manages another's property; official managing race meeting, assembly etc.; attendant on ship or aircraft

**stick** n long, thin piece of wood; anything shaped like a stick ~v **sticking**, **stuck** pierce, stab; place, fasten, as by pins, glue; protrude; adhere; come to stop; jam; **sticker** n adhesive label, poster

**sticky** adj covered with, like adhesive substance; (of weather) warm, humid; Inf awkward, tricky

**stickleback** n small fish with sharp spines on back

**stickler** n person who insists on something

**stiff** adj not easily bent or moved; difficult; thick, not fluid; formal; strong or fresh, as breeze **stiffen** v **stiffness** n

**stifle** v smother, suppress

**stigma** n (pl **-mas**, **-mata**) mark of disgrace **stigmatize** v

**stile** n arrangement of steps for climbing a fence

**still**[1] adj motionless, noiseless ~v quiet ~adv to this time; yet; even ~n photograph, esp. of film scene **stillness** n **stillborn** adj born dead

**still**[2] n apparatus for distilling

**stilt** n pole with footrests for walking raised from ground; long post supporting building etc. **stilted** adj stiff in manner, pompous

**stimulus** n (pl **-li**) something that

──────── T H E S A U R U S ────────

**sterile** barren, empty, fruitless, unfruitful, unproductive; aseptic, disinfected, germ-free, sterilized

**sterilize** disinfect, fumigate, purify

**stern** forbidding, grim, hard, harsh, inflexible, rigid, serious, severe, strict, unyielding

**stick** v dig, jab, penetrate, pierce, poke, prod, spear, stab, thrust; adhere, affix, attach, bond, cement, cling, fasten, fix, glue, paste (with **out**, **up**, etc.) bulge, extend, jut, project, protrude; catch, clog, jam, lodge, stop

**sticky** adhesive, gluey, gummy, tacky, viscous; awkward, difficult, embarrassing, nasty, tricky, unpleasant

**stiff** firm, hard, inelastic, inflexible, rigid, unbending, unyielding; chilly, cold, formal, standoffish

**stiffen** congeal, harden, jell, set, solidify, thicken

**stifle** choke, smother, suffocate; check, curb, prevent, repress, smother, stop, suppress

**still** v calm, hushed, inert, motionless, peaceful, placid, quiet, serene, silent, stationary, tranquil ~v calm, hush, pacify, quieten, silence, soothe, subdue ~adv but, however, nevertheless, notwithstanding, yet

**stilted** artificial, forced, stiff, unnatural, wooden

**stimulate** arouse, fire, goad, impel, incite, instigate, provoke,

rouses to activity; incentive **stimulant** n drug etc. acting as stimulus **stimulate** v rouse up, spur **stimulation** n

**sting** v **stinging, stung** thrust sting into; cause sharp pain to; feel sharp pain ~n (wound, pain, caused by) sharp pointed organ, often poisonous, of certain creatures

**stingy** adj mean; niggardly

**stink** v **stinking, stank, stunk** give out strongly offensive smell; Sl be abhorrent

**stint** v be frugal, miserly ~n allotted amount of work or time; limitation, restriction

**stipulate** v specify in making a bargain **stipulation** n proviso; condition

**stir** v **stirring, stirred** (begin to) move; rouse; excite ~n commotion, disturbance

**stirrup** n loop for supporting foot of rider on horse

**stitch** n movement of needle in sewing etc.; its result in the work; sharp pain in side; least fragment (of clothing) ~v sew

**stoat** n small mammal with brown coat and black-tipped tail

**stock** n goods, material stored, esp. for sale or later use; financial shares

in, or capital of, company etc.; standing, reputation; farm animals, livestock; plant, stem from which cuttings are taken; handle of gun, tool etc.; liquid broth produced by boiling meat etc.; flowering plant; lineage ~adj kept in stock; standard; hackneyed ~v keep, store; supply with livestock, fish etc. **stockist** n dealer who stocks a particular product **stocky** adj thickset **stockbroker** n agent for buying, selling shares in companies **stock exchange** institution for buying and selling shares **stockpile** v acquire and store large quantity of (something) **stocktaking** n examination, counting and valuing of goods in a shop etc.

**stockade** n enclosure of stakes, barrier

**stocking** n close-fitting covering for leg and foot

**stodgy** adj heavy, dull

**stoic** adj capable of much self-control, great endurance without complaint ~n stoical person **stoical** adj **stoicism** n

**stoke** v feed, tend fire or furnace **stoker** n

**stole** n long scarf or shawl

**stolid** adj hard to excite

rouse, spur, urge

**sting** smart, tingle

**stipulate** agree, contract, covenant, require, settle, specify

**stipulation** agreement, clause, condition, provision, qualification, requirement, restriction, rider, specification, term

**stir** v (oft. with up) arouse, excite, incite, inflame, prompt, provoke, raise, rouse, spur, stimulate, urge ~n agitation, commotion, disorder,

flurry, fuss, to-do

**stock** n array, choice, fund, goods, hoard, range, selection, stockpile, store, supply, variety, wares; capital, funds, investment, property ~adj banal, conventional, customary, ordinary, regular, routine, set, standard, trite, usual, worn-out ~v (with up) amass, buy up, gather, hoard, save; deal in, keep, sell, supply, trade in

**stocky** dumpy, stubby, thickset

**stomach** n sac forming chief digestive organ in any animal; appetite ~v put up with

**stomp** v tread heavily

**stone** n (piece of) rock; gem; hard seed of fruit; hard deposit formed in kidneys, bladder; unit of weight, 14 pounds ~v throw stones at; free (fruit) from stones **stony** adj of, like stone; hard; cold **stone-deaf** adj completely deaf

**stooge** n person taken advantage of

**stool** n backless chair

**stoop** v lean forward or down; abase, degrade oneself ~n stooping posture

**stop** v **stopping, stopped** bring, come to halt; prevent; desist from; fill up an opening; cease; stay ~n place where something stops; stopping or becoming stopped; punctuation mark, esp. full stop; set of pipes in organ having tones of a distinct quality **stoppage** n **stopper** n plug for closing bottle etc. **stopcock** n valve to control flow of fluid in pipe **stopwatch** n watch which can be stopped for exact timing of race

**store** v stock, keep ~n shop; abundance; stock; place for keeping goods; warehouse; pl stocks of goods, provisions **storage** n

**storey** n horizontal division of a building

**stork** n large wading bird

**storm** n violent weather with wind, rain etc.; assault on fortress; violent outbreak ~v assault; take by storm; rage **stormy** adj like storm

**story** n account, tale; newspaper report

**stout** adj fat; sturdy, resolute ~n strong dark beer

**stove** n apparatus for cooking, heating etc.

**stow** v pack away **stowaway** n person who hides in ship to obtain

———————— THESAURUS ————————

**stomach** n belly, pot, tummy Inf; appetite, desire, inclination, taste ~v abide, bear, endure, swallow, take, tolerate

**stony** blank, chilly, expressionless, frigid, hard, hostile, icy

**stoop** v bend, bow, crouch, duck, incline, lean

**stop** v cease, conclude, cut short, desist, discontinue, end, finish, halt, pause, put an end to, quit, refrain, terminate; arrest, bar, block, break, check, close, hinder, hold back, impede, intercept, interrupt, obstruct, plug, prevent, restrain, seal, silence, staunch, stem, suspend ~n cessation, conclusion, end, finish, halt, standstill

**store** v hoard, keep, put aside, put by, reserve, save, stockpile ~n emporium, shop, supermarket; cache, fund, hoard, provision, reserve, stock, supply; repository, storeroom, warehouse

**storm** n blizzard, hurricane, squall, tempest, tornado, whirlwind; commotion, disturbance, furore, outburst, tumult; assault, attack, onslaught, rush ~v assail, assault, charge, rush; fume, rage, rant, rave

**stormy** blustery, inclement, raging, rough, turbulent, wild, windy

**story** account, anecdote, legend, narrative, romance, tale, urban legend, yarn; article, feature, news item, report

**stout** big, burly, fat, plump, portly, tubby; brawny, hardy, robust, stalwart, strapping, strong, sturdy; bold, brave, courageous, fearless,

free passage

**straddle** v bestride; spread legs wide

**straggle** v stray, get dispersed, linger **straggler** n

**straight** adj without bend; honest; level; in order; in continuous succession; (of spirits) undiluted; (of face) expressionless ~n straight state or part ~adv direct **straighten** v **straightaway** adv immediately **straightforward** adj open, frank; simple

**strain**[1] v stretch tightly; stretch to excess; filter; make great effort ~n stretching force; violent effort; injury from being strained; great demand; (condition caused by) overwork, worry etc. **strained** adj **strainer** n filter, sieve

**strain**[2] n breed or race; trace

**strait** n channel of water connecting two larger areas of water; pl position of difficulty or distress **strait-jacket** n jacket to confine arms of violent person **strait-laced** adj prudish

**strand**[1] v run aground; leave, be left in difficulties

**strand**[2] n single thread of string, wire etc.

**strange** adj odd; unaccustomed; foreign **strangeness** n **stranger** n unknown person; foreigner; one unaccustomed (to)

**strangle** v kill by squeezing windpipe; suppress **strangulation** n strangling **stranglehold** n

**strap** n strip, esp. of leather ~v **strapping, strapped** fasten, beat with strap **strapping** adj tall and well-made

**strategy** n overall plan; art of war **stratagem** n plan, trick **strategic**

─────── THESAURUS ───────

plucky, resolute, valiant

**straight** adj direct, near, short; erect, even, horizontal, level, plumb, right, smooth, upright, vertical; in order, neat, orderly, organized, shipshape, tidy; consecutive, continuous, nonstop, solid, successive; neat, pure, unadulterated, undiluted, unmixed ~adv at once, directly, immediately, instantly

**straightaway** at once, directly, immediately, instantly, now, right away

**straighten** arrange, neaten, put in order, tidy (up)

**straightforward** candid, direct, forthright, honest, open, upfront Inf; easy, easy-peasy Sl, elementary, simple, uncomplicated

**strain** v distend, stretch, tauten, tighten; pull, sprain, tear, twist, wrench; filter, separate, sieve, sift;

bend over backwards Inf, break one's neck Inf, knock oneself out Inf, labour, strive, struggle ~n tautness, tension; effort, exertion, struggle; injury, pull, sprain, wrench; anxiety, pressure, stress, tension

**strained** artificial, awkward, difficult, false, forced, stiff, tense, uneasy, unnatural

**strait-laced** prim, proper, prudish, puritanical

**strand** n fibre, filament, length, string, thread

**strange** bizarre, curious, eccentric, extraordinary, odd, off-the-wall Sl, peculiar, queer, rare, rum Brit sl, uncanny, weird; alien, exotic, foreign

**stranger** alien, foreigner, incomer, newcomer

**strangle** choke, throttle; inhibit,

*adj* **strategist** *n*

**stratosphere** *n* layer of atmosphere high above the earth

**stratum** *n* (*pl* **strata**) layer, esp. of rock; class in society **stratification** *n* **stratify** *v* **-fying, -fied** form, deposit in layers

**straw** *n* stalks of grain; long, narrow tube used to suck up liquid

**strawberry** *n* creeping plant producing red, juicy fruit; the fruit

**stray** *v* wander; digress; get lost ~*adj* strayed; occasional; scattered ~*n* stray animal

**streak** *n* long line or band; element ~*v* mark with streaks; move fast; run naked in public **streaker** *n* **streaky** *adj*

**stream** *n* flowing body of water or other liquid; steady flow ~*v* flow; run with liquid **streamer** *n* (paper) ribbon, narrow flag

**streamlined** *adj* (of car, plane etc.) built so as to offer least resistance to air **streamlining** *n*

**street** *n* road in town or village, usu. lined with houses **streetwise** *adj* adept at surviving in dangerous environment

**strength** *n* quality of being strong; power **strengthen** *v*

**strenuous** *adj* energetic; earnest

**stress** *n* emphasis; tension ~*v* emphasize

**stretch** *v* extend; exert to utmost; tighten, pull out; reach; have elasticity ~*n* stretching, being stretched; expanse; spell **stretcher** *n* person, thing that stretches; appliance on which disabled person is carried

**strew** *v* **strewing, strewed, strewed** *or* **strewn** scatter over surface, spread

**stricken** *adj* seriously affected by disease, grief etc.

**strict** *adj* stern, not lax or indulgent; precisely defined; without exception

**stricture** *n* critical remark

——————— THESAURUS ———————

repress, stifle, suppress

**strategy** approach, plan, policy, programme

**stray** *v* drift, range, roam, rove, wander; deviate, digress, diverge, ramble ~*adj* abandoned, homeless, lost

**streak** *n* band, layer, line, slash, strip, stripe; dash, element, strain, touch, trace, vein

**stream** *n* brook, burn, course, current, flow, river, rush, surge, tide, torrent, tributary ~*v* cascade, course, flood, flow, gush, issue, pour, run, shed, spill, spout

**street** avenue, lane, road, row, terrace

**strength** brawn, fortitude, might, muscle, robustness, stamina, stoutness, sturdiness, toughness; energy, force, intensity, potency, power

**strengthen** brace up, fortify, hearten, invigorate, toughen; augment, bolster, brace, reinforce, steel, support

**strenuous** arduous, demanding, hard, laborious, taxing, tough; determined, earnest, resolute, spirited, strong, tireless

**stress** *n* emphasis, force, importance, significance, urgency, weight; anxiety, pressure, strain, tension, worry ~*v* accentuate, dwell on, emphasize, rub in, underline

**stretch** *v* extend, put forth, reach, spread; distend, draw out, elongate, expand, lengthen, pull, strain, tighten ~*n* area, distance, expanse,

**stride** v **striding, strode, stridden** walk with long steps ~n single step; length of step

**strident** adj harsh, loud **stridently** adv **stridency** n

**strife** n conflict; quarrelling

**strike** v **striking, struck** hit (against); ignite; attack; sound (time), as bell in clock etc.; affect; enter mind of; cease work as protest or to make demands ~n act of striking **striker** n **striking** adj noteworthy, impressive

**string** n (length of) thin cord or other material; series; fibre in plants; pl conditions ~v **stringing, strung** provide with, thread on string; form in line, series **stringed** adj (of musical instruments) furnished with strings **stringy** adj like string; fibrous

**stringent** adj strict, binding **stringency** n

**strip** v **stripping, stripped** lay bare, take covering off; undress ~n long, narrow piece **stripper** n **striptease** n

cabaret or theatre in which person undresses

**stripe** n narrow mark, band **striped, stripy** adj marked with stripes

**strive** v **striving, strove, striven** try hard, struggle

**strobe** also **stroboscope** n instrument producing bright flashing light

**stroke** n blow; sudden action, occurrence; apoplexy; chime of clock; mark made by pen, brush etc.; style, method of swimming; act of stroking ~v pass hand lightly over

**stroll** v walk in leisurely or idle manner ~n leisurely walk

**strong** adj powerful, robust, healthy; difficult to break; noticeable; intense; emphatic; not diluted; having a certain number **strongly** adv **stronghold** n fortress **strongroom** n room for keeping valuables

**stroppy** adj Sl angry or awkward

**structure** n (arrangement of parts in) construction, building etc.; form

extent, spread

**strict** firm, rigid, rigorous, severe, stern, stringent; accurate, exact, faithful, meticulous, precise, scrupulous, true

**strike** v beat, buffet, cuff, hit, knock, punch, slap, smack, thump; assail, assault, attack, hit, set upon; come to, hit, occur to, seem; down tools, walk out

**striking** conspicuous, dazzling, impressive, memorable, noticeable, outstanding

**string** n cord, fibre, twine; chain, line, procession, row, sequence, series, succession

**strip** v bare, denude, divest, peel, skin; disrobe, unclothe, undress ~n

band, belt, ribbon, shred, slip

**strive** attempt, bend over backwards Inf, break one's neck Inf, endeavour, fight, give it one's best shot Inf, knock oneself out Inf, labour, strain, struggle, toil

**stroke** n blow, hit, knock, rap, thump; apoplexy, attack, fit, seizure ~v caress, fondle, pet, rub

**stroll** v amble, ramble, saunter, wander ~n promenade, ramble, walk

**strong** athletic, brawny, muscular, powerful, stout, strapping, sturdy, tough; hale, hardy, healthy, robust, sound; durable, hard-wearing, sturdy, tough, unyielding; deep, fervent, fierce, firm, intense, keen;

~v give structure to **structural** adj

**struggle** v contend; fight; proceed, work, move with difficulty and effort ~n struggling

**strum** v strumming, strummed strike notes of guitar etc.

**strut** v strutting, strutted walk affectedly or pompously ~n rigid support; strutting walk

**strychnine** n poisonous drug

**stub** n remnant of anything, e.g. pencil; counterfoil ~v stubbing, stubbed strike (toes) against fixed object; extinguish by pressing against surface **stubby** adj short, broad

**stubble** n stumps of cut grain after reaping; short growth of beard

**stubborn** adj unyielding, obstinate

**stucco** n plaster

**stud**[1] n nail with large head; removable double-headed button ~v studding, studded set with studs

**stud**[2] n set of horses kept for breeding

**studio** n (pl -dios) workroom of artist, photographer etc.; building, room where film, television or radio shows are made, broadcast

**study** v studying, studied be engaged in learning; make study of; scrutinize ~n effort to acquire knowledge; subject of this; room to study in; book, report etc. produced as result of study; sketch **student** n one who studies **studied** adj carefully designed, premeditated **studious** adj fond of study; painstaking; deliberate

**stuff** v pack, cram, fill (completely); eat large amount; fill with seasoned mixture; fill (animal's skin) with material to preserve lifelike form ~n material; any substance; belongings **stuffing** n material for stuffing **stuffy** adj lacking fresh air; Inf dull, conventional

**stultify** v -fying, -fied make dull by boring routine

**stumble** v trip and nearly fall; falter ~n stumbling

**stump** n remnant of tree, tooth

---

concentrated, pure, undiluted

**structure** n arrangement, conformation, design, form, formation, make-up, organization; building, construction, edifice, erection ~v arrange, assemble, build up, design, organize, shape

**struggle** v bend over backwards Inf, break one's neck Inf, knock oneself out Inf, labour, strain, strive, toil, work; battle, compete, contend, fight, wrestle ~n effort, exertion, labour, pains, toil, work; battle, combat, conflict, contest, tussle

**stubborn** dogged, inflexible, intractable, obdurate, obstinate, pigheaded, unyielding

**student** apprentice, disciple, learner, pupil, scholar, undergraduate

**studious** academic, bookish, diligent, earnest, scholarly, serious

**study** v consider, contemplate, examine, learn, pore over, read, read up; analyse, examine, investigate, peruse, research, scrutinize, survey ~n analysis, contemplation, inquiry, investigation, perusal, review, scrutiny, survey

**stuff** v cram, crowd, fill, force, jam, pack, push, ram, shove, wedge ~n essence, matter, substance; belongings, effects, equipment, gear, kit, tackle, things

**stuffy** airless, close, heavy, muggy, oppressive, stale, stifling, unventi-

etc., when main part has been cut away; one of uprights of wicket in cricket ~v confuse, puzzle; walk heavily, noisily **stumpy** adj short and thickset

**stun** v stunning, stunned knock senseless; amaze **stunning** adj

**stunt**[1] v stop growth of

**stunt**[2] n feat of dexterity or daring

**stupefy** v -fying, -fied make insensitive, lethargic; astound **stupefaction** n

**stupendous** adj astonishing; amazing; huge

**stupid** adj slow-witted; silly **stupidity** n

**stupor** n dazed state

**sturdy** adj robust, strongly built; vigorous

**sturgeon** n fish yielding caviare

**stutter** v speak with difficulty; stammer ~n tendency to stutter

**sty** n place to keep pigs in

**stye** n inflammation on eyelid

**style** n design; manner of writing, doing etc.; fashion; elegance ~v design **stylish** adj fashionable **stylist** n one cultivating style

**stylus** n (pl -li, -luses) (in record player) tiny point running in groove of record

**suave** adj smoothly polite

**sub** n short for SUBMARINE, SUBSCRIPTION, SUBSTITUTE

**subconscious** adj acting, existing without one's awareness ~n Psychology part of human mind unknown, or only partly known, to possessor

**subdivide** v divide again **subdivision** n

**subdue** v overcome **subdued** adj cowed, quiet; not bright

**subject** n person or thing being

——————— THESAURUS ———————

lated; dull, staid, stodgy

**stumble** fall, lurch, stagger, trip

**stun** astonish, astound, knock out, overcome, overpower, stagger, stupefy

**stunning** dazzling, marvellous, sensational *Inf*, spectacular, striking, wonderful

**stunt** n act, deed, exploit, feat, trick

**stupendous** amazing, astounding, breathtaking, colossal, enormous, gigantic, huge, marvellous, sensational *Inf*, staggering, superb, vast, wonderful

**stupid** brainless, dense, dim, dull, half-witted, moronic, obtuse, simple, simple-minded, slow, slow-witted, thick, witless; asinine, idiotic, inane, ludicrous, mindless, senseless, unintelligent

**stupidity** brainlessness, denseness,

dimness, dullness, imbecility, obtuseness, slowness, thickness; folly, idiocy, inanity, lunacy, madness, silliness

**sturdy** athletic, brawny, durable, firm, hardy, hearty, muscular, powerful, robust, secure, solid, substantial, vigorous, well-built

**style** n cut, design, form , manner; approach, manner, method, mode, way; fashion, mode, rage, trend, vogue; chic, dash, elegance, flair, panache, polish, smartness, sophistication ~v adapt, arrange, cut, design, fashion, shape

**stylish** chic, dapper, fashionable, modish, polished, smart

**subconscious** adj hidden, inner, latent, subliminal

**subdue** break, conquer, crush, defeat, overcome, overpower, quell, vanquish

dealt with or studied; person under rule of government or monarch ~*adj* owing allegiance; dependent; liable (to) ~*v* cause to undergo; subdue **subjection** *n* act of bringing, or state of being, under control **subjective** *adj* based on personal feelings, not impartial; existing in the mind **subjectivity** *n*

**subjugate** *v* force to submit; conquer **subjugation** *n*

**sublet** *v* -**letting, -let** rent out property rented from someone else

**sublime** *adj* elevated; inspiring awe; exalted

**subliminal** *adj* relating to mental processes of which the individual is not aware

**submarine** *n* craft which can travel below surface of sea and remain submerged for long periods ~*adj* below surface of sea

**submerge** *v* place, go under water

**submersion** *n*

**submit** *v* -**mitting, -mitted** surrender; put forward for consideration; defer **submission** *n* **submissive** *adj* meek, obedient

**subnormal** *adj* below normal

**subordinate** *n/adj* (one) of lower rank or less importance ~*v* make, treat as subordinate **subordination** *n*

**subscribe** *v* pay, promise to pay (contribution); give support, approval **subscription** *n* money paid

**subsequent** *adj* later, following or coming after in time

**subservient** *adj* submissive, servile

**subside** *v* abate; sink **subsidence** *n*

**subsidiary** *adj/n* secondary (person or thing)

**subsidize** *v* help financially; pay grant to **subsidy** *n* money granted

**subsist** *v* exist, sustain life **subsist-**

——————— THESAURUS ———————

**subject** *n* affair, business, issue, matter, object, question, theme, topic; dependent, subordinate ~*adj* answerable, bound by, dependent, inferior, subordinate; conditional, contingent, dependent; disposed, liable, open, prone, susceptible ~*v* expose, lay open, submit, treat

**subjective** biased, emotional, personal, prejudiced

**submerge** dip, duck, engulf, flood, immerse, overflow, plunge, sink, swamp

**submission** capitulation, surrender, yielding

**submissive** acquiescent, compliant, docile, meek, obedient, passive, pliant, tractable, unresisting, yielding

**submit** accede, bend, bow, capitulate, defer, give in, succumb, sur-

render, yield; hand in, present, tender

**subordinate** *n* inferior, junior, second, underling ~*adj* inferior, junior, lesser, lower, minor, secondary

**subscribe** contribute, donate, give, pledge, promise

**subscription** donation, dues, gift, membership fee

**subsequent** after, ensuing, following, later, succeeding, successive

**subside** abate, decrease, diminish, dwindle, ebb, lessen, recede, wane

**subsidiary** ancillary, assistant, auxiliary, lesser, minor, secondary, subordinate, supplementary

**subsidize** finance, fund, promote, sponsor, support

**subsidy** aid, allowance, assistance, grant, support

ence *n* the means by which one supports life

**substance** *n* (particular kind of) matter; essence; wealth **substantial** *adj* considerable; of real value; really existing **substantiate** *v* bring evidence for, prove

**substitute** *v* put, serve in place of ~*n* thing, person put in place of another ~*adj* serving as a substitute **substitution** *n*

**subsume** *v* incorporate in larger group

**subterfuge** *n* trick, lying excuse used to evade something

**subterranean** *adj* underground

**subtitle** *n* secondary title of book; *pl* translation superimposed on foreign film ~*v* provide with subtitle or subtitles

**subtle** *adj* not immediately obvious; ingenious; crafty; making fine distinctions **subtlety** *n* **subtly** *adv*

**subtract** *v* take away, deduct sub-

traction *n*

**suburb** *n* residential area on outskirts of city **suburban** *adj* **suburbia** *n* suburbs and their inhabitants

**subvert** *v* overthrow; corrupt **subversion** *n* **subversive** *adj*

**subway** *v* underground passage; *US* underground railway

**succeed** *v* accomplish purpose; turn out satisfactorily; follow; take place of **success** *n* favourable accomplishment, attainment, issue or outcome; successful person or thing **successful** *adj* **succession** *n* following; series; succeeding **successive** *adj* following in order; consecutive **successor** *n*

**succinct** *adj* brief and clear

**succour** *v*/*n* help in distress

**succulent** *adj* juicy; (of plant) having thick, fleshy leaves ~*n* such plant **succulence** *n*

**succumb** *v* give way

**such** *adj* of the kind or degree men-

——————— THESAURUS ———————

**substance** fabric, material, stuff; essence, gist, import, matter, meaning, significance, subject, theme; assets, means, property, resources, wealth

**substantial** big, important, large, significant, sizable, worthwhile

**substitute** *v* change, exchange, interchange, replace, switch ~*n* agent, deputy, locum, makeshift, replacement, reserve, stopgap, sub ~*adj* acting, alternative, replacement, reserve, surrogate, temporary

**subtle** faint, implied, indirect, slight; deep, delicate, ingenious, profound, sophisticated; artful, crafty, cunning, shrewd, wily

**subtlety** delicacy, nicety, refinement, sophistication; craftiness, cunning, guile, wiliness

**subtract** deduct, diminish, remove, take away

**subversive** destructive, overthrowing, riotous, seditious

**succeed** crack *Inf.* flourish, make good, prosper, triumph, work; come next, ensue, follow

**success** fortune, luck, prosperity, triumph

**successful** flourishing, fruitful, lucrative, profitable, prosperous, thriving, unbeaten, victorious

**succession** chain, course, order, progression, run, sequence, series, train

**successive** consecutive, following

**succinct** brief, concise, laconic, pithy, terse

**succulent** juicy, luscious, lush

**succumb** capitulate, submit, sur-

tioned; so great, so much

**suck** *v* draw into mouth; hold in mouth; draw in ~*n* sucking **sucker** *n* person, thing that sucks; shoot coming from root or base of stem of plant; *Inf* one who is easily deceived

**suckle** *v* feed from the breast **suckling** *n* unweaned infant

**suction** *n* drawing or sucking of air or fluid; force produced by difference in pressure

**sudden** *adj* done, occurring unexpectedly; abrupt **suddenly** *adv*

**suds** *pl n* froth of soap and water

**sue** *v* suing, sued prosecute; seek justice from; make application or entreaty

**suede** *n* leather with soft, velvety finish

**suet** *n* hard animal fat

**suffer** *v* undergo; tolerate **suffering** *n*

**suffice** *v* be adequate, satisfactory (for) **sufficiency** *n* adequate amount **sufficient** *adj* enough, adequate

**suffix** *n* group of letters added to end of word

**suffocate** *v* kill, be killed by deprivation of oxygen; smother **suffocation** *n*

**suffrage** *n* vote or right of voting

**suffuse** *v* well up and spread over

**sugar** *n* sweet crystalline substance ~*v* sweeten, make pleasant (with sugar) **sugary** *adj*

**suggest** *v* propose; call up the idea of **suggestible** *adj* easily influenced **suggestion** *n* proposal; insinuation of impression, belief etc. into mind **suggestive** *adj* containing suggestions, esp. of something indecent

**suicide** *n* act of killing oneself; one who does this **suicidal** *adj*

**suit** *n* set of clothing; garment worn for particular event, purpose; one of four sets in pack of cards; action at law ~*v* make, be fit or appropriate for; be acceptable to (someone) **suitability** *n* **suitable** *adj* fitting, convenient **suitcase** *n* flat rectangular travelling case

**suite** *n* matched set of furniture; set of rooms; retinue

——————————— THESAURUS ———————————

render, yield

**sudden** abrupt, quick, rapid, swift, unexpected

**sue** charge, indict, prosecute, summon

**suffer** bear, endure, experience, feel, sustain, tolerate, undergo

**suffering** *n* agony, anguish, distress, hardship, misery, ordeal, pain, torment

**sufficient** adequate, enough

**suffocate** asphyxiate, choke, smother, stifle

**suggest** advise, move, prescribe, propose, recommend; hint, imply, insinuate, intimate

**suggestion** motion, plan, proposal, proposition; breath, hint, intimation, trace, whisper

**suggestive** bawdy, blue, improper, indecent, racy, ribald, risqué, rude, smutty, titillating

**suit** *n* costume, dress, ensemble, habit, outfit; *Law* action, case, cause, lawsuit, proceeding, prosecution, trial ~*v* accommodate, adapt, adjust, fashion, fit, modify, tailor; do, gratify, please, satisfy; agree, answer, become, befit, match, harmonize, tally

**suitable** applicable, appropriate, apt, becoming, befitting, due, fit, fitting, pertinent, proper, relevant, right; convenient, opportune

**suitor** n wooer; one who sues

**sulk** v be silent, resentful ~n this mood **sulky** adj

**sullen** adj unwilling to talk or be sociable, morose

**sully** v -lying, -lied stain, tarnish

**sulphur** n pale yellow nonmetallic element **sulphuric** adj **sulphurous** adj

**sultan** n ruler of Muslim country **sultana** n kind of raisin

**sultry** adj (of weather) hot, humid; (of person) looking sensual

**sum** n amount, total; problem in arithmetic ~v **summing, summed** add up; make summary of main parts

**summary** n brief statement of chief points of something ~adj done quickly **summarily** adv speedily; abruptly **summarize** v make summary of

**summer** n second, warmest season

**summit** n top, peak

**summon** v demand attendance of; bid witness appear in court; gather up (energies etc.) **summons** n call; authoritative demand

**sumo** n Japanese style of wrestling

**sumptuous** adj lavish, magnificent **sumptuousness** n

**sun** n luminous body round which earth and other planets revolve; its rays ~v **sunning, sunned** expose to sun's rays **sunless** adj **sunny** adj like the sun; warm; cheerful **sunbathe** n lie in sunshine **sunbeam** n ray of sun **sunburn** n inflammation of skin due to excessive exposure to sun **sundown** n sunset **sunflower** n plant with large golden flowers **sunrise** n appearance of sun above the horizon **sunset** n disappearance of sun below the horizon **sunshine** n light and warmth from sun **sunstroke** n illness caused by prolonged exposure to hot sun

**sundae** n ice cream topped with fruit etc.

**Sunday** n first day of the week **Sunday school** school for religious instruction of children

**sunder** v separate, sever

**sundry** adj several, various **sundries** pl n odd items, not mentioned in detail

**sup** v supping, supped take by sips; take supper ~n mouthful of liquid

**super** adj Inf very good

**super-** comb. form above, greater, exceedingly, as in **superhuman, supertanker**

**superannuation** n pension given on retirement; contribution by employee to pension

**superb** adj extremely good or

**sulk** brood, look sullen, pout

**sulky** churlish, cross, huffy, ill-humoured, moody, petulant, resentful, sullen

**sullen** brooding, gloomy, heavy, moody, morose, surly, unsociable

**sultry** close, humid, oppressive, sticky, stuffy

**sum** aggregate, amount, quantity, tally, total, whole

**summarize** encapsulate, epitomize, outline, sum up

**summary** digest, outline, précis, résumé, review, rundown, synopsis

**summit** apex, crown, head, height, peak, pinnacle, top, zenith

**summon** bid, call, convene, convoke, rally

**sumptuous** grand, lavish, luxurious, opulent, rich, splendid, superb

**sunny** bright, brilliant, clear, fine, summery, unclouded; blithe, cheer-

impressive

**supercharger** n device that increases power of engine **supercharged** adj

**supercilious** adj displaying arrogant pride, scorn

**superficial** adj of or on surface; not careful or thorough; without depth, shallow

**superfluous** adj extra, unnecessary **superfluity** n

**superhuman** adj beyond normal human ability or experience

**superimpose** v place on or over something else

**superintend** v have charge of; overlook; supervise **superintendent** n senior police officer

**superior** adj greater in quality or quantity; upper, higher in position, rank or quality; showing consciousness of being so ~n supervisor, manager **superiority** n

**superlative** adj of, in highest degree or quality; surpassing; *Grammar* denoting form of adjective, ad-

verb meaning *most*

**supermarket** n large self-service store

**supernatural** adj being beyond the powers or laws of nature; miraculous

**supernumerary** adj exceeding the required or regular number

**superpower** n extremely powerful nation

**supersede** v take the place of

**supersonic** adj denoting speed greater than that of sound

**superstition** n religion, opinion or practice based on belief in luck or magic **superstitious** adj

**superstructure** n structure above foundations; part of ship above deck

**supervise** v oversee; direct; inspect and control **supervision** n

**supervisor** n **supervisory** adj

**supine** adj lying on back with face upwards

**supper** n (light) evening meal

**supplant** v take the place of

———————————— THESAURUS ————————————

ful, genial, happy, pleasant

**superb** excellent, fine, first-rate, grand, magnificent, marvellous, splendid, superior, unrivalled, world-class

**superficial** exterior, external, shallow, skin-deep, slight, surface; casual, cursory, perfunctory, sketchy, slapdash

**superfluous** excess, extra, left over, needless, redundant, remaining, spare, surplus, uncalled-for, unnecessary, unrequired

**superintendent** chief, controller, director, governor, manager, overseer, supervisor

**superior** adj better, grander, greater, higher, paramount; choice, de

luxe, excellent, exceptional, first-class, first-rate, surpassing, unrivalled; condescending, disdainful, haughty, lofty, lordly, patronizing, snobbish ~n boss *Inf*, chief, director, manager, senior, supervisor

**superiority** advantage, excellence, lead, supremacy

**supernatural** miraculous, mystic, occult, paranormal, psychic, uncanny, unearthly

**supervise** administer, conduct, control, direct, look after, manage, oversee, run, superintend

**supervision** administration, charge, control, direction, guidance, management

**supervisor** administrator, chief,

**supple** *adj* pliable; flexible **supply** *adv*

**supplement** *n* thing added to fill up, supply deficiency, esp. extra part added to book etc. ~*v* add to; supply deficiency **supplementary** *adj*

**supplicate** *v* beg humbly, entreat **supplicant** *n* supplication *n*

**supply** *v* -plying, -plied furnish; make available; provide ~*n* (*pl* -plies) stock, store; food, materials needed for journey etc.

**support** *v* hold up; sustain; assist ~*n* supporting, being supported; means of support **supporter** *n* adherent **supporting** *adj* (of role in film etc.) less important **supportive** *adj*

**suppose** *v* assume as theory; take

for granted; accept as likely **supposed** *adj* assumed; expected, obliged; permitted **supposedly** *adv*

**supposition** *n* assumption; belief without proof; conjecture

**suppress** *v* put down, restrain; keep or withdraw from publication **suppression** *n*

**suppurate** *v* fester, form pus

**supreme** *adj* highest in authority or rank; utmost **supremacy** *n* position of being supreme **supremo** *n* person in overall authority

**surcharge** *v/n* (make) additional charge

**sure** *adj* certain; trustworthy; without doubt ~*adv* *Inf* certainly **surely** *adv* **surety** *n* person, thing acting as guarantee for another's obligations

**surf** *n* waves breaking on shore ~*v*

———— T H E S A U R U S ————

foreman, manager, overseer

**supple** elastic, flexible, limber, lithe, pliable, pliant

**supplement** *n* addition, appendix, codicil, extra, insert, pull-out ~*v* add, augment, extend, fill out, reinforce, top up

**supplementary** additional, auxiliary, extra, secondary

**supply** *v* afford, contribute, endow, furnish, give, grant, provide, stock, yield ~*n* fund, quantity, reserve, source, stock, store; (*usu. pl*) equipment, provisions, rations, stores

**support** *v* bear, brace, buttress, carry, hold, prop, reinforce, sustain, uphold; finance, fund, keep, maintain, provide for; sustain; aid, assist, back, champion, defend, help, promote, second, side with ~*n* aid, approval, assistance, backing, blessing, encouragement, help, patronage, promotion; brace, foun-

dation, pillar, post, prop, stay

**supporter** adherent, advocate, champion, fan, follower, patron, sponsor, well-wisher

**suppose** assume, conjecture, expect, imagine, infer, judge, presume, surmise, think; believe, conceive, conjecture, consider, fancy, imagine, pretend

**supposition** conjecture, guess, hypothesis, idea, presumption, speculation, surmise, theory

**suppress** check, conquer, crush, extinguish, overpower, quash, quell, quench, stop, subdue

**suppression** check, clampdown, crackdown, prohibition, quashing

**supremacy** ascendancy, dominance, mastery, predominance, primacy, sovereignty, sway

**supreme** chief, first, foremost, greatest, head, highest, leading, paramount, pre-eminent, prime, principal, top, ultimate, utmost

ride surf **surfer** n **surfing** n sport of riding over surf **surfboard** n board used in surfing

**surface** n outside face of object; plane; top; superficial appearance ~adj involving the surface only ~v come to surface

**surfeit** n excess; disgust caused by excess ~v feed to excess

**surge** n wave; sudden increase ~v move in large waves; swell

**surgeon** n medical expert who performs operations **surgery** n medical treatment by operation; doctor's, dentist's consulting room **surgical** adj

**surly** adj cross and rude

**surmise** v/n guess, conjecture

**surmount** v get over, overcome

**surname** n family name

**surpass** v go beyond; excel; outstrip **surpassing** adj excellent

**surplus** n what remains over in excess ~adj spare, superfluous

**surprise** n something unexpected; emotion aroused by being taken unawares ~v cause surprise to; astonish; take, come upon unexpectedly

**surrealism** n incongruous combination of images **surreal** adj

**surrender** v hand over, give up; yield; cease resistance ~n act of surrendering

**surreptitious** adj done secretly or stealthily; furtive

**surrogate** n substitute **surrogate mother** woman who bears child on behalf of childless couple

**surround** v be, come all round, encompass; encircle ~n border, edging **surroundings** pl n conditions, scenery etc. around a person, place, environment

**surveillance** n close watch, supervision

**survey** v view, scrutinize; inspect, examine; measure, map (land) ~n

─────── THESAURUS ───────

**sure** certain, confident, convinced, decided, definite, positive; accurate, dependable, foolproof, indisputable, infallible, precise, trustworthy, undeniable, undoubted, unerring, unfailing; guaranteed, inescapable, inevitable, irrevocable

**surface** n covering, exterior, face, outside, plane, side, top, veneer

**surfeit** n excess, glut, plethora, superfluity ~v cram, fill, glut, gorge, overfeed, stuff

**surge** gush, heave, rise, rush, swell

**surly** churlish, cross, morose, sulky, sullen, uncivil, ungracious

**surpass** beat, eclipse, exceed, excel, outdo, outshine, outstrip, transcend

**surplus** n balance, excess, remainder, surfeit ~adj excess, extra, remaining, spare, superfluous, unused

**surprise** n bombshell, jolt, revelation, shock; amazement, astonishment, incredulity, wonder ~v amaze, astonish, astound

**surrender** v abandon, cede, concede, give up, part with, relinquish, renounce, waive, yield; capitulate, give in, give way, submit, succumb, yield ~n capitulation, resignation, submission

**surreptitious** covert, furtive, secret, sly, stealthy, underhand

**surround** encircle, enclose, encompass, envelop, ring

**surroundings** background, location, milieu, setting

**surveillance** inspection, scrutiny, supervision, watch

act of surveying; inspection; report incorporating results of survey **surveyor** n

**survive** v continue to live or exist; outlive **survival** n continuation of existence **survivor** n one who survives

**susceptible** adj yielding readily (to); capable (of); impressionable **susceptibility** n

**suspect** v doubt innocence of; have impression of existence or presence of; be inclined to believe that ~adj of suspicious character ~n suspected person

**suspend** v hang up; cause to cease for a time; keep inoperative; sustain in fluid **suspenders** pl n straps for supporting stockings

**suspense** n state of uncertainty, esp. while awaiting news, an event etc.; anxiety, worry **suspension** n state of being suspended; springs on axle of body of vehicle

**suspicion** n suspecting, being suspected; slight trace **suspicious** adj

**sustain** v keep, hold up; endure; keep alive; confirm **sustenance** n food

**svelte** adj gracefully slim

**swab** n mop; pad of surgical wool etc. for cleaning; taking specimen etc. ~v **swabbing, swabbed** clean with swab

**swag** n Sl stolen property

**swagger** v strut; boast ~n strutting gait; boastful manner

**swallow¹** v cause, allow to pass down gullet; suppress ~n act of swallowing

**swallow²** n migratory bird with forked tail

**swamp** n bog ~v entangle in swamp; overwhelm; flood

**swan** n large, web-footed water bird with curved neck

**swap** v **swapping, swapped** exchange; barter ~n exchange

———————— THESAURUS ————————

**survey** v contemplate, examine, eye up, inspect, observe, scan, scrutinize, study, view; appraise, assess, estimate, size up ~n examination, inquiry, inspection, overview, review, scrutiny, study

**survive** endure, exist, last, live, live on, outlast, outlive, remain alive

**susceptible** (usu. with to) disposed, given, inclined, liable, prone, subject; easily moved, impressionable, sensitive, suggestible

**suspect** v distrust, doubt, mistrust; believe, conjecture, consider, fancy, guess, speculate, suppose, surmise ~adj doubtful, dubious, iffy Inf, questionable

**suspend** dangle, hang; arrest, cease, cut short, defer, delay, discontinue, interrupt, postpone, put off, shelve

**suspense** anxiety, apprehension, doubt, insecurity, tension, uncertainty

**suspicion** distrust, doubt, misgiving, mistrust, scepticism, wariness; glimmer, hint, shade, suggestion, tinge, touch, trace

**suspicious** doubtful, sceptical, unbelieving, wary; dodgy Brit, Aust, & NZ inf, doubtful, dubious, funny, queer, questionable

**sustain** bear, carry, support, uphold; bear, endure, experience, suffer, withstand; approve, confirm, maintain, ratify

**swallow** absorb, consume, devour, drink, eat, gulp

**swamp** n bog, fen, marsh, morass, quagmire ~v drench, engulf, flood,

**swarm¹** n large cluster of insects; vast crowd ~v (of bees) be on the move in swarm; gather in large numbers

**swarm²** v climb (rope etc.) by grasping with hands and knees

**swarthy** adj dark-complexioned

**swashbuckler** n daredevil adventurer **swashbuckling** adj

**swastika** n symbol of cross with arms bent at right angles

**swat** v **swatting, swatted** hit smartly; kill, esp. insects

**swathe** v cover with wraps or bandages

**sway** v swing unsteadily; (cause to) vacillate in opinion etc. ~n control; power; swaying motion

**swear** v **swearing, swore, sworn** promise on oath; cause to take an oath; declare; curse **swearword** n word considered obscene or blasphemous

**sweat** n moisture oozing from, forming on skin; Inf state of anxiety ~v (cause to) exude sweat; toil **sweaty** adj **sweatshirt** n long-sleeved cotton jersey

**sweater** n woollen jersey

**swede** n variety of turnip

**sweep** v **sweeping, swept** clean with broom; pass quickly or magnificently; extend in continuous curve; carry away suddenly ~n act of cleaning with broom; sweeping motion; wide curve; one who cleans chimneys **sweeping** adj wide-ranging; without limitations **sweepstake** n lottery with stakes of participants as prize

**sweet** adj tasting like sugar; agreeable; kind, charming; fragrant; tuneful; dear, beloved ~n small piece of sweet food; sweet course served at end of meal **sweeten** v **sweetener** n sweetening agent; Sl bribe **sweetness** n **sweet corn** type of maize with sweet yellow kernels **sweetheart** n lover **sweet pea** plant of pea family with bright flowers **sweet-talk** v Inf coax, flatter

**swell** v **swelling, swelled, swollen** or **swelled** expand; be greatly filled with pride, emotion ~n act of swelling or being swollen; wave of sea **swelling** n enlargement of part of body, caused by injury or infection

**swelter** v be oppressed by heat

---

### THESAURUS

inundate, overwhelm, submerge

**swap, swop** v barter, exchange, interchange, switch, trade, traffic

**swarm** n army, crowd, drove, flock, herd, horde, host, mass, multitude, shoal, throng ~v crowd, flock, throng (*with* with) abound, crawl, teem

**sway** v lurch, rock, roll, swing, wave; affect, control, govern, influence, persuade ~n authority, command, control, influence, jurisdiction, power, rule, sovereignty

**swear** affirm, assert, attest, avow, declare, promise, testify, vow;

blaspheme, curse

**sweaty** clammy, perspiring, sticky

**sweep** v brush, clean, clear, remove ~n arc, bend, curve, stroke, swing

**sweeping** all-embracing, all-inclusive, broad, comprehensive, global, wide; blanket, indiscriminate, unqualified, wholesale

**sweet** adj cloying, honeyed, sweetened, treacly; affectionate, agreeable, amiable, appealing, charming, cute, engaging, kind, likable *or* likeable, lovable

**sweetheart** beloved, boyfriend,

**swerve** v swing round, change direction during motion; turn aside (from duty etc.) ~n swerving

**swift** adj rapid, quick ~n bird like a swallow

**swig** n large swallow of drink ~v **swigging, swigged** drink thus

**swill** v drink greedily; pour water over or through ~n liquid pig food; rinsing

**swim** v **swimming, swam, swum** support and move oneself in water; float; be flooded; have feeling of dizziness ~n spell of swimming **swimmer** n **swimmingly** adv successfully

**swindle** n/v cheat **swindler** n

**swine** n (pl **swine**) pig; contemptible person

**swing** v **swinging, swung** (cause to) move to and fro; (cause to) pivot, turn; hang; be hanged; hit out (at) ~n act, instance of swinging; seat hung to swing on; fluctuation (esp. in voting pattern)

**swingeing** adj punishing, severe

**swipe** v strike with wide, sweeping or glancing blow

**swirl** v (cause to) move with eddying motion ~n such motion

**swish** v (cause to) move with hissing sound ~n the sound

**switch** n mechanism to complete or interrupt electric circuit etc.; abrupt change; flexible stick or twig; tress of false hair ~v change abruptly; exchange; affect (current etc.) with switch **switchboard** n installation for connecting telephone calls

**swivel** n mechanism of two parts which can revolve the one on the other ~v **-elling, -elled** turn (on swivel)

**swoop** v dive, as hawk ~n act of swooping

**sword** n weapon with long blade **swordfish** n fish with elongated sharp upper jaw

**swot** Inf v **swotting, swotted** study hard ~n one who works hard at lessons

**sycamore** n tree related to maple

**sycophant** n one using flattery to gain favours **sycophantic** adj

**syllable** n division of word as unit for pronunciation

**syllabus** n (pl **-buses, -bi**) outline of course of study

**syllogism** n form of logical reasoning consisting of two premises

———————— THESAURUS ————————

darling, dear, girlfriend, love, lover

**swell** v balloon, billow, bloat, bulge, distend, enlarge, expand, grow, increase, rise

**swelling** n bulge, bump, enlargement, lump, protuberance

**swerve** v bend, deflect, deviate, diverge, stray, swing, turn, turn aside, veer

**swift** fast, fleet, prompt, quick, rapid, speedy, sudden

**swindle** n deception, fraud, racket, scam Sl, sting Inf, trickery ~v cheat, deceive, defraud, dupe, fleece,

overcharge, skin Sl, sting Inf, trick

**swindler** charlatan, cheat, fraud, impostor, mountebank, trickster

**swing** v fluctuate, oscillate, sway, vary, veer; dangle, hang, suspend ~n fluctuation, stroke, sway

**swirl** v churn, eddy, twist

**switch** n alteration, change, exchange, reversal, shift, substitution ~v change, deflect, deviate, exchange, shift, substitute, trade

**swoop** v descend, dive, pounce, stoop, sweep ~n drop, pounce, rush

**syllabus** course, course of study,

**symbol** n sign; thing representing or typifying something **symbolic** adj **symbolism** n **symbolize** v

**symmetry** n proportion between parts **symmetrical** adj

**sympathy** n feeling for another in pain etc.; compassion, pity; sharing of emotion etc. **sympathetic** adj **sympathize** v

**symphony** n composition for full orchestra

**symposium** n (pl **-siums, -sia**) conference

**symptom** n change in body indicating disease; sign **symptomatic** adj

**synagogue** n Jewish place of worship

**sync** n Inf synchronization

**synchromesh** adj (of gearbox) having device that synchronizes speeds of gears before they engage

**synchronize** v make agree in time; happen at same time **synchronization** n

**syncopate** v accentuate weak beat in bar of music **syncopation** n

**syndicate** n body of persons associated for some enterprise ~v form syndicate; publish in many newspapers at the same time

**syndrome** n combination of several symptoms in disease

**synod** n church council

**synonym** n word with same meaning as another **synonymous** adj

**synopsis** n summary, outline

**syntax** n arrangement of words in sentence

**synthesis** n (pl **-ses**) putting together, combination **synthesize** v make artificially **synthesizer** n electronic keyboard instrument reproducing wide range of musical sounds **synthetic** adj artificial; of synthesis

**syphilis** n contagious venereal disease

**syringe** n instrument for drawing in liquid and forcing it out in fine spray ~v spray, cleanse with syringe

**syrup** n thick solution obtained in process of refining sugar; any liquid like this

**system** n complex whole; method; classification **systematic** adj methodical

——————— THESAURUS ———————

curriculum

**symbol** badge, emblem, figure, image, representation, sign, token

**symbolize** denote, mean, personify, represent, signify, stand for, typify

**symmetrical** balanced, proportional, regular

**symmetry** balance, evenness, harmony, proportion

**sympathetic** caring, compassionate, concerned, kind, kindly, pitying, supportive

**sympathize** commiserate, feel for, pity

**sympathy** compassion, pity, tenderness, understanding; affinity, agreement, harmony, rapport, union

**symptom** indication, mark, sign, token, warning

**synthetic** artificial, fake, manmade, mock

**system** method, practice, procedure, routine, technique; arrangement, classification, organization, scheme, structure

**systematic** efficient, methodical, orderly, organized

# T t

**ta** *interj Inf* thank you

**tab** *n* tag, label, short strap

**Tabasco** *n Trademark* hot red pepper sauce

**tabby** *n/adj* (cat) with stripes on lighter background

**table** *n* flat board supported by legs; facts, figures arranged in lines or columns ~*v* submit (motion etc.) for discussion **tablespoon** *n* spoon for serving food

**tableau** *n* (*pl* **-leaux**) group of persons representing some scene

**tablet** *n* pill of compressed powdered medicine; cake of soap etc.; inscribed slab of stone, wood etc.

**table tennis** ball game played on table

**tabloid** *n* small-sized newspaper with many photographs and usu. sensational style

**taboo** *adj* forbidden ~*n* prohibition resulting from social conventions etc.

**tabulate** *v* arrange (figures etc.) in tables

**tacit** *adj* implied but not spoken

**taciturn** *adj* habitually silent

**tack¹** *n* small nail; long loose stitch; *Naut* course of ship obliquely to windward; approach, method ~*v* nail with tacks; stitch lightly; append; sail to windward

**tack²** *n* riding harness for horses

**tackle** *n* equipment, esp. for lifting; *Sport* physical challenge of opponent ~*v* undertake; challenge

**tacky¹** *adj* sticky; not quite dry

**tacky²** *adj* vulgar, tasteless

**tact** *n* skill in dealing with people or situations **tactful** *adj* **tactless** *adj*

**tactics** *pl n* art of handling troops, ships in battle; methods, plans **tactical** *adj* **tactician** *n*

**tactile** *adj* of sense of touch

**tadpole** *n* immature frog

**taffeta** *n* stiff silk fabric

**tag¹** *n* label identifying or showing price of (something); hanging end ~*v* **tagging, tagged** add (on)

**tag²** *n* children's game where one chased becomes the chaser upon

---

## THESAURUS

**table** *n* chart, diagram, graph, index, list ~*v* move, propose, put forward, submit, suggest

**taboo** *adj* banned, forbidden, outlawed, prohibited, proscribed, unmentionable ~*n* anathema, ban, prohibition, proscription

**tacit** implicit, implied, silent, understood, unspoken, unstated

**taciturn** quiet, reserved, reticent, silent, unforthcoming

**tack¹** *n* nail, pin; approach, bearing, course, direction, line, method, path, way ~*v* affix, attach, fasten, fix, nail, pin

**tackle** *n* apparatus, equipment, gear, tools, trappings; block, challenge, stop ~*v* attempt, essay, have a stab at *Inf*, undertake; block, bring down, challenge, halt, stop

**tact** delicacy, diplomacy, discretion, judgment

**tactful** careful, considerate, delicate, diplomatic, discreet, sensitive, thoughtful

**tactical** artful, clever, cunning, shrewd, smart

**tactless** careless, clumsy, gauche, inconsiderate, indiscreet, insensitive, thoughtless, unfeeling

being touched ~v **tagging, tagged touch**

**tail** n flexible appendage at animal's rear; hindmost; lower or inferior part of anything; pl reverse side of coin ~v remove tail of; Inf follow closely **tailback** n queue of traffic stretching back from obstruction **tailboard** n hinged rear board on lorry etc. **tail coat** man's evening dress jacket **tail off** diminish gradually **tailspin** n spinning dive of aircraft **tailwind** n wind coming from rear

**tailor** n maker of clothing, esp. for men **tailor-made** adj well-fitting

**taint** v affect or be affected by pollution etc. ~n defect; contamination

**take** v taking, took, taken grasp; get; receive; understand; consider; use; capture; steal; accept; bear; consume; assume; carry; accompany; subtract; require; contain; hold; be effective; please ~n (recording of) scene filmed without break **takings** pl n earnings; receipts **take after** resemble in face or character **takeaway** n shop, restaurant selling meals for eating elsewhere; meal bought at this place **take in** understand; include; make (garment etc.) smaller; deceive **take off** remove; (of aircraft) leave ground; Inf go away; Inf mimic **take-off** n **takeover** n act of taking control of company by buying large number of its shares

**talc** also **talcum powder** n powder, usu. scented, to absorb body moisture

**tale** n story, narrative

**talent** n natural ability **talented** adj gifted

**talisman** n object supposed to have magic power

**talk** v express, exchange ideas etc. in words; discuss ~n lecture; conversation; rumour; discussion **talkative** adj

**taint** v contaminate, corrupt, dirty, foul, infect, pollute, spoil ~n defect, disgrace, dishonour, fault, flaw, smear, smirch, stain

**take** v clutch, grasp, grip, seize; acquire, get, obtain, receive, secure, win; appropriate, filch, nick Sl, chiefly Brit, pocket, purloin, steal; accept, book, buy, engage, hire, lease, purchase, rent; abide, bear, endure, stand, stomach, suffer, swallow, tolerate; consume, drink, eat, ingest, inhale, swallow; bear, bring, carry, convey, fetch, transport; accompany, bring, conduct, escort, guide, lead; deduct, remove, subtract

**take in** absorb, assimilate, comprehend, digest, grasp, understand; cheat, deceive, fool, hoodwink, swindle, trick

**take off** discard, doff, drop, peel off, remove, strip off; Inf caricature, imitate, lampoon, mimic, mock, parody, satirize

**tale** n account, anecdote, fable, fiction, legend, saga, story, urban legend

**talent** ability, aptitude, faculty, flair, genius, gift

**talented** able, artistic, brilliant, gifted

**talk** v chat, chatter, converse, gossip, say, speak, utter, confer, discuss, have a confab Inf, hold discussions, negotiate ~n address, discourse, lecture, oration, sermon, speech; chat, chatter, chitchat, con-

**tall** *adj* high; of great stature

**tally** *v* **tallying, tallied** correspond one with the other; count ~*n* record, account

**talon** *n* claw

**tambourine** *n* flat half-drum with jingling discs of metal attached

**tame** *adj* not wild, domesticated; uninteresting ~*v* make tame

**tamper** *v* interfere (with)

**tampon** *n* plug of cotton wool inserted into vagina during menstruation

**tan** *adj/n* (of) brown colour of skin after exposure to sun etc. ~*v* **tanning, tanned** (cause to) go brown; (of animal hide) convert to leather

**tannin** *n* vegetable substance used as tanning agent

**tandem** *n* bicycle for two

**tandoori** *adj* (of Indian food) cooked in a clay oven

**tang** *n* strong pungent taste or smell **tangy** *adj*

**tangent** *n* line that touches a curve **tangential** *adj*

**tangerine** *n* (fruit of) Asian citrus tree

**tangible** *adj* that can be touched;

real **tangibility** *n*

**tangle** *n* confused mass or situation ~*v* confuse

**tango** *n* (*pl* **-gos**) dance of S Amer. origin

**tank** *n* storage vessel for liquids or gases; armoured motor vehicle on tracks **tanker** *n* ship, lorry for carrying liquid

**tankard** *n* large drinking cup

**Tannoy** *n* Trademark type of public-address system

**tantalize** *v* torment by appearing to offer something

**tantamount** *adj* equivalent, equal (to)

**tantrum** *n* outburst of temper

**tap**[1] *v* **tapping, tapped** strike lightly but with some noise ~*n* tapping **tap dance** dance in which the feet beat out elaborate rhythms

**tap**[2] *n* valve with handle, plug etc. to regulate or stop flow of fluid ~*v* **tapping, tapped** draw off with tap; use, draw on; make secret connection to telephone wire to overhear conversation on it

**tape** *n* narrow strip of fabric, paper etc.; magnetic recording ~*v* record

──────── THESAURUS ────────

versation; gossip, hearsay, rumour; conference, congress, consultation, dialogue, discussion, meeting, seminar, symposium

**talkative** chatty, garrulous, long-winded, loquacious, verbose, voluble, wordy

**tall** big, giant, high, lanky, lofty

**tally** *v* accord, agree, correspond, match, square; count, mark, reckon, total ~*n* count, mark, reckoning, score, total

**tame** *adj* cultivated, disciplined, docile, obedient; bland, boring, dull, flat, insipid ~*v* break in, do-

mesticate, pacify, train

**tamper** interfere, meddle, muck about *Brit slf*, tinker

**tangle** *n* coil, confusion, knot, mass, mesh, snarl; complication, labyrinth, maze, mess, mix-up ~*v* coil, knot, mat, mesh, snarl

**tantalize** taunt, tease, torment, torture

**tantrum** fit, ill humour, outburst, storm, temper

**tap**[1] *v/n* beat, knock, pat, rap, touch

**tap**[2] *n* spigot, spout, stopcock, valve ~*v* draw on, exploit, milk,

(speech, music etc.) **tape measure** tape marked off in centimetres, inches etc. **tape recorder** apparatus for recording sound on magnetized tape **tapeworm** long flat parasitic worm

**taper** v become gradually thinner ~n thin candle

**tapestry** n fabric decorated with woven designs

**tapioca** n beadlike starch made from cassava root

**tar** n thick black liquid distilled from coal etc. ~v tarring, tarred coat, treat with tar

**tarantula** n (pl **-las**, **-lae**) large (poisonous) hairy spider

**tardy** adj slow, late

**target** n thing aimed at; victim

**tariff** n tax levied on imports etc.; list of charges

**Tarmac** n Trademark mixture of tar etc. giving hard, smooth surface to road

**tarn** n small mountain lake

**tarnish** v (cause to) become stained or sullied ~n discoloration, blemish

**tarot** n pack of cards used in fortune-telling

**tarpaulin** n (sheet of) heavy hard-wearing waterproof fabric

**tarragon** n aromatic herb

**tarry** v tarrying, tarried linger, delay; stay behind

**tart¹** n small pie or flan filled with fruit, jam etc.; loose woman

**tart²** adj sour; sharp; bitter

**tartan** n woollen cloth woven in pattern of coloured checks

**tartar** n crust deposited on teeth

**task** n piece of work (esp. unpleasant or difficult) set or undertaken **taskmaster** n overseer

**tassel** n ornament of fringed knot of threads etc.; tuft

**taste** n sense by which flavour, quality of substance is detected by the tongue; (brief) experience of something; small amount; liking; power of discerning, judging ~v observe or distinguish the taste of a substance; take small amount into mouth; experience; have specific flavour **tasteful** adj with, showing good taste **tasteless** adj bland, insipid; showing bad taste **tasty** adj pleasantly flavoured **taste bud** small organ of taste on tongue

**tattered** adj ragged **tatters** pl n

mine, use, utilize

**tape** n band, ribbon, strip ~v record, video

**taper** come to a point, narrow, thin

**target** aim, end, goal, intention, mark, object, objective; butt, quarry, scapegoat, victim

**tariff** duty, excise, levy, rate, tax, toll

**tarnish** dim, dull, rust, smirch, stain, sully, taint

**tart¹** harlot, loose woman, prostitute, scrubber Brit & Aust sl, slag Brit sl, slut, strumpet, trollop,

whore

**tart²** acid, bitter, pungent, sharp, sour, tangy; biting, caustic, sharp, short, snappish

**task** n assignment, chore, duty, job, mission

**taste** n flavour, relish, savour, smack; bit, bite, dash, drop, morsel, mouthful, sample, sip, swallow; appetite, bent, desire, fancy, inclination, leaning, liking, penchant, preference; appreciation, cultivation, culture, discernment, discrimination, judgment, refinement,

ragged pieces

**tattle** *v/n* gossip, chatter

**tattoo**[1] *n* beat of drum and bugle call; military spectacle

**tattoo**[2] *v* tattooing, tattooed mark skin in coloured patterns etc. by pricking ~*n* pattern made thus

**tatty** *adj* shabby, worn out

**taunt** *v* provoke with insults etc. ~*n* scornful remark

**taupe** *adj* brownish-grey

**taut** *adj* drawn tight; under strain

**tavern** *n* inn, public house

**tawdry** *adj* showy, but cheap

**tawny** *adj/n* (of) light yellowish-brown colour

**tax** *n* compulsory payments imposed by government to raise revenue; heavy demand on something ~*v* impose tax on; strain **taxation** *n* levying of taxes **tax return** statement of income for tax purposes

**taxi** *also* **taxicab** *n* (*pl* **taxis**) motor vehicle for hire with driver ~*v* **taxiing**, **taxied** (of aircraft) run along ground

**taxidermy** *n* art of stuffing animal skins **taxidermist** *n*

**TB** tuberculosis

**tea** *n* dried leaves of plant cultivated esp. in Asia; infusion of it as beverage; meal eaten in afternoon or early evening **tea bag** small porous bag of tea leaves **teapot** *n* container for making and serving tea **teaspoon** *n* small spoon for stirring tea etc. **tea towel** towel for drying dishes

**teach** *v* **teaching**, **taught** instruct; educate; train **teacher** *n*

**teak** *n* (hard wood from) E Indian tree

**team** *n* set of animals, players of game etc. ~*v* (*usu.* with up) (cause to) make a team **teamwork** *n* cooperative work by team

**tear**[1] *n* drop of fluid falling from eye **tearful** *adj* inclined to weep; involving tears **teardrop** *n* **tear gas** irritant gas causing temporary blindness

**tear**[2] *v* **tearing**, **tore**, **torn** pull apart; become torn; rush ~*n* hole or split **tearaway** *n* wild or unruly

sophistication, style ~*v* sample, savour, sip, test, try

**tasteful** beautiful, charming, cultivated, elegant, exquisite, polished, refined, smart, stylish

**tasteless** bland, boring, dull, flat, insipid, thin, uninteresting, vapid, weak; cheap, coarse, crass, crude, flashy, gross, improper, indelicate, low, naff *Brit sl* rude, tacky *Inf*, tawdry, uncouth, vulgar

**tasty** appetizing, delectable, delicious, luscious, palatable

**taunt** *v* deride, insult, jeer, mock, ridicule, tease ~*n* dig, gibe, insult, jeer, ridicule

**taut** rigid, strained, stretched, tense, tight

**tax** *n* charge, customs, duty, excise, levy, rate, tariff, toll, tribute ~*v* charge, impose; burden, drain, exhaust, load, overburden, push, sap, strain, stretch, try

**teach** advise, coach, direct, educate, guide, inform, instruct, school, show, train, tutor

**teacher** coach, guide, instructor, lecturer, master, mentor, mistress, professor, schoolmaster, schoolmistress, trainer, tutor

**team** *n* band, body, bunch, company, crew, gang, group, side, squad, troupe *v* (*usu.* with up) cooperate, couple, get together, join, link

person

**tease** v tantalize, torment, irritate **~n** one who teases

**teat** n nipple of breast; rubber nipple of baby's bottle

**technical** adj of, specializing in industrial, practical or mechanical arts; belonging to particular art or science; according to letter of the law **technicality** n point of procedure **technician** n one skilled in technique of an art **technique** n method of performance in an art; skill required for mastery of subject

**Technicolor** n Trademark colour photography, esp. in cinema

**technology** n application of practical, mechanical sciences; technical skills, knowledge **technological** adj

**teddy** also **teddy bear** n child's soft toy bear

**tedious** adj causing fatigue or boredom **tedium** n monotony

**tee** n Golf place from which first stroke of hole is made; small peg supporting ball for first stroke

**teem** v abound with; swarm; rain heavily

**teens** pl n years of life from 13 to 19 **teenage** adj **teenager** n young

**teeter** v seesaw, wobble

**teeth** n pl of TOOTH

**teethe** v (of baby) grow first teeth **teething troubles** problems, difficulties at first stage of something

**teetotal** adj pledged to abstain from alcohol **teetotaller** n

**Teflon** n Trademark substance used for nonstick coatings on saucepans etc.

**telecommunications** pl n (with sing v) communications by telephone, television etc.

**telegram** n formerly, message sent by telegraph

**telegraph** n formerly, electrical apparatus for transmitting messages over distance **~v** send by telegraph

**telepathy** n action of one mind on another at a distance **telepathic** adj

**telephone** n apparatus for communicating sound to hearer at a distance **~v** communicate, speak by telephone **telephonist** n person operating telephone switchboard

**telephoto** adj (of lens) producing magnified image

**teleprinter** n apparatus for sending and receiving typed messages

———————————————————— T H E S A U R U S ————————————————————

**tear** v claw, rend, rip, scratch, shred **~n** hole, rent, rip, rupture, scratch

**tearful** crying, sobbing, weeping

**tease** annoy, badger, bait, chaff, goad, mock, needle Inf, pester, provoke, taunt, torment, wind up Brit sl

**technique** fashion, means, method, mode, procedure, style, system, way; art, artistry, craft, knack, proficiency, skill, touch

**tedious** banal, boring, dreary, dull, ho-hum Inf, laborious, mind-numbing, monotonous, unexciting, uninteresting, wearisome

**tedium** banality, boredom, dreariness, dullness, monotony, routine, tediousness

**teem** abound, brim, bristle, overflow, swarm

**telepathy** mind-reading, sixth sense, thought transference

**telephone** v call, call up, phone, ring Inf, chiefly Brit

by wire

**telescope** *n* optical instrument for magnifying distant objects ~v slide together **telescopic** *adj*

**teletext** *n* electronic system which shows information, news on subscribers' television screens

**television** *n* system of producing on screen images of distant objects, events etc. by electromagnetic radiation; device for receiving this; programmes etc. viewed on television set **televise** *v* transmit by television; make, produce as television programme

**telex** *n* international communication service ~v send by telex

**tell** *v* **telling, told** let know; order; narrate, make known; discern; distinguish; give account; be of weight, importance **teller** *n* narrator; bank cashier **telling** *adj* effective, striking **tell off** reprimand **telltale** *n* sneak ~*adj* revealing

**telly** *n Inf* television (set)

**temerity** *n* boldness, audacity

**temp** *n Inf* one employed on temporary basis

**temper** *n* frame of mind; angry state; calmness, composure ~v restrain, moderate; harden (metal)

**temperament** *n* natural disposition; emotional mood **temperamental** *adj* moody; erratic

**temperate** *adj* (of climate) mild; not extreme; showing moderation

**temperance** *n* moderation; abstinence, esp. from alcohol

**temperature** *n* degree of heat or coldness; *Inf* high body temperature

**tempest** *n* violent storm **tempestuous** *adj* stormy; violent

**template** *n* pattern used to cut out shapes accurately

**temple**[1] *n* building for worship

**temple**[2] *n* flat part on either side of forehead

**tempo** *n* (*pl* **-pos, -pi**) rate, rhythm

**temporal** *adj* of time; of this life or world

**temporary** *adj* lasting only a short time

**tempt** *v* try to persuade, entice, esp. to something wrong or unwise **temptation** *n* **tempter** *n* (*fem*

**tell** announce, communicate, confess, disclose, divulge, express, impart, inform, notify, proclaim, reveal, say, speak, state; bid, command, direct, instruct; order; depict, describe, narrate, recount, relate, report

**temper** *n* attitude, disposition, humour, mood, nature, vein; anger, annoyance, fury, heat, irritability, petulance, rage, tantrum

**temperament** bent, character, constitution, humour, make-up, nature, personality

**temperamental** emotional, excitable, moody, passionate, sensitive,

touchy, volatile; erratic, unreliable

**temperance** moderation, restraint, self-control, self-restraint; abstinence, teetotalism

**temperate** balmy, fair, mild, pleasant; calm, mild, moderate, reasonable, sensible, stable

**tempestuous** blustery, inclement, raging, squally, stormy, turbulent; emotional, heated, impassioned, intense, passionate, stormy, turbulent, uncontrolled, violent, wild

**temple** church, sanctuary, shrine

**temporary** brief, ephemeral, fleeting, interim, momentary, passing, provisional, transient

**temptress**) **tempting** adj attractive, inviting

**ten** n/adj cardinal number after nine **tenth** adj ordinal number

**tenable** adj able to be held, defended, maintained

**tenacious** adj holding fast; retentive; stubborn **tenacity** n

**tenant** n one who holds lands, house etc. on rent or lease **tenancy** n

**tench** n freshwater fish

**tend¹** v be inclined; be conducive; make in direction of **tendency** n inclination **tendentious** adj controversial

**tend²** v take care of

**tender¹** adj not tough; easily injured; gentle, loving; delicate

**tender²** v offer; make offer or estimate ~n offer or estimate for contract to undertake specific work **legal tender** currency that must, by law, be accepted as payment

**tendon** n sinew attaching muscle to bone etc.

**tendril** n slender curling stem by which climbing plant clings

**tenement** n building divided into separate flats

**tenet** n belief

**tennis** n game in which ball is struck with racket by players on opposite sides of net

**tenor** n male voice between alto and bass; general course, meaning

**tenpin bowling** game in which players try to knock over ten skittles with ball

**tense¹** n form of verb showing time of action

**tense²** adj stretched tight; taut; emotionally strained ~v make, become tense **tensile** adj of, relating to tension **tension** n stretching; strain when stretched; emotional strain; suspense; *Electricity* voltage

**tent** n portable shelter of canvas

**tentacle** n flexible organ of some animals (e.g. octopus) used for

——————— THESAURUS ———————

**tempt** allure, attract, coax, draw, entice, invite, lure, seduce

**temptation** allurement, attraction, coaxing, draw, inducement, invitation, lure, pull, seduction

**tempting** alluring, attractive, enticing, inviting, seductive

**tenable** defendable, defensible, justifiable, maintainable, plausible, rational, reasonable, sound, viable

**tenacious** clinging, fast, firm, immovable, strong, tight; determined, dogged, firm, immovable, inflexible, obstinate, persistent, resolute, stiff-necked, stubborn, unyielding

**tenancy** holding, lease, occupancy, possession, residence

**tenant** holder, inhabitant, leaseholder, lessee, occupier, resident

**tend¹** gravitate, incline, lean

**tend²** cultivate, keep, look after, maintain, nurse

**tendency** inclination, leaning, partiality, penchant, predilection, predisposition, propensity

**tender** aching, bruised, delicate, inflamed, irritated, painful, raw, sensitive, smarting, sore; affectionate, amorous, caring, fond, gentle, kind, loving, warm

**tense** rigid, strained, stretched, taut, tight; edgy, fidgety, jumpy, keyed up, nervous, restless, strained, twitchy *Inf*, wired *Sl*; stressful, worrying

**tension** stiffness, stress, tautness, tightness; pressure, strain, stress, unease

grasping, feeding etc.

**tentative** *adj* experimental; cautious

**tenterhooks** *pl n* **on tenterhooks** in anxious suspense

**tenuous** *adj* flimsy; thin

**tenure** *n* (length of time of) possession of office etc.

**tepee** *n* N Amer. Indian cone-shaped tent

**tepid** *adj* moderately warm

**tequila** *n* Mexican alcoholic drink

**term** *n* word, expression; limited period of time; period during which schools are open; *pl* conditions; relationship ~*v* name

**terminal** *adj* at, forming an end; (of disease) ending in death ~*n* terminal part or structure; point where current enters, leaves battery etc.; device permitting operation of computer at distance

**terminate** *v* bring, come to an end **termination**

**terminology** *n* set of technical terms or vocabulary

**terminus** *n* (*pl* **-ni**, **-nuses**) finishing point; railway station etc. at end

of line

**termite** *n* wood-eating insect

**tern** *n* sea bird like gull

**terpsichorean** *adj* of dancing

**terrace** *n* raised level place; row of houses built as one block; (*oft. pl*) unroofed tiers for spectators at sports stadium ~*v* form into terrace

**terracotta** *n/adj* (made of) hard unglazed pottery; (of) brownish-red colour

**terrain** *n* area of ground, esp. with reference to its physical character

**terrapin** *n* type of aquatic tortoise

**terrestrial** *adj* of the earth; of, living on land

**terrible** *adj* serious; *Inf* very bad; causing fear **terribly** *adv*

**terrier** *n* small dog of various breeds

**terrific** *adj* very great; *Inf* good; awe-inspiring

**terrify** *v* frighten greatly **terrifying** *adj*

**territory** *n* region; geographical area, esp. a sovereign state **territorial** *adj* **Territorial Army** reserve army

**tentative** experimental, indefinite, provisional, speculative; cautious, diffident, hesitant, timid, uncertain, unsure

**term** *n* denomination, designation, expression, name, phrase, title, word; period, season, space, spell, time; course, session ~*v* call, denominate, designate, dub, entitle, label, name, style

**terminal** *adj* deadly, fatal, incurable, killing, lethal, mortal

**terminate** axe *Inf*, cease, close, conclude, cut off, discontinue, end, expire, finish, lapse, run out, stop, wind up

**termination** cessation, close, conclusion, discontinuation, end, ending, expiry, finish

**terrible** bad, dangerous, extreme, serious, severe; *Inf* abysmal, awful, bad, dire, dreadful, frightful, godawful *Sl*; awful, dreadful, fearful, frightful, gruesome, horrible, horrifying, monstrous, shocking

**terrific** enormous, extreme, great, huge, intense, tremendous; *Inf* amazing, breathtaking, brilliant, cracking *Brit inf*, excellent, fine, marvellous, mean *Sl*, outstanding, superb, wonderful

**terrify** frighten, intimidate, petrify,

**terror** n great fear; Inf troublesome person or thing **terrorism** n use of violence to achieve ends **terrorist** n/adj **terrorize** v oppress by violence; **terrify**

**terse** adj concise; abrupt

**tertiary** adj third in degree, order etc.

**Terylene** n Trademark synthetic yarn; fabric made of it

**test** v try, put to the proof; carry out examination on ~n examination; means of trial **testing** adj difficult **test case** lawsuit viewed as means of establishing precedent **test match** international sports contest, esp. one of series **test tube** tubelike glass vessel

**testament** n Law will; (with cap.) one of the two main divisions of the Bible

**testate** adj (of dead person) having left a valid will

**testicle** also **testis** n either of two male reproductive glands

**testify** v -fying, -fied declare; bear witness (to)

**testimony** n affirmation; evidence

**testimonial** n certificate of charac-

ter etc.; gift expressing regard for recipient

**testy** adj irritable

**tetanus** n (also called **lockjaw**) acute infectious disease

**tête-à-tête** n private conversation

**tether** n rope for fastening (grazing) animal ~v tie up with rope

**tetrahedron** n solid contained by four plane faces

**text** n (actual words of) book, passage etc.; passage of Bible **textual** adj **textbook** n book of instruction on particular subject

**textile** n any fabric or cloth, esp. woven

**texture** n structure, appearance; consistency

**than** conj introduces second part of comparison

**thank** v express gratitude to; say thanks **thankful** adj grateful **thankless** adj unrewarding or unappreciated **thanks** pl n words of gratitude

**that** adj refers to thing already mentioned; refers to thing further away ~pron refers to particular thing; introduces relative clause ~conj introduces noun or adverbial

——————— THESAURUS ———————

shock, terrorize

**territory** area, country, district, land, patch, province, region, turf US sl, zone

**terror** fear, fright, horror, intimidation, panic, shock

**terrorize** browbeat, bully, intimidate, menace, oppress, threaten

**terse** brief, clipped, concise, crisp, laconic, pithy, short, succinct; abrupt, brusque, curt, short

**test** v analyse, check, experiment, investigate, prove, research, try, verify ~n analysis, check, examination, investigation, research, trial

**testify** affirm, assert, attest, bear witness, certify, corroborate, declare, state, swear, vouch

**testimonial** certificate, commendation, endorsement, tribute

**testimony** affidavit, attestation, corroboration, deposition, evidence, statement

**text** body, matter, wording, words

**texture** consistency, feel, grain, structure, surface, tissue

**thankful** appreciative, grateful, indebted, obliged

**thanks** acknowledgment, appreciation, credit, gratefulness, gratitude,

clause

**thatch** *n* reeds, straw etc. used as roofing material ~*v* build roof with this

**thaw** *v* melt; (cause to) unfreeze ~*n* melting (of frost etc.)

**the** *adj* the definite article

**theatre** *n* place where plays etc. are performed; dramatic works generally; hospital operating room **theatrical** *adj* of, for the theatre; exaggerated

**thee** *pron Obs* object of THOU

**theft** *n* stealing

**their** *adj* of, belonging to them **theirs** *pron* belonging to them

**them** *pron* object of THEY **themselves** *pron* emphatic or reflexive form of THEY

**theme** *n* main topic of book etc.; subject of composition; recurring melody **thematic** *adj* **theme park** leisure area designed round one subject

**then** *adv* at that time; next; that being so

**thence** *adv Obs* from that place or time

**theology** *n* systematic study of religion and religious beliefs **theologian** *n* **theological** *adj*

**theorem** *n* proposition which can be demonstrated

**theory** *n* supposition to account for something; system of rules and principles, esp. distinguished from practice **theoretical** *adj* based on theory; speculative

**therapy** *n* healing treatment **therapeutic** *adj* of healing; serving to improve health **therapist** *n*

**there** *adv* in that place; to that point **thereby** *adv* by that means **therefore** *adv* that being so **thereupon** *adv* immediately

**therm** *n* unit of measurement of heat **thermal** *adj*

**thermodynamics** *pl n* (*with sing v*) science that deals with interrelationship of different forms of energy

**thermometer** *n* instrument to measure temperature

**Thermos** *n Trademark* vacuum flask

**thermostat** *n* apparatus for regulating temperature

**thesaurus** *n* (*pl* **-ruses**) book containing lists of synonyms

**these** *pron pl* of THIS

**thesis** *n* (*pl* **theses**) written work submitted for degree, diploma; theory maintained in argument

**thespian** *adj* of the theatre ~*n*

───── THESAURUS ─────

recognition, thanksgiving

**thaw** *v* defrost, melt, warm

**theatrical** affected, artificial, camp *Inf*, dramatic, exaggerated, histrionic, mannered, overdone, showy, stagy

**theft** larceny, pilfering, robbery, stealing

**theme** idea, keynote, matter, subject, topic

**theoretical** abstract, academic, impractical, notional, speculative

**theory** assumption, guess, hypothesis, speculation, surmise

**therapeutic** corrective, curative, healing, remedial

**therapy** cure, healing, remedial treatment, remedy, treatment

**therefore** accordingly, consequently, ergo, so, thus

**thesis** composition, dissertation, essay, paper, treatise; hypothesis, idea, line of argument, opinion, theory, view

actor, actress

**they** *pron* pronoun of the third person plural

**thick** *adj* fat, broad, not thin; dense; crowded; viscous; (of voice) throaty; *Inf* stupid ~*n* busiest part **thicken** *v* make, become thick; become complicated **thickness** *n* dimension through an object; layer **thickset** *adj* sturdy, stocky

**thicket** *n* thick growth of trees

**thief** *n* (*pl* **thieves**) one who steals **thieve** *v* steal

**thigh** *n* upper part of leg

**thimble** *n* cap protecting end of finger when sewing

**thin** *adj* of little thickness; slim; of little density; sparse; fine; not close-packed ~*v* **thinning, thinned** make, become thin

**thing** *n* (material) object; fact, idea

**think** *v* **thinking, thought** have one's mind at work; reflect, meditate; reason; deliberate; believe

**third** *adj* of number three in a series ~*n* third part **third degree** violent interrogation **third party** *Law, Insurance etc.* person involved by chance in legal proceedings etc.

**thirst** *n* desire to drink; feeling caused by lack of drink; craving ~*v* have thirst **thirsty** *adj*

**thirteen** *adj/n* three plus ten **thirteenth** *adj*

**thirty** *adj/n* three times ten **thirtieth** *adj*

**this** *adj/pron* denotes thing, person near or just mentioned

**thistle** *n* prickly plant

**thither** *adv Obs* to or towards that place

**thong** *n* narrow strip of leather, strap

**thorax** *n* part of body between neck and belly

**thorn** *n* prickle on plant; bush noted for its thorns **thorny** *adj*

**thorough** *adj* careful, methodical; complete **thoroughly** *adv* **thoroughbred** *n* pure-bred animal, esp. horse **thoroughfare** *n* road or passage; right of way

**thick** broad, deep, fat, solid, wide; compact, dense, heavy, opaque; bristling, bursting, chock-a-block, chock-full, covered, crawling, crowded, full, packed, swarming, teeming; dense, heavy, soupy, viscous; guttural, hoarse, husky, throaty; *Inf* braindead *Inf*, brainless, dense, dozy *Brit inf*, dull, obtuse, slow, stupid, thickheaded **thicken** cake, clot, condense, congeal

**thin** *adj* fine, narrow; bony, lanky, lean, meagre, skinny, slender, slight, slim, spare; diluted, runny, watery, weak; deficient, meagre, scanty, scarce, skimpy, sparse; delicate, filmy, fine, flimsy, sheer, un-

substantial

**thing** article, entity, item, object; affair, aspect, detail, facet, fact, factor, feature, idea, item, matter, point

**think** brood, cogitate, consider, deliberate, meditate, muse, ponder, reason, reflect; believe, conceive, conclude, consider, deem, esteem, estimate, guess *Inf, chiefly US & Canad,* imagine, judge, reckon, regard, suppose

**thirst** *n* dryness, thirstiness; appetite, craving, longing, passion, yearning

**thorough** careful, complete, conscientious, exhaustive, full, intensive, painstaking, scrupulous; abso-

**those** *pron pl of* THAT

**thou** *pron Obs* the second person singular pronoun

**though** *conj* even if *~adv* nevertheless

**thought** *n* process, product of thinking; what one thinks; meditation **thoughtful** *adj* considerate; showing careful thought; reflective **thoughtless** *adj* inconsiderate; careless

**thousand** *n/adj* ten hundred **thousandth** *adj*

**thrash** *v* beat; defeat soundly; move in wild manner

**thread** *n* yarn; ridge cut on screw; theme *~v* put thread into; fit film etc. into machine; put on thread; pick (one's way etc.) **threadbare** *adj* worn, shabby; hackneyed

**threat** *n* declaration of intention to harm, injure etc.; dangerous person or thing **threaten** *v* make or be

threat to

**three** *adj/n* one more than two **three-dimensional** *adj* having height, width and depth **three-ply** *adj* having three layers or strands **threesome** *n* group of three

**thresh** *v* beat to separate grain from husks; thrash

**threshold** *n* bar of stone forming bottom of doorway; entrance; starting point

**thrice** *adv* three times

**thrift** *n* saving, economy **thrifty** *adj* economical

**thrill** *n* sudden sensation of excitement and pleasure *~v* (cause to) feel a thrill; tremble **thriller** *n* suspenseful book, film etc. **thrilling** *adj*

**thrive** *v* thriving, throve *or* thrived, thriven *or* thrived grow well; prosper

**throat** *n* front of neck; passage from mouth to stomach **throaty** *adj*

———— THESAURUS ————

lute, complete, deep-dyed *usu derog*, downright, perfect, pure, sheer, total, utter

**though** *conj* allowing, even if, notwithstanding, tho' *US or poet*, while

**thought** cogitation, consideration, contemplation, deliberation, meditation, musing, reflection; belief, concept, idea, judgment, opinion, thinking, view

**thoughtful** attentive, caring, considerate, kind, solicitous; contemplative, meditative, musing, pensive, rapt, reflective, serious

**thoughtless** inconsiderate, insensitive, selfish, tactless; careless, foolish, heedless, mindless, silly, stupid, unthinking

**thrash** beat, belt *Inf*, birch, cane, clobber *Sl*, flog, leather, lick *Inf*, spank, whip; beat, clobber *Brit sl*,

crush, defeat, lick *Inf*, run rings around *Inf*, trounce

**threadbare** down at heel, frayed, old, shabby, worn, worn-out

**threat** intimidation, menace, warning

**threaten** endanger, jeopardize; browbeat, bully, cow, intimidate, menace

**threshold** door, doorway, entrance; beginning, brink, dawn, opening, outset, start

**thrift** carefulness, economy, saving

**thrifty** careful, economical, frugal, provident, saving, sparing

**thrill** *v* arouse, electrify, excite, move, stimulate, stir

**thrilling** exciting, gripping, sensational, stimulating, stirring

**thrive** bloom, boom, flourish, grow, increase, prosper, succeed

hoarse; deep, guttural

**throb** v **throbbing, throbbed** quiver strongly, pulsate ~n pulsation

**throes** pl n violent pangs, pain etc. **in the throes of** in the process of

**thrombosis** n clot in blood vessel or heart

**throne** n ceremonial seat; power of sovereign

**throng** n/v crowd

**throttle** n device controlling amount of fuel entering engine ~v strangle; restrict

**through** prep from end to end; in consequence of; by means of ~adv from end to end; to the end ~adj completed; Inf finished; continuous; (of transport, traffic) not stopping **throughout** adv/prep in every part (of) **throughput** n quantity of material processed

**throw** v **throwing, threw, thrown** fling, cast; move, put abruptly, carelessly; cause to fall ~n act or distance of throwing. **throwaway** adj designed to be discarded after use; done, said casually **throwback** n person, thing that reverts to earlier type

**thrush** n songbird

**thrust** v **thrusting, thrust** push, drive; stab ~n lunge, stab; propulsive force or power

**thud** n dull heavy sound ~v **thudding, thudded** make thud

**thug** n violent person

**thumb** n shortest, thickest finger of hand ~v handle with thumb; signal for lift in vehicle

**thump** n (sound of) dull heavy blow ~v strike heavily

**thunder** n loud noise accompanying lightning ~v make noise of or like thunder **thunderbolt, thunderclap** n lightning followed by thunder; anything unexpected

**Thursday** n fifth day of the week

**thus** adv in this way; therefore

**thwart** v foil, frustrate

**thy** adj Obs of or associated with you **thyself** pron emphatic or reflexive form of THOU

**thyme** n aromatic herb

**thyroid gland** gland controlling body growth

**tiara** n coronet

**tibia** n (pl **tibiae, tibias**) shinbone

**tic** n spasmodic twitch in muscles,

———————— THESAURUS ————————

**throb** v beat, pound, pulsate, thump ~n beat, pounding, pulsation, pulse, thumping

**through** prep between, during, in, in the middle of, throughout; by means of, by way of, using, via ~adj Inf completed, done, ended, finished

**throughout** everywhere, the whole time

**throw** v cast, heave, hurl, pitch, send, shy, sling, toss ~n cast, fling, heave, pitch, shy, sling, toss

**thrust** v drive, force, jam, plunge, propel, push, ram, shove; jab, lunge, pierce, stab, stick ~n lunge, push, shove, stab; impetus, momentum

**thug** heavy Sl, hooligan, ruffian, tough

**thump** n bang, blow, knock, smack, thud, whack ~v bang, batter, beat, hit, knock, pound, strike

**thunder** n boom, crash, pealing, rumble, rumbling ~v boom, crash, peal, resound, reverberate, roar, rumble

**thus** like this, so; accordingly, consequently, ergo, hence, then, therefore

esp. of face

**tick¹** *n* slight tapping sound, as of watch movement; small mark (Pt); *Inf* moment ~*v* mark with tick; make slight tapping sound

**tick²** *n* small insect-like parasite living on blood

**ticket** *n* card, paper entitling holder to admission, travel etc.; label ~*v* attach label to

**tickle** *v* touch, stroke (person etc.) to produce laughter etc.; amuse; itch ~*n* act, instance of this **ticklish** *adj* sensitive to tickling; requiring care

**tiddler** *n Inf* very small fish **tiddly** *adj* tiny; *Inf* slightly drunk

**tiddlywinks** *pl n* game of trying to flip small plastic discs into cup

**tide** *n* rise and fall of sea happening twice each day **tidal** *adj* **tidal wave** great wave, esp. produced by earthquake **tide over** help someone for a while

**tidings** *pl n* news

**tidy** *adj* orderly, neat ~*v* put in order

**tie** *v* **tying**, **tied** fasten, bind; restrict; equal (score of) ~*n* that with which anything is bound; restraint;

piece of material worn knotted round neck; connecting link; contest with equal scores; match, game in eliminating competition **tied** *adj* (of public house) selling beer etc. of only one brewer; (of cottage etc.) rented to tenant employed by owner

**tier** *n* row, rank, layer

**tiff** *n* petty quarrel

**tiger** *n* (*fem* **tigress**) large carnivorous feline animal

**tight** *adj* taut, tense; closely fitting; secure, firm; not allowing passage of water etc.; cramped; *Inf* mean; *Inf* drunk **tighten** *v* **tights** *pl n* onepiece clinging garment covering body from waist to feet **tightrope** *n* taut rope on which acrobats perform

**tile** *n* flat piece of ceramic, plastic etc. used for roofs, floors etc. ~*v* cover with tiles

**till¹** *prep/conj* until

**till²** *v* cultivate

**till³** *n* drawer for money in shop counter; cash register

**tiller** *n* lever to move rudder of boat

**tilt** *v* slope, slant; take part in medieval combat with lances; thrust (at)

**tick** *n* click, tap; dash, mark, stroke ~*v* choose, indicate, mark, select; click, tap

**ticket** card, coupon, pass, slip, token, voucher; card, label, slip, sticker, tag

**tide** course, current, ebb, flow

**tidy** *adj* methodical, neat, orderly, shipshape, spruce, trim, wellordered ~*v* neaten, order, straighten

**tie** *v* attach, bind, connect, fasten, join, rope, secure; bind, confine, hamper, hinder, limit, restrain ~*n*

band, bond, cord, fastening, link, rope, string; affiliation, affinity, bond, connection, kinship, relationship; dead heat, deadlock, draw, stalemate

**tier** bank, rank, row, series

**tight** rigid, stretched, taut, tense; close, compact, snug, fast, firm, fixed, secure; impervious, proof, sealed, sound, watertight; constricted, cramped, narrow; *Inf* close, mean, miserly stingy

**tighten** stretch, tense; fasten, screw, secure; close, cramp, narrow

~*n* slope; *Hist* combat for mounted men with lances

**timber** *n* wood for building etc.; trees

**timbre** *n* distinctive quality of voice or sound

**time** *n* past, present and future as continuous whole; hour; duration; period; point in duration; opportunity; occasion; leisure ~*v* choose time for; note time taken by **timeless** *adj* changeless, everlasting

**timely** *adj* at appropriate time **timer** *n* person, device for recording or indicating time **time bomb** bomb designed to explode at prearranged time **time-lag** *n* period between cause and effect **timetable** *n* plan showing times of arrival and departure etc.

**timid** *adj* easily frightened; shy **timorous** *adj* timid; indicating fear

**timpani, tympani** *pl n* set of kettledrums

**tin** *n* malleable metal; container made of tin ~*v* **tinning, tinned** put in tin, esp. for preserving **tinny** *adj* (of sound) thin, metallic **tinpot** *adj Inf* worthless

**tinder** *n* dry easily-burning material used to start fire

**tinge** *n* slight trace ~*v* colour, flavour slightly

**tingle** *v/n* (feel) thrill or pricking sensation

**tinker** *n* formerly, travelling mender of pots and pans ~*v* fiddle, meddle (with)

**tinkle** *v* (cause to) give out sounds like small bell ~*n* this sound or action

**tinsel** *n* glittering decorative metallic substance

**tint** *n* (shade of) colour; tinge ~*v* give tint to

**tiny** *adj* very small, minute

**tip**¹ *n* slender or pointed end of anything; small piece forming an extremity ~*v* **tipping, tipped** put tip on

**tip**² *n* small present of money given for service rendered; helpful piece of information; *also* **tip-off** warning, hint ~*v* **tipping, tipped** reward with money; *also* **tip off** give tip to

**tip**³ *v* **tipping, tipped** tilt, upset; touch lightly; topple over ~*n* place where rubbish is dumped

——————————— THESAURUS ———————————

**till** cultivate, dig, plough, work

**tilt** *v* cant, heel, lean, slant, slope, tip ~*n* angle, cant, incline, pitch, slant, slope

**timber** beams, boards, logs, planks, trees, wood

**time** *n* age, date, epoch, era, generation, hour, interval, period, season, spell, stretch, term; allotted span, day, duration, life, season ~*v* schedule, set; clock, count, measure

**timeless** abiding, ageless, changeless, deathless, endless, enduring, eternal, everlasting, immortal, last-

ing, permanent, undying

**timely** convenient, opportune, prompt, punctual, seasonable

**timetable** curriculum, list, programme, schedule

**timid** afraid, bashful, cowardly, fearful, nervous, retiring, shy

**tingle** *v* itch, prickle, sting, tickle ~*n* itch, itching, prickling, stinging, tickling

**tinker** *v* dabble, meddle, play, toy

**tint** *n* cast, colour, hue, shade, tone ~*v* colour, dye, rinse, stain

**tiny** diminutive, little, minute, pygmy *or* pigmy, slight, small, teensy-

**tipple** v drink (alcohol) habitually ~n drink

**tipsy** adj (slightly) drunk

**tiptoe** v walk on ball of foot and toes; walk softly

**tiptop** adj of the best quality or condition

**tirade** n long angry speech or denunciation

**tire** v reduce energy of, weary; bore; become tired, bored **tired** adj weary; hackneyed **tireless** adj not tiring easily **tiresome** adj irritating, tedious **tiring** adj

**tissue** n substance of animal body, plant; soft paper handkerchief

**tit** n small bird

**titanic** adj huge, epic

**titanium** n light metallic element

**titbit** n tasty morsel of food; scrap (of scandal etc.)

**tithe** n (esp. formerly) tenth part of income, paid to church as tax ~v exact tithes from

**titillate** v stimulate agreeably

**title** n name of book; heading; name, esp. denoting rank; legal right or document proving it; Sport championship

**titter** v/n snigger, giggle

**titular** adj pert. to title; nominal

**TNT** SEE TRINITROTOLUENE

**to** prep denoting direction, destination; introducing comparison, indirect object, infinitive etc. ~adv to fixed position **to and fro** back and forth

**toad** n animal like large frog **toady** n servile flatterer ~v be ingratiating

**toadstool** n fungus like mushroom

**toast** n slice of bread browned on both sides by heat; tribute, proposal of health etc. marked by people drinking together; person or thing so toasted ~v make (bread etc.) crisp and brown; drink toast to; warm at fire **toaster** n electrical device for toasting bread

**tobacco** n (pl -cos) plant with leaves used for smoking **tobacconist** n one who sells tobacco products

**toboggan** n sledge for sliding down slope of snow

**today** n this day ~adv on this day; nowadays

**toddle** v walk with unsteady short steps **toddler** n young child begin-

———————— THESAURUS ————————

weensy, teeny-weeny, wee

**tip**[1] apex, crown, end, head, peak, point, top

**tip**[2] n hint, pointer, suggestion also **tip-off** forecast, hint, warning, word ~v remunerate, reward also **tip off** advise, caution, warn

**tip**[3] v cant, incline, lean, slant, spill, tilt, upset

**tire** drain, exhaust, fail, flag, weary

**tired** drained, drowsy, exhausted, fatigued, sleepy, spent, weary, worn out

**tireless** determined, energetic, industrious, resolute, vigorous

**tiresome** dull, exasperating, flat, laborious, tedious, trying, wearing, wearisome

**tiring** arduous, fatiguing, strenuous, tough, wearing

**titbit** dainty, delicacy, goody, juicy bit, morsel, snack, treat

**title** n caption, heading, label, name; designation, epithet, name, nickname, pseudonym, term; claim, entitlement, ownership, privilege, right

**toady** n hanger-on, lackey, parasite, sycophant, yes man ~v crawl, creep, flatter, grovel

ning to walk

**to-do** *n* (*pl* **-dos**) *Inf* fuss, commotion

**toe** *n* digit of foot; anything resembling this **toe the line** conform

**toffee** *n* chewy sweet made of boiled sugar etc.

**toga** *n* garment worn in ancient Rome

**together** *adv* in company; simultaneously

**toggle** *n* small peg fixed crosswise on cord etc. and used for fastening

**toil** *n* heavy work or task ~*v* labour

**toilet** *n* lavatory; process of washing, dressing; articles used for this **toiletries** *pl n* objects, cosmetics used for cleaning or grooming

**token** *n* sign, symbol; disc used as money; gift card, voucher exchangeable for goods ~*adj* nominal

**tolerate** *v* put up with; permit **tolerable** *adj* bearable; fair **tolerance** *n*

**tolerant** *adj* forbearing; broad-minded **toleration** *n*

**toll** *v* ring (bell) slowly at regular intervals ~*n* ringing

**toll** *n* tax, esp. for use of bridge or road; loss, damage

**tom** *n* male cat

**tomahawk** *n* fighting axe of N Amer. Indians

**tomato** *n* (*pl* **-toes**) plant with red fruit; the fruit

**tomb** *n* grave; monument over one **tombstone** *n*

**tombola** *n* lottery with tickets drawn from revolving drum

**tomboy** *n* girl who acts, dresses like boy

**tome** *n* large book

**tomfoolery** *n* foolish behaviour

**tomorrow** *adv/n* (on) the day after today

**tom-tom** *n* drum beaten with hands

─────────────── THESAURUS ───────────────

**together** closely, in concert, in unison, jointly, mutually; concurrently, en masse, in unison, simultaneously

**toil** *n* drudgery, effort, exertion, hard work, industry, labour, pains, slog, sweat ~*v* break one's neck *Inf*, drudge, labour, slave, slog, strive, struggle, work

**toilet** bathroom, can *US & Canad sl*, closet, convenience, john *Sl*, chiefly *US & Canad*, latrine, lavatory, loo, outhouse, privy, urinal, washroom, W.C.); ablutions, bathing, dressing, grooming, toilette

**token** *n* badge, mark, proof, sign, symbol ~*adj* nominal, superficial, symbolic

**tolerable** acceptable, bearable, endurable, supportable; acceptable, adequate, average, fair, middling,

O.K. *or* okay *Inf*, ordinary, unexceptional

**tolerance** charity, magnanimity, patience, sympathy; endurance, fortitude, resilience, resistance, stamina, toughness

**tolerant** charitable, fair, liberal, open-minded, patient, unbigoted, unprejudiced; indulgent, lenient, permissive, soft

**tolerate** abide, bear, endure, stand, stomach, suffer, swallow, take; accept, allow, permit, stand for

**toll¹** *v/n* chime, clang, knell, peal, ring

**toll²** charge, customs, duty, fee, levy, payment, rate, tariff, tax; cost, damage, inroad, loss

**tomb** crypt, grave, sepulchre, vault

**tombstone** gravestone, head-

**ton** *n* (*also* **long ton**) measure of weight, 1016 kg (2240 lbs.); *US* (*also* **short ton**) measure of weight, 907 kg (2000 lbs.) **tonnage** *n* carrying capacity of ship

**tone** *n* quality of musical sound, voice, colour etc.; general character ~*v* blend, harmonize (with) **tone-deaf** *adj* unable to perceive subtle differences in pitch

**tongs** *pl n* apparatus for handling coal, sugar etc.

**tongue** *n* organ inside mouth, used for speech, taste etc.; language, speech

**tonic** *n* medicine etc. with invigorating effect; *Mus* first note of scale ~*adj* invigorating, restorative **tonic water** mineral water etc. containing quinine

**tonight** *n* this (coming) night ~*adv* on this night

**tonne** *n* metric ton, 1000 kg

**tonsil** *n* gland in throat **tonsillitis** *n* inflammation of tonsils

**tonsure** *n* shaving of part of head as religious practice; part shaved

**too** *adv* also, in addition; overmuch

**tool** *n* implement or appliance for mechanical operations; means to an end ~*v* work on with tool

**toot** *n* short sound of horn, trumpet etc.

**tooth** *n* (*pl* **teeth**) bonelike projection in gums of upper and lower jaws of vertebrates; prong, cog **toothless** *adj* **toothpaste** *n* paste used to clean teeth **toothpick** *n* small stick for removing food from between teeth

**top**[1] *n* highest part, summit; highest rank; first in merit; garment for upper part of body; lid, stopper of bottle etc. ~*adj* highest in position, rank ~*v* topping, topped cut off, pass, reach, surpass top; provide top for **topmost** *adj* highest **topping** *n* sauce or garnish for food **top brass** important officials *sp* hat man's tall cylindrical hat **top-heavy** *adj* unbalanced **top-notch** *adj* excellent, first-class **topsoil** *n* surface layer of soil

**top**[2] *n* toy which spins on tapering point

**topaz** *n* precious stone of various colours

**topiary** *n* trimming trees, bushes into decorative shapes

**topic** *n* subject of discourse, conversation etc. **topical** *adj* up-to-date, having news value

stone, memorial, monument

**tone** modulation, pitch, sound, timbre; air, aspect, attitude, character, manner, mood, note, quality, spirit, style, temper, vein; cast, colour, hue, shade, tinge, tint ~*v* blend, go well with, harmonize, match, suit

**tongue** dialect, idiom, language, speech, talk, vernacular

**tonic** cordial, refresher, stimulant

**too** also, as well, besides, further, likewise, moreover, to boot; exces-

sively, extremely, unduly

**tool** appliance, contrivance, device, gadget, implement, instrument, utensil; agent, means, medium, vehicle

**top** apex, crest, crown, head, height, peak, pinnacle, summit, vertex; head, lead; cap, cork, cover, lid ~*v* beat, best, better, outdo, surpass ~*adj* crowning, highest, superior, topmost, upper; best, chief, elite, finest, first, greatest, head, lead, prime, principal, ruling,

**topography** n (description of) surface features of a place **topographic** adj

**topple** v (cause to) fall over

**topsy-turvy** adj in confusion

**tor** n high rocky hill

**torch** n portable hand light containing electric battery; burning wooden shaft; any apparatus burning with hot flame

**toreador** n bullfighter

**torment** v torture in body or mind; afflict; tease ~n suffering, agony of body or mind; pest **tormentor, -er** n

**tornado** n (pl **-does, -dos**) whirlwind; violent storm

**torpedo** n (pl **-does**) self-propelled underwater missile with explosive warhead ~v strike with torpedo

**torpid** adj sluggish, apathetic **torpor** n torpid state

**torrent** n rushing stream; downpour **torrential** adj

**torrid** adj parched; highly emotional

**torsion** n twist, twisting

**torso** n (pl **-sos**) (statue of) body without head or limbs

**tortilla** n thin Mexican pancake

**tortoise** n four-footed reptile covered with shell of horny plates **tortoiseshell** n mottled brown shell of turtle

**tortuous** adj winding, twisting; involved, not straightforward

**torture** n infliction of severe pain ~v inflict severe pain

**Tory** n member of conservative political party

**toss** v throw up, about; be thrown, fling oneself about ~n tossing

**tot¹** n very small child; small quantity, esp. of drink

**tot²** v **totting, totted** add (up); amount to

**total** n whole amount; sum ~adj complete, absolute ~v **totalling, totalled** amount to; add up **totality** n **totally** adv

**totalitarian** adj of dictatorial,

——————————— THESAURUS ———————————

sovereign, superior

**topic** issue, matter, point, subject, theme

**topical** current, popular, up-to-date

**topple** fall, fall headlong, fall over, keel over, knock down, overbalance, overturn, tip over, upset

**topsy-turvy** chaotic, confused, disorderly, inside-out, jumbled, messy, untidy

**torment** v agonize, distress, harrow, pain, rack, torture; aggravate *Inf*, annoy, harass, hassle *Inf*, persecute, pester, trouble ~n agony, anguish, distress, hell, misery, pain, suffering, torture; hassle *Inf*, nuisance, pest, plague, scourge, trouble

**tornado** cyclone, gale, typhoon, whirlwind

**torrent** flood, flow, gush, rush, spate, stream

**torture** v agonize, distress, pain, persecute, torment ~n agony, anguish, distress, hell, misery, pain, suffering, torment

**toss** v cast, fling, hurl, pitch, shy, sling, throw ~n cast, fling, pitch, shy, throw

**tot** v add up, calculate, count up, reckon, tally, total

**total** n all, amount, entirety, mass, sum, whole ~adj all-out, complete, consummate, deep-dyed *usu derog*, downright, entire, full, outright, perfect, sheer, thorough, unqualified, utter ~v add up, amount to,

one-party government

**totem** *n* tribal badge or emblem
**totem pole** carved post of Amer.
Indians
**totter** *v* walk unsteadily; begin to
fall
**toucan** *n* large-billed tropical
Amer. bird
**touch** *v* come into contact with;
put hand on; reach; affect emotions
of; deal with; (with *on*) refer to ~*n*
sense by which qualities of object
etc. are perceived by touching;
touching; characteristic manner or
ability; slight contact, amount etc.
**touching** *adj* emotionally moving
~*prep* concerning **touchy** *adj* easily
offended **touch down** (of aircraft)
land **touchline** *n* side line of pitch in
some games **touchstone** *n* criterion
**touché** *interj* acknowledgment that
remark or blow has struck target
**tough** *adj* strong; able to bear
hardship, strain; strict; difficult;

needing effort to chew; violent ~*n*
*Inf* rough, violent person **toughen** *v*
**toupee** *n* wig
**tour** *n* travelling round; journey to
one place after another ~*v* make
tour **tourism** *n* **tourist** *n*
**tournament** *n* competition, contest usu. with several stages
**tourniquet** *n* bandage, surgical instrument to stop bleeding
**tousled** *adj* ruffled
**tout** *v* solicit custom ~*n* person
who sells tickets at inflated prices
**tow** *v* drag along behind, esp. at
end of rope ~*n* towing or being
towed **towpath** *n* path beside canal
or river
**towards** *prep* (*also* **toward**) in direction of; with regard to; as contribution to
**towel** *n* cloth for wiping off moisture after washing
**tower** *n* tall strong structure, esp.
part of church etc.; fortress ~*v*

————————————— THESAURUS —————————————

reach, reckon

**totally** absolutely, completely, entirely, fully, perfectly, quite, thoroughly, unconditionally, utterly,
wholeheartedly, wholly
**totter** stagger, stumble, sway, teeter, walk unsteadily
**touch** *v* brush, caress, feel, finger,
fondle, handle, stroke; affect, melt,
move, soften, stir ~*n* feel, feeling;
brush, caress, contact, pat, stroke;
approach, manner, method, style,
way; ability, adroitness, artistry,
flair, knack, mastery, skill, virtuosity; bit, dash, drop, hint, jot, pinch,
speck, spot, taste, trace
**touching** affecting, melting, moving, stirring
**touchy** bad-tempered, cross, easily
offended, grouchy *Inf*, grumpy,

irascible, irritable, oversensitive,
quick-tempered, ratty *Brit & NZ
inf*, testy
**tough** *adj* durable, firm, hard,
leathery, solid, stiff, strong, sturdy;
brawny, hardy, stout, strong, sturdy; firm, resolute, severe, stern,
strict, unbending; difficult, hard,
knotty, thorny, uphill; rough, ruffi-
anly, vicious, violent ~*n Inf* brute,
heavy *Sl*, ruffian, thug
**tour** *n* excursion, journey, outing,
trip; circuit, course, round ~*v* explore, holiday in, journey, sightsee,
visit
**tourist** holiday-maker, sightseer,
traveller
**tow** *v* drag, haul, lug, pull, trail, tug
**towards** almost, nearing, nearly;
about, concerning, for, regarding;

stand very high; loom (over)

**town** n collection of dwellings etc. larger than village and smaller than city **township** n small town

**toxic** adj poisonous; due to poison

**toxicity** n strength of a poison **toxin** n poison

**toy** n something designed to be played with ~adj very small ~v trifle **toy boy** much younger lover of older woman

**trace** n track left by anything; indication; minute quantity ~v follow course of; find out; make plan of; draw or copy exactly **tracing paper** transparent paper placed over drawing, map etc. to enable exact copy to be taken

**trachea** n (pl **tracheae**) windpipe

**track** n mark left by passage of anything; path; rough road; course; railway line; jointed metal band as on tank etc.; separate song, piece on record ~v follow trail or path of **track events** athletic sports held on running track **track record** past accomplishments **tracksuit** n loose-

fitting suit worn by athletes etc.

**tract**[1] n wide expanse, area

**tract**[2] n pamphlet, esp. religious one

**traction** n action of pulling

**tractor** n motor vehicle for hauling, pulling etc.

**trade** n commerce, business; skilled craft; exchange ~v engage in trade **trader** n **trade-in** n used article given in part payment for new

**trademark, trade name** n distinctive legal mark on maker's goods **trade-off** n exchange made as compromise **tradesman** n dealer; skilled worker **trade union** society of workers for protection of their interests

**tradition** n unwritten body of beliefs, facts etc. handed down from generation to generation; custom, practice of long standing **traditional** adj

**traffic** n vehicles passing to and fro in street, town etc.; (illicit) trade ~v **trafficking, trafficked** trade **traffic lights** set of coloured lights at road junctions etc.

———————— THESAURUS ————————

**tower** n castle, citadel, fort, keep, refuge, stronghold ~v loom, overlook, rear, rise, soar, top

**toxic** harmful, noxious, poisonous, septic

**trace** n evidence, mark, record, remnant, sign, token; bit, dash, drop, hint, shadow, suggestion, touch ~v detect, determine, discover, find, follow, pursue, seek, track, trail, unearth; chart, copy, draw, map, outline, sketch

**track** n footmark, footprint, footstep, mark, path, scent, trace, trail, wake; course, line, path, pathway, road, track, way ~v chase, dog, fol-

low, pursue, trace, trail

**trade** n barter, business, commerce, dealing, exchange, traffic, truck; business, calling, craft, job, line, occupation, profession, skill; deal, exchange, swap ~v bargain, barter, deal, exchange, peddle, traffic; exchange, swap, switch

**tradesman** dealer, merchant, purveyor, seller, shopkeeper, supplier, vendor; craftsman, workman

**tradition** custom, customs, habit, institution, ritual

**traditional** conventional, customary, established, fixed

**traffic** n transport, vehicles; barter, business, commerce, dealing, ex-

**tragedy** n sad event; dramatic, literary work dealing with serious, sad topic **tragedian** n actor in, writer of tragedies **tragic** adj of, in manner of tragedy; disastrous; appalling

**trail** v drag behind one; lag behind; track, pursue ~n track or trace; rough path **trailer** n vehicle towed by another vehicle

**train** v educate, instruct, cause to grow in particular way; follow course of training; aim (gun etc.) ~n line of railway vehicles joined to locomotive; succession, esp. of thoughts etc.; procession; trailing part of dress **trainee** n one training to be skilled worker **trainer** n **training** n

**traipse** v walk wearily

**trait** n characteristic feature

**traitor** n one who is guilty of treason **traitorous** adj

**trajectory** n line of flight

**tram** n vehicle running on rails laid on roadway

**tramp** v travel on foot; walk heavily ~n (homeless) person who travels about on foot; walk; cargo ship without fixed route

**trample** v tread on and crush under foot

**trampoline** n tough canvas sheet stretched horizontally with elastic cords etc. to frame

**trance** n unconscious or dazed state; state of ecstasy or total absorption

**tranche** n portion

**tranquil** adj calm, quiet; serene **tranquillity** n **tranquillize** v make calm **tranquillizer** n drug which induces calm state

**trans-** comb. form across, through, beyond

change, trade, truck ~v barter, deal, exchange, market, peddle, trade

**tragedy** affliction, calamity, disaster, misfortune

**tragic** appalling, awful, catastrophic, dire, disastrous, dreadful, grievous, miserable, pathetic, sad, shocking, unfortunate, woeful, wretched

**trail** v drag, draw, haul, pull, tow; dawdle, follow, lag, loiter, straggle; chase, follow, hunt, pursue, trace, track ~n footsteps, mark, path, scent, trace, track, wake; beaten track, footpath, path, road, route, track, way

**train** v coach, educate, guide, instruct, school, teach, tutor; aim, direct, level, point ~v chain, course, order, series, set, string; caravan, convoy, procession

**training** discipline, education,

guidance, instruction, tuition, upbringing; exercise, practice, preparation

**trait** attribute, feature, mannerism, quality, quirk

**traitor** betrayer, deceiver, informer, quisling, turncoat

**tramp** v hike, march, slog, trek, walk; march, plod, stamp, toil, trudge ~n bag lady chiefly US, bum Inf, vagabond, vagrant; hike, march, slog, trek

**trample** crush, squash, stamp, tread

**trance** daze, dream, rapture, reverie, spell, stupor

**tranquil** calm, composed, peaceful, placid, quiet, restful, serene, still

**tranquillity** calm, calmness, composure, peace, peacefulness, placidity, quiet, quietness, restfulness,

**transact** v carry through; negotiate

**transaction** n performing of business; single sale or purchase; pl proceedings

**transcend** v rise above; surpass

**transcendence** n **transcendent** adj

**transcendental** adj surpassing experience; supernatural; abstruse **transcendentalism** n

**transcribe** v copy out; record for later broadcast **transcript** n copy

**transfer** v -ferring, -ferred move, send from one person, place etc. to another ~n removal of person or thing from one place to another **transference** n transfer

**transfigure** v alter appearance of

**transfix** v astound, stun; pierce through

**transform** v change shape, character of **transformation** n **transformer** n Electricity apparatus for changing voltage

**transfuse** v convey from one to another, esp. blood from healthy to ill person **transfusion** n

**transgress** v break (law); sin

**transgression** n

**transient** adj fleeting, not permanent

**transistor** n Electronics small, semiconducting device used to amplify electric currents; portable radio using transistors

**transit** n passage, crossing **transition** n change from one state to another **transitive** adj (of verb) requiring direct object **transitory** adj not lasting long

**translate** v turn from one language into another; interpret **translation** n **translator** n

**translucent** adj letting light pass through, semitransparent

**transmit** v -mitting, -mitted send, cause to pass to another place, person etc.; send out (signals) by means of radio waves **transmission** n transmitting; gears by which power is communicated from engine to road wheels

**transmute** v change in form, properties or nature

**transparent** adj letting light pass

———————— THESAURUS ————————

**transaction** affair, bargain, business, deal, matter, proceeding, undertaking

**transcend** eclipse, exceed, excel, go above, go beyond, leave behind, outdo, outshine, outstrip, surpass

**transcribe** copy, reproduce, rewrite

**transfer** v carry, change, convey, move, shift, transport, turn over ~n change, handover, move, shift

**transform** alter, change, make over, remodel

**transformation** change, conversion

**transient** brief, fleeting, momen-

tary, passing, short, temporary

**transit** n carriage, crossing, passage, shipment, travel

**transition** change, conversion, passage, passing, shift

**transitional** changing, fluid, passing

**translate** convert, decode, transcribe; explain, interpret, paraphrase, simplify

**translation** decoding, gloss, paraphrase, version; paraphrase, simplification

**transmission** broadcasting, relaying, sending, showing; broadcast, programme

**transmit** broadcast, radio, relay,

without distortion; that can be seen through **transparency** *n* quality of being transparent; photographic slide

**transpire** *v* become known; *Inf* happen; (of plants) give off water vapour through leaves

**transplant** *v* move and plant again in another place; transfer organ surgically ~*n* surgical transplanting of organ

**transport** *v* convey from one place to another; deport ~*n* system of conveyance; vehicle used for this **transportation** *n* transporting; *Hist* deportation to penal colony

**transpose** *v* change order of; put music into different key

**transverse** *adj* lying across; at right angles

**transvestite** *n* person who wears clothes of opposite sex

**trap** *n* device for catching game etc.; anything planned to deceive, betray etc.; arrangement of pipes to prevent escape of gas; movable opening ~*v* **trapping, trapped**

catch; trick **trapper** *n* one who traps animals for their fur **trapdoor** *n* door in floor or roof

**trapeze** *n* horizontal bar suspended from two ropes for acrobatics etc.

**trapezium** *n* four-sided figure with two parallel sides of unequal length

**trappings** *pl n* equipment, ornaments

**trash** *n* rubbish; nonsense

**trauma** *n* emotional shock; injury, wound **traumatic** *adj* **traumatize** *v*

**travail** *v/n* labour, toil

**travel** *v* **-elling, -elled** go, move from one place to another ~*n* act of travelling; *pl* (account of) travelling **traveller** *n* **travelogue** *n* film etc. about travels

**traverse** *v* cross, go through or over ~*n* traversing; path across

**travesty** *n* grotesque imitation ~*v* **-estying, -estied** make, be a travesty of

**trawl** *v* fish at deep levels with net dragged behind boat **trawler** *n* trawling boat

send, send out

**transparent** clear, diaphanous, filmy, limpid, translucent; apparent, evident, manifest, obvious, patent, plain, visible

**transpire** *Inf* arise, befall, chance, happen, occur

**transport** *v* bear, bring, carry, convey, fetch, move, ship, take, transfer; banish, deport, exile ~*n* conveyance, vehicle; carriage, conveyance, shipment, shipping

**transpose** change, exchange, reorder, swap *Inf* switch

**trap** *n* ambush, net, pitfall, snare; device, ruse ~*v* ambush, catch, corner, ensnare, snare; deceive, dupe,

ensnare, trick

**trappings** adornments, dress, equipment, finery, fittings, fixtures, gear

**trash** garbage, junk *Inf* litter, refuse, rubbish; balderdash, bosh *Inf* bunkum *or* buncombe *chiefly US*, crap *Sl*, drivel, garbage *Inf*, hogwash, hot air *Inf* nonsense, rot, rubbish, tripe *Inf* twaddle

**traumatic** damaging, disturbing, painful, scarring, shocking, upsetting, wounding

**travel** go, journey, move, proceed, progress, tour, voyage

**traveller** explorer, gypsy, nomad, tourist, voyager, wayfarer

**tray** n flat board, usu. with rim, for carrying things

**treachery** n deceit, betrayal **treacherous** adj disloyal; unsafe

**treacle** n thick syrup produced when sugar is refined

**tread** v **treading, trod, trodden** or **trod** walk; trample (on) ~n treading; fashion of walking; upper surface of step; part of tyre which makes contact with ground **treadmill** n dreary routine

**treadle** n lever worked by foot to turn wheel

**treason** n violation by subject of allegiance to sovereign or state; treachery

**treasure** n riches; valued person or thing ~v prize; cherish **treasurer** n official in charge of funds **treasury** n place for treasure; government department in charge of finance **treasure-trove** n treasure found with no evidence of ownership

**treat** n pleasure, entertainment given ~v deal with, act towards; give medical treatment to; provide with treat **treatment** n method of counteracting disease; act or mode of treating

**treatise** n formal essay

**treaty** n signed contract between states etc.

**treble** adj threefold; Mus high-pitched ~n soprano voice ~v increase threefold

**tree** n large perennial plant with woody trunk

**trek** n long difficult journey ~v **trekking, trekked** make trek

**trellis** n lattice or grating of light bars

**tremble** v quiver, shake; feel fear ~n involuntary shaking

**tremendous** adj vast, immense; Inf exciting; Inf excellent

——————— THESAURUS ———————

**treacherous** deceitful, disloyal, faithless, false, perfidious, unfaithful, unreliable, untrue; dangerous, hazardous, perilous, risky, tricky, unsafe

**treachery** betrayal, disloyalty, duplicity, infidelity

**tread** v pace, plod, stamp, step, tramp, walk; squash, trample ~n footstep, gait, pace, step, walk

**treasure** n gold, jewels, riches, valuables ~v adore, cherish, esteem, love, prize, value

**treasury** bank, cache, hoard, store, vault

**treat** n banquet, entertainment, feast, party; delight, enjoyment, fun, joy, pleasure ~v deal with, handle, manage, use; attend to, care for, doctor, nurse; buy for, give, lay on, pay for, provide, regale

**treatise** dissertation, essay, paper, study, thesis, tract, work

**treatment** care, cure, healing, medicine, remedy; conduct, dealing, handling, reception, usage

**treaty** agreement, alliance, compact, concordat, contract, covenant, pact

**trek** n hike, journey, march, slog, tramp ~v hike, journey, march, plod, slog, tramp

**tremble** v quake, quiver, shake, shiver, shudder, teeter, totter, vibrate ~n quake, quiver, shake, shiver, shudder, trembling, tremor, vibration

**tremendous** colossal, enormous, great, huge, immense, monstrous, towering, vast; Inf amazing, brilliant, excellent, exceptional, great, incredible, marvellous, sensational

**tremor** n quiver; shaking

**tremulous** adj quivering slightly

**trench** n long narrow ditch **trench coat** double-breasted waterproof coat

**trenchant** adj cutting, incisive

**trend** n direction, tendency; fashion **trendy** adj Inf consciously fashionable

**trepidation** n fear, anxiety

**trespass** v intrude on property etc. of another ~n wrongful entering on another's land; wrongdoing **trespasser** n

**tress** n long lock of hair

**trestle** n board fixed on pairs of spreading legs

**trews** pl n close-fitting tartan trousers

**tri-** comb. form three

**trial** n test, examination; Law investigation of case before judge; thing, person that strains endurance or patience

**triangle** n figure with three angles

**triangular** adj

**tribe** n race; subdivision of race of people **tribal** adj

**tribulation** n trouble, affliction

**tribunal** n lawcourt; body appointed to inquire into specific matter

**tributary** n stream flowing into another

**tribute** n sign of honour; tax paid by one state to another

**trice** n moment, instant

**trick** n deception; prank; feat of skill or cunning; knack; cards played in one round ~v deceive, cheat **trickery** n **trickster** n **tricky** adj difficult

**trickle** v (cause to) run, flow, move in thin stream or drops ~n trickling flow

**tricolour** n three-coloured striped flag

**tricycle** n three-wheeled cycle

**trident** n three-pronged spear

**trifle** n insignificant thing or matter; small amount; pudding of

———————————— THESAURUS ————————————

Inf, super, wonderful

**tremor** quaking, quiver, shaking, shiver, trembling, vibration

**trench** channel, ditch, drain, furrow, gutter, pit

**trend** bias, course, current, drift, leaning, tendency; craze, fashion, mode, rage, style, thing, vogue

**trespass** v encroach, intrude ~n encroachment, intrusion

**trial** n audition, check, experiment, probation, proof, test, testing; contest, hearing, litigation, tribunal; adversity, affliction, burden, hardship, load, ordeal, pain, suffering, tribulation, trouble; bother, drag Inf, irritation, nuisance, pest, vexation

**tribe** blood, clan, class, family,

people, race, stock

**tribute** acknowledgment, applause, compliment, honour, praise, recognition, respect; charge, homage, offering, payment, tax

**trick** n artifice, deceit, deception, device, dodge, fraud, ploy, ruse, scam Sl, stratagem, swindle, trap; hoax, jape, joke, prank, stunt; art, gift, knack, secret, skill, technique ~v cheat, deceive, delude, dupe, fool, hoax, mislead, trap

**trickery** cheating, con Inf, deceit, deception, double-dealing, fraud, hoax, swindling

**trickle** v drip, drop, exude, ooze, seep ~n dribble, drip, seepage

**tricky** complicated, delicate, difficult

sponge cake, whipped cream etc.
~v toy (with)

**trigger** n catch which releases
spring, esp. to fire gun ~v (oft. with
off) set in action etc. **trigger-happy**
adj tending to be irresponsible

**trigonometry** n branch of mathematics dealing with relations of
sides and angles of triangles

**trilby** n man's soft felt hat

**trill** v/n (sing, play with) rapid alter-
nation between two close notes

**trillion** n one million million, $10^{12}$;
Obs one million million million,
$10^{18}$

**trilogy** n series of three related (literary) works

**trim** adj neat, smart; slender; in
good order ~v **trimming, trimmed**
shorten slightly by cutting; prune;
decorate; adjust ~n decoration; order, state of being trim **trimming** n
(oft. pl) decoration, addition

**trinitrotoluene** n powerful explosive

**trinity** n the state of being threefold; (with cap.) state of God as
three persons, Father, Son and

Holy Spirit

**trinket** n small ornament

**trio** n (pl **trios**) group of three; music for three parts

**trip** n (short) journey for pleasure;
stumble; Inf hallucinatory experience caused by drug ~v **tripping,
tripped** (cause to) stumble; (cause
to) make mistake; run lightly

**tripe** n stomach of cow as food; Inf
nonsense

**triple** adj threefold ~v treble **triplet**
n one of three offspring born at one
birth

**triplicate** adj threefold ~n state of
being triplicate; one of set of three
copies

**tripod** n stool, stand etc. with three
feet

**trite** adj hackneyed, banal

**triumph** n great success; victory;
exultation ~v achieve great success
or victory; rejoice over victory **tri-
umphal** adj **triumphant** adj

**trivia** pl n petty, unimportant
things **trivial** adj of little consequence **triviality** n

**troll** n giant or dwarf in Scandina-

**trifle** n nothing, triviality; bit, jot,
little, spot, touch, trace ~v amuse
oneself, play, toy

**trim** adj dapper, neat, orderly,
smart, spruce, tidy, well turned-
out; fit, shapely, sleek, slender,
slim, streamlined ~v clip, crop, cut,
pare, prune, tidy; adorn, array, bedeck, decorate, dress, embellish,
garnish, ornament

**trimming** n adornment, decoration,
embellishment; pl accessories, ex-
tras, frills, garnish, trappings

**trip** n excursion, expedition, jaunt,
journey, outing, run, tour, travel,
voyage ~v blunder, err, fall, lapse,

slip, stumble, tumble

**trite** adj banal, commonplace, hackneyed, routine, stale, stock, tired

**triumph** n accomplishment,
achievement, attainment, coup,
feat, success, victory; exultation,
joy, rejoicing ~v celebrate, exult,
gloat, glory, rejoice, revel

**triumphant** adj conquering, dominant, successful, victorious

**trivia** n details, minutiae, petty details, trivialities

**trivial** adj inconsequential, inconsiderable, insignificant, little, meaningless, minor, negligible, paltry, petty,
slight, small, trifling, unimportant

vian mythology and folklore

**trolley** *n* small wheeled table for food and drink; wheeled cart for moving goods etc.; *US* tram

**trollop** *n* promiscuous woman

**trombone** *n* deep-toned brass instrument **trombonist** *n*

**troop** *n* group of persons; *pl* soldiers ~v move in troop **trooper** *n* cavalry soldier

**trophy** *n* prize, award

**tropic** *n* either of two lines of latitude N and S of equator; *pl* area of earth's surface between these lines

**tropical** *adj* pert. to, within tropics; (of climate) very hot

**trot** *v* trotting, trotted (of horse) move at medium pace; (of person) run easily with short strides ~n trotting, jog **trotter** *n* horse trained to trot in race; foot of pig etc.

**troubadour** *n* medieval travelling poet and singer

**trouble** *n* state or cause of mental distress, pain, inconvenience etc.; care ~v be trouble to; be inconvenienced, be agitated; take pains trou-

**blesome** *adj* **troubleshooter** *n* person employed to deal with problems

**trough** *n* long open vessel, esp. for animals' food or water; hollow between waves

**trounce** *v* beat thoroughly, thrash

**troupe** *n* company of performers **trouper** *n*

**trousers** *pl n* garment covering legs

**trousseau** *n* bride's outfit of clothing

**trout** *n* freshwater fish

**trowel** *n* small tool like spade

**truant** *n* one absent without leave **truancy** *n*

**truce** *n* temporary cessation of fighting

**truck**[1] *n* wheeled (motor) vehicle for moving goods

**truck**[2] *n* dealing, esp. in **have no truck with**

**truculent** *adj* aggressive, defiant

**trudge** *v* walk laboriously ~n tiring walk

**true** *adj* in accordance with facts;

—————— THESAURUS ——————

**troop** n band, body, company, crowd, gang, group, horde, multitude, squad, team, unit; *pl* armed forces, army, men, military, soldiers ~v crowd, flock, march, parade, stream, swarm

**trophy** award, cup, laurels, prize

**tropical** hot, humid, steamy, sultry, torrid

**trot** v canter, jog, lope, run ~n brisk pace, canter, jog, lope

**trouble** n anxiety, distress, hardship, misfortune, pain, sorrow, suffering, vexation, woe, worry; discord, disorder, disturbance, hassle *Inf*, row, strife, tumult; ailment, complaint, defect, disease, disor-

der, illness; danger, difficulty, dilemma, mess, problem, spot *Inf*, tight spot; bother, care, effort, exertion, labour, pains, work ~v afflict, annoy, bother, distress, disturb, fret, harass, hassle *Inf*, pain, perturb, pester, plague, torment, upset, vex, worry; bother, burden, incommode, inconvenience, put out

**troublesome** annoying, bothersome, difficult, hard, taxing, tiresome, wearisome; disorderly, rowdy, turbulent, uncooperative, undisciplined, unruly, violent

**truce** armistice, break, ceasefire, interval, lull, respite

faithful; correct; genuine **truism** *n* self-evident truth **truly** *adv* **truth** *n* state of being true; something that is true **truthful** *adj* accustomed to speak the truth; accurate

**truffle** *n* edible underground fungus; sweet flavoured with chocolate

**trump** *n* card of suit ranking above others ~*v* play trump **trump up** *v* invent; concoct

**trumpet** *n* metal wind instrument like horn ~*v* blow trumpet; make sound like one; proclaim **trumpeter** *n*

**truncate** *v* cut short

**truncheon** *n* short thick club

**trundle** *v* move heavily, as on small wheels

**trunk** *n* main stem of tree; person's body excluding head and limbs; box for clothes etc.; elephant's snout; *pl* man's swimming costume **trunk call** long-distance telephone call **trunk road** main road

**truss** *v* fasten up, tie up ~*n* support; medical supporting device

**trust** *n* confidence; firm belief; reliance; combination of business firms; care; property held for another ~*v* rely on; believe in; expect, hope; consign for care **trustee** *n* one legally holding property for another **trustful**, **trusting** *adj* **trustworthy** *adj* **trusty** *adj*

**try** *v* **trying**, **tried** attempt; test, sample; afflict; examine in court of law ~*n* attempt, effort; *Rugby* score gained by touching ball down over opponent's goal line **tried** *adj* proved **trying** *adj* troublesome

**tryst** *n* arrangement to meet, esp. secretly

**Tsar** *see* CZAR

**T-shirt**, **tee-shirt** *n* informal (short-sleeved) sweater

**tub** *n* open wooden vessel like bottom half of barrel; small round container; bath **tubby** *adj* short and fat

**tuba** *n* valved brass wind instrument of low pitch

**tube** *n* long, narrow hollow cylinder; flexible cylinder with cap to hold pastes; underground electric railway **tubular** *adj*

**tuber** *n* fleshy underground stem of some plants

**trudge** *v* plod, slog, stump, tramp ~*n* footslog, haul, slog, tramp

**true** *adj* accurate, actual, authentic, bona fide, correct, exact, factual, genuine, precise, real, right, valid, veracious, veritable; devoted, faithful, loyal, staunch, steady, trusty

**trunk** body, torso; box, case, chest, coffer; proboscis, snout

**trust** *n* belief, certainty, confidence, faith, hope, reliance; care, charge, custody ~*v* believe, rely upon; assume, believe, expect, hope, presume, surmise; commit, consign, entrust, give

**trusty** dependable, faithful, reli-

able, staunch, true, trustworthy

**truth** accuracy, exactness, genuineness, legitimacy, reality, veracity; axiom, fact, law, maxim, reality, truism

**truthful** candid, honest, reliable, sincere; accurate, correct, exact, faithful, honest, literal, precise, realistic, reliable

**try** *v* aim, attempt, bend over backwards *Inf*, break one's neck *Inf*, endeavour, essay, give it one's best shot *Inf*, make an all-out effort *Inf*, strive; examine, inspect, sample, test; adjudge, adjudicate, examine, hear ~*n* attempt, effort, endeavour,

**tuberculosis** n communicable disease, esp. of lung **tubercular** adj **tuberculin** n bacillus used to treat tuberculosis

**tuck** v push, fold into small space; gather, stitch in folds ~n stitched fold; Inf food

**Tuesday** n third day of the week

**tuft** n bunch of feathers etc.

**tug** v tugging, tugged pull hard or violently ~n violent pull; ship used to tow other vessels **tug-of-war** n contest in which two teams pull against one another on rope

**tuition** n teaching, esp. private

**tulip** n plant with bright cup-shaped flowers

**tumble** v (cause to) fall or roll, twist etc.; rumple ~n fall **tumbler** n stemless drinking glass; acrobat **tumbledown** adj dilapidated **tumble dryer** machine that dries laundry by rotating it in warm air

**tummy** n Inf stomach

**tumour** n abnormal growth in or on body

**tumult** n violent uproar, commotion **tumultuous** adj

**tuna** n (pl **-na**, **nas**) large marine food and game fish

**tundra** n vast treeless zone between ice cap and timber line

**tune** n melody; quality of being in pitch; adjustment of musical instrument ~v put in tune; adjust machine to obtain efficient running; adjust radio to receive broadcast **tuneful** adj **tuner** n

**tungsten** n greyish-white metal

**tunic** n close-fitting jacket forming part of uniform; loose hip-length garment

**tunnel** n underground passage, esp. as track for railway line ~v **-nelling**, **-nelled** make tunnel (through)

**turban** n headdress made by coiling length of cloth round head

**turbine** n rotary engine driven by steam, gas, water or air playing on blades

**turbocharger** n propulsion unit driven by turbine

**turbot** n large flatfish

**turbulent** adj in commotion; swirling; riotous **turbulence** n

**tureen** n serving dish for soup

**turf** n (pl **turfs**, **turves**) short grass

———— THESAURUS ————

essay, go Inf, stab Inf

**tuck** v fold, gather, insert, push ~n fold, gather, pinch, pleat

**tug** v/n drag, haul, heave, jerk, pull, tow, yank

**tuition** education, instruction, lessons, schooling, teaching, training

**tumble** v drop, fall, pitch, plummet, roll, topple ~n collapse, drop, fall, plunge, roll, spill

**tumult** bedlam, brawl, commotion, din, disorder, riot, row, strife, turmoil, uproar

**tune** n air, melody, strain, theme; concert, concord, harmony, unison

~v adapt, adjust, attune, pitch, regulate

**tuneful** catchy, harmonious, melodic, melodious, musical

**tuneless** cacophonous, discordant, dissonant, unmelodic, unmelodious, unmusical

**tunnel** n burrow, channel, hole, passage, shaft ~v burrow, dig, excavate, mine

**turbulence** agitation, commotion, disorder, roughness, storm, turmoil

**turbulent** agitated, rough, swirling, unsettled, unstable; riotous, rowdy, unruly, violent, wild

with earth bound to it by matted roots ~v lay with turf **turf account-ant** bookmaker **turf out** Inf throw out

**turgid** adj swollen, inflated; bombastic

**turkey** n large bird reared for food

**Turkish** adj of Turkey **Turkish bath** steam bath **Turkish delight** jelly-like sweet coated with icing sugar

**turmoil** n confusion, commotion

**turn** v move around, rotate; change, alter position or direction (of); (oft. with **into**) change in nature; make, shape on lathe ~n turning; inclination etc.; period; short walk; (part of) rotation; performance **turning** n road, path leading off main rout **turncoat** n person who deserts party, cause etc. to join another **turn down** reduce volume or brightness; refuse **turnout** n number of people appearing for some purpose **turnover** n total sales made by business; rate at which staff leave and are replaced **turn-stile** n revolving gate for controlling admission of people **turntable** n revolving platform **turn up** v appear

**turnip** n plant with edible root

**turpentine** n oil from certain trees

used in paints etc. **turps** n Inf turpentine

**turquoise** n bluish-green precious stone; this colour

**turret** n small tower; revolving armoured tower on tank etc.

**turtle** n sea tortoise

**tusk** n long pointed side tooth of elephant etc.

**tussle** n/v fight, wrestle, struggle

**tutor** n one teaching individuals or small groups ~v teach **tutorial** n period of instruction

**tutu** n skirt worn by ballerinas

**tuxedo** n (pl **-dos**) US dinner jacket

**TV** television

**twang** n vibrating metallic sound; nasal speech ~v (cause to) make such sounds

**tweak** v pinch and twist or pull ~n tweaking

**twee** adj Inf oversentimental

**tweed** n rough-surfaced cloth used for clothing

**tweet** n/v chirp

**tweezers** pl n small forceps or tongs

**twelve** adj/n two more than ten **twelfth** adj ordinal number

**twenty** adj/n twice ten **twentieth** adj ordinal number

——————— THESAURUS ———————

**turmoil** agitation, bedlam, chaos, disorder, strife, tumult, upheaval, violence

**turn** v circle, gyrate, pivot, revolve, roll, rotate, spin, swivel, twirl, twist, wheel, whirl; go back, return, reverse, shift, switch, veer, wheel; alter, become, change, convert, mutate, transfigure, transform ~n circle, curve, gyration, spin, twist, whirl; bend, curve, departure, deviation, shift; chance, go, opportunity, shift, spell, stint, try; act, ac-

tion, deed, service

**turn down** diminish, lessen, lower, quieten, reduce the volume of; decline, rebuff, refuse, reject, say no to, spurn

**turning** side road, turn, turn-off

**turn up** appear, arrive, attend, come, show Inf; discover, find, unearth

**tutor** n coach, guide, instructor, lecturer, master, mentor, schoolmaster, teacher ~v coach, direct, educate, guide, instruct, lecture,

twerp, twirp n Inf stupid person

twice adv two times

twiddle v fiddle; twist

twig n small branch, shoot

twilight n soft light after sunset

twill n fabric with surface of parallel ridges

twin n one of two children born together ~v **twinning, twinned** pair, be paired

twine v twist, coil round ~n string, cord

twinge n momentary sharp pain; qualm

twinkle v shine with dancing light, sparkle ~n twinkling; flash

twirl v turn or twist round quickly; whirl; twiddle

twist v make, become spiral, by turning with one end fast; distort, change; wind ~n twisting

twit n Inf foolish person ~v **twitting, twitted** taunt

twitch v give momentary sharp pull or jerk (to) ~n such pull; spasmodic jerk

twitter v (of birds) utter tremulous

sounds ~n tremulous sound

two n/adj one more than one **two-faced** adj deceitful

tycoon n powerful, influential businessman

type n class; sort; model; pattern; characteristic build; specimen; block bearing letter used for printing ~v print with typewriter **type-cast** v repeatedly cast (actor, actress) in similar roles **typescript** n typewritten document **typewriter** n keyed writing machine **typist** n one who operates typewriter

**typhoid fever** acute infectious disease, esp. of intestines

typhoon n violent tropical storm

typhus n infectious feverish disease

typical adj true to type; characteristic **typically** adv

typify v **-fying, -fied** serve as model of

typography n art of printing; style of printing

tyrant n oppressive or cruel ruler **tyrannical** adj despotic; ruthless

— THESAURUS —

school, teach, train

twilight n dusk, evening, half-light

twin n counterpart, double, fellow, match, mate ~adj double, dual, identical, matching, paired

twine v braid, knit, plait, twist, weave; coil, curl, loop, spiral, twist, wind, wrap ~n cord, string, yarn

twirl v gyrate, revolve, rotate, spin, turn, twist, whirl, wind

twist v coil, curl, wind, wring; contort, distort ~n coil, curl, spin, wind; arc, bend, convolution, curve, turn

twitch v jerk, pluck, pull, snatch, tug, yank ~n jerk, jump, pull, spasm, tic

tycoon industrialist, magnate, mogul, potentate

type category, class, form, group, kind, order, sort, species, strain, variety; example, model, norm, pattern, personification, standard

typical average, characteristic, classic, normal, orthodox, standard, usual

typify embody, epitomize, exemplify, illustrate, personify

tyrannical autocratic, cruel, despotic, dictatorial, domineering, high-handed, oppressive, overbearing, ruthless, severe

tyranny authoritarianism, autocracy, cruelty, despotism, dictatorship,

**tyrannize** *v* exert ruthless or tyrannical authority (over) **tyrannous** *adj* **tyranny** *n* despotism

**tyre** *n* (inflated) rubber ring over rim of wheel of road vehicle

oppression, reign of terror
**tyrant** autocrat, despot, dictator, oppressor, slave-driver

# U u

**ubiquitous** *adj* everywhere at once
**udder** *n* milk-secreting organ of cow etc.
**UFO** unidentified flying object
**ugly** *adj* unpleasant to see, hideous; threatening
**ukulele** *n* small four-stringed guitar
**ulcer** *n* open sore on skin
**ulterior** *adj* lying beneath, beyond what is revealed
**ultimate** *adj* last; highest; fundamental **ultimatum** *n* (*pl* **-tums**, **-ta**) final terms
**ultra-** *comb. form* beyond, excessively, as in **ultramodern**
**ultraviolet** *adj* (of electromagnetic radiation) beyond limit of visibility at violet end of spectrum
**umbilical cord** cordlike structure connecting fetus with placenta of mother
**umbrage** *n* offence, resentment
**umbrella** *n* folding circular cover of nylon etc. on stick, carried in hand to protect against rain
**umpire** *n* person chosen to decide question, or to enforce rules in game ~*v* act as umpire
**umpteen** *adj Inf* very many
**un-** *comb. form* indicating not, reversal of an action
**unaccountable** *adj* that cannot be explained
**unanimous** *adj* in complete agreement **unanimity** *n*
**unassuming** *adj* modest
**unaware** *adj* not aware **unawares** *adv* unexpectedly
**uncanny** *adj* weird, mysterious
**unceremonious** *adj* without ceremony; abrupt, rude
**uncertain** *adj* not able to be known; changeable **uncertainty** *n*
**uncle** *n* brother of father or mother, husband of aunt
**unconscious** *adj* insensible; not aware ~*n* set of thoughts, memories etc. of which one is not normally aware

---
## THESAURUS
---

**ugly** no oil painting *Inf*, plain, unattractive, unprepossessing, unsightly; frightful, hideous, horrid, monstrous, repugnant, repulsive, shocking, vile; baleful, dangerous, menacing, ominous, threatening
**ulterior** concealed, covert, hidden, secret
**ultimate** end, eventual, final, furthest, last; extreme, greatest, highest, paramount, superlative, supreme, utmost
**umpire** *n* arbiter, arbitrator, judge, referee ~*v* adjudicate, judge, referee
**unanimous** agreed, common, like-minded, of one mind, united

**unassuming** humble, modest, quiet, reserved, retiring
**unaware** heedless, ignorant, unconscious, uninformed, unsuspecting
**unawares** by surprise, off guard, suddenly, unexpectedly
**uncanny** eerie, mysterious, queer, strange, supernatural, unnatural, weird
**uncertain** doubtful, dubious, iffy *Inf*, questionable, risky, speculative; hazy, irresolute, unclear, unconfirmed, undecided, unsettled, unsure, vague
**uncertainty** ambiguity, confusion,

**uncouth** adj clumsy, boorish

**unction** n anointing **unctuous** adj excessively polite

**under** prep below, beneath; included in; less than; subjected to ~adv in lower place or condition ~adj lower

**under-** comb. form beneath, below, lower, as in **underground**

**underarm** adj from armpit to wrist; Sport with hand swung below shoulder level

**undercarriage** n aircraft's landing gear; framework supporting body of vehicle

**undercurrent** n current that is not apparent at surface; underlying opinion, emotion

**undercut** v charge less than (another trader)

**underdog** n person, team unlikely to win

**undergo** v -going, -went, -gone experience, endure, sustain

**undergraduate** n student member of university

**underground** adj under the ground; secret ~adv secret but organized resistance to government in power; railway system under the ground

**undergrowth** n small trees, bushes growing beneath taller trees

**underhand** adj secret, sly

**underlie** v lie, be placed under; be the foundation, cause, or basis of

**underline** v put line under; emphasize

**underling** n subordinate

**undermine** v wear away base, support of; weaken insidiously

**underneath** adv below ~prep under ~adj lower ~n lower surface

**underpants** pl n man's underwear for lower part of body

**underpass** n road that passes under another road or railway line

**underpin** v give strength, support to

**understand** v -standing, -stood know and comprehend; realize; infer; take for granted

———————— T H E S A U R U S ————————

doubt, hesitancy, indecision

**unconscious** insensible, numb, out, senseless, stunned; heedless, ignorant, oblivious, unaware, unknowing

**uncouth** awkward, boorish, clumsy, coarse, crude, graceless, gross, loutish, rough, rude, uncultivated, vulgar

**under** prep below, beneath, underneath , governed by, secondary to, subject to, subservient to ~adv below, beneath, down

**undercurrent** riptide, undertow; feeling, flavour, hint, sense, suggestion, tendency, tinge, undertone, vibes Sl

**undergo** bear, endure, experience, stand, suffer, sustain, withstand

**underground** adj buried, covered, subterranean, clandestine, concealed, covert, hidden, secret

**underhand** deceitful, dishonest, fraudulent, furtive, secret, sly, sneaky, stealthy

**underline** mark, underscore; accentuate, emphasize, highlight, stress

**undermine** sabotage, sap, subvert, threaten, weaken

**understand** appreciate, comprehend, fathom, follow, get, grasp, know, make out, perceive, realize, recognize, see, take in; assume, believe, conclude, gather, hear, infer, learn, presume, suppose, think

**understudy** n one prepared to take over theatrical part ~v act as understudy

**undertake** v -taking, -took, -taken make oneself responsible for; enter upon; promise **undertaker** n one who arranges funerals **undertaking** n

**undertone** n dropped tone of voice; underlying suggestion

**underwear** n (also **underclothes**) garments worn next to skin

**underworld** n criminals and their associates; *Myth* abode of the dead

**underwrite** v -writing, -wrote, -written agree to pay; accept liability in insurance policy **underwriter** n

**undo** v -doing, -done, -did untie, unfasten; reverse; cause downfall of

**undulate** v move up and down like waves

**unearth** v dig up; discover

**uneasy** adj anxious; uncomfortable

**unemployed** adj having no paid employment, out of work **unemployment** n

**unexceptionable** adj beyond criticism

**unfold** v open, spread out; reveal

**ungainly** adj awkward, clumsy

**uni-** comb. form one, as in **unicycle**

**unicorn** n mythical horselike animal with single long horn

**uniform** n identifying clothes worn by members of same group, e.g. soldiers, nurses etc. ~adj not changing; regular **uniformity** n

**unify** v -fying, -fied make or become one **unification** n

**unilateral** adj one-sided; (of contract) binding one party only

**union** n joining into one; state, result of being joined; federation; trade union **unionize** v organize

**understudy** n replacement, reserve, sub, substitute

**undertake** agree, bargain, contract, guarantee, pledge, promise; attempt, begin, commence, endeavour, tackle, try

**undertaking** assurance, pledge, promise, vow, word; affair, attempt, business, enterprise, operation, project, task, venture

**undertone** murmur, whisper; feeling, flavour, hint, tinge, touch, trace

**underwear** lingerie, underclothes, underthings, undies, unmentionables *Humorous*

**underworld** criminals, gangsters; Hades, hell, the inferno

**undo** loose, open, unbutton, unfasten, untie, unwrap; annul, cancel, neutralize, offset, reverse; defeat,

destroy, ruin, shatter, upset, wreck

**unearth** dig up, excavate, exhume; discover, expose, find, reveal, uncover

**uneasy** anxious, edgy, nervous, twitchy *Inf*, worried; awkward, insecure, precarious, shaky, strained, tense, uncomfortable

**unemployed** idle, jobless, laid off, redundant

**unfold** open, undo, unfurl, unravel, unroll, unwrap

**ungainly** awkward, clumsy, gawky, inelegant, lumbering, uncouth

**uniform** n costume, dress, garb, habit, livery, outfit, regalia, suit ~adj consistent, even, regular, smooth, unchanging

**uniformity** consistency, evenness, homogeneity, regularity, sameness

(workers) into trade union

**unique** *adj* being only one of its kind; unparalleled

**unison** *n Mus* singing etc. of same notes as others; agreement

**unit** *n* single thing or person; group or individual being part of larger whole; standard quantity

**unite** *v* join into one; associate; become one; combine **unity** *n* state of being one; harmony; agreement

**universe** *n* all existing things considered as constituting systematic whole; the world **universal** *adj* relating to all things or all people

**university** *n* educational institution that awards degrees

**unkempt** *adj* untidy

**unless** *conj* if not, except

**unlike** *adj* dissimilar, different ~*prep* not typical of **unlikely** *adj* im-

probable

**unravel** *v* -elling, -elled undo, untangle

**unrest** *n* discontent

**unruly** *adj* badly behaved, disorderly

**unsavoury** *adj* distasteful

**unscathed** *adj* not harmed

**unsightly** *adj* ugly

**unthinkable** *adj* out of the question; inconceivable; unreasonable

**until** *conj* to the time that; (with a negative) before ~*prep* up to the time of

**unto** *prep Obs* to

**untoward** *adj* awkward, inconvenient

**unwell** *adj* not well, ill

**unwieldy** *adj* awkward; bulky

**unwind** *v* slacken, undo, unravel; become relaxed

——— THESAURUS ———

**union** amalgamation, blend, combination, conjunction, fusion, mixture, uniting; accord, agreement, concord, harmony, unison, unity; alliance, association, coalition, confederacy, federation, league

**unique** lone, only, single, solitary; incomparable, inimitable, matchless, peerless, unequalled, unmatched, unparalleled, unrivalled

**unison** accord, agreement, concert, concord, harmony

**unit** entity, group, section, whole; item, member, part, portion, section, segment

**unite** amalgamate, blend, combine, couple, fuse, join, link, merge, unify; ally, associate, band, close ranks, cooperate

**unity** singleness, undividedness, union, wholeness; accord, agreement, assent, concord, consensus, harmony, peace, solidarity, unison

**universal** common, general, widespread, worldwide

**universe** cosmos, creation, nature

**unlike** different, dissimilar, distinct, diverse

**unlikely** doubtful, faint, improbable, remote, slight

**unravel** disentangle, free, undo, unwind

**unrest** agitation, discontent, dissension, rebellion, sedition, strife

**unruly** disobedient, lawless, mutinous, rebellious, rowdy, wayward, wild, wilful

**unsightly** hideous, horrid, repulsive, ugly, unattractive

**unthinkable** implausible, inconceivable, incredible, unimaginable

**unwell** ailing, ill, sick, sickly, unhealthy

**unwieldy** awkward, cumbersome, inconvenient, unmanageable

**unwind** uncoil, undo, unreel, un-

**unwitting** *adj* not knowing; not intentional

**up** *prep* from lower to higher position; along *~adv* in or to higher position, source, activity etc.; indicating completion **upward** *adj/adv*

**upwards** *adv* **upbeat** *~adj Inf* cheerful **up-to-date** *adj* modern, fashionable

**upbringing** *n* rearing and education of children

**update** *v* bring up to date

**upfront** *adj Inf* open, frank

**upgrade** *v* promote to higher position; improve

**upheaval** *n* sudden or violent disturbance

**uphold** *v* **-holding, -held** maintain, support etc.

**upholster** *v* fit springs, coverings on chairs etc. **upholstery** *n*

**upkeep** *n* act, cost of keeping something in good repair

**upon** *prep* on

**upper** *adj* situated above; of superior quality, status etc. *~n* upper part of boot or shoe **upper case** capital letters **upper hand** position of control

**upright** *adj* erect; honest, just *~adv* vertically *~n* thing standing upright, e.g. post in framework

**uprising** *n* rebellion, revolt

**uproar** *n* tumult, disturbance

**uproot** *v* pull up, as by roots; displace from usual surroundings

**upset** *v* **-setting, -set** overturn; distress; disrupt *~n* unexpected defeat; confusion *~adj* disturbed; emotionally troubled

**upshot** *n* outcome, end

**upside down** turned over completely; *Inf* confused

**upstage** *v* overshadow

**upstart** *n* one suddenly raised to wealth, power etc.

───── THESAURUS ─────

roll; relax, take it easy

**unwitting** ignorant, innocent, unaware, unknowing, unsuspecting; accidental, chance, involuntary, unintended, unplanned

**upbringing** breeding, education, rearing, training

**upgrade** advance, better, enhance, improve, promote, raise

**upheaval** disorder, disruption, revolution, turmoil

**uphold** aid, back, champion, defend, maintain, stick up for *Inf*, support

**upkeep** keep, maintenance, running, subsistence; expenditure, outlay, overheads

**upper** high, higher, top, topmost

**upper hand** advantage, edge, mastery, supremacy

**upright** erect, straight, vertical;

ethical, good, honest, just, principled, righteous, virtuous

**uprising** insurgence, insurrection, mutiny, rebellion, revolt, revolution, rising

**uproar** commotion, disturbance, furore, mayhem, racket, riot

**upset** *v* capsize, overturn, spill; agitate, bother, disconcert, dismay, distress, disturb, fluster, trouble, unnerve; disorder, disrupt, disturb, spoil *~n* agitation, bother, confusion, distress, disturbance, shock, trouble, worry *~adj* ill, queasy, sick; agitated, bothered, dismayed, distressed, disturbed, hurt, troubled, worried

**upshot** end, end result, finale, outcome, result

**upside down** inverted, overturned, upturned; confused, disor-

**uptight** *adj Inf* tense; repressed

**uranium** *n* white radioactive metallic element

**urban** *adj* relating to town or city

**urbane** *adj* elegant, sophisticated

**urchin** *n* mischievous, unkempt child

**urge** *v* exhort earnestly; entreat; drive on ~*n* strong desire **urgency** *n* **urgent** *adj* needing attention at once

**urine** *n* fluid excreted by kidneys to bladder and passed as waste from body **urinal** *n* place for urinating **urinate** *v* discharge urine

**urn** *n* vessel like vase; large container with tap

**us** *pron* object of WE

**use** *v* employ; exercise; exploit; consume ~*n* employment; need to employ; serviceableness; profit; habit **usable** *adj* fit for use **usage** *n* act of using; custom **used** *adj* second-hand; accustomed **useful** *adj* **useless** *adj* having no practical use; *Inf* inept

**usher** *n* (*fem* **usherette**) doorkeeper, one showing people to seats etc. ~*v* introduce, announce

**usual** *adj* habitual, ordinary **usually** *adv* as a rule

**usurp** *v* seize wrongfully

**utensil** *n* vessel, implement, esp. in domestic use

**uterus** *n* (*pl* **uteri**) womb

**utility** *n* usefulness; benefit; useful thing ~*adj* made for practical purposes **utilitarian** *adj* useful rather than beautiful **utilize** *v*

**utmost** *adj* to the highest degree; extreme, furthest ~*n* greatest possible amount

─────────── THESAURUS ───────────

dered, muddled, topsy-turvy

**urban** city, civic, metropolitan, municipal, town

**urchin** brat, gamin, ragamuffin, waif

**urge** *v* beg, beseech, entreat, exhort, implore, plead; drive, encourage, force, impel, incite, induce, press, push, spur, stimulate ~*n* desire, drive, impulse, longing, wish, yearning

**urgency** importance, necessity, need, pressure, stress

**urgent** critical, crucial, imperative, immediate, important, pressing

**usable** functional, practical, serviceable, valid, working

**usage** control, employment, management, operation, running; convention, custom, habit, practice, rule, tradition

**use** *v* apply, employ, exercise, operate, practise, utilize; exploit, manipulate; consume, exhaust, expend, run through, spend ~*n* application, employment, exercise, operation, practice, usage; advantage, benefit, good, help, profit, service, value, worth; custom, habit, practice

**used** cast-off, second-hand, shop-soiled, worn

**useful** advantageous, effective, fruitful, helpful, practical, profitable, valuable, worthwhile

**useless** disadvantageous, fruitless, futile, ineffective, pointless, profitless, unproductive, vain, valueless, worthless *Inf* hopeless, ineffectual, inept

**usual** common, customary, everyday, general, normal, ordinary, routine, standard, stock, typical

**utmost** *adj* chief, extreme, greatest, highest, maximum, paramount, supreme; extreme, final, furthest,

**Utopia** *n* imaginary ideal state

**utter**[1] *v* express, say **utterance** *n*

**utter**[2] *adj* complete, total **utterly**
*adv*

——— THESAURUS ———

last, remotest

**utter**[1] *v* articulate, express, pronounce, say, speak, voice

**utter**[2] *adj* absolute, complete, deep-dyed *usu derog,* downright,

outright, sheer, stark, total, unqualified

**utterly** absolutely, entirely, extremely, fully, thoroughly, totally

# V v

**vacant** *adj* empty, unoccupied **vacancy** *n* untaken job, room etc.

**vacate** *v* quit, leave empty **vacation** *n* time when universities and law courts are closed; *US* holidays

**vaccinate** *v* inoculate with vaccine **vaccination** *n* **vaccine** *n* any substance used for inoculation against disease

**vacillate** *v* waver; move to and fro **vacillation** *n*

**vacuous** *adj* not expressing intelligent thought

**vacuum** *n* (*pl* **vacuums**, **vacua**) place, region containing no matter and from which all or most air, gas has been removed **vacuum cleaner** apparatus for removing dust by suction **vacuum flask** double-walled flask with vacuum between walls, for keeping contents hot or cold

**vagabond** *n* person with no fixed home; wandering beggar or thief

**vagaries** *pl* *n* unpredictable changes

**vagina** *n* passage from womb to exterior

**vagrant** *n* vagabond, tramp **va-**grancy *n*

**vague** *adj* indefinite or uncertain; indistinct; not clearly expressed

**vain** *adj* conceited; worthless; unavailing

**vale** *n Poet* valley

**valentine** *n* (one receiving) card, gift, expressing affection, on Saint Valentine's day

**valet** *n* gentleman's personal servant

**valiant** *adj* brave, courageous

**valid** *adj* sound; of binding force in law **validate** *v* make valid **validity** *n*

**Valium** *n Trademark* drug used as tranquilliser

**valley** *n* low area between hills; river basin

**valour** *n* bravery

**value** *n* cost; worth; usefulness; importance; *pl* principles, standards ~*v* estimate value of; prize **valuable** *adj* precious; worthy ~*n* (*usu. pl*) valuable thing **valuation** *n* estimated worth **value-added tax** tax on difference between cost of basic materials and cost of article made from them

**valve** *n* device to control passage of

--- THESAURUS ---

**vacancy** job, position, post, situation

**vacant** available, empty, free, unfilled, untenanted

**vacuum** emptiness, gap, space, void

**vague** dim, doubtful, hazy, ill-defined, imprecise, indefinite, indistinct, obscure, shadowy, uncertain, unclear, unknown, unspecified, woolly

**vain** arrogant, conceited, egotistical, proud, swaggering, vainglorious; empty, fruitless, futile, idle, pointless, unproductive, unprofitable, useless, worthless

**valiant** bold, brave, heroic, plucky, stouthearted, worthy

**valid** authentic, bona fide, genuine, lawful, legal, legitimate, official

**valuable** *adj* costly, dear, precious; esteemed, important, prized, treasured, useful, valued, worthy

**value** *n* cost, rate; advantage, ben-

fluid etc. through pipe; *Anat* part of body allowing one-way passage of fluids

**vampire** *n* (in folklore) corpse that rises from dead to drink blood of the living **vampire bat** bat that sucks blood of animals

**van**[1] *n* covered vehicle, esp. for goods; railway carriage for goods and use of guard

**van**[2] *n* short for VANGUARD

**vandal** *n* one who wantonly and deliberately damages or destroys **vandalism** *n* **vandalize** *v*

**vane** *n* weathercock; blade of propeller

**vanguard** *n* leading, foremost group, position etc.

**vanilla** *n* tropical climbing orchid; its seed pod; essence of this for flavouring

**vanish** *v* disappear

**vanity** *n* excessive pride or conceit

**vanquish** *v* conquer, overcome

**vantage** *n* advantage **vantage point** position that gives overall view

**vapid** *adj* flat, dull, insipid

**vapour** *n* gaseous form of a substance; steam, mist **vaporize** *v* convert into, pass off in, vapour **vaporizer** *n*

**variable** *see* VARY

**varicose** *adj* (of vein) swollen, twisted

**variegated** *adj* having patches of different colours

**variety** *n* state of being varied or various; diversity; varied assortment; sort or kind

**various** *adj* diverse, of several kinds

**varnish** *n* resinous solution put on surface to make it hard and shiny ~*v* apply varnish to

**vary** *v* varying, varied (cause to) change, diversify, differ **variability** *n* **variable** *adj* changeable; unsteady or fickle ~*n* something subject to variation **variance** *n* state of discord, discrepancy **variant** *adj* different ~*n* alternative form **variation** *n* alteration; extent to which thing varies; modification **varied** *adj* diverse; modified

**vase** *n* vessel, jar as ornament or for holding flowers

**Vaseline** *n* *Trademark* jelly-like petroleum product

**vast** *adj* very large

**VAT** value-added tax

**vat** *n* large tub, tank

**vault**[1] *n* arched roof; cellar; burial chamber; secure room for storing

efit, importance, merit, use, worth; *pl* ethics, principles, standards ~*v* account, assess, estimate, price; esteem, prize, regard highly, respect

**vanguard** forefront, front rank, leaders, spearhead, trendsetters, van

**vanish** disappear, evaporate, fade

**vanity** conceit, egotism, vainglory

**vapour** fog, fumes, haze, mist, smoke, steam

**variation** alteration, change, de-

parture, deviation, difference, diversity

**variety** change, difference, diversity, variation; assortment, collection, medley, mixture, range; brand, breed, category, class, kind, make, sort, species, strain, type

**various** assorted, different, diverse, miscellaneous, sundry

**varnish** *v* adorn, decorate, gild, glaze, gloss

**vary** alter, change, depart, fluctu-

valuables

**vault²** v spring, jump over with the hands resting on something ~n such jump

**VDU** visual display unit

**veal** n calf flesh as food

**vector** n Maths quantity that has size and direction

**veer** v change direction; change one's mind

**vegan** n one who eats no meat, eggs, or dairy products

**vegetable** n plant, esp. edible one ~adj of, from, concerned with plants

**vegetarian** n one who does not eat meat or fish ~adj suitable for vegetarians

**vegetate** v (of plants) grow, develop; (of people) live dull, unproductive life **vegetation** n plants collectively

**vehement** adj marked by intensity of feeling

**vehicle** n means of conveying

**veil** n light material to cover face or head ~v cover with, as with, veil

**vein** n tube in body taking blood to heart; fissure in rock filled with ore

**veined** adj

**Velcro** n Trademark fabric with tiny hooked threads that adheres to coarse surface

**velocity** n rate of motion in given direction; speed

**velvet** n silk or cotton fabric with thick, short pile **velvety** adj of, like velvet; soft and smooth

**vend** v sell **vendor** n **vending machine** machine that dispenses goods automatically

**vendetta** n prolonged quarrel

**veneer** n thin layer of fine wood; superficial appearance ~v cover with veneer

**venerable** adj worthy of reverence **venerate** v look up to, respect, revere **veneration** n

**venereal** adj (of disease) transmitted by sexual intercourse

**Venetian blind** window blind made of thin horizontal slats

**vengeance** n revenge **vengeful** adj

**venison** n flesh of deer as food

**venom** n poison; spite **venomous** adj

**vent** n small hole or outlet ~v give outlet to; utter

ate, modify

**vault¹** n arch, ceiling, roof; cellar, crypt; depository, strongroom

**vault²** v bound, clear, hurdle, jump, leap, spring

**veer** be deflected, change, change course, change direction, sheer, shift, swerve, tack, turn

**vegetate** idle, moulder, stagnate

**vehement** eager, earnest, fervent, fierce, forceful, intense, passionate, strong, violent

**veil** n cloak, cover, curtain, disguise, film, mask, screen, shade ~v cloak, conceal, cover, disguise,

hide, mask, screen, shield

**vein** course, current, seam, streak, stripe; dash, hint, strain, streak, thread

**vendetta** feud, quarrel

**veneer** n appearance, façade, front, gloss, pretence

**vengeance** reprisal, retaliation, retribution, revenge

**venom** poison, toxin; acrimony, bitterness, hate, malice, rancour, spite, spleen

**vent** n aperture, duct, hole, outlet ~v air, emit, express, release, utter, voice

**ventilate** v supply with fresh air

**ventilation** n **ventilator** n

**ventricle** n cavity of heart or brain

**ventriloquist** n one who can so speak that the sounds seem to come from some other person or place **ventriloquism** n

**venture** v expose to hazard; risk; dare; have courage to do something or go somewhere ~n risky undertaking

**venue** n meeting place; location

**veracious** adj truthful **veracity** n

**verandah, veranda** n open or partly enclosed porch on outside of house

**verb** n part of speech used to express action or being **verbal** adj of, by, or relating to words spoken rather than written **verbatim** adj/adv word for word

**verbose** adj long-winded

**verdant** adj green and fresh

**verdict** n decision of jury; opinion reached after examination of facts

**verge** n edge; brink; grass border along road ~v come close to; be on the border of

**verger** n church caretaker

**verify** v -ifying, -ified prove, confirm truth of; test accuracy of **verifi-** cation n

**veritable** adj actual, true

**vermilion** adj/n (of) bright red colour

**vermin** pl n harmful animals, parasites etc.

**vernacular** n commonly spoken language or dialect of particular country or place ~adj of vernacular; native

**verruca** n (pl -cae, -cas) wart, esp. on the foot

**versatile** adj capable of, adapted to many different uses, skills etc. **versatility** n

**verse** n stanza or short subdivision of poem or the Bible; poetry **versed** in skilled in

**version** n description from certain point of view; translation; adaptation

**versus** prep against

**vertebra** n (pl **vertebrae**) single section of backbone **vertebrate** n/ adj (animal) with backbone

**vertical** adj at right angles to the horizon; upright; overhead

**vertigo** n giddiness

**verve** n enthusiasm; vigour

**very** adv extremely, to great extent ~adj exact, ideal; absolute

─── THESAURUS ───

**venture** v chance, hazard, risk, speculate, stake, wager ~n chance, endeavour, enterprise, gamble, hazard, risk

**verbal** literal, oral, spoken

**verbatim** exactly, precisely, word for word

**verdict** conclusion, decision, finding, judgment, opinion

**verge** n border, brim, brink, edge ~v approach, border

**verification** authentication, confirmation, proof

**verify** attest, authenticate, check, confirm, prove, support, validate

**vernacular** n dialect, idiom, parlance, patois, speech ~adj common, informal, local, native, popular, vulgar

**versatile** adaptable, flexible, resourceful

**version** account, portrayal, reading, rendering, translation

**vertical** erect, on end, upright

**very** absolutely, decidedly, exceedingly, extremely, greatly, highly,

**vespers** pl n evening church service

**vessel** n any object used as a container, esp. for liquids; ship; large boat; tubular structure conveying liquids (e.g. blood) in body

**vest** n undergarment for upper body ~v place; confer **vestment** n robe or official garment

**vestibule** n entrance hall, lobby

**vestige** n small trace, amount

**vestry** n room in church for keeping vestments, holding meetings etc.

**vet** n short for VETERINARY SURGEON ~v **vetting, vetted** check suitability of

**veteran** n one who has served a long time, esp. in fighting services ~adj long-serving

**veterinary** adj of, concerning the health of animals **veterinary surgeon** one qualified to treat animal ailments

**veto** n (pl **-toes**) power of rejecting piece of legislation; any prohibition ~v enforce veto against

**vex** v annoy; distress **vexation** n cause of irritation; state of distress

**VHF** very high frequency

**via** prep by way of

**viable** adj practicable; able to live and grow independently

**viaduct** n bridge over valley for road or railway

**vibrate** v (cause to) move to and fro rapidly and continuously; give off (light or sound) by vibration; oscillate; quiver **vibrant** adj throbbing; vibrating; appearing vigorous **vibration** n

**vicar** n clergyman in charge of parish **vicarage** n vicar's house

**vicarious** adj obtained, enjoyed or undergone by imagining another's experiences

**vice¹** n evil or immoral habit or practice; criminal immorality, esp. prostitution; fault, imperfection

**vice²** n appliance with screw mechanism for holding things while working on them

**vice³** adj serving in place of

**viceroy** n ruler acting for king in province or dependency

**vice versa** Lat conversely, the other way round

**vicinity** n neighbourhood

**vicious** adj wicked, cruel; ferocious, dangerous **vicious circle** sequence of problems and solutions

——————— T H E S A U R U S ———————

**vessel** container, pot, receptacle, utensil; boat, craft, ship

**vet** v appraise, check, examine, investigate, look over, review, scan, scrutinize

**veteran** adj expert, long-serving, proficient, seasoned

**veto** n ban, boycott, embargo, interdict, prohibition ~v ban, boycott, forbid, prohibit, reject, rule out, turn down

**vex** v agitate, annoy, bother, distress, exasperate, get on one's nerves Inf,

harass, hassle Inf, irritate, pester, plague, provoke, rile, tease, torment, trouble, upset, worry

**viable** feasible, operable, practicable, usable, workable

**vibrant** alive, animated, colourful, dynamic, sparkling, spirited, vivacious, vivid

**vibrate** pulsate, quiver, shake, shiver, throb, tremble

**vibration** pulse, quiver, shaking, throb, trembling, tremor

**vice** corruption, depravity, evil, evildoing, immorality, iniquity, sin,

which always leads back to original problem

**victim** n person or thing killed, injured etc. as result of another's deed, or accident, circumstances etc.; person cheated; sacrifice **victimization** n **victimize** v punish unfairly; make victim of

**victor** n conqueror; winner **victorious** adj winning; triumphant **victory** n winning of battle etc.

**video** adj relating to or used in transmission or production of television image ~n video cassette recorder; cassette containing video tape ~v **videoing, videoed** record on video **video cassette recorder** tape recorder for recording and playing back TV programmes and films on cassette **video tape** magnetic tape used to record TV programmes

**vie** v **vying, vied** (with with or for) contend, compete against or for someone, something

**view** n survey by eyes or mind; range of vision; picture; scene; opinion; purpose ~v look at; survey; consider **viewer** n one who views; one who watches television; optical device to assist viewing of photographic slides **viewfinder** n window on camera showing what will appear in photograph **viewpoint** n way of regarding subject; position commanding view of landscape

**vigil** n keeping awake, watch **vigilance** n **vigilant** adj watchful, alert

**vigilante** n person who takes it upon himself or herself to enforce the law

**vignette** n concise description of typical features

**vigour** n force, strength; energy, activity **vigorous** adj strong; energetic; flourishing

**vile** adj very wicked, shameful; disgusting; despicable

**vilify** v **-fying, -fied** unjustly attack

turpitude, wickedness

**vicious** bad, cruel, fiendish, foul, monstrous, savage, vile, violent, wicked; cruel, malicious, mean, spiteful, vindictive

**victim** casualty, fatality, martyr, scapegoat, sufferer; dupe

**victimize** persecute, pick on

**victor** champion, conqueror, winner

**victorious** champion, successful, triumphant, winning

**victory** conquest, laurels, success, triumph, win

**view** n sight, vision; outlook, panorama, picture, prospect, scene, vista (sometimes pl) attitude, belief, feeling, opinion, sentiment, thought ~v behold, check out Inf, examine, eye, get a load of Inf, inspect, look at, observe, regard, scan, survey, take a dekko at Brit sl, watch; consider, deem, judge, regard, think about

**viewer** observer, onlooker, spectator, watcher

**viewpoint** angle, perspective, position, slant, stance, standpoint, vantage point, view

**vigilant** alert, attentive, watchful

**vigorous** active, brisk, energetic, flourishing, forceful, intense, lively, lusty, powerful, spirited, strong, vital

**vigour** activity, animation, dash, dynamism, energy, force, gusto, liveliness, might, power, spirit, strength, verve, vitality

the character of

**villa** n large, luxurious country house; detached or semidetached suburban house

**village** n small group of houses in country area

**villain** n wicked person **villainous** adj

**vindicate** v clear of charges; justify **vindication** n

**vindictive** adj revengeful; inspired by resentment

**vine** n climbing plant bearing grapes **vineyard** n plantation of vines

**vinegar** n acid liquid obtained from wine and other alcoholic liquors

**vintage** n gathering of the grapes; the yield; wine of particular year; time of origin ~adj best and most typical **vintner** n dealer in wine

**vinyl** n plastic material with variety of domestic and industrial uses;

record made of vinyl

**viola** n see VIOLIN

**violate** v break (law, agreement etc.); rape; outrage, desecrate **violation** n

**violent** adj marked by, due to, extreme force, passion or fierceness; using excessive force; intense **violence** n

**violet** n plant with small bluish-purple or white flowers; bluish-purple colour ~adj of this colour

**violin** n small four-stringed musical instrument **viola** n large violin with lower range **violinist** n

**VIP** very important person

**viper** n poisonous snake

**viral** adj see VIRUS

**virgin** n one who has not had sexual intercourse ~adj without experience of sexual intercourse; uncorrupted; (of land) untilled **virginal** adj **virginity** n

**virile** adj (of male) capable of

───────── THESAURUS ─────────

**vile** bad, base, contemptible, corrupt, debased, degrading, depraved, evil, impure, loathsome, low, mean, perverted, shocking, sinful, ugly, vicious, wicked; disgusting, foul, horrid, loathsome, nasty, repellent, repugnant, repulsive, sickening

**villain** blackguard, criminal, reprobate, rogue, scoundrel, wretch

**villainous** bad, base, criminal, debased, evil, fiendish, mean, sinful, vicious, wicked

**vindicate** absolve, acquit, clear, defend, excuse, exonerate, justify

**vindication** defence, excuse, justification, plea, support

**vindictive** malicious, revengeful, spiteful, vengeful

**vintage** n crop, era, harvest, ori-

gin, year ~adj best, choice, prime, select, superior

**violate** break, disobey, disregard, infringe, transgress; abuse, assault, debauch, defile, desecrate, dishonour, invade, outrage

**violation** abuse, breach, contravention, infringement, transgression, trespass; defilement, desecration, profanation, sacrilege, spoliation

**violence** bloodshed, brutality, cruelty, ferocity, force, frenzy, fury, passion, savagery, wildness

**violent** brutal, cruel, fierce, flaming, furious, passionate, powerful, raging, rough, savage, strong, tempestuous, vehement, vicious, wild; devastating, powerful, raging, strong, tempestuous, tumultuous,

copulation or procreation; strong, forceful **virility** n

**virtual** adj so in effect, though not in appearance or name **virtually** adv practically, almost

**virtue** n moral goodness; good quality; merit **virtuous** adj morally good

**virtuoso** n (pl **-sos**, **-si**) one with special skill, esp. in music **~adj** showing great skill **virtuosity** n

**virulent** adj very infectious, poisonous etc.; malicious

**virus** n infecting agent that causes disease **viral** adj

**visa** n endorsement on passport permitting bearer to travel into country of issuing government

**visage** n face

**vis-à-vis** prep in relation to, regarding

**viscount** n (fem **viscountess**) Brit. nobleman ranking below earl and above baron

**viscous** adj thick and sticky

**visible** adj that can be seen **visibility** n degree of clarity of vision

**vision** n sight; insight; dream; hallucination **visionary** adj marked by vision; impractical **~n** mystic; impractical person

**visit** v go, come and see; stay temporarily with (someone) **~n** stay; call at person's home etc. **visitation** n formal visit or inspection; affliction or plague **visitor** n

**visor, vizor** n movable front part of helmet; eyeshade, esp. on car; peak on cap

**vista** n extensive view

**visual** adj of sight; visible **visualize** v form mental image of

**vital** adj necessary to, affecting life; lively; animated; essential **vitality** n life, vigour

**vitamin** n any of group of substances occurring in foodstuffs and essential to health

———— THESAURUS ————

turbulent, wild

**virgin** chaste, fresh, immaculate, maidenly, pure, undefiled, untouched

**virtually** as good as, effectually, in effect, nearly, practically

**virtue** excellence, goodness, incorruptibility, integrity, morality, rectitude, uprightness; advantage, asset, attribute, credit, merit, strength

**virtuoso** n artist, genius, maestro, master **~adj** brilliant, dazzling, masterly

**virtuous** blameless, good, honest, incorruptible, moral, pure, righteous, squeaky-clean, upright

**visible** apparent, clear, detectable, discernible, evident, manifest, noticeable, observable, obvious, perceivable, plain, unconcealed

**vision** eyes, eyesight, perception, seeing, sight, view; discernment, foresight, imagination, insight; concept, daydream, dream, fantasy, idea, image

**visionary** adj idealistic, romantic **~n** dreamer, idealist, mystic, prophet, seer

**visit** v inspect, stay with **~n** call, sojourn, stay, stop

**visitor** caller, company, guest

**visual** optic, optical; discernible, observable, perceptible, visible

**visualize** envisage, imagine, picture

**vital** animated, dynamic, energetic, forceful, lively, spirited, vivacious, zestful; basic, essential, indispensable, requisite

**vitality** animation, energy, life,

**viva** *interj* long live

**vivacious** *adj* lively, sprightly **vivacity** *n*

**vivid** *adj* bright, intense; true to life

**vivisection** *n* dissection of, or operating on, living animals

**vixen** *n* female fox

**vizor** *see* VISOR

**vocabulary** *n* list of words, usu. in alphabetical order; stock of words used in particular language or subject

**vocal** *adj* of, with, or giving out voice; outspoken, articulate **vocalist** *n* singer **vocals** *pl n* singing part

**vocation** *n* (urge, inclination, predisposition to) particular career, profession etc. **vocational** *adj*

**vociferous** *adj* shouting, noisy

**vodka** *n* spirit distilled from potatoes or grain

**vogue** *n* fashion, style; popularity

**voice** *n* sound given out by person in speaking, singing etc.; quality of the sound; expressed opinion; (right to) share in discussion ~*v* give utterance to, express

**void** *adj* empty; destitute; not legally binding ~*n* empty space ~*v* make ineffectual or invalid; empty out

**vol.** volume

**volatile** *adj* evaporating quickly; lively; changeable

**volcano** *n* (*pl* -**noes**, -**nos**) hole in earth's crust through which lava, ashes, smoke etc. are discharged; mountain so formed **volcanic** *adj*

**vole** *n* small rodent

**volition** *n* exercise of will

**volley** *n* simultaneous discharge of weapons or missiles; rush of oaths, questions etc.; *Sport* kick, stroke etc. at moving ball before it touches ground ~*v* discharge; kick, strike etc. in volley **volleyball** *n* game where ball is hit over high net

**volt** *n* unit of electric potential **voltage** *n* electric potential difference expressed in volts

**voluble** *adj* talking easily and at length

**volume** *n* space occupied; mass; amount; power, fullness of voice or sound; book; part of book bound in

————————————————— THESAURUS —————————————————

liveliness, sparkle, vivacity

**vivacious** lively, spirited, vital

**vivid** bright, brilliant, glowing, intense, rich; clear, distinct, graphic, lifelike, memorable, powerful, strong

**vocabulary** dictionary, glossary, language, lexicon, wordbook, words

**vocal** *adj* clamorous, eloquent, expressive, forthright, frank, noisy, outspoken, strident

**vocation** business, calling, career, job, post, profession, trade

**vociferous** loud, noisy, shouting, strident

**vogue** craze, custom, fashion,

mode, style, trend, way; currency, favour, popularity, prevalence, use

**voice** *n* language, sound, tone, utterance, words; decision, part, say, view, vote ~*v* air, articulate, assert, declare, enunciate, express, utter

**void** *adj* empty, free, unfilled, unoccupied, vacant; invalid, useless, worthless ~*n* blank, emptiness, gap, space, vacuum ~*v* discharge, drain, emit, empty, evacuate

**volatile** changeable, erratic, fickle, inconstant, mercurial, temperamental, unsettled, unstable, unsteady, up and down *Inf*, variable

**volley** *n* barrage, burst, discharge,

one cover **voluminous** *adj* bulky, copious

**voluntary** *adj* having, done by free will; done without payment; supported by free-will contributions

**volunteer** *n* one who offers service, joins forces etc. of his or her own free will ~*v* offer oneself or one's services

**voluptuous** *adj* of, contributing to pleasures of the senses; sexually alluring because of full, shapely figure

**vomit** *v* eject (contents of stomach) through mouth ~*n* matter vomited

**voodoo** *n* religion involving ancestor worship and witchcraft

**voracious** *adj* greedy, ravenous **voracity** *n*

**vortex** *n* (*pl* **-texes, -tices**) whirlpool; whirling motion

**vote** *n* formal expression of choice; individual pronouncement; right to give it; result of voting ~*v* express, declare opinion, choice, preference

etc. by vote

**vouch** *v* (*usu. with for*) guarantee

**voucher** *n* document to establish facts; ticket as substitute for cash

**vow** *n* solemn promise, esp. religious one ~*v* promise, threaten by vow

**vowel** *n* any speech sound pronounced without stoppage or friction of the breath; letter standing for such sound, as *a, e, i, o, u*

**voyage** *n* journey, esp. long one, by sea or air ~*v* make voyage

**vulcanize** *v* treat (rubber) with sulphur at high temperature to increase its durability **vulcanization** *n*

**vulgar** *adj* offending against good taste; common **vulgarity** *n*

**vulnerable** *adj* capable of being physically or emotionally wounded or hurt; exposed, open to attack, persuasion etc. **vulnerability** *n*

**vulture** *n* large bird which feeds on carrion

———————— THESAURUS ————————

hail, salvo, shower

**volume** amount, body, bulk, capacity, mass, quantity, total; book, publication, title, tome, treatise

**voluntary** free, intentional, spontaneous, unforced, unpaid, willing

**volunteer** *v* advance, offer, present, proffer, propose, suggest

**vomit** *v* be sick, chuck (up) *Sl, chiefly US*, disgorge, heave, regurgitate, retch

**voracious** devouring, gluttonous, greedy, hungry, ravenous

**vote** *n* ballot, franchise, poll, referendum, suffrage ~*v* ballot, elect, opt

**vouch** (*usu. with for*) answer for, back, certify, confirm, guarantee,

support, uphold

**vow** *n* oath, pledge, promise ~*v* affirm, dedicate, devote, pledge, promise, swear

**voyage** *n* crossing, cruise, journey, passage, travels, trip

**vulgar** boorish, coarse, common, crude, dirty, gross, ill-bred, impolite, improper, indecent, indelicate, low, nasty, ribald, rude, tasteless, unmannerly, unrefined

**vulgarity** bad taste, coarseness, crudeness, grossness, indelicacy, rudeness

**vulnerable** assailable, defenceless, exposed, susceptible, weak, wide open

# W w

**wacky** *adj Inf* eccentric, funny

**wad** *n* small pad of fibrous material; thick roll of banknotes ~*v* **wadding, wadded** pad, stuff etc. with wad

**waddle** *v* walk like duck ~*n* this gait

**wade** *v* walk through something that hampers movement, esp. water **wader** *n* person or bird that wades

**wafer** *n* thin, crisp biscuit

**waffle¹** *n/v Inf* (use) long-winded and meaningless language

**waffle²** *n* kind of pancake

**waft** *v* convey smoothly through air or water ~*n* breath of wind; odour, whiff

**wag** *v* **wagging, wagged** (cause to) move rapidly from side to side ~*n* instance of wagging; *Inf* witty person **wagtail** *n* small bird with long tail

**wage** *n* (*oft. pl*) payment for work done ~*v* carry on

**wager** *n/v* bet

**waggle** *v/n* wag

**wagon, waggon** *n* four-wheeled vehicle for heavy loads; railway freight truck

**waif** *n* homeless person, esp. child

**wail** *v/n* cry, lament

**waist** *n* part of body between hips and ribs; various narrow central parts **waistcoat** *n* sleeveless garment worn under jacket or coat

**wait** *v* stay in one place, remain inactive in expectation (of something); be prepared (for something); delay; serve in restaurant etc. ~*n* act or period of waiting **waiter** *n* (*fem* **waitress**) attendant on guests at hotel, restaurant etc.

**waive** *v* forgo; not insist on **waiver** *n* (written statement of) this act

**wake¹** *v* **waking, woke, woken** rouse from sleep; stir up ~*n* vigil; watch beside corpse **waken** *v* cry, lament

**wake²** *n* track or path left by anything that has passed

**walk** *v* (cause, assist to) move,

---

## THESAURUS

**wade** ford, paddle, splash

**wag** *v* bob, flutter, nod, quiver, rock, shake, stir, wave ~*n* bob, flutter, nod, oscillation, quiver, shake, toss, wave

**wage** *n also* **wages** allowance, compensation, earnings, fee, hire, pay, payment, remuneration, reward, stipend

**wager** *n* bet, gamble, stake ~*v* bet, chance, gamble, hazard, lay, punt *chiefly Brit,* risk, stake

**wail** *v* bawl, bemoan, cry, grieve, howl, lament, weep ~*n* complaint, cry, grief, howl, lament, moan, weeping

**wait** *v* abide, dally, delay, hang fire, hold back, linger, pause, remain, rest, stay, tarry ~*n* delay, halt, interval, pause, rest, stay

**waiter, waitress** attendant, server, steward, stewardess

**waive** abandon, defer, forgo, give up, postpone, put off, relinquish, remit, renounce, resign, surrender

**wake¹** *v* arise, bestir, get up, rouse, stir; activate, animate, arouse, awaken, enliven, excite, fire, galvanize, kindle, provoke, quicken, rouse, stimulate, stir up

**wake²** backwash, path, slipstream, track, trail, train, wash, waves

travel on foot at ordinary pace; cross, pass through by walking; escort, conduct by walking ~n act, instance of walking; path or other place or route for walking **walking stick** stick used as support when walking **Walkman** n Trademark small portable cassette player with headphones **walkover** n Inf easy victory

**wall** n structure of brick, stone etc. serving as fence, side of building etc.; surface of one; anything resembling this ~v enclose with wall; block up with wall **wallflower** n garden plant **wallpaper** n paper, usu. patterned, to cover interior walls

**wallaby** n Aust. marsupial similar to and smaller than kangaroo

**wallet** n small folding case, esp. for paper money, documents etc.

**wallop** Inf v beat soundly; strike

hard ~n stroke or blow

**wallow** v roll (in liquid or mud); revel (in) ~n wallowing

**walnut** n large nut with crinkled shell; tree it grows on; its wood

**walrus** n large sea mammal with long tusks

**waltz** n ballroom dance; music for it ~v perform waltz

**wan** adj pale, pallid

**wand** n stick, esp. as carried by magician etc.

**wander** v roam, ramble; go astray, deviate ~n wandering

**wane** v/n decline; (of moon) decrease in size

**wangle** v Inf get by devious methods

**want** v desire; lack ~n desire; need; deficiency **wanted** adj being sought, esp. by police **wanting** adj lacking; below standard

**wanton** adj dissolute; without mo-

— THESAURUS —

**waken** activate, arouse, enliven, fire, galvanize, get up, kindle, quicken, rouse, stimulate, stir

**walk** v advance, go, hike, move, pace, promenade, saunter, step, stride, stroll, tramp, trek, trudge; accompany, convoy, escort, take ~n hike, march, promenade, ramble, saunter, stroll, tramp, trek, trudge, turn; alley, avenue, footpath, lane, path, pathway, pavement, promenade, sidewalk, trail

**wall** divider, enclosure, panel, partition, screen; barrier, block, impediment, obstacle

**wallet** case, holder, notecase, pouch, purse

**wallow** lie, splash around, tumble, welter; bask, delight, glory, luxuriate, relish, revel

**wand** baton, rod, stick, twig

**wander** v cruise, drift, meander, ramble, range, roam, rove, straggle, stray, stroll; depart, digress, diverge, err, lapse, veer ~n meander, ramble

**wane** v abate, decline, decrease, dim, drop, dwindle, ebb, fade, fail, lessen, sink, subside, weaken, wind down, wither

**want** v covet, crave, desire, eat one's heart out over, need, require, wish, yearn for; be short of, be without, call for, demand, lack, miss, need, require ~n appetite, craving, demand, desire, fancy, hankering, hunger, longing, need, thirst, wish; destitution, need, penury, poverty; absence, dearth, deficiency, famine, lack, scarcity, shortage

**wanting** absent, incomplete, lack-

tive; unrestrained

**war** n fighting between nations; state of hostility; conflict, contest ~v warring, warred make war **war-like** adj of, for war; fond of war **warrior** n fighter **warfare** n hostilities **warhead** n part of missile etc. containing explosives

**warble** v sing with trills **warbler** n any of various kinds of small song-birds

**ward** n division of city, hospital etc.; minor under care of guardian **warder** n (fem **wardress**) jailer **ward off** avert, repel

**warden** n person in charge of building, college etc.

**wardrobe** n piece of furniture for hanging clothes in; person's supply of clothes

**ware** n goods; articles collectively; pl goods for sale **warehouse** n storehouse for goods

**warm** adj moderately hot; serving to maintain heat; affectionate; en-thusiastic ~v make, become warm **warmth** n mild heat; cordiality; in-tensity of emotion **warm up** v make or become warmer; do preliminary exercises

**warn** v put on guard; caution; give advance information to **warning** n

**warp** v (cause to) twist (out of shape); pervert or be perverted

**warrant** n authority; document giving authority ~v guarantee;

ing, less, missing, short, shy; defec-tive, faulty, imperfect, patchy, poor, sketchy, substandard, un-sound

**wanton** adj abandoned, dissolute, fast, immoral, lewd, libertine, licen-tious, loose, shameless, unchaste; cruel, evil, gratuitous, malicious, motiveless, needless, senseless, spiteful, unjustified, unprovoked, vicious, wicked, wilful

**war** n battle, bloodshed, combat, conflict, contest, enmity, fighting, hostilities, strife, struggle, warfare

**ward** n area, district, division, pre-cinct, quarter, zone; charge, minor, protégé, pupil

**warden** n administrator, caretaker, curator, guardian, janitor, keeper, ranger, steward, warder, watchman

**warder, wardress** n gaoler, guard, jailer, keeper, prison officer

**ward off** avert, avoid, block, de-flect, forestall, parry, repel, thwart

**wardrobe** n closet, clothes cup-board; apparel, attire, clothes, out-fit

**warehouse** n depository, depot, stockroom, store, storehouse

**warfare** n arms, battle, blows, com-bat, conflict, contest, discord, fight-ing, hostilities, strife, struggle, war

**warlike** adj aggressive, belligerent, combative, hawkish, hostile, jingo-istic, martial, militaristic, pugna-cious, warmongering

**warm** adj balmy, pleasant, sunny; affable, affectionate, amiable, amo-rous, cheerful, congenial, cordial, friendly, genial, happy, hearty, kindly, likable or likeable, loving, pleasant, tender ~v heat, melt, thaw

**warmth** n heat, warmness; affability, affection, cordiality, happiness, heartiness, kindliness, love, tender-ness

**warn** v admonish, advise, alert, cau-tion, forewarn, inform, notify, tip off

**warning** n admonition, advice, alarm, alert, caution, hint, notice, notification, omen, premonition,

authorize, justify **warranty** n guarantee of quality of goods; security

**warren** n (burrows inhabited by) colony of rabbits

**warrior** n see WAR

**wart** n small hard growth on skin **wart hog** kind of Afr. wild pig

**wary** adj watchful, cautious, alert

**was** past tense, first and third person sing. of BE

**wash** v clean (oneself, clothes etc.) with water, soap etc.; be washable; move, be moved by water; flow, sweep over, against ~n act of washing; clothes washed at one time; sweep of water, esp. set up by moving ship **washable** adj capable of being washed without damage **washer** n one who, that which, washes; ring put under nut **washing** n clothes to be washed **washout**

n Inf complete failure **wash up** wash dishes and cutlery after meal

**wasp** n striped stinging insect resembling bee

**waste** v expend uselessly; fail to take advantage; dwindle; pine away ~n act of wasting; rubbish; desert ~adj worthless, useless; desert; wasted **wasteful** adj extravagant

**watch** v observe closely; guard; wait expectantly (for); be on watch ~n portable timepiece for wrist, pocket etc.; state of being on the lookout; spell of duty **watchful** adj **watchdog** n dog kept to guard property; person or group guarding against inefficiency or illegality **watchman** n man guarding building etc., esp. at night **watchword** n password; rallying cry

**water** n transparent, colourless,

sign, signal, threat, tip

**warrant** n assurance, authority, authorization, commission, guarantee, licence, permission, permit, pledge, sanction, security ~v affirm, assure, attest, avouch, certify, declare, guarantee, pledge, underwrite, uphold; approve, authorize, commission, demand, deserve, empower, entitle, excuse, justify, license, permit, require, sanction

**warrior** combatant, fighter, soldier

**wary** alert, attentive, careful, cautious, chary, distrustful, guarded, heedful, prudent, suspicious, vigilant, watchful

**wash** v bath, bathe, clean, cleanse, launder, moisten, rinse, scrub, shower, wet; (with away) carry off, erode, move, sweep away, wash off ~n ablution, bath, cleaning, rinse, scrub, shampoo, shower, washing; flow, roll, surge, sweep, swell, wave

**washout** disappointment, disaster, failure, fiasco, mess

**waste** v dissipate, lavish, misuse, squander; consume, corrode, crumble, decay, decline, disable, drain, dwindle, exhaust, fade, gnaw, perish, sink, undermine, wane, wither ~n extravagance, loss, misapplication, misuse, prodigality, squandering, wastefulness; debris, dregs, dross, garbage, leavings, litter, offal, refuse, rubbish, scrap, trash; desert, void, wilderness ~adj superfluous, unused, worthless; bare, barren, desolate, empty, unproductive

**wasteful** extravagant, lavish, prodigal, ruinous, spendthrift, thriftless, uneconomical

**watch** v check out Inf, contemplate, eye, get a load of Inf, look, mark, note, observe, regard, see, stare at, view; guard, keep, look af-

odourless, tasteless liquid, substance of rain, river etc.; body of water; urine ~v put water on or into; irrigate or provide with water; salivate; (of eyes) fill with tears **watery** adj wet; weak **water closet** sanitary convenience flushed with water **watercolour** n paint thinned with water; painting in this **watercress** n plant growing in clear ponds and streams **waterfall** n vertical descent of waters of river **water lily** plant that floats on surface of fresh water **waterlogged** adj saturated, filled with water **watermark** n faint translucent design in sheet of paper **watermelon** n melon with green skin and red flesh **water polo** team game played by swimmers with ball **waterproof** adj not letting water through ~v make waterproof ~n waterproof garment **watershed** n line separating two river systems; divide **water-skiing** n sport of riding over water on skis towed by speedboat **watertight** adj preventing water from entering or escaping; with no weak points

**watt** n unit of electric power

**wave** v move to and fro, as hand in greeting or farewell; signal by waving; give, take shape of waves (as hair etc.) ~n ridge and trough on water etc.; act, gesture of waving; vibration, as in radio waves; prolonged spell; upsurge; wavelike shapes in hair etc. **wavy** adj **wavelength** n distance between the same points of two successive waves

**waver** v hesitate, be irresolute; be, become unsteady

**wax**¹ n yellow, soft, pliable material made by bees; this or similar substance used for sealing, making candles etc.; waxy secretion of ear ~v put wax on **waxy** adj like wax **wax²** v grow, increase

**way** n manner; method; direction; path; passage; progress; state or condition; room for activity **wayfarer** n traveller, esp. on foot **waylay** v -laying, -laid lie in wait for and accost, attack **wayside** n/adj (by) side or edge of road **wayward** adj capricious, perverse, wilful

**WC** water closet

-ter, mind, protect, tend ~n chronometer, timepiece; eye, lookout, notice, surveillance, vigil, vigilance

**watchful** alert, attentive, guarded, heedful, observant, suspicious, vigilant, wary, wide awake

**watchman** caretaker, custodian, guard, security man

**water** n aqua, H₂O ~v dampen, drench, flood, hose, irrigate, moisten, soak, spray, sprinkle

**waterfall** cascade, cataract, fall

**watertight** sound, waterproof; airtight, firm, flawless, foolproof, impregnable, sound, unassailable

**watery** adulterated, diluted, insip-

id, runny, tasteless, thin, washy, weak

**wave** v beckon, direct, gesture, indicate, sign, signal; brandish, flourish, flutter, oscillate, quiver, ripple, shake, stir, sway, swing, undulate, wag ~n billow, breaker, ripple, roller, sea surf, swell; current, drift, flood, movement, outbreak, rush, stream, surge, sweep, tendency, trend, upsurge

**waver** dither *chiefly Brit*, falter, hesitate, seesaw, vacillate; flicker, fluctuate, quiver, reel, shake, sway, undulate, vary, wave, weave, wobble

**we** *pron* first person plural pronoun

**weak** *adj* lacking strength; irresolute; (of sound) faint; (of argument) unconvincing; unprotected, vulnerable; lacking flavour **weaken** *v* **weakling** *n* feeble creature **weakly** *adj* weak; sickly ~*adv* in weak manner **weakness** *n*

**weal** *n* streak left on flesh by blow of stick or whip

**wealth** *n* riches; abundance **wealthy** *adj*

**wean** *v* accustom to food other than mother's milk; win over, coax away from

**weapon** *n* implement to fight with

**wear** *v* **wearing, wore, worn** have on the body; show; (cause to) become impaired by use; harass or weaken; last ~*n* act of wearing; things to wear; damage caused by use; ability to resist effect of constant use

**weary** *adj* tired, exhausted, jaded; tiring; tedious ~*v* -**rying, -ried** make, become weary **weariness** *n*

———————— THESAURUS ————————

**way** approach, fashion, manner, means, method, mode, plan, practice, procedure, process, scheme, system, technique; access, avenue, channel, course, direction, lane, path, road, route, street, track, trail; advance, approach, journey, march, passage, progress

**wayward** contrary, disobedient, headstrong, incorrigible, mulish, obdurate, obstinate, perverse, rebellious, self-willed, stubborn, ungovernable, unruly, wilful

**weak** anaemic, debilitated, delicate, exhausted, faint, feeble, fragile, frail, infirm, puny, shaky, sickly, spent, tender, unsteady, wasted; cowardly, impotent, indecisive, ineffectual, infirm, irresolute, pathetic, powerless, soft, spineless; feeble, flimsy, hollow, invalid, lame, pathetic, shallow, slight, unconvincing, unsatisfactory; defenceless, exposed, helpless, unprotected, unsafe, untenable, vulnerable, wide open; diluted, insipid, tasteless, thin, watery

**weaken** abate, diminish, dwindle, enervate, fade, fail, flag, impair, invalidate, lessen, lower, reduce, sap, tire, undermine, wane; cut, debase, dilute, thin

**weakling** doormat *Sl*, drip *Inf*, milksop, sissy, wimp *Inf*

**weakness** faintness, feebleness, frailty, impotence, infirmity, powerlessness, vulnerability; blemish, defect, deficiency, failing, fault, flaw, imperfection, shortcoming

**wealth** affluence, assets, capital, cash, estate, fortune, funds, means, money, opulence, possessions, property, resources, riches, substance; abundance, bounty, plenty, profusion, richness

**wealthy** affluent, comfortable, opulent, prosperous, rich, well-off

**wear** *v* clothe *Inf*, don, have on, put on, sport *Inf*; display, exhibit, show; abrade, corrode, deteriorate, erode, fray, grind, rub; annoy, drain, get on one's nerves *Inf*, harass, irk, pester, tax, vex, weaken, weary ~*n* apparel, attire, clothes, costume, dress, garments, gear *Inf*, habit, outfit; abrasion, attrition, damage, erosion, use; employment, mileage *Inf*, service, use, utility

**weariness** drowsiness, exhaustion, fatigue, lassitude, lethargy, tiredness

**weasel** *n* small carnivorous mammal with long body and short legs

**weather** *n* day-to-day meteorological conditions, esp. temperature etc. of a place ~*v* affect by weather; endure; resist; come safely through

**weathercock** *n* revolving object to show which way wind blows

**weave** *v* **weaving, wove, woven** form into texture or fabric by interlacing, esp. on loom; construct; (*past tense* **weaved**) make one's way, esp. with side to side motion

**web** *n* woven fabric; net spun by spider; membrane between toes of waterfowl, frogs etc.

**wed** *v* **wedding, wedded** marry; unite closely **wedding** *n* marriage ceremony **wedlock** *n* marriage

**wedge** *n* piece of wood, metal etc. tapering to a thin edge ~*v* fasten, split with wedge; stick by compression or crowding

**Wednesday** *n* fourth day of the week

**wee** *adj* small; little

**weed** *n* plant growing where undesired ~*v* clear of weeds **weedy** *adj* full of weeds; weak

**week** *n* period of seven days **weekly** *adj/adv* happening, done, published etc. once a week **weekday** *n* any day of the week except Saturday or Sunday **weekend** *n* Saturday and Sunday

**weep** *v* **weeping, wept** shed tears (for); grieve

**weigh** *v* find weight of; consider; have weight; be burdensome **weight** *n* measure of the heaviness of an object; quality of heaviness; heavy mass; object of known mass for weighing; importance, influence ~*v* add weight to **weighting** *n* extra allowance paid in special circumstances

**weir** *n* river dam

**weird** *adj* unearthly, uncanny, strange, bizarre

**welcome** *adj* received gladly;

——————— THESAURUS ———————

**weary** *adj* dead beat *Inf*, drained, drowsy, exhausted, fatigued, flagging, sleepy, spent, tired, wearied, worn out; arduous, laborious, taxing, tiring, wearing ~*v* burden, drain, enervate, fatigue, sap, tax, tire, wear out

**weather** *n* climate, conditions ~*v* endure, overcome, stand, suffer, surmount, survive, withstand

**weave** blend, braid, entwine, intermingle, intertwine, knit, plait, twist; build, construct, contrive, create, fabricate, make, spin; wind, zigzag

**web** cobweb; lattice, mesh, net, network, weave

**wed** join, make one, marry, unite

**wedding** marriage, nuptials, wed-lock

**wedge** *n* block, chunk, lump ~*v* cram, force, jam, lodge, pack, squeeze, stuff

**weep** bemoan, bewail, cry, lament, mourn, snivel, sob, whimper

**weigh** consider, contemplate, evaluate, examine, eye up, ponder, study; burden, oppress, prey

**weight** *n* burden, gravity, heaviness, load, mass, pressure, tonnage; ballast, load, mass; authority, consequence, consideration, emphasis, impact, importance, influence, power, substance, value ~*v* ballast, charge, freight, load

**weird** bizarre, eerie, freakish, ghostly, grotesque, mysterious, odd, queer, strange, uncanny, un-

freely permitted ~n kindly greeting ~v -coming, -comed greet with pleasure; receive gladly

**weld** v unite metal by softening with heat; unite closely ~n welded joint **welder** n

**welfare** n wellbeing **welfare state** system in which government takes responsibility for wellbeing of citizens

**well**[1] adv better, best in good manner or degree; suitably; intimately; fully; favourably; kindly; to a considerable degree ~adj in good health; satisfactory ~interj exclamation of surprise, interrogation etc. **wellbeing** n state of being well, happy, or prosperous **well-disposed** adj inclined to be friendly **well-mannered** adj having good manners **well-off** adj fairly rich **well-read** adj having read much

**well**[2] n hole sunk into the earth to reach water, gas, oil etc.; spring ~v spring, gush

**wellies** pl n Inf wellingtons

**wellingtons** pl n high waterproof boots

**welter** v roll or tumble ~n turmoil, disorder

**wench** n young woman

**wend** v go, travel

**went** past tense of GO

**were** past tense of BE (used with you, we and they)

**werewolf** n in folklore, person who can turn into a wolf

**west** n part of sky where sun sets; part of country etc. lying to this side ~adj that is toward or in this region ~adv to the west **westerly** adj/adv **western** adj **westernize** v adapt to customs and culture of the West **westward** adj/adv **westwards** adv

**wet** adj wetter, wettest having water or other liquid on a surface or being soaked in it; rainy; (of paint, ink etc.) not yet dry ~v wetting, wetted make wet ~n moisture, rain **wet suit** close-fitting rubber suit worn by divers etc.

earthly, unnatural

**welcome** adj acceptable, agreeable, desirable, gratifying, wanted ~n acceptance, greeting, hospitality, reception ~v embrace, greet, hail, meet, receive

**welfare** advantage, benefit, good, happiness, health, interest, profit, prosperity, success, wellbeing

**well**[1] adv agreeably, nicely, pleasantly, satisfactorily, smoothly, splendidly, successfully, ably, adeptly, admirably, effectively, efficiently, expertly, proficiently, skilfully; correctly, easily, fairly, fittingly, justly, properly, readily, rightly, suitably; abundantly, amply, completely, considerably, fully, greatly,

heartily, highly, substantially, thoroughly, very much ~adj able-bodied, fit, hale, healthy, hearty, robust, sound, strong

**well**[2] n bore, hole, pit, shaft; pool, source, spring ~v exude, flow, gush, ooze, pour, rise, run, seep, spout, spring, spurt, stream, surge, trickle

**well-off** comfortable, flourishing, fortunate, lucky, successful, thriving

**wet** adj damp, dank, dripping, moist, saturated, soaking, sodden, soggy, sopping, waterlogged; drizzling, misty, pouring, raining, rainy, showery, teeming ~v damp, dip, drench, irrigate, moisten, saturate,

**whack** *v* strike with sharp resounding sound *~n* such blow

**whale** *n* large fish-shaped sea mammal

**wharf** *n* (*pl* **wharves**) platform at harbour, on river etc. for loading and unloading ships

**what** *pron* which thing; that which; request for statement to be repeated *~adj* which; as much as; how great, surprising etc. *~adv* in which way **whatever** *pron* anything which; of what kind it may be **whatsoever** *adj* at all

**wheat** *n* cereal plant yielding grain from which bread is chiefly made

**wheedle** *v* coax, cajole

**wheel** *n* circular frame or disc revolving on axle; anything like a wheel in shape or function; act of turning *~v* (cause to) turn as if on axis; (cause to) move on or as if on wheels; (cause to) change course, esp. in opposite direction **wheelbarrow** *n* barrow with one wheel **wheelchair** *n* chair mounted on large wheels, used by invalids

**wheeze** *v* breathe with whistling noise *~n* this sound

**whelk** *n* edible shellfish

**when** *adv* at what time *~conj* at the time that; although; since *~pron* at which time **whenever** *adj/conj* at whatever time

**whence** *adv/conj Obs* from what place or source

**where** *adv/conj* at what place; or to the place in which **whereabouts** *adv/conj* in what, which place *~n* present position **whereas** *conj* considering that; while, on the contrary **whereby** *conj* by which **whereupon** *conj* at which point **wherever** *adv* at whatever place **wherewithal** *n* necessary funds, resources etc.

**whet** *v* **whetting**, **whetted** sharpen; stimulate

**whether** *conj* introduces the first of two alternatives

**whey** *n* watery part of milk left after cheese making

**which** *adj* used in requests for a selection from alternatives *~pron* person or thing referred to **whichever** *pron*

**whiff** *n* brief smell or suggestion of; puff of air

**while** *conj* in the time that; in spite of the fact that, although; whereas *~v* pass (time) idly *~n* period of time

**whilst** *conj* while

**whim** *n* sudden, passing fancy **whimsy, whimsey** *n* fanciful mood **whimsical** *adj* fanciful; full of whims

**whimper** *v* cry or whine softly; complain in this way *~n* such cry or complaint

**whine** *n* high-pitched plaintive cry;

soak, splash, spray, sprinkle, steep *~n* dampness, humidity, liquid, moisture

**wheeze** *v/n* cough, gasp, hiss, rasp, whistle

**whereabouts** location, position, site, situation

**whet** edge, file, grind, hone, sharpen

**whiff** aroma, breath, draught, hint, odour, scent, smell, sniff

**whim** caprice, craze, fancy, impulse, notion, quirk, urge

**whimper** *v/n* cry, moan, snivel, sob, whine

**whimsical** capricious, eccentric, fanciful, freakish, funny, odd, peculiar, quaint, queer, unusual, weird

peevish complaint ~v utter this

**whinge** v complain ~n complaint

**whinny** v -nying, -nied neigh softly ~n soft neigh

**whip** n lash attached to handle for urging or punishing ~v **whipping, whipped** strike with whip; beat (cream, eggs) to a froth; pull, move quickly

**whippet** n dog like small greyhound

**whirl** v swing rapidly round; move rapidly in a circular course; drive at high speed ~n whirling movement; confusion, bustle, giddiness **whirlpool** n circular current, eddy **whirlwind** n wind whirling round while moving forwards ~adj very quick

**whirr, whir** v **whirring, whirred** (cause to) fly, spin etc. with buzzing sound ~n this sound

**whisk** v brush, sweep, beat lightly; move, remove quickly; beat to a froth ~n light brush; egg-beating implement

**whisker** n any of the long stiff hairs at side of mouth of cat or other animal; pl hair on a man's face

**whisky** n (Irish, Canad, US **whiskey**) spirit distilled from fermented cereals

**whisper** v speak in soft, hushed

tones, without vibration of vocal cords; rustle ~n such speech; trace or suspicion; rustle

**whist** n card game

**whistle** v produce shrill sound by forcing breath through rounded, nearly closed lips; make similar sound; utter, summon etc. by whistle ~n such sound; any similar sound; instrument to make it

**white** adj of the colour of snow; pale; light in colour; having a light-coloured skin ~n colour of snow; white pigment; white part; clear fluid round yolk of egg; (with cap.) white person **whiten** v **whitewash** n substance for whitening walls etc. ~v apply this; cover up, gloss over

**whither** adv Obs to what place; to which

**whittle** v cut, carve with knife; pare away

**whizz, whiz** n loud hissing sound ~v **whizzing, whizzed** move with such sound, or make it

**who** pron what or which person or persons; that **whoever** pron who, any one or every one that

**whodunnit** n Inf detective story

**whole** adj containing all elements or parts; not defective or imperfect; healthy ~n complete thing or sys-

---

THESAURUS

**whine** n cry, moan, sob, wail ~v cry, moan, sob, wail; bleat, complain, grouch Inf, grumble

**whip** n birch, cane, crop, horsewhip, lash, scourge, switch ~v beat, cane, flog, lash, scourge, strap, thrash

**whirl** v circle, pirouette, pivot, revolve, rotate, spin, turn, twirl, twist, wheel ~n circle, pirouette, revolution, rotation, spin, turn, twist, wheel; confusion, daze, flurry,

giddiness, spin

**whirlwind** adj hasty, lightning, quick, rapid, speedy, swift

**whisper** v breathe, murmur; hiss, murmur, rustle, sigh ~n low voice, murmur, undertone; breath, fraction, hint, shadow, suggestion, suspicion, tinge, trace; hiss, murmur, rustle, sigh, sighing

**white** ashen, bloodless, pale, pasty, wan

**whitewash** v conceal, suppress

tem **wholly** *adv* **wholehearted** *adj* sincere; enthusiastic **wholesale** *n* sale of goods in large quantities to retailers *~adj* dealing by wholesale; extensive **wholesome** *adj* producing good effect, physically or morally

**whom** *pron objective form of* WHO

**whoop** *n/v* (make) shout or cry expressing excitement etc.

**whooping cough** infectious disease marked by convulsive coughing with loud whoop or drawing in of breath

**whopper** *n Inf* unusually large thing **whopping** *adj*

**whore** *n* prostitute

**whose** *pron* of whom or which

**why** *adv* for what cause or reason

**wick** *n* strip of thread feeding flame

of lamp of candle with oil, grease etc.

**wicked** *adj* evil, sinful; very bad

**wicker** *adj* made of woven cane

**wicket** *n* set of cricket stumps; small gate

**wide** *adj* having a great extent from side to side, broad; having considerable distance from the mark; spacious; vast; far from the mark; opened fully; *adv* to the full extent; far from the intended target **widen** *v* **width** *n* breadth **widespread** *adj* extending over a wide area

**widow** *n* woman whose husband is dead and who has not married again *~v* make a widow of **widower** *n* man whose wife is dead and who has not married again

**wield** *v* hold and use

—————————— THESAURUS ——————————

**whole** *adj* complete, entire, full, total; intact, perfect, sound, unbroken, unimpaired, uninjured, unscathed, untouched; able-bodied, fit, hale, healthy, robust, sound, strong, well *~n* aggregate, all, everything, lot, sum total, total, totality; entity, unit

**wholehearted** committed, dedicated, determined, devoted, earnest, enthusiastic, genuine, real, sincere, true, unreserved, unstinting

**wholesale** *adj* broad, extensive, indiscriminate, mass, sweeping

**wholesome** beneficial, good, health-giving, healthy, nourishing, nutritious; clean, decent, honourable, moral, pure, respectable, righteous, virtuous, worthy

**wholly** all, altogether, completely, comprehensively, entirely, fully, heart and soul, in every respect, one hundred per cent *Inf*, perfectly,

thoroughly, totally, utterly

**whore** call girl, harlot, hooker *US sl*, loose woman, prostitute, scrubber *Brit & Aust sl*, slag *Brit sl*, streetwalker, strumpet, tart *Inf*, trollop

**wicked** abandoned, amoral, bad, corrupt, debased, dissolute, evil, heinous, immoral, iniquitous, nefarious, shameful, sinful, unrighteous, villainous

**wide** *adj* broad, comprehensive, encyclopedic, expansive, general, immense, inclusive, large, sweeping, vast; ample, commodious, full, roomy, spacious

**widen** broaden, dilate, enlarge, expand, extend, stretch

**widespread** broad, common, extensive, general, popular, prevalent, rife, universal, wholesale

**width** breadth, compass, diameter, extent, range, span

**wield** handle, manage, manipulate,

**wife** *n* (*pl* **wives**) man's partner in marriage, married woman

**wig** *n* artificial hair for the head

**wiggle** *v* (cause to) move jerkily from side to side ~*n* wiggling

**wild** *adj* not tamed or domesticated; not cultivated; sav²age; stormy; uncontrolled; random; excited; rash **wildcat** *n* any of various undomesticated feline animals **wildgoose chase** search that has little chance of success **wildlife** *n* wild animals and plants collectively

**wildebeest** *n* gnu

**wilderness** *n* desert, waste place

**wildfire** *n* raging, uncontrollable fire; anything spreading, moving fast

**wile** *n* trick **wily** *adj* crafty, sly

**wilful** *adj* obstinate; self-willed; intentional

**will¹** *v* (*past tense* **would**) forms future tense and indicates intention or conditional result

**will²** *n* faculty of deciding what one will do; purpose; volition; determination; wish; directions written for disposal of property after death ~*v* wish; intend; leave as legacy **willing** *adj* ready; given cheerfully **willingly** *adv* willingness **willpower** *n* ability to control oneself, one's actions, impulses

**will-o'-the-wisp** *n* elusive person or thing

**willow** *n* tree with long thin flexible branches; its wood **willowy** *adj* slender, supple

**willy-nilly** *adv*/*adj* (occurring) whether desired or not

**wilt** *v* (cause to) become limp, lose strength etc.

**wimp** *n* *Inf* feeble person

**wimple** *n* garment framing face, worn by nuns

**win** *v* winning, won be successful, victorious; get by labour or effort ~*n* victory, esp. in games **winner** *n*

———————— THESAURUS ————————

ply, use; apply, exercise, exert, have, hold, maintain, possess, utilize

**wife** helpmate, mate, partner, significant other *US inf*, spouse

**wild** *adj* ferocious, fierce, savage, untamed; free, native, natural; barbaric, brutish, ferocious, fierce, primitive, savage, uncivilized; boisterous, chaotic, disorderly, lawless, noisy, riotous, rough, turbulent, uncontrolled, undisciplined, unrestrained, unruly, violent; berserk, crazy, delirious, demented, excited, frantic, frenzied, hysterical, mad

**wilderness** desert, jungle, waste

**wilful** headstrong, inflexible, obstinate, self-willed, stubborn, unyielding; conscious, deliberate, intentional, voluntary

**will** *n* choice, decision, option; aim, determination, intention, purpose, resolution, resolve; desire, fancy, mind, pleasure, wish; testament ~*v* choose, desire, elect, opt, prefer, see fit, want, wish; bequeath, confer, give, leave, pass on, transfer

**willing** agreeable, amenable, consenting, content, eager, enthusiastic, game, happy, prepared, ready

**willingly** eagerly, freely, gladly, happily, readily

**willingness** agreement, consent, desire, inclination, volition, will, wish

**willpower** determination, drive, grit, resolution, resolve, self-control

**wilt** droop, sag, shrivel, wither

**wily** artful, astute, crafty, cunning, designing, foxy, scheming, sharp,

**winning** adj charming **winnings** pl n sum won in game, betting etc.

**wince** v flinch, draw back, as from pain etc. ~n this act

**winch** n machine for hoisting or hauling using cable wound round drum ~v move (something) by using a winch

**wind**[1] n air in motion; breath; flatulence ~v render short of breath, esp. by blow etc. **windward** n side against which wind is blowing **windy** adj exposed to wind; flatulent **windfall** n unexpected good luck; fallen fruit **wind instrument** musical instrument played by blowing or air pressure **windmill** n wind-driven apparatus with fanlike sails for raising water, crushing grain etc. **windpipe** n passage from throat to lungs **windscreen** n protective sheet of glass etc. in front of driver or pilot **windsurfing** n sport of sailing standing up on board with single sail

**wind**[2] v winding, wound twine; meander; twist round, coil; wrap; make ready for working by tightening spring ~n act of winding; single

turn of something wound

**window** n hole in wall (with glass) to admit light, air etc.; anything similar in appearance or function; area for display of goods behind glass of shop front **window-shopping** n looking at goods without intending to buy

**wine** n fermented juice of grape etc.; purplish-red colour

**wing** n feathered limb used by bird in flying; organ of flight of insect or some animals; main lifting surface of aircraft; side area of building, stage etc.; group within political party etc. ~v move, go very fast; disable, wound slightly **winger** n Sport player positioned at side of pitch

**wink** v close and open (one eye) rapidly, esp. to indicate friendliness or as signal; twinkle ~n act of winking

**winkle** n edible sea snail **winkle out** extract, prise out

**winsome** adj charming

**winter** n coldest season ~v pass, spend the winter **wintry** adj of, like winter; cold

——————— T H E S A U R U S ———————

**win** v be victorious, come first, conquer, overcome, prevail, succeed, triumph; accomplish, achieve, acquire, attain, earn, gain, get, obtain, procure, receive, secure ~n Inf conquest, success, triumph, victory

**wince** v blench, cower, cringe, draw back, flinch, quail, recoil, shrink, start

**wind**[1] n air, breath, breeze, draught, gust, zephyr; breath, puff, respiration

**wind**[2] v coil, curl, loop, twine,

twist, wreathe; meander, ramble, twist, zigzag

**windy** adj blustery, breezy, gusty, inclement, squally, stormy, wild

**wing** n annexe, extension; arm, branch, circle, clique, coterie, faction, group, schism, section, side

**wink** v bat, blink, flutter; flash, gleam, sparkle, twinkle ~n blink, flutter; flash, gleam, glimmering, sparkle, twinkle

**winner** champion, conqueror, first, victor

**winnings** booty, gains, prize(s), proceeds, profits, spoils, takings

**wipe** v rub so as to clean ~n wiping **wiper** n one that wipes; automatic wiping apparatus (esp. **windscreen wiper**) **wipe out** erase; annihilate; Sl kill

**wire** n metal drawn into thin, flexible strand; something made of wire, e.g. fence; telegram ~v provide, fasten with wire; send by telegraph **wiring** n system of wires **wiry** adj like wire; lean and tough **wire-haired** adj (of various breeds of dog) with short stiff hair

**wireless** n Obs radio, radio set

**wise** adj having intelligence and knowledge; sensible **wisdom** n (accumulated) knowledge, learning **wisdom tooth** large tooth cut usu. after age of twenty

**wish** v desire ~n expression of desire; thing desired **wishful** adj folly optimistic

**wishy-washy** adj Inf insipid, bland

**wisp** n light, delicate streak, as of smoke; twisted handful, usu. of

straw etc.; stray lock of hair **wispy** adj

**wistful** adj longing, yearning; sadly pensive

**wit** n ability to use words, ideas in clever, amusing way; person with this ability; intellect; understanding; humour **witticism** n witty remark **wittingly** adv on purpose; knowingly **witty** adj

**witch** n person, usu. female, who practises magic; ugly, wicked woman; fascinating woman **witchcraft** n **witch doctor** in certain societies, man appearing to cure or cause injury, disease by magic

**with** prep in company or possession of; against; in relation to; through; by means of **within** prep/adv in, inside **without** prep lacking; Obs outside

**withdraw** v -drawing, -drew, -drawn draw back or out **withdrawal** n **withdrawn** adj reserved, unsociable

**wither** v (cause to) wilt, dry up,

———————— THESAURUS ————————

**wintry** chilly, cold, harsh, icy, snowy

**wipe** v brush, clean, mop, rub, sponge, swab ~n brush, lick, rub, swab

**wipe out** annihilate, destroy, eradicate, erase, massacre, obliterate

**wiry** lean, sinewy, strong, tough

**wisdom** astuteness, discernment, enlightenment, foresight, insight, intelligence, judgment, prudence, reason, sagacity, sense, smarts Sl, chiefly US

**wise** aware, clued-up Inf, discerning, enlightened, informed, intelligent, judicious, perceptive, prudent, rational, reasonable, sage,

sensible, shrewd, sound

**wish** v crave, desire, hanker, hunger, long, need, thirst, want, yearn ~n desire, hankering, hunger, longing, thirst, urge, want, will, yearning

**wistful** longing, melancholy, mournful, sad, yearning

**wit** banter, fun, humour, levity, pleasantry, repartee; comedian, humorist, joker, wag; brains, cleverness, discernment, insight, intellect, judgment, perception, reason, sense, smarts Sl, chiefly US, wisdom

**witch** crone, enchantress, sorceress

**witchcraft** enchantment, magic, sorcery, wizardry

**withdraw** extract, remove; absent

decline **withering** *adj* (of glance etc.) scornful

**withhold** *v* **-holding, -held** restrain; refrain from giving

**withstand** *v* **-standing, -stood** oppose, resist, esp. successfully

**witness** *n* one who sees something; testimony; one who gives testimony ~*v* give testimony; see; attest; sign (document) as genuine

**wizard** *n* sorcerer, magician; *Inf* virtuoso **wizardry** *n*

**wizened** *adj* shrivelled, wrinkled

**wobble** *v* move unsteadily; sway ~*n* unsteady movement **wobbly** *adj*

**woe** *n* grief **woebegone** *adj* looking sorrowful **woeful** *adj* sorrowful; pitiful; wretched

**wok** *n* bowl-shaped Chinese cooking pan

**wolf** *n* (*pl* **wolves**) wild predatory doglike animal ~*v* eat ravenously

**wolverine** *n* carnivorous mammal inhabiting Arctic regions

**woman** *n* (*pl* **women**) adult human female; women collectively **womanish** *adj* effeminate **womanize** *v* (of man) indulge in many casual affairs **womanly** *adj* of, proper to woman

**womb** *n* female organ in which young develop before birth

**wombat** *n* Aust. burrowing marsupial with heavy body, short legs and dense fur

**won** *past tense and participle of* WIN

**wonder** *n* emotion excited by amazing or unusual thing; marvel, miracle ~*v* be curious about; feel amazement **wonderful** *adj* remarkable; very fine **wondrous** *adj* inspiring wonder; strange

━━━━━━━━━━━━━━━━ THESAURUS ━━━━━━━━━━━━━━━

oneself, back out, cop out *Sl*, depart, drop out, go, leave, pull out, retire, retreat

**withdrawal** extraction, removal; departure, exit, exodus, retirement, retreat

**withdrawn** aloof, detached, distant, introverted, quiet, reserved, retiring, shy, silent, taciturn

**wither** decline, dry, fade, languish, perish, shrink, wane, waste

**withering** hurtful, scornful, snubbing

**withhold** conceal, hide, hold back, keep, keep back, refuse, reserve, restrain, retain, suppress

**withstand** bear, brave, combat, cope with, endure, face, hold off, hold out against, oppose, resist, stand up to, suffer, take, take on, weather

**witness** *n* observer, onlooker, spectator, viewer, watcher ~*v* mark,

note, notice, observe, perceive, see, view, watch; attest, bear out, confirm

**witticism** clever remark, epigram, one-liner *Sl*, play on words, pleasantry, pun, quip, witty remark

**witty** amusing, brilliant, clever, epigrammatic, funny, humorous, original

**wizard** enchanter, magician, necromancer, sorcerer; adept, buff *Inf*, expert, genius, maestro, master, prodigy, virtuoso

**woe** anguish, distress, grief, misery, pain, sadness, sorrow, suffering, wretchedness

**woman** female, girl, lady, lass, lassie *Inf*, maid, maiden, wench *Facetious*

**womanly** female, feminine, ladylike

**wonder** *n* admiration, astonishment, awe, curiosity, fascination;

**wont** n custom ~adj accustomed

**woo** v court, seek to marry

**wood** n substance of trees, timber **firewood** tract of land with growing trees **wooded** adj having many trees **wooden** adj made of wood; without expression **woody** adj **woodland** n woods, forest **woodpecker** n bird which searches tree trunks for insects **wood pigeon** large pigeon of Europe and Asia **woodwind** adj/n (of) wind instruments of orchestra **woodworm** n insect larva that bores into wood

**woof** n barking noise

**wool** n soft hair of sheep, goat etc.; yarn spun from this **woollen** adj **woolly** adj of wool; vague, muddled ~n woollen garment

**word** n smallest separate meaningful unit of speech or writing; term; message; brief remark; information; promise; command ~v express in words, esp. in particular way **wordy** adj using too many words **word processor** keyboard, computer and VDU for electronic organization and storage of text

**wore** past tense of WEAR

**work** n labour; employment; occupation; something made or accomplished; production of art or science; pl factory; total of person's deeds, writings etc.; mechanism of clock etc. ~v (cause to) operate; make, shape; apply effort; labour; be employed; turn out successfully; ferment **workable** adj **worker** n **workaholic** n person addicted to work **working class** social class consisting of wage earners, esp. manual **working-class** adj **workman** n manual worker, **workmanship** n skill of workman; way thing is finished **workshop** n place where things are made

———— THESAURUS ————

curiosity, marvel, miracle, prodigy, rarity, sight, spectacle ~v ask oneself, conjecture, meditate, ponder, puzzle, query, question, speculate

**wonderful** amazing, astounding, extraordinary, marvellous, miraculous, remarkable, staggering, surprising; admirable, brilliant, cracking Brit inf, excellent, magnificent, mean Sl, outstanding, sensational, stupendous, superb, terrific, tremendous

**wood** also **woods** coppice, copse, forest, grove, thicket, trees, woodland; timber

**word** n expression, name; term; bulletin, dispatch, information, intelligence, latest Inf, message, news, notice, report, tidings; assurance, guarantee, oath, pledge, promise, solemn oath, vow ~v express, phrase, put, say, state, utter

**wordy** garrulous, long-winded, loquacious, rambling, verbose

**work** n drudgery, effort, exertion, industry, labour, slog, sweat, toil; business, calling, craft, employment, job, occupation, profession, trade; composition, creation, handiwork, opus, piece, production ~v function, go, operate, perform, run; control, direct, drive, handle, manage, manipulate, operate, ply, use, wield; drudge, labour, slave, sweat, toil

**workman** artisan, craftsman, employee, hand, labourer, mechanic, tradesman

**workmanship** art, artistry, craft, craftsmanship, expertise, handicraft, handiwork, skill, technique

**workshop** factory, mill, plant,

**world** n the universe; the planet earth; sphere of existence; mankind; any planet; society **worldly** adj earthly; absorbed in pursuit of material gain

**worm** n small limbless creeping snakelike creature; anything resembling worm in shape or movement; pl (disorder caused by) infestation of worms, esp. in intestines ~v crawl; insinuate (oneself); extract (secret) craftily; rid of worms

**worn** past participle of WEAR

**worry** v **-rying, -ried** be (unduly) concerned; trouble, pester, harass; (of dog) seize, shake with teeth ~n (cause of) anxiety, concern **worried** adj

**worse** adj/adv comparative of BAD or BADLY **worsen** v make, grow worse
**worst** adj/adv superlative of BAD or BADLY

**worship** v **-shipping, -shipped** show religious devotion to; adore; love and admire ~n act of worshipping **worshipful** adj **worshipper** n

**worsted** n woollen yarn ~adj made of woollen yarn

**worth** adj having or deserving to have value specified; meriting ~n excellence; merit, value; usefulness; quantity to be had for given sum **worthless** adj **worthwhile** adj worth the time, effort etc. involved **worthy** adj virtuous; meriting

**would** v expressing wish, intention, probability; past tense of WILL **would-be** adj wishing, pretending to be

**wound¹** n injury, hurt from cut, stab etc. ~v inflict wound on, injure; pain

— **THESAURUS** —

**world** earth, globe, planet; area, domain, environment, field, kingdom, province, realm, sphere; everybody, everyone, humanity, man, mankind, men

**worldly** earthly, mundane, physical, secular, temporal, terrestrial; avaricious, grasping, greedy, materialistic

**worn** frayed, ragged, shabby, tattered, tatty, threadbare; exhausted, fatigued, spent, tired, weary

**worried** afraid, anxious, bothered, concerned, nervous, perturbed, tense, troubled, uneasy, upset

**worry** v agonize, annoy, bother, brood, disturb, fret, harass, hassle Inf, perturb, pester, trouble, unsettle, upset, vex ~n annoyance, care, hassle Inf, problem, trial, trouble, vexation

**worsen** aggravate, decline, degen-

erate, deteriorate, exacerbate, get worse, go downhill Inf, go from bad to worse, sink

**worship** v adore, exalt, glorify, honour, love, revere, venerate ~n adoration, devotion, exaltation, glorification, glory, homage, honour, love, reverence

**worth** n credit, estimation, excellence, goodness, importance, merit, quality, value, virtue; cost, price, value

**worthless** insignificant, meaningless, paltry, pointless, rubbishy, trashy, trifling, trivial, unimportant, useless

**worthwhile** beneficial, good, helpful, productive, profitable, useful, valuable

**worthy** commendable, creditable, decent, deserving, estimable, good, honest, laudable, meritorious, reputable, respectable, righteous,

**wound²** past tense and past participle of WIND²

**wove** past tense of WEAVE **woven** past participle of WEAVE

**wow** interj exclamation of astonishment

**wraith** n apparition

**wrangle** v quarrel (noisily); dispute ~n noisy quarrel; dispute

**wrap** v wrapping, wrapped cover, esp. by putting something round; put round ~n loose garment **wrapper** n covering **wrapping** n material used to wrap

**wrath** n anger

**wreak** v inflict (vengeance); cause

**wreath** n something twisted into ring form, esp. band of flowers etc. as memorial or tribute on grave etc. **wreathe** v form into wreath; surround; wind round

**wreck** n destruction of ship; wrecked ship; ruin ~v cause wreck of **wreckage** n

**wren** n kind of small songbird

**wrench** v twist; distort; seize forcibly; sprain ~n violent twist; tool for twisting or screwing; spanner

**wrest** v take by force; twist violently

**wrestle** v fight (esp. as sport) by grappling and trying to throw down; strive (with); struggle ~n wrestling **wrestler** n **wrestling** n

**wretch** n despicable person; miserable creature **wretched** adj miserable, unhappy; worthless

**wriggle** v move with twisting action, squirm ~n this action

**wring** v wringing, wrung twist; extort; squeeze out

**wrinkle** n slight ridge or furrow on skin etc. ~v make, become wrinkled **wrinkly** adj

**wrist** n joint between hand and arm

**writ** n written command from law court or other authority

**write** v writing, wrote, written mark paper etc. with symbols or words; compose; send a letter; set down in words; communicate in writing **writer** n one who writes; author **writing** n **write-off** n Inf something damaged beyond repair **writhe** v writhing, writhed twist,

upright, virtuous

**wound** n cut, gash, harm, hurt, injury, slash ~v cut, damage, gash, harm, hurt, injure, pierce, slash; distress, grieve, hurt, offend, pain, sting

**wrap** v bind, cover, encase, enclose, enfold, envelop, fold, pack, shroud, surround, wind

**wrapper** case, cover, envelope, jacket, paper

**wreath** band, coronet, crown, festoon, garland, ring

**wreck** v break, demolish, destroy, devastate, ravage, ruin, shatter, smash, spoil; founder, shipwreck

**wreckage** debris, fragments, pieces, remains, rubble, ruin

**wrench** v twist, wrest, wring; rick, sprain, strain

**wrestle** battle, combat, contend, fight, grapple, struggle

**wretched** abject, dismal, hopeless, miserable, pitiful, poor, unhappy

**wriggle** v/n squirm, turn, twist, writhe

**wrinkle** n crease, crow's-foot, crumple, fold, furrow, line, pucker, rumple ~v crease, crumple, fold, furrow, ruck

**write** compose, copy, create, draft, inscribe, pen, record, scribble, take

squirm in or as in pain etc.

**wrong** *adj* not right or good; not suitable; incorrect; mistaken; not functioning properly ~*v* do wrong to; think badly of without justification **wrongful** *adj* **wrongly** *adv*

**wrote** *past tense of* WRITE

**wrought** ~*adj* (of metals) shaped by hammering or beating

**wrung** *past tense and past participle of* WRING

**wry** *adj* turned to one side, contorted; dryly humorous

———————— THESAURUS ————————

down, transcribe

**writer** author, columnist, essayist, hack, novelist, scribe

**writhe** squirm, twist, wriggle

**writing** calligraphy, hand, handwriting, print, scrawl, scribble, script; book, composition, document, letter, opus, publication, title, work

**wrong** *adj* bad, criminal, crooked, dishonest, evil, illegal, illicit, immoral, sinful, unlawful, wicked, wrongful; improper, inapt, incorrect, not done, unacceptable, unfit-

ting, unseemly, unsuitable; erroneous, fallacious, false, faulty, inaccurate, incorrect, mistaken, untrue; amiss, askew, awry, defective, faulty ~*n* abuse, crime, injury, injustice, misdeed, offence, sin, transgression ~*v* abuse, harm, hurt, illuse, injure, malign, maltreat, mistreat

**wrongful** blameworthy, illegal, illegitimate, illicit, immoral, improper, reprehensible, unfair, unjust, unlawful

**wry** dry, ironic, mocking, sardonic

# X x

**xenophobia** *n* hatred, fear, of strangers or aliens

**Xerox** *n Trademark* machine for copying printed material ~*v* copy with Xerox

**Xmas** *n short for* CHRISTMAS

**X-ray** *n* stream of radiation capable of penetrating solid bodies ~*v* photograph by X-rays

**xylophone** *n* musical instrument of wooden bars which sound when struck

# Y y

**yacht** n vessel propelled by sail or power

**yak** n ox of Central Asia

**yam** n sweet potato

**yank** v jerk; tug; pull quickly ~n quick tug

**yap** v **yapping, yapped** bark (as small dog); talk idly

**yard**¹ n unit of length, .915 metre **yardstick** n standard of measurement or comparison

**yard**² n piece of enclosed ground, oft. adjoining building and used for some specific purpose

**yarn** n spun thread; tale

**yawn** v open mouth wide, esp. in sleepiness; gape ~n act of yawning

**yd.** yard

**ye** pron Obs you

**year** n time taken by one revolution of earth round sun, about 365 days; twelve months **yearling** n animal one year old **yearly** adv every year, once a year ~adj happening once a year

**yearn** v feel longing, desire

**yeast** n substance used as fermenting agent, esp. in raising bread

**yell** v/n shout; scream

**yellow** adj of the colour of lemons, gold etc.; Inf cowardly ~n this colour **yellow fever** acute infectious tropical disease

**yelp** v/n (produce) quick, shrill cry

**yen** n Inf longing, craving

**yeoman** n Hist farmer cultivating his own land

**yes** interj expresses consent, agreement, or approval

**yesterday** n/adv (on) day before today; (in) recent past

**yet** adv now; still; besides; hitherto ~conj but, at the same time, nevertheless

**yeti** n apelike creature said to inhabit Himalayas

**yew** n evergreen tree with dark leaves; its wood

**yield** v give or return; produce; give up, surrender ~n amount produced

**yob** also **yobbo** n Inf bad-mannered aggressive youth

**yodel** v -**delling, -delled** warble in falsetto tone

**yoga** n Hindu system of certain physical and mental exercises

**yogurt, yoghurt** n thick, custard-like preparation of curdled milk

**yoke** n wooden bar put across the necks of two animals to hold them together; various objects like a yoke in shape or use; fitted part of garment, esp. round neck, shoulders; bond or tie; domination ~v put yoke on; couple, unite

**yokel** n (old-fashioned) country dweller

**yolk** n yellow central part of egg

**yon** adj Obs or dial that or those

---

## THESAURUS

**yearly** annual, annually, every year, once a year, per annum

**yearn** ache, crave, desire, eat one's heart out over, hunger, languish, long, pine

**yell** v bawl, holler Inf, howl, scream, shout, shriek ~n cry, howl, scream, screech, shriek

**yet;** already, now, right now, so soon; however, still; as well, besides, further, moreover, still, to boot

over there **yonder** *adj* yon ~*adv*
over there, in that direction
**Yorkshire pudding** baked batter
made from flour, milk and eggs
**you** *pron* (*second person*) refers to
person or persons addressed; refers
to unspecified person or persons
**young** *adj* not far advanced in
growth, life or existence; not yet old
~*n* offspring **youngster** *n* child

**your** *adj* of, belonging to you **yours**
*pron* **yourself** (*pl* **yourselves**) *pron*
emphatic or reflexive form of YOU
**youth** *n* state or time of being
young; young man; young people
**youthful** *adj*
**Yule** *n* Christmas season
**yuppie** *n* young highly-paid professional person ~*adj* of, like yuppies

———————————— T H E S A U R U S ————————————

**yokel** countryman, peasant, rustic
**young** *adj* early, new, recent; adolescent, green, growing, immature,
infant, junior, little, youthful
**youngster** boy, girl, juvenile, lad,
lass, teenager

**youth** boyhood, girlhood, immaturity; adolescent, boy, kid *Inf*, lad,
stripling, teenager, youngster
**youthful** boyish, childish, immature, juvenile, puerile, young; active, fresh, spry, vigorous

# Z z

**zany** *adj* comical, funny in unusual way

**zap** *v* **zapping, zapped** *Sl* attack, kill or destroy

**zeal** *n* fervour; keenness, enthusiasm **zealot** *n* fanatic; enthusiast **zealous** *adj*

**zebra** *n* striped Afr. animal like a horse

**zenith** *n* point of the heavens directly above an observer; summit; climax

**zephyr** *n* soft, gentle breeze

**zero** *n* (*pl* **-ros, -roes**) nothing; figure 0; point on graduated instrument from which positive and negative quantities are reckoned; the lowest point

**zest** *n* enjoyment; excitement, interest, flavour; peel of orange or lemon

**zigzag** *n* line or course with sharp turns in alternating directions ~*v* **-zagging, -zagged** move along in zigzag course

**zinc** *n* bluish-white metallic element

**zip** *also* **zipper** *n* fastener with two rows of teeth that are closed and opened by a sliding clip; short whizzing sound; *Inf* energy, vigour ~*v* **zipping, zipped** fasten with zip; move with zip

**zither** *n* flat stringed instrument

**zodiac** *n* imaginary belt of the heavens along which the sun, moon and chief planets appear to move

**zombie** *n* person appearing lifeless

**zone** *n* region with particular characteristics or use

**zoo** *n* (*pl* **zoos**) place where live animals are kept for show

**zoology** *n* study of animals **zoological** *adj* **zoologist** *n*

**zoom** *v* move, rise very rapidly; move with buzzing or humming sound

─── THESAURUS ───

**zero** naught, nil, nothing, nought

**zest** appetite, enjoyment, gusto, keenness, relish, zeal; flavour, kick *Inf*, piquancy, pungency, savour, spice, tang, taste

**zone** area, belt, district, region, section, sector, sphere

# CHEMICAL ELEMENTS

actinium
aluminium *or*
  *(U.S.)* aluminum
americium
antimony
argon
arsenic
astatine
barium
berkelium
beryllium
bismuth
boron
bromine
cadmium
caesium *or*
  *(U.S.)* cesium
calcium
californium
carbon
cerium
chlorine
chromium
cobalt
copper
curium
dysprosium
einsteinium
erbium
europium
fermium
fluorine
francium
gadolinium
gallium
germanium
gold
hafnium

helium
holmium
hydrogen
indium
iodine
iridium
iron
krypton
lanthanum
lawrencium
lead
lithium
lutetium *or*
  lutecium
magnesium
manganese
mendelevium
mercury
molybdenum
neodymium
neon
neptunium
nickel
niobium
nitrogen
nobelium
osmiumoxygen
palladium
phosphorous
platinum
plutonium
polonium
potassium
praseodymium
promethium
protactinium
radium
radon

rhenium
rhodium
rubidium
ruthenium
samarium
scandium
selenium
silicon
silver
sodium
strontium
sulphur *or*
  *(U.S.)* sulfur
tantalum
technetium
tellurium
terbium
thallium
thorium
thulium
tin
titanium
tungsten *or*
  wolfram
unnilennium
unnilhexium
unniloctium
unnilpentium
unnilseptium
unniquadium
uranium
vanadium
xenon
ytterbium
yttrium
zinc
zirconium

# GROUP NAMES AND COLLECTIVE NOUNS

barren of mules
bevy of quails
bevy of roes
brace or lease of bucks
brood or covey of grouse
brood of hens or chickens
building or clamour of rooks
bunch, company, or knob of wigeon (in the water)
bunch, knob, or spring of teal
cast of hawks
cete of badgers
charm of goldfinches
chattering of choughs
clowder of cats
colony of gulls (breeding)
covert of coots
covey of partridges
cowardice of curs
desert of lapwings
dropping of sheldrakes
down or husk of hares
drove or herd of cattle (kine)
exaltation of larks
fall of woodcocks
field or string of racehorses
flight of wigeon (in the air)
flight or dule of doves
flight of swallows
flight of dunlins
flight, rush, bunch, or knob of pochards

flock or flight of pigeons
flock of sheep
flock of swifts
flock or gaggle of geese
flock, congregation, flight, or volery of birds
gaggle of geese (on the ground)
gang of elk
haras (stud) of horses
herd of antelopes
herd of buffaloes
herd, sedge, or siege of cranes
herd of curlews
herd of deer
herd of giraffes
herd or tribe of goats
herd or pod of seals
herd or bevy of swans
herd of ponies
herd of swine
hill of ruffs
host of sparrows
kindle of kittens
labour of moles
leap of leopards
litter of cubs
litter of pups or pigs
litter of whelps
murmuration of starlings
muster of peacocks
nest of rabbits
nye or nide of pheasants

# GROUP NAMES AND COLLECTIVE NOUNS

pace or herd of asses
pack of grouse
pack, mute, or cry of
  hounds
pack, rout, or herd of wolves
paddling of ducks
plump, sword, or sute of
  wild fowl
pod of whiting
pride or troop of lions
rag of colts
richesse of martens
run of poultry
school or run of whales
school or gam of porpoises
sedge or siege of bitterns
sedge or siege of herons
shoal or glean of herrings
shoal, draught, haul, run,
  or catch of fish

shrewdness of apes
skein of geese (in flight)
skulk of foxes
sloth of bears
sord or sute of mallards
sounder of boars
sounder or dryft of swine
stand or wing of plovers
stud of mares
swarm of insects
swarm or grist of bees or flies
swarm or cloud of gnats
tok of capercailzies
team of ducks (in flight)
troop of kangaroos
troop of monkeys
walk or wisp of snipe
watch of nightingales
yoke, drove, team, or herd
  of oxen

# PLANETS OF THE SOLAR SYSTEM

Earth  Jupiter  Mars  Mercury  Neptune  Pluto  Saturn
Uranus  Venus

# CHARACTERS IN CLASSICAL MYTHOLOGY

Achilles
Actaeon
Adonis
Aeneas
Agamemnon
Ajax
Amazons
Andromeda
Antigone
Aphrodite
Apollo
Arachne
Ares
Argonauts
Ariadne
Atalanta
Athena
Atlas
Aurora
Bacchus
Boreas
Calypso
Cassandra
Cassiopeia
Castor
Charon
centaurs
Circe
Cronus
Cupid
Cybele
Cyclopes
Daedalus
Diana

Dido
Dionysus
dryads
Echidna
Echo
Electra
Europa
Eurydice
Galatea
Ganymede
Gorgons
Harpies
Hector
Hecuba
Helen
Hera
Hercules
Hermaphroditus
Hermes
Hippolytus
Hyacinthus
Hydra
Icarus
Iris
Ixion
Jason
Jocasta
Janus
Jason
Jocasta
Juno
Jupiter
Leda
Mars

Medea
Medusa
Menelaus
Mercury
Midas
Minerva
Minos
Minotaur
Muses
Narcissus
Nemesis
Neptune
Nereids
Niobe
Oceanids
Odysseus
Oedipus
Orestes
Orion
Orpheus
Pallas
Pan
Pandora
Paris
Penelope
Persephone
Perseus
Pleiades
Pluto
Pollux
Polydeuces
Polyphemus
Poseidon
Priam

| | | |
|---|---|---|
| Prometheus | satyrs | Titans |
| Proserpina | Selene | Triton |
| Psyche | Semele | Ulysses |
| Pygmalion | Sibyl | Uranus |
| Pyramus | Sirens | Venus |
| Remus | Sisyphus | Vulcan |
| Romulus | Tantalus | Zeus |
| Saturn | Thisbe | |

## The Fates

| | | |
|---|---|---|
| Atropos | Clotho | Lachesis |

## The Graces

| | | |
|---|---|---|
| Aglaia | Euphrosyne | Thalia |

## The Muses

| | |
|---|---|
| Calliope | epic poetry |
| Clio | history |
| Erato | love poetry |
| Euterpe | lyric poetry and music |
| Melpomene | tragedy |
| Polyhymnia | singing, mime and sacred dance |
| Terpsichore | dance and choral song |
| Thalia | comedy and pastoral poetry |
| Urania | astronomy |

# WEDDING ANNIVERSARIES

| YEAR | TRADITIONAL | MODERN |
|---|---|---|
| 1st | Paper | Clocks |
| 2nd | Cotton | China |
| 3rd | Leather | Crystal, glass |
| 4th | Linen (silk) | Electrical appliances |
| 5th | Wood | Silverware |
| 6th | Iron | Wood |
| 7th | Wool (copper) | Desk sets |
| 8th | Bronze | Linen, lace |
| 9th | Pottery (china) | Leather |
| 10th | Tin (aluminium) | Diamond jewellery |
| 11th | Steel | Fashion jewellery, accessories |
| 12th | Silk | Pearls or coloured gems |
| 13th | Lace | Textile, furs |
| 14th | Ivory | Gold jewellery |
| 15th | Crystal | Watches |
| 20th | China | Platinum |
| 25th | Silver | Sterling silver jubilee |
| 30th | Pearl | Diamond |
| 35th | Coral (jade) | Jade |
| 40th | Ruby | Ruby |
| 45th | Sapphire | Sapphire |
| 50th | Gold | Gold |
| 55th | Emerald | Emerald |
| 60th | Diamond | Diamond |

# BOOKS OF THE BIBLE
## (including the Apocrypha)

Acts of the
 Apostles
Amos
Baruch
Chronicles
Colossians
Corinthians
Daniel
Daniel and
 Susanna
Daniel, Bel and
 the Snake
Deuteronomy
Ecclesiastes
Ecclesisticus
Ephesians
Esdras
Esther
Exodus
Ezekiel
Ezra
Galatians
Genesis
Habakkuk

Haggai
Hebrews
Hosea
Isiah
James
Jeremiah
Job
Joel
John
Jonah
Joshua
Jude
Judges
Judith
Kings
Lamentations
Leviticus
Luke
Maccabees
Malachi
Manasseh
Mark
Matthew
Micah

Nahum
Nehemiah
Numbers
Obadiah
Peter
Philemon
Philippians
Proverbs
Psalms
Revelation
Romans
Ruth
Samuel
Song of Solomon
Song of Songs
Song of the
 Three
Thessalonians
Timothy
Titus
Tobit
Zechariah
Zephaniah

# COUNTRIES, CURRENCIES AND CAPITALS

| COUNTRY | CURRENCY | CAPITAL |
|---|---|---|
| Afghanistan | Afghani | Kabul |
| Albania | Lek | Tirana |
| Algeria | Dinar | Algiers |
| American Samoa | U.S. Dollar | Pago Pago |
| Andorra | French Franc; Spanish Peseta | Andorra la Vella |
| Angola | Kwanza | Luanda |
| Antigua and Barbuda | East Caribbean Dollar | St John's |
| Argentina | Argentine Peso | Buenos Aires |
| Armenia | Dram | Yerevan |
| Australia | Dollar | Canberra |
| Austria | Schilling | Vienna |
| Azerbaijan | Manat | Baku |
| Bahamas | Bahamanian Dollar | Nassau |
| Bahrain | Dinar | Manama |
| Bangladesh | Taka | Dhaka |
| Barbados | Barbadian Dollar | Bridgetown |
| Belarus | Dukat | Minsk |
| Belgium | Franc | Brussels |
| Belize | Belizean Dollar | Belmopan |
| Benin | CFA Franc | Porto Novo |
| Bermuda | Bermuda Dollar | Hamilton |
| Bhutan | Ngultrum | Thimphu |
| Bolivia | Boliviano | Sucre/La Paz |
| Bosnia and Herzegovina | Dinar | Sarajevo |
| Botswana | Pula | Gaborone |
| Brazil | Real | Brasilia |
| British Virgin Isles | U.S. Dollar | Road Town |
| Brunei | Brunei Dollar | Bandar Seri Begawani |
| Bulgaria | Lev | Sofia |
| Burkina-Faso | CFA Franc | Ouagadougou |
| Burundi | Burundi Franc | Bujumbura |
| Cambodia | Riel | Phnom Penh |
| Cameroon | CFA Franc | Yaoundé |
| Canada | Canadian Dollar | Ottawa |

# COUNTRIES, CURRENCIES AND CAPITALS

| Country | Currency | Capital |
|---|---|---|
| Cape Verde | Cape Verdean Escudo | Praia |
| Cayman Islands | Cayman Islands Dollar | Georgetown |
| Central African Republic | CFA Franc | Bangui |
| Chad | CFA Franc | N'djamena |
| Chile | Peso | Santiago |
| China | Yuan | Beijing |
| Colombia | Peso | Bogotá |
| Comoros | CFA Franc | Moroni |
| Congo Republic | CFA Franc | Brazzaville |
| Costa Rica | Cólon | San José |
| Côte d'Ivoire | CFA Franc | Yamoussoukro |
| Croatia | Kuna | Zagreb |
| Cuba | Peso | Havana |
| Cyprus | Lira; Cypriot Pound | Nicosia |
| Czech Republic | Koruna | Prague |
| Denmark | Danish Krone | Copenhagen |
| Djibouti | Djibouti Franc | Djibouti |
| Dominica | East Caribbean Dollar | Roseau |
| Dominican Republic | Peso | Santo Doming |
| Ecuador | Sucre | Quito |
| Egypt | Egyptian Pound | Cairo |
| El Salvador | Cólon | San Salvador |
| Equatorial Guinea | CFA Franc | Malabo |
| Eritrea | Birr | Asmara |
| Estonia | Kroon | Tallinn |
| Ethiopia | Birr | Addis Ababa |
| Faeroe Islands | Danish Krone | Thorshavn |
| Fiji | Fiji Dollar | Suva |
| Finland | Markka | Helsinki |
| France | Franc | Paris |
| French Guiana | French Franc | Cayenne |
| Gabon | CFA Franc | Libreville |
| Gambia | Dalasi | Banjul |
| Georgia | coupons | Tbilisi |
| Germany | Deutschmark | Berlin |
| Ghana | Cedi | Accra |

# COUNTRIES, CURRENCIES AND CAPITALS

| | | |
|---|---|---|
| Gibraltar | Gibraltar Pound | City of Gibraltar |
| Greece | Drachma | Athens |
| Grenada | East Caribbean Dollar | St George's |
| Guadeloupe | Franc | Bass-Tenne |
| Guam | U.S. Dollar | Agaña |
| Guatemala | Quetzal | Guatemala City |
| Guinea | Guinea Franc | Conakry |
| Guinea-Bissau | Peso | Bissau |
| Guyana | Guyana Dollar | Georgetown |
| Haiti | Gourde | Port-au-Prince |
| Honduras | Lempira | Tegucigalpa |
| Hong Kong | Hong Kong Dollar | Victoria |
| Hungary | Forint | Budapest |
| Iceland | Krona | Reykjavik |
| India | Rupee | New Delhi |
| Indonesia | Rupiah | Jakarta |
| Iran | Rial | Tehran |
| Iraq | Dinar | Baghdad |
| Ireland | Punt | Dublin |
| Israel | Shekel | Tel Aviv |
| Italy | Lira | Rome |
| Jamaica | Jamaican Dollar | Kingston |
| Japan | Yen | Tokyo |
| Jordan | Dinar | Amman |
| Kazakhstan | Tenge | Alma-Ata |
| Kenya | Kenya Shilling | Nairobi |
| Kirghizia | Som | Pishpek |
| Kiribati | Australian Dollar | Tarawa |
| Kuwait | Kuwaiti Dinar | Kuwait City |
| Laos | New Kip | Vientiane |
| Latvia | Lat | Riga |
| Lebanon | Lebanese Pound | Beirut |
| Lesotho | Loti | Maseru |
| Liberia | Liberian Dollar | Monrovia |
| Libya | Libyan Dinar | Tripoli |
| Liechtenstein | Swiss Franc | Vaduz |
| Lithuania | Litas | Vilnius |
| Luxembourg | Luxembourg Franc | Luxembourg-Ville |

# COUNTRIES, CURRENCIES AND CAPITALS

| Country | Currency | Capital |
|---|---|---|
| Macao | Pataca | Macao City |
| Macedonia | Denar | Skopje |
| Madagascar | Malagasy Franc | Antananarivo |
| Malawi | Kwacha | Lilongwe |
| Malaysia | Ringgit | Kuala Lumpur |
| Maldives | Rufiyaa | Malé |
| Mali | CFA franc | Bamako |
| Malta | Maltese Lira | Valletta |
| Marshall Islands | U.S. Dollar | Majuro |
| Martinique | French Franc | Fort-de-France |
| Mauritania | Ouguiya | Nouakchott |
| Mauritius | Mauritius Rupee | Port Louis |
| Mexico | Peso | Mexico City |
| Micronesia | U.S. Dollar | Palikir |
| Moldova | Leu | Kishinev |
| Monaco | Franc | Monaco-Ville |
| Mongolia | Tugrik | Ulan Bator |
| Montenegro | Dinar | Podgorica |
| Montserrat | East Caribbean Dollar | Plymouth |
| Morocco | Dirham | Rabat |
| Mozambique | Metical | Maputo |
| Myanmar | Kyat | Yangon |
| Namibia | Namibian Dollar | Windhoek |
| Nauru | Australian Dollar | Yaren |
| Nepal | Nepalese Rupee | Kathmandu |
| Netherlands | Guilder | Amsterdam/ The Hague |
| Netherlands Antilles | Guilder | Willemstad |
| New Zealand | New Zealand Dollar | Wellington |
| Nicaragua | Córdoba | Managua |
| Niger | CFA Franc | Niamey |
| Nigeria | Naira | Abuja |
| North Korea | North Korean Won | Pyongyang |
| Norway | Krone | Oslo |
| Oman | Rial Omani | Muscat |
| Pakistan | Pakistani Rupee | Islamabad |
| Palau | U.S Dollar | Koror |
| Panama | Balboa | Panama City |

# COUNTRIES, CURRENCIES AND CAPITALS

| | | |
|---|---|---|
| Papua New Guinea | Kina | Port Moresby |
| Paraguay | Guarani | Asunción |
| Peru | New Sol | Lima |
| Philippines | Philippine Peso | Manila |
| Pitcairn Island | Pitcairn Dollar | Adamstown |
| Poland | Zloty | Warsaw |
| Polynesia, French | CFA Franc | Papeete |
| Portugal | Escudo | Lisbon |
| Puerto Rico | U.S. Dollar | San Juan |
| Qatar | Riyal | Doha |
| Réunion | French Franc | St Denis |
| Romania | Leu | Bucharest |
| Russia | Rouble | Moscow |
| Rwanda | Rwanda Franc | Kigali |
| San Marino | Italian Lira | San Marino |
| São Tomé and Príncipe | Dobra | São Tomé |
| Saudi Arabia | Riyal | Riyadh |
| Senegal | CFA Franc | Dakar |
| Serbia | Dinar | Belgrade |
| Seychelles | Seychelles Rupee | Victoria |
| Sierra Leone | Leone | Freetown |
| Singapore | Singapore Dollar | Singapore |
| Slovakia | Koruna | Bratislava |
| Slovenia | Tolar | Ljubljana |
| Solomon Islands | Solomon Islands Dollar | Honiara |
| Somalia | Somali Shilling | Mogadishu |
| South Africa | Rand | Pretoria/Cape Town |
| South Korea | South Korean Won | Seoul |
| Spain | Peseta | Madrid |
| Sri Lanka | Rupee | Colombo |
| St Christopher and Nevis | East Caribbean Dollar | Basseterre |
| St Lucia | East Caribbean Dollar | Castries |
| St Vincent and Grenadines | East Caribbean Dollar | Kingstown |
| Sudan | Sudanese Pound | Khartoum |

# COUNTRIES, CURRENCIES AND CAPITALS

| | | |
|---|---|---|
| Suriname | Suriname Guilder | Paramaribo |
| Swaziland | Lilangeni | Mbabane |
| Sweden | Krona | Stockholm |
| Switzerland | Swiss Franc | Berne |
| Syria | Syrian Pound | Damascus |
| Taiwan | Taiwan Dollar | Taipei |
| Tajikstan | Rouble | Dushanbe |
| Tanzania | Tanzanian Shilling | Dodoma |
| Thailand | Baht | Bangkok |
| Togo | CFA Franc | Lomé |
| Tonga | Pa'anga | Nuku'alofa |
| Trinidad and Tobago | Trinidad and Tobago Dollar | Port of Spain |
| Tunisia | Tunisian Dinar | Tunis |
| Turkey | Turkish Lira | Ankara |
| Turkmenistan | Manat | Ashkhabad |
| Turks and Caicos Islands | U.S. Dollar | Grand Turk |
| Tuvalu | Australian Dollar | Funafuti |
| Uganda | New Ugandan Shilling | Kampala |
| Ukraine | Gryvna | Kiev |
| United Arab Emirates | Dirham | Abu Dhabi |
| United Kingdom | Pound Sterling | London |
| Uruguay | New Uruguayan Peso | Montevideo |
| U.S. Virgin Islands | U.S. Dollar | Charlotte Amalie |
| United States of America | Dollar | Washington |
| Uzbekistan | Som | Tashkent |
| Vanuata | Vatu | Vila |
| Vatican City | Italian Lira | Vatican City |
| Venezuela | Bolívar | Caracas |
| Vietnam | Dong | Hanoi |
| Western Sahara | Peseta | Laâyoune |
| Western Samoa | Tala | Apia |
| Yemen | Riyal; Dinar | Sana'a |
| Zaïre | Zaïre | Kinshasa |
| Zambia | Kwacha | Lusaka |
| Zimbabwe | Zimbabwe Dollar | Harare |

# TYPES OF CALENDAR

The number of days in a year varies among cultures and from year to year.

## GREGORIAN

The Gregorian calendar is a 16th-century adaptation of the Julian calendar devised in the 1st century BC. The year in this calendar is based on the solar year, which lasts about 365¼ days. In this system, years whose number is not divisible by 4 have 365 days, as do centennial years unless the figures before the noughts are divisible by 4. All other years have 366 days; these are leap years.

Below are the names of the months and number of days for a non-leap year.

| | |
|---|---|
| January 31 | July 31 |
| February 28* | August 31 |
| March 31 | September 30 |
| April 30 | October 31 |
| May 31 | November 30 |
| June 30 | December 31 |

\* 29 in leap years

## JEWISH

A year in the Jewish calendar has 13 months if its number, when divided by 19, leaves 0, 3, 6, 8, 11, 14 or 17; otherwise, it has 12 months. The year is based on the lunar year, but its number of months varies to keep broadly in line with the solar cycle. Its precise number of days is fixed with reference to particular festivals that must not fall on certain days of the week.

Below are the names of the months and number of days in each for the year 5471, a 12-month year (1980 AD in Gregorian).

| | |
|---|---|
| Tishri 30 | Nisan 30 |
| Cheshvan 29* | Iyar 29 |
| Kislev 29* | Sivan 30 |
| Tevet 29 | Tammuz 29 |
| Shevat 30 | Av 30 |
| Adar 29 | Elul 29 |

30 in some years

13-month years, the month Veadar, with 29 days, falls
tween Adar and Nisan.

## USLIM

year in the Muslim calendar has 355 days if its number,
hen divided by 30, leaves 2, 5, 7, 10, 13, 16, 18, 21, 24,
5 or 29; otherwise it has 354 days. As in the Jewish
lendar, years are based on the lunar cycle.

low are the names of the months and numbers of
ys in each for the Muslim year 1401 (1980 AD in
regorian).

| | |
|---|---|
| Muharram 30 | Rajab 30 |
| Safar 29 | Sha'ban 29 |
| Rabi'I 30 | Ramadan 30 |
| Rabi'II 29 | Shawwal 29 |
| Jumada I 30 | Dhu 1-Qa'dah 30 |
| Jumada II 29 | Dhu 1-Hijja 30* |

* 29 in some years